A Garland Series

British Philosophers and Theologians of the 17th & 18th Centuries

A Collection of 101 Volumes

Edited by

René Wellek

Samuel Clarke

THE WORKS,
1738

MIDDLEBURY COLLEGE LIBRARY

In four volumes
Vol. I

Garland Publishing, Inc., New York & London

1978

Bibliographical note:

this facsimile has been made from a copy in the
Yale University Library
(Mhc9.C556.1738)

The volumes in this series have been printed on
acid-free, 250-year-life paper.

Oversize

BX
5037
C5
1976
V. I

Library of Congress Cataloging in Publication Data

Clarke, Samuel, 1675-1729.
  The works, 1738.

    (British philosophers and theologians of the
17th and 18th centuries)
    Reprint of the 1738 ed. printed for J. and
P. Knapton, London, under title: The works of
Samuel Clarke.
    CONTENTS: v. 1. Sermons on several subjects.
--v. 2. Sermons on several subjects. Eighteen
sermons on several occasions. Sixteen sermons
on the being and attributes of God, the obligations
of natural religion, and the truth and certainty of
the Christian revelation. [etc.]
    1. Church of England--Sermons. 2. Sermons,
English. 3. Bible. N.T. Gospels--Paraphrases,
English. 4. Church of England--Doctrinal and
controversial works--Collected works. 5. Trinity
--Early works to 1800--Collected works. 6. Clarke,
Samuel, 1675-1729. I. Series.
BX5037.C5 1978   230'.3   75-11207
ISBN 0-8240-1762-5

Printed in the United States of America

T. Gibson pinx.^t

Samuel Clarke D.D.

G. Vertue Sculp^t

THE
WORKS

OF

SAMUEL CLARKE, D.D.

Late Rector of St James's Weftminfter.

In Four VOLUMES.

VOLUME the First.

CONTAINING

SERMONS on Several Subjects:

WITH A

PREFACE, giving fome Account of the Life, Writings, and Character of the Author: By BENJAMIN, now Lord Bifhop of Winchester.

LONDON:

Printed for John and Paul Knapton in Ludgate-Street.
MDCCXXXVIII.

SERMONS

ON

SEVERAL SUBJECTS.

BY

SAMUEL CLARKE, D.D.

Late Rector of St James's Westminster.

Published from the AUTHOR's Manuscript by
JOHN CLARKE, D.D. Dean of SARUM.

LONDON:

Printed for JOHN and PAUL KNAPTON in Ludgate-Street.
MDCCXXXVIII.

TO THE

QUEEN.

M A D A M,

I BEG leave, in the moſt humble manner, to preſent to Your
MAJESTY, a Body of Sermons, not unworthy, I truſt, of
Your Royal Countenance and Protection.

THE near Relation in which the Author of Them ſtood to
Me, makes it almoſt impoſſible for Me to know How to ſpeak,
upon this occaſion, either of Him, or of His Writings.

I AM ſenſible, It would ill become Me to mix my private Griefs
with the Duty I am now performing to his Memory : and much
worſe, to pretend to paſs a Judgment upon His Works, for which
I may juſtly be thought to have too defective a Capacity, and too
tender a Partiality. They will All be ſoon before the World, to

VOL. I.   (a)   ſpeak

DEDICATION.

speak for Themselves: And then, the Character which They deserve, will certainly attend upon Them, with a much better Grace, from the Consent of the Learned, the Judicious, and the Disinterested Part of Mankind.

BUT in one Point I must be allowed to be the most proper Judge: And to mention it will justify Me in the present Address to Your MAJESTY: That had Dr *Clarke* himself been to direct, To Whom these Discourses of His should be inscribed; He would have named no Other, than That QUEEN, in whose Favour He himself had lived; from whose Patronage He had enjoyed so much Honour; and of whose high Accomplishments He had conceived so great an Opinion.

UPON these Subjects, MADAM, I have a Right to speak: And it would indeed, be Injustice to his Memory for Me to be silent, who was, thro' so many Years, a Witness to the Sentiments He express'd upon Them. He would often be speaking of Them, not so much with the Pleasure of a Person highly distinguish'd by the frequent Attendances upon your MAJESTY, to which He was admitted; as with the Satisfaction of a truly Philosophical and well-disposed Mind, delighted with the Sight and Prospect of Something of Universal Good Influence.

COMPLIMENT and Courtliness towards the Appearances of Grandeur; an Undue Elevation of Heart upon the Uncommon Share of Favor He enjoyed; or a Selfish Application of Soul to make it subservient to his own Gain or Advancement: These were far removed from the Turn of his Mind; and never once appeared either in his Discourse, or in his Behaviour. The Satisfaction which used to shew itself in Him, was Manly and Christian: and the Personal Honour done to Himself was the Least part of it. If indeed, He had not entertained and express'd a due Sense of Your MAJESTY's particular Regard to Himself; He had been Unworthy of it: But This was not the Agreeable part of the Subject to Him.

YOUR uncommon Capacity, and Extensive Understanding; Your Quickness in apprehending the Force of Evidence, and Your

Sagacity

DEDICATION.

Sagacity in difcovering the Failures in the moft plaufible Pretenfes to it; Your Impartial Regard to Truth, and Conftant Enquiry after it; Your Univerfal Charity and Tendernefs to All, amidft our Various and Contradictory Opinions; Your Generous Concern for Religious and Civil Liberty, and Abhorrence of Every Sort and Every Degree of Perfecution and Oppreffion; Your Love of the Happinefs of Mankind in General, and Your Paffion for the Interefts of this Nation in particular: —— Thefe were the Topics, upon which He would with pleafure enlarge. From Thefe He prefaged great Good to Religion itfelf; and Happinefs to All who fhould live within the Influence of fo many Excellencies placed in fo Exalted a Station.

AND as Thefe Expreffions of Regard to Your High Accomplifhments, are the Teftimony of a Perfon, who formed his Judgment upon Experience; and a Teftimony often given in private, where He could have no Temptation either to difguife his Real Thoughts, or to profefs any Other; it is impoffible that Flattery can be fuppofed to have had any part in Them. They were the Sentiments of his Heart: And from the Remembrance of Them I receive this fatisfaction, That, in what I am now doing, I have His Voice and Concurrence; and that, as Thefe Difcourfes are His, fo the Dedication of Them to Your MAJESTY may, in no improper fenfe, be faid to be His alfo.

NAY, if I may be permitted to go a little farther, I will add That, if Dr *Clarke* himfelf were to chufe, under what Character He would be defcribed and known to Pofterity, He would wifh That from Other Points it might rife at laft into This, That whilft He lived He was honoured with the frequent Converfations of a QUEEN, as much diftinguifhed by Her Capacity and Taft of Good fenfe, as by Her Excellent Behaviour in Every Relation of Life.

PERMITT therefore, MADAM, his Works now to reft under the fame Patronage, which He himfelf once enjoyed. Suffer thefe Remains of His to be confecrated to that Great Perfon who efteem'd and cherifh'd their Author; and to fhelter Themfelves under that Royal Name which was the Glory of His laft Years.

AND

DEDICATION.

AND permitt Me, MADAM, at the fame time to acknowledge, with all the Sentiments of a Gratefull Heart, the Many Expreſſions of Your Regard to His Memory, as well as Your Generous Goodneſs and Beneficence to Myſelf, ſince His death: and to profeſs Myſelf, with all poſſible Reſpect and Duty,

MADAM,

Your MAJESTY's

Moſt Devoted and

Moſt Humble Servant,

Catharine Clarke.

THE

PREFACE,

Giving fome Account of the LIFE, WRITINGS, and CHARACTER of the AUTHOR.

D R. *SAMUEL CLARKE* was born at *Norwich*, *Oct.* 11. *A.D.* 1675. His Father was *Edward Clarke*, Efq; Alderman of That City, and One of the Reprefentatives of It, in Parliament, for feveral Years : A Perfon of an Excellent Natural Capacity, and of an untainted Reputation for Probity and all Virtue. His Mother was *Hannah*, the Daughter of Mr. *Samuel Parmenter*, Merchant, of the fame City. He received the firft Rudiments of Learning in the Freefchool at *Norwich*, from the Reverend Mr. *Burton*, under whofe Care He made a very Uncommon Proficiency in the Learned Languages. In the Year 1691, He was removed to *Cambridge*, and placed at *Caius College*, under the Tuition of Mr. *Ellis*, afterwards Sir *John Ellis*. And here, His Impatient Thirft after true Knowledge, and his Great Capacity both for difcovering and improving it, prefently began to fhew Themfelves.

THE Philofophy of *Des Cartes* was then the *Eftablifhed Philofophy* of that *Univerfity*; and the Syftem of Nature hardly allowed to be explained any otherwife than by *His* Principles: Which, at beft, were evidently no more than the Inventions of a very Ingenious and Luxuriant Fancy; having no Foundation in the Reality of Things, nor any Correfpondency to the Certainty of Facts. His *Tutor* himfelf though a Learned Man, and for ever to be honoured for his Confcientious Care of All under Him, was a Zelot for this Philofophy; and as He was Moft Diligent in reading to his Pupils, without doubt gave Them the moft favourable Impreffions of what He had fo clofely embraced Himfelf; and but little Encouragement to ftrike out any Light in another way of thinking. The Great Sir *Ifaac Newton* had indeed then publifhed his *Principia*. But this Book was but for the Few : both the Manner and Matter of it placing it out of the Reach of the Generality even of Learned Readers; and ftrong Prejudice, in favour of what had been received, working againft It. But neither the Difficulty of the Tafk, nor the Refpect He paid to the Director of his Studies; nor the Warmth and Prejudice of All around Him, had any Effect upon his Mind. Not at all fatisfied, therefore, with *Hypothefes* arbitrarily adapted to Appearances; He fet himfelf immediately to the Study of what was Real and Subftantial : And in This Study He made fuch uncommon Advances, that He was prefently Mafter of the Chief parts of the *Newtonian Philofophy*; and, in order to his Firft *Degree*, performed a Publick Exercife in the Schools, upon a *Queftion* taken from thence, which furprized the Whole Audience, both for the Accuracy of Knowledge, and Clearnefs of Expreffion, that appeared through the Whole. Such an Example could not but be of great ufe, to animate All around him. But He was not content with the Service He could do to *True Philofophy*, by his Example only.

As soon as He had taken that first *Degree*, Young as He was, He made an Effort for the Service of the Students, which ought not to be forgotten. The System of *Natural Philosophy* then generally taught in the *University*, was That written by Monf. *Rohault*; entirely founded on the *Cartesian* Principles; and very ill translated into *Latin*. He justly thought that Philosophical Notions might be exprefs'd in pure *Latin*: And if He had gone no farther than This, He would have merited of All Thofe who were to draw their Knowlege out of that Book. But His Aim was much higher than the making a Better Tranflation of it. He refolved to add to It fuch Notes, as might lead the Young Men infenfibly, and by degrees, to Other and Truer Notions than what could be found there. And this certainly, was a More Prudent Method of introducing Truth unknown before, than to attempt to throw afide this Treatife entirely, and write a New one inftead of it. The Succefs anfwered exceedingly well to His Hopes: And He may juftly be ftiled a Great Benefactor to the *University*, in this Attempt. For, by this Means, the True Philofophy has without any Noife prevailed: and to this Day, His *Tranflation* of *Rohault* is, generally fpeaking, the Standing Text for *Lectures*; and His *Notes*, the firft Direction to Thofe who are willing to receive the Reality and Truth of Things in the place of Invention and Romance. And thus before he was much above Twenty Years old, He furnifhed the Students with a *Syftem* of Knowledge, which has been ever fince, and ftill continues to be, a Publick Benefit to All who have the happinefs of a Liberal and Learned Education in that *University*.

I MMEDIATELY after this, His Thoughts were turned to *Divinity*; which he propofed to make the peculiar Study and Profeffion of his Life: For the profecution of which Defign He foon met with a very favorable Opportunity. Dr *John Moore*, then Lord Bifhop of *Norwich*, the greateft Patron of Learning and of Learned Men, that this Age has produced, had already fix'd his Eyes upon Mr. *Clarke*, as a Young Man, of a Genius much exalted above the Common rank, and promifing Great Things to the World in his riper Years. He refolved to make Him his *Chaplain*, as foon as He fhould be Old Enough to take Orders, And when He did fo, at the fame time He received Him into His Familiarity and Friendfhip, to fuch a remarkable degree, that He lived for near twelve Years in that Station, with All the decent Freedoms of a Brother and an Equal rather than an Inferior. The whole Family counted Themfelves happy in Him, as an Intimate Friend. The Bifhop's Value for Him increafed every day, as his Knowledge of Him increafed. There was no mark of Confidence, as well as Efteem, which that Prelate did not fhew Him, as long as He lived: And at his death, the higheft Mark of Confidence He could give Him, was the Leaving all the Concerns of his Family folely in His hands; a Truft, which He executed with the moft faithful Exactnefs, and to the Entire Satisfaction of Every Perfon concerned. To return,

H IS firft Studies, in order to fit Himfelf for the Office He propofed to undertake, were, The *Old Teftament* in the Original *Hebrew*; The *New* in its Original *Greek*; and the *primitive* Chriftian Writers. The *Firft* of Thefe He then read with that Exactnefs of Judgment, which very few have fhewn after a much longer Application; and which furnifhed Him with Many Obfervations written at that time with his own hand in the *Margen*, relating to the Miftakes of the Common *Tranflation* of it. The *New Teftament* he read with a true Critical Accuracy: And, with great Care, purfued his Defign farther, through the Writers of the Earlieft Ages, in order to difcover, if poffible, the Genuine Sentiments and Cuftoms of Antiquity; as well as to fupport the Authority and True Interpretation of the facred Books. The Refult of all this Application appeared fo early as the Year 1699, in *Two Treatifes*. The one was defigned for the promoting of the Practice of Religion, under the Title of *Three Practical*

tical

tical Effays upon *Baptifm, Confirmation,* and *Repentance.* The other, without his Name, was entitled, *Some Reflexions* on (a Book call'd) *Amyntor,* relating to the *primitive Fathers,* and the *Canon* of the *New Teftament.* I mention Them here, not to put them upon the level with his Other Performances; but only as having upon them the plain Marks of a Chriftian Frame of mind; and as Proofs of his Knowledge in the Writings of thofe Early Ages, even at his firft fetting out into the World.

FROM thefe Attempts, He proceeded, without Intermiffion, to Others of ftill greater Importance: making Ufe of the Leifure and Freedom He enjoyed in his Patron's Family, and of one of the Nobleft Private Collection of Books which ever appeared in *England,* for the Purpofe He had chiefly in his Eye; the Underftanding the Phrafeology of the *Holy Scriptures,* and the Explaining the Meaning of Them fo, as to make Them ufeful to All who are concerned in them. The firft *Effay,* in this Defign, was His *Paraphrafe* upon St *Matthew*'s Gofpel, publifhed in the Year 1701: and foon followed by *Paraphrafes* upon the *Gofpels* of St *Mark, Luke,* and *John.* Thefe were written with a manly plainnefs and perfpicuity; and accompanied with a very few fhort *Notes,* where Any Critical Explication was neceffary. Of how great benefit Thefe have been, and always will be, to Thofe *Englifh* Readers, who have Senfe and Goodnefs enough to be pleafed with a juft Reprefentation of the True Meaning of what is recorded in the Gofpel; I need not fay. Experience has already faid enough of the Ufefulnefs of fuch a Manner of Interpretation, from fo mafterly an Hand. It were highly to be wifhed that He had purfued his Original Defign, and completed the Work upon the Whole *New Teftament:* in many Books of which, the Intricate *Connexion* of the Parts; the feeming Perplexity of the *Argument*; and the *Obfcurity* of the *Style* at this diftance of Time, particularly call'd for the Affiftance of fo Critical an Underftanding, capable of finding out the True Ideas annexed to the old Words; and of difcovering the hidden Force of Thofe Reafonings, which would otherwife efcape the view of Common Readers. He had indeed, actually begun his *Paraphrafe* upon the *Acts* of the *Apoftles,* immediately after the Others were publifh'd; and had certainly propofed to Himfelf to go through All the remaining Books. But fomething accidental interrupted the Execution: and it is now only to be lamented that Any thing firft diverted Him from it; or that He did not afterwards prevail upon Himfelf to refume and compleat fo Excellent a Work; which His Friends often prefs'd upon Him; and to which He would fometimes anfwer, That it was made lefs neceffary by the Labours of feveral Worthy and Learned Perfons, fince the appearance of his Work upon the *Four Gofpels.*

BISHOP *Moore,* who was every day confirmed in the high Opinion of his Superior Talents, and Excellent Qualifications, very juftly thought that there was No place fo deferving of fuch a perfon, and fo fit for Such Abilities to exert Themfelves in, for the Good of Mankind, as the *Metropolis* of the Kingdom: And it very foon became his Settled Refolution, to make ufe of all his Intereft, which at that time was very confiderable amongft the Greateft Men of the Nation, in order to fix Him in the moft remarkable Scene of Action. But, in the mean while, He gave him the Rectory of *Drayton* near *Norwich,* and procured for Him a *Parifh* in that *City*; both together of very inconfiderable value: and Thefe He ferved himfelf in the Seafon, when the *Bifhop* refided at *Norwich.* His preaching at firft was without Notes; and fo continued till He was *Rector* of St *James*'s: A Method, in which He was peculiarly happy; not by trufting to his Memory entirely, and fpeaking a Sermon compofed before, in which fome have excelled; nor by heating himfelf gradually into Any fort of Paffion, to which *Others* have owed all their Fluency of Language; but by a Certain Strength and Coolnefs of Head, which could not eafily be furprized or deceived; and a Certain Faculty of Expreſſion, which was hardly ever at a loſs for plain and proper words.

I N the Year 1704. He was call'd forth to an Office worthy of ſuch an Underſtanding. It was to preach Mr *Boyle*'s Lecture, founded by that Honourable Gentleman, to aſſert and vindicate the Great Fundamentals of Natural and Reveled Religion. This was a Province, for which if ever Any one was peculiarly fitted by Natural Parts, and Learning; He was the Man. And He executed this Truſt in ſuch a Manner, that He at once ſurprized, and inſtructed, his moſt Underſtanding Hearers. He exceded the Expectations, even of thoſe who knew Him enough to expect Great Things from Him: and laid the Foundations of True Religion too deep and ſtrong to be ſhaken either by the Superſtition of Some, or the Infidelity of Others. The Subject of his Diſcourſes was, The Exiſtence of G O D, or of a Being of All poſſible Perfections. And in the Demonſtration of This, He choſe particularly to conſider the Arguings of *Spinoza* and *Hobbes*, the moſt plauſible Patrons of the Syſtem of *Fate* and *Neceſſity*; a *Syſtem*, which by deſtroying All true Freedom of Action in Any Intelligent Being, at the ſame time deſtroys All that can be ſtyled Virtue, or Praiſeworthy. This being a *Subject*, into which all the Subtilties and Querks of Metaphyſics had entred, and thrown their uſual Obſcurity and Intricacy; the Difficulty lay in clearing away this Rubbiſh of Confuſion; in introducing a Language that could be underſtood; in clothing the cleareſt Ideas in this plain and Manly Language; and in concluding Nothing, but from ſuch Evidence as amounts to *Demonſtration*. And thus it was that the Maſterly hand appeared. He began with Self-evident *Propoſitions*. From them He advanced to Such as received their Proof from the Former. In theſe He took no Step till he had ſecured the Way before Him. Throughout the Whole, No Word is uſed, but what is Intelligible to All who are at all verſed in ſuch *Subjects*, and what expreſſes the Clear Idea in the Mind of Him who makes uſe of it: and All is one Regular Building, erected upon an Unmoveable Foundation; and riſing up, from One Stage to Another, with equal Strength and Dignity.

H I S Labours ſucceded ſo well in This Great Attempt, that He was appointed to preach again, the next Year. And here He went on with the ſame Method, Clearneſs, and Strength, to deduce from What He had before proved, and to ſtrengthen with all proper Arguments, *The Evidences of* Natural *and* Reveled *Religion.* In theſe Diſcourſes He laid the Foundations of Morality deep, in the mutual Relations of Things and Perſons, one to Another; in the Unalterable Fitneſs of ſome Actions, and the Unfitneſs of Others: and in the Will of the Great Creator of All things, evident from his making Man capable of ſeeing theſe Relations, and this Fitneſs; of judging concerning Them; and of acting agreeably to that Judgment. He then proceded to demonſtrate the Chriſtian Religion to be worthy of God, from the *Internal* Evidence, taken from the perfect Agreeableneſs of It's Main Deſign to the Light of Nature; and to All the Moral Obligations of Eternal Reaſon; without which Agreeableneſs, All the Arguments in the World could never conclude in it's favor: And, after this, to prove It to be actually recommended to the World by G O D, from All the *External* Evidence, of Prophecy going before it, and Miraculous Works performed expreſſly for the honour and propagation of it. All which He executed with ſuch Maſterly Senſe, and perſpicuity of Expreſſion, as recommended both the Preacher and the Subject to All who heard Him. Theſe two Courſes of *Sermons* were ſoon printed in Two Continued *Treatiſes*: which was thought to be the moſt uſeful Way of publiſhing them to the World. Several *Editions* of them have already been printed; in Every One of which the *Author* did not ſcruple to make ſuch Alterations and Additions, as ſeem'd to Him neceſſary either for the preventing any Miſtakes, or the farther

ther

ther Clearing up the Important Subjects of Them. I shall say nothing farther about Them, but that Every Christian in *this* Country, in which They first saw the Light, ought to esteem Them as *His Treasure*; as They contain the True Strength not only of *Natural*, but of *Reveled* Religion: Which, if ever it be removed from such a Foundation; or separated from such an Alliance with Reason and uncorrupted Nature, will not long subsist in the Belief of Understanding Persons, after such a separation. And therefore, *What God hath joined together, let no man put asunder*.

SOON after the preaching of these *Sermons*, Bishop *Moore* found an Opportunity of bringing Him to Town; and procured for Him, by his Interest, the Rectory of St *Bennet's Paul's-Wharf*. Many in that Parish still remember how Instructive and Acceptable his Preaching was to All in it: And He Himself never forgot, but frequently with pleasure recounted, the very particular Civilities He received from the *Gentlemen* of *Doctors Commons*, who made the most considerable Part of his Audience.

ABOUT this time the Learned Mr *Dodwell* published a very remarkable Discourse: in which, in order to exalt the Powers and Dignity of the *Priesthood*, in that *One Communion*, which he imagined to be the *Peculium* of GOD, and to which He had joined Himself, He endeavour'd to prove, with his usual perplexity of Learning, That the Doctrine of the Soul's *Natural Mortality* was the True and Original Doctrine; and that *Immortality* was only at *Baptism* conferr'd upon the Soul, by the Gift of GOD, thro' the hands of One Sett of regularly-ordained Clergy. The Mischievous Tendency of these Doctrines, thus blended together, as it was back'd by the Great Name of the Author in the *Learned* World, made it more necessary that an Answer should be given to What might from Another hand perhaps have been received as a Design'd Banter and Ridicule both upon Natural and Instituted Religion. Mr. *Clarke* was thought the most proper Person for this Work. And He did it in so excellent a Manner, both with regard to the *Philosophical* part, and to the Opinions of some of the *Primitive Writers*, upon Whom these Doctrines were fixed; that It gave Universal Satisfaction. Nor did He stop here. For, a very Ingenious *Gentleman*, having laid hold on this favorable opportunity of coming into this Controversy, as a Second to Mr *Dodwell*, went much farther into the *Philosophy* of the Dispute; and indeed seemed to produce All that could plausibly be said against the *Immateriality* of the *Soul*, as well as the *Liberty* of *Human Actions*. This enlarged the Scene of the *Dispute*: into which Mr *Clarke* enter'd, and wrote with such a Spirit of Clearness, and Demonstration, as at once shew'd Him greatly superior to his Adversaries in *Metaphysical* and *Physical* Knowledge; and made Every Intelligent Reader rejoyce that Such an Incident had happen'd, to provoke and extort from Him that Plenty of strong Reasoning, and Perspicuity of Expression, which were indeed very much wanted upon this Intricate and obscure Subject. And I am persuaded that, as What He has writ in this Controversy, comprehends the Little that the Antients had said well; and adds still more Evidence than ever clearly appear'd before; and all in Words that have a Meaning to them: It will remain the Standard of Good Sense on That side of the Question on which He spent so many of his Thoughts, as upon One of his Favorite-Points.

ABOUT this time, His Worthy Patron brought Him to *Court*, and procured Him to be made One of the *Chaplains* in *Ordinary* to Queen *ANNE*; to whose greater Favor His own Excellent Qualifications recommended Him so soon and so powerfully, that, upon the Vacancy of St *James's Westminster*, She immediately consented to the Request of the *Bishop* and presented Him to that *Rectory*. In this Station, which placed Him in the observation of Many of the *Noblest* part of our World, How He conducted Himself for above *Twenty years*; What an Undisturbed Unanimity there was between Him, and all his Parishioners, thro' the whole Time; What his Preaching, and What his Conversation were; how inſtructive *Both*, and how acceptable, to All of Every Sort and Party into which We are diſtinguiſh'd; Let *Them* teſtify who were Eye-Witneſſes and Ear-Witneſſes to Them: who all equally rejoyced in his Diſcourſes and in his Preſence whilſt He was alive; and equally lamented their own Loſs, at his Death. As ſoon as He was ſettled in this Pariſh, He left off his former Way of preaching without the aſſiſtance of Notes; and made it one of his chief Studies to compoſe, and write down, as accurate *Sermons* as He could. Not, as I believe, becauſe He could not proceed in the former Method, with a Copiouſneſs of Good Senſe and Clear Expreſſion, which the Nobleſt Audience might with pleaſure have attended to; but chiefly, becauſe from that Time It became his Reſolution to prepare his Sermons in ſuch a Manner, that they might hereafter be as Uſefull from the *Preſs*, as He wiſhed Them then to be from the *Pulpit*.

U p o n his Advancement to ſuch a Station, it was eſteemed a Piece of Decency for Him to take the *Degree* of *Doctor* in *Divinity*, for which He was now of ſufficient Standing in the *Univerſity*. For this purpoſe, He went down to *Cambridge*, and propoſed his Two Queſtions; and performed a long *publick Exerciſe* upon Them; the Memory of which will, I believe, remain, and be delivered down from one Succeſſion of the *Learned* in that Univerſity to Another. The Queſtions were Theſe:

1. *Nullum Fidei Chriſtianæ Dogma, in S. Scripturis traditum, eſt Rectæ Rationi diſſentaneum.*

2. *Sine Actionum humanarum Libertate nulla poteſt eſſe Religio.*

1. *No Article of the Chriſtian Faith, delivered in the Holy Scriptures, is Diſagreeable to Right Reaſon.*

2. *Without the Liberty of Humane Actions there can be No Religion.* Two *Queſtions*, worthy of ſuch a Divine and ſuch a Philoſopher, to propoſe for *Publick Debate!*

T h e *Royal Profeſſor* of Divinity, Dr *James*, who was a Learned, Ready, and very Acute Diſputer, exerted Himſelf, beyond what was his Common Practice, in order to oppoſe and try Him to the Utmoſt. By the Help of a Great Memory, and Fluency of Words, and a certain Knack in the Art of Diſputing, He firſt went into a long *Examination* of Dr *Clarke*'s *Theſis*, (which was an Elaborate Diſcourſe upon the *Former* of theſe two *Queſtions*,) ſifting Every part of it with the ſtricteſt Nicety; and afterwards, preſs'd Him with all the Force of *Syllogiſm*, in it's various Forms, thro' the Courſe of the *Diſputation*. Here was an *Adverſary* worthy of ſuch a Reſpondent. To the *former* Dr *Clarke* made an *Extempore* Reply, in a continued Diſcourſe for near half an hour, in which, without any heſitation either for Thoughts or for Language, He took off the Force of All that the *Profeſſor* had ſaid, in ſuch a Manner, that Many of the Auditors declared Themſelves aſtoniſhed; and own'd that, if They had not been within Sight of Him, They ſhould have ſuppoſed Him to have read Every word of this *Reply* out of a Paper. After this, thro' the Courſe of the *Syllogiſtical* Diſputation, He guarded ſo well againſt the Arts which the *Profeſſor* was Maſter of, in perfection; He replied ſo readily to the greateſt Difficulties that ſuch an *Objector* could propoſe; and preſs'd upon the *Profeſſor* ſo cloſe and ſo hard with his Anſwers, clear and intelligible to All; that perhaps Never was ſuch a Conflict heard in thoſe *Schools*; never ſuch a Diſputation kept up for ſo long a time with ſuch Spirit; nor ever Any, which Ended with greater, if Equal honour, to the *Reſpondent*. The *Profeſſor* himſelf, who was a Man of *Humour* as well as *Learning*, ſaid to Him aloud, towards the End of the Diſputation, (an Accidental Debate having ariſen, as I have been informed, about the meaning of the word *Exacuo*,) *Profecto, Me probé exacuiſti*: which I hardly know how to interpret to the *Engliſh Reader*, unleſs by a phraſe of a low kind, *In truth You have thoroughly rubb'd me up*. Others think the word was *Exercuiſti*. They remember that the Profeſſor uſed often to ſpeak to a *Reſpondent*, after a long Difputation, *Finem jam faciam*; *Nam* Te *probé* exercui: *I will now make an End; for I have fufficiently* work'd *You*: and fay, That He was going to ufe the fame Expreffion to Dr *Clarke*; but after the word *Te*, ftop'd and corrected Himfelf, and faid,——*Nam* ME *probé* Exercuifti.——*For You have* work'd *Me thoroughly*. This was look'd upon as a very high Compliment, in *His* humorous way of fpeaking. And the Learned Members of that Body, who had with pleafure attended to Every part of the whole *Difputation*, went away difcourfing to one another of the Unufual Entertainment They had had in the Schools; not a little pleafed with fuch an Ornament to their own Univerfity: and admiring particularly, That, after an Abfence of fo many Years, and a long courfe of Bufinefs of quite Another Nature, They heard Him now handling the Subjects He undertook, in fuch a mafterly Manner, as if This fort of Academical Exercife had been his Conftant Employment; and with fuch a Fluency and Purity of Expreffion, as if he had been accuftomed, thro' this whole Time, to no other Language in Converfation but *Latin*.

Soon after this, Another Scene opened. He had for a confiderable time employed his Thoughts and Studies upon a Subject of a very high Nature, which had exercifed the Pens of Many of the greateft Divines; I mean, The Doctrine of the *Trinity*: and was now come to a fettled Judgment about it. But, let Every Man of fenfe be Judge with how much Wifdom, and in how Chriftian a Method, He proceded to form his own Sentiments upon fo Important a Point. He knew, and All men agreed, That it was a Matter of *Mere Revelation*. He did not therefore, retire into his Clofet; and fet himfelf to invent and forge a plaufible *Hypothefis*, which might fit eafily upon his own Mind. He had not recourfe to Abftract and *Metaphyfical* Reafonings, to cover or patronize any *Syftem* He might have embraced before. But, as a Chriftian, He laid open the *New Teftament* before Him. He fearch'd out *Every Text*, in which Mention was made of the *Three Perfons*, or of Any *One* of them. He accurately examined the Meaning of the Words ufed about Every one of Them: and by the beft Rules of *Grammar* and *Critique*, and by his Skill in Language, He endeavor'd to fix plainly What was declared about Every Perfon; and What was Not. And what He thought He had difcover'd to be the *Truth*, He publifh'd, under the *Title* of The *Scripture-Doctrine* of the *Trinity*.

I am far from taking upon Me to determine, in fo difficult a Queftion, between Him, and Thofe who made Replies to Him. The Debate foon grew very warm: and in a little time feem'd to reft principally upon *Him*, and *One* particular Adverfary, very fkilful in the Management of a Debate, and very Learned and well-verfed in the Writings of the Antient Fathers. The *Controverfy* has been long before the World: and All who can read what has been alledged on both Sides, ought to judge for Themfelves. But This, I hope, I may be allowed to fay, That Every Chriftian Divine, and Layman, ought to pay his Thanks to Dr *Clarke*, for the Method into which He brought this Difpute; and for that Collection of *Texts* of the *New Teftament*, by which at laft it muft be decided; on which fide foever the Truth be fuppofed to lie. And let Me add this one word more, That, fince Men of fuch Thought and fuch Learning, have fhewn the World, in their own Example, how widely the moft honeft Enquirers after *Truth* may differ, upon fuch Subjects: This methinks, fhould a little abate our Mutual Cenfures; and a little take off from our Pofitivenefs, about the Neceffity of explaining, in *this* or *that* one determinate Senfe, the Antient Paffages relating to Points of fo Sublime a Nature.

I pass over the Complaint made, in Convocation, Againft this Treatife concerning the *Scripture-Doctrine* of the *Trinity*: becaufe it foon ended, upon the *Right Reverend*, the Members of the *Upper-houfe*, having declared Themfelves fatisfied with the Explanations which the *Author* delivered in to Them, upon the *Subject* of the *Complaint*.

ONE Matter of Fact I will add, That from the Time of his publishing this *Book*, to the Day of his *Death*, He found no reason, as far as He was able to judge, to alter the Notions which He had there professed, concerning the *Father*, *Son*, and *Holy Ghost*, towards Any of Those *Schemes* which seem'd to Him to derogate from the *Honour* of the *Father*, on one side; or from That of the *Son*, and *Spirit*, on the other. This I thought proper just to mention, as what All his Friends know to be the *Truth*. And indeed, nothing to the Contrary can be alledged, without contradicting many Express Sentences, scattered through All his Works which have followed, or will follow, the fore-mention'd *Treatise*; evidently setting forth, or implying, the same Doctrine.

FROM the Time of his taking possession of St *James's*, His Residence was where his Heart and his Employment were; in the *Rectory-House*, in the midst of his Parishioners; seldom leaving the Place at all, unless for a few Weeks, in the *long Vacation*, when the Town was Empty: which He spent in visiting his Friends at *Norwich*, and other places; and, towards the latter part of his Life, in doing his Duty as Master of *Wigston's Hospital* at *Leicester*: a *Post* of no very great profit, but made agreeable to Him by the handsome Manner in which the late Lord *Lechmere* invited Him into it; and by the Method of taking possession of it, free from some of those Circumstances which by Law attend upon most other Preferments.

DURING the Time of his being *Rector* of St *James's*, besides the regular performance of All the other Offices of his Profession, He followed the Custom of his *Predecessors*, in reading *Lectures* upon the *Church-Catechism*, every *Thursday* morning, for some months in the Year. In the latter part of his Time, He revised These with great Care; and left Them, under the *Title* of An *Exposition* upon That *Catechism*, completely prepared for the *Press*. This *Exposition* has been published, according to his own express Desire, since his Death. The *Remarks* of a *Learned* Man followed it, as soon as it could well be read in the World. An *Answer* has been made to these *Remarks*: and the World must judge on which side Truth and Light appear.

BUT though *Divinity*, and the Studies peculiar to his Profession, were his great Employment; yet this did not hinder his Genius from shewing itself in Other sorts of Learning, worthy of a Man, and of a Clergyman. The first Specimen He gave the World of his Knowledge in the *Profane Authors*, was his Edition of *Cæsar's Commentaries*, 1712. in *Folio*, dedicated to his Grace the Duke of MARLBOROUGH, at a Time, when his Unequal'd Victories and Successes had raised his Glory to the highest pitch abroad, and lessen'd his Interest and Favor at Home. Of this I shall only say, That there are few Books in the World, that excell It, either for Beauty or Correctness; and that the *Notes* added shew the *Accuracy* of their Author.

THE last Instance of his *Critical* and *Classical* Learning was the Last Piece He published: The first *Twelve Books* of *Homer's Ilias*, with an almost New *Translation*, and *Notes*. *Homer* was his Admired Author, even to a degree of Something like *Enthusiasm* hardly natural to his Temper. In this He went a little beyond the Bounds of *Horace's* Judgment: and was so unwilling to allow the *Favorite-Poet* ever to *Nod*, that He has taken remarkable pains to find out and give a Reason for Every Passage, Word, and Tittle, that could create any suspicion. The Translation, with his Corrections, may now be styled Accurate: and his *Notes*, as far as They go, are indeed a Treasury of *Grammatical* and *Critical* Knowledge. He was called to this Task, by Royal Command: and He has performed it in such a Manner, as to be Worthy of the *Young Prince*, for whose Use it was laboured. The Praises given to this Excellent Work, by the Writers abroad in their *Memoirs*; as well as by the Learned Masters of the Three principal Schools of *England*; Those of *Westminster*, *Eaton*, and St *Paul's*; and the Short Character, That the Performance was *Supra omnem invidiam*, bestowed by One

whom

whom Dr *Clarke* himfelf had long before ftyled, *Criticos unus omnes longé longéque——— antecellens*, and whom Every one will know by that Title without my naming Him, make it unneceffary to add a Word upon this Subject.

In the midft of his Other Labours, He found time alfo to fhew His Regard to the *Mathematical* and *Phyfical* Studies; and his Exact Knowledge and Skill in them. For *thefe* indeed, He had a fort of a Natural Affection, and Capacity; which were greatly improved by the particular Friendfhip of the Incomparable Sir *Ifaac Newton*, whofe Death only put an End to it; and by the Light communicated to Him from his Writings and Converfation. At Sir *Ifaac*'s Requeft, He tranflated His Treatife of *Optics*, into that pure and intelligible *Latin*, which has fent it all over *Europe* in a plainer and lefs ambiguous Style, than the *Englifh Language* will fometimes permitt. And after the death of that Great Man, He vindicated his Doctrine about the Proportion of *Velocity* and *Force* in *Bodies* in *Motion*, from the Objections of fome late Mathematicians, in a fhort, plain, and Mafterly Letter, printed in the Tranfactions of the Royal Society, N° 401. 1728. and in a manner fufficient to fhew the excellent Greatnefs of his *Genius* for thefe *Subjects* as well as Others.

I MUST not pafs by a very remarkable Controverfy, which lafted long, in a private manner, between Him and the learned Mr. *Leibnitz*; and afterwards was publifhed, and infcribed to Her prefent MAJESTY, who was pleafed to have it pafs through Her hands: and was the Witnefs and Judge of every Step of it. It related chiefly to the Important and Difficult Subjects of *Liberty* and *Neceffity*. This *Liberty*, or *Moral Agency*, was a *Darling Point* to Him. He excelled always, and fhewed a Superiority to All, whenever it came into Private Difcourfe, or Publick Debate. But He never more excell'd, than when He was prefs'd with the Strength this *Learned Adverfary* was Mafter of: which made Him exert All his Talents to fet it once again in a Clear light; to guard it againft the Evil of *Metaphyfical Obfcurities*; and to give the finifhing Stroke to a *Subject*, which muft ever be the *Foundation* of Morality in Man; and is the Sole Ground of the Accountablenefs of Intelligent Creatures for all their Actions. And as This was the laft of Dr *Clarke*'s Works relating to a Subject which had been, by the Writings of Cloudy or Artfull Men, render'd fo intricate; I fhall take the Liberty to fay, with regard to All of the fame Tendency, from his Firft Difcourfe about the Being of G O D, to thefe Letters; That what He has written to clear and illuftrate this Caufe, does now ftand, and will for ever remain, before the World, a lafting Monument of a *Genius*, which could throw in Light where Darknefs ufed to reign; and force Good Senfe and Plain Words, into what was almoft the *Privileged place of Obfcurity*, and Unintelligible Sounds. For fuch indeed, had the *Subject* before Us been, under the hands of Moft who had written upon it; either through a *defire* of darkening it by Words without Meaning, or through an *Inability* of difcourfing clearly and confiftently about it.

SUCH was the Conduct, and fuch was the Life, of Dr. *Clarke*; full of Defigns and Works, becoming a Truly Great Man, intimately concern'd for his own Real Happinefs; and for That of All Intelligent Creatures and Moral Agents around Him. And, in the midft of All thefe *Studies* and Labours, His Natural *Conftitution* of *Body* was in appearance fo good; and his Care of his health was fo conftantly and regularly prudent; that All the Friends to his Perfon, and to True Knowledge, promifed Themfelves and the World a much longer Enjoyment of fuch Ufeful Accomplifhments, than it pleafed G O D to afford Them. He pafs'd his Life, without any Indifpofition bad enough to confine Him, except That of the *Small-Pox* in his Youth, till his laft Illnefs: though, fince his Death, many little Particulars, and Complaints have been call'd to mind, which feem to have been Evident *Symptoms* of fome Weaknefs, or Somewhat wrong, which He ufed to feel within. On *Sunday, May* 11, 1729. He went out in the Morning, to preach before the *Judges* at *Serjeant's-Inn* : and there was feized with a *Pain* in his Side, which made it impoffible for Him to perform the Office He was called to ; and quickly became fo violent that He was obliged to be carried home. He went to bed ; and thought Himfelf fo much better in the Afternoon, that He would not fuffer Himfelf to be blouded : againft which Remedy He had indeed entertained ftrong prejudices. But the Pain returning very violently about Two the next Morning, made the Advice and Affiftance of a very Able Phyfician abfolutely neceffary : Who, after twice bleeding Him, and other applications, thought Him, as He alfo thought Himfelf, to be out of all Danger ; and fo continued to think, till the *Saturday* Morning following : When, to the inexpreffible Surprize of All about Him, the *Pain* removed from his *Side* to his *Head* ; and, after a very fhort Complaint, took away his Senfes, fo as that They never returned any more. He continued breathing till between feven and eight in the Evening of that Day, *May* 17. 1729. and then died ; and by his Death (Let me be permitted to fay it) left the World deftitute of as Bright a *Light*, and as Mafterly a Teacher of *Truth* and *Virtue*, as ever yet appeared amongft Us.

HE married *Catharine*, the only Daughter of the Revered Mr. *Lockwood*, Rector of *Little Maffingham* in the County of *Norfolk* ; in whofe Good Senfe and Unblameable Behaviour He was happy to his Death. By Her, He had *Seven* Children ; *Two* of which died before Him, and *One*, in a few weeks after Him.

HE was a Perfon of a *Natural Genius*, excellent enough to have placed Him in the Superiour rank of Men, without the Acquirements of *Learning* : and of *Learning* enough, to have render'd a much lefs Comprehenfive *Genius* very confiderable in the Eyes of the World. But in *Him* They were both united, to fuch a degree, that Thofe who were of his intimate Acquaintance, knew not which to admire moft. The Firft Strokes of Knowledge, in fome of its Branches, feem'd to be little lefs than *Natural* to Him : For They appeared to lie right in His Mind, as foon as Any thing could appear ; and to be the very fame which afterwards grew up with Him, into perfection, as the Strength and Cultivation of his Mind increafed. He had one Happinefs very rarely known amongft the Greateft Men, That his *Memory* was almoft equal to his *Judgment* : which is as Great a Character as can well be given of it. It did not indeed, appear in Trifles ; nor in every part of Knowledge : But in Thofe particularly which regarded the Claffical and pureft Writers of the Antients ; or Any Part of Real and Experimental Philofophy ; as well as what can truly be called *Theology*, It was furprizingly excellent ; and of wonderful Ufe to Him, through all his Studies, and all his Converfation.

IN *Divinity*, it was his great Aim to fettle beyond all Contradiction what muft be the Support of True Religion ; and then to fhew the Evidences for what muft rely upon That Support. The *neceffary Exiftence* of *One* only GOD, and the Impoffibility of the *Exiftence* of More Than One, He juftly efteem'd as the *Foundation* of All. This neceffary *Unity* of the Supreme Being appears throughout His Writings to have been ever uppermoft in his Thoughts : a Subject, which, though often excellently handled, and made as Evident as any Arguments and Illuftrations *à Pofteriori* could make it ; yet had never I think, before his Time, been attempted in the Way of *ftrict Demonftration à Priori* : which certainly is the Strongeft, and therefore, the moft defirable of *All* Proofs, where it can be had. *He* undertook the Tafk : and Many of the Beft Judges, after a great deal of Confideration, have allowed that He has executed it in a Mafterly and Satisfactory Manner : with fo much Evidence indeed, as generally to convince Thofe who are capable of entring into this fort of Queftions.

I fay,

I fay, *Generally*; becaufe I am fenfible, There are fome very Underftanding Perfons who do not yet fee this *Evidence* fo clearly as Others do.

In *Morality*, It was His Great and Principal View to do lafting fervice to the Eternal Obligations of *Virtue*; that is, of Every Inftance of Practice and Conduct towards GOD, our Neighbour, and Our Selves, which refults from the Nature and Relations of Things: and this He has done in the plaineft and moft intelligible Manner.

In the Caufe of *Chriftianity* He labour'd as fincerely; and, with the fame Clearnefs and Strength, produced and illuftrated All the *Evidences* peculiar to it: not indeed, confidering It, as it has been taught in the Schools or Difcourfes of Modern Ages; but as it lies in the *New Teftament* itfelf.

And throughout All this, As his *Firft Principle* was the *Unity* of GOD, which He efteemed the Only Guard againft *Idolatry*, as well as the *Bafis* of All Moral Obedience; fo next to This, Nothing Seem'd to be more ftrong within Him, than his Inclination to Settle the True Notions of *Neceffity* and *Liberty* in what is called *Action*. This He has done in a very convincing Manner; and at the fame time demonftrated, beyond all reafonable doubt, That Freedom of *Action* in *Man*, which only can make Him at all *Accountable* to his *Creator*, as a Judge of his Behaviour. Such was the Courfe He ran, in the Caufe of That Religion, which alone can be ftyled worthy of GOD to propofe, or of *Man* to embrace!

In *Natural Philofophy*, and the *Mathematical* Knowledge neceffary to It, amidft All his other Employments, He excelled, as if Thefe had been his *Darling Study*. Not that He could poffibly find Time Himfelf to make all the proper *Experiments*, to neceffary *Calculations*. But He had I know not what happinefs of Genius, by which he immediately comprehended what coft Others a great deal of Pains; and fuch a Faculty of judging of any New *Syftems*, or *Propofitions*, from what He knew certainly before; and thefe fupported by a *Memory* which hardly ever failed Him upon thefe Subjects; That He was efteemed, by the *Knowers*, to be One of the Beft Judges, to apply to, for a Quick Determination about the Force or Failure of any Arguments, or appearing Demonftrations, in thefe Studies.

His *Critical* Skill in the learned Languages was like the Gift of Nature; fo ftrong and fo eafy in Him, that it appeared plainly, to what a Wide Extent This would have gone, had not his other Affairs and Studies put a neceffary Stop to what He was fo exquifitely framed for. Great as the Impediments were; We See, His *Memory* and his Judgment in this part of Learning were fo Strong and Powerful, that They fhone through them all in a few Inftances; and thefe fufficient to make All Men of Letters wifh that He could have fpent more of his Time this way. It is for his honour to obferve That he made this Critical Skill fubfervient to the *Caufe* of *Religion*, as well as *Polite Learning*; and gave a Noble Specimen of applying it to the difcovery of the True Meaning of Words and Phrafes ufed in the *Sacred Writings*: without which, We do but wander in the dark, when We pretend to fpeak upon many of the *Subjects*, contained in thofe Books.

As much as I have faid already of his Excellencies in Learning; There is ftill *One* behind, which was (I had almoft faid) ftrictly peculiar to Him: I mean The manner of his handling Subjects of a *Metaphyfical* and *Abftract* Nature. In this Skill, He had a Superiority fo vifible; that, I think, the Greateft Mafters of it ought to yield it up to Him. This Superiority appeared by his fhewing that He had always clear and diftinct Ideas; by clothing them with plain and Intelligible Words; by going no farther than thefe *Ideas* and *Words* could go together; and by arguing as clofely upon the abftrufeft Points which He pretended to underftand, as is ufual in *Mathematical Deductions* themfelves.

If

IF in *Any One* of thefe Many Branches of *Knowledge* and *Learning* He had excelled only fo much, as He did in *All*; This alone would have juftly intitled Him
to the Name of a *Great Man*. But there is fomething fo very extraordinary, that
the fame Perfon fhould excel, not only in thofe Parts of Knowledge which require
the Strongeft *Judgment*, but in thofe which want the help of the Strongeft *Memory*
alfo; and It is fo feldom Seen, That One, who is a Great Mafter in *Theology*, is at
the fame time fkilfully fond of all *Critical* and *Claffical* Learning; or Excellent in the
Phyfical and *Mathematical* Studies; or well framed for *Metaphyfical* and *Abftract* Reafonings: That it ought to be remarked, in how particular a Manner, and to how
high a degree, *Divinity* and *Mathematics*, *Experimental Philofophy* and *Claffical Learning*, *Metaphyfics* and *Critical Skill*, All of them, (Various and different as They are
amongft Themfelves,) united in Dr. *Clarke*.

THIS way of fpeaking of Him, with regard to All thefe, may Sound fo high;
that Many perhaps who were Strangers to Him, and to His Real Excellencies, may
think, I have faid too much. But I am confident, (and this is my Satisfaction) That
In All that I have faid upon thefe Subjects, I have the Confent and Teftimony of
Many of the moft Judicious and Learned Men, of All Denominations amongft Us; as
well Thofe who did not come into All his Sentiments, as Thofe who did.

HIS *Preaching* was what One would naturally expect from a Perfon of fo Critical a
Genius, and fo fedate a *Judgment*. The Defign and Tendency of it was not to
move the Paffions: nor had he any *Talent* this way. He wifely never attempted it,
becaufe He was fenfible He fhould not fucceed if He did. And if This was a *Defect*;
it was a *Defect* in his original Frame and Conftitution. But then, His Sentiments
and Expreffion were fo mafterly; His way of explaining the *Phrafeology* of *Scripture*,
by collecting, and comparing together, all the Parallel Places truly relating to any
Subject, was fo extraordinary and Convincing; that fuch a Delight of Satisfaction
went along with it, as more than made amends for the Want of the *Other*. And
in this Method of Preaching, He was fo univerfally acceptable, that perhaps there
was not a *Parifhoner* He had, of any Rank, (whatever might be his way of thinking in our divided World,) who was not always pleafed at his coming into the Pulpit;
or, who was ever weary of his Inftructions from thence. *However We differ in Some
matters, We defire to See No other Perfon in the Pulpit*; was, I know, a Saying a-
mongft Them. And it is for their honour, that I mention it.

THESE Accomplifhments of *Nature* and *Learning* not only made his *Preaching*
thus Excellent; but render'd his *Converfation* amongft his Friends in fo high a degree
Ufeful and Inftructive, that it might be ftyled An Eafy Continuation of his own
Studies, and a School of Knowledge to thofe who partook of it. Indeed, if I might
be allowed to judge in What that peculiar Excellence lay, which moft diftinguifhed
Him from other Great Men; I would place it in That Readinefs of Thought, and
Clearnefs of Expreffion, which hardly ever fail'd Him, when His Opinion was afked,
upon All forts of Important and Trying Queftions. The Pleafure and Satisfaction
which appeared where He converfed with any Freedom, could not but be very great;
to hear Many of the Difficulties which had perplexed very Able Men in their feveral
Profeffions and Studies, though ftarted all on a fudden, vanifhing almoft as fuddenly;
leffening continually as faft as He fpake, and generally ending with his Difcourfe.
Here indeed, it was That He triumph'd without a Rival. They who fancied Themfelves in Doubts never to be fatisfied, often found Light from Him, after having vainly tried to find it elfewhere: and They who did not fee to the End of their Difficulties immediately, yet had This Comfort, That they always underftood Him, as
far as He went; and at leaft that Satisfaction which is the next to finding out the
Whole Truth, I mean The Satisfaction of being convinced that it was in vain to Expect

it. Thofe who knew Him, have been daily Witneffes to what I now fay, in *Mathematical* and *Critical*, as well as *Theological* and *Metaphyfical* Subjects: Upon the laft of which indeed, He was One of the *very Few*, who could, or would, always talk intelligibly. His Difcourfe of this fort was without one Word or Term, which He was not as ready to give a plain Senfe to, as He was to make ufe of it; and in a Style which He would take as great a pleafure to adapt to the Underftanding of All perfons of Senfe, as Many would do, to raife their Language even out of their own reach, as well as that of Others. For He judged, That, as the Ufe of Language was to exprefs Thoughts; fo *Thofe founds* could not be juftly called *Language*, which reprefented No Thoughts at all. Such was his *Converfation* amongft his Friends: always far removed from *Pedentry*; and never arifing from his own *affectation* of introducing *Learning* into it; but from the Enquiries of *Others*, or the *Occafions* which naturally and unavoidably led to it.

WHAT added a Force to his *Preaching*, and Inftructive *Difcourfe*, was his own Unblameable Example, and Perfonal Conduct, in All the Duties of a Man, and a Chriftian. His Piety was Manly and Unaffected; built upon the moft folid Grounds, and free from all Pomp and Shew. The *Charity* of his Temper and Good-will was as Extenfive as the Whole Rational Creation of God. The *Charity* of his Affiftance and Beneficence, as Extenfive as the Circumftances of his Family would prudently admitt. His Love of the Religious and Civil Liberties of Mankind, was a Ruling and Powerful Principle in His Heart and Practice. In a word, His Morals, from the firft of his Days, to the laft, were without Reproach. There was an Innocence and Inoffenfivenefs remarkable thro' his whole Behaviour: And his *Life*, when He came into the View of the Great World, was an Ornament and Strength to that Religion which his *Pen* fo well defended.

No wonder that a Perfon of fuch a *Genius*, and fuch *Acquirements*, was fought after by the Greateft Lovers of Virtue and Knowledge. This was his Cafe, to fuch a Degree, that, thro' his laft Years, He could command but very little time for his own Studies, even in the *Morning*; and after the *Morning* was over, He was almoft Every day invited and prefs'd amongft his Friends abroad; not only Thofe of his own Parifh, who were equally defirous of his Company; but Many in all the other parts of the Town.

THE *Chief Perfons* of the *Law* will forgive Me, if I can't pafs over the Singular Regard They paid to this Great Man: which was fo remakable, that it feem'd to be a fort of Conteft amongft Them, who fhould fhew it moft. The *Lord High Chancellor*, The *Mafter* of the *Rolls*, The Lord *Chief Baron*, and feveral of his Brethren the Learned *Judges*, (not to mention *Others*) will, I am confident, efteem it their Honour to have it faid, fince it can be faid with Truth, That there never yet appeared a Divine amongft Us, (not related to *Them* by his Office,) who received fuch continued and fuch particular Marks of the higheft Refpect from fo many Ornaments of that *Honourable Profeffion*, as He did, from the Day of his being firft known amongft Them, to That day, on which fome of Them were Witneffes to the approaches of his laft Illnefs.

THE Regards paid to Him by the Beft of the Powerfull and Noble part of Our World, were as Conftant and as Remarkable. Above all, It ought ever to be remember'd, wherever the Name of Dr *Clarke* is remember'd, That her Prefent *MAJESTY*, from her firft Acquaintance with his Character to the Day of his Death, exprefs'd the high Eftem She had of his Comprehenfive Capacity, and Ufefull Learning, by very frequent Converfations with Him, upon Many of the moft Important and Entertaining Points of True Philofophy, and Real Knowledge. And feldom a Week pass'd in which SHE did not with pleasure receive some proof of the Greatness of his Genius, and of the Force of his Superior Understanding.

Iꜰ Any One should ask, as it is natural to do, How it came to pass that this Great Man was never raised higher in the *Church?* I must answer, That it was neither for want of Merit, nor Interest, nor the Favor of Some in whose Power it was to have raised Him. But He had *Reasons* within his own Breast, which hinder'd Him either from seeking after, or accepting any such Promotion. Of These He was the proper, and indeed the only Judge: and therefore I say no more of Them. He was happy in that Station, in which it had pleased GOD to fix Him before Those *Reasons* took place: and He had not in Him, either the Desire of Dignity, or Love of Riches, strong enough to make Him uneasy for Any thing more than what afforded Him and his Family a Decent appearance and place in Life. And, agreeably to this Character, As He sought after no promotion in the *Church*; so, He refused the offer of a very beneficial *Civil* Office.

Tʜᴜs adorned with the most Valuable of All Moral and Intellectual Accomplishments, He lived in the Esteem of the Wise and Good and Great; and died sincerely lamented by Every Friend to Learning, Truth, and Virtue.

I ʜᴀᴠᴇ thus paid that last Duty to the Memory of this Excellent Man, which I could not but esteem a Debt to such a Benefactor to the Cause of *Religion* and *Learning* united. And, as These Wᴏʀᴋs of His must last as long as Any Language remains to convey them to future times; perhaps I may flatter Myself That this Faint and Imperfect Account of Him may be transmitted down with Them. And I hope, It will be thought a pardonable piece of Ambition, and Self-Interestedness; if, being fearfull lest Every Thing else should prove too weak to keep the Remembrance of Myself in being, I lay hold on *His* Fame, to prop and support *My own.* I am sure, As I have little Reason to expect that Any thing of mine, without such an Assistance, can live: I shall think Myself greatly recompensed for the want of Any other Memorial, if *My* Name may go down to Posterity thus closely joyned to *His*; and I myself be thought of, and spoke of, in Ages to come, under the Character of *The FRIEND* of Dr. *CLARKE.*

BENJ. SARUM.

CONTENTS

CONTENTS.

CONTENTS.

I

CONTENTS.

I

S E R M.

SERM.

CONTENTS.

1

SERM.

CONTENTS.

SERM.

CONTENTS. xxiii

SERM.

SERMON

S E R M O N I.

Of Faith in GOD.

HEB. XI. 6.

But without Faith, it is impoffible to pleafe him : For he that cometh to God, muft believe that he is, and that he is a rewarder of them that diligently feek him.

THE foregoing Chapter is a very earneft and affectionate Exhortation to the Duty of *Faith*, Ver. 22. *Let us draw near with a true heart, in full affurance of Faith.* Ver. 23. *Let us hold faft the profeffion of our* Faith *without wavering.* Ver. 37. *For yet a little while, and he that fhall come will come, and will not tarry : Now the juft fhall live by* Faith. That This exhortation might not be ineffectual, for want of men's clearly underftanding *What* the *Nature* of the Duty was, to which they were here fo earneftly exhorted ; the Apoftle in the 1ft verfe of This chapter, proceeds to define diftinctly *what* Faith is, and wherein it confifts. *Faith,* faith he, *is the fubftance of things hoped for,* (in the original it is, *the firm and affured expectation* of things hoped for,) *the evidence of things not feen.* And *what* thofe *Things* are, which being *not feen* by *Senfe,* are yet made manifeft by *Faith,* he declares in the words of the Text. They are, faith he, the *Being of God,* and the *Rewards of the Life to come.* He that cometh to God, *muft believe that he is, and that he is a Rewarder of them that diligently feek him.* There has prevailed in *modern* times, a very different and enthufiaftick Notion of *Faith* ; as if Faith, under the Gofpel, was nothing but a Confident Reliance upon the Merits of Chrift, to do all That for us, which he on the contrary exprefsly requires that we fhould do for our felves. When we have heartily endeavoured to obey the Commandments of God ; and have performed our Duty really and fincerely, though very imperfectly ; to rely *Then* upon the Merits and Interceffion of Chrift, for the acceptance of thofe imperfect though fincere Endeavours ; This *is* indeed the *Duty,* and the *Comfort* of a Chriftian ; but it *is not* what the Scripture ufually calls *Faith. Faith,* is that firm Belief of things at prefent not feen ; that conviction upon the Mind, of the Truth of the Promifes and Threatnings of God made known in the Gofpel ; of the certain reality of the Rewards and Punifhments of the Life to come ; which enables a man, in oppofition to all the Temptations of a corrupt World, to obey God in expectation of an invifible Reward hereafter. This is that *Faith,* which in Scripture is always reprefented as a *moral Virtue,* nay as the *principal* moral Virtue, and the *root and fpring* of all *other* Virtues ; Becaufe it is an Act, not of the *Underftanding* only, but alfo and chiefly of the *Will,* fo to confider impartially, to approve and embrace the Doctrine of the Gofpel, as to make it the great Rule of our Life and Actions. By *This Faith* it is, that *We* muft be juftified ; and by *This* it is, that the *Antients* whofe example is celebrated in this xi[th] chapter, *obtained,* as the Apoftle expreffes it, *a good Report.* The Faith of *Abraham* was, that *he looked for a City which hath foundations,* even the heavenly *Jeru-*

S E R M. *falem* fpoken of in the Prophecies, *whofe Builder and Maker is God*, ver. 10. The Faith
I.   of the *other Patriarchs* was that *confeffing themfelves ftrangers and pilgrims on the Earth,*
they *declared plainly* that they *fought a better Country*, that is, *an heavenly,* ver 13, 16.
The Faith of *Mofes* was, that he *chofe rather to fuffer affliction with the people of God,
than to enjoy the pleafures of Sin for a feafon* ; For *he had refpect unto the recompence
of Reward* ; and *endured, as feeing Him who is invifible*, ver. 25, 26, 27. The
Faith of the *Martyrs* was *that they chofe to be tortured, not accepting deliverance, that
they might obtain a better Refurrection*, ver. 35. This is a very eafy and intelligible
Notion of *Faith* ; and fuch a Notion, as fhows plainly, how Faith is not a mere
fpeculative Act of the Underftanding, but a fubftantial practical moral Virtue.

'T I S true; This is *not* indeed the *only* Senfe of the word, *Faith*, in Scripture;
but 'tis the *Principal* and moft *important* fenfe of it. As may appear by confidering,
that all the Variety of fignifications, in which the word is ufed in different places of
Scripture, may properly be reduced, for memory and diftinctnefs fake, to thefe which
follow. *1ft*, The word, *Faith*, in fome places fignifies That earneft Truft and Confidence in the Power of God, to which in the Apoftles Times was annexed the Gift
of working Miracles. Thus *Matt.* xvii. 20. *If ye have* Faith (fays our Lord to his
Apoftles) *as a grain of muftard-feed* ; (if ye have That *Truft* in God, That particular
Kind of Faith or Dependance on him, That affured Reliance on his Power without
Doubt or wavering, required of *you* peculiarly at *This time* ; if you have *This Faith,*
though ever fo fmall in comparifon, anfwerable in *any meafure* to your prefent Office
and Advantages;) *ye fhall fay to this mountain, remove hence to yonder place, and it
fhall remove.* This was a Faith required of the Apoftles at *That particular* Time, and
of *Them* only. *2dly*, In other Paffages, the word, *Faith*, fignifies the duty of Veracity, Faithfulnefs, or Truth. Thus *Matt.* xxiii. 23. *Ye have omitted the weightier
matters of the Law* ; *judgment, mercy, and* Faith ; Faith, that is, *Fidelity, Truth,* or
Faithfulnefs, in the difcharge of any *Truft* repofed in Men. Analogous to which,
it is alfo fometimes ufed for the *Truft itfelf*, or the *thing* committed to our charge;
Thus *Rom.* xii. 6. *Having then Gifts differing according to the Grace that is given to
us; whether prophecy, let us prophefy according to the proportion of* Faith ; *Or Miniftry,
let us wait on our miniftring* ; [The phrafe in our modern language is very difficult,
and cannot well be underftood without This obfervation :] *According to the proportion
of Faith*, that is, according to the nature and degree of the *Gift* of the *Truft* repofed
in us, (whether it be *prophecy* or *miniftration* or any other Office which requires *Faithfulnefs* in the performance of it) fo let every one of us difcharge his refpective Duty.
3dly, Another and much more ufeful fignification of the word, *Faith*; is to denote
the *whole Gofpel of Chrift*, or the *Chriftian religion*, in oppofition to the ritual Works
of the Law of *Mofes*. Thus *Acts* vi. 7. *The number of the Difciples multiplied in Jerufalem greatly, and a great company of the Priefts were obedient to the* Faith; that is,
embraced the *Gofpel*. Again, *Rom.* iii. 28. *A man is juftified by Faith, without the
deeds of the Law* ; by *Faith*, that is, by the condition of the *Gofpel*. And *Rom.* x. 8.
The word of Faith, which we preach ; That is to fay, the Doctrine of the *Gofpel*.
And indeed *generally* throughout all the *Epiftles*, and in the Book of the *Acts*, this is
the conftant fignification of the word, *Faith*. And the reafon *why* the whole *Gofpel* is
fo often expreffed by that Name, is very obvious ; [namely] becaufe the great Motives
and Promifes of the Gofpel, are *the invifible things of a Future State*, which can be
difcerned by *Faith* only. *4thly* and *Laftly*, in *other* places of Scripture, the word,
Faith, fignifies plainly and literally and in its moft natural Senfe, *a firm Belief* and
Perfwafion ; a firm Belief, of the *Being*, and *Attributes*, and *Promifes* of God.
Not, (as *Some* underftand it,) a confident *Credulity* in they know not *what*, in whatever their Teachers require them to believe ; and *That* perhaps with fo much the greater

                                                            Affurance,

Affurance, as the things are more abfurd and unreafonable to be believed. Neither does *Faith* fignify, (as *Others* have contended,) a groundlefs imaginary Affurance, and confident Reliance on our being unalterably, we know not *why*, in the Favour of God. But it is a rational Perfwafion and firm Belief, of his Attributes difcovered by *Nature*, and of his Promifes made known in the *Gofpel*; fo as thereby to govern and direct our lives. Thus the word is ufed in the 1ft verfe of this chapter, *Faith is the Subftance (a Subftantial well-grounded expectation) of things hoped for, the evidence of things not feen.* And in the words of the Text; *Without Faith it is impoffible to pleafe God; For He that cometh to God, muft believe that he is, and that he is a rewarder of them that diligently feek him.*

To *come to God*, fignifies, according to the Nature of the Jewifh language, *making Profeffion of Religion*; undertaking to live a holy and virtuous Life, in obedience to God's commands, and in expectation of his Rewards. And it anfwers to another phrafe of the like import, walking *with God*; which fignifies *continuing and perfevering* in that religious practice, whereof *coming to God* is the *Beginning or Entrance.* Thus *Gen.* v. 22. *Enoch* walked *with God*; and, vi. 9. *Noah was a juft man, and perfect in his generation, and Noah* walked *with God.* *Walking with God*, is being *perfect* or *ftedfaft* in that religious courfe of Life, whereof *Coming to God*, is making the *firft Profeffion.* He that *cometh to* God, is as much as to fay, *whofoever will be a virtuous or religious man*: In like manner, as, he that *cometh to* Chrift, fignifies more particularly, *he that will take upon him to be a* Chriftian. *No man can* come to Me, fays our Saviour, *Joh.* vi. 44. (that is, he cannot *become a good Chriftian*,) *except the* Father *which hath fent me, draw him;——Every man that hath learned of the Father*, cometh unto Me. The phrafe, *except the* Father *draw him*, is in our *prefent* manner of fpeaking, difficult and unufual; But it is explained by what follows, *He that hath* learned *of the Father.* The Meaning is: No man can effectually believe in *Chrift*, except he firft believes in *God.* *Natural* Religion, is the beft Preparative for the reception of the *Chriftian.* The Love of Truth and *Virtue* in *general*, is the Difpenfation of the *Father*; And the Doctrine of the *Gofpel* in *particular*, is the Difpenfation of the *Son.* Now as no man can receive *Chrift*, who has not firft heard, and is thus drawn by the *Father*; as no one can be a good *Chriftian*, who is not firft refolved to be a good *Man*; fo no one can hear the *Father*, can *come to God*, unlefs he firft have *Faith*, and *believes in* Him. The Difpenfation of the *Father*, That of Creation or Natural Religion, is a neceffary Preparative for the Difpenfation of the *Son*, that is, for the Gofpel: And it muft *itfelf* have *preparation made for it* by *Faith going before*, as by the *Firft Foundation of all.* He that cometh to God, muft believe that he is, and that he is a Rewarder of them that diligently feek him.

The Senfe therefore of the Text is This. 'Tis in vain to make Profeffion of Religion, without being firft well inftructed and firmly perfwaded of *This* Foundation; *the Being and Attributes of God.* There is no *Chriftian*, who is not well apprized of This; and may be apt to think perhaps, that 'tis needlefs to remind him of it. But there are few who confider thefe firft Principles of Religion, fo *ferioufly* and fo *frequently* as they ought to do; and in *fuch* a manner, as to caufe them to produce their proper Effect, by influencing their whole Lives and Converfations. For *Knowledge* is but a dormant Habit, if not excited by conftant Meditation; and *Powers* are of no Ufe, if not produced into *Act.* Right Notions of the Being and Attributes of God, every one knows are the Foundation of all Religion: But then This Knowledge muft not be a bare Speculation; but a ferious, practical, affecting impreffion, and deep Senfe upon the Mind; of a Supreme Being, who created the World by his Power, preferves and governs it by his Goodnefs and Wifdom, and will judge it with Juftice, Mercy, and Truth: Of *fuch* a Supreme Being; whofe Glory, no Eye can behold; whofe Majefty,

jefty, no Thought can comprehend; whofe Power, no Strength can refift; from whofe Prefence, no Swiftnefs can flee; from whofe Knowledge, no Secret can be concealed; whofe Juftice, no Art can evade; whofe Goodnefs, every Creature partakes of. This is That *Faith*, without which it is *impoffible to pleafe God*. It is *impoffible* to pleafe him without *it*; not that Virtue and Righteoufnefs, if it were poffible to find them *without* Faith, could be in themfelves unacceptable to God; but that, becaufe *without* fuch Faith there *can be no* Righteoufnefs, therefore neither without it can God poffibly be pleafed. *Righteoufnefs* is the only means, by which rational Beings can obtain the Favour of God; And therefore fince *Faith* is neceffary in order to Righteoufnefs, 'tis *confequently* neceffary to the obtaining of the Favour of God. He that will *pleafe* God, muft *come to him* in the Ways of Virtue and true Holinefs; and he that *cometh to God*, muft firft *believe that he is*.

FROM what has been faid upon This head, we may eafily diffipate the vain Fears of many pious and fincere perfons, who are very apt to be fufpicious of themfelves that they want true *Faith*, and confequently that their Religion is vain. Now this Fear, in fuch Perfons, evidently arifes from want of having a diftinct Notion what *Faith* is. They are poffeffed of the *Thing*; but for want of clearly underftanding the *Notion*, they are not able to judge rightly whether they have it or not. From the explication which has Now been given of that Matter, men may eafily examine themfelves, whether they *have* that Faith, which I have been defcribing, or no. And without entring into the *definition* at all, there is yet a plainer Rule given us by our Saviour; by its *Fruits* we may know it. Whereever the *Fruits* of Righteoufnefs and true Virtue are found, *there* cannot be wanting the *Root* of Faith, from which thofe Fruits proceeds: For he that *cometh* to God, *does* certainly believe that he *is*; and gives the beft Proofs in the World that he does fo. On the contrary, whofoever upon examination finds not in his Life the Fruits of Righteoufnefs; whatfoever his *fpeculative* Underftanding may be, yet in the *Chriftian* fenfe he may be fure he has no Faith. For if the Spring, the Caufe, the active Principle were prefent; there would not be wanting its proper Effect. Such as the Root is, fuch *will* be the Branches. He who ferioufly *believes* that God is; *will* indeavour to *come unto him*, in the ways of Truth and Righteoufnefs.

HAVING thus briefly explained the *former* part of the words; and fhewn both *what* Faith is, and how abfolutely *neceffary*; as *without which* it is *impoffible* to pleafe God, or to come unto him; It remains that I confider, in the *latter* part of the words, thofe *Two* fundamental inftances or primary *objects* of Faith, laid before us by the Apoftle; namely, the *Being of God*, and his *Relation to* Us; that he *Is*, and that he is a *Rewarder of them that diligently feek him*. The firft foundation of all, and the *primary* object of Faith, is the *Being* of God; *He that cometh to God, muft believe that he* Is. Now the *Grounds* or *Arguments*, upon which our Faith in *This particular* is built; befides the Evidence and Authority of *Revelation*; are, from *Reafon it felf*, and from the very *Nature of Things*, many and various: there being hardly any thing in Nature, from whence the Certainty of the Being of God, may not juftly and reafonably be deduced. Some of the Arguments are abftrufe, and require Attention; but, when thoroughly confidered, conclude moft ftrongly to the Conviction of obftinate Unbelievers. Others are plain, eafy and obvious, fuited to all Capacities; always ready at hand to confirm the Faith even of the meaneft Underftandings; and yet differing from the former, not in *ftrength*, but in being more *common only*. It would be tedious to repeat at length upon This Head a great Number of Arguments, among Chriftians to whom they have been fo often urged, and are fo well underftood. But by a brief recapitulation, to remind our felves frequently of things already known, for the better affifting of our meditations; cannot but in many cafes be very ufeful. For

me,

me, faith St. *Paul*, to repeat unto you the *fame* things, is not grievous, and for *You* it
is fafe. To this purpofe, the numerous Arguments, which prove (in particular) *the*
Being *of God*, may be naturally reduced to the *Two* which follow.

Firft, THAT 'tis evident, both We our felves, and all the other Beings we know
in the World, are weak and dependent Creatures; which neither gave our felves Being,
nor can preferve it by any Power of our own : And that therefore we entirely owe
our Being to fome Superiour and more Powerful Caufe; which Superiour Caufe, either
muft be it felf the *firft Caufe*, which is the Notion of *God*; or elfe, by the fame Argument as before, muft derive *from* him, and fo lead us to the Knowledge *of* him. If
it be faid, that we received our Being from our Fore-Fathers by a continued natural
Succeffion, (which however would not in any ftep have been poffible, without a perpetual Providence;) yet ftill the Argument holds no lefs ftrong concerning the *Firft* of
the whole Race; that *He* could not but be made by a Superiour Intelligent Caufe. If
an Atheift, contrary to the Truth of all Hiftory, fhall contend that there may have
been, without any Beginning at all, an *eternal* Succeffion of Men; yet ftill it will be
no lefs evident, that fuch a perpetual Succeffion could not have been without an eternal
Superiour Caufe; becaufe in the Nature of Things themfelves there is manifeftly no *Neceffity*, that any fuch Succeffion of tranfient Beings, either temporary or perpetual, fhould
have exifted at all.

Secondly, THE *other* Argument, to which the greateft part of the Proofs of the Being of God may briefly be reduced, is the *Order* and *Beauty* of the World; That exquifite Harmony of Nature, by which (as St *Paul* expreffes it, *Rom.* i. 20.) *the invifible things of God from the creation of the World are clearly feen, being underftood by the
things that are made*. And This Argument, as it is infinitely ftrong to the moft accurate Philofophers, fo it is alfo fufficiently obvious even to the meaneft Capacities. *Whofe* Pf. civ. 2.
Power was it, that framed this beautiful and ftately Fabrick, this immenfe and fpacious
World? *that ftretched out the North over the empty place, and hanged the Earth upon nothing?* Job xxvi. 7. That formed thofe vaft and numberlefs Orbs of Heaven, and dif- Pf. xix. 1.
pofed them into fuch regular and uniform Motions? that appointed the Sun to rule the cxlvii. 4.
Day, and the Moon and the Stars to govern the Night? that fo adjufted their feveral Pf. civ. 19.
diftances, as that they fhould neither be fcorched by Heat, nor deftroyed by Cold?
that encompaffeth the Earth with *Air* fo wonderfully contrived, as at one and the fame
time to fupport Clouds for Rain, to afford Winds for Health and Traffick, to be proper
for the Breath of Animals by its Spring, for caufing Sounds by its Motion, for tranf-
mitting Light by its Tranfparency? that fitted the Water to afford Vapours for Rain,
Speed for Traffick, and Fifh for Nourifhment and Delicacy? that weighed the Mountains in Scales, and the Hills in a Ballance; and adjufted them in their moft proper
places for Fruitfulnefs and Health? that diverfified the Climates of the Earth into fuch
an agreeable Variety, that in that great Difference, yet each one has its proper Seafons,
Day and Night, Winter and Summer? that clothed the Face of the Earth with Plants
and Flowers, fo exquifitely adorned with various and inimitable Beauties, that even *Solomon* in all his glory was not arrayed like one of them? that replenifhed the World with
Animals, fo *different* from each other in *particular*, and yet All in the *whole* fo much
alike? that framed with exquifite workmanfhip the Eye for Seeing, and other parts of
the Body, neceffarily in proportion; without which, no Creature could have long fub-
fifted? that beyond all thefe things, indued the *Soul of Man* with far fuperior Faculties, with Underftanding, Judgment, Reafon and Will; with Faculties whereby in a
moft exalted manner *God teaches us more than the Beafts of the Field, and maketh us
wifer than the Fowls of Heaven?* Job xxxv. 11.

'TIS commonly alledged by Unbelievers, that all thefe things are done by *Second
Caufes*. And fuppofe they *were*, (which however is not univerfally true : But fuppofe

they *were* effected by Second Caufes,) yet *How* would *That* diminifh the Neceffity of acknowledging the *Firft* Caufe ? If among *Men,* many things are performed by the Ufe of *Inftruments*; are thofe things therefore ever the lefs juftly afcribed to the *Hands* which *ufed* the Inftruments ? Becaufe every Wheel in a *Watch* moves only *naturally,* according to the Frame of its parts, and the Strength which the Spring impreffes upon it ; is therefore the Skill of the Workman the lefs to be acknowledged, who adjufted thofe very things ? Or becaufe 'tis *natural* for the Wheels of a Watch, or for the Rooms of a Houfe, to be of fuch particular Shapes and Dimenfions, does This make it poffible, that therefore they may have been formed fo without any Artificer ? All *Natural,* All *Second* Caufes, are nothing elfe, but either the *inanimate* Motions of fenfelefs Matter, or the voluntary Motions of dependent Creatures. And What are thefe, but *One* of them the direct Operation; and the *Other,* only the free Permiffion, of Him who ruleth over all ? Mens neglecting therefore to infer the Being of God, from every thing they fee or think of every day, is in reality as great a ftupidity as if from the conftant and regular continuance of the *day-light,* men fhould ceafe to obferve, that there is fuch a thing as the *Sun* in the Heavens, from whence That Light proceeds. Nor would it be more abfurd to imagine, that the Light would continue, tho' the Sun, which caufes it, were extinguifhed; than that the Effects of Nature can regularly go on, without the Being of God who caufes thofe Effects. To evade this Argument there is no other poffible way, but to affirm either that all things were produced by *Chance,* or that they are all *Eternal neceffarily of themfelves.* As to *Chance,* 'tis evident That is nothing but a *mere Word,* or an *abftract Notion* in our manner of conceiving things. It has itfelf no real Being ; it is Nothing, and can *do* nothing. Befides, in the works of *God,* the *further* men fearch, and the more difcoveries they make, the *greater exactnefs* they conftantly find ; whereas in things done either by the Art of *Man,* or by what we call *Chance,* the *contrary* always is true ; the *more* they are underftood, the *lefs accurate* they appear. Beyond all credulity therefore is the creduloufnefs of Atheifts, whofe Belief is fo abfurdly ftrong, as to believe that Chance could make the *World,* when it cannot build a *Houfe* ; that Chance fhould produce all *Plants,* when it cannot paint one *Landfkip*; that Chance fhould form All *Animals,* when it cannot fo much as make a *lifelefs Watch.* On the other hand therefore, if they will affirm that all things are *eternal*; yet ftill the Argument holds as ftrong as before, that things which cannot for any *time* exift without a caufe, can much lefs without a caufe exift through all *time.* Unlefs they will affirm, that All things exift by an internal *abfolute Neceffity in their own Nature.* Which that they do *not,* is evident from hence; that there exifts in the World an infinite Diverfity of Things, whereas *Neceffity* is *uniform and without Variation.*

HAVING thus briefly fhown that God *Is*; it will eafily follow in the *next* place, that he *is* and muft be *a Rewarder of them that diligently feek him.* For he that governs the Motions of every even the fmalleft particle of *lifelefs Matter,* and by whofe Providence every *Vegetable* and every the meaneft *Animal* is perpetually preferved; without whom not a *Sparrow* falls to the ground; and with whom, even the very *hairs of our head* are all numbred; fhall he not much more take care of *Us,* O We of little Faith ? Now the proper and principal Care or Government over *Rational* Creatures, is the *Rewarding* or *Punifhing* them according to their refpective Deferts. If therefore God *Is,* (as hath before been proved,) and is Governour of the World; it follows that he muft be alfo, (fince therein principally all Government confifts; he muft be) *a Rewarder of them that diligently feek him.*

THE Application of what has been faid, is briefly, 1ft to Scepticks, and 2dly to Believers.

1st, To fuch as are Scepticks or Unbelievers of the Being of God, 'tis advifeable in
the firft place, that they confider how *uncomfortable* their Opinion is. 'Tis plain, fuch
is the condition of human Nature in This Life, that we are continually furrounded
with *Evils* which we cannot *prevent*, with *Wants* which we are not able to *fupply*,
with *Infirmities* which we cannot *remove*, with *Dangers* which we can no way *efcape*.
Our *injoyments* are fuch, as are *not* for one moment *fecure*; our *expectations*, of fuch
things as are *not in our own Power to accomplifh*. We are apt to *grieve*, for things we
cannot help; and to be tormented with *Fears*, of what we *cannot prevent*. And in all
thefe cafes, there is no fubftantial Comfort, but in the Belief of God; and in the fingular Satisfaction of having Him our Friend. Had the thing therefore really in itfelf
any *uncertainty*, (which is by no means the cafe,) yet it could not but be what every
wife and reafonable man muft *defire* and *wifh* might be true, that the World were governed by a wife and juft and merciful God. So that even *Scepticks themfelves* cannot
but be felf-condemned, when they *mock* and *fcoff* at Religion; when they refufe to hear
Arguments for the Truth of the moft defirable thing in the World; and will not examine thofe Evidences and Proofs of Religion, which are really much ftronger than
thefe perfons can before-hand imagine. And if the Proofs were much *weaker* than they
are, yet they would deferve at leaft to be ferioufly *confidered*; becaufe the hazard on
one fide is infinitely great, if Religion which they reject, be true; whereas on the
other fide there is no hazard at all, if, being received as true, it could poffibly prove to
be a miftake.

2dly, To fincere Believers, the Ufe of what has been faid, is; that being once fatisfied in the *main and great* Truths of Religion, they fuffer not themfelves to be
moved, and their Faith in this *Great* point, fhaken, by nice and uncertain difputes
about particular Queftions of lefs moment. For, which way foever many fuch Controverfies of an abftrufe and difficult nature, be determined; yet the great Foundation of
Religion, upon which a Wife Man may always act fteddily, is laid deep and fure in
this plain Propofition, that *God Is, and that he is a Rewarder of them that diligently
feek him.*

S E R M.
I.

Quid habet ea
res lætabile auf
gloriofum?

S E R M O N II.

Of the UNITY of GOD.

MATT. IV. 10. latter part.

Thou fhalt worfhip the Lord thy God, and Him only fhalt thou ferve.

THE Practice of True Religion, confifts principally in Two Great Branches;
giving *Honour* to God, and doing *Good* to Men. *Thou fhalt love the Lord thy
God with all thy Heart, and with all thy Soul, and with all thy Mind; This*
(fays our Saviour) *is the firft and great Commandment: And the fecond is like unto it,
Thou fhalt love thy Neighbour as thyfelf.* Under this *Second* Branch, the Duty of *Loving our* Neighbour or *Doing Good to Men*; are comprehended likewife thofe Duties
which more particularly refpect mens *Selves*, fuch as are *Sobriety, Temperance, Humility,*

S E R M.
II.

S E R M. *lity*, and the like. The *former* Branch, the Duty of *loving* God *with our whole Heart*,
II.   is by our Saviour expreſſed in *Other* words in the *Text* now read unto you, *Thou ſhalt*
     worſhip the Lord thy God, and Him only ſhalt thou ſerve. In diſcourſing upon which im-
portant Words, I ſhall obſerve the following Method.   1*ſt*, I ſhall conſider the *Suppoſi-*
tion laid down in the Text; that there is *One*, and *One Only*, True *God* or Supreme
Lord of all things; *The Lord thy God.* 2*dly*, I ſhall ſhew *What* that *Duty* towards
him is, which is expreſſed in *theſe* words, *Thou ſhalt* worſhip *the Lord thy God.* And
3*dly*, it being added, *Him* Only *ſhalt thou ſerve*; I ſhall thence take occaſion to explain
diſtinctly, the nature of the ſeveral Species of *Idolatry :* Which conſiſts, either in ſetting up *Idol-Gods*, in oppoſition to, or in conjunction with, the True God; or in worſhipping the *True God himſelf*, after an *idolatrous manner*; either repreſenting him under viſible and corporeal *Images*, or applying to him through falſe and *Idol-Mediators*,
in diminution of the Honour of the One *True Mediator*, whom God himſelf has expreſsly appointed to be Alone our Advocate, Interceſſor, and Judge.   The

I. 1*ſt*, T H I N G to be obſerved, is the *Suppoſition* laid down in the Text; that there
is *One*, and *One Only*, True *God* or Supreme *Lord* of all things ; *The Lord thy God.*
One *God :* That is, One Eternal and Infinite, One Supreme and Independent, One
All-powerful and All-wiſe, One perfectly Juſt and Merciful and Good Being.   The
God who created all things for his Own good pleaſure, and on whoſe Will depends
every Moment the continuance of their Being : *By the word of the Lord were the Hea-*
vens made, and all the Hoſt of them by the Breath of his Mouth, Pſ. xxxiii. 6.   The God
by whoſe Providence every thing is governed, ſo that *without him not a Sparrow falls*
to the ground, but even the *very hairs of our head are all numbred*, Matt. x. 29.   The
God who *hath made of one blood, all nations of men, for to dwell on all the face of the*
Earth, and hath determined the times before-appointed, and the bounds of their habita-
tion, Acts xvii. 26.   The God who, in times paſt, particularly manifeſted himſelf to
our Fathers, to *Abraham, Iſaac* and *Jacob*, and the Patriarchs : Who brought the
children of Iſrael out of *Egypt*, with an high hand and with an out-ſtretched Arm :
Who delivered the *Law* to *Moſes :* Who, in a Succeſſion of Ages, inſtructed his people
from time to time by the *Prophets :* and who, in theſe *laſt days*, hath *ſpoken unto us by*
his Son.   According to That declaration of St *Peter*; in his diſcourſe to the *Jews*,
Acts iii. 13. *The God of Abraham, and of Iſaac, and of Jacob, the God of our Fathers,*
hath glorified his Son Jeſus : And that of St *Paul*, 2 Cor. i. 3.   *God, even the Father*
of our Lord Jeſus Chriſt, the Father of Mercies, and the God of all comfort ; and ch. xi.
31. *The God and Father of our Lord Jeſus Chriſt, which is bleſſed for evermore.*

T H I S Doctrine, of the whole World being under the Government of *One God*,
is the *Natural* Notion, which the Light of *Reaſon it ſelf* has univerſally implanted in
the Minds of Men.   And had not perſons of vain and conceited Imaginations, *profeſ-*
ſing themſelves Wiſe, become Fools : Had not men of corrupt Manners, *diſliking to re-*
tain God in their Knowledge, and having *their fooliſh heart darkned*; Deifying the Souls
of their *deceaſed* Kings, out of Flattery to the *Living*; filled the minds of the ignorant
and deluded Vulgar, with a ſuperſtitious Belief of Many Gods having Rule over particular Places and Countries; The True Notion of God, ſo agreeable to the plain and
natural Dictates of unprejudiced Reaſon, might well have been preſerved among the
Nations of the Earth.   For the plain connexion, and dependence of one thing upon
another, through the whole material Univerſe ; through all parts of the Earth, and in
the viſible Heavens; The Diſpoſition of the Air, and Sea, and Winds; The Motions
of the Sun, and Moon, and Stars : and the uſeful Viciſſitudes of Seaſons, for the regular production of the various Fruits of the Earth ; have always been ſufficient to make
it evidently appear even to *mean* Capacities, (had they not been perpetually prejudiced
by wrong Inſtruction,) that all things are under the Direction of *One* Power, under

                                                                                                    the

1

the Dominion of *One* God, to whom the whole Univerſe is uniformly ſubjeᶜt. And
in faᶜt, notwithſtanding the ſtrongeſt Prejudices of long-eſtabliſhed Superſtitions and
inforced Idolatry, yet the *wiſeſt and Beſt Men,* in All *heathen-nations,* have ever ſeen
and in good meaſure maintained this Great Truth; as a Teſtimony to a degenerate and
corrupt World, that God never *left himſelf* wholly *without Witneſs,* notwithſtanding all
the provocations of Idolaters; but continually manifeſted himſelf to all reaſonable Underſtandings, *in that he did good, and gave us rain from heaven, and fruitful Seaſons,
filling our hearts with Food and Gladneſs.* But 'tis with greater *Clearneſs* from all appearance of Doubt, and with greater Aſſurance of *Authority* confirming the Diᶜtate of
Reaſon, that the *Scripture* ſets forth to us This Firſt Principle of religion. *Deut.* vi. 4.
Hear, O Iſrael, The Lord our God is One Lord; [ch. iv. 39.] *He is God in Heaven
above, and upon the Earth beneath; there is none elſe.* Again, *Iſ.* xliv. 6. *I am the
Firſt, and I am the Laſt, and beſides me there is no God;* [——*Is there a God beſides
me? yea, there is no God; I know not any.*] And in the New Teſtament, 1 *Cor.* viii. 4.
We know——*that there is none other God but One : For though there be that are* called
Gods, whether in Heaven or in Earth, (as there be many Gods;) *yet to Us there is but
One God, the Father, of whom are all things, and we in Him; and One Lord* (that is,
One Mediator.) *Jeſus Chriſt, by whom are all things, and we by Him.* This is the
Firſt thing I propoſed to conſider; The *Suppoſition* laid down in the Text, that there is
One, and *One Only* True *God* or Supreme *Lord* of all things; *The Lord thy God.*

II. 2*dly,* I A M to ſhew in the *next* place, *What* That *Duty* towards him is, which
is expreſſed *in theſe* words, *Thou ſhalt* worſhip *the Lord thy God.* And here the word,
Worſhip, muſt be underſtood in its largeſt Extent; to ſignify every religious, every virtuous Aᶜt or Habit, by which Regard is ſhown to God, either in the *Affeᶜtions* of our
Mind, or in the *Expreſſions* of our *Mouths,* or in the *Aᶜtions* of our *Life.*

1*ſt,* T H E *Worſhip* of God, as it denotes That Regard we are to bear to him in the
Affeᶜtions of our *Minds,* implies, as the Firſt Ground and Foundation of All, a firm
belief of his *Being : For he that cometh to God, muſt firſt believe that he Is, and that he
is a Rewarder of them that diligently ſeek him.* That is : Our Belief of his Exiſtence,
muſt not be a Careleſs ſpeculative acknowledgment of him, barely as a Being infinitely perfeᶜt in himſelf; but it muſt be a rational, conſiderate, and praᶜtical perſwaſion,
firmly impreſſed and fixed upon our Minds, of his being truly and literally the original
Author, and the continual Preſerver, Governour, Direᶜtor and Ruler of the Univerſe,
and of all things that are therein, by his immediate, real, living, aᶜtive Preſence, Authority and Dominion; in oppoſition to all ſceptical Notions concerning blind *Chance,*
or unintelligent *Fate.* From ſuch a Belief as This, of the Being of God; there *will*
ariſe juſt and worthy Notions of his Perfeᶜtions and Attributes. And a juſt Senſe, and
due Conſideration, of each of his Perfeᶜtions reſpeᶜtively; *will* naturally excite in us
That conſtant and proper Regard towards him in the correſpondent Affeᶜtions of our
Mind, or That internal habitual Honour and Senſe of Duty towards him, which, to
Him who ſees the Heart, is the moſt valuable and acceptable part of Worſhip. In
This Senſe therefore, the Worſhip, This internal Worſhip of God, includes the following particulars, and Others of the like nature. It implies our *fearing* his *Power*; ſo as
to be much more ſollicitous not to offend *Him,* than to fall under the Diſpleaſure of
any *Other* Perſon whatſoever : According to That Admonition of our Saviour, *Fear
not them which kill the Body, and after That have no more that they can do; But I will
forewarn you, whom ye ſhall fear; Fear Him, who, after he has killed, hath power to
caſt into Hell; yea, I ſay unto you, Fear him.* It implies our *revering* and ſtanding in
awe of His *Juſtice*; who, as *Moſes* deſcribes him, is a *Great God, mighty and terrible,* Deut. x. 17.
which regardeth not perſons, nor taketh Reward : or, as 'tis expreſſed in the book of
Job, ch. xxxiv. 19. *He accepteth not the Perſons of Princes, nor regardeth the Rich more*

SERM. *than the Poor ; for they are All the work of His hands.* It implies, our *Trusting* and
II. *Relying* upon his *Faithfulness* and *Veracity*, in all cases of Difficulty and Distress whatsoever; that, how little appearance soever there may be, in the *present* State of the
World, that *Truth* and *Righteousness* should prevail, yet the Hope of those things,
which *God, who cannot lie,* hath promised since the World began, stands for ever firm
and unshaken : So that 'tis with great reason, as well as with noble eloquence, that the
prophet *Habakkuk* expresses himself, ch. iii. 17. *Altho' the Fig-tree shall not blossom,
neither shall Fruit be in the Vines;* tho' *the labour of the Olive shall fail, and the
fields shall yield no meat;* tho' *the flock shall be cut off from the fold, and there shall
be no Herd in the Stalls; yet will I rejoice in the Lord, I will joy in the God of my
Salvation.* The *Last* instance I shall mention of the Particulars, wherein consists the
Internal Worship of God, or the proper Regard we are to bear to him in the *Affections*
of our *Minds,* is that of *Loving* him for his *Goodness. Goodness,* is the Proper Motive
and Object of *Love :* And therefore, as, comparatively speaking, *there is none* Good,
but One, that is God; He being the Alone Author of ever good thing we enjoy : so
He alone likewise, comparatively speaking, is consequently the Proper Object of *Love.*
By which *Love towards God,* we ought always carefully to observe, is Never meant
That Enthusiastick Warmth of Imagination, which is the essential character of *Fanati-
cism;* but (which is the just and proper Affection of a rational Creature towards its beneficent Author,) 'tis a *Desire* of *pleasing* him, a *Desire* of performing his Will, a *Defire* of being acceptable to him, a *Desire* of partaking of his Favour and Rewards, rather
than of the unreasonable Pleasures of Unrighteousness. This is the True Notion of *Loving* God. From whence, by the way, it clearly appears, that the Love of *Virtue* and
Truth, the Love of *Righteousness* and *Goodness,* is truly and indeed Loving of *God.* From
hence also at the same time 'tis very manifest, that mens doing their Duty with a Hope
and Prospect of *Future Rewards,* is not (as some have ridiculously argued,) a Mercenary
Temper. For the Rewards which God has promised to them that love and obey him,
are of such a Nature, as either themselves consist in, or are essentially conjoined with,
the Perfection of *Virtue.* The Rewards prepared for Them who shall be thought worthy to obtain That Life and the Resurrection from the Dead, are new Heavens and a
new Earth, wherein dwelleth *righteousness,* 2 *Pet.* iii. 13 ; where the *People shall be All
righteous,* If. lx. 21 ; in the City of God, whereinto *there shall in no wise enter any thing
that defileth, neither whosoever worketh abomination, or maketh a Lie,* Rev. xxi. 27. This
is a Reward, the Prospect and Desire whereof, in the performance of our Duty, is no
Diminution from the most exalted Love of *God,* or even of *Virtue* for Virtue's sake; but
is indeed the very same thing, or entirely coincident with, the Love of Virtue and the
Love of God. For which reason, not only *Moses;* who, *when he was come to years,
refused to be called the Son of Pharoah's Daughter ; chusing rather to suffer affliction
with the people of God, than to enjoy the Pleasures of Sin for a Season ; Esteeming the
reproach of Christ greater Riches than the Treasures in Egypt;* not only *Moses,* I say, is
in Scripture recorded, without any mark of Blame, to have *had Respect,* in all this, *to
the Recompence of Reward,* Heb. xi. 26; and *Abraham,* that he *looked for a City which
hath Foundations, whose Builder and Maker is God,* ver. 10. and the Martyrs of old,
that they endured what they did, in hopes of *obtaining a better Resurrection,* ver. 35 :
But even of our *Saviour himself* 'tis expresly affirmed, ch. xii. 2. that *for the joy which
was set before him, he endured the Cross, despising the Shame, and is sat down at the right
hand of the Throne of God.*

    2dly, THE *worshipping the Lord our God,* as it denotes primarily That *Internal* Re-
gard we are to bear towards him in the *Affections of our Minds;* so it implies likewise,
in the *next* place, our making suitable *Confession* with our *Mouths,* Rom. x. 10. *With
the Heart Man believeth unto Righteousness, and with the Mouth Confession is made unto
                                                    Salvation.*

Salvation. For 'tis our Duty, not only to have a conſtant Senſe of God upon our S E R M. own *Minds,* but to *honour* him alſo *before men,* and to promote the Knowledge of *Him* II. and his *Truth* in the World. And This Obligation, includes *Many* Particulars. The firſt and moſt obvious, is, our obligation to *make profeſſion* of the *True Religion,* how detrimental ſoever ſuch profeſſion may prove to our preſent temporal Intereſt. This is the Foundation of all the Slanders and Calumnies, of all the Reproaches and Perſecutions, which the beſt and moſt virtuous men have in all Ages and in all Nations ſuffered, upon account of their adhering to the Cauſe of Truth and Righteouſneſs. *Whoſoever,* ſays our Saviour, *ſhall confeſs me before men, him will I confeſs alſo before my Father which is in Heaven : But whoſoever ſhall deny Me before men, him will I alſo deny before my Father which is in Heaven,* Matt. x. 32. And ſtill more diſtinctly, *Mark* viii. 38. *Whoſoever ſhall be aſhamed of Me and of my Words, in this adulterous and ſinful generation, of him alſo ſhall the Son of Man be aſhamed, when he cometh in the glory of his Father with the Holy Angels.* This therefore is the firſt and principal Inſtance of *Confeſſing God* with our *Mouths ;* The making conſtant *Profeſſion* of the True Doctrine of Religion, how much ſoever we may poſſibly ſuffer thereby in our temporal Intereſt. Nor need I here to have added the word *poſſibly ;* Since indeed it can ſcarce poſſibly be otherwiſe, but that mens ſtedfaſtly adhering to what is True and Right, will always be more or leſs hurtful to their Temporal Intereſt. For though *in the general,* the Profeſſion of Chriſtian Religion does not now expoſe men to perſecution, as in the Apoſtles Days ; but on the contrary, Chriſtianity is in Some Countries publickly ſupported and encouraged : yet in the *particular* circumſtances of life, ſuch is the Ignorance and Superſtition, ſuch the Prejudices, Paſſions, and Animoſities of Men ; that whoſoever will not ſuffer himſelf to be ſwayed, according to the Cuſtoms of a corrupt Age, by Other Arguments than thoſe of Truth and Right ; will certainly loſe very many Advantages ; and perhaps be deſpiſed and ill-ſpoken of for ſo doing : *yea, and All that will live godly in Chriſt Jeſus,* ſays the Apoſtle, ſhall *ſuffer perſecution,* 2 Tim. iii. 12. *Next* therefore to the *Profeſſion* of True Religion in *general,* there is *further* implied in this Duty of *Confeſſing God with our Mouths,* an obligation not to be aſhamed of *Truth and Right,* of *Virtue* and *Goodneſs,* in all *particular* Caſes wherein they may happen to be conteſted. St. *Paul,* as he declared in *general,* that he was *not aſhamed of the Goſpel of Chriſt,* Rom. i. 16 ; ſo, when in a *particular circumſtance* he judged St. *Peter* to have departed from the Simplicity of the Goſpel, he *withſtood him to the Face,* Gal. ii. 11. And 'tis accordingly excellent Advice which is given by the Son of *Sirach,* Eccluſ. iv. 20. *Beware of Evil, and be not aſhamed when it concerns thy Soul : For there is a ſhame that bringeth Sin, and there is a ſhame which is glory and grace : Accept no perſon againſt thy Soul, and let not thy Reverence of any man cauſe thee to fall : Refrain not to ſpeak, when there is occaſion to do good : ſtrive for the Truth unto death, and the Lord ſhall fight for thee.* Promoting ſteddily the Intereſt of Truth and Virtue, is making confeſſion of *God,* who is the Author of Truth, and whoſe Glory and Honour is the eſtabliſhment of Virtue and Righteouſneſs. In theſe things conſiſts the Kingdom of God ; in theſe conſiſts the excellency of rational Creatures : And when men of corrupt Minds deſpiſe every thing as Folly and Enthuſiaſm, that happens not to ſerve the Intereſts of Covetouſneſs and Ambition ; *then* to adhere ſtedfaſtly to Truth and Virtue, notwithſtanding all the Contempt that may be caſt upon them, is what our Saviour calls, *not being aſhamed of Him, and of his words, in an adulterous and perverſe generation.* The remaining particulars included in this Duty of *confeſſing God with our mouths,* are, *ſpeaking honourably* of him, or reverencing his Name, in all *private* converſation ; and paying him Solemn *Worſhip* in *publick.* And *Theſe* Inſtances of Duty, will not eaſily be neglected by Such perſons, whoſe Minds have made natural to themſelves the fore-mentioned Habits of Virtue. For in like manner as our Saviour argues

in

SERM. in Another cafe, *Mark* ix. 39. *There is no man which fhall do a Miracle in my Name,*
II. *that can lightly fpeak evil of Me* ; fo here likewife, there is no man who habitually
loves *Truth and Virtue*, that can eafily fpeak difhonourably of *God*, the Supreme Good,
or lightly take his Name in vain, or that will not take pleafure in promoting his *Pub-lick Honour* and *Worfhip*, But

3*dly*, and laftly : T H E *Worfhip* of God, as it denotes the Regard we are to bear to
him in the *Affections* of our *Minds*, and in the *Expreffions* of our *Mouths* ; fo it includes
likewife, and that principally and chiefly, the Honour we are to pay him in all the
Actions of our *Lives*. It includes This, I fay, *principally* and *chiefly*. For, worfhip-ping God with our *Lips*, unlefs accompanied with Obedience in our *Lives*, is nothing
more than a Solemn Hypocrify, and is an Abomination before God. And the Regard
we bear to him in the Affections of our *Minds*, can by This only Proof be fhown, ei-ther to Others or to Ourfelves, to be real and fincere ; if it caufes us to *imitate* him,
and to endeavour to *pleafe* him, by a *Life* of *Virtue* and *true Holinefs*. For by the
Fruit only, as our Saviour directs, can we poffibly make a right judgment of the Good-nefs of the *Tree*. The Sacrifice therefore *moft acceptable* unto God, is that which St
Paul elegantly ftiles, *Rom.* xii. 1. *the prefenting* Our felves *a* Living *Sacrifice, Holy,
acceptable unto God, which is our Reafonable Service*. *Other* things are not to be left
undone, and the *external* Worfhip of God is by no means to be neglected ; But the
End and Great Defign of All, is the uniform Practice of *Virtue and Righteoufnefs*, in
the whole Courfe of our Lives. In all *comparative* Speaking, *Behold, to* obey, *is bet-ter than Sacrifice* ; *and to hearken, than the Fat of Rams* : Or, as it is expreffed by the
Scribe, whom our Lord commends, in the Gofpel, *Mark* xii. 33. *To love God with all
the Heart,*——*and his Neighbour as himfelf, is more than all whole burnt-offerings and
Sacrifices.*

A N D Now, having thus largely and diftinctly explained, [1*ft* the *Suppofition* laid
down in the Text ; that there is *One*, and *One Only*, True *God* or Supreme *Lord* of all
things ; and 2*dly*, *What* That *Duty* towards him is, which is expreffed in] *thefe* words,
Thou fhalt worfhip *the Lord God* : I fhould in the

III. N E X T place, from the following words, *And him* Only *fhalt thou ferve*, have
proceeded to explain the nature of the feveral Species of *Idolatry* : Which is the Great
Breach of this fundamental Commandment. But the Time will not permit me to enter
upon the Confideration of This matter, till a further opportunity.

SERMON

S E R M O N III.

Of the UNITY of GOD.

MATT. IV. 10. latter part.

Thou fhalt worfhip the Lord thy God, and Him only fhalt thou ferve.

IN difcourfing upon thefe important words of our Saviour; I propofed, *1ft*, to con- S E R M.
fider the *Suppofition* laid down in the Text; that there is *One*, and *One Only*, True   III.
God or Supreme *Lord* of all things; *The Lord thy God*. *2dly*, to fhow *What* That
Duty towards him is, which is expreffed in *thefe* words, *Thou fhalt* worfhip *the Lord
thy God*. And *3dly*, it being added, *Him Only fhalt thou ferve*, from thence I propofed to take an occafion of explaining diftinctly, the nature of the feveral Species of *Idolatry*: Which is the Great Breach of this fundamental Commandment.

THE two Former of thefe Heads I have already gone through; Having largely
fhown, that there is *One*, and *One Only*, True *God*, or Supreme *Lord* of all things;
ftiled here by our Saviour, *The Lord thy God*: And that our *Duty* towards him, expreft in *Thefe* words, *Thou fhalt* worfhip *the Lord thy God*; denotes every religious,
every virtuous Act or Habit, by which Regard is fhown to God, either in the *Affections*
of our *Minds*, or in the *Expreffions* of our *Mouths*, or in the *Actions* of our *Lives*.

IT remains, that I proceed at this time from the latter part of the Text, *And Him
Only fhalt thou ferve*, to explain diftinctly the Nature of the feveral Species of Idolatry. Which Sin confifts, either in fetting up *Idol-Gods*, in oppofition to, or in conjunction with, the True God; or in worfhipping the *True God himfelf*, after an *idolatrous manner*; either reprefenting him under vifible and corporeal *Images*, or applying
to him through falfe and *Idol-Mediators*, in diminution of the Honour of the One *True
Mediatour*, whom God himfelf has exprefsly appointed to be Alone our Advocate, Interceffor, and Judge.

1. THE *Firft* and Higheft Degree of Idolatry is, when men totally cafting off all
Belief of the True God, fet up, in direct *oppofition* to Him, fome imagination of their
own, if not as a formal Object of Worfhip, yet at leaft as That to which Alone they
afcribe all thofe great Effects, which are indeed the bountiful Gifts of God to Mankind, and the fovereign Benefits of his Government over the World. Of This kind
are the Notions which Some men frame to themfelves, of *Nature, Fate, Chance*, and
the like; when they afcribe the Being and Order, the Beauty and Ufefulnefs of the
World and all things that are therein, to Thefe as their real Caufes; which in Truth
are nothing but mere empty words, mere abftract Notions, mere Fictions or *Idols* of
the Imagination, which have no real Exiftence, or (as St *Paul* expreffes himfelf in a
like cafe) are *Nothing in the World*. For, What is *Nature*? What is *Fate*, or *Chance*?
Are they any real Beings, or Agents? or can That be truly the Caufe of any thing,
which itfelf has really no fubfiftence? or are not thefe Notions plainly the mere Re-
fuges of Ignorance, and the thin Cover of affected Perverfenefs? Lefs unreafonable of
the two, were thofe antient Idolaters, who ftopping fhort at the immediate and vifible

SERM.
III.

Caufes of the Life and Food and Plenty they injoyed, worfhipped the Sun and Moon and Stars of Heaven, as the *Authors* of That Good, whereof they were really and undeniably the *Inftruments*. Lefs unreafonable, I fay, was even *This*, than to attribute the caufes of all things, to the efficiency of a mere abftract Nothing. And yet the worfhipping thefe glorious and moft noble parts of the vifible Univerfe, was a Folly altogether without Excufe, even in the darkeft Times of heathen-ignorance; Becaufe Reafon itfelf, without Any Revelation, was abundantly fufficient to lead men from the wonderful operations of unintelligent and lifelefs Matter, to the Knowledge of an Intelligent, Living, and All-wife Caufe. For, *the invifible things of God from the creation of the World are clearly feen, being underftood by the things that are made, even his eternal Power and Godhead*, Rom. i. 20. So that *Job* (who appears not to have had any knowledge of the Jewifh religion) could fay: *If I beheld the Sun when it fhined, or the Moon walking in brightnefs; and my Heart hath been fecretly inticed, or my mouth hath kiffed my hand: This also were an iniquity to be punifhed by the judge; for I fhould have denied the God that is above.* Which natural knowledge of God, when men had once fuffered to be corrupted; and had *changed the Truth of God into a Lye, worfhipping and ferving the Creature inftead of the Creator, who is Bleffed for ever*; Idolatry quickly fpread itfelf into *Many Branches*: And as Some worfhipped the Hoft of Heaven, the Sun and Moon and Stars, becaufe of their Beauty and Ufefulnefs; fo Others, carried away with Flattery towards their Kings and Governours, deified and worfhipped, after their Deaths, thofe who in their life-time, for exercifing Lordfhip over them, had been ftiled Benefactors. This latter was the Idolatry of the Antient *Greeks* and *Romans*; thofe *Learned* Nations, who in all *other* refpects improved and civilized themfelves to fuch a degree, and cultivated all Arts and Sciences to fo high a Pitch, that all Countries in the World, in comparifon of *Them*, were ftiled and juftly accounted *barbarous*. But their *Religion*, thefe Learned and Famous Nations received in the blindeft and moft ftupid manner, by Tradition from their ignorant and barbarous Anceftors; their *Jupiter* himfelf, the Object of their moft folemn Worfhip, being no other than a *King*, who, in the antient dark and fabulous Ages, had reigned in the Ifle of *Crete*. Of the fame kind, feems to have been the idolatry of the *Chaldeans*, at the time when *Abram*, in order to fet up the worfhip of the True God, departed *out of his country, and from his Kindred, and from his Father's houfe*, Gen. xii. 1. And afterwards in the kingdom of Ifrael, *Baal*; concerning whom we find *Elijah* thus fpeaking to the people; *If Jehovah be God, follow him; but if Baal, then follow him*; This *Baal* (I fay) was no other than [*Belus*] an antient King of *Affyria*, whofe Worfhip *Ahab* had eftablifhed in fuch direct oppofition to the Worfhip of the *God of Heaven*.

1 Kings xviii. 21.

2. THE *next* Species of Idolatry, is, when men fet up falfe Gods, not indeed totally in *exclufion of*, but in *conjunction with* the Worfhip of the One True God of the Univerfe. Of *This* kind was the idolatry of thofe *Heathens*, who though they knew and acknowledged the True God, from that Light of Nature and Reafon and the Works of Creation, which the before-mentioned more ftupid Idolaters had no regard to; yet at the fame time they worfhipped alfo many Other imaginary Deities, as *Parts* or *Branches* or particular *Manifeftations* of the Supreme Being, in particular *Places* or upon particular *occafions*. Not much unlike to which, was the Practice of thofe *Samaritans*, 2 Kings xvii. 33 and 41. who *feared the* Lord, *and* yet at the fame time, as the Text tells us, *ferved* alfo *their* own Gods *after the manner of the Nations*. Under the fame Head, may be reduced the opinion of the *Syrians* in *Ahab's* time; who fancied that different parts of the World, were under the dominion and government of different Gods: Concerning whom we read, 1 *Kings* xx. 28, that *the Syrians faid, The Lord is God of the Hills, but he is not God of the Valleys.* Laftly, of the fame kind was the idolatrous notion of the *Manichees* in later times, even fince the times of

Habentes phantafma idololatriæ, fays Irenæus of the Valentinian Emanations.

the

the Gofpel; who taught that *Good* proceeded from a Supreme Almighty *Good* Being, S E R M.
and that at the fame time *Evil* proceeded from another equally Supreme All-powerful   III.
Evil Being.

3. A *Third* Sort or Degree of Idolatry, is, when men worfhip indeed the *True God*,
and Him Only, but yet after an *idolatrous manner*; reprefenting him under *vifible and
corporeal Images*.   God is a *fpiritual* Being; a Being of infinite *Greatnefs, Power* and
Majefty; whom the Heavens, and the Heaven of Heavens cannot contain.   And 'tis
the greateft indignity imaginable to conceive, that he who *made the World and all
things that are therein*, who *giveth unto All Life and Breath*, and whofe *Offspring* (or
the *Work of whofe hands*) even *Men* and all rational *Spirits* are, fhould himfelf be *like
unto* (or can be reprefented by) *gold, or filver, or ftone, graven by Art and Man's De-* Acts xvii 29.
vice.   And therefore 'tis with great Juftice that St *Paul* reproves even the Heathen-
world, in that, *when they knew God* by the Light of Nature and Reafon, yet, contrary
to reafon, *they changed the glory of the uncorruptible God, into an Image made like to
corruptible man, and to birds, and fourfootted beafts, and creeping things*, Rom. i. 23.
To the *Jews*, God, in the *Second Commandment*, confirmed this Law of Nature, by a
literal and exprefs prohibition, that they fhould not make to themfelves any image or
reprefentation of *him*, under the fimilitude of any creature whatfoever; of any thing
either in the *Heavens, Earth,* or *Water*; of Sun, Moon, or Stars; of *Men, Beafts,*
or *Fifhes*.   To reprefent God, the invifible Author of all Good, under the likenefs of
thofe moft *excellent* of all the vifible parts of the creation, thofe moft *beneficial* inftruments and conveyers of his Bleffings to Mankind, the *Sun, Moon,* and *Stars*; which
in Scripture is called *worfhipping the Hoft of Heaven*:   To *This*, I fay, one *may poffibly*
conceive, how in the days of ignorance there *might be* fome Temptation: And therefore, not without very apparent reafon, the Scripture is diftinct and particular, in fetting forth how all thefe things were brought into Being, *merely* by *His* Will and
Power; that for *His* pleafure *alone* they *Are, and were created*; that the *Heavens* are
the Work of His *hands*, and that 'tis His *Sun that fhineth on the evil and on the good.*
Alfo, *Man* being the Lord of this lower world; that weak minds fhould be tempted to
reprefent God under a *Humane* fimilitude, *This* likewife may eafily be accounted for.
But that any one fhould ever be *fo abfurd*, as to reprefent the Almighty Lord and Father of the Univerfe, under the likenefs of *Birds, and Beafts, and creeping things*;
This is a degree of ftupidity that would be altogether incredible, did not *profane hiftory*
affure us of the Folly of the *Egyptians* in this kind, and the *facred hiftory* give us a very
particular Account how the *Jews themfelves* in the wildernefs *changed their glory into
the fimilitude of a calf that eateth hay*; faying, This *is the God that brought thee out of
the land of Egypt*, and *proclaiming a Feaft* to it under the Sacred Name of *Jehovah*;
And *Jeroboam*, in after times, caufed *Ifrael to fin* again the fame Sin, by fetting up
Calves in *Dan* and *Bethel*, as Reprefentatives of the God of Heaven, who had commanded himfelf to be worfhipped without any Image in the Temple of *Jerufalem.*
Nay, even after the greater Light of the *Gofpel*; Chriftians, as they ftile themfelves, in
the Church of *Rome*, have not been a whit behind the groffeft antient Idolaters, in
their corruptions of This kind; making Pictures and Images of the Invifible God, even
of the Father Almighty, in exprefs oppofition to the Second Commandment.   And in
the matter of Tranfubftantiation; fancying the elements to be changed into the Body of
Chrift, and knowing the Body of Chrift to be in union with his Divinity, and his Divinity to be in union with that of his Father; from hence, by three or four fteps of
multiplied idolatry, they pay to the mere elements of bread and wine, That Worfhip
which indeed is due only to the God and Father of All, even to Him who *fo loved the*
World, *as to give his only begotten Son, that whofoever believeth in him, fhould not
perifh, but have everlafting Life.*   In which and the like cafes, an unaccountable Ty-

ranny

SERM. ranny has for many Ages compelled Learned men to employ their whole skill and abi-
III. lities, not in getting a right understanding of things, but in defending implicitly what
ignorant and unlearned Persons had decided for them before.

4. Another *Kind* or *Species* of Idolatry, is when Men apply themselves to God
through *False* and *Idol-Mediators*, in diminution of the Honour of the *One True Mediator*, whom God himself has expressly appointed to be *Alone* our Advocate, Intercessor and Judge. *God who at sundry times and in divers manners spake in times past
unto the Fathers by the Prophets, hath in these last days spoken unto us by his Son*; who,
*when he had by himself purged our Sins, sat down on the right hand of the Majesty on
High*; where *he ever liveth, to make intercession for us.* To Us Christians therefore, as

1 Cor. viii. 6. *there is* (if we will use St *Paul's* expression) *One God, even the Father, of whom are
all things*; so there is also *One Lord, even Jesus Christ, through whom are all things.*
For there is One God, and One Mediator between God and Men, the Man Christ Jesus,
1 Tim. ii. 5. As therefore the setting up any Idol or *False God*, in opposition to, or in
conjunction with the *True God*, is Idolatry with regard to *God*; so the setting up any
Idol or *False Mediator*, in opposition to, or in conjunction with the *One True Mediator*,
is Idolatry with regard to *Christ*. Which most evidently shows, that the Worship paid
by the Church of *Rome* to *Angels*, and to *Saints departed*, to *Images* and *Relicks*, and
to the *Blessed Virgin*, whom they profanely stile the *Mother of God*; is truly and properly *Idolatry*: And that the Excuse they plead, that the Worship thus paid, is not
Divine, but only *Mediatorial* Worship; is nothing to the purpose, and alters not at
all the *Nature*, but only a *Circumstance* of the Crime: An *Idol*-Mediator being as
truly and plainly an *Idol*, and a departing from *Christ* our only true *Mediator* and *Advocate*; as the worshipping an *Idol*-God, is a departure from the *Living and True God.*
St *Paul* argues in this manner expressly and most prophetically; *Col.* ii. 18; *Let no man
beguile you of your Reward, in a voluntary humility* [or *will-worship*, ver. 23.] *and
worshipping of Angels*; *intruding into those things which he hath not seen, vainly puffed
up by his fleshly mind, And not holding the Head*, which is Christ. And the same thing
was long before prophesied of by *Daniel*, ch. xi. 38; when speaking of *Antichrist*, he
foretells concerning him, that not only *a God whom his Fathers knew not, should he honour*, that is, should corrupt the true Notion and Worship of God; but moreover, that
he should *honour* also *Gods of Forces*, or (as it is more rightly rendred in the *Margin* of
the Bible) should worship divers *Gods-Protectors*, that is, Saints, and Angels, and
Images, on whom men should rely for Protection and Salvation.

5. *Fifthly* and *Lastly*; Besides, all these several Kinds and Degrees of Idolatry,
literally and strictly so called; there are also several *other* things, which because they
are, in different ways and manners, a departing in some measure from God, and placing
our reliance or our affections upon some wrong Object; they are therefore in Scripture
figuratively, and by way of analogy or proportion, represented as *Idolatrous* Practices.
Thus St *Peter* describes those *Jewish Proselytes*, who had indulged themselves in being
present, though not perhaps at the actual Worship, yet at the *Idol-Feasts* of the Heathen; he describes them as having *wrought the Will of the Gentiles*——*in revellings,
banquetings, and abominable* idolatries, 1 *Pet.* iv. 3. And St *Paul*, speaking of *Jews*,
who never had *literally* been idolaters, but, neglecting the true Will of God, had
placed their whole Trust upon what he there calls *the weak and beggarly elements* of a
formal and ceremonious religion, namely, their Superstitious observation of *days and
months and times and years*; he thus expresses his censure of them, *Gal.* iv. 8; *then
when ye knew not God, ye did service unto Them* [unto those things] *which by nature are
no Gods.* And among *Christians*, mens taking delight in promoting Corruptions of Religion introduced by human power and violence, the Scripture calls *falling down and
worshipping the wild Beast*, that is, paying more regard to the Will of oppressive and un-

reasonable

reafonable *Men*, than to the Will of *God*; [And worſhipping *the* Image *of the Beaſt*, SERM. that is, (with ſome alluſion perhaps to *Nebuchadnezzar's* golden Image,) being fond   III. of falſe and ſuperſtitious religions, ſet up for the ſake of Worldly Power, Dominion and Grandeur, by Popes and Papal Councils, thoſe *Images* of Authority ſitting in the Seat and Temple of God, deceiving the Rulers and Nations of the Earth.] Further yet : Becauſe men who have no right Senſe of God upon their Minds, are very apt to place That Whole *Truſt* and *Reliance* upon the *Riches* and *Power* of this preſent World; which ought to be placed upon God Alone; hence St *Paul*, by a very elegant figure, thus expreſſes himſelf; *Covetouſneſs, which is Idolatry*; and *Covetous man, who is an* Col. iii. 5. *Idolater*: And *charges them who are rich in this World,*——*not to* Truſt *in uncertain* Eph. v. 5. Riches, *but in the Living* God. And our Saviour himſelf, in the ſame figure and man- 1 Tim. vi. 17. ner of ſpeaking, declares, *Matt*. vi. 24, *No man can ſerve* (no man can worſhip) *two Maſters,*——*ye cannot ſerve God and Mammon.* Laſtly : Becauſe very *vicious* and *debauched* perſons, have no regard, no intention, no deſire of *pleaſing God*; but are wholly intent upon *pleaſing* and gratifying their own *corrupt inclinations*, and entirely *Servants* and *Slaves* to their *pleaſures*; therefore the Apoſtle elegantly repreſents *Theſe* alſo, as figurative Idolaters; *whoſe God is their Belly*, Phil. iii. 19; and who *ſerve not our Lord Jeſus Chriſt, but their own Belly*, Rom. xvi. 18.

HAVING thus at large explained the *Nature, Kinds,* and *Degrees* of Idolatry in the *literal* ſenſe; and in what manner 'tis ſometimes applied alſo *figuratively* to *Other Vices* : I ſhall conclude with a general Obſervation, or two, upon the whole. And

1ſt, I OBSERVE, that *Idolatry* is a Crime which all men hugely deteſt the *Name* of, and yet it is very apt to grow upon ſuperſtitious perſons by inſenſible degrees. Thus the *Jews*, tho' God had given them the moſt expreſs Command in the World, that as they had never ſeen any ſimilitude of him, ſo they ſhould never repreſent him by any Image, or by the Likeneſs of Any Creature whatſoever; yet firſt they ſet up in the wilderneſs the *golden Calf*, upon a *particular occaſion*; and afterwards they *eſtabliſhed Jeroboam's calves*, in *Dan* and *Bethel*, for a *conſtancy*; as *repreſentations* of the *True God* : And from thence they fell to worſhip the Image of *Baal*, who was a Falſe *God* : And, by degrees, the *Gods of the Nations*, whom the Lord had caſt out from before them, crept in amongſt them ; Till at length they proceeded to that Heighth of Impiety, as to *Sacrifice even their own Children to Moloch.* In like manner among *Chriſtians*, departed *Saints* were at firſt very honourably ſpoken of, as having been Martyrs *for the Word of God and for the Teſtimony of Jeſus*; and their *Relicks* began to be had in eſteem, as *Memorials* of them. Afterwards, This veneration towards them increaſed, to the ſetting them up as *Advocates* and *Interceſſors* with God ; which was directly idolizing them, to the great diminution of the Honour due to *Chriſt* our *Only Mediatour.* In order to preſerve the *Remembrance* of theſe Saints the better, *Pictures* and *Images* were introduced ; firſt as *hiſtorical* repreſentations only, to aſſiſt the Memory : But after a while, peculiar *Favours* and *Bleſſings*, and a ſingular *efficaciouſneſs of Prayers*, were believed to be annexed to the *places* wherein ſuch *Images*, or ſuch or ſuch a particular *Image* was ſet up : Juſt as *Balaam*, when God would not permit him to curſe *Iſrael* from *One hill*, fanſied he might curſe them from *Another.* And at laſt, when This corruption arrived at its heighth, the *Worſhip* came to be paid directly to the *Images themſelves*, even to *wood and ſtone*; men who call themſelves Chriſtians, *falling down to the ſtock of a Tree* ; to idols that *have eyes and ſee not, and ears and hear not : They that make them, are like unto them, and ſo are all ſuch as put their truſt in them*, Pſ. cxv. 8.

2dly, I OBSERVE, that, in the whole Scripture-hiſtory, there is no Crime attended with a greater *general corruption of manners*, or conſtantly threatned with a *ſeverer puniſhment*, than this of *idolatry* in every kind and degree of it. Among the *Heathens, for* This *cauſe*, ſays St *Paul*, (for their departing from the Law of Nature in

S E R M. This point,) *God gave men up unto vile affections, and ——— to a reprobate mind,*
III.   Rom. i. 26, 28. And for *This* cause originally, did God root out the seven nations of
the *Canaanites* from before the children of *Ifrael.* The *Jews,* whenever They fell into
any degree of this Crime, immediately the confequences became intolerable. When
they had erected the golden calf, *the people fat down to eat and drink, and rofe up to
play,* i. e. to *debauch* themfelves. And *Balaam* tempted them to *idolatry* and *fornication* together : And then *God gave them up to worfhip the Hoft of Heaven.* And at
length (as I before obferved) they came to *facrifice even their children to Moloch.* To
prevent thefe Evils, God, at the firft giving of the Law, ftrictly forbad all Approaches
to this vice ; and by his Prophets conftantly declared, that he *would not give his Honour to another, nor his Praife to graven Images.* He commanded, not only *actual
idolatry,* but even mens *tempting* each other to it, to be punifhed with *Death.* He
threatned, that, for *This* Crime, he would *vifit the Sins of the Fathers upon the children unto the third and fourth generation ;* That is, Upon a People under a *national*
covenant, and Bleffed or *beloved* (as St *Paul* fpeaks) for *the Fathers fakes,* he would,
for their *national* irreligion, fend down very *Long* temporal Judgments. And This
threatning has actually been fulfilled upon them in fuch a captivity and fuch a difperfion, as never happened to any other nation upon the Face of the Earth.

A m o n g *Chriftians,* (for the greater part even of *Thofe alfo* who call themfelves
Chriftians, have for many Ages been *Idolaters,* as the Kingdom of *Ifrael* had been be-
fore;) Among *Chriftians,* I fay, the introducing This Vice, has not only corrupted the
Simplicity of the Gofpel, but has alfo greatly encouraged all immorality, by making
Superftition an equivalent inftead of a virtuous Life ; and particularly it has been the
caufe of infinite Cruelties and Perfecutions among Chriftians, in order to fupport tyranny and Superftition ; infomuch that even of the *Chriftian Church* it is prophefied in
Scripture, that *in her fhould be found the blood of Saints and of Prophets, and of all
that are flain upon the Earth.* For our deliverance from this tyranny by the Reformation, we can never be too thankful ; nor ever fufficiently careful, to guard againft every
appearance of approaching towards it again.

SERMON

SERMON IV.

Of the ETERNITY of GOD.

REV. I. 8.

I am Alpha and Omega, the Beginning and the Ending, faith the Lord ; which is, and which was, and which is to come, The Almighty.

THESE words are a defcription of the Perfon of the *God* and *Father* of All, from the *Primary Attributes* of his *Nature*, and from the *Part* which he is reprefented to bear peculiarly in *delivering This Prophecy*. In the *giving of* This *Prophecy*, he is *Alpha and Omega*, the Firft Author and the laft End of all. For the whole Prophecy is, *The Revelation of Jefus Chrift, which* God, [that is, the *Father*,] *gave unto him*, ver. 10. And the *manner* of his giving it, is very elegantly defcribed, *ch.* iv. and v. by a reprefentation of God fitting upon a Throne, Supreme over all ; and giving unto the Lamb a Book, which none other but He, in Heaven or on Earth, was worthy to open. Likewife *abfolutely*, with regard to his Proper *Nature*, the primary Attributes of the God and Father of All, are ; He is *Alpha and Omega, the Beginning and the End*, the firft Author and Fountain from whom all things originally proceed, and the ultimate End in whom all things finally terminate ; He is, " *which is, and which was, and which is to come*," eternal of himfelf by abfolute neceffity of Nature, being derived from None, begotten of None, proceeding from None. Laftly, He is, *The Almighty*, Supreme abfolutely over all ; For fo the word in the Original Properly fignifies ; including every *one* of the Divine Attributes, and not, as the *Englifh* word founds, all Power *only*. The former part of this Defcription, *viz.* the words, *I am Alpha and Omega, the Beginning and the End*, are alfo applied to *Chrift*, ver. 11. of *This* chapter, and ver. 13. of the xxiid chapter ; In which places they fignify, that our Saviour, by the good pleafure of the Father, *(all things* being *delivered unto him of the Father*, Matt. xi. 27.) is the *Beginner* and *Completer* of our Salvation ; the *Alpha* and the *Omega, the* Author *and the* Finifher *of our Faith*, as St *Paul* paraphrafes the words, *Heb.* xii. 2. But in the *Text*, 'tis evident thefe words are fpoken of *the Father* ; both from their being joined immediately with the following words, *which is, and which was, and which is to come*, which in the 4th verfe are ufed exprefs as a periphrafis, or diftinguifhing Defcription of the *Perfon of the Father* ; And the fame thing appears alfo from the whole Thread and Connexion of the Difcourfe. For the *Three* Divine Perfons, as bearing fo many Diftinct parts in the delivering of This prophecy, are *Thrice* diftinctly mentioned in This chapter. Firft, in the Preface or Title, ver. 1. *The Revelation of* Jefus Chrift ; *which* God *gave unto him* ;——*and he fent and fignified it by his* Angel, [*his Meffenger*,] *unto his Servant John.* Then *again* in the Salutation, ver. 4, *Grace be unto you, and Peace from him which is, and which was, and which is to come*, (that is, from the *Father* ;) *and from the feven Spirits which are before his Throne*, (that is, from the Holy Ghoft, whofe Minifters all the prophetick

S E R M. Spirits are;) *and from Jesus Christ, who is the Faithful Witness.* The Salutation is the
V.   same, (only in sublime words according to the prophetick Style,) with That of St *Paul*;
The Grace of our Lord Jesus Chrift, *and the Love of* God, *and the Fellowship of the
Holy Ghost.* Then the *third* time, in the Body of the Difcourfe, or in the entrance of
the defcription of the Vifion it felf, he refumes his mention of *the Father,* ver. 8. *I am
Alpha and Omega, the Beginning and the Ending, faith the Lord; which is, and which
was, and which is to come, the Almighty;* And his mention of the *Holy Ghost,* ver. 10.
I was in the Spirit; And of the *Son,* ver. 13, 18. *I faw one like unto the Son of Man,
——faying,——I am he that liveth and was dead, and behold I am alive for evermore.*

T H E Occafion and Connexion of the words being thus explained; the Doctrine from
thence arifing to be difcourfed upon at this time, is That primary Attribute of the Divine Nature, his abfolute and independent *Eternity. I am Alpha and Omega, the Beginning and the Ending, faith the Lord; which is, and which was, and which is to
come.*

I N difcourfing upon which Subject, I fhall 1*ft*, briefly fet forth in general the feveral
Significations we find in Scripture of the words *eternal, immortal,* and *everlafting.*
2*dly*, I fhall offer fome Obfervations, concerning the *Eternity of* God in particular.
And 3*dly*, (which is the moft material,) I fhall confider of what *Ufe* this Meditation
may be to us in *Practice.*

I N the *Firft* place, 'tis very neceffary in general, for preventing Confufion in our
Notions, and for the more diftinct explication of feveral Paffages in Scripture, to obferve
the different Senfes in which the words *eternal, immortal* and *everlafting,* are ufed by the
facred Writers.

S O M E T I M E S, (which is the *loweft* Senfe they are ever taken in, and yet a very
frequent one,) they fignify nothing more but only a *long* duration. Thus *Gen.* xvii. 8.
I will give unto thee the land wherein thou art a ftranger, for an everlafting *poffeffion;*
the meaning is, to him and his Heirs for a *long,* unlimited fucceffion. *Num.* x. 8. *The
Sons of Aaron fhall blow with the Trumpets, and they fhall be to you for an Ordinance* for
ever: for ever, that is, as long as your government and eftablifhment fhall laft. *Gen.*
xlix. 26. The *Hills* are called *Everlafting;* And *Hab.* iii. 6. the *everlafting Mountains;*
By which words all that is intended to be exprefs'd, is, their being ftrong and permanent
as the frame and conftitution of the Earth. 1 *Sam.* iii. 13. *I have told Eli, that I will
judge his houfe* for ever: It fignifies only, for many fucceffive generations. And *Exod.*
xxi. 6. *He fhall ferve his Mafter for* ever. The meaning is, He fhall not go free at the
end of the ufual Term of feven years, but fhall continue with him till his Mafter's
Death, or till the year of Jubilee. This is the firft and loweft Senfe of the words *eternal*
and *for ever;* to fignify only, after a figurative manner of fpeaking, a certain *long*
Period.

T H E *next* Senfe they are ufed in, is to denote a Duration continuing as long as the
Subject exifts, and then putting it in a State out of which it fhall never be reftored.
Thus *Num.* xxiv. 20. *Amalek was the firft of the Nations, but his latter End fhall be,
that he perifh for ever;* The meaning is, He fhall never recover to be again a mighty
Nation. *Deut.* xiii. 16. *That City fhall be an Heap* for ever; the Senfe is, as it follows
in the very next words, *it fhall not be built again.* But the moft remarkable Paffage of
all, to our prefent purpofe, is that expreffion of St *Jude,* ver. 7. *Even as Sodom and
Gommorrha, and the Cities about them,——are fet forth for an Example, fuffering the
vengeance of eternal Fire.* 'Tis plain the Apoftle does not here mean *Hell-Fire,* becaufe *That,* being at prefent *invifible,* cannot be faid to be *fet forth for an* Example,
but as a *Threatning* only. Whatever is *fet forth for an Example,* muft be fomething
that is *already* prefent, or paft: And therefore *the Vengeance of eternal Fire,* muft in

                                                                   this

this place fignify only *That Fire*, which irrecoverably deftroyed the Cities of *Sodom*, and ended in their final or eternal overthrow.

IN *other* places of Scripture, the words *eternal* and *for ever*, fignify in a *higher* Senfe, a Duration, not figuratively, but *properly and literally everlafting* ; without *End*, though not without *Beginning*. Thus *Angels* and the Souls of Men are *eternal*, or *immortal* ; and the *Happinefs* they enjoy in Heaven, is *everlafting* Life, an *endlefs* and *eternal* weight of Glory.

Laftly, THE Laft and *higheft* and moft abfolutely perfect Senfe of the words, *eternal*, and *everlafting*, is when they fignify a Duration of inexhauftible and never-failing permanency, both without *Beginning*, and without *End* ; And not only fo, but including alfo *Neceffary* and *Independent* Exiftence, fo as in *no* manner whatfoever to *derive* from any other. He who Thus exifts, exifts *of himfelf* abfolutely, as the Firft Fountain and Origin of all Being, totally felf-fufficient, and independent of Any. And this is the peculiar property and diftinguifhing *perfonal* character, of the *Father only* ; [of Him, by whofe good pleafure all Creatures were created ; of Him, from whom the Holy Spirit [it felf] proceedeth ; of Him, by whom the Son [himfelf] was begotten ; of Him, who in the higheft and moft fuperlative Senfe of the words, is *He which is, and which was, and which is to come.*

HAVING thus briefly in the *firft* place, for preventing Confufion in our Notions, and for the more diftinct explication of feveral paffages in Scripture, fet forth in general the different fenfes in which the words *eternal*, *immortal* and *everlafting*, are made ufe of by the facred Writers : I proceed now, in the *Second* place, to offer fome Obfervations concerning this Doctrine of the *Eternity of* God in particular ; concerning *That* Eternity defcribed in the Text, by the words, *Which is, and which was, and which is to come*.

AND 1*ft* we may obferve, that This Eternity is a Perfection, Attribute, or Character, by which God is *very frequently* defcribed in *Scripture* ; in order to raife in our Minds a juft Awe and Veneration of his divine Majefty. *Deut.* xxxiii. 27. *The* Eternal *God*. *Rom.* xvi. 26. *The* everlafting *God*. *If.* lvii. 15. The Holy One, *that inhabiteth Eternity*. 1 Sam. xv. 29. *The Strength of Ifrael*, (in the original it .is, *the* Eternity *of Ifrael*,) *will not lie nor repent*. 1 Tim. i. 17. *The King eternal, immortal*, ch. vi. 16. *who Only hath Immortality*. In the words of the Text, *He which is, and which was, and which is to come*. And, to mention but one paffage more, *Pf.* cii. 24. *Thy years are throughout all generations. Of old haft thou laid the foundations of the Earth, and the Heavens are the work of thy hands. They fhall perifh, but Thou fhalt endure ; yea, all of them fhall wax old like a garment ; and as a vefture fhalt thou change them, and they fhall be changed. But Thou art the fame, and Thy Years fhall have no End.* Of which laft words it is remarkable, that in the firft chapter of the epiftle to the *Hebrews* they are alfo in a very proper Senfe applied to *the Son*, as the perfon *by* whom the Father *made*, and by whom he *governs* all things through *all Ages* ; by *whom God made the worlds*, ver. 2, and 10.

2*dly*, 'TIS to be obferved, that not only in *Scripture* is God frequently defcribed by this Attribute of Eternity, but even under the *Light of Nature* alfo is he reprefented to us after the fame Manner. For the very *Heathen Writers themfelves*, have fpoken very juftly and honourably of God in this particular. And not to *Philofophers* only, but even to the *meaneft capacities*, are there obvious Arguments in *Reafon*, to prove clearly the Neceffity of this divine Perfection, and to fet it before them in a practical and ufeful Light. For fince 'tis in *Some* degree a Perfection, *to Be* ; and a greater *Degree* of that Perfection, *to continue in Being :* 'tis evident, when we conceive of God the *moft perfect* Being, we muft conceive him to be infinite in *This* perfection alfo, as well as in others ; and that, as his Power is not bounded by any oppofite Strength, nor his Immenfity terminated by any Bounds of *Place*, fo neither is his Duration limited by any Periods of Time; but that he exifts and lives and governs all things, from everlafting to everlafting, without beginning and without end.

AGAIN: 'Tis evident even to the meaneft Capacity, which confiders things at all; that He who firft gave Being to all *other* things, could not poffibly have any Beginning *himfelf*, and *muft* therefore neceffarily have exifted from all Eternity; and that he who hath already exifted *from* all eternity, *independently* and *of Himfelf*; cannot poffibly be liable to be deprived of his Being, and muft therefore *neceffarily* exift for an Eternity to come.

3*dly*, 'TIS worthy of Obfervation, as to the *Manner* of our conceiving the Eternity of God; that the Scholaftick Writers have generally defcribed it to be, not a *Real* Perpetual *Duration*, but *One Point* or *Inftant* comprehending Eternity, and wherein all things are really co-exiftent at once. But unintelligible Ways of Speaking, have (I think) never done any Service to Religion. The true Notion of the Divine Eternity, does not confift in making paft things to be ftill prefent, and things future to be already come; [which is an exprefs contradiction:] But it confifts in *This*, and in *This* it infinitely tranfcends the manner of exiftence of all created Beings, even of *thofe* which fhall continue for ever; that whereas *Their* finite Minds can by no means comprehend all that is paft, or underftand perfectly the things that are prefent, much lefs know, or have in their power, the things that are to come; but their Thoughts and Knowledge and Power, muft of neceffity have degrees and periods, and be fucceffive and tranfient as the Things themfelves; The eternal, fupreme Caufe, on the contrary, has fuch a perfect, independent, and unchangeable comprehenfion of all things; that in every Point or Inftant of *his* eternal Duration, all things paft, prefent, and to come, muft be, not indeed themfelves prefent at once, (for That is a manifeft contradiction;) but they muft be as entirely known and reprefented to him in one fingle Thought or View, and all things prefent and future be as abfolutely under his Power and Direction; *as if* there was really no Succeffion at all, and *as if* all things *had been*, (not that they really *are*,) actually prefent at once. *A Thoufand years in thy fight, are but as yefterday*, Pf. xc. 4. And 2 *Pet*. iii. 8. *One day is with the Lord as a Thoufand years, and a Thoufand years as one day*. Not, a Thoufand years *are* one day; but are to *Him*, as *if* they were only one day.

HAVING premifed thefe few Obfervations concerning the Nature, Manner, and Proof of the Eternity of God; it remains in the *Third* and laft place, (which is the moft material,) that we confider of what *Ufe* this Meditation may be to us in Practice.

AND 1*ft*, This Attribute of *Eternity*, abfolute, neceffary, and *independent*; is one of the principal Characters, by which the *True God of the Univerfe*, the One Maker and Governour of all things, the alone Author and Fountain of all Being and Power, is diftinguifhed from *falfe Deities*, from falfe Gods, worfhipped in *oppofition to him*, without any *Power from him*, without any Authority whatfoever either in Nature or Reafon, either inherent in themfelves, or communicated from *him* that has it of *himfelf*. Idols, are Gods but of yefterday, and which perifh to morrow: Beings, which have no Authority and Dominion over us; or perhaps, not real Beings at all, but mere Fictions and Imaginations only: *Lying Vanities*, as the Scripture elegantly ftiles them; that is, mere Nothings; having nothing of reality in them; either no Being, or at leaft no Dominion and Authority over men. But the *True God of the Univerfe* thus defcribes himfelf, *If*. xliii. 10, *I am He: Before me there was no God, neither fhall there be after* *me*. He was *before* all things, and he fhall be *after* all things, Eternal, Immutable, and Self-fufficient. He is *Alpha and Omega, the Beginning and the End; which is, and which was, and which is to come.*

The High and Lofty One, that inhabiteth Eternity.

2*dly*, THE

2*dly*, THE confideration of the *Eternity* of God, is an Argument why his *Pro-*vidence ought not to be cavilled at, nor his *Promifes* doubted of; even though there be no prefent appearance of the Performance of his *Promifes*; and no prefent way of explaining, the Methods of his *Providence*. All *other* Beings, having Command only of the *prefent* Time; if they cannot *immediately* accomplifh what they undertake, 'tis never certain but fome Change in their *own* ftate, or fome alteration in the Nature and Courfe of *Things*, may prevent them from being able to accomplifh it *at all*. But *God* having in his hands the Power of *all* Time alike, can never be involved in any difficulty, nor hindred by any intervening accidents, nor perplexed by any change of things or circumftances, nor influenced by any Length or Periods of Time; fo as either to become unable or unwilling to perform his remoteft Promifes, fo as to find any difficulty in extricating the moft perplexed appearances in the Methods of his Providence. Senfelefs therefore is the objection of thofe *Scoffers*, who the Apoftle foretells fhould *come in the laft days, walking after their own lufts, and faying, Where is the Promife of his coming ? For fince the Fathers fell afleep, all things continue as they were, from the Beginning of the creation*, 2 Pet. iii. 4. The Apoftle returns the true and plain Anfwer, ver. 8. *Beloved, be not ignorant of this one thing, that one day is with the Lord as a Thoufand years, and a Thoufand years as one day.*

3*dly*, THE confideration of God's *Eternity*, is a fure ground of *Truft and Confidence*, of *hope and cheerfulnefs*, to *good* Men at all times ; feeing his protection may be relied on and depended upon *for ever*. This is the excellency defcribed by the Pfalmift, *Pf.* xc. 1. *Lord, thou haft been our Refuge from one generation to another ; Before the Mountains were brought forth, or ever the Earth and the World were made, thou art God from everlafting, and World without End.* His Power, his Goodnefs, his Mercy, and other Perfections, are all eternal and unchangeable as his Being. On This Security, the mind of man (after a Life of Virtue) may rely with full Satisfaction ; and they who love righteoufnefs will be joyful therein. *Truft ye in the Lord for ever ; for in the Lord Jehovah, is evelafting Strength*, If. xxvi. 4. and *Deut* xxxiii. 26. *There is none like the God of Jefurun ; who rideth upon the Heavens in thy help, and in his excellency on the Sky : The* eternal *God is thy refuge, and underneath are the* everlafting *Arms ; and he fhall thruft out the Enemy from before thee.* The fame Argument is made ufe of likewife by the Apoftle, with regard to the Interceffion and Mediation of Chrift ; Heb. vii. 25. *He is able to fave Them to the uttermoft, that come unto God by him, feeing he ever liveth to make Interceffion for them.* Other fecurity there is no where to be found ; nor any thing that can afford fufficient comfort and fupport, in the days of adverfity and trouble. The Power of *Men* will fail, and their Friendfhip is fallible and uncertain. The *Pleafures* of Life are fhort ; and the time will come, when there fhall be no relifh in them. At leaft, *Death* puts an end to all the injoyments, and all the hopes of this prefent Life. And therefore a Wife man will above all things endeavour, to fecure to himfelf the Favour of Him who liveth for ever ; who alone can unloofe the Bands, even of Death itfelf ; and crown him with Immortality, and eternal Life. *Hearken unto me*, faith the Prophet, *ye that know righteoufnefs ; the people, in whofe heart is my Law. Fear ye not the reproach of men, neither be afraid of their reviling. For the Moth fhall eat them up like a garment, and the worm fhall eat them like wool. But my righteoufnefs fhall be* for ever, *and my falvation from generation to generation*, If. li. 7, 8. And ch. ii. 22, *Ceafe ye from man, whofe breath is in his Noftrils* ; (whofe *Life* depends on fo fmall a thing as a Breath ;) *For wherein is he accounted of ?* The Pfalmift in like manner, *Pf.* cxlvi. 2. *O put not your Truft in Princes, nor in any Child of man ; for there is no help in them. For when the Breath of Man goeth forth, he fhall turn again to his earth, and then all his thoughts perifh.*

Bleffed

SERM.
IV.

Blessed is he, that hath the God *of* Jacob *for his help, and whose Hope is in the Lord his* God.

4thly, THE Confideration of This divine Perfection, the *Eternity* of God, is a ground for frail and mortal man to hope for *Pity* and *Compassion* from him. This is the Ufe the Prophet *Isaiah* makes of this Meditation, ch. lvii. 16. *I will not contend for ever, neither will I be always wroth : For the Spirit should fail before me, and the Souls which I have made.* The Pfalmift likewife, *Pf.* cii. 24. *I said, O my God, take me not away in the midst of my Days; Thy years are throughout all Generations.* And *Pf.* cvii. 13. *Like as a Father pitieth his children, so the Lord pitieth them that fear him; For he knoweth our Frame, he remembreth that we are but dust. As for man, his days are grass; as a flower of the Field, so he flourisheth : For the wind passeth over it, and it is gone; and the place thereof shall know it no more. But the mercy of the Lord, is* from everlafting to everlafting, *upon them that fear him; and his righteousness unto childrens children.*

5thly, THE Confideration of God's being *eternal*, leads us to a right Knowledge and juft Senfe of the *Excellency of that Reward*, wherewith he will finally crown thofe who obey his Commandments. The Greatnefs of which Reward confifts principally in This, that it is an Inheritance which fadeth not away, *eternal* in the Heavens. This is a Reward, worthy of *Him* to beftow, whofe Kingdom ruleth over all; and which *He alone* is capable of beftowing, who *Himself* liveth and reigneth *for ever. Behold I come quickly,* fays our Lord, invefted with his Father's Power and Eternal Dominion; (in *the glory of his Father*, as 'tis expreffed, *Mat.* xvi. 27;) *behold,* (faith he,) *I come quickly, and my Reward is with me, to give every man according as his Work shall be,* Rev. xxii. 12. The *reason* is annexed, ver. 13. *I am Alpha and Omega, the Beginning and the End, the First and the Last.* God who liveth for ever, hath promifed to reward his Servants eternally; And therefore moft elegantly follows in the next verfe That affectionate exclamation, ver. 14. *Blessed are they that do his commandments, that they may have right to the* Tree of Life. *God* is eternal, by Neceffity of Nature : But *Man's* immortality, is of free Grace. This therefore his dependent Immortality, or his Poffibility of attaining to be Immortal, was excellently reprefented *at first* by that Figure of *the Tree of Life* growing in Paradife; And his condemnation to *Mortality*, by his exclufion from the Benefit of that Tree. And his *restoration* to Immortality again by the Will of God, is no lefs properly defcribed, by his being again admitted to the Tree of Life; *Rev.* ii. 7. *To him that overcometh, will I give to eat of the* Tree of Life, *which is in the midst of the Paradise of God.*

Lastly; IF God is *Eternal*, this confideration ought to be matter of infinite Terror to all impenitent and incorrigible Sinners; that he who liveth for ever, as he will reward his Servants *eternally*, fo he can *punish his Enemies as* long *as he pleases*; for there is no End of his Power. This Argument is excellently urged by the Apoftle, *Heb.* x. 31. *It is a fearful thing to fall into the hands of the* Living *God*; to fall under the final Difpleafure of Him, who liveth for ever, and can make his Punifhments as *durable* as he thinks fit. The fame confideration is likewife laid before us by our Saviour, *Matt.* x. 28. *Fear not them that kill the Body, and after That have no more that they can do; But I will forewarn you whom ye shall fear : Fear Him, who after he has killed, can destroy both Soul and Body in Hell; yea I say unto you, Fear him.* The Particulars of This Punifhment, are beft fet forth in the words of Scripture; in thofe words, which God himfelf has thought moft proper to work upon our Fear, in fuch manner as it ought to be worked upon. St *Mar.* ix. 44. It is, *The Worm that dieth not,* and *the Fire that is not quenched.* Rev. xx. 10. It is, *The lake of Fire and Brimstone, where* the Devil and *the false Prophet are, and shall be tormented day and night for ever and ever.* And *ch.* xiv. 11. *The smoke of their Torment ascendeth up for ever and ever, and they*

have

have no reft day nor night. What the full purport and literal meaning of thefe figurative S E R M. expreffions is, we do not perfectly know. But thus much is evident, that they fignify IV. the greateft Severity of Punifhment, which the Juftice and Wifdom and Goodnefs of Him who has infinite and eternal Power, *can* think fit to inflict. *From* which *Wrath to come*, the Gofpel exhorts us to *flee*; and *from which*, God of his infinite mercy grant, *&c.*

S E R M O N V.

Of the SPIRITUALITY of GOD.

J O H. IV. 24.

God is a Spirit, and they that worfhip him, muft worfhip him in Spirit and in Truth.

THESE Words are part of our Saviour's Difcourfe with the Woman of *Sama-* S E R M. *ria*; for the fake of making which Difcourfe to *Her*, and of the confe- V. quent opportunity *That* gave him to inftruct the reft of her City, he feems to have taken his Journey *on purpofe* into That Country. For when the Difciples, during the Time of his being employed in This Work, would have interrupted him by defiring him to take fomewhat to eat; he replied unto them, ver. 34. *My Meat is to do the Will of him that fent me, and to finifh his Work.* After which he adds immediately in the very next Words, ver. 35. *Say ye not, there are yet four Months, and then cometh Harveft. Behold, I fay unto you, Lift up your Eyes, and look on the Fields, for they are white already to harveft.* Which Words, being a *Similitude* only, without the interpretation, and their connexion being fomewhat difficult; they deferve briefly to be explained by the way. The true Senfe of them depends, upon what the Evangelift had before related, *ver.* 30. that a great number of the *Samaritans*, upon the Wo- man's report, were coming out of the City to fee Jefus. Whom when Jefus beheld at a diftance, coming towards him; he fhows them to his Difciples, and fays; *The Hufbandman fupports himfelf under the Labour of his imployment, with a diftant hope of Harveft after four Months to come: But behold, our Harveft is at hand, and ready to be reaped:* meaning the *Samaritans*, who were ready to receive his Doctrine; and whom upon That account he here compares, as he ufually does all well-difpofed Per- fons in the whole courfe of his Preaching, to *good Wheat.* And that This Paffage, which would otherwife be very obfcure, ought to be underftood in this figurative fenfe, which thus makes it very eafy and intelligible; appears likewife further, from the very next words, *ver.* 36. *And he that reapeth receiveth Wages, and gathereth Fruit unto Life eternal; that both he that foweth, and he that reapeth, may rejoice together.* The words, *Fruit unto Life eternal*, fhow evidently *what Harveft* it is he was fpeaking of. But to return to the more immediate occafion of the words of the Text. Our Saviour, in

SERM. his Difcourfe with the *Samaritan* woman, having proved himfelf to her to be a *Pro-*
V. *phet*, by difcovering to her that he knew all the moft fecret actions of her Life; the
immediately, as was natural to an inquifitive perfon, afks his Opinion concerning that
great Queftion between the *Jews* and the *Samaritans*, which of the Two profeffed
the truer Religion, *ver.* 20. To This, our Saviour gives her a twofold Anfwer. Firft,
that the *Jewifh*, and not the *Samaritan*, was the true Religion, *ver.* 22. for that in
Jerufalem God had chofen to place his name; and, in matters of Religion, the Command of *God* only, and *not* the Inftitutions of *Men*, are the Rule of Right. But then
Secondly he tells her in the next place, that neither the one nor the other of thefe Religions were to continue long, but that Both of them were quickly to give place to
the more excellent and fpiritual Inftitution of the Gofpel: *ver.* 21, 23, 24. *The Hour*
cometh, fays he, *when ye fhall neither in this mountain, nor yet at Jerufalem, worfhip*
the Father; But——the true worfhippers fhall worfhip the Father in Spirit and in
Truth; For the Father feeketh fuch to worfhip him: God is a Spirit; and they that
worfhip him, muft worfhip him in Spirit and in Truth. In the following Difcourfe upon
which Words, I fhall *1ft* endeavour to explain, *what* is meant by *God*'s being a *Spirit*;
or *how* we are to underftand That Attribute of the divine Nature, which we call his
Spirituality: And *2dly* I fhall confider what our confequent *Duty* is, of *worfhipping*
him accordingly *in Spirit and in Truth.*

    I. I am to endeavour to explain, *what* is meant by God's being a *Spirit*; or *how*
we are to underftand that Attribute of the divine Nature, which we call his *Spiritu-*
ality. And here 'tis to be obferved, that the Scripture, as it does not much infift upon
proving to us the *Being* of God, but rather always *fuppofes That to be already known* by
the Light of Nature; fo alfo, when it mentions any of the *natural* Attributes of the
Divine Effence, it does not ufually inlarge either upon the Proof or Explication of
them, but generally makes mention of them *occafionally* only, and as prefuppofing them
beforehand well known by mens Reafon. Wherefore though the Scripture no where
exprefsly ftiles God a Spirit, but in this one fingle Paffage only; yet fince in numberlefs places it does by *confequence* fuppofe him to be fo, and founds our *Duty* to him often upon That Suppofition; 'tis very reafonable for us to inquire, fo far as our Faculties enable us, into the True Notion of fo excellent an Attribute of the divine Nature.
And

    1ft, The *firft and loweft particular* that is included in the Notion of God's being
a *Spirit*, is, that we are to conceive of him as of a Being infinitely removed from all
thofe grofs Properties, which conftitute the Nature of *Matter* or *Body.* Thus, for
Inftance, the nature of *Matter* or *Body*, is, that it is *Tangible*, and may be felt, or
difcerned by the Touch; which a *Spirit* cannot be: This Diftinction our Saviour takes
notice of, *Luk.* xxiv. 39. Handle *me, and fee; for a Spirit hath not Flefh and Bones,*
as ye fee me have.

    The Nature of *Matter* is, to be *Divifible* into *Parts*, and to have its Frame *dif-*
folved; which a *Spirit* cannot be: This alfo is taken notice of by our Saviour, *Matt.*
x. 28. *Fear not them which kill the* Body, *but are not able to kill the* Soul.

    The Nature of *Matter* is, to be *Vifible* to the *Eyes:* But a *Spirit*, is abfolutely
Invifible.

    The Nature of *Matter* is, to be *paffive* only, or act *only by neceffity*, that is, (pro-
perly fpeaking) not to *act at all*, but only to be *acted upon:* But a *Spirit*, is in its nature a *Living, Intelligent, Active* Being.

    And This is the *firft and loweft particular*, included in the Notion of God's being
a Spirit.

    2dly, By the Scripture's affirming God to be a *Spirit*, we are directed to conceive
of him, as of a Being not limited by *human fhape*, or included under any *other Form*

                                                whatfoever.

whatfoever.   In the darker and more ignorant Ages of the Church, there was a fect of S E R M.
men, who received their denomination from the Notion they had, that God was to   V.
be underftood as having *really* a *Human Form*.   Yet perhaps it was not their intention
to fet up a particular Sect, but might poffibly be merely an effect of their *Ignorance*
and *want of Learning*, or of their *inability* only to *exprefs* themfelves properly.   Or
perhaps, more probably, it was nothing more, but that other *people* mifunderftood their
manner of expreffing themfelves, and afcribed to them an opinion which they meant
not to maintain.   However That be, it is certain that there are None *Now* fo ignorant,
(who are arrived at years of any Underftanding,) as to think that God has *really* a *human* or any *other Shape*.   Yet becaufe in expreffing the feveral *Powers* of God, and his
different *manners* of acting, all language is fo deficient, that we are forced to make ufe
of figurative ways of fpeaking, and of fimilitudes drawn from *our own* manners of acting, to reprefent our conceptions of *thefe* divine Powers, to which the Faculties of Man
bear but a very fmall and imperfect Analogy; it is therefore very neceffary, for preventing miftakes in this matter, that we attend with fome Care to the true Meaning
of thofe many paffages in Scripture, which, in condefcenfion to the Vulgar, do fpeak
concerning God after this figurative manner.   For Example; When the Scripture,
fpeaking of Him, who, being an infinite Mind, is therefore really prefent in every
place alike, yet reprefents him as *being in Heaven*, as *dwelling* or *fitting* there, and
having the *Earth* for his footftool; This ought to be underftood only as a Defcription
of his Supreme *Authority and Dominion over all*.   When mention is made of the *Eyes*,
of Him who has *no* Parts; This muft be underftood of his perfect *Knowledge* and *Difcernment* of all things; who, having *made* the Eye, cannot but have *in himfelf* That
Power in a much perfecter and higher manner, of which the Eye made by him is only
an Inftrument proportionate to the other fhort Faculties of weak and finite Creatures.
His *looking down* upon the Earth, fignifies, not any *Pofture*, (which is the Property of
Bodies only,) but his *watchful Providence* and *continual Infpection* over all Events.
When mention is made of his *Ear*, and of his *bowing down his ear* towards men;
This fets forth to us his Willingnefs and Readinefs to be moved by the Prayers of his
Servants; which Prayers, he, who made the Ear, knows and underftands by the
fame perfect Power, by which he difcerns the *Heart* as well as the *Mouth*; which
Power neverthelefs, we, through defect of Language, can no otherwife exprefs, than
by faying that he *hears us*.   *Arms* and *Hands*, being in *Men* the inftruments of Action, and the Seat of Strength, fignify, when applied to *God*, his *Power and Might*.
Smelling a fweet favour, is nothing but a *Hebrew* phrafe, drawn from the Law of Sacrifices, to exprefs God's *Acceptance* of the Services of his fincere Worfhippers.   And
the mention of his *Mouth*, or *Lips*, fo frequently found in Scripture, is evidently nothing elfe but a familiar Metaphor, to fignify his *Revealing*, in what manner foever it
be, *his Will* to his Servants.   Indeed, fuch figurative ways of fpeaking, as thefe, are fo
common in all Languages, and fo well underftood upon numberlefs occafions even in
common Speech, that the bare mention of them is fufficient to prevent their being
miftaken, even by the meaneft Capacities.   There is much *greater* Difficulty in explaining *thofe* paffages of the *Old* Teftament, wherein God is reprefented as *appearing
vifibly*, and as it were *face to face*, to Holy men of old; when yet both in the *nature of
Things*, 'tis certain that the Effence of a pure Spirit is abfolutely impoffible to be feen;
and moreover *in Scripture* the God and Father of all, is peculiarly diftinguifhed by that
particular Attribute, that he is the *Invifible God*, whom *no man has feen at any time*,
whom *no man hath feen or can fee*, and of whom our Saviour affirms to the *Jews*, that
they *had neither feen his fhape nor heard his voice*, Joh. v. 37.   Concerning the *appearance* therefore of God in the Old Teftament, 'tis obfervable that *generally and for the
greater part*, in order to prevent miftakes, and that men might not imagine it was *God
himfelf*

S E R M. *himself* that appeared, but only *a Glory* to reprefent his appearance; there was *no* parti-
V. cular Shape or Form, feen in that Glory.   Thus to *Mofes* at the burning Bufh, there
feems to have been the appearance *only of Fire* : To the whole people of *Ifrael* in the
Wildernefs, the glory of the Lord that appeared in the tabernacle of the congregation
and upon the Mount, was the appearance *only of a cloud and Fire* ; and therefore *Mofes*
exhorts them, *Deut.* iv. 15. *Take good heed unto yourfelves, left you make a graven image,
the fimilitude of any figure ; for ye faw no manner of fimilitude on the day that the Lord
fpake unto you in Horeb, out of the midft of the fire :* To *Mofes*, defiring to fee the Face
of God, it was denied as a requeft impoffible to be granted, *Exod.* xxxiii. 20. To *Abraham*, the word of the Lord feems to have come moft frequently without *any* vifible appearance at all : And in the *Temple* between the Cherubims, which was the Seat wherein he had placed his Name, and the Throne where he would receive the Worfhip and
Homage of his people ; there never was any other appearance but of a *Cloud and Fire*.
This (I fay) was *generally and moft ufually* the Cafe, of the appearances of God under
the Old Teftament.   But yet, becaufe it *fometimes* was plainly otherwife ; and the Lord,
that appeared, is *in* fome *places* undeniably reprefented as under a human fhape ; As
when *Adam* heard the *voice of the Lord God* walking *in the garden in the cool of the day*,
Gen. iii. 8 ; And *Abraham* talked with the Lord, as with one of the three *men*, whom
he faw going towards *Sodom*, Gen. xviii ; And of *Mofes* it is related, *Exod.* xxxiii. 11.
That the Lord fpake unto him face to face, as a man fpeaketh unto his Friend ; And of the
Elders of *Ifrael*, Exod. xxiv. 10. that *they faw the God of Ifrael, and there was under his
feet as it were a paved-work of Sapphire-ftone, and as it were the Body of Heaven in its
clearnefs* ; And the Prophets, *Micaiah*, *Ifaiah*, and *Daniel*, faw in their Vifions *the
Lord fitting upon his Throne, and all the hoft of Heaven ftanding about him, on his right
hand and on his left* : For the full explication therefore of this matter, and the clear reconciling Thefe Texts of Scripture with other exprefs Texts and with the Reafon of
Things, which do both of them undeniably prove that the Effence of the God and Father of all, cannot but be *abfolutely invifible* ; 'tis here further to be obferved, that all
thefe appearances of God in the Old *Teftament*, wherein he feems to have been reprefented as in a human Form ; and all thofe other appearances alfo, wherein there was
feen only a Glory ; were in reality no other than the *Angel of the Covenant*, even *Chrift
himfelf* ; who from the Beginning appeared in a bodily Glory, having (as St *Paul* expreffes it) *the Form of God*, and being the vifible *Image of the Invifible God*, reprefenting the Supreme Majefty of the Father, and acting *in his Name* and *as his Word*.
Thus St *Stephen* exprefsly, *Acts* vii. 30. *There appeared to Mofes in the Wildernefs, the
Angel of the Lord in a flame of fire in a Bufh* ; The *Angel of the Lord*, that is, the
Angel of his Prefence, the great Meffenger of his Covenant ; as our Saviour is ftiled,
Mal. iii. 1. and *Gal.* iv. 14. And This, 'tis very probable, was not altogether unknown
to thofe eminent Prophets under the Old *Teftament*, to whom God was pleafed to reveal
himfelf more diftinctly ; that the perfon who appeared to *Adam* in Paradife, was that
fecond Adam who is the Lord from Heaven ; that the Lord who talked familiarly with
Abraham, was He *whofe day Abraham earneftly defired to fee, and he faw it and was
glad*, Joh. viii. 56. and that the Lord who fpake *to Mofes face to face, as a Man talketh
with his friend*, was He in whom at length was fulfilled the Law and the Prophets, by
whom was revealed openly *Grace and Truth*, Joh. i. 17.

   3dly, As by God's being a Spirit, is *meant* that he has no human, or other bodily
fhape ; fo thereby is not *meant*, that he is fuch a Spirit as are the Souls of Men. For
the word, *Spirit*, does not fignify, as the word, *Body*, does ; *one* only determinate *fort*
or *kind* of Beings ; But, thro' the defect of Language, and alfo for want of more diftinct Notions, we by one common Name call *every* Being *a Spirit*, which is *not Body* ;
tho' probably fome of thofe Intelligent Natures we call Spirits, are as much fuperior to,

     and

and different from, other Spirits, as thofe others are different from Matter or Body. When therefore we affirm *God* to be a *Spirit*, we muft not thereby mean only to dif-tinguifh him from *Bodily Subftance*; but, in like manner as our Soul, by very great Proportion excels the Body, in the fuperior Powers of Life, Underftanding, Know-ledge, Activity, and the like; fo we muft conceive of *Him*, as of a Being excelling in an infinitely higher proportion, not only the *Souls of Men*, but alfo all *other* Intellectual Natures or Spirits whatfoever.

4thly and *Laftly*, When we affirm that God is *a Spirit*, we muft thereby under-ftand that he is *abfolutely and perfectly fuch*; that is, that he is wholly void of all thofe Paffions, Affections, and Commotions, fuch as Love, Hatred, Anger, Grief, Repent-ance, and the like, which are the Properties of embodied *Spirits*: And that He, determining all his Actions, with infinite Calmnefs and undifturbed Serenity in Himfelf, according to the Rules of perfect Right and unerring Reafon; has thefe Paffions of *Mind* afcribed to him in Scripture, only after the fame figurative man-ner of fpeaking as the Senfitive Organs of the *Body* likewife are; becaufe thereby to *Us* are beft reprefented fuch Actions of *His*, as in their *Effect upon* other *things*, not in their *nature within* Him, bear fome Analogy to the like Paffions or Affec-tions in *Us*.

Having thus at large explained, *what* is meant by God's being a *Spirit*; or *how* we are to underftand That Attribute of the divine Nature, which we call his *Spiritu-ality*: It remains that I proceed now in the

II*d* place to confider, *what* our confequent *Duty* is, of *worfhipping* him accordingly *in Spirit and in Truth*. And This phrafe plainly fignifies, worfhipping him with the real Subftantial Worfhip of the *Heart and Mind*, in oppofition to mere *ceremonial and external Forms*; worfhipping him in a *Manner*, worthy of God; with the inward fin-cere Devotion of the *Soul and Affections*, evidencing itfelf in the whole Life and Con-verfation by the true and acceptable Fruits of *Obedience and Imitation*. This is wor-fhipping God *in Spirit and in Truth*. But more particularly; The full and diftinct Meaning of this Phrafe, will beft be underftood, by confidering what are in Scripture the *contrary* Characters, to which *Spirit and Truth* are fet in oppofition. Now *Spirit* is fometimes oppofed *literally* to the *Body*, and fometimes 'tis oppofed *figuratively* to *Flefhly* or *Carnal* Ordinances. *Truth* alfo in like manner is oppofed fometimes literally to *Faljhood*, and fometimes figuratively to *Types or Shadows*. Confequently *worfhipping God* in Spirit, when 'tis oppofed to worfhipping him with the *Body* only, fignifies *Sin-cerity*, as oppofed to *Hypocrify*; and when 'tis oppofed to *Flefh* or carnal *Ordinances*, then it fignifies *Morality* or *real Holinefs*, in oppofition to *ritual* or *ceremonial* perfor-mances. In like manner; *worfhipping God* in Truth, when 'tis oppofed to Falfe *Wor-fhip*, fignifies worfhipping him according to the rules of the true *Religion*, in op-pofition to *Idolatry*; and when 'tis oppofed to *Types or Figures*, then *Truth* like-wife fignifies, as *Spirit* did before, *Morality* or *real Holinefs*, in oppofition to *ri-tual* or *ceremonial* performances. This precept therefore, of worfhipping God in *Spirit and in Truth*, is tranfgreffed, 1*ft*, by all *Idolaters*, who are guilty of *Falfe* worfhip, in oppofition to the *Truth*; and 2*dly*, by all thofe, who placing the chief of Religion in *external Forms and Ceremonies*, which may be performed without True Virtue, worfhip God (as the Scripture expreffes it) in the *Flefh* and not in the *Spirit*.

I. They are guilty of tranfgreffing this Precept in the higheft and *moft* prefump-tuous manner, who fet up *Falfe and Idolatrous* worfhip, in oppofition to the *Truth*. By *Idolatry*, in this place, I underftand, not the Worfhip of *Falfe* Gods; (For *That*, is not only not worfhipping God *in Spirit and in Truth*, but indeed *not worfhipping him*

S E R M. at all;) But, by *Idolatry*, in this place, I would be underftood to mean, worfhipping
V. the True God *in an Idolatrous* manner, and by *Falfe Mediums* of Worfhip; in oppofition to what our Saviour calls (in the words before the Text) *the True worfhippers Worfhipping him in Truth*.   Now *This* fort of Falfe worfhip, is That which thofe *Heathens*
are charged with, *Rom.* i. 21. who *when they* knew God, *yet glorified him not* as God,
——*but became vain in their imaginations,*——*and changed the Glory of the uncorruptible God, into an* Image *made like to corruptible man, and to Birds and four-footed Beafts
and creeping things*.   And the *Jews* were ftill *more inexcufably* guilty of it, when in the
wildernefs they worfhipped the Golden Calf, moft abfurdly, as an Emblem or reprefentation of the God of Heaven; and in *Jerufalem* itfelf, when they fet up *high places*,
not in oppofition indeed to the *True God*, but in oppofition to the *Temple*, in oppofition
to that *Place* of worfhip, which he Himfelf had chofen to place his Name there.   And
when in *Dan and Bethel* they fet up Calves, not indeed as Falfe Gods, like the Worfhippers of *Baal*; but as falfe and abfurd reprefentations of the God of *Ifrael*.   And the
Samaritans, 2 *Kings* xvii. 24. when they worfhipped God, not as the Supreme Lord
of all things, but as *the God of the Land,* the God of That particular Country.   And
corrupt Chriftians, ftill the *moft inexcufably of all*; when, notwithftanding fo many repeated Declarations of the Will of God to the contrary, they yet continue to worfhip
him thro' *Falfe Mediators,* thro' the pretended Interceffion of Saints and Angels and of
the Bleffed Virgin, whom he hath *not* appointed to any fuch Office: And when moreover, by introducing *Images,* not only of Chrift, but even of God himfelf, they totally
deftroy the Spiritual Purity of the Gofpel-worfhip.

N o w the *reafons why* this *particular Species of Idolatry,* this worfhipping the *True
God* under *Falfe Images,* is fo feverely condemned in Scripture; are principally thefe
Two.

1*ft*, B E C A U S E it tends to fubvert the Great and Primary Foundation of all Religion,
by giving men *mean and unworthy Notions of God,* confining his Prefence, and falfly
fuppofing that there can be any fuch Thing as a Similitude or Reprefentation of him.
Forafmuch (faith the Apoftle) *as we are the off-fpring of God,* (forafmuch as even *we
ourfelves* are rational Beings, and our Minds far fuperiour to any corporeal reprefentation,) *we ought not* (faith he) *to think that the* Godhead *is like unto* (that is, can in
any manner be reprefented by,) *Gold or Silver, or Stone graven by Art and Man's
device,* Acts xvii. 29.   The Heathens, knowing that God was every where prefent,
firft worfhipped him in *the Sun and Stars,* as the moft illuftrious Inftruments, of his
Power, and the beft Vifible Reprefentations of his glorious Greatnefs and Goodnefs.   *Then* they foon fell to worfhip the *Sun and Stars* themfelves, inftead of the
God who *made* thofe bright Luminaries, and whom they fuppofed to be *in them.*
And from thence by degrees they defcended to worfhip the meaneft plant; and at
laft Wood and Stone, even the workmanfhip of their own hands.   The *Jews* in like
manner, I wifh it could not be faid that *Chriftians* alfo, from beginning to make
imaginary reprefentations of God, quickly fell by degrees from more refined Idolatry, to worfhipping at laft, in the moft ftupid manner, even Stocks and Stones.   This
being in the higheft degree contrary to the Precept of worfhipping God according to
Truth, 'tis with great Elegancy and juft Sharpnefs of Reproof, that, in the Old
Teftament, Idols are frequently ftiled *Falfhood,* and *Lyes,* and *Lying Vanities*; and
the Makers thereof, *Teachers of* Lyes; and in the New Teftament likewife, *Idolaters* are called, by way of Eminence, *Lyars,* Rev. xxi. 8. and *whofoever loveth or
maketh a* Lye, ch. xxi. 27. xxii. 15; and that they *turn the Truth of God into a*
Lye, *Rom.* i. 25.   To prevent fo great a corruption of the firft Principles of Religion
in the Notion of a Deity, the fecond Commandment is delivered in larger and more

Jer. x. 14.
Am. ii. 4.
Jon. ii. 8.
Hab. ii. 18.

I   explicit

explicit Terms, than any of the reft: *Thou ſhalt not make to thyſelf any graven Image, nor the Likeneſs of any thing that is in Heaven above, or in the Earth beneath, or in the Waters under the Earth*; that is, Thou ſhalt not think ſo meanly and unworthily of God, as to imagine that He who made all things, can be repreſented by any Similitude of the things, that are made. And 'tis with great elegancy of Expreſſion, that the Prophet *Iſaiah* derides the Makers of Images, ch. xl. 18. *To whom will ye liken God, or what likeneſs will ye compare unto him? The workman melteth a graven Image, and the goldſmith ſpreadeth it over with gold, and caſteth ſilver chains.*

2*dly*, T H E other reaſon, why This Idolatry is ſo ſeverely condemned in Scripture, is becauſe it always tends to *corrupt mens Manners*, and to introduce all ſort of Wickedneſs. St *Paul*, in his whole *firſt chapter to the* Romans, largely ſhows, how the *Heathens*, when *they changed the Truth of God into a Lye*, were conſequently *given up unto vile affections among themſelves*; and their own Hiſtories ſhow, that departing from the natural Notion of God, they came at length even to *human Sacrifices*, and ſuch other Cruelties, as no other principle, how corrupt ſoever, but only This of *Idolatrous Superſtition*, could have led men to. The *Jews* in like manner, whenever they fell into Idolatry, their whole Hiſtory ſhows, how it totally deſtroy'd all Senſe of Virtue out of their minds, and they came at laſt to *ſacrifice even their own* children *to Moloch*. And ſad it is to obſerve, how *Chriſtian Idolatry* alſo has had the ſame Effect; cauſing men to rely on *Saints*, and even on the *Relicks* of Saints, inſtead of the practice of Righteouſneſs and true Virtue; and teaching them, inſtead of Chriſtian Charity, and univerſal Love, and Good-will towards all men, to be on the contrary guilty of ſuch *inhuman Cruelties*, as men could never have thought of, who had never heard of any Religion at all.

> Tantum religio potuit ſuadere malorum.

T H U S the Precept in the Text, of *worſhipping God in Spirit and in Truth*, is tranſgreſſed in the Firſt and Higheſt manner, by the *Practice of Idolatry*.

II*dly*, I T is in the Next place tranſgreſſed by thoſe, who place the chief of Religion *in external Forms and Ceremonies*. But of This, hereafter.

SERMON

SERMON VI.

Of the SPIRITUALITY of GOD.

JOH. IV. 24.

*God is a Spirit, and they that worſhip him, muſt worſhip him in
Spirit and in Truth.*

S E R M.
VI.

THE Nature and Manner of the Worſhip we are to pay to God, depends upon
the conſideration of the *Nature of* Man, who is to pay that Worſhip ; of
the *Nature of* God, to whom the Worſhip is to be paid ; and of the Will *of
God*, which is the Rule and Meaſure of our Obedience, when we conſider him as our
Governor, our Lord, and our Judge. The *Nature of* Man is, that he is a *reaſonable
and intelligent* Creature ; and therefore the Worſhip *he* is to pay to God, muſt be a *reaſonable and intelligent* Worſhip. The *Nature of* God is, that he is a *ſpiritual Being,
infinitely perfect* ; and therefore the only Worſhip *he* can delight to receive, is that *ſpiritual worſhip* which proceeds from the Heart and Affections, from a *ſincere Mind*, and
from a *righteous Intention*. The Will *of God*, as revealed in Scripture, is only a Confirmation and Illuſtration of the *Precepts of Nature*, with greater Clearneſs and with
ſtronger Authority ; excepting only, that in condeſcenſion to the *Infirmity* of the *Jews*,
He gave *them* for a Time, Precepts which in themſelves were not good, but ſuited to
the then preſent Circumſtances of that people ; and, in condeſcenſion to the *Neceſſities*
of *Chriſtians*, he has appointed *us* Two Sacramental Rites, not as in Themſelves eſſential to Religion, but as *external Helps* to bind ſtronger upon us the Obligation of thoſe
Moral Duties wherein the eſſence of Religion truly conſiſts, and as *inſtituted Means* of
conveying and applying to good men in this imperfect State, and upon true Repentance,
the requiſite Benefit of a Saviour. Theſe *latter*, the Inſtitutions given to *Chriſtians*, are
indeed of *perpetual* obligation ; becauſe the Duties, to which theſe outward Rites are
our ſolemn obligation, are themſelves of Neceſſity eternal : Yet has the Scripture taken
exceeding great care to inſtruct us, that not in the performance of theſe outward Rites,
but in thoſe Spiritual Duties of Righteouſneſs, Juſtice, Charity and Holineſs, to which
the outward Rites are but Helps and Obligations, does the Life and Spirit of true Religion conſiſt. The *former*, *viz.* the Inſtitutions given to the *Jews*, were declared not
only to be inferiour to the Duties of Morality, and wholly ſubordinate to them ; but
moreover that they were alſo of temporary *appointment* only, ſuited to the preſent Infirmities of that people, and to give place in due time to a more ſpiritual and more acceptable Form of Worſhip. The Time of eſtabliſhing which better Religion, being
then juſt accompliſhed, when our Saviour ſpake the words of the Text ; 'tis evident
they are to be underſtood as a *Reaſon* given, from the Attributes of God and from the
Nature of Things, *why* the Spiritual Religion of the Goſpel, which conſiſts in the
practice of Univerſal Righteouſneſs, Charity, Holineſs and Truth, ſhould be more acceptable to God, than the *ceremonious* performances of the *Jewiſh* Law, or any *outward* Devotions of *Chriſtian* Hypocriſy. *God*, ſays he, *is a Spirit ; and they that wor-*

1

ſhip

ſhip him, muſt worſhip him in Spirit and in Truth. In a Foregoing Diſcourſe upon which words, I propoſed *1ſt* to explain, *what* is meant by *God's* being a *Spirit*; or *how* we are to underſtand That Attribute of the Divine Nature, which we call his *Spirituality*; And *2dly* to conſider, *what* our conſequent *Duty* is, of worſhipping him accordingly *in Spirit and in Truth.* In explication of the *Former* of Theſe, *what* is meant by God's being a *Spirit*; or *how* we are to underſtand That Attribute of the Divine Nature, which we call his *Spirituality*; I have ſhown, *1ſt,* That the *firſt and loweſt particular* included in the Notion of God's being a *Spirit,* is that we are to conceive of him as of a Being infinitely removed from all thoſe groſs Properties, which conſtitute the Nature of *Matter* or *Body.* *2dly,* That by the Scripture's affirming God to be a *Spirit,* we are directed to conceive of him, as of a Being not limited by *human Shape,* or included under any *other Form* whatſoever. *3dly,* That ſince the word, *Spirit,* does not ſignify, as the word, *Body,* does, *one* only determinate *Sort* or *Kind* of Beings; but, on the contrary, Every *kind* of Beings, which are *not Body* ; therefore we muſt not hereby mean only to diſtinguiſh God from *Bodily Subſtance* ; but, in like manner as our Soul by very great Proportion excells the Body, ſo we muſt conceive of *Him,* as excelling, in an infinitely higher Proportion, not only the Souls of Men, but alſo all *other* intellectual Natures or Spirits whatſoever. *4thly* and *laſtly,* that when we affirm God to be *a Spirit,* we muſt thereby underſtand that he is in all reſpects *abſolutely, and perfectly* Such; that is to ſay, that he is wholly void of all thoſe Paſſions, Affections and Commotions, ſuch as Love, Hatred, Anger, Grief, Repentance, and the like, which are the properties of *embodied Spirits* ; and that therefore all theſe things are aſcribed to him in Scripture *figuratively* only, and not *literally.* As to the *Second* general Head, *what* our conſequent *Duty* is, of worſhipping him accordingly *in Spirit and in Truth* ; I have ſhown that it conſiſts, in worſhipping him *1ſt,* with *True* worſhip, after ſuch a *manner* as is worthy of God and ſuitable to his Nature, in oppoſition to all *falſe* or *idolatrous* worſhip; and *2dly,* That it conſiſts in worſhipping him with *Spiritual* worſhip, That of the Heart and Mind and morally virtuous Actions, in oppoſition to merely *ritual and ceremonial Forms :* And that therefore the Precept in the Text is principally tranſgreſt, *1ſt,* by all *Idolaters,* who are guilty of *Falſe* Worſhip in oppoſition to the *Truth* ; and *2dly,* by all thoſe, who placing the chief of their Religion in *external Forms and Ceremonies,* worſhip God (as the Scripture expreſſes it) in the *Fleſh,* and not in the *Spirit.* The *former* of theſe, I inlarged upon in my laſt Diſcourſe, and ſhowed how Idolatrous or *Falſe* worſhip, in oppoſition to the *Truth,* tends *1ſt* to ſubvert the Great and Primary Foundation of all Religion, by giving men *mean and unworthy Notions of God* ; and *2dly* how it tends to *corrupt mens manners* in *other* reſpects, and to introduce all ſorts of Wickedneſs. It remains that I proceed Now, to conſider,

II. In the *Next* place, how *all* They are likewiſe guilty of tranſgreſſing the Precept in the Text, who (though they are *not* indeed guilty of *Falſe* worſhip, yet) placing the chief of their Religion in *outward Forms and Ceremonies,* worſhip God, that is, worſhip the True God, in the *Fleſh* (as the Scripture expreſſes it) and not in the *Spirit.* God is a Being, of infinite Holineſs, Juſtice, Righteouſneſs, Goodneſs and Truth; and 'tis his Will and Pleaſure that all reaſonable Creatures, according to their ſeveral Capacities, ſhould conform themſelves to his Likeneſs by the Imitation of theſe great and excellent Perfections. In *This,* conſiſts the Eſſence of Religion ; Theſe Diſpoſitions of Mind, are the moſt excellent *Virtues* upon *Earth :* and the *Foundation of the Happineſs of Heaven.* Theſe Qualifications are the Great *End and Deſign,* for the *promoting* of which, all religious Inſtitutions were intended ; and no external Performances whatſoever, are any otherwiſe of any Value, than as *Means* to promote theſe Great *Ends.* When therefore Men invert this natural Order of Things, and ſeparate the *Means* from the *End*; when they take up wholly with thofe external Obfervances, which in themfelves are of no value, but only as they tend to, and promote that Subftantial Virtue and Righteoufnefs, which is finally good and intrinfically in its own Nature profitable unto men; their religion in fuch cafe, like a Shadow without a Subftance, is vain; and like a Body without a Spirit, is dead. Of This great and fundamental Fault were guilty

1*ft*, **The** *antient Jews*; who, miftaking the Defign of their own Law, which was by *Sacrifices and Expiations* to remind them of the Neceffity of *true Repentance and Amendment of Life*; on the contrary, neglected the *End*, which was *Repentance and Amendment*; and contented themfelves with the bare *Means*, which were the *ritual Obfervations of the Law*; being defirous that *Sacrifices and Expiations* fhould ferve *inftead of*, and make amends for the *want of*, That Purity of Life and Manners, which in reality they were intended only as *Means* to promote; and from the Care of which, all *atonements and propitiations* were fo far from difcharging men, that indeed they were of no other Ufe, and defigned for no other purpofe, than to bind upon men more ftrongly their obligations to That *inward and real Holinefs*, of which all *legal and external Purifications* were but *Types and Figures*. The not rightly underftanding this Matter, was the great Error of the antient *Jews*: And an Error of fuch importance it was, affecting even the very Effence of Religion, that one of the main defigns of the preaching and writings of all the Prophets, was to reprove them for, and draw them off from, fo fatal a miftake. *Hath the Lord as great delight*, fays God by the Prophet *Samuel*, (1 Sam. xv. 22.) *Hath the Lord as great delight in burnt-offerings and Sacrifices, as in obeying the voice of the Lord? Behold, to obey, is better than Sacrifice, and to hearken than the Fat of Rams.* By the Prophet *David*, Pf. l. 13. *Will I eat the Flefh of Bulls, or drink the Blood of Goats? Nay, but Offer unto God Thankfgiving, and pay thy Vows unto the moft High.* By the Prophet *Ifaiah*, ch. i. 11. *To what purpofe is the Multitude of your facrifices unto me, faith the Lord; ——while your hands are full of Blood*, that is, of murder and unrighteous oppreffion: *But wafh ye, make you clean, put away the evil of your doings from before mine eyes, ceafe to do evil, learn to do well, feek judgment, relieve the oppreffed, judge the fatherlefs, plead for the widow:* Otherwife, *He that killeth an ox,* [ch. lxvi. 3.] *is as if he flew a man; and——he that burneth incenfe, as if he bleffed an Idol.* By the Prophet *Amos*, ch. v. 21. *I hate, I defpife your Feaft-days,——your burnt-offerings and your meat-offerings; ——But let judgment run down as water, and righteoufnefs as a mighty ftream.* Laftly, by the Prophet *Micah*, ch. vi. 7. *Will the Lord be pleafed with thoufands of Rams, or with ten thoufands of rivers of oyl?——Nay, but He hath fhewed thee, O man, what is good; and what doth the Lord require of thee, but to do juftly, and to love mercy, and to walk humbly with thy God?* And in a paffage ftill more remarkable than all thefe, *Jer.* vii. 22. *I fpake not unto your Fathers, nor commanded them in the day that I brought them out of the land of Egypt, concerning Burnt-offerings or Sacrifices; but This thing commanded I them, faying, Obey my voice.* There is here a confiderable difficulty in the expreffion, becaufe it feems in the *Englifh Tranflation*, as if it were a *denial* of God's having inftituted Sacrifices *at all*; which would be a direct contradiction to the whole Hiftory of Scripture. But 'tis a very remarkable Idiom in the *Original*, and deferves therefore to be obferved carefully, for the right underftanding of This and many other the like places; that what in modern languages is always expreffed in one Sentence by words comparative, the *Hebrew* ufually expreffes in two diftinct periods, by affirming concerning *one* thing, and denying of *another*, what is intended to be only comparative between *Both*. The Senfe therefore of thefe words, *I fpake not to your Fathers concerning Sacrifices,* is; I fpake not concerning *them*, as if they were of the fame importance with *moral obedience*. That This is the true interpretation of the Phrafe, there is an

evident

evident proof in the parallel place, *Hof.* vi. 6; where the prophet ufing that very fame expreffion, *I defired mercy, and* not *Sacrifice*; explains it comparatively in the very next words, *and the knowledge of God,* more than *burnt-offerings.* And from This idiom of the *Hebrew* language, the fame manner of fpeaking has been fometimes derived into the New Teftament. Thus *Mat.* xv. 24. *I am* not *fent,* faith our Saviour, *but to the loft fheep of the Houfe of Ifrael*: His meaning is not abfolute, that he was *not* fent *at all* to any other than the *Jews* only; but that he was not fent fo *foon,* fo *immediately* fo *principally*; his Miffion was not to be made known fo *early,* to any other Nation, as to the *loft fheep of the Houfe of Ifrael.* Again, *Joh.* xii. 44. *He that believeth on* Me, *believeth* not *on* Me, *but on* Him *that fent me,* that is, not fo *much,* not fo *properly* on *Me,* as on *Him that fent me.* Joh. xvii. 9. *I pray* not *for the World, but for* them *which thou haft given me :* Thefe words have fometimes been alledged in proof of the *abfolute reprobation* of the greateft part of mankind : But from what has been now faid concerning the nature of the *Jewifh* Language, it fufficiently appears that our Saviour's meaning, was only to pray for his Difciples *more efpecially,* and in a *more particular manner,* than for the reft of the World. *Acts* v. 4. *Thou haft* not *lied unto* Men, *but unto* God; that is, not only unto Men, not *fo much* to mere Men, as to God *himfelf,* who infpired them with his Holy Spirit. 1 *Cor.* i. 17. *Chrift fent me,* not *to baptize, but to preach the Gofpel*; that is, the Proper Office of an Apoftle, was not *fo much* to baptize, to perform the Ceremony Himfelf with his own hands, but rather to attend conftantly the Work of preaching the Gofpel. 1 *Cor.* vi. 12. *All things are lawful for me, but all things are not expedient :* The meaning is not, that all things were alike lawful ; but that all *thofe* things which *are* lawful, are not therefore confequently expedient. And, to mention, but *one* place more, 1 *Tim.* ii. 14. Adam *was* not *deceived, but the* Woman *being deceived was in the tranfgreffion :* The Meaning is not that *Adam* was *not deceived at all,* but that *his* Deception was *confequent* upon the *Woman*'s being deceived *firft,* and that it was brought upon *him* by *her* means. The Apoftle had faid in the verfe foregoing; *Adam was* firft formed, *then Eve :* And he adds; but *Adam was* not deceived, that is, was *not* firft *deceived*; The Deception began not at *him,* but at *her.* From all thefe, and from other the like paffages which might be alledged, 'tis abundantly evident, that when God tells the *Jews* by the Prophet, *I fpake* not *to your Fathers in the day that I brought them out of the land of Egypt concerning burnt-offerings or Sacrifices, but This thing commanded I them, faying, Obey my voice*; though the manner of the expreffion feems *Now* unufual to *Us,* yet in the language of the *Jews at that time* it was very eafy, and the meaning obvious, that hereby was not denied God's having commanded Sacrifices *at all,* but their *comparative value* only is denied, when diftinguifhed from the Practice of moral Virtue and Righteoufnefs.

I T may here perhaps by fome be inquired; if the inftitutions of the *Jewifh* Law, were matters comparatively of fo fmall importance ; *Statutes* (as the Prophet expreffes it) *which were not good, and Judgments whereby men fhould not live*; for *what reafon* then was That Law given by divine appointment at all ? To This queftion, the Scripture intimates to us feveral Anfwers. In the *firft* place, it was given That People, to preferve them from Idolatry ; to keep them from running after the Cuftoms of the Idolatrous Nations round about them ; by employing them in the continual Service of the True God. This reafon is hinted at in feveral places of the Law ; and particularly, *Deut.* v. 22, where, at the time of the *original* delivering of the *Ten Commandments* from God to the Children of *Ifrael,* 'tis affirmed that *he added no more* ; but after their pronenefs to Idolatry fhown in the cafe of their fetting up the *golden calf,* the whole ceremonial Law with all its burdenfome rites was immediately injoyned them. In the *next* place, *another reafon* of appointing thofe numerous Sacrifices and Expiations, Wafhings, Purifications, and the like ; was to remind that Stiff-necked people, of their

Obligation

S E R M. Obligation to Purity and true Holinefs of life, by fuch corporeal Figures and Emblems,
VI.   as might always be vifibly before their Eyes; fuited to their capacities, and prejudices:
⌇⌇⌇⌇   proper to withdraw them from the Pollutions of their neighbouring Nations; to admo-
nifh them conftantly, of their being the peculiar People of the True God, the Holy
One of *Ifrael*; and confequently to keep them under a perpetual Senfe, of their obli-
gation to be Holy even as He was Holy. *Laftly, Another reafon* of God's giving the
Law of *Mofes*, was to be a prophetick Typifying of the Meffiah to come; and a
Schoolmafter, (as St *Paul* expreffes it, *Gal.* iii. 24. iv. 1.) *to bring Men unto Chrift.*

Joh. i. 17. For *the Law*, (faith St *John*,) *was given by Mofes, but Grace and Truth, came by Je-*
fus Chrift; The meaning is; The *Law*, was only a *Type* or *Shadow* of That *Truth*,
and an *Emblem* of That *Grace* or *Mercy* of God, which was to be clearly and fully
revealed in the *Gofpel.* And for That Reafon, the Law was not of *perpetual*, but only

Heb. vii. 18. of *temporary* inftitution: *There is verily* (fays the Apoftle) *a difannulling of the Com-*
ix. 9, 10. *mandment going before, for the Weaknefs and Unprofitablenefs thereof*; it being *only a*
x. 1. figure *for the Time then prefent,——impofed upon them till the time of* Reformation;
——*a Shadow of good things to come, and not the very Image* (the Senfe is, *not the very*
Subftance) *of the things themfelves*, Heb. x. 1. The not attending to thefe *Ends* of the
Inftitution of the Law of *Mofes*, which yet are very plainly hinted in the Law itfelf
and in the Writings of the Prophets; was a principal Caufe of the *antient Jews* falling
into that fundamental Error, of laying greater ftrefs upon the bare *ritual and ceremonial*
performances, than upon that *real Virtue and true Righteoufnefs* whereof thefe outward
Obfervances were but Types and Figures; Contrary to the perpetual Exhortations of all
their own Prophets, and contrary to that great Duty enforced in the Text from *natural*
Reafon itfelf, that God, being a Spirit, ought confequently to be worfhipped in Spirit
and in Truth.

2*dly*, T H E *next* remarkable Example, of perfons erring fundamentally from this
great Rule of *worfhipping God in Spirit and in Truth*, were thofe *Jewifh* Converts
among the Primitive Chriftians, who contended that *after* their Converfion it was ftill
neceffary to obferve the *Law* together with the *Gofpel.* Which opinion of theirs, was
the occafion of much Controverfy in the Apoftles times; as may be feen at large, in
th xv^th chapter of the *Acts*, and in the whole Epiftle to the *Galatians.* Which Con-
Particularly, troverfy being Now long fince at an End; it would no longer have been of any Ufe to
ch. vi. 12. *Us* to inquire into the State of it, were it not that accidentally 'tis ftill very neceffary to
the right underftanding two of St *Paul's* Epiftles, That to the *Romans*, and That to
the *Galatians*; many erroneous and hurtful Doctrines in Chriftianity, having been occafioned by mens ignorantly applying feveral Phrafes in thofe Epiftles, according to the
modern Senfe of words among Chriftians at this day; when in reality they were by the
Apoftle ufed only according to the Signification of the words in *thofe* days, relating to
This controverfy with the *Jewifh* Chriftians about the neceffity of ftill retaining the
Law of *Mofes.* For againft *Thefe* mens opinions it is, that St *Paul* argues, and *not at*
all in the way of comparing one Chriftian virtue with another, when he earneftly in
thefe Epiftles magnifies *Faith* in oppofition to the *Law*, *Grace* in oppofition to *Works*,
and the *Spirit* in oppofition to *Flefh* or *carnal Ordinances.* Thus when he tells his
converts, *Rom.* iii. 28, and *Gal.* ii. 15, iii. 2. that they are *juftified by* Faith, *with-*
out the deeds of the Law; and that they *received* the Holy Ghoft, *not by the works*
of the Law, *but by the Hearing of* Faith; his meaning is not, (as fome in later Ages
have unreafonably underftood him,) that men are juftified barely by *Faith* or *Believing*,
as diftinguifhed from *Virtue* or *Righteoufnefs of Life*; but that men are juftified by the
Obedience of the *Gofpel*, (fo the word *Faith* always fignifies in St. *Paul's* epiftles,) and
is therefore fometimes exprefsly called *The obedience of Faith*, Rom. xvi. 25; and *obe-*
dience to the Faith, Rom. i. 5; and *Acts* vi. 7. they are juftified (he faith) by the Obedience

3

dience of the *Gospel* only, by That *Fidelity* or *Sincerity* in religion, which the Gospel requires, without obferving the ceremonies of the Law of *Mofes*. In like manner, when he tells them that their Salvation is not of *works*, but of *Grace*, Rom. xi. 5; and *Gal.* v. 4. he does not mean that God faves them without the *works of Virtue and Righteouf-nefs*; but that they are faved by the gracious *difpenfation of the* Gospel, (That is always the meaning of the word, *Grace*, in thefe Epiftles,) they are faved by the gracious *difpen-fation of the Gospel*, by the merciful Terms of Repentance declared through Chrift, and not by the *ritual and rigorous Obfervations of the Mofaick Law*. Further; becaufe one great End of This Laft Difpenfation of the Gofpel, was to teach men to worfhip God with pure worfhip, *in Spirit and in Truth*, with all Holinefs and Righteoufnefs of the *Heart and Mind*; in oppofition to *external Forms and carnal Ordinances*, Such as Cir-cumcifion, Bodily Wafhings, Purifications, and the like; which affect the *Body* only : therefore St *Paul* frequently expreffes the Gofpel of Chrift by the figurative Name of *Spirit*, and the Law of *Mofes* by that of *Flefh* : Gal. iii. 3. *Are ye fo foolifh? Having be-gun in the* Spirit, *are ye now made perfect by the* Flefh? Thefe Phrafes, which otherwife might feem very difficult becaufe different from modern ways of fpeaking; do, from what has been faid, appear plainly to fignify This only, that the *Galatians* were worthy of reproof, for that fince their embracing the Religion of *Chrift*, they imagined they could ftill become *more perfect*, by continuing the practice of *Jewifh* obfervances. And that This is his true and only meaning may be fhown yet more evidently from the follow-ing parallel places; *Rom.* ii. 29. *Circumcifion, is that of the* Heart, *in the* Spirit, *and not in the* letter : And *ch.* vii. 6. *We are delivered from the* Law;—*that we fhould ferve in newnefs of* Spirit, *and not in the oldnefs of the* letter : And *Phil.* iii. 3, We *are the circum-cifion, which worfhip God in the* Spirit,—*and have no confidence in the* Flefh. *Spirit*, in all thefe places, is the *fpiritual worfhip* of the Gofpel; and what he here ftiles *Flefh*, is the fame as what he elfewhere calls a *carnal commandment*, Heb. vii. 16; and *ch.* ix. 10. *car-nal ordinances*, namely, *meats and drinks and divers wafhings*. Thefe, where there is no true Virtue and Righteoufnefs of Life, are the Forms *of Godlinefs* without the Power *of it*; the corruption, which our Saviour principally meant to reform in the words of the Text; and which St *Paul* cautions againft, when he declares, that *the Kingdom of God is not meat and drink, but righteoufnefs, and peace, and joy in the Holy Ghoft*; Rom. xvi. 17 : *that we are minifters of the New Teftament, not of the* letter, *but of the* Spirit, 2 Cor. iii. 6: that *Circumcifion is nothing, and uncircumcifion is nothing, but Faith which worketh by Love* : And inftanceth in *Abraham*, Rom. iv. 3, 10. that *before* his receiving the Seal of Circumcifion, he *believed* in God, and obeyed his commandments, *and it was counted unto him for Righteoufnefs* : The Religion of *Abraham*, was the fame as the Spiritual Religion of the *Gospel*; He lived *before* the Law, as our Saviour requires that *Chriftians* fhould do *after* the law; *worfhipping God in Spirit and in Truth*.

3*dly*, As Some among the *Antient Jews*, and *Antient Chriftians*, were, in the manner already fhown, guilty of tranfgreffing this great Precept of *worfhipping God in Spirit and in Truth*; fo among Chriftians of all *later* Ages likewife, there are Many too juftly chargeable with being guilty of the fame Fundamental Fault in different re-fpects. In the

1*ft* PLACE, Thofe of the Church of *Rome*, do in the Higheft degree tranfgrefs this great Commandment of our Saviour, when inftead of that *Spiritual Worfhip*, which our Lord intended to eftablifh, they on the contrary fill their Religion with more *rites and ceremonies*, than even the *Law of Mofes itfelf* was burdened withal; And (which of all other things is the moft profane,) compell Men by force, to make external and hypocritical Profeffions in matters of Religion; which yet, they well know, if it is not feated in the Heart, is no Religion at all.

SERM. VI.

2dly, OF tranfgreffing this precept in the Text, *thofe* Chriftians alfo are guilty in *All* communions, who place the chief of their Religion in the *Form* of Godlinefs, in barely *going to Church*, and *in receiving the Sacrament*, and in fuch other *outward Performances*, which ought not indeed to be *left undone*, but which are *Then only* acceptable to God and ufeful to the Souls of Men, when they are means of producing that True Holinefs, Charity, and Righteoufnefs of life, which is, in Heaven, as well as upon Earth, the eternal and unchangeable effence of Religion. Such perfons as Thefe therefore are well reproved by the Prophet *Jeremy?* ch. vii. 4. *Truft ye not in lying words, faying, The Temple of the Lord, the Temple of the Lord, the Temple of the Lord are thefe*; But *throughly amend your ways and your doings; throughly execute judgment between a man and his neighbour; opprefs not the ftranger, the fatherlefs and the widow.*

3dly, THEY alfo cannot be faid to worfhip God in Spirit and in Truth, who place religion chiefly in matters of *opinion, fpeculation, and difpute*; in Doctrines hard to underftand, and of no ufe in practice. *Though I underftand all* myfteries, faith the Apoftle, and *all* Knowledge; *and have not charity: I am nothing,* 1 Cor. xiii. 2. There follows in the next verfe an expreffion ftill more remarkable; *though I beftow all my goods to feed the* poor, *and have not charity, it profiteth me nothing.* From this paffage it appears, that the word *Charity*, in the New Teftament, does not fignify (as we *now* ufe it) only *Alms to the poor*; but *That* univerfal Love and Good-will towards all men, which includes both *It* and *all other* Virtues; The conftant practice of *which* univerfal Charity, is *indeed* Worfhipping God *in Spirit and in Truth.*

4thly, OF tranfgreffing this Precept in the Text, *They* alfo are guilty, who are over-zealous and contentious about *fmall* things, which withdraw the affections and the attention from *greater*. Their fuperftitious *zeal* about which things, is like the unprofitable excrefcencies of fruitful plants, eating out and deftroying the life of religion. In our Saviour's phrafe, *they tithe mint, anife and cummin, and neglect the weightier matters of the law, judgment, mercy and truth.*

Laftly, ALL fuch perfons are very far from worfhipping God in Spirit and in Truth, who living in the practice of *any* known fin, ferve not God with the *whole* Heart and *Spirit, cleanfing themfelves from all filthinefs of Flefh and Spirit, perfecting Holinefs in the fear of the Lord.*

SERMON

SERMON VII.

Of the IMMUTABILITY of GOD.

MAL. III. 6.

For I am the Lord; I change not.

IN difcourfing upon thefe words of the Prophet, I fhall *firft* indeavour to fhow *in* what refpects God muft be acknowledged to be *Unchangeable*, or *wherein* this Attribute of *Immutability* confifts. And *2dly*, I fhall confider, what *Ufes* may be made of This meditation, in the government of our Life and Practice.

I. IN order to explain the Nature of This divine Attribute of Immutability, and fhow diftinctly *wherein* it *confifts*; it is to be obferved, that both in Reafon and Scripture God is confidered as Unchangeable, upon *different Accounts* and in very *different Refpects*.

1ft. IN refpect of his *Effence*, God is abfolutely unchangeable, becaufe his Being is neceflary, and his Effence Self-exiftent: For whatever *neceffarily* Is; as it cannot but *Be*, fo it cannot but *continue* to be *invariably what it is*. That which depends *upon* Nothing, can be affected *by* Nothing, can be *acted upon* by Nothing, can be *changed* by Nothing, can be *influenced* by no *Power*, can be *impared* by no *Time*, can be *varied* by no *Accident*. The Scripture does not often enter into the philofophical part of This Speculation, but yet very emphatically expreffes it in the *Name* which is given to God both in the Old Teftament and in the New. In the Old Teftament, God himfelf declared it to *Mofes*, Exod. iii. 14. *Thus fhalt thou fay unto the children of Ifrael,* I AM *has fent me unto you.* And in the New Teftament, St *John* fets it forth in the beginning of his Prophecy, *Rev.* i. 4. *Grace be unto you and peace, from Him which is, and which was, and which is to come.* *Other* things alfo *Are*, and have been, and *fhall be :* But becaufe what they *have been*, might have been *otherwife*; and what they *Are*, might as poffibly *not have been at all*; and what they *fhall be*, may be very *different from what Now is*; therefore of *Their* changeable and dependent effence, which to day may be *one thing*, and to morrow *another thing*, and the next day poffibly *nothing at all*; of fuch a dependent and changeable effence, compared with the invariable Exiftence of God, it *fcarce* deferves to be affirmed that it Is. And 'tis very remarkable, that in the paffage now cited, *He which is, and which was, and which is to come,* the words in the Original are placed in a very unufual conftruction, a conftruction no where elfe found in the whole New Teftament, nor perhaps in any other Book; but very fuitable to fuch a fingular occafion; fo as to fignify, Not barely, He which *is, and was, and is to come,* (for *That may* perhaps, in *Some* fenfe, be affirmed alfo of fome *other* Beings;) but it fignifies, *He* whofe Being (or whofe proper *Name* and *Character*) is, effentially and invariably, *which Is, and Was, and is to come:* And This expreffion is ὁ ὢν ὁ ἦν &c. very agreeable to the Sublimity of the Prophetick Style. In *other* places, the Scripture fets forth the fame thing, only in *more eafy and popular* expreffions: Stiling God, *the King immortal,* 1 Tim. i. 17; Which *only hath immortality,* ch. vi. 16. that is, who only hath it *immutably and independently :* The *incorruptible* God, Rom. i. 23. and, ἀφθάρτῳ

from

SERM. *from everlafting to everlafting,* (that is, by an unchangeable effence,) thou art *God,*
VII. Pf. xc. 2. All *other* things are changeable and perithable; even the Frame of the Hea-
Pf. cii. 26. vens themfelves above, and the Foundations of the Earth beneath; *They all fhall perifh,
yea all of them fhall wax old like a garment; as a vefture fhalt thou change them, and
they fhall be changed; But* Thou *art the Same,* the *Same* through *all* generations, and
beyond all generations ftill unchangeably the *fame.*

2*dly.* IN refpect of his *Perfections* likewife, as well as his *Effence,* God is abfolutely *unchangeable.* Concerning *thofe* Perfections which flow *neceffarily* from his Effence, and depend not on his *Will,* this is Self-evident; becaufe whatever *neceffarily*
flows from any Caufe or Principle, muft likewife of neceffity be as invariable, as the
Caufe or Principle from which it neceffarily proceeds. Of This kind are the Power, the
Knowledge, the Wifdom, and the other *natural* Attributes of God; which having no
dependence even upon his *own Will,* any more than his very Being itfelf has; 'tis plain
they can *much lefs* be fubject to any Alteration, from any *other* Caufe or Power whatfoever. Concerning thofe *other* Perfections, the Exercife whereof depends upon his
Will; fuch are his Juftice, Veracity, Goodnefs, Mercy, and all other *moral* Perfections; the absolute Immutability of *thefe,* is not indeed fo obvious and felf-evident;
becaufe it depends on the unchangeablenefs, not only of his *Effence,* but of his *Will*
alfo. Neverthelefs, upon careful confideration, the unchangeablenefs of *Thefe* likewife,
will no lefs certainly appear: becaufe in a Being who always knows what is right to be
done, and can never poffibly be deceived, or awed, or tempted, or impofed upon; his
general Will or *Intention,* of doing always what is beft and moft fit and right, will in
reality, though not upon the *fame* ground of natural *Neceffity,* yet in event, and upon
the whole, be as *certainly and truly unchangeable,* as his very Effence itfelf. With
great reafon therefore does the Scripture thus fpeak of his *Juftice and Veracity,* Pf. cxvii. 2.
The Truth *of the Lord endureth* for ever; and *Pf.* cxi. 3, 5, 7, 8. *His* righteoufnefs
endureth for ever; *he will ever be mindful of his* covenant; *The works of his hands are
verity and judgment, all his commandments are* fure; *They ftand* faft *for* ever and ever,
and are done in Truth *and Uprightnefs.* And concerning his *Mercy and Goodnefs,*
Pf. xxxvi. 5. *Thy Mercy, O Lord, is in the Heavens, and thy Faithfulnefs reacheth unto
the clouds; Thy* righteoufnefs *is like the ftrong mountains, thy judgments are like the great
deep.* And the Apoftle St *James* reprefents this to us under a very elegant Similitude,
ch. i. 17. *Every good and perfect Gift,* faith he, *cometh down from the Father of Lights,
with whom is no variablenefs neither* fhadow of turning. The Comparifon is extremely
elegant, drawn from the confideration of That which in corporeal things is the leaft fubject to change, *viz.* the Sun fhining in the Heavens. The *Sun,* is the greateft, the
moft regular, the moft ftable and conftant Difpenfer of Light and Heat and fruitful influences, upon the whole Face of This inferor World; yet is his influence varied by
different Motions, by Days and Nights, by Winter and Summer, by Clouds and
Shadows, and by alterations within its own Body. But *God,* the *Father* of fpiritual
Light, the Author and Difpofer of all good and perfect Gifts, has in him no Motion,
no Uncertainty, no Alteration of any of his Perfections, *no Variablenefs neither fhadow
of turning.*

3*dly,* As God is unchangeable in his *Effence,* and in the *general Perfections* of his
Nature; fo is he alfo in the *particular Decrees and Purpofes* of his *Will;* and fo likewife in his *Laws,* in his *Promifes,* and in his *Threatnings.* The Reafon is; becaufe,
having all *Power* and all *Knowledge,* he can never refolve upon any thing, which fhall
be either not *poffible,* or not *reafonable,* to be accomplifhed. All *finite* Beings, are frequently forced to change their Defigns; becaufe they often find it *impoffible* to finifh
what they begin, or *unreafonable* to purfue their firft Intention: But in *God,* thefe
things have no place.

1   HE

HE is unchangeable in all his *Decrees and Purposes*; because having all things in his Power, and comprehending all things in his Fore-knowledge, he can by no Force be over-ruled; he can by no surprize or unexpected accident be prevented; he can by no unforeseen Alteration in the reasons of things be himself changed in his Purpose. *The Counsel of the Lord standeth for ever, and the thoughts of his Heart from generation to generation,* Pf. xxxiii. 11. *He is in one mind, and who can turn him? and what his Soul desireth, even That He doth,* Job xxiii. 13. Some have from these passages attempt-ed to deduce the doctrine of absolute Predestination; that because the Decrees and Pur-poses of God are unchangeable, therefore Men's Salvation, or Condemnation, does not at all depend on any Works in their own Power. And indeed, were there any such Decree, it could not be denied but it would be unchangeable, and consequently that All Religion were vain. But the *Truth* is, that the Scripture mentions no *such* Decree at all; and therefore men need not be concerned about the Unchangeableness of That, which has no Being. The Decree of God, is not that This or That particular person, shall necessarily be saved or perish; (For then What Need, or what Use would there be of a day of Judgment?) But his Decree is, that Faith and Obedience, in whomsoever it is found, shall lead to Salvation; and Disobedience on the contrary, to Destruction: And *This* Decree is indeed, like all his other Purposes, absolutely unalterable.

AGAIN, in his *Laws* likewise, that is, in the uniform Intention of all his Com-mandments, God is perfectly *unchangeable*; because they are always founded on the same immutable *reasons*, the eternal Differences of Good and Evil, the original nature of Things, and universal Equity; and they always tend to the same regular *End*, the Order and Happiness of the whole Creation. Of This, the Law of *Nature* was the primary Institution; the Law of *Moses*, was the typical or figurative Representation; and the Gospel of *Christ*, its completion or perfect Restoration. And this is the mean-ing of that passage of the Apostle, *Heb.* xiii. 8. *Jesus Christ, the same yesterday, and to day, and for ever.* That this is here spoken, not of the *Person*, (though in *That* sense also it is true; but that it is *here* spoken, not of the *Person*) but of the *Law* of Christ, appears from the words immediately following, with which it is connected; *Be not carried away with divers and strange* doctrines; *for Jesus Christ is the same yesterday, and to day, and for ever*; his Doctrine is, eternally and unchangeably, One and the same. *The Gospel,* faith the same Apostle, *Gal.* iii. 8. was *preached before unto Abra-ham*: which *Gospel, the Law that was given four hundred years after, could not dif-annul*; but was *added* only *because of Transgression,* (that is, because of the infirm and childish state of the people of the *Jews,*) *till the promised Seed should come*: till the more explicit declaration of that Faith, by which alone both *Abraham* and all good men from the beginning of the world *were,* as all good Christians *shall be* even unto the End, uniformly justified; that is, by the *everlasting Gospel,* Rev. xiv. 6. the eternal and *un-changeable Law of God.*

FURTHER; in his *Covenants or Promises,* (such as are not declared to be condi-tional, and annexed to certain particular Qualifications,) God is likewise perfectly *un-changeable.* The Reason is, because *Covenants or Promises of this kind* are founded upon such grounds as cannot be altered; even upon the original, fixt and permanent Designs and Intentions of all-wise Providence. Thus, concerning the Promise made to *Abraham*; God, faith the Apostle, *Heb.* vi. 13. *because he could swear by no greater, sware by himself;* —— *confirming it by an Oath, to show unto the heirs of Promise the immutability of his Counsel.* The reason of which unchangeable resolution was, because the giving that land to *Abraham* and to his Seed after him, included the Promise both of the *temporal Jerusalem* for an Habitation of the true Worshippers of God *here,* and of the *heavenly Jerusalem,* wherein both *Abraham* himself personally and all his spiri-tual Posterity were to be made happy *hereafter.* Of the same Nature is That Declara-

SERM. tion concerning *all Ifrael*, Num. xxiii. 19. *God is not a man, that he fhould lye ; neither*
VII. *the Son of Man, that he fhould repent : Hath he faid, and fhall he not do it ? or hath he*
fpoken, and fhall he not make it good ? Behold, I have received commandment to blefs ;
and he hath bleffed, and I cannot reverfe it. The reafon of This, is, becaufe it was a
declaration of the whole Scheme of Providence in eftablifhing a Standard of true Religion among that People : which was a matter not to be altered by any mens future
behaviour : It was one of thofe things, which God might juftly, and without wrong to
any man, determine *at firft* by his abfolute Supreme Power ; (as in the cafe of *Jacob*
and *Efau*, he declared, *before either of them was born or had done either good or evil,*
that the pofterity of *the elder fhould ferve* that of *the younger* ;) and which Defign *after-*
wards, in the *whole courfe* of his Providence, he might *continue* to accomplifh in the
fame manner, however *different* mens behaviour might be under the feveral periods of
That difpenfation. And This is the true Meaning of that other difficult Text in St. *Paul*,
Rom. xi. 28, 29. *As concerning the Gofpel, they* (the Nation of the *Jews*) *are Enemies*
for your fake ; but as touching the election, they are beloved for the Fathers fakes ; For
the Gifts (thefe Gifts) *and Calling of God are without Repentance.* Some have applied
Thefe words alfo to the doctrine of Predeftination : But their being fpoken exprefsly of
whole Nations, and not of *fingle perfons*, evidently demonftrates the contrary ; and fhows
at the fame time the reafon of the immutability of thefe Gifts of God, namely becaufe
they are not moral Gifts or Graces to particular Perfons, but parts of the general
Scheme and Defign of Providence in the Government of the World through fucceffive
Ages. Of the fame kind, is that promife of God to *David*, Pf. lxxxix. 21. *I have*
found David my Servant, with my Holy oil have I anointed him ;——my mercy will I
keep for him for evermore, and my Covenant fhall ftand faft with him ;——If his children
forfake my Law, and walk not in my judgments ; Then will I vifit their tranfgreffion with
the rod, and their iniquity with ftripes ; Neverthelefs my loving kindnefs will I not utterly
take from him, nor fuffer my Truth to fail ; my covenant will I not break, nor alter
the thing that is gone out of my lips ; Once have I fworn by my Holinefs, that I will not
lye unto David. Thefe Promifes, were unalterable Prophecies, of a Meffiah to arife out
of the Seed of *David* ; As had in like manner before been promifed to *Adam* and the
Patriarchs, to *Abraham*, to *Ifaac*, and to *Jacob.* And therefore 'tis a weak thing in
the modern *Jews*, to alledge that their *Sins* have prevented the coming of the Meffiah ;
which was one of the original great Conftitutions of Providence, and a Promife of God
not to be repented of.

Laftly, GOD is *unchangeable* likewife in his *Threatnings* ; that is to fay, in fuch
Threatnings, as are not *merely perfonal* ; For of *Thofe* I fhall have occafion to fpeak prefently : But in his *general Threatnings*, as well as in his *Promifes*, God is abfolutely *un-*
changeable. The Reafon is, becaufe, as his Love to Virtue and Goodnefs is unalterable,
fo his Hatred to Vice is irreconcileable ; and alfo becaufe thefe Threatnings are often
Prophetick parts of the general Scheme of Providence. Thus in the cafe of *Saul* ; tho'
upon his repenting in fome meafure, the Prophet confented to honour him for the
prefent before the Elders of his people ; yet in the matter of the Kingdom as to the
Time to come, the Threatning of God, being more a Prophecy of the great Counfels
of Providence, than a perfonal Threatning to *Him*, could not be reverfed : 1 *Sam.* xv. 28.
The Lord has rent the Kingdom of Ifrael from thee this day, and hath given it to a
Neighbour of thine, that is better than Thou ; And alfo the Strength of Ifrael will not lye,
nor repent ; for he is not a man, that he fhould repent. In like manner, the Difperfion
and Captivity of the *Jewifh* Nation for fome Ages before and after the Coming of the
Meffiah ; at the fame time that it was a juft Punifhment for *their particular* Sins, being moreover *in general* one of the great Events or Difpenfations of Providence in the
whole Oeconomy or Government of Mankind upon Earth ; is always fpoken of by the

I

Prophets,

Prophets, as a Judgment which God would indeed *put an* end *to* upon the Repentance of that Nation, but the *Sentence and* Execution *whereof he would not reverse*, Jer. iv. 27. *Thus hath the Lord said, The whole Land* shall *be desolate :——I have purposed it, and will not repent, neither will I turn back from it.* And *Ezek.* xxiv. 14. *I the Lord have spoken it, it* shall *come to pass, and I will do it ; I will not go back, neither will I spare, neither will I repent.* And therefore very remarkable is the Answer that was given to good King *Josiah*; when, being grieved at these Threatnings, he sent to inquire of the Lord; 2 *Kings* xxii. 15. *Thus saith the Lord God of Israel, Tell the man that sent you, ——I* will *bring evil upon this place, and upon the* inhabitants thereof ;——*But to the King* himself —— *thus shall ye say ;——Because thine Heart was tender, and thou hast humbled thy self before the Lord, behold therefore I will gather* Thee *unto thy Fathers ——in peace, and* thine *eyes shall not see all the Evil that I will bring upon this place.* And the Account given of this matter in the following chapter, is no less remarkable ; *ch.* xxiii. 25 ; and *ch.* xxiv. 4. *Like him was there no King before him, that turned to the Lord with all his Heart,——neither after him arose there any like him ; Notwithstanding, the Lord turned not from the fierceness of his great wrath, wherewith his Anger was kindled against Judah, because of all the provocations that Manasseh had provoked him withal,——and for the innocent blood that he shed, which the Lord* would not *pardon.*

AGAINST all that has been hitherto said, concerning the Unchangeableness of God ; there is One very obvious, and great *Objection*; drawn from those Texts of Scripture, which seem to speak of God in a very different manner from those already cited, and to represent him on the contrary as very frequently repenting and changing his Purpose. Thus 'tis recorded, *Gen.* vi. 5. that when *God saw that the wickedness of man was great in the Earth,——it* repented *the Lord that he had made man on the Earth, and it grieved him at his Heart* ; and 1 *Sam.* xv. 35. that *the Lord* repented, *that he had made Saul King over Israel*; and *Num.* xiv. 30, 34. concerning a whole generation of the people of *Israel, Doubtless* (saith he) *ye shall* not *come into the land, concerning which I sware to make you dwell therein, and ye shall know my breach of promise,* or (as it is better rendred in the margin) *Ye shall know the altering of my Purpose :* And *Jer.* xxvi. 13. *Amend your ways and your doings,——and the Lord will* repent *of the evil that he hath pronounced against you :* And *Jonah* iii. 10. *God saw their works, that they turned from their evil way ; and God* repented *of the Evil that he had said he would do unto them, and he did it not.* These passages (I say) may at first fight seem to be a very strong *Objection*, against what has been before laid down concerning the Unchangeableness of God in all his Purposes. But the *Answer* likewise, from what has been before said, is plain and obvious. *Those* Declarations of the Designs and Purposes of God, which are *Prophetick* of the great Events of Providence, are *in themselves* absolutely *fixt and unalterable* ; because the Wisdom of God could not possibly be deceived, in the original Design and Intention of appointing them. But *these* Promises and Threatnings, which are merely *personal*, either to any particular man, or to any Number of men, are always *conditional* ; because the Wisdom of God thought fit to make *These* depend on the Behaviour of Men ; and the Immutability of God with regard to *These*, does not consist in the unalterableness of the Things themselves, but in the unchangeableness of *the Condition* upon which they are to be performed. The *Rule*, is universal and unchangeable ; *Jer.* xviii. 7. *At what instant I shall speak concerning a Nation,—— to pull down and to destroy it ; if that nation——turn from their evil, I will repent of the evil that I thought to do unto them : And at what instant I shall speak concerning a Nation,——to build and to plant it ; If it do evil in my sight,——then I will repent of the good, wherewith I said I would benefit them.* The *Expressions*, of God's *repenting, grieving,* and the like ; are only *figurative*, in condescension to the weakness of our Apprehensions ;

S E R M.   prehenfions; fignifying, not any *Change* in *God* himfelf, but only a *Difference of the*
VII.   *Event* with regard to *Us*.   God's Affection towards Good or Evil, towards Virtue or
Vice, is *therefore* uniform and unchangeable; becaufe his Promifes and Threatnings *in-*
variably follow thefe Difpofitions, through all the Changes of mens perfonal behaviour.
Thus Good Parents and Princes, without any Change in *Themfelves*, encourage or difcourage their refpective children, or fubjects, according as *They* change their behaviour
for the better or the worfe.   Thus *Laws themfelves*, which can have no *Affection*, nor
Change of *Affection*, towards one perfon or another; yet vary their *Effect*, themfelves
remaining unvaried; and bring rewards or punifhments, according to the different behaviour of the perfon upon whom they are executed.   The only difference in This cafe,
is; that Laws made by the beft *human* Wifdom, can take *no* notice of the *Repentance*
of great Malefactors in the cafe of capital Crimes; becaufe 'tis impoffible for human
Wifdom to difcern when fuch Repentance is fincere, and confequently 'tis altogether
unfafe to truft to any pretences of That kind : But God who fees the inmoft Difpofitions of Mens Hearts, judges always according to the reality of thofe Difpofitions, and
difpenfes his Rewards or Punifhments accordingly.   And in This, he acts uniformly,
without Change or Variation.   As the fame Fire, with one unvaried Action, confumes
combuftible matter, but purifies and refines Gold; and the fame Sun, with one continual Heat, melts one fort of Bodies, and hardens another; fo God, without any
change or alteration in himfelf, punifhes the wicked when they fo continue, and fhows
compaffion towards the fame perfons when they become truly and fincerely penitent.

II. THE *Ufes* of this Difcourfe, by way of Application, concerning the Immutability of God, are briefly as follows.

1*ft*, THE *Unchangeablenefs* of God's *natural Perfections*, and the *Promife* of Him to
whom thofe Perfections fo invariably belong, is to *good men* at all times the greateft
poffible fecurity, that they fhall not finally fail to be Happy.   When the World, and
all things that are therein, fhall fail; the Power of God, his Wifdom, his Goodnefs,
his *Love* of Virtue, are Perfections which can never fail in *themfelves*; and his *Promife*
fecures the Application of them to *Us*; if we continue to live in obedience to his Commands.   *Heb*. vi. 13, 17.   *When God made Promife to Abraham ; becaufe he could fwear*
by no greater, he fware by himfelf ;——Wherein God willing more abundantly to fhew
unto the heirs of Promife the immutability of his counfel, confirmed it with an Oath ;
That by two immutable things, in which it was impoffible for God to lye, we might have
a ftrong confolation, who have fled for refuge to lay hold upon the hope fet before us.   And
Tit. i. 2.   *The Hope of eternal life, which God, that* cannot lye, *promifed before the world*
began.   The fame Inference is drawn by the Prophet in the words of the Text; *I am*
the Lord, I change not, (my Compaffion, my Promife, is immutable;)   therefore *ye*
Sons of Jacob are not confumed.   And by the Pfalmift, *Pf*. xxxiii. 11, 12.   *The Counfel*
of the Lord ftandeth for ever ;   Therefore *Bleffed is the Nation whofe God is the Lord,*
and the people whom he has chofen for his own inheritance.   And *Pf*. xxxvi. 6, 7.   *Thy*
righteoufnefs is like the ftrong mountains ;——Therefore *the children of men put their truft*
under the fhadow of thy wings.

2*dly*, THE *Threatnings* of him whofe nature and perfections are *unchangeable*, ought
to be a perpetual Terror to *impenitent Sinners*.   He will by no means clear the Guilty,
nor can by any application be reconciled to Sin.   No Bribe, no Force, no Artifice, no
Interceffion, no length of Time, can change his Hatred towards unrighteous *Actions* ;
or hinder him, without true Repentance and effectual Amendment, from punifhing unrighteous *Men*.   His Wifdom, his Honour, his Goodnefs, obliges him to preferve the
Dignity of his Laws and Government; and 'tis therefore a dreadful thing for wilful
Sinners to fall into the hands of the ever-living, ever-unchangeable God.

3*dly*, ON

3dly, On the contrary, the confideration of the *Mercy* of Him, who is *unchange-* S E R M.
able in his Perfections, ought to be a no lefs conftant incouragement to fuch as are truly VII.
penitent, and fincerely defirous to amend. Men, are oftimes weak and paffionate, and
implacable when provoked : But the Mercy and Compaffion of *God*, is, like all the
other perfections of his Nature, unchangeably ready to extend itfelf towards thofe, who
at any time become capable Objects of it. And from the fame confideration, appears
likewife the abfolute and indifpenfable *Neceffity of Repentance* : For as the Mercy of
God is always open *to* the penitent, fo *from* it the impenitent are irreverfibly excluded.
'Tis impoffible, that *God* fhould change : The Sinner *may* change, and *muft* do fo, or
perifh.

4thly and *Laftly* ; As *Unchangeablenefs* is an Excellency and Perfection in *God* ; fo in
Man, on the *contrary*, to *change* his opinion and manner of acting, when there is juft
caufe fo to do, is one of *his* greateft Commendations. And the Reafon in Both, is the
fame ; namely, that Right and Truth are to be followed unchangeably. As therefore
God, who *never can* err in his judgment of Right and Truth, muft confequently be
unchangeable in his acting according to it ; fo, for the very fame Reafon, frail and fallible *Man*, whenever he finds he *has* erred from what is True and Right, muft immediately return unto it. But in things certainly and demonftrably *True* ; or which, upon
the fulleft and moft careful examination, are found evidently and undeniably *Good* ; in
thefe things, men ought to be firm and ftedfaft without wavering ; and *not like children,*
toffed to and fro with every wind of doctrine, by the flight of men, and cunning craftinefs
whereby they lie in wait to deceive. For *Jefus Chrift*, i. e. the Doctrine or Gofpel of
Chrift, *is the fame yefterday, and to day, and for ever* ; *Be not* therefore (fays the
Apoftle) *carried about with divers and ftrange doctrines* ; *for it is a good thing that the*
heart be eftablifhed with grace. And our Saviour himfelf, *Rev.* iii. 15. *I would thou wert*
cold or hot, and not *luke-warm* : The meaning is ; If men pretend to make profeffion
of Religion at all, they ought to be, not *luke-warm*, not carelefs and indifferent, in matters of Religion ; but they ought to be *zealous*, that is, not *hot in their* paffions, not,
fierce and contentious about difputable opinions, about things *uncertain and indifferent* ; but
zealous and ftedfaft in the purfuit and practice, of what is clearly and indifputably Juft
and Right. I conclude with the exhortation of St *Paul*, 1 Cor. xv. 58. *Therefore, my*
beloved brethren, be ye ftedfaft, unmoveable, always abounding in the work of the Lord, for-
afmuch as ye know that your labour is not in vain in the Lord.

SERMON VIII.

Of the Omnipresence of God.

1 KINGS VIII. 27.

But will God indeed dwell on the Earth? behold, the Heaven, and Heaven of Heavens, cannot contain thee :------

SERM.
VIII.

AS the *Eternity* of God fignifies his continued exiftence, through all the periods of boundlefs *Duration*: fo his *Immenfity* or *Omniprefence*, fignifies his being equally prefent in every Part of the infinite *Expanfion* of the Univerfe. In difcourfing upon which Attribute of the Divine Nature, I fhall 1*ft*, indeavour briefly to prove the Truth of the Doctrine itfelf, that God *muft be* immenfe or omniprefent. 2*dly*, I fhall offer fome particular Obfervations concerning the Nature and Circumftances of This Divine Perfection. And 3*dly*, I fhall confider (which is the *moft* important of all,) how This Meditation, may become ufeful to us in influencing our Practice.

Firft, IN order to prove the Truth of the Affertion itfelf, that God muft of Neceffity be Omniprefent; 'tis to be obferved, (and it may eafily be apprehended even by the meaneft Capacities,) that if Being or Exiftence be at all a Perfection, (as it manifeftly *is* the Foundation of all other Perfections,) it will follow, that in like manner as *continuing* to exift through larger periods of *Time*, fo alfo *Extent* of Exiftence (and confequently of Power) through larger portions of *Space*, is the having a greater degree of this Perfection. And as That Being, which is abfolutely perfect, muft with regard to Duration be *Eternal*; fo, in refpect of *Greatnefs*, it muft likewife be *Immenfe*. Otherwife, its Perfections will be limited; which is the Notion of *Imperfection*: And, by being fuppofed to be *Finite* in *Extent*, the Perfection of its Power will as totally be deftroyed, as it would be, fuppofing it to be *Temporary* in *Duration*. For as Any Being, which is not *Always*; at the *time* when it is not, is as if it never was; fo whatever Being is not *every-where*; in *thofe* places where it is not, is (to all the purpofes of Power and Activity) as if it had no Being in any place at all. For no Being can act *Where* it is not, any more than *When* it is not. Power, without Exiftence, is but an empty word without any reality; and the fcholaftick Fiction of a Being *acting* in all places, without being *prefent* in all places, is either making the Notion of God an exprefs contradiction, or elfe a fuppofing him *fo* to act by the miniftry of Others, as not to be Himfelf Prefent to underftand and know what they Do. He therefore that will frame to himfelf a true Idea of this Divine Attribute, (fo far as finite Underftanding can comprehend what is Infinite;) muft in This, as in others of the divine Perfections, form in his Mind the *Notion* at the fame time, and by the fame fteps, by which he afcends to the *Proof* of it. And That, in the prefent cafe, is more diftinctly as follows. All *created* Beings are, by the neceffary condition of their Nature, finite and circumfcribed. They can be prefent but in one certain determinate place at once, and they can move but within certain bounds in certain periods of time. The larger thofe Limits are, in

which

which any Creature can *be* and *act*; which it can either at once fill with its presence, or supply with its activity, swiftness and vigour; so much the greater share has it of this Kind of Perfection: And, by inlarging this perfection to its utmost Possibility, we must consequently ascribe to God, the *most Perfect* Being, *Infinity* or *Immensity*: That is, we must conceive of him, as of a Being that fills all things, and that contains all things within its own boundless Nature; that is not defined or circumscribed by any Space, but co-exists with, and is present with all things, and infinitely beyond whatever we can imagine, without limits and without bounds; *in whom* (as the Apostle expresses it,) *we live, and move, and have our Being*, and in whom all things subsist.

Again: I T cannot but be evident, even to the *meanest* Capacity, upon *careful* consideration; that He who *made* all things, as he could not but be *before* the things that he made, so it is not possible but he must be *present* also, with the things that he made and governs. For things could not be made without the actual presence of the Power that made them; nor can things ever be governed with any Certainty, unless the Wisdom, that governs them, be present with them. Whatever Arguments therefore prove the *Being* of God, and his unerring *Providence*; must all be understood to prove equally likewise his actual *Omnipresence*.

Lastly: H E who exists by *Necessity of Nature*, (which is the Character of God;) 'tis manifest must exist in all places alike. For absolute Necessity, is at *all times* and in *all places* the same. Whatever can be absent at *any* time, may be absent at *all* times; and whatever can be absent from *one* place, may be absent from *another*; and consequently can have no Necessity of existing at all. He therefore, who exists necessarily, must necessarily exist *Always and Every-where*: that is, as he must in duration be Eternal, so he must also in Immensity be Omnipresent.

T H E Truth of the Doctrine itself, that God must of Necessity be Immense or Omnipresent, being thus briefly proved by such Arguments as are most obvious and universally intelligible; I proceed now in the

IId place, T o offer some particular *Observations*, concerning the Nature and Circumstances of this divine Attribute. And

1*st*, 'T I S to be observed, that this Attribute of *Omnipresence*, as 'tis constantly ascribed to God in *Scripture*, so is it in *Reason* likewise so plain and obvious, that the generality of moral Writers even among the *Heathens* themselves, have not been wanting to assert it clearly and without hesitation. The only difficulty has been, in explaining the particular *Manner* of our apprehending or conceiving it. Concerning which, the Schoolmen have presumed to assert with great Confidence, that the Infinity of God is a *Point* only, and not a proper Immensity; just as they fancy his Eternity to be an *Instant* only, and not a proper everlasting Duration. But these Notions of theirs, as they are absurd and unintelligible, so they are frivolous and vain. For the Excellency of the Perfections of God, does not consist in impossible and contradictory Notions; but in true Greatness, Dignity, Majesty and Glory. And vain men, while they have affected to clog Religion with Absurdities which could not be understood, have made its Doctrines, (as far as in Them lay,) not venerable, but ridiculous. The *Eternity* of God, does not consist in making time past to be still present, and future Time to be already come, (which is a manifest Inconsistency and Impossibility;) but it consists in a true proper everlasting duration, without Beginning and without End: And in like manner the *Immensity* of God, does not consist in making things to be where they are not, or not to be where they are, (which is the Effect of confounding the Notion of Place:) But it consists in This; that whereas all finite Beings can be present but in One determinate Place at once; and corporeal Beings even in that One Place very imperfectly and unequally, to any Purpose of Power or Activity, only by the successive Motion of different Members and Organs; The Supreme Cause on the contrary, being

SERM.
VIII.

an uniform Infinite Effence, and comprehending all things perfectly in himfelf, is at all times equally prefent, both in his real Effence, and by the immediate and perfect Exercife of all his Attributes, to *every Point* of the boundlefs Immenfity, *as if it* were (not that it really *is*) all *but One fingle Point.* And Thus the Scripture itfelf always reprefents this matter. *Jer.* xxiii. 24. *Can any hide himfelf in fecret places, that I fhall not fee them, faith the Lord?* Do not I fill Heaven and Earth, [faith the Lord?] Acts xvii. 27. *He is not far from every one of Us; For in Him we live, and move, and have our Being,* Job xxiii. 8. *Behold, I go* forward, *but he is not there; and* backward, *but I cannot perceive him; On the* left hand, *where he doth work, but I cannot behold him; he hideth himfelf on the* right hand, *that I cannot fee him.* And, in the words of the Text; *Will God indeed dwell on the Earth? Behold, the Heaven, and Heaven of Heavens cannot contain thee.*

2dly, T I S worthy of Obfervation, that this right Notion of the Omniprefence of God, will very much affift us to form a juft apprehenfion of the Nature of that *Providence,* which attends to and infpects, not only the great Events, but even the minuteft Circumftances of every the fmalleft Action and Event in the World : Even *That* Providence, *without which not a Sparrow falls to the ground,* and by which *the very hairs of our Head are all numbred.* There have been Many, who though they fully acknowledged God's Government of the World, that is, his Power and Dominion over *all* things, and his *actual* Care and Concern for all the *great* and (as they think) moft *material* Tranfactions in the Univerfe; yet have been apt to imagine, that *fmall* and (as they fancy) *inconfiderable* things, are beneath his Care, and unworthy of his Attention. But This is a Miftake arifing from the Want of having a true Notion of the Divine Omniprefence. For, That Perfection being once rightly underftood, it cannot but be evident, that *all* things are alike eafy to be infpected by him as *any,* and the *minuteft* things as much fo as the *greateft*; Nay, it will appear, that not only the fmalleft things are *not unworthy* his infpection, but that even in the Nature of things 'tis abfolutely *impoffible,* that He who is every where alike prefent, fhould not obferve and attend to every thing alike.

THERE is a certain determinate number or quantity of things, which every intelligent Creature, according to the proportion of its fphere of Power and Activity, is able to attend to. And by This we may judge, that as Creatures of larger Capacities can obferve a much greater number of things at one and the fame time, than Beings of a lower rank can imagine it poffible they fhould; fo God, who is prefent every where, can with infinitely greater Eafe direct and govern *all things in the World at once,* than we can attend to thofe *few* things which fall within the compafs of our fhort obfervation. By This alfo is removed the Objection of Thofe, who think *Man* fo fmall and inconfiderable a part of the immenfe Univerfe, as that 'tis *beneath* the infinite Majefty of God to take fuch particular care of fo mean a part of the Creation; to fhow fo great condefcenfion towards fuch inconfiderable Beings, as to fend his own Son into the World on purpofe for their Redemption and Salvation. For they who thus object, do not confider, that though Man is indeed a very inconfiderable part of the Works of God, when compared with the *whole* Creation; yet in *This Place,* and upon *this Earth,* he is the greateft and moft valuable of all. Wherefore while the Omniprefence of God takes fuitable care of all his *other* Creatures through the whole Univerfe, each in their proper ftate; *in This place,* there is nothing *more* worthy of his care, than Man; nothing, *befides* Man, capable of being taught to ferve him, of being brought to Happinefs and Glory by him.

3dly, 'T I s here proper to obferve, how weak have been the Scruples of fuch perfons, who have been afraid to acknowledge the true Notion of the Divine Omniprefence, leaft they fhould feem to diminifh from the Glory and Majefty of God, by fuppofing

him

him to be always actually present in all, even in *impure*, places. For They, who have
raised to themselves This difficulty, have not been aware, that as the Beams of the
Sun are not at all foiled by the Matter they shine upon, and as the Purity and Holiness
of the Divine Nature is not in the least diminished by beholding all the *Wickedness* and
moral Impurity which is acted in the World; so the Omnipresent Essence of God is
not at all affected, by any *Natural Impurity* of Things or Places whatsoever; it being
the superlative Excellency and Prerogative of his Nature, to *act* always upon all things
every where, and itself to *be acted upon* by Nothing. All the *sensible* Qualities of Matter, are merely *relative* to *Us* in our present state, depending on the frame of *our* bodily Organs, and not being any thing really inherent in the Things themselves. *We*
behold only the outward Surfaces of things, and are affected only by the various Motions and Figures of certain small parts of Matter; which, by the Help of *Microscopes*,
appear even to *Us* to be really very different in Themselves from what our Senses represent them; And to a Spirit, which sees the inward real Essences of Things, and not
the external sensible Images which affect *Us*, they have no similitude at all with our
Imaginations.

4*thly*, I*t* will be here necessary to observe, How and in what sense, God, who is
every where necessarily alike present, is yet in Scripture so frequently represented to *be
in Heaven* : As if He who is in *All* places, could be confined in *Any*; or any proper
Habitation could be ascribed to *Him*, whom (as *Solomon* declares) *the Heaven of Heavens cannot contain.* The True meaning therefore of God's being *in Heaven*, is to express his *Height and Dignity*, not in *place*, but in *Power* : It being only a *similitude*
drawn into common Speech, from the Situation of things in Nature. As the Heavenly
Bodies, the Sun and Stars, are High above us in *place*; and all Earthly Blessings depend on the Sun and Rain and the Descent of kindly Influences *literally from above* :
so, by an easy *figure* of speech, whatsoever is above us in *Power*, we are from hence
used to represent as being above us in *Place*. Our Saviour, speaking of the Pride and
Greatness of *Capernaum*; *And thou Capernaum*, says he, *which art exalted unto Heaven, shalt be brought down to Hell*, Matt. xi. 23. The *Power and Dominion* of the
King of *Babylon*, is thus set forth by the Prophet *Isaiah*, ch. xiv. 13, 14. *Thou hast
said in thine heart, I will ascend above the heights of the clouds, I will ascend into Heaven, I will exalt my Throne above the stars of God* : And the *Destruction* of his Monarchy is described after the like manner, *ver.* 12. *How art thou fallen from Heaven !*
The Greatness and Dignity of *our Saviour*'s Kingdom, is represented in Scripture, by
his *sitting* at the right hand *of God in the heavenly places*. We know that God has no
Hands, nor any Shape or Figure; But the meaning of Christ's sitting on his right hand,
is his being exalted next to him in Authority and Power. Thus therefore when we
speak likewise of God, even the invisible Father himself, as being *in Heaven*; it must
be understood to express his *Supremacy*, not in *Place*, but in *Power and Dominion*;
that He is the High and Holy One, Great and Glorious and Supreme above All. But
there is also *another* reason of this expression, of God's *being in Heaven* : And That is,
To signify, that though of his real actual Presence there is indeed no Confinement, yet
of his Glory and Majesty there is in that Place a particular and extraordinary *Manifestation.* Thus the Angel in the Book of *Tobit* represents it, *ch.* xii. 15. *I am* (saith
he) *one of the seven holy Angels, which go in and out before the* Glory *of the Holy One* :
And the Salutation to the Churches, which begins the Book of the *Revelation*, ch. i. 4.
*Grace be unto you, and Peace from him which is, and which was, and which is to come,
and from the seven spirits which are before his* Throne. The real and proper *Presence* of
God, is equally in *all places* : But his *Throne*, his *Glory*, the place where the righteous
shall see his *Face*, where they shall behold a more particular glorious Manifestation of
his Power and Majesty, is in *Heaven*. In like manner, here upon *Earth*; in places,

A*cts* xvii. 27.

SERM. where God has been pleafed more particularly to manifeft his Glory, to place his
VIII. Name There, to receive There the Homage of his Servants; in thofe places God in
Scripture-phrafe is faid to *Be*: Not as if at the fame time he was not equally in all other
places alfo; but that in thefe places he chofe to manifeft himfelf to his Servants, and There
to receive homage from them. The Patriarch *Jacob*, concerning the place where he firft
faw the Vifion of Angels afcending and defcending out of Heaven; *Surely*, fays he, *the
Lord is in this place*, Gen. xxviii. 16; *and it fhall be the Houfe of God*, ver. 22. In like manner in the Temple at *Jerufalem*, the *Glory* of God *appeared* vifibly, 2 *Chron.* vii. 1. and
there it alfo *was*, when it did *not* appear: and how He whom the Heaven, and the
Heaven of Heavens cannot contain, did thus at that time dwell on Earth in a Temple made with hands, is well expreffed by *Solomon*, 1 Kings viii. 30. *Hearken thou
to the Supplication of thy Servant, and of thy people Ifrael, when they fhall pray in,
or towards, this place; and hear thou in heaven, thy dwelling-place*: The fenfe is;
God, who is prefent in *every place*, had appointed in *That place* to receive his Tribute
of worfhip. And upon this Account, the *place* was efteemed Holy, and refpected accordingly: *Ecclef.* v. 1. *Keep thy foot, when thou goeft to the houfe of God*, What the
meaning is, of that unufual Phrafe, *Keep thy foot*; is explained *Exod.* iii. 5. where God,
appearing to *Mofes* in the Bufh, fays thus unto him; *Put off thy fhoes from off thy Feet,
for the place whereon thou ftandeft is holy ground.* The Cuftom or Manner in thofe
Eaftern countries of fhowing Honour or Veneration, was by uncovering the *Feet*, as
our prefent method of fhowing refpect, is by uncovering the *Head*. Yet *God* himfelf
was not prefent even then in the Bufh, any more than in all other places; but the
place was made Holy by God's manifefting his *Glory* there; for fo St *Stephen* expreffly
tells us, *Acts* vii. 30. *there appeared to Mofes an Angel of the Lord, in a flame of Fire
in the Bufh.* In like manner, God is faid in Scripture to *dwell in the* Hearts of good
men: *(with him that is of an humble and contrite Spirit*, as the Prophet, *If.* lvii. 15.
expreffes it;) And that the *Bodies* of them which are fanctified, are *Temples* of the Holy
Ghoft, and *Temples* of God. Not by any confinement of the *Prefence* of God; but by
his being pleafed to fhow forth his *Power and Influence*, in particular places, and to particular perfons.

THESE Obfervations being premifed, it remains in the
IIId and *laft* place, THAT I proceed to draw fome ufeful inferences from what
has been faid; and to fhow (which is the *moft* material of all,) how this Meditation
upon the divine Omniprefence, may become ufeful to us in influencing our practice. And

1*ft*, BY This character of Omniprefence, the *True God of the Univerfe* is diftinguifhed from all Falfe Deities; and the Vanity of *Idolatry*, made plainly to appear.
The Gods of the Nations, *pretended* to be but Gods of *particular Countries*; as the
Gods of *Henah, Ivah*, and *Sepharvaim*, 2 Kings xviii. 34. Or, of particular *parts* of
the *fame* Country; as *Gods of the Hills, and not of the Valleys*, 1 Kings xx. 28. That
is, at moft, Beings only of a limited prefence and power: in reality, of no power or
dominion at all; and commonly not fo much as *any* Beings at all, but indeed mere
Fictions and Imaginations of men: *Lyes*, and *Lying Vanities*, as the Scripture frequently ftiles them. But the True God, who *made* Heaven and Earth and all things
that are therein, does by his prefence and power *infpect alfo and govern* all things,
in the *Whole* Heavens and in the *Whole* Earth.

AND from the fame confideration, appears alfo the Vanity of making any Image
of the *True* God, as well as of worfhipping *falfe* Gods. For by what Likenefs
can *he* be reprefented, the Majefty of whofe Prefence fills all things? And how foolifh is it to think, that He *in whom we live and move and have our Being*, and

whofe

whofe *offspring we* all (even all *rational* Beings) *are,* fhould himfelf be *like unto Gold* S E R M. or *Silver* or *Stone graven by art and man's device?* Acts xvii. 28, 29.   **VIII.**

FROM hence likewife appears the Folly, of fuch *Superftitions* as that of *Balak;* who when *Balaam* was not permitted to curfe *Ifrael* from *one place,* carried him to *another;* faying, *Come, I pray thee, I will bring thee unto* another place; *peradventure it will pleafe God, that thou mayft curfe me them* from thence, *Num.* xxiii. 27. As if *God* faw things *differently* in *different places;* and would curfe *Ifrael* from *One* place, when he had bleffed him from another.

FROM the fame reafon appears alfo the Vanity of *Saint-worfhip,* among Chriftians: As if God, who being Omniprefent hears all Prayer *Himfelf,* fhould either need or regard the Interceffion of Others, whom he hath *not exprefsly,* (as in the cafe of *our Saviour,) appointed* to that High and Singular Office.

2*dly,* IF God is Omniprefent; from hence it follows that he is to be worfhipped and reverenced *every where,* in *private* as well as in publick. Honour is to be paid him, not only by *Angels* before his Throne in *Heaven,* and by the *congregation* publickly in his *Temple* on Earth, but alfo by *every man* fingly in his moft *private retirements. God dwelleth not in Temples made with hands,* Acts vii. 47; and xvii. 24. that is, he is not prefent *there only,* but fees alfo that more retired part of our behaviour, which is concealed from the world; and moft of all approves that *private* piety and virtue, which cannot but proceed from a fincere mind, becaufe it is not capable of the applaufe of Men. *When Thou prayeft,* faith our Saviour; *enter into thy clofet, and pray to thy Father which is in fecret; and thy Father, which feeth in fecret, fhall reward thee openly,* Mat. vi. 6.

NAY further; he beholds, not only our moft private retirements, but alfo That which is ftill much *more* fecret than thefe, even the very Thoughts and Intents of our Hearts; that inward frame and difpofition of the mind, which may be diffembled and entirely concealed from Men. Hence he is ftiled in Scripture, the *Searcher of the Hearts and Reins.* Nor are there any Paffages in Holy Writ, which do more worthily and magnificently reprefent him, than thofe which thus defcribe him, fitting in the circuit of Heaven, and beholding at one view, all the Actions and all the Thoughts of all men throughout the whole World. 2 *Chron.* xvi. 9. *The eyes of the Lord run to and fro throughout the whole Earth, to fhow himfelf ftrong in the behalf of them, whofe* Heart *is perfect towards him.* Prov. xv. 3. *The eyes of the Lord are in every place, beholding the Evil and the Good:* and ver. 11. *Hell and deftruction are before him;* how much more then, the Hearts of the children of Men! And *Job* xxvi. 6. *Hell is naked before Him, and Deftruction has no covering.* Which confideration ferioufly meditated upon, will teach us to behave ourfelves at all times, and in all places, with circumfpection and care, as in the prefence of our Judge, who continually obferves us, and in due time *will bring to light the hidden things of darknefs, and will make manifeft the counfels of the Hearts,* 1 Cor. iv. 5. It will teach us to be as much afraid of committing any Sin or Impurity in Secret, as in the Face of the Sun and in the prefence of all mankind; confidering that our moft private mifdeeds are fet before him, and *our fecret fins in the Light of his countenance,* Pf. xc. 8. and that all the wickednefs men now commit in private, fhall one day be publifhed before all the Inhabitants of Heaven and Earth. Laftly, it will oblige us to govern even our very Thoughts and Defires, and indeavour to keep them in continual Subjection to the law of God; feeing that He who is of purer eyes than to behold iniquity, fearches even our very Hearts and Reins with his intimate prefence and all-feeing Eye. *O Lord, thou haft fearched me out, and known me; thou knoweft my down-fitting and mine up-rifing; thou underftandeft my Thoughts long before: Thou art about my path, and about my bed, and fieft out all my ways;* Pf. cxxxix. 1. And *Heb.* iv. 12. *The word of God is*
quick

quick and powerful, and sharper then any two-edged sword, piercing even to the dividing asunder of Soul and Spirit, and of the joints and marrow; and is a discerner of the
Thoughts and Intents of the Heart: Neither is there any Creature that is not manifest
in his Sight; but all things are naked and opened unto the eyes of Him with whom we
have to do.

3dly, and to conclude; FROM the consideration of God's being Omnipresent, it follows that his *Power* (as well as Knowledge) is unlimited; to be *every where* relied on
by Good men, and to be feared by Bad. As there is no *Time*, so neither is there
any *Place*, where he is not at hand to protect his Servants. *Ps.* xlvi. 1. *God is our refuge and strength, a very* present *Help in Trouble; Therefore will we not fear, though
the Earth be removed, and though the Mountains be carried into the midst of the Sea.*
And *Hab.* iii. 17. *Tho' the fig-tree shall not blossom, neither shall fruit be in the vines;
tho' the labour of the olive shall fail, and the fields shall yield no meat; though the flock
shall be cut off from the fold, and there shall be no herd in the stalls: yet will I rejoice
in the Lord, I will joy in the God of my salvation.* But the most affectionate instance
in the whole Scripture, of relying on the *omnipresent* power of God, is that of *Jonah*
in the Whale's belly, ch. ii. 2. *Out of the belly of Hell I cried, and thou heardest my
Voice: In the midst of the seas, the floods compassed me about; all thy billows and thy
waves passed over me: The depth closed me round about, the weeds were wrapt about my
Head: I went down to the bottoms of the Mountains, the Earth with her bars was a-
bout me for ever;* (It should not have been translated, *was about me* for ever; For
That was not so; But, *the Earth with her everlasting bars was about me:*) yet *I remembred the Lord, and my prayer came unto thee.* The same consideration ought likewise on the contrary, to be a Terror to wicked and impenitent Sinners; that there is
no possible place, where they can escape God's justice, or avoid the vengeance of
omnipresent wrath. The Anger of Man, as it is but of short duration, so it can be
but of small *extent*, and may generally be fled from: But *from the judgment of God,*
Plato. says an excellent *Heathen-writer, let no man hope to be able to escape: For though you
could descend into the very depth of the Earth, or fly on high to the extremities of the Heavens; yet should you never escape the just judgment of God, either before or after Death.*
The very same thing is expressed more emphatically by the Holy Ghost in Scripture.
Ps. cxxxix. 6. *Whither shall I go then from thy Spirit, or whither shall I go then from
thy presence? If I climb up into heaven, thou art there; if I go down to Hell, thou art
there also: If I take the wings of the morning,* that is, if I could flee as swift as the
morning-light, which darts in a moment from under one end of Heaven to the
other; *and remain in the uttermost parts of the sea: even there also shall thy hand lead
me, and thy right hand shall hold me.* Again; *Amos* ix 2. *Though they dig into Hell,
thence shall mine hand take them; tho' they climb up to Heaven, thence will I bring
them down: Tho' they hide themselves in the top of Carmel, I will search them out thence;
and though they be hid in the bottom of the sea, thence will I command the serpent and
he shall bite them.* And *Job* xxxiv. 21. *His eyes are upon the ways of man, and he
seeth all his goings; There is no darkness nor shadow of Death, where the workers of iniquity may hide themselves.* And to mention but one place more; *Ecclus.* xvi. 17. *Say
not thou, I will hide my self from the Lord: Shall any remember me from above? I shall
not be remembred among so many people: for what is* my *soul among such an infinite number of Creatures?* Say not thou *thus,* saith he; For *behold, the Heaven, and the Heaven of Heavens, the Deep and the Earth, and all that therein is, shall be moved when
he shall visit; The mountains also and foundations of the Earth shall be shaken with trembling, when the Lord looketh upon them: No heart* (says he) *can think upon these things
worthily; and Who is able to conceive his ways?*

SERM.

SERMON IX.

Of the OMNIPOTENCE of GOD.

PSAL. CXLVII. 5.

Great is our Lord, and Great is his Power.

THIS Pſalm is an eloquent *compariſon* of the Greatneſs of the Power of God **S E R M.**
ſhown forth in the works of *Creation*, with the Greatneſs of the ſame **IX.**
Power ſhown forth in the works of *Providence* towards his Church and
People. The works of *Creation* are ſet forth, ver. 4, 8, 16. *He telleth the number of
the Stars, and calleth them all by their Names*; he *covereth the heaven with clouds,
and prepareth rain for the Earth; he giveth ſnow like wool, and ſcattereth the hoar-
froſt like aſhes.* The works of *Providence* are ſet forth, ver. 3, 6, 19. *The Lord doth
build up Jeruſalem, and gather together the outcaſts of Iſrael; The Lord ſetteth up the
meek, and bringeth the ungodly down to the ground; He ſheweth his word unto Jacob,
his ſtatutes and ordinances unto Iſrael.* The *concluſion* drawn from *Both,* is, ver. 7.
and in the words of the Text, *O ſing unto the Lord with thankſgiving, ſing praiſes
upon the harp, unto our God; For Great is our Lord, and Great is his power.* In diſcourſing upon which words, I ſhall firſt endeavour to ſhow briefly, that God *muſt
of neceſſity be* All-powerful. 2*dly,* I will give ſome faint and imperfect repreſentations, ſome general and inadequate Idea, *wherein* the *Perfection* of this Power
conſiſts. 3*dly,* I ſhall conſider *what* particulars are *not* included in the true notion
even of *Omnipotence itſelf.* And 4*thly,* I ſhall draw ſome practical *Inferences* from the
whole.

I. THAT God *muſt* of neceſſity be *All-powerful,* is ſelf-evident. For ſince *all
things* in the Univerſe were made by him, and depend upon Him for their very
Being; and all the *Powers* of all things are derived from him, and muſt conſequently
be entirely ſubject to him; 'tis manifeſt that nothing can make any difficulty or reſiſtence
to the execution of his Will, and therefore his Power muſt be abſolutely infinite. Where
there is no *Being,* 'tis plain there can be no *Power*: Now *all* things that *are* in the
World, have *no other Being* than what depends on His pleaſure: There is therefore,
and can be, in the Univerſe, *no Power* againſt *His.* This *precarious* Being, which *all*
things derive from the mere Will of God, the Apoſtle elegantly deſcribes, *Rom.* iv. 17.
by his *calling thoſe things which be not, as tho' they* were: And the unlimitedneſs of
his Power *over* them, may on the contrary as truly be deſcribed, by his *looking on all
things that* Are, *as tho' they* were not. But the truth of this Attribute of the divine
Omnipotence, (that mighty *working, whereby he is able to ſubdue all things to himſelf,*)
is ſo evident to the common reaſon of mankind, that we need not ſo much ſeek for
Arguments to prove and demonſtrate its reality, as we ought to endeavour to give lively
and affecting deſcriptions of it, ſuch as may be proper to fill mens minds with a juſt

S E R M. fenfe of the fupreme Majefty of God, and to excite in them accordingly refolutions of
IX. Obedience to him. Such defcriptions as thefe, the Scripture frequently affords us;
great and moving defcriptions of the Power of God, and fuch as are naturally apt to
produce in us the profoundeft Humility and Reverence towards him. Thus *Job* ix. 4.
*He is wife in heart, and mighty in ftrength; Who has hardened himfelf againft him, and
has profpered? which removeth the mountains, and they know not; which overturneth them
in his anger: which fhaketh the earth out of her place, and the pillars thereof tremble:
Which commandeth the Sun, and it rifeth not, and fealeth up the Stars: Which alone
fpreadeth out the Heavens, and treadeth upon the waves of the Sea: Which doth great
things, paft finding out, yea and wonders without number.* And ch. xxvi. 6. *Hell is
naked before him, and deftruction hath no covering: He ftretcheth out the north over the
empty place, and hangeth the earth upon nothing: He bindeth up the waters in his
thick clouds, and the cloud is not rent under them: The Pillars of Heaven tremble, and
are aftonifhed at his reproof: He divideth the Sea with his Power, and by his Underftanding he fmiteth thro' the Proud: Lo, thefe are part of his ways, but how little a portion is heard of him? but the thunder of his Power, who can underftand?* So likewife
the eloquent prophet *Ifaiah*, ch. xiv. 27. *The Lord of Hofts hath purpofed, and who fhall
difannul it? his hand is ftretched out, and who fhall turn it back?* And ch. xl. 12. *Who
hath meafured the waters in the hollow of his hand? and meted out Heaven with the fpan?
and comprehended the duft of the Earth in a meafure? and weighed the mountains in fcales,
and the hills in a balance? Who hath directed the fpirit of the Lord, or, being his Coun-
feller, has taught him? Behold, the Nations are as a drop of the bucket, and are counted
as the fmall duft of the balance; behold, he taketh up the Ifles as a very little thing:
All nations before him are as nothing, and they are counted to him lefs than nothing and
vanity: To whom then will ye liken God, or what likenefs will ye compare unto him?*
To mention but One paffage more; *Dan.* iv. 34. *He that liveth for ever, whofe dominion is an everlafting dominion, and his kingdom from generation to generation; And
all the inhabitants of the earth are reputed as nothing; and he doth according to his Will
in the Army of Heaven, and among the inhabitants of the Earth; and none can ftay
his hand, or fay unto him, what doft thou?* Thefe are lively defcriptions of *arbitrary*
Power indeed; *arbitrary*, not in the Senfe that the *Tyrants* of This World have occafioned that word to be ufed, when it fignifies a Power of doing unreafonable and
unjuft things, a Power of Violence and unrighteous oppreffion, a Power of acting according to mere Will and Pleafure without Right or Reafon; but in *God*, arbitrary or
irrefiftible Power, tho' it *is* indeed a Power of doing all things abfolutely without controul, yet it is *fo* a Power of doing them, as that at the fame time there is always with
the notion of That Power, neceffarily and infeparably connected, an Idea of infinite Reafon, Wifdom, and Goodnefs. And the reafon *why* thefe notions are always infeparably connected, when we think rightly of God; is becaufe, in *Him*, Acting according
to his fupreme *Will and Pleafure*, does not fignify, as it does among corrupt *men*, acting according to Will and Inclination without reafon, but on the contrary it fignifies
always, acting according to *That* Will, which is influenced by *nothing* but the moft
perfect *Reafon* only; which is the fame thing, as if Will and Pleafure could be fuppofed to have no place at all, and the Univerfe were governed by mere abftract Reafon
and the Right of Things. For in *God*, Will and Reafon are *one and the fame* thing;
or at leaft go always fo together, *as if they* were but one thing; whereas in the Rulers of *this* World, they too often fignify things *contrary* to each other: Governing
according to *Law or Reafon*, and governing according to *abfolute Will or Pleafure*, being on *Earth* the two moft *oppofite* forms of Government; while in *Heaven* they are
nothing but two different *Names*, of one and the fame *Thing*.

I

IF it be asked, *whence* this difference arises; the reason of it will appear, by considering *what* we mean, when we affirm that whatever *God* does, we are sure is Right; because He does it. Which is too often so understood, as if the *Power and Will* of God *made* that *to be* Right, which *is* so; and as if it might as easily have made the contrary *to become* Right. The Consequence of which is, that there is really no difference between good and evil in the *Nature* of Things, but that *Will and Power* makes all the distinction : From whence tyrannical *Men*, who have *Power* to do what they *will*, think that *They* also consequently have a Right to do so. But now This is not only not true with regard to *Men*, but even with regard to *God himself also* it is plainly a Mistake : For, not *Power or Will*, but the Reason of Things only, is the Foundation of *Right* : And tho' 'tis indeed certainly true, that whatever God does, we are sure 'tis Right, because he does it; yet the meaning of This, is not, that God's *doing or willing* a thing, *makes* it to be Right ; but that *his* Wisdom and Goodness is such, that we may depend upon it, even *without* understanding it, that whatever he wills, was *in itself* Right, *antecedent* to his willing it ; and that he *therefore* willed it, *because* it was Right. Wherefore though among *Men*, whose Wills are not always righteous, absolute or arbitrary Power is the thing in the world the most to be detested, dreaded, and abhorred, as being the Sum total of the greatest Calamities that God ever inflicted upon sinful men in *This* World ; yet the Notion of irresistible and uncontroulable Power in *God*, where 'tis in conjunction with a perfect Understanding and with a righteous Will, justly excites in us *nothing* but such a *Veneration and Awe*, such a *Sense* of *adorable* and incomprehensible *Majesty*, as naturally leads us to that *Adoration and Fear*, that *Honour*, *Duty*, and *Obedience* towards him, which is the great Principle and Foundation of all Religion.

HAVING thus briefly shown *in general*, that God *must* of necessity *be All-powerful*; I proceed now in the

II*d* place, To give *in particular* some faint hints and representations, some little imperfect Idea, *wherein* the peculiar Exercise of this most perfect Power *consists*, and *in what Instances* it has principally displayed itself. And

I*st*, THE Perfection of this Power appears, in its *giving* Being *originally* to *all* things, and in its governing *them continually* while they are in Being. That the World was not made by *Chance*, appears from the *Beauty and Usefulness* of the things that are in it ; and that it does not exist by *Necessity*, is evident from their *Variety* : For in the Necessity of *Fate*, there is no *Variety* ; and in the confusions of *Chance*, there is no *Beauty or Usefulness*. The *Being* therefore of the World, is the *Effect* of the *Power* of God ; and the *Variety* of finite Powers communicated to different *Creatures*, are a glorious demonstration of the *infinite* Power of the *Creator*. And there is no better way, by which we can frame to ourselves some faint Idea or representation of the *perfection* of that Power, than by considering in one general view the Number and Variety of *Effects*, it has produced in the Creation ; how it has given *Being*, to all things ; how it has *diversified* that Being, under innumerable *Forms*, in the Compositions and Motions of *inanimate Matter* ; how it has exalted the products of Matter, beyond all the imaginable Powers of its unactive nature, in the *Vegetation* and *Growth* of *Plants*; how it has indued with a *higher Principle*, than can arise from Mechanism, the *Brute-creatures*, furnished with the Powers of Self-motion and the sensitive Life ; how it has, in a much *more* wonderful manner, implanted in *Men* the Image of the divine Nature, even those high Faculties of Understanding, Reason, and Will ; and, beyond all these, which is the Supreme excellency of created Nature, made them capable of *Religion*, of knowing, worshipping, obeying, and imitating their Maker. *Wonderful*, O Lord, are all thy works ; and worthy *art thou to receive glory and honour and power ; for thou hast created all things, and for thy pleasure they Are, and were created*, Rev. iv. 11.

NOR

Heb. i. 2.
Col. i. 17.

NOR does the Perfection of the divine Power appear more in having *created* things, than it does in *governing* them continually while they are in being: For he *upholdeth* all things by the word of his Power, and by his Providence does the Universe *subsist*. This is that Kingdom of God, which the Psalmist describes, *Ps.* ciii. 19. *The Lord has prepared his Throne in Heaven, and his Kingdom, ruleth over all*; and *Ps.* cxlvii. 15. *He sendeth forth his commandment upon Earth, and his Word runneth very swiftly.* And to this *natural* Kingdom of God, may well be applied those words of St *John* concerning his *spiritual* Kingdom, *Rev.* xix. 6. *I heard as it were the voice of a great multitude,——saying, Alleluia, for the Lord God omnipotent reigneth.* To frame to ourselves any *just* idea of this Power by which God *ruleth* over all, is absolutely impossible; because our conceptions are altogether finite, and our imagination extends but to a very few either objects or degrees of Power. But the best representation we can form of it in our own minds, is by considering, that the Powers of all things in the World put together, bear no proportion to His; and that the Resistance of Universal Nature at once, would to Him be no Resistance at all; who can withdraw from all things the foundation of all Power, even their very Being itself; so that all things are to *him*, as

ch. xl. 17.

the Prophet *Isaiah* elegantly expresses it, by the *highest possible*, and yet not *too high* a figure; they are to *him*, saith he, less *than nothing and Vanity*. The disproportion, can be set forth by no similitude: For, to the greatest Strength, even the thin Air makes some resistance; and the finest web gives some impediment, even to the greatest swiftness: But to the Power of *God*, nothing makes *any* opposition: Nothing, except the perverse *Will* of wicked Spirits and wicked Men; whom, being indued with freedom, God does not think fit to influence by *Power*, but by the *moral and* rational *motives only of Promises and Threatnings.* Where-ever his *Power* interposes; all things, as they were at first made out of *nothing*, so with regard to any power of opposing his government, they still continue *as nothing.*

BUT this Perfection of the divine Power in *Ruling over all*, as it appears *demonstrably* to *considerate and inquisitive persons*, in that general *Providence* which presides over and directs the *whole course of Nature*; so to the *greater part of mankind*, it manifests itself *more* conspicuously in those remarkable Events, which we usually stile particular *Providences*: Which, when they are directly *miraculous* interpositions, are apt indeed most strongly to affect men; but, *without* That, are sufficient Evidences of the Supreme Power by which the World is governed. Instances of this kind, are, the *Flood* wherewith God destroyed the old World; The bringing the *Jews* out of *Egypt*, with a mighty hand and with a stretched-out arm; The judgment upon *Nebuchadnezzar*, that great King of *Babylon*, (*Dan.* iv.) who while he was vaunting himself in the pride of his heart, and saying to himself, *Is not This great Babylon which I have built?* suddenly he was struck with with such a distemper from Heaven, that his Understanding was taken from him, and he seemed *to himself* to be driven from among men, and to eat grass with the Beasts of the field, till the Pride of his Heart was humbled, and his reason returned unto him, and he gave glory to the God of Heaven. And, to mention no more Instances; of This kind was the destruction of *Sennacherib*, 2 Kings xix. 35. *when an Angel smote in one night in the camp of the Assyrians an hundred fourscore and five thousand men.* These Princes called themselves *Supreme*, and looked upon themselves as *Lords of the World*; and behaved themselves accordingly, as having no superiour; not considering, in the midst of their Power and Glory, that *he that is Higher than the Highest regarded*, and that *there were Higher than They*, Eccles. v. 8. The *greatest* mortal power, (of men *whose Breath is in their nostrils*, that is, whose Life depends upon so small a circumstance as a Breath of Air,) being *nothing* in comparison to the power of the *meanest* ministring Spirit in the Armies of the Angels of God; *who* (as the Psalmist expresses it) *refraineth the Spirit of Princes, and is wonderful among*

I

the

the Kings of the Earth. This is the *Firſt* particular, wherein the Perfection of the divine Power conſiſts; its *giving* Being *originally* to *all* things, and ruling *them abſolutely* while they *continue* in Being.

2dly, THE *ſecond* particular, wherein the perfection of the divine Power conſiſts, is this; that it not only extends to the doing all *things* in the government of the whole Univerſe, and That without any the leaſt oppoſition from the *things themſelves*; but that it does them alſo without any *difficulty in itſelf*; without *any* pains, or labour of operation; with ſuch abſolute and perfect *eaſe,* as not only not *Men,* but probably *no finite Beings whatſoever,* do even *thoſe* things, which are the moſt *eaſily* done by them. This Notion is ſublimely expreſt by *Iſaiah,* ch. xl. 28. *Haſt thou not known, haſt thou not heard, that the everlaſting God, the Lord, the creator of the ends of the Earth, fainteth not, neither is weary?* There was a certain Sect among the antient Philoſophers, who, pretending they durſt not think God ſhould take upon him the *Trouble* of governing the World; covered their Atheiſm by aſſerting, that to the *Happineſs* of God it was neceſſary to ſuppoſe him unconcerned *for,* and removed at an infinite diſtance *from,* the World. But this Exemption of the infinitely bleſſed God, from ſo mean an imperfection as *Care and Sollicitude*; which the *Epicureans* provided for, by making him *abſent* from the World; does on the contrary *really* ariſe, from his being *preſent,* actually *Omnipreſent,* to *every* part of the Univerſe; ſo as to be able to direct and govern the *Whole* with *leſs* difficulty to himſelf, (if *That* may with any propriety be ſo called, which indeed is *no* difficulty *at all*;) he governs, I ſay, and directs the whole World with *leſs* difficulty, than any finite creature can ſo much as *behold* or *view* any part of it. *He ſitteth upon the circle of the Earth, and the inhabitants thereof are as graſhoppers; he ſtretcheth out the Heavens as a Curtain, and ſpreadeth them out as a Tent to dwell in,* Iſ. xl. 22.

3dly, THE *third and laſt* particular, wherein the perfection of the divine Power conſiſts, is, its doing not only *all* things, and doing them *without difficulty,* but its doing them alſo perfectly *at once,* without ſtanding in need of any *Time* to do them in. The original ſubſtances of all things, were probably created *in a moment: In the Beginning God created the Heaven and the Earth,* Gen. i. 1. And though the conſequent formation of This Earth out of a Chaos, is indeed repreſented to *us* as having been performed gradually in certain *periods of time*; yet the reaſon of this, is not that the *Power of God* required any ſuch *number of days* (with regard to *itſelf*) to accompliſh this work in; but only to repreſent more diſtinctly to *our* conception, the harmony and beauty of the ſeveral parts of this wonderful Fabrick of the World; which the divine Power could as eaſily have ſet in order in *one ſingle moment,* as in *ſix days* or *years.* The Notion of *This* Perfection of the divine Power, in doing things thus *inſtantly,* or *in a moment*; is ſet forth in Scripture by God's cauſing things to be produced, as it were without any operation at all, by his mere Will or Command. *God who* commanded *the Light to ſhine out of Darkneſs,* 2 Cor. iv. 6. ſaying, Let there be *Light, and there was Light,* Gen. i. 3. And Pſ. xxxiii. 6, 9. *By the* word *of the Lord were the Heavens made, and all the hoſt of them by the* Breath *of his mouth; He* ſpake *the word, and it was done; he* commanded, *and it ſtood faſt.* The meaning of all which expreſſions is not to be taken literally, as if lifeleſs Matter were capable of obeying any *Law*; much leſs, that That which had no Being, could by obeying a *command,* come into Being: But the meaning is, that the *Actions of God* are as ſwift as *Thought*; and the *Effects* of his operations, as *immediate,* as if *Willing and Acting* were *really* in *Him* (what they are figuratively repreſented to *Us,)* one and the ſame *Thing.* And This alſo is the true meaning, if there be any meaning at all, of what the School-Authors ſay, when they affirm that God is a *mere* or *ſimple* Act: Not that the *Action itſelf,* is the *Perſon who acts,* (which is very unintelligible and very abſurd;) But that the *Actions of God* are ſo inſtantaneous

S E R M. and perfect, that to *Us* they are scarce distinguishable from his *Will* or *Mind itself*.
IX. Having thus briefly endeavoured to give some faint hints and representations, some
little inadequate Idea, *wherein* the peculiar Perfection of this divine Power *consists*, and
in what instances it has principally displayed itself; I proceed in the

III*d* place, To consider *what* particulars are *not included* in the true Notion of *Om-*
nipotence itself. And

1*st*, 'T I S evident *Infinite Power* must be understood to reach to all *possible* things,
but cannot be said to extend to the working any thing which implies a *Contradiction* :
As, that a thing should *be* and *not be* at the same time; that the same thing should *be*
made, and *not be made* ; or *have been*, and *not have been* : That the same Body should
be in *two places at once*, or *not be in the place where it is* : That things should be *equal*
and *not equal* at the same time; or the same thing *greater* or *less* than *itself*. These and
the like, are, in the Nature of Things, absolutely impossible; and to ascribe to God a
Power of doing what can't be done, is not *magnifying*, but *mocking* his Power. And
the Reason is plain : Because a Power of causing a thing to *be*, at the same time that
it *is not*, is only a Power of doing that which is Nothing, that is, no Power at all.

2*dly*, T H E *Infinite* Power of God, cannot be said to extend to such things, as are
naturally *evil* absolutely with respect to *himself*; that is to say, which imply *natural*
imperfection in the Being *itself*, to whom such Power is ascribed. Such would be, a
Power of *destroying his own Being, weakening or diminishing his own Power*, or limit-
ing it any otherwise than by the free determinations of Wisdom and Goodness. For,
any *capacity*, or *possibility* of being *diminished*, even tho' by the unlimited Power *itself*
working upon itself, would be *Imperfection or Weakness*, and not *Power*.

3*dly*, I N F I N I T E Power, *cannot* be understood to include a possibility of doing
such things as are morally *evil*, with regard to *Others*. Such are whatever things are
unjust, unrighteous, cruel, contrary to Promise, and the like. A possibility of doing
any of which things, is (as before) a Mark, not of *Power*, but of *Impotency or Weak-*
ness. Hence the Scripture frequently uses such expressions as these; *God which* cannot
lye, Tit. i. 2; he cannot *deny himself*, 2 Tim. ii. 13. And *Heb*. vi. 13, 18. *Because*
God could swear by no greater, he sware by himself,——confirming the immutability of his
counsel by an Oath; that by two immutable things, in which it was impossible *for God*
to lye, we might have a strong consolation. The *Ground* indeed or *Reason* of the impossibility of God's doing any of these things, is not the same as the impossibility of working contradictions. For *contradictions* are impossible *absolutely*, in the nature of the
things themselves; but *doing evil* is impossible *relatively* only, with respect to the *Na-*
ture of a perfectly *good Being*. But tho' the *ground* or *reason* of the impossibility is
different, yet the *impossibility itself* is *in Event* the *same*. For God can no more act in
contradiction to the *moral perfections* of his *own* Nature, than he can act in contradiction to the *absolute Nature of Things* : Nor is it any more possible, that a Being of infinite *Justice, Goodness*, and *Truth*, should do any thing *unjustly, unrighteously, or false-*
ly; than that a Thing should *be* and *not be* at the same time. The *Rectitude* of his
Will, is as unalterable, as the *Necessity* of his *Nature* : and 'tis as truly a contradiction,
that the *Will* of an infinitely *Good* Being, should *chuse* to do any thing contrary to
Right; as that the *Power* of an infinitely *powerful* Being, should be *able* to do any
thing inconsistent with *Power*. For in like manner as 'tis *for This Reason* manifest,
that infinite Power cannot extend to *natural* contradictions, *because* they imply a destruction of *that very Power*, by which they must be supposed to be worked; so 'tis
also *for the like reason* evident, that the same infinite Power cannot extend to *moral*
contradictions, *because* These imply a destruction of some *other* Attributes, as necessarily
belonging to the divine Nature as Power.

IV. T H U S.

IV. **T H U S** have I endeavoured briefly, *1ſt,* to prove, that God *muſt* of neceſſity *be* all-powerful; *2dly,* to give ſome general and inadequate idea, *wherein* the Perfection of this Power *conſiſts;* and *3dly,* to ſhow what *particulars* are *not included* in the true Notion even of *Omnipotence itſelf.* What remains, is, to draw ſome uſeful *Inferences* from the ſeveral parts of the foregoing Diſcourſe. And theſe inferences will be of two ſorts; *1ſt,* ſuch as may aſſiſt us to make a right judgment of the Truth or Falſhood of ſeveral *Doctrines* which have been taught in Divinity; And *2dly,* ſuch as may tend more immediately to direct and influence our *Practice.* But the conſideration of Theſe, muſt be referred to a following opportunity.

S E R M. IX.

S E R M O N X.

Of the OMNIPOTENCE of GOD.

PSAL. CXLVII. 5.

Great is our Lord, and Great is his Power.

IN a former Diſcourſe upon theſe words, I propoſed *1ſt,* to endeavour to ſhow that God *muſt* of neceſſity *be* All-powerful; *2dly,* to give ſome faint hints and repreſentations, ſome general and inadequate idea, *wherein* the *Perfection* of this Power conſiſts, and *in what inſtances* it has principally diſplayed itſelf: *3dly,* to conſider *what* particulars are *not included,* in the true Notion even of *Omnipotence* itſelf. And *4thly,* to draw ſome practical *Inferences* from the whole. The *Three firſt* of theſe general Heads, I have already gone through. That God *muſt* of neceſſity *be* All-powerful, I have ſhown from *this* conſideration, that the Powers of all things that Are, are derived from *Him,* and depend continually upon him. The peculiar *Perfection* wherein this divine Power conſiſts, and the *Inſtances* wherein it has principally diſplayed itſelf, I have ſhown to *be;* its *giving Being* originally to *all* things, and its *governing* them continually while they are in Being; its doing all things with abſolute and perfect *Eaſe,* without any *difficulty* in *itſelf,* or *oppoſition* from any *other* thing; and its doing things perfectly *at once,* without ſtanding in need of any *Time* to do them in. *Laſtly,* the particulars *not included* in the true Notion even of *Omnipotence itſelf,* I have ſhown, *are,* whatever things are *Contradictory* abſolutely in their *own Nature;* whatever things are *naturally evil* and imply *weakneſs or imperfection* in the *Being itſelf* to whom the Power of doing them is aſcribed; and whatever things are *morally evil* and imply *injuſtice or unrighteouſneſs* towards *Others:* The Power of doing *theſe* things is not included even in *Omnipotence itſelf;* and the aſcribing to *God* any ſuch poſſibility, would not be a *magnifying* but *mocking* his Power.

IV. **T H A T** which remains at this Time, is to draw ſome uſeful and proper *Inferences,* from the conſideration of this *whole* Doctrine of the *divine Omnipotence.* And Theſe Inferences may be of *two* ſorts. *Firſt,* ſuch as will aſſiſt us to make a right judgment of the Truth or Falſhood of ſeveral *Doctrines* which have ſometimes been

S E R M. ·X.

taught

SERM.
X.
taught in Divinity: and *Secondly*, such as may tend more immediately to direct and influence our *Practice*.

I. THOSE Inferences from the Notion of the divine Omnipotence, which may assist us in making a right judgment of the Truth or Falshood of several *Doctrines* that have sometimes been taught in Divinity, are such as follow.

1*st*, IF the Power of God be absolutely Supreme and Infinite, then 'tis evident that *no Power* can possibly be *contrary* to *His*, *no Kingdom oppofite to His*; any farther than He himself, in the infinite and unsearchable Wisdom of his Supreme Government, thinks fit to permit and suffer it *should* be so. When therefore we read of the *Devil's* setting up a Kingdom in opposition to the Kingdom of God; great care must be taken that we do not so understand it, as if the Devil had, properly speaking, *any Power* against *God*. But the Meaning is *This* only; that, in like manner as *Wicked Men* set up themselves against *God*, and resist his *Will*, and exalt themselves in opposition to *God's Kingdom*; and yet really have *no Power* at all, any further than God thinks fit to permit them: So *the Devil* likewise opposes the Kingdom and the Will of God, not by any *natural*, but by a *moral* Power only; not by being able to resist the Will of God by *Force*, but by being suffered to do things wicked and displeasing to God, through that natural *liberty of chusing and acting*, which is essential to the Being of a rational Creature. One of the greatest and noblest Effects of God's *creating power*, is his producing rational Creatures, such as are Angels and Men. Without These, all the rest of the whole Creation had lost its beauty; because *These only* are capable of discerning what That Beauty is, and of praising their Creator for it. Yet in order to make them capable of returning him this Praise and Adoration worthily, by delighting to obey his Commands and imitate his Nature; it was essentially necessary they should be indued with that Liberty or Freedom of Will, which at the same time that it made them capable of Virtue, could not but make them likewise capable of Vice. Such of them therefore, as abused that Liberty of Will to the Choice of *Wickedness*, (which God gave them on the contrary to make them capable of *Virtue*;) became thereby Enemies to *God*, and Deceivers one of *another*. And the opposition they make to God by the Practice of Wickedness, is no other, than what originally by the Freedom of an intellectual nature it was necessary they should be capable of making; and for the preventing of which, it is not proper that the absolute Power of God should interpose, before the final day of Retribution. For the Kingdom of God, which wicked Men and wicked Spirits set themselves in opposition to, is not the Kingdom of his *Power*, but his Kingdom of *Righteoufnefs*; and the very nature and essence of a Kingdom of *Righteoufnefs*, is, to prevail, not by *Force*, but by the Victory of *Virtue* over the opposition and the Deceits of Wickedness. This observation may be of considerable Use, both for the right apprehending the nature of God's Supreme Government, and for the true understanding of several parts of Scripture. When we read of the Devil's first rebelling against the Almighty, and exalting his throne above the Stars of God, and presuming to be like the most High; for which offence he was cast down from Heaven; 'tis evident the meaning is not, (as some have childishly supposed, or poetically represented,) that he rebelled against God, as hoping to prevail by *Force*. No; Those Angelic Spirits, had their Knowledge been *but equal* to *ours*, as indeed it was *far superior*; but had it been *equal only* to that of *Men*, yet they could not possibly have been so absurdly ignorant, as to imagine that Finite could prevail *by Force* against Infinite, or not know that the Almighty could, if he pleased, annihilate them as swift as Thought, and withdraw their very Being from them in a moment, and destroy them for ever with the least blast of his mouth. *Force* therefore, 'tis evident, they could not think of; But the meaning of the Devil's rebelling, is; that he presumptuously transgressed the Law of the most High; and preferred his own Will, as wicked *Men* also do, before the Command-

ments

ments of God; and probably firſt deceivèd *himſelf* with the very ſame Temptation, S E R M. wherewith he afterwards deceived our Firſt Parent; *In the day thou doſt this Thing,* X. *ſurely thou ſhalt not die.* We read indeed, *Rev.* xii. 7. that *there was War in Heaven*; *Michael and his Angels fought againſt the dragon, and the dragon fought and his Angels; And prevailed not, neither was their place found any more in Heaven; And the great dragon was caſt out, that old Serpent, called the Devil and Satan, which deceiveth the whole world; and his Angels were caſt out with him.* But the meaning of this paſſage is not literal, as if the Devil had Power to *fight againſt* the Angels or Miniſters of God's government; But according to the ſublimity and loftineſs of the prophetick ſtyle, 'tis evident it muſt be underſtood as a highly figurative deſcription, how wonderfully *the Goſpel of Chriſt* prevailed in the primitive times, by the courage and conſtancy of the Martyrs, againſt *Heathen Idolatry* then poſſeſſed of the Powers of the whole Earth. For ſo the careful and attentive Reader may clearly ſee it explained in the very next words, *ver.* 10. *Now is come ſalvation and ſtrength, and the Kingdom of our God, and the Power of his Chriſt; For the Accuſer of our Brethren is caſt down;——And they overcame him by the Blood of the Lamb, and by the word of their Teſtimony; and they loved not their lives unto the Death.* 'Tis therefore a great Error in *good men*, to magnify the Power of the Devil, (as has ſometimes been done) to ſuch a degree, as to become either an *Objection* againſt the Truth of Religion, or too great a *Diſcouragement* in the practice of it: Whereas on the contrary our Saviour declares to his Diſciples, St *Luk.* x. 18. *I beheld Satan as Lightning fall from Heaven; Behold, I give unto you Power over all the Power of the Enemy, and nothing ſhall by any means hurt you*: And St *Jude* aſſures us, *ver.* 6. that *the Angels which kept not their firſt eſtate, but left their own habitation, he hath reſerved in everlaſting chains under darkneſs, unto the judgment of the great day*: And St *Paul* hath taught us, 1 *Cor.* x. 13. that *God is faithful, who will not ſuffer us to be tempted above That we are able, but will with the temptation alſo make a way to eſcape, that we may be able to bear it*: And St *James* accordingly exhorts, *ch.* iv. 7. *Reſiſt the Devil, and he will flee from you.* The apprehenſion therefore that many melancholly *pious* perſons have ſometimes entertained, of the great Power of the Devil, is very erroneous and groundleſs. But 'tis a much greater Fault in *bad* men, to magnify the Devil's power, as they are very apt to do, in order to *excuſe* their *own* Crimes: As if, becauſe the *Devil tempted* them to do ill Things, therefore the *doing* thoſe ill things was a leſs fault in *themſelves.* Which is an Error ariſing from a very falſe Notion of the Devil's temptations. For had the Devil any Power at all over mens Will or Actions, it would indeed be, if not an Excuſe for their Wickedneſs, yet at leaſt an extenuation of it in the Sight both of God and Man, to be able to allege they were influenced by ſome ſuperiour Power. But if the Devil's power of tempting men, be nothing more, but like that of wicked *mens* tempting one another; *viz.* the ſetting before them *opportunities* of doing evil, and repreſenting to them the unrighteous *pleaſure or profit* they may be maſters of thereby; 'tis evident this is no excuſe for a man to allege in his own behalf, that he *did* a wicked action, becauſe a fair *opportunity* of doing it was laid before him, or becauſe he ſaw it would bring him ſome *pleaſure or profit.* And yet This is plainly all the Power the Devil generally has over Men. *Let no man ſay,* (ſays St *James*) *when he is tempted, I am tempted of God*; that is, let no man think that God permits the Devil to have properly any Power or Influence over him; For *every man* (ſaith he) *is then only tempted, when he is drawn away of his own Luſt and enticed,* Jam. i. 13. The Devil *did* indeed enter into *Judas,* when he reſolved to betray our Saviour; but 'twas the Covetouſneſs of his *own Heart* only, that gave him admiſſion. And St *Paul* tells us of perſons in *the ſnare of the devil, who are taken captive by him at his Will*; but 'tis becauſe they are ſlaves by their own conſent, to thoſe *Habits* of Wickedneſs which are the ſnares of the Devil. And

SERM. 'twas *Satan* filled *Ananias's* heart to lye to the Holy Ghoft; yet this in Scripture is fo
X. far from being efteemed an *Excufe*, that on the contrary the Apoftle urges it as an
aggravation of his Crime; *Why* has Satan filled thine Heart? *why* have you been fo
wicked, as to commit fo abominable a Crime, which you *knew* could be nothing but a
fuggeftion of the Devil?

WHAT has been faid upon This Head, will hold yet *more* ftrongly, againft that ftill
more abfurd and wicked opinion, taught by fome Antient Corrupters of Religion in the
primitive Times, called by the name of *Manichees*: Who from the Many Evils and
Wickedneffes which are in the World, concluded there was a *Supreme Evil Principle*,
Zoroaftres,&c. originally oppofite unto, and independent upon, the Power of God. Which blafphe-
mous opinion, was firft taught by the *Perfian* Philofophers, who called the Good Principle *Light*, and the Evil Principle *Darknefs*. And againft This abfurd opinion it is,
that *Ifaias* in his Prophecy to *Cyrus* King of *Perfia*, *(If.* xlv. 6, 7.) thus declares; *I
am the Lord, and there is none elfe*; *I form the Light, and create Darknefs*; *I make
Peace, and create Evil*; *I the Lord, do all thefe things*, That is; Thofe Powers,
which the *Perfians* looked upon as original Supreme Principles of Good and Evil, calling them by the figurative Name of *Light and Darknefs*, are nothing but the Creatures
of God, acting always either by *His* appointment, or at leaft by his Permiffion; and
there is *No Power* independent upon *His*. If it be here afked; fince God is the Supreme Infinite Good, and there is no Power independent upon *His*; why then are not
all things made good? for, *who hath refifted his Will?* the Anfwer has already been
given *in part*; that Freedom of Will, is effential to the Being of rational Creatures;
So that Abfolute Power over-ruling that Freedom, would be deftroying that Nature
which it had created; And therefore That poffibility of Evil, which is confequent upon Freedom, is reafonable to be permitted. And This holds, both with regard to Evil
Spirits and Evil *Men*. But then, with regard to *Men*, it may ftill *further be anfwered*;
that, befides its being inconfiftent with moral government to over-rule their Wills by
Power, there arifes moreover from thofe Evils, which could not reafonably be prevented, a various manifeftation of the *Wifdom of God* in bringing Good frequently out
of Evil; of the *Mercy and Goodnefs and Compaffion of God* in bearing with Sinners unto
Repentance; and finally of the *Juftice of God* in deftroying thofe who will by no
means be amended. And This is the Anfwer St *Paul* gives to a like difficulty, *Rom.* ix.
22. *What if God, willing to fhow his Wrath, and to make his Power known, indured
with much long-fuffering the Veffels of Wrath fitted to deftruction? fitted to deftruction*,
by their *own* Wickednefs; yet, at the fame time, indured on *God's* part *with much
long-fuffering*, that they might have fpace of Repentance.

2*dly*, FROM what was faid concerning the *Extent* of the divine Power, that it muft
by no means be underftood as including a Poffibility of working *Contradictions*; the *Inference* naturally to be drawn, is, that we ought to lay it down as a *Rule*, always to reject with Indignation, thofe who would impofe upon our Faith any plain Impoffibilities, under colour and pretenfe of the *Omnipotence of God*. For if Contradictions really
deftroy themfelves, and are Nothing; and a Power of working them is but a Power
of doing nothing; and confequently the afcribing to God any fuch Power, is not magnifying, but mocking his Omnipotence; it follows plainly, that whofoever indeavours
to impofe any fuch thing on mens Faith, howfoever in words he may pretend to exalt
and think highly of the divine Power, yet in reality he does but reproach the *Reafon*
of Mankind, and turn *Religion* into Ridicule. For if the Religion a man teaches be
confeffedly *unreafonable*; with what Arguments can he apply ferioufly to Another man's
Reafon to believe and embrace it? And if it be repugnant to the *Attributes* of God;
what *Authority* can be able to fupport it? The *Effect* of fuch Doctrines is nothing elfe,
but expofing ourfelves to the Scorn of Unbelievers; and giving too juft occafion to

Atheiſtical and profane Spirits to blaſpheme the Sacred Names of God and Religion. Of This nature is the doctrine of *Tranſubſtantiation*; that great Reproach of the Common Senſe of *Men*; and great Profanation of that divine Attribute, the Omnipotence of *God*. And of the ſame Nature and Tendency in proportion, are all falſe and fooliſh Explications of the plain and true doctrines of Religion ; Such Explications, as are frequently to be found in ſubtle and ſcholaſtick writers, and ſometimes in Others from whom ſuch things ſhould not be expected; which make religion unintelligible, and conſequently not really and heartily believed, even by thoſe who Themſelves fancy that they do believe it. For nothing influences mens *practice*, but what they underſtand : And whatever religion has no effectual influence upon the conſtant courſe of men's Lives and Actions, to eſtabliſh Virtue, Righteouſneſs and Charity in their whole behaviour; is a Religion for which men are certainly nothing the better, and may very poſſibly be much the worſe.

3dly, IF the Power of doing *Evil* be not included in the true Notion of Omnipotence ; then from hence we may learn not to regard ſuch Doctrines, as, under pretenſe of God's Sovereignty, ſupreme uncontroulable dominion, and abſolute Power, aſſert *hard* things concerning him, *inconſiſtent* with his moral Perfections. Of This kind, are all thoſe Doctrines, which make *God* the Author of *Sin and Death :* The Doctrines of abſolute *Predeſtination* and *unconditionate Decrees*; the Doctrines which ſubject *Men* to unavoidable *Fatality*, and repreſent *God* capable of the greateſt *Cruelty*. Theſe Doctrines muſt of Neceſſity be falſe. And the Scriptures upon which they are built, though to the careful Reader they have plainly enough another meaning, yet even if we could not tell how to interpret them otherwiſe, we might neverthelefs be certain that their ſenſe was miſtaken ; becauſe we are beforehand ſure from the nature of God, that 'tis altogether as impoſſible for him to do what is *Evil* or *Unjuſt*, as to be able to work even *Contradictions themſelves*. The Authors of the contrary Opinion allege, that whatever God does, is *therefore Juſt and Good*, becauſe *He* does it. Which is indeed very true : But not, unleſs it be rightly underſtood. For the meaning of that Aſſertion, is not, that the nature of Things would be altered by God's acting otherwiſe than he does ; or that What is Evil and Unjuſt would become Juſt and Good by ſuppoſing God to do it ; but the right meaning of it is, that becauſe from our Knowledge of the divine Attributes we are beforehand Sure *in general* that God *will* do nothing but what is *in itſelf* Juſt and Good, therefore whenever we know of any thing *in particular* that *God does* it, we may ſafely from thence and for that reaſon depend upon it, that the Thing is *in its own Nature* Juſt and Good; for that, otherwiſe, *He* would not have done it. But now if men hence take occaſion to contend, that things in their *own Nature* hard and unrighteous, may, by being aſcribed to *God*, be taught and defended; what is this, but abuſing mens Reaſon with a pretenſe of God's abſolute Power and Dominion ? As if, becauſe what a known *juſt man* or *juſt governour* at any time *does*, may well be depended upon to be in itſelf a *juſt Thing*; therefore, tho' ſuch a Perſon ſhould *change* his character, and do a thing plainly *unjuſt*, it might ſtill be imagined to follow that it was *juſtly* and *rightly* done. Is not this plainly *ſpeaking deceitfully for God*; and having recourſe to his Supremacy and Omnipotence, to deſtroy all the other Perfections of the Divine Nature ? The Foundation of all erroneous opinions in theſe Matters, is the Notion of *Dominion's* being founded in *Power*, and that *Omnipotence only* is the Ground of God's *abſolute Right* over his Creatures. But the Falſity of this Notion appears from hence, that if *Power* was the Meaſure of *Right*, it would follow that all the other Perfections of God were of no moment; and that, whatever the worſt Being in the World did, provided he had but abſolute Power, would be as juſt and righteous as the Actions of the All-merciful and Good God : Which is manifeſt Blaſphemy. The Truth therefore is evidently This: In things merely *poſitive*, which

in

in their own nature are neither good nor evil, *Dominion or Power* is indeed the Foundation of *Right*; and *Superiour Authority* is the only *Measure*, by which the *Fitness or Goodness* of such things is to be judged of. But matters of *Moral* consideration, derive their Goodness or Badness, not from *Will or Power*, but from the unchangeable *nature of things themselves*; from that eternal Reason, the unalterable conformity to which, is one of the principal internal Perfections of the divine Nature; And therefore in *these* things, the *Power of God* ought no more to be conceived capable of making *Evil Good*, than in *natural* things it can be imagined to produce *Contradictions*. If This were not the case, any sort of Wickedness might come to be taught under pretense of Religion.

But II. T H E R E is *another* sort of Inference to be drawn from the consideration of the Divine Omnipotence; which may still more immediately influence and direct our *Practice*. And

1*st*, I F God has infinite and irresistible *Power*, hence arises an evident necessity of fearing and obeying him. The *Rule* indeed of his Government, is not *Power*; but *Equity*. But as his Commands are always in themselves *Just and Righteous*, so his *Power* will exact Obedience to those Commands. *There is one Law-giver*, (says the Apostle, St *James* iv. 12.) *who is able to save and to destroy.*

2*dly*, T o *wicked men* therefore, who have lived in disobedience to the Laws of God, presumptuously and impenitently; the consideration of the Greatness of the Divine *Power*, is *just* matter of *Terror*. Ps. xc. 11. *Who knoweth the Power of thine Anger?* And the Apostle, Heb. x. 31. *It is a fearful thing to fall into the hands of the living God:* And our Saviour himself, St *Luke* xii. 5. *I will forewarn you, whom ye shall fear; Fear Him, who, after he hath killed, hath Power to cast into Hell; yea, I say unto you, Fear Him.* The most enormous Offenders *may* possibly escape the Punishment of Men, and evade the stroke of human Justice; They may perhaps conceal their Crimes from the Eye of the World; or by Number, or Strength, be too great to be punished by any temporal Authority. But from the *Power of God*, there is no escaping; from *His Justice*, there is no appeal; from *His Wrath*, no Strength, no Fraud, no Policy, no Wisdom or Artifice can deliver them. This therefore is a very strong Argument, to perswade wicked men to Repentance; that they may appease his *Wrath*, whose *Power* they cannot resist; and become Objects of his *Mercy*, from whose *Justice* otherwise there is no escaping.

3*dly*, T H E consideration of the Greatness of the Divine Power, is a sure ground of *Trust and Confidence* to virtuous and *good men*, at all times and under all distresses. Ps. lxii. 8. *O put your trust in God always, ye people; pour out your hearts before him, for he is our hope:*———*God spake once, and twice I have also heard the same, that Power belongeth unto God.* And Ps. xci. 1. *He that dwelleth in the secret place of the most High, shall abide under the shadow of the Almighty;*——— *Surely he shall deliver thee from the snare of the fowler, and from the noisom pestilence;*——— *Thou shalt not be afraid for any terror by night, nor for the Arrow that flieth by day; For the pestilence that walketh in darkness, nor for the destruction that wasteth at noon-day.* This is also excellently expressed in the book of *Job*, ch. v. 19. *He shall deliver thee in six troubles, yea in seven there shall no evil touch thee; In famine he shall redeem thee from Death, and in War from the Power of the Sword:*——— *At destruction and famine thou shalt laugh, neither shalt thou be afraid of the Beasts of the Earth; For thou shalt be in league with the stones of the field, and the Beasts of the field shall be at Peace with thee.* And by the Prophet *Habbukkuk*, ch. iii. 17. *Tho' the fig-tree shall not blossom, neither shall fruit be in the Vines; tho' the labour of the olive shall fail, and the fields shall yield no meat; tho' the flock shall be cut off from the fold, and there shall be no herd in the stalls; yet will I rejoice in the Lord, I will joy in the God of my Salvation.* All the

afflictions

afflictions and calamities of *This World* may possibly in the course of things, fall S E R M. upon the *best* of Men; but he that *made the world* is their defence and deliverance. X. *Oppressors and Tyrants* may hate and persecute them for a time; But *mortal men,* whose breath is in their nostrils, wherein are they to be accounted of? For God breaketh the Arms of the Mighty, and bringeth the Counsel of the wicked to nought. The *Devil* may assault them with variety of Temptations, and stir up against them all the Enemies of God and Virtue; But God is infinitely superiour to all the Powers of Wickedness, and has reserved those Apostate Spirits in chains under Darkness, unto the judgment of the great Day. Such persons saith our Saviour, *shall never perish,* *neither shall Any pluck them out of* my hand; For *my Father which gave them me, is* *greater than all,* Joh. x. 28. And St *Paul,* 2 Tim. i. 12. *I know,* says he, *whom I* *have believed, and I am persuaded that he is able to keep that which I have committed* *unto him, against That day.* This is that Faith and Trust in God, for which the Patriarch *Abraham* is so justly commended, *Rom.* iv. 17. *Who,* relying on *God who* *quickneth the dead, and calleth those things which be not as though they were; Against* *Hope, believed in Hope; and——staggered not at the Promise of God thro' Unbelief;* *but was strong in Faith, giving Glory to God; and being fully perswaded, that what* *he had promised, he was Able also to perform.* And *Heb.* xi. 8, 10, 17. 19. *By Faith* *Abraham when he was called,——went out, not knowing whither he went; and sojourned* *in the land of Promise as in a strange country;——for he looked for a City which hath* *foundations, whose builder and maker is God.——By Faith, when he was tried,——* *he offered up his only begotten Son;————accounting that God was able to raise him up* *even from the dead, from whence also he had received him in a figure;* (He had *before* *received him from the dead in a figure;* that is, the *Birth* of his Son in his old age, Heb. xi. 12. when his own body was *now* already *as good as dead,* was even as great a Miracle as and Rom. iv. That which he afterwards expected, of his being *raised again.*) This also is That 19. Faith of *Moses,* ver. 24, by which, *when he was come to years, he refused to be called* *the Son of Pharoah's daughter; choosing rather to suffer affliction with the people of God,* *than to injoy the pleasures of Sin for a Season; Esteeming the reproach of Christ greater* *riches than the treasures in Egypt;* *for he had respect unto the recompence of re-* *ward,——and indured as seeing Him who is invisible.*

4*thly* and *Lastly*; The consideration of the Omnipotence of God, ought to teach vain Mortals *Humility,* and that the *Potsherds of the Earth* (as the *Prophet* elegantly stiles men) should not proudly insult and domineer over each other. *Pride was not* *made for Man, nor furious Anger for them that are born of a Woman,* Eccluf. x. 18. Whatever power any man has, he received it from God; and God, who gave That Power, is infinitely Higher than all; Nay, the meanest ministring Spirit in the Armies of the Angels of God, is far superiour to all the Power of all the Potentates of the Earth together. Yet even *God Himself,* uses not arbitrary and absolute Power to Evil; nor does wrong, even to the meanest of his creatures. *Be wise now therefore, O* *ye Kings,* Pf. ii. 10. *be instructed, ye that are Judges of the Earth.* For 'tis the greatest Glory of the greatest Men, to imitate in This Particular the Great King and Sovereign of the Universe.

S E R M O N XI.

Of the OMNISCIENCE of G O D.

JOB XXXVII. 16. laſt part.

Of Him that is perfeſt in Knowledge.

SERM.
XI.

THESE words are a Declaration of That Divine Attribute, the Perfection of *Knowledge.* In diſcourſing upon which Subjeſt, I ſhall *1ſt* endeavour to prove plainly and intelligibly, that God who is the Governour and Judge of all, *muſt* be a Being indued with *perfeſt Knowledge.* 2*dly,* I ſhall offer ſome Obſervations concerning the *particular Nature and Circumſtances* of the divine Knowledge. And 3*dly,* I ſhall make ſome *praſtical Refleſtions* upon the whole.

I. IN order to prove plainly and intelligibly, that God is a Being which muſt *of* *Neceſſity* be indued with *perfeſt Knowledge;* 'tis to be obſerved, that *Knowledge* is a Perfeſtion, without which the foregoing Attributes are no Perfeſtions at all, and without which *thoſe which follow* can have no Foundation. Where there is no *Knowledge,* Eternity and Immenſity are as nothing; and Juſtice, Goodneſs, Mercy, and Wiſdom can have no place. The Idea of *Eternity and Omnipreſence* devoid of *Knowledge,* is as the Notion of *Darkneſs* compared with That of *Light;* 'tis as a Notion of the *World,* without the Sun to illuminate it; 'tis as the Notion of *inanimate Matter,* (which is the Atheiſt's ſupreme Cauſe,) compared with That of *Life and Spirit.* And as for the *following* Attributes, *Juſtice, Goodneſs, Mercy, and Wiſdom;* 'tis evident that, without *Knowledge,* there could not *poſſibly* be any ſuch thing as Theſe *at all.*

AGAIN: That God *muſt* be himſelf a Being indued with *perfeſt Knowledge,* appears from his having to *other* Beings communicated certain degrees of that Perfeſtion. For whatever Perfeſtion is in any *Effeſt,* muſt of Neceſſity have been *much more,* in the *Cauſe* that produced it. Nothing can give to *Another,* that which it hath not *itſelf:* And therefore from the Figure and Motion, from the Compoſitions and Diviſions of lifeleſs Matter, 'tis evident nothing could ever have ariſen, *but* lifeleſs Matter. Wherefore ſince in Created Beings there *are* many degrees of *Knowledge,* it follows neceſſarily that the *Perfeſtion of Knowledge* muſt be in Him that created them: *Pſ.* xciv. 8. *Ye Fools, when will ye be wiſe? He that planted the Ear, ſhall He not hear? He that formed the Eye, ſhall He not ſee?*——*he that teaches man Knowledge, ſhall not He know?* In the caſe of *Imperfeſtions* indeed, the Argument lies *otherwiſe:* Theſe *may be* in the Effeſt, tho' they were *not* in the Cauſe: And the reaſon is evident; Becauſe tho' nothing can give what it has not, yet any cauſe may forbear to give *all* that it has; Tho' nothing can communicate *more,* than it has itſelf; yet it may communicate as much *leſs,* as it pleaſes. Finiteneſs therefore, which is but a Negation; and all the conſequences of being Finite, ſuch as Figure, Motion, Compoſition, Diviſion, and the like; *may* be in the Creature, tho' they are not in the Creator. But whatſoever is a real poſitive Perfeſtion, as *Knowledge* is; *muſt* have been firſt and perfeſt in the original Cauſe, or elſe it could never have been tranſmitted to any thing that was produced.

Laſtly,

Lastly, to conclude this First Head, as needing not much enlargement; From the *Immensity* or *Omnipresence* of God, may the same Truth be likewise clearly evinced: For from thence it follows, if he is an Intelligent Being at all, (as has already been proved by the foregoing Arguments;) it follows, I say, from his *Omnipresence*, that his *Knowledge must be* Infinite and Perfect. For where-ever *Himself* is, his *Knowledge* is, which is inseparable from his Being, and must therefore be *infinite*; And where-ever his infinite *Knowledge* is, 'tis plain it must necessarily have a thorough prospect of the inmost nature and essence of every thing; so that nothing can be concealed from his Inspection.

HAVING thus briefly proved, that God must of Necessity be a Being indued with *perfect Knowledge*; I proceed now in the

IId place, To offer some Observations, concerning the *particular Nature and Circumstances* of this divine Knowledge. And this I shall do distinctly, with regard to the *Object*, the *Manner*, and the *Certainty* of this Knowledge.

1*st*, WITH regard to the *Object* : 'Tis a Knowledge of *All* things absolutely, without exception. *Our* Knowledge and comprehension of things, is short as our Duration, and narrow as our Extent. Our *Senses* inform us of the Surfaces and external Properties of a *few* things, within the reach of our imperfect Organs. Our *Reason* leads us a little further, to the Knowledge of some few *more* things than our Senses take in, and to the Discovery of some few of the inward and more hidden Properties of the things about us. Our *Imagination and Conjectures* extend a little further yet, to a *greater Number* of Things; but with more Uncertainty, and less Distinctness. *Angels* according to the greater Activity of their Nature, and higher Perfection of their Faculties, comprehend still *more* things than We; more in number, and with a more clear insight; yet limited and bounded as strictly within *their* proper Sphere, as *we* within *ours*. But the Knowledge of *God* is absolutely unlimited, and perfectly universal; infinite as his Duration, and boundless as his Immensity; extending to all things every where, without exception; and to all the Properties and Powers of things, without restriction.

BUT, to be more particular: The Knowledge of God, with respect to the *Object* of it, is a Knowledge of all the *Actions* of Men; a Knowledge of all their *Thoughts and Intentions*; a Knowledge of what seems yet more difficult, even of *future and contingent Events*.

THE most obvious, the first, and most manifest Object of the divine Knowledge, is, *All the* Actions *of all Men, Prov.* v. 21. *The ways of Man are before the Eyes of the Lord, and he pondereth all his goings*: and *Job* xxxiv. 21. *His eyes are upon the ways of Man, and he seeth all his goings*. *We* behold but a *small* part of each other's behaviour; and can observe only a *few* of the Actions, even of those with whom we converse most intimately. But God sees *all* the Actions of every man, and compares and weighs them together; and cannot by *one part* of our behaviour, be led into any false judgment concerning any *other* part of it. He understands the *Quality and Circumstances* of every Action, and exactly observes every *degree* of Good or of Evil in it; even degrees as secret and imperceptible to *Us*, or which *we* may be apt to fancy of as small importance, as the falling of a sparrow to the Earth, or a hair of our head falling short in number. And This Exactness of Knowledge, is necessary to the Judge of all the Earth, in order to his doing that which is right, in the final decision of mens eternal state; where every the least variation in the degree of Happiness or Misery, cannot but be of the utmost importance, because it will be from thenceforth unchangeable and everlasting. *God shall bring every work into judgment, with every secret thing, whether it be good, or whether it be evil*, Eccles. xii. 14. And *Luk.* xii. 2, 3. *There is nothing covered, that shall not be revealed; neither hid, that shall not be known: What-*

soever

SERM. *foever ye have spoken in darkness, shall be heard in the light; and that which ye have*
XI. *spoken in the ear in closets, shall be proclaimed upon the house-tops.* And 1 Tim. v. 24, 25.
Some mens Sins are open beforehand, going before unto judgment; and some men, they fol-low after: Likewise also the good works of some, are manifest beforehand; and they that are otherwise connot be hid. They that are otherwise, cannot be hid; That is; Not, as it is generally underſtood, *those works that are otherwise than good, cannot be hid;* For That is what was affirmed in the foregoing verſe: But the meaning is; *those good works, which are not now manifest, yet shall not always be hid:* For ſo the Apoſtle's ſimilitude, is compleat and elegant: *As* ſome mens *sins* are open *before-hand,* and others they fol-low *after;* ſo alſo the *good* works of ſome, are manifeſt beforehand; and *those good* works which are now *otherwise,* which are now *not manifest,* yet ſhall not *always* be hid. This exactneſs of the divine Knowledge, in order to the final and univerſal judg-ment, is elegantly deſcribed in Scripture by that figurative expreſſion, of Men's Actions being all *written in a Book*: Pſ. lvi. 8. *Thou tellest my wandrings;——Are they not written in thy* Book? Mal. iii. 16. *The Lord hearkned and heard it, and a* Book *of Re-membrance was written before him, for them that feared the Lord, and that thought upon his Name.* Dan. vii. 10. *The judgment was set, and the* Books *were opened.* And *Rev.* xx. 12. *The* Books *were opened,——and the dead were judged out of those things that were written in the* Books, *according to their works.* The meaning of all theſe places is, that every action of every man, is more certainly known to *God,* and remembred unto judgment; than things are made certain to be remembred among *men,* by being written down in *Books.* And from hence it appears, that mens *names being written in the book of life from the foundation of the World,* does not ſignify their being predeſti-nated by an abſolute decree to eternal Life; but their being recorded before God in all ages from the beginning, as thoſe who are judged worthy of eternal Life. For when a good man turns wicked, God threatens to blot *his Name out of his Book,* Rev. iii. 5. Which could not poſſibly be, if it was meant of an abſolute Predeſtination. And on the contrary, *Acts* iii. 19. the Sins of them that repent, are ſaid to be *blotted out*; that is, they ſhall not appear or be remembred againſt them in judgment. And This con-cerning the *Actions* of Men.

    T H E next, and more wonderful, Object of the divine Knowledge, is, *the Hearts, the Thoughts and Intentions* of Men. *We,* and perhaps all created Beings, can judge of Perſons, *Only* by their words and actions, and *by* the outward appearances in their be-

Heb. iv. 12.   haviour: But God, is *a Discerner of the Thoughts and Intents of the Heart.* 1Chr. xxviii. 9. *The Lord searcheth all Hearts, and understandeth all the Imaginations of the Thoughts.* And 1 Sam. xvi. 7. *The Lord seeth not as Man seeth; For Man looketh on the outward appearance; but the Lord looketh on the Heart.* Where-ever we are, he is always with us, and ſurrounds us with his boundleſs preſence; he includes and penetrates every part of our Subſtance, ſees into our inmoſt Thoughts and Purpoſes, and ſearches the moſt ſecret receſſes of our Hearts and Souls, with his un-erring and all-ſeeing Eye. And *This* alſo is a Power neceſſary, in order to his judging the World with Equity. For Wickedneſs lies in the *Heart,* as well as in the *Actions*; And, *Thou shalt not covet,* is a Command, as well as Thou ſhalt not *do* ill. *Whosoever* looketh *on a woman to lust after her,* that is, with an ill *intention,* tho' without opportunity of any ſinful *act*; *hath already* (ſaith our Saviour) *committed adultery with her in his heart,* Matt. v. 28. And ch. xv. 19. *Out of the* Heart, ſaith he, *proceed evil Thoughts, Murders, Adulteries, Fornications, Thefts, False-witness, Blasphemies.* In order therefore to the paſſing a righteous judgment concerning men's final ſtate, 'tis neceſſary that the Judge be able to ſearch the Hearts. And both Scripture and Reaſon, and the juſt and unavoidable Fears of ill-deſigning men, do ſufficiently bear teſtimony to the Truth of the doctrine, that God *is* able to do This infallibly and without Error. Nay there are caſes, wherein the

Heart

Heart being deceitful, not only to others, but even to a man's *self* alfo by fecret partia- S E R M. lity and imperceptible prejudices ; no perfect and unerring judgment can be made of a XI. man by *any other*, than by God only. 1 *Cor.* iv. 4. *Yea, I judge not mine* own felf, faith St *Paul* ; *For I know nothing by myfelf*, (I am *not* confcious *of any thing to myfelf*, fo the words ought to be rendred ;) *yet am I not hereby juftified* ; *but he that judgeth me, is the Lord*. And 1 *Joh*. iii. 20. *If our Heart condemn us, God is greater than our hearts, and knoweth all things*.

But there is a further, and ftill *more* wonderful Object of the Divine Knowledge, than even the Hearts or Thoughts of Men ; and That is, *Future Events*. He that gave all things thofe Powers and Faculties which they injoy, muft be acknowledged to forefee what each of thofe Powers and Faculties will produce ; and, thro' an infinite feries of Caufes, perceive at one View all things that ever *fhall be*, as if they *at prefent were*. Even the moft contingent Futurities, the actions of free Agents, cannot be conceived to be hidden from *his* forefight, who gave to his Creatures thofe very Powers of Will, and Choice, by which they are free agents. *Known unto God are all his works, from the Beginning of the World*, Acts xv. 18. The many predictions of future events, which have been in the World, were convincing evidences of the Truth of this Attribute, to the heathen philofophers ; And even the common reafon of the vulgar taught them, that it could not be imagined, that the Knowledge of the infinite and eternal God fhould be in any refpect finite. There is in this Matter, *one* Difficulty only, which has in all Ages employed the Speculation of confidering perfons : Namely the following queftion, *How Fore-knowledge in* God, *can be confiftent 'with Liberty of Action in* Men. In order to remove which difficulty, it may not be improper to premife two things ; 1*ft*, That our finite Underftandings may very reafonably be allowed, not to be able to comprehend all the ways of infinite Knowledge ; *Job* xi. 7. *Canft thou by fearching find out God? canft thou find out the Almighty unto Perfection? It is as High as Heaven, what canft thou do? deeper then Hell, what canft thou know? The meafure thereof is longer than the Earth, and broader than the Sea*. But This Acknowledgment of the Incomprehenfiblenefs of the Ways of God, muft always be underftood with relation to fuch things only, as do not imply any exprefs Contradiction : For whenever *That is* the cafe, it cannot be faid concerning *fuch* things, that they are incomprehenfible, or what we cannot underftand ; but on the contrary, that they *are fuch* things which we *do* clearly and diftinctly underftand, that they cannot poffibly *be :* The neceffary Falfity of all *Such* things being as clear to our Underftandings, as the Self-evidence of the plaineft Truths. Alfo, it muft be obferved, that this acknowledgement ought to be underftood *only* of things *exprefsly revealed*, not of any *humane* doctrines.

2*dly*, It is further neceffary to premife, that in the matter before us, the Queftion is not, *whether Mens Actions be free* ; but *whether or no, and How, that Freedom of Action, which makes Men to be Men, can be confiftent with Fore-knowledge of fuch Actions*. For if thefe two things were really inconfiftent, and could by no means be reconciled ; it would follow, not, that *Mens Actions were not Free* ; (for That would deftroy *All* religion, and take away *all* the moral Attributes of God at once ;) But on the other fide it would follow that *fuch free Actions* as *Mens* are, and without which Rational Creatures could not *be* Rational Creatures, were not the Objects of the Divine Fore-knowledge. And in fuch cafe, it would be no more a Diminution of God's *Omnifcience*, not to *know* things impoffible and contradictory to be known ; than 'tis a diminution of his *Omnipotence*, not to be able to *do* things impoffible and contradictory to be done. But This is *not* the Cafe : For, thefe two things being premifed, we may Now to the Difficulty itfelf, *How Fore-knowledge in* God *can be confiftent with Liberty of Action in* Men, anfwer directly ; that they *are therefore* confiftent, becaufe Foreknowledge has *no Influence at all* upon the Things fore-known ; and it has *therefore* no

SERM. Influence upon them, becaufe Things would be juft as they Are, and no otherwife,
XI. tho' there was no Fore-knowledge. Fore-knowledge, does not caufe things to be ; but
Things that are to be hereafter, whether neceffarily or freely, are the caufe of its being
fore-known that they *fhall* fo, whether neceffarily or freely, be. The *Futurity* of free
Actions, is exactly the *fame*, and, in the nature of things themfelves, of the like *cer-*
tainty in *Event*, whether they *can*, or *could not* be, fore-known. And as *Our* knowing
a thing to be, when we fee it is ; does not hinder an Action from being *Free*, notwithftanding that it is then certain and cannot *but* be, when it is : fo God's *forefeeing*, that
any Action will freely be done ; does not at all hinder its being Free, tho' he knows it
certainly ; becaufe *His Fore-feeing* things to come, does no more influence or alter the
Nature of things, than our *feeing* them when they are. The *Manner* of God's knowing *future free Actions*, muft not indeed be, like his Fore-knowledge of things *neceffary* ;
I fay, it muft not be by forefeeing a continued *Chain of Caufes* ; For That would indeed
deftroy their Freedom : But it muft be a Power, quite of another kind : A Power,
whereof we can only have an obfcure glimpfe, in fome fuch manner as That which
follows. What *one man* will freely do upon any particular occafion, *another man* by
obfervation and attention, may in fome meafure judge ; and the wifer the perfon be,
who makes the obfervation, the more probable will his Judgment be, and the feldomer
will he be deceived. An Angel, in the like cafe, would make a judgment of the future event, as much nearer to Certainty than that of the wifeft man, as the Angelic Nature and Faculties are fuperiour to the humane. In God himfelf, whofe Powers are all
in every refpect infinitely tranfcending thofe of the higheft Creatures, *This* Judgment of
future free actions, muft needs be infallible, that is, as truly certain, (though entirely of
a different kind,) as *That* Fore-knowledge which he has of neceffary events by feeing
their neceffary chain of caufes. Nor ought it to feem ftrange, that this divine Fore-
knowledge of future *free* Actions, fhould be entirely of a different Nature, from his
Fore-knowledge of *neceffary* events. For there is a not unlike diftinction in fome *others*
alfo of the divine Attributes. The *Omniprefence* of God, is an Attribute *neceffarily* belonging to him, by abfolute Neceffity of *Nature*, and altogether independent of his
Will : The *Goodnefs* of God is likewife a *neceffary* Attribute ; yet not in the fame manner as his Omniprefence, by a mere abfolute neceffity of Nature, but by the unalterable
Rectitude of his *Will* ; Which is the true reafon, why we properly return him *Thanks*
for being *Good*, but not for being *Omniprefent*. Thus *Both* are neceffary ; and yet by a
Neceffity of a totally different fort or kind. In like manner the *Fore-knowledge* of God,
both That of *Neceffary* and that of *free* Events, is in the iffue of Things, equally *cer-*
tain ; Yet in the one cafe This Certainty is entirely of a different nature, from That in
the other ; It arifing in the cafe of *neceffary* events, from God's own fore-appointing a
neceffary chain of caufes to produce thofe events ; but in the cafe of *free* events, it arifes
from, and depends upon, the mere futurity of the things themfelves.

To illuftrate this matter by an Example. That *Chrift fhould die for the Sins of*
Men, God not only fore-knew, but fore-appointed it alfo, and fent him into the world
on purpofe for that End. That *Judas fhould betray our Saviour*, God fore-knew, but
did not fore-appoint it ; only he chofe on purpofe into the number of his difciples One
fuch perfon, the wickednefs of whofe *own* Heart, he *faw* would prompt him to accomplifh that Event.

THAT *Ahab* fhould fall at *Ramoth-Gilead*, God forefaw, and forewarned him of it ;
yet God's foreknowledge did not make it neceffary for him to go up and perifh there ;
but the mere wickednefs of his own Will, defpifing the divine admonition, as it was the
only Caufe of the Event, fo was it likewife the only ground of the Fore-knowledge :
And had *Ahab* been difpofed to repent at the Advice of the Prophet, it was in his own

Power

Power to have prevented his deftruction; and the Fore-knowledge of God, would Then
have been accordingly, the Fore-knowledge of a contrary Event.

THE fame may be underftood in general concerning *all* exhortations offered to wicked perfons, which God beforehand knows that they will not obey. Concerning which
if it be inquired, to what purpofe then are they offered at all; the unreafonablenefs of
this objection will appear by confidering, that according to the fame argument, fince
God knew beforehand *every thing* in the whole Creation, therefore he fhould never have
created any thing at all. The true Anfwer plainly is: Whatever is in itfelf, and in the
nature of Things, *reafonable to be done*, 'tis fit *fhould actually* be done: And 'tis never
the more nor the lefs reafonable, for things being known or not known beforehand. The
reafon of God's fending exhortations to wicked men, is not that *he himfelf* is ignorant
what they *will* do, but that upon *their own account* 'tis reafonable they fhould be fo exhorted: And if the thing be reafonable *in itfelf*; it cannot *ceafe* to be fo, upon the account of Fore-knowledge. And This, concerning the *Object* or *Extent* of the divine
Knowledge: 'Tis a Knowledge of *all things* abfolutely, without exception; a Knowledge of all the *Actions* of Men, a Knowledge of all their *Thoughts*, a Knowledge of all
future and even *contingent Events*.

2*dly*, WITH regard to the *Manner* of this divine Knowledge; tho' it is moft unreafonable to imagine we can in any meafure poffibly explain *in particular*, all the
Ways, Manners, and Circumftances of infinite Knowledge; yet fome few *general* obfervations, fuch as thefe which follow, may be very ufefully made by us upon this Head.
That the divine Knowledge is not, for inftance, as Ours, and probably that of Angels
alfo, is; a knowledge of things *by degrees and parts*; feeing we can fix on but one fide
of a thing, and confider it only in one view at once; But 'tis a *perfect* comprehenfion
of every thing, in all poffible refpects *at a time*, and in all poffible Circumftances *together*. Again; it is not, as Ours, and poffibly that of higher Beings than we, only a
fuperficial and external knowledge of things, but an *intimate and thorough profpect of
their very inmoft nature and effences*, all things being *naked and opened* (as the Apoftle
expreffes it) *to the eyes of Him with whom we have to do*. Further; it is not, as Ours,
and probably that of the higheft created Beings more or lefs is, *confufed and general*;
but a *clear, diftinct, and particular* knowledge of every even the minuteft thing or circumftance; a knowledge, which not *a hair of our head* efcapes, and without which
not a *fparrow falls to the ground*. Laftly, it is not, as Ours, *acquired with difficulty,
confideration, attention, and ftudy*; but a Knowledge *neceffarily and perpetually arifing
of itfelf*, and infeparable even from the very exiftence of him whofe Effence is Omniprefent. And This briefly with regard to the *Manner* of the divine Knowledge.

3*dly*, As to the *Certainty* of it, (which was the laft Circumftance I propofed to
fpeak to,) I need but juft mention, that whereas *Our* Knowledge, (even of thofe things
which we are *well capable* of underftanding,) is difturbed and hindred by innumerable
caufes, by education and prejudice, by temper and intereft, by cuftom, humour, and
diforders of mind or body; All which we muft conftantly endeavour to conquer; and
may fo far do it, as to efcape all *fatal* errors, tho' we cannot avoid numberlefs miftakes:
And whereas the Knowledge even of the Higheft *Angels*, is always mixed with *fome*
degree of Uncertainty; as in that remarkable expreffion of the *Archangel* to *Tobias*,
Moreover I fuppofe (fays he;) he was not *certain*; but, *I fuppofe* (faith he) *that fhe
fhall bear thee children*: The divine *Knowledge* on the contrary is in all things abfolutely
infallible, without the *leaft poffibility* of any *degree* of being *deceived*.

III. IT remains, that I conclude with a few Practical Inferences from the whole.

And, 1*ft*, IF the divine Knowledge is *perfect*, it is a proper Object of our Admiration and Honour. Of our *Praifes* indeed and *Thankfgivings*, his Goodnefs, Mercy,
and Compaffion are more properly the Grounds: But to be *admired and adored*, is

what

SERM.
XI.

what every Perfection in the divine Nature equally claims. The *small glimpses* of Knowledge which appear in *Men*; if they be skilled in languages, that fictitious Learning which arises merely from our Dispersion and Confusions; if they have improved themselves in the study of Philosophy, History, or other Sciences; even *these small glimpses* of Knowledge, cannot but raise in us *some* proportion of Esteem. What Veneration then is due to *Him*, whose Knowledge is *in Himself* infinite, and who is the sole Author of whatever Knowledge is found in *Any Other*. And how should this teach us to think humbly and meanly of ourselves, and of all Creatures, and of all their possible acquirements! to consider, that we *have* and *know* nothing, but what we have received! (*For who has put Wisdom in the inward parts? or who has given Understanding to the Heart?* Job xxxviii. 36.) That *Knowledge*, and all other Faculties in created Beings, not only in *Men*, but even in the Highest *Angels* also, are but little *Images* and *Shadows* of Perfection; faint and derivative rays of Light, from the incomprehensible fountain of Glory! in comparison of whom, our Knowledge itself is Ignorance, and our Light as Darkness!

Ἥλιθ᾽ ὃς πάντ᾽ ἐφορᾷ κὴ πάντ᾽ ἐπακούει.

2*dly*, IF God knows all, even our most *secret actions*; then ought we constantly to live under the Power of this Conviction, in all holy and godly conversation, both publickly and in private. 'Twas with great *Elegancy*, that the antient Heathen Poets described the *Sun* in the Firmament, as overseeing and beholding all things; but the Description is *True*, in propriety and strictness of Speech, only of the all-seeing Eye of the *Father of Lights*. And hence appears the Vanity, of worshipping Saints and Idols, or any other Beings which know not all things. Which Folly *Elijah* excellently ridiculed, when he told the prophets of *Baal*, that their God was *pursuing, or talking, or in a journey, or perhaps he sleepeth, and must be awaked.*

3*dly*, IF God knows, not only our most secret Actions, but also even our *Hearts and Thoughts*; This shows us, the Folly of all *Hypocrisy*; the Obligation, to Purity of Heart; the reasonableness of the Command, *thou shalt not covet*; and the true Comfort of secret unaffected Piety.

Mat. vi. 31, &c.
Nos cæcâ magnaq; cupidine ducti, Conjugium petimus partumque uxoris, at illis Notum qui pueri qualisque futura sit uxor.
Ζεῦ Βασιλεῦ, τὰ μὲ ἐσθλὰ ἓ εὐχομένοις κὴ εὐνύκτοις Ἅμμι δίδν τὰ ᾗ λυγρὰ κὴ εὐχομένοις ἀπαλέξειν.

4*thly*, IF God knows all *future events*, then may we safely depend and trust on his Providence, without being *over-sollicitous* for the time to come. *We* are very apt to covet Riches, Honour, or Power; But *God* sees how perhaps these very things we so earnestly desire, would be hurtful to us; or how ill we should bear it, when perhaps they were again on a sudden taken from us.

FOR the same reason therefore, neither ought we on the contrary to *boast ourselves of to morrow, for we know not what a day may bring forth*; Prov. xxvii. 1. xix. 21. *Jam.* iv. 13. Nor can wicked men *at all excuse* themselves, upon account of God's *Foreknowledge* of their *Actions*; For it has been before shown, that between these things there is no connexion.

5*thly*, IF God *Alone* knows future events, as appears by the prophets challenging false Gods to foretel such events; then hence appears the Wickedness and Folly of pretending to foreknow things by the Help either of Men or Devils. 'Tis observable that no persons are *less careful* to ascribe to *God* his due Honour, than those who are very ready to ascribe to *other* Powers, to delusive Impostures or Diabolical Artifices, *more* than their due. And God accordingly describes himself, as taking Delight in *frustrating the tokens of the Liars, and making diviners mad*, as *turning wise men backward, and making their knowledge foolish*, Is. xliv. 25.

Lastly, IF God *Alone* knoweth the Thoughts of Men, then neither ought *We* to be forward in judging *others*, any further than their Actions give plain reason so to do; For *who art thou that judgest another man's servant? to his own Master he standeth or falleth*, Rom. xiv. 4; and 1 *Cor.* iv. 5. neither should we be too much concerned at *Others* judging uncharitably concerning *Us*, if in our Consciences we stand innocent before God, and have not by indiscreet behaviour given men just occasion of offence.

SERMON

SERMON XII.

Of the WISDOM of GOD.

COL. II. 3.

In whom are hid all the Treasures of Wisdom.

IN the foregoing chapter, the Apoſtle having very eloquently magnified the *Grace* (that is, the gracious and merciful Declarations) of God in the Goſpel, *ver.* 6 and 12. and having ſet forth in the loftieſt Expreſſions the Dignity of the Perſon of Chriſt, *ver.* 15. and the glorious *Effects* of his Sufferings, upon thoſe who thro' Repentance and renewed Obedience were made partakers of the reconciliation purchaſed by his Blood, *ver.* 21. concludes with a joyful mention of *his own* Sufferings alſo, after the example of Chriſt, *ver.* 24. Of this Goſpel, ſays he, I *Paul* was made a Miniſter, *Who now rejoice in my Sufferings for you, and fill up that which is behind of the Afflictions of Chriſt in my Fleſh, for his Bodies ſake which is the Church.* The Church of *Rome* has found, in this expreſſion of the Apoſtle, the doctrine of the *Merit of the Saints* : For if St *Paul* filled up that which was behind of the Sufferings of Chriſt, for his Body the Church ; it follows, they think, that the Sufferings of St *Paul* muſt conſequently be in proportion a Stock of Merit for the Church. But the real Meaning of the Apoſtle's words is very different from what they vainly conceive. For, *to fill up that which is behind of the Afflictions of Chriſt*, does not ſignify to *compleat* any thing that lacked to be *added* after the Sufferings of Chriſt, as if the Sufferings of Chriſt were not in point of Merit ſufficient of themſelves ; but it ſignifies, to *accompliſh* that which remained to be *fulfilled* of thoſe prophecies, which foretold that after the Sufferings of Chriſt, his Servants likewiſe ſhould therein follow his example. And theſe Sufferings of the Apoſtle's, *were* alſo indeed *for his Bodies ſake which is the Church* ; that is, for the Benefit indeed, not of the Church in *future Ages*, by way of *Merit* ; but of the Church *then preſent*, by way of *Example* and *Encouragement* and *bearing Teſtimony* to the Truth ; On which greatly depended the propagation of the Goſpel.

In this *2d* chapter, the Apoſtle proceeds to expreſs his great *Concern* for the *Coloſſians*, and his earneſt deſire of their *Improvement* both in the *Knowledge* and in the *Practice* of Religion ; *ver.* 1 and 2. *how great Conflict I have for you,*——*that your hearts* may be——*knit together in* love, *and unto all riches of the full Aſſurance of* Underſtanding ; *to the acknowledgment of the myſtery of God, and of the Father, and of Chriſt* ; *In whom are hid all the Treaſures of Wiſdom.*

To the acknowledgment of the myſtery of God ; that is, to the publick advancement of the Goſpel, and of the Glory of God therein manifeſted ; and that all men may acknowledge the myſterious or wonderful Love of God towards mankind, Now revealed by the preaching of his Son. The words next following, *of God, and of the Father, and of Chriſt*, are not rightly rendred ; For they found in that tranſlation, as if *God* and *the Father* were two diſtinct perſons ; Whereas they ought to be rendred, *of God, even the Father* ; *and alſo of Chriſt*. *In* whom, adds the Apoſtle, (ſumming up his

U whole

SERM. whole Argument by way of Exclamation in the words of the Text,) *are hid all the*
XII. *Treasures of Wisdom.* The word, *In whom,* may by the construction equally be referred, either to *God,* or to *Christ : God even the Father, and Christ;* in whom, in
each or either of whom, *are hid all the Treasures of Wisdom.* If it be understood as
referring to *God, even the Father ;* then it will be a declaration or acknowledgment of
his *Wisdom in* general; that He, is the Author and Fountain of *all* Wisdom. But if it
be applied to *Christ ;* then it must be understood of the *Wisdom of the Gospel in* particular; that in Him was treasured up all *that* Wisdom of God, which was to be manifested to mankind by the Gospel. In *either* way of understanding it, the Sense is not
much different; and in *Both,* it is a very useful Subject for our Meditations; *the Wisdom of God* more *generally,* or *the Wisdom of God manifested in Christ* more *particularly.*

WISDOM, is the right Use or Exercise of Knowledge ; and differs from Knowledge, as the *Use* of a Power or Faculty differs from the *Faculty itself.* 'Tis therefore,
in the divine Nature, a distinct Attribute from that of *Knowledge ;* and, as such, I shall
accordingly consider it in the following Discourse. And herein, for Method's sake, I
shall *1st* endeavour to show briefly in general, that God *must* of Necessity be infinitely
Wise ; 2*dly,* I shall consider more distinctly and in particular, the different *Manifestations* of this divine Wisdom, in his *Works,* in his *Government,* and in his *Laws :* and
3*dly,* I shall show of what *Use* these Meditations may be unto us in Practice.

I. In the *First* place, that God must of Necessity be infinitely Wise, appears from
hence; that, being Himself the Alone original Cause and Author of all things; and
knowing what each of their Powers and Faculties can produce; and seeing at one
View all the possible Circumstances and Disposition of things, all their mutual Relations and Dependencies, all their possible Compositions or Divisions, their Variations
and Changes, their Fitness or Suitableness each to certain respective Ends and Purposes ;
beholding (I say) all these things at once, 'tis evident he cannot but of Necessity always know, without possibility of Error, *what* is the *Best and Properest End* to be
brought about, in each one of the possible infinite cases or methods of disposing things;
and *which* are the fittest *Means* to that End ; and *how* those Means may best be *ordered
and directed,* to accomplish it accordingly : And, having no wrong Inclination possibly
to change his Will, any more than opposition possibly to withstand his Power; 'tis
plain he will always actually effect, what in right and reason is fittest to be done. Now
This is infinite or perfect Wisdom ; To know always the Best *End ;* to see always the
Means that will produce that End; to understand exactly *how to apply* those means to
the accomplishing that End; and to have always a right and invariable *Inclination or
Will,* to act accordingly.

AGAIN; every Unwise Action, or circumstance of Action, must necessarily proceed, either from shortness of Understanding, or from defect of Power, or from Faulti-
ness of Will; Either that the Agent *knows* not, or that he *can* not, or that he *will* not
do what is best. But now from each of these Defects, the Perfection of the divine
Nature is infinitely removed. Therefore every Action of God, must of Necessity,
(meaning in the *moral* sense of the word *Necessity,*) be what is *absolutely* and *in itself*
and *upon the whole* most Wise.

FROM *some* or *other* of these Defects, in *some* Degree, or in *some* Circumstances, no
Other Being can be exempt. *No other Being* therefore is perfectly Wise : But the Per-
fection, as *in* God it is complete and absolute, so *to* him Alone it is confined : The
Apostle frequently stiling him, with the greatest Justice and Truth, *God Only Wise.*
Yet *Vain man* would *be Wise ;* Wise *without,* and Wise *in opposition to,* his Maker :
Profanely sometimes, and Atheistically Wise ; *though man be born like a wild asses colt,*
Job xi. 12. that is, tho' being short-lived as the Beasts that perish, he could neither

give

give himſelf Being, nor *continue* it to himſelf when he had it; neither knows what S E R M. things have been before him, not what ſhall be after him, nor the millionth part of XII. the things that are preſent with him. Philoſophers, when beyond an humble Admi- ration of the Works of God, and a ſober inquiry into the nature and operations of ſe- cond cauſes under the direction of the firſt, they indulge themſelves in feigning Schemes out of their own Imagination, and attempt in *explaining Nature* to exclude the God *of Nature*; *profeſſing themſelves wiſe, they become Fools*, Rom. i. 22. and un- der the Notion of Science, vent the moſt ridiculous extravagancies. Politicians, Ty- rants, the great Oppreſſors and Deſtroyers of the Earth, lay what they call Wiſe and long fore-caſted Deſigns. But yet, as *Elihu* well obſerves, *Job* xxxii. 9. *Great men are not always wiſe*: For God often turneth their Wiſdom backward, and maketh their Counſel Fooliſhneſs; blaſting their deepeſt projects with the Breath of his Mouth, and diſperſing them as a Spider's web; by Storms and Tempeſts, by Fire and Earthquakes, by Diſeaſes and Death, by potent Enemies or treacherous Friends, and innumerable other unforeſeen or unavoidable Accidents. But what need we mention theſe greater and more enormous Follies? The true Wiſdom even of the *beſt* and moſt *reaſonable* men is mixt with perpetual Weakneſs; and our wiſe Actions bear no proportion to our Infirmities. Nay, even Angels themſelves, thoſe great and glorious Spirits, who al- ways behold the Face of God, and ſurround the Throne of infinite Wiſdom; yet even of theſe it is elegantly affirmed in the Book of *Job*, ch. iv. 18. that *he puts no truſt in his Servants, and his Angels he chargeth with Folly*: With *Folly*; Not like the Fol- lies of Vain *Men*; But with ſuch *Imperfections* as are *comparatively Folly*, in the Eyes of Him who alone is Wiſdom and Perfection itſelf.

Having thus briefly ſhown in general, that God *muſt* of Neceſſity be infinitely Wiſe, and that *He Only* is ſo; I proceed Now in the

II*d* place, To conſider more diſtinctly and in particular, the different *Manifeſta- tions* of this divine Wiſdom, in his *Works*, in his *Government*, and in his *Laws*. The Wiſdom of God in his *Works*, is the Demonſtration of his *Being*; The Wiſdom of God in his *Government*, is the great Confirmation of the Truth of his *Providence* with regard to Men; and the Wiſdom of God in his *Laws*, is the Excellency and recom- mendation of *Religion*.

1*ſt*, If we conſider the *Works* of God, and view this ſtately Fabrick which his hands have made; we ſtill find, that from the brighteſt Star in the firmament of Hea- ven, to the meaneſt Pebble upon the face of the Earth, there is no part of Matter, great or ſmall, wherein the Wiſdom of the Creator does not more clearly and unde- niably appear, than the Skill of an Architect is manifeſted by a Building, or the Judg- ment of an Artificer by the completeneſs of his Work. In almoſt every part of the Creation, the *Variety* of *Things themſelves* is *greater*; and the *different* Uſes which *every ſingle thing* is with the utmoſt exquiſiteneſs fitted to ſerve at once, are *more in Number*, than the Wiſeſt and and Greateſt Philoſophers, aſſiſted by the perpetually growing diſcoveries of increaſing ages, are ever able to exhauſt or enumerate. So that preſent and future Times, after employing the Sagacity of all Generations, ſhall ſtill with the ſame Truth as at firſt, repeat the words of *Job*; who, having at large deſcribed the Great- neſs of the Works of God in Heaven and in Earth, concludes ch. xxvi. 14. *Lo, theſe are* part *of his ways; but how* little *a portion is heard of him!* Or, as, *Salomon* expreſſes it, *Ecclef.* xi. 5. *As thou knoweſt not what is the way of the Spirit*; (Of *the Wind*, it ſhould be tranſlated; according to that of our Saviour, *Thou heareſt the Sound thereof, but knoweſt not whence it cometh, nor whither it goeth;*) *As thou knoweſt not what is the way of the Spirit, nor how the bones do grow in the womb of her that is with child; even ſo thou knoweſt not the works of God who maketh all.* Or, as the wiſe Author of the book of *Eccleſiaſticus*; who, having given a noble deſcription of all the parts of the

SERM. visible Creation known in *his* time, sums up all at last with this judicious exclamation,
XII. ch. xliii. 32. *There are still hid greater things than these, and we have seen but a few
of his Works.* Nevertheless, while to the *largest* Understandings, the Number of Things,
and the Variety of the Uses to which each of them is fitted, are more than can *in particular* be possibly comprehended; 'tis yet at the same time, even to the *meanest*
capacities, made most obviously apparent in *general*, through the *whole* frame of Nature, that every thing is with consummate Wisdom adapted to the best and noblest
Uses. *The invisible things of God from the Creation of the World are clearly seen, being understood by the things that are made.* The *Heavenly* Bodies, by their being fitly
placed to communicate to us in a due proportion their Heat and Light and other
Influences, by never-failing Vicissitudes of Day and Night, Winter and Summer, Seed-time and Harvest, *declare*, even to the most vulgar Understandings, *the Glory of God;
and the firmament showeth his handy-work*, Pf. xix. 1. For, had these Bodies been of
any other Bigness, at any other Distance, or in any other Motion than they Now are;
(which shows their present constitution to be the effect of perfect Wisdom;) the
world could by no means have subsisted. By the *Sun*'s being bigger or nearer than
it is, we had necessarily been consumed with Heat; By its being either smaller or
farther off, we had as unavoidably been destroyed with Cold; By any inequality in its
Motion, a Succession of *Both* extremes, Heat and Cold after each other, would
have brought upon us the same destruction, as a Perpetuity of *Either*. The *Earth*
whereon we dwell, being so beautifully adorned with Plants and Animals, so bountifully furnished with Seas and Rivers, Air and Winds, Clouds and Rain, Metals and
Minerals, for Use, for Ornament, for Delight; gives daily demonstration, even to
persons of the lowest capacity, if not perverted and stupified thro' Vice and Debauchery; that *the Lord by* Wisdom *founded the Earth*, that *by Understanding he established
the Heavens*; that *by his Knowledge the depths are broken up, and the clouds drop down
dew*, Prov. iii. 19: Or, as the Prophet expresses it, *Jer.* li. 15. that *he made the Earth
by his Power, established the World by his* Wisdom, *and stretched out the Heaven by
his Understanding.* Had any of these things been disposed in any *other* manner or
proportion than they are, the Earth had been no place of Habitation: With more
Waters, the whole had been made unserviceable by moisture: with *less*, it had been
destroyed thro' drought. The Air, with the violence of *stronger Winds*, would have
overturned all things: and without *Any*, it would have putrified by stagnation. Nay,
even those *inconvenient* things, as they may seem at first sight; by removing of which,
some profane Philosophers of old pretended that they could have mended the structure
of the World; even *these very things* themselves, which have been brought as objections against the Wisdom of the Creator, are found upon a closer view to be by no
means useless or unnecessary. *Wide Seas* are necessary for the producing of Rain;
Mountains and barren lands for preserving the Air healthful; and *Storms and Tempests* for purifying it when corrupt; and other particular things still *more noxious,*
if they have not likewise their more secret Uses, yet at least they are proper instruments in the hand of Providence for correcting and awakening a careless and irreligious World.

　　IF now from the World itself, we turn our eyes more particularly upon *Man*, the
principal visible Inhabitant whom God has placed therein, and the numberless *other
Creatures* wherewith he hath replenished it; no understanding can be so low and
mean, no Heart so stupid and insensible, (unless infatuated with the absurd prejudices
and witchcraft of Atheism,) as not to see plainly, that nothing but infinite and perfect Wisdom, could have produced that *infinite Variety of Living Creatures,* so *like*,
and at the same time so *unlike* to each other, that in That boundless Diversity, the
innumerable particulars wherein each creature differs from all others, should yet eve-

ry

ry one of them have its proper Beauty, and its peculiar, adequate, and singular Use. And over all These, is placed *Man*, the Lord of all, made in the Image of God; made capable *Himself* of adoring his great Creator, and of turning *all other things* likewise to his Praise. The *inanimate* part of the World, being void of *Sense*; the *animate* part, being void of *Reason*; cannot praise God any otherwise, than through the Mouth of *Man:* Without *Him*, the Heavens could not declare the Glory of God, nor the Earth shew forth his handy-work. But *by and through Man, all things* extol their Maker; and, by affording materials for *Our* Songs of Praise, *they themselves* may justly be said, not only without any impropriety of speech, but on the contrary indeed by a most elegant and lively Figure, as it is exemplified in the *Song of the Three Children;* *they themselves*, even the *inanimate* creatures, even all *the works of the Lord*, may themselves be said to praise him, to *praise him and magnify him for ever*. In the *Body* of Man, the Wisdom of God has manifested itself in so putting together an inconceivable number of different minute parts, as that none of them could be spared or otherwise placed, but to the great damage, if not destruction, of the whole. *O Lord, I will give thanks unto thee, for I am fearfully and wonderfully made; marvellous are thy works, and That my Soul knoweth right well. My Bones are not hid from thee, though I be made secretly, and fashioned beneath in the Earth. Thine eyes did see my Substance, yet being unperfect, and in thy Book were all my Members written; Which day by day were fashioned, when as yet there was none of them*, Ps. cxxxix. 13. But still *more* than in all these, more admirably and in a more exalted manner, appears the Divine Wisdom in the creation of the *Soul* of Man; a Substance endued with those wonderful Faculties, of *Thinking, Understanding, Judging, Reasoning, Chusing, Acting*, and, which is the End and Excellency of all, *Religion*; the Power of knowing, obeying, imitating, and praising its Creator; Which, yet neither It, nor still superiour Beings, Angels and Archangels, or the whole Host of Heaven, can worthily or sufficiently do; for, *who can express the mighty acts of the Lord, or shew forth all his Praise?* Ps. cvi. 2.

THE *more* all these works of God are studied, and the more diligently they are inquired and searched into, the more and the clearer Marks of Wisdom continually appear in them. And perhaps this very thing itself, is none of the smallest instances of the divine Wisdom in the contrivance of the whole; that whereas in the language of Scripture, and to the common sense and obvious judgment of pious persons of the *meanest* capacities among the Vulgar, God himself appears to be the immediate Author of all the operations of Nature; but by those who have gained some small conceited Knowledge in Philosophy, these things are generally so ascribed to the efficiency of second Causes, that God is represented either as not interposing at all, or so remotely as hardly to be taken notice of; it has again by those, who have made the *greatest* and truest improvements in natural Knowledge, been discovered and clearly proved, that all second Causes, (excepting Men and Angels, which are free Agents,) all *other* second Causes, (as they are usually stiled,) are really no Causes, and have no efficiency at all, but are *mere Instruments* by which God perpetually acts, and is Himself the constant (if not Only) Agent in what we vulgarly call the *Course of Nature.* So that the best and perfectest Philosophy, has ended where the natural Sense of Mankind began; strongly confirming and rescuing That Truth out of the hands of half-learned vain Scepticks, which was originally the universal Voice of Nature, and the first and most obvious Manifestation of God. And the Wisdom of the great Creator has in *This*, as in all other matters, illustriously appeared; that in order to our *true Knowledge of God*, wherein All men both learned and ignorant are equally concerned, all *other* sorts of Learning and Knowledge, (tho' very useful and valuable,) yet are so far from being absolutely *necessary*, that, provided there be not wanting an honest and sincere intention, it will at least, with regard to all thefe *other* things, be found true in proportion, that *he who gathered much, had nothing over, and he who gathered little, had no lack.*

AND thus much concerning the Wifdom of God, as made known by his *Works.*

2. I AM in the next place to confider, the Manifeftations of the fame divine Wifdom in his *Government* of the World. By which I do not now underftand *That Providence* by which he preferves and governs the *natural World*; For This was included under the former Head; But by his *Government of the World*, I would here be underftood to mean, his *Government of rational Creatures*, of *Angels* and of *Men.* Now concerning the Wifdom of Providence in *This* Government, 'tis not reafonable to make any pofitive judgment, from only a partial Knowledge of a few of its proceedings in fome fmall portions of Time. For, not of the Government of a *Kingdom* or a *Family*, much lefs of the Government of the *Univerfe*, can any one make a right and true judgment, without feeing the Iffue and Defign of the *Whole.* Yet even in all the *fingle* parts of the divine Oeconomy, if we confider the Hiftory of Providence, we fhall find fufficient marks of Wifdom, to convince and fatisfy us, that the Difpofition of the whole, will in the end appear as much wifer than can now be conceived; as the Structure of the natural World, after the Difcoveries of many Ages, has been found greater and nobler, than the mean conjectures and narrow Notions of the Antient Philofophers apprehended. *Angels*, having been at firft created in fo perfect a ftate, that nothing lefs than a total and incorrigible corruption, could make them chufe to *leave their own Habitation, Jude* vi. it was therefore fit that no place fhould be left for their Return, but that they fhould be *referved in chains under darknefs, unto the judgment of the great day.* The State of *Man* in *Innocence* was in great Wifdom furnifhed abundantly with all things neceffary, to the Happinefs of fuch a Creature in fuch a State: Yet, that his Obedience fhould be tried by God's referving *one* homage to himfelf, in acknowledgment of his being Author and Lord of all, cannot but be confeffed to be more becoming a Wife and Supreme Governour, than if he had appointed no fuch trial, nor required any inftance of Obedience at all. For This feems to be the meaning of the forbidden Tree; poffibly not that in its own nature, it was better or worfe than the other Fruits of the Earth; but that God referved it, as an inftance of homage to himfelf: And the curiofity of trying what was forbidden, and curiofity of knowing good and evil, became to our firft Parents a Temptation to Sin. By complying with which Temptation, when Men had actually finned; he who before was immortal, juftly became fubject to Death. Not that his Body was, *before* the Fall, *naturally Immortal*; (which can hardly be conceived:) but that God, either by tranflating him, or by glorifying him, or by *any other* means unknown to us, (but in general aptly figured by the *Tree of Life*;) would have preferved him from Death, which by Sin only was to come actually upon him. Neverthelefs even from That Mortality, which he brought upon himfelf by Sin, God ftill left him a Hope of reftitution; becaufe in his nature he was more frail and fallible than Angels, and fell not like them through incorrigible malice, but with a mixture of Weaknefs. The Light of *Nature*, and the Tradition of God's revealing himfelf in Paradife, were fufficient Guides to the Pofterity of *Adam* in the firft Ages. In oppofition to which Light when men had by degrees corrupted themfelves more and more, even to an univerfal Defection; the Wifdom of God manifefted itfelf in deftroying that generation by a Flood, for an Example to all future Ages; and yet not deftroying them fo utterly, but that a few Witneffes were left, for a better Teftimony to thofe that fhould come after, than if a total Deftruction had made neceffary a new Creation. After This, the Wifdom of God fhewed forth itfelf in inflicting proper particular judgments for particular crying Sins; deftroying the inhabitants of *Sodom*, for their unnatural Lufts, by Fire from Heaven; punifhing the *Jews*, as often as they fell into Idolatry, with *that recompenfe of their error which was meet*, by fuffering them to be

carried

carried captive into Idolatrous Nations, and difperfed in fo unexampled a manner, as to S E R M. remain a ftanding inftance of Providence in the fight of all Nations even at This day; XII. and frequently requiting alfo *particular* eminent perfons in Hiftory, fuch as *Agag,* *Adonibezek,* and the like, with the fame meafure that they had meted unto Others: Yet at the fame time more generally *forbearing* wicked perfons, that they might have fpace for *Repentance*; and on the contrary, frequently *difciplining* the good, chaftifing whom he loved, and weaning them from the World. So that even thofe very pro-ceedings of Providence, which were vulgarly looked upon as the chief objections againft it, his afflicting the good and fparing the evil, appeared, when rightly confidered, to be on the contrary none of the fmalleft inftances of its Wifdom.

Upon the whole; the Patriarchs and the *Jews* were a ftanding Theocracy, and perpetual Teftimony againft Idolatry; as a *Light* of true Religion, *upon a Hill,* held forth unto all Nations. And the Wifdom of that *Jewifh* inftitution appeared particu-larly in This, that by a number of rites in the worfhip of the *true* God, they were pre-ferved from running after falfe Gods ferved by their neighbouring nations; and thofe rites were at the fame time, both emblems of moral Purity, and Types of Chrift: By whofe coming at laft in the fulnefs of Time, the Wifdom of God moft of all confpicuoufly manifefted itfelf, in bringing Life and Immortality to Light, and difcovering plainly how all the various Scenes and Difpenfations of Providence through the courfe of all Ages in this World, fhould at the final Judgment terminate in a juft retribution of re-ward and punifhment to every fingle perfon according to his defert. But this belongs more properly to the next Head, *viz.* the manifeftation of the Wifdom of God in his *Laws.*

S E R M O N   XIII.

Of the W I S D O M of G O D.

C O L. II. 3.

In whom are hid all the Treafures of Wifdom.

IN a former Difcourfe upon thefe Words I have fhown, I*ft* in general, That God S E R M. muft of Neceffity be infinitely Wife; and II*dly,* I propofed to confider, more dif- XIII. tinctly and in particular, the different *Manifeftations* of this divine Wifdom, in the *Works* of God, in his *Government,* and in his *Laws.* The Two former of thefe con-fiderations, *viz.* the *Works* of God, and his *Government* of the World by Providence, I have already gone through: The

3*d* and *laft,* Which is the Manifeftation of the Wifdom of God in his *Laws,* will be the Subject of the prefent Difcourfe. Now the *primary* and *original Law* of God, is the *Law of Nature*; That eternal and unchangeable Law of Morality, which
neceffarily

SERM. XIII. necessarily arises from the *Nature* of Creatures, and from their *Relation* to God and to each other. And the Wisdom of *This* Law, is the very same as the Wisdom of God's Creation itself; being nothing else, than the universal Benefit and Happiness of all reasonable Creatures, arising from their acting according to that *Nature* which God has given them, and according to the respective *Relations* wherein they are placed thereby.

THE *next Law* of God given to Men, was the *Mosaick* Institution: (For the several Appearances of God to the *Patriarchs*, were but so many revealed confirmations of the Law of Nature:) And the *Wisdom* of *That* Institution given to the *Jews* by *Moses*, appeared by its being fitted, by a number of Rites and Ceremonies used in the Service of the *True* God, to preserve them from the numerous Temptations of that idolatrous worship paid to *False* Gods, wherewith all the Nations were overspread around them. Which Rites were also at the same time, both apt Emblems of moral Purity, and Types of what was after to be accomplished by Christ. Upon which account, St *Paul* elegantly describes the Use of *the Law*, that *it was their* School-master *to bring them unto Christ, that they might be justified by Faith*, Gal. iii. 24. *by Faith*, that is, not by bare *Belief* in opposition to *Obedience*, but by the obedience of that Christian *Religion* which was by way of eminence called by the name of *Faith*, as the Jewish *Religion* had been stiled *the Law*. But These things I do but just mention, as preparatory to what follows.

THE *Last* and *Great* Manifestation of the Wisdom of God in his *Laws*, is *the Gospel itself*; that plenary and final Revelation of the Will of God by Christ, upon account of which, Christ is stiled *the* Wisdom *of* God, 1 *Cor.* i. 24: And the words of the Text itself, tho', they be indeed of such ambiguous construction, that they may possibly enough be understood of *the Wisdom of* God *the* Father, as one of the divine Attributes, in *general*; or of *the Wisdom of* Christ, *in general*, as being that divine Person *in whom dwelt the fulness of the Godhead bodily*; yet, considering the occasion and manner upon which they are introduced, it seems to be their most natural meaning and intent to affirm, with regard only to *the Gospel in* particular, that *in Christ are hid all the Treasures of Wisdom*. For the Apostle having in the foregoing verse, been speaking concerning *the acknowledgment of the* Mystery, *of God the Father and of Christ*; by which mystery he plainly means the Gospel; must reasonably be understood, when he adds immediately these next words, *all the Treasures of Wisdom*, to intend still to express thereby the same mystery. The Gospel therefore is here stiled by the Apostle, Col. ii. 3. *all the Treasures of Wisdom*; that is, all the treasures of *That* Wisdom, which God intended to make known to the World by Christ. And because it is *That* particular instance of the divine Wisdom, *in which*, of all others, we are *most* concerned; 'tis therefore fit we should more distinctly inlarge upon it. Now in order to set forth more clearly, the Wisdom of God in this Dispensation; 'tis necessary to observe in the first place, that *Wisdom* consists principally in two things; in choosing to pursue the most excellent *Ends*; and in accomplishing those Ends by the best and fittest, tho' oftentimes the most unlikely, *means*. Now the *Ends* of the Gospel are, in the first place That great and *universal* Design, which both *This* and *in general all* Other actions of God, do ultimately tend to and terminate in; *viz.* the establishing *universal Righteousness* and *Happiness* through the whole World, which is the Kingdom of God. But then *more particularly*, and *in order to That* general *Design*, the principal Ends of *This Dispensation in* particular, are: 1*st*, To vindicate the Justice of God, and the Honour of his Laws and Government; and to show his irreconcileable Hatred against Sin: 2*dly*, To manifest at the same time, and in a consistent manner, his Mercy and Compassion towards Sinners: 3*dly*, To show the absolute Necessity of Repentance to Sinners, and of their effectual Amendment and Reformation; and the Impossibility of Pardon without it: and 4*thly*, To give to Them who are in This manner truly Penitent, an assured

Hope

Hope, that they ſhall be Objects of the Divine Mercy ſo illuſtriouſly manifeſted in the Goſpel; and to inſtruct and aſſiſt them in their Duty accordingly. Theſe are *Ends*, well becoming the Wiſdom of the Supreme Governour of the World, to intend and profecute. And in the *accompliſhing* theſe Ends through *the Goſpel*, by *Means* in reality ſo excellently fitted to their reſpective Ends; and yet ſome of them ſo *unexpected*, and others to humane Judgment ſo *improbable of Succeſs*, has the divine *Wiſdom* more illuſtriouſly appeared, than in any other diſpenſation of Providence known to us. In the

1ſt place; the *firſt* End or Deſign of the Goſpel, is to vindicate the *Juſtice* of God, and the *Honour* of his Laws and Government; and to ſhow his irreconcileable *Hatred againſt Sin*. When Man had preſumptouſly ſinned by tranſgreſſing a plain Command of his Supreme Governor; 'tis manifeſt God could not but be diſpleaſed at ſo unreaſonable an Action, and his Juſtice would neceſſarily call for Puniſhment: Neceſſarily; Not perhaps by any abſolute neceſſity of *Nature*; as if God by his ſupreme dominion and authority *could not* have forgiven Offenſes committed againſt himſelf, freely and without any Satisfaction, if he had ſo pleaſed: For every Prince *upon Earth*, every *Superiour* whatſoever, every *private* offended perſon, *has That* Power, if he *thinks fit* to exerciſe it: Nay, in ſome caſes, we are *commanded* to forgive offenſes, without requiring any Satisfaction at all: But the meaning is, when we ſay the *Juſtice* of God *neceſſarily* called for Puniſhment, that it was very *Fit*, very *right*, very *reaſonable*, and in the Wiſdom of Government, really *neceſſary*, that the pernicious and deſtructive Nature of Sin, ſhould be made apparent; that *His* indignation againſt it, who is of purer eyes than to behold iniquity, ſhould be fully manifeſted; and that the Honour and Dignity of the eternal Laws of his righteous Government ſhould be ſupported and vindicated, the Greatneſs and Weight of his Commands preſerved, and the neceſſity of Holineſs and true Virtue evidenced. Now *This End*, the Wiſdom of God accompliſhed even *more effectually*, by the Death of his Son; than it would have been even by the Deſtruction of the Offender himſelf. For ſince God *would* not paſs over the Sins of Men, without ſo great a perſon's ſuffering in the Nature of Man; that is, ſince he *did not* think any *other* method ſo *proper* of declaring his mercy and compaſſion towards Sinners, as that of ſo ſingular and extraordinary a Diſpenſation; This ſhows, in the ſtrongeſt and moſt affecting manner, the greatneſs of his Indignation againſt Sin, and his real Concern to preſerve the Laws of everlaſting Righteouſneſs from being deſpiſed or lightly tranſgreſſed. Rather than This ſhould not be effectually taken care of, he permitted *his own Son* to become a Sacrifice for Sin: He *permitted* him, I ſay; (For one perſon cannot *juſtly* be appointed to ſuffer for another, but by his *own conſent* :) He *permitted*, that *his own Son* ſhould, *for Sin, condemn Sin in the fleſh*, Rom. viii. 3. that is, ſhould himſelf by ſuffering in the Fleſh as a Sacrifice for Sin, become the great and ſtanding condemnation of Sin for ever; ſhould become an everlaſting example and demonſtration, how neceſſary the Wiſdom of God thought it in the government of the World, that Sin ſhould be ſeverely and exemplarily condemned. And This is the plain meaning of all thoſe phraſes of Scripture, wherein the Death of Chriſt is repreſented as our *redemption, ranſom,* or *purchaſe*; or his *buying* us *with a price*, and the like. His making *ſatisfaction* for us, was not by way of exact *equivalent*, which God was *bound* to accept; as in the caſe of one man's paying a debt for another: For in That caſe, no Ackowledgments are due to *him, to* whom the debt is paid, but to *him* only, who pays it; Neither could it with Truth have been affirmed, (as the Scripture always takes care to affirm with great earneſtneſs,) that God forgives mens Sins freely *and out of mere* grace and mercy, if *Satisfaction* were made for them in *That* ſenſe: But the plain meaning of Chriſt's making *Satisfaction* for us, is, that God was pleaſed freely to appoint, and freely to accept, and, of his mere grace and mercy, to be *ſatisfied with* what

S E R M. Chriſt did and ſuffered, in vindication of the divine Juſtice, and of the Honour of
XIII. God's Laws and Government, and for the manifeſting his irreconcileable Hatred againſt
Sin.

2dly, THE ſecond End or Deſign of the Goſpel, is to manifeſt at the ſame time,
and in a conſiſtent manner, God's *Mercy and Compaſſion* towards Sinners. *Mercy*, is
an Attribute as eſſential to the divine Nature, as Juſtice; and *its* proper Office, is to
ſhow forth itſelf in all truly compaſſionate caſes. Man, tho' an actual Sinner by the
corrupt Choice indeed of his *Will*, yet in his very *Nature* was frail and fallible, and
liable to be deceived. His caſe therefore, was, upon That conſideration, a proper object of compaſſion : For God *knew whereof we were made, and remembred that we
were but duſt*, Pſ. ciii. 14. That which in This caſe became infinite Wiſdom to do,
was to extend mercy and compaſſion unto ſinful Man ; and yet to do This in ſuch a
manner, as might at the ſame time be perfectly conſiſtent with his unalterable Juſtice
and Indignation againſt Sin. Now *This End* would not have been ſo compleatly anſwered, by God's making uſe of his abſolute Sovereignty and Supreme Authority *alone*,
in the forgiveneſs of Sin. But it was perfectly anſwered by the All-wiſe diſpenſation of
the Goſpel, when God manifeſted his *Love* to the *World* by *ſending his only-begotten
Son*, that *in* him *we* might *have redemption thro' his blood, even the forgiveneſs of Sins,
according to the riches of his grace, wherein he has abounded towards us in all Wiſdom
and Prudence*, Eph. i. 7, 8. Theſe laſt words, *in all Wiſdom and Prudence*, ſeem de-
ſignedly added by the Apoſtle, to expreſs the wonderful Fitneſs of the Goſpel, fully to
anſwer the End I am now ſpeaking of. For nothing could poſſibly be a greater Inſtance and Aſſurance of God's Love and Compaſſion towards Men, than This ſending
of his own Son for their Redemption ; *He that ſpared not his own Son, but delivered
him up for us all ; how ſhall he not with Him alſo freely give us all things ?* Rom. viii.
32. And yet at the ſame time, in this diſpenſation, the heinouſneſs of Sin, and God's
irreconcileable Anger againſt it, is ſet forth in the *ſtrongeſt* manner ; in the very circumſtances of Mercy itſelf, even while he is pardoning and accepting of Sinners. So that
we may juſtly ſay with the Pſalmiſt, *Mercy and Truth*, (that is, *Mercy and Juſtice)
are* here *met together ; Righteouſneſs and Peace*, (that is, *Juſtice and Forgiveneſs*) *have
kiſſed each other*. The only conſiderable difficulty in this matter, is to conceive how ſo
great a Perſon as the *Son of God*, ſhould condeſcend *ſo far*, in taking care of ſuch *mean*
perſons as the *Sons of Men*. But This difficulty ariſes only from our Narrowneſs of
Thought. For if 'tis not beneath the incomprehenſible Majeſty of *God himſelf*, to inſpect, direct, and over-rule the Motions of every even the ſmalleſt particle of inanimate
Matter in the Univerſe; as his Providence in the courſe of Nature demonſtrates that it
is not ; (ſince not only not a ſparrow falls to the ground without our Father, but even
the very Hairs of our head, as our Saviour aſſures us, are all numbred by him :) I ſay,
If 'tis not beneath the incomprehenſible Majeſty of God himſelf to inſpect, direct, and
over-rule the Motions of every particle of inanimate Matter in the Univerſe, much leſs
is it any Diſparagement to the Dignity of the Son *of God*, (tho' a very wonderful *condeſcenſion* indeed *it is*,) to redeem the immortal Souls of Men.

3dly, THE *third* End of the Goſpel, is to ſhow the abſolute Neceſſity of *Repentance* to Sinners, and of their effectual Amendment and Reformation ; and the Impoſſibility of Pardon without it. That *men* cannot otherwiſe become happy, than by the
Practice of Virtue ; and that *Sinners* cannot become capable of Pardon, but by forſaking their Sins ; is evident both from what we know by Reaſon, concerning the nature of God, of Men, and of Things; and from all former Revelations of the divine
Will. But by the *Goſpel*, the Wiſdom of God has in a more illuſtrious manner, and
with *greater Weight* of Arguments, ſet forth the indiſpenſable neceſſity of *Repentance*
and *Amendment*, and the impoſſibility of obtaining Pardon *without* it ; when even *with*

it,

it, he did not think fit to manifeſt his mercy to Sinners directly, but through the Inter- S E R M.
ceſſion of Chriſt, and by the merits of his Death; Appointing that the *Manner* of ac- XIII.
cepting even *Repentance itſelf*, ſhould be through the Mediation of his beloved Son, by
men's being *baptized into his Death*, and *waſhing their robes in the blood of the Lamb :*
In *This very* Diſpenſation of mercy, *revealing* more *expreſsly* his *wrath from Heaven
againſt all ungodlineſs and unrighteouſneſs of Men ;* and commanding us in the ſtricteſt
manner, to walk worthy of ſo great a vocation, behaving ourſelves exemplarily, as
children of the Day and of Light, in all Holineſs and godly converſation : For that,
whereas *God winked at the former times of ignorance, he now* peremptorily *commands all
men every-where to repent, becauſe he has appointed a day wherein he will judge the world
in righteouſneſs :* (Acts xvii. 30.) and *if judgment muſt* begin *at the houſe of God, what
will the End be of them that obey not the Goſpel ?* This is the ſtrongeſt reproof in the
World to all the vain Contrivances, by which wicked men deceive themſelves; by
Pilgrimages and Abſtinences, by Purifications and Oblations, by the Merits of Saints,
by Death-bed Sacraments, by the Abſolutions of the Prieſt, or Any other means of reconciliation whatſoever, beſides that One *of cleanſing themſelves from all filthineſs both of
fleſh and ſpirit, and perfecting Holineſs in the Fear of God.*

4thly, T H E *fourth* and *laſt* End or Deſign of the Goſpel, is to give to ſuch as are
truly Penitent *a full Aſſurance of Hope,* that they *ſhall be* Objects of the divine Mercy;
and to inſtruct and aſſiſt them in their duty accordingly. And *This End,* the Goſpel
has anſwered in the wiſeſt and moſt perfect manner. For though there was indeed,
even under the Light of *Nature,* very *good* ground of *Hope,* that God *would* accept the
Repentance of Sinners; yet 'tis a ſtrong *additional* aſſurance, which the divine Wiſdom
has now vouchſafed us, in *not ſparing his own Son, but delivering him up for us all.*
This is *indeed* an *effectual* encouragement to all ſincere Penitents, to All who have *really*
forſaken every vicious courſe ; to *draw near* and apply themſelves to the Throne of Heb. x. 22.
grace *with a true heart, in full aſſurance of Faith*; having *boldneſs and acceſs with con-* Rom. v. 1, 2.
fidence, to enter into the Holieſt by the blood of Jeſus, by a new and living way which Eph. iii. 12.
he has conſecrated for us. And the more ; becauſe he has *not only* opened unto us the Heb. x. 19.
Temple in Heaven by his Blood, but *continues conſtantly* to *make interceſſion for us,* to Heb. vii. 25.
be our *Advocate with the Father,* and a perpetual *High-Prieſt* for us *over the houſe of* 1 Joh. ii. 1.
God : And, that we might live worthy of theſe great privileges, hath himſelf *left us* Heb. x. 21.
an example of all Holineſs and Purity, *that we ſhould follow his Steps :* And, that we 1 Pet. ii. 21.
might not want *Motives* to engage us to imitate him, has made to us a clear and diſtinct Diſcovery of a Judgment to come. And, becauſe it was Wiſe and Fit, that
That doctrine which was to be an *univerſal* Law and Rule of Life, which was to be
the condition of Salvation to perſons of *all* capacities, ſhould be very eaſy and intelligible to *All*; therefore he has delivered it to us with all Plainneſs and Simplicity, not
in the abſtruſe *words of Man's Wiſdom,* (not in Terms hard to be underſtood, ſuch as
are Thoſe wherewith Later Ages have corrupted his Doctrine ;) *but in demonſtration of
the Spirit and of Power,* 1 Cor. ii. 4. *Teaching us, that denying ungodlineſs and worldly
luſts, we ſhould live ſoberly, righteouſly and godly in this preſent World,* in expectation of
being judged according to our works. And he is to be *himſelf* our Judge; who, as
St *Paul* expreſſes it, *that he might be a merciful and faithful High-Prieſt,* has *himſelf* Heb. ii. 17.
firſt *ſuffered in all things like his brethren*; and *can be touched with the feeling of our in-* iv. 15. & v. 2.
firmities, having himſelf been *in all points tempted like as we are*; and *can have compaſſion on the ignorant and on them that are out of the way, for that he himſelf alſo had
been compaſſed with infirmity.*

T H E S E are ſome of the principal *Ends* and Deſigns of the Goſpel. On account of
the *Excellency* of which *Ends,* and the wonderful *Fitneſs* of the reſpective *Means,*
made uſe of by the divine Wiſdom in the manner I have now diſcours'd of, to accompliſh

SERM. plifh them; Chrift is called, (in 1 *Cor.* i. 24. *and* 30.) *the* Wifdom *of God*; and in
XIII. the *Text*, Col. ii. 3. it is expreffed, that in Him *are hid all the* Treafures of Wifdom;
and *Eph.* i. 8. that, by this difpenfation, the Grace of God has *abounded towards us, in
all* Wifdom and Prudence; and *Phil.* iii. 8. that *all* other *things* are to be *accounted as
Lofs, for the* Excellency of the Knowledge *of Chrift Jefus our Lord.* This is the *firft*
mark of Wifdom; the *Excellency of the Ends propofed*, and the *Fitnefs of the refpective
Means* to accomplifh them.

THE *next* Circumftance wherein the Wifdom of God has particularly fhown forth
itfelf in the accomplifhing of the fore-mentioned Ends, is; that the Incarnation of
Chrift, as, *after* it was revealed, it appeared to be plainly in all refpects the *fitteft* poffible Means; fo, *before* it was revealed, it was on the contrary fuch an *unexpected* Method, and fo *undifcoverable* by any *finite* Wifdom, as to be an infcrutable Myftery, not
only to Men, (upon which account St *Paul* calls it in the words before the Text, *the*
Myftery *of God, even the Father, and of Chrift*; and in 1 *Cor.* ii. 7. *the wifdom of God
in a* myftery, *even the* hidden *wifdom which God ordained before the world unto our
glory, which none of the princes of this world knew*; and *Col.* i. 26. *the* myftery *which
hath been* hid *from ages and from generations, but now is made manifeft to his Saints*;)
but it was moreover a myftery which even the *Angels* alfo *defired to look into*, 1 Pet. i.
12. and fuch an inftance of Wifdom, *Eph.* iii. 9, 10. that thereby not only all Men
may *fee, what is the fellowfhip of the myftery which from the beginning of the world has
been hid in God, who created all things by Jefus Chrift*; but even to the higheft Angels
alfo, *to the principalities and Powers in heavenly places, may be known by the Church the
manifold Wifdom of God.*

THE *laft* circumftance I fhall take notice of, wherein the Wifdom of God has remarkably manifefted itfelf in the Gofpel, is his caufing it to prevail in the World by
unlikely inftruments, by the preaching of mean and unlearned perfons, in oppofition
to all the human Power and Wifdom of the World. The *Jews*, fond of eftablifhing
their own righteoufnefs, oppofed with all their Might *the righteoufnefs of God*, that is,
That new doctrine, that new method of Religion and Righteoufnefs, which God eftablifhed in the Gofpel. The *Gentiles*, conceited of *their own human Wifdom and Philofophy*, oppofed with all their Learning and artfulnefs of difpute, the *divine Wifdom manifefted in the fame doctrine of Chrift.* Againft *Both* thefe Oppofers at once, a few
mean and unlearned Perfons were wonderfully inabled to prevail. And the Wifdom of
God in caufing them fo to do, in *deftroying the Wifdom of the Wife, and bringing to nothing the underftanding of the prudent*, is moft elegantly defcribed by St *Paul*, in 1 *Cor.*
i. 21. *After that, in the Wifdom of God, the World by Wifdom knew not God, it pleafed
God by the foolifhnefs of preaching to fave them that believe.* For the *Jews require a
Sign, and the Greeks feek after Wifdom*; *But we preach Chrift crucified, unto the Jews
a ftumbling-block, and to the Greeks foolifhnefs*; *but unto them which are called, both
Jews and Greeks, Chrift the Power of God and the Wifdom of God*: *For——God hath
chofen the foolifh things of the World to confound the wife, and the weak things of the
world to confound the things that are mighty*; *——That no flefh fhould glory in his prefence.* And in the 11*th* to the *Rom.* ver. 30. he illuftrates and ftrengthens the fame
Argument ftill further, by obferving another and more *particular* inftance of Wifdom,
in God's fo difpofing *this whole matter*, as that the unbelief of the *Jews* at firft, and
the converting of the *Gentiles*, would finally terminate in the more illuftrious Reducing
of the *Jews* likewife, and the Salvation of *Both*: *For as ye*, faith he, ye *Gentiles, in
times paft have not believed God, yet now have obtained mercy through Their* [the *Jews*]
unbelief; *Even fo have Thefe alfo* [the *Jews*] *now not believed, that through your* [the
Gentiles] *mercy They alfo may obtain mercy.* *For God hath concluded them All in unbelief, that he might have mercy upon All*: *O the depth of the Riches both of the Wifdom
and*

and *Knowledge of God! how unsearchable are his judgments, and his ways paft finding* S E R M, *out !* XIII.

III. T H E *Ufes* we are to make of this *Whole* Difcourfe, concerning the Wifdom of God confidered either in general, or as more particularly manifefted in his Works, his Government, and in his Laws; are briefly fuch as follow. *That* from hence we con-fute the Folly of *Atheifts*, by fhowing them that the *more* the Works of God are ftu-died, the *more* marks of Wifdom are continually difcovered in them. *That* we who are *already* convinced of this truth, be continually *praifing* God for all his works of Wifdom; *who by his excellent Wifdom made the Heavens, for his mercy endureth for ever; and ftretched out the Earth above the Waters,* Pf. cxxxvi. 5, &c. and particularly for his works feen in *ourfelves;* whether with regard to our *bodies,* Pf. cxxxix. 14. *I will praife thee, for I am wonderfully made;* or with refpeƈt to the Faculties of our *Minds,* for his having *taught us more than the Beafts of the Earth, and made us Wifer than the Fowls of Heaven,* Job xxxv. 11. *That* tho' the Inftances of Wifdom we *can* difcover, are numberlefs; yet we are not to wonder, if we *cannot* find out *All* the ways of *infinite* wifdom, nor comprehend *All* the fecrets of Providence : For, *canft thou by fearching find out God? canft thou find out the Almighty unto perfeƈtion? It is as high as heaven, what canft thou do? deeper than hell, what canft thou know? The mea-fure thereof is longer than the Earth, and broader than the Sea.* Job. xi. 7. This Excel-lent man *Job himfelf,* who once thought he could underftand the ways of God, and argue with him, yet confefſed afterwards, *ch.* xlii. 5, 6. *I have heard of thee by the hearing of the Ear, but Now mine Eyes fee thee; wherefore I abhor my felf, and repent in Duft and Afhes.* *That* therefore it becomes *Us* to apply ourfelves to our *own* plain Duty, and leave *Secret things* to the Lord our God; confidering, whenever the Diffi- Deut. xxix. culties of Providence are greater than we can explain, that if the well-laid Defigns of 29. a Wife and potent Prince, cannot by the firft Scene of Aƈtion poffibly be difcovered; much more may it be impoffible for *Us,* from our very fhort view of a few events of Providence, to be able to explain the Defigns of the Supreme and All-wife Governour of the World; which yet in the End, (when we know the *whole,*) fhall appear moft evidently Wife and Excellent : *Seek not out the things that are too hard for thee, nei-ther fearch the things that are above thy ftrength : But what is commanded thee, think thereupon with reverence; for it is not needful for thee to fee with thine eyes, the things that are in fecret,* &c. Eccluf. iii. 21. For the fame reafon, we are, in all *affliƈtions,* Ecclef. ii. chearfully to *fubmit* to him; confidering that the Divine Wifdom knows infinitely *tot.* better what is fit for us, than we can judge for ourfelves; and is able to find out un- Nos cæcâ expeƈted means of deliverance for us, when he pleafes; and make *all things work toge-* pidine duƈti, ther *for good* to them that love and fear him. And in all *Exigencies,* where there ap- &c. pear no vifible means of efcape, yet we may depend on him without anxious follicitude; confidering, that He whofe Providence attends even to the minuteft things; who feeds the Fowls of the Air, and clothes the Lillies of the Field; without whom not a fpar-row falls to the ground, or a hair of our head perifhes; will certainly much more take care of *Us :* And that no counfel can take place, and no device can ftand, how deeply or wifely foever it may feem to be laid to human Underftanding, if it be not agreeable to his All-wife Will : For even *the Foolifhnefs of God,* as St *Paul* expreffes it, 1 *Cor.* i. 25. that is, thofe things which to *Us* feem the moft improbable, and wherein God makes ufe of the moft *unlikely* means and inftruments; even *This is wifer than men; and the weaknefs of God is ftronger than men.* Laftly, If *God* is infinitely and Only wife, let *Us* in *Our* proportion *feek* true Wifdom, by *Imitation of* him, and by *Obedi-* Jam. i. 5. *dence to* his Commands, *Prov.* ii. 3, &c. *If thou cry after knowledge, and lift up thy* Job xxvii 28. *voice for underftanding; if thou feek her as Silver, and fearch for her as hid Treafure; Then fhalt thou underftand the fear of the Lord, and find the knowledge of God : For*

SERM. *the Lord giveth Wifdom, out of his mouth cometh Knowledge and Underftanding : He*
XIII. *layeth up found Wifdom for the righteous, he is a buckler to them that walk uprightly;*
He keepeth the Paths of judgment, and preferveth the way of his Saints; Then fhalt thou
underftand righteoufnefs and judgment and equity, yea every good path.

S E R M O N   XIV.

Of the GOODNESS of GOD.

PSAL. CXLV. 9.

The Lord is Good to All; and his tender Mercies are over all his
Works.

SERM.
XIV.

THO' *every one* of the Divine Perfections in *particular*, affords moft juft ground of Adoration and Honour; yet That which to *Us* completes the Idea of God, and reprefents him under the Notion of the *Father* as well as *Lord* of the Univerfe, and makes the Supreme Being and Governour of all things, to be no lefs the Object of our *Hope and Love*, than of our *Admiration and Fear*; is This *glorious* Attribute, of *Goodnefs*. Eternity and Immenfity *amaze* our Thoughts: Infinite Knowledge and Wifdom fill us with *Admiration* : Omnipotence or irrefiftible Power is *great and adoreable*; but at the fame time, if confidered fingly by itfelf, 'tis alfo *dreadful and terrible* : Dominion and Majefty clothed with perfect and impartial *Juftice*, is worthy of the *Higheft Praifes*; but ftill to *Sinners* it appears rather *awful and venerable*, than the Object of Defire and Love : *Holinefs and Purity* are inexpreffibly beautiful and amiable Perfections; but of too bright a Glory, for *Sinners* to contemplate with Delight. 'Tis *Goodnefs* that *finifhes* the Idea of God; and reprefents him to us under that *lovely* Character of being the *Beft*, as well as the *Greateft*, Being in the Univerfe. *This* is That Attribute, which both *in itfelf* is infinitely amiable, and, as a ground-work interwoven with all the *Other* Perfections of the Divine Nature, makes every one of *Them* alfo to become Objects of our *Love* as well as of our Adoration. Immenfe and Eternal Goodnefs, Goodnefs All-powerful and All-wife, Goodnefs invefted with Supreme Dominion, and tempering the rigour of unrelenting Juftice; This is *indeed* a Defcription of a *Perfect* Being; a Character, *truly worthy* of God. This is That inexhauftible Fountain of Beneficence, from which the *whole Frame of Nature* derives its Being; by which *all Creatures* in the Univerfe, are continually fupported and preferved; from which *Man* derives his *prefent* Injoyments, and his *future* Hopes; which *Angels*, and Archangels, and the Spirits of juft men made perfect, adore with never-ceafing Praifes in the regions of eternal Happinefs; and of which *our Saviour himfelf*, who, having been in the Bofom of his Father, knew infinitely better than All Thefe, what was his True and Effential Nature : affirms by way of Eminence and High

Diftinction,

Diftinction, that *there is None Good, but One, that is God.* The Pfalmift defcribes this **S E R M.** Attribute elegantly in the words of the Text; *The Lord is Good to All, and his tender* **XIV.** *Mercies are over All his Works.*

IN the following Difcourfe upon which words, I fhall *1ft*, endeavour to fhow briefly *in general*, What *Goodnefs* is: *2dly*, I fhall prove that *God is* and *cannot but be Good*, according to this *general* Notion of Goodnefs: *3dly*, I fhall endeavour to fet forth diftinctly in *what particular* Inftances, the divine Goodnefs has more peculiarly difplayed itfelf: *4thly*, I fhall confider the *Difficulties* or *Objections* which may be raifed againft this important doctrine, which is the Foundation of true Religion, and the great Guard againft Superftition: And *Laftly* I fhall draw fome ufeful *Inferences* from the Whole.

IN the *1ft* place, 'tis neceffary to fhow briefly *in general*, What *Goodnefs* is. For unlefs we clearly and diftinctly underftand *what* Goodnefs *is*, 'tis evident we mean *nothing*, when we fay *God is Good*; and confequently cannot be certain whether we *honour* him, or *difhonour* him, in giving him an unknown Character. Nothing therefore can be more abfurd, than the doctrine which has fometimes been advanced; that *Goodnefs* in *God*, is not the fame thing as Goodnefs in *Men*; but fomething altogether tranfcendent, and which we underftand not. This I fay, is highly abfurd: Becaufe, if This were the cafe, it would plainly follow, that when we affirm God to be *Good*, we fhould only affirm *we know not what*; that is, in reality we fhould affirm *nothing at all*. There *is* indeed *This* difference; that Goodnefs in *Men*, even in the *Beft* of men, is *fhort and imperfect, frail* and *mutable, unfteady* and always *mixt* more or lefs with Evil; and even in *Angels* and *Archangels* themfelves, 'tis *finite* and *deficient*; whereas in *God* alone, it is *effential* and *perfect*. But ftill the *Thing itfelf* is every where the *fame*. Goodnefs is every where of the fame *Nature*, tho' not in the fame *proportion*; and in All Beings whatfoever, in whom it is found at all, it is the fame in *Kind*, tho' not in *Degree*. If Goodnefs in *God*, were (as Some have imagined,) we know not what; how could we be commanded to *imitate*, what we do not underftand? or how fhould any man know, whether he were likely to fare the *better* or the *worfe*, by means of That which he knows not what it is? What *Comfort* can any man draw from the confideration of the Divine *Goodnefs*, if he means thereby only he knows not what; any thing that Power, any thing that Dominion, any thing that Sovereignty can do, whether it be Beneficent or not? The True Notion therefore of the Goodnefs of *God* muft be learnt by confidering what Goodnefs is in *Men*; And by adding, to the Idea of a good *Man*, boundlefs *Perfection* in the *Degree* of thofe Qualifications which denominate him fuch, we arrive at the neareft Conception, that 'tis poffible for Us to frame, of the *Divine Goodnefs*. Thus our Saviour himfelf teaches us to argue; St *Matt.* vii. 11. *If ye then, being evil, know how to give good Gifts unto your children; how much more fhall your Father which is in Heaven, give good things to them that afk him.* Now *Goodnefs* in *Men* fignifies a *Benevolent Difpofition*; a Difpofition to do good to others, even more extenfively, and with greater Benignity, than is required by That Virtue which we call *Juftice*, or *Righteoufnefs*. According to That accurate Diftinction of the Apoftle, *Rom.* v. 7. *For a righteous* [or Juft] *man, fcarcely will one die; yet peradventure for a* Good *man, fome would even dare to die. Righteoufnefs*, or *Juftice*, is doing all that Good to Others, which *They* have any Claim of *Right* to demand; But *Goodnefs* is, further, doing them All That Good, which, whether *They* have any Right to expect or not, is in any wife *fit*, or *reafonable*, for Us to beftow. Thus therefore the *Goodnefs of* God, is That *Beneficent* Difpofition of the divine Nature, which moves him to diffufe upon All his Creatures thro' the Immenfe Univerfe, and thro' a Boundlefs Eternity, every good thing that is *proper* for them, every thing that tends to their *True* Happinefs, every good which either *They* are in their own Nature *capable* of re-

3 *ceiving,*

ceiving, or which for *Him*, in his All-wife Government of the Whole, is *fit and rea-sonable* to give.

AND from hence, by the way, 'tis evident demonstrably, that there *is* not, there *cannot be* any such thing, as *absolute and unconditionate Reprobation*. For, This being a matter wholly contradictory to all our Notions of Goodnefs; if absolute and irrefistible *Sovereignty* could fuffice (as fome Sects of men have imagined) to make fuch a thing become *Good*, it would follow that the word, *Goodnefs*, had no fignification at all; and confequently, that it was neither *in itfelf* of any importance, nor of any confequence to *Us*, whether the Almighty God was Good or no. Than which, nothing can be affirmed more *unworthy* of the Creator of all things; or be more defervedly reckoned among thofe *hard Speeches*, which if not *unrighteous*, yet at leaft rafh *inconfiderate* men, *have fpoken againft him.*

Jude 15.

2dly, HAVING thus therefore briefly explained in general *What* Goodnefs is, it will now be eafy in the 2d place to prove, that *God* actually *is and cannot but be Good*, according to this *general* Notion of Goodnefs. For, Goodnefs being nothing elfe but a fixt Difpofition, to do always what in the Whole is *Beft*, and (fo far as is confiftent with *Right* and *Juftice*) what is *moft beneficial* to All; 'tis evident that the Supreme Being, having all *Knowledge*, fo that his *Underftanding* can never *err* in *judging* what is Beft; and having *no Want* of any thing to complete his *own Happinefs*, fo that his *Will* can never be influenced by any *wrong Affection*, or have any poffible *Temptation* laid before it to act otherwife than according to what he knows Beft; 'tis from hence, I fay, very evident to Reafon, that the Supreme Caufe, being thus neceffarily Happy in the eternal injoyment of his own infinite Perfections, and altogether incapable of being tempted with Evil, could not poffibly have any other Motives to make any Creatures at all, but only that he might communicate to them his own Perfections, Goodnefs and Happinefs; according to *their different* Capacities, arifing from that *Variety of Natures*, which 'twas fit for *infinite Wifdom* to produce; and according to *their different* Improvements, *and Deferts*, arifing from that *Liberty*, which is effentially Neceffary to the Conftitution of *Intelligent and active Beings*. God therefore is *Neceffarily* and *Effentially Good*. And yet, even *This neceffity* arifing wholly from the unalterable Rectitude of his *Will*, (whereas his *natural* Attributes, fuch as Knowledge and Power, arife immediately from abfolute *Neceffity of Nature*;) there is therefore *This difference*, that, whilft for his *Power, Knowledge*, and the like, we can only *admire and adore* him, for his *Goodnefs* we return him moreover *Praife and Thanks*. For which reafon, the Scripture not only conftantly confirms, what natural Reafon teaches us, that God *is* Good; but reprefents it alfo as the Attribute wherein he chiefly *delights*; and defcribes it always in the tendereft and moft affectionate expreffions. *Like as a* Father *pitieth his children, fo the Lord pitieth them that fear him*, Pf. ciii. 13. *I am the Lord, which exercife loving-kindnefs, judgment and righteoufnefs in the Earth; for in thefe things I* delight, *fays the Lord*, Jer. ix. 24. and If. xlix. 15. *Can a woman forget her fucking-child, that fhe fhould not have compaffion on the Son of her womb? yea, they may forget, yet will I not forget thee.* In the fecond *commandment*, when God had threatned *judgments* to the *third and fourth* generation of them that *hate* him; To fhow how much *more* he delights in *rewarding* than in *punifhing*, he promifes *mercy* unto *Thoufands* of them that *love* him and keep his commandments. And 'tis not without a very *fignificant and expreffive emphafis*, that our Saviour fo remarkably affirms, St *Mar.* x. 18. *There is none Good but One, that is God.* But This *in general*.

3dly, I PROPOSED in the 3d place to fet forth diftinctly, in *what particular Inftances* the Divine Goodnefs has more peculiarly difplayed itfelf. And here, to go through all the works, of Creation, Providence, and Redemption, is a Subject which the Tongues of Men and Angels, fhall never be able to exhauft. For the Goodnefs of

God

God is *boundless* as his univerfal Works, and *endlefs* as the Ages of Eternity. *Who can* S E R M.
exprefs the noble acts of the Lord, or fhow forth all his Praife ? Pf. cvi. 2. By the *Good-* XIV.
nefs of God, was that incomprehenfible Variety of Creatures brought into *Being*, which
of themfelves would never have exifted : And a *further* Mark of the *Fountain* from
which they all proceed, is that Character given things upon their firft production, that
God beheld every thing which he had made, and, in their refpective kinds and degrees,
they were *each* of them *very Good*. By the fame *Goodnefs*, is fuitable Provifion made
for the *Prefervation* of all things, for their proper *Continuance* and *Well-being* : Pf. civ.
27. They *all wait upon Thee, that thou mayeft give them their meat in due feafon ; Thou* Pfal. cxlv. 15.
openeft thine hand, and fatisfieft the defire of every living Thing ; He maketh the grafs to cxlvii. 9.
*grow upon the mountains, and giveth to the beaft his food, and to the young ravens which
cry unto him.* And *Mat.* vi. 26. *The fowls of the Air*, faith our Saviour, *neither fow,
nor reap, nor gather into Barns ; yet your heavenly Father feedeth them. And the lillies
of the field toil not, neither do they fpin ; and yet I fay unto you, that even Solomon in all
his glory, was not arrayed like one of Them :* Like *one* of *Them*, whom *Nature* has a-
dorned with what *no Art* can exprefs, and clothed them with *inimitable* Beauty. In
Man ftill *more particularly*, has the *Goodnefs of* God appeared, in giving him fo excellent and noble a Being : *Thou madeft him a little lower than the Angels, and crownedft
him with glory and honour ; Thou madeft him to have Dominion over the works of thy
hands, and haft put all things in fubjection under his Feet*, Pf. viii. 5. He has indued
us with *Reafon, Underftanding*, and *Knowledge*, not only fufficient to preferve our Dominion over the *Creation* ; but fuch as moreover inables us to contemplate, to adore,
and to imitate, our great *Creator himfelf*. The Apoftle alleges This, as a particular inftance of the divine Goodnefs, *Jam.* i. 17, 5. *Every Good and every perfect Gift* (that
is, every *perfection* of our nature, and efpecially every *religious qualification*,) *is from
above, and cometh down from the Father of Lights,——who giveth to all men liberally
and upbraideth not.* In the *whole courfe* of our lives, his *Goodnefs* prevents numberlefs
Evils from falling upon us ; which, with all our Reafon and Underftanding, we could
by no means either prevent or avoid. And under *actual* Evils, which the Wifdom of
his unerring Providence thinks fit *not* to prevent, he relieves and comforts and fupports
men under them ; And frequently affords a Remedy, by *Temporal* Deliverances : Or if
he fees *That* not fit, yet (which is a much *greater* Inftance and Exercife of Goodnefs)
he always makes provifion for mens *eternal Happinefs*, if by their own Perverfenefs
they neglect not the Means which he has afforded them for That End. He has indued them with *Reafon* and *natural Confcience*, to diftinguifh between Good and Evil ;
and to forewarn them, as it were by an inward and perpetual Inftinct, of the certainty
of a future Judgment. He has *confirmed* this natural Confcience, with the additional
Help of an exprefs *Revelation* ; and has declared, that according to the feveral *Degrees*
of mens Knowledge in thefe matters, he will require of them a feverer, or lefs fevere
Account, in fuch manner as becomes the Judge of the whole Earth to do right. And
in the mean time, that Sinners may, if poffible, be brought to Repentance ; he, with
much long-fuffering and forbearance, defers their Punifhment ; and, if they *do* repent,
he forgives and pardons them, as a *Father* receives a returning Child ; nay, even as a
Shepherd rejoyces over a Sheep that had been loft. And This is That *Part* of *Goodnefs*, which is ftrictly and properly diftinguifhed by the Name of *Mercy*. God being
our Creator and Supreme Governour, and it being our neceffary and moft reafonable
Duty to obey at all times his Laws in every particular ; 'tis plain that every wilful Tranfgreffion juftly deferves Punifhment ; And *after* fuch Tranfgreffion, our beft Obedience
being nothing more than was our Duty *before* it, 'tis evident that in ftrict *Juftice* God
is not obliged, in confideration of what is *to come*, to forgive what is *paft :* In *ftrictnefs
of Juftice*, I fay, God was under *no* obligation to pardon Sinners upon their Repen-

S E R M. tance; but his Goodnefs *only* moved him to have compaffion upon them; And the *Ef-*
XIV. *fect* of That compaffion, was the Coming of Chrift. It has fometimes been apprehended otherwife, that the interpofition of Chrift was the *Caufe* of God's mercy and compaffion towards Sinners: But the *Scripture* always reprefents this matter the *other* way,
more to the Honour and Exaltation of the divine Goodnefs; that 'twas the *original*
Mercy and free Compaffion of God, which moved him to fend his Son to mediate on
our Behalf. Thus our Saviour himfelf expreffes it, *Joh.* iii. 16. *God fo loved the world,*
that he gave *his only-begotten Son:* He does not fay, *the only-begotten Son prevailed*
with God to love the world; but, the *Love and Compaffion* of God towards his Creatures,
prevailed with him to *fend* his *Son* into the world. *God,* of his own original eternal
effential Goodnefs, *fo* loved *the world, that,* in pity towards fallen Mankind he appointed This *method* of recovery, and gave *his only-begotten Son, that whofoever believeth in*
him, fhould not perifh, but have everlafting Life. Thus alfo St *Paul; God,* faith he,
(that is, *God the Father,) commendeth his* Love *towards us, in that while we were yet*
Sinners, Chrift died for us, Rom. v. 8. And St *John,* in his firft epiftle, ch. iv. 8, 9.
God, faith he, *is Love;* and *In This was manifefted the Love of God towards us, becaufe*
that God fent his only-begotten Son into the world, that we might live through him.

Thefe declarations of Scripture are fo exprefs, that they feem intended on *pur-*
pofe to prevent all poffibility of Miftake in this Matter. And thofe men (of whatfoever
Sect they be) who fpeak otherwife, fpeak not honourably enough of the divine Goodnefs, while they reprefent the Supreme Majefty of Heaven as an object of *Fear and*
Dread only, and not of *Love;* Invefting him, in the conceptions they frame of him,
with Dominion, and Power, and the Terrors of unrelenting Juftice, but not fufficiently
attending to his effential *Goodnefs;* which is the Attribute wherein he chiefly delights;
and which he always exercifes, *fo far* as is confiftent with Juftice and Wifdom and
good Government; and *of* which, the fending a Perfon of fuch Dignity as his only begotten Son, to reconcile Sinners to Himfelf confiftently with Juftice, by his exemplary
Humiliation, by his Life and Doctrine, by his Sufferings and Death, by his Exaltation
and Interceffion for us; of the *Goodnefs,* I fay, of *God the Supreme Father and Lord of*
all, This is an unparallelled and everlafting Inftance.

But 4*thly,* Against this *whole* Notion of the divine Goodnefs, there are *two* very
great *Objections,* which deferve diftinctly to be confidered; Namely, the *Evils* which
God *permits* to happen in the *prefent* Life, and the *Punifhments* which he *inflicts* in
that which is *to come.*

As to the *Evils* which happen in the *prefent* Life; the antient *Perfian* Philofophers
(and after Them the *Manichees* in later Ages) fancied, that there was an infinite *Evil*
Principle, independent *upon,* and oppofite *to* the infinite *Good* one. Againft Thefe,
Efaias declares, in his prophecy to *Cyrus* King of *Perfia,* If. xlv. 7. *I form the Light*
and create Darknefs, I make Peace, and create Evil; I the Lord do all thefe things.
The meaning is: There is no *Evil* happens in the world, but what for wife ends
is permitted by the Providence of the One infinitely *Good* God.

To inftance in particulars. *All* that we call *Evil* in the prefent Life, is either merely an *Evil of Imperfection,* fuch as the Want *of certain Faculties and Excellencies*
which other Creatures enjoy; Or *Natural Evil,* fuch as *Pain, Death,* and the like;
Or *Moral Evil,* fuch as are all kinds of *Debauchery, Sin and Vice.* The *Firft* of
Thefe, *viz.* mere *Imperfection,* is not properly an *Evil.* For every Power, Faculty,
or Perfection, which Any Creature enjoys, being the *Free* Gift of God, which he
was no more obliged to beftow, than he was to confer Being or Exiftence itfelf; 'tis
plain, the mere *Want* of any certain Faculty or Perfection in Any kind of Creatures,
which *Never* belonged to their Nature, is no more an *Evil* to *Them,* than their never
having been created, or brought into Being at all, could properly have been called an
               Evil.

Evil. The *Second* kind of Evil, which we commonly call *Natural Evil*, is either a SERM. neceſſary Conſequence of the Former; as *Death*, to a Creature on whoſe Nature Im- XIV. mortality was never conferred; And then 'tis no more properly an *Evil*, than the Former: Or elſe 'tis balanced in the whole, with as great or greater Good; as the *Afflictions and Sufferings of good men*; And *Then alſo* 'tis not properly an Evil: Or elſe, laſtly, 'tis a *Puniſhment*; And then 'tis a neceſſary conſequent of the *Third* and laſt ſort of Evil, *viz. Moral Evil*, which is *Debauchery, Sin, and Vice.* And this ariſes wholly from the Abuſe of that *Liberty*, which God gave to his Creatures for the moſt excellent Purpoſes; and which 'twas *reaſonable and fit and neceſſary* to give them for the Perfection and Order of the whole Creation: But they Themſelves, contrary to God's intention and command, have abuſed what was *neceſſary* for the Perfection of the *whole*, to the corruption and depravation of *Themſelves*; And thus all ſorts of *Evils* have entered into the world, without any diminution to the infinite *Goodneſs* of the Creator and Governour thereof.

As to the *Puniſhments* which God will inflict *in the Life to come:* Since all men acknowledge proportionable Puniſhments to be *neceſſary* in all *Governments whatſoever*; and ſince the Kingdom and Government of *God* over the whole Univerſe, continues in the *future* ſtate as well as in the *preſent*; 'tis plain we can have no juſt reaſon to preſume, that the Puniſhments of incorrigible Sinners will be leſs uſeful to the Ends and Reaſons of God's infinite Government *There*, than they are neceſſary in the Wiſdom of his Providence *here*. Nor can the Goodneſs of God be more obliged to preſerve wilful men from *perdition hereafter*, than he is bound to preſerve the careleſs from a *Precipice at preſent*. The exact *Nature and Manner* indeed of the future Puniſhment of the Wicked, any further than is in general neceſſary to deter us from Sin, is not diſtinctly revealed to us. But concerning it there are *two* things moſt clearly declared in Scripture, abundantly ſufficient to vindicate the Divine Goodneſs. *Firſt*, that the *Degrees* of Puniſhment in that final and eternal ſtate, ſhall be exactly proportionate to the Degree of mens Demerits; and even Damnation itſelf ſhall by the righteous Judge be inflicted in weight and meaſure. And *Secondly*, that the *Puniſhment itſelf*, abſolutely ſpeaking, ſhall at the day of judgment, in the nature and reaſon of the thing, appear ſo juſt and neceſſary, that *every mouth*, even of *Sinners* themſelves, *ſhall be ſtopped before God*; ſtopped, not by Force and Power, but by the clear evidence of Right and Reaſon. And God, when he *cometh with ten thouſand of his Saints to execute Judgment upon All*, ſhall convince *ungodly Sinners*, not only of their *ungodly deeds* which they have committed, but of their *hard Speeches* alſo which they have *ſpoken againſt him*, Jude 15. And when the Puniſhment of the wicked ſhall be *actually* inflicted upon them in the place of Torment, even *This* ſhall be, not only in the preſence of *God*, but in the preſence of the *Holy Angels* alſo, and in the preſence of *the Lamb*, Rev. xiv. 10. That is; it ſhall be ſuch as is, not only *appointed* by the *infinite Majeſty of God the righteous Judge of all*, but *approved* moreover by *Men* and *Angels*, and by *Him alſo himſelf, who loved us unto Death, even Chriſt our merciful and compaſſionate High-Prieſt.*

5*thly*, IT remains in the 5*th* and *laſt* place, that I draw ſome *practical Inferences* from this whole Doctrine, concerning the Divine Goodneſs.

And 1*ſt*, THE Goodneſs of God, is a Ground of perpetual *Praiſe and Thankfulneſs.* Pſ. ciii. 2. *Bleſs the Lord, O my Soul, and forget not all his Benefits. Who forgiveth all thy Sin, and healeth all thy infirmities. Who ſaveth thy Life from deſtruction, and crowneth thee with mercy and loving-kindneſs.*

2*dly*, IF God is infinitely *Good*; this makes him the moſt perfect Object of our *Love*, as well as of our *Fear*. And tho' Obedience that proceeds from *Fear*, will be accepted

to

S E R M. to Salvation; yet when it proceeds from *Love*, it is more eafy and pleafant, more free
XIV.   from the danger of Superftition, and from erroneous Circumftances of all kinds.

3*dly*, A juft Senfe of the *Goodnefs* of God, is apt to raife in generous minds a very
ftrong hatred and indignation againft Sin; when they confider that 'tis an offence, not
only of Indignity againft their Supreme Governour, but of *Ingratitude* alfo againft their
Benefactor; Whofe commands are all given them, not for *his own* Sake, but for *theirs*;
Not that their Obedience is of any Advantage to *Him*, but for *their own* Benefit only,
and everlafting Happinefs.

4*thly*, Though the *Goodnefs* of God be, like all his other Attributes, truly infinite;
yet let not Sinners *prefume* upon it to their own deftruction. For, infinite as it is,
it extends not to *Devils*; it extends not to *impenitent Sinners*, it extends not to the
deftruction of Juftice and Virtue and good Government: Even as infinite *Power*, extends
only to the *Objects of Power*, not to *Impoffibilities*. God *loves* his Creatures, beyond
the Love of the tendereft and moft compaffionate Father; but ftill always with this *one*
exception, that he loves Virtue, Righteoufnefs, and Goodnefs, ftill better than them.
And againft *no* fort of Sinners does the Scripture fpeak with greater *Indignation of Severity*, than againft thofe who prefumptuoufly make the *Goodnefs* of God an occafion of
finning, and turn even the *Grace* of God *itfelf* into Wantonnefs. *Deut.* xxix. 19. *If it
come to pafs, when a man heareth the words of this curfe, that he blefs himfelf in his heart,
faying, I* fhall *have peace, though I walk in the imagination of my heart: The Lord
will not* fpare *him, but the Anger of the Lord fhall fmoke againft that man, and all the
Curfes that are written in this book fhall lie upon him.* And 'tis recorded in the book
of *Kings* for an everlafting memorial, that when God pardoned *Manaffeh* upon his
true Repentance after *many* years wickednefs, and he reigned in *Jerufalem fifty and
five years*, his Son *Amon* prefuming upon the *Goodnefs* of God to imitate his Father's
wickednefs, was cut off in his Sin after only *two years* reign.

5*thly*, The *Goodnefs* of God, is an *example* for *Us* to imitate. Does *He* who has
all *Power* abfolutely in his own hands, *caufe his Sun to fhine on the Evil and on the
Good, and fend his rain on the juft and on the unjuft*, doing good to All, and extending his mercy over all his works? And fhall frail *mortals*, fhall vain and finful men,
tyrannize over each other? Shall *God* forgive *us* freely ten thoufand talents? and fhall
We not forgive *each other* our one hundred pence? efpecially when, in our *daily* Prayer,
our Lord has taught us to make This the exprefs condition of our own defiring Forgivenefs? And the *Reafon* of the thing, is elegantly expreffed by the *Son of Sirach*,
Ecclus. xxviii. 3, 4. *One man beareth hatred againft another, and doth he feek pardon
from the Lord? He fheweth no mercy to a man which is like himfelf, and doth he ask
forgivenefs of his own Sins?*

Laftly, The confideration of the *divine Goodnefs* is an incouragement to Repentance;
feeing he requires of us no *impoffible*, no *hard* condition; but only faith unto us, *Wafh
and be clean*, Amend and be forgiven. Yet at the fame time it fhows alfo to Sinners the
abfolute *Neceffity* of their Reformation; feeing, *without* fuch Reformation, even infinite
Goodnefs itfelf *will not* pardon them, tho' it waits with much long-fuffering for their
Repentance and Amendment.

S E R M O N

SERMON XV.

Of the PATIENCE of GOD.

ECCLES. VIII. 11.

Becauſe ſentence againſt an evil work is not executed ſpeedily, there-fore the Heart of the Sons of Men, is fully ſet in them to do Evil.

CONCERNING the *Goodneſs* of God *in general,* I have diſcourſed already upon another occaſion: Concerning that *particular Branch* of Goodneſs, which conſiſts in deferring the Puniſhment of evil-doers, and is properly diſtinguiſhed by the Name of *Patience* or *Long-ſuffering,* I intend at this time to treat, from the words now read unto you. In which, it is obvious to obſerve; *iſt,* the *Character,* or *Deſcription* given, of the divine *Patience and Long-ſuffering;* It conſiſts in *This,* that *Sentence againſt an evil work is not executed ſpeedily.* *2dly,* The *ill Uſe* that wicked and profane Men are too apt to make of the divine forbearance; Their *Heart is* thereby *fully ſet in them to do evil.* *3dly,* The *Folly and Abſurdity* of thus abuſing the Patience of God; foraſmuch as *Sentence* againſt every evil work, tho' it be not *ſpeedily executed,* yet is *certainly paſſed;* and, if the Sinner amends not, will alſo *certainly be executed;* and That, the more *ſeverely* too, becauſe *not ſpeedily.*

I. HERE is a *Character* or *Deſcription* given, of the divine *Patience and Long-ſuffer-ing;* It conſiſts in *This,* that *Sentence againſt an evil work is not executed ſpeedily.* The *Deſign* and *Reaſon* of which Delay, is declared to us by St *Paul, Rom.* ii. 4. *The Riches of the Goodneſs and Forbearance and Long-ſuffering* of God, which *leadeth thee to Re-pentance;* And St *Peter,* 2 *Pet.* iii. 9, 15. *The Lord is not ſlack concerning his Promiſe, as ſome men count ſlackneſs, but is long-ſuffering to us-ward, not willing that Any ſhould periſh, but that All ſhould come to Repentance;* —*wherefore, beloved,* — *account that the long-ſuffering of our Lord, is Salvation.* The *Reaſon* of God's delaying Puniſhment, is to bring Men to *Repentance;* and to vindicate his Juſtice and *Goodneſs* in their de-ſtruction, if, after all his forbearance, they continue finally impenitent: *Rom.* ix. 22. *He endureth with much long-ſuffering the veſſels of wrath fitted to deſtruction;* fitted to deſtruction, by their own wickedneſs; and making that deſtruction *neceſſary* and inevi-table, by their deſpiſing the Patience and Long-ſuffering of God. The incomprehenſi-ble Majeſty of God, ſtands in need of none of our Services, nor receives any Advantage from our Amendment and Return to him: yet he bears with us much more, than frail and paſſionate Men are willing to bear with men like themſelves, tho' their well-being entirely depends on the Services which they do each other. There is *no obligation* upon God in ſtrictneſs to ſpare Sinners at all; but, if he pleaſed, he might *with juſtice* cut them off immediately; and could *with eaſe* even out of the Stones of the Street raiſe up children unto *Abraham;* that is, create new and better creatures, who ſhould obey him in bringing forth the Fruits of Righteouſneſs: Yet, in great compaſſion, he chuſes ra-ther to invite *Sinners* to Repentance; and with much unwillingneſs inflicts at laſt That

S E R M. Punifhment, which their incorrigiblenefs makes *neceffary* even for *Goodnefs* itfelf, in the
XV. adminiftration of the Supreme Government of the Univerfe, to inflict. *How fhall I*
give thee up, Ephraim? how fhall I deliver thee, O Ifrael? how fhall I make thee as
Admah? how fhall I fet thee as Zeboim? mine heart is turned within me, my repentings
are kindled together, Hof. xi. 8. And Jer. ix. 7. *I will melt them and try them; for*
how *fhall I do for the daughter of my people?* Thefe are very cloquent and affectionate
defcriptions of what the Pfalmift declares in a direct and lefs figurative manner,
Pf. ciii. 8. *The Lord is full of Compaffion, and Mercy, Long-fuffering, and of great*
Goodnefs;——He hath not dealt with us after our Sins, nor rewarded us according to
our Wickedneffes;——Like as a Father pitieth his own children, even fo is the Lord
merciful unto them that fear him; For he knoweth whereof we are made, he remembreth
that we are but duft. Pf. lxxxi. 12. *My people would not hear my voice, and Ifrael*
would not obey me; So I gave them up unto their own hearts lufts, and let them fol-
low their own imaginations. O, that my people would *have hearkned unto me; for*
if Ifrael had walked in my ways, I fhould foon have put down their Enemies, &c.
The particular *Inftances* which the Scripture gives us of this Patience and Forbearance of God towards Sinners, are very remarkable; and fuch as may give us a *truer*
Notion of this divine Attribute, than can be done by any verbal Defcription. When
God had threatned to *Adam,* that in the day he eat of the forbidden Fruit, he
fhould furely die; he did indeed accordingly, in that very day, become inevitably
fubject to Mortality; being from thenceforward excluded the Benefit of the Tree of
Life. But the actual execution of That fentence of Death was deferred for many
years, that by Repentance and better obedience for the future, he might efcape
the much feverer Punifhment of Death eternal. When the whole World had corrupted
themfelves in the days of *Noah,* and God refolved to deftroy them all with a Flood;
yet St *Peter* obferves, 1 Pet. iii. 20. that *the Long-fuffering of God* waited, *while the*
Ark was preparing; in all which time, *Noah* was unto them a *Preacher of Righteouf-*
nefs, to have deterred them (if poffible) from their difobedience. After this, in the cafe
of *Sodom and Gomorrha,* God fent *Lot* into thofe Cities, to be unto them a Teacher
and an Example of Righteoufnefs: Whofe righteous Soul when they had vexed day
by day with their Impieties, and the Cry of their Wickednefs was become exceeding
great before God; yet, to fet forth the Greatnefs of the Divine Patience, God reprefents himfelf to *Abraham,* as refolving to refpite the Deftruction of thofe Cities, if he
could find even but *ten* righteous Perfons therein. The meaning of which, is not that
God will always fpare a wicked Nation, whenever there fhall be found therein a *certain*
determinate Number of good men; but only to fhow in general God's unwillingnefs to
deftroy, where-ever there appears Any *Hope,* or Foundation of Amendment. And becaufe thefe Cities, *when* deftroyed, were fet forth to *Us* as *an example, fuffering the*
Vengeance of eternal Fire, that is, of That Fire which finally confumed them, fo that
they never were built again: therefore 'tis reafonable to believe, that his Willingnefs to
have faved them from That Deftruction, was intended as a *Type,* to fhow us how unwilling he is, that Sinners fhould finally fall under That condemnation, of which the
Fire of *Sodom* is fet forth as a Refemblance. In following Ages: When the feven Nations of *Canaan* were to be difpoffeffed before the children of *Ifrael,* in order to bring
Them into the promifed Land which he had fworn to their Fore-fathers; *one* reafon
why they entred not in fooner, was *not only* becaufe the *Jews* were not worthy to be fo
bleffed, but becaufe the *Canaanites* had not yet made it neceffary for themfelves to be fo
curfed. The iniquity of the Amorites, fays the Scripture, *was not yet full;* and the Patience of God towards them, was not yet worn out. He who even out of the *Stones,*
if need were, could have raifed up *children* unto *Abraham;* could much more, if he
had fo pleafed, have provided a *Country* for the children of *Abraham* to dwell in,

3　　　　　　　　　　　　　　　　　　　　　　　　　　　　　　　　　　　　without

without difpoffeffing for them any other people. But *herein* was difplayed the Wifdom of the Great Governour of all things, that when the fulnefs of the iniquity of the *Amorites*, made it neceffary for *them* to be difpoffeffed ; *then*, and not till *then*, did he bring the *Ifraelites* to the borders of the promifed Land. At the fame time did the Divine Patience bear with the provocations of the *Jews in the Wildernefs, forty years :* Pf. lxxviii. 41, 38, 39. cvi. 23, 42, 43, 44. *Many a time did they provoke him in the wildernefs, and grieved him in the defert : But he was fo merciful, that he forgave their mifdeeds, and deftroyed them not : Yea, many a time turned he his wrath away, and would not fuffer his whole Difpleafure to arife : He faid, he would have deftroyed them, had not Mofes his chofen ftood before him in the gap. Many a time were they brought down in their wickednefs ; neverthelefs, when he faw their Adverfity, he heard their Complaint ; He thought upon his Covenant ; and pitied them.* In following Ages ; That fevere, and as they had *Then* reafon to apprehend, *unalterable* fentence againft *Nineveh* ; *yet forty days and Nineveh fhall be deftroyed* ; was on the contrary intended in the wife Counfels of Providence, to be a ftanding Example of God's Patience towards Sinners. For the *Ninevites*, in that time of refpite, turned from their evil deeds ; and *the Lord alfo repented him of the Evil which he faid he would do unto them, and he did it not,* Jonah iii. 10. Laftly, in the Cafe of *Jerufalem*, that perpetual Type of the whole Church ; how *affectionately* and with what a *moving* eloquence does our Saviour exprefs the Patience, and the Long-fuffering of God. *O Jerufalem, Jerufalem, thou that killeft the Prophets, and ftoneft them which are fent unto thee ; how often would I have gathered thy children together, even as a hen gathereth her chickens under her wings, and ye would not !* Matt. xxiii. 37. And with what a mixture of tender compaffion and forbearance, is that Threatning denounced againft *all* wicked men in general, Rev. ii. 21. *I gave her fpace to repent of her fornication, and fhe repented not : Behold, I will caft her into a bed, and them that commit adultery with her into great Tribulation, except they repent of their Deeds.* This therefore is the Character of the Divine Patience : Generally fpeaking, *Sentence againft an evil work is not executed fpeedily.*

II. THE Text reprefents unto us, the *ill Ufe* that wicked men are too apt to make of this divine forbearance : therefore *the Heart of the Sons of Men is fully fet in them to do evil.* Therefore ; That is, not that there is any *reafon*, not that there is any juft *ground*, not that any good *Argument* to encourage Men in their Difobedience, can be drawn from the Long-fuffering of God : But that in *Fact*, and by fad *experience*, it appears too frequently *True* ; that wicked men are apt to deceive themfelves, with fo *abfurd*, fo *groundlefs*, fo *unreafonable* a Proceeding. *Becaufe* God punifhes them not *immediately*, but gives them fpace of repentance ; therefore they abfurdly *prefume*, or carelefsly go on *as if they prefumed*, that he would not punifh them at all. *Where is the Promife,* (where is the *Threatning) of his Coming ? For fince the Fathers fell afleep, all things continue as they were, from the beginning of the Creation.* Upon this ground ; *Come ye, fay they* (as the prophet *Ifaiah* elegantly reprefents them,) *I will fetch wine, and we will fill ourfelves with ftrong drink ; and to morrow fhall be as This day, and much more abundant.* And *Wifd.* ii. 6. *Come on therefore, let us enjoy the good things that are prefent ; and let us fpeedily ufe the Creatures like as in youth.* Thus wicked and debauched perfons, in the days of riot, are apt to flatter themfelves ; *He hath faid in his Heart, tufh, I fhall never be caft down, there fhall no harm happen unto me,* Pf. x. 6. or, as it is in the new tranflation, *I fhall never be in adverfity.* That *Thus* it was in *antient* days, the Prophet *Ifaiah* complains, ch. xxvi. 10. *Let favour be fhowed to the Wicked, yet will he not learn righteoufnefs ; in the land of uprightnefs will he deal unjuftly, and will not behold the Majefty of the Lord.* And that *Thus* it will *continue* to be, among incorrigible Men, to the *end* of the World ; our Saviour plainly declares, Matt. xxiv. 38. *As in the days that were before the Flood, they were eating and drink-*

2 Pet. iii. 4.

If. lvi. 12.

ing,

SERM.
XV.

ing, marrying and giving in marriage, untill the day that Noah entred into the ark, And knew not untill the Flood came, and took them all away; So shall also the Coming of the Son of Man be. This is the ill *Use,* that wicked men are too apt to make of the divine forbearance. Instead of being led thereby to repentance, (which is what God gives them space for;) they on the contrary thence promise themselves final impunity, and their *heart is more fully set in them to do evil.* How absurd This their Conclusion is; and how foolish their Practice, in thus abusing the Patience and Long-suffering of God; is the

IIId HEAD I proposed to speak to : And it will abundantly appear, from the following Considerations.

1st, SIN is not therefore the less *evil in itself,* because *not* always *punished immediately.* All Wickedness, is an endeavouring to confound the *natural order and reason of Things :* 'tis a dishonouring of *ourselves,* as we are created rational and intelligent Beings; 'tis injurious to other *Men,* as tending always to subvert that Peace and Happiness of the World, which the Wisdom of Providence has appointed to consist, in the Practice of universal Righteousness, of Justice, Truth, and Charity among Men; 'Tis, finally, offering the highest Affront to *God* the *Supreme Governour of All;* who is of *purer eyes than to behold iniquity;* and whose *principal* Concern it is, not to suffer that *Great* Distinction of Things, the Difference of Good and Evil, to be for ever neglected and despised. *Flee* therefore *from Sin,* says the wise Author of the Book of *Ecclesiasticus,* ch. xxi. 2. *Flee from Sin, as from the Face of a Serpent; The Teeth thereof are as the Teeth of a Lion, slaying the Souls of Men; All iniquity is as a two-edged Sword, the Wounds whereof cannot be healed :* Cannot; that is, cannot without *much greater Difficulty* be healed, than careless Sinners are willing to perswade themselves.

2. As *Sin* is not in *itself* the less *evil,* because *not* always *punished immediately;* so neither ought it to be imagined, that *God* is therefore the less *provoked,* because there appear not in *Him,* as in vain Mortals, any *sudden Transports* of hasty Passion. God, is pure and unmixt Reason; and, as all his *other* Actions are without any emotion in himself, so he *punishes* also, not that he has any *pleasure* in so doing, but that the thing is in itself right and necessary to be done. When therefore he has born with Sinners, as long as Wisdom and Goodness thinks reasonable to bear with them; his Patience, after That, *will* have an End : *Luke* xiii. 7. *Then said he to the dresser of his Vineyard, behold these three years I come seeking fruit on this fig-tree, and find none; cut it down, why cumbereth it the ground?* The *Spirit* of God, *will not always strive with man;* neither will he suffer himself to be *mocked,* and his Laws finally to be *trampled upon.* The *Holy Spirit of Discipline will flee* from *Deceit,* (Wisd. i. 5.) *and will remove from Thoughts that are without understanding, and will not abide when unrighteousness cometh in.* Long did the Patience of God bear with the *Jews* in the Wilderness, in the day of their provocation; but at length, *he sware unto them in his wrath, that they should not enter into his rest,* Ps. xcv. 11. In *Ps.* cvi. 26. 'tis thus expressed; *he lifted up his hand against them, to overthrow them in the Wilderness :* He *lifted up his hand,* that is, *he sware unto them;* so That phrase signifies in the *Hebrew;* and so it ought therefore to have been translated in *one* Psalm, as well as in the *other;* and cannot otherwise be rightly understood. Again, When God had threatned by *Jonah,* that *yet forty* days *and Nineveh shall be destroyed;* and after That, upon their repentance, *God* also *repented of the evil he had said he would do unto them, and he did it not :* yet *forty* years after, when they relapsed again, *Nineveh was* destroyed: and the prophecy, which *Jonah* murmured to see disappointed, as *he* thought; was in its time, according to the exactness of the Prophetick style, punctually accomplished : as is observed in the last chapter of the book of *Tobit,* ver. 8 and 15. Lastly, *Jerusalem itself,* over which our Saviour had expressed such tender and affectionate compassion, yet had at length, for its impeni-

tency,

tency, that *final* Sentence pronounced againſt it, *Matt.* xxiii. 38. *Behold, your Houſe is left unto you deſolate*; and ch. xxiv. 2. *There ſhall not be left one ſtone upon another, that ſhall not be thrown down.* The Application of theſe examples to every one of *Us*, is made by St *Paul* in that earneſt Admonition, *Rom.* ii. 4. *Deſpiſeſt thou the riches of his goodneſs and forbearance and long-ſuffering, not knowing that the goodneſs of God leadeth thee to Repentance? But after thy hardneſs and impenitent heart, treaſureſt up to thyſelf wrath againſt the day of wrath, and revelation of the righteous judgment of God?* The *natural* and *proper* effect of the divine forbearance, is to lead Sinners to Repentance: And if it has not that effect, but they on the contrary abuſe his Patience, and deſpiſe his admonitions, adding to their Sin perverſe ingratitude, and moſt diſingenuous Obſtinacy to their Rebellion; the Scripture aſſures us that the Time *will* come, when *they* ſhall cry, and ſhall not be heard; but He *alſo ſhall laugh at their calamity, and mock when their Fear cometh*; *when their Fear cometh as deſolation, and their deſtruction as a whirlwind.* Upon which Account, exellent is the Advice of the Son of *Sirach*, Eccluſ. v. 4. *Say not, I have ſinned, and what harm has happened to me? for* though *the Lord is long-ſuffering, he will in no wiſe let thee go*:——*Say not, his mercy is great, he will be pacified for the multitude of my Sins*; *For mercy and* Wrath *come from him, and his indignation reſteth upon Sinners.*

3*dly*, As it does not follow that *God* is *leſs* Angry with Sinners, becauſe he *defers* puniſhing them; ſo neither can it be inferred, that the Puniſhment of Sin is at all the *leſs Certain and Unavoidable*, for not being inflicted *immediately.* Among Men, every *delay* is a poſſibility of *Eſcaping*; becauſe *Time and Chance happeneth to them all*: And whatever is at *a diſtance*, is for that very reaſon proportionably *uncertain* whether it ſhall ever come to paſs at all. But with *God*, Time makes no difference in the Certainty of Events; neither can any intervening Accidents ever diſappoint *His* purpoſe. *Though a Sinner do evil an hundred times, and his days be prolonged*; *yet ſurely* (ſays the Wiſeman) *I know that it ſhall be well with them that fear God*; *But it ſhall* not *be well with the Wicked*, Eccleſ. viii. 12. And St *Peter* elegantly confutes this fooliſh Hope of Sinners, 2 Ep. iii. 4. *There ſhall come Scoffers, walking after their own luſts, and ſaying, Where is the Promiſe of his Coming? for ſince the Fathers fell aſleep, all things continue as they were, from the beginning of the Creation*:——*But, beloved, be not ignorant of this one thing, that one day is with the Lord as a thouſand Years, and a thouſand years as One day.* (Not that the one is with God *literally* no longer a Duration than the other, as the Schoolmen have fooliſhly taught, who love to make abſurdities even out of the plaineſt things; But the meaning is, that What is at a thouſand Years diſtance, is with God as *Certain*, as if it was to be effected the very next moment.) *The Lord is not ſlack concerning his Promiſe, as ſome men count ſlackneſs*; *but is long-ſuffering to us-ward, not willing that Any ſhould periſh, but that All ſhould come to Repentance. But the day of the* Lord *will come, as a Thief in the Night.*

4*thly*, As the Puniſhment of Sin is not the *leſs* Certain for being delayed, ſo neither will it be the *leſs* Severe. *Juſtice* (as all the *other* Attributes alſo are) is in the Divine Nature *Neceſſary.* That is: Not that Supreme Power has not a *natural Right* to pardon freely whom he pleaſes, (as ſome have vainly imagined;) but that, *morally* ſpeaking, it is as *Neceſſary* in the Government of the Univerſe, that infinite *Wiſdom* ſhould finally *puniſh* the *incorrigible*; as that infinite *Patience* ſhould *bear with* ſuch as are *capable of Amendment*, and infinite *Mercy* ſhould *pardon* ſuch as do *actually amend.* The Puniſhment of the *Fallen Angels*, the bringing in of the general *Flood*, and the *Overthrow of Sodom and Gomorrah*, are *Examples* of this kind, written on purpoſe for our Admonition. *Jude* 6. *The Angels which kept not their firſt eſtate, he has reſerved in chains under darkneſs, unto the judgment of the great day.* And the Application is expreſsly made by St *Peter*, 2 Ep. ii. 4,——9. *If God ſpared not the Angels that ſinned,*

SERM. *but caſt them down to hell;*——*And ſpared not the Old world,*——*but brought in the*
XV. *Flood upon the world of the ungodly* ; *And turned the Cities of Sodom and Gomorrah into*
aſhes ; *making them an example unto thoſe that after ſhould live ungodly* : *If* God did
theſe things of old ; the Inference is, *The Lord* ſtill *knoweth how*——*to reſerve the un-*
juſt unto the day of judgment to be puniſhed. And of *all* unjuſt perſons, *none* more exemplarily than thoſe, who *therefore* preſume to abuſe the Patience of God, becauſe *Sen-*
tence againſt an Evil work is not executed ſpeedily. Deut. xxix. 19. *If, when a man*
heareth the words of this Curſe, he bleſs himſelf in his heart, ſaying, I ſhall have peace,
though I walk in the imagination of my heart ; *The Lord will not ſpare him, but the*
anger of the Lord ſhall ſmoke againſt that man, and all the Curſes that are written in
this book ſhall lie upon him. *Jeruſalem,* and the Nation of the *Jews,* are at this day a
ſtanding Inſtance of this great Truth : Whom, after long forbearance and repeated admonitions, God at laſt overthrew with ſuch a total Deſtruction, as never befel any *other*
Nation under Heaven.   Beſides : From the Sufferings even of *good* men, the *profane*
and impenitent may well collect, that the divine Patience will not permit them to go for
1 Pet. iv. 17. ever unpuniſhed.   *Judgment,* ſays the Apoſtle, *muſt begin at the houſe of God* ; *and if*
it firſt begin at us, what ſhall the end be of them that obey not the goſpel of God.   And
if the righteous *ſcarcely be ſaved, where ſhall the Ungodly and the Sinner appear ?* The
Judgments of God in this *preſent* Life, which fall upon *mixt multitudes* of *good and bad,*
are frequently very terrible : *Who* then ſhall bear the vengeance of his *final* Wrath, when
he ſhall have ſeparated entirely the Goats from the Sheep, into the *proper place of*
Torment ? Tho' even *There* alſo, exact *Juſtice* ſhall reign ; and *Damnation itſelf* ſhall
be inflicted, with perfect accuracy of *Weight and Meaſure.*

5thly and *laſtly* ; As the Puniſhment of Sin neither *is* the leſs *certain,* nor *will be*
the leſs *ſevere,* for being uſually *delayed* ; ſo neither can a Sinner from thence at any
time depend, that it ſhall not overtake him the very next moment.   For *whenever* it
comes upon an impenitent Debauchee, it ſurprizes him *as a Thief in the Night* ; and
the *Execution* of *Sentence againſt an evil work,* how *long* ſoever delayed, yet *when* it
comes, ſeems as ſpeedy as if *no Space* had intervened.   *As the Fiſhes that are taken in*
an evil Net, and as the birds that are caught in the ſnare ; *ſo are the ſons of men ſnared*
in an evil time, when it falleth ſuddenly on them.   Vain therefore and fooliſh, beyond
all other Inſtances of Folly, is the behaviour of *thoſe* impenitent Sinners, whoſe heart is
therefore ſet in them to do evil, becauſe *their Lord delayeth his coming.* Of which Divine Forbearance if they make not That Uſe for which it was deſigned, ſo as to be led
thereby to Repentance ; their Lord will *come in a day when they think not of it, and at*
an hour which they are not aware of, and will cut them in ſunder, and appoint them
their portion with Unbelievers ; *there ſhall be weeping and gnaſhing of Teeth.* Thus the
Juſtice and *Mercy,* the *Severity* and the *Patience* of God, are perfectly conſiſtent with
each other ; and together with *all the other* Attributes of the Divine Nature, unite uniformly in one and the ſame point ; which is, the promoting everlaſting Righteouſneſs
and true Virtue through the whole Creation.   Which matter whoſoever ſeriouſly and
wiſely conſiders ; will neither ſuperſtitiouſly dread the Power, nor deſpair becauſe of the
Juſtice, nor preſume upon the Patience and Mercy of God ; but will ſerve him with
Fear, and adore him with Love, and be led to Repentance by Hope, and improve daily
more and more in the Practice of all Chriſtian Virtues and Graces, till the time comes
that he ſhall be made perfectly like unto God, becauſe he ſhall ſee him as he is.

SERMON

S E R M O N XVI.

Of the JUSTICE of GOD.

JOB XXXIV. 10, 11, 12.

Therefore hearken unto Me, ye men of Understanding : Far be it from God, that He should do wickedness ; and from the Almighty, that He should commit iniquity : For the work of a Man shall he render unto him, and cause every man to find according to his Ways : Yea, surely God will not do wickedly, neither will the Almighty pervert Judgment.

THESE words are a very lively and emphatical Description of the *Justice and* S E R M. *Righteousness* of the Supreme Governour of all things; *introduced* with an   XVI. affectionate Appeal to the common Reason of Mankind, for the *Truth* of the Assertion ; and *closed*, with an eloquent repetition of the *Assurance* of its Certainty. The *Assertion* of the Justice of God is in *these* words : *Far be it from God, that He should do wickedness ; and from the Almighty, that He should commit iniquity.* The *Description, wherein* this Justice consists, is in the words which follow : *The Work of a Man shall he render unto him, and cause every man to find according to his Ways.* The Whole is *introduced* with an Appeal to the *common Sense and Reason of Mankind,* for the Truth of what is here affirmed : Hearken unto Me, ye men of understanding ; *Far be it from God, that He should do wickedness.* And the Proposition is *closed,* with an elegant repetition of the same Assurance : Yea, surely *God will not do wickedly, neither will the Almighty pervert judgment.* There are and will be *difficulties* in the administration of Providence ; But these *difficulties* affect only such as are *careless* in matters of Religion ; and they can never make *reasonable and considerate persons,* men *of attention and understanding,* to doubt concerning the *Righteousness* of the Divine Government: *Hearken unto Me, ye men of* Understanding ; *Far be it from God, that He should do Wickedness.* A righteous and just Man may be depended upon that he will not do an unjust thing : Much *more* therefore, far be it from the Almighty, far be it from the Supreme *Lord* and *Governour* of *all* things, that *He* should commit iniquity. Many things *mysterious,* many things *incomprehensible,* there needs must be in the nature of the Supreme Being : But *Injustice or Iniquity, Hard or Unrighteous Dealing* with any of his Creatures ; This, above all things, *far be it from* him ; This, *whatever* we do, *far* ought we to keep it from all our Notions and Conceptions of him. *Objections* will be started, and *Difficulties* (in particular cases) cannot but arise : But whether we can answer them or no, we are *sure* they must be false ; because no evidence can be *so strong,* in proof of any *particular* doctrine inconsistent with this Notion, *as* are the Arguments which prove in *general* the truth of the divine Justice. However therefore our short understanding may perhaps fail in reconciling things, yet the *Foundation* must be stood to as being *demonstrably* true, and what can *never* be moved ; yea, surely *God will not do wickedly, neither will the Almighty pervert judgment.*

My

4

SERM.
XVI.

MY Defign in the following Difcourfe upon thefe words is to *prove* briefly, that God *is* and *cannot but be* Juft; to *explain wherein* the Nature of that Juftice confifts; to *remove* the *Objections* arifing from *particular* cafes againft this *general* Truth; and finally, to *apply* what fhall be faid, by fome *ufeful Inferences* in Practice. And

I*ft*, THAT the Supreme Lord and Governour of all things, *is* and *cannot but be* Juft *in all his Actions*, may be made appear in the following manner. There being neceffarily in Nature a *Difference* of Things, which is what we call *Natural* Good and Evil; and a Variety in the Difpofitions and Qualifications of Perfons, which is what we call *Moral* Good and Evil; from the due or undue adjuftment of thefe *Natural Qualities* of *Things* to the *moral Qualifications* of *Perfons*, arife unavoidably the Notions of *Right* and *Wrong*. Now the *Will* of every intelligent Agent being always directed by fome *Motive*; 'tis plain the *natural Motive of Action*, where nothing irregular interpofes, can be no other than This *Right, or Reafon of Things*. Whenever therefore This *Right and Reafon* are not made the *Rule of Action*; it can only be, either becaufe the Agent is *ignorant* of what is Right, or wants Ability to purfue it, or elfe is *knowingly and willingly diverted from it* by the *Hope of fome Good*, or *Fear of fome Evil*. But now None of thefe caufes of Injuftice, can poffibly have any place in God: His Actions therefore muft always neceffarily be directed by *Right and Reafon and Juftice only*. For, having *all Knowledge*, 'tis impoffible he can be *deceived* in judging what is Right: having no *Want* of any thing, his *Will* cannot poffibly be *influenced* by any *wrong Affection*; and having no *Dependence*, his *Power* can never be limited by any *fuperiour Strength*. 'Tis very evident therefore, that He who *knows* thus *perfectly* the *Rule of Equity*, and neceffarily *judges of things as they really Are*; who has *complete Power* to execute Juftice according to that Knowledge, and *no poffible temptation* to deviate in the leaft therefrom; who can neither be *impofed upon* by any *Deceit*, nor *moved* by any *Biafs*, nor *awed* by any *Power*; 'tis very evident (I fay) that fuch a Being will always do what is *Right*; without iniquity, and without partiality; without prejudice, and without refpect of Perfons.

THERE is a fhorter way, which has frequently been made ufe of, to prove that all the Actions of *God* muft *needs* be *Juft*; by alledging, that whatever *He* does is *therefore* Juft, becaufe *He* does it. Which Argument is not *proving*, but *fuppofing*, the thing in Queftion: For, the *Reafon why* God's doing a thing proves it to be Juft, is only upon This foundation, that, knowing him to be a perfectly Juft Being, we are fure, if the thing had not been in itfelf Juft, he *would not* have done it. And in *This* fenfe indeed the Argument is very good and reafonable. But thofe who ufe it have generally turned it to a very different and very falfe Meaning: As if, becaufe whatever *God* does is certainly *Juft*; therefore, whatever *Unjuft and Unreafonable* things they in their Syftems of Divinity afcribe to him, were made *juft and reafonable* by their fuppofing *God* to be the Author of them: Or, becaufe the *Effence* of God is *incomprehenfible*, and all his *Attributes* infinitely *tranfcending* the Perfections of any finite Beings; that therefore *Juftice* in *Him*, was not the fame Thing, nor to be judged of by the fame Notions, as Juftice among *Men*: Or that, God being *All-powerful*, and having no Superiour to render an account to of what he does; therefore *whatever* is afcribed to *Him*, though *in itfelf* it may feem *unjuft*, and *would be* Unjuft among Men, yet by *Supreme Power* is made *Juft and Right*. And upon *This* kind of Reafoning is built the Doctrine of *abfolute Reprobation*, and fome other the like Opinions. But now, in reality, *What* is this elfe, but fpeaking deceitfully for God, and deftroying the Truth of his divine Attributes, under the appearance of defending them? For if every thing that *Power* can do, is Juft; *What* then is *Juftice*, but *mere* Power only, and not any thing *really* in the *Nature* of Things? And fo, the worft and moft cruel Being in the World, with fufficient *Power* annext, would in thefe men's Senfe, be as *Juft*, as Supreme

preme

preme Goodnefs itfelf. The alleging in this manner the *Power of God*, to the deftroy-ing our moral Notion of *Juftice*, is like alleging the fame Power, in the cafe of Tranfubftantiation, to the deftroying the natural Truth of *Things*. The Effect of *Both* is the confounding the whole Nature of Truth and Falfhood, of Right and Wrong; and making every thing to be unintelligible and without Meaning. One *fenfe* indeed there is, in which *Supreme Power may* be faid to be the Foundation of *Juftice* : And That is, becaufe *fuch Power* fets the Perfon, who poffeffes it, above all poffibility of being *tempted*, or *compelled* by any *Fraud*, or by any *Force*, to do an unjuft thing. And in *This* fenfe, the Argument feems to be ufed by *Elihu* in the Text; *Job* xxxiv. 10. *Far be it from* God, (from Him who is Supreme over All,) *that* He *fhould do* Wickednefs; *and from the* Almighty, (from Him who has *Power* over All,) *that* He *fhould commit iniquity.* And by the Author of the Book of *Wifdom*, very elegantly; ch. xii. ver. 12, 15, 16, 18. *Who fhall fay, what haft* Thou *done?*——*or Who fhall accufe Thee for the Nations that perifh, whom thou haft made ? or Who fhall come to ftand againft thee, to be revenged for the unrighteous men ? For, feeing thou art righteous thyfelf, thou ordereft all things righteoufly; thinking it not agreeable with thy* Power, *to condemn him that hath not deferved to be punifhed : For thy* Power *is the beginning of Righteoufnefs; and, becaufe thou art Lord of All, it maketh thee to be gracious unto all.* For *Thou, maftering thy* Power, *judgeft with equity, and ordereft us with great favour; for Thou mayeft ufe Power when thou wilt.* In *This* fenfe, I fay, *Power may* be affirmed indeed to be the foundation of *Juftice*; as fetting the Perfon who is poffeffed of it, far above all temptation of doing wrong. But in any *other* fenfe; to make *Power*, the Meafure of *Juftice*; and to imagine that Juftice in *God*, is not the fame thing as Juftice among *Men*; but fomething tranfcendent, and we know not what; is in reality fubverting the Nature of Things, taking away the intrinfick difference between Good and Evil, and overturning the ground of all Religion. For, tho' the *Effence* of God, which it is *not* our bufinefs to underftand, is really incomprehenfible; as indeed are the *Effences* of *all other* things; yet the Notion of his moral *Attributes muft* be eafy and familiar; and, if we could not underftand *Thefe*, the *whole Doctrine* of the Gofpel would be *infignificant* to us. For, all Revelation from God *fuppofeth* us to *know beforehand* what is meant by *Juftice*, Goodnefs, and the like. So that no man can reafonably entertain any Notion of God, contradictory to Thefe, upon any pretenfe whatfoever. And 'tis very abfurd for any one to pretend, that we cannot underftand what *Juftice in God* is : For if we underftand not This, 'tis all one to us whether God be juft or not. Neither would it be poffible for us to *imitate* his Juftice : For he who *imitates*, endeavours to be *Like* fomething that he *Knows*; and muft of neceffity underftand, *what* 'tis he aims to be like. So that if we had no certain and fettled Notion of the Juftice and other Moral Attributes of God ; Religion, which confifts in the imitation of him, would be altogether unintelligible to our Minds and impoffible to our Practice.

A N D All This is in Scripture fo conftantly fuppofed to be True, that God There perpetually *appeals* to the common Reafon and natural Judgment of Mankind, for the Equity of his Dealings with them : For the Equity, not of *particular Providences*, which 'tis impoffible men in this fhort period of Life fhould be capable of obferving; but he appeals to them for the Equity of his *general Laws* or Rules of Government. *O Houfe of Ifrael, are not my ways equal, are not your ways unequal?* Ezek. xviii. 29. *Judge, I pray you, betwixt Me and my Vineyard; What could have been done more to my Vineyard, that I have not done in it?* If. v. 3. St *Paul* in like manner, fpeaking of the Judgments of God, declares that *all Mouths fhall be ftopped before him*, not by the irrefiftiblenefs of his *Power*, but by the conviction of the *righteoufnefs* and juftice of his Sentence ; Rom. iii. 4. cited from the 51ft Pfalm, *That thou mighteft be juftified in thy*

sayings, and mightest overcome when thou art judged. These are very plain and full declarations, both that God is *Just,* and that men are well capable of understanding *What*
that Justice is, which is so eminent a Perfection of the divine Nature. And to this
natural Sense and Knowledge of Right it is, that our Saviour himself appeals, when he
says, *Luc.* xii. 57. *Yea, and why even of* yourselves *judge ye not what is right?* and
when he so often repeats it in his Preaching to the *Jews, He that hath* Ears *to hear,
let him hear.*

HAVING thus proved *in general,* that God *is* and *cannot but be* Just; which was
the *first* thing proposed: I proceed now in the

II*d* place, To endeavour to explain *more particularly,* wherein the Nature of that
Justice consists. And here it may be necessary to *premise,* that *Justice* is of two sorts;
There is a Justice which consists in a distribution of *Equality.* The *former sort* belongs
to such Persons, as have no other Authority, but only a Power of distributing to several
persons *equally* their respective Dues: The *Latter sort* of Justice belongs to such a person, as having complete Right and Authority to do what he wills with his own, and distributing his free Gifts *variously* in *what proportion he pleases,* afterward dispenses *equitably* Rewards and Punishments, according to the different Use each man makes of the
different Gifts he is respectively intrusted with. And of This *latter* sort, is the *Justice
of God.* God is the Supreme Lord and Author of all; and as all his Gifts are free,
'tis evident he is under no more obligation to distribute them *equally,* than he was originally obliged to distribute them at all. He gives to one man after This manner, and
to another after That; and then his Justice consists in dealing with every one proportionably, according to the Analogy of their different behaviour under such different
Circumstances. In the matter of *Punishment;* his Justice requires that it should always be apportioned with the most strict exactness, to the Degree or Demerit of the
Crime: That is to say, that no man must be punished *more* than he deserves; though,
on the contrary, He that is supreme over all, may accept of as much *less* punishment,
or may *remit* punishment upon any such *free* conditions of his own gracious appointment, as he himself in the Wisdom and Goodness of his Government shall think fit
and reasonable: And This is the True foundation of the Gospel-Mercy, made known
to us from God by and through Christ. As to the Matter of *Reward;* Justice *originally* is not concerned at all; because at the best, men, even if they were sinless Creatures, are but unprofitable Servants; and, doing only what is their Duty to do, however they would have a right to escape Punishment, yet they *could* have *no* claim of
Merit to a Reward. But *in consequence of God's free Promise,* good men *have* a *just*
title to the Reward promised them; And the *Justice of God* in the distribution of this
Reward consists in *This,* that they who by the *Grace of God,* and according to the
merciful Tenor of the Gospel-Covenant, shall be found to have *obeyed the Law of Righteousness,* shall, according to the *proportion* of the good Use they have made of their
respective Gifts, have a *proportionably greater* share bestowed upon them of that future
Happiness; the *whole* of which is merely God's *free Gift* indeed and undeserved Bounty,
and yet at the same time *such* is good mens *Title* to it upon account of the Promise,
that the Apostle thought it not an improper expression, to say, *God is not* unrighteous,
to forget your work and labour of Love, Heb. vi. 10.

NOW this observation being *premised,* for the preventing any mistake in the General Notion of the Divine Justice; the Particulars *wherein* this Justice consists, or
which it principally *includes,* are these which follow; 1*st,* an *Impartiality,* with regard
to Persons; and 2*dly,* an *Equity* of Distribution, with regard to Things. To the *Persons* of men he has *no Respect;* but, in the final issue of Things, he will *upon the whole*
deal equitably with *all* his creatures; and in the distribution of *Rewards and Punishments in particular,* he will observe strictly an exact and righteous *proportion.* 1*st,* The

Notion

Notion of divine Juſtice, includes an abſolute *Impartiality* with regard to *Perſons.* All men are alike the Work of God's hands; and therefore as 'tis evident he could origi- nally have no regard to one more than to another, ſo when the various diſpenſations of infinite Wiſdom ſhall at the great Period and Conſummation of Nature have ac- compliſhed and unfolded *the myſtery of God,* it will manifeſtly appear, that finally alſo he has been *no Reſpecter of Perſons.* There are indeed in Scripture many particular *in- ſtances,* which at firſt ſight may ſeem not eaſily reconcileable with this great Truth: But the *general Rule itſelf* is ſo clearly and expreſsly laid down, and ſo perpetually re- peated and appealed to upon every occaſion; that no obſcurity or difficulty in the explication of particular caſes, can be oppoſed to the Evidence of ſo plain a Rule. The *general* Propoſition we may depend upon as certain, however difficult it may ap- pear at preſent to reconcile the *particulars;* and whatever *Clouds and Darkneſs are round about him, yet* we are ſure *Righteouſneſs and Judgment* are *the Habitation of his Seat.* 'Tis an obſervation of great importance, and neceſſary to be attended to in This, as in moſt other Doctrines of Religion; that obſcurer paſſages of Scripture are always to be interpreted by the plain ones, and not the plain ones made doubtful by thoſe that are more obſcure. And the Reaſon is evident: Becauſe that which is at preſent obſcure, may very eaſily in the event of things, and in the unfolding of Providence, have the difficulties removed, and make a final Harmony and Conſiſtency of the whole; But if that which is once clearly and plainly revealed, in words expreſs and full, and with- out ambiguity, is ever in any wiſe to be ſhaken by any after-diſcovery; or if a *general* perpetual Rule can be made in any degree uncertain, by the preſent difficulty of application of any *particular* caſe: there can Then never be *any* certain Aſſurance of the Truth of *Any* Doctrine or Revelation at all. To apply this to our preſent Subject: Whatever difficulty there may be at preſent, in reconciling God's being no Reſpecter of Perſons, with the many ſeeming Advantages we find in Scripture granted at any time to one particular Nation, Family, or Perſon, more than to other Nations, Families, or Perſons; (which Difficulty will come to be conſidered under my *Third* general head, wherein I propoſed to remove the *Objections* that may be alledged againſt the Impar- tiality of the divine Juſtice;) Whatever Difficulty, I ſay, there may poſſibly be at pre- ſent in reconciling theſe Things to each other; yet the general *Declaration,* or the univerſal Truth of the *Doctrine* itſelf, that *God is no Reſpecter of Perſons,* is ſo clearly and diſtinctly, ſo expreſsly and fully, ſo conſtantly and with ſuch earneſtneſs laid down and inculcated in every part of the Scripture, as a *Foundation never to be departed from* in all queſtions of Religion; that we may be very ſure, God will thoroughly juſtify it in the end; and ſhow us, that whatever now appears to us as an exception to this Rule, was nothing elſe but our beholding in an imperfect and broken View, only ſome ſmall portions of his All-wiſe Proceedings. In the *infancy* of the world, the Patriarch *Abra- ham,* when he took upon him to plead with God for *Sodom,* lays down this as a Rule or Foundation, upon which *every* Argument muſt for ever be built, *Shall not the Judge of all the Earth do right?* Gen. xviii. 23. In the book of *Job, Elihu,* diſputing with *Job's* friends, argues in like manner from the Light of Nature and common Reaſon; ch. xxxiv. 1,——19. *Hear my words, O ye wiſe men; and give ear unto me, ye that have knowledge;* ——God *accepteth not the perſons of Princes, nor regardeth the Rich more than the Poor, for they* all *are the work of* His *hands.* In the revelation God made of himſelf to *Moſes,* the character he commanded *Moſes* to give of him to the *Iſraelites,* is exactly agreeable to the ſame *Natural* Notion; *Deut.* x. 14, 17. *Behold, the Heaven and the Heaven of Heavens is the Lord's thy God, the Earth alſo with all that therein is;——he is a great God, a mighty and a terrible, which regardeth not perſons, nor taketh reward; He doth execute the judgment of the fatherleſs and widow, and loveth the ſtranger, in giving him food and raiment.* In the book of *Pſalms,* wherein are devoutly

celebrated

SERM. celebrated all the divine Attributes, the Juſtice of God is Thus likewiſe ſet forth;
XVI. *Pſ.* xcviii. 9. *With righteouſneſs ſhall he judge the World, and the people* (that is, all
nations) *with Equity.* In the Inſtructions given by good King *Jehoſhaphat* to the
Judges which he appointed through all the Cities of *Judah*; the ſame Notion of
the impartiality of the divine Juſtice is ſtill preſerved; 2 *Chr.* xix. 7. *Let the fear of
the Lord,* (ſays he) *be upon you; take heed, and do righteouſneſs; for there is no iniquity
with the Lord our God, nor reſpect of perſons, nor taking of Gifts.* In the Writings of
the *Prophets,* this Juſtice of God, in oppoſition to all Reſpecting of perſons, is ſtill
more emphatically expreſt; *Jer.* xxii. 24. *As I live, ſaith the Lord; Though Coniah the
Son of Jehoiakim King of Judah, were the* ſignet upon my right hand, *yet would I pluck
thee thence.* And concerning the *whole nation of the Jews,* that peculiar people of God;
elect, and beloved for the Fathers ſakes; to whom in a ſingular manner, were committed the divine oracles; and of whom it was written, that God *did not deal ſo with any
other nation, neither had the Heathen knowledge of his laws;* yet even concerning *This*
people, when they tranſgreſſed the Law that had been given them, *Will he regard your*
Perſons, ſaith the Divine Juſtice? *Mal.* i. 9. *I have no pleaſure in you, ſaith the Lord
of Hoſts, neither will I accept an offering at your hand; For from the riſing of the Sun
even unto the going down of the ſame, my name ſhall be great among the* Gentiles,——
and *my name ſhall be great among the* Heathen, *ſaith the Lord of Hoſts.* In the New-
Teſtament, our Saviour in *the Goſpel* repeats the ſame doctrine to the *Phariſees,* Matt. xxi.

Ch. viii. 43. *the Kingdom of God ſhall be taken from you, and given to a nation bringing forth
11, 12. the fruits thereof: And I ſay unto you, that many ſhall come from the eaſt and from the
weſt, and ſhall ſit down with Abraham, Iſaac, and Jacob, in the Kingdom of Heaven;
But the children of the Kingdom ſhall be caſt out into outer darkneſs; there ſhall be weep-*
Ch. vii. 21. *ing and gnaſhing of Teeth.* For, *Not every one that ſaith unto me, Lord, Lord;* (not
every Profeſſor of the true Religion, not every member of the People or Church of God,)
ſhall enter into the Kingdom of Heaven; but he that doth *the Will of my Father which
is in Heaven. Many will ſay to me in that day, Lord, Lord, have we not propheſied
in thy Name, and in thy Name have caſt out devils, and in thy Name done many wonderful works? And then will I profeſs unto them, I never knew you; depart from Me,
ye that work iniquity.* In the Acts of the *Apoſtles,* ch. x. 34. *Of a Truth,* ſaith St
*Peter, I perceive that God is no reſpecter of Perſons; But in every Nation, he that
feareth Him and worketh righteouſneſs, is accepted with him.* In their *Epiſtles,* the ſame
doctrine is perpetually inculcated as the Foundation of all religion: *Rom.* ii. 6,——10.
God will render to every man according to his deeds,——to the Jew *firſt, and alſo to the*
Gentile; *For there is no reſpect of perſons with God. For as many as have ſinned without law, ſhall alſo periſh without law; and as many as have ſinned in the law, ſhall be
judged by the law;——In the day when God ſhall judge the Secrets of Men by Jeſus
Chriſt.* Again, *Epheſ.* vi. 8. *Whatſoever* good *thing any man doth, the ſame ſhall he receive of the Lord, whether he be bond or free,——for there is no reſpect of perſons with*
Col. iii. 25. *him;* Likewiſe, *he that doth* wrong, *ſhall receive for the wrong that he hath done; and
there is no reſpect of perſons.* Theſe repeated Declarations of Scripture from one End
of the *Bible* to the other, are ſo full and plain, that, were the difficulties which ariſe
from *particular* caſes, to *our* apprehenſion altogether unanſwerable, (as I ſhall ſhow in
its proper place they by no means are, when I come to conſider the ſeveral Objections that may be alledged;) yet the *general Doctrine itſelf* would nevertheleſs be certain and eſtabliſhed as a *firſt Principle,* as a fundamental *Rule* of interpretation, to
which every thing elſe muſt of neceſſity be underſtood to agree; *viz.* that God, with-
1 Pet. i. 17. out reſpect of perſons, *judgeth according to every man's work.*

3

AND

AND this is the *firſt* particular, included in the Notion of divine Juſtice; an *Impar-* S E R M.
tiality with regard to Perſons. The *ſecond*, is an *Equity* of diſtribution, with regard to 　XVI.
Things; That is, the obſerving an exact proportion in the ſeveral *particular* degrees of
Reward and Puniſhment, as well as an Impartiality and determining *what* Perſons ſhall
be in *general* rewarded or puniſhed. But the inlargement upon *This* Head muſt be referred to a farther opportunity.

S E R M O N XVII.

Of the JUSTICE of GOD.

JOB XXXIV. 10, 11, 12.

Therefore hearken unto Me, ye men of Underſtanding : Far be it from
God, that He ſhould do Wickedneſs ; and from the Almighty, that He
ſhould commit iniquity : For the work of a Man ſhall he render unto
him, and cauſe every man to find according to his Ways : Yea, ſure-
ly God will not do wickedly, neither will the Almighty pervert Judg-
ment.

IN my laſt Diſcourſe I propoſed to treat of the *Divine Juſtice* after the follow- S E R M.
ing Method : 1ſt, to *prove*, that God *is* and *cannot but be* Juſt; 2dly, to *explain* 　XVII.
wherein the Nature of that Juſtice conſiſts: 3dly, to *remove* the Objections ariſing
from *particular* caſes againſt this *general* Truth: And finally, to apply what ſhall be
ſaid, by ſome *uſeful Inferences* in Practiſe. In the *firſt* place, that God *is and cannot*
but be Juſt, I have already proved at large: *Secondly*, in explaining *wherein* the Nature of this divine Juſtice conſiſts, I obſerved that it includes, (1ſt) an *Impartiality*
with regard to *Perſons*, and (2dly) an *Equity* of Diſtribution, with regard to *Things*.
Concerning the *Impartiality* of the divine Juſtice with regard to *Perſons*, I have already diſcourſed. That which I am now to proceed to in the next place, according
to the Method propoſed, is to ſhow that it denotes likewiſe an *Equity* of diſtribution
with regard to *Things*. That is to ſay; it includes the obſerving an exact proportion
in the ſeveral *particular* degrees of Reward and Puniſhment, as well as an Impartiality
in determining what Perſons ſhall be *in general* rewarded or puniſhed. And of This,
the Scripture gives us a very clear and diſtinct Account: Aſſuring us, that *they that be* Dan. xii. 3.
wiſe, that is, who *Themſelves* obey the commandments of God, *ſhall ſhine as the Bright-*
neſs of the Firmament; and *they that turn* many *to righteouſneſs*, which is ſtill a more
excellent pitch of Virtue, ſhall be *as the* Stars, the diſtinguiſhed Glory of the Firmament itſelf, *for ever and ever*: And that, even among *Theſe*, as *one ſtar differeth from* 1 Cor xv. 41.
another ſtar in glory, ſo ſhall it be alſo at the Reſurrection of the dead: That, one

VOL. I.　　　　　　　　　　　　E e　　　　　　　　　　　　　man

SERM.
XVII.
~~~~~~
Mat. x. 41.

Luke xix. 17.
1 Cor. iii. 8.
2 Cor. ix. 6.
1 Cor. iii. 13.

1 Cor. iii. 15.

man fhall receive a *Prophet's reward*; and another the *reward of a righteous man*; and a third, in a rank ftill inferiour to Both of thefe, yet for *giving to drink* but *a cup of cold water to one of* Chrift's *little ones*, that is, to a perfon any way perfecuted for confcience fake, *fhall in no wife lofe his Reward*: That according to men's different improvements of the Talents committed to their charge, One fhall be made *Ruler over five Cities*, and another over ten: That, *every man fhall receive his* own *reward, according to his* own *labour*; *reaping fparingly* or *bountifully*, accordingly, as he hath *fparingly* or *bountifully fown*, or if he has *built hay and ftubble*, that is, needlefs and unprofitable Doctrines upon the foundation of Chrift; fo as in great meafure to *lofe* his Reward, becaufe his Work was ufelefs; yet, if he was truly *fincere and upright* in his intention, for the integrity of his Heart *He himfelf fhall be faved*, tho' *fo as by Fire*; that is, with great Difficulty, as a man efcapes with his Life out of a houfe on Fire, wherein his Goods are confuming. Laftly, the different Degrees of the Reward of good men, are moft elegantly fet forth by St *John* in his Defcription of the heavenly *Jerufalem*, as of a royal City; *the City*, as our Saviour himfelf ftyles it, *the City of the Great King*; within which, the *Glory of God's* prefence did more immediately fhine, *and the Lamb was the Light thereof*; and without, the *Nations of them that are faved* did *walk in the Light of it*, Rev. xxi. 23; and ch. xxii. 2. *In the midft of it was the Tree of Life, which yielded her* Fruit *every Month, and the Leaves of the Tree were for the Healing of the Nations.*

AGAIN on the other fide, as in the diftribution of *Rewards*, fo in the allotment of the Degrees of *Punifhment* likewife, does the Scripture clearly fet forth to us the exact Impartiality of the Divine Juftice. The words of our Saviour are exprefs and full, St *Luke* xii. 47. *That Servant which* knew *his Lord's Will, and prepared not himfelf, neither did according to his Will, fhall be beaten with* many *ftripes; But he that* knew not, *and did commit things worthy of ftripes, fhall be beaten with* few *ftripes*: For *unto whomfoever much is given, of him fhall be much required; and to whom men have committed much, of Him they will ask the more.* Accordingly, againft the *Pharifees*, who had the beft opportunities of feeing and confidering his mighty Works, our Saviour always denounces his *feveret* Judgments for their Hypocrify and Unbelief. *Other* forts of Sinners he always reproved with fingular Tendernefs, and exhorted to Repentance with all Meeknefs and Compaffion; But the *Pharifees*, who finned againft the cleareft Light, and with the greateft Obftinacy, he conftantly challenged with the utmoft fharpnefs, as incorrigible hypocrites, as a generation of Vipers. *To him that* knoweth *to do good, and doth it not, to Him it is Sin*, Jam. iv. 17. The *Pharifees* had a learned and a religious education; and they defpifed the reft of the people, as, in comparifon with themfelves, blind and ignorant: Yet their Lives were vitious, notwithftanding that Knowledge; and then, the very thing they boafted of, was their great Condemnation. *Jefus faid unto them, If ye were blind, ye fhould have no Sin; but Now ye fay, We fee; Therefore your Sin remaineth*, John ix. 41. It *remaineth*; that is, you ftand moft clearly and moft inexcufably convicted of it. Their Learning and Knowledge in the Law and the Prophets qualified them to hear the words of Chrift, and to obferve his Works, with greater Advantage: And therefore he fays unto them, *Joh.* xv. 22. *If I had not come and fpoke unto them, they had not had Sin*; (that is, *comparatively* fpeaking their Sin had been nothing to what it Now is;) *But Now, they have no cloak for their Sin:—If I had not done among them the works which none other man did, they had not had Sin; but Now they have both feen and hated, both Me and my Father.* And in proportion to This aggravation of their Fault, does he accordingly enhance the Severity of their Punifhment; *Thefe*, faith he, *fhall receive* greater *Damnation*; Mar. xii. 40. He does not only threaten them with God's final wrath in general, in common with all other wicked men; *O ye generation of vipers, how can ye efcape the Damnation of Hell?* Matt. xxiii. 33. but he adds moreover in particular, ver. 14. *Ye fhall receive a greater Damnation*: In

the

the original it is, a *more abundant* condemnation ; a Meaſure of Wrath, *over and above* the general Sentence which ſhall paſs upon the World of the Ungodly.

IN like manner, comparing the *whole Nation* of the unbelieving *Jews* with the infidel Heathen World ; and conſidering how wilfully and with what aggravating circumſtances They rejected thoſe means of Salvation, which perhaps many of the Heathen would in the like caſe gladly have accepted ; he accordingly declares concerning them, Mat. x. 15. *Verily I ſay unto you, it ſhall be more tolerable for the land of Sodom and Gomorrha in the day of judgment, than for that City.*

Laſtly, IN that ſublime and affectionate deſcription of the great judgment, *Rev.* xx. 11, *and* 19, 20. there is made a very remarkable diſtinction of This kind : *I ſaw a great white throne, and him that ſat on it ; from whoſe face the Earth and the Heaven fled away, and there was found no place for them : And I ſaw the dead, ſmall and great, ſtand before God ; and the books were opened,* —— *and the dead were judged out of thoſe things which were written in the Books, according to their Works : And whoſoever was not found written in the book of Life, was caſt into the lake of Fire.* But *the Beaſt* and ——*the falſe Prophet,*——which *deceived* the Nations,——*theſe Both were caſt* Alive *into the Lake of Fire burning with Brimſtone.* The Diſtinction made by *Moſes* in the caſe of the *firſt* Death, *Num.* xvi. 29. *If theſe men die the common death of all men, or if they be viſited after the viſitation of all men ; then the Lord hath not ſent Me ; But if the Lord make a new thing, and the Earth open her mouth and ſwallow them up,*—— *and they go down* Quick [*or Alive*] *into the pit ; then ye ſhall underſtand that theſe men have provoked the Lord :* The *ſame* diſtinction (I ſay) ſeems to be made by St *John* in the caſe of the *ſecond* Death ; *Theſe* Two (ſaith he) *were caſt* Alive *into the lake of fire, burning with Brimſtone ;* That is, they were repreſented to be ſo diſtinguiſhed in the degree of a *ſeverer Puniſhment,* as they had been in the guilt of a more *provoking Wickedneſs.*

FROM all theſe paſſages of Scripture it abundantly appears, that the true and complete Notion of the Divine Juſtice, includes his obſerving an exact Proportion in the ſeveral *particular* Degrees of Reward and Puniſhment, as well as an Impartiality in determining what Perſons ſhall be *in general* Rewarded or Puniſhed.

NOW This *Juſtice* of God, as it will in the *End* certainly exert itſelf according to this exact Proportion in the final Diſtributions of the Great day ; ſo in the *preſent* intermediate Time, that God might not leave himſelf wholly without Witneſs, he has frequently in the courſe of his Providence given remarkable Preludes, or *particular* Inſtances and Significations of his *general* Intention, in extraordinary *Deliverances* of *Good Men,* and exemplary *Puniſhments* of the Bad, in all generations. His bringing in the *Flood* upon the World of the Ungodly, was a temporal Inſtance of his Juſtice : And our Lord tells us, that *as the days of Noah were, ſo ſhall alſo the coming of the Son of Man be ; For as in the days that were before the Flood, they were eating and drinking, marrying and giving in marriage, until the day that Noah entred into the Ark ; And knew not until the Flood came, and took them all away ; So ſhall alſo the coming of the Son of Man be,* Matt. xxiv. 37. And as righteous *Noah* was then delivered in the Ark from *temporal* Deſtruction by the divine Juſtice ; ſo by *a like figure,* ſays the Apoſtle, *Baptiſm alſo,* that is, *not the putting away of the filth of the Fleſh,* not the bare external Form or Ceremony, *but the Anſwer of a good Conſcience towards God,* ſhall finally ſave *Us* from everlaſting Perdition. Again : The overthrow of *Sodom and Gomorrha,* was another *temporal* Inſtance of the divine Juſtice, by which thoſe Cities were *ſet forth for an Example, ſuffering the Vengeance of eternal Fire :* Of *eternal Fire ;* that is, not the Jude 7. Fire of *Hell,* for That, being inviſible, cannot yet be ſaid to be *ſet forth for an example ;* But thoſe Cities were made an Example by that *temporal* fire, the *Effect* whereof was *eternal,* bringing upon them remedileſs and endleſs Deſtruction. And This, was an

Emblem

SERM. *Emblem* or *Earneſt* of God's *final* Juſtice. For ſo our Saviour argues, St *Luk.* xviii.
XVII. 28. *As it was in the days of Lot, they did eat, they drank, they bought, they ſold, they*
planted, they builded; But the ſame day that Lot went out of Sodom, it rained Fire and
Brimſtone from Heaven, and deſtroyed them all; Even Thus ſhall it be in the day when
the Son of Man is revealed. And as juſt *Lot* was then delivered from *temporal* Death,
by God's immediate miraculous interpoſition; ſo in the infliction of *eternal* Death, it
Gen. xviii. 23. may be depended upon, that *the Judge of all the Earth will do what is right,* and will
not deſtroy the righteous with the wicked. In *This* ſenſe, the plea of *Abraham* was undoubtedly juſt, and will finally be verified without exception; though in the *preſent*
mixt ſtate of things, the Nature of God's government of this world is ſuch, that (unleſs in extraordinary caſes, for particular ſtanding examples;) the righteous for the
more part are indeed involved in common calamities with the wicked, and the wicked
enjoy the Bleſſings of Providence in common with the Righteous.

THERE have been *ſome* perſons ſo unreaſonable, as, from the general Notion of
the Divine *Goodneſs,* to frame to themſelves an imagination, that God ſhould *finally*
puniſh no Offenders at all; but, in the *future* ſtate reward thoſe who are capable of it,
and deſtroy the reſt immediately without any puniſhment at all. But if Puniſhment
is in the *preſent* ſtate, for the ſupport of Laws and of good Government, juſt and righteous; nay, and no leſs conſiſtent with *Goodneſs* too, than requiſite in *Juſtice:* For
the ſame reaſon, in the *future* ſtate likewiſe, it is juſt and righteous; nay, and conſiſtent with *Goodneſs* too; For the univerſal Laws and Government and Kingdom of
God, continue for ever. In their *own* caſe, when they themſelves are the Parties offended, men always think it reaſonable that Offenders ſhould be puniſhed; nay, and
often complain of Providence for not puniſhing them ſooner. And ſhall it not be
thought reaſonable in the Government of the Univerſe, that in the future *eternal* ſtate,
as well as in the preſent *temporary* one, ſuch Puniſhment ſhould be inflicted on impenitent Offenders, as infinite Power, Wiſdom, Juſtice, and Goodneſs in Conjunction,
judges exactly proportional to the demerit of each Criminal, and moſt proper to anſwer
the Ends of the divine Government, in ſupporting the Honour and Dignity of the
eternal and univerſal Laws of God's boundleſs and everlaſting Kingdom?

III. I PROCEED now in the *Third* place, to conſider the *Objections* ariſing from
particular caſes, againſt the *general* Doctrine of the Divine Juſtice.

And *firſt*; THAT great and *general* Objection, which has in all Ages been drawn
from the unequal Diſtributions of Providence in the *preſent* life, is ſufficiently anſwered
by the Belief of a *Future ſtate*; wherein, by the exactneſs and preciſe equity of the
final Determinations of the Great Day, ſhall be abundantly made up all the little Inequalities of this ſhort life, which is but for a moment. Beſides which *general* and full
Anſwer, there are alſo many *ſpecial* reaſons of theſe ſeeming Inequalities; which ſhow
them to be not only *conſiſtent* with, but even to be beautiful *Parts* of the All-wiſe Deſign of Providence, in governing the World, through all variety of circumſtances with
final Equity and exactneſs of Juſtice. God frequently afflicts the Righteous, for the
trial and improvement of their virtue; for the exerciſe of their patience; for the correction of their faults; and for purging them that they may bring forth more and more
fruit. *I will refine them, as ſilver is refined; and will try them as gold is tried,* Zech.
xiii. 9. *And ſome of them of underſtanding ſhall fall, to try them and to purge, and to*
make them white, Dan. xi. 35; and ch. xii. 10. *Many ſhall be purified and made white*
and tried. Having been a little chaſtiſed, they ſhall be greatly rewarded; for God
proved them, and found them worthy for himſelf: As gold in the furnace has he tried
them, and received them as a burnt-offering, Wiſd. iii. 5. And 1 *Pet.* i. 6, 7. *Ye are in*
heavineſs through manifold temptations; that the trial of your Faith being much more
precious, than of gold that periſheth, though it be tried with Fire, might be found unto

praiſe

praife and honour and glory, at the appearing of Jefus Chrift. On the other hand, God frequently, for no lefs wife reafons, defers punifhing the wicked; nay, as the Pfalmift complains, makes them remarkably profperous in the World: Sometimes, to make them inftruments in the hands of Providence for the Punifhment of Others; as in the cafe of Tyrants, and publick Oppreffors: Sometimes, to caufe their Punifhment, when it comes finally upon them, to be more exemplary and remarkable; as in the cafe of *Pharaoh*, and of thofe profane perfons, whofe *End* cleared the Pfalmift's mind of thofe doubts, which their Profperity had raifed in him at the *Beginning*: At other times, God does it to fhow his Mercy and Forbearance, and to give men Time and Space for Repentance; *enduring with much long-fuffering, the veffels of wrath fitted to deftruction.* Therefore, fays the Author of the book of *Wifdom, chaftenest thou them by little and little, that offend;——that leaving their Wickednefs, they may believe on Thee: ——Not that thou waft unable——to deftroy the ungodly at once;——But executing thy judgments upon them by little and little, thou gavest them place of repentance,—— whereby they might be delivered from their malice,* ch. xii. 2, 9, 10, 20.

B U T befides this obvious and *general* Objection againft the Juftice of Providence, in the diftribution of *temporal* good things; there are alfo *particular* difficulties arifing from *fingular* inequalities even with regard to fpiritual advantages, which deferve to be diftinctly confidered. Thus, fince God is the common Creator and Lord of all men; fince *the heaven is his, and the earth alfo, with all that therein is*; fince he declares that he *regardeth not perfons, nor taketh reward*; but *loveth the ftranger, in giving him food and raiment*; and has promifed to *judge the* World *with righteoufnefs, and the Na*tions *with equity*: Well may it be inquired how is *That which follows* confiftent with impartial Juftice, when in fo *diftinguifhing* a manner, in the very fame place which fome of thefe *general* declarations are made, 'tis faid to the *Jews in particular,* ver. 15. *Only the Lord had a delight in thy Fathers to love them, and he chofe their feed after them, even* you *above all people:* He *did not deal fo with any other nation, neither had the Heathen knowledge of his Laws:* And all This, not for any *merit* in the perfons themfelves; For he faith, *Rom.* ix. 11. concerning *children not yet born, neither having done any good or evil;——Jacob have I loved, but Efau have I hated;* that is, (as the Apoftle himfelf explains it,) *the Elder fhall ferve the Younger;* the *Pofterity* of *Jacob* have I chofen to be my peculiar people, and not the *Pofterity* of *Efau.* Now the true Anfwer to this difficulty, is This. As God may very juftly exercife his Power and Wifdom in making great Variety of Creatures, and was not at all obliged to make *Men Angels:* fo neither is he obliged to indue all *Men* with all the *fame* Faculties and Advantages; to make them *all* capable of the very *fame Kind* and *Degree* of Happinefs; or to afford *all of them* all the very *fame* means and opportunities of obtaining it. *Impartial Juftice* confifts, not in dealing with all perfons *alike*, but in dealing with all perfons *proportionably.* And *Wifdom* appears even much *more*, in that diverfity of diftributions; which at the fame time diminifhes nothing from Juftice. 'Tis as juft with God, to intruft one man originally with two talents, as another with ten; And he that with the improvement of thofe two talents, gains to himfelf two more, has as much Juftice done him, as he that with the improvement of ten talents gains to himfelf other ten. God divides to every *Man*, and to every *Nation* what Advantages and Favours he himfelf pleafes, with great Wifdom, and without any Injuftice: And when he comes finally to judge the whole Earth, it will appear in that great Variety of Circumftances in all kinds, that, upon the whole, *he that gathered much, had nothing over, and he that gathered little, had no lack.* This is what the Apoftle excellently expreffes, in the whole 2d chapter to the *Romans*; and particularly, *ver.* 6. *God will render to every man according to his deeds,——to the* Jew *firft, and alfo to the* Gentile; *For there is no refpect of Perfons with God; But as many as have finned without the Law, fhall*

SERM.
XVII.

Pf. lxxiii

Rom ix. 22.

Deut. x. 14;
17, 18.

Pf. cxlvii. 20.

SERM. *also perish without Law; and as many as have sinned in the Law, shall be judged by the*
XVII. *Law,——in the day when God shall judge the secrets of men by Jesus Christ.*   But there
is also, besides This, another *particular* reason of God's different dispensations towards
the *Jews* and *Gentiles*, expressed at large by St *Paul* in the 11th to the *Romans*, and
summed up briefly in the following words, *ver.* 12. and 30. *If the Fall of them* [of the
Jews] *be the Riches of the World, and the Diminishing of them, the Riches of the Gentiles,
how much more their Fulness ?——For as ye* [Gentiles] *in times past have not believed God,
yet now have obtained mercy through their unbelief;* [the unbelief of the Jews;] *Even so
have These also now not believed, that through your mercy They also may obtain mercy;
For God hath concluded them all in unbelief, that he might have mercy upon all : O the
depth of the Riches both of the Wisdom and Knowledge of God !*

AGAIN, if it be objected against the Impartiality of the Divine Justice, that since
our Saviour declares, if the same means had been used with the inhabitants of *Tyre* and
Sidon, that had been used towards the cities of the *Jews,* they would have repented;
why then were not those means offered them ? and since in the Parable he sets forth,
that some worked in the Vineyard much longer than others, *why* then did they receive
but all equally a penny ? The answer to these difficulties is plain, both from what has
been already said, and from what our Saviour suggests in the places themselves.   As the
inhabitants of *Tyre* and *Sidon* were of a less obstinate disposition, than some of the
Jewish Cities; so he declares it should fare proportionably better with them at the day
of Judgment: *I say unto you; it shall be more tolerable for Tyre and Sidon at the day
of judgment, than for you :* And elsewhere; *Many* (says he) *shall come from the east
and from the west, and shall sit down with Abraham, Isaac, and Jacob, in the Kingdom of God; and ye yourselves (the children of the Kingdom) shall be shut out into outer
darkness.*   Then as to the Parable of the Labourers in the Vineyard; if it be understood of the different Ages of the *World,* concerning the *Jews* and *Gentiles,* as 'tis plain
it was *primarily* meant; there is then no difficulty in it.   But if it be understood of the
different periods of mens *lives,* (as it *may* also be;) yet still the penny given equally to
them all, may be understood of *Heaven in general,* not exclusive of very different degrees *in* that One state of Happiness which shall itself in the whole be common to
them all.   Or lastly, If the penny given to them that came in in the last period of
their lives, were to be understood even of an equality in *degree,* with those who came
in first; yet even *still* there would be no injustice in this matter; because God may do
what he pleases with the abundance of what is his own, and wrongs no man by giving to others his free and undeserved Gifts.   Nevertheless, though God *may justly* act in
these cases as he pleases, without giving *us* any reason of his acting; yet in reality, 'tis
most reasonable to suppose he never *does* act arbitrarily, without a reason which *he* sees,
though we do *not.*   To Him that sees the *Heart,* a true Penitent, even after many
and long transgressions, may possibly come to *exceed* in Virtue, even those who have
from the Beginning lived more regularly and innocently.   The antient *Jews* had a Proverb, that no man could equal the Zeal of a sincere Penitent; and St *Paul's* description of such a person is very emphatical, 2 *Cor.* vii. 11. *Behold, this self-same thing,
that ye sorrowed after a godly sort, what carefulness it wrought in you; yea, what clearing of yourselves; yea, what indignation; yea, what fear; yea, what vehement desire;
yea, what zeal; yea, what revenge !*

THE *Uses* of this whole Discourse concerning the Justice of God, are;

1. LET us acknowledge and submit to the Divine Justice, and show forth our due
Sense and Fear of it in the course of our Lives.   This is St *Peter's* inference, 1 *Pet.* i.
17. *If ye call on the Father, who without respect of Persons judgeth according to every
man's work; pass the time of your sojourning here in Fear.*

Marginal notes:
Luk. x. 13.
Mat. xi. 21.

Mat. xx.

Mat. xi. 22.

2. A right Notion of the Juſtice of God, is matter of *Comfort* to *good* men; who, if they ſincerely endeavour to perform their duty, know that with a juſt and righteous God there can be no ſecret Decree to exclude them from Happineſs. *God is not un-*righteous, (ſo the Apoſtle expréſſes it, *Heb.* vi. 10.) *to forget your work, and labour of love.* Wherefore however dark the ways of Providence may ſeem at preſent, yet *Let not thine heart envy Sinners, but be thou in the Fear of the Lord all the day long; For ſurely there is a reward, and thine expeɛtation ſhall not be cut off,* Prov. xxiii. 17.

3. THE Juſtice of God is matter of *Terror* to all *wicked* and *unrighteous* men, how great and powerful ſoever they may be. He *accepteth not the perſons of Princes, nor regardeth the rich more than the poor; for they All are the work of his hands,* Job xxxiv. 19. *He which is Lord over all, ſhall fear no man's perſon, neither ſhall he ſtand in awe of any man's greatneſs; for he hath made the ſmall and great, and careth for all alike,* Wiſd. vi. 7. And *Rev.* vi. 15. *The Kings of the Earth, and the great men, and the rich men, and the chief captains, and the mighty men,——hid themſelves in the dens and in the rocks of the mountain,——from the face of him that ſitteth on the throne, and from the wrath of the Lamb.*

4. FROM the conſideration of the Juſtice of God, who has Power freely to forgive, and puniſhes None but where the higheſt *Reaſon* requires it; ariſes a True Notion of the heinouſneſs of Sin, and of the inexcuſableneſs and ſelf-condemnation of ſinners; *who knowing the* righteous *judgment of God, that they who do ſuch things are worthy of death, not only do the ſame, but have pleaſure in them that do them.*

Laſtly, and to conclude; If God, who is All-powerful and Truly Supreme, and Ac-countable to None for what he does, yet always confines himſelf to what is juſt and righteous, and appeals even to *Us* alſo, to judge of his ſo Doing; ſaying, *Judge, I pray you, between Me and my Vineyard;* how then dare mortal men inſult and tyrannize over each other, and think themſelves by Power and Force diſcharged from all obliga-tions of Equity towards their Fellow-creatures? *Be wiſe now therefore: O ye Kings,* ſays the experienced Preacher *Solomon, be inſtruɛted, ye that are Judges of the Earth.*

SERMON

SERMON XVIII.

Of the GLORY of GOD.

1 COR. X. 31.

Whether therefore ye eat or drink, or whatsoever ye do, do all to the Glory of God.

SERM. **T**HE Design of the Apostle in this chapter, is to press upon Christians the great
XVIII. Obligation they are under, to walk *worthy of their holy vocation*; to walk *worthy of God*, as he elsewhere expresses it, (1 *Th*. ii. 12.) to live as becometh *the
Gospel of Christ*; to behave themselves in such a manner, as may do *honour* to their
religion, may give *Credit and Reputation* to their Profession; In a word, that they be
sollicitous above all things to promote the *Glory of God*, and the *Salvation of Men*; to
bring over *Unbelievers*, to the acknowledgment of the Truth; and to prevent, as far as
possible, those who *Do believe*, from being in any manner offended and discouraged in
their Duty, or by any means tempted and seduced into Sin.

THE Great Temptation in the Apostles days was that of relapsing into the Heathen
Idolatry; either *directly*, into the gross Acts of this Sin, through Fear of Persecution;
or *consequentially*, into the Snare of a defiled Conscience, by presumptuously misunder-
standing the true Bounds of what was lawful and innocent. Against *Both* these, St *Paul*
gives diligent Caution in This chapter. Against falling into *direct* Idolatry through fear
of Persecution, he exhorts the *Corinthians* by the following Argument, *ver*. 13. *There
has no Temptation*, says he, *taken you, but such as is common to Man : But God is
Faithful, who will not suffer you to be tempted above what ye are able; but will with the
Temptation also make a way to escape, that ye may be able to bear it : Wherefore, my
dearly beloved, flee from Idolatry*. To strengthen which Argument, he proceeds in the
next Verses, to represent to them the *Greatness* of the Sin; by showing them distinctly,
under a plain and obvious Similitude, what *Idolatry* was. *Ver*. 15. *I speak*, saith he,
as to Wise men; judge ye what I say. He does not insist merely upon his own *Authority*,
though it was no less than Apostolical; as Others, who have no such Claim, are frequently too apt to do : He does not require of them to submit implicitly to what he
says, without first considering whether it was right or no : But he exhorts them to
make use of their own Reason and Understanding : *I speak*, says he, *as to Wise*, (that
is,) to *Sensible and Reasonable* Men; *Judge ye what I say* : Consider, if what I now
propose to you, be not a reasonable and conclusive Argument. *The Bread which we
break, is it not the Communion of the Body of Christ ?* that is, is it not a professing ourselves to be Disciples of *Christ ?* to be *Members* of his *Body ?* ver. 16. For we, says he,
being Many, are one Bread and one Body. In like manner, he speaks of *Israel after the
flesh, Are not they which eat of the Sacrifices partakers of the Altar ?* that is, is not
This a declaring themselves to be Disciples of *Moses ?* ver. 18. By the same Argument
therefore; being *partakers*, saith he, *of the Table of Devils*, by eating of the Sacrifices

I

in

in the Idol-Temple, *ver.* 21; is, in reality, to communicate in the Guilt of the Hea-then-Idolatry.

AGAINST the *next* danger, *viz.* that of falling *confequentially* into the Snare of a defiled Confcience, by prefumptuoufly mifunderftanding the true Bounds of what was lawful and innocent; Againft *This*, he cautions them in the remaining part of the chapter. An *Idol*, every well inftructed Chriftian knew to be *Nothing in the World*: As to *Meats* therefore offered in facrifice to Idols; the *good Creatures of God* could not be defiled, by the imaginary Superftitions of *vain Men*. And therefore Chriftians, pro-vided *They themfelves* bore no part in the Heathen-*worfhip*, were not obliged to make any Inquiry, whether Meats fold in the Markets, or fet before them at any Friend's houfe, had by *Others* been dedicated to Superftitious Ufe, *ver.* 25, 27. Neverthelefs, though as to Thofe who *had* this Underftanding, the Matter was clear; yet, if any *fcrupulous and weaker* Brother was diffatisfied as to the Lawfulnefs of This Practice, in *fuch cafe* they were bound to abftain : Bound, not by any obligation upon their *own* Confcience, but out of Tendernefs and Regard to *His*, *ver.* 28, 29. left by *Their* need-lefsly doing what was innocent to *Themfelves*, *He* fhould be incouraged to do the fame thing which was *not* innocent to *Him* : In which cafe, it was much more *material*, and of *greater importance to the Honour of Religion*, that they fhould *avoid* offending his *Confcience*, than that they fhould unfeafonably affert *their* own *Liberty*. *Ver.* 23. *All things are lawful for me, but all things are not expedient ; all things are lawful for me, but all things edify not.* The Meaning is ; All things that are *lawful for a man to do*, 'tis not confequently for the Intereft of Religion that he *fhould do* them, if it fo happens that *other* Mens Confciences be not therein fatisfied as well as his *own*. For *That* is moft for the True intereft of Religion, which tends moft towards making all men act with a good confcience. *Ver.* 24. *Let no man* therefore *feek his own, but every Man another's Wealth* : That is; be not fo much follicitous to keep up the full Extent of your own innocent Liberty, as to do That which will more generally and effectually prevent Men's falling into Sin. This ought always to be the main End, the great and prevailing confideration, in every Action of a good Chriftian ; *what* will moft tend to promote the Kingdom of God, the Practice of univerfal Righteoufnefs and Truth amongft Men. In order to *This* End, it is not indeed Lawful to do any thing that is *Evil*, but it is at any time very commendable to forbear doing what is *innocent*. *This* End, all our *Great and Religious* Actions ought always *actually and directly* to aim at ; and all our *fmaller and indifferent* Actions, ought by a *general and habitual* intention, to have the fame Tendency. For fo the Apoftle concludes his *whole* Difcourfe, in the words of the Text; *Whether therefore ye eat or drink, or whatfoever ye do, do All to the Glory of God : Give none Offenfe, neither to the Jews, nor to the Gentiles, nor to the Church of God : Even as I pleafe all men in all things, not feeking mine own Profit, but the Profit of Many, that they may be faved.*

THE words of the Text, contain a Doctrine of the higheft importance in Religion; And therefore, in the following Difcourfe upon them, I fhall more largely and diftinctly confider; *1ft*, What is the true meaning, and full Intent, of that Phrafe which we fo often meet with in Scripture, *The Glory of God :* And *2dly*, What it is, that is required of men in Practife, in order to their fatisfying the Precept in the Text; *Whether ye eat or drink, or whatever ye do, do All to the Glory of God?*

I. As to the true meaning, of that Phrafe which we fo often meet with in Scrip-ture, *The Glory of God :* 'Tis to be obferved that the

1ft and original Signification of it, is to denote to us the *Effence*, the *Perfon*, or the *Majefty* of God; that is, *God himfelf*, who is the *Fountain of Glory*. Thus 2 *Pet.* i. 17. *There came to him*, (to our Saviour at his Baptifm,) *fuch a Voice from the* Excellent Glory : From the *Excellent Glory*, that is, from *God*, his *Father* ; as 'tis literally ex-

S E R M. preffed, in the very fame Verfe. In *This* fenfe, the Name *of God*, the *Majefty on*
XVIII. *High*, and fome other fuch Phrafes, are alfo ufed in the like manner, to fignify *God himfelf*. And, *fitting on the right hand of* Power, Matt. xxvi. 64. is, fitting at the right hand of *God*, who Alone has properly *All Power*.

2*dly*, This phrafe, *the Glory of God*, fignifies in the *next* place, the Manifeftation of God's Perfections or Attributes, by the *external Exercife* of them towards his *Creatures*. God was effentially Happy before any thing was created, in the enjoyment of his own unfpeakable Perfections: But the *Manifeftation* of the Glory of thofe Perfections, and the *Communication* of Good to *Others*, could not be till the Creation of Things. Hence the Prophet *Ifaiah*, reprefents God Thus fpeaking, *(ch.* xliii. 7.) *I have created him for my Glory, I have formed him, yea I have made him.* In *Allufion* to which expreffion it may probably be fuppofed to be, that St *Paul* fays, 1 Cor. xi. 7. that *Man is the Image and* Glory *of God*.

And becaufe in *every one* of the divine Perfections *in particular*, when manifefted *fingly* in their proper and refpective Acts, there is fomething *diftinctly* worthy of Adoration and Praife; 'tis therefore not unfrequent in Scripture, to exprefs any *one* of thofe Perfections fingly, by the Title of the *Glory of God*. Thus concerning the Divine Power, *Pf.* xix. 1. *The Heavens declare the* Glory *of God*, (that is, they fhow forth unto Men the *Power* of God in *creating*, and his *Wifdom* in *difpofing* things;) *and the Firmament fheweth his handy-work*. And *Joh.* xi. 4, 40. *This Sicknefs* of Lazarus, faith our Lord, *is not unto Death, but for the* Glory *of God*,——that *thou fhouldeft fee the* Glory *of God*——*and that the* Son of God *might be* glorified *thereby*: The Meaning is; It was intended for a manifeftation of God's *Power* to raife the dead, and of his having *communicated* That Power alfo to the *Son of Man*. And here we may obferve, by the way, that the Tyranny indeed of *weak and vain Mortals*, is apt to take pleafure in *Power for Power's fake*; and their great Complacency and *Glory* is, in being able to exercife it arbitrarily and without reafon. But *God*, whofe Power is truly *infinite*, makes it His *Glory* to exercife Power, *only in doing Good*; (for almoft *all* our Saviour's Miracles were Acts of *Beneficence*, as well as of *Power*;) or at leaft, if the Subject is not capable of *Good*, yet the Exercife of his Power, even in Acts of *Severity*, is according to *Juftice* always. Rom. ix. 22. *What if God, willing*——*to make his* Power *known, endured with much long-fuffering the veffels of Wrath fitted to deftruction!* He did not fhow his abfolute *Power*, in *fitting* a certain Number of men *to deftruction*; as fome have abfurdly underftood this Text, directly contrary to the words themfelves; but he fhowed his *Power* in *juftly* punifhing Thofe, who after *much long-fuffering* and forbearance with them, appeared finally *fit* for nothing but *Deftruction*.

Again: Becaufe Mercy *and* Goodnefs are reprefented in Scripture, as the Attributes wherein God *chiefly delights*; according to that of St *James*, ch. ii. 13. *Mercy rejoiceth againft Judgment*; or, as it is in the Original, *Mercy glorieth over Judgment*: therefore *This* alfo is, in a particular and *emphatical* manner, called *the Glory of God*. Rom. ix. 23. *That he might make known the Riches of his* Glory, *on the veffels of Mercy*: And *Ephef.* iii. 16. *That he would grant you, according to the Riches of his* Glory, *to be ftrengthned*——*by his Spirit in the inner man*.

In purfuance of which *fame* manner of fpeaking, *Grace* or *Mercy* is by the Evangelift called likewife the *Glory* of Chrift; Joh. i. 14. *We beheld his* Glory, *the* Glory *as of the only-begotten of the Father, full of Grace*, (that is, of *Mercy*,) *and Truth*. And even of a *Man*, Prov. xix. 11. *It is his* Glory, faith Solomon, *to pafs over a Tranfgreffion*. And the *Thanks*, which men are bound to return to God for his *free Goodnefs and Compaffion* towards them, is expreffed to be accordingly *to the Praife of his* Glory; Eph. i. 14. *The redemption of the purchafed Poffeffion, unto the Praife of his* Glory. In *This* particular fenfe, is fometimes meant That general Obfervation, that the *End* to
which

which God directs All his Actions, is *his own* Glory; Rom. xi. 32. *God hath concluded* S E R M. *All under Sin, that he might have* Mercy *upon All.*   XVIII.

THUS God's *manifesting* the several Attributes and Perfections of his Divine Nature, and Gal. iii. in the *external Exercise* of them towards his *Creatures*; is frequently what the Scripture 22. means by the *Glory of God.*

3dly, FROM hence, on the other side, the *Return* or *Acknowledgment*, which *Creatures* make again to *God*, for *His* manifestations of his Goodness to *Them*; is likewise in Scripture stiled *The Glory of God*, or *their* giving *Glory to Him.* To *give Glory to God*, is to promote his *Honour* in the World; or to contribute what we can towards keeping up in All men's minds, a just *Sense* of him, and *Regard* towards him.

AND This is done, particularly; by *Worshipping* him, with *constant* and perpetually-returning Acts, of solemn *publick Devotion, Pf.* xxix. 1. *Give unto the Lord,* glory *and strength; give unto the Lord the* glory *due unto his Name;* worship *the Lord, in the Beauty of Holiness.* Thus the *Saints in* Heaven, (Rev. iv. 11.) are represented as *worshipping* God, and saying, *Thou art worthy, O Lord, to receive* Glory *and Honour and Power; for Thou hast created all things, and for thy pleasure they Are, and were Created.* And the *Nations of the* Earth are directed accordingly, (ch. xix. 7.) *Fear God, and give* Glory *to him, and worship him that made Heaven and Earth.* Which Worship because the Heathen World gave to *Others* instead of the True God, even to *Gods which did not make the Heaven and the Earth,* as the Prophet describes them; therefore St *Paul* Thus Jer. x. 11. charges them, *Rom.* i. 21. that *when they knew God,* yet *they* glorified *him not as God.*

Again: BY *Thanks particularly returned for special Mercies or Benefits received,* by which we profess our Sense of God's being the Author of those Benefits; is the Honour of God promoted among Men, or *Glory* given unto him. Thus *(Luke* xvii. 18.) when of the ten Lepers that were healed, one only, who was a *Samaritan,* was truly Thankful for the Mercy shown him; *There are not found,* says our Saviour, *that returned to give* Glory *to God, save This Stranger.*

Further: G L O R Y is in like manner said to be given to God, by *Acknowledgment of his Government and Supreme Dominion in the World:* Phil. ii. 11. *That every tongue should confess, that Jesus Christ is Lord, to the* Glory *of God the Father;* that is, to the *Honour* of God who exalted him, and who gave him a Name which is above every Name, by *setting him at his own right hand in the Heavenly places.* Thus also *Rev.* xi. 13. when great Judgments of God fell upon the idolatrous World, the *remnant* (says the Text) *were affrighted, and gave* Glory *to the God of Heaven;* that is, they then acknowledged the True God to be indeed Supreme Governor of the World. For *not acknowledging* of which, but proudly assuming to *himself* the cause of his own Grandeur and Riches, King *Belshazzar* is thus reproved by *Daniel,* ch. v. 22.) *Thou, O Belshazzar, hast not humbled thine heart, but hast lifted up thy self against the Lord of Heaven; and——the God in whose hand thy Breath is, and whose are all thy ways, thou hast not glorified.* And King *Herod,* when, being *arrayed in royal apparel,* he *sat upon his Throne; immediately the Angel of the Lord smote him,* Acts xii. 23. *because he gave not God the* Glory; that is, because forgetting his dependance upon God, he suffered the People to applaud him as being *himself* a God, and the Author of his own Greatness.

UPON the same Ground, *Confession of past Sins,* with true *Humiliation,* and a just Sense of the *Unworthiness* and *Ungratefulness* of Sin, is in Scripture stiled *giving* Glory *to God.* Josh. vii. 19. *Joshua said to Achan,* who had stolen some of the accursed things, and indeavoured to dissemble it; *My Son, give, I pray thee,* glory *to the Lord God of Israel, and make confession unto him:* That is; Acknowledge, that nothing can be concealed from *His* all-seeing Eye; and that to *Him* there is no secret nor Shadow of Darkness, where the Workers of Iniquity may hide themselves.

3   *Actual*

SERM.
XVIII. *Actual Repentance*, and *Forsaking* of Sin, by *real Amendment*, is still in a higher degree *giving* Glory *to God*, or promoting his Honour. *Rev.* xvi. 9. *Men blasphemed the Name of God, who hath Power over these plagues; and they* repented *not, to give him* Glory.

HABITUAL *Holiness*, or a *constant established Practice* of Virtue, *in the course of our Lives*, is yet further, in the *highest* degree we are capable, *giving* Glory *to the God* of all Righteousness and Holiness, who is of purer Eyes than to behold iniquity. 1 *Cor.* vi. 20. Glorify *God in your Body, and in your Spirit: Being filled with the Fruits of righteousness, which are by Jesus Christ, unto the* Glory *and Praise of God.* (Phil. i. 11.)

Phil. iv. 8. IN a word: *Whatever* tends to the true Honour of Religion, to the promoting and establishment of Virtue and Goodness among Men; *Whatsoever things are true, whatsoever things are honest, whatsoever things are just, whatsoever things are pure, whatsoever things are lovely, whatsoever things are of good report, if there be any Virtue, if there be any Praise, these* are the things which promote the *Glory* of God. God is *himself* a Being of infinite Holiness and Goodness; a perfectly just and righteous, as well as Supreme, Governour of the Universe: And the Glory of *such* a Governour, is the establishment of his *Moral Kingdom*, the universal establishment of the *Dominion and Power of Virtue*, in the Wills of all reasonable and intelligent Creatures. His *natural* Kingdom is by *Necessity*; for the material World *cannot but* obey him: But his *moral* Kingdom which is his *greatest Glory*, is the Dominion of *Righteousness* and *Virtue*. Hence the Apostles, in their Exhortations to the Practise of *Any Virtue* whatsoever, frequently urge *This* Argument, that it will be *to the Glory of God*: (Rom. xv. 5.) *God—grant you to be* like-minded *one towards another,—that ye may* with one mind glorify *God, even the Father of our Lord Jesus Christ.* And in the words of the Text; *Whether ye eat or drink, or whatsoever ye do, do all to the* glory *of God*: Do every thing, even the most *common* actions of Life, in such a manner, as may *become* the Professors of the Gospel of Christ, and may promote the Honour and Interest of Religion. The words are of the same import, with those in *Col.* iii. 17. *Whatsoever ye do in word or deed, do all in the name of the Lord Jesus;* do every thing so as becomes the Disciples of Christ, *giving Thanks to God, even the Father, by Him*; that *God in* all *things may be* glorified, *through Jesus Christ*, 1 Pet. iv. 11; or, as 'tis expressed, *Tit.* ii. 10. that ye may adorn *the Doctrine of God our Saviour in all things.* To *adorn* the Doctrine of God; is, by your Practise to cause it to appear *lovely* and *beneficial* to mankind; to show how *glorious* 'tis in its Effects, and how *worthy* to be embraced, and practised by all men. This is what the Scripture elsewhere calls, glorifying *the* word *of the Lord*, Acts xiii. 48; *glorifying it*, and causing it to *have its* free course; so St *Paul* explains it, 2 *Th.* iii. 1. 'Tis promoting the interest of Religion and Virtue, and the general Salvation of Men; 'Tis spreading the *Knowledge* of God, and bringing men over to the *Obedience* of his Commands, in order to their becoming capable of being Partakers of his *Happiness.* Which *Happiness and Perfection* of rational Creatures, being the great *End and Design* of God's Creation, and what both Nature and Scripture calls the Kingdom *of God*; therefore whatever tends to the promoting of Virtue and True Religion in the World, is promoting the Honour and the Glory of God. When Many of the Jews, convinced by our Saviour's Miracles, embraced the Truth of his Doctrine: the Scripture thus expresses it, *Mat.* xv. 31. that they glorified *the God of Israel.* When our Saviour promises his Disciples, for the further confirmation and establishment of their Faith, that God would certainly grant them the Petitions they should rightly put up in his Name; he does it in the following manner, *that the Father*, says he, *may be* glorified *in the Son*, Joh. xiv. 13. In the 21st chapter of the same Gospel, *ver.* 19; because the Testimony and the Sufferings of the Martyrs, are one of the principal Means of propagating the True Religion, therefore our Saviour's foretelling in what manner St *Peter* should *die*, is by the Evangelist thus exprest, that our Lord *signified by what*

Death

Death Peter fhould glorify God. For the fame reafon, the Spreading of the Knowledge of the True God, among the Nations of the World, is by the Prophet called, *fetting his* Glory *among the Heathen*, Ezek. xxxix. 21. And becaufe Nothing does This
more effectually, than the virtuous *Lives*, and good *Examples* of thofe who profefs the
Truth; therefore the Apoftle tells the *Corinthians*, (2 Cor. iv. 15.) that *the abundant
grace* which was in them, did *thro' the thankfgiving of Many, redound to the* Glory of
God. And our Saviour, exhorting his Difciples to be bright Examples of Virtue to the
World, does it in this manner, (Matt. v. 16.) *Let your Light*, fays he, *fo fhine before
Men, that they may fee your good works, and* glory *your Father which is in Heaven*.

A L L that has been faid upon This Head concerning the *Glory of God*, is ftill further
confirmed by the confideration of the Contrary, what is meant by the *Difhonour of God*.
Literally and ftrictly fpeaking, 'tis evident God *cannot be difhonoured*, becaufe his effential *Honour* or Glory is *immutable*. But as the *promoting of Virtue and Righteoufnefs*, is
glorifying God; fo the bringing any *Reproach* upon *Religion and Goodnefs*, is *difhonour-
ing of God*, who is the Author of true Religion and the Fountain of Goodnefs. Thus,
under the *Old* Teftament, the Wickednefs of *Eli's* Sons, [1 *Sam.* ii. 17.] caufed *men to
abhor the offering of the Lord*. And the Sin of *David*, (2 *Sam.* xii. 14.) gave *great
occafion to the Enemies of the Lord to blafpheme*. Upon This ground, *Nehemiah* thus
exhorts the Jews at their return from the captivity, (ch. v. 9.) *Ought ye not to walk in
the Fear of our God, becaufe of the* Reproach *of the Heathen our Enemies?* And God
complains by the Prophet *Ifaiah*, ch. lii. 5. *They that rule over* my people, opprefs
them, *faith the Lord, and* my Name *continually every day is* blafphemed. And again,
by *Ezekiel*, ch. xxxvi. 20. *When they entered unto the Heathen whither they went, they*
profaned my Holy Name, *when they faid, Thefe are the people of the Lord*.

I N the *New* Teftament, the fame Argument is urged by St *Paul*, *Rom.* ii. 23.
Through breaking the Law, difhonoureft thou God? For the Name of God is blafphemed
among the Gentiles, through You, as it is written. And in his *particular Directions* to
perfons in *particular Stations*, his exhortation to *young* women is, that by fober converfation they *give none occafion to the Adverfary to fpeak reproachfully*, 1 Tim. v. 14:
and that they be *chafte* and *difcreet, that the word of God be not blafphemed*: Tit. ii. 5.
And to *young* men, *ver.* 8. that by their *uncorruptnefs, gravity* and *fincerity,——he
that is of the contrary part may be afhamed, having no evil thing to fay of them*. And
to *Servants*, that they behave themfelves well towards their Mafters, *that the Name of
God and his Doctrine be not blafphemed*, (1 Tim. vi. 1.)

T H U S have I briefly explained what is in Scripture meant by This phrafe, *The
Glory of God*, and our *giving glory* to him. 'Tis promoting the intereft of *True Virtue
and Righteoufnefs* in the World. For as the natural *Kingdom of God* over the *inanimate*
Creation, confifts in his Exercife of *Power and Wifdom*; fo the fpiritual *Kingdom of God*
over the *rational* World, confifts in the *Obedience of the Wills* of reafonable Creatures to
the *moral and eternal Laws of Righteoufnefs*: And the *Glory of God*, as of *every Good
Governour in Proportion*, is the *Goodnefs and Happinefs of his Subjects*. When therefore we fay that God *does every thing for his own Glory*, and that This is his *Ultimate
End*; the meaning is, that his Defign in all things is the final eftablifhment of his
Kingdom of univerfal *Righteoufnefs* in the whole Creation. And accordingly when a
Man does any Action *becaufe it is good and right*, or forbears it *becaufe it is evil and
immoral*; *then* only, and not when he acts upon any *enthufiaftick* principles, does he
truly *intend the Glory of God*.

T H I S in *General*. I fhould now have proceeded in the 2d place, to fhow *more par-
ticularly*, what it is that is required of men in Practife, in order to their fatisfying the
Precept in the Text, *Whether ye eat or drink, or whatfoever ye do, do all to the Glory of
God*. But This, hereafter.

SERMON XIX.

Of the GLORY of GOD.

1 COR. X. 31.

Whether therefore ye eat or drink, or whatsoever ye do, do all to the Glory of God.

SERM.
XIX.
IN Discoursing upon these words, I have proposed to consider, *1st*, what is the True Meaning, and full Intent, of that Phrase which we so often meet with in Scripture, *The Glory of God* : And *2dly*, What it is, that is required of Men in Practice, in order to their satisfying the Precept in the Text.

I. As to This Phrase, which we so often meet withal in Scripture, *The Glory of God*; I have shown, that it denotes, in its *1st* and original Signification, the *Essence*, the *Person*, or the *Majesty* of God; that is, *God Himself*, who is the *Fountain of Glory*. *2dly*, It signifies the *Manifestation* of God's Perfections or Attributes, in the *external Exercise* of them towards his *Creatures*. And from hence, *3dly*, on the *other* side, the *Return* or *Acknowledgment*, which *Creatures* make again to *God*, for *His* manifestations of his Goodness to *Them*, is likewise in Scripture stiled, *The Glory of God*, or *Their* giving *Glory to Him*.

Thus far I have *already* proceeded *in general*. That which *Now* remains, is,

II. To consider distinctly and *particularly*, in the several Cases and Circumstances of Life, *what* it is that is required of men in Practise, in order to their satisfying the Precept in the Text; *whether ye eat or drink, or whatsoever ye do, do all to the Glory of God.*

And *1st*, He who will in all things promote the *Glory of God*, must in the first place show forth the Sense he has of God upon his Mind, by *Acts immediately and directly religious*; by *such* Acts, as are *Professed Acknowledgments* of our own Dependence upon God, and *exemplary* to provoke other men, (as the Apostle elegantly expresses it, *Heb.* x. 24.) *unto Love and to good Works*. Of this Kind, are *publick Prayer* and *Thanksgiving* : Ps. cvii. 31. *O that men would therefore praise the Lord for his Goodness, and* declare *the Wonders that he doth for the Children of Men ! That they would exalt him also in the Congregation of the people, and praise him in the Seat of the Elders !* By this *publick* Worship of God, are made the properest *Expressions* of the Sense we have of our Dependence upon him; and by this manner of Expressing it, is That *Sense itself*, the Sense of God and of Religion upon the Minds of Men, most effectually kept up and preserved. Very emphatical is the Description St *John* gives us, of the whole Universe joining, in their several Capacities, to give *Glory* in This manner to their Common Lord : *Rev.* v. 13. *Every Creature, which is in Heaven, and on the Earth, and under the Earth, and such as are in the Sea, and All that are in them heard I, saying, Blessing, and Honour, and Glory, and Power, be unto him that sitteth upon the Throne.*

2dly, He who, according to the Direction in the Text, will do all things to the *Glory of God*; as he must be constant in *Acts immediately and directly religious*, so he

must

muſt reſolve againſt being at Any time guilty of *Any Action* which is *directly irreli-* S E R M.
gious. Of this Kind, is *every deliberate Sin,* every Act which is *againſt a man's own*   XIX.
Conſcience, every *known Tranſgreſſion of a Commandment.* Which things, whoſoever is at
any time guilty of; far from *doing all to the Glory of God,* he on the contrary, as much
as in him lies, *diſhonours* and reproaches him. For wilful Sin, ſinning *preſumptuouſly* or
with a high hand, (as the Scripture expreſſes it;) is in the Nature of Things a *Diſho-*
nour to God : *Rom.* ii. 23. *Thou that makeſt thy boaſt of the Law, through breaking the*
Law diſhonoureſt *thou God?* 'Tis *reproaching* the Lord; or contending, in effect, that
his Commandments are not wiſe, juſt, and good : *Num.* xv. 30. *The Soul that doth*
ought preſumptuouſly, the ſame reproacheth *the Lord, and that Soul ſhall be cut off from*
among his people. 'Tis caſting *Contempt* upon his Laws; *Iſ.* v. 24. They have caſt
away *the Law of the Lord of Hoſts, and* deſpiſed *the word of the Holy One of Iſrael.*
'Tis *defying* his *Power*; 1 *Cor.* x. 22. *Do we* provoke *the Lord to jealouſy? are we*
ſtronger *than He?* In a word; 'tis profeſſing that we know better what is right and fit
for us *ourſelves,* than *he* can judge for us; and therefore that *we will not have* Him *to*
reign over us. This is the caſe of preſumptuous Sins; of all Actions, known to be
directly and in their own nature *irreligious.*

  B U T, not only by Actions *intrinſically* and *in their own* Nature immoral, is God
diſhonoured; but alſo by every thing, which in its *Circumſtances* is Evil; by every Act,
which either the *Perſon who commits* it, *judges* to be unlawful: or which needleſly
gives *Offence to Others,* and becomes to *Them* the Cauſe or the Occaſion of Sin. For,
the Kingdom of God conſiſting in the Prevalency of univerſal Righteouſneſs, Sincerity,
and Truth; it follows, that not only by the Practiſe of whatever is *intrinſically immo-*
ral, but alſo by whatever *wounds and defiles the conſcience* either of him who does the
Action, or of Others who by the Example of it are led into the Commiſſion of what
to Them is Sin; by *every ſuch thing* is God's Kingdom of Righteouſneſs diminiſhed,
and the Dominion of Virtue over the Hearts and Wills of Men, (which is the *Glory*
and the *Delight* of God) is weakened and impaired. For whoever does any thing with
a Senſe or Judgment in his own mind of its being unlawful when he does it; however
otherwiſe the Act might poſſibly have been innocent in its own Nature; yet he ſins at
That time againſt his own *Conſcience,* and conſequently againſt *God.* And whoever
does any thing with a probable Knowledge or Expectation, that his doing it will be a
means of deceiving or tempting his *Neighbour* into Sin; however otherwiſe the Action
might have been not only innocent *in itſelf,* but innocent alſo to *Him,* becauſe he
knew it to be ſo; yet in This caſe, by Uncharitableneſs, he ſins againſt his *Brother,*
and conſequently againſt *God.* For, ſince the promoting of Virtue and Goodneſs in
the World, is the moſt important of all things; it becomes us at all times, and in all
our Actions, to look upon it as our main End. And though the *Perverſeneſs* of *mali-*
cious perſons, who are apt to *miſrepreſent* things, is by no means an Obligation upon
any Good man, to forbear doing any thing that he *himſelf* knows to be innocent; yet
the *Weakneſs of ſincere* and *well-meaning* perſons, who by relying upon *His* Example,
might be led to do what would in *Them* be Sin, is a very ſtrong reaſon, (unleſs he has
otherwiſe ſome *Great* Occaſion or Neceſſity of Acting,) it is (I ſay) in point of *Cha-*
rity a very ſtrong reaſon, why he ſhould forbear doing that which would be ſo hurtful
to *Them.* Where the thing that gives Offence to Others, and either drives or leads
them into Sin is ſuch, as not only upon account of this *Circumſtance* or *Conſequence,*
but *intrinſically* alſo and *in its own Nature* is *unlawful*; there the Scripture denounces
againſt the Offender the utmoſt *Severity* of Woe, as againſt a preſumptuous Diſho-
nourer of God : *Matt.* xviii. 6. *Whoſo ſhall* offend *one of theſe little ones that believe in*
Me, it were better for him that a milſtone were hanged about his Neck, and that he
were drowned in the Depth of the Sea : Woe unto the World, becauſe of Offences; for it

I   *muſt*

muſt needs be that Offences come, but Woe to that man by whom the Offence cometh. But where the thing done is innocent in itſelf, and only by accidental *conſequence* proves an occaſion of Sin to Others; yet even There, he who foreſees this conſequence and takes not care to prevent it; is in Scripture charged with *Uncharitableneſs* towards the Soul of his *Brother,* if it be a *Fellow-chriſtian* whom he ſo cauſes to offend; or with want of true Concern for the *Glory of God,* if the Offence be given to an *Unbeliever.*

A s to the Caſe of *Unbelievers*; the Apoſtles thus exhort, 1 *Pet.* ii. 12. *Have your converſation honeſt among the Gentiles; that——they may by your good works which they ſhall behold, glorify God in the day of Viſitation.* Again, 2 *Cor.* viii. 21. *Provide for honeſt things,* (that is, things of *good reputation,* as well as lawful,) *not only in the ſight of the Lord, but alſo in the ſight of men. Abſtain from all* Appearance *of Evil,* 1 *Th.* v. 22. *Provide things honeſt,* that is, reputable, *in the ſight of all men,* Rom. xii. 17. *Walk honeſtly towards them that are without,* 1 *Th.* iv. 12. *Honeſtly,* that is, *wiſely, circumſpectly,* ſo as to afford them *no Objection againſt your religion;* Thus the ſame Apoſtle explains himſelf, *Col.* iv. 5. *Walk in* Wiſdom *towards them that are without.*

A s to the caſe of *Fellow-chriſtians*; how the *Glory of God* is to be promoted, by our behaviour towards *Them*; by our taking care to avoid even ſuch *innocent* things, as we ſee likely to lead any of *Them* into Sin, and may be forborn without any *great* inconvenience to *Ourſelves*; the Apoſtle explains himſelf at large, by putting a particular and very remarkable inſtance, in the *chapter whereof my Text is a part*; and in the *eighth chapter of this Epiſtle,* and in the *fourteenth chapter to the* Romans.

T h e Caſe he puts, is, whether it was lawful for Chriſtians to eat of ſuch meats, as the Heathen had ſacrificed to their Idols. In the *preſent chapter,* whereof my Text is a part, he thus reſolves the queſtion, *ver.* 25, 27. *Whatſoever is ſold in the ſhambles, or ſet before you at a friend's houſe, That eat, asking no queſtion for conſcience ſake*; i. e. Care not, whether the Heathens have ſuperſtitiouſly offered it to their Idols, or not; *For the Earth is the Lord's, and the Fulneſs thereof*; ver. 26. The Meaning is; *God* made *all* things, and every creature of His is good, if it be received with Thankſgiving; nor can any man's Folly and Superſtition make That to be *unclean,* which God has made *clean* to us. *But if any man ſay unto you, This is offered in ſacrifice unto Idols,* ver. 28. *then eat* not, *for his ſake that ſhewed it*; that is, *forbear* Then, *out of charity to* Him, leaſt *Your* Liberty cauſe *Him* to ſtrain his Conſcience, and ſo fall into Sin. And then he ſums up all in the words of the Text, *Whether therefore ye eat or drink, or whatſoever ye do, do all to the Glory of God: Give none Offence, neither to the Jews, nor to the Gentiles, nor to the Church of God.*

I n the *eighth chapter* of this epiſtle, he again propoſes and reſolves the *ſame* queſtion: Ver. 4. *As concerning the eating things offered in Sacrifice unto Idols, we know that an Idol is nothing in the World, and that there is none Other God but One. Howbeit,* ſaith he, ver. 7. *there is not in every man That knowledge: For ſome with conſcience of the Idol unto this hour, eat it* as *a thing offered unto an Idol; and their Conſcience, being weak, is defiled.* Wherefore, though in reality, and to a man of underſtanding, the good creatures of God are not at all the worſe, for having by other mens vain and ſenſeleſs ſuperſtition been offered to an Idol; yet *take heed,* ſays the Apoſtle, ver. 9. *leſt by any means this Liberty of yours become a ſtumbling-block to them that are weak: For if any man ſee Thee which haſt knowledge, ſit at meat in the Idols temple, ſhall not the conſcience of him that is weak, be emboldened,* (in the original it is expreſſed very emphatically, *ſhall he not be* edified,) *to eat thoſe things which are offered to Idols?* And *through* Thy *knowledge, ſhall the weak Brother periſh, for whom Chriſt died.* And then he concludes, *ver.* 12. *When ye ſin ſo againſt the Brethren, and wound their weak conſcience, ye ſin againſt Chriſt: Wherefore if Meat make my Brother to offend, I will eat no meat while the World ſtandeth, leſt I make my Brother to offend.*

I

Laſtly,

Laſtly, T H E *ſame* queſtion he again determines, in the *fourteenth chapter* to the S E R M. *Romans: I know*, ſaith he, ver. 14. *and am perſwaded by the Lord Jeſus, that there is*   XIX. *nothing unclean of itſelf*; *but to him that* eſteemeth *any thing to be unclean, to Him it is unclean: But if thy Brother be grieved with thy meat, Now thou walkeſt not* charitably :——*All things indeed are pure, but 'tis evil for that man who eateth with offence: It is good* therefore, *neither to eat fleſh, nor to drink wine, nor any thing whereby thy Brother ſtumbleth, or is made weak: Haſt thou Faith? have it to thyſelf before God.* His meaning, in theſe *laſt* words, is; not, (as ſome have wickedly perverted the words,) that provided a man has right notions of religion *himſelf*, he need not openly own and profeſs them before *Others:* But his meaning is, that in things of an *indifferent* nature, (of *which only* he was here ſpeaking,) men of underſtanding had better keep *to themſelves* their lawful Liberty, than run the hazard of incouraging *others* to venture further than their conſciences will innocently permit them. *Haſt thou Faith?* i. e. haſt thou *aſſurance* of the innocency of what thou doſt? *have it to thyſelf before God.*

T H E Sum is This: To *do* any *Evil Action*, that *Good* may come of it, is *not lawful:* But to *forbear* any *innocent* action, when ſuch forbearance is the likelieſt means to prevent another man's falling into Sin, is both *lawful* and *commendable.* Nay, the acting otherwiſe, is, in ſuch caſe, *Uncharitableneſs* towards our Brother: *Rom.* xiv. 15. *If thy Brother be* grieved *with thy Meat, Now walkeſt thou* not charitably.

To apply this to *Other* caſes. We affirm, and with great reaſon, that ſuch Uſe of *Images* in religious Worſhip, as the Church of *Rome* injoins, is *direct Idolatry.* But ſuppoſe it were *not*; yet, ſo long as the generality of the people cannot poſſibly pray otherwiſe amongſt them, than *with* Conſcience *of the Idol*, as St *Paul* expreſſes himſelf, 1 *Cor.* viii. 7. 'twould be the greateſt Injuſtice in the world, for *Them* to cauſe their Brethren to periſh, for whom Chriſt died; by impoſing upon them needleſly, and without warrant of Scripture, ſo manifeſt a ſtumbling-block, and ſo evident a cauſe of falling into Sin. And the like may be ſaid in proportion, concerning the Violent and Obſtinate Impoſition of *any* dubious doctrine, or *any* dangerous Ceremony, beyond the original Plainneſs and Simplicity of the Goſpel. 'Tis chuſing to hazard the Salvation of Men, and to cauſe Diviſions and Strifes, and unneceſſary Difficulties of Conſcience among the Servants of Chriſt, for the ſake of Pride and Vanity and Love of Dominion over men. Whoever is ſincerely deſirous to *do all things to the Glory of God*; as he will be heartily ſorry for all his *own* Sins and Offences, ſo he will really endeavour, as much as in him lies, to prevent the Sins of *Others*; He will avoid every thing, that may lead them into Sin; he will ſet them an example of Virtue, in the Practice of his own life; he will recommend to them in his Diſcourſe, upon all fair and proper occaſions, the excellency and the reaſonableneſs of Religion; he will rejoice and be truly pleaſed, to ſee Virtue, Righteouſneſs, and univerſal Charity, and Good-will, prevail and proſper in the World; he will lead no man into Error, nor be eaſy to ſee any man continue in it; but will wiſh with *Moſes*, that *all* the Lord's people were Prophets; and contribute, as much as in him lies, towards enabling them to be ſo. And, if he be in Power or Authority, he will deſire not to grieve or burden the Conſciences of Men; but will eſteem it of much more importance to unite Chriſtians in the plain Simplicity of the Goſpel, and in the bonds of Righteouſneſs and true Charity; than to eſtabliſh for Himſelf Any Power or Dominion over the Conſciences of his Brethren, either by preſumptuouſly claiming to himſelf a falſe *ſpiritual* Authority which Chriſt has not given him, or antichriſtianly and atheiſtically making uſe of *Temporal Power* to compel or awe men in matters of *Religion.*

T H U S have I briefly explained the Two *Primary* and Great Inſtances, wherein conſiſts a man's *doing All things to the Glory of God.* It implies *firſt*, that he regularly ſhow forth the Senſe he has of God upon his Mind, by *Acts immediately and directly*

SERM. *religious*; and 2*dly*, that he refolves againſt being *at* Any *time* guilty of Any *Aƈtion*
XIX. which is *direƈtly* Irreligious. But further,

     3*dly*, I N all *great* Aƈtions, Aƈtions of *moment and conſequence* in the main courſe of
a man's life; although they be *not* ſuch, as have any direƈt *relation to* Religion; yet
ought he *expreſly* to *intend* the *Glory of God*, as his chief *and* main *end*. He ought
to intend the *Glory of God*; that is, the promoting of *Truth and Right, of Juſtice and
Goodneſs* in the World. For whatever is *Therefore* choſen, *becauſe* it tends to the promoting of *Virtue and Goodneſs*, is (in the Scripture-ſenſe) done *for the Glory of God :*
And whatever is *for That reaſon* avoided, *becauſe* it has, in any manner, a *Tendency to
Evil*; is avoided *for the Glory of God*. Now there is no *conſiderable* Aƈtion in any
man's Life, no Aƈtion of *conſequence* and *importance* in the World; but which, even
though it has *not any* direƈt *relation to* Religion, yet ſome way or other has in the
whole a Tendency, to promote the Cauſe either of Virtue or of Vice. Such is, for inſtance, a man's chooſing his *Profeſſion*, imployment, or manner of Life in the World.
Whatever Profeſſion, though *not* in itſelf direƈtly *unlawful*, yet leads men needleſsly
into many and ſtrong *Temptations* to Sin ; will always, if poſſible, and if he is not under any *preſſing* neceſſity, be avoided by a Man who is ſincerely deſirous to do all things
to the Glory of God. Every *innocent* Profeſſion, may *equally* and *indiƈerently* be choſen
by any good Man; But yet, even in *That* Choice, his *main and ultimate* End, will be
the Exerciſe of Right and Truth, and the mutual comfortable Support of Men, in
Juſtice, Faithfulneſs and Charity. Profit, Power, Credit, Reputation, and the like,
may very innocently, and very juſtly be aimed at, by Men in Any buſineſs or imployment whatſoever : But theſe things muſt Always be deſired, with a due Subordination
to the Intereſt of Virtue; which is the *Glory of God*, and the only true and final *Happineſs* of *Men*. Whoever, in the Great *Lines* and main *Courſe* of his Life, aims merely
or principally at worldly and temporal Ends; in the attainment of Thoſe Ends, he *has
his Reward*.

     4*thly* and *Laſtly*; As in all *Great* Aƈtions, a good Chriſtian ought aƈtually ; ſo in all
even the *ſmalleſt* and moſt *inconſiderable* Aƈtions of Life, he ought habitually to intend
the *Glory of God*. *Whether ye eat or drink, or whatſoever ye do, do all to the Glory of
God*. The Scripture repreſents all, even *irrational* and the very *inanimate* creatures,
(*Pſ.* cxlviii. 2, &c.) *Beaſts and all cattle, worms and feathered fowls ; the Sun, the Moon
and Stars ; Mountains and all Hills, fruitful Trees and all Cedars ; Fire and Hail,
Snow and Vapours, Wind and Storms*; The Scripture, I ſay, repreſents even All *Theſe*
as *glorifying God*, becauſe they aƈt *regularly*, according to the *Nature* he has given
them, and by *his* Command. Much *more* then, may even the moſt *common* aƈtions of
Men, be juſtly ſaid to be *done to the glory of God* ; when they are done *decently and ſoberly, regularly and innocently* ; as becomes *Men*, and *Chriſtians*, and ſuch as have upon their minds, even when they are not direƈtly thinking of it, an *habitual* Regard to
God and Religion. In a *Journey* ; to a *diligent* Man, and one whoſe mind is really
bent upon his journey's End, *every thing* he does, as well as *aƈtual travelling*, tends
truly to the ſame End. His *Reſt* and *Sleep*, his *Stops* and *Refreſhments*, nay even his
very *Diverſions and Digreſſions*, ſtill tend uniformly, towards enabling him to arrive at
his intended Home. And thus likewiſe, in the courſe of a Religious Life; to a Man
truly and ſincerely Virtuous, every *Aƈtion* of his Life promotes the Honour of Religion,
which is the Glory of God; and every *thing* he does, is ſanƈtified by a Habit of Virtue : His *worldly buſineſs and imployment*, by *Juſtice and Charity* running uniformly
through all the parts of it; The *common* Aƈtions of his Life, by *decency and inoffenſive-
neſs* ; His very *Pleaſures and Diverſions*, by *Innocency and right Intention*. In a word;
whatſoever he is doing, he ſtill Always habitually *remembers the End*, *and* therefore he
never does amiſs, Eccluſ. vii. 36.

                                        III. T H E

III. The *Uſes*, which may be drawn by way of Inference from what has been ſaid, are :

1*ſt*, From hence we may learn how *ſevere* a Reproof thoſe perſons juſtly deſerve, who far from doing *all* things, as the Apoſtle directs, *to the Glory of God*; do, on the contrary, by *Profaneneſs, Unrighteouſneſs and Debauchery*, directly *diſhonour* Him whom they profeſs to ſerve ; bringing a *Reproach and Infamy* upon our moſt Holy Religion, and cauſing the Name of God and the Doctrine of Chriſt to be through *Their* means *blaſphemed* among Unbelievers.

2*dly*, Those deſerve in the *next* place to be rebuked ſharply, who, though they do not diſhonour God by Acts directly *irreligious*, yet are *careleſs and negligent* in matters of Religion ; not much regarding whether *Truth* or *Errour* prevails in the World ; nor being ſollicitous to do *honour* to their religion, and to promote the *ſpreading* of the Doctrine of Chriſt, by ſhowing the *reaſonableneſs* of it, by preſerving the Simplicity and *Purity* of it, and by exhibiting the *Beauty* of it to all Mankind.

3*dly*, After Theſe, are to be reproved ſuch as *have* indeed a *Zeal* for Religion, but *not according to Knowledge* ; placing the main Streſs of Religion in *Forms* and *Ceremonies* unworthy of God ; or in *Opinions* and *Notions*, which either through their *obſcurity and unintelligibleneſs*, or by their *diſagreeableneſs* to the *Everlaſting Goſpel, to natural Religion and to the Divine Perfections*, hinder, inſtead of promoting, the Glory of God.

4*thly*, Even the *Beſt* of Men have need to be admoniſhed, and to be *put in remembrance, that they* ſtir up *the Gift of God that is in them*, 2 Tim. i. 6. That they *purge* themſelves continually from every evil work, *that they may bring forth* more *fruit*, Joh. xv. 2. that they be *more and more diligent* in all their Actions, to do every thing to the Glory of God : Not with a ſuperſtitious Anxiety, or burdenſom Preciſeneſs, in things of little moment ; but with a cheerful Application of every thing that occurs in Life, to the promoting of Truth and Right, of Reaſon and Virtue among Men. Rejoicing in the Glory of God, and in the eſtabliſhment of his Kingdom of Righteouſneſs ; as That wherein conſiſts the Happineſs of the whole Creation, both in This World and in That which is to come.

Laſtly, From hence we may learn to comfort and ſatisfy the minds of ſome *weak* Chriſtians ; who, not having a right Notion *What* the Glory of God is, can never aſſure themſelves that they are *True* Promoters of it. They read that *Moſes* prayed to God to blot *Him* out of his book, if thereby the children of *Iſrael* might be ſaved ; and that St *Paul* even *wiſhed* Himſelf *accurſed from Chriſt*, if thereby the Nation of the *Jews* could be converted. And hence *ſome* have put the queſtion to *Themſelves*, and *others* have been ſo weak as to put it in their *Writings* ; whether a Chriſtian ought to be *content* to periſh finally, for the Glory of God. The queſtion is abſurd and contradictory ; and has *no* foundation in the Texts referred to. *Moſes*, and St *Paul*, in the circumſtances they were Then in, might charitably, and without any extravagancy, be willing to have born the *temporal* Curſe then coming upon the *Jews*, (which is all that their words mean ;) if thereby it could have been poſſible to have ſaved the whole Nation. But ſuch High Expreſſions of Affection are always well underſtood, in *all* books and in *all* languages, to have, not a literal, but a figurative Meaning. A *Chriſtian's* Duty, of doing all things to the *Glory of God*, ſignifies plainly *This only* ; that he ought always to prefer the Intereſt of *Religion and Virtue*, before all *Worldly conſiderations* whatſoever. Which that We may All do, *&c.*

SERMON

SERMON XX.

Of GOD's being the FATHER of Mankind.

MATT. XXIII. 9.

And call no man your Father upon the Earth; For One is your Father which is in Heaven.

SERM. XX.

IN the following Difcourfe upon thefe words, I fhall endeavour to fhow diftinctly, 1*ſt*, in what Senfe God is in Scripture ufually ftyled Our *Father*. 2*dly*, What we are to underftand, when we find it affirmed of him, that he *is in Heaven*. 3*dly*, What is meant, by *calling any man our Father upon the Earth*. And 4*thly*, Why we are forbidden to *call any man Father on the Earth*, upon account of there being *One which is our Father in Heaven*.

I. In the *Firſt* place; there are *two* Senfes, wherein God is in Scripture ufually ftiled our *Father*.

1. THE *firſt* is, as he is the *Father* or Author of *all things*, by originally *creating* or giving them Being. In *This* Senfe, the wifeft of the Antient *Philofophers* among the *Heathen*, ftyled God, *the Father of the Univerſe*. And the *Scripture* fometimes ufes expreffions of the fame Nature. Thus when St *Paul* had declared, 1 *Cor.* viii. 6. that *To Us there is but One God*; he immediately in the very next words gives a Defcription who That One God is, by adding, *the Father, of whom are all things*; that is to fay, *from* whom all things derive their exiftence, and are brought into Being by his Will and Power. The like manner of fpeaking we find again, *Eph.* iv. 6. *One God and Father of all, who is above all, and through all, and in all: Father of all*, that is, Author and Creator of all things. So the word is ufed in the *Creed*, when we declare we believe in God, *the Father Almighty*, or, *the Almighty Father*, the Maker of Heaven and Earth. And This is the utmoft latitude of fignification, to which the word can poffibly be extended: it reaching, in *This* fenfe, to things both *rational* and *irrational, animate* and *inanimate*; making God truly and properly, in the fulleft and moft literal Senfe, *the Father of the Univerſe*. But *more commonly*, the word is ufed in Scripture in a Senfe fomewhat more reftrained, with regard to rational and intelligent Beings; God being peculiarly ftiled Father, with refpect to Thefe to whom he has given *Life and Underſtanding*; but Creator *or* Maker only, with refpect to *inanimate* things, to whom he has communicated only *Simple Being*. Thus *Heb.* xii. 19. The *Father of Spirits:* And *Eph.* iii. 15. *The* Father;——*of whom the whole* Family *in Heaven and Earth is named. Father*, and *Family*, are relative Terms; And 'tis a noble Idea, which This Text gives us of God; reprefenting the *whole Univerſe* as the Houfe of God, framed and preferved by his Power; and all Orders of *intelligent* Beings, as the Family of God, under the Government of his Wifdom, Juftice, and Goodnefs, in their feveral and refpective Stations. In *This* fenfe, *Angels* are ftiled the *Sons of God*; Job xxxviii. 7. *The morningſtars fang together, and all the* Sons *of God ſhouted for joy*; that is, the *Angels* rejoiced and praifed God, at the time of the creation of the vifible World. And the fame Affembly,

bly,

4

bly, who are ftiled the *Hoft* of Heaven, 1 *Kings* xxii. 19. (*I faw the Lord fitting on his throne, and all the* Hoft of Heaven *ftanding by him on his right hand and on his left*;) are, in another defcription of the like vifion, called the *Sons of God,* Job i. 6. *There was a day when the* Sons of God *came to prefent themfelves before the Lord.* Again, *Dan.* iii. 25. *Nebuchadnezzar* faw *four men loofe, walking in the midft of the fire*; and *the Form of the Fourth,* fays he, *is like the Son of God*; or like a *Son of God,* that is, like *an Angel*; as the fame perfon is ftiled, *ver.* 28. of that chapter. Upon the fame account; namely, upon account of having received *Life* from the hands of God, *the Life of an intelligent and rational Being*; our firft Father *Adam* is called, *The Son of God,* Luke iii. 38. which was the Son of *Adam,* which was the Son of *God.* And *all mankind,* confidered as Creatures endued with Reafon and Underftanding; in oppofition to *Idols,* which have neither Underftanding, Senfe, nor Life; are faid to be *The Off-spring* of God, *Acts* xvii. 29. This therefore is the *firft* and original Senfe, wherein God is in Scripture ftiled our *Father.* It fignifies our deriving from him, our *Being* and our *Life.* *All* things are his *Creatures*; but *Intelligent* Beings only are his *Sons.*

2*dly,* Thus far, God is our *Father* by *Nature.* But 2*dly,* there is ftill a higher and more peculiar fenfe, wherein the Scripture reprefents God as being our *Father fpiritually,* by *religion and grace.* Concerning which St *Paul* thus fpeaks, *Rom.* viii. 15. *Ye have received the Spirit of Adoption, whereby we cry Abba, Father.* The true explication of which Notion, may (I think) rightly be fet forth in the following manner. As God is in *general* the Father of all *intelligent* and rational Beings, fo he is in a more *particular* and exalted manner the Father of Him, who in Scripture is ftiled *The Only-begotten Son*; the *Brightnefs of his* Father's *Glory, and the exprefs Image of his Perfon*; the *Image of the Invifible God, and the Firft-born of every Creature,* Col. i. 15. By the interpofition of this divine perfon, the only-begotten Son, *it pleafed the Father,* faith St *Paul, to reconcile all things unto himfelf,* Col. i. 19. *By Him,* faith he, *to reconcile all things,* ver. 20. *whether they be things in Earth, or things in Heaven.* The Meaning is: The whole World of rational Creatures being confidered as the *Family* of God, (according to that Text before-cited, which declares that *Of Him the whole* Family *in Heaven and in Earth is named*;) the government of this Houfe of God is reprefented by the Apoftle, as adminiftred by the only-begotten Son; whom the Father has *given to be the Head over all things,* that *he might gather together in One all things in Chrift,* Eph. i. 22. *both which are in Heaven and which are on Earth, even in Him,* Eph. i. 10. By *Sin,* men reject themfelves; and in the divine Juftice, are rejected out of This houfehold of God, and are no more worthy to be called his Sons. But by True Repentance and Amendment of Life, made available through the Interceffion of Chrift our great High-Prieft; they who *were fometimes alienated, and Enemies in their Minds by wicked Works,* are again *reconciled,* Col. i. 21. and, *Through Him have accefs* again *by one Spirit unto the Father*; and *are no more ftrangers and foreigners, but fellow-citizens with the Saints, and of the* Houfehold *of God,* Eph. ii. 18. This Reftoring of Sinners by Repentance and Reformation of Life, through the Mediation of Chrift, to the Favour of God, is elegantly ftiled by St *Paul, God our Father's* Adoption *of Children by Jefus Chrift to Himfelf,* Eph. i. 2, 5. The Effect of which reconciliation, to thofe who by the Practice of Virtue and Righteoufnefs, continue to live worthy of their moft Holy Calling; the Effect of it is, that *Chrift is not afhamed to call them Brethren,* Heb ii. 11. that *God himfelf* vouchfafes them the Denomination of *Sons,* 1 *Joh.* iii. 1. *Behold, what manner of Love the Father has beftowed upon us, that we fhould be called the Sons of God*; and that accordingly they have *accefs* with confidence to the Throne of Grace, as to a merciful and reconciled *Father*; *Gal.* iv. 5. Ye have *received the Adoption of Sons*; *And becaufe ye are Sons,* God *hath fent forth the Spirit of his Son into your heart, crying Abba, Father*; *wherefore thou art no more a Servant, but a Son.* In confequence of this State

S E R M. of Reconciliation, our Saviour in all his Difcourfes conftantly reprefents God, as having
XX.   the tender care and affection of a *Father* towards us : teaches us to acknowledge him
and look up to him as our Father, upon account of his continual *Providence* in preferving us ; his *Love*, in revealing himfelf to us by his Son ; his *Goodnefs*, in being ready
to affift us with his Spirit ; his *Mercy* in forgiving our Offences; his *Authority*, mixt
with the greateft *Patience*, in correcting us, not, as earthly parents, *after their own
pleafure, but for* Our *Profit*, Heb. xii. 10. And, to incourage us to pray to him, he
lays before us That moving and moft pathetick Argument, *Matt.* vii. 11. *If ye being
evil, know how to give good Gifts unto your children ; how much more fhall your Father
which is in Heaven, give good things to them that ask him?* In the Writings indeed of
Some Authors, God feems fometimes to be reprefented to us under a different character ;
as a *hard mafter, expecting to reap where he has not fown, and to gather where he has not
ftrawed.* But fuch reprefentations are confequences only of mens own private Opinions ;
and not taught, but *reproved*, in Scripture. For God *is* Love ; and he loves, and does
good to, all his Creatures ; and his tender mercies are over all his works. Only againft
wilful *wickednefs*, he is indeed irreconcileably fevere, and *unrighteoufnefs* is his abhorrence
and abomination.

     II. Having Thus, briefly explained what the Scripture means, when it ftyles God
our *Father*, I proceed now in the 2d place to fhow *what* we are to underftand, when
we find it affirmed of him that he *is in Heaven.* As if He who is equally in *all* places,
could be confined in *Any* ; or any proper Habitation could be afcribed to *Him*, whom
2 Kings viii. *the Heaven, and the Heaven of Heavens cannot contain*, If. lxvi. 1. *Thus faith the Lord,
27. The Heaven is my Throne, and the Earth is my Footftool ; Where is the Houfe that ye
build unto me? and Where is the place of my Reft?* The true meaning therefore, when
God is faid to *Be in Heaven*, is to exprefs his *Height and Dignity* ; not in *place*, but in
Dominion and *Power* : It being only a *fimilitude* drawn into common Speech, from the
fituation of things in Nature. As the Heavenly Bodies, the Sun and Stars, are High
above us in *place* ; and all Earthly Bleffings depend on the Sun and Rain and the Defcent of kindly Influences *literally from above* : fo, by an eafy *figure* of Speech, what-
foever is above us *in Power*, we are from hence ufed to reprefent as being above us *in
Place.* The Power and Dominion of the King of *Babylon*, is thus fet forth by the
Prophet *Ifaiah*, ch. xiv. 13. *Thou haft faid in thine Heart, I will afcend above the
Heights of the clouds, I will afcend into Heaven, I will exalt my Throne above the Stars
of God* : And the *Deftruction* of his Monarchy is defcribed after the like manner, ver. 12.
How art thou fallen from Heaven! Thus likewife our Saviour fpeaking of the *Pride*
and *Greatnefs* of *Capernaum* ; *And thou Capernaum*, fays he, *which art exalted unto
Heaven, fhalt be brought down to Hell*, Matt. xi. 23. And with Us *Now*, Men's being
High or *Low* in *Place*, is not meant to exprefs their *habitation* upon *Hills* or in *Vallies*,
but the Dignity of their Station in the World. The Greatnefs and Dignity of *our* Saviour's own Kingdom, is reprefented in Scripture, by his *fitting at the* right hand *of God
in the* heavenly *places* : We know that God has no Hands, nor any Shape or Figure ;
But the meaning of Chrift's fitting on his right Hand, is, his being exalted next to him
in Authority and Power. Thus therefore when we fpeak likewife of *God*, even the
invifible Father himfelf, as being *in Heaven* ; it muft always be underftood to exprefs
his *Supremacy*, not in *Place*, but in *Power and Dominion* ; that He is the High and
Holy One, Great and Glorious and Supreme above All.

     But there is alfo *another* reafon of this expreffion, of God's being *in Heaven* ; To
fignify, that tho' of his real actual *prefence* there is indeed no Confinement, yet of his
Glory and Majefty there is in That place a particular and extraordinary *Manifeftation*.
Thus the Archangel in the Book of *Tobit* reprefents it, ch. xii. 15. *I am* (faith he)
one of the Seven Holy Angels, which go in and out before the Glory *of the Holy One* ;
3   and

and the Salutation to the Churches, which begins the Book of the Revelation, is of the same Nature, ch. i. 4. *Grace be unto you and Peace, from him which is, and which was, and which is to come, and from the seven Spirits which are before his Throne.* The *real* and proper *Presence* of God is equally and necessarily in *All* places: But his *Throne*, his *Glory*, the place where the righteous shall see his *Face*, that is, a more particular glorious manifestation of his Power and Majesty; this, is in *Heaven*. In like manner here upon *Earth*; in places where God has been pleased more particularly to manifest his Glory, to place his Name There, to receive There the Homage of his Servants; in those places God in Scripture-Phrase is said to *Be*. Not as if at the same time he was not equally in all *other* places also: *For in Him we live and move and have our Being,* Acts xvii. 28. And as *Job* elegantly expresses it, ch. xxiii. 8. *Behold, I go forward, but he is not there; and backward, but I cannot perceive him; On the left hand, where he doth work, but I cannot behold him; he hideth himself on the* right *hand, that I cannot see him*: But the Meaning of God's being said to *Be* in *particular places*, is, that in those places he chose to *manifest* himself to his Servants, and to receive *Homage from* them. The Patriarch *Jacob*, concerning the place where he first saw the Vision of Angels, ascending and descending out of Heaven; *surely*, saith he, *the Lord is in this place*, Gen. xxviii. 16; *and it shall be the house of God*, ver. 22. In like manner in the Temple at *Jerusalem*, the *Glory* of God *appeared visibly*, 2 Chr. vii. 1. and There it also was, when it did *not* appear: And how He, whom the Heaven, and the Heaven of Heavens cannot contain, did thus at that time dwell on Earth, in a Temple made with hands, is in a lively manner expressed by *Solomon*, 1 Kings viii. 30. *Hearken thou to the Supplication of thy Servant, and of thy people Israel, when they shall pray in,* or *towards, this place; and hear thou in* Heaven *thy dwelling-place*: The meaning is; God, who is present in *every* place, had appointed in *That* place to receive his Tribute of Worship. Again; when the Lord appeared to *Moses* in the Bush; *the place*, says he, *whereon thou standest, is Holy Ground*, Exod. iii. 5. Not that *God* himself was present even Then in the Bush, any more than in all other places; but the place was made Holy, by God's manifesting his *Glory* there; For so St *Stephen* expresly tells us, Acts vii. 30. *There appeared to Moses an* Angel *of the Lord, in a flame of Fire in the Bush.*

In like manner, God is said in Scripture to *dwell in the* Hearts of good men: And that the *Bodies* of them which are sanctified, are *Temples* of the Holy Ghost; God dwelling in them *by* his Holy Spirit: Not by any Confinement of the *Presence* of God; but by his being pleased to show forth the *Power and Influences* of his Holy Spirit, in particular places, and to particular persons.

III. Having thus shown at large, what the Scripture means by stiling *God* our *Father*, and by affirming him to *be in Heaven*; I am in the 3d place to consider, what we are to understand by *calling any* man *our Father upon the Earth*. And this plainly appears in the Context, from the whole Scope and Design of our Saviour's discourse, in the directions he gives to his Disciples. *The Scribes and Pharisees*, says he, *sit in Moses's seat;—But do not ye after their work: For they—love greetings in the Markets, and to be called of men, Rabbi, Rabbi: But be not ye called Rabbi; for One is your Master, even Christ: And call no man your Father upon the Earth; for One is your Father, which is in Heaven: Neither be ye called Masters; for One is your Master, even Christ.* From whence it clearly appears, that *calling any man our Father upon Earth*, signifies paying to any Earthly Teacher, (not a due regard and attention, but) That *deference*, which the Scribes and the Pharisees were by our Saviour reproved for unjustly claiming. And the Deference or Regard they claimed, was, that men should follow them ignorantly and *implicitly*, in the Traditions they taught. In the Histories of the Antient *Jews* 'tis observed, that they frequently preferred the Traditions of their Rabbi's, even before the Writings of the Prophets themselves. And this Account of them we find confirmed in Scripture. God

complained

SERM. complained *of old* by the Prophet *Iſaiah*, ch. xxix. 13. *Their Fear towards me is taught*
XX. *by the Precept of men*; i. e. Humane Authority had *too much* weight among them, in
matters of Religion. In our *Saviour's time*, things were grown to a ſtill higher degree
of Corruption in this reſpect: *In vain*, ſays our Lord to the Phariſees, *do they worſhip*
God, *teaching for Doctrines the Commandments* (or Inventions) *of* Men, *Mar.* vii. 7.
For, laying aſide the Commandment of God, ye hold the Tradition of Men, ver. 8. And
he repeats it again in the next verſe; *Full well ye reject the Commandment of God, that*
ye may keep your own Tradition, ver. 9. *Making the word of God of none effect, through*
your Tradition which ye have delivered, ver 13. The Profeſſors of *Chriſtianity* itſelf
quickly began, even in the *earlieſt* times, to fall into ſome degrees of the ſame Fault; as
appears by the inſtructions St *Paul* gives to *Titus*, ch. i. 14. *Rebuke them ſharply, that*
they———may not give heed to———Fables and Commandments of Men. Some of theſe
Commandments of Men, he particularizes, *Col.* ii. 18. *Let no man beguile you of your*
reward, in a voluntary humility, and worſhipping of Angels, intruding into thoſe things
which he hath not ſeen, vainly puſt up by his fleſhly mind. In *after-times*, theſe *Com-*
mandments of Men (as is the nature of all Superſtition) continually multiplyed and
increaſed; according to the Apoſtle's Prophecy, 2. *Tim.* iv. 3. *The Time*, ſays he, *will*
come, when they will not endure ſound doctrine, (that is, they will not be content with
the Form of Sound words delivered by Chriſt and his Apoſtles;) *but after their own*
luſts ſhall heap up to themſelves Teachers.———and ſhall turn away their ears from the
Truth, and ſhall be turned unto Fables. And the only poſſible way to prevent this
Evil, is to conſider, that this aſſumed Authority *of Men* in matters of Faith, prevailed
from time to time more and more, till at length it ended in the eſtabliſhment of that
Kingdom of This World, which we call *Popiſh Religion.* And here I cannot omit to
obſerve, that the word *Pope*, the original of which is the old *Greek* word πάππα, ſignifies *Father*; and it ſignifies *Father* in that *very* ſenſe, wherein the Text forbids us
to *call any man Father upon Earth.* For by calling a man *Father*, here, our Saviour
plainly means *having regard to* humane *Authority in matters of Faith, or in Doctrines*
of Religion. Which thing is altogether inconſiſtent with true Chriſtianity; becauſe the
revealed Will of God, or whatever is *additional* to the law of Nature, is *at once* made
known to us *Whole* and *Entire* in the Writings of the Evangeliſts and Apoſtles. The
adhering immoveably to which Rule, the Law of Nature and of the Goſpel; is acknowledging that *One* only *is our Father, which is in Heaven*; and *one* only *our Maſter,*
which is Chriſt. All *we*, are *brethren* only; and have *no* Authority to *make* any doctrines
of Religion, but only to perſwade and earneſtly exhort men to practiſe what Chriſt has
already taught. The *Apoſtles themſelves*, did not take upon them to exceed their Maſter's inſtructions: Much *more* inexcuſable are vain men, who in *later* Ages have been
guilty of ſo great and high a preſumption. The Power which the Church of *Rome* has
aſſumed, of impoſing Doctrines of Faith, by the Authority of *Popes*, and of *general Coun-*
cils, and *Armies*, and *Inquiſitions*; is moſt elegantly deſcribed in Scripture under the character of a *man of Sin, ſitting in the Temple of God*; that is, in his Church; *exalting him-*
2 Theſſ. ii. 4. *ſelf above God, ſhowing himſelf that He is God, ſpeaking great words againſt the moſt*
Dan. vii. 25.
Rev. xiii. 8. *High*, and taking upon himſelf to *change Times and Laws*, and commanding *all the*
World to worſhip him; that is, impoſing upon men by Force, his own Religion. This
is the deſcription given us of the Church of *Rome*, in the Prophecies of *Scripture*; and
whoſoever *taketh from*, or *addeth to*, the *words of* that inſpired Rule, by endeavouring
to ſet up *any* humane Authority in matters of Faith; makes himſelf in proportion a partaker of the Sin, of that great Corruptneſs of the World.

IV. AND now, having ſufficiently explained what is meant by *calling any man Fa-*
ther upon the Earth; it will be very obvious to underſtand, in the 4th and laſt place,
how the *ground and reaſon* of this prohibition is aſſigned to be This, that *One is our*

Father.

Father which is in Heaven. For, our *Father in Heaven* having clearly, and fully, pre-
ſcribed to us the conditions of Salvation through Chriſt; It follows evidently that They
who *call* men *Fathers upon Earth,* that is, who of their own Fancies make *other* conditions of Salvation, thereby cauſing Diviſions and Contentions among their Brethren;
do in effect ſubvert all true Religion. For, *other Foundation can no man lay, than that*
which is laid, even Jeſus Chriſt; that is, the *doctrine* already taught, by *Chriſt Himſelf*
and his Apoſtles. If any man *departs from This* foundation, and teaches for doctrines
the Commandments of Men; he *forſakes the Fountain of Living waters, and hews him*
out ciſterns, broken ciſterns that can hold no water, Jer. ii. 13. Or, as St *Paul* expreſſes
it, *Col.* ii. 19. *not holding the Head, from which all the Body has nouriſhment miniſtred,*
his religion conſequently is vain. Or if *upon* this true Foundation, he *builds the Hay and*
Stubble of unintelligible Speculations, and doctrines uſeleſs in Practice, he at leaſt *loſes*
great part of his *Reward,* 1 *Cor.* iii. 12, 15. For *This* reaſon, it highly imports all
Chriſtians to *take heed* how *they hear,* Luk. viii. 18; and diligently to *ſearch the Scrip-*
tures, wherein are *the words of eternal Life.* And they who have Power and Influence
over *others,* can never too often recollect, how God complains by the Prophet, concerning the Shepherds of *Iſrael,* that *with Force and with Cruelty have ye ruled.* Ezek.
xxxiv. 4. and how our Saviour inſtructs *his* Diſciples, ſaying, *Ye know that the Princes*
of the Gentiles exerciſe Dominion over them, and they that are great, exerciſe Authority
upon them: But it ſhall not be ſo among you; but whoſoever will be great among you, let
him be your Miniſter; and whoſoever will be chief among you, let him be your Servant;
For even *the Son of Man* himſelf *came not to be miniſtred unto, but to miniſter, and to*
give his life a ranſom for many, Matt. xx. 25, 26, 28. The Head of the Church of
Rome profanely ridicules this Text, by ſtiling himſelf the *Servant of the Servants of*
Chriſt, at the ſame time that he imperiouſly impoſes upon their Faith his own Doctrines
and Creeds, and perſecutes them to death if they ſubmit not to *Him* and his general
Councils as *Fathers upon the Earth.* But the *True* Apoſtles of our Lord, did not *ſo*
learn Chriſt. We preach not ourſelves, ſaith St *Paul, but Chriſt Jeſus the Lord:* Neither *have we Dominion over your Faith, but are Helpers of your Joy,* 2 Cor. i. 24. Thus
ſpake the Apoſtles concerning *themſelves,* even though they were *inſpired* perſons, and
had a juſt claim to infallibility in Doctrine. How much *more* ought All, who have
no pretenſe to ſuch miraculous Gifts, to be of the ſame *meek* Spirit; following the Admonition of St *Peter,* 1 Pet. v. 3. *Feed the flock of God,——not as being* Lords *over*
God's heritage, but as being enſamples to the Flock: And That of St. *James,* ch. iii. 13.
Who is a wiſe man, and endued with knowledge amongſt you? let him ſhow, out of a good
converſation, his works with meekneſs *of Wiſdom;* and ver. 1. of the ſame chapter, *My*
Brethren, be not many Maſters: The word in the original, is, *many* Teachers; but our
Tranſlators very rightly render it, *Maſters;* becauſe the Apoſtle there ſpeaks of the very
ſame kind of haughty and imperious Teachers, againſt whoſe Practices our Saviour
warns his Diſciples in the Text, and in the words next following: *Be not ye called, Ma-*
ſters; for One is your Maſter, even Chriſt; and *call no man your Father upon the Earth:*
for One is your Father which is in Heaven. Which admonition, that *All* among us may
conſtantly attend to, both who *Teach* and *Hear* the Simplicity of the Goſpel; God of
his infinite mercy grant, *&c.*

Margin notes: S E R M.
XX.

1 Cor. iii. 11.

2 Cor. iv 5.

S E R M O N XXI.

Of being the CHILDREN of GOD.

ROM. VIII. 16, 17.

The Spirit itself beareth witness with our Spirit, that we are the Children of God : And if Children, then Heirs ; Heirs of God, and Joint-Heirs with Christ.

SERM.
XXI.

IN difcourfing upon thefe words of the Apoftle, I fhall endeavour to explain briefly 1*ft*, What is here meant by our being *Children of God.* 2*dly*, What is to be underftood, by our being ftiled *Heirs of God*, and *joint-heirs with Chrift.* And 3*dly*, How the *Spirit of God*, the *Spirit itfelf beareth witnefs with our Spirit*, if we be good Chriftians, that thefe Charaƈters do truly belong to us.

1*ft*, I AM to confider what is here meant by our being *children of God.* God is in Scripture ftiled, *The Father of All* ; Eph iv. 6. *One God and Father of All, who is above all, and through all, and in us all.* Here, the title *Father* is applied to him, in refpeƈt of his giving *Being* to all things, as they are his *Creatures* and the Work of his hands. For though inanimate or irrational creatures can in no Senfe be ftiled the *Children* of God ; yet God, confidered as the Author of All Being, may properly enough be ftiled *the Father of the Univerfe.* In a Senfe fomewhat more reftrained, and with regard to fuch Beings, to whom he has given *Life* and *Reafon* and *Moral* Faculties, God is ftiled the *Father, of whom the Whole Family in Heaven and Earth is named*, Eph. iii. 15. The *Whole Family* of *rational* creatures, *Angels* and *Men.* And Thefe in like manner, upon account of the *living* and *rational* nature he has given them, are frequently in Scripture ftiled *the Sons of God.* By *Sin*, Men forfeit the Benefit of this natural relation to God their Father, and become *Strangers* and *Aliens* and *without God* in the World ; being rejeƈted by him, and no longer looked upon as his Sons, but caft off as Objeƈts of his Wrath and Difpleafure. By *Repentance* and *renewed Obedience*, they who are effeƈtually convinced of the Folly and Unreafonablenefs of Sin, return, as far as in them lies, to their Father's houfe, and defire to have Accefs again to his Favour and Mercy. And God, by accepting their Repentance, and pardoning their paft Sins, according to the gracious Terms and Declarations of the Gofpel ; and giving them the affiftance of his Holy Spirit to fanƈtify them for the future ; receives them again, as a gracious Father, and *adopts* them for his Sons ; (in St *Paul's* language, gives them *the Spirit of Adoption, whereby they cry, Abba Father* ;) and they become again *Fellow-citizens with the Saints, and of the Houfhold of God.* This is what the Scripture elfewhere calls *Regeneration*, or the *New Birth* ; and fometimes, the *New Creation* ; Defcribing fuch perfons, as being in a fpiritual fenfe, Created anew *unto good works* ; and Born, *not of blood, nor of the Will of the Flefh, nor of the Will of Man, but of God*, Joh. i. 13. *Being* born again, *not of corruptible feed, but of incorruptible, by the word of God which liveth and abideth for ever*, 1 Pet. i. 23. *The God and Father of our Lord Jefus Chrift*, having, *according to his abundant mercy*, begotten us again *unto a lively*

hope,

hope, ver. 3. And the plain Meaning of all thefe figurative expreffions, is; that when a Sinner fincerely returns to a Senfe of his Duty, and effectually amends his Life; God, who confidereth whereof we are made, and remembreth that we are but Duft, pitieth him even as a *Father* pitieth his children; and, though in ftrictnefs of eftimation he be indeed no more worthy to be called his Son, yet, upon this his true Repentance, he receives him again to the Arms of his Mercy, and fays, *Rev.* xxi. 7, *I will be his God, and he fhall be my Son.* Anfwerable to which account of this relative character on *God*'s part, 'tis manifeft that the Title on *Our* part, of being *Children of God*, is expreffive of the higheft obligations of *Duty* and *Obedience*, and of our ftedfaftly perfevering in the practice of all *Virtue* and *Righteoufnefs.* The departing from which originally, as it caufed thofe who *by creation*, were naturally the Sons of God, to become Strangers and Enemies to him; fo by returning to it again, and by no other method whatfoever, can they, who through wicked works have been ftrangers and enemies to God, become again, through the divine Mercy, the Sons of God *by adoption*, and continue to preferve That character by their perfeverance therein. *In This, the children of God are manifeft, and the children of the Devil: Whofoever does not righteoufnefs, is not of God.*

H A V I N G thus explained briefly, what the Apoftle in the Text means, by ftiling us the *Children of God*; the next thing I propofed to confider, was

2. W H A T we are to underftand by the following characters; being *Heirs of God, and joint-heirs with Chrift: If children, then Heirs; heirs of God, and joint-heirs with Chrift.* The word, *children*, being a Title of Affection and Love, implies, when ufed in the *figurative* Senfe, an expectation of *favour*, and a dependance for *Support*, Gal. iv. 7. *Wherefore thou art no more a Servant, but a Son; And if a Son, then an Heir of God through Chrift.* The expreffion is exactly the fame with That in the Text; *We are the children of God, and, if children, then Heirs.* If the relation of *children* be acknowledged, the very Notion of that relation carries along with it in courfe a Promife, or Affurance of a Bleffing. And becaufe *God* is infinitely *more able* to provide for thofe who rely on *Him*, than *earthly Parents* are to make provifion for their natural Pofterity; and the portion of *God*'s children can by no poffible misfortune, by no Accident, by no Force, by no Fraud, be taken from them, unlefs by departing from the commandments of their Heavenly Father, they voluntarily caft themfelves out of *His* Favour. Therefore the inheritance of thofe *on whom the Father has beftowed fuch manner of love, that they fhould be called the Sons of God*, is in Scripture ftiled *a Kingdom which cannot be moved, the things which cannot be fhaken, a City which hath foundations, a continuing city, an inheritance among them that are fanctified, the inheritance of the Saints in Light, an inheritance incorruptible and undefiled that fadeth not away.* And God himfelf, in St *John*'s vifion, fpeaking from the throne of his glory, thus declares, *Rev.* xxi. 7. *He that overcometh, fhall inherit all things, and I will be his God, and he fhall be my Son.* Here the Title of *Son* or *Child of God*, being ufed as of the fame import with One that is to inherit *all things*, that is, all thofe things which God has promifed to them that love him; is exactly correfpondent to the Apoftle's manner of fpeaking in the Text, *If children, then* Heirs. And becaufe the Promife of God, who cannot lie, ftandeth always fure; fo that the Reward of Virtue, however at prefent diftant and invifible, is yet in reality as Certain in the determinations of the Divine Counfel, as if it was already actually in poffeffion; hence St *Paul*, carrying the fame figure ftill *Higher*, in his defcription of the Happinefs of thofe fincerely religious perfons, whom in the Text he ftiles Heirs *of God*, thus expreffes himfelf, *Eph.* ii. 5. *God hath quickned us together with Chrift, and hath raifed us up together, and made us fit,* (hath *already* made *us fit*) *together in heavenly places in Chrift Jefus.* And elfewhere he calls *them, fellow-citizens with the Saints, and of the houfhold of God:* And tells them

Heb. xii. 28.
27.
xi. 10, 13, 14

Acts xx. 32.
Col i. 12.
1 Pet. i. 3.

SERM them that they *are come*, (that they are already come) *unto Mount Sion, unto the City*
XXI. *of the living God, the heavenly Jerusalem*; and *to an innumerable company of Angels,*
and to the Spirits of just men made perfect, and to Jesus the Mediatour of the New Co-
venant, and to God the Judge of All.

THIS is the full meaning of that *Second* character, given in the Text to sincere
Christians; that they are *Heirs of God*; Heirs of his *Promises*, and *Kingdom*.

IT follows; *And Joint-Heirs with Christ: Heirs with God, and Joint-heirs with*
Christ. The sense of which expression is this. Though *Men*, as well as all superiour
rational Creatures, are originally by Creation the Children of God; and so long as they
continue to obey the Law of their Nature and the Commands of God, cannot fail
consequently to continue in his Favour; And though *Sinners*, when they sincerely repent and amend, have good and reasonable Grounds, from the consideration of God's
natural Perfections, to hope for Mercy and Compassion at his hands: Yet neither to
Sinners is God under any obligation of *Justice*, to restore them upon their Repentance
to the *same state of Favour* as if they had never sinned; nor even to the most *innocent*
and perfectly *Sinless* Creatures, (if any such there were,) is he under Any natural obligation to confer *Immortality*, and an *eternal Kingdom of Glory*. All, that *Justice* in
That case requires, is, to distinguish them according to their Deserts, in That rank of
the Creation wherein their natural Capacities placed them, and for such a Space of
Time as the original good pleasure of the Creator allotted them. The Being which
God freely gave, he may at any time without any injustice take away: And no Creature, even *without* consideration of *Sin*, has any more claim of Right to continue for
ever, or even for any limited time to be exalted above the natural improvement of its
original capacities, than it had any Right to be created *Before* it was, or to have been
made in Any *Higher* Species of Creatures. *Eternal Life* therefore, or the *Kingdom of*
Heaven, is the *Gift* of God; not due to Mankind by *Nature*; not a Claim of *Right*;
no, not even if they had continued Innocent; much less, to returning *Sinners*; but 'tis
the *Gift*, the *Free Gift* of God, originally in the State of *Innocence*; and to *Penitents*
still much more, is it merely a *Free Gift*, in and through *Christ*. *That which is born of*
the Flesh, is Flesh; and has no title, no claim of Right, *naturally*, to the *Spiritual*
Kingdom of God. But the Father has appointed unto his Son Jesus Christ a Kingdom,
and *I*, says our Lord to his Disciples, *appoint unto You a Kingdom, even as my Father*
appointed unto Me: That *whosoever overcometh*, (that is, whosoever prevails over the
sinful Temptations of the World,) may *sit down with Me in My Throne, even as I also*
overcame, and am sat down with my Father in His *Throne*. By *Nature*, we are only
in general the *Creatures* of the Almighty, and the *Works* of his Hands. By *Sin*, we
were become Objects of his *Wrath* and *Displeasure*. By obeying the gracious Terms
of the *Gospel of Christ*, we are *not only* restored again to the Favour of God, as of a
merciful and tender Father; but our nature is moreover *exalted* by him to some similitude with *His*, who was in a singular manner the *Son of God*, and yet condescended to
become our Elder Brother, by being made in the likeness of *Men*. *He* voluntarily became himself the *Son of* Man; and *as many as received him, to them gave he power*
that They *should become the* Sons of God. He has received them as *Joint Heirs* with
himself, in his Father's Kingdom; And God, even *the God and Father of our Lord Je-*
sus Christ, has begotten *them again* (as St Peter expresses it) *unto a lively hope*, (that
is, unto the Hope of eternal Life,) *by the resurrection of Christ from the dead*. He hath
caused them to be *conformed to the Image of his Son, that he might be the First-born*
among Many Brethren. And *for this cause*, saith St *Paul, Heb*. ii. 11. Christ *is not*
ashamed to call them brethren. Nay, the same Apostle, in a most elegant and lively
manner, carrying the same figure of speech still higher, *Eph*. v. 30. *We are members,*
says he, *of his Body, of his Flesh, and of his Bones*. Those who never had the Knowledge

ledge of the Gofpel, are God's children by *creation*; in fuch a fenfe as St *Luke* fays of S E R M. *Adam*, that he was the *Son of God*. And with regard to Thefe, the *Judge of the whole* XXI. *Earth will do what is Right*, and *with Equity fhall he judge the Nations*. But as to his *Free Gifts*, he is ftill always at liberty to do what he pleafes with his own : And in that Kingdom which he has appointed to his Son Jefus Chrift, he may appoint whom he himfelf thinks fit to fit on his right hand and on his left. He may *have mercy on whom he will have mercy, and compaffion on whom he will have compaffion*. The meaning is ; not that God will act arbitrarily and without Reafon ; as fome have abfurdly underftood thefe words : But that He, and He only, is the competent, proper, and unerring Judge, upon what Perfons, and on what Conditions, 'tis fit for him to beftow his Favours. And in and through Chrift, he may give power, upon what Terms and Conditions he pleafes, to fuch as fhall attain to thofe Conditions, to become in a *peculiar* manner the *Children of God*; and *if Children, then Heirs* ; *Heirs of God*, and *Joint-Heirs with Chrift*.

I T remains, in the

3d and laft place, T H A T I confider in what fenfe the Apoftle here affirms, that the *Spirit of God*, the *Spirit itfelf, beareth witnefs with Our Spirit*, if we be good Chriftians, that thefe Characters do truly belong to us. For the clearer explication of which affertion, I obferve

1ft, T H A T nothing can be more abfurd, nothing can be more contrary to the whole Tenour of the Gofpel, than the Notions of thofe men, who take their own *Enthufiaftick imaginations* to be the Teftimony of the Spirit of God. Such perfons judge not of the Tree, by its Fruit ; They compare not the Courfe of their Lives, with the Rule of God's Commandments ; They judge not of their being fpiritual perfons, or having the Spirit of Chrift, by their practice of thofe Virtues, which the Scripture calls *bringing forth the Fruits of the Spirit :* But they have a ftrong, confident Conceit, that they are the elect, the chofen people of God ; and the mere ftrength of this groundlefs imagination, they apprehend to be *the Spirit of God bearing witnefs with their Spirit, that they are the Children of God*. But This is fo fenfelefs a notion, fo manifeftly deftructive of all Virtue, and of all the true difference between Good and Evil ; that it needs barely be mentioned among perfons of common Underftanding, to expofe the Folly of it. Wherefore

2dly, I N the *Apoftles days*, the *miraculous Gifts* and *Graces of the Spirit*, made evident by their *real* and *vifible* Effects, as in That great Inftance of the Gift of Tongues beftowed as upon This day, were undeniable Teftimonies, of the Spirit of God being given to thofe perfons, in whom thofe Effects appeared. Not that all who were endued even with miraculous Gifts, were confequently good and fincere Chriftians : But thefe Gifts, to thofe who beheld them, were evident Atteftations of the Spirit, to the Truth of the *Gofpel :* And to the *Perfons themfelves*, on whom thofe Gifts were beftowed, if they were confcious in their own Hearts of their being fincere in their Profeffion, and virtuous in their Practice, then thefe Gifts were indeed *the Spirit of God bearing witnefs with Their Spirit, that they were the Children of God*. But

3dly, B O T H in the *Apoftles days*, and in *all fucceeding generations*, even to the end of the World ; the feveral *Declarations* which the Spirit of God hath made, by the *Prophets* in the *Old* Teftament, and by *Chrift and his Apoftles* in the *New* ; compared with the verdict of our own Confciences, concerning the agreeablenefs of our Actions to thofe declarations ; thefe are the Teftimony of *the Spirit itfelf bearing witnefs with our Spirit, that we are the Children of God*. The Promifes of God made to men in Chrift, and eftablifhed upon the Terms of the Gofpel, are reprefented in the *New Teftament* as being *Sealed*, or *confirmed by Covenant*, to us in Baptifm : And therefore, fpeaking concerning Baptized Converts, 2 *Cor*. i. 22. *God*, faith St *Paul, hath alfo* Sealed *us*, *and given the Earnest of the Spirit in our Hearts.* Confequently they who *make good* This obligation, by bringing forth the fruits of the Spirit in the fuitable Practice of a Virtuous Life; Thefe *have* the *Seal* or *Earnest* of the Spirit: 2 *Tim.* ii. 19. *The Foundation of God ftandeth fure, having This* Seal,——*Let every one that nameth the Name of Chrift, depart from iniquity:* And, *Grieve not the Holy Spirit of God, whereby ye are* Sealed *unto the day of Redemption.* The Teftimony of a good Confcience, is, in the language of the text, the *Witnefs of our* own *Spirit*; And the Agreement of this Teftimony of our own Confcience, with the Revealed Declarations of the Will of God, when carefully and duly compared together, is what the Apoftle here ftiles the *Spirit of God bearing witnefs with Our Spirit, that we are the Children of God.*

BY this *One* obfervation, the whole Difcourfe of the Apoftle in this chapter becomes very plain and intelligible: And at the fame time, by the *whole* tenour of his difcourfe in this chapter, is *this* clearly confirmed to be the true meaning of the Text. *Ver.* 1. *There is now,* fays he, *no condemnation to them which are in Chrift Jefus; who walk not after the Flefh, but after the Spirit:* That is, who are guilty of no debauchery or vicious Practices, but live in the regular practice of thofe moral virtues, which he elfewhere by name calls the *Fruits of the Spirit. For to be carnally* (that is, vicioufly) *minded,* (ver. 6.) *is death; but to be fpiritually* (that is, virtuoufly) *minded, is life and peace.* Ver. 8. *So then they that are in the Flefh,* (they that are under the power, and

Ver. 9. live in the practice of any known Sin,) *cannot pleafe God:* And *if any man have not the Spirit of Chrift,* (that is, if any man who profeffeth the Name of Chrift, yet *departeth not from iniquity,* which is the *Seal* upon which the *Foundation* or Covenant *of God ftandeth fure;* If any man in This fenfe *hath not the Spirit of Chrift,) he is none of his. For if ye live after the Flefh,* ver. 13. *ye fhall die; but if ye through the Spirit do mortify the deeds of the body, ye fhall live. For as many as are led by the Spirit of God,* (that is, as many as are prevailed upon by the Motives of the Gofpel to live anfwerably to their Holy profeffion,) *they are the Sons of God,* ver. 14. And that they *are* fo, they may certainly know, by thefe Fruits *of the Spirit* appearing in the whole courfe of their *lives,* compared with the Declarations *of the Spirit* made in the *Gofpel*; even as certainly as a Tree is known by its Fruit. For Thus, adds the Apoftle in the Text, *the Spirit itfelf beareth witnefs with our Spirit, that we are the Children of God; and if Children, then Heirs, Heirs of God, and Joint Heirs with Chrift; if fo be that we fuffer with him, that we may be alfo glorified together.*

THE reafon of his annexing thefe *laft* words concerning our *Suffering* with Chrift, is, becaufe in the whole Syftem of moral Virtues which are the Fruits of the Spirit, there is no one that affords a more certain Mark or Teftimony of Sincerity; there is no one, to which a man's own *Spirit* or Confcience beareth witnefs with more confidence, or to which All the Declarations of the *Spirit of* God bear witnefs with greater Clearnefs and Affurance; than to this virtue of Chufing to run the hazard of Suffering at any time for Truth and Righteoufnefs. 2 Tim. ii. 11. *It is a* faithful *Saying, If we be dead with him, we fhall alfo live with him; If we fuffer, we fhall alfo reign with him.*

1 Pet. iv. 13. Wherefore, *think it not ftrange,* —— faith St *Peter,* but *rejoice, in as much as ye are partakers of Chrift's Sufferings, that when his glory fhall be revealed, ye may be glad alfo with exceeding Joy.* In the Apoftles days, *Suffering for* or *with Chrift,* fignified being *perfecuted* for the Profeffion of *Chriftianity* in *general.* In later Ages, fince the religion of Chrift has in *Name* and *Form* been profeffed among the Nations, Perfecution has more frequently been brought upon men for adhering to fome *particular* Truths, and for oppofing fome *particular* Corruptions in practice. For, not only the Apoftles fuffered in *Their* days, but many alfo of the Beft men in *our* days; yea, *and All,* in *All* days, fays the Apoftle St *Paul, that will live godly in Chrift Jefus,* fhall *fuffer perfecution.* But whether they be perfecuted by *men,* or no; yet if by ftedfaftly refifting the

Temptations of Sin, they *be planted together* with Chrift *in the likenefs of his Death, they* S E R M.
fhall be alfo in the likenefs of his refurrection. Knowing this, that our old man is crucified XXI.
with him, that the Body of Sin might be deftroyed, that henceforth we fhould not ferve
Sin. Now if we be dead with Chrift, we believe that we fhall alfo live with him,
Rom. vi. 5, 6, 8. This is what the *Spirit of God* conftantly and uniformly declares and
teftifies, through the whole Scripture. And therefore they who by *thefe* declarations,
and by the confideration of *thefe* religious motives, are influenced to live in fuch manner,
as that they can fay with St *Paul, Our rejoicing is This, the teftimony of our confcience,*
that in Simplicity and godly Sincerity——we have had our converfation in the world;
Thefe, as often as they compare their *own* hearts and actions, with the things that *God*
has revealed unto us by his *Spirit*; have, according to the expreffion in the Text, the
Spirit of God bearing witnefs with Their *Spirit, that they are the Children of God.*

S E R M O N XXII.

Of Loving G O D.

MATT. XXII. 37, 38.

Jefus faid unto him, Thou fhalt love the Lord thy God, with all
thy Heart, and with all thy Soul, and with all thy Mind; This
is the Firft and Great Commandment.

IN thefe words there is obfervable; *1ft,* The *Duty* injoined; *Thou fhalt love the* S E R M.
Lord thy God: *2dly,* The *Circumftances* requifite, to make the performance of this XXII.
Duty *acceptable and complete;* Thou fhalt love him, *with all thy Heart, and with*
all *thy Soul, and with all thy Mind: 3dly,* The *Weight,* and *Importance,* of the Duty;
It is *the Firft and Great Commandment.*

I. THE Duty injoined, is, *Thou fhalt love the Lord thy God.* A Duty, in *every*
man's mouth, of *all* Religions, and in *all* Sects: But, upon *what* Ground *its Obligation*
is founded, and in *what* particulars the rational *Practice* of it confifts; is not fo clearly
and univerfally underftood. Men often talk very earneftly of *loving* God, while at the
fame time they in their doctrine reprefent him as the moft *hateful* Being in the Univerfe;
cruel and partial; arbitrary, and tyrannical; fhowing favour to fome, and making
others miferable, for no other reafon, but becaufe he has abfolute and irrefiftible Power.
But what fuch perfons fpeak concerning *loving* of God, is evidently nothing but *mere*
Forms of *empty words,* without *any meaning* or *fignification* at all; becaufe there is in
their Minds *no real Object, upon which* the Love they fpeak of can be fixt. And where
the *Root* thus is *rottennefs*; (to ufe the Prophet *Ifaiah's* Comparifon,) what wonder if
the *Bloffom,* and the *Fruit,* accordingly goes up as *Duft?* what wonder if the expreffions

S E R M. sions of their *Love* towards *God*, end in nothing but peevishness, contentiousness, and
XXII. perhaps *Hatred* towards their *Brethren*? A True *Love* of *God*, must be founded upon a
right Sense, of his *Perfections* being really *amiable* in *themselves*, and *beneficial* to *Us*:
And such a *Love* of *God*, will of Necessity show forth itself, in our endeavouring to
practise the *same* virtues ourselves, and exercise them towards *others*, which we profess
to *love* and admire in Him.

ALL *Perfection* is *in* itself lovely, and amiable in the very *nature* of the Thing:
The Virtues and Excellencies of *Men remote* in History, from whom we can receive *no
personal* Advantage, excite in us an *Esteem* whether we will or no: And every *good*
mind, when it reads or thinks upon the character of an *Angel*, loves the Idea, though
it has *no* present communication with the Subject, to whom so lovely a character belongs:
Much more, the inexhaustible Fountain of *All* Perfections; of Perfections without
number, and without limit; the Center, in which *All* Excellencies unite, in which
All Glory resides, and from which *every good thing* proceeds; cannot but be the Supreme Object of *Love*, to a reasonable and intelligent Mind. Even *supposing* we ourselves received no Benefit therefrom, yet infinite *Power, Knowledge, and Wisdom* in
conjunction, are lovely in the very *Idea*, and amiable even in the *abstract Imagination*.
But That which makes these Perfections most *truly and substantially*, most *really and
permanently*, the Object of our Love; is the *Application* of them to *ourselves*, and our
own more immediate *Concerns*; by the consideration of their being joined also with
those *relative and moral* Excellencies, which make them at the same time no less *beneficial* to Us, than they are excellent *absolutely in their* own Nature. Then is God the
Complete Object of Love, when together with the Notion of Infinite Power, Knowledge, and Wisdom, we consider him moreover as actually *governing the World*; and
when, in the *exercise* of that Dominion over us, we consider his *Truth and Faithfulness*, his *Justice and Impartiality*, his *Equity, Mercy, and Goodness* towards his Creatures; When we consider his Goodness in giving us *Being*, and a *Being so excellent*;
his *Care*, in making such plentiful Provision for our *temporal Preservation*, and for our
eternal Happiness; his Mercy, in sending his Son to redeem us from Death, and to
procure Pardon even for the *greatest* of Sinners upon their true Repentance: When we
consider *these* things, I say, *Then* is it that God truly appears the complete Object of
Love: For so our Saviour himself teaches us to argue; *Luke* vii. 47. To whom *much*
is forgiven, he will love the *more*; and the Apostle St *John*, 1 Joh. iv. 19. We (says
he) *love* Him, *because He first loved* Us.

THIS therefore is the true Ground *and* Foundation of our Love towards God. But
wherein this love towards God *consists*, and by what *Acts* it is most properly exercised,
has sometimes been very much misunderstood. Men of strong Passions and warm Imaginations, have been too apt to place it in a mere *Enthusiastick zeal of Affection*, a sort
of Scholastick Speculation, unintelligible and fruitless; seated in the *Fancy* only, instead
of the *Understanding*; and having no Effect upon the *Will*, or *Actions*, in the *general
course* of a Man's Life. By which means, they make the *Love of God*, a thing entirely
distinct from the *Love of Virtue and Righteousness*: Whereas the Scripture always speaks
of them as being One and *the same*; judging of Men constantly by that *never-failing*
Rule, of discerning the Tree by its Fruits; and always representing men to have just so
much *Love* towards *God* in their *Hearts*, as they pay *Obedience* to his *Laws* in their
Actions. The *only* Distinction found in Scripture, is, that our *Love of God*, is *sometimes*
used in a more *restrained* Sense, as distinguished from the *Love of our* Neighbour; and
then it signifies, that which is usually called our *Duty towards* God; worshipping the
True *God*, and *Him Only*, in opposition to all False *Gods*; and placing our *whole Faith
and Trust* in him accordingly. At *other* times 'tis used in a more *general* sense, as including our whole Duty *both* towards *God* and towards *Men*; righteousness towards

Men

4

Men being infeparable from a true Love towards *God* ; and it being impoffible that he S E R M. who loveth *God,* fhould not love his *Brother* alfo. But in *Both* thefe Senfes, whether XXII. it be underftood according to the more *limited* or the more *general* interpretation, it always fignifies a moral Virtue, not a *Paffion or Affection* ; and is therefore in Scripture always *with great* Care explained and *declared* to mean, the *Obedience of a virtuous Life,* in oppofition to the *Enthufiafm of a vain imagination.* In the *old* Teftament, *Mofes* in his *laft* exhortation to the *Ifraelites,* thus expreffes it ; *Deut.* x. 12. *And now Ifrael, what doth the Lord thy God require of thee, but to fear the Lord thy God, and to love him?* And *what is loving him?* why, he tells them in the very next words, 'tis *to walk in all his ways, and to ferve the Lord thy God with all thy heart and with all thy Soul, to keep the* Commandments *of the Lord, and his Statutes which I command thee this day for thy good.* In the *New Teftament,* our *Saviour* ftill more *diftinctly* expreffes the fame thing, inculcating and repeating it in fuch a manner, as fhows plainly his *Forefeeing* at that time, in his own mind, how apt men would be to mifunderftand it : *Joh.* xiv. 15, 21. *If ye* love *me,* faith he, keep *my Commandments* : *He that* hath *my Commandments, and* keepeth *them* ; he *it is that* loveth *me.* And in his prophecy concerning the Signs of the End of the World, he puts *Love towards God,* as the *oppofite* to *iniquity* ; thereby plainly declaring it to mean the *fame* as *Virtue* : Matt. xxiv. 12. *Becaufe* iniquity *fhall abound, the* Love, faith he, *of Many fhall wax cold.* And the beloved Difciple, who, as he leaned more nearly upon his Mafter's Breaft, fo he feems in this matter to have been more particularly infpired with his Mafter's Sentiments ; *Whofo,* fays he, keepeth *his word, in* Him, *verily is the Love of God perfected* ; 1 Joh ii. 5. *Hereby know we, that we Are in Him* : *For* This *is the Love of God, that we keep his Commandments,* 1 Joh. v. 3. And again, 2 *Joh.* vi. 6. This, fays he, *is* Love, *that we walk after his Commandments.* And, effectually to prevent fuch Men's enthufiaftick Notions of Religion, as judge of their *Love towards God* by *any* empty Speculation, by *any* Warmth of Zeal in matters of Opinion, by *any* Paffion or Affection whatfoever, wherewith the Mind or Imagination may, without any real Fruit of Virtue and Righteoufnefs, fancy itfelf tranfported ; the fame Apoftle frequently gives us this *one fure* rule, in which there can be *no* Deception ; that we meafure the Truth of our Love towards *God,* by the extent and proportion of our Love towards our *Neighbour.* 1 Joh. iii. 17. *Whofo feeth his* Brother *have need, and fhutteth up his compaffion from him, how dwelleth the Love of* God *in him?* Again, ch. iv. 12, 20. *No Man hath feen* God *at any time* ; *If we love* one another, *God dwelleth in Us, and his Love is perfected in us* : *If any man fay, I love* God, *and hateth his* Brother, *he is a Liar* ; *For he that loveth not his* Brother *whom he hath feen, how can he love* God, *whom he hath* not *feen?* The Argument is : God, who is *invifible,* can *no otherwife* be fhown to be the Object of our Love, than by our *delighting* to obey and imitate him, in Acts of Righteoufnefs and Charity and univerfal Good-Will, towards Mankind who are *vifible* and always *with us.* This *Commandment have we from* Him, *that he who loveth* God, *love his* Brother *alfo* : That ver. 21. is, that whofoever pretends to love *God,* fhould *prove* the *Truth* of what he profeffes by his behaviour towards *Men.* For by This *we know,* (as the fame Apoftle goes on, ch. v. 2.) *that we love the* children *of God, when we love God and keep his Commandments.* The words from their connexion with what went before, feem to be tranfpofed ; and that they fhould not be read thus, *that we love the children of God,* when *we love* God ; but on the other fide, *by* This *we know that we love* God, *when we love the children of* God, *and keep his Commandments.* Thofe who place the Sum of their religion, in impofing upon men blind Notions and unintelligible Opinions ; and *hate* and *perfecute* All who differ from them ; and, by indeavouring to *compel* Others into their own hypocrify, fill the World with cruelty, violence and oppreffion ; Thefe perfons, I fay, do in one *refpect* act extreme wifely ; that they difcourage men, as much as they can, from read-

SERM. ing and ſtudying the Scriptures with their own eyes; leaſt they ſhould There ſee it ſet
XXII.   forth, in ſo *plain*, ſo *clear*, ſo *bright*, ſo *perpetual* and *unavoidable* a *Light*, how *dif-*
ferent, how *Contrary*, Their Spirit is to the Spirit of *Chriſtianity*, which is the Spirit of
Love. For, if they who *rightly* teach the *true* doctrine of Chriſt, ſhall *yet* be bid to *de-*
part from him, if in their own private lives they be *workers of iniquity*; much *more*
ſhall the ſame Sentence be pronounced on thoſe, the manner of whoſe very *teaching* is
itſelf a work of unrighteouſneſs, violence and oppreſſion. But to proceed: As the
Scripture thus *expreſsly*, ſo the *reaſon and nature of the thing itſelf* no leſs *plainly*, ſhows,
in oppoſition to all Superſtitious Notions; that *Love towards God*, and *Virtue* or *Righte-*
ouſneſs of Life, are in reality only two different *Names* of One and the Same *Thing*.
For, *What* is rational *Love*, but a *Deſire to pleaſe* the perſon beloved, and a *Compla-*
cency or Satisfaction *in* pleaſing him? To *love* God therefore, is to have a ſincere *De-*
ſire of obeying his Laws, and a *Delight or Pleaſure* in the *Conſcience of That Obedience*.
Whereever *This Obedience* is not found; Men may talk what they pleaſe, of *ardent*
Love and Devotion towards God, of the *higheſt Zeal* and even *Fury* for his Service; it
is *all* nothing but moſt *certain* hypocriſy. For whatever ſpecious pretenſes the Wit of
Man may invent, our Saviour's Argument will for ever ſtand good; *men do not gather*
grapes of thorns, nor figs of thiſtles. The Tree *will* always be known by its Fruit. Love
towards God, *will* always ſhow forth itſelf in doing his Will. *If a man* love *me*, ſaith
our Saviour, *he* will *keep my words*, Joh. xiv. 23. To love *God*, is to love *Goodneſs,*
Righteouſneſs, Charity and Truth: If therefore to *love* theſe Virtues, and live at the ſame
time in the Practice of all the *contrary Vices*, be a Contradiction; for the ſame reaſon it
follows, that, to pretend to *love* God, and at the ſame time practiſe the *Vices which he*
hates, is a Contradicton alſo. As *He only who* doth *righteouſneſs, is righteous*; ſo *He only*
who doth *what is pleaſing to God*, can be ſaid to *love* him. To *love* God, and yet delight to *diſobey* him, is a manifeſt inconſiſtency: And therefore the Pſalmiſt's Admonition, is both an *Argument* of *Reaſon*, and a *Rule* by which to *Try* men; Pſ. xcvii. 10.
Ye that love *the* Lord, *ſee that ye* hate *the Thing which is* Evil. In Scripture, wicked
men and evil Spirits, are elegantly ſtiled Enemies *and* Haters *of God*: not that they oppoſe or withſtand his *Power*; for That is impoſſible; but becauſe they *hate* his Laws,
and *delight* in what he forbids: In like manner therefore on the *other* ſide, Love *to-*
wards God, is alſo impoſſible to be expreſſed by any *Benefit* we can do to *Him*, but
can be teſtified only by our *Love of Righteouſneſs* and by our *Practice of Virtue*. Even
to an *Earthly* Superiour, to a *Parent*, or a *Prince*, *Love* can no otherwiſe be ſhewn
from a *Child* or a *Servant*, than by chearfully obſerving the *Laws*, and promoting the
true *Intereſt*, of the Government he is under. There is *This* difference only; that
Earthly Superiours are *then* only to be obeyed, when they command what we ſee to be
juſt and right: But God, who, being infallible, can *never* command what is wrong, is
for that reaſon abſolutely to be obeyed in *all* things: Only, to prevent the Errors and
the Frauds of *Men*, whether *impious* or *pious* Frauds, very *great* heed is to be taken, in
matters of weight and importance, that whatever is pretended to be a Command of *God,*
be really and indeed Such.

Laſtly: THAT the *Love of God*, and the *Practice of Righteouſneſs*, are one and the
ſame thing, appears from thoſe Texts, wherein all *Relation* of *Men to God*, is declared
to be founded upon *Virtue* only. Thus the Title of *Sons* of God, Rom. viii. 14. *As*
many as are led by the Spirit of God, they are the Sons of God, and Phil. ii. 15. *That*
ye may be blameleſs and harmleſs, the Sons of God. The Title of *Friendſhip* likewiſe:
Jam. ii. 23. *It was imputed unto Abraham for righteouſneſs, and he was called the*
Friend *of God*: He was *called*; that is, he was ſo ſtiled in the *old Teſtament* by God
himſelf, *Iſ.* xli. 8; and 2 *Chr.* xx. 7. *Thou, Iſrael, art my Servant, the Seed of Abra-*
bam my Friend. Our Saviour gives the *ſame* Title to his *Apoſtles*, upon the *ſame* ground;

Joh.

Joh. xv. 14. *ye are my* Friends, *if ye do whatfoever I command you.* And ftill more emphatically, *Mat.* xii. 50. *Whofoever fhall* do the Will *of my Father which is in Heaven, the fame is my* Brother *and* Sifter *and* Mother. *Chrift* acknowledges *no relation*, but what arifes from *religion only*; nor regards *any* declaration of *Love* towards him, other than that of Obedience to his Commands in the Gofpel. St *Paul* elegantly purfues the fame Similitude, 2 *Cor.* v. 16. *Henceforth know we no man after the Flefh*; *yea, though we have known* Chrift *after the Flefh, yet now henceforth know we him no more:* His meaning is; All temporal perfonal Knowledge and Friendfhip, fuch as was between Chrift and his natural Relations here upon Earth, now difappears; and no man knows Chrift, or is known of him, any otherwife than in proportion as he obeys his Laws. The like is to be obferved, concerning That Title given to the *Jews,* of being *God's peculiar people :* For *They only* were fo in the fpiritual and *religious* fenfe, who in *Practice,* not who in *Profeffion,* ferved the True God. *Gal.* iii. 28; and *Col.* iii. 11. *There is neither Jew, nor Greek; there is neither male, nor female; neither Barbarian, Scythian, bond nor free; but Chrift,* (that is, Obedience, to Chrift,) *is all in all.* And ch. v. 6; and 1 *Cor.* vii. 19. *Circumcifion is nothing, and Uncircumcifion is nothing, but the Keeping of the Commandments of God.* And the fame is fully expreffed in that declaration of *John the Baptift,* when he fays, that even out of the *Stones of the ftreet, God could raife up children unto Abraham :* Children unto *Him,* in the fpiritual and beft fenfe, who for his exemplary obedience had this Teftimony given him, that he is *called* in Scripture, (*Rom.* iv. 16.) *the Father of the Faithful.*

Now from this Account which has been given of the *true* Nature of *Love towards God*; it will be eafy for us to correct the Errors; which Men have fometimes fallen into in Both Extremes. *Some* have been very confident of their Love *towards God*, from a mere warmth of fuperftitious zeal and enthufiaftick affection, without any great care to bring forth in their Lives the Fruits of Righteoufnefs and true Holinefs. And the Error of *thefe men* may be corrected, by confidering, that God being effentially juft and good, holy and true, and of all other moral Perfections; 'tis confequently evident, that unlefs they confider him under *Thefe Characters* which are infeparable from his Nature, and unlefs they accordingly love (and themfelves imitate) thefe Virtues; 'tis not *God* whom they are zealous for, but a mere *abftract Notion*, a *Phantom only* of their own Imagination.

On the contrary; Others there are, who though they really *love,* and fear, and ferve God, in the courfe of a virtuous and religious life; yet, becaufe they feel not in themfelves that *warmth* of affection, which many Enthufiafts pretend to; therefore they are afraid and fufpect, that they do not *love God* fincerely, as they ought. Now the Errour of thefe pious perfons is to be corrected, by confidering, that there is *no* other Mark fo infallible of the Goodnefs of a Tree, as the *Fruit* which it brings forth. If they live in *Obedience* to the Commands of God, they need *no other* evidence of the Sincerity of their Hearts towards him: For all *other* Signs may poffibly be erroneous; but *This,* is the *very thing fignified* itfelf. Love of *Goodnefs, Righteoufnefs and Truth*; is Love of *God:* For *God is Goodnefs and Truth :* And He who loves thefe Virtues, which are the moral Perfections of the divine Nature, does therefore love God moft perfectly; becaufe he loves *thofe* Excellencies, for the *Sake* of which God expects that we fhould love him above all things.

But further: There are *Some* perfons of This fort, who are fearful that their Love towards God is not entire and perfect, and that they do not love God as the Chief Good, if they obey and ferve him for the hope of *Reward.* But This alfo is a great miftake: For *as* Happinefs, no lefs than *Holinefs,* is *effential* in the divine Nature; *fo* in all *inferiour* Beings, the proper Reward *of Virtue* is infeparably defirable with *Virtue itfelf :* And not the Defire of *Heaven,* which is the Perfection of Virtue; but only the Defire

of

SERM. of Sinful *Pleasure*, which is deftructive of Virtue, is inconfiftent with, and diminiſhes
XXII. from, our *Love of God.* The Scripture expreffly declares, that he who cometh to God,
not only *may*, but *muft* believe him to be a *Rewarder* of them that diligently feek him:
That *Abraham* accordingly, That great Father of the Faithful, *looked for a City which
hath foundations, whofe Builder and Maker is God:* That *Mofes*, had *refpect unto the
recompence of Reward:* That the *Martyrs* fuffered in hope, *that they might obtain a
better Refurrection:* That our Lord *himfelf*, endured the Crofs, *for the joy that was fet
before him:* And that the *end* of All good mens *faith*, is *the Salvation of their Souls*, even
joy unfpeakable and full of Glory. The *Hope of* which *Joy*, the Apoftle in That very
Verfe, not only fuppofes to be *confiftent with*, but fpeaks of it as being, *itfelf*, our
Love of Chrift.

II. Having thus at large explained the *Duty* injoined in the Text, *Thou fhalt love
the Lord thy God:* I proceed now in the 2d place, to confider briefly the *Circumftances*
requifite, to make the performance of this Duty *acceptable and complete:* Thou fhalt
love him *with all thy Heart, and with all thy Soul, and with all thy Mind.* In St *Luke*
it is, fomewhat *more diftinctly;* with all thy *Heart*, with all thy *Soul*, with all thy
Strength, and with all thy *Mind.* Which words, though fometimes indeed ufed *promifcuoufly*, yet, when thus put together in *Order*, feem intended to exprefs after a more
diftinct manner, the requifite *Circumftances* of That *Obedience*, which is the proper E-
vidence of our Love towards God. And

1ft, It muft be *Sincere:* We muft love, or obey him with all our Heart. 'Tis not
the *external Action* only, but the *inward Affection of the* Mind principally, that God regards: An affection of Mind, which influences all a man's actions *in fecret*, as well as
in publick; which determines the perfon's *true* Character, or denomination; and diftinguifhes *him* who really *is* a Servant of God, from *him* who only *feems* or *appears* to
be fo. It was the character of the *Jews* of *old*, and is *now* of too great a part of Chriftians, *Ezek.* xxxiii. 31. *With their* Mouth *this people fhews much love, but their* Heart
goeth after their Covetoufnefs; i. e. after their Sinful Pleafures.

2dly, Our Obedience muft be *Univerfal:* We muft love God with all our Soul, or
with our whole *Soul. He* does not love God, in the Scripture-fenfe; who obeys him in
fome inftances only and not in *all. No man*, fays our Saviour, *can ferve two Mafters:*
And, *if any man love the* World, *the love of the* Father *is not in him*, 1 Joh. ii. 15.
And *Jam.* iv. 4. *Whofoever will be a Friend of the* World, *is the Enemy of God.* The
meaning of thefe paffages, is not, that he who Truly loves *God*, muft confequently
wholly neglect, and have *no regard at all* to any thing elfe; but, that nothing elfe muft
fo poffefs our affections as to *interfere* with our Duty, when they come in competition;
and thereby render our Hearts (as the Scripture expreffes it,) *not right* or *not whole* with
the Lord. Thus *Saul* was tempted to fpare the *beft* of the *Amalekite's* Goods, expreffly contrary to God's Command: And the *Jews*, under Pretenfe of the *Corban*, of giving fomewhat to the fervice of the *Temple*, excufed themfelves from providing for their
neceffitous *Parents:* And *Many* who have zealoufly *taught* the doctrine of Chrift,
fhall at the day of Judgment be bid to *depart from him*, becaufe they have allowed themfelves in the practice of fome unforfaken *iniquities.* The Pfalmift places his confidence
in *This* only, that he *had refpect unto* All God's *commandments*, Pf. cxix. 6. Generally
fpeaking, moft men's Temptation lies principally in fome One *Particular* Inftance:
And *This* is the proper *Tryal* of the perfon's *Obedience*, or of his *Love* towards God. If
he overcomes in *This* inftance, then may he *have confidence towards God;* But if he
fails *here*, and *continues* fo to do, he is guilty of *all.* By forfaking the Sin that *moft
eafily* befets us, we muft endeavour to improve daily and grow in grace; aiming at the
character given in the Gofpel to *Zacharias*, that he was *perfect, walking in all the Commandments of the Lord blamelefs.* The meaning is, not that our Obedience can in this

1

Side notes:
Heb. xi. 6.
ver. 10, 14.
ver. 26.
ver. 35.
ch. xii. 2.

1 Pet. i. 8, 9.

c. 27.

Mat. vi.

Mat. vi. 24.

life be *indeed finlefs*; but that we muft be *fincere* in endeavouring to avoid *all Sin*, according to the meafure and poffibilities of our *prefent* frailty; till at laft we be prefented really *faultlefs, before the prefence of his glory, with exceeding Joy.*

3*dly,* Our Obedience muft be *conftant* and *perfevering in* Time, as well as *Univerfal* in its *Extent:* We muft love God with all our Strength; *perfevering* in our Duty, *without fainting. He that endureth to the* end, faith our Saviour, *the fame fhall be faved*; and *He that* overcometh, *fhall inherit all things*; and, *we are made partakers of Chrift, if we hold the beginning of our confidence ftedfaft unto the* end. The Scripture-notion of Obedience is, walking *in holinefs and righteoufnefs before him* all the days of our life, *Luk.* i. 75. The meaning is, not fo as never to fall into any *Sin*, but fo as never to apoftatize from our Duty by falling finally into *any* courfe *of Sin. The juft fhall live by faith*; but *if any man draw back*, fays God, *my Soul fhall have no pleafure in him.* For Chriftianity is a *warfare*, wherein we muft *not only fight*, but *fo* fight as to *overcome*; and a *race*, wherein we muft *not only run*, but *fo* run as to *obtain.*

4*thly,* Our Obedience to God, ought to be *willing and chearful:* We muft love him with all our Mind. *Pf.* v. 12. *They that love thy Name, will be* joyful *in thee:* And St *Paul*, among the fruits of the Spirit, reckons up peace, and joy *in the Holy Ghoft.* Neverthelefs, This ought not to be matter of fcruple to any *weak* and fincere mind: For Obedience to the Commands of God, *whatever* principle it proceeds from, even though it be but *Fear* only, will be accepted unto Salvation. But Virtue becomes *more perfect*, when 'tis made eafy by Love, and by habitual Practice incorporated as it were into a man's very nature and temper. For fo the Scripture reprefents *Angels*, as *rejoycing* and *delighting* to perform their Lord's pleafure; and our Saviour declares 'twas his *meat and drink* to do the Will of his Father which is in Heaven. Which Examples when we can in any *tolerable* degree imitate, then is fulfilled in us the obfervation of St *John*, that *perfect Love cafteth out Fear*; and That of St *Paul, Rom.* viii. 15. that [1 Joh. iv. 18.] we have not received the Spirit of bondage to Fear, but the Spirit of adoption, whereby we cry, Abba, Father*; and 2 Tim. i. 7. *God hath not given us the Spirit of* fear, *but of* love, *and of a found mind.*

These are the *Circumftances* requifite to make the performance of this Duty acceptable and complete: We muft love the Lord our God, with all our *Heart*, with all our *Soul*, with all our *Strength*, and with all our *Mind.* The

IIId and laft thing obfervable in the Text, is the *Weight and Importance* of the Duty; It is the *Firft and great Commandment.* The Reafon is, becaufe 'tis the *Foundation of all*; and, without *Regard to God*, there can be *no Religion.* Not that Virtue, at *any* time, or in *any* perfon whatfoever, can be *not praife-worthy*; much lefs, that, in thofe who have *not* a right knowledge of God, even virtuous Actions themfelves are (as fome have very *unreafonably* affirmed) only *fplendid Sins*; but that there is no *fecurity*, no certain *depending* upon fuch virtues, as arife merely accidentally from *natural goodnefs of Temper*, and are not built upon a firm and fettled perfwafion, that God does Now govern, and will finally judge the World. The Houfe, is good; but it is built (according to our Saviour's comparifon) upon the *Sand only*, and not upon a *Rock.* 'Tis *Faith* only that *overcomes the World:* Nothing but a fteddy Belief of a Judgment to come, and of God's being a Rewarder of them that diligently feek him, can be effectual to conquer the Temptations of Sin. *This* Faith therefore, that we may all hold faft, God of his infinite Mercy grant, *&c.*

SERMON XXIII.

Of the FEAR of GOD.

JOB XXIII. 15.

Therefore am I troubled at his presence : When I consider, I am afraid of him.

SERM
XXIII.

IN This Chapter *Job* gives a noble Description of the Sense he had upon his Mind, of the invisible Omnipresence and Omniscience of God. Ver. 8. *Behold, I go forward, but he is not there : and backward, but I cannot perceive him : On the left hand where he doth work, but I cannot behold him ; he hideth himself on the right hand, that I cannot see him : But he knoweth the way that I take.* To a man of Virtue and Integrity, the consideration of This great Truth is a solid Ground of real and lasting Satisfaction. *He knoweth the way that I take————My foot hath held his steps ; his way have I kept, and not declined : Neither have I gone back from the Commandment of his Lips : I have esteemed the Words of his Mouth, more than my necessary Food,* ver. 11. In times of *Affliction* particularly, it is an inexpressible Support, if a man can be able to say with this exemplary person, ver. 3. *O that I knew where I might find him ! that I might come even to his Seat ! I would order my Cause before him, and fill my Mouth with Arguments.————Will he plead against me with his great Power ? No ; but he would put Strength in me.————He knoweth the Way that I take : When he hath tried me, I shall come forth as Gold.* Nevertheless, though the Hope signified by these high Ex-

1 Joh. iii. 19. pressions, is indeed a well-grounded Hope ; and what the Apostle St *John* calls, an *assuring* of *our Hearts before God* ; Yet considering the infinite Purity of the Divine Nature, and the Frailness of this our mortal State, and the unprofitableness even of our best Services, and our aptness to impose upon ourselves, and to deceive through carelessness even our Own Hearts ; so that though a man be not conscious to himself of

1 Cor. iv. 4. any Great Wickedness, yet is he *not hereby justified, but he that justifies* him, *is the Lord* : And considering also, that, in the nature of Things, there cannot but be many Secrets in the Dispensations of Providence, and in God's Government of the Universe, unsearchable to our short and limited Understandings ; 'Tis not without great reason that *Job* immediately corrects himself in the words next following ; ver. 13. *But he is in One Mind, and who can turn him ?————For he performeth the thing that is appointed for me ; and many such things are with him. Therefore am I troubled at his presence ; when I consider, I am afraid of him.* The Expressions are of the same import, as those in the *Ninth* chapter, ver. 11 ; *Lo, he goeth by me, and I see him not ; he passeth on also, but I perceive him not. Behold, he taketh away ; who can hinder him ? Who will say unto him, what dost thou ?————Whom, though I were righteous, yet would I not answer ; but I would make Supplication to my Judge.*

THE words of my Text ; *I am troubled at his Presence ; when I consider, I am afraid of him* ; have, in the place, they stand, a *particular* Reference to *These* Considerations. But I shall take them at this time in their *larger* sense, as containing this

more

more *general* and very important Propofition; that the *Fear of God* is the Refult of
Confideration, the Refult of *Attention*, and true *Reafon*; not of empty *Imagination*,
and vain *Apprehenfions*. *When I Confider, I am afraid of him.*

By the *Fear of God*, I would be underftood to mean, not the Superftitious *Dread*
of an *arbitrary* or *cruel* Being; but That *Awe* and *Regard*, which neceffarily arifes in
the Mind of every man, who believes and habitually confiders himfelf as living and
acting in the fight of an Omniprefent Governour, of perfect Juftice, Holinefs and Purity; who fees every Thought, as well as every Action; who cannot be impofed upon,
by Any Hypocrify; who, as certainly as there is any Difference between Good and
Evil, cannot but approve the one, and deteft the other; and whofe Government, as
certainly as he has any Power at all, confifts in rewarding what he approves, and punifhing what he hates. Of fuch a Governour as This, though we are fure he is indued
with infinite Goodnefs, yet may it juftly be faid, with the greateft Reafon, and without any tendency to Superftition; *When I confider, I am afraid of him.*

This *Fear of God*, is the *Foundation* of *Religion*. For though Virtue *is* indeed
amiable, *abfolutely*, in its own Nature; and, if the World could poffibly be fuppofed
to fubfift without the *Government*, and even without the *Being* of God, ftill the nature of *Good and Evil* would be what it is, and Virtue would be *in itfelf* unalterably
excellent, and Vice for ever blame-worthy; Yet the great *Support* of Virtue among
Men, is the Senfe upon their Minds of a Supreme Governour and Judge of the Univerfe,
who will finally and effectually *reward* what is in itfelf effentially *worthy of reward*,
and *punifh* what is *worthy of punifhment*. To a *perfect* and *unerring* Mind, incapable
of being deceived, and which is exalted above all poffible temptation; to fuch a one,
the *intrinfic Reafon* of Things, the *effential Excellency* of Truth and Right, is in itfelf a
fteady and always fufficient Motive of Action. But *Men*; who, when they *know* what
is Right, and neceffarily *approve* it, yet at the fame time find *another Law in their
Members warring againft the Law of their Mind*, urging them with ftrong *Paffions*, and
uneafy *Appetites*; and thefe follicited moreover with perpetual Temptations from *without*, with Allurements of *Pleafure* and *Profit*, with *Baits* of *Power* and *Ambition*, with
Examples of a degenerate and corrupt World, and with *Threatnings* alfo of perpetual
Perfecutions in different kinds, if they adhere ftedfaftly to the Interefts of Truth and
Virtue: To *fuch* Beings as thefe, I fay; to finite, changeable and fallible Creatures;
'tis very neceffary, that the *eternal intrinfic Reafon of Things*, the *effential and unalterable Excellency of Truth and Right*, confidered as a *Motive* of Action, fhould be *fupported* and *ftrengthened* by a conftant and lively Senfe upon their Minds, of an univerfal
Supreme Governour; who being effentially the Fountain of all Perfection, the *Truth
and Reafon of Things* and the *unalterable Right of every Cafe* are confequently the eternal *Laws* of his Kingdom: Which, by his univerfal Power and Government over all,
he will as certainly fupport and maintain; finally rewarding Virtue, and punifhing
Vice; as 'tis certain there *Is* a Difference between Good and Evil, and that infinite
Wifdom cannot be *infenfible* of That Difference. A firm and fettled Perfwafion of the
reality and certainty of this great Truth, that we are continually under the infpection
of *fuch* a Supreme Governour and Judge; of an omniprefent Spirit, *in whom we live
and move and have our Being*, and to whom our very Thoughts are open as our Actions; cannot but fill the mind of every *confiderate* Perfon, with a juft Awe and *Fear*
of him: *When I confider, I am afraid of him:* Afraid, not as of an arbitrary and tyrannical Power; but as of a juft and powerful and wife Governour, whofe Laws are
reafonable and neceffary to be obeyed, and from whofe juft difpleafure the Difobedient
can by No Power or Artifice be protected.

The *Ground of This Fear*, the Text tells us, is *Reafon and Confideration: When I
Confider, I am afraid of him.* Atheiftical and profane men fuppofe on the *contrary,*
that

SERM.
XX

that the *Ground* of this Fear is *Timorousness of Temper, Superstition, Customary Tradition*, or *political Fiction*. 'Tis of infinitely great Moment, to determine *which* of these two is the *Truth* ; And therefore I shall consider distinctly the very different *Grounds, Characters*, and *Effects*, of *Religion* and *Superstition*; and how these Two things, which Atheistical and corrupt Minds would fain imagine to be the same, may be *distinguished* from each other.

1. IN the *first* place, as to the *Ground* and *Foundation* of Religion. That there is an essential Difference between Good and Evil, between Virtue and Vice ; is what every man as clearly discerns by the natural and necessary Perception of his own Mind and Conscience, as his Eyes see the Difference between Light and Darkness. 'Tis not a man's *particular Timorousness of Temper*, 'tis not *Customary Tradition* from his *Ancestors*, 'tis not the *imaginary Speculation* of *Philosophers*, 'tis not the *political Fiction* of *Governours*, that makes him see when he is *oppressed, defrauded, cheated*, treated *unjustly* and *injuriously* ; that these *Actions* are in their own nature *unrighteous*, and the *Person* who is guilty of them *worthy of Punishment*. Every man, of every degree of capacity, in every Age, and in every Nation, sees and feels this to be the Truth of Things ; And no *accidental Variety* of *Temper*, no *Tradition*, no *Philosophy*, no *Form of Government*, can either *alter* or *abolish* these Notions. The *Reasonings* and *Speculations* of *Men*, do not *make* things to be what they are ; but only help men to *discover* with greater Clearness, or to a deeper degree, what their *real intrinsic* Natures are. *Laws* likewise, do not *make* Virtue to be Virtue, or Vice to be Vice ; but only *inforce* or *discourage* the Practice of such things, as the very *making of a Law* always and necessarily *presupposes* to have been Fit or Unfit *before* the making of the Law : Because otherwise *all Laws* about *moral* matters would be *professedly* to *no Purpose*, and of *no Use*. There *may* perhaps be in some *Men*, and possibly in some whole *Nations*, for want of Attention and Consideration, a very great degree of *Ignorance*, in many *particular Instances*, of this natural and essential difference of Good and Evil ; (Though, I believe, no person, who had at all the use of his Reason, ever was so *universally* ignorant, as not to dislike and think *really blame-worthy* a wilful *Breach of Faith*, or an Act of *causeless Cruelty*.) But the *Ignorance*, be it in what degree it will, either of any *Man* or of any *Number of men*, makes no alteration at all, in the *Nature* and *Truth* of *Things* ; nor affords any Argument, against the *reality* of their *essential Differences*. Were there in nature *no real* and *unalterable* Difference between Moral Good and Evil ; it would follow, not only that whole Nations might possibly be *ignorant* of This Distinction ; which is nothing to the purpose ; (for so they may be of the plainest Mathematical Truths, and yet those Truths not be at all the less certain :) But it would follow, that whole Nations might as *possibly*, with a full perswasion within themselves of the Strength and Clearness of their manner of reasoning and arguing, determine in all instances universally Virtue to be Vice, and Vice to be Virtue, as *We* think we with reason determine the contrary : Nay, it would be as *easy*, and as *natural*, and as *probable* they should so determine, as that Nations should differ in the *Fashion* or *Colour* of their *Cloaths*, or in any other Circumstances of things by nature indifferent. Which since no man (I think) has ever been so absurd as to affirm ; it follows undeniably, that That First *Ground* and *Foundation* of *Religion*, the essential Difference between Virtue and Vice, is laid *immutably* and *universally* in the *Nature* and *Reason* of Things : Whereas all *Superstitions*, various always as the Motion of the Winds and Clouds, are notoriously founded only in *accidental Temper, customary Tradition*, or *political Fiction*.

AGAIN : That there is an *invisible Power* presiding over the Universe, (which is *Another* part of the prime *Ground* and *Foundation* of Religion ;) The Belief, I say, of an *invisible Power* ruling over the Universe, and which will finally *support* Virtue and

punish

punifh Wickednefs; is a Belief arifing from *Reafon and Confideration*; which is directly contrary to the Effence of *Superftition*. The *vifible Works* of Nature, every man by his own experience every day, perceives evidently to be the Effects of an *invifible Power*. The more *extenfive*, and the more *exact*, any man's Obfervations are; the more Evidences he continually finds of the *reality*, and of the *Greatnefs*, of this *invifible Power*: But even to the *meaneft Capacities*, and in the moft *obvious Occurrences* of life, God has by no means *left himfelf without Witnefs, caufing his Sun to fhine, and fending us Rain and fruitful Seafons, filling our Hearts with Food and Gladnefs.* The *Marvelloufnefs* of the Works of Nature fhows the *Greatnefs* of this Power; and the *Regularity* and *Uniformity* of them fhows it to be the Power of *One and the Same* Agent, acting or directing every where. The *Underftanding* of this univerfal Governour, which is fufficient to direct the whole Frame of *Nature*; cannot be infenfible of that Difference of *Moral* Good and Evil, which even to *Us* appears neceffarily and effentially demonftrable. To expect therefore that this Supreme Being will judge according to *Right*, that is, according to the *neceffary nature* of Things; In other words, To *fear* that he will punifh us if we act unreafonably, and to *hope* for his Favour if we be Followers of Truth and Right; is the Voice of *Reafon*, and not of *Superftition*.

Superftitious Apprehenfions, arifing in *particular* from *Timoroufnefs of Temper*, teach men to fear they know not *what*, or to be afraid of *God* they know not *why*; to *fear* him, not as a *juft and righteous Judge*, but merely as vefted with *irrefiftible Power*; to *fear* him, not fo as by That Fear to be deterred from unrighteous Practices, but fo as to be perpetually commuting for a vicious Life with the repetition of unprofitable Ceremonies without number. *Superftitions* founded upon *Cuftomary Tradition*, teach men to be afraid of things which have *no exiftence*, or of *Beings* which have *no Power and Dominion* over us; to place *Religion* in Practices which have *no* Tendency to *Virtue*; to lay Strefs upon *Opinions*, which have no *Senfe*, or no *Truth* in them; upon things, whereof no man can give a rational Account, or, in St *Peter's* language, *give an Anfwer to* any one *that asketh a Reafon of the Hope*, or of the *Fear that is in him*. *Superftitions* derived from *political Fiction*, teach men to make *Religion*, confift in *Parties and Factions*; in things which, in *different countries*, are contrary to each other, and, in the *fame country*, contrary at *different Times*; in things which promote not at all the Honour of *God*, nor univerfal Meeknefs and Good-will towards *Men*; but on the contrary, fometimes are directly *deftructive* both of *Truth* and *Charity*.

INSTANCES of *all* thefe feveral kinds of Superftitions in the *Heathen* World, were their worfhipping of *fictitious* Deities, inftead of the Great God and Governour of the Univerfe, of whom by the Light of Nature and Reafon they were not ignorant: And more particularly, their mixing fometimes *barbarous* and *cruel*, fometimes *beaftly* and *impure* Rites, even amongft their facred and religious Performances. In the *Jewifh* Nation, the general and prevailing Superftition always was, their relying upon outward *Forms* and *Ceremonies*, (which ought *not* indeed to be left undone,) and laying the ftrefs of Religion upon *them*, more than upon *the weightier matters of* the *Law*, Juftice, Mercy, and Fidelity; of which, all *external* Purifications were but Shadows and Memorials. In the *Chriftian* World, Inftances of no lefs fhameful Superftitions, are, mens departing from *the Everlafting Gofpel*, which requires us (*Rev.* xiv. 6, 7.) to *worfhip him that made Heaven and Earth*; and fetting up the Worfhip of the *Hoft*, and of the *Bleffed Virgin*, and of *Angels*, and *Saints*, and *Relicks*, and *Images*: Alfo relying upon *Indulgencies*, *Pilgrimages*, *Proceffions*, *Maffes for the Dead*, and the like: Nay, and upon the moft ridiculoufly extravagant *Abfurdities* in *Belief*, and the moft *inhuman Perfecutions and Barbarities* in *Practice*. All which things have no Foundation in *Reafon*, nor any Appearance of being commanded of *God*. The true *Religion of Chrift*, as taught by Himfelf and his Apoftles, has nothing of This Sort in it; requiring no-

S E R M. XXIII.

Mat. v. 45. Acts xiv. 17.

1 Pet. iii. 15.

Mat. xxiii. 23.

SERM.
XXIII.
thing of us, but This moft *reafonable Service*, that, in expeftation of a righteous Judgment to come, we continually *worſhip* the *God of the Univerſe* ; living in *Sobriety*, *Righteouſneſs*, and *Charity towards All men* ; and making conftant *Acknowledgments* of the Divine *Goodneſs and Compaſſion*, in receiving *Sinners* to *Repentance* through the *Atonement* and *Interceſſion* of Chrift. Than which Doctrine, nothing can be more *firm* in its *Foundation*, or more *excellent* in its *Effects*.

2. AND This is the *Second* great or charafteriftick Mark, by which *Religion* and *Superftition* may be *diſtinguiſhed* from each other. As they differ entirely in their *Ground and Foundation*, fo do they likewife in their *Effects*. *By their Fruits ye ſhall know them*, Matt. vii. 20. *Religion*, which is founded in *Truth*, always makes men impartially *inquiſitive* after *Truth*, Lovers of *Reaſon*, *Meek*, *Gentle*, *Patient*, *Willing to be informed* : *Superftition*, on the contrary, naturally makes men *blind* and *paſſionate*, defpifers of *Reaſon*, carelefs in *inquiring* after *Truth*, *Haſty*, *Cenſorious*, *Contentious*, and *Impatient of inſtruction*. *Religion* teaches men to be exactly *juſt*, *equitable*, and *charitable* towards all men : *Superftition*, on the contrary, frequently puts men upon undervaluing the eternal Rules of *Morality*, and upon preferring the Intereft of particular *Sects and Parties*, the prevalency of fome *uncertain Opinions*, and the practice of fome *needleſs Ceremonies*, before the unalterable Precepts of the *everlaſting Law* and the *everlaſting Goſpel*. Laftly, True *Religion*, the Religion of *Nature* in general, and the Religion of *Chriſt* in particular, by fecuring the Belief of a *future Judgment*, tends greatly to promote the Happinefs of *Nations* and *good Governments*, in obliging the *Conſciences* of men to *real Fidelity*, *Juſtice*, and the *ſincere Practice* of *every Virtue*, which the *very beſt human Laws* can but *imperfectly* fecure, by compelling merely the *External* Action : But *Superftition*, on the contrary, frequently produces *Wars*, and *Tumults*, and *Perſecutions*, and *Tyrannies* without end ; there being nothing fo *wicked*, which men of *Superftitious Principles* will not think *pious* and *neceſſary*, and which men of *No Principles* will not upon occaſion bring themfelves to fubmit to.

I SHALL conclude This Head, with obferving that there are *Two* Particulars, wherein *True Religion*, the Religion taught by *Chriſt himſelf*, (for the Religion profeſſed by many Nations who *call* themfelves *Chriſtian*, is palpably nothing but *Superftition* ;) the *true* Religion, I fay, as taught by *Chriſt himſelf*, has in *Two* Particulars principally, by men who receive not the Goſpel, been objected to as encouraging *Superftition*. One is, that it teaches men to be *obſtinate* and *wilful*, in parting with all Advantages, even with *Life* itfelf, for the fake of Religion. The Other is, that by teaching men to *deſpiſe* the *World*, it hinders them from attending to the *Good of the Publick*. But the Anfwer to Both thefe Objections is not difficult. Without a *ſtedfaſtneſs* which cannot be moved by Temporal Inconveniencies, there is *no Virtue* to be depended upon, in *natural* Religion, any more than in *Chriſtian* : Is therefore *All Virtue*, nothing but *Superftition* ? And as to *deſpiſing* the *World*, in the Senfe of *withdrawing from* the *Buſineſs* of the World, Chriftianity no where teaches this, but only in Times and Places of general *Perſecution*. In *Other* Cafes, defpifing the *World*, does not fignify defpifing the *Buſineſs* of the World, or neglecting to attend the *Publick Good*, but defpifing all Temptations to the *Wickedneſs* of the World, the Temptations of *lawleſs* Pleafure, the Temptations of *unjuſt Gains*, the Temptations of *corrupt Ambition*. Thefe only, are, in the Scripture-fenfe, That *World* which is an Enemy to God.

SERMON XXIV.

Of the WISDOM of being Religious.

PROV. IX. 10, 11.

The Fear of the Lord is the beginning of Wisdom, and the Knowledge of the Holy is Understanding; For by me thy days shall be multiplied, and the years of thy Life shall be increased.

THERE is no Desire which God has so deeply fixed and implanted in our Nature, as that of Preserving and Prolonging our Life. Life and Health, are the Foundation of all other enjoyments : and are therefore of greater value than all other Possessions put together, because they are necessary in order to the Enjoyment of those Possessions; And without These, all other things that are the Objects of Men's Hopes and Desires in the World, have with regard to Us, no Being, no Subsistence. *For, what shall it profit a man, if he gain the whole World, and lose his own Life? Or what shall a man give in exchange for his Life?* The principal Point of Wisdom therefore in the Conduct of Human Life, is so to use the enjoyments of this present World, as that they may not themselves shorten that Period, wherein 'tis allowed us to enjoy them. And if any part of Knowledge deserves a steddier attention, than other, and has of all others the justest pretence to be esteemed invaluable; 'tis unquestionably *That* Knowledge, by which, as the Wiseman here expresses it, our *days may be multiplied, and the Years of our Life may be increased.*

Let us eat and drink, for to morrow we die; was the reasoning of the Epicure, mentioned by St *Paul*, 1 Cor. xv. 32. But it was very false reasoning, to make the melancholy consideration of the Shortness of Life an Argument for Debauchery, when that very Debauchery is evidently the Cause of making Man's Life still shorter. Temperance and Sobriety, the regular Government of our Appetites and Passions, the promoting Peace and good Order in the World, are, even *without* regard to any Arguments of Religion, the greatest instances of Human Wisdom; because they are the most effectual means of preserving our Being, and Well-being in the World; of prolonging the Period, and inlarging the Comforts and Enjoyments of Life. *Religion*, has added Strength to these Considerations; and, by annexing the Promise of God's immediate Blessing, to the natural Tendency and Consequences of Things, has made the Wisdom of choosing Virtue infinitely more conspicuous; and the Folly of Vice, more apparently absurd. *Length of Days* upon *Earth*, is in the *Old Testament* frequently promised to the *Righteous*; And the principal intent of that promise, was to be an Emblem or Signification of a *longer Life*, even of *Eternity*, more expressly promised in the *New*. The Land of *Canaan* was a Type of Heaven, the true Land of Promise; And the *days* of the righteous being *long in the Land which the Lord their God had given them*, was a figurative præsignification of that future and more complete State of Happiness, wherein their *days should be multiplied* without number, and *the years of their Life should be increased without End*. This is a Demonstration *indeed*, of the Wisdom of being Religious;

S E R M.
XXIV.

3

gious;

SERM
XXIV.

gious; and of the happy Effects of having always before our Eyes the Fear of the Lord. *The Fear of the Lord is the beginning of Wisdom, and the Knowledge of the Holy is Understanding; For by me thy Days shall be multiplied, and the Years of thy Life shall be increased.*

The *Fear of the Lord*, and the *Knowledge of the Holy*, are two synonymous Expressions, each of which signifies in Scripture Phrase, *the Practice of Virtue and true Religion.* For so it is very usual in all good Authors, to express the *Whole* by some *principal Part.* Thus, when 'tis said, *The* Soul *that sinneth, it shall die*; because the Soul is the principal and most excellent part of Man, 'tis of the same import, as if it had been expressed, *The* Man *that sinneth, shall die.* And *Gen.* xlvi. 27. *All the* Souls *of the House of Jacob which came into Egypt;* that is, all the *Persons, were threescore and ten.* In like manner, because the *Fear* or *Love* of God, the *Knowledge* or *Study* of his Will, *Faith* or *Trust* in him, the *Remembrance* of him, or *frequent Meditating* upon his Laws, are *principal Parts* of Religion; and such as are apt to have so great an influence upon Men, that One of these Virtues can hardly be supposed to be found any where separate from the rest, or without producing its true and genuine Effects in the general course of a religious and Holy Life; therefore *each* of these are frequently put *singly* in Scripture for the *Whole* of Religion, and to express the Practice of Virtue in general. Thus, to Remember our *Creator in the days of* our *Youth,* is the Wiseman's description of an early Piety; and with *the Wicked* that shall *be turned into Hell,* in the Psalmist's language, are joined *all the Nations that* forget *God.* In like manner *Believers,* or they that have *Faith* in God, signifies always in the *New Testament* good *Christians,* or such as are endued with *all* virtues and graces of the Spirit; and on the contrary *every* kind of *Wickedness,* as well as *Infidelity,* is represented under the Character of *Unbelief.* The Love *of God,* is by St *John* and by our Saviour himself, defined to be *this, that we keep his Commandments,* 1 Joh. v. 3; and Joh. xiv. 15. The *Knowledge* of God, is in the writings of the same Apostle explained by the very same Phrase of *keeping his Commandments,* 1 Joh. ii. 3, 4: and they that know not *God,* are by St *Paul* described as Persons nothing differing from those *that obey not the Gospel.* 2 Th. i. 8. Lastly, Because *Fear* is of all other Passions the most deeply rooted in our Nature; and is more apt to be strongly moved by Apprehensions of the Divine displeasure, than the milder Passions of Desire and Hope are to be worked upon by Representations of the Excellency of Virtue and of the Greatness of its Reward; therefore the Fear *of God* is the *most* frequently of all these figurative Expressions, put in Scripture for the Whole of Religion; and Persons of Universal Piety and remarkable Holiness, are by no character more usually described than by This, that they fear *the Lord,* or *have the* Fear *of God before their Eyes.* And because *each one* of these Phrases singly, signifies thus, properly enough, the *Summ of Religion*; therefore any *Two* of them may likewise be used, as synonymous to *each other*; As, in the Text, the *Fear* and the *Knowledge* of the Lord: *The* Fear *of the Lord is the beginning of Wisdom, and the* Knowledge *of the Holy is Understanding; For by me thy Days shall be multiplied, and the Years of thy Life shall be increased.*

IN the Words we may observe,

1*st,* THAT the Practice of Religion is *in general* Man's truest Wisdom: *The Fear of the Lord is the beginning of* Wisdom; *and the Knowledge of the Holy is* Understanding.

2*dly,* THAT the Practice of Religion is *in particular* Wise in *this respect,* that it tends to prolong our Life and lengthen our days: *For by Me thy Days shall be multiplied, and the Years of thy Life shall be increased.* And

3dly, IT

3

3*dly*, IT may be reafonable to inquire, how far this Bleffing of long Life promifed S E R M. to Obedience under the *Old Teftament*, is proper to be defired by Chriftians under the XXIV. Gofpel-State.

1*ft*. THE Words contain this univerfal Propofition; That *the Practice of Religion is* in general *Man's trueft* Wifdom : The *Fear of the Lord is the beginning of* Wifdom, *and the Knowledge of the Holy is Underftanding*. And here, the whole Tenor of Scripture, in Conjunction with the Reafon of Things, concurs in fetting forth the Wifdom of being virtuous and religious. The Books of *Solomon* efpecially, whofe *Human* Judgment was fuperior to all others, even feparate from his Knowledge in things *Divine*, are fo full of this Notion; that, throughout all his Writings, the Words feem never to be ufed in any other Signification, but that Wifdom is always put for true Virtue and Piety, and Folly or Madnefs for the Habit of Sin. As if there were *no other* Folly in the World, but that of Wickednefs ; nor *any* true Wifdom, but that of Religion; becaufe, in the *comparative* Senfe, no other things fo *eminently* deferve thofe Names. And indeed, if Wifdom confifts in ftudying thofe things which are of the greateft Ufe and Neceffity for us to Know ; If it be wife to imploy our Thoughts about things *in their own Nature* the moft Excellent, and, in *their relation to us*, of the utmoft importance ; If it be Wife to purfue the nobleft *Ends*, and in the purfuit thereof to ufe the beft and propereft *Means* ; If it be Wife to confult our own real Happinefs ; and to be more concerned for the improvement of our Minds in practical Knowledge, than for amufing them with vain and empty Speculations ; If Eternity be of more importance than Time, and a never-ceafing Duration than a tranfitory Moment ; If the Favour of God be infinitely more valuable than the Friendfhip of the World ; and it be more advifable to pleafe an Almighty Benefactor, than mortal Men whofe Breath is in their Noftrils ; If Joy and Satisfaction of Mind be truly more defirable, than endlefs Anxiety, Horrour and Defpair ; If Peace and Love, Charity and univerfal Good-Will, be more eligible than Wars, Confufions and Defolations ; and it be wifer to promote the Happinefs of the World, than that Men fhould make each other miferable without Caufe and without End ; In a word ; If Wifdom confifts in knowing and diftinguifhing, in choofing and in adhering to, *whatfoever things are true,*——*honeft,* ——*juft,*——*pure,*——*lovely,*——*of good report* ; things that promote the Health of our Bodies, and fecure the Peace and Quiet of our Minds ; things that eftablifh the Order of the World, and make Other Men Happy as well as ourfelves ; things that make our prefent enjoyments, eafy, and the remembrance of what is paft, comfortable ; and the Hopes and Expectations of what is to come, fecure ; If the choofing *Thefe* things, be the Part of a Wife Man ; then is Religion evidently Man's trueft Wifdom. For, where are thefe things to be found, but in the Practice of Virtue and true Religion ?

THERE *is* a Wifdom in the underftanding of *Arts* and ufeful *Sciences*; which are beneficial to Mankind in this prefent State: and are in Scripture afcribed to the infpiration of the Almighty : But *this* is a Wifdom confined to particular Perfons, and its ufefulnefs limited to a very fhort Duration. There *is* a Wifdom, which men place in being able to over-reach and defraud each other, confifting in the *Skill and cunning Craftinefs of them that lye in wait to deceive:* But this is a Wifdom falfely fo called ; and the End of it appears always to be the extremeft Folly. There *is* a Wifdom, of thofe who by *Political Skill* manage fecretly the great Affairs of the World, and by deep Counfels bring about unexpected Changes in the States and Kingdoms of the Earth ; But *This* Wifdom is often a great Snare, and a dangerous Temptation to Men's Virtue ; giving extraordinary Opportunities indeed to the brighter Virtue of fome very few Heroick Spirits, to fhine forth illuftrioufly, to the Glory of Religion in fingular Acts of Moderation and Juftice, of Piety and great Goodnefs, for the Publick Peace and Security of

SERM. Mankind; but much more ufually joined with great Wickedneſs, and ſeldom men-
XXIV. tioned in Scripture, but with the Marks of an evil or fuſpicious Charaċter. There *is* a
Wiſdom, in *Words*, and artful *Repreſentations* of Things; called by St *Paul the en-
ticing Words of Man's Wiſdom*: But *This* alſo in Scripture, is always ſpoken of with an
ill Charaċter; being that *Philoſophy and vain Deceit*, That Art of confounding Truth
and Falſhood, which St *Paul* warns us againſt; and which vain Pretence to Wiſdom,
God choſe the weak things of the World, the plain unaffeċted ſimplicity of the Doċtrine
of the Goſpel, on purpoſe to confound.   Laſtly, There *is* a Wiſdom in ſearching out
the Secrets of *Nature*, and underſtanding the Variety of the Works of God: And this
indeed, ſo far as 'tis praċtical, and leads to the knowledge of the Author of Nature, is
an excellent Wiſdom, and worthy of great Commendation: But where 'tis *merely Speculative*, 'tis of more Difficulty than Uſe, and lies level to the Capacity of but few men's
Underſtandings.   The *only Wiſdom*, that *all* Men are capable of, and that *all* Men are
indiſpenſably obliged to attain, is the *Praċtical Wiſdom* of being truly Religious; the
Wiſdom of underſtanding, and of ſteddily purſuing, their own true Temporal and Eternal Intereſt.   The compariſon between *Speculative* and this *Praċtical Wiſdom*, is moſt
elegantly made by *Job*, in his xxviiith chapter: *Surely*, ſays he, *there is a Vein for the
Silver, and a place for Gold where they fine it*, ver. 1.   *There is a Path which no Fowl
knoweth, and which the Vulture's Eye has not ſeen; The Lion's whelps have not trodden
it, nor the fierce Lion paſſed by it*; ver. 7.   *But where ſhall* Wiſdom *be found, and
where is the Place of Underſtanding?* ver. 12.   *Man knoweth not the price thereof, neither is it found in the Land of the living; The depth ſaith, It is not in Me; and the
Sea ſaith, It is not with Me; It cannot be gotten for Gold, neither ſhall Silver be weighed for the price thereof*, ver. 15.   *Whence then cometh Wiſdom? and where is the place
of Underſtanding?* ver. 20.   The Reply follows; God, ſaith, he, *underſtandeth the
Way thereof, and He knoweth the place thereof; For He looketh to the Ends of the Earth,
and ſeeth under the whole Heaven*, ver. 23.   But *unto* Man *he ſaid; Behold, the Fear
of the Lord, That is his Wiſdom, and to depart from Evil, that is his Underſtanding*,
ver. 28.   His Meaning is; The Secrets of *Nature*, God only knoweth perfeċtly; but
the Knowledge of *Religion*, is the proper Wiſdom of *Man*.   *The Secret things belong
unto the Lord our God; but the things that are revealed, belong unto Us and to our
Children for ever; that we may do all the Works of the Law*, Deut. xxix. ult.   This is
very affeċtionately expreſſed likewiſe by *Moſes* in his exhortation to the *Iſraelites*,
Deut. iv. 6; *Behold, I have taught you ſtatutes and judgments, even as the Lord my
God commanded me; ——Keep therefore and do them; for This is your Wiſdom and
Underſtanding in the ſight of the Nations.*   This is that which alone can make men
truly great, truly admirable and praiſe-worthy; *The Fear of the Lord is the beginning
of Wiſdom; a good Underſtanding have all they that do thereafter; the Praiſe of it in-
dureth for ever*, Pſ. cxi. 10.   I conclude this Head, that *the Praċtice of Religion is* in
general *Man's trueſt Wiſdom*, with the excellent Words of the wiſe Author of the Book
of *Eccluſ.* ch. i. 14, 16, 26, 27.   *To fear the Lord, is the beginning of Wiſdom; and
it was created with the faithful in the Womb: To fear the Lord, is fulneſs of Wiſdom;
and filleth men with her fruits: If thou deſire Wiſdom, keep the commandments; and the
Lord ſhall give her unto thee; For the Fear of the Lord, is Wiſdom and Inſtruċtion; and
Faith and Meekneſs are his Delight.*

   2*dly*, THE Praċtice of Religion, as it is man's trueſt Wiſdom *in general*, ſo *in particular* the Text aſſures us 'tis wiſe in *this Reſpeċt*, that it tends to prolong our Life and
lengthen our Days: *The Fear of the Lord, is the beginning of Wiſdom; and the Knowledge of the Holy, is Underſtanding; For by Me thy days ſhall be multiplied, and the
years of thy Life ſhall be increaſed.*   There is nothing in the *Old* Teſtament more frequent, than Promiſes of Health and Life, of a longer and more comfortable Subſiſtence,

to them that live in Obedience to the Commands of God.   In the delivery of the Law, S E R M.
God himſelf annexes to the Fifth Commandment a Promiſe, that *the Days of thoſe* XXIV.
that obſerved it, ſhould *be long in the Land which the Lord their God had given them :*
And St *Paul* takes notice of it as the *firſt*, and indeed the *only* Commandment, *with*
an expreſs and particular *Promiſe* annexed.   *Solomon*, in his Book of *Proverbs*, among
a great variety of Arguments to perſwade men to the Practice of Virtue, always mentions *Length of Days*, as a principal Motive propoſed by God in the perſon of Wiſdom; *My Son, forget not my Law, but let thine Heart keep my Commandments*; *For
length of Days, and long Life, and Peace ſhall they add unto thee*, Prov. iii. 1. *They
ſhall be Life unto thy Soul*, ver. 22; and ver. 13. *Happy is the Man that findeth Wiſdom,
and the Man that getteth Underſtanding*; *For Length of Days are in her right hand,
and in her left hand Riches and Honour*, ver. 16.   And accordingly the Pſalmiſt in his
exhortation to Obedience, cited by St *Peter* in his firſt Epiſtle; *Come ye children*, ſays
he, *hearken unto me, I will teach you the Fear of the Lord*; *What man is he that deſireth Life, and loveth many Days, that he may ſee good?* *Keep thy Tongue from evil,
and thy Lips that they ſpeak no guile*; *Depart from evil, and do good*, Pſ. xxxiv. 11.
And in the prophetical deſcription of the final happy reſtoration of *Jeruſalem*, among
other bleſſings it is added, *Iſ.* lxv. 20. *There ſhall not be* in it *an old man that hath
not filled his days*.   On the contrary, among the various Threatnings denounced in the
Old Teſtament againſt Sinners, 'tis very uſual to make this declaration, that their *Days
ſhall be ſhortned*.   Prov. x. 27. *The Fear of the Lord prolongeth Days*; *but the Years of
the wicked ſhall be ſhortned.*   And *Job* xv. 31. *Let not him that is deceived, truſt in
Vanity*; *for Vanity ſhall be his recompenſe.*   *It ſhall be accompliſhed before his Time, and
his Branch ſhall not be green.* *He ſhall ſhake off his unripe Grape as the Vine, and ſhall
caſt off his Flower as the Olive.*   The Application of which Obſervation, is made by
the Wiſeman, *Eccleſ.* vii. 17. *Be not overmuch Wicked, neither be thou fooliſh*; *why
ſhouldeſt thou die before thy Time?* There is *ſomething* in the *Nature of Things*, that
tends to verify this Doctrine; and there is *More* in the *poſitive Appointment and Conſtitution of Providence.*   In the *Nature of Things*, men deſtroy themſelves and ſhorten
their Days by many kinds of Wickedneſs: By Wars and Deſolations they depopulate
whole Countries; by private Quarrels they bring each other to untimely Ends; by capital Crimes they bring themſelves to be cut off by the Hands of Juſtice; by Luxury and
Intemperance they deſtroy their Bodies; the riotous and unclean perſon going (as *Solomon* very elegantly expreſſes it) like *as an ox goeth to the ſlaughter, or as a Fool to the
correction of the ſtocks*; *'Till a dart ſtrike through his Liver*; *as a Bird haſteth to the
ſnare, and knoweth not that it is for his Life*, Prov. vii. 22.   By Envy and Malice they
conſume themſelves, and pine away in the midſt of their iniquity; This alſo is elegantly expreſſed by *Solomon*, Prov. xiv. 30. *A ſound Heart is the Life of the Fleſh, but
Envy the Rottenneſs of the Bones.*   Laſtly, by the Terrors of their own Minds are they
eaten up, and gnawed upon by the Worm of Conſcience till they are conſumed:
Pſ. xxxix. 11. *When thou with Rebukes doſt chaſten Man for Sin, thou makeſt his Beauty
to conſume away, like as it were a Moth fretting a garment.*   In like manner on the
other hand, according to the ſame natural Tendency of Things, by Peace and Charity
are men preſerved from Deſtruction; by Temperance are their Bodies maintained in
Health; by Quiet of Conſcience and Satisfaction of Mind, is a new Life added to their
Spirits; *Prov.* iii. 7. *Fear the Lord, and depart from Evil*; *It ſhall be Health to thy
Navel, and Marrow to thy Bones.* Which Notion is ſtill more fully expreſt by the Author
of the Book of *Eccleſiaſticus*, ch. i. ver. 11, 12, 20. *The Fear of the Lord is honour,
and glory, and gladneſs, and a crown of rejoycing*; *The Fear of the Lord maketh a merry
Heart, and giveth joy and gladneſs, and a long Life*; *The Root of Wiſdom is to fear the
Lord, and the Branches thereof are long Life.*

AND

AND This, in the *Natural Order and Tendency of Things.*

IN the *positive Appointment and Constitution of Providence*, there was yet *more* Assurance of the Doctrine; God, under the Old Testament, wherein these Promises were made, *usually* preserving the Righteous by a singular Care and Protection; (so that *Job*'s Friends could appeal to experience, *Whoever perished being innocent? or when were the righteous cut off?* Job iv. 7.) and on the contrary, the same Providence *generally* cutting off the Wicked, by extraordinary judgments, in the present Life. Even of those who prospered *longest*, so that it was *hard* for the Psalmist to *understand* the reason of it, and reconcile it with Providence, *Ps.* lxxiii. 16; yet even of *These* at length he observed upon better consideration, *Surely thou didst set them in slippery places, thou castedst them down into Destruction; How are they brought into Desolation as in a moment! they are utterly consumed with Terrors*, ver. 18, 19. But, most frequently, evil Doers were cut off *sooner*, and destroyed suddenly in the midst of their carriere. *Hast thou marked the old way, which wicked men have trodden? which were cut down* out of Time, *whose foundation was overflown with a Flood?* Job xxii. 15. *Bloody and deceitful Men, shall not live out half their days*, Ps. lv. 23. Upon account of the Profaneness of *Eli*'s Family, God threatens him, 1 *Sam.* ii. 32. *There shall not be an old man in thy house for ever.* And the Psalmist, as being sensible what the usual Effect of Wickedness was, prays thus, *Ps.* cii. 24. *O my God, take me not away in the midst of my Days.* Indeed, in the whole Book of *Psalms* the wicked are perpetually threatned with being cut *off* before their Time: And That Threatning is paraphrased with great Variety and Elegancy of Expression, in the Book of *Job*; *The Flag, whilst it is yet in its greenness, and not cut down, it withereth before any other Herb; So are the Paths of all that forget God, and the Hypocrites Hope shall perish*, ch. viii. ver. 12. *Yea, the Light of the Wicked shall be put out; and the spark of his Fire shall not shine*, ch. xviii. ver. 5. *His roots shall be dried up beneath, and above shall his branch be cut off*, ver. 16. *They are exalted for a little while, but are gone and brought low,——and cut off as the tops of the ears of Corn*, ch. xxiv. ver. 24.

NEVERTHELESS, after all This; forasmuch as general Threatnings are not executed always without exception; neither were the Wicked constantly cut off, even under the Times of the *Old* Testament, but sometimes prospered for a long time; and Sudden Cutting off was not itself always a judgment, but sometimes a *taking away from the Evils to come*; and righteous Persons themselves, were not always preserved from every Destruction; but in some cases, God threatned to *cut off the Righteous·with the wicked*; and Preservation itself, or Length of Days, was not always a Mercy; but only when it was promised and granted as an Emblem or Præsignification of a longer, even of an eternal Life; and the Temporal Promises of the Old Testament, cannot Now be applied with any Certainty under the New; where eternal Life is so much more clearly revealed: For these reasons, in the

3*d* place, IT may be worthy our Inquiry, *how far* this Blessing of long Life, promised to Obedience under the Old Testament, is proper to be desired by Christians under the Gospel State. And here it is certain, the Gospel gives us so mean a Notion of the present Life, and so glorious a representation of the Happiness of that to come; that no Man who firmly believes the Scriptures, and has lived so religiously as to have secured to himself a good Foundation against the Time to come, but must needs wish rather, (whenever he seriously meditates upon these things,) to be *delivered from the miseries of this sinful World*, and *to be present with the Lord, which is far better.* But alas! there are few, extremely few, whose Lives have either been so innocent, or their Repentance and Amendment so complete, as not to have Reason to wish for *more years*, wherein to root out more perfectly their former ill Habits, or to improve the good Dispositions they have already in some measure attained. And it were very well, if even Years and Ex-

perience

perience could, in thefe latter degenerate Ages of the World, produce but the fame S E R M. Effect which the Belief of the Gofpel, in the primitive and pureft Times, accomplifhed XXIV. frequently as it were in a Moment. But if the generality of Chriftians *were* fo perfect, as not to need to defire longer Space of Time for their *own* Amendment and Improvement; yet at leaft for the fake of *others*, with whom they are concerned either in private Friendfhips, or in natural Relation, or in publick Affairs, 'tis reafonable men fhould defire for themfelves, and others for them, the Bleffing of Length of Days. *For none of us liveth to Himfelf, and no man dieth to Himfelf*, Rom. xiv. 7; and St *Paul*, though for his own part he defired rather to *be prefent with the Lord*; yet, becaufe for him *to live* was *Chrift*, that is, was needful for the propagation of the Gofpel, and more beneficial to the Perfons he had converted; therefore he defired rather to continue with them; and This he calls the *Fruit of his Labour*. Phil. i. 22. Further; fince God has placed Us in this World, for Ends and Purpofes of his all-wife Providence; and we know not beforehand what Duties he intends to call us to; and he has implanted in us a natural and neceffary Defire of Life, in order to accomplifh his wife Defigns in the Government of the World; 'tis therefore natural and reafonable for us to look upon Length of Days as a Bleffing; and that *the hoary head is a crown of glory, if it be found in the way of righteoufnefs.* But when any perfon through difcontent defires, not to continue in the World, nor to fulfil that Duty which God has appointed him here; 'tis like defiring that he had never come into it; which is murmuring and finding fault with God's Creation, and repining at God for making us fuch Creatures as he has been pleafed to make us. However the very longeft Life here, is but a Moment in Comparifon of Eternity; And the greateft Length of Days is then only really a Bleffing, (as I before obferved,) when 'tis a Type or Emblem of a happy Eternity, of God's *giving men indeed a long Life, even for ever and ever*, Pf. xxi. 4. We ought therefore to make it the main Care of our Lives, to fecure our Eternal Happinefs hereafter; and then Length of Days here will be a Bleffing, not only upon their own Account, but much more fo upon account of their affording us Opportunity, of preparing ourfelves by ftill greater Care and Watchfulnefs, and continual improvement of ourfelves in the Practice of all Virtues, for a more perfect and complete Degree of Happinefs in the Life to come. If This be not done, Length of Days will, like all other Bleffings, be turned into a Curfe; and become only a ftronger Evidence againft us of our incorrigible Impenitency. If we be not *fo taught to number our Days, as to apply our Hearts unto Wifdom*; If, as our Years pafs on, we think not more and more intenfely on the Preparations for Eternity; but defer our Repentance from *day to day*, and put off our defigns of being religious from one *year* to another; it will nothing profit us, (nay, on the contrary, it will be a great Aggravation of our Mifery,) that *our Days have been multiplied, and that the Years of our Life have been increafed.* For, when *all thefe things are paffed away as a Shadow, and as a Poft that hafteth by*; (which is the cafe even of the longeft Life here upon Earth;) then fudden and fo much heavier deftruction will come upon us unawares, even as Pain upon a Woman in Travail, and we fhall not efcape. Then the expectations of the delaying Sinner fhall appear *thin as the Spider's web*; and his *Hopes as the light Chaff, which the wind fcattereth away from the Face of the Earth.* Then they who fpend the Day in Riot and Debauchery, and fay *To morrow fhall be as this Day and much more abundant*, fhall have their Soul required of them in a moment; and *the Servant that fays in his Heart, My Lord delayeth his Coming; and fhall begin to beat the men-fervants and maidens, and to eat and drink, and to be drunken; the Lord of that fervant will come in a day when he looketh not for him, and at an hour when he is not aware, and will cut him in funder, and will appoint him his portion with the Unbelievers;* and how *much* foever the Mafters delay, *i. e,* how *long* foever that wicked Servant's *Life* be, yet his deftruction, when it comes, furprizes him unprovided as in a moment.

SERM. But He, on the other hand, who in a ſhort Life makes ſpeedy proviſion for Eternity;
XXIV. though he be prevented with early death, yet, *being made perfect in a ſhort Time, he fulfilleth a long time;* as the Son of *Sirach* excellently expreſſes it; *For honourable Age is not that which ſtandeth in length of Time, nor that is meaſured by numbers of Years; But* Wiſdom *is the gray hair unto men, and an unſpotted life is old Age.*

S E R M O N   XXV.

Of imitating the HOLINESS of GOD.

1 PET. I. 15, 16.

But as he which hath called you, is Holy; ſo be ye Holy, in all manner of Converſation; Becauſe it is written, Be ye holy, for I am holy.

SERM. NOTWITHSTANDING the natural Proneneſs of Mankind to Superſtition;
XXV. and the ſtrong Bent which is in all corrupt Minds, to endeavour to make a-
mends, by formal and external Services, for the want of true Virtue and Ho-
lineſs of Life; yet even in the *Heathen* World itſelf, under the bare Light of *Nature* alone, the beſt and wiſeſt men were ſenſible of this great Truth, that the moſt acceptable Service which could be paid to God, was to indeavour to become *like* him by a righteous Temper and Diſpoſition of Mind. The *Revelation* which God has been pleaſed to make to us of himſelf in Scripture, does every where confirm this Notion; and almoſt the whole Deſign, both of the antient Prophets under the Law, and of all our Saviour's Diſcourſes in the Goſpel, is to eſtabliſh the ſame Doctrine: *As he which hath called you, is Holy; ſo be Ye Holy, in all manner of Converſation.* In the following Diſcourſe upon which words, I ſhall *1ſt* briefly ſet forth the *Obligations* we are under to *imitate* the God whom we worſhip. *2dly,* I ſhall conſider the true *Extent,* and proper *Limitations* of This Duty. And *3dly,* I ſhall draw ſome uſeful *Obſervations* from the whole.

Iſt, I SHALL briefly ſet forth the *Obligations* we are under, to *imitate* the God whom we worſhip. The *Difference* of *moral.Good and Evil,* is, in the nature of things, eternally, eſſentially, and unchangeably neceſſary. Juſt as *Light* and *Darkneſs* are of neceſſity always contrary to each other, and can by no Power be made to be the ſame. With regard to this neceſſary and unalterable difference of Good and Evil; the *Will of God,* who can never be impoſed upon by any Errour, is conſtantly and invariably determined to do always what in the whole is *beſt and fitteſt* to be done, according to the everlaſting Rules of Juſtice, Equity, Goodneſs and Truth. This, is the Ground and Foundation of all God's *own Actions* in the Government of the Univerſe. Now the ſame intrinſick Excellency of *Right* and *Good,* which always determines the Will of *God Himſelf,* ought alſo in Proportion to govern the Actions of all *other* rational Beings likewiſe;

likewife; according to the degree of their *Knowledge* of what is right, and of their *Power* to perform it. That is to fay; All *rational and intelligent* Beings are, by the Law of their Nature, obliged to indeavour to become in their feveral degrees and proportions *like* unto *Him*, who alone is *Perfect* Reafon and Underftanding. This is an *original* Obligation, founded in *Nature itfelf*, *requiring* us to *imitate* what it *neceffitates* us to *admire*. And this Obligation is confirmed by the fame Light of Reafon, teaching us further, that *Imitation of God*, as 'tis moft *fit* in *itfelf*, fo it cannot but be likewife moft acceptable unto *Him*, and agreeable to his *Will*. For, the *fame abfolute Perfection* of the Divine Nature, which makes us certain that God muft *Himfelf* be of Neceffity infinitely Holy, Juft and Good; makes it equally certain that he cannot poffibly approve Iniquity in *Others* : And the fame *Beauty*, the fame *Excellency*, the fame *Weight and Importance* of the Rules of everlafting Righteoufnefs, with regard to which God is always pleafed to make thofe Rules the Meafure of all his *Own* Actions, neceffarily prove, that it muft likewife be his *Will*, that all rational Creatures fhould proportionably make them the Meafure of *Theirs*. Even among *Men*, there is no *Earthly* Father, but in thofe things which he efteems his *own* Excellencies, *defires* and *expects* to be imitated by his *children*. How much *more* is it neceffary that *God*, who has the tendereft Concern for all his Creatures, and who is infinitely far from being fubject to fuch Paffions and Variablenefs as frail *Men* are, fhould defire to be imitated by his Creatures in thofe Perfections, which are the foundation of his own unchangeable Happinefs !

PARTICULARLY, If God is *himfelf* effentially of infinite Holinefs and Purity; it plainly follows, that 'tis impoffible but he muft likewife be of *purer Eyes than to behold* with Approbation any manner of *Impurity* or *Immorality* in his *Creatures*. And confequently it muft needs be his *Will*, that they fhould All (according to the Meafure of their frail and finite nature) be *Holy as He is Holy*.

Hab. i. 13.

IF God is *himfelf* a Being of infinite Juftice, Righteoufnefs and Truth; it muft needs be his *Will*, that all *rational Creatures*, whom he has created after his own Image, whom he has endued with excellent Powers and Faculties to enable them to diftinguifh between Good and Evil; fhould imitate him in the Exercife of thofe divine Perfections, by conforming all their Actions to the eternal and unalterable Law of Righteoufnefs.

IF God is *himfelf* a Being of infinite Goodnefs; *making his Sun to rife on the Evil, and on the Good, and fending Rain on the Juft and on the Unjuft*; having *never left himfelf wholly without Witnefs*, but *always doing Good, giving men Rain from Heaven and Fruitful Seafons, and filling their Hearts* with Food and Gladnefs : it cannot but be his *Will*, that all *reafonable creatures* fhould, by mutual Love and Benevolence, permit and affift each other to injoy in particular the feveral Effects and Bleffings of the divine univerfal Goodnefs.

IF God is *himfelf* a Being of infinite Mercy and *Compaffion*; as 'tis plain he bears long with men before he punifhes them for their Wickednefs, and often freely forgives them his *ten thoufand Talents*; it muft needs be his *Will*, that they fhould forgive one another their *hundred pence*; being *merciful* one to another, *as he is merciful* to them All; and *having Compaffion* each *on his Fellow-fervants*, as God *has pity on Them*.

Again : IF *Love* towards God, be an obvious and principal Duty of Natural Religion, in thofe who believe God to be the Supreme Good; it follows of neceffity, that *Imitation* of him alfo muft equally be a Duty of indifpenfable Obligation. For God, being effential Goodnefs, Righteoufnefs and Truth, can no otherwife have *Love* expreft towards him from his Creatures, than by their loving and imitating thofe Virtues in *their* Practice, which in *His* Nature are effential Perfections. Love of God, in any

3

other

SERM
XXV.
other fenfe than This, is nothing elfe but unintelligible Enthufiafm. Laftly: If *Happinefs* is Man's chief End; and *perfect Happinefs* is, in the divine nature, in *effential* conjunction with perfect *Holinefs and Goodnefs*; it follows neceffarily, that *fo far only* can any creature poffibly become *like* to God in the injoyment of *Happinefs*, as he is firft made *like* to him in the participation of *Goodnefs*.

THESE are the *Obligations* we are under, to *imitate* the God whom we worfhip; drawn from the confideration of the Nature *of things*; and of the *Will of God made known to us by the Light of* Reafon only. In the *Revelation* which God has been pleafed to make to us of himfelf in *Scripture*, the neceffity of the fame Duty, is more exprefsly and more clearly enforced. At the delivery of the *Law to Mofes*, the *particulars* of Duty, by which the Worfhippers of the True God were to be diftinguifhed from all other Nations, are introduced with this *general* Preface to the *whole*, Levit. xix. 1. *The Lord fpake unto Mofes, faying, Speak unto all the Congregation of the children of Ifrael, and fay unto them, Ye fhall be Holy, for I the Lord your God am Holy.* And ch. xi. 44. *I am the Lord your God; ye fhall therefore fanctify yourfelves; and ye fhall be holy, for I am Holy.* By the *citation* of which words, fpoken thus from the Mouth of God *himfelf* to *Mofes*; the *Apoftle* confirms his *own* Argument in the words of the Text; *As He which hath called you, is Holy; fo be Ye Holy, in all manner of Converfation:* Becaufe *it is written, Be ye Holy, for I am Holy.* Man, was originally created in the *Image* of God, *Gen.* i. 27; that is, he was made in his *natural* capacity a rational and intelligent creature, capable of diftinguifhing between Good and Evil, and of being Lord over the inferiour Creation. By a right ufe of thefe Powers and Faculties, in imitation of God, he is declared likewife in the *moral* fenfe, to be *after God, created in righteoufnefs and true Holinefs,* Eph. iv. 24. *After God;* that is, after the *pattern and fimilitude* of God, *after the* Image *of Him that created him,* Col. iii. 10. By Debauchery and Corruption of manners, by the Practice of Any wickednefs whatfoever, men are *alienated,* faith St *Paul, from the* Life *of God,* Eph. iv. 18: And when again by true Repentance and real Amendment of Life, they return to their Duty, and improve in the Practice of Virtue; the Apoftle reprefents them as being reftored and *made partakers of the* Divine Nature. 2 *Pet.* i. 4. The manner of fpeaking is figurative, and very elegantly expreffive of that *moral* likenefs to God, which is elfewhere ftiled literally, being *partakers of his* Holinefs, *Heb.* xii. 10; and, in the Text; being *Holy,* as *He is Holy:*

Heb. xii. 14.
Without which *Holinefs,* the Scripture plainly declares, *no man fhall fee the Lord.* A *Likenefs* to God *here,* by the habitual Difpofition of a virtuous mind, is indifpenfably neceffary to the enjoyment of *Glory* and *Happinefs hereafter.* And the Perfection even of *That* Glory and Happinefs itfelf, principally confifts in our becoming ftill *more and more* like him, by the total abolifhing of all Sin: *We fhall be like him, for we fhall fee him as he is,* 1 Joh. iii. 2. What the *full* meaning of This is, the Apoftle tells us, *does not yet* clearly *appear.* But, though *God* is *himfelf* invifible; yet both by the *Light of Nature,* we have a *competent* Knowledge of his *moral* Attributes; and in the Life of *Chrift,* who is the *vifible* Image of the invifible God, we have a complete Example, and Pattern of moral *Perfection,* fet before us to imitate. *Learn of Me,* faith our Saviour, *for I am meek and lowly in Heart,* Matt. xi. 29. And again in another place,

Joh. xiii. 15.
I have given you an Example, faith he, *that ye fhould do as I have done to you.* The Apoftles accordingly, in their exhortations to the practice of Virtue, do frequently remind us of this Divine Pattern: 1 *Pet.* ii. 21. Chrift has *left us an* Example, *that ye fhould follow his Steps; who did no Sin, neither was guile found in his mouth:* And 1 *Joh.* ii. 6. *He that faith, he abideth in Him, ought himfelf alfo fo to walk, even as he walked.* This is the higheft Excellency and Perfection of a Chriftian; to be *conformed*

Rom. viii. 29.
to the Image of the Son of God, by a Life of Virtue and Righteoufnefs *here:* Which

2 Cor. iii. 18.
whofoever is, fhall *hereafter* alfo be changed into the fame Image, from glory to glory; when

when our Lord fhall *prefent* his Servants *faultlefs before the prefence of his* Father's *glory, with exceeding Joy*; and they *fhall fee his Face, and his Name fhall be in their foreheads*; and they *fhall ferve him day and night in his Temple*, and enjoy his uninterrupted Favour for ever and ever.

THESE are the *Obligations* we are under, to imitate God: Which was the *firft* Head I propofed to fpeak to.

II*dly*, I AM in the next place to confider the true *Extent*, and proper *Limitations* of this Duty. And here 'tis very evident,

1*ft*, THAT All imitation of God, muft be underftood to be an imitation of his *moral* Attributes only, and not of his *natural* ones. In the exercife of his Supreme *Power*, we cannot imitate him: In the Extent of his unerring *Knowledge*, we cannot attain to any Similitude with him: We cannot at all *Thunder with a Voice like Him*, Job xl. 9; nor are we able to fearch out and comprehend the leaft part of the depth of his unfathomable *Wifdom*. But his *Holinefs and Goodnefs*, his *Juftice, Righteoufnefs*, and *Truth*, his *Mercy* and *Compaffion*; thefe things we *can* underftand; in thefe things we *can* imitate him; nay, we cannot approve ourfelves to him as obedient Children, if we do not imitate him therein.

THE Holinefs of God; that is, *in* general, That difpofition of the Divine Nature, by which he is infinitely removed from all *moral Evil whatfoever*, is in an emphatical manner propofed to our imitation in the words of the Text; *As he which has called you is Holy, fo be* Ye *Holy, in all manner of Converfation*. The word, *Holinefs*, is perpetually in the mouths of Chriftians; but what it properly *means*, This they have often but a very imperfeft and confufed Notion of. It fignifies originally, in the Jewifh language, *Separation from Common Ufe*: And in *That* Senfe, all the Veffels and Furniture of the Temple are, in the Old Teftament, ftiled, *Holy*. In the fame Senfe, 'tis ufed of *Perfons* alfo imployed in the Service of God; who are intitled to this *external* and *nominal Holinefs*, whether they really anfwer their charafter or no. But the word is ufed in a *better* Senfe, when 'tis transferred from this *literal* to a *moral* fignification; expreffing a man's being *feparated*, by true Religion, from the *common Praftices* of a vicious and corrupt World; And, when applied to *God*, it fignifies his *infinite* Diftance, from every *kind* and *degree* of *moral Evil* whatfoever.

IN the Text therefore is propofed to our imitation the Example of the Divine *Holinefs*, or his *Hatred to Sin and Wickednefs* in general; *Be ye Holy, for I am Holy*. In *other* paffages of Scripture, particular moral Attributes are laid before us as Patterns to walk by. The words immediately following the Text, fet forth the Juftice of God; *ver*. 17. *Calling on the Father, who, without refpeft of Perfons, judgeth according to every man's work*. In the *fifth* chapter of St *Matthew*, our Saviour direfts us to imitate the Goodnefs of God, as the moft effeftual means to obtain a fhare in his Favour, and a part in his moft perfeft Happinefs: *Love your Enemies*, faith he, (that is, *not*, make them equal with your Friends, *but*, defire and promote their amendment, and then be ready to forgive them;) *do good to them that hate yov, and pray for them which defpitefully ufe you: That ye may be the children of your Father which is in Heaven*, (that is, that ye may be *like* unto *Him*,) who *maketh his Sun to rife on the Evil and on the Good, and fendeth Rain on the Juft and on the Unjuft*. And, to mention no more Inftances, the *Mercy* of God is by our Saviour in a very affeftionate manner propofed as an Example to excite us to Charity; *Luk*. vi. 35. *Do good, and lend, hoping for nothing again; and your Reward fhall be great, and ye fhall be the children of the Higheft; for He is kind unto the Unthankful and to the Evil; Be ye therefore merciful, as your Father alfo is merciful*. Which laft words, are remarkably varied by St *Matthew*, in his narration of the *fame* Difcourfe of our Lord. For what in St *Luke* we read thus, *Be ye therefore* merciful, *as your Father alfo is merciful*, is by St *Matthew* fet down in the

S E R M. following manner; *Be ye therefore* perfect, *even as your Father which is in Heaven is*
XXV. *perfect.* As if *Perfection,* and *Mercy or Charity,* were one and the same thing; and
as if he that was truly indued with this virtue of *Charity,* might *consequently* be sup-
Mat. v. 48. posed to be perfect in all *other* virtues likewise. This is the *first* necessary limitation,
of this Duty of imitating God; It must always be understood to be an imitation of his
moral Perfections only.

2*dly,* E v e n in these *moral* Excellencies, 'tis evident further, that it must necessarily mean an imitation of *likeness* only, and not of *Equality.* One would think, there
could be no great *need* of this Observation. Yet some Enthusiasts there have been, who
have vainly boasted themselves to be altogether without Sin; and being puffed up with
spiritual pride, and thinking themselves *above* the Duties of what they call *common Mo-*
rality, have by a Neglect of true Virtue, *fallen into the snare* and *condemnation of the*
Devil. Of This kind there seem to have been Some in St *John*'s time, against whom
he directs his Discourse, in his First Epistle, ch. i. 8. *If we say that we have no Sin,*
we deceive ourselves, and the Truth is not in us. But in our *present* Age, men are apt
to run much rather into the *contrary* extreme; not *pretending* to a perfection *above*
what is humane, but *neglecting* to endeavour after what *is* their *Duty* to obtain. They
know God to be a Being of infinite Holiness; that he *charges even his* Angels *with*
Folly, and the Heavens are not pure in his Sight: And therefore they think *frail men*
may be excused from attempting to imitate him at all. But This is a very wicked and
profane Suggestion. For though the Goodness indeed of such imperfect creatures as
we are, can be but in a very mean and low degree; yet *in* that proportion and degree,
we are indispensably bound to follow after it. And as a Finite *can* resemble infinite, so
we are to resemble God, by partaking of the same moral excellencies in *kind,* though
they cannot but be infinitely inferiour in *degree.* The Light of a *Star,* though it bears
no proportion at all to the glorious Beauty of the *Sun,* yet *Light* it is nevertheless, and
directly contrary to *Darkness:* So the Virtues of *Angels and of Men,* though they bear
no proportion to the adorable Perfections of *God,* yet, in their proper *measure and de-*
gree, they resemble them, as being of the same *nature and kind*; opposite and contrary to *wickedness,* just as every degree of *Light* is contrary to *Darkness.* The Apostle
aptly expresses This, by the similitude of a *Child* learning to imitate the Virtues of a
wise man and an' *affectionate* Parent; *Eph.* v. 1. *Be ye therefore* Followers *of God,* saith
he, *as Dear* Children.

3*dly,* B u t though our Imitation of the moral Perfections of God is always to be
understood with these great Limitations; as signifying an imitation of *Likeness* only,
and not of *Equality*; suitable to the weak nature of such frail, imperfect, and fallible
Creatures : Yet ought we *also* to consider, that even in the *Degrees* of Goodness it is
our Duty *continually* to improve, if we will at all answer the Precept in the Text, *Be*
ye Holy, for I am Holy. A perfect and most complete Example is set before us to imitate, that aiming always at That which is most excellent, we may grow continually
and make a perpetual Progress in the ways of Virtue : And though we can never come
up to our Pattern itself, yet, by such imitation as our frail and mortal nature is capable
of, we may attain to what St *Peter* calls being *made Partakers of the Divine Nature.*
Which participation of true Holiness *after the Image of him who created us,* is truly
and in a proper Sense the *comparative* Perfection of our *Humane* nature, as *absolute*
Perfection is the Perfection of the *Divine.* Which clearly explains the meaning and
extent of St *Paul*'s exhortation, 2 *Cor.* vii. 1. that we should perfect *Holiness in the*
Fear of God; and That Advice of our Saviour himself, St *Matt.* v. 48. *Be ye* perfect,
even as your Father which is in Heaven is perfect.

III. I t remains now in the *last* place, that I draw some useful *Observations* from
the Whole of what has been said; and so conclude. And

1*st,* I f

1ft, IF true Religion confifts in the imitation of God; and all imitation of God, is SER M. of neceffity confined to his *moral* Perfections only; then it thence evidently follows, XXV. that *moral Virtue* is the chief End of Religion; and that, to place the main ftrefs of Religion in any thing elfe befides true Virtue, is Enthufiafm or Superftition. When our Saviour gave his Apoftles Power over unclean Spirits, he thought it neceffary to add at the fame time the following Caution, *Luke* x. 20. *Notwithftanding in This rejoice not, that the Spirits are fubjeét unto you; but rather rejoice, becaufe your Names are written in Heaven :* your *Names are written in Heaven,* that is, your Repentance and Obedience is acceptable to God : For fo, in Scripture-phrafe, they who *keep the Commandments of God,* are faid to be *written in the Book of Life ;* and thofe who *Sin* againft him, he threatens that he will *blot* out of his *Book,* Exod. xxxii. 33. Again : In his defcription of the day of Judgment, *Many,* fays our Saviour, *will fay to me in That day, Lord, Lord, have we not prophefied in thy Name, and in thy Name have caft out devils, and in thy Name done many wonderful works? And then will I profefs unto them, I never knew you, Depart from Me ye that work iniquity ;* That is, all ye who have lived vitioufly and immorally. St *Paul* in like manner, 1 *Cor.* xiii. 1. *Though I fpeak,* fays he, *with the Tongues of Men and Angels; and though I have the gift of Prophecy, and underftand all myfteries, and all knowledge ; and though I have all Faith, fo that I could remove Mountains, and have not Charity,——it profiteth me nothing.* The greateft part of the *Rulers* of this World are ftrangely guilty of *This* Errour; when they affeét rather to be like God in *Power,* which is *not* an imitable Attribute, than in *Goodnefs,* wherein alone 'tis their Glory to be like him.

2dly, IF true Religion confifts in the imitation of God ; and that which is imitable in God, be his *moral* Perfections; hence it follows neceffarily, that *moral* Excellencies, *Juftice, Goodnefs, Truth,* and the like, are of the *fame kind* in God as in Men. For otherwife, if (as fome have imagined in order to maintain unintelligible doétrines,) *Juftice, Goodnefs, and Truth* in God, did not anfwer our common and natural Notions of thofe Virtues; but were of a kind quite different, and inconceivable to us; how then could men be obliged to *imitate* they knew not what? or how could it become poffible in *any* fenfe to be *holy as he is Holy,* if it could not be underftood by us *What* Holinefs is ? The Truth therefore plainly is; As Light is Light, *wherefoever* and in what *degree* foever it appears, and has no communion or fimilitude with Darknefs : fo Goodnefs, in *whomfoever* and in what *degree* foever it be found, ftill always carries along with it the fame Idea of Goodnefs, and has no communion or Fellowfhip with Wickednefs.

3dly and *Laftly;* FROM hence it appears, of how great importance it is to Men to frame to themfelves right and worthy Notions of *God.* For fuch as are the Conceptions Men have of the *Objeét of their Worfhip;* fuch alfo will proportionably be *their* own *Behaviour and Praétice.* The *Gentiles,* who worfhipped *vile and impure Deities,* were *themfelves* accordingly *given up to work all Uncleannefs with Greedinefs.* The *Jews,* when they fell from the Worfhip of the True God, to ferve the Idols and Images of really or fiétitioufly *cruel Dæmons ;* were *themfelves* accordingly devefted of humanity, and facrificed even their own Children to *Moloch.* And among *Chriftians* likewife, it is too fad and true an obfervation; that in proportion as they have departed from the Simplicity of the Gofpel, and feigned to themfelves either *ridiculous* or *wicked* notions of the infinitely wife and good God ; fo has their *religion* accordingly been changed either into a *ridiculous,* or into a *barbarous* and *cruel* Superftition. The only poffible remedy for which Evil, is to adhere ftedfaftly and immoveably to the natural and unchangeable notions of *righteoufnefs and holinefs* in *God,* and the indifpenfable neceffity of true *righteoufnefs and holinefs* among *Men.*

SERMON

4.

SERMON XXVI.

Of the LOVE of GOD towards Sinners.

St JOHN III. 16.

For God so loved the World, that he gave his only-begotten Son, that whosoever believeth in him, should not perish, but have everlasting Life.

SERM.
XXVI.

THESE Words are *part* of that Excellent Discourse, wherein our Saviour instructed *Nicodemus*, giving him a short Account of the Doctrine of the Gospel; And the Words themselves, are a brief Summary of that whole Discourse. *Nicodemus* was a Man of Learning and Authority among the *Jews*, and, as it seems, of a better and more pious Disposition, than the generality of those of his own Rank. Moved therefore by the Greatness of our Saviour's Miracles, and probably also having studied the Prophecies, which foretold the coming of the Messias about That Season; he thought himself bound to enquire what That Doctrine was, which our Saviour began so publickly and with so great Authority to teach; And accordingly he goes to him by Night, to converse privately about it. Our Saviour, addressing himself to him as to a Man of Understanding, begins at the Foundation of the Whole; and represents to him the Necessity of entring upon a religious Course of Life, according to the perfecter and more spiritual Principles of the Christian institution : *ver.* 3. *Except*, says he, *a man be born again, he cannot see the Kingdom of God.* Which Expression, *Nicodemus* at first not understanding; our Saviour further explains it to him, *ver.* 5. *Except*, says he, *a Man be born of Water and of the Spirit*; Except he be baptized into the Profession of the true Religion, and, suitable to this external Obligation, be inwardly renewed and purified from all wicked Dispositions in the Spirit of his Mind; *he cannot enter into the Kingdom of God.* For, *whatsoever is born of the Flesh*, can be but *Flesh*; *That which is born of the Spirit*, That only *is Spirit.* By *natural* Birth, a Man can have no other Title than only to the injoyments of this *Natural and Mortal Life* : To *Immortality* and a share in the *Kingdom of God*, he cannot be intitled, but by a New and *Spiritual* Birth, by being delivered from the Dominion of Fleshly Lusts, and living under the more perfect Law of Reason and Religion. To make this still more intelligible, and to take off the Difficulty of apprehending the meaning of that Phrase of being *Born again*, our Saviour proceeds to illustrate it by an easy similitude, *ver.* 7; that, as in the Course of *Nature* some of the greatest and most sensible Effects are produced by secret and imperceptible Causes; so it ought not to be wondred at, if some of the greatest *Moral* Effects, and most important Changes in the Mind of Man be wrought likewise by degrees invisible, and by means not discernable to Sense : *Marvel not that I said unto thee, ye must be born again : The* Wind *bloweth where it listeth, and thou hearest the Sound thereof, but canst not tell whence it cometh, and whither it goeth; so is every one that is born of the Spirit.*

HAVING

HAVING thus prepared the Way, by explaining the Foundation; our Saviour from hence makes a Tranfition, *ver.* 12. to the higher and more fublime Doctrines of the Gofpel; *If I have told you,* fays he, *earthly things, and ye believe not; how fhall ye believe if I tell you of heavenly things?* If ye believe me not even in thefe plain and more obvious matters, which I have fuited to your Capacities, and delivered in eafy Comparifons, drawn from the moft natural and common things here upon Earth; how much lefs will ye believe me, when I tell you more fublime and heavenly myfteries? when I declare to you the Dignity of my Perfon and Office, the fpiritual Nature of my Kingdom, and the Sufferings I muft firft undergo for the Redemption of Mankind? And yet thefe things are true and certain as the others; and the Works which I do, are fufficient Arguments, why ye fhould believe me even in Thefe things alfo. Now thefe fublimer Doctrines he begins to enumerate, *ver.* 13. *No man,* fays he, *hath afcended up to Heaven, but he that came down from Heaven, even the Son of Man which is in Heaven:* That is; Chrift, the *Son of Man,* the promifed Meffias, *That Son of Man* defcribed in the Prophet *Daniel* as *coming in the clouds of Heaven* to receive an everlafting Dominion; *This* Son of Man came forth from God, fo as no other Prophet, no not *Mofes* himfelf, ever did; For he was with God before he came amongft Men; and when he firft appeared in this World, he had before had a Being in Heaven in the Bofom of his Father, in which Dignity he ftill continues. And 'tis the Prerogative of *him* only, who came thus from God as no other ever did, throughly to underftand and to reveal to Men, the yet fecret Counfels of God concerning the eftablifhment of his Kingdom, and the Method of Men's Salvation. *No man hath afcended up to Heaven, but he that came down from Heaven, even the Son of Man which is in Heaven.* What this Method of Men's Salvation was, he proceeds more diftinctly to declare, *ver.* 14 and 15, *As Mofes lifted up the Serpent in the Wildernefs, even fo muft the Son of Man be lifted up; That whofoever believeth in him, fhould not perifh, but have eternal Life.* That is: That the Meffiah, by his Sufferings and Death fhould accomplifh the Redemption and Salvation of Men, opening an entrance into the Kingdom of Heaven, to all thofe who fhall fincerely obey him; *This* (fays our Saviour) ye ought not to be furprized at, as a new and ftrange Doctrine; fince ye have a reprefentation and prediction of it, even in your own Law. For as *Mofes* fet up in the Wildernefs the Figure of a Serpent, which being indeed the Likenefs of a venomous Beaft, yet was fo far from having any thing of its poifonous Nature, that on the contrary all thofe which had been bitten by real Serpents, were immediately healed by looking up towards this Reprefentation: So the *Son of Man,* the *Angel of the Covenant,* being made in the likenefs of finful Flefh, yet having really no Sin in him, fhall be lifted up on the Crofs, that by the Power of his Death, finful men believing in him, and being enabled to conquer and forfake their Sins, may obtain remiffion of Sin, and Everlafting Life. *For* thus he adds in the Words of the Text, fumming up his whole Difcourfe; *God fo loved the World, that he gave his only-begotten Son, that whofoever believeth in him, fhould not perifh, but have everlafting Life.*

Mal. iii. 1:
If. lxiii. 9.

THE Connexion of our Lord's Difcourfe being thus explained; we may in the Words themfelves confider 1*ft,* how and in what fenfe it is fuppofed, that without the coming of Chrift into the World, Men could not but have perifhed: 2*dly,* in what Senfe it is affirmed, that all who believe in him, fhall not perifh, but have everlafting Life: and 3*dly,* we may take Notice, that this Salvation of Men by the Coming of Chrift is afcribed to the antecedent Love of God, the original Goodnefs and Mercy of the Father Almighty. *God fo loved the World, that he gave his only-begotten Son, that whofoever believeth in him, fhould not perifh, but have everlafting Life.*

1*ft,* WE are to confider, how it is *fuppofed* in the words of the Text, that without the Coming of Chrift into the World, Men could not but have perifhed. And for the clearer explaining the ground of this Suppofition, it may be proper to obferve in the *firft* place, that when God originally created Man in the State of *Innocence*, and feated him in the Garden of Paradice, there was no *Obligation* upon *God* to indue him with Immortality. 'Twas not by Virtue of any Claim of *Right*, or by any *Neceffity* in the Nature of the Thing, but an Effect of his unbounded *Goodnefs* only, and a mere *free Gift*, that *God created Man to be Immortal, and made him to be an Image of his own Eternity*. He might juftly have created him for what Time he pleafed ; and even in the State of *Innocence*, might without any Wrong have put a Period to That Being, which at firft 'twas nothing but his own good Pleafure, that moved him to give Beginning to at all. And if This was the Cafe even in the State of *Innocence* itfelf, how much more when Man by Sin had forfeited all Title to the Divine Favour! If God was under no obligation to give Immortality to the immediate Work of his own Hands, how much lefs to the Pofterity of a fallen Sinner! and what claim could *They* have to the perpetual injoyment of Paradice, which to their Firft Parent himfelf, even in his moft perfect State of Innocence, was but a Free Gift! Undoubtedly nothing is more evident, than that God might without any Wrong have left them All to the natural Confequences of their own Mortality, and without any Injury to them might have forborn to make that Promife of eternal Life in Chrift, which the World would have had no Right to demand, even though there had never been in it any Sin. But then we are alfo to obferve *further*, that All the Sons of *Adam* are moreover Sinners *themfelves* ; and as by the Sin of *Adam* they became in the *Courfe of Nature* excluded out of Paradice, and from the Tree of Life, and from the Hopes of Immortality ; fo by their *own* Sins they became farther, and in a more proper Senfe, liable to the Wrath of God ; and fubject, not only to *Death*, which came *equally* and *univerfally* upon All ; but alfo to *actual Punifhments* in the future State, *proportionable* to every man's *private* Sin and *perfonal* Demerit. From which *common Death*, coming *equally* upon *All* ; and from which *proportionable Punifhment*, due to *every* man's *particular* Sins : nothing, that Sinners themfelves could do, could avail to refcue them, or to prevent their *perifhing* according to the Courfe of Nature, and the righteous Judgment of God. For God, whofe Promife of Immortality even to *Innocent* Creatures, was but a Free Gift of mere Bounty, was much lefs under any Obligation to provide a Place of eternal Happinefs for the Pofterity of a finful Parent ; themfelves alfo actual Sinners, and at the beft but very imperfect and undeferving Penitents ; whofe greateft Endeavours of Repentance, could at the moft but afford ground of Hope for an Abatement of Punifhment, and not any expectation of Reward. The Suppofition therefore in the Text is by no means difagreeable to Reafon ; that, without the Coming of Chrift into the World, Men could not but have *perifhed* : Thofe who *themfelves* had finned after the fimilitude of *Adam*'s tranfgreffion, being neceffarily liable to the wrath of God, and to the proportionable *actual Punifhment* of their Sins ; and thofe who had not finned in their own Perfons, being yet unavoidably in the Courfe of Nature involved in that *common Death*, from which *God* was not under any Obligation to refcue them ; feeing it was his *Free* Gift to give them Being at all, and that even in the State of *Innocence* itfelf He had been under no Obligation to indue them with Immortality.

THIS feems, ftrictly and accurately fpeaking, to have been the True State of *All Mankind*, when confidered as antecedent to the Promife of Chrift's Coming. But it deferves alfo to be taken Notice of, that as in moft other places, fo in the Text likewife, 'tis probable that when men's *Perifhing* is fpoken of, it is not fo much to be underftood in that *ftrict Senfe*, wherein *Every man whatfoever* is liable, more or lefs, to the Wrath of God ; as in that more *general and ufual Senfe*, wherein both *Jews* and *Gentiles* are reprefented as being for the *greateft part* by an univerfal Corruption of Manners loft in Sin, and utterly fallen *fhort of the Glory of God*. The *Jews* had in

their

their Law itfelf, no Expiation appointed for great and wilful Tranfgreffions; And there- S E R M.
fore *through* Chrift was *preach'd unto* them *the forgivenefs of Sins*; that *by him all that* XXVI.
believe might be *juftified from all things, from which they could not be juftified by the*
Law of Mofes, Acts xiii. 39. And Rom. viii. 3. *What the Law could not do, in that it*
was weak through the Flefh, God fending his own Son in the likenefs of finful Flefh, and
for Sin, condemned Sin in the Flefh. The *Gentiles* are juftly reprefented by St *Paul*, as
being *Enemies* to God, *walking* generally *in the Vanity of their Mind*; *Having the Un-*
derftanding darkened, being alienated from the Life of God, through the ignorance that is
in them, becaufe of the blindnefs of their Heart; *who being paft feeling*, (having loft all
fenfe of the natural and effential Difference of Good and Evil,) *have given themfelves*
over——to work all Uncleannefs with greedinefs, Eph. iv. 18. This was too plainly the
cafe of the greateft part of the *Gentile*-World in the Apoftles Time. And though there
be among *Us*, fome Deniers of the Gofpel of Chrift, who pretend that by the Light of
Reafon, without any Belief of Revelation, they can make out the Obligations of Morality, and teach men the Practice of Virtue, and their natural Duty both towards God
and Man; yet the beft and principal of thofe Reafonings they are inabled to make ufe
of even concerning *natural* Religion itfelf, are evidently owing to that Light and Improvement, which has arifen from the Preaching of the *Gofpel of Chrift*. Had the Knowledge of the Chriftian Religion never been propagated amongft Us, we had ftill, like our
barbarous Anceftors, been Worfhipping of Stocks and Stones in the Darknefs of moft
ftupid Ignorance: And thofe very Perfons, who now endeavour to turn againft Chriftianity, thofe Arguments for the Reafonablenefs of Natural Religion, which without
the Knowledge of the Gofpel they would never have been able to difcover; far from
improving themfelves, as they fondly imagine, under the Light of Nature, had then in
all probability been deftitute of the common Principles even of Civility and Humanity.
'Tis to the Mercy of the Gofpel therefore, that thefe Perfons owe their being *Now* in a
State fo different from that of the *Gentiles* in the Apoftles Times, who, by their total
Corruption, were in a State of abfolute *Enmity againft God*, and liable to his fevereft
Wrath. Without the Knowledge of Chrift, it cannot be doubted but the greateft part
of *Us*, who now are apt to think fo highly of our own Improvements, would have been
in the Cafe of thofe, who *not liking to retain God in their Knowledge*, were *given up*
unto vile Affections, and *received in themfelves That recompence of their Error, which was*
meet, being drowned in Deftruction and Perdition. And thofe who, by efcaping the
greater Pollutions, would not indeed have been involved in the fame *degree of Perdition*
with the reft, (for the Judge of all the Earth will always do what is Right,) yet would
have had *no Title* to that eternal Inheritance, that heavenly Kingdom, which is the *Free*
Gift of God in Chrift; an undeferved Gift, which nothing that Men could do of themfelves, even when they had done their whole Duty, could at all have merited, or
(without the Sanctification of the Spirit of God,) have qualified them for. For, *Except*
a man be born from above (fo the words are in the original, which we render, *Except*
a man be born again;) *Except a man be born* from above, *except he be born of Water and*
of the Spirit, *he cannot enter into the Kingdom of God*, Joh. iii. 3, 5. *Neither is there*
Salvation in any other, Acts iv. 12. *For there is none other Name under Heaven given*
among men, whereby we muft be faved; i. e. whereby we can attain *that* Kingdom of
Heaven, *that* free Gift of eternal Life, *that* Place peculiarly *prepared* by Chrift for his
Difciples out of the *Many Manfions in his Father's Houfe, that* Weight of Glory and
unfpeakable Reward, undeferved even by our beft Performances. Very *agreeable* to
Reafon therefore is the Suppofition in the Text, that, without the coming of Chrift into
the World, men, in the manner before explained, could not but have *perifhed*.

2*dly*, THE Second thing to be confidered in the Text, is; in what Senfe 'tis affirmed, that *All who* believe *in* Chrift, *fhall not perifh, but have everlafting Life.* Of which

Kind,

SERM. Kind, there are frequent *general* Aſſertions in Scripture. *Acts* x. 43. *Through his*
XXVI. *Name, whoſoever* believeth *in him, ſhall receive Remiſſion of Sins*; and ch. xiii. 39. *By*
him, all that believe, *are juſtified from all things, from which they could not be juſtified by*
the Law of Moſes. St *John* in like manner in his Firſt Epiſtle, ch. v. 12. *He that hath*
the Son, hath life; and he that hath not the Son of God, hath not life; Theſe things have
I written unto you that believe *on the Name of the Son of God, that ye may know that*
ye have eternal Life. And our Saviour himſelf, in the Goſpel, St *John* iii. 36. *He*
that believeth *on the Son, hath everlaſting Life*; and in the words immediately before
thoſe of the Text, ver. 14. *As Moſes lifted up the Serpent in the Wilderneſs, even ſo*
muſt the Son of Man be lifted up; That whoſoever believeth *in him, ſhould not periſh, but*
have eternal Life. There have been ſome ſo abſurd, as from theſe and other the like
paſſages in the New Teſtament, to conclude that by *Faith* only, *viz.* by a bare Aſſent
to the Truth of the Chriſtian Doctrine, or by a confident Perſwaſion of their belonging
to Chriſt, they ſhould not fail of Obtaining Salvation. But the contrary is plain both
from the Reaſon of the thing itſelf, and from numberleſs other paſſages of Scripture:
That, when it is affirmed, that whoſoever *believeth* in Chriſt, *ſhall not periſh, but have*
everlaſting Life; the meaning is not, whoſoever *profeſſeth* or *pretends* to believe in him,
but whoſoever *really* believes in him, and *with Effect*; whoſoever is ſo perſwaded of
the Truth of his Doctrine, as to embrace the *Terms* propoſed by the Goſpel, and to
make them the Rule of his Life and Actions. For as, in all other caſes, things are
judged of not by their *mere Denomination* and *external Appearances*, but by their *in-*
ward Powers or Qualities, and by their *real Effects*; and *Shadows* are not taken for
Subſtances, nor *Pictures* for the *Things themſelves* which they repreſent, notwithſtanding
their being called perhaps by the ſame *Names*: So, *believing in Chriſt*, is not barely profeſſing *to believe in him*, but *believing in him* indeed; believing his Doctrine to be *True*;
conſidering it accordingly as of the utmoſt *Importance*; endeavouring conſequently to
underſtand it *ourſelves*, and not truſting ourſelves to be impoſed upon by *Others*; and
finally, *governing our ſelves by it* in all our Actions, in the whole Courſe of our Lives.
For the word *Faith*, always contains in it the Notion of *Faithfulneſs* or *Fidelity*. And
though the plain Reaſon of the Thing itſelf might be ſufficient in ſo evident a Caſe; yet
the Scripture is not wanting to explain it alſo in variety of Words. *He that believeth,*
(ſays our Saviour in another place,) *and is* baptized, *i. e.* and enters into an obligation
to *live ſuitably* to that Belief; *he* ſhall be ſaved. For, *not every one that ſaith unto me,*
Lord, Lord, ſhall enter into the Kingdom of Heaven, but he that doth *the Will of my*
Father which is in Heaven. And *being baptized*, ſaith St *Peter*, is not *the waſhing*
away of the filth of the Fleſh, but the Anſwer of a good Conſcience towards God. And
the Anſwer of a good Conſcience towards God, is the *Faith* which *worketh*, or evidences
itſelf, *by Love*: For *the End of the Commandment*, ſaith St *Paul*, is *Charity, out of a*
pure Heart, and of a good Conſcience, and of Faith unfeigned, 1 Tim. i. 5.

ALL that *believe* therefore, are *All* that *embrace* and *obey* the Goſpel. For Theſe,
Chriſt came into the World on purpoſe, that they *might not periſh, but have everlaſting*
Life: And becauſe the Goſpel was commanded to be preached to *every Creature*, that
is, to all mankind; and God has expreſſly declared that he would have *all men* to be
ſaved; and deſireth not that *any* ſhould periſh, but that *All* might come to Repentance;
therefore we may reaſonably underſtand the Words in the Text, *whoſoever believeth in*
him, as if it had been thus expreſſed: God gave his Son, that *Every one by believing*
in him; that *every man*, by *his* means, and by accepting the advantage and gracious
Terms of the Goſpel, might avoid periſhing, and obtain everlaſting Life. And This
Senſe of the Phraſe is juſtified by the Words immediately following the Text, ver. 17.
For God ſent not his Son into the World to condemn the World, but that the World, that
the whole World, *through him might be ſaved.* Thoſe to whom the Goſpel is actually

I   preached

preached, have this Salvation *clearly* offered them, unlefs they rejeĉt it by their wilful Impenitence. The Jews and Patriarchs had it no lefs *certainly*, though more obfcurely, repofited in the expeĉtation of him that was to come : And thofe who never heard either of the Law or the Gofpel, yet have it *effeĉtually* laid up for them, (though without their having any prefent Knowledge of it,) in that declaration of the Apoftle, that *they which have not the Law, are a Law unto themfelves*; and that *their uncircumcifion*, if they *keep the Law*, fhall (through the blood of Chrift, though not explicitly made known amongft them,) *be counted to them for circumcifion*, if they *keep the Law*, fhall (through the blood of Chrift, though not explicitly made known among them,) *be counted to them for Circumcifion.* Thus God fhall univerfally be juftified, when he appears in Judgment; and *All mouths* fhall be ftopped before him.

And This may fuffice for Explication of the 2*d* particular that was to be confidered in the Text, *viz.* in what Senfe it is affirmed, that *all who* believe *in Chrift, fhall not perifh, but have everlafting Life.*

3*dly*, We are in the laft place to take Notice, that this Salvation of Men by the Coming of Chrift, is afcribed to the antecedent Love of God, the original Mercy and Goodnefs of the Father Almighty. God *fo loved the World, that he gave his only-begotten Son, that whofoever believeth in him, fhould not perifh, but have everlafting Life.* It is a falfe Notion which fome men have taken up of God, and very injurious to Religion, to conceive *God* in his own Nature to be a fevere and mercilefs Punifher; to look upon him as a Cruel Exercifer of irrefiftible Power, as an Objeĉt only of dread and horror; to imagine, that, contrary to his own Inclination, and as it were *againft* his Will, he was prevailed upon by Chrift to take Pity on his Creatures, as a Cruel and Paffionate Man is fometimes over-ruled by his Friend, to be better than his Intention. No: All this is a very unjuft Reprefentation of God; The hard Speeches which ignorant or unrighteous men have fpoken againft him. The *Scripture* on the contrary, as well as *Natural Reafon*, always fets forth God as the Supreme Fountain of Goodnefs; the Preferver, not the Enemy and Deftroyer, of his Creatures. 'Twas not the interpofition of Chrift which *changed* the Mind of God; but 'twas the original Goodnefs and Love of God, which *appointed* for us the Interpofition of Chrift. To punifh Sinners, and deftroy Wickednefs out of his Kingdom, is indeed the neceffary Office even of That Governour who is Goodnefs itfelf; and therefore, in order to difcourage Sin, he thought fit it fhould be pardoned by no eafier a Method, than by the Incarnation and Death of his Son. Yet 'twas his Goodnefs only that moved him to contrive that Method; and his original Love to his Creatures, that put him upon fo reconciling Mercy with Juftice. God did not *hate* the World, and fuffer the Interceffion of Chrift to prevail over that Hatred; but God *loved* the World, and *therefore gave* his only-begotten Son, that whofoever believeth in him fhould not perifh, but have everlafting Life. And hence it is, that the *Father* is ftiled (by way of eminence) *God our Saviour:* Tit. iii. 4, 6. *The Kindnefs and Love of* God our Saviour,——*which he fhed on us abundantly through Jefus Chrift our Saviour.* But this is a Subjeĉt of fuch importance, that it deferves to be treated of more particularly in a following Difcourfe.

S E R M O N XXVII.

Of the L o v e of GOD towards Sinners.

St J O H N III. 16.

For God so loved the World, that he gave his only-begotten Son, that whosoever believeth in him, should not perish, but have everlasting Life.

SERM. XXVII.

IN discoursing upon these Words, I have proposed to consider the following particulars; *1st,* how and in what sense it is *præsupposed* in the Text, that without the Coming of Christ into the World, men *could not but* have perished. *2dly,* In what Sense it is affirmed, that *All* who *believe* in him shall not perish, but have everlasting Life. And *3dly,* that this Salvation of Men by the Coming of Christ, is ascribed to the Antecedent Love of God, the Original Mercy and Goodness of the Father Almighty. *God so loved* the World, that he *gave his only begotten Son,* that whosoever believeth in him, should not perish, but have everlasting Life. The Two former of these Propositions I have already discoursed of; and shall therefore at this Time proceed directly to the *Third*; namely, to observe, that in the Words of the Text, the Salvation of Men by the Coming of Christ, is expressly ascribed to the Antecedent Love of God, the original essential Mercy and Goodness of the Father Almighty. *God so loved* the World, that *he gave* his only-begotten Son. And This is necessarily to be observed, in Vindication of the essential *Goodness of God,* which is one of the primary Attributes of the Divine Nature; and in opposition to those, who while they think they magnify the Redemption purchased by the Blood of Christ, (which can never indeed be too much magnified in a *consistent* manner,) seem to forget the equal Necessity, of maintaining at the same Time all the original Attributes of God; and are not sufficiently aware of the Danger of representing *one* Method of God's acting, as inconsistent with *another*; or *any* of God's actions *so,* as to be *contradictory* to his *Nature* or any of his *Attributes.* For since Truth cannot be contrary to itself; and *every* true Doctrine must of Necessity be agreeable, and in perfect harmony on all sides with every *other* true Doctrine whatsoever; 'tis of the utmost importance to Religion, that we take Care never to represent any *one* part of its Doctrine in such a manner, as to destroy *another*; least *That* also in its turn destroy the *present* Notion; and so *Both* give Advantage to the sceptical Unbeliever. 'Tis not easy to imagine, *how much* Religion has frequently suffered by this very means; and what occasion has been given to the profane Adversary to blaspheme, whilst the unwary carrying *particular* Doctrines too far, and pressing them by Arguments not well consistent with *other* Doctrines of equal Necessity, have afforded too plausible Grounds of Objecting against the *Whole.* What I am now speaking of will best be understood, by *instancing* in *particular Instances.* The *Justice* of God may seem to be most highly magnified, by supposing that it puts an absolute *Necessity* upon him, either of inflicting an infinite Punishment, or of demanding an infinite Satisfaction. But they who so speak, ought at the same time to consider on the other hand, that they leave no room either for Goodness or Mercy: And that the Scripture

3

on the contrary always fpeaks, even of the Satisfaction of *Chrift*, not as a Price or Equi- S E R M.
valent which made our Pardon *due* by a Claim of *Right* ; but as a Means *freely* appoint- XXVII.
ed, and *freely* accepted, by the mere Mercy and Compaffion of the Father ; who, as
Supreme Governour of all things, remits voluntarily of his own Right, in what Meafure
and upon what Terms he pleafes.

I n like manner the *Grace* of God, fome Men imagine they greatly magnify, when
they afcribe to its operation the *whole* and *entire* Progrefs of every good work. But if
they would look at the fame time on the other part of the Queftion, they might find,
that by leaving nothing at all for the *Will of Man* to do, they make him to be a Subject no more capable of Religion, than the Beafts that perifh, or even than lifelefs
Matter itfelf.

A g a i n ; The Merit *of good Works*, which the Church of *Rome* boafts of, is indeed
effectually deftroyed, by making good Works to be *of no importance at all* towards Juftification, and by afcribing the Whole to *Faith only*. But they who fo deftroy Merit,
fhould not be ignorant, that at the fame time and with the fame Argument, taking
away the Neceffity of Virtue and of good Manners, they deftroy alfo the very Foundation of *all Religion*.

T o give an inftance or two of another kind. The *Authority of Councils*, or of *any
humane Power*, to determine Matters of Faith, is indeed a moft effectual Means of
putting a perpetual ftop to all kinds of Schifm, and to all Divifions whatfoever in Matters of Religion : But he that ufes this Argument againft an Adverfary *before* him, ought
not to be unaware, that there is another *behind* him, who makes ufe of the very fame
Argument even with greater Force againft *Him* ; For the Church of *Rome* has plainly
the greateft and the moft univerfal Weight of *humane Authority*, which God ever permitted to opprefs fair and impartial Inquiry after the Truth.

A g a i n ; the *Divinity of Chrift*, may feem to be moft earneftly and zealoufly contended for, by thofe who confound it with the Supreme Independency and Self-exift-
ence of the Perfon of the Father : But if they confidered on the other hand, how in fo
doing they either deftroyed the moft fundamental Principle of *all* Religion, the *Unity*
of God ; or elfe the firft Principle of *Chriftian* Religion, the *Being* of the Son of God ;
it would appear that they knew rightly, neither the Father nor the Son.

Laftly : T o inftance in the Doctrine of the Text, the *Coming of Chrift* into the
World for the *Redemption of Mankind* ; It may feem indeed at firft fight to be a pious
extolling the Love of our Saviour, and the Greatnefs of the Work he undertook ; to
aggravate the natural Mifery of Mankind, to reprefent in the terribleft Colours the Severity of the Juftice of an incenfed God, and to defcribe the Supreme Father and Creator
of all things, as having no Thoughts of Pity or Compaffion towards his perifhing Creatures, till moved thereto as it were *againft* his original Intention, by the Interpofition of
Chrift. But they who thus argue, ought on the other hand to be aware, that 'tis no
lefs injurious to Religion, to diminifh the original Goodnefs and Compaffion of the *Father of Mercies*, than 'tis pious to be worthily fenfible of the greatnefs of the Redemption purchafed by the Blood of Chrift. A true and fincere Chriftian will after a confiftent manner magnify the Love of *Chrift* in *dying* for our Sins ; and the Mercy of
God, in *fending* him to die for that Purpofe, in choofing and in accepting that Atonement. God *fo loved the World, that* he gave *his only-begotten Son* ; (and the *only-begotten Son* fo loved the World, that he was *willing to be given* for our Redemption ;) that
whofoever believeth on him, fhould not perifh, but have everlafting Life. The Salvation
of Men therefore, is owing *both* to the *Redemption* of *Chrift*, who gave himfelf for us ;
and to the antecedent *Love* and original effential Goodnefs of *the Father Almighty*, who
was pleafed to appoint and to accept that Sacrifice. Nor is it fo great an Argument of
the *Severity* of God, that he would not pardon Sinners without the Death of his Son ;

S E R M. as it is of his essential *Goodnefs* and *Compassion*, that he would rather appoint his Son to
XXVIII. die, than that sinful man should not be pardoned.   He that appoints the *Means*, thereby
declares his Choice and Approbation of the *End* : And if God had not been by Nature,
originally and essentially Good and Merciful, he would no more have *accepted* any Propitiation *for* Sin, than he would have pardoned it *without* any.   Most unjustly therefore, and with great injury to Religion, is God sometimes represented as an implacable
and cruel Judge, delighting in the destruction of Sinners, till they were *taken* (as it
were) out of his Hands by the Interposition of Christ ; This (I say,) is a very injurious
Representation of the Great God and Father of Mercies : For, the Coming of Christ
was not the first Cause of the Goodnefs and Love of God towards us ; but the essential and eternal Goodnefs of God was the cause and reason of the Coming of Christ.
God so loved *the World*, says our Saviour, *that he* gave *his only-begotten Son*.   It became the Supreme Governour of the Universe, to punish Sin : And yet he so loved
the World, and had such Compassion upon the Work of his Hands, that he was willing to find an Expedient by which sinful man might be pardoned and saved, without
giving encouragement to Sin ; and therefore *he* gave *his only-begotten Son, that whosoever believeth on him, should not perish, but have everlasting Life*.

T H E words of the Text, are Each of them very emphatically significant, and
strongly expressive of that glorious Attribute of the Divine Nature, his essential and
eternal Goodnefs.   *God*, even the Father and Lord of all things, who disposes all
things according to the pleasure of his own Will, and whose Actions can be determined by Nothing Without Himself ; *He so* loved *the World*, was so moved by the
original and eternal Goodnefs of his own Nature, to have Compassion upon the Work
of his Hands ; that he *gave*, freely and out of mere Bounty, without any Obligation,
and without any Constraint ; he gave *his* Son out of his Bosom, his *only-begotten Son,*
the *Son of his Love*, to die for the Sins of Men ; that so, though it was not fit, in his
Wisdom and Government of the World, that *Sin* should pass unpunished ; yet by this
means, *Sinners* believing on him, and being by him brought to Repentance, might not
perish, but have everlasting Life.   He might justly have sent his Son to take *Vengeance*
upon a sinful World ; to *destroy* it *totally*, as he did before *in part* at the overthrow of
Sodom ; and to do it *finally*, as he had before done it *for a Time* at the general Deluge.
But on the contrary our Saviour declares, that *Mercy* prevailed over Judgment ; that
God so loved *the World*, (that is, was so moved by his own internal Goodnefs to have
compassion upon Sinners,) that he *sent his Son into the World, not to condemn the World,
but that the World through him might be saved*, Joh. iii. 17. In *later* Ages, many have
been used to speak otherwise ; and to represent God as clothed with the mere Severity
of a rigorous and strict Judge, till his Wrath was, (as it were, *contrary* to his own Intention,) appeased and pacified by the Intercession of Christ.   And This has made some
very pious Persons look upon God as an Object of the greatest *Terror*, who on the
contrary ought above all things to be *Loved* as the most perfect Good : For, comparatively speaking, *There is None Good*, saith our Saviour, *but One, that is, God*.   To
Sinners, indeed, so long as they continue *Impenitent*, *God* cannot but be very justly an
Object of the utmost Dread.   And so also indeed is even *our Saviour himself*, who died
for them : For thus the Scripture emphatically represents their Case, *Rev*. vi. 16, that
they shall *say to the Mountains and to the Rocks, Fall on us ; and hide us from the face
of him that sitteth on the throne, and from the Wrath of the* Lamb.   To *impenitent* Sinners, the Wrath of the *Lamb* himself is no less terrible, than even the Face of him that
sitteth upon the Throne.   But on the contrary, to Sinners truly *penitent*, and to All
who sincerely endeavour to obey the Will of God ; not only the Love of *Christ*, which
is the *mediating* Cause, but the antecedent Love and essential Goodnefs of *the Father
Almighty*, which is the *primary and original* Cause of their Salvation, is always in

3   Scripture

Scripture reprefented and laid before them as a *Motive of Gratitude*, and as a principal
Argument to excite in *Them* fuitable Returns of Love and Obedience to *Him*. In the
twentieth chapter of the *Acts*, ver. 24. St *Paul* calls his Apoftlefhip *the Miniftry which
he had received of the Lord Jefus, to teftify the Gofpel of the Grace of God*: The Gofpel
of the Grace of God, i. e. the gracious declaration of *God's* Love and Favour towards
Mankind, manifefted by *Chrift*. In his Epiftle to the *Romans*, ch. i. ver. 1, 3, 5. he
ftiles it the *Gofpel of God, concerning his Son Jefus Chrift our Lord, by whom we have received grace*; *Grace*, that is, the gracious Manifeftation of *God's* Compaffion towards
Sinners in the Gofpel. *Ch.* iii. 22, 25. he calls it the righteoufnefs *of God, which is by
Faith of Jefus Chrift*; *whom God hath fet forth to be a propitiation through Faith in his
Blood, to declare his* righteoufnefs *for the remiffion of Sins that are paft, through the forbearance of God,* The Righteoufnefs *of God*, in fending Chrift for the remiffion of our
Sins, is a phrafe that founds harfh in modern language: But in the Jewifh Speech, becaufe *righteous and good* men are *apt* to be moved with *compaffion*, therefore they have
but one and the fame Word to exprefs both *Righteoufnefs* and *charitable Pity*.   From
whence, both in the Old and New Teftament, the Word *Righteoufnefs* muft frequently
be underftood to fignify, not ftrict *Juftice*, but *Equity, Charity, Forbearance*, and
Compaffion : And particularly in the place now cited, the Righteoufnefs *of God* in fending Chrift, fignifies, not any *Obligation* upon him in *Juftice* fo to do, but his *Goodnefs*
and *Mercy* moving him him to do it.   In the fame Epiftle to the *Romans*, ch. v. 5, 6,
8, 15. he Thus defcribes the ftate of the Gofpel; that the Love of God *is fhed abroad
in our Hearts*, becaufe *when we were yet without ftrength, in due time* Chrift *died for
the Ungodly*; And, that God *commendeth his* Love *towards us, in that while we were
yet Sinners*, Chrift *died for us*; And that, as *through the offence of One*, viz. by the Occafion of *Adam's* Sin, *Many be dead*; fo, and *much more, the* Grace *of* God *and the
Gift by Grace*, i. e. the Love and Favour of God, *by one Man Jefus Chrift, hath a-
bounded unto Many*. And ch. viii. 32. He draws an Argument of *further* Hope, from
this very confideration; *He that* fpared not *his own Son, but delivered him up for us all,
how fhall he not, with Him, alfo freely give us all things?* 'Tis the fame Argument,
which the Wife of *Manoah* had of old made ufe of, *Judg.* xiii. 23. *If the Lord were*
pleafed *to kill us, he would not have received a burnt-offering at our Hands*. Again,
in the Second Epiftle to the *Corinthians*, ch. v. the Apoftle reprefents God, not only as
confenting to our redemption by Chrift, and being the *original Author* of it, *ver.* 18.
All things are of God, who hath reconciled us to himfelf by Jefus Chrift; but he carries
it ftill much further, *ver.* 20. *As though God did* befeech *you by Us, we pray you*,
(faith he) *in Chrift's ftead, be ye reconciled to God*. This is not the Character of a
mercilefs and Cruel Judge; to be himfelf not only the *Author* of man's Redemption
by *Sending* his Son, but even to *befeech* us alfo to accept him when he is fent.   *As I
live*, faith the Lord God, *I have no pleafure in the Death of him that dieth, but rather that he fhould turn from his Ways and live*. Nor are thefe *figurative* Expreffions,
or the incidental reprefentations of Single Texts; but they are the *whole Tenour* of Scripture, inculcating This Notion perpetually, as of the *greateft importance* to Religion.
Thus the fame Apoftle St *Paul* again, in his Epiftle to the *Ephefians*, ch. ii. 4, 5, 7,
10, 11, 12, 13. God, faith he, *who is rich in Mercy, for his great* Love *wherewith
he* loved *us, even when we were dead in Sins, hath quickned us together with Chrift*;—
*That in the Ages to come he might fhew the exceeding Riches of his Grace, in his Kind-
nefs towards us through Chrift Jefus*:——*For we are His workmanfhip, created in
Chrift Jefus unto good works, which God hath before ordained that we fhould walk in
them; Wherefore remember that ye being in time paft Gentiles in the flefh, who are called
Uncircumcifion by that which is called the Circumcifion in the flefh made by hands, that
at that time ye were without Chrift, being aliens from the commonwealth of Ifrael, and*

Strangers from the covenants of Promise, having no hope, and without God in the world; But now in Chrift Jefus ye who fometimes were far off, are made nigh by the blood of Chrift. And in 2 *Theff.* ii 13, 14. *We are bound to give thinks always to God for you,———becaufe God hath from the beginning chofen you to Salvation,———whereunto he called you by our Gofpel, to the obtaining of the Glory of our Lord Jefus Chrift :* And *ver.* 16. *Our Lord Jefus Chrift himfelf, and* God, even our Father, *which hath loved us and hath given us everlafting confolation, and good hope through grace——ftablifh you in every good Word and Work.* Again, 2 *Tim.* i. 9. God——*hath faved us, and called us——according to his own Purpofe and Grace, which was given us in Chrift Jefus before the World began :* And *Tit.* iii. 4, 6. *After that the* Kindnefs *and* Love *of* God our Saviour *toward* Man *appeared ;——which* He *fhed on us abundantly through* Jefus Chrift our Saviour : The expreffion is *very* remarkable, that fpeaking of the *Love* of *the Father* towards us, he calls *Him* by the Title of *Saviour* in the *firft* place : *The Kindnefs and Love of* God our Saviour, *which he fhed on us through* Jefus Chrift our Saviour. The Apoftle St *John* in like manner, 1 *Joh.* iii. 1, 16. *Behold* (faith he) *what manner of* Love, *the* Father *hath beftowed upon us, that we fhould be called the Sons of God: Hereby perceive we the* Love of God, *becaufe* He (that is, *Chrift*) *laid down his Life for us :* And ch. iv. 9. very nearly repeating the Words of our Saviour in the Text, *In This* (faith he) *was manifefted the* Love of God *towards us, becaufe that God fent his only-begotten Son into the World, that we might live through Him.* Thefe and numberlefs other the like paffages in Scripture, do fufficiently declare, what I at firft propofed to prove in Vindication of the Divine Attributes, *viz.* that the Salvation of men by the Coming of Chrift, is and ought to be afcribed primarily to the Antecedent Love, and Original effential Goodnefs of the Father Almighty. God *fo loved the World, that he gave his only-begotten Son, that whofoever believeth in him, fhould not perifh, but have everlafting Life.*

I T remains that I conclude, with drawing fome ufeful Inferences from what has been faid upon This Subject.

And 1*ft*, F R O M hence we may obferve, that every Doctrine of Truth is confiftent both with *itfelf,* and with every *other* Truth; and ftands clear of Objections, equally on *All* fides. Upon *fome Reprefentations* of the *Severity* of *God,* and of the *Mifery* of *Men,* Unbelievers have been encouraged to object : If perfect Goodnefs be an effential Attribute of the Divine Nature, how then could God, who is infinitely Good, leave all men to perifh, antecedently to the confideration of the Coming of Chrift ? The Anfwer is obvious : *God* did not caufe men to perifh, but their *own Wickednefs* made it neceffary for the Wifdom of a perfectly Good Governour to punifh and deftroy them. And yet his Juftice and Wifdom were not more fpeedy in condemning them, than his Goodnefs in moving him to find a means of bringing them to *Recovery* by Repentance, and to *Salvation* by Chrift. And This Goodnefs did not firft manifeft itfelf at the Coming of Chrift ; but the Apoftle affures us it was *given us in Chrift Jefus* before the World began, 2 Tim. i. 9. It was promifed to *Adam,* it was repeated to the Patriarchs, it was declared by the Prophets ; it was fulfilled in Chrift : And both *before* and *fince* the Coming of Chrift, it has been made good to thofe, who obferved the *Law,* and who obeyed the *Gofpel,* and to thofe who (without the Knowledge of Either) have been (as St *Paul* defcribes them) *a Law unto themfelves.* In this whole Tranfaction, the *Goodnefs* of God has manifefted itfelf abundantly, in doing what he was by no means *bound* to do, what no Power could have *conftrained* him to do, what to *Himfelf* was no *Benefit* or Advantage ; (For he could as eafily out of the *Stones* have raifed up Children unto *Abraham,* according to the elegant expreffion of St *John the Baptift,* as have prevailed with the real Children of *Abraham* to bring forth Fruits meet for Repen-

tance :)

ta•ace :) Laftly, 'twas doing That, which brought the *greateft Sufferings*, (not indeed S E R M. neceffarily, for That would not have been juft ; but *freely* and *voluntarily*,) *upon the* XXVII. *Perfon who was moft dear* to him, even his only-begotten and moft beloved Son. And What greater Inftance of Goodnefs and Bounty than This, can poffibly be conceived ? Had God, *without* requiring any Propitiation at all, freely forgiven all Sins upon Repentance; This (no doubt) would by all have been efteemed an Act fufficiently evidencing that perfect Goodnefs and Mercy which is an effential Attribute of the Divine Nature : But now, freely and of his own meer Bounty, to *find out and appoint* a Propitiation ; is, with regard to his *Goodnefs* towards *Us*, the very fame thing, as *requiring no Atonement at all* would have been ; and, at the fame time, 'tis more *agreeable* to the Exercife of his *Other* Attributes, in the Government of the World. Neither therefore is the *effential Goodnefs* of God, in any wife inconfiftent with that *Severity* againft Sin, which made the Incarnation of Chrift neceffary to mens Salvation ; Nor on the other fide is that *Severity*, wherewith God condemns men antecedent to their redemption by Chrift, at all inconfiftent with the moft perfect Notion of effential Goodnefs.

2dly, F R O M what has been faid, we may obferve, of how great Importance it is to Religion, to frame right and worthy Notions concerning the *Attributes* and the *Actions* of God. The Foundation of Religion is the *Love* of God; and no man can love whom he does not think well of. The Service of a Tyrant, is Slavery : And where there is not a Reverence, mixt with the Affection of *Love* as well as Fear, there the Obedience can be but Formal and External, without the Heart and without Life. 'Tis therefore of the greateft Confequence in Religion, that men entertain not hard and difhonourable Thoughts of Cod. To reprefent God, as choofing and delighting to make Men extremely miferable, or as being originally and of Himfelf mercilefsly fevere, may indeed at firft Sight to inconfiderate Perfons feem to magnify the Redemption purchafed by Chrift : But in reality, by deftroying our natural Notion of God's effential Goodnefs, it deftroys the firft Principle and Foundation of Religion. God is, of Himfelf, the Father of Mercies : But becaufe, in the All-wife government of the World, it was fit and neceffary that Sin fhould not go unpunifhed, therefore this Mercy could not be manifefted to us, but thro' the Son of his Love. Yet ftill it was the fame God, who moved by his *own* Compaffion, fhowed us mercy in his Son; And the Scripture is againft no perfons more fevere, than againft thofe who fpeak hardly, and unworthily, of God. One part of the great snd final judgment, as reprefented by St *Jude*, is to *convince men of all their* hard fpeeches *which they have fpoken againft him*, ver. 15. And fevere is the reproof given upon this Account in the flothful Servant in the Parable, St *Luk*. xix. 22. *Out of thine own Mouth will I judge thee ;——Thou kneweft that I was an auftere man, taking up that I laid not down, and reaping that I did not fow.* And 1 *Sam*. ii. 2, 3. *There is none Holy as the Lord ;——let not arrogancy* (in the original it is, *let not Hard words*) *come out of your Mouth*. And *Mal*. iii. 13. *Your Words have been ftout againft me, faith the Lord; Yet ye fay, What have we fpoken fo much againft thee ? Ye have faid, It is vain to ferve God, and what profit is it that we have——walked mournfully before* him ? 'Tis therefore plainly injurious to religion, to entertain *hard* Thoughts of God, in diminution of his original and effential Goodnefs. Neverthelefs on the contrary it ought alfo to be obferved, that 'tis equally dangerous for Sinners to prefume on the *other fide* unreafonably upon his *Love and Mercy*. For as, *before* the Coming of Chrift, men ftood condemned for their *Sins*; fo, *after* his Coming alfo fhall they be condemned for their *impenitency*. And as the *Juftice* of God did not prevent his *Mercy* from fending a Redeemer to fave all true *Penitents*; fo his *Love in Chrift* will not prevent his *Juftice*, from becoming to all *incorrigible* Sinners a confuming Fire.

3dly, F R O M

4

S E R M.   *3dly*, F r o m what has been faid, we may learn how vain That diſtinction is,
XXVII.   which has fometimes been made between *Nature* and *Grace*, as if the Gifts of *Na-*
ture and thofe of *Grace* were oppofite to each other ; when in reality they are nothing
elfe but the Gifts of the *fame* God, *derived* to us *originally* from the *effential* Goodnefs of his Nature, and *improved* in us by his *reconciled* Goodnefs and Mercy through
Chriſt.

4thly, F r o m hence we may obferve, how the *Satisfaction of Chriſt* is by no
means inconfiſtent with the Notion of God's *Free Pardon* of Sin. For it was not, that
the *Satisfaction of Chriſt* did in Strictnefs of Juſtice *oblige* him to pardon ; but on the
contrary, his Refolution to pardon Sin determined him *freely to appoint and accept that
Satisfaction.*

5thly, I f *God* fo loved *Us*, the Application is eafy, that *We* ought alfo to love *Him*.
And *how* we are to do *That*, the Apoſtle St *John* tells us, 1 *Joh.* v. 3. *This is the Love
of God, that we keep his Commandments.* *Love* towards a Superiour confiſts properly in
taking pleafure to do his Will : in delighting to obey him and to do things acceptable
to him. *Whofo* therefore keepeth *his* Word, *in Him verily is the Love of God perfected ;
hereby know we that we Are in Him,* 1 Joh. ii. 5.

Laſtly, I f *God* fo loved *us*, then ought *We* alfo, after *His* example, to love *one another*. And This is the Inference of the fame Apoſtle St *John*, 1 Joh. iv. 7—21 ;
wherewith I fhall conclude : *In this was manifeſted the love of God towards us, becaufe
that God fent his only-begotten Son into the World, that we might live through Him ;——
Beloved, if God fo loved Us, We ought alfo to love one another.——If a man fay, I love
God, and hateth his Brother, he is a Liar ; for he that loveth not his Brother whom he
hath feen, how can he love God whom he hath not feen? And this commandment have we
from Him, that He who loveth God, love his Brother alfo.*

SERMON

SERMON XXVIII.

Of BELIEVING in GOD.

ROM. IV. 3.

Abraham believed *God, and it was counted unto him for Righteoufnefs.*

BELIEF in *God* is the Foundation of all Religion both Natural and Revealed. For, *he that cometh to God muft believe that He Is, and that he is a Rewarder of them that diligently feek him.* Good Temper and Humanity *may be,* and often *is* the caufe of many virtuous Actions; which, wherever they are found, ought never to go without their juft commendation : But the *fteddy courfe* of a virtuous and religious life, uniform in all its parts and upon all occafions, refifting all the temptations of the World, overcoming all difficulties, and perfevering to the End under all difcouragements; this is a Superftructure which cannot be built upon a lefs ftrong Foundation than a firm Belief of a future State, and an Expectation of the righteous Judgment of God.

Now, as *without* Belief in God, there *can* be *no Religion;* fo, where there *is* fuch Belief in God, the Scripture always in courfe fuppofes it accompanied with every *other* part of true Religion. The *Root* is *always* fuppofed to have the *Branches* joined with it; and where a *Tree* is mentioned, 'tis always underftood to be a Tree bearing its proper *Fruit.* A *Man,* never fignifies the dead *Body* of a Man without the *Soul* or *Life*; neither does *Faith* in Scripture-phrafe ever mean the bare *Profeffion* of men's Belief, without *evidence* of its *reality* by its *Effects*; except only where it is declared to be *dead* and ufelefs. *As the Body,* faith St *James, without the Spirit, is dead; fo Faith without Works, is dead alfo,* Jam. ii. 26. As, in *natural* things, to *feparate* Caufes and Effects, to feparate things in their own nature infeparable, to fuppofe the *Sun* to be without *Light,* or the *Fire* without Heat, is unnatural and abfurd : fo, in matters of *Religion and Morality,* to feparate *Belief* and *Practice,* to feparate the *Obligation* to any Duty from the *Performance* of it, is, morally fpeaking, monftrous and impoffible : the *one* being as contrary to *Reafon,* which is the Rule of *Morality,* as the *other* is contrary to the courfe and poffibilities of *nature.* For *this* reafon both in Scripture and in common Speech, the Name of any *One* eminent Virtue is very ufually put for the *Sum* of *All*; and he that in the infpired Writings is commended particularly for *One* Virtue, is not thereby fo much intended to be diftinguifhed for *That,* as fuppofed to be thereupon endued with *all others* likewife. *Righteoufnefs,* which properly fignifies the *particular* Duty of fair and equitable Dealing between Man and Man, is in Scripture generally ufed for the *whole* Practice of true Religion in general. And the Character given to *Noah,* Gen. vi. 9. that he *was a* juft *man;* is in the very fame verfe explained to be, that he was a man perfect *in his generation,* and that he *walked with God.* In like manner, *believing* in God; becaufe 'tis the Foundation of *Obedience* to him, and wherever it is fincere, will naturally be *attended with* fuch Obedience, fignifies therefore

SERM. the fame as living *religioufly*. Which, as it is True concerning *Religion in* general, fo
XXVIII. in *Chriſtianity in* particular it is ſtill *more* uſual, to put *Faith* for the *whole* Practice of
Virtue and Religion; becauſe, as the *Foundation of Religion in* general is Believing in
God; ſo the Foundation of *Chriſtianity in* particular, is the Belief of that great *Act* of
God, the raiſing his Son from the Dead, in order to judge the World in Righteouſ-
neſs. Which is what the Apoſtle obſerves, ver. 23. of this chapter: *It was not written,*
ſays he, *for Abraham's ſake alone, that his Faith was imputed to him for Righteouſneſs:*
But for Us *alſo, to whom it ſhall be imputed, if we believe on Him that raiſed up Jeſus*
our Lord from the Dead. This is the Reaſon, why the *whole* Goſpel is, in the *New*
Teſtament, ſo frequently called by the Name of *Faith.* The *Jewiſh* Religion is, on
the contrary, through the whole *New Teſtament*, uſually ſtiled by the Name of *Works*;
upon account of the numerous external Ceremonies and ritual Obſervations, which,
though not in reality, yet, in the opinion and practice of the greater part of that Nation,
were the main Body of their Religion, or that which they chiefly and moſt eagerly
contended for. For ſo indeed, both in *antient* and in *modern* time, the corrupt diſpoſition of Mankind generally leads them to this one conſtant Errour; to value *moſt* in
every Religion that which is of *leaſt* importance in it; *opinions or ceremonies*, which
diſtinguiſh them into different *Parties*; and not *true Virtue, Righteouſneſs and Goodneſs*,
wherein all, who are indeed religious, do neceſſarily agree. The *great* Queſtion at the
firſt preaching of the Goſpel, was, whether the Practice of Virtue required by Chriſt in
his Religion, was ſufficient to Salvation, without the continuation of the *Jewiſh* Ceremonies. The Argument uſed by the Apoſtle to prove that it *was* ſufficient, was, that
Abraham their Father was *himſelf* ſaved, not by the Obſervation of the *Rites They* laid
ſuch ſtreſs upon; but by the Practice of the very *ſame* Virtues which the *Goſpel* now requires; inſomuch that the Scripture expreſſly affirms, that the *Goſpel* was before preached
unto *Abraham, Gal.* iii. 8. And this Argument is at large urged in *Rom.* iv. 3. the preſent chapter, whereof my Text is a part. *Abraham's* Faith, ſays the Apoſtle, was *reck-*
oned unto him for righteouſneſs; and it was ſo reckoned unto him, not only *after*, but
before his circumciſion, *ver.* 10. The acceptableneſs of his Faith therefore did not depend upon the covenant of circumciſion, as the *Jews* imagined; but upon that right and
worthy *Notion of God* from which his Faith proceeded; and upon that *conſequent Obe-*
dience, of which his Faith was the cauſe; *ver.* 20. *He ſtaggered not at the promiſe of*
God through Unbelief; but gave Glory to God; being fully perſwaded, that what he had
promiſed, he was able alſo to perform; *and therefore it was imputed to him for righteouſ-*
neſs. And the Application is; that *it was not written for his ſake alone, but for* Us *alſo,*
to whom it ſhall likewiſe be imputed, if we believe on Him that raiſed up Jeſus our Lord
from the Dead; *who was delivered for our offences, and roſe again for our Juſtification.*
Which laſt words are added to ſet forth the True Nature of Faith in Chriſt. For if the
End of Chriſt's Death was to deliver us from *Sin*; and the End of his *Reſurrection*, to
bring us unto *Righteouſneſs*; 'tis evident that Faith in Chriſt is no otherwiſe of Benefit to
us, than as it tends to deſtroy *Sin*, and eſtabliſh *Virtue.* Which ſhows the extreme
Folly and moſt dangerous Errour of Thoſe, who ſet up Faith in oppoſition to Moral
Virtue; and make the Goſpel of Chriſt a Form of *Words* only, and an *imaginary Specu-*
lation, inſtead of being (what the Scripture always repreſents it) the *way of Righteouſ-*
neſs and the *Holy Commandment.*

   HAVING thus briefly explained the nature and ground of the Apoſtle's Argument
in general; we may now eaſily underſtand the meaning of the words of the Text *in*
particular: Abraham believed *God, and it was counted unto him for righteouſneſs. Abra-*
ham was the great Example of Righteouſneſs, ſo as to be ſtyled in Scripture (by way of

Rom. iv. 16.   eminence) *the Friend of God*, and the Father *of the Faithful.* Eccluſ. xliv. 19. *He was*
a great Father of many people; in glory was there none like unto him, who kept the law

                                                                of

of the most High, and was in covenant with him. Now *This* Righteousness, which the Son of *Sirach* calls keeping *the Law of the most High,* the Apostle calls the righteousness of *Faith,* in opposition to that of *Works.* By the *Works* therefore which he disparages, 'tis plain he means *Rites and Ceremonies,* not the *Practice of Virtue;* and by *Believing in God,* which he so highly commends, he means *True Religion.* By adhering to this true Religion, *Abraham* made proof of his believing in God, which was counted to him for righteousness; and *We,* if we *so* believe in God, shall have it imputed for righteousness unto *Us* likewise.

IN order therefore to make this observation of the Apostle useful to us in Practice, it may be proper to consider distinctly, *1st,* wherein consisted that *Faith* of *Abraham,* which the Text says was counted to him for righteousness; and *2dly, What* it is, that is particularly required of *Us,* when *we* likewise are in Scripture commanded to *believe in God.*

I. Now the Account which the Scripture gives us of the *Faith* of *Abraham* is this:

1st, IT consisted in his believing the *true* God, the Maker and Governour of the Universe, the Lord of Heaven and Earth. The Nations among whom he sojourned, were all Idolaters; Worshippers of dead men, worshippers of the Kings who had reigned over them in their life-time: For *That* was the original of all the Heathen-Idolatry. Every City or Territory had its own Prince, and the World was divided into small Kingdoms. These Kings were honoured by their Flatterers with Honours, during their *Lives* too nearly divine; and after their *Deaths,* they were by the ignorant people worshipped as Gods. The Worship paid to such Gods of their own making, was accordingly superstitious; and the corruption of their *manners* was answerable to the absurdity of their *religion.* From these, *Abraham* separated himself, and believed in the true God the Maker of all things; and for the sake of that Belief, forsook his native country. Heb. xi. 8. *By Faith Abraham went out, not knowing whither he went, and sojourned in the land of Promise as in a strange country; for he looked for a City which hath foundations, whose Builder and maker is God.* He believed that the God of the whole World, whom alone he worshipped, was able to *preserve* him in the present Life, or *reward* him in another that should come; and This *Faith was counted unto him for righteousness.* Some have *disputed,* whether the Patriarchs under the old Testament had any express knowledge of the Life to come. But that they *had,* the Apostle's Argument is a plain *demonstration,* Heb. xi. 13. They who having *seen the promises afar off, confessed themselves to be Strangers and Pilgrims in the Earth, declare plainly that they seek a——better country,* ver. 16.

2dly, As *Abraham*'s Faith consisted *in general* in believing the *True God,* so *in particular* it manifested itself in such *Acts* of Dependence upon him, as became a person who had *just and worthy Notions* of the True God whom he served; And for This, it was counted unto Him for righteousness. Thus St *Paul* expressly argues, in the case of *Abraham*'s receiving the promise of a Son, *Rom.* iv. 17. *Before him whom he believed, even God who quickneth the dead, and calleth those things which be not, as though they were, He against Hope believed in Hope,——giving glory to God, and being fully persuaded, that what he had promised, he was able also to perform;* and therefore (saith he) *it was imputed to him for righteousness.* Thus likewise in the case of offering up his *Son,* the excellency of his Faith consisted in This, that it was founded upon that Great Principle of Religion, the expectation of a Resurrection from the dead. *He accounted,* saith St *Paul, that God was able to raise him up even from the dead, from whence also he received him in a Figure,* Heb. xi. 19. These last words, *from whence also he received him in a Figure,* are by Expositors understood to signify, *Isaac*'s near escape from Death, when he was just upon the point of being offered. But This being an Event not foreseen by *Abraham* before it came to pass, could not be to him an Argument at That Time, to

confirm

confirm his Faith. And therefore I think the words will bear *another* fenfe, much more pertinent to the Apoftle's intention. *Abraham*, faith he, *accounted, that God was able to raife him up even from the Dead*; and he had the more reafon fo to account, be-caufe he had already once before *received him* from the dead *in a figure*; namely, at the time of his *Birth*, when he fprang from Parents *as good as dead*; as the fame Apoftle ex-preffes in the very fame chapter. *Abraham's* Reafoning was This; (and it was very pertinent and ftrong;) The fame God who could caufe *Ifaac* to receive life at firft from *Parents already dead through Age*, could as eafily the fecond time raife him to life again, when he *himself* fhould be *dead*.

3*dly*, The Faith of *Abraham* was not a Speculation or mere Credulity, but a Prin-ciple of Obedience and True Holinefs. Gen. xviii. 19. *I know Abraham, that he will command his children and his houfhold after him, and they fhall* keep *the way of the Lord, to do juftice and judgment; that the Lord may bring upon Abraham that which he has fpc-ken of him.* Thefe words of *God Himfelf* in the Old Teftament, are fufficiently clear. But becaufe there arofe afterwards fome miftakes about this matter; St *James*, in ex-prefs decifion of a point of controverfy in *His* time, alledges the very fame example: Ch. ii. 21. *Was not Abraham our Father juftified by Works, when he offered Ifaac his Son upon the Altar? Seeft thou how Faith wrought with his Works, and by Works was his Faith made perfect! And the Scripture was fulfilled which faith, Abraham believed God, and it was imputed unto him for Righteoufnefs.* 'Tis very remarkable that thefe laft words, which in the Text are cited by St *Paul* for the magnifying the efficacy of *Faith*, are at the fame time cited by St *James*, to fhow the *equal* neceffity of *Works of Righte-oufnefs*. *Abraham believed God, and it was imputed unto him for Righteoufnefs.* A-braham was juftified by *believing* in God; but the Reafon why his Faith was fo highly accepted, was becaufe the *Effect* of it was Righteoufnefs of Life.

4*thly*, and *Laftly*, The *Faith* of *Abraham* is oppofed in Scripture, juft as the Faith of Chriftians is, not to the Works of *Virtue*, but to the *Rites and Ceremonies* of the Law of *Mofes*. *Gal.* iii. 7. *They that are of Faith*, faith St *Paul*, that is, they who believing in Chrift expect Salvation through the real Holinefs of the Gofpel, and not by fuch outward Forms and Ceremonies as the *Jews* obferved; *the fame* (faith he) *are the children of Abraham*; ver. 6. *Even as* Abraham *believed God, and it was accounted to him for righteoufnefs.* And *Rom.* iv. 13. *The Promife was not to Abraham or to his Seed through the Law, but through the righteoufnefs of Faith:——To the end the Promife might be fure to* all *the Seed, not to that only which is of the Law, but to That alfo which is of the Faith of Abraham, who is the Father of us all.* His meaning is: The Promifes of God to *Abraham*, the Promife of giving him a better Country than that which he went out from; the Promife of being his God and his exceeding great Re-Rom. iv. 12. ward; the Promife of making him *Heir of the World*; (all which, the reafon of the thing fhows, and the Apoftle in the eleventh to the *Hebrews* expreffly declares, to be meant of the heavenly *Canaan*, the new *Jerufalem*, whereof the Land of Promife was but a Type and a Shadow;) Thefe Promifes were made to *Abraham*, not as circum-cifed, not as the Father of the Nation of the *Jews*; but as having *that* exemplary Faith, *that* firm Belief in the One true God the Maker of all things, *that* readinefs to obey him in oppofition to the univerfal corruption of an idolatrous World, and *that* depen-dence upon God's being finally a Rewarder of them who diligently ferve him without Any Profpect of temporal Advantage; which made this great man to be defervedly efteemed the Father of all Faithful and Holy Men, who fhould acceptably ferve the fame God, in all Ages and in all Nations of the World.

This is the Account the Scripture gives us of that *Faith of Abraham*, which *was accounted to him for Righteoufnefs*. The right Underftanding of which matter removes at once all the Difficulties concerning the Notion of Faith and Works, which has

occafioned

occasioned so many vain controverfies in the Chriftian World; and at the fame time S E R M. may ferve to inftruct us, (which was the XXVIII.

II. *Second* thing I propofed to fpeak to;) *what* it is, that is particularly required of Us, when *We* likewife are in Scripture commanded to *believe in God.* And this evidently implies,

1*ft*, BELIEVING his *Being:* That is; not only, in a Speculative manner, believing that there *is* an infinitely Perfect Being, in the notional way wherein Philofophers defcribe him, which may eafily be feparate from any religious Affection; but 'tis having upon our Minds a conftant Senfe of his being, in the moral fenfe, the Supreme Governour, and righteous Judge of the World. *This* Belief of the Being of God, is That only, which becaufe it will certainly produce the Fruits of Virtue, fhall therefore certainly be accounted unto us for Righteoufnefs.

2*dly*, THE Duty of Believing in God implies, not only our believing his Being, and his being Governour and Judge of the World; but alfo that we have *worthy and honourable Apprehenfions* of his *Nature and Attributes.* For when any man thinks he believes in God, without attending at the fame time to thofe Perfections and Excellencies, which conftitute the true and real Notion of God, he deceives himfelf with that empty fallacy of putting *Words* for *Things*; and inftead of placing his Religion in obeying the Commands of the True Governour of the Univerfe, by the Practice of all Holinefs, Righteoufnefs, and Virtue; he will be apt to content himfelf with worfhipping he knows not *what,* and he knows not *how,* with a blind Superftition, without Underftanding, and without any real improvement in Goodnefs. This is naturally the Effect of afcribing *Abfurdities* to God, as thofe of the Church of *Rome* do in the matter of *Tranfubftantiation*; or of teaching things concerning him contrary to the common and obvious Notions of *Righteoufnefs and Goodnefs,* as thofe have done, who contend for the Doctrine of abfolute and unconditionate *Predeftination.* The Religion of fuch men ufually confifts more in an ufelefs amazement of Mind, than in any real Practife of Virtue: Than which, nothing can be more difhonourable to God, or more injurious to Religion. For if a wife and good *man* had rather his Name fhould not be mentioned at all, than that there fhould be joined with it a Character contrary to Wifdom and Goodnefs; much more muft it needs be unacceptable to God, that Men fhould *frame* of him fuch Notions as are not honourable to *Him*; and *ferve* him with fuch a Religion, as is of no True Benefit to *Them.* God governs the *natural* World with abfolute Power and Wifdom; and the *moral* World with perfect Righteoufnefs, Juftice, and Goodnefs. In the imitation and Practice of thefe Virtues confifts the true Effence of Religion towards *men*; and in the acknowledgment of, and dependence upon, thefe Perfections of the Divine Nature, confifts True Faith towards *God.* Herein confifted the Faith of *Abraham*; that, in the midft of an Idolatrous World, he conftantly retained this Notion of the One invifible God of the whole Univerfe; and trufted in him, and ferved him, and obeyed him accordingly, in all Holinefs and Righteoufnefs of Life; depending upon a remote and invifible Reward; and therefore he was ftyled, the *Friend* of God, and was fet forth as a perpetual Example of True Faith to all fucceeding generations. *Look at the generations of old,* faith the Son of *Sirach, and fee; did ever any truft in the Lord, and was confounded? or, did any abide in his fear, and was forfaken? or whom did he ever defpife, that called upon him?*

3*dly,* BELIEVING in God, fignifies believing his *Revelations* alfo, as well as what *Nature* teaches concerning Him. The Obligations of *revealed* Religion are founded upon the fame Ground as the obligations of *natural* Religion; and they mutually ftrengthen and confirm each other. By the dictates of *Nature* it was reafonable to expect that God would vouchfafe to make more clear to men his Will by *Revelation*; and in all true *Revelation* is contained a fuller enforcement and more ftrong confirma-

S E R M. tion of the Law of *Nature.* Men therefore who in Chriſtian countries, where the Goſ-
XXVIII. pel is preached, pretend to believe in the *God of Nature,* and yet at the ſame time reject the revelation of the *Goſpel,* which is ſo *agreeable to* and *perfective of* the Law of
Nature; do, generally ſpeaking, in *pretenſe* only, and not in *reality,* ſhow any more
regard to *natural* than to *revealed* Religion; falling for the moſt part into abſolute Atheiſm. Whereas they who ſeriouſly believe, and practiſe the Duties of *natural* Religion,
are generally diſpoſed to embrace alſo conſequently the *Revelation* of the *Goſpel.* Thoſe
whom *the Father,* the God of *Nature,* draweth, come eaſily to *Chriſt,* who is the Author of the Goſpel. The only thing neceſſary here to be obſerved, is, that for preventing with due care the *Frauds* and Impoſitions of men, who have ſometimes attempted,
(as particularly in many Inſtances in the Church of *Rome*) to impoſe their own Inventions inſtead of Divine Revelation; diligent inquiry ought always to be made into the
evidence of the *Facts,* and into the *nature and reaſon* of the *thing.* For a doctrine, even
not unreaſonable in itſelf, yet is not to be admitted as a divine Revelation without good
evidence of the *Fact:* Neither on the contrary can any pretenſe of evidence of Fact, be
ſufficient for the admiſſion of a Doctrine *impoſſible or abſurd in itſelf.* Tranſubſtantiation has no evidence of being revealed: But had there been never ſo great an appearance
of Evidence for it, yet it could not be received, becauſe the manifeſt *Abſurdity of the
thing,* would always be a ſtronger Argument *againſt* its being an Object of Faith, than
any other evidence could be *for* it. Every Revelation *muſt* be agreeable to the *Nature
of God,* and to the *poſſibility of things.* Our Saviour himſelf alledges it as an Argument,
for the Proof of the Truth even of his *Miracles* themſelves; that his Doctrine was directly contrary to the Power and Intereſt of evil Spirits, and tended in its own Nature
to the Glory of God, and to the Benefit of Men: Otherwiſe the Objection of the Phariſees would have been of ſome force, that he caſt out Devils by the Prince of the Devils. In the *Old Teſtament,* the greateſt Difficulty of This kind, is the Inſtance of *A-
braham* offering up his Son; which if it was a thing unalterably evil in itſelf, it may
be objected could never be a Revelation from God. For the clearing of which it is
therefore to be obſerved, that of things Evil or Immoral there are three ſorts. Some
things are Evil, only becauſe prohibited by a poſitive Law; and theſe it is evident are no
longer evil, than the Law which forbids them continues in Being. Other things are
Evil unalterably in their own Nature; even ſo as that it would be a direct contradiction
and abſolute impoſſibility to ſuppoſe, that God ſhould at *any time* whatſoever, or upon
any occaſion, command them: Such are *Hatred of God and Goodneſs,* the *worſhip of
Falſe Gods,* a *malicious or cruel Temper of Mind;* and the like. Now between theſe two
ſorts of Evils there is a third; which is not only evil, becauſe contrary to any poſitive
Law, but contrary alſo even to the Law of Nature itſelf: Yet *not ſo unalterably,* but
that in ſome particular circumſtances, when expreſſly commanded by the God of Nature, it *may* ceaſe to be contrary to that Law. And of this kind, is the taking away
the Life of an innocent man; as in the caſe of *Abraham* and his Son. Which though
contrary to the Law of Nature, to be done by the Will of Man, or of any Power on
Earth; yet may without any inconſiſtency be in a particular caſe commanded by God:
Becauſe God who *gave* life, may *take it away* when he pleaſes, either by a natural Diſeaſe, or by any other Inſtrument which he thinks fit. Only he who in ſuch a caſe
ſhall pretend to be an Inſtrument in the hand of God, muſt ſhow a Commiſſion or
Revelation, as *clear* as was that to *Abraham:* Otherwiſe all Impiety and Superſtition
may be brought in the place of Religion; as thoſe of the Church of *Rome,* under pretence of doing ſervice to God, are perpetually deſtroying the beſt of his Servants.

　　4thly and *Laſtly;* As believing in God, ſignifies believing his *Revelations,* as well
as his *Nature and Attributes;* ſo it always includes *Obedience* to him likewiſe, when
it means That Faith which ſhall be counted to us for Righteouſneſs. *Abraham's Faith,*

I

faith

faith St *James*, *wrought with his Works, and by Works was his Faith made perfect*. S E R M.
And concerning *Ours* in like manner St *Paul* declares, *Rom.* x. 10. *With the Heart* XXVIII.
man believeth unto Righteoufnefs, and with the Mouth confeſſion is made unto Salva-
tion.

S E R M O N XXIX.

Of the GRACE of GOD.

T I T. II. 11, 12.

*For the Grace of God, that bringeth Salvation, hath appeared to all
men : Teaching us, that denying Ungodlinefs and Worldly Lufts, we
fhould live foberly, righteoufly and godly, in this prefent World.*

IN the *Firſt* Chapter of This Epiftle, the Apoftle inftructs *Titus* in the particulars S E R M.
of his *own* Duty; exhorting him to be diligent in *ftudying*, ftedfaft in *holding faſt*, ·XXIX.
painful in *teaching*, and, above all things, exemplary in *practiſing* the Chriftian
Doctrine. In the *ſecond* chapter, he directs him what inftructions he fhould give to *Others*;
to perfons in every circumftance of Age, and in every Station of Life; That men of all
Ranks and Conditions whatfoever, of all degrees and of all capacities, might know how,
by a fuitable Behaviour, to *adorn in all things the Doctrine of* God our Saviour; whofe
kindneſs and Love has been *ſhed on us abundantly, through* Jefus Chrift our Saviour,
ch. iii. 6. The Apoftle, I fay, having in *This*, and in the *foregoing* Chapter, inftructed
both *Titus himſelf*, and thofe who were *under his charge*, in the Great *Branches of
Moral Duty*; he proceeds in the words of the Text to *inforce* the *Practiſe* of thofe
Duties by this *emphatical Argument*; that the very *End* and *Deſign of the Goſpel of
Chriſt* was to *teach* men the neceffity of fuch Practife: To *teach* them, that *denying
ungodlineſs and worldly Lufts, they ſhould live foberly, righteoufly and godly, in this preſent World*; *Looking for that Bleſſed Hope, and the Glorious appearing of the Great God,
and our Saviour Jeſus Chriſt; Who gave himſelf for us, that he might redeem us from
all iniquity, and purify unto himſelf a peculiar people, zealous of good Works.*

SOBRIETY, Righteoufnefs, and Godlinefs, are the *Ends* for the promoting whereof,
Chrift came into the World. Whatever therefore in Any Profeffion of Religion *tends
not to promote* thefe Ends, is *uſeleſs and deceitful:* Whatever tends in any degree to *fruf-
trate* them, is *pernicious and deftructive*. By This Rule, may eafily be tried the real
and intrinfick *Value* of every *doctrine*; by This, may be weighed the degree of *dange-
roufneſs* of every *Errour*, in Religion. Every Notion and Speculation whatfoever, every Form and Ceremony of Any Kind, every external Rite, every inward Opinion, concerning *Faith*, or *Grace*, or the *Merits of Chriſt*, or *any other* Doctrine whatever it
be:

be: So far as it leads and influences Men to be more truly *virtuous* and *good*, to have a
more conftant Senfe of *God* upon their Minds, to be more *fober and temperate*, to have
a more ftrict Regard to *Truth, Juftice, Equity* and *Charity*, in the whole Courfe of
their Actions; fo far it makes them *better Chriftians*. But if, on the contrary, any of
thefe things be (as they too frequently are, among *All* Profeffions of Men; If they be)
at any time looked upon as *Equivalents*, to be accepted of God in the *room* and in
the *ftead* of true Virtue ; they are Then really deftructive of all Religion. For *whofoever* (fays our Lord) *fhall break one of thefe Leaft Commandments,* (fpeaking of the
eternal Duties of the *Moral* Law,) *and fhall teach men fo,* (that is, fhall upon Any
pretenfe whatfoever teach men to look upon Other things as of more importance than
thefe;) *he fhall be called the leaft in the Kingdom of Heaven;* that is, he fhall of all
men be the fartheft from ever entring therein. The *Reafon* why Chrift *gave himfelf for
us,* was, *that he might redeem us from all iniquity, and purify unto Himfelf a peculiar
people, zealous of good Works.* The *Caufe,* for which was revealed *that Bleffed Hope,
and the glorious Appearing of the Great God, and our Saviour Jefus Chrift,* was, that
it might be an effectual *Support* to men in the *Practife of Virtue,* under the various
Temptations of a vitious and unrighteous World. The *End and Defign,* for which
God's *gracioufnefs* towards men in the *Forgivenefs of Sins,* was declared in the Gofpel;
was to *teach* us the *neceffity* of Obedience for the future, and to *incourage* us in our *fincere Endeavours* after it. *The Grace of God, that bringeth Salvation, hath appeared to
all men ; Teaching us, that denying Ungodlinefs and Worldly Lufts, we fhould live foberly,
righteoufly and godly, in this prefent World.*

IN the following Difcourfe upon Thefe Words, I fhall 1*ft* explain *What* is meant by
the Grace of God. And 2*dly,* I fhall confider, *How* This *Grace of God* Teaches *us;*
teaches us in a *peculiar* and *emphatical* manner; that, *Denying ungodlinefs and Worldly
Lufts, we fhould live foberly, righteoufly and godly, in this prefent World.*

I. IN the *Firft* place, the *proper* Signification of the word *Grace,* is *Favour: Favour* in *fuch* a fenfe, as denotes *Mercy* and *Goodnefs* in a *Superiour,* either *remitting*
fomewhat of his *Own Right,* or *conferring* fomewhat Beneficial upon *Others*; freely,
and without Any obligation of Debt. And becaufe *This* may be done after *various
manners,* and in a great *diverfity* of *Inftances*; hence the word *Grace* in Scripture, is
accordingly applied, in a *proportionable diverfity* of *Significations.*

SOMETIMES it fignifies thofe *extraordinary Gifts and Powers* of the Holy Ghoft,
by which the Apoftles were inabled to *demonftrate* the *Truth* of their *Commiffion,* to
preach their *Doctrine* with *Authority,* to *convince Gainfayers* with *Evidence,* to *govern
the Churches* by a proper diftribution of different *Trufts and Offices.* And the *Gifts* or
Powers, by which the Apoftles were enabled to do all thefe things with extraordinary
Efficacy and Succefs, are *Therefore* called *Grace,* becaufe they are not at all *Natural
Acquifitions,* but *Free Gifts of God*; diftributed to every one feverally, not according
to the Will of *Man,* but *at* fuch *times,* and *in* fuch *proportions,* and *to* fuch *Perfons,*
and *for* fuch *Purpofes,* as God *himfelf* pleafed. Thus *Rom.* i. 5. *By whom we have re-
ceived* Grace *and* Apoftlefhip, *for Obedience to the Faith among all Nations.* That is;
Who has *gracioufly* been pleafed to *fend forth* Us the Apoftles, to preach with mighty
Works and Demonftration of the Spirit, in order to bring back the Nations to the
Knowledge of God and to the Practife of Virtue, by the Arguments and Motives of
the Gofpel of Chrift. In like manner, ch. xii. 6. *Having then* Gifts, *differing according
to the* Grace *that is given to us,* (that is, according to the good pleafure of God in dif-
tributing thofe Gifts;) *whether it be prophecy, let us prophefy,* (or whatever Gift it be,
let us imploy it diligently,) *according to the proportion of Faith,* i. e. according to the
Nature and Ufe of the Gift or Power or *Truft* committed to our Charge or *Fidelity*:
So the word *Faith* evidently fignifies in This place; and above, in *ver* 3. *according as*
                                                                                        God

God has dealt to every man the Measure of Faith, *i. e.* according to the nature and degree of the Power committed to every man's *Trust* or *Faithfulness.* Had *This* signification of the word been generally attended to, which is manifestly the Apostle's true meaning; it might have prevented abundance of weak and unintelligible things, which have sometimes been spoken concerning *God's giving* men *Faith,* and the like. But This, by the way. Another remarkable Passage of the same Apostle, where the word *Grace* plainly signifies again the *extraordinary Gifts of the Spirit,* is in *Eph.* iv. 7. 11. *Unto every one of us is given* Grace, *according to the Measure of the Gift of Christ:——— And he gave Some Apostles, and Some Prophets, and Some Evangelists, and Some Pastors and Teachers.* This therefore is the *First* Sense, wherein the word *Grace* is frequently used in the *New Testament:* It denotes the *extraordinary Powers* wherewith God was *graciously* pleased to indue the Apostles, in order to inable them to propagate the Gospel with Authority and Success.

I N *Other* Passages, the same word is made use of to signify That extraordinary *Assistance and Support,* which God has sometimes been pleased to afford his Servants, under extraordinary *Difficulties and Trials.* And *This* is called *Grace,* because considered as given *particularly* upon *extraordinary* occasions, over and above the *general Supports,* arising from the Considerations of *Reason,* and from the *Motives and Promises of the Gospel* in *general.* Thus when St *Paul* under some *particular* Affliction and Distress, which he calls *The Messenger of Satan to buffet* him, prayed with repeated importunity to have this Trouble removed from him ; The Lord said unto him, 2 *Cor.* xii. 9. *My* Grace *is sufficient for thee.* And when our Saviour foretells his disciples, that they should be *persecuted* and *brought before Kings and Rulers for* His *name's sake*; he tells them at the same time, which is another Instance of This *Grace* or *Gracious Goodness* of God, which *will not suffer* men *to be tempted above what* they *are able*; He tells them they need not be sollicitous, *what Answer* to make; For *the Holy Ghost* should *teach them* in *That Hour,* and *He himself* would *give* them *a Mouth and Wisdom, which all their Adversaries* should *not be able to gainsay or resist*; Luke xii. 11; and xxi. 14.

A *Third* sense, wherein the word *Grace* is sometimes made use of in the *New Testament,* is to express such *Moral Virtues,* as are the *Effects* of men's being influenced by the *Spiritual Motives of the Gospel*; and the *Practice* of which, preserves men in the *Favour* of God, and recommends them to his *Gracious Acceptance.* Thus *Eph.* iv. 29. *Let no corrupt Communication proceed out of your Mouth, but that which is good to the Use of edifying ; that it may minister* Grace *unto the Hearers*; That is, that it may promote the Practice of *Virtue* in the World. And 2 *Pet.* iii. 18. *Grow in* Grace ; That is, improve more and more in all *virtuous* Behaviour, which may render you *Acceptable* in the *Sight of God.* After the same manner of speaking, the Apostle St *Paul,* 2 *Cor.* viii. 1, stiles the extraordinary *liberality* of the *Macedonian Churches* to the Poor, *the* Grace *of God bestowed on them.* And his direction to *Titus,* to *perswade* the *Corinthians* to *imitate* that exemplary liberality, he *thus* expresses, *ver.* 6. *We desired Titus, that, as he had begun, so he would also finish in* you *the same* Grace *also.* And then he adds his *Own* exhortation, still in the *very same* Style, *ver.* 7. *Therefore as ye abound in every thing, in Faith, in Utterance, and Knowledge, and in all Diligence, and in your Love to Us ; see that ye abound in* This Grace *also,* the Grace of Liberality and Charity. In these Passages, 'tis as evident as possible, that the word *Grace* denotes the *very same,* as *Christian* or *Moral Virtue.* And *Moral Virtues* are plainly *for This reason* called by the name of *Grace,* because they *proceed from* and are *founded in* a *Regard to God* in *general,* and in *particular* to his *Will* revealed under the *Gracious Dispensation of the Gospel of Christ.* They are the *Effects* of men's *Conversion to God*; the *Effects* of all the *external* and *internal Influences* of the Gospel; the *Fruits of the Spirit.* And not only in the Language of *Scripture,* in the *Apostles* times; but even at *This day,* in

SERM. *common Speech*, the word *(Grace) still retains* in many Cafes the *fame* Signification.
XXIX. Thus when *abandoned* and *debauched* perfons are vulgarly ftiled *Gracelefs*; the Intent of
That denomination never is to *excufe*, but always to *aggravate* the Fault of the perfons
fo ftiled. It never means any Defect on *God's* part, as if *He* afforded them not the
Capacities of Religion and Virtue; but always on *their own* part only, that All the
Means and Affiftances of Religion are beftowed on them *in vain*, and *have not In-
fluence* fufficient to *reform* them.

To proceed: *Another* Signification of the word *Grace* in Scripture, is to exprefs
that *merciful Acceptance* of *Repentance and Amendment*, whereby *God* is pleafed, not
out of any *obligation of Juftice*, but *in gracious Goodnefs*, to reftore men to his Favour.
1 Cor. xv. 9. In *This* fenfe, St *Paul* fays of *Himfelf*, *I am not meet to be called an Apoftle, becaufe I
perfecuted the Church of God*: But by the Grace of God, (that is, by his *gracious Acceptance* of my fincere Intentions,) *I am what I am*. In like manner, when the *Doctrine*
Joh. i. 17. of Chrift, as diftinguifhed from the *Law of* Mofes, is by the Evangelift ftyled Grace
Acts xiv. 3. *and Truth*; and when the *Apoftles Preaching*, is by St *Luke* called *The Word* (or De-
Rom. iii. 24. claration) *of God's* Grace; and when St *Paul* declares, that repenting Sinners *are juftified freely by his* Grace; and blames thofe, as the moft *pernicious Perverters* of his
Rom. vi. 1. Doctrine, who think they may *continue in Sin, that* Grace *may abound*: 'Tis evident
the word *Grace*, in all thefe Paffages, fignifies That *merciful* and *compaffionate* difpofition of the Divine Nature, whereby God freely *remits* of his *Right of Punifhment*;
and receives penitent Sinners upon *more gracious Terms*, and to *greater degrees of his
Favour*, than he was bound to do by *any obligation* of *Juftice*.

AND *hence* it is, that in the *Laft* place, the *Gofpel itfelf*, as being the *Great* and
Standing Declaration of God's *Mercy and Goodnefs* towards men, fhown forth in the
free Pardon and Forgivenefs of Sin, upon the *gracious Terms* of Repentance and Amendment; hence the *Gofpel itfelf*, I fay, is in the *New Teftament* very frequently meant by
This Phrafe, *the Grace of God*. Thus *Col.* i. 6. *Since the day ye heard of it, and knew
the Grace of God in Truth*: That is, from the Time ye were inftructed in the *Doctrine of the Gofpel*. And 2 *Thef.* ii. 16. *Our Lord Jefus Chrift himfelf, and God even
our Father,*——*hath given us*——*good Hope through* Grace; that is, through the *gracious Promifes of the Gofpel*. Again; 2 Tim. ii. 1. *Thou therefore, my Son, be ftrong
in the* Grace *that is in Chrift Jefus*, (that is, Be Faithful and Diligent, in preaching
the Gofpel;) *And the things that thou haft heard of Me,* —— *the fame commit thou to
Faithful men, who fhall be able to teach Others alfo*. In like manner; *the Prophets*——
1 Pet. i. 10. *prophecying of the* Grace *that fhould come*, is, their foretelling the Revelation of *the
Gal. v. 4. Gofpel*. And Some among the *Galatians, falling from* Grace; means their rejecting
the Privileges of the *Gofpel of Chrift*, when they claimed to be *juftified by* their obferving the Ceremonies of the *Jewifh Law*. To give but one Inftance more: The Queftion St *Paul* puts, *Rom.* vi. 15. *Shall we fin, becaufe we are not under the Law, but
under* Grace? is, in fenfe, plainly This: Shall the *Mercy*, the *Compaffion and Gracious
Goodnefs* of God, declared in the *Gofpel* much more exprefsly than under the *Mofaick
Law*; fhall it be an incouragement to us to continue in Sin? God forbid. And Thus
therefore likewife in the words of the Text: *The* Grace *of God*, that is, the *gracious
Doctrine of the Gofpel*, has been declared *to all men*; *Teaching us, that Denying Ungodlinefs*, and fo on. The Apoftle here very *exprefsly* explains his own words. He is
not fpeaking of *That Grace* of God, which *operates in* or *upon* men; but of *That
Grace* which Teaches them, that *Denying Ungodlinefs and Worldly Lufts*, they *fhould
live foberly, righteoufly, and godly in this prefent World*.

THE *Additional* words, *(which bringeth Salvation,)* are, in the Original, of ambiguous conftruction; and may equally fignify, either, as we render them, *The Grace of
God that bringeth Salvation, hath* appeared *to* all *men*; or, *The Grace of God hath appeared*,

4

peared, bringing Salvation *unto* all *men*. If we underſtand them in the *former* ſenſe, S E R M. *(The Grace of God that bringeth Salvation, hath* appeared *to* all *men ;)* they are *Then* XXIX. of the ſame import with thoſe *other* expreſſions, *Rom.* x. 18. *Their Sound is gone forth into all the Earth, and their Words unto the Ends of the World*; and *Col.* i. 23. *The Hope of the Goſpel which ye have heard, and which was preached to every creature under Heaven.* If they are underſtood in the Latter ſenſe ; *(The Grace of God hath appeared, bringing* Salvation *unto* all *men ;)* the meaning of them *Then* is the ſame, as in the *following* Expreſſions of Scripture ; that Chriſt *has aboliſhed Death, and hath brought Life and Immortality to Light through the Goſpel*; that God *will have All men to be ſaved, and to come to the Knowledge of the Truth*; being *not willing that Any ſhould periſh, but that All ſhould come to Repentance.* In whichſoever of *theſe two ſenſes* the words of the Text be taken ; the *Meaning* of them, upon the whole, amounts to the *Same* ; that the Deſign of God in the gracious Declarations of the Goſpel, is to bring *all men*, by the Promiſe of Pardon, to Repentance and Amendment *here*, and thereby to eternal Salvation *hereafter.*\ The *Senſe* of the Propoſition is *plain :* The only *difficulty* here, is that which ariſes, and indeed very obviouſly, from comparing the *actual Event* of things, with the *Declarations* of God's gracious *Intention and Deſign.* If God *deſigned* by the gracious Terms of the Goſpel to bring *all men* to Salvation ; how comes the *Extent* of it to be confined within ſo *narrow* a Compaſs, and the *Effect* of it to be in experience ſo inconſiderable, even where in Profeſſion it ſeems to have nniverſally prevailed ? The *Anſwer* to This, is ; that in all *moral* matters, the *Intention* or *Deſign* of God, *never* ſignifies (as it does *Always* in *Natural* things) an *Intention of the Event, actually* and *neceſſarily* to be accompliſhed ; but (which *Alone* is *conſiſtent* with the *nature of Moral* things,) an *Intention* of all the *Means*, neceſſary on *His* part, to the putting That Event into the Power of the proper and immediate Agents. For inſtance : With *intention* that *all men* ſhould act *reaſonably*, God indues them with the *Faculty* of *natural Reaſon.* The *Event*, whether after This they will *act reaſonably* or no, *muſt* depend upon *their own* Choice and Care : Becauſe *the very Faculty* or *Power* of acting *reaſonably*, does *neceſſarily* and *eſſentially* include in it a *Power* of acting likewiſe *unreaſonably.* The caſe is the *very ſame*, with reſpect to the Method of bringing men to Salvation by the *Goſpel.* God has commanded the Goſpel to be preached to the *whole World.* The merciful *Conditions*, and the gracious *Means and Aſſiſtances* of the Goſpel, are *ſufficient* to bring *all men* to Salvation ; except ſuch as either wilfully *reject* it, when fairly and reaſonably propoſed to them ; or who *profeſſing* to *embrace* it, yet *obey* it *not.* For, as for Thoſe to whom it was either never *at all*, or (which is much the ſame thing,) never *reaſonably* preached, their caſe is exactly the ſame with regard to the *Goſpel*, as the caſe of *ſuch others* is with regard to *Natural Reaſon*, who either totally or in great meaſure want That natural Faculty. Every man ſhall be *accepted according to what he* Hath, *and not according to what he* hath not, 2 *Cor.* viii. 12. God therefore *willeth all men to be ſaved*; (juſt in the ſame manner as he willeth all men to act rationally :) And yet This does not hinder them from *deſtroying themſelves* by wilfully *rejecting* That Salvation. For tho' *the Grace of God has* indeed *appeared to all men*, and is *ſufficient* alſo to *bring all men to ſalvation* ; yet it effects This no otherwiſe than by *Teaching them*, as the Apoſtle *proceeds* in the Text, (which is the *Second Particular* I propoſed to conſider ;) *teaching them*, in a *peculiar* and *emphatical* manner, *that denying Ungodlineſs and worldly Luſts, they ſhould live ſoberly, righteouſly, and godly, in this preſent World.*

II. N o w *How* the Goſpel does This, is not a point which needs much *inlargement.* 'Tis what our Saviour and his Apoſtles inculcate in the *whole New Teſtament*, from the One End to the Other. The *Practiſe of Virtue*, or *Living ſoberly, righteouſly, and godly*; is the *End* and *Deſign* of all Religion. God is Himſelf a Being of infinite *Holineſs*

SERM.
XXIX.

ness and _Goodness_; and by no other way than by _imitating_ these Perfections, can Any Creature become acceptable in his Sight. By the Light of _Nature and Reason_ therefore, men are bound to the Practice of these Virtues. But because their very _Best_ Performances are always _defective_; and Those who have _transgressed_ in any plain Instances, stand in need of particular _Pardon_; and Methods of mens own Invention to appease the Anger of God, had continually introduced numberless vain and delusive _Superstitions_; therefore, in compassion to the Weakness of Mankind, and to cure these Great Evils, God was pleased to send them an Instructor from Heaven, to _teach_ them in a _more effectual_ manner, than any ever _before_ discovered, how that _denying Ungodliness and worldly Lusts, they should live soberly, righteously, and godly, in this present World._ The Gospel, I say, teaches us _This_, in a method _more effectual_ than _Any_ foregoing: By giving, even to the _Meanest_ Capacities, the plainest and fullest, the perfectest and most distinct Account, of the Excellency and Extent of _Moral Virtue_; as in our Saviour's Sermon upon the Mount. By giving, even to persons of the _Lowest_ Abilities, clearer Instructions concerning the _Nature_ and _Perfections_ of God, than were usually attained even by the most _Learned Philosophers_ amidst the dark Superstitions of the _Pagan_ World. By showing to all men, that God is a Being _of purer Eyes than to behold iniquity_; So far _hating Wickedness_, as that he did not think fit to pardon Sin without so great a Testimony against it as the Death of his Son; And yet, at the same time, of such essential _Mercy and Goodness_, that he would rather give his own Son a Ransom for Sinners, than not find a method of pardoning them, consistent with the Wisdom of his infinite and eternal Government. By giving us consequently the _Example_ of _Christ_, in his Life, and in his Sufferings; the _Assistances_ of his _Spirit_; the Assurance of a _Reward for Virtue_, in a happy immortality; and a more express declaration of his _Wrath from Heaven, against all Unrighteousness and Ungodliness of men._ By _These Means_ does the Gospel in the most effectual manner _Teach us, That denying Ungodliness and worldly Lusts, we should live soberly, righteously, and godly in this present World._ And to _Them_ who are thus taught by it, and to _Them_ only, it is _the Grace of God which bringeth Salvation._ 'Tis unto _Them_, as the same Apostle elsewhere expresses it, _the Savour of Life unto Life_; but unto the Wicked, _the Savour of Death unto Death._

SERMON

S E R M O N XXX.

Of the GRACE of GOD.

PHIL. II. latter part of the 12th, and the 13th verfe.

Work out your own Salvation with Fear and Trembling ; For it is God which worketh in you, both to will and to do, of his good pleafure.

THERE is no one Queftion in the whole Syftem of Divinity, which has raifed greater Controverfies in the Church of God, than That concerning the Extent of the *Grace of God* and the *Power of Man. Some,* in order to vindicate God from being the Author of Sin, have been fo follicitous to maintain the perfeƈt Freedom of *Men's* Faculties, and their Liberty of choofing Good or Evil ; that they either *have,* or have been thought *to have,* diminifhed from the Abfolutenefs of the Sovereignty, or from the Efficacy of the Grace of *God.* They have been *thought,* I fay, to diminifh from the Grace of God. For whether they have *really* done fo, or only by their Adverfaries been *reprefented* as doing fo ; is not very evident. In almoft *all* Controverfies, what Men *fay* for *Themfelves,* and what their *Adverfaries* infer or *reprefent* them as faying, are generally two very different things : And they who will not be at the pains to confider diftinƈtly what *each* fide alledges for *itfelf,* but will judge of *Either* by the charaƈter or reprefentation made of it by the *Other* only ; will for ever be led into erroneous judgments concerning Men and Things, and continue unavoidably ignorant of the True State of the Matter in Queftion, whatfoever it be. Whether therefore They who in Antient Times were reprefented as *Deniers* of the *Grace of God,* were rightly charged with fo doing or no, does not certainly appear ; becaufe the *Ground* of that charge, was only their afferting the *Freedom of the Will of Man ;* which though their *Adverfaries* judged to infer a Denial of the Sufficiency of the Power or Grace of God, yet perhaps *They Themfelves* faw no fuch Confequence of it. However That be ; *Others,* in the contrary Extreme, that they might be fure not to afcribe too little to the Efficacy of the Divine Grace, have fuppofed men to have *no natural Powers at all* of Aƈting or Willing, *no Ufe* of the original Faculties given them at their Creation, *no Liberty of Will* or Freedom of Choice, in matters of Morality and Religion. By which Doƈtrine they have *confequently,* (even themfelves *feeing* and acknowledging the confequence,) introduced an abfolute *Neceffity* or *Fatality* upon Men's Aƈtions. From whence it follows, in the next ftep of deduƈtion, (though This indeed they are not fo willing to fee ;) but in Truth it *does* neceffarily and unavoidably follow ; that *God Himfelf,* and not *Man,* will be the Author of Sin.

SOMETHING not unlike to This, has happened in *another* Queftion concerning the *Liberty* of the Will of *Man,* and the *Prefcience* or *Foreknowledge* of God. *Some,* confidering that without Liberty of the Will, there can be no Religion, no Virtue or Vice, no juft Punifhment or reafonable Reward ; have, in order to remove an Objection which they judged would otherwife lie hard againft fo important a Truth, *denied,* or feemed *to deny*, God's foreknowledge of future and free Events. *Others* on the contrary, intent upon magnifying the Glory of the Divine Attributes, and follicitous to fecure the including all poffible future Events within the Compafs of God's Foreknowledge, have affirmed all the Actions of Men to be Neceffary and Determined abfolutely, by a Chain of certain and unalterable Caufes. The Confequence of which unavoidably is, that Man in reality is no more capable of Morality or Religion, than a Beaft that perifhes, or than a lifelefs Machine.

T H E *Truth*, in *Both* thefe Controverfies, is; that there is Something in *Each* part of the Queftion, which muft needs be acknowledged to be True; and yet 'tis equally neceffary that it *be always fo only* acknowledged, and *fo only* underftood, as to be confiftent with what on the *Other* part of the Queftion muft at the fame Time, and for the fame Reafons, of Neceffity be acknowledged too. For otherwife, we do but indeavour to eftablifh *One* Truth at the Expence of *Another*; which, at the conclufion of the Argument, is not indeed confirming *Either* of them, but deftroying *Both*. Thus, for inftance, the *Freedom of Men's Will*, whatever be the Nature and the Degree of that Freedom, muft upon no account be any thing in any wife inconfiftent with any of the *Perfections of God*; becaufe the Attributes of the Divine Nature are *Neceffary* in themfelves, abfolutely and unalterably, and antecedent to the Production of all created Beings. And on the other fide, *no Attribute of the Divine Nature*, fuch as *Foreknowledge* in particular, can poffibly be fuch as to take away the *Liberty of the Will of Man*; becaufe then it would confequently deftroy fome of the Other equally neceffary Perfections of God, fuch as Juftice and Goodnefs, which cannot poffibly be deftroyed. Since therefore neither the *Foreknowledge* of God, nor the *Liberty of Man*, can without a plain contradiction be denied; it follows unavoidably, that the *Foreknowledge* of God muft be *of fuch a Nature*, as is not inconfiftent with the *Liberty of Man*. That is to fay; it cannot be a Knowledge of the fame fort or Species, as is the Knowledge of neceffary and determined Events, arifing from a View of the whole Chain or Series of Neceffary Caufes producing thofe Events : but it muft be a Knowledge quite of another Nature ; a Power, difficult indeed for Us to frame a *clear* conception of, but yet not impoffible to have a Notion of in general. For as a *Man* who has no Influence over Another perfon's Actions, can yet often perceive beforehand what That Other will do; and a *wifer* and more experienced Man, will ftill with greater *probability* forefee what Another, whofe Difpofition he is perfectly acquainted with, will in certain Circumftances do; and an *Angel*, with ftill much lefs *degrees of Errour*, may have a farther Profpect into Men's future Actions, fo 'tis very reafonable to apprehend, that *God*, without influencing Men's Wills by his Power, yet by his Forefight cannot but have as much *Certainer* a Knowledge of future Free Events, than either Men or Angels can poffibly have, as the *Perfection* of *His* nature is greater than that of *Theirs*.

I N like manner, in that *Other* queftion, which is the Subject-matter of my Text ; Whatever Power Men be fuppofed to have in the Ufe of their *natural Faculties*, 'tis evident it cannot be fuch as in any wife to diminifh the Senfe they ought to have of their continual *Dependence* upon *God*; becaufe thofe *very* Powers and *natural* Faculties, are *themfelves* entirely the Gift of *God*, and not any thing at all of *our own* procuring, *as of our felves*. So that thofe who have been charged with afcribing *the moft* to the Power of Men's own Wills, did not perhaps (as their *Adverfaries* conceived) *intend* to derogate any thing from Men's true Dependence upon God : For it cannot be imagined that any reafonable Men fhould contend, (neither did their Argument require it,) that any One fhould in any Action, or in any Degree, be Independent on his Maker. On the other fide ; whatever be fuppofed to be the Power and Efficacy of the *Grace of God*, even where it has the moft *effectual* Influence ; yet it muft upon no account be underftood to be fuch as to over-rule the Liberty of Men's Will and Choice, and render their Actions *neceffary*; becaufe This would be to remove the whole Foundation of Religion, by entirely deftroying the Morality of Men's Actions, and taking away the very Nature of Virtue and Vice. Since therefore neither the Influence of the *Divine Grace*, nor the proper *Power of Men* in the ufe of their *natural* Faculties, can without an evident contradiction be denied; it follows unavoidably, that the *Grace of God* muft of neceffity always be underftood, to have the nature of a *moral Affiftance only*, which does perfectly agree with Men's *Free ufe of their Faculties*; and that it is *not* in the nature of a *phyfical compulfion*, which is altogether inconfiftent with Men's doing any thing *themfelves*. The Apoftle perfectly expreffes this whole Notion, in the Words of the Text: *Work out* your own *Salvation with Fear and Trembling*; *for it is* God *that worketh in you both to will and to do, of his good pleafure*. He does not fay, *Work out your own Salvation* yourfelves, *as having* no Need *of the Grace of God*: Neither does he fay on the contrary, *The Grace of God worketh* All *in you, and therefore ye need not to do any thing* yourfelves: But, afcribing to each part its proper Office, he fays, *Work* ye *out your own Salvation, becaufe* the Grace of God (the Motives and Affiftances of the Gofpel) *gives you Power fo to do*.

T H E principal Argument alledged by Thofe, who think the Influence of the Divine Grace to be *fo* efficacious as to *neceffitate* Men's Actions, is, that it feems to Them *unworthy* of the Supreme Power, Sovereignty and Majefty of God to do any thing *ineffectually*, or to permit Any Act of His to be *refifted and fruftrated* by the Power of frail and mortal Men. And, were the Power *of God* the matter in queftion, This Argument would indeed be undoubtedly good. But in *Moral* matters, where whatever is not done *voluntarily and without Compulfion*, is not done *at all*; the cafe is very different. For in *thefe* matters, to influence a Moral Agent with fuch an Efficacy as *cannot be refifted*, is entirely to deftroy the Morality of the Action, to take away the whole Nature of Virtue and Vice, and to make all Reward or Punifhment impoffible or unjuft. So far therefore is it from being unworthy of God, to *forbear* exerting his irrefiftible Power in *thefe* Cafes; that, on the contrary, it would be altogether unworthy of him to *exercife* That Power; becaufe it would be a fubverting of his whole Defign, in creating rational and intelligent Beings at all. *Moral Agents*, muft be influenced only by *Moral Motives*; by Reafon and Argument, by Perfuafion and Conviction, by Hopes and Fears. The *Efficacy* therefore of the Grace of *God*, *can* confift *only* in laying before men *ftrong Arguments* for their *Conviction*, and giving them fufficient *Helps* and *Affiftances* to overcome whatever would hinder them from acting according to fuch conviction. Any *other* influence than what is of this *moral* nature; any Influence that amounted to *Force*, and could not be refifted; far from being truly *efficacious* to make Men *good and virtuous*, would on the contrary make it as *impoffible* for them to have any Virtue or Goodnefs at all, as it is that a *Clock* or a *Watch* fhould be virtuous and praife-worthy.

T H E Summ is This: In order to give *God* his due Honour and Glory, and to keep up in Men's Minds a juft Senfe of their continual Dependence upon him; 'tis neceffary that we at all times acknowledge, that all our Powers and *natural* Faculties *themfelves* are entirely at firft *derived* to us from God's free Goodnefs, and continually *preferved* to us merely by the fame good pleafure; and that neither our *Being*, nor *any Power* we have, is in any wife owing to Ourfelves: That, much more, every *fupernatural* Sufficiency, every *extraordinary* Degree of Affiftance, every *revealed* Means of Knowledge, every *New* Motive to Virtue or Determent from Vice, every *Direction or Guidance in the way of Life* which we receive from the Knowledge of Things *invifible*, and from the kind Influence of the *Divine Spirit*; is wholly the *Gift* or *Grace* of *God*: That the *Promife* of *Heaven* and of *eternal Happinefs* at all, as the Reward of our beft *En-*

deavours

SERM. deavours and most perfect *Services*, if such were *possible* to be performed by us; that
XXX. even *This* also is merely God's *free Bounty*, and *undeserved Gift*, to unprofitable Servants : All This, I say, is of necessity to be acknowledged, in order to give God his *due Honour* and *just Glory*.

A T the same time, that the *Nature of Virtue and Vice* may not be taken away ; 'tis also of no less necessity to be acknowledged, that as the natural *Faculties* wherewith God hath originally endowed Men, are in their own Power either to *make use of* or to *neglect* ; so the supernatural *Assistances* afforded Men by the Revelation of the Gospel, and by the Influence of the Divine Grace, are still *but* in the Nature of *Assistances*, which may either be *complied with* or *rejected* : And the Gift of eternal Life, as it is the *free* Gift of God, which Men could not possibly deserve, or claim, by Virtue of any Work or Duty which they were capable of performing ; so it is *not* a *forced* Gift, *imposed* upon them whether they will or no ; but *such* a *free* Gift, as requires the *concurrence* of their *own Endeavours*, in *applying* and *making Use of* the Divine Assistance which enables them to obtain it. For this reason, the Apostle St *Peter* exhorts men to *grow in Grace*, as a Duty depending upon their *own Endeavours*, 2 *Pet.* iii. 18 ; and St *Paul* admonishes Men, *not to quench* or *grieve* the *Holy Spirit of God*, who *will not* forcibly *strive* with Those which resist his good Motions ; and Men are frequently blamed in Scripture for *receiving the Grace of God* in vain ; for resisting *the Holy Ghost*, and for rejecting *the Counsel of God against themselves*.

T H E *Cause* of erroneous Opinions, in This and most other questions about which there have at any time been raised any Controversies, is generally This ; that Men attending to *One* point only, and being sollicitous to oppose strongly some *particular* Errour, have been apt to do it in such a manner, as has carried them out beyond the Truth of the Argument, and prevented them from guarding against being exposed to Errour in some contrary Extreme. Thus in disputing against the Errours of the Church of *Rome*, incautious persons have frequently been betrayed by an unwise Zeal to make use of such Arguments, as they were not aware might at the same time be alledged by Others of an opposite Perswasion, with the same Force against themselves. And nothing is more common, than for Others on the contrary, in the heat of Controversy with some of their Brethren who differ from them, to draw such Arguments from Church-Authority, and General Councils, and the like ; as they are not enough sensible may on any other occasion be used against Themselves by Those of the Church of *Rome*, with at least as Great and perhaps Greater Force. Thus in like manner in the present case ; If Any persons, sollicitous to maintain the Liberty of Man's Will, have at any time asserted such a Power in Men's Use of their natural Faculties, as to make them *not dependent* upon God; or such as may *of Right* claim the Reward of Heaven, and not of *Free Grace* and *undeserved Promise* ; These indeed, (if any Such have been, and they have not rather been *mistaken* by their Adversaries,) These, I say, *going about to establish* their own *righteousness*, (in the Sense St *Paul* blames, *Rom.* x. 3.) and *not submitting themselves unto the righteousness of God*, have indeed *frustrated the Grace of God*, (as the same Apostle speaks again, *Gal.* ii. 21 ;) *For if righteousness comes by* This way, *then* undoubtedly *Christ is dead in vain*. But then Others on the *contrary part*, sollicitous (as they conceived) to maintain God's absolute Sovereignty in all things, and the Efficacy of Divine Grace ; to magnify the work of God in Men, and to depress and humble the Vanity of Those who assume Any thing to themselves as *of themselves* ; have almost perpetually urged such Arguments against their Adversaries, as they were not aware might by the Enemies of all Religion, the Asserters of Necessity and Fate, be with equal Strength alleged against *Themselves*. And by *exalting* (as They thought) the Grace of God into an *irresistible Efficacy*, they have consequently made it, in truth and reality, to be of *No Efficacy at all*. For, in matters of morality and religion, That

3   *only*

only is of any Effect, which makes Men, in the *moral* fenfe, *better* than they would otherwife be: And then *only* are they morally *Better*, when by *moral* Motives, by conviction of *Truth* and *Reafon*, by well-grounded *Hopes* and juft *Fears*, they are perfwaded and prevailed upon to love and to chufe freely what is *Right* and *Good*. If by any *irrefiftible* Influence they are *compelled* to do it, the beft Action in the World has no longer any Goodnefs in it; being not done by *Them*, any more than by any *material* or *unintelligent Inftrument*, to which no man ever afcribes either *Good* or *Evil*. The *Truth* therefore is plainly This: If we will frame to ourfelves right Notions of Religion, Notions which truly tend to the Glory of *God*, and to promote Virtue and Obedience in *Men*; the *Power* afcribed to *Men*, muft neither on the one fide be fuppofed to be fuch, that thereby men can *Merit* any thing, as of *themfelves*; neither on the other fide muft the Influence of the *Power* or *Grace of God* be imagined to be fuch, as will make vain and needlefs our own Endeavours. But the *Grace of God*, manifefted in the *merciful Terms of the Gofpel*, in the *clear Revelation of a Future State, and of a Judgment to come*, in God's *declared Acceptance of Repentance through Chrift*, and in the *promifed Affiftance of the Holy Spirit*; This *Grace of God*, I fay, effectually *enables* men to perform their Duty. And the *Power and Will of Man*, applying and making *Ufe* of that Affiftance to an actual Improvement in Virtue, brings forth on *its* part, thofe acceptable Fruits of the Spirit, which wicked men are *therefore* juftly condemned for not bringing forth, becaufe *They alfo* had the means of Grace offered and propofed to them, but wilfully and obftinately refufed to be amended thereby. God hath, *of his good pleafure*, or of his free Grace, *given them both to will and to do*; and yet, through their own perverfenefs and obftinate difobedience, they *work* not *out their own Salvation*.

WHEN therefore the Scripture tells us that *by Grace we are faved*, and yet that at the fame time we *work out our own Salvation*; 'tis plain that thefe *different Phrafes* are only *different reprefentations of one and the fame thing*, under *different refpects*: Juft as *Heighth* and *Depth* are *one and the fame thing*, confidered only in *different Pofitions*. Men are faved *by Grace*, becaufe without God's gracious Affiftance and Acceptance of their imperfect Endeavours, they could not of themfelves attain unto Salvation; and at the fame time 'tis no lefs true, that they *work out their own Salvation*, becaufe without their leading a Life of Virtue and Obedience through a diligent Ufe of thofe means which the Grace of God affords them, the *Grace of God* alone will in no wife force them to be faved. Thus *God's working in* or *with Us*, and *our working together with God*, are promifcuoufly expreffed in Scripture, as Caufes concurrently producing the fame Effect. And mens being *hardened*, or *wicked*; *hardened of* God, or *hardening* themfelves, are phrafes ufed in like manner to fignify one and the fame thing under different Refpects. They harden *themfelves*; becaufe 'tis by their own Obftinacy and Perverfenefs only, that they become obdurate. And they are hardened of *God*, not by any proper Act or Efficiency of his, (except perhaps in fome extraordinary judicial Cafes;) but by his juftly ceafing to ftrive with them any longer, giving them up *unto their own hearts lufts*, (as the Scripture expreffes it,) *letting them follow their own imaginations, and* giving them over *to a reprobate mind, to work all unrighteoufnefs with greedinefs*. Laftly; 'Tis very remakable to This purpofe, that the very *fame* Acts and Habits, which are known by the Name of *Moral Virtues*, are alfo in Scripture ftiled *Graces* or *Gifts of the Spirit*: Moral Virtues, as they are feated in the Mind of Man, directing his Intentions, and appearing in his Practice: And, at the fame time, *Gifts or Fruits of the Spirit*; as they are promoted by the *Arguments of revealed Religion*, by the *Affiftance of the Spirit of God*, and by being *practifed in exprefs Obedience to the Divine Commands*. The Fruit of the Spirit, (faith St *Paul*, Eph. v. 9.) *is in all* Goodnefs *and* Righteoufnefs *and* Truth. And Gal. v. 22. *The Fruit of the* Spirit, *is Love, Joy,*

SERM.
XXX.
Peace, *Long-suffering, Gentleness, Goodness, Faith, Meekness, Temperance; against
Such, there is No Law.*

AND Now, having *premised* a large explication of the *general* Doctrine, upon which
the exhortation in the Text is founded; I should in the *next* place have proceeded to
consider *distinctly,* the several *particular* expressions made use of in the Text: *What* is
meant, by *working out our Salvation*; *what* it is, to work it out *with Fear and Trembling*; and *why*, in *That* manner: *What* is meant by God's *giving us both to will and
to do, of his good pleasure*; and *how This* consideration is a Motive to *Us*, to endeavour to
work out our own *Salvation.* But the distinct Consideration of these particulars, must
be referred to a following opportunity.

SERMON XXXI.

Of the GRACE of GOD.

PHIL II. latter part of the 12th, and the 13th verse.

*Work out your own Salvation with Fear and Trembling; For it is God
which worketh in you, both to will and to do, of his good pleasure.*

SERM.
XXXI.
IN a foregoing Discourse upon these words, I premised a large Explication of the
general Doctrine, upon which the Exhortation in the Text is founded. I shall
now proceed to consider *distinctly*, the several *particular* Expressions made use of
in the Text: *What* is meant by *working out our Salvation*; *what* it is, to work it out
with Fear and Trembling; and *why*, in That manner; *what* is meant by God's *working
in us both to will and to do, of his good pleasure*; and *How This* consideration is a Motive to *Us*, to endeavour to *work out* our own *Salvation.*

I. IN the *first* place I am to consider *what* is meant, by *working out our* Salvation.
The word, *Salvation*, originally and in its *general* Notion, signifies *Deliverance* from
any great and imminent Danger; especially *such* Deliverance or Escape, as is accomplished not without labour and hazard.   And from hence it comes in Scripture to be applied in the *Spiritual* sense, to signify *particularly* and by way of *eminence*, the *Great
and Final Deliverance* of virtuous and good men from that *general* Destruction, which,
in the nature of Things, and by the righteous appointment of God, must at last over-
whelm a wicked and incorrigible world. *The whole World*, saith St. *John, lieth in Wickedness*, or, as the Original has it, *under the Power of the wicked One*, 1 ep. v. 19; that
is, The greater part of Mankind, through their easiness in yielding to the Temptations
of Unrighteousness, their negligence in not correcting the Corruptions of their Nature,
and their Perverseness in chusing wilfully the Ways of Wickedness and Debauchery;
are altogether incapable of that State of Happiness, which is in Scripture stiled *The
Kingdom of God.*   For, what St *Paul* affirms in the *literal* Sense, that *Flesh and Blood,*
mortal and corruptible Bodies, *cannot inherit the Kindom of God;* is in the *spiritual* Sense

still

ftill *more* neceffarily true, that *wicked and corrupt* Minds fhall in no cafe enter therein. S E R M·
The new Heavens and new Earth, which *we look for according to his Promife*, are fuch XXXI.
wherein *dwelleth* only *Righteoufnefs*; that is, Meeknefs and Juftice, Purity and Holinefs, Faithfulnefs and Truth.   And therefore our Saviour, fpeaking of the refurrection
of the Saints unto eternal Life, elegantly ftiles it *The Refurrection of the* Juft, *Luk.* xiv. 14.
God is *of purer eyes, than to behold Iniquity*; and therefore into the heavenly *Jerufa-*
lem there fhall in no wife enter any thing that defileth, neither whatfoever worketh abomi-
nation or maketh a Lie: There fhall be admitted no Fraud or Violence, no Arbitrarinefs or Injuftice, no Debauchery or Impurity whatfoever; but *the Spirits of* Juft *men*
only, *made perfect* by the Practice of *Virtue*, and by the influences of the good *Spirit*
of God.   Now the Bulk of the wicked and corrupt World, being (in the nature of
Things) incapable of inheriting This Kingdom of Righteoufnefs, muft of neceffity, not
by any Cruel and Severe Decree of God, but of neceffity in point of Wifdom and Good
Government, they muft be excluded out of Heaven, and, by the righteous and impartial Sentence of the unerring Judge, be in fuch a manner, as fhall be exactly fuitable to each of their refpective Demerits, fent into Deftruction.   *From* which Deftruction, *They who* (as our Lord expreffes it,) *fhall be thought* worthy *to obtain that Life,*
and the Refurrection from the Dead, fhall be Saved.   Not that all *Others* alfo fhall not
equally rife from the Dead; but that *That only* deferves to be truly and *emphatically*
ftiled the *Refurrection from the Dead*, which is a *Refurrection unto* Life *and Glory.*
This Deliverance therefore of all juft and good men, by the Mercy of God, and through
the Interpofition of Chrift, from that final Deftruction which muft naturally and of
neceffity, under the Government of a Wife and Righteous Judge, fall upon a wicked
and corrupt World; this, I fay, is what the Scripture calls *Salvation.*   The *Confequence*
of which Salvation is indeed moreover mens being admitted into That incorruptible *In-*
heritance, that unfpeakable and never-fading *Happinefs*, which is the Free Gift of God
through Chrift, to Thofe whom in his unerring Judgment he fhall think fit to advance beyond their natural and original capacities, to be *Heirs of God*, and *Joint-*
Heirs with Chrift, in his eternal Kingdom of Glory.

   B U T the *Primary* Notion of *Salvation*, according to the *proper* fignification of the
word, is *Deliverance from Deftruction.*   And the *Greatnefs* of this Deliverance is, in
the *New Teftament*, lively reprefented unto us by feveral remarkable Types.   'Tis
reprefented *firft*, by the Salvation of *Lot* out of *Sodom*; when God with Fire from Heaven overthrew thofe wicked Cities, *fetting them forth for an example*, having deftroyed
them with an irreparable Deftruction, which St *Jude* calls *the Vengeance of eternal*
Fire, ver. 7.   'Tis reprefented in the *next* place, by the Salvation of the *children of*
Ifrael out of *Egypt*; when God overthrew *Pharaoh* and his whole Army in the Sea,
but led his own people fafely through the Sea and through the Wildernefs, into the promifed *Canaan.*   'Tis reprefented *again*, by the Salvation of thofe who efcaped at the
final deftruction of *Jerufalem*; concerning which our Saviour foretold, *Matt.* xxiv. 40.
that *then fhould two* men *be together in the field; the one fhould be taken, and the other*
left; And that *two women fhould be grinding* together *at the mill; the one fhould be taken,*
and the other left.   *Laftly*, 'Tis reprefented by the Salvation of *Noah* and his Family
in the Ark; when God deftroyed at once the whole impenitent World with a Deluge
of Water.   For fo St *Peter* expreffly applies the fimilitude, 1 ep. iii. 20. *The like figure*
whereunto, even Baptifm (faith he) *doth alfo Now fave Us.*   Only, leaft by *Baptifm* any
man fhould be fo weak as to think he meant the bare outward Form or Ceremony, the
mere Name or Profeffion of a Chriftian; he adds in the very fame verfe this moft important caution, that thereby he underftands, *not the putting away of the Filth of the*
Flefh, (not *the mere Wafhing* or the *Ceremony* of Baptifm,) *but the Anfwer of a good*
Confcience towards God in the courfe of a virtuous and a Chriftian Life.

Now

SERM.   Now This being the true Notion of the word *Salvation*, the Duty of working out
XXXI.   *this Salvation*, which is what we are so earneftly exhorted to in the Text, muft con-
fequently fignify the making ufe of thofe *Means* which are proper and fufficient to ob-
tain This *End:* That is, it muft fignify the *whole Progrefs* of our Deliverance, by a
Life of *Virtue* and true *Religion*, from *the Power and Tyranny of the Devil*, from the
Dominion and Slavery of Sin, and from the *Punifhment of Death*.

   MEN, in the State of Heathen *ignorance and wickednefs*, being as it were habitually
fubject to a Spirit of Delufion, of Impiety, and of all kinds of Debauchery, are in Scripture reprefented as being in *Slavery to Satan*; who is therefore ftiled the *Prince of This
World*, and the God *of This World*, the *Prince of the Power of the Air*, the *Spirit that
worketh in the children of difobedience*. From This *Tyranny of the Devil* men are faved,
by forfaking the *Idolatry of the Nations*, and returning to the *worfhip of the true God of
the Univerfe*, as taught in the *Gofpel of Chrift*: Being *delivered*, as St *Paul* exprefles it,
from the Power of Darknefs, and tranflated into the Kingdom of God's dear Son,
Col. i. 13.

   LIKEWISE thofe, who having embraced the *Gofpel of Chrift*, yet live unworthy of
their Holy Profeffion, by means of *Any Habit of Unrighteoufnefs or Debauchery*, are reprefented in Scripture, as being *Slaves to Sin*, and ftill *in the Snare of the Devil*. The
expreffions of This kind are very frequent and elegant; that fuch perfons are *Servants
of Sin*; that *Sin has the Dominion over them*: that they are *overcome by it*; and *brought
in bondage to it*; that they are the *Servants of Corruption*, and the like. And becaufe
the Devil is the *Head* of this Corruption, who *Tempts* men into it, and *delights* in it;
therefore, whofoever lives in Sin, notwithftanding his profeffing himfelf a *Difciple of
Chrift*, is ftill in reality *the Servant of Satan:* 1 Joh. iii. 8. *He that committeth Sin, is
of the Devil; for the Devil finneth from the Beginning*. Whofoever is fo falfe to himfelf, as not to be able to refift the Temptations of Unrighteoufnefs, imitates, and is
fubject to, the Great Enemy of God and Goodnefs; is *in the Snare of the Devil, and
taken captive by him at his Will*. Now the Defign of Chrift's coming into the World
was to *deftroy thefe works of the Devil*; to fave *men from their Sins*, Mat. i. 21. to
perfuade them, and to *enable* them, to fave *themfelves from* amongft a wicked and *corrupt generation*; to *deliver them from the bondage of corruption into the glorious Liberty
of the children of God*. *Working out our own Salvation* therefore, (confidered as an Exhortation given to fuch as are already Chriftians,) fignifies *making a* diligent ufe of the
Means and Encouragements which God has afforded us in the Gofpel, to affift and enable us, *effectually to reform every evil Habit*, and to improve in the Practice of every
Virtue, *perfecting Holinefs in the Fear of God*. The *Confequence* of which *Salvation
from* Sin, is *Salvation alfo from the* Punifhment which God has denounced againft Sinners. And not only fo, but upon them who *fhall be thought worthy to efcape all thefe
things that fhall come to pafs, and to ftand before the Son of Man*, fhall be conferred
moreover God's free Gift of Eternal Life and Happinefs.

   THE Exhortation therefore in the Text, to *work out our own Salvation*, is of the fame
import with That of St *Peter*, 2 ep. i. 10. *Brethren, give diligence to make your Calling and Election fure; for if ye do thefe things, ye fhall never fall: for fo an Entrance
fhall be miniftred unto you abundantly into the everlafting Kingdom of our Lord and Saviour Jefus Chrift*. From which Admonition of St *Peter*, compared with This in the
Text, it follows plainly and undeniably, that Men (by God's Affiftance) have a *Power*,
as well as an *Obligation*, to *work out their own Salvation*; and that their *election*, that
is, their being *chofen* and *approved* of God, depends upon That *diligence* and *fincere endeavour* of their *own*, which the Apoftle exprefsly exhorts them to make ufe of to this
purpofe, that thereby they may *fecure* their being *elected* of God.

II. I AM to confider in the *fecond* place, *what* is meant by working out our Salvation S E R M.
with *Fear and Trembling*; and *why* it muft be done in That manner. XXXI.

Now the words *Fear and Trembling*, are not put here to exprefs a *Paffion*, but to
denote *Care and Diligence* in our *Actions*, in oppofition to *Prefumption, Remiffnefs*, or
negligent Confidence. According to thofe *other* Admonitions in Scripture; *be not high-
minded, but fear*; and, *let hm that* thinketh *he ftandeth, take heed left he fall.* The
wife man obferves, Prov. xxviii. 14. *Happy is the man that* feareth, that is, who is
cautious, *always*; *but he that* hardeneth *his Heart*, that is, who is carelefs and negligent, *fhall fall into Mifchief.* And, *To This man will I look*, faith God himfelf by the
Prophet, If. lxvi. 2. *even to Him that is poor and of a contrite Spirit, and trembleth at
my word.* St *Paul*, though fo eminent an Apoftle, yet fpeaks thus concerning his *own
Practife* upon This Head: *I keep under my Body*, fays he, *and bring it into Subjection*,
1 Cor. ix. 27, *left by any means, when I have preached to Others, I my felf fhould become
a caft-away.* And *Phil.* iii. 11. *If by any* means, fays he, *I might attain unto the
Refurrection of the dead*; *Not as though I had already attained, or were already perfect;——But this One thing I do; forgetting thofe things which are behind, and reaching
forth unto thofe things which are before, I prefs towards the Mark for the prize of the
high calling of God in Chrift Jefus.*

THE *Reafons why* we are exhorted to work out our Salvation after this manner, with
Fear and Trembling; that is, with *Caution and Diligence*, with *Care and Earneft Application*; are,

1*ft*, BECAUSE 'tis of *all* others the thing of the *greateft importance* to us. 'Tis
the *One thing neceffary*; the Prefervation of *ourfelves*, of our *Souls*, of our *Life*,
of our *Happinefs for ever.* What *Naaman*'s Servant faid to his Mafter upon
another occafion, is *much more* applicable *here*; *My Father, if he had bid thee do
fome* Great *thing, wouldft thou not have done it? how much rather then, when he faith
unto thee, Wafh and be clean? Skin for Skin, and all that a man has, will he give for
his Life*; for the prefervation of this *fhort*, this *tranfitory* life: *What then fhall he give
in Exchange for his Soul*, in Exchange for his portion in *Eternity*? If therefore no wife
Man, according to our Saviour's Argument in the Parable, attempts to *build a Tower*,
without *firft fitting down and counting the Coft* of it; how much more does it behove every
reafonable perfon to be follicitous before all things, that he be well affured in his *own*
Underftanding, and not by mere hap-hazard rely blindly upon *Others*, in order to find
which is the True Way of *Salvation*; and that he be accordingly *diligent*, in walking
in That Way!

2*dly* ANOTHER reafon why we are required to work out our Salvation *with Fear*,
is becaufe of the *Difficulties* we muft expect to meet with in the Work. *Difficulties*,
not in the Nature of the *thing it felf*: For Chrift's *Yoke is eafy, and his Burden light.
Virtue* is of all things *the moft natural and the moft reafonable*; and the *Commandments of
God*, in themfelves *no way grievous. But great Difficulties* often arife, by the perverfe
oppofition of *wicked men* from *without*, and the corrupt inclination of *unreafonable and
ungoverned Appetites* from *within.* Infomuch that even *the righteous*, faith St *Peter*,
fcarcely are faved: And St *Paul* fpeaks of Men being *faved, fo as by fire*; that is, efcaping with difficulty, as out of a Houfe which is in Flames: *faved with Fear, pulled
out of the Fire*, fo St. *Jude* expreffes it, *ver.* 23. The *Flefh* lufteth againft the Spirit;
warring againft the reafon and law of our Minds; fo that we cannot, without fome
Pains and Care, do the things that are moft reafonable. And when we have perfectly
conquered *ourfelves*; yet ftill, through the Difficulties brought upon us by *Others*, by the
Profane Perfecutor, or the *Superftitious Bigot*; by the Blenders of *humane* Authority
with *Divine*; and thofe who mingle and confound together the *Powers of* This World
and the *Doctrines of* Men, with the *Commands of* God; by Thefe is the *Gate* often made

SERM. *ſtrait*, and the *Way narrow*, ſo that through *tribulation only* can we poſſibly *enter into*
XXXI. *the Kingdom of God.*

3*dly*, A *third* reaſon, why we are directed to work out our Salvation *with Fear*, is,
becauſe it is a Work that can be done but *Once*; and if we *Once* miſcarry, we have loſt
ourſelves for ever. *It is appointed for Men* Once *to die, and after That, the Judgment:*
And *when* Once *the maſter of the Houſe is riſen up and hath ſhut to the door*, there is
no more Admiſſion. This Argument is repreſented to us under a very elegant Similitude
by one of the moſt *antient* Writers next to the Apoſtles times: *As a Potter*, ſays he,
*while the Clay is moiſt and ſoft, moulds it over and over again, if it pleaſes him not at
firſt; but after it has been once hardened in the Fire, its ſhape can be mended no more:
So in the preſent life, God affords Men from time to time Space and Means of Repentance;
but after Death and Judgment has once paſſed upon them, and they be caſt into the Fire,
there is no more Remedy for ever.*

4*thly*, WE are exhorted to work out our Salvation *with Fear*, and to be *perpetually*
upon our *guard*, becauſe we are *continually* in danger of *New Temptations*, and *at* no
time ſecure from their Aſſaults. Temptations of one ſort or other, perpetually ſurround
us; and the Negligent, or Preſumptuous, cannot fail of being frequently betrayed into
Sin. From hence are thoſe repeated Admonitions of our Saviour and his Apoſtles, to
watch and to be *ready always, to ſtand faſt in the Faith*, to *quit ourſelves like men*, to
be ſtrong, to be ſober and *vigilant, to take heed leſt there be in any of us an evil heart of
unbelief;* and to *exhort one another daily, while it is called to day, leſt, a promiſe being
left us of entring into his Reſt, any of us ſhould ſeem to come ſhort of it.*

Laſtly: ANOTHER reaſon why we are required to work out our Salvation *with
Fear*, is, becauſe whatever progreſs in Virtue we have already made, yet if hereafter
we fall back into unrighteous Practices, we loſe our reward. *The Juſt*, ſaith God, *ſhall
live by Faith;* but *if any Man draws back, my Soul ſhall have no pleaſure in him:* For
*no Man putting his hand to the plough, and looking back, is meet for the Kingdom of
God.* As in a *Race*, All run, but he only that perſeveres, obtains the Prize; and in a
warfare, All fight, but he only that overcomes gains the Crown of Victory; ſo, in
the *ſpiritual* Combat, *he that endures to the End*, ſaith our Lord, *the ſame ſhall be ſaved.*
For to them who by *patient Continuance* in well-doing ſeek for glory and honour and
immortality, to *Them* only is made the Promiſe of eternal Life. Wherefore, as St *Paul*
admoniſhes, *we ought to give the more earneſt Heed to the things which we have heard,
left at any time we ſhould let them ſlip*, Heb. ii. 1.

III. THE *Third* thing I propoſed to conſider in the Text, was, *what* is meant by
God's *working in us both to will and to do of his good pleaſure.* Now the plain and full
meaning of This, is;

1*ſt*, THAT *God* is to us the only *Author* of all thoſe *Powers and Faculties*, which
we vulgarly call *Natural. In Him we Live, Move, and have our Being.* From *Him*
we are indued with *Reaſon and Underſtanding*, with the *Faculty of diſcerning between
Good and Evil*, with the *Power of Willing and Chooſing what is Right.* We are not
ſufficient of ourſelves to think *any thing as of ourſelves; but our Sufficiency is of God,*
2 Cor. iii. 5. Weak therefore is That diſtinction ſo often found in the Writings of
Divines, between *Nature* and *Grace;* as if *One* was not equally the Gift of God, as
the *Other.*

2*dly*, GOD's giving us *both to will and to do*, ſignifies his affording us moreover *Supernatural* Helps. Such is, the *Revelation of the Goſpel;* which is therefore frequently
in Scripture called, *The Grace of God;* Tit. ii. 11. *The Grace of God which bringeth
Salvation, hath appeared to all men.*

UNDER which *general* Grace, are included more *particularly*, the following Supernatural Helps. A *clear and diftinct Knowledge of our Duty*, more diftinct than could be difcovered by the Light of Nature alone. A more plain and exprefs *bringing of Life and Immortality to Light*, by the particular Revelation of a *judgment to come*. *Exceeding Great and precious Promifes*; by the Faith and expectation of which, we are enabled to *overcome the World*, to *quench all the Fiery darts of the Devil*, and to become *partakers of the Divine Nature*, by perfecting Righteoufnefs and true Holinefs. An *Affurance of the Forgivenefs of paft Sins upon Repentance*; which is what the Scripture emphatically calls *Grace*; *The* Law *came by Mofes, but* Grace *and Truth came by Jefus Chrift*. The *Affiftance of the Divine Spirit* in the *conftant and ordinary* practife of our Duty; by which we are *renewed, juftified, fanctified,* and have *the Love of God fhed abroad in our Hearts*. Not that the Spirit of God acts upon us by way of neceffary *compulfion*, forcibly and irrefiftibly; (for the exhortations given us, not to *quench* and *grieve* and drive him from us, evidently fhow the contrary;) But he *helps our Infirmities*, in the way of *Moral Affiftance, Perfwafion, Direction* and *Concurrence*; but *will not always ftrive with men* who obftinately refift his good Motions. *Wifd.* i. 4. *Into a malicious Soul Wifdom fhall not enter, nor dwell in the body that is fubject unto Sin*; *For the Holy Spirit of Difcipline will flee deceit, and remove from Thoughts that are without Underftanding, and will not abide when unrighteoufnefs cometh in.*

Laftly, UNDER *Extraordinary Trials*, the Gofpel affures us of ftill more *particular and extraordinary Supports*: that God *will never leave us, nor forfake us*; but *will with the Temptation* always *make a way to efcape, that we may be able to bear it*; and particularly, that in time of great Perfecution, *it fhall be given us in that fame Hour what we fhall fpeak* and *what we fhall do*.

THESE are, over and above our *natural* Powers and Faculties, the *Supernatural* Helps and Affiftances afforded us by the Gofpel: *Both* of which are included in the Affertion in the Text, that *'tis God which worketh in us both to will and to do*.

THE *laft* words added in the Text, ὑπὲρ τῆς εὐδοκίας, *of his good pleafure*, do not fignify, as *Some* have imagined, that God works all thefe things *arbitrarily*, without any regard to the Difpofitions and Qualifications of Men. But the True meaning of the words is, that he does all thefe things *through his* Goodnefs; That is the Senfe, of the word which we render *good pleafure*. 'Tis God's *Goodnefs* which moves him to *work in us both to will and to do*; to give us both the *Faculties of Nature*, and the *Supernatural Affiftances of the Gofpel*, to lead us unto Life and Happinefs.

IV. THE *Fourth* and *Laft* thing I propofed from the Text, was, to fhow *How* This confideration of God's *working in us both to will and to do*, is an Argument or Motive to Us to *work out our own Salvation*. *Work out your own Salvation, For it is* God *that worketh in you both to Will and to Do of his good pleafure*. The Meaning plainly is; not, that *God* does *All* for us; For then the *Contrary* confequence muft needs have been true, that we could do *nothing* for *ourfelves*: But *God*, of his great Goodnefs gives us *Power*; therefore *We may* and *ought* to *Act*. And we may depend alfo, that if we be fincere in the Ufe of the Powers he has given us, our Endeavours fhall not be in vain. For, *Greater is He that is in Us, than He that is in the World*; and *if God be for us, who can be againft Us?* The Exhortation therefore in the Text, is of the fame Import with that in *Eph.* vi. 10. *Finally, my Brethren, be ftrong in the Lord, and in the Power of his might.*

THE *Inferences* proper to be drawn from the whole of what has been faid, are:

I. FROM hence we may obferve, how little Foundation there is in Scripture for thofe Men's Opinion, who underftanding figurative Expreffions literally and abfurdly, contend that wicked Men have no Power to do any thing towards their own Converfion;

SERM. fion; and confequently afcribe the Caufe of Men's Impenitency, to *God's* not giving
XXXI. them (as they call it) the *Grace to Repent.* Which is a very great Abufe of a Scrip-
ture-expreffion. For, God's *giving* or *granting* Men *Repentance,* fignifies (in Scripture) his granting them the Favour to have their Repentance *accepted* to the Forgivenefs of paft Sins, or *allowed* inftead of Innocence; and not his *conferring* Repentance
upon them, as an external Donation: Which is altogether unintelligible. Nor is it lefs
abfurd, from thofe paffages where very bad Men are faid to be dead in *trefpaffes and
fins;* and that when they amend, *God* creates *in them a new Heart;* to conclude literally, that wicked Men have no more Power to *amend their manners* than to *raife themfelves from the dead,* or to *create themfelves anew.* Which Doctrine, muft of neceffity
make Men very *flothful* Servants.

2*dly,* THE *fecond* Ufe proper to be made of the explication now given of the words
of the Text, is to Exhort Men to be *diligent* in working out their own Salvation by the
Ufe of thofe Means which God has worked or implanted in them. Which exhortation cannot be better expreffed, than in the words of the Author of the Book of *Wifdom,*
ch. i. 12. *Seek not Death in the Errour of your life; and pull not upon yourfelves deftruction with the works of your own hands. For God made not Death, neither has he pleafure
in the deftruction of the living. But ungodly Men with their works and words called it
unto them.* And Eccluf. xv. 11. *Say not thou, the Lord has caufed me to err; for he
hath no need of the finful man. The Lord hateth all abomination; and they that fear
God, love it not. He himfelf made Men from the beginning, and left them in the hands
of his counfel; if thou wilt, to keep the Commandments, and to perform acceptable Faithfulnefs. He hath fet fire and water before thee; ftretch forth thy hand unto whether thou
wilt. Before man is Life and Death; and whether him liketh fhall be given him. For
the Wifdom of the Lord is great; and he is mighty in Power, and beholdeth all things.
And his Eyes are upon them that fear him, and he knoweth every work of Man. He hath
commanded no man to do wickedly, neither has he given any man licence to fin.*

SERMON

S E R M O N XXXII.

Of the KINGDOM of GOD.

MATT. VI. 10.

Thy Kingdom come.

THOUGH *every Christian* acknowledges this Prayer of our Lord's composing to be a complete Pattern and Direction, as to the *Subject-matter* of the things we are to pray for; yet Many, very Many, 'tis to be feared, perpetually repeat the *Words*, with very little Attention to the *Sense* expressed by them: Not considering, that All Devotion confists entirely in the Application of the *Mind* to God, with an *Understanding* of what it defires; and not at all in the mere repeating with the *Lips* certain customary *Forms of Words*.

OUR Lord in the *former* part of this Prayer, after having taught us that the True and Proper Object of Worship, to whom our Petitions ought constantly/(through *His* Mediation) to be directed, is *the Father which is* in Heaven; (that is, *the Most* High; he who, not in *Place or Situation*, but in *Dignity and Dominion*, is *Supreme over All:*) Our Lord, I say, in the *former* part of this Prayer, after directing us to the True Object of Worship, our *Heavenly Father*, instructs us to pray in the *first* place, for Blessings *spiritual and eternal*; and then, in the *following* part of the Prayer, to ask for the *Comforts and Necessaries* of this *present Life*. In the *former* part, among the Petitions for Blessings of a *Spiritual* nature, and one of the *Principal* of Those Petitions, are the *Words of the Text :* Words of a very large and extensive signification; comprehending in brief almost *the Whole Notion* of True Religion; and, therefore, *particularly* worthy to be the Subject of our Meditations: *Thy Kingdom come.*

GOD is *by Nature King* over All; and his *Kingdom* is the *Universe*. His *Dominion* is infinite and everlasting, his *Power* absolute and irresistible, his *Glory* inexpressible and inconceivable. *Of him, and Through him, and To him, are all things*, Rom. xi. 36. That is, *For his Pleasure*, all things were *created*; *By* his *Providence*, all things are *preserved*; *To* his *Glory*, all things *terminate*. The *Heavens declare the Glory of God, and the Firmament sheweth his Handy-work*. The whole Frame of Nature obeys his Commands; and all the Powers of the Universe depend entirely upon the Word of his Mouth.

BUT because the True Greatness and Dignity of a Governour confists chiefly in the Obedience of them that can *disobey :* Because 'tis more *excellent* to be obeyed by *Reason and Understanding*, by *Will and Choice*, than by mere *necessity of Nature :* Because 'tis more *noble* to govern *Free Agents* by *moral considerations*, by the *Knowledge* of what is intrinsically *Good or Evil*, by a *Sense* of the Excellency of *Truth and Virtue*, by the *Wisdom* of reasonable and useful *Laws*, and by the *Views* of proper *Rewards and Punishments*, than to have *Power* over infinite Systems of *inanimate Matter*, which has no Sense of the Regularity of its own Motions, nor capacity to perceive the Wisdom and Glory of its Creator : Therefore the *Kingdom* of God *principally* confists, in his

S E R M. Government of *reasonable and intelligent* Creatures; in his being *served and obeyed* by
XXXII. those, who at the same time are capable of *disobeying*; who by their own *Actions* set
forth his Glory, and not merely in their being *Acted upon* by *Him*; who in their several Stations and Degrees, according to the Light that is afforded them, *discern* what
is *Right*, and *approve* what is *Good*, and *act* by their *Free Power*, and are *conscious* of
the Excellency of *Virtue*, and *Love* him whom they Obey, and are made *Happy* by
the Participation of his Perfections.   This is That, wherein *principally* consists the
Kingdom of God : A Kingdom, wherein shines forth the *Goodness*, and *Justice*, and
Wisdom, and *Holiness*, of the Supreme Governour, as clearly as his *Power and Domi-*
nion does in his ruling the whole material Universe.

B Y *Sin*, This Kingdom of God, This his Government over the *Hearts* and *Wills* of
the rational part of the Creation, is *opposed* and *withstood*.   For his *natural Kingdom*,
the Kingdom of his *Power*, cannot be resisted.   In *This* respect, the whole World is
in his Hand as a Dust of the Ballance; He can withdraw from all things their very
Being itself, and, with a Blast of his mouth, whenever he pleases, reduce them all
into Nothing in a Moment.   So that 'tis a very *absurd* Notion, which some have entertained, from certain figurative expressions of Scripture very much misunderstood;
as if the Devil had attempted to oppose the Almighty with *Force*, and had contended
with him for the *Dominion of the Universe*.   No : Such representations as These are
only the Fictions of Poets.   But indeed the *Devil rebelled* against God, in the same
Sense wherein *wicked* men *rebel* against him.   Not by thinking to resist his *Power*, but
by presumptuously venturing to disobey his *Will*, in those things wherein the Nature of
Virtue and Vice, and the very Essence of Moral Government, necessarily requires that
they should not be over-ruled and compelled by Force.   For here, the Thing that God
requires is the *Free Consent of the Will*; which, in the nature of things is not subject to
Compulsion; *Obedience itself* being *No obedience*, where there was no possibility of having *disobeyed*.   By *Sin* therefore this *Moral Kingdom of God* began to be opposed; by
the *Sins* of *Evil Angels*, and by the *Sins* of *Wicked men* : Among whom, as they corrupted themselves by degrees, in departing from the Living God; the Devil set up a
Kingdom of Idolatry and Great Wickedness, in opposition to the Righteous Kingdom
of God.   In order to *destroy* which *Works of the Devil*; (to *destroy* them, not by the
exercise of *Omnipotence*, but by the establishment of *Virtue and True Religion*, which
is the *Proper* and the Only *proper* Destruction of Immorality and Vice;) God was
pleased to give assistance and strength to the Light of Nature and Reason, by making
Revelations of himself from time to time to the degenerate world, and of the true manner of worshipping him; first by the *Patriarchs*, whom he appointed to be *Preachers*
of Righteousness both before and after the Flood; and then by *Moses* and the *Prophets* ;
and at last by his *Own Son*; who came into the World, and was *manifested* (as St *John*
assures us) *for* This *Cause*, that *he might destroy the Works of the Devil*; that is, that he
might root out Idolatry and Superstitious Worship, and reform men from Debauchery
and all Unrighteous Practices; that by the Knowledge, Worship, and Love of the
One True God and Maker of all things, in Purity and Holiness of Life, in Justice,
Meekness, and universal Charity and Good-will towards each Other, he might bring
them back, from a state of general corruption, to become Worthy and Obedient Subjects
of his Father's Kingdom of Righteousness.

F O R This reason, the *State* of the *Gospel*, the *Religion* of *Christ*, the *Obedience* of
Faith, is in Scripture perpetually stiled the *Kingdom of God* : That Kingdom of God,
which we are commanded to *seek* in the *righteousness thereof* : That Kingdom, which
our Saviour told the *Jews*, when he began to preach, was Then *come unto them* :
Which he elsewhere declared to the *Pharisees*, *cometh not with observation*; *neither shall*

i

they

they say, Lo here, or lo there ; for behold, the Kingdom of God is within *you :* Which, he affured his Difciples, *whofoever did not receive* with the Meeknefs and Inoffenfivenefs of *a little child, fhould not enter thereinto* at all : and which, he threatens, in cafe of mens unworthinefs, fhould be *taken from* One Nation, and *given to Another* that would *bring forth the Fruits* thereof : That Kingdom, which, in his *Parables,* our Lord reprefents under *various fimilitudes* of a *moral* fignification ; fetting forth, by apt and proper Comparifons, its different States in the prefent World ; and *out of which,* he tells us, fhall finally be *gathered All Offences, and they which do iniquity :* That Kingdom, which *God Thus* defcribed of old to *Mofes,* Exod. xix. 6. *Ye fhall be unto me a* Kingdom *of Priefts, and an Holy Nation :* And the *Prophet Thus,* Pf. xlv. 6. *A Sceptre of Righteoufnefs is the Sceptre of thy Kingdom :* And the *heavenly Hoft* in the Revelation *Thus,* ch. xii. 9, 10. *Now is come Salvation and Strength, and the* Kingdom *of our God ;* for *That old Serpent——which deceiveth the whole World,* (that is, the Devil, the Spirit of Errour, the Spirit of Idolatry and Debauchery in All Nations,) *was caft into the Earth,* (that is, was thrown down low, and deftroyed,) *and his Angels were caft out with him :* Laftly, That Kingdom, which the *Apoftle* St *Paul* tells us, *is not in Word, but in Power ; is not Meat and Drink* (Forms and Ceremonies,) *but Righteoufnefs, and Peace, and Joy in the Holy Ghoft.*

THIS, in the *New Teftament,* is the frequent and ufual acceptation of this Phrafe, *The Kingdom of God ;* It fignifies the *State of the Gofpel,* or the eftablifhment of *true Religion* in the World. From which Ufe of the Phrafe in Scripture, we may by the way obferve, how greatly all fuch *Enthufiaftick* perfons err, who under the Notion of the *Kingdom of God,* reprefent to themfelves either the *Saints* exercifing *Temporal Authority and Dominion* in *This World,* or God *himfelf* influencing the Minds of Men by his *abfolute and irrefiftible Power.* As to the former Notion, That of the *Saints* exercifing *Temporal Authority and Dominion* in *This World ;* in *This* Senfe, our Saviour has exprefsly declared, that his Kingdom is *not* of *This World ;* And the True Profperity of the Church of God, 'tis plain, does not at all confift in the Increafe of *Temporal Grandeur,* which tends always to corruption ; but in the Increafe of *True Holinefs and Virtue* only, in the Hearts and Lives of Men. And as to the *Other* Notion, That of God's influencing the Minds of Men by his *abfolute and irrefiftible Power ; This* alfo is a very erroneous apprehenfion concerning the manner of God's *ruling* over *Moral Agents :* For the True Greatnefs and Glory of a Prince reigning in his Kingdom, is the Willing *Obedience* of his Subjects, not their *Weaknefs and Incapacity of refifting him :* And in all things relating to *Religion and Morality,* 'tis not magnifying the Glory and Majefty of God, to fuppofe *Him* acting upon and over-ruling mens *Wills* by his *Power,* but to fuppofe *Them* (like *reafonable* creatures) *chufing* to obey his Commands by their *Wills,* and *loving* the Practife of *Virtue and Goodnefs.*

THIS therefore is the *ufual* Meaning of the *Kingdom of God* in Scripture : It denotes the *State of the Gofpel,* or the Prevalency of *True Religion* among Men.

NEVERTHELESS, Since, at the Beft, *all* that can *here* be done in this *imperfect* State towards eftablifhing God's Kingdom of Virtue and Righteoufnefs, and confequently of True Happinefs among his Creatures : Since, I fay, All that *can* be done towards thefe great Ends in this prefent *frail and imperfect* State, is *only in order* to a more *complete and perfect* State hereafter, when God fhall have *put down all Rule and all Authority and Power ;* and when *All Enemies,* Satan and Sin, and Death, fhall be entirely *deftroyed ;* and his *Saints* fhall *reign* with him in *Glory* for ever : Therefore to *That future and perfect* State it is, that This phrafe, *The Kingdom of God,* always has *reference,* even when 'tis applied to the *ftate of the Gofpel Here :* And *That Heavenly State* it is, which *ultimately and properly* is ftiled *the Kingdom of God ;* Wherein the

Righteous

Righteous ſhall ſhine forth as the Sun, in the Kingdom of their Father; Into which Kingdom, *there ſhall in no caſe enter any thing that defileth, neither whatſoever loveth or maketh a Lye*; but they who *overcome*, (that is, they who ſo reſiſt the Temptations of Covetouſneſs, Ambition, and Senſual Pleaſure, as in the midſt of a degenerate and debauched World, to follow Truth, and Right, and Charity, fearing God, and keeping his Commandments;) *Theſe* ſhall *receive the Kingdom prepared for them from the beginning of the World,* and (according to the gracious Promiſe of their Father) ſhall inherit it for ever. This *Heavenly State,* I ſay, it is, to which That phraſe, *The Kingdom of God,* always has *reference,* even when 'tis expreſsly applied to *the State of the Goſpel here.* And 'tis with Great Propriety of expreſſion, that *Both* theſe States are, as well *ſeparately* as *jointly,* included under this One Denomination: They being indeed, not *Two diſtinct* States, but One the *continuation only* of the Other; differing from each other no otherwiſe, than as Seed-time from Harveſt, or as Childhood from the perfection of Man's eſtate: *Virtue,* and *Goodneſs,* and the *Love of God,* and *Obedience* to him at *preſent,* being the *Beginnings of Happineſs here*; and the *Glories of Heaven* hereafter being nothing elſe but the ſame *Virtue,* and *Goodneſs,* and *Love of God,* and *Obedience* to him, completed and made perfect *There,* by an aſſurance of his uninterrupted Favour and Preſence for ever. And This Notion, by the way, ſhows the extreme Folly and Abſurdity of All Thoſe, who (fundamentally erring from the Truth and Nature of Things,) found their *Religion here,* and their *expectations of Happineſs hereafter,* in any thing elſe (whatſoever it be) *diſtinct* from *Virtue,* and *Righteouſneſs,* and *Charity,* and *True Holineſs*; which things are, not only the *Characters* and *Marks* of, but they are themſelves neceſſarily and immutably the *Very Eſſence* of the *Kingdom of God.*

FROM what has been hitherto ſaid in explication of this Phraſe ſo very frequently met with in the *New Teſtament,* it appears therefore, that there are *Three* Senſes, to which the full Notion of the *Kingdom of God* extends. There is his *Kingdom of Nature,* by which he ruleth with irreſiſtible Power, abſolutely over *All*: There is his *Kingdom of Grace* or *Virtue*; by which he reigneth in the *Hearts of Moral Agents,* who obey him *willingly* or of *Free Choice*: And there is his *Kingdom of Glory*; wherein he ſhall finally be for ever adored by Thoſe, who, through a Life of Virtue and True Holineſs, ſhall be found *meet to be Partakers of That Inheritance of the Saints in Light.*

AND according to theſe *ſeveral* ſenſes of the Phraſe, muſt the Petition in the Text, *Thy Kingdom come,* be in like manner underſtood, to extend to different Significations.

1. IN the *firſt* place, as to the Natural *Kingdom of God*; *This* indeed we cannot with *Any Propriety* pray that it *may come,* becauſe, *by Neceſſity of Nature,* it always *is,* and *cannot but be,* actually *preſent.* 'Tis *neceſſarily,* from *everlaſting* to *everlaſting*; a Kingdom of abſolute and irreſiſtible Power; without *Limits,* and without *Interruption*; In *all* Places alike, without diſtinction; and that cannot *come* at *one* Time, more than at *another.* Nevertheleſs, though the Kingdom of God, in *This* ſenſe, is what we cannot pray *may come*; yet we *may* and *ought* to rejoice in the Thoughts of its being always Preſent: *Pſ.* xcvii. 1. *The Lord reigneth, let the Earth rejoice; let the multitude of the Iſles be glad thereof.* 'Tis matter of great and juſt ſatisfaction to reaſonable Minds, to conſider that the Government and Sovereignty of the Univerſe, the Alone Truly abſolute and uncontrolable Power, is in the hands of unerring Wiſdom and of perfect Goodneſs; and that things are not under the uncomfortable Dominion of Blind Chance, or of inexorable and unrelenting Fate. But

2dly, THAT therefore which our Saviour principally directs us to deſire and pray for in This Petition, is the eſtabliſhment of God's Kingdom of *Grace* or *Virtue.* That as his *Kingdom of* Nature ruleth *Always abſolutely* over All *things,* ſo his *Kingdom of* Grace or *Virtue* may *in due Time* be *univerſally* eſtabliſhed over its *proper Subjects*: As his *natural*

Power

Power is *abſolute and uncontrolable*, ſo his *ſpiritual* Dominion over the Hearts and Wills of rational Creatures, may *prevail* finally againſt all the Oppoſition of Sin and Satan : As his *Glory* eſſentially is *infinite* and *immutable* ; ſo *relatively* alſo, it may in due time be promoted and acknowledged by all reaſonable Creatures. *This* is the *principal* ſenſe of our praying for the *Kingdom of God to come*. 'Tis expreſſing our earneſt Deſire, that the Goſpel of Chriſt, the true Religion of God, in its native and uncorrupted Simplicity, may ſpread and prevail over the whole Earth, as the *Waters cover the Sea* ; and that *all the Kingdoms of the World may become the Kingdoms of our Lord and of his Chriſt* : May *become his Kingdoms*, not by conqueſt of Temporal Power, but by Perſwaſion and Force of Truth, by the Power and Demonſtration of the Spirit. And that all they who *have* embraced the Goſpel in Profeſſion, may *let the Kingdom of God rule in their Hearts*, by *living* as *worthy* Subjects of it. For 'tis in the *willing Subjection* of the Mind to *Truth and Right*, and in the regulating conſequently all *Actions*, *Paſſions*, *Appetites*, and *Affections*, according to the Divine Laws; in *This* it is, that this *Kingdom of God* principally conſiſts. By his *Power*, he can *at all times* ſubdue all *things* unto himſelf; and by This irreſiſtible Dominion, the whole material unintelligent World is perpetually governed, and obeys it *neceſſarily*, without *any poſſibility* of *diſobeying* : But 'tis the *Will* of God, that *Intelligent* and *Rational* Beings ſhould not obey *his* Will, but by *their own*; ſhould not obey by *neceſſity of nature*, but by the *free Choice and unconſtrained Compliance* of the *Will*. The *material Univerſe* therefore, the whole *Frame of Nature* is ſubject to the Power of God ; but reaſonable *Creatures only* are ſubject to his Laws. By This they become *accountable*, and *capable of* being *judged* : By This, they are rendred either *acceptable* to him, and capable of *Reward*; or *obnoxious*, and *liable to* be *puniſhed*. This Trial, This Probation he puts upon them ſuitable to their rational Nature : And 'tis the *Perfection* of their *Nature*, and the *higheſt Improvement* of their *Virtue*, to *chuſe* to obey him *cheerfully and readily*. The more *excellent* the *Nature*, and the more *perfect* the *Virtue* of any *reaſonable Creature* is, the more does it delight in obeying the moſt perfect Will of God, who is *Perfection* and *Goodneſs itſelf*. For this reaſon, the *Angels in Heaven* are ſtiled in Scripture, by way of eminence, *thoſe Servants of His that do his Pleaſure*. And our Saviour as it were by way of *explication* of this Petition, *Thy Kingdom come*, directs us to proceed in the following words, *Thy Will be done in Earth as it is in Heaven* : And elſewhere ſets before us, to the ſame End, his *Own* ſtill *more perfect* Example, *Joh.* iv. 34. *My Meat is to do the Will of Him that ſent me, and to finiſh his Work*. But

3*dly* and *Laſtly*, THERE is ſtill *another* ſenſe of this Petition, which was very much inſiſted on in the Primitive Church : And That is, that God's *Kingdom of* Glory might *come ſpeedily* ; and that being *quickly* delivered from the Miſeries of this ſinful and corrupt World, they might *ſoon* attain to That *Bleſſed Hope* of the *Reſurrection from the Dead*. It was an Opinion which *prevailed generally* in thoſe early Ages, that at the Reſurrection every man ſhould ariſe *in Order* according to the *degree* of his Goodneſs; and that they who were raiſed and judged *firſt*, ſhould *themſelves* have a part in *judging* thoſe which followed. Whether there was *juſt* ground for this opinion, or not, I ſhall not here take upon me to determine : But the *Texts* on which they built it were theſe which follow; 1 *Cor.* xv. 23. *Every man in his own order* ; *Chriſt, the Firſt-fruits* ; *afterward they that are Chriſt's, at his coming : and Then cometh the end*. 1 Theſ. iv. 16. *The dead in Chriſt ſhall riſe firſt*. Rev. xx. 6. *Bleſſed and holy is He that has part in the firſt Reſurrection*. 1 Pet. iv. 17. *Judgment muſt begin at the Houſe of God*, 1 Cor. vi. 2. *Do ye not know that the Saints ſhall judge the World?* ——*and that we ſhall judge Angels?* Jude 14. *The Lord cometh with ten thouſand of his Saints to execute Judgment*. Matt. xix. 28. *Jeſus ſaid unto them, Verily I ſay unto you, that ye which have followed me in the Regeneration, when the Son of Man ſhall ſit in the Throne*

SERM.
XXXII.
*of his Glory, ye also shall sit upon twelve thrones, judging the twelve tribes of Israel:
And every one that hath forsaken houses, or brethren, or sisters, or father, or mother, or
wife, or children, or lands, for my Name's sake, shall receive an hundred-fold, and shall
inherit everlasting Life:* In St *Luke* it is, *shall receive manifold more in This Present
time, and, in the World to come, Life everlasting,* ch. xviii. 30. Lastly, *Rev.* xx. 4.
*I saw Thrones, and they sat upon them, and Judgment was given unto them; and I saw
the Souls of them that were beheaded for the testimony of Jesus, and for the word of God,
and——they lived and reigned with Christ a thousand years.* 'Tis remarkable, the
Text does not say, that *Christ* came down and reigned *upon Earth* a thousand years;
as Many have imagined without *Any* ground: But only that the Martyrs *reigned with
Christ* a thousand years; *whatever* be the meaning of that Prophetical, and perhaps
figurative, period of Time. These are the Texts upon which in the Primitive times was
built That general Opinion, that at the Resurrection every man should arise *in Order*
according to the *degree* of his Goodness; and which made them therefore in their
Prayers petition for an early Resurrection. Whether there was in the Text sufficient
foundation for the Opinion in *This particular* or no, (which 'tis not at all needful for
Me here to determine,) yet *in the general* 'tis certain, that they who lived in such continual State of Persecution as the Primitive Christians did, and had such a lively sense
as they always had upon their Minds of the Glory and Happiness of Heaven, had very
good reason to pray earnestly and constantly, that the *Kingdom of God* (in this Last and
most perfect Sense of the phrase) might speedily *come*; that it would please God *shortly
to accomplish the Number of his Elect, and to hasten his Kingdom*: According to that
pathetick conclusion of the book of the *Revelation,* ch. xxii. 20. *He which testifieth
these things, saith, Surely I come quickly: Amen; even so come, Lord Jesus.* And
though (God be Thanked) *We* are not *Now* under such *continual* and such *severe* Persecution, as the *Primitive and Better* Christians were; yet whosoever has a just sense
of the *Vanity* and *Disorders* of this *present* World, and the *Glory* of the World *to come*;
whosoever observes what St *Paul* foretels, 2 *Tim.* iii. 12. *Yea, and All that will live
godly in Christ Jesus* shall *suffer persecution*; and considers the Difficulties continually
arising to *upright and sincere* men in *Every* Station of Life, from the numerous Errors and Corruptions, evil Customs and debauched Practices, of an *ignorant, superstitious and tyrannical* World; will see reason to think it *still* and *ever,* a most natural and proper part of the Prayer of every Good Christian, that the *Kingdom of
God may come*; even That *New Heavens and New Earth, wherein dwelleth righteousness.*

    To which, that we may All at length arrive, *God of his infinite Mercy grant,* &c.

SERMON XXXIII.

Of the KINGDOM of GOD.

St MAT. VI. 33.

But feek ye firft the Kingdom of God, and his Righteoufnefs, and all thefe things fhall be added unto you.

OUR Saviour in the 24*th* verfe of this chapter, warns his Difciples of the abfo- lute Impoffibility, of their being at the fame time fervants of God, and flaves to the pleafures of this prefent corrupt World. *No man*, fays he, *can ferve two Mafters*; No man can at one and the fame time obey two Perfons of a contrary dif- pofition; The Judgment and Affections of his Heart and Soul cannot at once be fixt and fettled upon things of a different and inconfiftent nature : *For either he will hate the one, and love the other ; or elfe he will hold to the one, and defpife the other.* He muft of neceffity, by obeying the one, difobey and neglect the other ; and then, *his* Ser- vant only he is, to whom he obeys. *Ye cannot ferve God and Mammon* ; ye cannot be truly religious and fincere fervants of God, while your Hearts and Affections are too intently and infeparably fixt upon the vanities of the prefent finful World ; For in all probability there *will* fometime or other arife a competition between them ; and then he that cannot part with thofe injoyments of the World, which are inconfiftent with his Religion, *muft* neglect his duty towards God; and he that will upon no Account neg- lect his Duty towards God, muft be content to part with all the contrary Interefts in the prefent World.

THIS therefore being the cafe, that we cannot attend wholly to two contrary things at once; and that it cannot be imagined, but that one or the other of them muft in many circumftances and upon many occafions be poftponed ; our Saviour pro- ceeds to advife us, *ver. 25. which* of the two oppofite Interefts 'tis of the greateft im- portance for us to fecure. He admonifhes us, that our main and principal Intentions ought always to be fixed upon our Chief, that is, our future Happinefs; without being unreafonably and anxioufly follicitous, concerning the tranfitory Injoyments of this pre- fent life ; *Therefore I fay unto you, Take no thought for your life, what ye fhall eat, or what ye fhall drink ; nor yet for the body, what ye fhall put on.* With refpect to the *Apoftles*, to whom thefe words were more immediately directed, they are to be under- ftood in the *ftrict* and *literal* Senfe ; that being in a perpetual Progrefs from one place to another to preach the Gofpel, they were not to make any provifion at all for their own maintenance, but to rely entirely upon the Providence of God, by whofe appoint- ment they were employed in that fpiritual work. But as the words exprefs the duty of *Chriftians at all times and in all places*, they muft be underftood in a larger and lefs ftrict Senfe ; to fignify, that, after we have ufed a reafonable induftry to attain the ne- ceffaries of this prefent life, we ought not to be any further anxious and follicitous about them; but to rely on the Providence of God for a continual fupply of thefe things by

SERM. XXXIII.

3

his

S E R M. his bleffings upon our *juft* Endeavours, and to be content with what proportion of them
XXXIII. he is pleafed to beftow upon us in the ways of Righteoufnefs.

T H E Reafons or Arguments, *why* we ought thus contentedly to rely upon the Providence of God, our Saviour adds in the 25th and following verfes: *Is not the Life more than meat, and the Body than raiment ?* He that firft gave you Life and Being, without your contributing any thing towards it yourfelves; will he not much more beftow upon you, in the ways of Virtue and Integrity, things neceffary for the fupport and prefervation of that Life ? *Behold the fowls of the Air ; for they fow not, neither do they reap, nor gather into barns;* they forefee not their own Wants, nor are able to make any provifion againft them; *yet your heavenly Father feedeth them; Are ye not much better than they ? And why take ye Thought for raiment ; Confider the Lillies of the Field how they grow ; they toil not, neither do they fpin ; and yet* God gives them a continual increafe, and clothes them with inimitable Beauty ; fo that *even Solomon himfelf in all his glory, was not arrayed like one of thefe : Wherefore if God fo clothe the grafs of the Field, which to day is, and to morrow is caft into the oven, fhall he not much more clothe you, O ye of little Faith?*

A F T E R which Reafonings he repeats again the admonition itfelf, *ver.* 31. *Therefore take no Thought, faying, What fhall we eat, or what fhall we drink ? or wherewithal fhall we be clothed ? (for after thefe things do the Gentiles feek;) for your heavenly Father knoweth that ye have need of all thefe things;* (Which admonition, if it be applied, not to the then prefent circumftances of the Apoftle's only, but to all Chriftians in general ; it muft be underftood with fome limitations in the fenfe before explained ;) And then he adds, in the Words of the Text, *But feek ye firft the Kingdom of God, and his righteoufnefs, and all thefe things fhall be added unto you.*

T H E *Kingdom of God,* in Scripture-phrafe, fignifies, fometimes the Glory and Happinefs of *Heaven;* fometimes the ftate of the Gofpel, the eftablifhment of the Religion of Chrift upon *Earth* ; and very frequently *Both* of them together ; they being in reality one and the fame thing, differing only in time and in degree. For God carries on one uniform and regular defign of bringing all his Creatures to Righteoufnefs and Happinefs; and thefe are infeparable the one from the other. Righteoufnefs is the only poffible foundation of true Happinefs; and Happinefs is, both in the nature of things and by the appointment of God, the Fruit and the Effect of Righteoufnefs. They differ only as Seed-time and Harveft, as Childhood and the State of a Man; *Grace or Virtue,* being the beginning, the ground and principle of *Happinefs,* growing up and improving towards the Perfection of *Glory.* The *Kingdom of God* therefore, when it fignifies *Both,* is not ufed in different Senfes, but in its moft proper and natural fignification : On the contrary, when it feems reftrained to *One fignification,* it is *then rather* taken figuratively, and put only as a Part for the Whole. In the Text, it is of little importance in *which* of the two Senfes we underftand it : For, if by the *Kingdom of God,* be meant the ftate of the Gofpel or the Religion of Chrift here ; yet without doubt 'tis principally with regard to its final iffue and perfection in Heaven : And if thereby be meant the Glory and Happinefs of Heaven, yet this always prefuppofes the foregoing eftablifhment of true Righteoufnefs and Holinefs upon Earth. Or, they may feem *Both* to be expreffed in thefe words of our Saviour, The *Kingdom of God* and *his Righteoufnefs* ; the *Glory of Heaven,* and the *Way* that leads to it; the *End* to be ultimately aimed at, and the neceffary and indifpenfible *Means* of attaining it.

To *Seek* thefe things, is to value and efteem them; to fix our Thoughts and Meditations upon them ; to propofe them to ourfelves as the moft valuable End, towards which all our Actions ought to be directed; to be diligent in inquiring and ftudying the Means, by which they may beft be attained; and to be as zealous and hearty, as fincere and fteddy in our indeavours after them, as the *Gentiles,* i. e. as worldly men, are, in

feeking

feeking after the Pleafures and Profits, in purfuing the Intereft and Injoyments of S E R M. the prefent Life. This is to *feek* the *Kingdom of God*, and his *Righteoufnefs*: Ufing XXXIV. out utmoft Endeavours, imploying all our Powers and Faculties, to promote the In- terest of true Religion and the Practice of Virtue among Men, which is the beginning of the *Kingdom of God* on *Earth*; in order to fecure to Ourfelves and Others a portion in that eternal ftate of Happinefs, which is the final eftablifhment of his *Kingdom* in *Heaven*.

SEEK ye *firft*; i. e. feek thefe things *before*, and in *preference to* all other things; feek them with greater diligence and more earneft labour, with fteddier zeal and with a warmer affection, with greater care and deeper concern, with a more conftant and un- wearied application: Seek them as things of greater moment, even of infinite importance; fo as in competition always to prefer them clearly before all other Interefts and Defigns whatfoever: Confidering that there is no proportion between things finite and infinite, no comparifon between things temporal and eternal: that it will be unfpeakably a great- er Happinefs to be judged worthy of the meaneft portion of that eternal inheritance, where *neither moth nor ruft doth corrupt, and where thieves do not break through and fteal*, than to be put in poffeffion of all the fhort-lived empires of this World, and of all thofe tranfitory Riches, which of themfelves moulder away in few years into that duft from whence they were originally taken: that 'tis *even here* infinitely a greater pleafure to *fave a Soul from Death by converting a Sinner from the Error of his Ways*, than Senfual and Voluptuous Perfons ever find in the higheft gratifications of Senfe, or worldly minds in the poffeffion and injoyment of the largeft Treafures.

SEEK ye *firft* the Kingdom of God; *i. e.* not fo as wholly to exclude the care of other things; For That is impoffible in this prefent Life, and to pretend to it, is but Enthufiafm, and hinders the fpreading of true Religion: But feek *this* chiefly and in the firft place; Make *this* your principal and main care; Suffer nothing to interfere or come in competition with it: Do this *above* and *before* all other things, and yet other things need not to be left undone. The very Command itfelf of feeking this *firft*, implies that other things alfo may be fought *afterwards*; that other things likewife may be taken care for, in their proper *place*, and *fubordinate* Rank; with a due and moderate degree of affection, fuch as may always be confiftent with this ultimate and great defign. And with *This Limitation*, if not to the *Apoftles themfelves*, yet at leaft fo far as they can be a general precept to *all Chriftians at all times*, muft the Words, (as I before hinted) of neceffity be underftood.

THE Words being thus explained, we may obferve in them thefe three things:

I. A *Precept*, or the *Duty* commanded, *Seek ye the Kingdom of God and his Righ- teoufnefs*.

II. THE *manner* and *degree* of the Obligation, *Seek it firft*.

III. THE *Promifes* even of a *temporal Reward* annexed. *And all thefe things fhall be added unto you*.

I. THERE is in the Words a *Precept*, or the *Duty* commanded, *Seek ye the Kingdom of God, and his righteoufnefs*. And here without doubt, there is no Man who with any the leaft degree of Sincerity calls himfelf by the Name of Chriftian, but *profeffes* and *thinks* that he feeks the Kingdom of God. The very title and pro- feffion of a Chriftian, implies as much as his being a Candidate for Heaven; And fo long as he continues a member of the Church of Chrift *here*, he is apt to believe that he retains his title, and is going forwards towards his inheritance in the glory that fhall be revealed *hereafter*; efpecially if he be conftant in his outward Profeffion; if he be zealous for Notions which perhaps he underftands not, and which tend not much to influence practice; and if he be diligent in attending the external rites and fervices of Re-

S E R M. ligion. But 'tis obferveable that our Saviour tells us, St *Luk.* xiii. 24. that there are *ma-*
XXXIV. *ny* that feek *to enter in,* who *fhall not be able;* and in the expreffion of the Text itfelf
he plainly enough intimates, that Men may *in vain* feek the Kingdom of God, if they
feek it not according to the righteoufnefs thereof. Since therefore there *is* fuch a thing
as *Seeking* without *Effect;* and to fall finally fhort of what we profefs to Seek for, is at
leaft an equal, perhaps a greater Mifery, than never to have fought after it at all; it
cannot but be a fubject worthy our moft ferious Confideration, to inquire into the full
meaning and extent of this precept of our Saviour; which unqueftionably is not obeyed
in its true Senfe, unlefs we *fo Seek* as to be able to *Find.* St *Paul,* 1 *Cor.* ix. 24. compares the life of a Chriftian to a *Race,* wherein *they that run, run all, but one receiveth
the prize;* and thereupon he exhorts his *Corinthians fo* to run, that they might *obtain.*
In like manner our Saviour in the Text, when he commands us to feek the Kingdom
of God, and directs us to feek it in the way of righteoufnefs, and elfewhere warns us
that many who feek it fhall not be able to find it; he cannot but be underftood as exhorting us to feek it earneftly and effectually and in *fuch* a manner, as that we may
not finally fail to attain it.

For our clearer direction therefore in obeying this precept, 'tis to be obferved, that
feeking any thing fincerely and effectually, implies in it the following particulars.

1. HAVING a juft *value and true efteem,* for the thing we profefs to feek after. For
the defires and endeavours after any object, muft of neceffity always be proportionable, not to the real and intrinfick value of the thing itfelf, but to the degree of the
impreffion it makes upon our mind, and of the affection it confequently excites in it.
There are great numbers of thofe who call themfelves Chriftians, who though they are
afraid indeed of the punifhment of Hell, and cannot bear the terror of eternal torments;
(which makes them therefore not dare to be openly profane;) yet they have no real
Efteem for the ftate of Heaven, no earneft defire after that Happinefs, which confifts
in the likenefs of God and in the Perfection of Virtue. To prevent the ill Effects of
which Remifsnefs, the Scripture ufes great variety of Arguments, to excite in us a juft
Regard and true Value, for the greatnefs of that Happinefs, which God has vouchfafed
to prepare for them that love and obey him; reprefenting it to us under the Notion of
a *Pearl* of fuch great price, that that Perfon is fpoken of as acting very wifely, who immediately fold all that he had to purchafe it; under the fimilitude of a *Crown* that never fades; of a *Kingdom* that will continue for ever; of a *Prize* which no Labour can
be too much in contending for; of a *Glory* fhining forth as the Sun, as the Brightnefs
of the Firmament, and as the Stars for ever and ever; of a *Treafure* that can never
wafte, nor be diminifhed either by violence or fraud; of *fulnefs of joy* without intermiffion, and *pleafures* that will laft for evermore; of *feeing the Face* of God, and being
made like unto him, and being affured of his Love and Favour for ever. And yet all
thefe are but figurative expreffions, Comparifons, and very imperfect reprefentations;
For, after all that is or can be faid, yet *Eye hath not feen, nor Ear heard, neither hath
entered into the Heart of man to conceive, the things that God hath prepared for them that
love him.* In which *One* elegant Image there is contained *much Variety* under a moft
beautiful Gradation. Great is the Diverfity of glorious Objects which entertain the *Eye*
in contemplating the beautiful Order and exquifite proportion of the Works of God;
and yet this is far exceeded by the hearing of the Ear, and by the larger compafs of
Other men's obfervations joyned with our own. Many are the Glories which the *Ear*
hath heard of, in the defcription of all parts of the World at prefent, and in the Hiftories of the Ages that have paft before us; and yet thefe likewife are ftill far excelled, by
what the Heart of man is able to conceive, and the Mind can reprefent to itfelf in the
Imaginations of the Thoughts. Vaftly great, and even unlimited are the Glories,
which a vigorous and comprehenfive *Imagination* can frame to itfelf as poffible; and yet

even

even thefe likewife (fays the Apoftle) are as far excelled by the glory that fhall be revealed in the *Kingdom of God*, as the Seeing of the Eye is by the Hearing of the Ear,
or the Hearing of the Ear by the Imagination of the Heart. But becaufe thefe things
after all are in their own nature *fpiritual*, and can only be *fpiritually difcerned*; 'tis ftill
a matter of confiderable Difficulty, and requires frequent and ferious Meditation, to poffefs our minds with a juft value and due efteem of them; which is abfolutely neceffary,
in order to our feeking them worthily, and with that earneftnefs and diligence they deferve. The Affections muft be drawn off from vain Imaginations, and the Mind reconciled to the Love of Truth and Goodnefs: We muft *hunger and thirft after righteoufnefs*, as our Saviour expreffes it; or, in the Pfalmift's Phrafe, *thirft after* it, even *as the
Hart panteth after the Water-brooks*. Otherwife, what wonder is it that men fall fhort
of the Kingdom of God, both here and hereafter; that they attain not to its Righteoufnefs here, and to the Glory of it hereafter; if their Defires after it be weak, their
indeavours carelefs, and they *feek* it as if they fought it not?

2. SEEKING any thing heartily and effectually, implies that we *fix our Attention*
continually, *i. e.* habitually upon it. 'Tis not fufficient that our judgment be convinced of the importance and neceffity of Religion, unlefs our Paffions and Affections likewife be in fome meafure interefted. Nor is it enough that our Affections be moved once
or feldom, but our zeal muft be renewed by frequent meditation. *We muft give earneft
heed to the things which we have heard, left at any time we fhould let them flip*, Heb. ii. 1.
For, as in matters of Senfe, Objects at a diftance appear fmall and imperfect; and nothing but reafoning and judgment, can correct the errors and deceptions of the Sight;
fo in matters of Religion and of fpiritual concern, nothing but frequent confideration
and earneft and ferious meditation, can reprefent thofe things as *prefent* to us, fo as to
caufe them to make vigorous and lafting impreffions upon our Minds, which yet we
all know *cannot be* very far *diftant* from Us: For *Death* is not remote from the longeft
Liver in this tranfitory World; and *That* conveys us if not immediately, yet without
any farther Change of our State, it conveys us unto Judgment. To prevent our Attention being diverted from thefe things, the Apoftles are perpetually exhorting us, to raife
our thoughts from the Vanities of this tranfitory and uncertain World, to the Glories
of that Heavenly and eternal Kingdom which we profefs to feek as our ultimate End:
to *fet our affections on things above, not on things in the Earth*. And our Saviour
in his parable of the Sower warns us, how the Word of the Kingdom, notwithftanding the
unfpeakable Weight and Importance of it, may yet very poffibly make no more impreffion on the Minds of carelefs and inconfiderate Perfons, than Seed caft upon the hard
high-way can enter into the Earth and grow; or if the Word preached *does* make fome
impreffion at firft, yet that it may eafily be drowned by the Cares and Bufinefs and Pleafure of a corrupt World, as Corn is choked and over-run, by a multitude of Weeds.
And This without queftion is the true Reafon, why in fo great a number of Chriftians
who feem in fpeculation to believe the great doctrines of Religion, and profefs zealoufly
to feek the Kingdom of God; yet in reality thefe things have little more influence upon
their Lives and Practice, than a Demonftration of any Truth laid afide and neglected
after it has once been underftood; or than a paffage of a Hiftory, forgotten after it has
been once read; than a Dream, when one awaketh; or than a paft Thought that is never recollected. This fort of Perfons, are excellently defcribed by *Ezekiel*, ch. xxxiii. 31.
*They come unto thee, as my people cometh, and they fit before thee as my people, and they
hear thy words, but they will not do them; for with their mouth they fhew much love, but
their Heart goeth after their Covetoufnefs. And lo, thou art to them as a very lovely
fong, of one that has a pleafant voice, and can play well on an inftrument; for they hear
thy words, but they do them not.*

3. SEEKING

3. SEEKING any thing heartily and effectually, implies, that we be *diligent and impartial in inquiring after the best and most certain means of attaining it*. He that in earnest seeks the Kingdom of God, must not be bent upon choosing his own ways and doing his own pleasure, upon gratifying his own inclinations and indulging his own Passions; but on the contrary must resolve to submit entirely to the Will of God, to embrace Truth where-ever he finds it, and to be always sincere in the Search after it. *Trust in the Lord with all thine Heart, and lean not to thine own Understanding*, Prov. iii. 5. Zeal without Knowledge, Heat in the Passions without Light in the Understanding, is like travelling in a wrong road; which the faster a man goes, and the further he proceeds in it, the farther he is from his journey's End, and with the greater difficulty will he return into the Way that truly leads to it. The first Disposition necessary in him that with Effect would *seek* the Kingdom of God, is, that with a Meek and unprejudiced Mind he consider and study the *Means* by which God has directed him to obtain it, and with simplicity and purity of Intention receive the *ingrafted Word, which is able to save his Soul:* following the Example of Holy *David*, whose study all the day long was in the Law of God, and in the night-season also he meditated on the same. For want of this desire of true instruction it is, that so many blind Superstitions, so many absurd unintelligible Doctrines, and so many unreasonable Practices, have in several Ages of the World crept in under pretense and in the room of Religion; making void the plainest Reason of things and the most express Commandment of God, through the Corruptions and Disputes of Men; and fulfilling that Prophecy of our Saviour, that many should *seek to enter in*, (seeking in vain and wrong ways, in ways of their own inventing and agreeable to their own corrupt affections,) many should in this manner *seek* to enter in, *and should not be able*. The only safe, certain, and general direction, by which persons of all capacities may guide themselves in this matter, in the midst of a divided and contentious World, is to adhere stedfastly to the *two great Rules* which God has given us to walk by; *viz.* never allowing our selves in any Action contrary to our *Reason* and Conscience, which (as the Wise man elegantly expresses it) is the *Candle of the Lord*; or contrary to *Scripture*, which is the brighter and clearer Light of Revelation. And herein we must first take care, not to fail in the *foundation*; in those *plain* and *certain* things, wherein no man can innocently mistake, but *he that runs may read them*; in those great commandments, those weightier matters of the Law, the Love of God and of our Neighbour : and then we may with more safety proceed to consider the *Superstructure*, of doctrines *more* speculative and *less* certain, of rites *more* difficult and of *less* importance. But for any man who is profane and a blasphemer of the Name of God, who is unjust and unrighteous towards his Neighbour, or who lives in the Habitual Practice of Intemperance and Debauchery; for such an One to pretend to *seek* zealously the Kingdom of God, in matters of external form, or in contending for Laws and Doctrines of Men, is like labouring to set in order the garments upon a *dead* Body; or like watering a Plant, whose very roots are dead. 'Tis contending about the *Name* of Religion, where the *Thing* is not; and for the *Shadow*, where there is no *Substance*. And here comes in that great and never-failing Rule of our Saviour, *By their Fruits ye shall know them*. Whoever is more concerned for particular Forms and Ceremonies, for Doctrines of a Sect or Party, for Dominion over other men's Consciences, for any thing that depends on temporal Authority, than for the Discovery of Truth and the Practice of Virtue; very sure we may be, that That Man's religion is Vain.

4thly and *lastly*, SEEKING any thing heartily, sincerely, and effectually, implies, that we immediately *Practise and put in Execution*, what we are once satisfied is the true Means to obtain it. Resting in the speculative part of Religion, is as if a man
should

fhould hope to arrive at his journey's end, merely by inftructing himfelf in the S E R M.
knowledge of the Way. No: He that in earneft *feeks the Kingdom of God,* muft not XXXIII.
only know and underftand, but muft in the courfe of his Life put in *Practice* alfo
the *Righteoufnefs thereof. Though I fpeak* (faith St *Paul) with the Tongues of Men and
of Angels, and have not Charity, I am become as founding brafs or a tinkling cymbal:
and though I have the gift of Prophecy and underftand all myfteries, and all knowledge;
and though I have all Faith, fo that I could remove mountains, and have no Charity,
it profiteth me nothing.* The *Pharifees* underftood, the *Scribes* difputed well about
the Law; and *many* at the day of judgment fhall fay, *Lord, have we not taught in
thy ftreets, and in thy name done many wonderful works?* and yet he will fay unto
them, *I know ye not; depart from me all ye workers of Iniquity:* For, not he that
knows, but he only that *does* righteoufnefs, *is righteous.* And this is evidently the Work,
not of a few hours, but of a whole life: So that they who put off their Repentance to
their Death-bed, far from feeking *firft,* do plainly feek only in the *laft* place *the
Kingdom of God and his righteoufnefs:* i. e. they are the greateft neglecters and
defpifers of it; And confequently they fhall be leaft in the Kingdom of Heaven;
i. e. in Scripture-phrafe, far fhall they be from ever arriving there. Which brings
me to the IId thing I propofed to fpeak to, *viz.* the *manner and degree* of the
Obligation; *Seek ye firft the Kingdom of God, and his righteoufnefs, and all thefe
things fhall be added unto you.*

S E R M O N XXXIV.

Of the KINGDOM of GOD.

MATT. VI. 33.

*But feek ye firft the Kingdom of God, and his Righteoufnefs, and all
thefe things fhall be added unto you.*

TIS a very lively and affecting defcription of Providence, which our Saviour S E R M.
gives us in his excellent difcourfe to his Difciples in this chapter: That our XXXIV.
heavenly Father knoweth what things we have need of before we ask him; and
is at all times able and willing to fupply us with what his infinite Wifdom knows to be
needful and convenient for us; that not only *men* who are endued with reafon and fore-
caft, and have the Advantage of their own labour and induftry; but even the *Ravens
and Fowls of the Air, which neither fow nor reap, which neither have ftorehoufe nor barn,*
have yet a plentiful provifion made for them, and are continually fed by his bountiful
Providence: Yet not a *Sparrow,* one of the meaneft of Birds, *falls to the ground without* him, *i. e.* without his direction or permiffion; *not one of them,* as St *Luke* expreffes
it, *is forgotten before God:* That not only Creatures endued with Life and Senfe, but

SERM. ftill further, even the *Grafs* and Flowers of the Field, which can contribute nothing to-
XXXIV. wards their own fupport, nor are at all fenfible of what is done for them, have yet in
them more and greater marks of the inimitable workmanfhip of the great Creator of all
things, than ever the Courts of the greateft Princes, even that of *Solomon* himfelf, had
of human artifice and earthly glory: Nay, further, that even things of a ftill lower degree than either Plants or Animals, thofe very things which of all others feem to us the
leaft valuable and leaft to be regarded, even thefe are not beneath the care and infpection of Providence, but the very *hairs of our head are all numbred* before God.

THE Ufe our Saviour makes of this lively Defcription of Providence, is to teach us
to rely at all times upon the Care and Protection of God, without unreafonable anxiety,
diffidence, and diftruft. And indeed, were not the noble Subject careleffly and inconfi-
derately paffed over in mens thoughts, without attention and ferious meditation; or
were there not fecretly in the breafts of men *an evil Heart of Unbelief,* it is not poffible but this excellent Argument would generally produce in the Minds and Lives of men,
its juft and natural effect. Men who ftudy and contemplate the *Phænomena* of *Nature,*
which are the Works of God, the further they carry their inquiries, and the deeper
difcoveries they make, the More, and the more undeniable Evidences they perpetually
find, that the Works of Nature are not the Blunders of Chance, or the blind Effect of
unintelligent Fate; but the continual Operations of God who governs all things, by the
uninterrupted care and interpofition of an All-wife Providence, which *neither flumbers
nor fleeps,* and from whofe direction nothing is exempted, at any time or in any place.
Chriftians, who according to their Profeffion, believe the *Scriptures,* find our Saviour in
the paffages now recited, declaring fully and in few words this great Truth, confirming
it by his Divine Authority to thofe who have not capacities or opportunities of obferving
it in the nature of the things themfelves; and making infinitely a better improvement of
it, to caufe us to put our Truft worthily in God who governs all things, than ever was
made by any of the Philofophers in any Age of the World: *If God,* faith he, *fo feeds
the Birds of the Air, and clothes the Grafs of the Field; how much more will he take* care
of *you, O ye of little Faith?*

BUT our Saviour's Argument does not end here: The confideration of the Care of
Providence over us, teaches us to truft in God for a fupply of all things neceffary *here*;
and This our Truft in him for things neceffary *here,* is in order to enable us with greater
earneftnefs and lefs diftraction of Thought, to attend upon the one thing neceffary, the
fecuring our portion in the eternal Happinefs of the Kingdom of God *hereafter*: That
our Hearts being weaned from an over-fond Love and Affection for the tranfitory enjoyments of this prefent World, may be *there* more furely and fteddily fixed, where is
laid up our true and lafting treafure; even *that treafure in the Heavens that faileth not,
where no thief approaches, neither moth corrupteth. Take no thought therefore,* fays our
Lord; *i.e.* be not eager and follicitous, anxioufly and unreafonably careful, for thefe
things which the *Nations of the World feek after,* even the *Gentiles which know not
God:* But rather *feek ye the Kingdom of God;* fo it is expreffed in St *Luke*; or in the
words of the Text, *Seek ye firft the Kingdom of God and his Righteoufnefs: You,* faith
he, who have the Happinefs to *know God,* and to whom his Glory has been particularly
revealed; *you* who are bleffed with the knowledge of his true Religion, of the Purity
and Excellency of his divine Laws, and the great and eternal Reward which will attend
the Practice of them; Live *ye* fuitably to fo excellent a Belief, and anfwerably to fo
great a degree of Knowledge: Let *your* affections be raifed above things earthly and
temporal, to thofe which are fpiritual, heavenly, and eternal; *Seek ye firft the Kingdom
of God and his Righteoufnefs*; and all thefe things, thefe earthly and temporal bleffings,
fo far as the Wifdom of God fees neceffary for your prefent comfortable fubfiftence,
fhall be added unto you.

IN

IN a foregoing Difcourfe upon thefe Words, I obferved in them thefe three things:

I. A Precept or Duty commanded ; *Seek ye the Kingdom of God and his Righteoufnefs.*

II. THE manner and degree of the Obligation ; *Seek it* firft.

III. THE Promife even of a *temporal* Reward annexed ; *And all thefe things fhall be added unto you.*

I. IN difcourfing upon the Precept or Duty commanded, *Seek ye the Kingdom of God and his Righteoufnefs* ; I obferved, that Seeking any thing heartily and effectually, implies thefe four things :

1ft, THAT we have a juft *value and efteem* for the thing we pretend to feek after.

2dly, THAT we *fix our Attention* continually, *i. e.* habitually upon it.

3dly, THAT we be *diligent and impartial in enquiring after the beft and certaineft means* of attaining it. And

4thly, THAT we *immediately practife thofe Means, and heartily put them in Execution.* And thefe I have already enlarged upon.

I proceed now in the II*d* place, to confider the particular *manner and degree* of our Obligation to this Duty, contained in the *comparative* expreffion, Seek ye *firft,* or (as 'tis expreffed in St *Luke,*) Seek ye *rather* the Kingdom of God. And here (as I before took notice in the Explication of the Text,) it is reafonable to obferve, that the Word *firft,* or *rather,* as in the *comparative* Senfe it *heightens* the Obligation of the Duty, and fignifies that we are bound to feek the Kingdom of God *more heartily, more earneftly, more zealoufly,* with *greater conftancy,* with *greater diligence,* with *ftronger and more intenfe affections,* than can reafonably be employed about any temporal concern ; fo, on the contrary, in the *abfolute* Senfe, 'tis a *relaxation* or *diminution* of the ftrictnefs and rigour of the Duty ; fignifying, that we are not obliged to feek the Kingdom of God *wholly* and *only,* in a *total and abfolute* exclufion of all other defires, (as fome melancholy well-difpofed perfons may be apt to imagine ;) but only that we are to feek it *chiefly* and in the *firft* place ; as being infinitely of more value and of greater importance to us, and confequently infinitely worthier of our higheft care and concern than any temporal and worldly affairs. But the very Word itfelf, Seek this *firft,* implies in the proper notion of it, that *other* things alfo may be defired *afterward,* i. e. in their due place, and with a fubordinate affection. The Words immediately foregoing, *Take no thought, faying, what fhall we eat, or what fhall we drink, or wherewithal fhall we be clothed,* feem indeed to be fpoken abfolutely and without reftriction : And perhaps to the Apoftles themfelves, the immediate Hearers of this Difcourfe of our Lord, who were to have no fettled habitation or abode, but were to preach the Gofpel from one Nation and Kingdom to another ; to *them* poffibly this inftruction was *intended* fo to be underftood, in the abfolute and unreftrained Senfe. But as the Circumftances of Chriftians in following times neceffarily made the ftrict and literal Senfe of thofe words altogether impracticable ; fo the Words of the Text immediately following them, evidently give us room to interpret them in fuch a manner, as to be a prohibition *only* of *immoderate* and *exceffive* Cares ; of *fuch* Cares and Sollicitude for the things of the World, as is unworthy of the Character, and inconfiftent with the Zeal and Diligence of thofe whofe Heart and whofe Treafure is in Heaven. 'Tis not forbidden us to defire and to ufe moderately the things of the World ; but we muft with our *firft* and *greateft* care, feek the Kingdom of God and his Righteoufnefs.

THE *Limitations* therefore of this Duty, or the particular *Degree and Manner* of the Obligation expreffed in the Text, may be fet forth in the following particulars.

1ft, SEEKING in the *firft* place the Kingdom of God, fignifies, in the leaft and loweft fenfe, that we muft *not delay and put off to the future* our defigns and intentions of

living

SERM.
XXXIV.

living religiously. The Apostles were obliged, when they were first called by our Saviour, to leave all that they had and follow him; and we find that some who desired only to take leave of their Friends, or to have time but for the burial of a nearest Relation, were not allowed the indulgence even of so short a delay. The Person who when he was commanded by our Saviour to *follow him*, answered readily, *Lord, I will follow thee ; but let me first go bid them farewell which are at home at my house*, St *Luke* ix. 61, was told, that *no man having put his hand to the plough, and looking back, is meet for the Kingdom of God* : The expression 'tis plain is *figurative* ; but the Sense is, He who, when he is convinced of the Truth of Religion, is not willing *immediately* to comply with the Obligations thereof, but desires still a longer and a little longer delay, is not worthy to be admitted to injoy the benefit of it at all. And this refusal to allow of any delay, was at a time when our Lord himself had not where to lay his Head ; and when the Circumstances of things were such, that no man could become a Disciple of Christ, but he must necessarily part with not only the *sinful*, but even all the *innocent* also and most allowable enjoyments and comforts of Life ; at a Time when a man that had kept all the commandments from his Youth, according to the usual extent and interpretation of the Law, was dismissed by our Saviour with a very severe intimation of the danger even of not-ill-gotten possessions ; because he was not willing to *sell all that he had, and give to the poor* : In a word, when no man could embrace the Christian Religion, but he must at the same time resolve to lose all that he had, and very probably even his life itself also for the sake of the Gospel. How much more *Now*, when God is pleased to require of us a much easier Obedience ; when we are required, not to part with *all* that we have, but only to retrench our vain and sinful expences ; not to sell *all* and give to the Poor, but to be charitable out of the Superfluities of our plenty and abundance ; not to lay down our *lives*, or leave even the *comfortable Enjoyments* of life, but only to forsake the unreasonable and unfruitful Pleasures of Sin, the Madness and Follies of Profuseness, the unprofitable Gains of Unrighteousness, the hurtful and mischievous extravagancies of Intemperance, the malicious and unmanly pleasures of Pride and Arbitrariness, of Oppression, Uncharitableness, and Revenge : *How much more*, I say, *in these days*, when God is pleased to exact of us only so easy an Obedience ; *how much more* unreasonable is it, that men should *delay* complying with so good, so gentle, so necessary an Obligation ? *How much more* unreasonable is it that men should *first* desire to satisfy themselves with the enjoyments of Sin, and then hope to mock God by *at last* desiring to enter into his Kingdom ? And how unworthy must they needs be *at the End of their lives* to be admitted into his Kingdom, who would not be persuaded to employ the *beginning and best* of their days in seeking the Righteousness thereof ? 'Tis no advantage to God if we are righteous and obedient to him, nor is there any accession made to *his* Self-sufficient Happiness, by *our* becoming Subjects of his Kingdom : 'Tis for our *own* benefit only, that he commands us to do Righteousness ; and therefore, if we slight and neglect and carelessly let slip the opportunities of preparing and qualifying ourselves to be members of his Kingdom, 'tis very just in *him* to exclude us therefrom. Not that any man, when he first comes to a true sense of Religion, how late soever it be, hath reason absolutely to despair ; but that those who are better instructed in their early days, should have no incouragement to defer their Obedience.

2*dly*, SEEKING *first* the Kingdom of God signifies, that though our *actual* intention may often lawfully be imployed upon the things of the World, yet our *habitual, principal*, and *greatest* regard must always be fixt upon the Life that is to come. I have *before* shown, that *seeking any thing heartily and effectually*, necessarily implies, among other things, that we *fix our attention continually*, i. e. *frequently and habitually upon it*. And now to apply this, in the *comparative* Sense, to the Precept in the Text : 'Tis manifest, that seeking the Kingdom of God *first*, or *before* the things of

the

the World, neceſſarily implies, that even *while* we are imployed in worldly affairs, in S E R M.
providing for the preſent neceſſaries of life; yet our principal and main Intention muſt XXXIV.
always habitually be directed towards our Ultimate and Great End. *Whatſoever thou*
takeſt in hand, (as the wiſe Son of *Sirach* excellently expreſſes it,) *remember the End,*
and thou ſhalt never do amiſs, Eccluſ. vii. 36. Thus a Traveller may imploy his *imme-*
diate and preſent Thoughts upon the conveniencies of his journey and the accommoda-
tions at his Inn; but yet at the ſame time, his *principal and chief* View will continually be upon the End of his Journey, and his ſafe arrival at home; and all other things
will in courſe be directed with a ſubordination to That chief Deſign. And in *this*
Senſe, a man may be *at all times* ſeeking the Kingdom of God; without any way
neglecting, or at all withdrawing himſelf from ſecular Buſineſs: Which was the original Error of thoſe who firſt ran into the Superſtition of a Monkiſh retirement; and,
in order (as they weakly thought) to become more religious towards *God*, put themſelves out of all capacity of doing any good amongſt *Men.* There is no imployment
wherein a Man may not perpetually be doing ſomething for the Honour of God, for
the Good of Men, or for the Improvement of the Virtues of his own Mind: There is
no Buſineſs, nay, there is no innocent Diverſion, wherein he may not make it his
chief and conſtant care to act always like a reaſonable man and a good Chriſtian.
There is no ſtate of life wherein he may not keep a conſtant Eye upon a future ſtate,
and ſo uſe the things of the preſent World, as that the great and ultimate ſcope of all
his Actions may always reſpect that which is to come: He may ſtedfaſtly propoſe to
himſelf one great deſign of his life, and endeavour to act always regularly upon that
Deſign: He may conſtantly fix his main Intention upon his chief and ultimate End;
and in every thing he does, be careful always to maintain a juſt regard to That. Every
thing he undertakes may be either directly conducive to that End, or at leaſt *not con-*
trary to and inconſiſtent with it. Which Method of acting, *ſanctifies* all the *Buſineſs,*
nay, even all the *Pleaſures* and *Diverſions* of life. And this is the

3*d* T H I N G, which the Phraſe, (Seeking *firſt* the Kingdom of God,) neceſſarily
implies, namely, that whenever there ariſes a *competition* between the Intereſt of Religion and that of the World, we always *prefer* the more important ſpiritual and eternal Intereſt, before any temporal and worldly concern. *If any man come to me*, ſaith
our Saviour, *Luk.* xiv. 26. *and hate not his Father, and Mother, and Wife, and Chil-*
dren, and Brethren, and Siſters, yea, and his own Life alſo, he cannot be my Diſciple.
If he *hate* not Father and Mother, is, in modern language, a very harſh expreſſion:
But the meaning is, (according to the well-known Uſe of ſuch ways of ſpeaking among
the *Jews,*) if he be not willing to part with *them,* when there is a Neceſſity ſo to do,
rather than with his *Religion.* So our Saviour himſelf explains it, St *Matt.* x. 37. *He*
that loveth Father or Mother more than Me, is not worthy of me;——*and he that*
taketh not his croſs, and followeth after me, is not worthy of me. We have reaſon to
bleſs God we are not *now* called to ſo ſevere a trial; neither are we required to part
with *all things* for his ſake, as the Diſciples in the primitive times were obliged to do:
But we are *at all times* under the ſame Obligation to be in *Readineſs* to loſe all, to have
an *indifferency* for the things of the World *comparatively* to our Religion; and to be
habitually in ſuch a Diſpoſition of Mind, as to be *always willing* to part with whatſoever ſhall at any time come in competition with our Duty. And of this there *are* Trials,
even in our preſent citcumſtances, by which Men *may* judge, in great meaſure, of
their own Sincerity or Inſincerity in this particular. For inſtance; If a man, rather
than deny himſelf the unlawful and unreaſonable pleaſure of a Debauch; if, rather
than part with the unjuſt gains of Fraud and Deceit, of Oppreſſion and unrighteous
Judgment; if, rather than reſtrain the fooliſh and unfruitful Vanity of a profane Jeſt,

S E R M. of mockery and fcoffing at Religion; he is willing *Now* to lay afide all his hopes of
XXXIV. Heaven (as every vicious man plainly does, notwithſtanding his profeſſion of Chriſtianity;) ſuch a perſon may very eaſily judge, *how* ready he would be to leave *all*, even
the *innocent* injoyments of life, and even *life itſelf*, for the ſake of that Religion which
he *now* ſo ſlightly and upon every trivial an occaſion openly diſhonours. *He* indeed
who *now* plucks out a *right eye*, or cuts off a *right hand*, who reſiſts great temptations
of unrighteouſneſs, and by the Spirit of Religion, mortifies violent Paſſions and ſtrong
corrupt inclinations; ſuch a one may reaſonably pretend, and has good evidence, has
juſt ground of hope within himſelf, that if it ſhould pleaſe God to call him to ſo ſevere
a trial, he *ſhould* be able to lay down even his life for his Religion. But if a man be
not faithful in that which is *leaſt*, if he cannot prevail with himſelf to go through the
ſmalleſt difficulty, what ground has he to pretend, that he would be faithful in that
which is *much*, and undergo the *ſevereſt and moſt difficult* trial?

I N theſe particulars ſeem to be contained the full meaning and intention of the Precept, Seek ye *firſt* the Kingdom of God, and his Righteouſneſs.

I T remains that I proceed briefly in the

IIId and laſt place; T O conſider the Promiſe annexed even of a temporal reward;
and all theſe things ſhall be added unto you. Now

F R O M this Promiſe we may ſeem reaſonably to infer theſe three things.

1. T H A T, *generally* ſpeaking, God bleſſes the endeavours of the righteous, and of
thoſe who truſt in him; at leaſt ſo far, as to ſupply them with the neceſſary ſupports
and conveniencies of Life. *I have been young, and now am old,* ſaith the Pſalmiſt, *and
yet ſaw I never the righteous forſaken, nor his ſeed begging their bread.* Which Obſervation, though it was indeed more univerſally true under the *Jewiſh* diſpenſation, than
in the Goſpel-ſtate; yet even *ſtill* for the more part, *Godlineſs*, as St *Paul* declares,
has the promiſe even *of the Life that now is:* And our Saviour, through his whole Argument in the Context, ſeems to ſuppoſe, that Providence, which ſecretly directs and
over-rules all Events, is particularly concerned to make proviſion for thoſe, who in the
faithful diſcharge of their duty rely upon him.

2. W H E N this happens *otherwiſe*, (as in the caſe of *Perſecution* it neceſſarily muſt;)
then from the Promiſe here annexed we may reaſonably conclude, that, what a righteous man loſes upon account of his Religion, ſhall by the care of Providence be,
Some other way, made good to him. *There is no man,* ſaith our Saviour, *that has left
houſe, or brethren or ſiſters, or father or mother, or wife or children, or lands, for my
ſake and the goſpel; but he ſhall receive an hundred fold now* in this time,——*with Perſecutions*; i. e. he ſhall either in the courſe of Providence be reſtored, to more than he
has loſt; or ſhall receive more than an equivalent in that peace and comfort and ſatiſ-
faction of mind, that joy in the Holy Ghoſt, which ariſes from a Senſe of a good
Conſcience and of the Favour of God.

3. W H E N *neither* of theſe are ſecured to a man, (as they can only be affirmed for
the *moſt* part;) then it may certainly be depended upon, that his reward *hereafter*,
ſhall be ſo much the greater. *Uſually* he ſhall in the *preſent time* receive an hundred
fold, *together with Perſecutions*; but in the End *infallibly* eternal life. It was a noble
Anſwer to this purpoſe, (wherewith I ſhall conclude,) which the three children of the
Jews gave to *Nebuchadnezzar* King of *Babylon*, when they were commanded to fall
down and worſhip the graven Image which he had ſet up, under pain of being caſt
alive into a burning fiery furnace; *Dan.* iii. 17. It was propoſed to them to forſake
the religion of their God for the Law of the King and the Religion of the Country;
and their Anſwer was; *If it be ſo; our God whom we ſerve, is able to deliver us from
the burning fiery furnace; and he* will *deliver us out of thine hand, O King: But if*

I   *not;*

1 Kings ili.
13.

not; (if he does *not* think fit to deliver us; *yet*) *be it known unto thee, O King, that* we will *not serve thy Gods, nor worship the graven Image which thou haft fet up.* They depended upon God, if he did *not* think fit to deliver them from *temporal* Death, that he would recompence it to them with Life and Happinefs *eternal.*

S E R M. XXXIV.

S E R M O N XXXV.

Of the Liberty of Moral Agents.

St J O H. VIII. 32.

And ye fhall know the Truth, and the Truth fhall make you Free.

THE Evangelift, in the foregoing part of this Chapter, having recorded a large Difcourfe of our Saviour's concerning his being *the Light of the World*, or, the *Teacher of true Religion*, ver. 12; concerning the Teftimony he bore of *himfelf* by the Nature and Tendency of his *Doctrine*; and the Teftimony *the Father* bore of him, by his miraculous *Works*, ver. 14 and 18; concerning his *Departure* out of the World, and the *Reafon* of the *Jews* refufing to believe on him, *ver.* 21 and 23; concerning the *manner* of his Death, and the great *Succefs* wherewith the Gofpel fhould afterward be propagated, *ver.* 28; The Evangelift, I fay, having at large recorded thefe *Difcourfes* of our Saviour, proceeds in the next place to relate the *Effect* thefe Difcourfes had upon the People, *ver.* 30; *As he fpake thefe Words, many believed on him* : Namely, Upon *Jefus's* foretelling feveral Things that were to happen to Himfelf and to the Nation of the *Jews*, many that heard him were difpofed to confider and compare what they had known and heard of him before; and being perfwaded that he was a Perfon fent from God, they declared that they *would* become his Difciples. But Jefus, knowing who thefe Converts were, and that their Faith was not firm and well-grounded; and that with thofe new Difciples many alfo of the unbelieving *Jews* hypo-critically joined themfelves, with intent to take fome private Opportunity of *killing* him; as appears from the following part of the Hiftory : He faid unto them, *ver.* 31. *If ye* continue *in my Word*, then *are ye my Difciples indeed*; If ye will be truly my Difciples, ye muft not only profefs by a fudden perfwafion to be convinced of the Truth of what I fay, but ye muft fo retain and fteddily adhere to my Doctrine, as to con-form your Lives and Practices thereto; *If ye* continue *in my Word*, then *are ye my Difciples indeed.* And then he adds in the Words of the Text; *And ye fhall know the Truth, and the Truth fhall make you Free.* The meaning is; And by fuch Practice, you will continually attain a more and more perfect *Knowledge* of the Truth; and *That Knowledge* will fecure to you the greateft and moft defirable *Freedom* in the World.

S E R M. XXXV.

THAT

SERM.
XXXV.

THAT by *Truth* in the *New Testament*, is meant the general Doctrine of the Gospel revealed to us by Christ, I suppose needs not any particular Proof in this place. That *continuing* in the Practice of Christ's Commandments, and sincerely endeavouring to obey the Will of God, is one of the best and greatest Helps to enable a man to understand perfectly, the *Truth* and *Reasonableness*, the *Necessity* and *Excellency* of the Doctrine of the Gospel; is also sufficiently evident, without farther Explication at This Time. The only Difficulty in the Words of the Text, is the Sense of that latter part, *And the Truth shall make you Free.* For what Relation there is between *Truth* in the *Understanding* and *Liberty* in the *Actions*, does not appear at first sight: And 'tis still in the reading of Scripture as great a Paradox to some Christians at This day, as it seemed to be to the *Jews* at the time when it was spoken; that it should be said of such Persons as had never been *Slaves*, that the Truth should make them *Free*. The Explication is given by our Saviour in the Words following the Text; and yet given in such a manner, as not to appear but to those who read with Attention. For the *Jews*, when our Saviour had spoken these Words, *The Truth shall make you Free*, taking them in the gross and literal Sense, replied, *ver.* 33. *We be Abraham's Seed*; we have by Descent a natural Right to Freedom, *and were never in bondage to any man; How sayest thou then, Ye shall be made Free?* Upon This, our Lord opens to them the true Sense of the Words, *ver.* 34. *Verily I say unto you, Whosoever committeth* Sin, *is the servant of Sin.* Which is to say: Ye fancy, because with respect to *Bodily* Service ye are not in bondage to any man, that therefore ye are really *Free men*. But forasmuch as *to whomsoever men yield themselves servants to obey, his Servants they are to whom they obey*; and *of whomsoever a man is overcome, of the same is he brought in bondage*; therefore, so long as you continue in your Sins, you are as really Slaves, as any person that is in bondage to the severest Master; For there cannot be a greater Slave, than he who is under the Power and Dominion of unreasonable Lusts. This is the evident meaning of that expression; *Whosoever committeth Sin*; not by inadvertency or surprize, not by mistake or sudden incursion, but deliberately and habitually, as was the Case of those *Jews* our Saviour discoursed with; *whosoever so committeth Sin, is the Servant of Sin.* And This will illustrate the meaning of that more difficult passage, which follows immediately in the next words, *ver.* 35; *And the Servant abideth not in the House for ever; but the Son abideth for ever : If the Son therefore shall make you Free, ye shall be Free indeed.* I know indeed, says our Lord, that you esteem yourselves highly, upon your belonging to the Family and House of God, which was first set in order by *Moses*; and that upon this account you will claim to yourselves even That spiritual Freedom, whereof I am now speaking. But, let me assure you, neither is that Privilege you boast of, your being the peculiar people of God, sufficient of itself to give you real Freedom from the Dominion and Guilt of Sin; neither, if it could, was the Authority of *Moses* intended to continue always, but only for a Time, like that of a *Servant*, and to give place at length to the Authority of the *Son*, whose Government in God's house is to continue for ever. Wherefore the only means, by which you can preserve to yourselves the Privilege of God's peculiar Family, and obtain a perfect Freedom from the Slavery of Sin, is, that ye submit to the Authority of the *Son* who is now come into the World, and that ye continue in Obedience to his Doctrine and Government. *The Servant abideth not in the House for ever; but the Son abideth for ever : If the Son therefore shall make you Free, ye shall be Free indeed.*

THE Design and Meaning of our Saviour's whole Discourse being thus explained, the Doctrine contained in the words of the Text, appears evidently to be This; That the *religious Restraints* laid upon men by the Gospel are really and truly the *greatest*

Liberty;

Liberty; and the *Service of God*, the moſt *perfect Freedom* : *If ye continue in my Word,* S E R M-
then are ye my Diſciples indeed : *And ye ſhall know the Truth, and the Truth ſhall make* XXXV.
you Free.

L I B E R T Y, all men are ſenſible, is a Jewel of ineſtimable Value; and therefore
there is nothing more earneſtly or more juſtly contended for, nothing more univerſally
or more reaſonably deſired. But alas ! As *Children* are often eagerly deſirous of what
they do not underſtand, and know not when they are in Poſſeſſion of what they deſire,
but are put off and pleaſed with falſe reſemblances of things, and hold faſt ſomething
really contrary to what they think they are fond of : So, in This particular, *Men* themſelves, even Wiſe men and Learned, the Rich and the Potent, the cunning and the moſt
ſenſible in other Affairs, are very frequently impoſed upon, (I ſhould ſay, impoſe upon
themſelves,) and love to be deceived, and take pains to abuſe their own Underſtandings ; and, while they love Liberty above all things, embrace Slavery in the ſtead thereof; ſhutting their Eyes, and calling things by falſe Names, and ſtiling Bondage Liberty,
and Liberty Bondage. For while *All* men contend for Liberty, wherein does the
greater part of the World imagine true Liberty to conſiſt ? Moſt men ſeem to place it
in being allowed to let looſe the Reins to all their Appetites and Paſſions without controul ; to be under no reſtraint either from the Laws of Men, or from the Fear of God.
Princes generally think it to conſiſt in having the Power of tyrannizing over the multitude of their Subjects, and ſacrificing the common Rights and Properties of Mankind
to their own ſingle and unreaſonable Ambition. The *common People* are apt to place it
in unbounded Licentiouſneſs, and having no ſuperiour but the Humour of the Multitude. The *Covetous perſon* would gladly be allowed to increaſe his Treaſure by ſome
ſhorter ſteps than thoſe of honeſt Induſtry and patient Labour. The *Debauchee* thinks
no Chains more troubleſome, than thoſe which would confine his Pleaſures from irregularity and exceſs. And oh ! how happy would the *revengeful ſpirit* be, might he but
have Liberty to ſatisfy his Malice, without preſent Shame or future Danger ! This, 'tis
to be feared, is the Notion too great a part of Mankind have of Liberty. And what a
Liberty is This ? Is it not like the Liberty a Madman deſires, of being permitted to
deſtroy himſelf ? Is it any thing more, than a Liberty to chuſe the worſt of Slaveries,
and to exchange the Government of a moſt reaſonable Maſter, for that of the worſt
and cruelleſt Tyrant ? For, *what* does the *Ambitious Prince* or the *Licentious Multitude* ; what does the *Covetous*, and *Revengeful*, or the *Debauched Sinner*; but only
chuſe to be a Servant to *Paſſion*, inſtead of a Follower of *Right Reaſon* ? What is it
that makes a *Beaſt* be a Creature of leſs Liberty than *Man*, but only that its natural
Appetites more neceſſarily govern all its Actions, and that it is not indued with a Faculty of Reaſon, whereby to exert itſelf, and gain a Power or Liberty of over-ruling
thoſe Appetites ? For if the true Liberty of a Moral Agent does not principally conſiſt
in the Power of over-ruling ſuch Appetites; *wherein* lies the Excellency of humane
Nature at all, above the inferiour Creation ? Or what ſuperiority has Man above the
Beaſts that periſh, in any *Moral regard*; if his greater Knowledge and Underſtanding
ſerves only to make him feel and be ſenſible of his Subjection to thoſe lower Appetites,
which the other Creatures are naturally ſubject to, without being ſenſible or having any
uneaſy Reflections that they are ſo ? Is not the Difference, in ſuch a Caſe, This only;
that the Man is really the greater Slave, or has the leſs Liberty of the Two, becauſe
He only is by his Reaſon capable of underſtanding that he wants it ? If a man's Body
be under confinement, or he be impotent in his Limbs, he is then deprived of his *bodily*
Liberty : And for the ſame Reaſon, if his *Mind* be blinded by ſottiſh Errors, and his
Reaſon over-ruled by violent Paſſions; is not This likewiſe plainly as great a Slavery and

SERM as true a Confinement? For, *to whomsoever men yield themselves servants to obey*, (as the
XXXV. Apostle excellently expresses it,) are they not *his servants to whom they obey*, Rom. vi.
16; and *of whomsoever a man is overcome, of the same* also *is he* not *brought in bondage*,
2 Pet. ii. 19?

BUT here it is obvious for the Libertine to reply, that he has no Notion of the
Slavery we speak of, nor is at all sensible that he is under any Restraint: For *what
greater Liberty can a man have, than to do what he pleases? or what can he desire
more, than to do what he wills without controul?* I answer: This is indeed the True
Definition of mere *physical* or *natural* Liberty; that is to say, of That Liberty which
is common to Man with every living Creature, with the savagest Lyon, and with the
meanest Insect. For *They* also do what they will, and go and come as they please,
and follow the Instinct, and gratify all the Appetites of Nature. But the Liberty of a
Moral Agent and of a *rational* Being, implies something more. It implies a Liberty of
doing what is *Right*; a Freedom of hearkning to what *Reason* dictates, and a Power of executing what the unprejudiced and improved *Understanding* judges to be fit;
fit and reasonable, fit for *Him* who is a rational Person, fit for any *Other* rational Person in *His* place, to do. And *this* Liberty the Sensual person parts with; and suffers
himself to be captivated, *against* his Reason, by the Law of Sin.

THE Licentious Sinner will still reply; He is not *sensible* of any such Captivity,
or any Slavery he is under; He gives himself his full Liberty to do what he thinks fit;
and greater Freedom than This how can he desire! But the Answer to This Fallacy
is evident. For as a Man while he sleeps in his Prison, is not sensible of his Confinement, and yet continues confined: Or a Madman imagines the Room he is shut up in
to be as spacious as the World; and yet receives no inlargement: Or an Idiot embraces and admires his Chain as the brightest Ornament, and yet it continues a Chain:
So the vitious Libertine, while his Eyes are blinded with Ignorance and Prejudice, his
Understanding darkned with false Representations, and his Will bribed perpetually
with deceitful Allurements; while he loves the Dominion of Sin, and takes pleasure in
the Practice of Unrighteousness, and silences the Voice of Reason and Conscience; he
fancies himself Master of the most unbounded Liberty, and yet at the same time is
really in bondage to the most unreasonable Service. The Scripture describes this State
by a most elegant similitude, of mens being dead *in Trespasses and Sins*; Eph. ii. 1, 5;
by their being inclosed *in the Snare of the Devil, and taken* captive *by him at his Will*;
2 Tim. ii. 26; by their being *brought into* Captivity *to the Law of Sin*; Rom. vii. 23.
By the History of *Samson*, who, after many repeated insults, yet would not see the
Bondage he was in, till his Strength was departed from him: And by the description
of a foolish young man led away with the inticements of a strange Woman; *Prov.*
vii. 21. *With her much fair Speech she caused him to yield, with the flattering of her
lips she forced him. He goeth after her straitway, as an Ox goeth to the Slaughter, or
as a Fool to the Correction of the Stocks; Till a dart strike through his liver, as a Bird
hasteth to the snare, and knoweth not that it is for his Life.*

BUT This, is not *generally* the Case of Sinners. *More usually*, they not only *are*
in Captivity to Sin, but *feel also and know* themselves to be so; and yet have not Courage to assert their Liberty. Their *Reason* is over-ruled; and their *Passions* govern them,
even *against* their Judgment. Which, in a figurative sense, is exactly what *Solomon*
literally complained of, *Ecclef.* x. 7; *I have seen Servants upon Horses, and Princes
walking as Servants upon the Earth.* When *Reason*, which ought to *govern*, is thus
dethroned; and the Fear of God, and all Sense of Religion laid aside; the man is then
under the Dominion of his Passions, as of many disagreeing Masters to be served at
once; and his Heart is *like the troubled Sea, when it cannot rest, whose Waters cast up
mire*

mire and dirt; If. lvii. 20. He is toffed to and fro with impotent and impatient *Defires*, S E R M. torn in pieces with eager and impetuous *Appetites*, pufh'd on by unruly and exorbitant XXXV. *Affections*, tormented with vain and difappointing *Hopes*, and as often with ground- lefs or too well grounded *Fears*; confumed with *Envy*, or fwelled with *Pride*; raging with *Anger*, or anxious after *Revenge*. This is the thraldom of a man enflaved to Sin; and *Who fhall deliver him from the Body of this Death?* The Scripture defcribes the miferable ftate of fuch Perfons, by many elegant ways of Expreffion: Telling us, that they are *Servants of Sin*; John viii. 34. *Servants to uncleannefs and to iniquity*; Rom. vi. 19; and *Servants of Corruption*; 2 Pet. ii. 19; that they *cannot ceafe from Sin*; 2 Pet. ii. 14; that *Sin* hath *Dominion over them*, and *reigns in their mortal Bodies*, Pf. xix. 13, while they *obey it in the Lufts thereof*; Rom. vi. 14. 12. That tho' in their mind they cxix. 133. approve the Law of God, yet they *fee another law* in their *members warring againft the law of* their *mind, and bringing* them *into captivity to the law of Sin*; *fo that* they *cannot do the things that* they *would*; Rom. vii. 22; and Gal. v. 17. That when at any time *to will is prefent with* them, yet *how to perform that which is good* they *find not*; *For the good that* they *would*, they *do not*; *but the evil which* they *would not, That* they *do*; Rom. vii. 18, and ver. 15; *That which* they *do*, they *allow not*; *For what* they *would, That do* they *not*; *but what* they *hate, That* they *do*. All which, is comprized in one expreffive word in the verfe foregoing, *ver.* 14; they are *fold* under Sin : That is, they have by long ill habits and corrupt practice, as it were *given up* themfelves, *parted with their Liberty*, and *yielded* themfelves abfolutely into the *Snare of the Devil, to be taken captive by him at his Will*. The Phrafe is twice applied in the *Old Teftament* to *Ahab*; 1 Kings xxi. 20, 25; that he *did* fell *himfelf to work wickednefs in the Sight of the Lord*. And twice, to the whole people of *Ifrael*; in the days of *Hofea*; 2 Kings xvii. 17; that they fold *themfelves to do evil in the Sight of the Lord*; and in the days of *Antiochus*; 1 Macc. i. 15; that they *were* fold *to do mifchief*.

AND now if this be the Cafe of habitual Sinners; we may well ask concerning *Li- berty*, in the words wherein *Job* put the Queftion concerning true *Wifdom*; *Where* then Job xxviii. 12. *fhall* Liberty *be found? and where is the place of* True Freedom? And the Anfwer may be returned in the Words of the fame excellent Author; *Behold, the Fear of the* Job xxviii. 28. *Lord, that is,* Freedom; *and to depart from Evil, is* True Liberty,

THE True liberty of a Rational and Moral Agent, confifts in his being able to follow *right Reafon only*, without Hindrance or Reftraint. It confifts in a clear unbi- affed Judgment, and in a Power of acting conformably thereunto. Man therefore is then *Free*, when his *Reafon* is not awed by bafe *Fears*, nor bribed by foolifh and fantaftick *Hopes*; when it is not tumultuoufly hurried away by *Lufts* and *Paffions*, nor cheated and deluded by falfe Appearances of prefent *Good*; but confiders *impartially*, and judges *wifely*, and acts *effectually* and with Refolution. This is the Liberty of a ra- tional Agent; the Freedom of a Man, of a Chriftian, of an Angel. Not that in this prefent frail ftate, we can ever actually arrive at fuch a perfect Freedom; but that by ftudying and practifing the Truth, the Truth of *Nature* and the Truth of *Religion*, we may and ought continually more and more to affert and improve our Freedom, till at length we arrive at the glorious Liberty of the children of God.

BUT here the profane Libertine will ask, as before; Is it not a greater Liberty, for him to follow abfolutely his own Pleafure, than to be under the direction of the Laws of right Reafon and Religion? I anfwer; It is by no means fo great a Liberty: For when a man follows *true Reafon*, his Will is directed by its natural and proper Motive, which is a right Underftanding; But when he follows what he calls his *own Pleafure*, his Will is then directed by a falfe and unnatural Motive; by *Error and Prejudice*, by *Obftinacy and falfe Appearances of Things*. Now it is very evident, that what *Impo- tency*

S E R M.　*tency or Bonds* are to the *natural Liberty* of the *Body*, that very fame thing is *Igno-*
XXXV.　*rance or Paſſion* to the *moral Liberty* of *the Mind.* Wherefore as the Body is then
　　　　free, when it is moved by the Natural Action of the Blood and Spirits, and not by the
Convulſive Motions and Violence of a Diſeaſe; ſo the Mind is then and then only Free,
when its Choice is directed by the natural Motive of right Reaſon, and not by the violent impetus of a blind and headſtrong Paſſion.

Th is Argument may further be illuſtrated in the following manner. God Himſelf
is a Being, as of all other Perfections, ſo particularly of the moſt perfect and complete
Liberty. Now *His* Liberty conſiſts in this, that being infinitely *Knowing* and infinitely *Powerful*, 'tis impoſſible he ſhould ever be influenced by any *Violence*, or by any
Deceit; but his *Will* is always directed by *abſolute Right and Reaſon only*: And This is
what we vulgarly call, his being neceſſarily *Juſt and Good.* Not that *Juſtice and Goodneſs* are *Neceſſary* in him by a phyſical, natural and immediate *Neceſſity*, excluſive of
Will and Choice, in the ſame Senſe as his *Omnipreſence* or *Eternity* is Neceſſary; (For
then it would be no more proper to return him *Thanks* for the Exerciſe of his *Juſtice and
Goodneſs*, than for being *Eternal or Omnipreſent*; Which is manifeſtly abſurd.) But
the meaning of his being Neceſſarily *Juſt and Good*, is This only; that the *Liberty*
by which he always *chooſes* what is eternally and abſolutely right and good, can never
poſſibly be infringed, no not in the leaſt degree, by any Error or Paſſion, by any
Violence or by any Deceit. The Liberty of *Man*, therefore, conſiſts proportionably
in the very ſame things; in his being free from all thoſe falſe Biaſſes and corrupt Inclinations, which would cauſe his Will to decline from the Direction of Right Reaſon.
And where This Liberty is preſerved by good men to any conſiderable degree of Perfection, there the Holy Ghoſt is pleaſed to expreſs itſelf in ſuch manner even concerning *Them* alſo, as to affirm that they *cannot ſin*; 1 Joh. iii. 9. Which expreſſion is
therefore ſo far from implying their having *no Liberty* of Will at all, as ſome have
vainly imagined; that on the contrary, it ſignifies their having their *Liberty ſo perfect*,
in Imitation of God, as (abating the unavoidable infirmities of human Nature) to be in
no danger of being biaſſed or ſeduced. This is what our Saviour promiſes in the Text,
John viii. 32.　that if men will continue in his Word, then they *ſhall know the Truth, and the Truth
ſhall make them free.* And it ſufficiently makes good the general Doctrine I at firſt
drew from the Words; namely, that the *Religious Reſtraints* laid upon men by the
Goſpel, are really and truly the *greateſt Liberty*; and the *Service of God*, the moſt
perfect Freedom.

There are ſome other Senſes in Scripture, of the Words *Liberty* and *Bondage*;
which for the fuller underſtanding of the Text, in which they are all directly or indi-
rectly comprehended, deſerve briefly to be mentioned in this Place.

And 1*ſt*, Christian *Liberty*, in many places of Scripture, and principally in
St *Paul's* epiſtles, ſignifies deliverance from the Obligation of the Ceremonial law;
Acts xv. 10.　from that Yoke, *which neither our Fathers, nor we*, as it is elſewhere expreſſed, *were
able to bear.* Of This it is that he ſpeaks, when he tells us that we *have not received*
Rom. viii. 15.　the *Spirit of* Bondage *again, but the Spirit of Adoption*; that, *when we were children,
we were* in bondage *under the Elements of the World*; Gal. iv. 3; that *the Lord is
That Spirit; and where the Spirit of the Lord is, there is Liberty*; 2 Cor. iii. 17. The
expreſſion is difficult, and has been much miſunderſtood: But the meaning is, that
the Goſpel is the Spirit and End of the Law; and where the Spirit, or thing ſignified is fulfilled, there the type, or bare letter, is ſuperſeded, *The Lord is that Spirit; and where the Spirit of the Lord is, there is Liberty.* Of *This* alſo he is to be
underſtood in thoſe places, where he adviſes Chriſtians to beware of falſe brethren
Gal. ii. 4.　that would *ſpie out their Liberty*, and *bring them* again *into bondage*; to *ſtand faſt in*
v. 1.　　　　　　　　　　　　　　　　　　　　　　　　　　　　　　　　　　　　　　　*the*

S E R M.
XXXV.

Gal. v. 13.
1 Cor. viii. 9.
ix. 21.

the Liberty wherewith Chriſt had made them free, and not be intangled again with the yoke of bondage; not to uſe Liberty for an occaſion to the Fleſh; to take heed leſt by any means this Liberty of theirs, became a ſtumbling-block to them that are weak: And accordingly concerning *himſelf* he declares in this reſpect, that *To them that are without law, he* became *as without Law, yet being not without Law to God, but under the Law to Chriſt.* The meaning is, that though men were delivered by Chriſt, from the bondage of the *ceremonial* Law; yet were they by no means diſcharged from any *moral* Obligations. And the ſame is the intent of St *Peter*'s Exhortation, 1 Pet. ii. 16. *As free, and* yet *not uſing your* Liberty *for a cloak of Maliciouſneſs, but as the* Servants *of God.*

2*dly.* I N other places of Scripture, the *Freedom* of Chriſtians, ſignifies their Deliverance from the Bondage of that *Fear,* which was the conſequence of the Curſe and Severity of the Law. Of the Wicked it is ſaid, that they *flee, when no man purſueth;* and *are in great Fear,* even *where no Fear is.* Not that they have *no juſt* Cauſe of Fear; but on the contrary, becauſe they have always *ſo much reaſon* to be afraid, that it often ſhows forth itſelf even upon *improper* occaſions.

Prov. xxviii. 1.
Pſ. liii. 5.

B U T further; even with regard to thoſe, who *are not* notoriouſly wicked; their being under the Law, is in general called the *Spirit of Bondage to Fear,* Rom. viii. 15. And their Deliverance from that Fear by the gracious Terms of the Goſpel, is ſtiled *the Spirit of Adoption, whereby they cry Abba Father;* whereby they apply to God, not as to a ſtrict and ſevere Judge, but as to a merciful and reconciled Father. And as our Lord is ſaid to have *delivered* them, Heb. ii. 15. *who through Fear of Death were all their Life-time ſubject to Bondage.*

3*dly.* T H E *Liberty* of a Chriſtian, may alſo ſometimes very properly ſignify, his Deliverance from the Slavery of endleſs *Superſtition.* Of the Prophets of *Baal* it is recorded; 1 *Kings* xviii. 28; that *they cried aloud, and cut themſelves with knives and lancets, till the Blood guſhed out upon them:* And of ſome other Idolaters; that they *cauſed their own Children, to paſs through the Fire to Moloch.* Thoſe among the Heathen, who were leſs Cruel; yet were in perpetual Fear, of *Dreams* and *Omens,* and vain *Preſages;* and in continual Bondage to tedious and uſeleſs Obſervations. The Corrupters of Chriſtianity, have after the ſame Example, introduced an intolerable Burden of Pilgrimages and Abſtinencies, and voluntary Humilities; which *Who has required at their Hands?* All which things, when a reaſonable man ſeriouſly conſiders, he may very properly ask himſelf that Queſtion, which *Naaman*'s ſervant put to his Maſter; 2 *Kings* v. 13; *If God had bidden thee to do ſome great thing, wouldſt thou not have done it? How much rather then, when he ſaith unto thee, Waſh and be clean;* when he *only* ſaith unto thee, Repent and amend.

B U T 4*thly,* and *laſtly,* That which it chiefly and above all ſignifies in Scripture-phraſe, is (what I have applied it to in the foregoing diſcourſe) *Freedom* from the Slavery of *Sin.* So the Apoſtle expreſſly; *Rom.* vi. 18; *Being then made* Free from Sin, *ye became the Servants of Righteouſneſs;* Rom. viii. 2; *The Law of the Spirit of Life in Chriſt Jeſus, has made me free from the law of* Sin *and* Death; and *ver.* 21; *delivered from the* bondage *of Corruption, into the glorious liberty of the children of God.* Where this *Liberty* is improved to any conſiderable degree, the perſon is ſaid to be *dead* to *Sin;* in oppoſition to thoſe who on the contrary, for want of any improvement at all, are repreſented as *dead* in *Sin,* Rom. vi. 7; *He that is dead,* (or as it is explained by an eaſier Phraſe in the verſe before, he in whom *the* body of Sin is *deſtroyed,*) is *free from Sin;* and 1 Pet. iv. 1. *He that has ſuffered in the Fleſh,*

S E R M. *(viz.* he that has conquered his corrupt affections;) *has ceased from Sin.* That the
XXXV. Words, *suffered in the Flesh*, must in this place be understood thus, not literally but
⌇⌇⌇ figuratively, appears evidently from the following Words; *ver.* 2. *That he no longer*
should live the rest of his Time in the Flesh, *to the Lusts of Men, but to the Will*
of God. The *highest* improvement and perfection of this Liberty in the present
Life, is, when a man not only obeys the Commands of God, but does it habitually with ease and pleasure; when the *Commandments* of God seem *not grievous*
to him, but the *yoke* of Christ *easy*, and his *burden* light; when he can *delight to*
know the *Ways* of God, and *call* his *Sabbaths* a *delight*; If. lviii. 2, 13; when he can
Pf. cxix. 14, say with *Job*, ch. xxii. ver. 26; that he *has his delight in the Almighty*; with the
16, 24, 35, Psalmist; *Pf.* i. 2. that *his delight is in the Law of the Lord, and in his Law doth*
47, 70, 77, *he exercise himself day and night*; and with our Saviour himself; *Joh.* iv. 34. *My*
174. *meat is to do the Will of him that sent me, and to finish his Work.* When *This* is the
Case, which is the highest pitch of Christian Perfection upon Earth; then may it be
said of such a Person, that he *continueth in the perfect Law of Liberty*, Jam. i. 25;
ii. 12. Then may he cry out with the Psalmist, *Pf.* cxvi. 16; *O Lord, I am thy*
servant and the son of thine handmaid, thou hast broken my Bonds in sunder; And *I*
will walk at Liberty, *for I seek thy commandments*; Pf. cxix. 45. Then is fulfilled
That Prophecy, *If.* lxi. 1, applied by our Saviour to Himself, *Luke* iv. 18; *He has*
anointed me to preach the Gospel to the Poor,——to preach deliverance to the cap-
tives,——to set at Liberty *them that are bruised.* Lastly, of such a Person, who
thus delights to do the Will of God, it may be declared, though he *be a Servant*,
that *yet he is the Lord's free Man,* 1 Cor. vii. 22; that because *the Son* has *made him*
free, therefore *he is free indeed*; Jo. viii. 36; or (as it is in the Words of the Text,)
that *he knows the Truth, and the Truth doth make him Free.*

S E R M O N

SERMON XXXVI.

A Virtuous Mind the beft Help to underftand True Religion.

DAN. XII. 10. latter part.

And none of the Wicked fhall underftand ; But the Wife fhall underftand.

TO feek a man's true and final Intereft, by parting with fome prefent and in- SERM. confiderable Advantages for the fake of more and much greater ones to come, XXXVI. is the proper Act of *Wifdom*; and the general Character of *Folly*, is the purchafing fome trivial prefent Benefit, at the hazard of much better and more valuable things in reverfion. For This reafon, in Scripture-phrafe, *Religion and Virtue* are almoft always fignified under the denomination of *Wifdom*; and *Folly*, is but another Name for *Sin*. The *Sinner* and *the Fool*, are always reciprocal Terms ; and no man is ftiled *Wife* by the Spirit of God, upon any other account than that of being *Religious*. For *unto man he faid ; The Fear of the Lord, That is Wifdom ; and to depart from Evil, is Underftanding* ; Job xxviii. 28. And This is fo much the *known* language of Scripture, that I need in this place but juft mention it. Thus *Ecclef.* ii. 13 ; *Then I faw*, fays Solomon, *that Wifdom excelleth Folly, as far as Light excelleth Darknefs* ; the meaning is, that Religion and Virtue is *as much more* excellent and more profitable to men than Wickednefs, as one thing can *be* preferable to another. And in the Words of the Text ; *None of the* Wicked *fhall underftand : But the* Wife, (thofe who are fuch in *oppofition to* the Folly of Wickednefs, that is, the *Righteous) fhall underftand*.

To *Underftand*, may be taken in two Senfes ; Either to fignify the underftanding of thefe *particular* Prophecies ; or the underftanding the true nature of Religion in *general*. In *Both* thefe Senfes, the Words are very proper and emphatical ; and in *Both*, they are very remarkably fulfilled. If we take them in the *former* Senfe ; *None of the Wicked fhall underftand* ; i. e. none of them fhall apprehend the true meaning and intent of thefe Prophecies ; *But the Wife*, viz. the *righteous* and well-difpofed, the careful and diligent inquirers, *fhall underftand them* : If we take them, I fay, in This Senfe, then They were very remarkably fulfilled upon the *Jews* in our Saviour's time ; who, notwithftanding that this Prophecy of *Daniel* contained as clear a Prediction as could be defired, of the *Time* and *Manner* of our Saviour's appearing in the Flefh ; yet through their obftinate prejudices againft *Him* and his *doctrine*, they refolved *not to fee* it : And becaufe there were other paffages in the Prophecy, more *obfcure*, and *difficult* to be interpreted ; therefore they would by no means be perfwaded to underftand what was *plain*. The like to which, has exactly happened among *Chriftians* alfo. For whereas in the New Teftament, there are very many Prophecies, and as exprefs as can be ; of a Man of Sin to be revealed ; of a general Defection and Apoftacy in the latter times ; of a Worldly Power fitting in the Seat of God, and prefuming to change Laws and Times, and compelling the *whole World* to worfhip him, by fubmitting to his ar-

3 bitrary

S E R M. bitrary and unreaſonable Power; and that the Head of this Corruption is that great
XXXVI. City which ruleth over the Kingdoms of the Earth: yet becauſe there are indeed other
paſſages in the Prophetick part of the New Teſtament, more obſcure and difficult;
therefore thoſe of the Church of *Rome*, and as many as favour their abſurd pretenſions,
reſolve they will not underſtand the cleareſt Deſcriptions of things; but *will* continue
to make Temporal Power, Riches and Grandeur, a Mark or Note of the *True* Church;
when the Scripture on the contrary expreſsly makes it a Mark of the *Falſe* one, perſecuting and ſcattering the true Worſhippers of God.

But *ſecondly*; if we take the Words of the Text in the *latter* ſenſe, to expreſs
Men's Underſtanding, not of theſe *particular* Prophecies, but of the true Nature of
Religion *in general*; they are then evidently fulfilled in the greater part of Men. *None
of the Wicked underſtand*; *But the Wiſe*, that is, the *Righteous*, do *underſtand*. And
This being the moſt *generally uſeful* Senſe of the Words, I ſhall in the following Diſcourſe conſider them according to *This* Interpretation. And ſo the Propoſition they
contain, is This: That a *virtuous Diſpoſition of Mind* is the *beſt Help*, and a *vitious
inclination the greateſt Hindrance*, to a *right Underſtanding* of the *Doctrine of True
Religion. None of the Wicked ſhall underſtand; But the Wiſe ſhall Underſtand.*

For the clearer Proof and Illuſtrating of which Propoſition, it may be proper to
conſider diſtinctly the Two following particulars: 1ſt, What there is in the *Nature
of Things themſelves*; and 2dly, What there is in the poſitive *Appointment of God*;
which makes a *virtuous Diſpoſition* ſo great a *Help*, and a *vitious Inclination* ſo great a
Hindrance, to a *Right Underſtanding* in *Matters of Religion*.

In the 1ſt place, there is ſomething in the *Nature of Things themſelves*, ſomething
in the very *Frame* and Conſtitution of the *Mind of Man*, ſomething in the *Nature and
Tendency* of all *Religious Truths*; which helps to verify the general Propoſition. In a
Mind virtuouſly diſpoſed, there is a native *agreeableneſs* to the *Principles of true Religion*; in like manner as in a healthful *Body*, the *Organs* are fitted to their proper *Objects*; and as in the Frame of the Material *World*, every thing is ſuited and adjuſted to
its proper *Uſe* and *Employment*. A *well-diſpoſed* Mind does as naturally entertain the
great *Truths* of Religion, as the *Eye* diſcerns *Colours*, and the *Palate* reliſhes *Taſtes*; or
as *good Ground* receives *good Seed*, and feeds and nouriſhes it till it brings forth much
Fruit. It is our Saviour's own Compariſon, St *Luke* viii. 15. *Thoſe on the* good ground
are they, who in an honeſt and good heart, *having heard the Word, keep it, and bring
forth Fruit with Patience.* And in other places of Scripture, perſons of ſuch a diſpoſition, are, upon the ſame account, ſaid to be, not *ordained*, as we falſely render the

Acts xiii. 48. Word, but *prepared* or *diſpoſed* for *eternal Life*; and that God daily added to his
Acts ii. 47.   Church, not *ſuch as* ſhould be *ſaved*, (though that alſo is true) but *ſuch as* were *ſaved*,
(ſo the original Word ſignifies;) namely, ſuch as were beforehand *qualified and well in-
clined*, to ſave themſelves from a wicked generation, by embracing the Doctrine of the
Goſpel of Chriſt. Our Saviour elſewhere calls ſuch Perſons his *Sheep, that will hear

Joh. x. 27.   his Voice*; and ſays of them, that they are *Drawn by* his *Father*, before they *come to
vi. 44.   Him*; that is, that by a Love to the Truth of God *in general*, they are fitted to receive
that Revelation of his Will, made by the Goſpel *in particular*. In the Study of every
Humane Science, there is ſome particular previous Temper, ſome certain Prediſpoſition
of Mind, which makes men fit for that particular Study, and apt to underſtand it with
Eaſineſs and Delight: Generally and Principally, a *Love* to that particular Science,
and a high Eſteem of its Value and Uſefulneſs. The ſame holds true in proportion,
in *Religious* Matters likewiſe. A general love of Virtue; an equitable, fair, and charitable Spirit; and a juſt Senſe of the Neceſſity and Reaſonableneſs of obeying God's
Commands, is the firſt Principle and Beginning of Religion; the beſt and great preparative to open the Underſtanding, to make men ſtudy with pleaſure, and comprehend

hend with Eaſe, and judge with right Diſcernment of Divine Truths. *The Fear of* S E R M
the Lord, ſays the Pſalmiſt, *is the* Beginning *of Wiſdom : A good Underſtanding have* XXXVI.
all they that do his Commandments ; *The Praiſe thereof endureth for ever.*; Pſ. cxi. 10.
And *Solomon,* who in his Knowledge of the Workings of the Mind of Man, as well as
in other Sciences, had no Superior, lays down the ſame Maxim, *Prov.* i. 7. *The
Fear of the Lord is the* Beginning *of Knowledge*; and repeats it again as the Foundation
of all Inſtruction, ch. ix. ver. 10. *The Fear of the Lord is the* beginning of *Wiſdom* ;
and the Knowledge of the Holy, is Underſtanding. The Author of the Book of *Ecclus.*
with the variation of One Word only, expreſſes likewiſe the ſame Senſe ; *ch.* i. *ver.* 14,
20. *The* Root *of Wiſdom, is to fear the Lord.* The *Root* ; that is to ſay, the firſt
Ground and Principle, the firſt Capacity and Diſpoſition to receive Religious Truths ;
that which makes the *Mind* ſuſceptible and apt to apprehend them ; that which makes
them eaſy and pleaſant to be underſtood. *For Wiſdom* goeth about, *ſeeking ſuch as are* Wiſd. vi. 16,
worthy of her ; *ſhe ſheweth herſelf favourably unto them in the Ways, and meeteth them* 17, 14.
in every thought : For the very true Beginning *of her, is the* Deſire *of Diſcipline*———
*And whoſo ſeeketh her early, ſhall have no great travel, for he ſhall find her ſitting at
his Doors.*

F U R T H E R ; as a *virtuous Diſpoſition of Mind* is the beſt *preparative* for *beginning*
the Study of Religion ; ſo *Practice and Experience* in the *courſe* of a Virtuous Life and
in the Obedience of God's Commands, is in *continuance* the beſt *information* and perpetual *improvement* of a man's *Underſtanding and Judgment* in the Knowledge of Divine
Truths. *He that* keepeth *the Law of the Lord, getteth the Underſtanding thereof,*
ſays the wiſe Son of *Sirach* ; *and the perfection of the Fear of the Lord, is Wiſdom,*
Eccluſ. xxi. 11. *Evil men underſtand not judgment* ; *but they that ſeek the Lord, underſtand all things,* Prov. xxviii. 5. He that practiſes what he knows, improves his Knowledge continually by that Practice ; and by Actions, even more than by Speculation and
Study, is the underſtanding of practical Truths inlarged. In the common Affairs of
the preſent Life, it is obvious that Men of Buſineſs, Experience and Diligence, are generally much better Judges in their proper Employments, than Others who for Parts
and Learning may perhaps in other reſpects be eſteemed much ſuperiour. And ſo it is
likewiſe in Matters of Religion. Not the Wiſe and Crafty, not the learned and profound, not the ſubtle Arguers in Speculation and Diſpute, are the beſt Inſtructors in the
Duty of a Chriſtian ; but, in theſe matters, rather *the mouth of the* Juſt, (ſays *Solomon,*)
bringeth forth Wiſdom, and the Lips of the Righteous *know what is acceptable,* Prov. x.
31, 32. There is a Spirit and a Life in the Diſcourſe of a Righteous Man, proceeding
from the Sincerity of an Upright Heart ; which no Skill nor Art can imitate. There
is a Knowledge and Diſcernment ariſing from virtuous Practice, which another man
cannot learn from him that has it, but by *going* himſelf and *doing likewiſe.* The Pure
in Heart ſee God *here,* as well as *hereafter,* after *another* manner, than vitious and profane Philoſophers argue about him. And as, with regard to *worldly* Employments,
men of Parts and Learning can diſpute and contend about them, without underſtanding them ; but Thoſe only are truly ſkilful, who have exerciſed themſelves in the
Practice of the particular Employments : So in *Religion,* there is no man truly wiſe
and knowing, but he that has *lived* like a Chriſtian, inſtead of diſputing about it. When
ſome of the *Jews,* moved with the Wiſdom and Excellency of our Saviour's Diſcourſes,
believed on him by a ſudden Impulſe of unexperienced Affection ; our Saviour, knowing the Weakneſs of the Ground of their Faith, ſaid unto them, *If ye* continue *in my
Word,* then—*ye ſhall know the Truth, and the Truth ſhall make you free,* St Joh. viii. 31 ;
free, from the ſlavery of unreaſonable Luſts and Paſſions ; *free,* from the Darkneſs of
Ignorance and Errors. *The Wiſe* ſhall *underſtand.*

V O L. I.   M m m   O N

SERM.
XXXVI.

On the contrary, in the Nature of *Vicious Inclinations*, and in the Practice of *all Wickedneſs*, there is ſomething *neceſſarily repugnant*, ſomething that in the *nature of things* will be a hindrance and impediment to a right Underſtanding in matters of Religion: *None of the Wicked ſhall underſtand*. A *vicious Diſpoſition* blinds mens Eyes, corrupts their Principles, and ſubverts their Judgment; it cauſes, that men have *Eyes and ſee not, Ears and hear not, Underſtandings* and yet *do not underſtand*. They *become vain in their Imaginations*, as St *Paul* expreſſeth it, *Rom.* i. 21. *and their fooliſh heart is darkned*. They have a *reprobate mind*, Rom. i. 28. The Word in the original ſignifies, an *injudicious mind*; a mind deſpoiled of its right Judgment, and of its natural Power of diſcerning. They have, as the ſame Apoſtle elſewhere elegantly deſcribes them, *their Underſtandings* darkned,——*becauſe of the Blindneſs of their Hearts*. A Perſon in *this* ſtate; *the natural man*, as St *Paul* calls him; (ſo we render the Word, 1 *Cor.* ii. 14. but it ought to be tranſlated, *the Senſual man*;) *a man wholly taken up with the Cares and Pleaſures of the preſent Life*; ſuch a one *receiveth not the things of the Spirit of God*, he underſtands them not, has no reliſh of them; *for they are fooliſhneſs unto him*; *neither* can *he know them, becauſe they are ſpiritually diſcerned*: ſpiritually *diſcerned*; i. e. diſcerned by *Thoſe* only, who have Faculties to diſcern them with; by *Thoſe*, whoſe Minds are not blinded with the Love of Wickedneſs. St *John* gives us an emphatical Inſtance of This in one particular Vice, that of *Hatred and Malice*; which whoſoever is addicted to, he tells us is no more capable of underſtanding the Doctrine of the Goſpel, that Doctrine of Love and univerſal Charity, than a man whoſe Eyes are ſhut, is able to diſcern the Light: *He that hateth his Brother, is in darkneſs, and walketh in darkneſs, and knoweth not whither he goeth, becauſe that Darkneſs has blinded his Eyes*, 1 *Joh.* ii. 11. No Words can expreſs in a more lively and emphatical manner, than this Deſcription does, the incredible ſtupidity of ſuch Chriſtians as think they do God good Service by perſecuting one another, and expect to propagate the peaceable and charitable Doctrine of Jeſus Chriſt by Arbitrarineſs, Violence and Force. And the ſame may be ſaid, in proportion, of all *other* Vices; Whoſoever is engaged in *Any* vitious habit, he is thereby made *blind*, and *walketh in Darkneſs*. Our Saviour repreſents to us the ſame thing, by another the like elegant ſimilitude; comparing vicious men to perſons that are *deaf* and *cannot hear*; St *Joh.* viii. 43. *Why do ye not underſtand my Speech? even becauſe ye* cannot hear *my Words*; For *Ye are of your Father the Devil, and the Luſts of your Father ye will do*. The meaning of this difficult Text, by comparing it with that now cited from St *John's* Firſt Epiſtle, appears very evident. For here our Saviour in a very expreſſive manner deſcribes the unfitneſs of the malicious *Phariſees* to receive his Doctrine, by ſaying that they were *deaf* and *could not hear his Words*; juſt as St *John* in the other place repreſents the incapacity of uncharitable men to underſtand the Goſpel, by declaring that they are *blind* and *walk in Darkneſs*. And when This is the Caſe, (as it is too plainly the Caſe of moſt Wicked men,) it is no wonder if they run into unaccountable Extravagancies. Hence, among the *Heathen*, thoſe who *knew God*, yet *glorified him not as God, but changed the glory of the uncorruptible God into an image made like to corruptible man, and to birds and beaſts and creeping things*, Rom. i. 21. Hence the *Jews in the* Wilderneſs, though they knew God, not only by the Light of *Nature*, but by clear *Revelation* alſo; yet even *They* likewiſe ſo far corrupted themſelves, as to *change their Glory*, i. e. the *True God*, whom They alone of all Nations upon the Face of the Earth had the Privilege more immediately to ſerve; even *They* changed this their Glory, *into the ſimilitude of a Calf that eateth Hay*, Pſ. cvi. 20. Hence the *Jews in our* Saviour's time, when they could not deny the Greatneſs of his Miracles, aſcribed them to *Beelzebub* the Prince of Devils; and, after they had ſaid, *Let him now come down from the Croſs and we will believe him*, yet, after his Reſurrection, which was a much *greater*

Miracle,

Eph. iv. 18.

Miracle, they ſtill continued to disbelieve. Thus through *Blindneſs* it comes to paſs, that *none of the Wicked do underſtand.*

B U T further : A Wicked diſpoſition not only *blinds* men, and hinders them from conſidering, prevents their examining things, and cauſes them to overlook even the ſtrongeſt Evidence; but it moreover *prejudices* them *Againſt* the Truth, and cauſes them even to *hate* it, and become profeſſed *Enemies* to it.   They hate *to be reformed*; and therefore *caſt God's words behind them*, Pſ. l. 17. Their *carnal mind is* even enmity *againſt God*; and therefore *is not ſubject to the Law of God, neither indeed can be,* Rom. viii. 7.   A perſon that gives them the beſt Advice in the World, may come to be looked upon as their *Enemy*, for that very reaſon, *becauſe he tells them the Truth,* Gal. iv. 16. They will knowingly chuſe and love *Darkneſs rather than Light, becauſe their deeds are evil*, St Joh. iii. 19. and reject the Truth for no other cauſe, but only becauſe they *have* pleaſure *in unrighteouſneſs*, 2 Theſſ. ii. 12.   And This is an effectual Reaſon indeed, why none of *ſuch* wicked perſons can *underſtand*.   But where This is *not* the caſe, yet at leaſt by any intervening worldly conſideration, working upon their Ambition, Covetouſneſs, or any other Paſſion; they will certainly be hindred from apprehending the Truth.   To the Queſtion propoſed, St Joh. vii. 48, *Have any of the* Rulers *or* Phariſees *believed on him?* the Anſwer is given, *ch.* xii. *ver.* 43, *They loved the praiſe of Men, more than the Praiſe of God;* and *ch.* v. *ver.* 44. *How can ye believe, which receive Honour one of another, and ſeek not the Honour which cometh from God only?* The Jews, to *this day*, have *the Veil remaining* upon their Heart, principally through their expecting a *temporal* Meſſiah, to exalt them in the ſplendor and glory of this World : And it is too ſad a Truth, that one of the principal *Hindrances* of the *Reformation* of erroneous Doctrines and Practices among Chriſtians; ſuch as *Tranſubſtantiation, Purgatory, Indulgences, Prayers for the Dead,* and the like; is their being *profitable* to, and tending to promote unreaſonable and unjuſt *Power in* thoſe that maintain them.   Where ſuch Worldly Intereſts and Paſſions interpoſe, it is no wonder that Men underſtand not the Force even of the ſtrongeſt reaſoning : *They are like the deaf Adder that ſtoppeth her ear; which refuſeth to hear the voice of the charmer, charm he never ſo wiſely,* Pſ. lviii. 4.   There is One thing further, and not ſo commonly taken notice of, by which an *Evil Diſpoſition* hinders right Underſtanding in matters of Religion; and That is, that it promotes *contentious Diſputes* about *needleſs Intricacies,* for the ſake of Pride, Vain-glory or Profit; and in order to impoſe upon other mens Belief uncertain Opinions, which confound and darken the plaineſt Truths.   Theſe St *Paul* calls *fooliſh queſtions*——and *contentious*——which are *unprofitable and vain; ſtriving about words to no profit, but to the ſubverting of the Hearers; profane and vain bablings, and oppoſitions of Science falſely ſo called,* and *which will increaſe unto more ungodlineſs; profane and old wives fables; Fables and commandments of Men, that turn from the Truth; fooliſh and unlearned queſtions, that gender ſtrifes; Fables and endleſs genealogies, which miniſter queſtions rather than godly edifying.*   And perſons who by Heat and Dogmaticalneſs, and by Zeal for uncertain Opinions without due inquiry and examination, cauſe or promote ſuch Contentions; he calls *proud, knowing nothing, but doting about queſtions and ſtrifes of words, whereof cometh envy, ſtrife, railings, evil ſurmiſings, perverſe diſputings of men of corrupt minds, and deſtitute of the Truth, ſuppoſing that gain is Godlineſs,* 1 Tim. vi. 4; and declares that they *have a Form* only *of Godlineſs, but deny the Power thereof*;——*reſiſting the Truth,* being *men of corrupt minds, and reprobate concerning the Faith,* 2 Tim. iii. 5, 8.   Which natural Effects of *Contentiouſneſs* and vain *Diſputes* in order to impoſe upon each other our own Opinions, are probably in great part the true reaſon from whence it comes to paſs, that *not many wiſe men after the Fleſh, not many mighty, not many noble are called; But God has choſen the fooliſh things of the world, to confound the wiſe;* and

the

2 Cor. iii. 14.

Tit. iii. 9.
2 Tim. ii. 14.
1 Tim. vi. 20.
2 Tim. ii. 16.
1 Tim. iv. 7.
Tit. i. 14.
2 Tim. ii. 23.
1 Tim. i. 4.

S E R M.
XXXVI. *the weak things of the world, to confound the things that are mighty;* 1 Cor. i. 26. *Not many wiſe men after the Fleſh;* i. e. not many of thoſe whom *the World* generally eſteemed *wiſe,* for their being able by ſubtle diſputes to perplex and make intricate even the plaineſt Truths; but the men of Integrity and Plainneſs, of Sincerity and Simplicity of Heart, men of fair and equitable Principles, univerſally charitable and Lovers of *1 Cor. iii. 18.* Mankind, *Theſe* were the Perſons that embraced the Goſpel of Chriſt. And this ſeems to be the Ground and Meaning of that affectionate Thankſgiving of our Saviour's, St *Matt.* xi. 25. *I thank thee, O Father, Lord of Heaven and Earth, becauſe thou haſt hid theſe things from the Wiſe and Prudent,* (that is, from the Cunning or Crafty,) *and haſt revealed them unto Babes;* (to Men of unprejudiced Plainneſs and uncorrupt Integrity;) *Even ſo, Father, for ſo it ſeemed good in thy ſight:* And of his declaring accordingly to his Diſciples, St *Luke* xviii. 17, *Verily I ſay unto you, Whoſoever ſhall not receive the Kingdom of God as a little Child, ſhall in no wiſe enter therein.*

A N D thus much concerning the *firſt* general Head, namely, what there is in the *Nature* of *Things Themſelves,* which makes a virtuous *Diſpoſition* ſo great a *Help,* and a *vicious Inclination* ſo great a *Hindrance,* to a *right Underſtanding* in matters of *Religion.*

T H E *ſecond* thing to be conſidered, was, What there is moreover in the *poſitive Appointment* and *Conſtitution* of God, by which we are aſſured that *None of the Wicked ſhall underſtand, but the Wiſe* (in oppoſition to the Folly of Wickedneſs, *i. e. the Righteous) ſhall underſtand.* And here the Scripture declares, 1ſt, *in general,* that by *ſome* means or other, by ſome or *other* Method of Providence in the Government of the World, God *will* take care, that righteous and piouſly-diſpoſed perſons *ſhall* attain to *ſo much* Underſtanding as is *neceſſary* for their own particular Salvation : That *the Meek, God* will *guide in Judgment;* and *ſuch as are gentle, them he* will teach *his way,* Pſ. xxv. 9. That *God* will *give to a man that is good in his ſight, Wiſdom and Knowledge, and Joy,* Eccleſ. ii. 26. That though *Heaven is his Throne, and Earth is his Footſtool,* yet on ſuch a one he *will* vouchſafe to *look,* even on *him that is poor and of a contrite Spirit, and trembleth at* his *Word,* Iſa. lxvi. 1, 2. That *if any man will do his Will, he* ſhall *know of the doctrine whether it be of God,* St *Joh.* vii. 17. And upon *this* are founded thoſe frequent exhortations in Scripture, *Prov.* ii. 1, 5; *My Son, if thou wilt* receive *my Words, and* hide my Commandments *with thee;*——then *ſhalt thou* underſtand *the fear of the Lord, and* find the Knowledge *of God;*——*For the Lord giveth Wiſdom,*——*he layeth up ſound Wiſdom for the Righteous.* Again, *Eccluſ.* i. 26, *If thou deſire Wiſdom,* keep the Commandments, *and the Lord* ſhall give *her unto thee; For the Fear of the Lord is Wiſdom and Inſtruction, and Faith and Meekneſs are his delight.* St *Jam.* i. 5, *If any of you lack Wiſdom, let him ask of God,*—— *and it* ſhall *be given him :* And *Epheſ.* v. 14; *Awake thou that ſleepeſt, and ariſe from the dead,* (viz. from the Death of *Sin,*) *and Chriſt* ſhall give *thee Light.* St *Paul* himſelf was a great example of this Doctrine; whom, becauſe of the ſincerity of his Zeal, God was pleaſed to convert even by a Miracle : For having been ſo impoſed upon as to think that Religion could be propagated by Perſecution and Violence, he juſtly ſtiled himſelf the greateſt of Sinners. But yet for the ſincerity of his Intention, the pious Centurion *Cornelius,* was inſtructed by an Angel ſent from Heaven ; and the *Ethiopian* Eunuch was taught by an Apoſtle ſent to him on purpoſe ; And concerning *all* the Diſciples, when one of them aſked our Lord, *How is it that thou wilt manifeſt thyſelf to Us, and not unto the World?* He replied, St *Joh.* xiv. 23. *If a man* love *me, he will keep my Words, and my Father will love him, and we will come unto him, and make our abode with him.*

But *2dly,* T H E Scripture declares further *in particular,* that, by the *ſecret aſſiſtance of his Holy Spirit,* God will peculiarly direct and enlighten thoſe that are truly ſincere.

1 *Joh.*

4

1 *Joh.* ii. 20, *Ye have an Unction from the Holy One, and ye know all things.* Again, **S E R M.**
Acts v. 32,—*the Holy Ghoſt, which God has given to them that* obey *him :*—the Holy **XXXVI.**
Ghoſt, who is the Spirit of *Truth,* the Spirit given firſt to the Apoſtles, and afterwards
to all good men in proportion, to lead them into *all* (that is, into *all neceſſary*) *Truth.*
And This, I ſuppoſe, is the meaning of thoſe paſſages of Scripture : *The froward is an
abomination to the Lord ; but his* Secret *is with the righteous.* Prov. iii. 32. *The* Secret
of the Lord is with them that fear him, and he will ſhow them his Covenant, Pſ. xxv. 14.
And *Many are in high places, and of renown : but Myſteries are revealed unto the
Meek,* Eccluſ. iii. 19.

On the contrary, where there is a *vicious Inclination* and an *Affection to Wickedneſs*;
there mens minds are not only blinded by the natural conſequence of ſuch a diſpoſition,
but God moreover withdraws his Spirit from them, and the Holy Ghoſt will not dwell
in a Heart that takes pleaſure in Unrighteouſneſs. *For into a malicious Soul Wiſdom
ſhall not enter, nor dwell in the Body that is ſubject unto Sin ; For the Holy Spirit of
Diſcipline will flee deceit, and remove from Thoughts that are without Underſtanding,
and will not abide when Unrighteouſneſs cometh in,* Wiſd. i. 4. Nay, not only ſo ; but,
where men are obſtinately incorrigible, God is repreſented in Scripture as juſtly giving
them up *in judgment* to be *deceived* by the *Evil One,* that for a deſerved puniſhment
they may increaſe unto more Ungodlineſs. Rev. xx. 8, *Satan* is deſcribed as being let
looſe, that he may *go out to deceive the Nations :* And the deſtruction of Wicked *Ahab,*
is thus eloquently repreſented in a moſt lively Image by the Prophet *Micaiah,* 1 Kings
xxii. 19, *I ſaw the Lord ſitting on his throne, and all the hoſt of Heaven ſitting by him
on his right hand and on his left. And the Lord ſaid, Who ſhall perſwade,* (in the original it is, *Who ſhall* deceive) *Ahab, that he may go up and fall at Ramoth-Gilead?
and one ſaid on this manner, and another ſaid on that manner. And there came forth a
Spirit, and ſtood before the Lord, and ſaid, I will perſwade him; and the Lord ſaid
unto him, Wherewith? And he ſaid, I will go forth, and be a lying Spirit in the mouth
of all his Prophets; And he ſaid, Thou ſhalt perſwade him and prevail alſo; Go forth,
and do ſo.* The Repreſentation is highly figurative, and by no means to be underſtood
literally ; But the meaning is, that God juſtly permits Wicked men when they obſtinately refuſe to hear *Him,* he permits them to be deceived by the *Evil One* to their
own deſtruction. The like expreſſion is uſed, *Judg.* ix. 23, God ſent *an Evil Spirit
between Abimelech and the men of Shechem :* The meaning is, as it is explained in the
following words, God permitted *Abimelech* to be *deceived* and *dealt treacherouſly with*
by the men of *Shechem,* that his *cruelty* and the *blood* which he had ſhed might *come
upon* him. 'Tis nothing more, but an acknowledgment of the Juſtice and Wiſdom of
Providence, in ſuffering Wicked men to be judicially blinded, that they may fall according to their deſerts. *With him is Strength and Wiſdom, the Deceived and Deceiver
are his ;——He removeth away the Speech of the Truſty, and taketh away the Underſtanding of the Aged* from them : *Job* xii. 16, 20. The Heathen World, becauſe they
did *not like to retain God in their Knowledge,* therefore *God gave them up* to *Uncleanneſs,*
and to *vile affections,* and to a *reprobate (i. e.* an *undiſcerning) mind,* Rom. i. 24, 26,
28. *Joſh.* xi. 20. *Deut.* ii. 30. *Pharaoh,* becauſe of his obſtinate Wickedneſs, *God
hardned his Heart,* i. e. ſuffered his Underſtanding to be more and more blinded, that
he ſhould not *ſee* the Tendency of God's wonderful Judgments worked in *Egypt.* The
ſame Phraſe is uſed of the people of the Jews, *If.* lxiii. 17, *Thou haſt* hardned *our
Heart from thy Fear ;* or, as it is, *ch.* vi. 10, Make *the Heart of this people fat——
leſt they underſtand with their Heart, and convert and be healed.* The *Meaning* is expreſſed at large, *ch.* xxix. 13, 10, *Foraſmuch as this people draw near me with their
mouth,——but have removed their Heart far from me ;* Therefore, *behold, I will proceed to do a marvellous work among this people ;——The Wiſdom of their Wiſe men ſhall*

SERM. *periſh, and the Underſtanding of their prudent men ſhall be hid;——The Lord has poured*
XXXVI. *out upon you the Spirit of deep ſleep, and has cloſed your Eyes.* And *Ezek.* xiv. 5, 6, 9,
Rom. xi. 8. *Becauſe they are all eſtranged from me by their Idols,* Therefore *ſay unto the houſe of
Iſrael,——If a prophet be deceived when he has ſpoken a thing; I the Lord have de-
ceived that prophet, and I will ſtretch out my hand upon him, and will deſtroy him from
the midſt of my people Iſrael.* The like Expreſſions are uſed in the *New Teſtament,* con-
Rev. xvii. 17. cerning corrupt *Chriſtians; He that is unjuſt, let him be unjuſt ſtill; and he which is
Rev. xxii. 11. filthy, let him be filthy ſtill; and he that is righteous, let him be righteous ſtill; and he
that is holy, let him be holy ſtill.* And *God ſhall* put *it into their hearts to deliver their
Kingdom and Power unto the Beaſt.* And 2 *Theſſ.* ii. 10, *Becauſe they received not the
Love of the Truth,——for this cauſe God ſhall ſend them ſtrong Deluſion, that they ſhould
believe a Lye; That they all might be damned who believed not the Truth, but had plea-
ſure in unrighteouſneſs :* And, 2 *Tim.* iii. 13, *Evil men and ſeducers ſhall wax worſe and
worſe, deceiving and being deceived.* All which paſſages, are as it were Paraphraſes and
Illuſtrations of the Words of the Text; *None of the Wicked ſhall underſtand, but the
Wiſe ſhall underſtand.*

FROM what has been ſaid, we may *infer,* 1*ſt,* That *Wicked* men have no *reaſon to
complain,* for their not being able to *underſtand* Religion; and *Infidels* no *Excuſe,* for
their not *believing* it. *For God who commanded the Light to ſhine out of Darkneſs, hath
ſhined in our Hearts, to give the light of the Knowledge of the glory of God, in the face of
Jeſus Chriſt : But if our Goſpel be hid, 'tis hid to them that are loſt; In whom the God
of this World has blinded the minds of them which believe not, leſt the light of the glorious
Goſpel of Chriſt, who is the Image of God, ſhould ſhine unto them.* 2 Cor. iv. 6, 3, 4.

2*dly,* FROM hence appears the Reaſon of our Saviour's ſpeaking ſo much in Parables. To the *Wiſe* and well-diſpoſed, it was *given to know the Myſtery of the Kingdom
of God; but to others (i. e. to the Wicked) he ſpake in Parables, that ſeeing they might
not ſee, and hearing they might not underſtand :* And thence our Saviour ſo frequently
at the end of his Parables cried out; *He that has Ears to hear, let him hear;* and, *He
that can receive it, let him receive it.* And *he that hath an Ear, let him hear, what
the Spirit ſaith unto the Churches.*

3*dly,* FROM what has been ſaid, we may obſerve, how it comes to paſs, that
Faith, which is generally looked upon as an Act of the *Underſtanding,* and ſo not in
our own Power, is yet in the *New Teſtament* always required and inſiſted upon as a
Moral Virtue. The reaſon is, becauſe *Faith,* in the Scripture-ſenſe, is not barely an
Act of the *Underſtanding,* but a mixt Act of the *Will* alſo; conſiſting very much in
that *Simplicity and Unprejudicedneſs* of Mind which our Saviour calls *receiving the
Kingdom of God as a little child;* in that freedom from *guile and deceit,* which was
the character of *Nathaniel,* an *Iſraelite* indeed; and in that *teachable diſpoſition* or *Deſire to know the Will of God,* for which the *Bereans* were ſo highly commended, who
ſearched the Scriptures daily, whether thoſe things the Apoſtle taught, *were ſo or not.*
They are commended for not believing on the *Authority* even of the Apoſtles. But

4*thly,* FROM hence it appears, that there is no need of an *Infallible Guide on Earth,*
or of an *unerring Church.* For all neceſſary Truth is ſufficiently made known in Scripture; and one great part of our Chriſtian Duty, is to *ſtudy* the Will of God with ſuch a
Diſpoſition of Mind, as may entitle us to the Promiſe given in the Text, that *the Wiſe*
ſhall *underſtand.*

5*thly* and *Laſtly,* YET This muſt be ſo underſtood, as to be a Security, not againſt
All, but againſt *Fatal Miſtakes.* The beſt and piouſeſt perſons, may in many things
err; but their *Errors* cannot be dangerous, or of final ill conſequence : For in things
abſolutely neceſſary to Salvation, the *Wicked* only can be void of Underſtanding. *None
of the Wicked ſhall underſtand; But the Wiſe ſhall underſtand.*

SERMON

SERMON XXXVII.

The Practice of Morality leads to the Practice of the Gospel.

JOH. VI. 44.

No man can come to Me, except the Father which has sent Me, draw him.

THE *Duty* and *Happiness* of rational Creatures, is the Practice of Righteouf-nefs and true Virtue, founded upon a Belief of the Being and Government of God; whofe *Kingdom* over rational Creatures confifts, in the conformity of their Wills and Actions to the Nature and Life of God; each in their feveral Stations, according to the Degree of Light and Knowledge which they injoy, indeavouring to approve themfelves to him by a chearful Obedience to his Commands; and conftantly promoting the Great Ends of his Government by preferving the Harmony of the *Moral* World, in like manner as the Wifdom of his Government over the *Natural and Material* World is fhown forth in the regularity of all its Motions. By *Sin*, Moral Agents oppofe and bring diforder into this Kingdom of God; which the inferior part of the Creation, having no Liberty of Choice, is not capable of doing. And they who thus oppofe God's Kingdom of Righteoufnefs, become thereby *Enemies* to God, and alienated from his Favour. Neverthelefs, man being a frail and fallible Creature, liable to be feduced, tempted and deceived; and there being, in the cafe of moft Sinners, many Circumftances that excite Pity and Compaffion; therefore God does not immediately caft them off, but generally allows them Space and Time for Repentance. And for this very End did he fend his Son, our Lord Jefus Chrift, into the World; that inviting men to Repentance, declaring to them more diftinctly the Malignity of Sin, giving them the fulleft Affurances of Pardon (upon their real and fincere Amendment) through the Merit of his own once offering himfelf a Sacrifice for ever, and revealing to them more clearly the Certainty of a future Judgment, and the Rewards and Punifhments of the Life to come, he might by thefe means reduce them to the Obedience of God's Commands, and confequently reftore them to the Divine Favour. *Chrift has once fuffered for Sins, the juft for the unjuft, that he might bring us to God,* 1 Pet. iii. 18. And Col. i. 21. *You that were fometimes alienated, and enemies in your mind by wicked works, yet now hath he reconciled in the body of his Flefh through death, to prefent you holy and unblameable and unreproveable in his Sight.* But then we muft here carefully obferve, that in like manner as God *originally* and *from the Beginning*, while the *inanimate* world obeys him abfolutely and by neceffity of Nature, would not compel the Obedience of *rational* Creatures by the irrefiftiblenefs of his Power, but exacted it only from the willing Compliance of their own Choice; fo now *likewife* in the *reftoration* of men *by Chrift*, he will have no one reduced to his obedience by *Force*, but by fuch Motives as work properly upon rational Agents, *Reafon* and *Arguments*, *Promife* and *Threatnings*, *Hopes* and *Fears*. Thus in the Old Teftament; *I taught Ephraim*

S E R M. *Ephraim to go*, fays God by the Prophet, *taking them by their arms, but they knew*
XXXVII. *not that I healed them*; *I drew them with Cords of a man, with bands of Love, and I*
～～～ *was to them as they that take off the yoke.* Hof. xi. 3. And in the Gofpel; *No man*,
fays our Saviour in the words of the Text, can *come to Me, except the Father, which has
fent me*, draw *him*: No Man can be a worthy Difciple of *Chrift*, if he has not firft upon his mind a due fenfe of *God*. No Man can be a fincere Follower of the *Son* of God,
who is not in a difpofition of being *drawn* to a Love of Virtue, and of being *prevailed
upon* to practife Righteoufnefs, by a Senfe of the *Goodnefs* and *Reafonablenefs* and *Excellency* of the eternal Laws of *God*, even the *Father*, who fent him.

F o r the clearer and more diftinct explication of which doctrine, and of our
Lord's full Meaning and Intention in thefe words; it will be proper to confider particularly,

Firft, W H A T is meant by the Phrafe of *Coming to Chrift*: No Man can *Come to
Me*, except *the Father which has fent me*, draw *him*. *Some* enthufiaftick perfons,
judging of the Senfe of this Phrafe merely from the conceptions of their own imagination, and not from its *Ufe* and clear Signification in *other* paffages of the fame Writings; (which indeed is the only poffible way of Underftanding the true meaning either
of Scripture, or of any book whatfoever:) and *Others* negligently following *Their* Interpretation, have fuppofed that *Coming to Chrift* means a *relying* or *depending* upon
His Merits and *Satisfaction*, to bring them to Salvation, whether they obey his Commandments by a virtuous Courfe of Life, or no. But whoever confiders the many
Paffages of Scripture, in which this expreffion is to be met with, cannot fail to obferve,
that it really fignifies quite another thing. *Heb.* xi. 6. *He that* cometh to God, *muft
believe that he Is, and that he is a Rewarder of them that diligently feek him*: Coming
to God here evidently expreffes the fame thing, *as diligently feeking him*: And, *diligently feeking him*, is the fame as fincerely defiring to *know and obey his Will*, in order
to *pleafe* him. Again, *ch.* vii. 2 5. Chrift *is able to fave to the uttermoft them that* come
unto God by him, *feeing he ever liveth to make interceffion for them*: Coming unto
God *by Chrift*, is, Sinners returning by Repentance and Real Amendment to the O-
bedience of God's Commands, in hopes of obtaining pardon for what is paft, through
the Interceffion of Chrift. In like manner therefore, *Coming unto* Chrift, fignifies alfo
ferving and obeying Him, *becoming* his *Difciples*, *believing* his *doctrine*, and *living according to it*, fincerely defiring to *underftand and practife* his *Will*: Joh. vi. 3 5. *He
that* cometh to me, *fhall never hunger*; he that believes and obeys the Gofpel, fhall
never want any thing necefiary towards his obtaining eternal Life. And thus likewife
in the words of the Text; *No man* can come to Me, No Man can be a worthy difciple of Chrift, no Man can be a true and fincere Chriftian; *except the Father which has
fent me, draw him*. And This is the

Second thing to be confidered in the Text; the meaning of thefe *latter* words, *except the Father which has fent me, draw him*. Which expreffion, many Writers in Divinity have fo underftood, as if thereby was fignified, that no man had it in his own
Power to become a good Chriftian, or to perform any good Action; but that every Act
of Virtue, was operated or produced in him by the immediate Power of God. And
thus much of Truth there *is* indeed in That Notion; that neither in any *religious*, nor
in any *natural* action, does any one perform any thing, but by a Power freely given
him from, and entirely depending upon, the good pleafure of God. *In Him*, and by
virtue of Powers and Faculties continually depending *upon* him, we *live and move,
and have our Being*, and perform all, even the *natural* Actions of Life. In the execution of civil *Power and* Authority, or of any *Office* whatfoever, there is ftill further,
not only a continual dependance upon the Will of God for the ufe of men's *natural Faculties;*

culties;

culties; but moreover a dependence upon God's general Providence in the Government of the World, to order things so, as that the *Authority*, whatever it is, may actually take place : Thus *Pilate* could have had *no Power* to judge or condemn our Lord, or any other person, except it were *given him from above*, Joh. xix. 11. And the *Baptist* in This sense well expresses the *Success* of his Own Ministry, *A man can receive nothing*, says he, *Joh.* iii. 27, *except it be given him from Heaven.* In *religious* matters still further, it is *not only* true, that *it is God who giveth us both to will and to do of his good pleasure*; that it is God from whom alone we receive the *rational Faculties*, or *Powers*, both of *chusing* and *acting*; but *moreover*, that it is owing to his superabundant *grace* and *favour*, to his *free Gift and undeserved Bounty in Christ*, that he has afforded us the *Benefit* of a *Revelation*, the *Advantage* of a clearer and more *express* declaration of his *Will*, the *Assistances* of his *Holy Spirit*, an *Authoritative Assurance* of *Pardon* upon *Repentance*, and a more *complete Discovery* of the *Rewards* and *Punishments* in the *future* State, than could be obtained by the bare Light of Nature. All This, I say, is unquestionably true; and ought to be continually and thankfully acknowledged, with a just and humble sense of our Dependence upon God in every thing that we Are, or Do. But it is *not* the Meaning of the *Text* before us, nor what our Saviour is at all here speaking of in this whole Discourse. For where any one is exhorting men to *act*, and pressing them to *perform their Duty*; it is not *there a proper Argument or Incitement to Diligence*, (though it is undoubtedly in itself a certain Truth,) to tell them they can do nothing at all, unless God give them Power; but the *proper Motive* is to assure them, that because God *has* actually given them *Power*, therefore he *expects* and *requires* it of them, that they should *act* accordingly. Thus St. *Paul* argues to the *Philippians*, ch. ii. 12. *Work out your own Salvation with Fear and Trembling; For it is God which worketh in you both to will and to do, of his good pleasure.* The meaning plainly is; God *has given* you Power to chuse and act, *therefore* work out your own Salvation. And for the same reason, when our Saviour, in the Text, tells the unbelieving *Jews*, by way of *Reproof* for their obstinate Infidelity, and not by way of *pitying* them for any Want of Power to do their Duty; when he tells them (I say) by way of *Reproof* for their unreasonable Infidelity, that *no man* can *come to* Him, *except the Father draw him*; it is very certain he does not by these words mean to express any *Act* of *God* upon *Them*, but some certain *affection* or *disposition* of *Theirs* with regard to *God*.

For the further clearing of which explication of our Lord's sense, it is to be observed in the general nature of language, that when *Any Person* or *Thing* is said to *draw* another, the word (*draw*) may with equal propriety of Speech, signify either the *Action* of *Him* who *draws* the Other, or the *Action* of the *Other* who is *drawn* by him. And that, both in Scripture and in vulgar language, it *much* more *frequently* signifies the Action of Him who *is drawn*, than of Him who *draws*, will appear most evidently, and beyond All contradiction, from the following considerations. Our Saviour discoursing with the *Jews*, *Joh.* xii. 32. *And I*, says he, *if I be lifted up from the Earth, will* draw *all men unto me*: His meaning clearly is, not to express any *Act* of *his own upon Men*; but that, after his crucifixion, many nations and people, convinced by the Excellency of his doctrine, and by the Miracles it was attended with, should by *their own Will and Act* embrace his Religion. In like manner when God by the Prophet declared concerning the *Israelites* of old, *Jer.* xxxi. 3. *With loving Kindness have I* drawn *thee*; and *Hof.* xi. 4. *I drew them with Cords of a man, with Bands of Love*; every one sees the Meaning to be This only, that the consideration of the kindness and love of God, shown forth to the *Israelites* in so many eminent Instances of Mercy, was a very strong reason to prevail with them to obey and serve him cheerfully. The sense is the very same, as in that of St *Paul*, 2 *Cor.* v. 14. *The Love of Christ* constraineth *us*; which is a stronger expression than that of *drawing* us : *The Love of*

SERM. *Chrift*, fays he, *conftrains* or *compels* us,——*that we fhould not henceforth live unto our-*
XXXVII. *felves, but unto Him who died for us, and rofe again.* A fenfe of *Gratitude, draws* Us;
Acts of *Kindnefs, Love* and *Good-will*, from One *Perfon* to another, do very ftrongly
draw men; The *Beauty* and *Excellency*, the *Goodnefs* and *ufefulnefs* of *Things, draws*
or perfwades them: We are *drawn*, by *Arguments* and *Reafons*, by *Promifes* and
Threatnings, by *Hopes* and *Fears*; Yet it is not that *thefe things* are *Agents*, but that
we ourfelves *act*, when we are faid to *be drawn* by them. Much after the fame manner of fpeaking, Men are faid to be *moved* (or drawn) with *compaffion*, Matt. ix. 36.
moved with *indignation*, Matt. xx. 24. *moved* with *Envy*, Acts vii. 9. *moved* with
Fear, Heb. xi. 7. And when St *Paul* had reckoned up the things which are generally
apt to affect Men moft ftrongly, yet *None* of thefe *things* (fays he) move *Me*,
Acts xx. 24. After the fame manner, in the *Ill* fenfe of the word, Men are defcribed
to be drawn *away with their own* Luft, *and enticed*, Jam. i. 14. and *David* is reprefented as having been moved *by* Satan *to number the people*, 2 Sam. xxiv. 1. And yet
neither the one nor the other expreffion were at all intended to fignify, that the *things
done* were not the perfons *Own Acts*. Directly on the contrary, the Scripture plainly
means, feverely to *blame* the One, *acting* upon the incitement of *Luft*; and the Other,
for *acting* upon the Suggeftions of the *Devil*. Thus therefore in the *Text* likewife,
when our Lord fays, *No man can come to Me, except the Father, which has fent me,*
draw *him*; it is reafonable and neceffary to underftand him as fpeaking, not concerning
any *Act* of God upon *men*, but concerning the *Affection* which *Some men* bear towards
God. For as it is not a *misfortune*, but a *Vice*, for a man to be *drawn away* by his
own *Luft*, and enticed; and St *Peter's* expoftulation with *Ananias, Why hath* Satan
filled thine heart, is not by way of *Excufe*, but by way of *aggravating* his crime: So
neither on the *other* fide, is it any declaration of *Fate*, but a high commendation of
Men's *Virtue*, to fay that they were *drawn* to their Duty, or prevailed with to perform it, by confideration of *God*. Indeed, *without* confideration of *God*, without a
continual *View* and *Regard* towards *Him*, as Governing the World, there *can* be no
fuch thing as *True Virtue*: No man *can* become a *true and good Chriftian*, without
firft having a Senfe of the original *natural* obligation he lies under, of *Love and Duty*
towards *God: No man can come to Me, except the Father, who has fent me, draw him.*
And *This* fenfe of the phrafe, our *Saviour himself* confirms by the words immediately
following: For fo he exprefsly adds in the very *next* verfe; *Every man that hath* heard,
and hath learned *of the Father, cometh unto Me*; Every one that has a juft fenfe, and
fuitable Practice, of *natural* Religion towards *God*; will be difpofed readily to embrace
the Doctrine of *Chrift*.

THERE is *another* expreffion very frequent in Scripture, which may help much to
illuftrate the manner of fpeaking in the Text. The fame Difciples of Chrift, who are
here faid to be *drawn* to him by the Father, are elfewhere frequently defcribed as being *given* to him of God. Heb. ii. 13, *I, and the children whom God has given me.*
And again, *Joh.* xvii. 2, *Thou haft given him power over all flefh, that he fhould give
eternal life to as many as thou haft given him*. Now that even *This phrafe* does not denote any *Action* of God upon *men*, but merely the *character* or *qualifications* of the perfons defcribed; is apparent from the *parallel* places of Scripture. *All that the Father*
giveth *me*, Joh. vi. 37, are, in the 40th verfe, *every one which feeth the Son, and* believeth *on him*; And they *to whom* it is not given *of the Father* to come to *Chrift*, ver. 65,
are they whom, in the *verfe before*, our Lord reproves for their *unreafonable obftinacy* in
not believing. And when in his Prayer to the Father, *ch.* xvii. 12, he fays, *thofe that
thou gaveft me, I have kept, and none of them is loft*, but *the Son of perdition*; it is plain
by That exception, that *Judas* was originally one of thofe, whom God had *given* to
Chrift, in the fame fenfe as he *gave* him the reft of his Difciples; and yet afterwards,

3   by

by his own Fault, by becoming a Son of Treachery, *i. e.* a wicked and traiterous per- S E R M.
fon, he ceafed to be of that number. Juft as, in *Acts* xxvii. 24; *God had* given to XXXVII.
St *Paul all thofe that failed with him,* and yet he declares, *ver.* 31; *Except thefe* abide
in the ship, ye cannot be faved.

By a not much unlike figure of Speech, fuch perfons as *voluntarily* undertake extraordinary Difficulties *for the Kingdom of Heaven's fake*; Matt. xix. 12; are, in the *verfe before*, ftiled *thofe to whom it is* given. And, *It is* given *unto you*, fays our Lord to his Difciples; *ch.* xiii. 11; *to know the myfteries of the Kingdom of Heaven*; becaufe *feeing ye fee*; (that is, ye fee without Prejudice;) and *hearing, ye hear and underftand*; ver. 13. And concerning thofe of a *contrary* Difpofition, the Scripture fays that they are *blinded*; that God *hath given them eyes that they fhould not fee, and ears that they fhould not hear*; nay, that God *fends them ftrong Delufion*. And *Mofes*, in a moft affectionate manner of expoftulation, complains of the *Ifraelites*; *Deut.* xxix. 4, that after all the *Great* things that their *eyes had feen, the Signs of thofe Great Miracles*, yet the Lord *had not given them an heart to perceive, and eyes to fee, and ears to hear, even unto That day*. Nothing is more evident, than that the meaning of thefe Complaints is, not that *God* was *wanting in his affiftance*, much lefs that he actually *operated upon men* to make them *ftupidly and ungratefully wicked*; but that, through their *own* Obftinacy and Perverfenefs, the Means which *God* had been pleafed to make ufe of to reclaim them, had always proved ineffectual; and all the great and marvellous things which he had done for them in *Egypt* and in the Wildernefs, had not prevailed with them to repent, had not *drawn* them (as our Saviour in the Text expreffes it) to the Obedience expected of them. And the fame thing may in the like fenfe too juftly be faid at this day, concerning many among *Us*, God has by a long feries of very marvellous Events delivered *Us* from That greateft of All Temporal calamities, the eftablifhment of Popery and Arbitrary Power, by which Other Great and (in other refpects) Wife nations have been reduced under the vileft Indignities of the moft irrational and inhuman Slavery: And yet *the Lord hath not given us an heart to perceive, and eyes to fee, and ears to hear, even unto This day.*

From what has been faid in explication of the phrafes made ufe of in the Text, the general *Doctrine* it contains is plainly this; that no man can *become* a true Difciple of *Chrift*, who is not affected with a fincere Love of *God and Virtue*; Nor can any one who *already profeffes* the Name of Chrift, behave himfelf as becomes that Holy Profeffion, by Any other Methods or Forms of Religion whatfoever, than by the Practice of Righteoufnefs and true Virtue, in Obedience to the moral Commands of God. When our Saviour had worked the Miracle of the Loaves, recorded in the Beginning of This chapter; many of the *Jews* believed on him; that is, they profeffed themfelves his Difciples, not out of any regard to the Excellency and Holinefs of his Doctrine, but in hopes of being fupported by him in the World. To thefe perfons he fays, *ver.* 26; *Ye feek me, not becaufe ye faw the Miracles, but becaufe ye did eat of the Loaves, and were filled: Labour not for the meat which perifheth, but for That meat which endureth unto everlafting life.* This Doctrine when they relifhed not, but began to *murmur*; he reproves them with fomewhat *more earneftnefs* in the words of the Text; *No man can come to Me, except the Father, which has fent me, draw him:* It is in vain to profefs to be my Difciples upon any other foot, than that of Regard to *God*, and to *the World to come.* Upon which when they murmured ftill more, *ver.* 61; he replied again, *ver.* 64, *There are fome of you that believe not;* —— therefore *faid I unto you, that no man* can *come to Me, except it were given unto him of my Father: Given unto him of my Father;* that is, in the *fame* fenfe, as he elfewhere tells the *Apoftles* that it was given to them *to know the myfteries of the Kingdom of Heaven*, becaufe they were unprejudiced, willing to *hear* and to *underftand*; and came to him, not upon any *temporal*

poral

SERM.
XXXVII.
poral Defign, but being perfwaded (as St *Peter* expreffes himfelf ; *ver.* 68 of this chapter) that he *had the words of eternal Life.*

UPON account of the neceffary and infeparable connexion of *thefe Two* things ; of a fteady *Regard* to the *eternal* obligations of the *moral law* of God, in every one who profeffes to embrace the *Revelation* of Chrift ; upon This account (I fay) it is, that our Lord declares, *Joh.* vii. 16, 17. *My doctrine is not mine, but His that fent me* ; *If any man will do His will, he fhall know of the doctrine whether it be of God, or whether I fpeak of myfelf.* And again, *ch.* viii. 42 ; *If* God, fays he, *were your Father, ye would love* Me ; *for I proceeded forth and came from God* ; *neither came I of myfelf, but he fent me.* Like to which, is that of the Apoftle St *John* ; 1 *Joh.* ii. 13 ; *I write unto you little children, becaufe ye have known the Father* ; *ver.* 24 ; *If that which ye have heard from the beginning, fhall remain in you, ye alfo fhall continue in the Son and in the Father.* 2 Joh. 9 ; *He that abideth in the* doctrine, (that is, he that *obeys the Laws) of Chrift,* he *hath both the Father and the Son.* On the contrary, to the immoral and hypocriti-cal *Pharifees,* who hated the doctrine of Virtue and Righteoufnefs ; *Ye neither know* me, fays our Lord, *nor my* Father ; *Joh.* viii. 19. And, fpeaking of the perfecutions which the vicious and debauched World would bring upon his difciples ; *Thefe things,* fays he, *will they do unto you, becaufe they know not him that fent me* ; Joh. xv. 21. *They have both feen and hated both* Me *and my* Father ; *ver.* 24. *And thefe things will they do unto* you, *becaufe they have not known the* Father, *nor* Me ; *ch.* xvi. 3 ; that is, they have no true Senfe, either of *natural* Religion, or *revealed.*

THE Sum therefore and application of the Whole, is This : The Great End and Defign of the Gofpel of Chrift, is to reftore Sinners to the Favour of *God,* by bringing them back to the Practice of *True Virtue.* Vicious and corrupt Minds therefore, who are enemies to the *Moral Laws* of God, *muft* always naturally be averfe to the Doctrine of the *Gofpel.* Confequently fuch perfons are very apt, either to oppofe and perfecute the true Difciples of Chrift ; or elfe, if in times of Profperity they themfelves embrace the Profeffion of Chriftianity, they always place their Religion in outward Forms and Ceremonies, or in certain Syftems of opinion, confiftent with unrighteous practice. For to a True Senfe of Chrift's Religion *no man* can come, *except the Father draw him,* that is, except the love of God and Virtue be his Motive.

SERMON

SERMON XXXVIII.

The Character of a Good Man.

GEN. XVIII. 19.

For I know Him, that he will command his children, and his houſe-
hold after him, and they ſhall keep the way of the Lord, to do
Juſtice and Judgment.

THESE words are part of the character, which God himſelf, in different places
of the Old Teſtament, has given of that Great and Good Man, the Patriarch
Abraham. And they are ſpoken in this place, as a ground or reaſon of the
great and laſting Bleſſings which God declared he intended to confer upon him. Ver. 18;
Abraham ſhall ſurely become a great and mighty nation, and all the nations of the Earth
ſhall be bleſſed in him : For I know Him, that he will command his children and his houſe-
hold after him, and they ſhall keep the way of the Lord, to do Juſtice and Judgment ;
that the Lord may bring upon Abraham, that which he hath ſpoken of him. Upon account of This character, and the Bleſſings conſequent upon it, he is elſewhere ſtiled in
Scripture *The Friend of God,* and the *Father of all them that believe.* And in the book
of *Eccleſiaſticus ;* ch. xliv. 19; his hiſtory is thus briefly and elegantly ſummed up ;
Abraham was a great Father of many people, in glory was there none like unto him :
Who kept the Law of the moſt High, and was in covenant with him ; he eſtabliſhed the
Covenant in his fleſh, and, when he was proved, he was found faithful : Therefore he
aſſured him by an Oath, that he would bleſs the nations in his Seed, and that he would
multiply him as the Duſt of the Earth, and exalt his Seed as the Stars, and cauſe them
to inherit from Sea to Sea, and from the River unto the utmoſt part of the Land.

THE *Virtues,* upon account whereof theſe great Bleſſings were promiſed to *Abra-*
ham, were *perſonal :* But the *Bleſſings themſelves,* 'tis evident, were, with regard to
Him, figurative only ; being fulfilled not till ſome *hundreds* of years *after,* upon his
Poſterity ; whereas *He himſelf* did but ſojourn *in the land of Promiſe, as in a ſtrange*
country, and *confeſſed that he was a Stranger and Pilgrim on the Earth.* From whence
the Apoſtle to the *Hebrews* very juſtly infers, That *Abraham* underſtood the promiſed
Bleſſing, with regard to *Himſelf,* to be of a *ſpiritual* and *better* kind. Ch. xi. 14, 16, 10;
For they that ſay ſuch things, declare plainly that they ſeek a country ; a better country,
that is, an heavenly ; For he looked for a City which hath foundations, whoſe Builder and
Maker is God.

THE *particular* Virtue which procured to *Abraham* the character given him in my
Text, was his *keeping the way of the Lord,* that is, his adhering to the *Belief* and
Worſhip of the One True God of the Univerſe, in oppoſition to the general corruption
of the idolatrous Nations among whom he lived ; and his *commanding his children and*
his houſehold after him, to do the like. 'Twas his exemplarily putting in Practice, what
Joſhua publickly declared before all the tribes of *Iſrael,* that *He* alſo would do in the
like caſe : Ch. xxiv. 15; *If it ſeem evil unto you to ſerve the Lord, chuſe ye this day*

VOL. I.   P p p   *whom*

SERM. *whom ye will ferve; whether the Gods which your Fathers ferved, that were on the other*
XXXVIII. *fide of the flood, or the Gods of the Amorites in whofe land ye dwell: But as for Me and*
my Houſe, we will ſerve the Lord. In the *New Teſtament,* This practice is ſtiled,
[ικᾶι ἐκ τᾶ Θηρία] *Rev.* xv. 2; not (as we render the words,) *getting the victory* over
the Beaſt; but, *getting the victory* (or *overcoming) from* out of the midſt of *the Beaſt;*
That is, adhering ſtedfaſtly to the *True Religion,* in the *midſt* of idolatrous and corrupt
Nations.

THE Great and Principal Deſign of every man's life, ought to be the promoting the
Glory of God; the encouraging of Virtue, and diſcouraging every kind of Vice. Not
that any man is obliged to be perpetually employed in actions that are *immediately* of a
religious nature; or that all his Thoughts and Diſcourſes are to be wholly confined to
things *Sacred:* But that his Principal and Final Aim, his General and Conſtant View,
the ſettled Temper and Diſpoſition of his mind, and the Habitual Tendency of all his
Actions, be the eſtabliſhing of Truth and Right in the World. And when once a man
has habitually fixt to himſelf this Great End, and it is become (as it were) his Natural
Temper; When he is *transformed* (as St *Paul* expreſſes it) *by the renewing of his Mind,*
and his *Meat and Drink* (as our Saviour ſpeaks concerning himſelf) is to *do the Will of*
his Father which is in Heaven: This Love of Goodneſs, will naturally, like all *Other*
Habits, influence even the moſt *common* actions of his life: Even when he is not
actually thinking of it, but employed perhaps in the moſt *vulgar* affairs, or even in
diverſions themſelves; yet ſtill *every thing* he does, will habitually have ſomewhat in it,
tending to promote a general ſenſe of Truth and Equity, a general Regard to God and
Virtue. And *whatever* his *particular* State, Relation, or Circumſtances of Life be;
he will particularly apply the proper Advantages and Opportunities, wherewith That
State or Thoſe Circumſtances more peculiarly furniſh him, to promote the ſame Ends
of Virtue and Goodneſs.

As a *Magiſtrate* or *Governour,* he will take care that That Weight, and Power of
influencing Others, which the Superiority of his Station gives to his *Example,* ſhall be
directed conſtantly to the Intereſt of Virtue. In the *execution* of *Laws,* (in which
matter there is room for great variety of Prudent or Imprudent exerciſe of Power,) he
will always endeavour to put the *Streſs* of Authority, upon urging men to *do* thoſe things
which will really make them *better,* and *deterring* them from ſuch Practices as are intrinſically in their own nature *evil* or *vicious;* That ſo the Laws of *God* and *Man* may
uniformly promote one and the ſame End, *for the Puniſhment only of Evil-doers, and*
for the Praiſe of them that do well: And with regard to *Ambition,* or the Increaſe of
his own *Power and Dominion;* he will take much more pleaſure in being able to be
publickly beneficial to Mankind, by maintaining their juſt Rights and Properties; than
in obtaining to *Himſelf* Power, for Power's ſake.

AGAIN: A perſon of this diſpoſition, if he be in his ſtation a *Preacher* of the *Goſ-*
pel; he will not have in his View the *temporal* Grandeur of any particular *Sect* or *Party*
of Men; but will always endeavour to ſet before men the Truth of God in That native *Simplicity,* and repreſent to them the religion of Chriſt (in the manner our Lord
himſelf repreſented it) to be ſuch a *reaſonable* Service, as that it may effectually *con-*
vince the Minds of Gainſayers, and, by the irreſiſtible force of Truth and Reaſon, compel them to ſubmit themſelves to the Obedience of Chriſt. And above all things he
will take care to give evidence in his whole behaviour, that He *himſelf* ſincerely believes and expects That Judgment to come, which he ſets forth to *Others* as the Great
Argument that muſt oblige them to embrace the Truths and to obey the Precepts of
the Goſpel: According to That direction of our Saviour; *Let your Light ſo ſhine before*
men, that they may ſee your good works, and glorify your Father which is in Heaven.

I

If

If he lives in a *corrupt* and degenerate *Age*, he will *principally* set himself, with all meekness and gentleness, to oppose the *particular corruptions* of the Age he lives in; endeavouring, by all fair and righteous methods, to bring as Many as possible to the acknowledgment of the Truth.

Lastly, Such a person, if he be in the capacity of a *Father* or *Master of a Family*, will take all proper occasions to instill right notions of Truth and Virtue, into those over whom the Circumstances of his State and Relation naturally give him an Influence. And by his *Private* Example, showing in his most free and retired conversation, that he has constantly upon his mind That *Real* Regard to God and Virtue, which 'tis more easy and usual to make Show of in Publick; he will with great efficacy promote the True Honour of God, and the advancement of sincere Religion. For, *formal Admonitions* and *Publick Declarations* concerning matters of *Religion*, are apt to be of very small force, either towards fixing in the *Mind Right Principles*, or forming in the *Manners* a Habit of *virtuous Practice*; if in the *private* life and conversation of those by whom Families are to be directed, there appear Prophaneness and Impiety, or Lewdness and Debauchery, or tyrannical Oppressiveness and violent and unreasonable Passions. How affectionate soever the Exhortations of the Preachers of the Gospel be, and how often soever repeated Instructions be given to young persons either in Schools or otherwise; yet if the Examples they find at home in the Practice of common Life, be vitious, debauched, and altogether contrary to the Precepts and Admonitions given them in form; the effect of all such instruction cannot but be, comparatively speaking, very inconsiderable. Nor is there any other *possible* way, by which there can be any Hope that the arguments of Religion should come to have their due Weight, and *general* Efficacy in the World; unless They, whose State, Relation, and Circumstances, give them a Natural Influence over Many, will show in the whole course of their private conversation, and in the freest and most retired part of common Life, that they have really upon their Minds a Sense and Concern for Religion; that they have habitually in all their Actions a constant Regard to God, and a sincere Desire to promote the Knowledge of Truth and the Practice of Virtue and Goodness amongst Men. This was the Temper of *Abraham*; Upon account of which, That Great character is given him in the Text, with a *repeated* Assurance of the Blessings designed him : *I know Him, that he will command his children and his houshold after him, and they shall keep the way of the Lord, to do Justice and Judgment; that the Lord may bring upon Abraham, That which he hath spoken of him.*

The words, *He will Command his Children and his houshold after him*, seem to imply, as if it was in *Abraham's* power to *undertake* for those that were to come after him, *what* they should do; and as if *They* were originally under an *obligation* to *perform* what he should require of them. Which in *general*, 'tis evident, cannot be true : Because then it would follow, that All *Other* Heads of Families had the same Authority likewise; and consequently, the posterity of *every* family, lying under the *same* obligation, would be under a necessity, wherever any *False* religion prevailed, to continue for ever in the profession of such false Religion : Directly contrary to *Abraham's own* Practice, who, being born among an idolatrous and corrupt people, *gat him out from his country, and from his kindred, and from his Father's house*; Gen. xii. 1. Neither, where the *Truth itself* prevails, is it sufficient that Those who come after, follow it barely upon the *Command* of those who went before : Because, though it be indeed, by Chance, the *Truth* only, which they follow; yet, They not knowing it to be so, but following it merely upon such a principle, as would equally have made them follow Any *Error*, 'tis, with regard to the Morality of *Their* Act, the very same thing as if they were *not* in the Truth. But in *Some* particular Cases, and with regard to *some*

particular

SERM. particular things, such Circumstances there *may* be, as may make it very reasonable for
XXXVIII. Parents and Governours to Command *their children and their houshold after them* ; and
very reasonable for *Thefe*, to be under the strictest Obligation to *obey* such Commands.
Where things are in their own nature absolutely and *confessedly* indifferent, there the
Command of proper Superiours is manifestly the *Only Rule* of Action. On the other
side ; where things are already made necessary by a superior obligation, as where there
is a clear and express Command of *God* ; or where things are *intrinsically and essentially
obligatory* in their own nature, as is the *Study of Truth with Sincerity and Impartiality*,
and the *Practice of all moral and eternal Virtues* ; there the instruction and direction,
and Example and Authority of natural Superiours, is the proper means of laying before
ignorant and *thoughtless* minds, and of inforcing upon them, those original and antecedent Obligations. This latter, was the case of *Abraham* in the Text : He was to command *his children and his houshold after him*, that they should *keep the way of the Lord,
to do Justice and Judgment* : that they should *worship* the *True God* in opposition to
Idols, and that they should practise *Justice and Righteousness* towards *Men*. The things
were *in themselves* necessarily, of *intrinsick eternal obligation* ; and the Command of
Abraham, was the setting That obligation before their eyes ; teaching them to see it,
and have a just sense of it, reminding them to attend to it, and pressing and inforcing
it upon their Minds. In This case therefore, *Abraham* might well undertake, (and it
is his great Commendation that he did so,) to command (as far as in him lay) *his children and his houshold after him* ; Because the *things themselves*, *together* with *His Command*, clearly carried along with them *their* own evidence and *conviction*. The *grounds
and reasons* of which conviction nevertheless, in the midst of universally corrupt and
idolatrous nations, might very possibly and probably, in *His* family, as well as in all
those around him, not have been attended to ; had they not been seconded by *His* Instruction, Example, and Command. *I know Abraham, that he will command his children and his houshold after him, and they shall keep the way of the Lord.*

Another Instance, wherein there seems to be an Obligation laid upon Posterity, by
an *Act* of those who went before them ; is the case of *Circumcision*. Gen. xvii. 9 ;
*God said to Abraham, Thou shalt keep my Covenant, thou and thy seed after thee, in their
generations :*——*Every man-child among you,*——*that is eight days old, shall be circumcised,*——*for an everlasting covenant : And the*——*man-child who*——*is not circumcised, that soul shall be cut off from his people ; he hath broken my Covenant.* Circumcision, was a *Token of the Covenant* between God and That people ; and an *Obligation*
upon the circumcised person, to keep the Law : Yet 'tis evident an infant at eight
days old, could not give his *Consent*, to take upon himself any such Obligation. The
Reason why the Obligation *was valid* upon him *notwithstanding*, was *This*. God was
pleased to promise to *Abraham* and his Posterity such and such particular Blessings, as
were entirely a *free Gift*, and which he was not in justice under any obligation to have
promised. These Blessings he limited to the Conditions of a particular Covenant ; and
the Seal or Token of That Covenant, was the ceremony of Circumcision. Now, if
the person who, without his own *consent*, was circumcised the eighth day, would not
afterwards perform the conditions of That Covenant ; there was no wrong done him,
if he received not those Blessings, which by *Free Gift only* were annexed to the performance of the conditions of That particular Covenant. And he might *moreover* very
justly be *punished*, for rejecting That Covenant ; because *God* has, without controversy,
a Right to require from All his Creatures Obedience to such Commands as he thinks
fit to impose upon them, whether they themselves give their *Assent* to his Commandments or no. I

By *Analogy* drawn from this Rite of *Circumcifion*, it has for very many Ages been S E R M.
a general Practice in the Chriftian Church, to receive Infants by *Baptifm* into the Obliga- XXXVIII.
tions of Faith and Obedience to the Gofpel; and to make Profeffion for them, what
they are to believe and obey. Whether this Analogy be *rightly* drawn, or no; and be a
fufficient and *adequate* foundation, for what has been built upon it; is a controverfy
which I fhall not at prefent enter into : But from what has been already faid upon the
Unqueftionable cafe of *Circumcifion*, and upon *Abraham's Command* in the Text to *his
children and to his houfehold after him*, and upon the *Nature* of thefe forts of Obligations in *general*; the proper *application* I fhall make, is, to confider briefly *what Obligation* lies upon *Thofe*, who, without their own Knowledge or Confent have been *baptized* in their *Infancy*, and have had a *Baptifmal Vow* made for them by *Others*; *What*
Obligation *really* lies upon *Them* to *embrace* and *obey* the *Gofpel*, in the *whole* courfe of
their *Lives*. Now it is very evident, *generally* fpeaking, that no man has a Right to
make any Promife for Another, without his own Confent; and no man is obliged to
make good any fuch Promife, if there lies upon him no *other* obligation, but what arifes
merely from *fuch* a Promife, made without his Knowledge or Confent. Neither is it
fufficient, that the things promifed to be done, are *really* for the perfon's own *Advantage* who is to perform them. For *every* perfon, when he arrives at years of understanding, has in all fuch cafes, a Right to judge for Himfelf *what is* his own Advantage;
and it is not what *Another* thinks, but what he himfelf is convinced to be for his own
Benefit, that muft finally determine him to chufe and act. Wherefore, indeed, All
Undertakings of this kind, fuch as are *Baptifmal Vows* made on the behalf of *Infants*,
are not to be efteemed as Promifes what the perfon *fhall* do, but what he fhall be
taught, what he fhall be *inftructed*, what he fhall be *reminded* and *called upon* to do,
and to take upon himfelf that he *will* do. For the true *Ground* of *obligation* in this
cafe is, that the things themfelves to be performed are in their own nature fuch, as
every Perfon, when he arrives at the full Ufe of his Reafon, would be indifpenfably
obliged to perform, whether Others had beforehand undertaken for him any fuch
thing, or no. To *inquire carefully* into the Will of God, to *believe* what God declares, and to *do* what he commands, are obligations abfolutely incumbent upon every
man, though they had never been bound upon him by any Vow or Promife : And
therefore the Vow made at Baptifm on the behalf of an Infant, is not fo truly the
Ground of his being obliged; as the *neceffary obligation* of the *Things themfelves*, is that
which makes the *Vow itfelf* to be valid upon him. Nor is any Promife made by
Others, fo properly with intention to lay any *obligation* upon the perfon, or tie him
up to any thing which he would not otherwife have been bound to perform; But the
true Defign is only in way of kindnefs and affiftance, to *remind* him of an obligation,
abfolute in itfelf, that he carefully *inquire after*, and *believe* and *obey* the *Will* of God.
And This may, very eafily, be of Great *Benefit* and *Ufefulnefs*. For every man being
obliged to *ftudy* impartially the *Will of God*, and to improve himfelf in the *Knowledge
of Truth* and in the *Practice of Virtue*, and to live up to the beft *Light* he can obtain; it is plainly of very great Advantage to Men, to be from the Beginning inftructed in the *way of Truth*, to have *Examples* fet before them of *Virtue and Righteoufnefs*, and to be *reminded* and *called upon* to *confider* and *attend to* thofe Obligations,
which are incumbent upon Men whether they attend to them or no. The Great and
Righteous Judge of the Whole Earth, knows how to have compaffion, upon the *ignorant*, and upon them that are *out of the way*; and *will* referve *mercy* in ftore, according to the exigency of *every* Man's cafe, for thofe who, through ill inftruction, wander in the ways of Error. But it is a mighty *Advantage*, and a particular *Bleffing*, to
be originally led into the way of *Righteoufnefs*. For fo in the Text, it is not only re-

SERM. corded in commendation of *Abraham*, that he would *command his children and his*
XXXVIII. *houfehold after him*; but it is taken notice of alfo in the way of confequent Benefit to
Them, that *They* would accordingly *keep the way of the Lord, to do Juftice and Judg-
ment.*

I SHALL conclude, with making this *One only* further Obfervation. Since *keeping
the way of the Lord*, fignifies clearly, in *Abraham's* cafe, believing *the True God*, as
well as doing *Righteoufnefs*; and fince under the *Gofpel* ftill more emphatically, fincere
Faith is always infifted upon, as well as *Virtuous Practice* : it may very naturally be
inquired, if *Believing* does not, like our *Actions*, depend upon the *Will*; but if Men
muft *believe* what they have good Evidence for, and cannot *believe* what they fee no
reafon to be convinced of ; *how* then can Believing be a Duty, which a Man fhould
be bound to perform ? The Anfwer plainly is ; that *That Believing*, which is the Duty
of a Chriftian, is not, in the ftrict fenfe of the word, That bare Affent of the Underftanding which is not in our Power to with-hold ; but it fignifies, in the *moral* fenfe,
that good Difpofition of the Mind and Will, by which a Man is difpofed to attend to,
and examine impartially, to confider and receive willingly, what upon due inquiry he
fhall find to be the Will of God; not careleffly and creduloufly, but upon fober Reafon, and proper Evidence.   And fo likewife on the contrary ; *Unbelief*, in Scripture,
does not fignify difbelieving what wants juft and fufficient proof ; but it always means,
either carelefsly and negligently rejecting without inquiry and without Reafon ; or elfe
rejecting wilfully and obftinately, through the love of Sin and Vice.   And this is evidently the cafe of all profane, loofe, and debauched Infidels ; who, merely becaufe
they hate to be reformed, pretend to difbelieve, what, if they ferioufly examined as
they ought to do, they would find all poffible reafon to embrace.

SERMON

SERMON XXXIX.

The Nature of Humane Actions.

LUKE XI. 35.

Take heed therefore, that the Light which is in Thee be not Darkness.

UPON our Lord's having worked a remarkable Miracle, *ver.* 14. The *Pha-* *rifees*, who were refolved not to be convinced by *Any* Evidence whatfoever, becaufe his Doctrine was a perpetual Reproof of their Hypocrify and Other Vices; alledged, fome of them, *ver.* 15. that *he caft out Devils through Beelzebub, the chief of the Devils.* Others, *tempting him,* ver. 16, *fought of him a fign from Heaven :* That is, Pretending to diftruft the Miracles which he worked on *Earth,* as if *Thefe* might poffibly be the Effect of fome *Magical* Power or Artifice ; they infifted that he fhould call for fome miraculous Sign directly from Heaven. Our Lord, know-ing the Wickednefs of their Hearts, *ver.* 17; and that they did not really defire to be convinced, but only fought for occafions of cavilling ; tells the people, *ver.* 29, *This is an evil generation ; They feek a Sign, and there fhall no Sign be given it.* And then he defcribes the *Incurablenefs* of the Malice and Hypocrify of thefe *Pharifees* ; in that their Notions even of *Religion itfelf,* the very Principle from which alone there is Hope of reformation of Manners ; their Notions even about *This very thing,* were *themfelves* the Great *Spring* and *Fountain* of Corruption. Their *Religion itfelf* was *Pride* and *Party, Popularity* and *External Show.* And if the *Guide* of men's Actions be *itfelf* thus *vicious,* how vicious muft their Actions be ! *Ver.* 34, *The Light* (fays he) *of the Body, is the Eye ; Therefore when thine Eye is fingle, thy whole Body alfo is full of Light ; But when thine Eye is Evil, thy Body alfo is full of Darknefs.* His meaning is : What the *Eye* is to the *Body ;* That very fame thing in proportion, the *Moral Judgment* and *Underftanding,* the Directing Principle, is to a man's *Mind.* If this *Moral Judgment* of the Underftanding be unbiaffed and uncorrupt, and hearkned to with Simplicity and Sincerity ; it *will* either direct and preferve men in the Paths of Truth and Right, or be perpetually calling upon them to return into them. But as, when a man's *Eyes* are blinded or put out, his whole Body muft of neceffity move in Darknefs : So, if the *Moral Judgment* of the Mind, the Principle which ought to guide and direct men's Actions, be *itfelf* perverted by unreafonable Prejudices, and cor-rupted by vicious Appetites and Paffions ; there is no hope, but fuch perfons muft con-tinue in Error and Wickednefs. *Take heed therefore,* adds our Lord in the words of the Text, *Take heed that the Light which is in thee, be not Darknefs :* Let every man above all things confider and take care, that this *Moral Judgment* of his Mind and Un-derftanding, be not corrupted with blind unreafonable Prejudices, and with vicious and wilfully indulged Affections. For in That cafe, his very *Guide* becomes his *Seducer ;* and his *Light* itfelf, is *Darknefs.*

IN the following Difcourfe upon thefe words, I fhall *1ft* confider briefly the *Nature of Humane Actions ;* and what *Dependence* they have upon the *directing Principle,*

upon

SERM. upon the *Light* or *Understanding* that is in the Mind of Man. *2dly*, I shall show *what*
XXXIX. *Power* men have over their own Actions, with regard to the *Influence* of That Light
or Understanding, by which they are to be directed. And *3dly*, I shall confider of
what *Consequence* it is in matters of Religion, that men fail not in this first and grand
Foundation of all; in the *Root*, the *Spring*, the universal *Guide* and *Director* of their
Actions. *Take heed, that the Light which is in thee, be not Darkness.*

I. I AM to confider the *Nature* of *Humane Actions*; and what *Dependence* they
have upon the *directing Principle*; upon the *Light* or *Understanding* that is in the
Mind of Man. The *Motions of Matter* being All *necessary*, it is evident that *Matter*
can in no fenfe poffibly be capable of *any Action at all*. It can neither begin to *move
itself* when *at Rest*, nor put any *Stop to itself* when *in Motion*, nor in any degree alter
its own *determination*, or its prefent *State* or *manner of Existence*. But whatever *impreffions* it receives from the *Impulfes* of other *Matter*, or from the *Influences* of external
Agents; by *Thefe*, and *Thefe only*, it is always neceffarily and invariably determined.
Senfitive and *Brute Animals* have in themfelves a *higher* Principle, a Principle of *Self-
motion*; by which they act and determine themfelves, according to the Influence of
certain *Appetites and Paffions*. But it is always according to That Influence and Direction *merely*. For over the *Appetites and Paffions themfelves*, they have *No Government*; no *moral Judgment* or *Difcernment* of the Difference of *Good and Evil*; no
fuperior Light or Direction, by which to *fuppress* a hurtful *Appetite*, or *over-rule* the
Inftincts of *Paffion* : And *therefore* they are not at all *accountable* for any thing they
do. This is the proper and peculiar Nature of *Humane* Actions; the diftinguifhing
character by which *Man*, as a *rational* and *moral Agent*, is diftinguifhed from the inferior Creation. He not only has in himfelf a *Power of Acting*, which is in common to
him with the irrational Creatures; but he has moreover a *ftill higher* Principle or Power
of *directing* his Actions, with fome *determinate Views*, and to fome certain and conftant *End*. He has a Power of judging *beforehand*, concerning the *Confequences* of his
Actions, concerning the Reafonablenefs or Unreafonablenefs of the End he aims at;
and he has a Power of recollecting, *after* the Action done, whether he acted with a
good or an evil View. He can either *follow* the irregular Motions of All his *Appetites
and Paffions*, as do the Beafts that perifh; or he can *reftrain* and *over-rule* their Sollici-
tations, by attending to the Guidance of a *Superior Light* of *Reafon* and *Religion*.
Nay, a man *cannot* indeed *but* have *fome* View and Defign in every thing he does.
Even when he abandons himfelf *moft implicitly* to the *Brutal* Guidance of *mere Appetite and Paffion*, ftill he does it with fome *View*; and with a *Confcioufnefs*, which *Beafts*
have not, that he knowingly and deliberately *chufes* to aim at fome mean and unworthy End. Hence arifes That *Judgment of Reflection* which we call *Confcience*; by
which a man either *approves* or *condemns* his own *paft* Actions, and apprehends that
he fhall accordingly be *approved* or *condemned* by *Him* alfo to whom he muft finally
give account of himfelf. *If* a man, in the general courfe of his Life, accuftoms himfelf to confider thefe things beforehand, that is, if he will behave himfelf as a rational
Creature; *If* he accuftoms himfelf in all his Actions to confider the Reafon and E-
quity of Things, to confider what is reafonable for *Himfelf* to do, or for *Him* to expect fhould be done by *Another*; to confider what is agreeable to the Will of God,
and likely to be approved at the Bar of an impartial and All-feeing Judge : *If* This
(I fay) be his main directing Principle, and the Point which he conftantly keeps in
View; his Actions, *generally* fpeaking, will not fail to be Virtuous and Good. For
fuch as is the Root or Caufe, fuch will be the Effect: Such as is the Fountain, fuch
will be the Streams that iffue from it. A Good tree, will not ufually bring forth Bad
fruit. A Good man, out of the good treafure of his heart, will naturally bring forth
Good

Good things. For out of the abundance of the Heart the Mouth will fpeak, and the S E R M. Hands will be accordingly directed to act.

O n the contrary ; *If* a man's Principles be loofe and Atheiftical ; *If* he has no Senfe of the Reafon and Equity of things, nor Apprehenfion of the righteous Judgment of God ; *If* his *Views* be no other than the fatisfying of his Appetites, the gratification of his Paffions, the purfuing his prefent Interefts, and pleafing his own unreafonable Self-will ; it cannot be, but his Actions will be *generally* immortal and vicious.

F u r t h e r yet ; *If* a man's Principles be *Superftitious*, that is, fuch as not only *fet him at liberty* from the great ties of Benevolence and Charity, but moreover lay upon him the ftrongeft *direct and pofitive Obligation* to unrighteous Practices ; in This cafe, his Conduct will neceffarily be as much worfe, than That of a perfon who has *no* Principles at all ; as One who follows a *Falfe Light* that leads directly to Deftruction goes more certainly out of the right way, than he who at all adventures walks in *Darknefs.* Such a one will act *wickedly*, not only when his *Pleafures*, his *Intereft*, or his *Paffions prompt* him ; which is the fartheft a Man of *no principles* will go ; But *This Man*, in *oppofition* to all his own natural Inclinations and Paffions, as well as to the Reafon and Truth of things, will, out of *Principle*, and in order to do *God* good Service, run zealoufly into the vileft barbarities of unrighteoufnefs. This is a confideration very neceffary to be diftinctly attended to, concerning the *Nature* and *Spring* of *Human Actions* ; and what *Dependence* they have upon the *directing Principle*, upon the *Light* or *Underftanding* that is in the Mind of Man.

II. I P r o p o s e to fhow *what Power* Men have over their own Actions, with regard to the *Influence* of That Light or Underftanding, by which they are to be directed. Every Action a Man does, Every Action of any confiderable importance in life, Every Action that is of a Moral or Immoral nature ; muft of neceffity be done with *fome View* or other, either upon a *Good Principle* or a *Bad* one. For when we fpeak of man's having *No Principles* at all, the Meaning is only that they have No *Good Principles* ; and that they act intirely upon this One *ill* Principle, of thinking themfelves at Liberty from all Obligation to regard the Effential Differences of Good and Evil. Every Action (I fay) of a rational Creature, every fuch Action as has any thing of Morality or Immorality in it, muft of neceffity be done with *Some View* or other, either upon a *Good Principle* or a *Bad* one. Now if Mens *Principles* were *neceffarily* implanted in their *Nature*, and their *Actions* by a like *natural Neceffity* followed from their *Principles* ; the Confequence then indeed would be, that Men had *no Power* at all over their Own Actions, and confequently could be no way *accountable* for what they do. But the Truth, plainly is This. As the *Eye*, or the *Faculty of Seeing*, is not at all formed by the Power of *Man* ; and the *Light*, which is the *Object* of Sight, is likewife what *God* has made it, and has no dependence on *Man's* Will or Pleafure ; and therefore Men are not anfwerable for having *better* or *worfe* Organs of Senfe, or for having *more* or *lefs* Light, but only for the *Ufe of thofe Eyes* and of *That Light* which they have : So, with regard to the *Mind* likewife, both the *internal Capacity of Underftanding*, and the *external Means of Information*, are what *God* pleafes to beftow on every Man, and have no dependence on the perfon's *own Will* ; And therefore no Man is anfwerable for having a *larger* or *fmaller Capacity*, or for having *more* or *fewer Means of Information* : But he is accountable for the *Ufe* of *That* degree of Underftanding, and for the *Ufe* or *Abufe* of *Thofe* Means of Knowledge, *whatfoever* they be, which God has thought fit to afford him. A Man may *fhut* his Eyes, and may *chufe* Darknefs rather than Light : Or he may, through *Wilfulnefs* or *Paffion*, chufe to follow a *Falfe Light* inftead of a *True one*, an *imaginary Spectre* inftead of a *Reality* : Or he may *put out* his Eyes, and bring himfelf under a fort of neceffity of blindly following fome *Guide*, who (as it happens) may equally lead him in the *Right*

Way or in a *Wrong* one. A Man may by *Negligence*, or by *Wilfulness*, or by *Love of Vice*, or by *Any customary* and *habitual ill Practice*, pervert or blind his own *Understanding*. He may, by *rejecting* the *Means* of discovering the Truth, through his own *Fault*, and not through Want of Capacity, form to himself *ill Principles* instead of *Good* ones. Or, if he had never so *good Principles*, yet, as *seeing the Way* is not necessarily *walking in it*, he may suffer himself to be *Tempted* to act *against* his Principles, to act *against* the Reason of his *own Mind*, as well as against the Reason and Truth of *Things*. Men therefore *have a Power* over their own Actions, notwithstanding *all the Influence* of that Light or Understanding, *by which they are to be directed*. Nevertheless; since, *generally* speaking, such as Men's *Principles* are, such will be Their *Actions*; and He whose Conduct is directed by settled *ill Principles*, will much more *constantly*, and in much *greater Instances*, and with Effects of much *higher Malignity*, do what is Wrong; than He who, having *virtuous and good Principles*, yet in particular Cases fails of keeping up to them in Practice; it is hence obvious,

III. IN the *Third* place, to observe, of what *Consequence* it is in matters of Religion, that Men fail not in this first and grand Foundation; in the *Root*, the *Spring*, the universal *Guide* and *Director* of their Actions: *Take heed, that the Light which is in thee, be not Darkness*. If a Man has the *Best* Principles that can be: If he be firmly perswaded in his own Mind, of the essential Difference of Good and Evil, of God's Government of the World, and of a Judgment to come: If he has right Notions of the true Nature of Religion, that it consists in living *soberly, righteously and godly*, under the Inspection of a righteous and all-seeing Judge: Still, such is the Deceitfulness of Sin, so many are the Temptations and Allurements of the World; so blind are the Appetites, so strong the Passions of Men; that nothing is more common, than to see even these *best of Principles* over-ruled, and the Force of them defeated, by the Strength and Prevalency of different Temptations. How much *more*, when Men's *Principles themselves* are *consistent* with Wickedness, must it be expected that *Degeneracy of Manners* will prevail! and still *more*, if their Principles be not only *consistent* with Vice, but such as moreover *directly lead* them, and even *lay the Obligations of Conscience* upon them, to unrighteous *Practices*! If the Salt itself has lost its Savour, wherewith shall things be seasoned? And if the Light itself which is in thee, be Darkness, how great is That Darkness? To instance in Particulars. If a Man's Religion consists chiefly, in a confident Presumption of his own unconditionate *Predestination*; will not This naturally lead him to be *stiff* and *censorious*, and to have too little Care of his *Moral* and *Equitable* Behaviour towards all Men? If a Man can perswade himself that a strong *Credulity*, or an imaginary *Belief of unintelligible Notions*, can be truly acceptable in the Sight of God; has not This an obvious and evident Tendency, to make him pride himself in the pretended *Rightness* of his *Faith*; and despise the real Virtues, of *Impartiality, Equity*, and *Love of Truth?* If Another can prevail with himself to believe, that after a *vicious and immoral Life*, he may at last upon a Bed of Sickness, by the *Absolution of the Priest*, or by the *Sacraments of the Church*, or by a *confident Reliance upon the Merits of Christ*, elude the Threatnings of the Almighty, and artfully escape the Wrath of the Just and Righteous Judge of the whole Earth; does not this plainly give him encouragement to defer his Repentance, to think Virtue and Goodness really needless, and to *continue in Sin, that Grace may abound?* Again: If a Man can fancy that the most important and fundamental point of Religion, is the adhering fiercely to some one particular *Sect, Party*, or *Denomination* of Men; and the contending violently *for* or *against* certain peculiar *Forms* or *Ceremonies* of Worship; has not This an evident Tendency to make him believe, that, by a great *Zeal* for these external Forms, he may commute or compensate for the Want of those Moral Virtues, which Alone are of *Real and Essential Goodness?* But

if,

if, beyond All This, a Man's very *Mind and Conscience* be so far defiled, as that he can S E R M. imagine Religion to lay a direct *Obligation* upon him to commit some of the greatest XXXIX. of *Wickednesses*, to make use of the *vilest Frauds* and the most *open Violences*, to break Faith against the most *Solemn Engagements*, and even *with the greatest Cruelty to destroy Men's Lives* in order *to do God good Service*; as Those of the Church of *Rome* have frequently done : Whenever This (I say) is the Case, so that Men can satisfy their very *worst Passions*, of *Ambition, Pride, Cruelty,* and *Tyranny,* not only *without the Reproach,* but even *with the highest Applause,* of their own Consciences; What Hope, what Possibility is there, for *Virtue and Goodness* here to take Any place ? *Take heed, that the* Light *which is in thee, be not Darkness.*

T H E *Light,* which God *originally* implanted in Men, is *Reason,* or their *Natural* Sense and Discernment of the Difference of Good and Evil. The Light of *Revelation,* is a Confirmation and Improvement of the *Natural Light* of Reason. And they are *Both of them* extinguished, by the *Darkness of Irreligion,* and (which is still of *worse* consequence) by the *False Lights of Superstition.*

T H E *Inferences* from what has been said, are briefly as follows.

1*st.* F R O M this exhortation of our Saviour given to all Christians, *Take heed, that the* Light *which is in thee, be not Darkness*; it is evident that persons even of the *meanest* capacities, *may* and *must* have a *clear Understanding* of their Christian *Duty,* so far as it is at any time to *Them* a *Duty.* To live *soberly, righteously,* and *godly,* with a constant Sense of God upon their Minds, and under a perpetual Expectation of the future Judgment ; is what the *Lowest* Capacities may *see clearly* and *distinctly* to be their Duty. This is *Fundamental* in Religion. Things of *greater Difficulty,* they cannot be obliged to understand or regard, any further than they meet with *particular Light* to direct them. If at any time they run on *implicitly,* and stop not at the things they *certainly know,* they run an *apparent hazard* either of walking in *Darkness,* or (which is still *more* dangerous) of following a *False and deceitful Light.*

2. W H O E V E R at any time speaks against *Reason,* in matters of Religion; *knows not,* or considers not, *whereof he Affirms.* All *Reason* and *Truth* is from *God*; And God does as truly *reveal* himself by the *Nature and Reason of Things,* as by *Inspiration of Words. Reason,* is the *Light* of God's *Creation* : And though Men, if they be not very careful and very sincere, *may* mistake their own *Fancies and Imaginations* for *Reason* ; yet the *Nature and Truth of Things,* is still really what it is ; and *Light* is always *discernable,* if Men would honestly attend to it. The Experience of all Ages and of all Nations hath shown, that no Errors have been of such wide Extent, and of such lasting Continuance, and so destructive of all Moral Virtue and Goodness ; as those which Men have been led into, by departing from the most *evident and rational Fundamentals* of Religion, to follow the *blind and false Lights* of *Superstition.*

3. F R O M what has been said, it is evident it never was our Lord's intention, that there should be among Men (what the Church of *Rome* pretends to be) an *Infallible Guide.* Had any such thing been appointed of God, our Saviour's Caution in the Text, and in numberless other places in his Gospel, had been needless and absurd. *Teachers* of Religion, are, in the nature of the thing, necessary ; and, in fact, expressly appointed of Christ. But all *Teaching,* supposes that persons are *capable of being taught*; and that *when* they *Are* taught, they *can Then see* and *know* the thing to be *right.* In the way to eternal life, a man may very well be supposed to *want* the direction of a *Guide* : Yet in the whole Course of That Way, he may by Many *very certain Marks and Tokens,* laid down *beforehand* in *Reason* and *Scripture,* distinguish clearly whether his *Guide* directs him *right* or no : And if his Guide leads him to a *Precipice,* he may easily enough discern it. *Take heed, that the Light which is in thee, be not Darkness.*

SERMON

S E R M O N XL.

How to judge of Moral Actions.

L U K. VI. 44.

For every Tree is known by his own Fruit : For of Thorns men do not gather Figs, nor of a Bramble-bush gather they Grapes.

THERE are *some Figures of Speech* founded upon Similitudes so obvious, so natural, so expressive, that whilst they convey into the minds even of Those who have the meanest capacities, a Notion or Doctrine altogether as *distinct* and as *easy* to be understood, as any *Literal* expression whatsoever; they at the same time *illustrate* it *moreover* with the *clearest Light*, and *confirm* the *Truth* of it with the *strongest Reason* or *Argument*. Of This kind, there is great Variety of Instances of Scripture.

THUS when St. *Paul* exhorts Christians to present their Bodies a *Living Sacrifice*, holy, acceptable unto God; and elsewhere tells them, that they themselves are the *Temple* of God; and threatens, that if any man defile the *Temple* of God, Him shall God destroy : Under the *strong image* of the Unfitness and Abominableness, the Detestableness and Profaneness of any Uncleanness or Impurity appearing in the *Temple of God*; the odiousness of all *moral* impurity, of all *debauched* Practices whatsoever in Any person who professes himself a Worshipper of God, is set forth after a *more lively and affecting manner*, than it could be by any *literal* description whatsoever; And, under the *obvious* and *sensible Idea*, that a *Sacrifice* offered to *God*, even of a *Beast slain*, could not, with *any* just sense of the Greatness of the Divine Majesty, but be *without Blemish*; is represented the Acceptableness of a *Living Rational Person*, dedicating himself to the Service of God by a *sober and virtuous course of life*, in opposition to every kind of Debauchery, *more strongly and pathetically*, than it could any way have been done in *plain and direct Terms, without* such a *figurative* expression.

IN like manner in the words of the *Text*, the necessary Connexion between the nature of mens *Actions*, and the *Principles* from which they flow; and the Absurdity of supposing, that *good Actions* can ever flow from *ill Principles*, or *ill Actions* from *good Principles*; is expressed with greater Clearness and Strength, under the *similitude* of the regular Productions of nature, than it could have been by the most *literal and direct* Assertion. *Every Tree is known by its own Fruit : For of Thorns men do not gather Figs, nor of a Bramble-bush gather they Grapes.*

OUR Saviour, in his Parable of the *Sower*, St *Matt.* xiii. under the similitude of *different sorts of ground*, wherein good Seed being sown, brought forth *fruit* according to the nature of the Soil, in some places plentifully, in others thinly, in others none at all; gives a very *emphatical* and *accurate* description of the different Effects, which the Doctrines of True Religion, or the Teaching and Exhortations of Virtue, have upon the Lives and Actions of different Sorts of men. As the *same Seed*, sown in a *good Soil* or a *bad*, brings forth *much Fruit* or *little*, or *perishes entirely* and never grows at all; so the Knowledge of Truth, and the Instructions of Righteousness, *according to* the *different*

3

ferent

ferent dispositions of the minds of Those, to whom the Arguments of Reason and the Mo-tives of Religion are propofed; are either entirely fuppreffed by them, and extinguished, or elfe, fometimes in a greater, fometimes in a lefs degree, they produce the Fruit of *Virtuous Acts and Habits*, in the courfe of a righteous and religious Life. And from hence, throughout the whole Scripture, by a figure of Speech grounded upon *the ana-logy of This Parable*, the Acts and Habits of every Moral Virtue, founded upon the Mo-tives of the Gofpel, and fpringing from the Principles of True Religion, from the Belief of God and of a Judgment to come; are very expreffively termed, *the* Fruits *of the Spi-rit*; the natural *Produce* of a Mind rightly inftructed in the Doctrines of *Truth*, and di-rected and influenced in all its Actings, by a juft Senfe of what is *Right in itfelf* and *Ac-ceptable to God*; Gal. v. 22; *The* Fruit *of the Spirit, is Love, Joy, Peace, Long-fuffe-ring, Gentlenefs, Goodnefs, Faith, Meeknefs, Temperance*. And They who by a vir-tuous courfe of Life in their whole converfation, and in every part of their Behaviour in the World, fhow that their Religion is not an *empty Notion* or external *Form of Godli-nefs*, a mere *Denomination* of a Sect or Party; but a real *Principle* and Ground of Action, a real *Rule and Guide* of life and manners; are by the Apoftle defcribed under *This* character, that they *bring forth* Fruit *unto God*; having *their* Fruit *unto Holinefs, and the End everlafting Life*, Rom. vi. 22; vii. 4. The *Figure*, is the *very fame* with *That* made ufe of in *the Text: Every Tree is known by his own* Fruit; *for of Thorns men do not gather Figs, nor of a Bramble-bufh gather they Grapes*. And the *literal* fenfe of it is explained by our Saviour himfelf in the very next words following; ver. 45: *A good man, out of the good Treafure of his Heart, bringeth forth that which is good; and an evil man, out of the evil treafure of his Heart, bringeth forth that which is evil; For of the abundance of the Heart, his Mouth fpeaketh*. Now according to *This* explication, it is evident that, whether by this figurative phrafe, *every Tree*, we underftand the *Perfon himfelf* who acts, or the *Principles* from which his Actions flow; the *Senfe* is, either way, *one and the fame*. By the *Actions* of a man's Life, by the whole *Courfe and Tenour* of his Behaviour in the World, and by *no other diftinction* whatfoever, can be af-certained the *True Character* of any *Perfon*, and the *Real Goodnefs* or *Badnefs* of his *Principles*. External *Names* and *Denominations*, either of *Things* or *Perfons*, are all *deceitful*. Pretences to *Opinions* and *Doctrines*, may be all *fallacious*. Forms and Ob-fervances of all kinds may be *hypocritical*. Any thing may be called by *Any Name*, and Any thing may appear under *Any Shape*. But never can it happen in Any cafe, that of *Thorns* men fhould *gather Figs*, or that of a *Bramble-Bufh* they fhould *gather Grapes*. Never can it happen in Any cafe, that men of *corrupt Principles* and *vicious Lives*, can really have any *True Religion*; or that Any *True Religion*; any *Doctrine* that is from God, fhould be the Parent of any *Vice* or of any *Folly*, of any *Abfurdity*, of any *Cruelty*, of any *Pride, Tyranny*, or *Contentioufnefs*, or of any thing *mifchievous* among men. The *Acknowledgement* and the rational *Worfhip* of *God* who ruleth over All; The *Univerfal Love* and *Goodwill* of *All* men towards *All*, in which our Lord de-clares *all the Law and the Prophets*, and all the *Gofpel* too, to be fummarily contained; The *Sobriety, Holinefs*, and *Virtuous Living*, which the Religion of Chrift requires in Thofe, who expect a Judgment to come, and who (*according to his Promife*) *look for* new Heavens *and a* new Earth, *wherein dwelleth Righteoufnefs*: Thefe things can *no more poffibly* be the real productive *Caufe* of any thing *hurtful* to Mankind, than a *Vine* can bring forth any *other Fruit* than *Grapes*, or a *Fig-tree* than *Figs*; or than *Sheep* (according to *another* of our Lord's fimilitudes) can juftly be charged with the Rapine committed by *Wolves in Sheeps-clothing*. There is *no Principle in Nature* of more *certain and neceffary Truth*, of more *evident Clearnefs*, of more *univerfal Extent* and *Ufefulnefs* than This. And for *This reafon* our Saviour, upon fo *many* occafions, and in *numerous Places* of the Gofpel, repeats this Maxim, and makes perpetual Allufions to

SERM. it. Thus *Matt.* vii. 15, *Beware of false Prophets, which come to you in Sheeps-clothing,*
XL. *but inwardly they are ravening Wolves: Ye shall know them by their* Fruits: *Do men
gather Grapes of Thorns, or Figs of Thistles? A good Tree cannot bring forth evil Fruit,
neither can a corrupt Tree bring forth good Fruit: Every Tree that bringeth not forth
good Fruit, is hewn down and cast into the Fire:* Or, as he elsewhere expresses himself concerning the hypocritical Pharisees, *Matt.* xv. 13, *Every Plant, which my heavenly Father hath not planted, shall be rooted up.* Again, *Matt.* xii. 33, 34. Concerning
the same hypocrites, when, under a pretence of Zeal for Religion, they *blasphemed*
both the *Doctrine* and the *Works* of the Holy Ghost; *O Generation of Vipers,* says he,
how can ye, being Evil, speak Good things? Either make the Tree *good, and his* Fruit
good; or else make the Tree *corrupt, and his* Fruit *corrupt; For the* Tree *is known by his*
Fruit: That is; Either forbear these wicked and unrighteous Practices, or pretend not to
make Profession of Religion at all. To mention but One place more; *Joh.* xv. 1; *I
am the true Vine,* saith our Lord, *and my Father is the Husbandman. Every Branch in
me that beareth not Fruit, he taketh away; and every Branch that beareth Fruit, he
purgeth it, that it may bring forth more Fruit.* The Meaning is: The Belief of the
Doctrine of Christ, and of a Judgment to come, is the Foundation, the Root or Principle of all Christian Virtues: Every man therefore who calls himself a Christian, and yet
lives not in the Practice of Christian Virtue; is rejected of God, as a Dead Branch; as
having no participation in that Vital Principle which alone unites him to Christ here, and
entitles him to a Share in his Kingdom hereafter.

THE Meaning of the figurative Expressions in the Text, being thus explained from
the *Nature and Reason of the Thing,* and from the *Use of the like manner of Speaking* in
other places of Scripture; the *Doctrine* contained in the words, appears plainly to be
This: That by the *Actions* of a man's Life, by his *virtuous* or *vicious Practice,* by the
whole *Course and Tenour* of his Behaviour in the World, and by *no other Mark or Distinction* whatsoever, can with any certainty be determined the *True Character* of *Any
Person,* and the *Real Goodness* or *Badness* of the *Principles* by which he is governed.
*Every Tree is known by his Own Fruit: For of Thorns men do not gather Figs, nor of a
Bramble-bush gather they Grapes.*

AND the *Use* of this Doctrine is of the *greatest Importance* and *Extent:* For, from
hence may be estimated the *Excellency* and *Weightiness* of Any particular *Truth,* and the
Measure or Degree of *Malignity* of every Sort of *Errour,* in matters of Religion. From
hence may be judged the *Nature* and *Quality* of every kind of *Materials,* built (according to the Apostle St *Paul's* similitude, 1 *Cor.* iii. 12.) *upon the Foundation of Christ;*
whether it be *Gold, Silver, Precious-stones, Wood, Hay,* or *Stubble.* Whether it be
Work of such a sort, as, when it comes to be *tried* by the *Fire* of the Divine Judgment,
it will *abide,* and the Builder shall *receive a Reward* for it. Or whether it *shall be burnt,*
and *He accordingly shall suffer loss;* and yet *he himself finally be saved,* but *so as by Fire.*
Or whether, lastly, it be such as is *destructive* of the very *Foundation itself,* on which it
is built; and Then That severe Threatning in the following words be applicable to him;
ver. 17. *If any man destroy the Temple of God, him shall God destroy.*

THE *End* and *Design* of all *Religion;* the Proper *Effect* and *Produce of Good Principles;* the Good *Fruit* of a Good *Tree;* the *ultimate View* and *Fundamental Intention
of all religious Truths,* implanted in men either by Nature or Teaching; is the Practice
of *Virtue.* For the word *Religion,* in its very *Notion* and *original Meaning,* signifies
an *Obligation:* an *Obligation* upon men, arising from the *Reason of Things* and from
the *Government of God,* to *do* what is *just* and *virtuous* and *good;* to live, in a constant
habitual Sense and Acknowledgment of *God,* in the practice of universal Justice and Charity towards *Men,* and in a regular and sober Government of *their Own* Passions; under
a firm perswasion and continual expectation of the righteous distribution of Rewards and
Punish-

Punishments at their proper Seafon, in the eternal Judgment of God. *This*, is the **S E R M.** Foundation of Religion; the *Fundamental* Doctrine; in all *Places*, and at all *Times*, **XL.** invariable and eternal. *This*, being corrupted by numerous *Superstitions* among the *Jews*, and by the abfurdeft *Idolatries* and moft enormous *Immoralities* among the *Heathens*, *Chrift* came into the World to *reftore*; and, by the preaching of *Forgivenefs* upon *True Repentance* and *effectual Amendment of Life and Manners*, to bring back Sinners to the Kingdom of God, through the Obedience of the Gofpel. *In proportion* therefore as *any Doctrine of Truth* has a greater or more proper and more immediate Tendency to *promote* This Great *End*, to *produce* This *Fruit of the Spirit*; exactly *the very fame proportion* has it of *Weight* and *Excellency*, in the religious eftimation of things: 'Tis *Gold*, or *Silver*, or *Precious Stones*, (in the Apoftle's Language,) *built upon the Foundation of Chrift*. And, on the *other* fide, any *Erroneous Opinion*; in *proportion* as it has *Any*, or *No Moral* Influence; in the *very fame proportion*, it is either *Faulty* or *Innocent*. 'Tis (in St *Paul*'s fimilitude) either *Wood*, *Hay*, *Stubble*; fomething that is merely *loft labour*, *ufelefs* only, and *infignificant*, and of *no Strength* in the Building: Or elfe it is *oppofite to*, and *deftructive of*, the very *Foundation* of the *Temple of God*. 'Tis (in the analogy of our *Saviour's* Parable,) That which denominates a Man either to be a *Vine*, in which are many *Fruitlefs* Branches; or that he is (according to the Comparifon in the *Text*) a *Thorn* or a *Bramble-bufh*, from which it is impoffible to expect there fhould ever at all *be gathered Figs* or *Grapes*.

By *This Rule* therefore (I fay) may certainly be diftinguifhed the *Meafure* or *Degree* of *Malignity* of *every Sort* of *Errour*, in matters of *Religion*.

By *This*, (to inftance in *Particulars*,) it appears *Wherein* confifted the *malignity* of the Heathen-*Idolatry*, and *how Great* the *Evil* of it was. For whereas the rational *Worfhip* of *the One True God* of *Nature*, and *Governour* of the *Univerfe*, and the *Acknowledgment* of his *True Perfections* and *Attributes*, taught by the original uncorrupted Light of Nature and Reafon, leads Men by a *direct* and *proper*, by an *immediate*, *natural*, and *perpetual Influence*, to the Imitation and *Practice* of thofe moral and eternal *Virtues*, which, in their higheft and complete Perfection, are the Excellencies of the Divine Nature itfelf; the *Worfhip* of *Wood* and *Stone*, on the contrary, by a no lefs natural and immediate Tendency, leads Men to place *empty fuperftitious* and *fenfelefs Obfervances* in the Room of all real Virtue and Goodnefs. And the *Worfhip* of *Fictitious Deities*, formed, by the Imaginations of *Corrupt Men*, like to *Themfelves* in the Practice of all *unrighteoufnefs and Debauchery*; This, ftill *much more*, leads Men into the moft *abominable Corruption* of Manners. According to the defcription St *Paul* gives of the Heathen-World, *Rom.* i. 21; *Becaufe that when they knew God, they glorified him not as God,———and did not like to retain God in their Knowledge*; therefore *God gave them over to a reprobate mind, to do thofe things which are not convenient*.

Again: By the *fame* meafure of Judging, may eafily be underftood the *Nature* of *That Errour*, and the *Degree* of its *ill Effect*, which the Nation of the *Jews* had very generally fallen into, in and before our Saviour's time; *viz.* their laying the great *Strefs* of *Religion*, more upon the exact Obfervance of certain Outward *Ceremonies*, than upon the habitual Practice of *Moral Virtue*. The *Ceremonies* of the *Jewifh* Law, befides their perpetual *typifying* of the *Meffiah* to come, and their *diftinguifhing* in a moft remarkable manner the *National Worfhippers of the God of Heaven* from all the *idolatrous Nations* of the Earth; were moreover appointed of God to be continual *Emblems*, and as it were *Memorials* of their Obligation to *Moral Holinefs*. *Sanctify yourfelves*, faith the Lord; *Levit.* xi. 44; *and ye fhall be Holy, for I am Holy*: And *if ye will obey my voice indeed, and keep my covenant, —ye fhall be unto me a Kingdom of Priefts*, **Ex. xix. 5:**

and

S E R M. *and a Holy Nation.* *So far* therefore as their Obfervance of the *Ceremonies* of the Law,
XL.   promoted the *End* for which thofe Ordinances were appointed ; *So far as* they kept
that people *fteddy* in their *Adherence,* to the *Worſhip* of the *True God,* and, by the
Care required in avoiding every *natural* Impurity, continually reminded them to be
much more fearful of whatever was *morally* fuch: *So far* thofe Ceremonies were of
real Eſteem in the Sight of *God,* and of *real* religious *Advantage* to Men. Whenfoever
the Obfervance of the fame *outward Ceremonies,* was feparate from the *internal Moral
Benefit;* the *Ceremony* then became *uſeleſs,* and the *Obſervation* of it *vain.* But when
at any time the *Ceremony* came *in competition* with the *Moral Duty,'* or was *preferred*
before it, or was prefumed to be *acceptable* in the *Stead* of it; in the *Stead* of the
weightier matters of the Law, Juſtice, Mercy, and Faithfulneſs; Then the *Ceremony,*
though of God's *own* appointment, became (as the *Prophets* in the *Old Teſtament,* and
our Saviour in the *Goſpel,* perpetually declare ; it became) *odious* to God, and *abominable* in his Sight.

Laſtly : By the *ſame* Rule may be judged the *degree* of *Malignity* of any *erroneous
Notions* or *Opinions* among Chriſtians. The *End* and *Deſign* of the *Goſpel of Chriſt,*
is to *reſtore Sinners* to the *Favour of God,* by bringing them back to the Practice of
Righteouſneſs and *True Holineſs.* So far as *Any Errour whatſoever,* hurts not and prevents not *This Deſign* ; fo far as it is merely *ſpeculative,* and produces no Fruit of evil
Confequences in *Practice*; fo far it is *innocent,* and may be afcribed to *Weakneſs.* But
in what *degree* foever its Influence is hurtful to *Virtue,* in the very *ſame* proportion it is
always *Faulty* in *Men,* and *blame-worthy* before God.

F o r inſtance : With regard to erroneous Notions concerning *God :* Every Opinion
concerning the Divine Nature or Perfections, which is in itfelf *abſurd* and *unintelligible,*
is juſt *ſo far* hurtful to Religion, as it *diverts* Men from the *Practice* of the *Law of
Righteouſneſs,* by filling them with a *childiſh* and *ſuperſtitious* imagination, that *God* is
pleaſed with their *pretending* or *fanſying* that they *believe* they *know not what.* Notions concerning *abſolute* and *unconditionate Predeſtination,* are juſt fo far faulty and
blame-worthy in Religion, as they *cut* the *Sinews* and *demoliſh* all the *Motives of Virtue,* by afcribing to God *ſuch* a *Sovereignty,* as *deſtroys* all the *Other Perfections* of his
Nature ; a *Sovereignty,* denoting a *Power* of acting, in *Moral* Matters, without regard
to *Moral* Reafon ; Which, in Truth and Reality, is no more an *Attribute of God,* than
the *Power* of acting in *natural* things, contrary to *Natural* Poffibility. Erroneous Notions concerning *Faith,* (taking it to fignify a mere *credulity* ; whereas in truth, when
fpoken of as a Chriſtian virtue, it always means *Fidelity,* or *Acting Faithfully* and fteddily *upon* Chriſtian *Principles* :) Errours concerning *Grace,* (taking it to fignify an
Operation of God upon *Men,* when indeed it denotes His *gracious Acceptance* of their
Repentance and *Amendment,* brought about by the *Motives* and *Aſſiſtances* of the *Goſpel:)*
Errours concerning the *Merits of Chriſt,* (when *vicious* and *debauched* perfons hope to
be faved by *His Merits,* inſtead of *reforming and amending their manners* in order to
obtain Forgivenefs through His Interceffion :) And, ſtill more than all thefe, Applications made to *Angels,* and to *Saints departed,* and to *Images* of Wood and Stone, and
Other the like *Inventions*; All Thefe things, are, upon One and the fame Account,
deſtructive of *true Religion*; in that they ſuppofe Obedience to the eternal and unchangeable Law of God, which is the Practice of *Moral Virtue,* may be commuted for
by any other Performances whatfoever : Which is indeed the *Eſſence* of all *Superſtition:*
'Tis, in the Allufion made by our Saviour in the Text, the Fruit of the *Thorn* or *Bram-
ble-buſh,* inſtead of *Grapes.*

A g a i n ; With regard likewife to erroneous Notions concerning our Duty towards
Men : Every Opinion that leads in Practice to *Contentiouſneſs, Pride, Cruelty,* and the
like ;

like; is evidently fo far *not innocent*, but *deftructive* of Religion, as it is *inconfiftent* with the Great and Eternal Law of *Charity* and *Good-will* towards *Mankind*. From whence may eafily be perceived the extreme *Malignity* of the *Romifh Doctrine* of *Perfecution*; by which all the *Authority*, wherewith God has invefted men for the *Incouragement of Virtue* and *Punifhment of Vice*, has been wickedly and perverfely imployed in *forcing* a *violent and hypocritical Pretenfe of Unity of Opinion*, in matters generally of *doubtful Speculation*, and oft-times of *Ungodly Practife* too; to the entire *Subverfion* both of *Truth and Charity*.

Laftly; W I T H regard to erroneous Notions concerning every man's own private Duty in the Government of *Himfelf*: Every Opinion that gives Licence to Any Sort of *Debauchery*; that gives men Incouragement to *fin*, in hopes *that Grace may abound*; *turning the Grace of God into Lafcivioufnefs*, as the Apoftle expreffes it, and *making Chrift the Minifter of Sin*; Every fuch opinion, I fay, is a *Root of Bitternefs*, and brings forth *Fruit unto Death*. Of This Sort is That defperate Notion which has prevailed fo much in the Church of *Rome*; a relying upon repeated *Confeffions* and *Abfolutions* for the *Pardon of Sins*, in the *Practice* of which they ftill however *continue*. And of the fame Kind is That dangerous expectation even among *Proteftants* too; when Men of *loofe and debauched Lives* flatter themfelves, that, without Any real Virtue or Holinefs, they fhall be accepted of God, upon their performing, on a Bed of Sicknefs and at the Approach of *Death*, fome of thofe external Duties, which were inftituted on purpofe to be *Obligations* and Affiftances to *Holinefs* of *Life*. But our Rule is One, and Plain: *He that doth Righteoufnefs, is Righteous*. Which is the *literal* Meaning of the *Figure* in the Text: *Every Tree is known by his own Fruit: For of Thorns men do not gather Figs, nor of a Bramble-bufh gather they Grapes*.

S E R M O N XLI.

The Nature of Religious Truths.

2 TIM. II. 25.

In Meekneſs inſtructing thoſe that oppoſe themſelves, if God perad-venture will give them Repentance to the acknowledging of the Truth.

SERM.
XLI.
AS *Light* is neceſſarily and eſſentially different from *Darkneſs*, notwithſtanding thoſe who are blind cannot diſtinguiſh That difference; ſo, notwithſtanding the Weakneſs and Blindneſs of mens Underſtandings, and the much worſe Confuſion ariſing from the Corruption and Perverſeneſs of their Wills; yet *Truth* is ſtill, in the Nature of Things, always Real and Invariable, and, for the moſt part, *diſtinguiſhable* alſo from *Error*. In *ſome kinds* of things, 'tis indeed very *difficult* for *Us* to diſcover where the Truth lies; the *Cauſes* of things, being abſtruſe; the *Ends and Deſigns* of them, remote; the *things themſelves*, often intricate; the *Manner* how they may poſſibly be, diverſe and various; and *our Underſtanding*, in itſelf finite and fallible. But This difficulty of finding out the Truth, is generally in things of That nature only; which are of no great importance for us to know. As the *Eyes* of our *Body*, are fitted only to diſcern things within the reach of ſuch a diſtance, as 'tis of Uſe to us in Life to comprehend within our View; ſo our *Underſtanding*, which is the *Eye* of the *Mind*, can very difficultly ſearch into the Truth of numberleſs things, which it does not concern us diſtinctly to know. But in All things of *importance*, in all things of *great and real Uſe* to us, ſuch as are the eternal Differences of Good and Evil, and all Matters fundamental in *Religion*; in *Theſe* things, Truth is always as diſtinguiſhable to the unprejudiced Underſtanding of a Perſon even of a *mean* Capacity, as Light is by the Eye diſtinguiſhable from Darkneſs.

THAT *God*, the Maker and Judge of all, is to be worſhipped, rather than the Fic-tions of Humane Folly. That the Worſhip moſt acceptable to him, is the *Obedience* of a virtuous and ſober Life, rather than an Endleſs Circle of mere external Ceremo-nies. That the Practice of *Juſtice, Righteouſneſs, Meekneſs* and *Charity*, is much more uſeful to men, *than their ſtirring up each other's Zeal for or againſt opinions*, of which they underſtand very little: Theſe great Lines of Truth, are ſo plainly, ſo brightly con-ſpicuous, both in Reaſon and Scripture, that *he who runs may read them*. Whoſoever is led into any Errour, contrary to theſe *Great and Fundamental Truths*, 'tis not by his *Underſtanding*, but by his *Will* that he is deceived; and therefore he is juſtly anſwer-able for his Folly. *God would have all men to be ſaved, and to come to the knowledge of the Truth*, 1 Tim. ii. 4. The Light held forth to them is clear and ſtrong; the Rules are Few and conſpicuous; that an unprejudiced perſon would hardly think it poſſible they ſhould be miſtaken. Yet ſo extenſive is *That kind* of *Error* which proceeds from Wilfulneſs and corrupt Affections, that in oppoſition to theſe Great and Plain Rules it is, that the *whole World lieth in Wickedneſs*, 1 Joh. v. 19. In oppoſition to the

Evidence

Evidence of This fhining Light it is, that the Devotion of the *Popifh* World is tranf-ferred from the God and Father of all things, and from the One only Mediator whom *He* has appointed; to Saints, and Angels, and Images, and fictitious Relicks. In oppofition to the fame plain and evident Truths it is, that, not in the *Popifh* World only, but in too great a part even of That alfo which calls itfelf *Proteftant*, mere outward and cuftomary Forms have by Many perfons a greater Strefs laid upon them, than the weightier matters of the Law, Practife of True Virtue: And men generally are more concerned to fupport uncertain Opinions, than to promote the Habits of Juftice, Goodnefs, Temperance, Meeknefs, and univerfal Good-will towards Mankind; upon which principally depends our Happinefs in *This* World, and our Title to *That which is to come.* This is the Great Corruption, the Great and Univerfal Error of All Ages in matters of Religion. And they who Thus *oppofe themfelves* to the Great End and Defign of the Gofpel, fubverting the Simplicity and Purity of the doctrine of Chrift; thefe, as well as the Atheiftical, debauched, and profane, are the Perfons whom we ought to be continually *inftructing in Meeknefs, if God peradventure will give them Repentance to the Acknowledgment of the Truth.*

In which words of the Apoftle, we may obferve diftinctly the following particulars. 1ft, A fuppofition laid down; That *Truth* is fomething *real* in *itfelf,* and of *importance* to *Men;* fomething that *may* be found, and which we *ought* to feek after. 2dly, An Obfervation made concerning the corrupt ftate and difpofition of Mankind, that Some there will always be, who *will* fet themfelves to *oppofe* the Truth. 3dly, A Direction given, concerning our *Own* Duty; that we ought to *inftruct* fuch perfons, in *Meeknefs.* And 4thly, A Reafon added, *why* we ought to do it in That manner; *if God peradventure will give them Repentance to the acknowledgment of the Truth.*

1ft. Here is a *Suppofition* laid down; that *Truth,* is fomething *real* in *itfelf,* and of *importance* to *Men;* fomething that *may* be found, and which we *ought* to feek after. I have already obferved, that where-ever the Scripture fpeaks of *Truth,* it always means *fuch* Truth as has relation to *Religion;* And I fhall ufe the word in *That* fenfe, thro' the whole following Difcourfe. *All* Truth, of what kind *foever* it be, is *real;* but *not* always of *importance. All* Truth, has its *Foundation in Nature;* but is *not* always neceffary, or of any great Ufe for Us to know. But Truth in matters of *Religion,* is always of the greateft *importance,* as being the *Foundation* and the *Support,* of *Right Practice.* Men, upon *erroneous Principles,* may do what is Right by *Chance;* or the general *Probity* of their Temper, may over-rule the ill influence of miftaken Principles: But there can be no 'certain, there can be no *fteddy* Rule of good Practice, without a Foundation of Truth. All *Error* is founded in *Imagination* only; 'Tis a Shadow, without a Subftance; 'Tis generally nothing elfe, but a carelefs following of *other* mens Opinions, or pretended Opinions; a lazy and formal Adherence to the *Cuftoms* of the Age men live in, or the *Notions* which *happen* to prevail, like *other Fafhions,* in *particular Places,* and among certain *Sects* or *Parties* of men. Principles of which kind, can be no better a Foundation of Practice, than mere Chance; And Religion built upon fuch quick-fand, is, in the feveral Nations of the Earth, nothing at all more than the *Cuftom* or *Fafhion of the Country.* Religion acceptable to *God,* who judges the Heart; muft be, in the *Mind* of every *particular* Perfon, a Love of *Truth* and *Right:* A Love of *That* Truth and Right, not which is efteemed fuch upon mere vulgar and cuftomary Acceptation, but which the Mind itfelf perceives and feels, and, upon Examination finds to be fo in reality. Of This, the Mind of *every* uncorrupt Man, is by the Author of Nature made as competent a Judge; as the Eyes of the Body, are made fit to difcern between Light and Darknefs. And the Righteoufnefs of God's future Judgment, (*That Judgment* wherein men fhall give an account of themfelves, not in the lump by Sects and Parties, but every man fingly and perfonally for himfelf;

S E R M. himfelf; the Righteoufnefs, I fay, of *that future Judgment)* muft of neceffity depend,
  XLI.   upon every man's underftanding for Himfelf the Rule he is to be judged by. *What*
~~~~~   This Rule is, can be of no difficulty for any man to difcover. *Natural Confcience,*
That *original Light,* That *Candle of the Lord,* which God has implanted in every
man's Breaft, tells him always *what* it is, with regard to the *eternal Truths* of *Morality :* And to them who live under the Light of the *Gofpel,* the additional *Precepts*
given by *Chrift* in *Scripture,* are no lefs clear and confpicuous. *Thefe Truths* of God,
are, like an immoveable *Rock,* the Bafis and Foundation of That True Religion,
which approves itfelf to every man's *Underftanding* by clear Reafon, and glorifies God
by making men like unto him through Virtue and Righteoufnefs in their *Practice.*
All *falfe* Religions confift, in *changing the Truths of God into a Lie,* Rom. i. 25.
Either corrupting the Truth of God's *Creation,* by introducing into Religion things oppofite to, or things which draw men from, the Practice of Virtue, of Juftice, Goodnefs and Charity. Or corrupting the Truth of God's *Revelation,* by mixing with the
plain fimplicity of the Doctrine of Chrift, Traditions and uncertain Notions of merely
Humane Invention. *Truth itfelf,* both *natural* and *revealed,* when feparate from all
corruptions of *Men,* appears always with a native Luftre and Beauty, with a Strength
and Clearnefs of Reafon, which the Scripture elegantly compares to *a Light fhining
in Darknefs;* which needs no *external Force,* no *Violence or Compulfion,* no *artificial
impofing* upon the Underftanding, (as the *Inventions of Men* do,) to caufe it to be received and embraced; But it requires only an *unprejudiced apprehenfion,* and an *uncorrupt Will,* in order to its being entertained univerfally in the Love thereof. It always tends alfo to promote mens *true Intereft:* their true Intereft, as well *Temporal* as
Eternal: The *Peace* and *Satisfaction,* of every man's *Own Mind* in particular; and,
in general, univerfal *Love and Good-will* towards all *Others.* For all the *Contentions*
and *Animofities,* all the *Hatred* and *Malice,* all the *Perfecution* and *Cruelties* which
have ever been exercifed in the World under pretenfe of zeal for Religion; have in
reality always arifen purely upon Account of zeal for matters of *mens own* Invention,
never out of concern for the plain *Laws* and *Commands* of God. And all the dark and
flavifh Bigottry, which has at any time tormented the Minds of particular men; has
been owing to the Superftitious Errors, wherewith the Weaknefs of Some, and
the Defigns of Others, have mifreprefented That *Truth of God,* which the Apoftle
ftiles *the perfect Law of Liberty;* and of which, our Saviour himfelf declares, *Joh.* viii.
32, *Ye fhall know the Truth, and the Truth fhall make you Free.* Not without the
greateft reafon therefore, is that Exhortation of the Wife man, *Prov.* xxiii. 23, *Buy
the Truth, and fell it not:* And ch. iv. 7, *Wifdom is the principal thing; therefore
get Wifdom; and with all thy Getting, get Underftanding.* St *Paul* in like manner,
Phil. iv. 8, in That elegant enumeration, wherein he reckons up every thing that can
be thought to be excellent, and exhorts the *Philippians,* in the moft earneft and affectionate manner, *If there be Any Virtue, if there be any Praife,* to *think upon* Thofe
things; not without a particular Emphafis, placeth at the Head of All, in the very
firft rank, *Whatfoever things are* True. And This may fuffice, for Explication of the
Firft Particular in the Text; the *Suppofition* laid down, that *Truth* is fomething *real*
in *itfelf,* and of importance to *Men;* fomething that *may* be found, and which we
ought to feek after.

    2*dly,* T H E *next* Obfervation collected from the Words of the Text, is; that fuch
is the corrupt State and Difpofition of Mankind, that *Some* there will *always be,* who
will fet themfelves to *oppofe* the Truth. Notwithftanding the Native *Excellency and
Beauty* of Truth, confidered *in itfelf;* notwithftanding the *Strength and Clearnefs of
Reafon,* with which it is generally accompanied; notwithftanding the apparent *Benefit
and Advantage,* which the Knowledge of Truth always brings to Mankind; yet fo
little

4

little fenfible are Men of the intrinfick Excellency of things, fo unattentive to the S E R M. Strength of the cleareft Reafon, fo apt to be impofed upon in judging concerning their XLI. own true Intereft; that nothing is more Common, than to fee the plaineft and moft ufeful Truths, in matters of Religion, violently and paffionately oppofed.

T H E principal *Caufes* of this Oppofition; are in particular, *Ignorance, Carelefsnefs, Prejudice,* and *Vice.*

T H E *Firft* caufe of Men's fetting themfelves in oppofition to the Light of Truth, is *Ignorance.* Meaning here, by *Ignorance,* not a bare *Want of Knowledge :* (For the natural and proper Effect of *bare Want of Knowledge,* is, that Men forbear to pafs Any judgment *at all,* upon what they underftand not; and that they neither contend *for* or *againft* any opinion, before they have fome *Reafon* to determine them fo to do :) But there is a *prefumptuous* Ignorance, which *defpifes* Knowledge; And This makes Men *oppofe* the Truth, before they underftand any thing of it. Seeft thou a man that *defpifeth* inftruction ? there is more hope of a *Fool,* than of Him.

A N O T H E R caufe of Men's oppofing the Truth, is *Carelefsnefs.* They blindly, and without any Confideration, follow the *Cuftoms* of the Place where they happen to live; And the Knowledge of Truth, feems to them to be of no great Importance. They take up their Religion at adventures, not from the confideration of the Laws of *Nature* or of *Revelation,* but merely from the *Company* they *chance* to be educated amongft; And thus *All Religions* are put upon an equal foot, varying according to the accidental Temper of the Perfons among whom they prevail. Men of This difpofi- tion, *carelefs* of finding out the Truth, and confequently having indeed no Religion at all, but barely the name and profeffion of it; generally prefer *Any degree* of *Ignorance,* before the carefulleft *Study* either of the *Nature* of *Things,* or of the Laws of *God.* To This Temper 'tis palpably owing, that fo many *whole Nations* at this day, *Pagans and Mahometans,* never give themfelves the Trouble to enquire at all, whether the *Chriftian* Religion be true or no; And even among the Profeffors of *Chriftianity,* (as they think themfelves to be,) many entire Nations, full of Men very Learned and of great Abili- ties, yet never fuffer any careful Inquiry to be made, whether the Worfhip of imagi- nary Saints, and of Images of Wood and Stone, and of Relicks, and of Bread; and innumerable other Doctrines and Practices, abfurd Notions and fuperftitious Ceremo- nies; they never (I fay) fuffer any careful Examination to be made, whether thefe things are agreeable to the Plainnefs and Simplicity, to the Holinefs and Purity of Chrift's Religion or no.

A *further* Caufe of Men's oppofing the Truth, is *Prejudice.* They are not perhaps naturally *ignorant;* nor yet of fo *lazy and carelefs* a Temper, as to oppofe the Truth merely to avoid the *Trouble* of ftudying it. But their *Prejudices* are fo ftrong, that the *cleareft Light* cannot overcome and diffipate fo thick a cloud. They have accuftomed themfelves to found their Belief entirely in an *implicit* Reliance upon *Other Men;* in- ftead of building it upon the Evidence of *Things themfelves,* which is the Foundation of Truth. And Then, the Traditions of the Scribes and Elders and Pharifees; the Decrees of *Popes,* or the Determinations of *Parties,* evidently governed by Worldly Motives; fhall have much more Weight with them, to perfwade them to *blind* or *fhut* their Eyes; than the *whole Scripture* of Truth, or the ftrongeft and *plaineft Reafon* in the World, fhall have to perfwade them to *open* them. So little do they confider Thofe Admonitions of our Saviour; *Search the Scriptures;* and, *He that hath Ears to hear, let him hear :* And That of St *Paul; I fpeak as unto wife men,* (that is, to intelligent perfons;) *judge ye what I fay,* 1 Cor. x. 15. And of St *Peter,* 1 Pet. iii. 15. *Be ready always to give an Anfwer to every man that afketh you a reafon of the Hope that is in you.*

SERM.   BUT the *Laſt* and *Greateſt* reaſon of Men's ſetting themſelves in oppoſition to the
XLI.   Truth, is the *Wickedneſs* and *Corruption* of their *Manners*; the Love of unrighteouſneſs and debauchery, the Deſire of Power and Dominion, the Concern they are under
for the Defenſe and Support of a Sect or Party, without having Any Knowledge how
far they are, or are not, in the Right. Theſe are things, which make men to *ſhut
their Eyes* againſt the Light, to *love* and chooſe *darkneſs rather than Light*, and wilfully to *ſtop their Ears* againſt all the Means of being better informed. Concerning
ſuch Perſons, St *Paul* propheſies, 2 *Tim.* iii. 2, 8, *In the laſt days——men ſhall be——
Boaſters,——Deſpiſers of thoſe that are good,——heady, high-minded, Lovers of pleaſure more than Lovers of God, Having a Form of godlineſs, but denying the Power
thereof,——reſiſting the Truth, men of corrupt minds.* And theſe things *muſt be*, ſaith
1 Cor. xi. 19. the ſame Apoſtle; (*i. e.* it is fit and juſt that the Providence of God ſhould *permit* it
Thus to be;) *that thoſe which are approved*, (i. e. that thoſe who ſeek and obey the
Truth and Simplicity of the Goſpel, ſeparate from all *worldly* and unjuſtifiable *Deſigns*,)
may be made manifeſt among you.

    3*dly*, THE *Third* thing obſervable in the Text, is the *Direction* given us concern-
ing *our own* Duty; that we ought in *Meekneſs* to *inſtruct* thoſe who oppoſe themſelves
againſt the Truth. He who *himſelf*, *ſuffers* for well-doing, and for the Teſtimony
of a good Conſcience, is ſure of being (at leaſt *ſo far*) in the *Right* : But he who
does Violence to *Others*; if *they*, whom he does violence to, be in a *right* cauſe, He
is an Enemy to God : But if they be in the *wrong*, yet He diſhonours the Truth, by
2 Tim. ii. 24. acting unrighteouſly for it, not knowing what Spirit he is of. *The Servant of the
Lord, muſt not ſtrive, but be gentle unto all Men, apt to teach, patient.* We cannot
always diſcern, *who* they are that err through *ignorance*, and *who* through a *vitious
diſpoſition.* (I ſpeak not here concerning matters of *Immorality*; for Faults of *This*
Gal. v. 23. kind, are evident to *all* men.) But if we *could*, yet *Meekneſs* is at all *times* neceſſarily
a *Fruit of the Spirit* ; And we are commanded to *be patient towards* All *men*, 1 Th.
v. 14; towards them that *oppoſe*, as well as towards them that are only *ignorant of*,
Jam. iii. 13. the Truth. *Who is a Wiſe man*, ſaith St *James*, and indued with Knowledge amongſt
you? let him ſhow out of a good converſation his works with Meekneſs of Wiſdom.* For
——the Wiſdom that is from above, is firſt pure, then peaceable, gentle and eaſy to be
intreated.* But *Anger, reſteth in the boſom of Fools*, Eccleſ. vii. 9. And the *Wrath
of Man worketh not the Righteouſneſs of God*, Jam. i. 20. being always a *certain*
Evidence, that Men are more concerned for ſome temporal Intereſt, than for the real
Honour of God and Goodneſs. Men of a true Chriſtian Spirit, ſincerely deſirous to
promote the Knowledge of Truth and the Practice of Virtue in the World, rather than
the obtaining of Temporal Power and Dominion for themſelves, are always willing to
conſider, that *they themſelves* are fallible ; and therefore conſtantly endeavour to convince *Others*, by the Methods of *Reaſon*, and not of *Paſſion* and *Violence*. *Shewing
all Meekneſs unto all Men, for* that *we ourſelves alſo were ſometimes fooliſh*, Tit. iii. 2, 3.
Which *Temper*, is much *more* reaſonable in point of *Truth and Error* ; when, even
with regard to Faults of the *Will*, St *Paul* admoniſhes, *if a man be overtaken in a
Fault——reſtore ſuch a one in the Spirit of Meekneſs, conſidering thyſelf, leſt Thou alſo
be tempted*, Gal. vi. 1. (He ſpeaks not of the *Crimes* of *Malefactors*, ſuch as muſt neceſſarily be puniſhed by the hand of *Juſtice* ; But he means *ſuch* Faults, as are to be
cured by Reproof.) Our *Saviour himſelf*, though infallible, and could *not err*; yet
Matt. xi. 29. was *meek and lowly in Heart* : And rebuked his Diſciples with great Severity, when
once upon high provocation they diſcovered an inclination to violent Methods ; *Ye
know not* (ſaid he) *what manner of Spirit ye are of*, Luke ix. 55. Plainly intimating to
all ſucceeding Generations, *wherein* would lie the principal Difference between the
Spirit of Chriſt and the *Spirit of Anti-Chriſt.*

I

4thly and *Laftly*; HERE is in the Text annexed a *particular Reafon*, with regard SERM.
to *the Perfons to be inftructed*; *why* our Inftruction to them, ought always to be ac- XLI.
companied with Meeknefs: *If God peradventure will give them Repentance to the ac-*
knowledgment of the Truth. In the Original, it is; Leaft *God peradventure fhould give*
them Repentance to the acknowledgment of the Truth. The Meaning is : We are to
inftruct them with Meeknefs; leaft peradventure by our Heat and Paffion, we raife
in them a juft Prejudice againft us; when by meek inftruction, they *might* poffibly
have been brought to Repentance, and to the acknowledgment of the Truth; And fo
we, by our ill behaviour, become anfwerable for *their* mifcarriage. For, nothing can
be a greater hindrance to men's being convinced, than the applying *Violence* and *Paf-*
fion inftead of *Reafon*: And nothing can give more Advantage to the Evidence of
Truth, than the meek Behaviour of thofe who profefs it. For *This* reafon, we fo
frequently find repeated in Scripture the following Admonitions, which may ferve for a
proper Application of this whole Difcourfe. *Be ready always to give an Anfwer to*
every man that afketh you a reafon of the Hope that is in you, with Meeknefs *and*
Fear, 1 Pet. iii. 15. *Give none Offence, neither to the Jews, nor to the Gentiles*,
1 Cor. x. 32. *Walk in Wifdom towards them that are without*, Col. iv. 5. *Have a* 1 Th. iv. 12.
good report of them which are without, left ye fall into reproach, 1 Tim. iii. 7. *Let your*
Moderation, your meek and exemplary good Spirit, *be known unto all men*, Phil. iv. 5.
Blamelefs and harmlefs, the Sons of God; without rebuke, in the midft of a crooked and
perverfe Generation, among whom ye fhine as Lights in the World, Phil. ii. 15. *Having*
your converfation honeft, that is, of good reputation, even *among the Gentiles; that*
whereas they fpeak againft you as Evil-Doers, they may by your good works which they
fhall behold, glorify God in the day of vifitation, 1 Pet. ii. 12. And in the words of
our Saviour himfelf, *Matt.* v. 16. *Let your Light fo fhine before men*; the Light of
your Meeknefs, Goodnefs, and Charity; the Light of your excellent Temper, and univerfal Virtue; that the whole World *may fee your good Works, and glorify your Father*
which is in Heaven.

SERMON

SERMON XLII.

Of CHRIST's calling Sinners to Repentance.

MAR. II. 17.

When Jesus heard it, he saith unto them, They that are whole, have no need of the Physician, but they that are sick: I came not to call the Righteous, but Sinners to Repentance.

SERM.
XLII.

THE Occasion of these words, was briefly This. Our Lord, having called his Apostle *Matthew* from the Receipt of Custom, and the Call being immediately obeyed; he thereupon went home with the Converted Disciple, unto That Disciple's house. *And it came to pass, that as Jesus sat at meat at his house,* (ver. 15.) *many Publicans and Sinners,* of That Disciple's former acquaintance, having followed them from the Receipt of Custom, *sat also together with Jesus and his Disciples;* our Lord being always ready, to take *every* occasion of exhorting Sinners to Repentance, and to *give* them every opportunity of receiving such Exhortations. *But the* conceited *Scribes and Pharisees,* ver. 16, *when they saw him eating with Publicans and Sinners;* not considering, according to the Reason and Truth of things, that, not the *conversing* with Sinners, but the *partaking* with them in their *Sins,* or *incouraging* them therein, is only *faulty;* nay, that conversing with such persons, not only may be *innocent,* but, when it is in order to their Amendment, very *praise-worthy* also: The *Scribes* and *Pharisees,* I say, not considering *This,* but being full of Vanity and Pride, and valuing themselves upon an *affected* appearance of *peculiar Holiness,* in despising and setting themselves *above* the conversation of those whom in contempt they called *Publicans and Sinners;* pretended to *wonder much,* when they saw Jesus sitting at meat with persons of That character; and asked his Disciples, saying, *How is it that he eateth and drinketh with Publicans and Sinners?* Jesus, hearing their question, and knowing their Wickedness and Pride of Heart, replies in the words of the Text; *They that are whole, have no need of the Physician, but they that are Sick: I came not to call the Righteous, but Sinners to Repentance.*

IN discoursing upon which words, I shall *1st* draw some Observations from the several *particular* expressions we meet with in the Text; and *2dly,* I shall consider the *general* Doctrine of *Repentance,* as therein laid down by our Lord.

I. THE *Observations* naturally arising from the several *particular* expressions made use of in the Text; are,

1st, THAT *Sin* is to the *Soul,* what *Disease* or *Sickness* is to the *Body:* The *Whole,* and they that are *Sick,* are here, in our Saviour's phrase, the *Righteous* and the *Sinners.* And the Analogy, is very obvious and elegant. For as the *natural* Health of the *Body,* consists in *This;* that every Part and Organ, regularly and duly performs its proper Function; and, when any of these are disordered or perverted in their operations, there ensues Sickness and Diseases: So likewise, with regard to the *Spiritual* or *Moral* State of the *Mind* and *Soul;* when every Faculty is employed in its natural and proper manner,

and

and with a juft direction to the end it was defigned for; when the *Underftanding* judges S E R M.
of things according to Reafon and Truth, without partiality and without prejudice; XLII.
when the *Will* is in its *actions* directed by this judgment of Right, without Obftinacy
or Wilfulnefs; and when the *Paffions* in their due fubordinate ftation, and the *Appetites*
under the Government of Sober intention, ferve only to *quicken* the execution of what
Reafon directs; then is the Mind of man Sound and whole; fit for all the operations of
a *rational* creature, fit for the employments of a *virtuous and religious* Life. On the
contrary, the *Abufe* or *mifimployment* of *Any* of thefe Faculties, is the *Difeafe* or *Sicknefs* of the Soul. And when they are *All* of them perverted, *totally* and *habitually*, by
a *general* corruption and depravation of Manners; then, as the *Body*, by an incapacity
of *all* its organs for the Ufes of *natural* Life, *dies*, and is diffolved; fo the man in his
moral capacity, by an *habitual* neglect and diflike of all virtuous Practices, becomes (as
the Scripture elegantly expreffes it) Dead *in Trefpaffes and Sins*. And as, in *Bodily*
Difeafes, Some are *more* dangerous, and more likely to prove *mortal*, than Others; in
which fenfe our Saviour fays concerning *Lazarus*, *This Sicknefs, is* not *unto Death*,
ch. xi. of St *John's Gofpel*; ver. 4; So, in the *fpiritual* fenfe, the fame Apoftle St *John*,
in his 1ft Epiftle, fpeaks of *Sins*, which, according as there be *Any* or *No Hope* of
mens recovering from them, either *are* or *are* not unto *Death*, 1 Joh. v. 16.

2. A *Second Obfervation* arifing from our Saviour's manner of expreffing himfelf in
the Text, is; that *Repentance*, is not an *Original* and *Primary* Duty of Religion; but
a Duty, only of *fecondary* intention, and of *confequential* Obligation: Our Lord *came
not to call the* Righteous, *but* Sinners *to Repentance*. The *Original* Duty of all rational
Creatures, is to *obey* the Commandments of God: And *Such* Intelligent Beings, as
have *always* lived in obedience to God's Commands, are *not* obliged to the Duty of
Repentance. It is *Sin* only, that brought in the obligation to this *fecondary* and confequential Duty. And to thofe who *Have* finned, This Duty is of *Such a* Nature, that
it is a particular *Privilege* to them to be *permitted* to perform it; *Acts* xi. 18. When
the *Jewifh* Chriftians at *Jerufalem*, firft heard of the Apoftles being *authorized* to preach
the Gofpel to the *Gentiles*, they faid, Then *hath God alfo to the Gentiles* granted *Repentance unto Life*. Granting *Repentance*, does not fignify, as Some Moderns have
underftood it, God's *working Repentance* in *men*, or *operating it* upon *them*; but
it means, his gracioufly *allowing them the* Benefit *of Repentance*, or, his accepting *their Repentance* fo as to render it available *unto Pardon*. Among fuch frail and
degenerate Creatures, as *Men* in this *prefent State* are; there are *None*, in *ftrictnefs* of Speech, *free from Sin*; and confequently *None*, but what are obliged to this
Duty of Repentance. Neverthelefs, according to the gracious eftimation of things
in the Gofpel, and according to the more ufual acceptation of words in Scripture;
they who, allowing for the general frailties and Infirmities of humane nature, fincerely
endeavour, in the conftant courfe and tenour of their Actions, to live in habitual O-
bedience to the Commands of God; are ftiled *Righteous* in *fuch* a manner, as that our
Saviour came not, *comparatively* fpeaking, to call *Them* to Repentance. In the prayer
of *Manaffeh* King of *Judah*, we find this Notion expreffed in very ftrong Terms:
Thou, O Lord, fays he, *that art the God of the Juft, haft not appointed Repentance to
the Juft, as to Abraham and Ifaac and Jacob, which have not finned againft thee; but—
of thine infinite Mercies thou haft appointed Repentance unto* Sinners, *that they may be
faved*. The word, *Sinners*, here, it is plain, is not ufed in *That* fenfe, wherein *All
men* are declared to be Sinners; but in *That* fenfe, wherein the Scripture declares that
the *Wicked* are *an* abomination to the Lord, and them that *work iniquity* his Soul hateth.
Againft *thefe* perfons it is, that the *Wrath of God* is denounced with *indignation*, and
the *Threatnings of his Law* are *thundred* with *Severity*. The Law (fays St *Paul*) *is not* 1 Tim i. 9.

S E R M. *made for a* righteous *man*, (for *againſt ſuch, there is no law*; Gal. v. 23) *but* it is made
XLII. *for the lawleſs and diſobedient, for the ungodly and for Sinners, for the unholy and profane,——for man-ſlayers, for whoremongers——for Liars, for perjured perſons, and if
there be any Other thing that is contrary to ſound doctrine.* In *compariſon* with *Theſe*;
men who *love Truth*, and *do Righteouſneſs*, and ſincerely *fear God*, however they be
incompaſſed with many infirmities, are yet ſtiled in Scripture not only *juſt* and *righteous*, but even perfect *in their generation, walking in* All *the commandments of the Lord*
blameleſs; *Iſraelites indeed, in whom there is No Guile*; *juſt perſons, that* need no Repentance : and of whom our Lord in the text declares, that he *came not to call* Them
to Repentance. There *is* a Repentance, to which even the *Beſt* of men are continually
obliged; a Senſe of their unworthineſs before God; an acknowledgment of their Weakneſſes and Follies; a continual uninterrupted Endeavour to amend what they find amiſs
in themſelves, and to improve more and more unto perfection. But *This* is *not* That
Repentance, to which our Saviour came to call *Sinners:* That *Total Change* of Life
and Manners, of which when our Lord ſaw an inſtance in *Zacheus*, he ſaid, This day
is Salvation come unto this Houſe; and in deſcribing of which, he calls it a *New* Birth,
a being Born again *of Water and of the Spirit.* In contradiſtinction to which, and under
the very ſame Figure of expreſſion, That *perpetual* Amendment of infirmities, which
is the Duty of *Good* men, may well be repreſented in the words of our Saviour to
St *Peter*, Joh. xiii. 10. *He that is waſhed, needeth not, ſave to waſh his feet, but is clean
every whit.*

3. A *Third* thing obſervable in our Saviour's manner of expreſſing himſelf in the Text,
is the juſt and ſharp *Reproof* contained in this his Anſwer to the Proud and Hypocritical
Phariſees. They were *Whole*, it ſeems, and therefore had no need of a *Phyſician*;
They were very *righteous*, they thought, and therefore had no need of being invited to
Repentance. They were the perſons, who St *Luke* tells us; *chap.* xviii. 9, *truſted in
themſelves that they were righteous, and deſpiſed Others*; And therefore our Lord rebuked
their Pride, by his Parable of the *Phariſee* and the *Publican*; telling them that the pe-
nitent *Publican* went down to his houſe juſtified, rather than the Boaſting *Phariſee*;
*For every one that exalteth himſelf, ſhall be abaſed; and he that humbleth himſelf, ſhall
be exalted.* They were the ſame perſons, to whom the ſame Evangeliſt tells us our
Lord ſaid upon *another* occaſion; *chap.* xvi. 15, *ye are they which juſtify yourſelves before Men, but God knoweth your Hearts; For That which is highly eſteemed amongſt
Men, is abomination in the Sight of God.* And thus likewiſe in the words of the
Text, when the ſame Hypocrites were finding fault with *Jeſus*, for keeping company
with Publicans and Sinners, which *They* thought it beneath *Themſelves* to do; the Anſwer he made them, contains in it this ſevere Sting; *Ye* who fancy yourſelves *whole*,
what need have *ye* of a Phyſician? *Ye* who truſt in your ſelves that ye *are righteous*,
what need have *ye* of being invited to *Repentance?*

THESE are the *Obſervations* naturally ariſing from the ſeveral *particular* expreſſions
made uſe of in the Text. That which remains is, to conſider, in the

II. *Second* place, the general Doctrine of *Repentance*, as here laid down by our Lord:
The Deſign of his Preaching, was *to call Sinners to Repentance.*

GOD being the *Author* and *Preſerver* of our Being, and our Supreme *Governour*;
it is manifeſt that his *Will*, however made known to us, whether by *natural Reaſon*, or
by additional *Revelation*, is the *Rule* and *Law* of our Actions. This *Law* or *Rule*, all
men, as they are rational Creatures, are originally obliged to obey at *all times* and in
all particulars; nor can there in *any caſe*, in the nature and reaſon of things, be *any
Excuſe* or *Diſpenſation* for tranſgreſſing it. Nevertheleſs *in fact*, in this preſent ſtate,
ſuch is the Frailty and Infirmity of our Nature, ſuch is the Blindneſs and Erroneouſneſs

of

of our Underſtandings, ſuch the Falſeneſs and Corruption of our Wills, ſuch the Power and Headineſs of our Paſſions, ſuch the Influences of innumerable Temptations ſurrounding us in a degenerate and unrighteous World; that there is *no man liveth, and ſinneth not.* Now of *Sin,* in proportion to the ſeveral degrees of its aggravation, the natural and juſt *Effect* is *Fear,* and *Looking for of Judgment,* and mens being conſequently *all their Life-time ſubject to Bondage,* Heb. ii. 15. By this Fear of the Divine Diſpleaſure, joined with a Senſe of paſt Follies, and of the unreaſonableneſs of Sin in the nature of the thing itſelf; they who have in them a root of *general* good Diſpoſition, and have not been corrupted with long and fixt *Habits* of Vice, are apt to be led to *Repentance :* And the conſideration of the nature and perfections of *God,* That *Goodneſs and Mercy* which the *Light of Nature* teaches us, muſt be found in the moſt perfect Being, gives them very reaſonable Grounds of *Hope,* that their Repentance and Amendment ſhall not be in vain. By Theſe conſiderations, many worthy and well diſpoſed Minds, even in the *Heathen World* itſelf, regulated their Behaviour; and, forſaking the Corruptions of the World around them, made very great Improvements in the ways of Virtue. Nevertheleſs, ſince a man's performing his Duty for the *future,* is nothing more, but doing what is *Then* his Duty to do, and makes no Expiation for *Paſt* Offences; there could not but remain upon the Minds of Penitents ſtill *Some* Uncertainty and uneaſy Doubts. In revealing himſelf to the people of the *Jews,* God was pleaſed *by degrees* to *clear* this matter; *aſcertaining* the Hopes, and *removing* the Suſpicions, of *natural Reaſon,* by expreſs *Promiſes* and *Declarations* of Mercy : Appointing *firſt,* in the *Law* itſelf, *Sacrifices* for *All* Offences, *except* the moſt *preſumptuous : Afterwards* ſignifying, by his *Prophets,* that, upon a *real Forſaking* and *effectual Amendment* even of Preſumptuous Faults, he would accept the *Sacrifice of a broken Spirit, a broken and contrite heart he would not deſpiſe :* Inviting men, as in the prophecy of *Iſaiah,* ch. lv. 7 ; *Let the wicked forſake his Way, and the unrighteous man his Thoughts; and let him return unto the Lord, and he will have mercy upon him; and to our God, for he will abundantly pardon :* And intimating, as in the liiid chapter of the ſame Book, that he had appointed an univerſal propitiation, to be revealed in his due ſeaſon, who was to be *wounded for our Tranſgreſſions, and bruiſed for our Iniquities,* and *by whoſe ſtripes we ſhould be healed.* At length, in the fulneſs of Time, by the actual Coming of Chriſt, this great Diſpenſation was completely opened; and *Repentance* and *Remiſſion of Sins,* was commanded to be preached, in *His* name, unto all the Nations of the Earth. *Come unto Me,* ſays he, *all ye that labour and are heavy laden, and I will give you Reſt.* And again : *Let him that is athirſt, come; and whoſoever will, let him take the water of life freely.* He has given us aſſurance, that God *wills not that Any ſhould periſh, but that All ſhould come to Repentance :* Nay, that as a Shepherd rejoices over a Sheep that had been loſt; ſo *it is not the Will of our Father which is in Heaven, that One of theſe little ones ſhould periſh.* Further; that *there is joy in the preſence of the Angels of God, over One Sinner that repenteth;* Nay, that *Joy ſhall be in Heaven over One Sinner that repenteth,* more *than over ninety and nine juſt perſons that need no Repentance.* The Meaning is; not that *Repentance* is in itſelf *more,* or *ſo much* valuable as *Innocence ;* or that a *returning Sinner* is *more* acceptable, or *ſo much* acceptable to *God,* as One that *never Sinned :* But that, in like manner as either a man's *Self,* or his *Friend's,* having eſcaped any extraordinary and very imminent *Danger,* cauſes a greater and more ſenſible preſent *Pleaſure,* than his having never fallen into any ſuch danger at all; and yet it does not at all follow, that *Danger* is in any caſe *deſirable :* So it may very reaſonably and conſiſtently be apprehended, how the *Repentance* of a Sinner may cauſe greater *immediate joy* in the preſence both of Men and Angels; than the *ſteddy Perſeverance* of One who, by the regular and uniform Practice of all Virtue, has nevertheleſs deſerved a far

higher

SERM.
XLII.

higher degree of *settled Esteem and Approbation*. Now this authentick declaration made by our Saviour, of the acceptableness of True Repentance in the Sight of God; is *That Glad Tidings*, which the word *Gospel*, [Ευαγγέλιον,] in its original Signification, properly denotes; That publication of *Peace on Earth and Good-will towards men*, which the Angel, in his congratulation to the Shepherds, calls *Tidings of great joy which shall be unto all people*; and which the Apostle St *Paul* stiles by the general name, of the *Grace of God which bringeth Salvation*. The *Means*, by which the Benefit of this gracious Dispensation is originally applied to Sinners, is *Baptism*: By which, they who were converted from unrighteous ways thro' the *Apostles* Preaching of the Gospel, having *their Hearts* (as the Scripture expresses it) *sprinkled from an evil conscience, and their Bodies washed with pure Water*, received assurance of the Pardon of their *past* Sins, and entred into a Solemn obligation to obey the Commands of God for the *future*; And by which *at all times*, they who are initiated into Christ's religion, are *admitted* to the gracious Terms of the Gospel-covenant, and *obliged* to live in obedience to those Terms: For the *Baptism* which *saves us*, the Apostle expressly declares, is not *the putting away the filth of the flesh*, but the Answer of a good *conscience towards God*. To those who *renounce* this Baptism by *total* and *final* Apostacy, the Benefit thereof is entirely vacated: For the *One Sacrifice* of Christ *once offered for us for ever*, being *totally and finally* rejected; *there remains no more Sacrifice for Sin, but a certain fearful looking for of judgment and fiery indignation, which shall devour the Adversary*. As to those who *never totally* apostatize, but yet, notwithstanding their *profession of Christianity*, fall into the habitual practice of *Any Wickedness* or *Debauchery*; their Sin, without doubt, is far more inexcusable; their Hearts more hardened; their Return to their Duty, much more difficult; than That of *such Sinners*, mentioned in the Text, whom our Saviour *came to call* originally *to Repentance*. For it is *better* for men *never to have known the way of righteousness, than after they have known it, to turn from the Holy Commandment delivered unto them*. Nevertheless, even to such *Offenders* as *These*, however unworthy, there still remains a gracious Call to Repentance; and the invitation which God has made by his Son in the Gospel, he in abundant mercy continues to repeat. Such persons, are to be *rebuked* very *sharply*, but not driven absolutely to Despair. *That which is lame*, ought not *to be turned* quite *out of the way*, but that it *rather be healed*. St Paul delivered a great Sinner *unto Satan*, to the end that *his Spirit might* finally *be saved in the Day of the Lord*: and gives caution, *least* even *such* an one should be *swallowed up of much Sorrow*. He speaks of many that *had sinned already*, even in the Instances of great Crimes; and threatens them upon Supposition they had not yet *repented*. The Apostle St *James* declares likewise; *If any of you do err from the Truth, and one convert him; let him know, that He who converteth a Sinner from the Error of his ways, shall save a Soul from Death, and shall hide a multitude of Sins*. And our Saviour himself, speaking even of *Great Corrupters* of religion, threatens that he will *cast* them *into a bed of Sickness, and kill their children* (that is, their Followers) *with death*, except *they repent of their Deeds*. Indeed, in cases of *This* nature, where men, notwithstanding their Knowledge of the Truth, have been guilty of Great and Presumptuous Wickedness; their *Repentance* ought to be *very exemplary*, and their *Amendment* thoroughly and conspicuously *effectual*. To *these* persons, the Scripture says; *Be afflicted, and mourn, and weep; let your laughter be turned to mourning, and your Joy to Heaviness; Humble yourselves in the Sight of the Lord, and he shall lift you up*. But for the *smaller* Failings, Infirmities and Surprizes, incident even to sincere and good men through the whole course of their lives; for the forgiveness of *these*, there is evidently *continual* provision made in the *whole Tenour* of the Gospel. Our Saviour directs us to pray *daily*, for the forgiveness of Trespasses of *This* kind; and, by commanding us to

forgive

forgive *each Other* fuch Trefpaffes, not only till Seven times, but even till Seventy S E R M. times Seven; gives reafon to thofe who conftantly and fincerely *indeavour* to obey his XLII. Will, to hope for proportionable favour at the hands of *God.*

The *Inferences* arifing from the foregoing Doctrine of Repentance, are:

1ſt. From what has been faid, appears the Folly of thofe corrupt Practices, of *Confeſſions, Penances, Abſolutions,* and the like; introduced in the Church of *Rome,* (inftead of true Amendment of life,) by the Vanity and Ambition of Men. For the Texts, concerning *retaining and forgiving* of Sins, on a mifunderftanding of which thefe corruptions have been founded; do not, in their true Meaning, put it into *Any* men's power, to fit in the Seat of God; but only appoint and authorize them *from* God, to preach and explain That Doctrine *unto* Men, by the *Terms* of which they muft finally be judged.

2*dly.* From what has been faid about the nature of True Repentance, it appears; that, among *Proteſtants,* and Chriftians of *all* denominations whatfoever; *Confeſſions of Sin*; and *profeſſions of Repentance,* made daily in our *Prayers* to God; if they be only *formal* and *ineffectual,* and produce not *real Amendment* of life; are altogether as vain and ufelefs, as the *Popiſh* Confeffions made to Men. For to pray continually that our *Life hereafter may be pure and holy,* and yet at the fame time return daily to the commiffion of *known Sins*; is the higheft hypocrify and mockery of God. Concerning *thefe* perfons it is, that our Saviour declares, *Luke* xiii. 24. *Many, I ſay unto you, will* Seek *to enter in, and ſhall not be able.* They will *Seek,* not in the way of true virtue and righteoufnefs of life, but in ways which they hope may be fubftituted in its place. That is, in the expreffion of our Saviour, they will build their Houfe upon the *Sand,* and not upon a *Rock.*

S E R M O N XLIII.

The Excellency of Moral Qualifications.

A C T S XI. 24.

For he was a good man, and full of the Holy Ghost.

SERM. **T**HERE is nothing in nature more amiable, than the character of a truly *Good*
XLIII. man; a Man, whose principal Business and Pleasure is to make all Men easy,
with whom he has any Concern, in the *present* life; and to promote, as far as
in Him lies, their Happiness likewise in That which is *to come.* Other Qualifications,
have their *Value*; and do, in their proportion, merit a just degree of Esteem. Great
Knowledge and Abilities, every where necessarily command Respect. Great Actions
never fail to fill Men with Admiration, and to procure Applause. But of *all* Charac-
ters, That of *Goodness* is the most *lovely*; and approaches nearest to the Similitude of a
Divine Perfection. *God* is the *Fountain of Goodness*, from which flows all the Happiness in the whole Creation: And there is no one Perfection in the Divine Nature,
which it is *so much* our *Duty* and our *Glory* to imitate. He who most excells in This
particular character, has the most of the *Divine Likeness*, that Man in this Mortal state
can possibly arrive at; And therefore in the description given of St *Barnabas* in my
Text, the expressions are used as Synonymous and of the *same* Meaning, that he was *a
Good Man*, and *full of the Holy Ghost.*

THE *Occasion* of the Character here given of *Barnabas*, was the *Concern and Desire*
he showed, that the Benefit of True Religion might spread *far* in the World; that
Men of *all* Nations might become partakers of the gracious Mercy of God declared in
the Gospel, by being brought to Repentance for the Remission of *Sins. Barnabas* was
the *first* person who ventured to introduce *Paul* among the Disciples at *Jerusalem*, immediately after his Conversion; when the rest of the Christians *were all afraid of him,
and believed not that he was a Disciple*, Acts ix. 26. Afterwards, when upon occasion
of *the persecution that arose about Stephen*, the Disciples *which were scattered abroad*
from *Jerusalem* for fear of the *Jews*, did some of them *speak unto the Grecians,
preaching the Lord Jesus*, ch. xi. 19, 20. *Barnabas* was the person chosen to be *sent
forth* from *the Church in Jerusalem, that he should go as far as Antioch*, ver. 22. *Who
when he came, and had seen the grace of God, was glad, and exhorted them all, that with
Purpose of Heart they would cleave unto the Lord*, ver. 23. And then it follows, in the
words of my Text; *For he was a good Man, and full of the Holy Ghost.*

'TIS plain this character given in the Text to *Barnabas*, was intended as a description of an *excellent* person; of a person *excellent*, not so much upon account of his *miraculous Gifts*, as of his *Moral Qualifications.* And therefore the character deserves to
be *particularly* considered, as a *Pattern* and *Example* to All who are desirous to improve in Christian Virtue. For though the Disciples of Christ are not *in All Ages* indued with *miraculous Powers*, yet they may and ought *always* to endeavour after those

Moral

Moral Qualifications ; which are, in Scripture-language, the *Fruits of the Spirit* ; and, S E R M. in St *Paul*'s opinion, the *more excellent* ones too.

XLIII.

THE word, *Good*, in this character of a *good* man, is ufed fometimes in a way ex- Eph. v. 9. preffive of *Virtue in general*, as oppofed to *all Wickednefs* or *Vice* ; and fometimes as 1 Cor. xii. 31. denoting a *particular Kind* or *Degree* of *Virtue*, as diftinguifhed by way of Excellency above *other* Virtues. In the *former* fenfe of the word, a *good man* ftands oppofed to a *vicious* or *bad* man : In the *latter* fenfe, a *good man* ftands diftinguifhed, by way of Eminence or Superiority, above *other* even *juft* and *righteous* perfons.

1. THE word, *Good*, is fometimes expreffive of *Virtue in general*, as oppofed to *all Wickednefs* or *Vice*. In *This* fenfe, what *Good* is, every one knows : It needs not be defined or explained in Many Words ; but every man's own Mind and Confcience may be appealed to, to tell him *what* it is. It is not any thing that is difputed or controverted among Men, which Some call Good, and Others Evil ; but what Mankind is well agreed in, and what even the Light of Nature itfelf univerfally approves. It is *real* and *fubftantial* in the nature of things, fo as not to be varied by any external Change of Time or Circumftances : And it is *unqueftionable* and *indifputable*, fo as to be acknowledged by men of all Parties and of all Opinions, how much foever they may differ among themfelves in Other matters, and how little Regard foever they may in Practice pay even to this undifputed Goodnefs itfelf. *Whatfoever things are True,* Phil. iv. 8. *whatfoever things are Honeft, whatfoever things are Juft, whatfoever things are Pure, whatfoever things are Lovely, whatfoever things are of good Report ; if there be any Virtue, and if there be any Praife* ; thefe are the things, in which This *Goodnefs* confifts. In the *Old* Teftament, it is thus defcribed by the Prophet, *Mic.* vi. 8. *He hath fhowed thee, O man, what is Good ; And what doth the Lord require of thee, but to do juftly, and to love Mercy, and to walk humbly with thy God?* In the *New* Teftament, it is by St *Paul* expreffed thus : that *denying ungodlinefs and worldly Lufts, we fhould live fober-* Tit. ii. 12. *ly, righteoufly and godly, in this prefent World*, under a fenfe and expectation of a Judgment to come. And by St *Peter* in the following manner ; 1 *Pet.* iii. 10 : That a Man *refrain his Tongue from evil, and his Lips that they fpeak no Guile* ; That he *efchew evil, and do good* ; that he *feek peace, and enfue it ;——for who is he that will harm you, if ye be* Thus *followers of that which is Good?* ver. 13. This *general* Practice of Virtue, which determines the perfon's whole character, and denominates a *Good* Man ; is what our Saviour reprefents in his Parable under the Similitude of *Good Ground*, wherein the Seed fown takes Root and grows, and brings forth Fruit, being neither hindred by Rocks and want of depth of Earth, nor choaked with Weeds, nor fcorched up and withered by the Heat of the Sun : That is, when neither Irrefolutenefs of Temper, nor Fear of Perfecutions, nor the Temptations and Allurements of Profit or Pleafure, the Cares and Bufinefs, the Deceits or Enticements of a corrupt World, withdraw a Man from the uniform Purfuit and Practice of what is juft and right. This is That *Sincerity*, or (in our Saviour's language) That *Honeft and Good Heart,* Luke viii. 15. which in the Scripture-ftyle is oppofed to *Hypocrify*. For *Hypocrify*, in the language of the facred Writers, does not generally fignify a folemn and formal *Pretence to Religion* without *Any real Belief of Religion* at all. This fort of Hypocrites, are but *Few* in number ; and no Man can be guilty in *This* kind, without exprefsly and diftinctly *condemning himfelf* in every part of his *own* Pretences. But the *Hypocrify* much more frequently fpoken of in Scripture, and fo generally oppofed to *real Goodnefs* ; is *That* Hypocrify, in which Men no lefs ufually impofe upon *Themfelves*, than *Others* ; *deceiving their own Hearts*, as St *James* expreffes it, ch. i. 26. It is *That* Deceit, by which Men fancy that they can become acceptable to God, by any external Profeffion of Religion, by Zeal for particular uncertain Opinions, by an exact Obfervation of any outward Ceremonies, by conftant Devotion even towards God himfelf ; without becoming

coming really *Good Men*; without governing their own unreasonable Passions; without being just, beneficent, and charitable, towards All Mankind; in a word, without living in the Practice of those Moral Virtues, which are the eternal and unalterable Commands of God, and which are the ultimate End of every religious Institution. The only *Evidence* therefore, or certain *Mark*, whereby That *Sincerity* which denominates a really *Good Man*, can be distinguished from such Profession of Religion, as the Scripture deems hypocritical; is when the Fruits of it appear in a *general* and *habitual* Influence over *all* his Actions: When the Arguments of Reason and Religion, are not only heard with Pleasure, and produce perhaps sudden and real Effects, in the Times and Places of publick Devotion; (which is what our Saviour expresses by *receiving* the *Word with joy*, like Seed speedily springing up in shallow ground, without having *Root* in itself;) But the true Evidence of *Sincere Goodness* is, when the Considerations of Reason and Religion influence Men habitually in the whole Course and Method of *Common Life*, in their *Business* and *Transactions* of all kinds, in their very *Freedoms* and *Diversions* themselves, in circumstances of *Temptation*, and in Cases attended with *Difficulties*, as well as in Seasons of professed Devotion: When the Precepts of Virtue, and the Doctrines of Practice, which true Religion teaches, are *imbibed*, *digested*, and converted as it were into the *Food* and *Nourishment* of Life: Which is what our Saviour, in the *Sixth* chapter of St *John*, calls *eating his Flesh, and drinking his Blood*: Just in the same sense, as *Wisdom* is introduced speaking; *Ecclus.* xxiv. 21. *He that eateth me, shall yet be Hungry; and he that drinketh me, shall yet be Thirsty.*

2. B E S I D E S this *larger* and more usual Sense of the word, *Good*, expressing *Virtue in general*, as opposed to *all Wickedness* or *Vice*; there is *another* sense of the word, as denoting a *particular Kind* or *Degree* of *Virtue*, by way of Excellency above *other* Virtues. And in *This* sense, a *good* man stands distinguished, by way of Eminence or Superiority, above *other* even *just* and *righteous* persons. *Goodness* in *This* sense, is universal Virtue, joined with a *singular* degree of *Benignity* and *Beneficence* in *particular*.

I N the describing or taking account of Actions; the phrase, *doing of Good*, is frequently applied *peculiarly* to the Virtue of *Beneficence* or *Charity*. Thus *Heb.* xiii. 16; *To do good, and to communicate, forget not.* Again, 1 *Tim.* vi. 17; *Charge them who are Rich in This World,——that they do Good, that they be rich in Good Works, ready to distribute, willing to communicate.* And from hence, in the Characters of Persons, a *Good man* very often signifies, not only One who leads *in general* a *virtuous* Life, but who moreover is *particularly* eminent for *Benignity* of Temper; One who always *does more for* the Benefit of Others, than could in strictness of justice be demanded of him; and *exacts less* for himself *from* Others, than in strict Right appears to be his due; and readily takes *greater Pains* for his Neighbour's Advantage, and voluntarily undergoes *more Troubles and Difficulties* for the Good of Mankind, than, according to the common Measures and Estimation of Duty, he could be understood to be obliged to. Concerning *This* Character it is, that St *Paul* declares, *Rom.* v. 7, *Scarcely for a Righteous man will one die; yet peradventure for a Good man, some would even dare to die.* And in *This sense*, the character of *Good* seems to be given to *Barnabas* in the Text. He was the person who *first* ventured to introduce *Paul* among the Disciples at *Jerusalem*, when the rest *were all afraid of him, and believed not that he was a Disciple*, ch. ix. 26. And *He* being the person chosen by the Church at *Jerusalem*, to travel as far as *Antioch*, and confirm the Faith of those *Grecian* or *Gentile* Converts, which had been brought over to Christianity by the preaching of Some of those Disciples, who, upon the Persecution that arose about *Stephen*, were *scattered abroad from Jerusalem* for fear of the *Jews*; he performed this Office with a singularly *good* and *charitable* Concern for the Happiness of Mankind. Having *seen the Grace of God*, that is,

I

having feen Evidences of God's univerfal Mercy and Compaffion towards the *Gentiles* S E R M.
as well as *Jews*, he *was glad, and exhorted them All, that with Purpofe of Heart they* XLIII.
would cleave unto the Lord, ch. xi. 23 : *For he was a Good man, and full of the Holy*
Ghoſt.

CONCERNING the *latter* part of This charaĉter, *full of the Holy Ghoſt* ; it is to
be obferved, that the *Holy Ghoſt*, in Scripture-language, fometimes fignifies the *Perfon*
of the Holy Ghoſt, fometimes his *Miraculous Gifts*, and fometimes the *Moral* Effeĉts
and Influences of the Doĉtrine delivered to us by the Spirit of God. In either of the
two former fenfes, a Prophet is fpoken of as being *full of the Holy Ghoſt*, when he is
aĉtually *infpired* by him, or miraculoufly *conduĉted and direĉted* by him either in *Words*
or *Aĉtions*. Thus *Jefus, being full of the Holy Ghoſt, was led by the Spirit into the*
Wildernefs ; Luke iv. 1 : And *Stephen, being full of the Holy Ghoſt,——faw the Glory*
of God, Aĉts vii. 55. In the *latter* fenfe of the word, a man is then faid to be *full of*
the Holy Ghoſt, when his mind, under the *Moral* Influences of the Spirit of God, and
of *the Doĉtrine which is according to Godlinefs*, is, in an eminent manner, zealous ᵢ Tim. vi. 3.
for the promoting of Truth, and for the Praĉtice of good Works. Thus the Seven
Deacons appointed by the Apoſtles, *Aĉts* vi. 3 : were *men of honeſt Report, full of the*
Holy Ghoſt and Wifdom ; Men of *honeſt Report*, that is, of known integrity, of virtuous and upright charaĉter, and of exemplary Zeal. And in the fame fenfe, *Barnabas*
is in my Text defcribed to have been a *Good man, Full of the Holy Ghoſt and of Faith.*
Upon a like account, and after the fame manner of fpeaking, very *wicked perfons*, or
men intending to attempt any very *wicked enterprize*, are in Scripture reprefented as
being *filled* with the Evil *Spirit*. Thus when *Ananias* had projeĉted within himfelf
to *defraud* the Apoſtles, St *Peter* reproves him in the following manner ; *Aĉts* v. 3 ;
Why hath Satan *filled thine Heart, to lie to the Holy Ghoſt ?* And when *Judas* refolved
in his own Mind to betray our Lord ; then, the Evangeliſt tells us, *Satan entered*
into him, *Luke* xxii. 3. The Meaning of which is not, that the *Thoughts* of the *Men*,
were the *Aĉtions* of the *Devil* ; But, that fubmitting to Temptation upon *ill* Principles, is being fubjeĉt to the *Devil* ; in like manner as aĉting upon *good* Principles, is
being under the Government of *God*, under the guidance and influence of the *Spirit of*
Holinefs.

THE words of the Text being thus explained, it is obvious from thence to obferve,

1ſt, THAT, with regard to a perfon's *moral* or *religious* charaĉter ; being a *good*
man, and being *full of the Holy Ghoſt*, are *one* and the *fame* thing. With regard to
the vifible *Works* or *Operations* of the Holy Ghoſt, the cafe is very different. A man
might *fpeak with the tongues of Men, and of Angels* ; might *have the Gift of Prophecy* ; ᵢ Cor. xiii. 1.
might *underſtand all Myſteries and all Knowledge* ; might *have all Faith, fo that he*
could remove Mountains ; and yet poffibly at the fame time, for want of real Goodnefs and true Virtue, might, in the *religious* eſtimation of things, be (as St *Paul* expreffes it) abfolutely *Nothing*. And our *Saviour himfelf* expreffly mentions Some,
who fhould be able to plead that they *had prophefied in his name, and in his Name had* Matt. vii. 22.
caſt out Devils, and in his Name done many wonderful works ; and yet, faith he, *will*
I profefs unto them, I never knew you ; depart from Me, ye that work iniquity. The
Reafon of the difference, is plain : Becaufe thefe *external* miraculous Works of the
Holy Ghoſt, being of Ufe *only* for the *conviĉtion* of men's *Underſtandings*, which is
not neceffarily followed with a *virtuous* difpofition of the *Will* ; hence thefe *outward*
Gifts may very poffibly be found in an *unrighteous* perfon, who is not himfelf in-
fluenced in his *own Praĉtice* by the Arguments wherewith he preaches to *Others*. But
the *internal* Effeĉts of the influence of the Spirit of God upon the perfon's *own Mind* ;
the Moral Effeĉts of the *Motives and Arguments of Religion* taught by the Holy
Ghoſt, and of the *Affiſtances* afforded by him ; thefe cannot poffibly be *feparate* or *dif-*

S E R M. *ferent* from true *Virtue*, becaufe Virtue is itfelf *effentially* the End of Religion, and the
XLIII. ultimate Defign of all religious Influences. And therefore to be in *This* fenfe *full of the*
Holy Ghoft, and to be a *good man*, muft neceffarily be *one* and the *fame thing*.

2*dly*, F r o m what has been faid, we may obferve; that *moral Virtues*, and what
the Scripture calls the *Fruits of the Spirit*, are *one and the fame thing* under different
Denominations. *The Fruit of the Spirit*, faith St *Paul*, *is in all Goodnefs and Righteoufnefs and Truth*, Eph. v. 9. And again, *Gal.* v. 22; *The Fruit of the Spirit, is
Love, Joy, Peace, Long-fuffering, Gentlenefs, Goodnefs, Faith* [Fidelity,] *Meeknefs,
Temperance*; *Againft Such, there is no Law*. Thefe things, when confidered in *themfelves*, in their own *abfolute* and *intrinfick nature*, as being *Difpofitions* of Mind *effentially* and unalterably *good*; are ftiled *Virtues*. When confidered with regard to their
Effects, in the vifible *Actions* and *Practice* of *men*; they are called *Morality*. When
confidered with refpect to the *Root* or *Spring*, the *Fountain* or *Principle* from which
they flow; namely, a right *Senfe* of the *Reafon* and *Truth* of Things, and a juft Regard to *God* the Judge of all; they are then ftiled *Religion*. Laftly, when confidered
with refpect to the *extraordinary* Supports they receive from the Revelation of the *Gofpel* in particular, as being therein explained with *clearer* and more *diftinct* Declarations,
inforced with *ftronger* and more *powerful* Motives, encouraged and promoted with all
the *Helps* and *Affiftances* of the *Spirit of God*; in *This* refpect, they are called *Fruits
of the Spirit*.

3*dly*, B y This Rule therefore, may eafily be difcovered and reproved, every kind
of *Enthufiafm* and *Superftition*. Whatever tends not to *promote* real Virtue and Goodnefs; much more, whatever (under the Appearance of Religion) tends to *deftroy* Virtue and Goodnefs; is the Produce either of *Atheifm*, or of *Enthufiafm* and *Superftition*.
The *Spirit of God*, is the *Spirit of Holinefs* and *Goodnefs*; and therefore whofoever lives
in the Practice of *Any Vice*, is certainly, in the *religious* fenfe, *void of the Spirit of
God*. All *other* Marks whatfoever, of *having the Spirit*; are but *vain* and *enthufi-
aftical*. If a man could *fpeak with the Tongues of Men and Angels*, (as St *Paul* expreffes
it,) and *had all Faith*, fo that he could work *All Miracles*; and be not a *virtuous*
man; All This would be only the Operation of the Spirit of God *by* Him, for the conviction of *Others*; but *To* himfelf, of no Advantage, any more than to a *Sounding
Brafs* or a *tinkling Cymbal*.

SERMON

SERMON XLIV.

Of HUMILITY.

LUKE XIV. 11.

For whosoever exalteth himself, shall be abased ; and he that humbleth himself, shall be exalted.

THERE is no Virtue in human Life, of more universal Usefulness than *Humility*; and yet none more difficult to be *practised* by a man's *self*, or to be rightly *stated* and defined to *others*. *Pride* grows upon Men insensibly by imperceptible degrees, and creeps in untaken notice of upon innumerable Occasions, and veils itself often under an affected Appearance even of *Humility* itself. For *true Humility*, as it is hard to define, so it is not always easy to know when a man has it : And whilst it is frequently described to be a man's having in appearance a meaner Opinion of himself, than it is *possible* for him to have in reality ; (for no man can *really think that* of himself, which he *knows* at the same time *not to be true* of himself;) it happens, not uncommonly, that there may be great *Pride*, in a man's *pretending so* to think of himself, as he knows every body believes there is no just reason to think of him ; and that there may be more and truer *Humility* in *Another* person, who without either *affected Humility* or *real Pride*, so thinks of himself as he ought to think, and so behaves himself as becomes his proper Station and Imployment in the World. For *true Humility* consists, not in *Imagination*, but in *Action* ; not in men's *appearing* to *think ill* of themselves, but in *behaving* themselves *well*; it consists in carrying themselves modestly in the Performance of their present Duty, not assuming to themselves any thing above the character of their proper Station, not putting *themselves* forward in an eager and indecent manner, but, by the Practice of real and useful Virtues, causing *Others* to be desirous of their Advancement in the World. This is the Behaviour of True Merit ; and the Method, which, in the Nature of Things, in the Judgment of the Wisest Men, and by the Appointment of God himself, leads modest and unaffected Virtue, to real Honour, and to a settled and established Esteem. *For whosoever exalteth himself, shall be abased ; and he that humbleth himself shall be exalted.* In the following Discourse upon which Words, I shall *1st* endeavour to show *what* True *Humility* is, and wherein it consists ; and *2dly*, propose some Arguments to perswade men to the Practice of it. Under which *same* Heads, it will appear at the same Time what *Pride* is, and by what Arguments men are to be warned against falling into it.

1st, I AM to consider *what* True *Humility* is, and wherein it consists. And here, because the Circumstances of men are infinitely various ; and the Practice of every moral Virtue, is diversified in as many different manners, as the Circumstances of the Case wherein it is to be exercised ; therefore either *general* Rules cannot be given at all, or, if they be, yet commonly they are but of small Use, because they are lost in the endless diversity of the Application. On the other hand, *particular* Rules for every single Case, are as impossible to be laid down ; because their *Number* would

2

wholly

S E R M. wholly confound the Memory, and fo become incapable of being applied at all. The
XLIV. middle and moft ufeful Way, is to mention the principal Heads only; which, being
Few, are eafy to be remembred; and yet to which all the reft, that are numberlefs,
may with eafe be occafionally reduced in Practice. In order therefore to explain diftinctly and intelligibly, what true *Humility* is; it may be proper to confider it, with
regard to the *Perfons* towards whom it is to be exercifed, and with regard to the *Things*
wherein thofe Perfons differ feverally from each other, The *Perfons*,. in our behaviour
towards whom the Virtue of *Humility* is to be exercifed, are either *Superiors, Equals,*
or *Inferiors :* and the *Things* wherein thefe feveral Perfons differ principally from each
other, are either their Civil *Stations* in the World, their different Natural *Abilities,* or
their Religious *Improvements.*

    1*ft,* W I T H regard to *Superiors* in *general,* true *Humility* confifts, in paying them
chearfully and readily all due Honour and Refpect, in thofe *particular Regards wherein* they are our Superiors,· notwithftanding any *other* accidental Difadvantages on *their*
fide, or Advantages on *ours.* More particularly; with regard to Superiors in Civil
Stations in the World, true *Humility* confifts, in obeying them willingly in all things
juft and lawful; in fubmitting to the Authority, even of the froward and unworthy;
in not defpifing their Perfons, expofing their Weakneffes, or infulting over their Infirmities; but being truly fenfible, that thofe of Us who think beft of our own Abilities,
might, in higher Stations, and under greater Trufts, find Difficulties we are not at
prefent aware of; and very poffibly not be able to fee, or at leaft not find means to
avoid, the Frailties we are generally fo apt to cenfure in the Behaviour of our Superiors. With regard to Superiors in Natural *Abilities,* true Humility confifts, not in
fubmitting our Underftandings to them blindly and implicitly, but in being willing and
defirous to be inftructed and informed by them; in not envying them the Advantages
God has given them above ourfelves; nor repining, but on the contrary *rejoycing,* at
their being preferred or honoured, according to the Proportion of their true Merit or
Capacity. With regard to Superiors in Religious *Improvements,* Humility confifts
likewife, in *rejoicing,* to fee the Practice of Virtue, and the Advancement of the Kingdom of God upon Earth; not grieving, but taking Pleafure, to find fuch Perfons
efteemed highly in the World, and propofing them to ourfelves as Examples and Patterns for our Imitation. This is the Virtue of Humility, in our Behaviour towards *Superiors* of all kinds.

    2*dly,* T O W A R D S our *Equals,* true Humility confifts, in civil and affable, in cour-
teous and modeft behaviour; not in formal Pretences of thinking very meanly and
contemptibly of ourfelves; (for fuch Profeffions are often very confiftent with great
Pride,) but in patiently permitting our Equals (when it fhall fo happen) to be preferred before us, not thinking ourfelves injured when Others but of equal Merit chance
to be more efteemed, but on the contrary rather fufpecting that we judge too favour-
rably of ourfelves, and therefore modeftly defiring that thofe who are reputed upon the
level with us, may have fhown unto them rather a greater Refpect. This is what
the Apoftle means; *Rom.* xii. 10; when he bids us *be kindly affectioned one to another,
with brotherly love, in honour* preferring *one another.* 'Tis what the Wife-man had
long before exhorted to, *Prov.* xxv. 6; *Put not forth thyfelf in the prefence of the King,
and ftand not in the place of great men; For better is it, that it be faid unto thee,
Come up hither; than that thou fhouldft be put lower in the prefence of the Prince whom
thine eyes have feen.* 'Tis what our Saviour ftill more largely and diftinctly recommends, in that Parable whereof the Text is the conclufion, St *Luk.* xiv. 7; *He put
forth a Parable to thofe which were bidden, when he marked how they chofe out the
chief rooms; faying unto them, When thou art bidden of any man to a wedding, fit not
down in the higheft room; left a more honourable man than thou, be bidden of him; And he*

that

that bade thee and him, come and say to thee, Give This man place, and thou begin with
shame to take the lowest room: But when thou art bidden, go and sit down in the lowest
room; that when he that bade thee cometh, he may say unto thee, Friend, go up higher;
Then shalt thou have worship in the presence of them that sit at meat with thee: The
Application of all which, he subjoins in the words of the Text, ver. 11. *For whosoever*
exalteth himself, shall be abased; and he that humbleth himself, shall be exalted. Further;
True Humility with regard to our *Equals*, consists, in willingly submitting, for Peace
sake, to many things, if *not very unreasonable*, yet otherwise such as in our own judgment we should not chuse or think best of. *Eph.* iv. 1; *I beseech you, that ye walk*
worthy of the Vocation wherewith ye are called; with all lowliness and meekness, with
long-Suffering, forbearing one another in love; Endeavouring to keep the Unity of the
Spirit in the bond of peace; —— For *unto every one of us is given grace, according to*
the measure of the Gift of Christ; i. e. men have different judgments, different inclinations, different Gifts and Talents from God, divided to every one severally as he pleases; and therefore, to prevent Confusion, where men otherwise are equals, the
Duty of Humility requires, that they should all be ready to submit to each other, with
all Meekness, Patience and Good-will. *Col.* iii. 12; *Put on, as the elect of God, holy*
and beloved, bowels of mercies, kindness, humbleness of mind, meekness, long-suffering;
Forbearing one another, and forgiving one another; ——*And above all these things, put*
on Charity, which is the bond of Perfectness; Charity, *i. e.* mutual Love and an affectionate desire of Peace and Agreement; For so it is explained in the words next immediately following; *And let the Peace of God rule in your Hearts, to which also ye*
are called in one Body. The like Exhortation we find, 1 *Pet.* v. 5, where the Apostle
not only directs, *Ye Younger, submit yourselves unto the Elder;* but he adds moreover,
Yea, all of you be subject one to another, and be clothed with Humility. And *Eph.* v. 21;
Submitting yourselves one to another in the Fear of God. This is the Character of true
Humility, in our Behaviour towards our *Equals*.

3*dly*; WITH regard to our *Inferiors*, Humility consists, in assuming to ourselves
no more than the Difference of Men's Circumstances, and the Performance of their respective Duties, for preserving the regularity and good Order of the World, necessarily
requires. Particularly, towards Inferiors in Civil *Stations* in the World, the Humility of a Governor consists, not in making his Authority despicable and subject to contempt, but in exercising it so, as to show that he is not puft up with the Love of
Power and Dominion, but looks upon it as a Trust committed to him, for the Benefit of those who are placed under his Inspection. He commands, without insulting; he
reproves, with meekness; he punishes unwillingly, and never without giving evidence of
Pity and Compassion. With regard to Inferiors in natural *Abilities* or Accidental *Ad-*
vantages in the World, such as Learning and Knowledge, Riches, Plenty, and the
like; Humility consists, in not despising and contemning those, upon whom God has
been pleased to bestow fewer Talents; but on the contrary in considering, that possibly
they have some *other* Gifts, which may be wanting in *us*; and in being willing to *com-*
municate to *them*, the Advantages *we* injoy; that *They* may be the better, for the
Things wherewith God has blessed *Us*. The true Humility of a *rich man* consists, not
in levelling himself with the Poor, but in being willing to assist them by relieving their
Necessities: not in confounding the Distinctions of Men's Condition, which God and
Nature has established; but in indeavouring to make the condition of the Meanest
easy, and supportable to themselves. And in like manner, the true Humility of Persons endued with more *Learning and Knowledge* than others, does not consist in making a Show of being ignorant, (which may be a conceited Vanity or foolish Affectation;)
but it consists in being willing to *communicate* what they know, and in sincerely desiring that all Others might attain the same Knowledge with themselves: After the ex-

ample

SERM. ample of *Mofes*, who, inftead of becoming haughty and infolent through the multitude
XLIV. of the Revelations wherewith God had been pleafed to honour him; and inftead of
difcouraging others, from feeking after the like Knowledge; on the contrary declared
publickly, *Numb.* xi. 29; *Would God that* All *the Lord's people were Prophets, and that
the Lord would put his Spirit upon them.* Laftly, Towards our Inferiors in refpect of
Religious *Improvements,* true Humility confifts, in being rightly fenfible of our *own
many* Infirmities, even *thofe* of Us who may be apt to imagine ourfelves to have made the
greateft Improvements; and in being fincerely follicitous, for the welfare, and the Salvation
of All meh; *Let nothing be done through Strife or Vain-glory, but in Lowlinefs of Mind
let each one efteem another better than themfelves; Look not every man on his own things, but
every man alfo on the things of Others,* Phil. ii. 3. It confifts in indeavouring to influence
Men towards Religion, by *Meeknefs* rather than by *Power: Jefus called his Difciples unto
him, and faid; Ye know that the Princes of the Gentiles, exercife Dominion over them; and
they that are great, exercife Authority upon them: But it fhall not be fo among you; but
whofoever will be great among you, let him be your Minifter; And whofoever will be chief
among you, let him be your Servant; Even as the Son of Man came not to be miniftred
unto, but to minifter, and to give his life a ranfom for many;* St Matt. xx. 25. It confifts, in not affecting to gain the empty *Applaufe* of Men, by an outward oftentation
of greater Piety than others: *All their Works,* They do, (fays our Saviour, fpeaking of the
proud Pharifees,) *they do for to be feen of men; They make broad their Phylacteries, and
inlarge the borders of their garments; And love the uppermoft rooms at feafts, and the
chief Seats in the Synagogues; And greetings in the markets, and to be called of men, Rabbi, Rabbi; But be not ye called Rabbi; for One is your Mafter, even Chrift; and all ye
are brethren: And call no man your Father upon Earth; For One is your Father,
which is in Heaven: Neither be ye called, Mafters; For One is your Mafter, even Chrift;
But he that is greateft among you, fhall be your Servant; And whofoever fhall exalt himfelf, fhall be abafed; and he that fhall humble himfelf, fhall be exalted,* St Matt. xxiii. 4.
It confifts, in *condefcending* to thofe beneath us, and not difdaining even to *yield* to them
in things indifferent: *Be of the fame mind one towards another; Mind not high things,
but condefcend to Men of low eftate: Be not wife in your own Conceits,* Rom. xii. 16. It
confifts, in *bearing* their infirmities patiently and without frowardnefs; *We then that
are ftrong, ought to bear the infirmities of the Weak, and not to pleafe ourfelves: Let every one of us pleafe his neighbour, for his Good to Edification: For even* Chrift *pleafed
not himfelf,* Rom. xv. 1. It confifts, in *forbearing* to *judge* or *defpife* thofe that differ
from us in opinion; *Let not him that eateth, defpife him that eateth not; and let not
him which eateth not, judge him that eateth,* Rom. xiv. 3. It confifts in taking care
not to *offend,* by haughty and prefumptuous behaviour, fuch perfons as by Meeknefs
might be prevailed upon to believe in Chrift, or fuch as by kind treatment might be
kept from departing into Divifions; *Take heed, that ye defpife not one of thefe little ones;
For whofo fhall offend one of thefe little ones that believe in me, it were better for him
that a millftone were hanged about his Neck, and that he were drowned in the depth of the
Sea,* St Matt. xviii. 10, 6. It confifts, in taking heed not to *impofe* needlefs *Difficulties*
upon thofe under our Power; For fo our Saviour defcribes the Pride of the Pharifees;
*They bind heavy burdens and grievous to be born, and lay them on men's fhoulders; but
they themfelves will not move them with one of their fingers,* St. Matt. xxiii. 4, and
1 Pet. v. 3; *Neither as being Lords over God's heritage, but being Examples to the Flock:*
Laftly, it confifts in ufing great *gentlenefs,* even to thofe that *have offended; Brethren,
if a man be overtaken in a Fault, ye which are fpiritual, reftore fuch a one in the Spirit of Meeknefs, confidering thyfelf, left Thou alfo be tempted,* Gal. vi. 1. And 2 Tim. ii.
25; *In* Meeknefs *inftructing thofe that oppofe themfelves, if God peradventure would
give them Repentance to the acknowledgment of the Truth.* Thefe are the Characters

I

and

and the Inſtances of True *Humility*, with regard to our Inferiors in Religious *Improve-* S E R M.
ments; which was the *laſt* of thoſe Caſes or Circumſtances, wherein for diſtinctneſs ſake, XLIV.
I propoſed to conſider This excellent Virtue. And indeed there are no caſes, wherein
the Practice of Humility is more difficult or more intricate, than when men are tempted
to Spiritual *Pride*, or to *deſpiſe* thoſe who are ſuppoſed to be their Inferiors in *religious
improvements.* Which Vice inſinuating itſelf into men upon *different* occaſions, and
branching forth itſelf into *many* Inſtances; a brief mentioning ſome of the principal of
them, may aſſiſt us ſtill further in underſtanding the nature of the contrary Virtue.
And *1ſt*, there is a *ſpiritual Pride* in *preſuming* to ſin, upon the Senſe of the Virtues
we are in other reſpects indued with. This was the Caſe of *Uzziah* King of *Judah*;
of whom the Scripture relates, 2 Chr. xxvi. 4, 16; that *he did that which was right in
the Sight of the Lord, according to all that his Father had done, And he ſought God
in the Days of Zechariah, who had underſtanding in the Viſions of God;——and God
made him to proſper:——But when he was ſtrong, his heart was* lifted up *to his deſtruction; for he tranſgreſſed againſt the Lord his God.* The ſame was in ſome degree the
caſe of *Hezekiah,* who having ſerved the Lord diligently, beyond all that his Fathers
had done; and having been accordingly bleſſed with great Proſperity; yet at length he
rendred not again according to the Benefits done unto him; For his Heart was lifted up;
Therefore there was wrath upon him, and upon Judah and Jeruſalem, 2 Chr. xxxii. 25.
And this is a Fault ſo incident even to otherwiſe *good* men, that St *Paul* declares even
concerning *himſelf,* 2 Cor. xii. 7. *Leſt I ſhould be exalted above meaſure through the
Abundance of the Revelations, there was given to me a Thorn in the Fleſh,* an Affliction,
the meſſenger of Satan to buffet me, leſt I ſhould be exalted above meaſure. The Duty of
Humility in *This* caſe, conſiſts, in being always ſenſible of our Fallibility and our Danger; in *working out our own Salvation with Fear and Trembling;* even when we think
we *ſtand* ſureſt, yet *taking heed leſt* we *fall;* being (as the Prophet expreſſes it, *Iſ.* lxvi. 2.)
of a poor and contrite Spirit, and trembling at God's Word. 2dly, There is a *ſpiritual
Pride of Vain-glory,* in affecting a *publick Appearance* of ſuch Actions, as in themſelves
are good and commendable. This was the great Fault of the Phariſees; who *loved to* Mat. xii. 38.
*go in long-clothing, and loved ſalutations in the market-places, and the chief Seats in the
Synagogues, and the uppermoſt rooms at feaſts;* who *when* they gave *their Alms, ſound-
ed a trumpet before* them *in the ſynagogues and in the ſtreets, that they* might *have* Matt. vi. 2.
glory *of men;* and when *they prayed,* did it *ſtanding in the ſynagogues, and in the corners* vi. 5.
of the ſtreets, that they might *be ſeen of Men;* and, *when they faſted,* put on *a ſad* vi. 16.
countenance, and disfigured their Faces, that they might appear unto men to faſt. In oppoſition to This, true Humility conſiſts, in being contented to let the World be ignorant of the particular good Works we do; in ſo diſpoſing our Alms, as *not to let our
left hand know what our right hand does;* and in avoiding all Affectation, and publick
Boaſting, of our private Virtues. All which neverthelesſs, is ſo far from being inconſiſtent with that *other* Precept of our Saviour, of *letting our Light ſo ſhine before men,
that they may ſee our good Works, and glorify our Father which is in Heaven;* that, on
the contrary, there is no greater and more effectual recommendation of Virtue, to the
imitation of *reaſonable* and *well-diſpoſed* Perſons; than when they find it ſincerely unaffected, and which *vaunteth not itſelf. 3dly,* There is a *ſpiritual Pride,* of men *confidently juſtifying themſelves,* and being wholly inſenſible of their *own* Failings, while
they are very cenforious in *judging* and *deſpiſing* others. Of This, our Saviour gives us
an excellent inſtance, St *Luke* xviii. 9. *And he ſpake this Parable unto certain which
truſted in themſelves that they were righteous, and deſpiſed others; Two men went up into
the Temple to pray; the one a Phariſee, and the other a Publican: The Phariſee ſtood
and prayed thus with himſelf, God, I thank thee that I am not as other men are, extortioners, unjuſt, adulterers, or even as this publican: I faſt twice in the week, I give
tithes,*

SERM. *tithes of all that I poſſeſs : And the Publican ſtanding afar off, would not lift up ſo much*
XLIV. *as his Eyes to Heaven, but ſmote upon his Breaſt, ſaying, God, be merciful to me a*
Sinner : I tell you, ſays our Saviour, *this man went down to his houſe juſtified rather*
than the other ; For every one that exalteth himſelf ſhall be abaſed ; and he that hum-
bleth himſelf, ſhall be exalted. The ſame Sort of Pride, is deſcribed by the Wiſe-man,
Prov. xxx. 12 : *There is a generation that are pure in their own eyes, and yet is not*
waſhed from their filthineſs ; There is a generation, O how lofty are their eyes, and their
eye-lids are lifted up. Again, by our Saviour, St *Luke* xvi. 15. *Ye are they which juſtify*
yourſelves, before men, but God knoweth your Hearts, for that which is highly eſteemed a-
mong men, is abomination in the ſight of God. And by St *Paul,* 2 Cor. x. 12. *We*
dare not make ourſelves of the number, or compare ourſelves with ſome that commend
themſelves ; but they meaſuring themſelves by themſelves, and comparing themſelves amongſt
themſelves, are not wiſe : But we *will not boaſt of things without our meaſure ;——For*
not he that commendeth himſelf is approved, but whom the Lord commendeth. And
Gal. vi. 3. *If a man think himſelf to be ſomething, when he is nothing, he deceiveth*
himſelf. And again, by our Saviour himſelf, *Rev.* iii. 17. *Thou ſayeſt, I am rich, and*
increaſed with goods, and have need of nothing ; and knoweſt not that thou art wretched
and miſerable and poor and blind and naked : ſpeaking of a corrupt and proſperous ſtate
of the Church. The *Humility* oppoſite to *This* ſort of Pride, is that of St *Paul,*
1 Cor. iv. 4. *I know nothing by myſelf ; yet am I not hereby juſtified ; but he that judg-*
eth me, is the Lord. And *Phil.* iii. 12. *Not as though I had already attained, either*
were already perfect ;——but this One thing I do ; forgetting thoſe things which are be-
hind, and reaching forth unto thoſe things which are before, I preſs towards the mark,
for the prize of the high calling of God in Chriſt Jeſus. And that of *Job,* ch. ix. 20.
and ch. xlii. 6. *If I juſtify my ſelf, my own mouth ſhall condemn me ; if I ſay, I am per-*
fect, it ſhall alſo prove me perverſe ;——Wherefore I abhor my ſelf, and repent in duſt
and aſhes. The meaning of all which, is ; not that good men ſhould ſpeak or *think* of
themſelves, in the ſame manner and ſenſe as wicked men ought to do, but that when
they conſider the infinite purity of God and the perfection of his law, they ſhould then
humble themſelves in a deep ſenſe of their own many Follies and imperfections.
4*thly,* There is ſtill a *further* degree of *ſpiritual Pride,* in pretending to *Merit* at the
hands of God ; as thoſe of the Church of *Rome* have preſumptuouſly aſſumed to themſelves to do. And in oppoſition to *This* ſort of Pride, Humility conſiſts in that Diſpoſition of Mind, which is recorded of the good *Centurion,* St *Luke* vii. 6, and Mat. viii. 8.
Lord, I am ι. t worthy, (I have no claim, no pretence to expect,) *that thou ſhouldſt*
come under my roof : Wherefore neither thought I my ſelf worthy to come unto thee ; but
ſpeak the word, and my Servant ſhall be healed. And of St *Paul,* Eph. iii. 8. *Unto me,*
who am leſs than the leaſt of all Saints, is this Grace given ; The expreſſion is hyperbo-
lical ; But the meaning is, that he had not any the leaſt claim of Right or Deſert to that
ſingular Favour, of being made the Apoſtle to the *Gentiles.* And in like manner, of
Abraham, Gen. xviii. 27. *I have taken upon me to ſpeak unto the Lord, which am but*
duſt and aſhes. And of *Jacob,* Gen. xxxii. 10. *I am not worthy of the leaſt of all thy*
Mercies. And accordingly our Saviour directs his Diſciples, St *Luke* xvii. 10. *When ye*
ſhall have done all thoſe things which are commanded you, ſay, We are unprofitable Ser-
vants ; we have done that which was our Duty to do. Nevertheleſs, upon This Head
of *Merit,* it is alſo to be obſerved, that there is a Fault even in the *contrary* Extreme ;
a pretended *Humility,* in imagining, that as we cannot *Merit,* ſo neither are we able to
Do any thing, but muſt leave the Grace of God to do All for us. Which opinion, does
as effectually deſtroy Religion in *one* extreme, as the doctrine of *Merit* does in the *other.*
For, as, according to the Doctrine of *Merit,* the *Reward* is not of *Grace,* but by *Claim*
of Right ; ſo, on the other ſide, if we are able to *do nothing at all,* then the *Puniſh-*

I   *ment*

ment cannot be by *Juſtice*, but by mere *arbitrary Power*, which is inconſiſtent with the Attributes of God. *5thly*, There is yet a *higher* degree of this *Spiritual Pride*, in pretending to Works of *Supererogation*. This alſo is a fond Pretence of the Church of Rome. And This ſeems to have been the Fault of the Young man in the Goſpel; who, when our Saviour had ſaid unto him, *If thou wilt enter into life, keep the Commandments*; would needs reply further; St *Matt.* xix. 20. *What lack I yet?* This alſo is what St *Paul* ſo juſtly reproves, *Col.* ii. 18. *Let no man beguile you of your reward, in a voluntary humility and worſhipping of Angels, intruding into thoſe things which he hath not ſeen, vainly puſt up by his fleſhly mind;* ——— *which things have indeed a* Show of Wiſdom, *in will-worſhip and humility:* But *True* humility, in oppoſition to this falſe and *proud* appearance of it, conſiſts, in making, not our *own* Will, but the *Will of God*, the Rule of our Duty; *caſting down imaginations, and every high thing, that exalteth itſelf againſt the knowledge of God; and bringing into captivity every Thought to the Obedience of Chriſt,* not, *of Men* but, *of Chriſt.* *Laſtly,* There is a *Spiritual Pride*, in ſeeking after and being fond of myſterious *and ſecret things*, to the neglect of our *plain* and manifeſt Duty; In alluſion to which, the corrupt Church in the *Revelations*, is ſtiled, *Myſtery, Babylon the Great.* And in oppoſition to This, *True Humility* is that which the Wiſeman deſcribes, *Prov.* iii. 7. *Be not wiſe in thine own eyes; Fear the Lord, and depart from evil:* And *Moſes,* Deut xxix. 29. *Secret things belong unto the Lord our God; but thoſe things which are revealed, belong unto us, and to our children for ever, that we may do all the Words of this Law:* And the Pſalmiſt, *Pſ.* cxxxi. 1. *Lord, mine heart is not haughty, nor mine eyes lofty; neither do I exerciſe myſelf in great matters, or in things too high for me:* And the wiſe Son of *Sirach,* Eccluſ. iii. 21. *Seek not out the things that are too hard for thee, neither ſearch the things that are above thy ſtrength: But what is commanded thee, think thereupon with reverence; for it is not needful for thee to ſee with thine eyes the things that are in ſecret: Be not curious in unneceſſary matters, for more things are ſhewed unto thee, than men underſtand: For many are deceived by their own vain opinion, and an evil ſuſpicion has overthrown their judgment.* The only caution here neceſſary to be given, is that this entire humble Submiſſion of our own judgment, is due to *God only,* in the Words of his own immediate and expreſs Revelation: The paying the like deference to any *humane doctrine* or *humane explication* of doctrine whatſoever, without thoroughly examining it and underſtanding it perfectly; is not *Humility,* but *Ignorance and Sloth.* And This may ſuffice upon the 1ſt particular, *what* True Humility is, and wherein it conſiſts.

S E R M O N XLV.

Of Humility.

LUK. XIV. 11.

For whosoever exalteth himself, shall be abased; and he that humbleth himself, shall be exalted.

SERM.
XLV.

IN a former Discourse upon these Words, I have endeavoured to show distinctly *What* the Virtue of true Humility *is*, and wherein it consists. It remains that I proceed at this Time, to propose some *Arguments* to perswade men to the *Practice* of it. And 1*st*, The Scripture frequently lays before us, the *natural* ill consequences of Pride; and the Advantages arising from true Humility, even in the *natural* Course and Order of Things.

PRIDE makes men foolish, and void of caution; and This puts them upon doing things that bring them to Dishonour : *When Pride cometh, then cometh Shame ; but with the lowly is Wisdom*, Prov. xi. 2.

IT makes men negligent, and improvident of the future; and this often throws them into sudden calamities; *The Turning away of the Simple,* (in the original it is, *the Ease, the* Negligence *of the Simple,) shall slay them ; and the Prosperity of Fools shall destroy them*, Prov. i. 32.

IT makes men rash and peevish, obstinate and insolent; and This seldom fails to bring down ruin upon them; *Pride goeth before destruction, and an haughty Spirit before a Fall; Better it is to be of an humble Spirit with the lowly, than to divide the Spoil with the Proud*, Prov. xvi. 18.

IT involves men perpetually in Strifes and Contentions; and These always multiply Sin, and are inconsistent with true Happiness; *He loveth transgression, that loveth strife, and he that exalteth his Gate, seeketh Destruction*, Prov. xvii. 19.

IT disobliges men's best Friends, and gives their Enemies perpetual Advantages against them; and This often draws great inconveniencies upon them: *Before destruction the Heart of Man is haughty, and before Honour is Humility*, Prov. xviii. 12.

IT makes men vain and lovers of Flattery, rejecting those about them who would do them most Kindness, and liking those best who do them the greatest injury; And This causes them to be insensible of their own Disease, till they suddenly fall under Contempt: *A man's Pride shall bring him low, but Honour shall uphold the humble in Spirit*, Prov. xxix. 23.

IT makes men impatient of good Advice and Instruction, and That renders them incorrigible in their Vices; *Seest thou a man wise in his own Conceit? there is more Hope of a Fool, than of him: The sluggard is wiser in his own conceit, than seven men that can render a reason*, Prov. xxvi. 12, 16; and xxxviii. 26. *He that trusteth in his own Heart, is a Fool; but whoso walketh wisely, he shall be delivered.*

Lastly, IT fills men full of vain-glorious Designs, employing all their Thoughts in self-confident Imaginations; and This makes them incapable of Religious improvements,

and

and to have no relifh of true Wifdom : *The full Soul loatheth the honey-comb,* Prov.
xxvii. 7 ; and xxv. 27. *It is not good to eat much honey ; fo for men to fearch their own*
glory, is not glory.

T H E S E are the elegant Obfervations of wife *Solomon,* upon the *natural* inconveniencies and difadvantages of Pride. In the *other* parts of Scripture we find likewife, feveral Remarks of the fame kind. That *Pride* hinders men from examining impartially,
into the Truth of Religion ; *How can ye believe,* fays our Saviour, *which receive honour
one of another, and feek not the honour which cometh from God only ?* Joh. v. 44. And,
have any of the Rulers, or of the Pharifees believed on him ? ch. vii. 48. That it makes
men *difdain* to leave their pleafing Vanities, and *think much* to condefcend to the mean
Reftraints and Confinements of Religion ; *Judges* ix. 9. *The Olive-tree faid,*———*Should
I leave my Fatnefs ?*———*And the Fig-tree faid,*———*Should I forfake my Sweetnefs, and
my good Fruit ?*———*And the Vine faid,*———*Should I leave my Wine which cheereth God
and Men, and go to be promoted over the Trees ?* ver. 13. That it caufes men to take
Offence at the Plainefs and Simplicity of the Gofpel, and thereby hinders it from
making due impreffions upon them ; *The Wifdom of God,*———*which none of the Princes
of This World knew,* 1 Cor. ii. 8. *Where is the Wife ? Where is the Scribe ? Where is
the Difputer of this World ?*———*For ye fee your calling, Brethren, how that not many
Wife men after the Flefh, not many mighty, not many noble are called,* ch. i. 20, 26.
*Therefore let no man glory in men : If any man among you feemeth to be wife in This
World, let him become a Fool, that he may be wife,* i. e. let him lay afide the Wifdom
of *Self-conceit,* in order to become *capable* of Inftruction in the *true Wifdom,* ch. iii. 21, 18.
That it hinders men from performing the Duty of Chriftian Charity, one towards another ; *Diotrephes, who loveth to have the preeminence among them, receiveth us not ;*
3 Joh. 9. Laftly, that in the execution of the *Offices* of Chriftian Authority, it turns
men from a due regard of the *Intent* of their Office, to *temporal* and worldly confiderations, and this leads them into a Snare, and brings them to Deftruction : *A Bifhop*
(fays the Apoftle) *muft not be a novice, left being lifted up with Pride, he fall into the
Condemnation of the Devil,* 1 Tim. iii. 6. Thefe are the *natural* ill confequences of
Pride, which the Scripture lays before us ; and which confequently difcover to us the
Advantages arifing from true Humility, even in the *natural* courfe and order of things.

2dly, T H E *next* Argument the Scripture makes ufe of, to perfwade men to the
Practice of Humility, is This ; that Pride, as it is ufually of *natural* ill confequence,
fo it is moreover *particularly hateful to* God ; who reprefents himfelf as taking *delight,*
to bring down the lofty, and to exalt the humble. It is the Obfervation of *Eliphaz* in
the book of *Job,* ch. xxii. 29 ; *When men are caft down, then thou fhalt fay, There is
lifting up ; and he fhall fave the Humble perfon :* And ch. xxxiii. 14, 17 ; *God fpeaketh
once, yea twice, yet man perceiveth it not ;*———*that he may withdraw man from his
purpofe, and hide Pride from man.* God himfelf by the Prophet *Ifaiah,* declares,
ch. ii. 11 ; *The lofty looks of man fhall be humbled, and the haughtinefs of men fhall be
bowed down, and the Lord alone fhall be exalted in that Day ; For the day of the Lord
of hofts fhall be upon every one that is proud and lofty, and upon every one that is lifted
up ; and he fhall be brought low.* The Wife man in like manner, *Prov.* iii. 34 ; *Surely*
(fays he) *he fcorneth the fcorners, but giveth grace unto the lowly.* Which paffage is,
almoft in the very fame words, quoted by St *Peter,* 1 Pet. v. 5, *Be clothed with humility ; For God refifteth the Proud, and giveth Grace unto the humble.* The Bleffed Virgin, after the Angel's annunciating to her the Conception of our Lord, inferts into her
hymn the fame general Obfervation : *He hath fhowed Strength with his Arm, he has
fcattered the proud in the imagination of their Hearts ; He hath put down the mighty
from their Seats, and has exalted the humble and meek,* St *Luke* i. 51. Our Saviour
himfelf, taking a little Child, and fetting it before his Difciples, when they were con-

I   *tending*

tending for pre-eminence; *Verily* (fays he) *I fay unto you ;——whofoever fhall humble himfelf as this little Child, the fame is greateft in the Kingdom of Heaven ;——But who-foever fhall offend one of thefe little ones that believe in me,* i. e. whofoever fhall by proud and contemptuous treatment difcourage the meaneft Chriftian, or drive him into any Sin ; *it were better for him that a milftone were hanged about his neck, and that he were drowned in the Depth of the Sea,* St Matt. xviii. 4, 6. And again, in the words of the Text, upon another not unlike occafion ; *Whofoever* (faith he) *exalteth himfelf, fhall be abafed ; and he that humbled himfelf, fhall be exalted.* The *Reafon why* Pride is always reprefented in Scripture, as being thus *particularly* hateful *to God* ; is becaufe it ufually fignifies, and always includes, fomething of that *Prefumptuoufnefs,* that *prefuming* to tranfgrefs infolently and with a high Hand, which is the greateft Aggravation of Sin, and the moft directly oppofite to that meek and humble Spirit, which *trembleth at God's Word,* which ftudies his Will, and is always fearful of difobeying it. *Wo unto them,* faith the Prophet, *that call evil good, and good evil ; that put darknefs for light, and light for darknefs,* If. v. 20 ; *i. e.* who are fo infolent as prefumptuoufly to deny, either in their Words or Actions, the moft evident moral Differences of Right

Ifa. v. 21.

and Wrong : For fo it is explained in the Words immediately following ; *Wo unto them,* (not, who miftake, or are guilty of any Error or falfe opinion in this matter, but) *unto them that are wife in their own eyes, and prudent in their own fight* ; who fay,

Jer. xviii. 12.

We will walk after our own devices, and we will every one do the imagination of his evil Heart : Who *fay unto God, Depart from us, for we defire not the knowledge of thy ways : What is the Almighty, that we fhould ferve him ? and what profit fhould we have if we pray unto him ?* Job xxi. 14. Concerning fuch perfons as *Thefe* it is, that the Scripture threatens ; *Every one that is proud in Heart, is an abomination to the Lord ; though hand join in hand, he fhall not be unpunifhed,* Prov. xvi. 5. It is generally fuppofed by Divines, that the original Sin even of the *Devil himfelf,* was *Pride* ; becaufe St *Paul* fpeaking of a man's being *lift up with Pride,* calls it *his falling into the condemnation of the Devil.* And this, is not at all improbable ; provided, by *Pride,* be underftood, not (with the vulgar) his attempting to *refift God Almighty by Force,* which is abfurd and impoffible and childifh to imagine ; but his prefuming, upon the Greatnefs and Dignity of his Nature, infolently to tranfgrefs fome of the Divine Commands. And fomething *like* this, is the Cafe of Powerful *Tyrannical Princes,* who proudly defpife the Thoughts and Expectation of God's righteous judgment. For which reafon, the Prophet *Ifaiah* fo defcribes the Deftruction of the King of *Babylon,* that the Words are, not without probability, thought to be an Allufion to the Fall of *Satan,* ch. xiv. 12, *How art thou fallen from Heaven, O Lucifer, Son of the morning ! how art thou cut down to the ground, which didft weaken the Nations ! for thou haft faid in thine Heart, I will afcend into Heaven, I will exalt my throne above the Stars of God, I will fit alfo upon the mount of the Congregation, in the fides of the North ; I will afcend above the heights of the clouds, I will be like the moft High. Yet thou fhalt be brought down to Hell, to the fides of the Pit.* And *They that fee thee fhall — fay, Is this the man that made the Earth to tremble? — that made the World as a wildernefs, and deftroyed the Cities thereof?* This is the manner wherein the Scripture reprefents God *delighting* to deftroy Tyrants, thofe *proud* and mighty Tranfgreffors.

ANOTHER inftance of which, is the defcription of the Haughtinefs and the Fall of *Nebuchadnezzar* ; Dan. iv. 30; *The King fpake and faid, Is not This great Babylon that I have built for the Houfe of the Kingdom, by the might of my Power, and for the honour of my Majefty?* But *when his Heart was lifted up, and his Mind hardned in Pride, he was depofed from his kingly throne, and they took his glory from him : and he was driven from the Sons of men ; and his Heart made like the Beafts, and his dwelling was*
with

with the wild Asses; ch. v. 20; that is, his Understanding was taken from him, and he *imagined* himself to be turned into a Beast.

AND the Instance of *Pharaoh*; Exod. v. 2. *Who is the Lord, that I should obey his Voice?* —— *I know not the Lord, neither will I let Israel go* : Therefore the Lord *sent all* his *plagues upon* his *Heart, and upon* his *Servants, and upon* his *People*; ch. ix. 14.

AND that of *Herod*; Acts xii. 21; *Upon a set day, Herod arrayed in royal apparel, sat upon his throne, and made an oration*; *And the people gave a shout, saying, It is the voice of a god, and not of a man*; *And immediately the Angel of the Lord smote him, because he gave not God the glory*; *and he was eaten of worms, and gave up the Ghost:* The *Angel of the Lord*, that is, a sudden disease, by the direction of Providence, came upon him: The Figure is the same as that which St *Paul* uses, when he calls a temporal Affliction the *Messenger* or *Angel* of Satan to buffet him; 2 *Cor.* xii. 7; So 1 *Th.* ii. 18.

ANOTHER Example, is that of *Haman* in the Book of *Esther*; who when he would have sacrificed a whole Nation to his Pride and Haughtiness, God justly suffered him to fall by the same ignominious Death which he had contrived for another.

AND that of *spiritual Babylon* or *Christian* Tyranny and the Spirit of *Persecution* in the *Revelation*; ch. xviii. 7; *How much she has glorified herself, and lived deliciously, so much torment and sorrow give her*; *For she saith in her heart, I sit a Queen, and am no widow, and shall see no sorrow*; *Therefore shall her plagues come in one day*; *death and mourning and famine*; *and she shall be utterly burnt with Fire*; *for strong is the Lord God who judgeth her.*

THE manner and reason of God's proceedings in all which and the like Instances, cannot be more elegantly expressed, than in the words of the wise Son of *Sirach*; Eccluf. x. 7; *Pride is hateful before God and Man, and by both doth one commit Iniquity*: —— *Why is Earth and Ashes proud?* —— *The beginning of Pride is, when one departeth from God, and his Heart is turned away from his Maker*: *For Pride is the beginning of Sin*; *and he that hath it, shall pour out abomination*; *and therefore the Lord brought upon them strange calamities, and overthrew them utterly*: *The Lord hath cast down the Thrones of proud Princes, and set up the meek in their stead*: *The Lord hath plucked up the roots of the proud Nations, and planted the lowly in their place*: *The Lord overthrew the Countries of the Heathen, and destroyed them to the Foundations of the Earth.* —— *Pride was not made for men, nor furious Anger for them that are born of a woman.* This therefore is the *second* Argument to deter men from Pride; the consideration of its being *particularly hateful to God*.

3dly, THE *third* and last motive the Scripture lays before us, to recommend the Practice of Humility, is the Example of *God* himself, and of our Lord and Saviour *Jesus Christ*. Properly and strictly speaking, *Humility* is not a Perfection that can be ascribed to *God:* Because where there is no room for *Pride*, there can never be properly any Exercise of *Humility*; and he whose Nature is of infinite and unlimited Excellency, can neither possibly assume to *himself*, nor have ascribed to him by *Others*, any thing beyond what is absolutely and necessarily due to him: Neither can he possibly *debase* himself, in the literal Sense; or in any wise *diminish* from his own superlative and unchangeable Excellency. Nevertheless, in a figurative manner of speaking, the Scripture *does* sometimes ascribe Humility to God, and recommends his Condescension as a Pattern for us to imitate. *The Lord, who dwelleth on high,* —— *humbleth himself to behold the things that are in Heaven, and in the Earth*; Ps. cxiii. 6: And Ps. cxxxviii. 6; *Though the Lord be high, yet hath he respect unto the lowly.* And the same manner of speaking is used by God himself; If. lvii. 15; *Thus saith the High and Lofty One, that inhabiteth Eternity*; ——*I dwell in the high and holy Place*; *with Him also, that is of a contrite and humble Spirit*; And ch. lxvi. 1; *Thus saith the Lord, The Heaven is my Throne,*

SERM. *and the Earth is my Footstool*; —— *yet to this man will I look, even to him that is poor*
XLV. *and of a contrite Spirit, and trembleth at my Word.* But the Example more accom-
modate to our Infirmities, and more generally alleged in Scripture, is that of *our Saviour*: Who, though he was Lord of all, yet was content *not to have where to lay his Head*;
St *Matt.* viii. 20. Before whom it was proclaimed; *Tell ye the Daughter of Zion, Behold, thy King cometh unto thee, meek and sitting upon an Ass*; St *Matt.* xxi. 5. Who,
though he was greater than All, yet declared concerning himself; *If I honour myself,
my honour is nothing*; *It is my Father that honoureth me, of whom ye say that he is your
God*; St *Joh.* viii. 54: Who, *though he was rich, yet for our sakes he became poor, that
we through his Poverty might be rich*; 2 Cor. viii. 9. Who, *glorified not* Himself, *to
be made an High Priest*; *but he that said unto him, Thou art my Son*; Heb. v. 5. Who,
when he was reviled, reviled not again; *when he suffered, he threatned not*; *but committed himself to him that judgeth righteously*; 1 Pet. ii. 23. Which Example of universal Humility in all Circumstances, he himself proposes to us for our Imitation:
Learn of Me, for I am meek and lowly in Heart; St *Matt.* xi. 29. *If I, your Lord
and Master, have washed your Feet, then I have given you an example, that ye should
do as I have done to you*; St *John* xiii. 15. *Whosoever will be chief among you, let him
be your Servant*; *Even as the Son of Man came not to be ministred unto, but to minister,
and to give his life a ransom for many*; St *Mark* xx. 28. And the same is urged by
the Apostle; Rom. xv. 2; *Let every one of us please his neighbour for his good to edification*; *For even* Christ *pleased not himself.* And Phil. ii. 5; *Let this mind be in you,
which was also in Christ Jesus*; *Who, though he was in the Form of God, yet was not
greedy to appear as God*; (so the words signify in the original;) *but made himself of no
reputation, and took upon him the Form of a Servant, and was made in the Likeness of
Men*; *And* —— *humbled himself, and became obedient unto Death, even the Death of the
Cross: Wherefore God also has highly exalted him.*

THESE are the Principal Arguments the Scripture makes use of, to perswade men
to the Practice of Humility *in general.* There are moreover *in particular*, as many
peculiar distinct Motives to practise this Duty, as there are different Circumstances and
varieties of Cases wherein it is to be exercised. Without practising it towards *Superiors*, there can be no Government; without exercising it towards *Equals*, there can
be no Friendship and mutual Charity. Then, with regard to *Inferiors*; besides the
general Example of Christ's singular and unspeakable Condescension towards us All,
there are proper Arguments to deter us from Pride upon account of *every particular
Advantage* we may seem to have over Others, whether in respect of our Civil *Stations*
in the World, or of our Natural *Abilities*, or of our Religious *Improvements.* If the
Advantages of our Civil *Stations* in the World, tempt us to proud and haughty Behaviour; we may do well to consider that Argument of *Job*; ch. xxxi. 13; *If I did despise the cause of my Man-servant, or of my Maid-servant when they contended with me;
What then shall I do, when God riseth up? and when he visiteth, what shall I answer
him? Did not he that made* Me *in the Womb, make* Him? *and did not One, fashion us
in the Womb?* And ch. xxxiv. 19; *He accepteth not the Persons of Princes, nor regardeth the Rich more than the Poor*; *for they are All the Work of his Hands.* Which same
Argument is urged also by the Wise-man; Prov. xiv. 31. *He that oppresseth the Poor,
reproacheth his Maker*: And ch. xxii. 2; *The Rich and Poor meet together*; *the Lord
is the Maker of them All.* It will become us also to think upon the *Vanity* and *Uncertainty* of these things, which are so apt to puff us up: *For all Flesh is as Grass*; *and
all the glory of Man, as the Flower of Grass*; *The Grass withereth, and the Flower thereof falleth away*; 1 Pet. i. 24. And Jam. i. 10; *Let the Rich rejoyce, in that he is made
low*; *because as a Flower of the Grass he shall pass away.* It may be proper likewise
to consider, that, if we are placed in High Stations, we have a *larger Account* to give,

to him that ruleth over All; and possibly, while we are honoured upon this single Ac- S E R M. count, others beneath us may be valuable for *better and more really excellent* Qualifica- XLV. tions; And it will not be long before Death and Judgment level all worldly Distincti- ons; And the greatest men, if they have been wicked, shall then be forced to cry out, *What hath Pride profited us? or what hath riches with our vaunting brought us? All these things are past away as a shadow, and as a Post that hasteth by.* Again: If we are apt to be puft up with the Advantage of Natural *Abilities,* such as Learning, Know- ledge, Wisdom, or the like; it may humble us to consider, how *small* a Degree of these things, we can attain to even at the best: seeing that *Knowledge,* as *Job* most elegant- ly expresses it, *is hid from all men, neither is it found in the land of the living.* And ch. xxviii. 21, if we could attain to *much more* of it, than we do; yet still there is something far more ¹³. Excellent than That: *For Knowledge puffeth up, but* Charity *edifieth; And if any Man think that he knoweth any thing, he knoweth nothing yet, as he ought to know;* 1 Cor. viii. 1. Wherefore, *Thus saith the Lord: Let not the Wise man glory in his Wisdom, neither let the mighty man glory in his Might; let not the rich man glory in his riches: But let him that glorieth, glory in This, that he understandeth and knoweth me, that I am the Lord which exercise loving-kindness, judgment and righteousness in the Earth; For in these things I delight, saith the Lord;* Jer. ix. 23. *Lastly,* If our Advantages even in Religious *Improvement* itself, tempt us to spiritual Pride and Vain-glory, to judge or to despise our weaker Brethren; the Scripture admonishes us to consider, *that all the members of Christ, are useful in their several Stations; I say to every man,* says the Apostle, *that is among you, not to think of himself more highly than he ought to think, but to think soberly, according as God has dealt to every man the measure of Faith, i. e.* according to the Station wherein God has placed him in the Church; *For, as* (in our natural capacity) *we have many Members in one Body, and all Members have not the same Office: so* (in our spiritual capacity) *we being many are one body in Christ, and every one members one of another;* Rom. xii. 3. that therefore *the Eye cannot say to the Hand, I have no need of thee; nor again the Head to the Feet, I have no need of you,* 1 Cor. xii. 21; that our Saviour himself refused not to be baptized by *John Baptist,* though a person infinitely meaner than himself; but on the contrary declared, that *thus it becomes us to fulfil all Righteousness:* that, how great soever our Abilities or Ad- vantages be, yet the means by which we arrive even at These, are, *not that we are suf-* 2 Cor. iii. 5. *ficient of ourselves to think any thing as of ourselves, but our sufficiency is of God;* that therefore we must *learn not to think of men, above that which is written, that no one of* 1 Cor. iv. 6, *us be puffed up for one against another; For who maketh thee to differ from another? and what hast thou, that thou didst not receive?* The meaning of which places, is not, that God acts upon Men as Machines, so as that They do nothing at all themselves, but that the Gifts whereby they are *enabled* to become eminent, (and that not so much in *moral* Virtues, as in *miraculous spiritual Powers* in the Church, mentioned at large by St *Paul,* 1 *Cor.* xii, These) are all, not their own, but received from God's free Goodness and Bounty. Further, we are admonished to consider, in abatement of spi- ritual Pride and Contempt of our weaker Brethren, and of those who differ from us in matters of opinion; and with whom we are apt to be angry for not complying with *our* Notions; that there is a day a coming which, distinguishing men by their Works of Piety, and true Holiness only, shall level them in all other respects, and set them up- on Even ground before an impartial Bar; where mens foolish pride and arrogance, shall be entirely confounded; and those who looked with scorn upon others as infinite- ly below them, shall find themselves placed upon an equal foot with them whom perhaps they most despised: *Who art thou,* therefore, *that judgest another man's ser- vant? To his own Master, he standeth, or falleth;* Rom. xiv. 4, and ver. 10. *Why dost thou judge thy Brother? and why dost thou set at nought thy Brother? For we shall all* stand

SERM.
XLV.

stand before the judgment-seat of Christ. That, how great foever our improvements be, even in *real* Virtue and Righteoufnefs; yet we have continual reafon to *take heed left we fall;* and Pride and Confidence, is the Security only *of a* blind *man,* who fees no danger: That even while we ftand the moft upright, we have nothing to glory of be-

Job. xxv. 4.
iv. 18.

fore God; For *how can man be juftified with God? Behold he put no truft in his Servants, and his Angels he charged with Folly; How much lefs in them that dwell in houfes of clay, whofe Foundation is in the Duft!* That the greateft and moft eminently pious men, have been exemplarily humble in This refpect; holy *Job* refufing to juftify himfelf

ix. 20. xiii. 6.

before God; and *Abraham* ftiling himfelf Duft and Afhes; and *Jacob* acknowledging himfelf lefs than the leaft of God's mercies; and St *Paul* calling himfelf lefs than the leaft of all Saints: not that he *then* was fo, but that he *had been* a Perfecutor of the Church of God. That Humility is the only means to entitle us to the Divine Affiftance and continual Direction, and the beft Help to a right Underftanding in matters of Religion; (meaning always by Humility, not a blind and carelefs Submiffion to the No-tions of *Men,* but an intire giving up ourfelves to the Will of *God;*) *Truft in the Lord with all thine Heart, and lean not unto thine own underftanding; In all thy ways ac-knowledge him, and he fhall direct thy Paths; Be not wife in thine own eyes; Fear the Lord, and depart from evil;* This is the Advice of *Solomon; Prov.* iii. 5. And the Pfalmift declares: *Pf.* xxv. 9. *Them that are meek will God guide in judgment, and fuch as are gentle, them will he learn his way;* And St *Paul* directs, 2 *Cor.* x. 5. to *caft down imaginations, and every high thing that exalteth itfelf againft the Knowledge of God, and to bring into Captivity every Thought to the Obedience of Chrift;* Not our *Underftandings* to the Opinions of *Men;* but our *Wills,* the Thoughts and Defigns of our Hearts to the Obedience of Chrift. And the wife Son of *Sirach* advifes; *Eccluf.* iii. 17. *My Son, go on with thy bufinefs in Meeknefs, fo fhalt thou be beloved of him that is approved; The greater thou art, the more humble thy felf, and thou fhalt find Favour before the Lord; Many are in high places, and of renown, but myfteries are revealed unto the Meek;* And our Saviour himfelf profeffes; St *Mat.* xi. 25. *I thank thee, O Father, Lord of Heaven and Earth, becaufe thou haft hid thefe things from the wife and prudent, and haft revealed them unto Babes; Even fo, Father, for fo it feemed good in thy fight.* Thefe are the Arguments the Scripture makes ufe of, to perfuade us to the Practice of Humility; And they are all briefly fummed up in the Words of the Text; *Whofoever exalteth himfelf, fhall be abafed; and he that hum-bleth himfelf, fhall be exalted.*

SERMON

S E R M O N XLVI.

Of Poverty of Spirit.

MATT. V. 3.

Blessed are the Poor in Spirit; for Theirs is the Kingdom of Heaven.

THE *Beatitudes*, or Declarations of Blessedness, with which our Saviour be- S E R M. gins his Sermon upon the Mount; though they seem each of them to be a XLVI. recommendation of some *singular Virtue*, and to contain each of them singly a Promise that such a *particular* Virtue shall have its *distinct*, *proper*, and *peculiar Reward*; yet this is not so to be understood, as if any of these Virtues singly specified, were to be taken *separately*, exclusive of *Other Virtues*; or as if any of the *Rewards* here distinctly mentioned, were to be looked upon as conferred *separately*, and *divided* from the *Other* Constituents of the Happiness of Heaven : But by a very usual and well-known manner of speaking, wherein a Part is figuratively put for the Whole; as, in *Other* places of Scripture, *Faith* or *Hope* or *Charity*, or *Repentance*, or the *Love* or *Fear* of God, do frequently stand for the *Whole Duty* of a Christian; and the single particulars of *seeing God*, or *being with God*, or of *living for ever*, are intended to include in general *All* the Blessings and Happiness, *All* the Glories and Enjoyments, of the *Heavenly State*; so *Here* likewise our Saviour, in each *Beatitude*, must be understood *in general* to annex the Promise of the Happiness of Heaven, to the *universal* Practice of our *whole* Christian Duty. And it is with singular Beauty and Elegancy, as well as with great Variety and Instructiveness of expression, that, in the *former* part of each Beatitude, he describes our *Christian Duty* under the character of some *particular eminent Virtue*; and, in the *latter*, he sets forth to us, under the like number of different *distinct* Views, the Glories of his heavenly Kingdom : Representing, in the *latter* part of each Beatitude, the *Happiness* of that eternal State, under *such a particular Figure*, and in *such a particular Light*, as is most agreeably correspondent to That *particular* Notion of Virtue under which he had in the *former* part represented our Christian *Duty*. Thus when the Life of a Christian is expressed under the character of being *poor in Spirit*, then his Reward is the *Riches* of the *Kingdom of Heaven* : *Blessed are the poor in Spirit, for theirs is the Kingdom of Heaven.* When his *present* State is represented as a temporary *Mourning*, then his *future* State is the *Comforts* and the Joys of Eternity: *Blessed are they that mourn, for they shall be comforted.* When his Virtue is described under the Notion of *Meekness*, in opposition to striving violently for Dominion and great Possessions; then his Recompence is the *Inheritance* of the whole *Earth*; even the inheritance of That *New Heaven and New Earth, wherein* Meekness *is to dwell* and reign for ever : *Blessed are the Meek, for they shall inherit the Earth.* When his steddy Love of Truth and Right, is set forth under the similitude of *hungring and thirsting after Righteousness*; then the Promise to him is, that he shall be fully *satisfied*, even to the utmost of his Desire: *Blessed are they that hunger and thirst after Righteousness, for they shall*

S E R M. *be filled.* When his Religion is confidered as confifting, (as to the main Branches of XLVI. it) in Acts of *Goodnefs*, *Charity*, and *Mercy* towards *Others*; then the Happinefs annexed is, that He *himfelf* fhall find *Mercy* and Compaffion from *God*: *Bleffed are the merciful, for they fhall obtain mercy.* And, to mention but one Inftance more; When the whole Moral Obedience of a fincere Difciple of Chrift, is emphatically comprehended under the fingle Title of *Purity of Heart*; then the Joys of Heaven are held forth to him correfpondently under *This* View, that he fhall be admitted to See, and to dwell for ever in the Prefence of, the *Fountain of Purity and Holinefs* itfelf: *Bleffed are the pure in Heart, for they fhall fee God.*

Of Thefe *Beatitudes*, the *Firft* is what will be the Subject of our prefent Meditations; *Bleffed are the Poor in Spirit, for theirs is the Kingdom of Heaven.* In difcourfing upon which words, I fhall *firft* endeavour to explain diftinctly the Meaning of the Phrafe, being *poor in Spirit*; And then, *Secondly*, I fhall draw fome *Obfervations*, from the confideration of the Nature of the *Virtue* here fpoken of, and of the *Reward* here declared to be annexed to it.

I. In order to explain diftinctly the Meaning of this phrafe, being *Poor in Spirit*; it is to be obferved, that thofe two different manners of expreffion, which we *Now* ufually call *literal* and *figurative*, were in the *Jewifh* language frequently denoted by the words *flefh* and *fpirit*. The *flefh*, fays our Saviour, *profiteth nothing*; *the words that I fpeak unto you, they are* Spirit *and they are Life*, Joh. vi. 63. His meaning is; He intended not to be underftood *literally*, but *figuratively*. To *Be* therefore, or *Do*, any thing *in* Spirit; fignifies *being* or *doing* that Thing *figuratively*, in the *fpiritual* or *moral*, in the *religious* or in the *abftract* fenfe; in oppofition to the *grofs* and more *literal* meaning, in which the fame words may at *other* times be underftood. Thus when the Angel in the Revelation *carried away* St John *in the* Spirit *into the wildernefs*, (ch. xvii. 3.) the Meaning is, he was not carried thither *really* and *literally*, but only in a *vifionary* Reprefentation. By the like figure of Speech, St. *Paul*, when he was *perfonally abfent*, yet, becaufe his *Name*, his *Commiffion* and *Authority*, was to be made ufe of, as if he had *Himfelf* been There; *I therefore*, fays he, *verily, as abfent in Body, but prefent in* Spirit, 1 Cor. v. 3. and again, (Col. ii. 5.) *Though I be abfent in the Flefh, yet am I with you in the* Spirit, *joying and beholding your Order.* And in a ftill more *fublime* Ufe of the fame Metaphor; *Acts* xx. 22. while he was yet at full liberty, and had no violence offered him, yet prophetically forefeeing that *Bonds and Afflictions* were coming upon him, *Behold*, fays he, *I go* Bound in the Spirit *unto Jerufalem.* Upon the fame ground of expreffion, *That Moral* Holinefs and Purity of the *Gofpel*, which is oppofed to the *ritual* and *ceremonious* Performance of the *Jewifh Law*, our Saviour calls *Worfhipping the Father in* Spirit *and in Truth*, John iv. 23. And That abfolute *departing from all unrighteoufnefs*, fo effentially required in the Gofpel, of which the *Jewifh Circumcifion* was but a Type or Emblem; is by the Apoftle moft elegantly ftiled, *Circumcifion in the Spirit*: Rom. ii. 28. *That is not Circumcifion, which is outward in the Flefh: But—Circumcifion is That of the Heart, in the* Spirit, *and not in the letter, whofe Praife is not of Men, but of God:* For We *are the Circumcifion*, (Phil. iii. 3.) *which worfhip God in the* Spirit,——*and have no confidence in the flefh.* We *Chriftians*, fays he, if, according to our Profeffion, we purify our felves from all Filthinefs both of Flefh and Spirit, We are the *True Circumcifion*; while the unbelieving *Jews*, if they continue impenitent, are, notwithftanding the Covenant of *literal* circumcifion, rejected as being, in the fight of God, *uncircumcifed in Heart*; Acts vii. 51.

Answerable therefore to this figurative manner of expreffion in fo many *other* places; the Phrafe in the *Text*, *Poor in* Spirit, in contradiftinction to *literal Poverty of* Eftate, fignifies a *Temper of* Mind, difingaged from, and fitting loofe to, the *Co-*

vetous

vetous and *Ambitious* Defires of the prefent World: That *moderate* and good Temper or S E R M.
Difpofition of mind, which caufes thofe who *have* Riches, not to fet their *Hearts* upon XLVI.
them, not to *abufe* them, not to *truft* in them, but to employ them virtuoufly to the glory of God, and to be at all times willing rather to part with them, than betray the Intereft of Truth and Virtue: And which, for the fame reafon, caufes thofe who have *no*
riches, to be *contented*, and not *murmuring*, nor *unthankful* towards God, but willing rather to continue *always* in a mean and low eftate, than to gain Riches by unrighteous and
unlawful Methods. This is being *poor in Spirit.* This is what the Prophet *Ifaiah* defcribes, ch. lxvi. 2. *To this man will I look, faith the Lord; even to him that is Poor;*
to him that is *of a contrite Spirit, and trembleth at my word.* This is the Temper of
thofe whom St *James* calls the *Poor of this World, Rich in Faith, and Heirs of the*
Kingdom: The Temper, of which St *Paul* declares, that *Godlinefs with Contentment is*
great Gain; and which our Saviour defcribes in his charaċter of the Church of *Smyrna*,
Rev. ii. 9. *I know thy works, and tribulation, and poverty; but thou art Rich:* Rich
in *Virtue*, Rich in *Good Works*, Rich *towards God.* According to *This* account of the
virtue of being *poor in Spirit*; an Eminent *Inftance* thereof was the Practice of *Mofes*,
when he *refufed to be called the Son of Pharaoh's daughter, chufing rather to fuffer af-*
fliction with the people of God, than to enjoy the pleafures of Sin for a Seafon. And the
contrary Spirit, is That which our Saviour fpeaks of, *Luke* xii. 21. *So is he that layeth*
up treafure for himfelf, and is not rich towards God.

AND now, having at large explained (which was the *Firft* thing propofed,) the
Meaning of this Phrafe, being *Poor in Spirit*; It remains in the

II. *Second* place, that I proceed to draw fome *Obfervations*, from the confideration
of the Nature of the *Virtue* here fpoken of, and of the *Reward* here declared to be
annexed to it: *Bleffed are the Poor in Spirit, for Theirs is the Kingdom of Heaven.*
And

1ft, FROM what has been faid, it appears, that perfons of *All* ranks, and conditions whatfoever, are *equally* concerned, in the *Admonition* included in the declaration
here made by our Lord. *Poor* and *Rich*, the *Meaneft* and the *Greateft*, are equally
Capable of being, and equally *obliged* to be, *Poor in Spirit.* A perfon of the *largeft*
and moft *plentiful* Poffeffions; if he has obtained them by *lawful*, and *honourable* Methods; if they make him not *infolent*, and *oppreffive* to his Neighbours; if he ufes
them with *Sobriety, Moderation* and *Temperance*; if he be willing to *relieve* the Neceffities of thofe that want, and be rich in *good* Works as well as in *Poffeffions*; if, being *Rich in this world*, he *be not high-minded, nor trufts in uncertain Riches, but in the*
Living God, who giveth us richly all things to enjoy; if he *does good*, and is *ready* to
communicate, laying up in ftore for himfelf a good Foundation againft the time to come,
that he may lay hold on eternal Life; In a word, if he prefers the *Commandments of*
God, before the Increafe of his *Worldly Intereft*; and is willing upon any occafion, to
run the hazard of *lofing* what he poffeffes, rather than depart from the Ways of *Truth*
and *Virtue:* This man, though he poffeffed the *Wealth* of the *Indies*, and exceeded
even *Solomon* in all his Grandeur; yet ftill he would be included in the defcription given by our Saviour in the Text, and would be intitled to the *Bleffednefs* of being *Poor*
in Spirit. On the *other* fide, One who is literally *poor*; if he be *unthankful*, and *com-*
plaining againft *God*; if his Poverty be brought upon himfelf, by *Debauchery* or *Idle-*
nefs; if he be *vicious* as far as his Circumftances inable him, and would ftick at *no*
unrighteous Practices to advance his Fortune : Such an one, though he be in the *Low-*
eft Poverty of *Eftate*, yet can in no wife come under the denomination of being *Poor*
in Spirit. It is evident therefore, that thefe words of our Lord in the Text, do not
relate to men's *external Circumftances* or *Condition* in the *World*, but to the *Temper* or
Difpofition of their *Minds*; and confequently that the *Advice* included in This *Beati-*
tude

S E R M. *tude* or *Declaration of Blessedness, equally* concerns persons of *All* Ranks and Estates
XLVI. whatsoever. The *Poor*, by Contentedness, Patience, Resignation to the Will of God,
and by the Exercise of such Other virtues as are more peculiarly proper to a mean and
low estate; and the *Rich*, by preferring at all times the Commands of God, before either the Increase or the Preservation of their Wealth; are (as I said) equally *Capable*
of being, and equally *obliged* to be, *Poor in Spirit*. Nevertheless, though the *Virtue*
here recommended, is undoubtedly the *Common Duty* of *Both*; yet, since the *Poor* are
in This particular under *Fewer* Temptations, and can withdraw their Affections from
such an Adherence to the World as is the chief Impediment of a Christian life, with
much less difficulty than the *Rich* can do; and since, upon *This* account, our Lord and
his Apostles do very *frequently* pronounce *absolutely* and *in general, Wo* to the *Rich*,
and *Blessedness* to the *Poor*, in such *large* and *unlimited* expressions, as may easily be
mistaken unless interpreted according to the Analogy of the *more distinct* manners of
speaking used in *Other* places : Therefore,

    2dly, I observe, that there is contained in the Text, a *particular* Ground of *Comfort*
and Support, to those who are *Poor* and *Destitute*, and under *Mean Circumstances* in
the World; and *particular* matter of *Caution*, to those who abound in *Riches* and
Power and the *Good things* of this *present Life*. The *Duty* here recommended by our
Lord, of being *Poor in Spirit*, is (as I have already observed) *equally* obligatory to
persons of *All* ranks and conditions whatsoever; and the *Promise* annexed, is to *All*, in
whatever station they be in the World, who shall attain That Good Temper and Disposition of Mind. But now this excellent Temper, this Virtue of being disingaged
from the *Covetous* and *Ambitious* Desires of the World, is what the *Poor* are *naturally*
led to by their very Circumstances; being under the Advantage of escaping Many
Temptations, which Others are continually subject to; and being perpetually called upon
by the *Afflictions* of *This* life, to turn their Thoughts to the expectation of a *Better*.
It ought therefore to be matter of Just *Comfort* and *Support*, nay even of *Thankfulness*
too, under many kinds of temporal Wants and Afflictions; to consider how great an
Advantage such circumstances give men, of obtaining this virtue of being *poor in Spirit* :
Which our Saviour looked upon as so *natural* and *easy*, and so *likely* to be practised by
Persons in That State, that, in places parallel to the Text, he sometimes uses that ge-

Luk. vi. 20.   neral and seemingly unlimited expression; *Blessed be ye poor, for yours is the Kingdom*
Matt. v. 4.   *of God*; and, *Blessed are they that mourn, for they shall be comforted*. For the same
reason, on the *other* side, to those who abound in *Riches* and *Power* and the *Good*
things of this present Life, the Text plainly suggests *particular* matter of *Caution*; in
annexing the heavenly Reward to *That* Temper and Disposition of Mind, which *They*
in particular are surrounded with so many Temptations to depart from, that our Sa-

Luk. vi. 24.   viour sometimes pronounces in words *seemingly absolute, Wo unto you that are rich, for*
ye have received your consolation. It is evident, his Meaning *cannot* be, to represent
Riches as a *Crime*; For he elsewhere expresly explains himself to his Disciples, that he
meant not to blame those who *have*, but those who (to the neglect of God and Virtue)
trust in Riches : But his Design clearly was, to admonish and put us in mind, how
dangerous a state, Great Prosperity generally is; how *full of Temptation*, how ready to
puff men *up*; how apt to make them *covetous, insolent* and *ambitious*; and to destroy
in them that *meek*, that *equitable*, that *moderate* disposition of mind, which in the
Text is stiled being *poor in Spirit*. St *Paul* gives us a remarkable instance of an ill effect in this kind, even of a *little* Prosperity; when the *Corinthians* falling into Divisions

1 Cor. iv. 8.   among themselves, began to be *puffed up for one against another* : Now, says he, *ye*
are full, now ye are Rich, ye have reigned as Kings without us. And our Saviour, in
his Admonition to the Church of *Laodicea*, hints at a *like* case, *Rev*. iii. 17. *Thou sayest,*

I am rich, and increased with goods, and have need of Nothing; and knowest not that *thou art wretched and miserable and poor and blind and naked.*

3dly, A *Third observation* which may be made upon the words of the Text, is; that from the *Reason* our Saviour here gives, *why* he pronounces the Poor in Spirit to be Bleſſed; (*Bleſſed are the Poor in Spirit*, for *Theirs is the Kingdom of Heaven:*) From *this Reaſon*, I ſay, here annexed by our Saviour, it evidently appears, that *however excellent* Virtue *really* is in itſelf, and *truly deſirable* even for its *own* ſake; yet neither are the higheſt Improvements in Religion, any way inconſiſtent with having reſpect to the recompenſe of Reward; nor is the Practice of Virtue (as ſome have abſurdly argued with a moſt *Vain* Affection) at all *mercenary*, when founded upon a View to the Happineſs of Heaven. *Mercenarineſs* ſuppoſes always that Something *Wrong* is done, for the ſake of ſuch *Lucre* as a virtuous man can never purchaſe upon *Such Terms.* But the Happineſs of *Heaven*, conſiſts *itſelf* in, and is eſſentially conjoined with, the perfection of *Virtue*; And the expectation and view of *This* Reward, is *itſelf* an immediate *Act*, of the *Virtue of depending upon God.* Were *Temporal Proſperity*, the *certain* and *conſtant* and at all times the *immediate Reward of Virtue*; it might indeed be alledged, *not* that the Practice of it was *mercenary*; becauſe *That* always ſuppoſes the doing of ſomething which is in itſelf *blame-worthy*; but it might indeed be alledged, in *diminution of the Excellency* of it, as we find it was in the caſe of *Job* in the time of his Proſperity, *Does Job ſerve God for nought?* But as the Practice of Virtue is in reality *far from* being *ſecure* of any *temporal Recompence*, and the *Reward* it principally relies upon is *ſpiritual* and *heavenly*; the expectation of *Such* Reward, far from being any diminution, is *itſelf* (as I now obſerved) a proper *Act* of *Virtue*, and of *Dependence upon God*. In the Antient *Heathen* World, the Virtue of the Beſt and Braveſt men, under the Light of Nature and Reaſon, conſiſted in their *Truſting* in God; in their *Truſting, without* any expreſs revealed Promiſe, that the *Judge of the whole Earth* would finally *do what was Right*, and would *not* ſuffer *Virtue* to *periſh* equally with *Vice.* Under the *Old Teſtament*, *Moſes*, being eminently what our Saviour in the Text calls *Poor in Spirit*, preferred the *Poverty* and *Affliction* of the People of God, before the *Riches* and *Honours* of *Pharaoh's* Court; and it is recorded of him, not in a way of *diminiſhing*, but of *extolling* his Virtue, that he *eſteemed this Reproach* to be *greater Riches than the Treaſures in Egypt*; *for he had reſpect unto the recompence of the Reward.* And when *Job*, in the time of his greateſt Diſtreſs, perſiſted in his Reliance upon God: (*though he ſlay me, yet will I truſt in him*;) it was not a *lower*, but a *higher* pitch of the *ſame virtue* in him, (becauſe it was fixing it upon a *rational* and *conſiſtent* Ground,) to declare that he *knew that his Redeemer lived, and that he ſhould ſtand at the latter day upon the Earth.* Under the *New Teſtament*, God *himſelf* has, in a more *expreſs* and *explicit* manner, declared himſelf to be, in the future and eternal ſtate, *a Rewarder of them that diligently ſeek him*; not thereby to *diminiſh*, but to *increaſe* That Virtue, the Practice of which is *rationally* and *conſiſtently* ſupported by ſo divine and glorious an Expectation. Accordingly, the Apoſtle St *Paul* declares concerning *himſelf*, that he *preſſed toward the Mark, for the* prize *of the high calling of God in Chriſt Jeſus.* And he perpetually exhorts all *other* Chriſtians; ſo to *run*, that they may *obtain an* incorruptible Crown; ſo to behave themſelves, as they who are continually *looking for that Bleſſed Hope and the glorious Appearance of the Great God and our Saviour Jeſus Chriſt*: *laying hold upon the* Hope *ſet before them*; even *the Hope which is laid up for them in Heaven*; *looking not at the things which are temporal, but at the things which are eternal*; and conſidering that their *light affliction which is but for a moment, worketh for them a far more exceeding and eternal Weight of Glory.* Our *Saviour* alſo himſelf, when his Diſciples asked him, ſaying, *Behold, we have forſaken all and followed thee, what ſhall we have therefore?* ſcrupled not to reply, *Matt.* xix. 28. *Verily I ſay unto you,*

Phil. iii. 14.

1 Cor. ix. 25.

Tit. ii. 13.

Heb. vi. 18.
Col. i. 5.
2 Cor. iv. 18.

SERM. —*when the Son of man shall sit in the throne of his glory, Ye also shall sit upon twelve*
XLVI. *thrones, judging the twelve tribes of Israel.* And elsewhere, in his exhortations to the
Mat. v. 12. same Disciples; *When men shall revile you,* says he, and *persecute you; rejoice, and be
exceeding glad; For great is your Reward in Heaven.* Nay, which is *more remarkable*
than all these; concerning our Lord's *own* practice, the Scripture declares, that *for the
Joy which was set before him, he endured the Cross, despised the Shame, and is set down
at the right hand of the Throne of God.* To imagine therefore, as Some *Enthusiastick*
Writers, and Others through a *vain and conceited affectation* have done; that the perfection of Virtue wholly excludes Self-love, and all Regards to any recompence of Reward; is taking upon themselves to reproach the *Greatest* and most eminently *Virtuous*
men, that have lived in All *Nations* and in All *Ages*; it is reproaching the *Apostles* of
our Lord; it is reproaching *our Saviour* in his *own* Practice; it is reproaching *God himself,* and the *Nature of things* which he has made; who hath *prepared for,* and *expressly
promised to,* them that love and obey him, such *good things* as pass man's Understanding,
*which Eye hath not seen, nor ear heard, neither hath it entred into the heart of man, to
conceive.* Through the expectation of which spiritual and eternal Happiness, whoever
is prevailed upon to live *virtuously,* has a Right to apply to himself upon account of
Religion *in general,* what our Saviour in the Text says *in particular* of those who are
poor in Spirit; Blessed are they, for theirs is the Kingdom of Heaven.

SERMON XLVII.

Of the Virtue of CHARITY.

1 COR. XIII. 3.

*And though I bestow all my goods to feed the poor, and though I
give my Body to be burned, and have not Charity, it profiteth me
nothing.*

SERM. IN the following Discourse upon these words, I shall *1st* explain *What* That Virtue
XLVII. is, which the Apostle here calls *Charity*; and *What* its opposite *Vice.* *2dly,* I shall
consider the excellent *Effect,* which the general Practice of this Virtue would have
in the World; and the great *Stress* which our Saviour and his Apostles accordingly do
constantly lay upon it, as being the *Principal Part* and the *main End* of Religion.
3dly, I shall take Notice of the incredible *Mischiefs* arising to Mankind, from the
Want of this Great Virtue. And *Lastly,* I shall draw some useful *Inferences* from the
whole.

I. I AM to explain *What* That Virtue is, which the Apostle here calls *Charity*;
and *What* its opposite *Vice.* And here it is evident at first sight to every attentive person,

fon, that the word in This place cannot poffibly mean, what in common Speech it is now generally ufed to fignify, *Alms* or *Charity to the Poor.* For it is exprefsly *diftin- guifhed* from That, in the very words of the Text itfelf: *Though I beftow all my Goods to feed the Poor, and have not Charity, it profiteth me Nothing.* Charity therefore muft needs here fignify fome Virtue or good Habit, of a *more general* and extenfive Nature. And indeed the Apoftle himfelf diftinctly defines it, in the verfes following my Text; *Charity*, fays he, *fuffereth long, and is kind; envieth not, vaunteth not itfelf, is not puffed up; doth not behave itfelf unfeemly, feeketh not her own, is not eafily provoked, thinketh no Evil; rejoiceth not in iniquity, but rejoiceth in the Truth; beareth all things, endureth all things;* and fo on; *ver.* 4, 5, 6, 7. From this defcription it is evident, that by the word *Charity* in the Text, is expreffed That *Chriftian Temper and Difpofi- tion,* That *Love and Good-Will towards Mankind,* which is the Great Foundation of All virtues; and concerning which the fame Apoftle elfewhere tells us, that the End *of the Commandment is Charity. Without* this *Good and Chriftian Temper of Mind,* no fingle *Action* is valuable in the Sight of God: *Though I beftow all my Goods to feed the Poor, and have not Charity, it profiteth me nothing:* That is, *Almfgiving,* or the Act of any *other* Virtue, if it proceeds only from fome accidental Caufe, and fprings not from a right Principle; if it be accompanied with, and made fubfervient to, Defigns of Pride and Ambition, of imperioufnefs and dominion, of Party, Faction and worldly Power in matters of Religion; it is of No Efteem in the Sight of God. Where *Love and Goodnefs and Chriftian Temper,* are not the *Governing Principle;* nothing is ac- ceptable, no not even Almfgiving itfelf. But where *Love* and *univerfal Charity,* (even That *Love* which St *Paul* declares to be *the fulfilling of the Whole Law;* Where *This)* is the *Root; There* indeed, one of its Faireft *Branches,* one of the goodlieft *Inftances* and *Effects* of it in *particular,* is *Liberality towards our Poor Brethren.* From whence it has come to pafs, that *Charity,* which properly fignifies *univerfal Love and Good-Will,* has by frequent ufe been confined, to the *particular* fenfe of *Charity to the Poor.* And Great indeed are the Promifes which are made in Scripture, to this *fingle Branch* of Charity, *in particular:* It is ftiled by our Saviour; St *Luke* xvi. 9; a *Making to our- felves Friends of the Mammon of Unrighteoufnefs, that when we fail, they may receive us into everlafting Habitations.* Upon which *Application* of the Parable of the Unjuft Steward, I cannot but obferve by the way, that his remitting to his Lord's Debtors a part of their Debt, ought not to be underftood (as it ufually is) to have been a de- frauding of his *Lord;* For it is only upon his *former* behaviour, that the Text charges him with *Injuftice:* But in this *laft* Action, he feems to be reprefented as obliging his Lord's Debtors out of what *He himfelf* was ftill to account for: For which reafon, our Saviour compares *his* fecuring to himfelf by a timely Bounty the Friendfhip of thofe Debtors, (he compares it) to *Our* laying up for ourfelves, by works of Charity and Beneficence here on *Earth,* a treafure hereafter in the *Heavens.* Very *Great* things therefore, I fay, are indeed fpoken in Scripture, concerning this *particular* Virtue of *Liberality to the Poor.* But it is evident This is *not* what is meant by the word *Cha- rity* in the Text, becaufe it is exprefsly diftinguifhed in the words themfelves, from *beftowing all our Goods to feed the Poor.* And indeed it deferves to be particularly taken notice of, that not only in *This* Text, but in all *Other* places alfo, without exception, through the whole *New Teftament;* the word *Charity* never once fignifies the *giving of Alms,* but always That *Univerfal Love,* That *Chriftian Temper* and *Goodwill to- wards All men,* of which *Alms-giving to the Poor* is but one fingle Branch, or one par- ticular *Effect.* And *Many other* Inftances there are, wherein the Signification of words in common Ufe being much changed by cuftom and courfe of Time, confiderable Er- rours and Miftakes are thence apt to arife among fuch as read the Scriptures carelefsly and without Attention: Which Errours can no otherwife be prevented, but by taking

3

care

S E R M. care to obferve, not the bare *Sound of fingle Words*, but the connexion and fenfe and
XLVII. meaning of the *whole Difcourfe*. To Him who thus reads and confiders with Attention, it is manifeft that the *Charity*, which the Apoftle here fuppofes a Perfon may be
wholly void of, though he *beftows all his goods to feed the Poor*; and which he at large
defcribes, in the following part of this Chapter; it is manifeft, I fay, that the Charity
here fpoken of, is That *Chriftian Temper*, That *univerfal Love* and *Benignity of Mind*,
which, in oppofition to all worldly Party and Faction, to all Hatred, Contentioufnefs
and Animofity, imperioufnefs and defire of impofing upon each other, teaches men
with meeknefs and patience, with gentlenefs and kindnefs, in imitation of Chrift, to
be follicitous for nothing elfe, to be earneftly bent upon no other Defign, comparatively fpeaking; but that of promoting univerfally the *Knowledge of Truth*, and the *Practice of Righteoufnefs*, for the general Benefit of Mankind.

T H E *Contrary* to which Virtue of univerfal Love and Charity, or the proper Vice
of *Uncharitablenefs*, is That Spirit of Violence and Arbitrarinefs, That Love of imperioufnefs and Dominion, That prefumptuous Hating and ill-treating of each other, upon
account of unavoidable Differences in opinion; things not effential to Religion; which
our Saviour fo earneftly warns us againft; St. *Matt.* vii. 1; *Judge not, that ye be not
judged; For with what Judgment ye judge, ye fhall be judged ——— And why beholdeft
thou the Mote that is in thy Brother's Eye, but confidereft not the Beam that is in thine
own Eye?* St *James* in like manner; ch. iv. 12; *There is one law-giver, who is able to
fave and to deftroy; Who art thou that judgeft another?* And St *Paul*; Rom. xiv. 4.
*Who art thou that judgeft another man's fervant? to his own mafter he ftandeth or fall-
eth:* And *Why doft thou judge thy Brother, or why doft thou fet at nought thy Brother?
for we fhall all ftand before the judgement-feat of Chrift*; ver. 10: *Let not him that eateth, defpife him that eateth not; and let not him which eateth not, judge him that eateth*;
ver. 3. *For the Kingdom of God is not meat and drink*, (that is, is not Forms and Ceremonies) *but righteoufnefs and peace and joy in the Holy Ghoft*; ver. 17. From the
two laft-cited Verfes it is evident, that this Duty of *Charity*, or of *not judging and cenfuring* each other, is not to be underftood as having place with regard to Inftances of
plain *wickednefs*; but with refpect either to fuch matters of *Speculation*, as are not in
men's own Power; or to things *indifferent* in *Practice*, which are not of moral Obligation. For all notorious *wickedneffes*; fuch as are Atheifm, and Prophanenefs; Oppreffion, Injuftice and Fraud, Rioting, and Debauchery; are *Sins* which (as the A-
poftle expreffes it) go before *unto Judgment*: They are fuch things, for which we *may*
and *ought* to judge ill of men, and to rebuke them fharply and feverely for them. But
the proper objects about which the Virtue of *Charity* is to be employed, are Things *indifferent*, concerning which God has given no plain Commandment; or fuch Matters
of *Opinion*, wherein fincere men may with equal regard to Truth and Virtue, follow their different judgments and confcience. Judging and cenfuring each other
about things of *This* nature, is what the Scripture declares to be altogether *Unchriftian*. And the experience of all corrupt Ages has abundantly fhown, that
prefumptuous reproaching each other upon account of fuch things as Thefe; has
been the great Caufe of all the Schifms and Divifions, of all the contentions
and animofities, which have over-run and in great meafure deftroyed the Chriftian world. For the Sins of Schifm and Divifion among Chriftians, are of a
much larger extent, and will be charged to the Account of *More* and of *other kind of*
perfons than carelelefs and prefumptuous men are apt to imagine. All imperioufnefs
and affectation of dominion, which St *Peter* calls *Lording it over the Heritage of God*;
all peevifhnefs and unreafonablefs; all contentioufnefs, fiercenefs, and animofity of
Spirit; all ill-Ufage of men, and cafting names of Reproach upon each other, on account of Matters either of *indifferent Practice* or of *fincere Opinion*; all *Parties and*

Factions

Factions in Religion, or *Incroachments* upon That Christian (and virtuous, *not* licen-S E R M.
tious) *Liberty wherewith* our *Lord has made his* Disciples *free*; Gal. v. 1. All these XLVII.
things are justly chargeable, with being each in their proportion, the Causes and sad
occasions of irreconcileable Divisions among Christians. From whence it plainly appears,
that not only *particular persons*, but even the greatest *Bodies of men*, may be guilty of
That Vice, which the Apostle in the Text calls *not having Charity*, or not having
That Christian Temper and universal Love, without which all other even the *greatest*
appearances of Goodness will *profit men nothing*. The Church of *Rome*, for Example,
is a stupendous Instance of This: who, excluding (as much as in them lies) from
Christian Communion and from the Hopes of Salvation, all men who cannot embrace
the Doctrines of Popes and Councils and other humane Inventions, as of like necessity
with the Gospel itself; do, by the Greatest Schism that ever was in the World, cut in
sunder (or rather cut themselves off from) That Spouse or Body or Universal Church
of Christ, which can possibly be but One, One Temple built upon the *Foundation*, and
upon the *Doctrine* of Christ and his Apostles only; and though consisting of different
parts, varying from each other in external Forms, as Members of the same living Body
differ in Shape from each other; yet all united in one Holy Band of *Righteousness* and
Charity.

II. HAVING thus at large explained *What* That Virtue is, which the Apostle in
the Text calls *Charity*, and *what* its opposite *Vice*; I proceed in the 2d place to consider the excellent *Effect*, which the general Practice of this Virtue would have in
the World; and the great *Stress* which our Saviour and his Apostles accordingly do
constantly lay upon it, as being the *Principal Part* and the *main End* of Religion.
That nothing is so much wanting, in order to set the World right, as a *charitable Spirit*
and *Christian Temper* among those who call themselves Christians, is evident to All
men. That the Gospel *may still* be propagated; nay, that it may *best* and most
effectually; nay, that indeed it *can only* be propagated, by the Same means with which
our Saviour *began* to propagate it; by *strength of Reason* and *clearness of Evidence*, by
good *Example of Virtue and Righteousness in Practice*, joined with *Love* and true
Charity towards the Persons of All men; is demonstrable from the Nature of *Things* and
of *Men*. The *Harvest* of persons capable of receiving the Truth, when laid before
them plainly and distinctly in the Spirit of Meekness and Charity, is very great:
The *Labourers* only, saith our Saviour, are too *few*; *Pray ye therefore the Lord of the*
Harvest, that he will send forth Labourers into his Harvest. Did Christians universally
labour, after This manner; the *Effect* could not but be, that the *Knowledge of the Lord*
would fill the Earth, as the Waters cover the Sea: The Vine which God's right hand has
planted, would *spread out her Branches unto the Sea, and her Boughs unto the River*:
Not by any *One Party* of Christians swallowing up and destroying all the rest; but by
each of them severally taking away their uncharitable Distinctions, removing their needless particularities, and the unchristian Bars and Confinements set up by humane Invention; and uniting upon the One immoveable Foot, of the everlasting Gospel of Truth
and Charity. Marvellous are the Promises of Blessings and Happiness, which in the
Prophetick Part of Scripture are made to the Church of God, when it shall *in This man-*
ner prevail upon the Earth. *With righteousness shall he judge the poor, and reprove with*
equity for the Meek of the Earth; and he shall smite the Earth with the rod of his mouth,
and with the breath of his lips, shall he slay the wicked: and righteousness shall be the
girdle of his loyns, and faithfulness the girdle of his reins: The wolf also shall dwell with
the lamb, and the leopard shall lie down with the Kid; and the Calf and the young Lion
and the fatling together, and a little Child shall lead them: —— They shall not hurt
nor destroy in all my holy Mountain; for the Earth shall be full of the Knowledge of
the Lord, as the Waters cover the Sea: —— And he shall set up an Ensign for the Na-
tions, and shall assemble the outcasts of Israel, and gather together the dispersed of Judah,

from

SERM. *from the four corners of the Earth*; Iſai. xi. 4, &c. And in the *Revelation of St John,*
XLVII. the like Prophecies are again repeated; ch. xiv. 6; xi. 15; *I ſaw an Angel having the*
Everlaſting Goſpel to preach unto Them that dwell on the Earth, and to every nation and
kindred and tongue and people: ——*And there were great Voices in Heaven, ſaying;*
The Kingdoms of this World are become the Kingdoms of our Lord and of his Chriſt;
and he ſhall reign for ever and ever. Whether theſe and the like Prophecies ſhall yet
finally have a *literal* Accompliſhment, by an univerſal Prevalency of the Goſpel of
Peace on Earth; or whether they ſhall have their full and literal completion, *only* in
That *New Heaven and New Earth*, *wherein Righteouſneſs* is to *dwell* for ever; is
ſtill a ſecret in the Breaſt of Providence, which we ought not to be over-confident in
explaining. But in *This* we cannot err; in exhorting in the mean time all Chriſtians continually, to put on that Spirit of Chriſt, That Spirit of Meekneſs and true
Humility, That Spirit of Love and univerſal Charity, That Chriſtian *Temper*
and diſpoſition of Mind; which *alone* can promote the Kingdom of God, and
His Righteouſneſs: Which, *ſo far* as it is in any time practiſed, cauſes Chriſtianity
to become in Fact *a Light ſhining before men*, inviting them *to glorify our Father*
which is in Heaven: And which, if it was the *Univerſal* Behaviour of Chriſtians, would
certainly cauſe the Goſpel *univerſally to prevail*, by means of that irreſiſtible Excellency and Beauty in which it would appear, when all Contentions and Animoſities, all
unreaſonable *Prejudices* againſt each other, all Parties and Factions and Names of Reproach among Chriſtians upon account of differences in opinion, were laid aſide; and
every man, making the Goſpel alone the Rule of his *own* Actions, and having no Deſire to have *dominion* over the Conſciences of his Brethren, but all of them inſtructing
and exhorting each other (according to the reſpective *Order* and Nature of their ſeveral
ſtations and *capacities*) with mutual Love and Forbearance, as Fellow-ſervants of one
common Lord by whom they muſt All at laſt be judged; bent their Whole Endeavours
towards *One only* uniform End, the promoting amongſt men the *Knowledge of Truth*
and the *Practice of Right.* Were This (I ſay) the *General* Behaviour of Chriſtians,
according to the Obligations of their moſt Holy Profeſſion; it could not fail but the
Goſpel would be embraced univerſally over all the Earth. And for This reaſon it ſeems
to be, that our Saviour in all his Diſcourſes conſtantly lays ſo peculiar a *Streſs* upon
this Duty of *Love and Charity and Good-will towards Men*; as if it was the *Principal*
Part and *Great Deſign* of Religion; and as if he had always a particular View to
that general Corruption and Deſtruction of true Chriſtianity, which he foreſaw would
for ſo many Ages together be the conſequence of *Want of Chriſtian Temper* among
thoſe who called themſelves the *Chriſtian World.* *A New Commandment*, ſays he, *I*
give unto you, that ye love one another; Joh. xiii. 34. A *New* Commandment; Not
that it was not *Always* men's Duty in general; but that it was to be, in a *New and*
diſtinguiſhing manner, the Character and Badge of Chriſtians; the Effect and the Support, the Life and Eſſence of true Chriſtianity. The *Jews* hated the *Samaritans*, and
the *Samaritans* hated the *Jews*; and by This means their Schiſm was kept up for ever.
But *Chriſtians*, were to love their Brethren; to love alſo thoſe that differed from them;
nay, to ſhow all gentleneſs even towards thoſe that moſt fiercely oppoſed them; that,
by this godlike behaviour, they might by degrees gain and win all men over to the
acknowledgement of the Truth. It was to be their diſtinguiſhing Character; *Joh.* xiii.
35; *By this ſhall all Men know that ye are my Diſciples, if ye have love one to another.*
As imperiouſneſs, and affectation of dominion, and perſecution, is eſſentially the Spirit
of *Antichriſt*; ſo the *Chriſtian* Spirit and Temper, is Meekneſs, Charity, Forbearance
and Love. The *True* Diſciples of Chriſt, are to be diſtinguiſhed from falſe prophets,
from wolves in ſheeps clothing; not by men's crying, *Lord, Lord*; not by their
fierceneſs for what *They* call the Temple of God, and which perhaps is nothing but

ſome

some Humane Invention: But *by their Fruits*, says our Lord, *ye shall know them.* By their *Fruits*; that is, by those *Christian virtues*, by those Good *works*, which the Scripture elsewhere stiles the *Fruits of the Spirit.* Our Saviour *himself*, desired to be judged of, by the *Goodness* as well as by the *Greatness* of his Works: And therefore, in his parable of a *Kingdom divided against itself*, the *Reason* he gives for asserting the unpardonableness of men's ascribing his mighty works to the assistance of the *Evil One*, is the *Goodness* and *Beneficence* of the Works. In another place, *comparing together* the Great and most important Duties of Religion; next to the Love of *God*, he makes Charity towards *Men*, the Grand Design of Religion: *Thou shalt love the Lord thy God with all thy Heart*; *This*, saith he, *is the first and great Commandment*; *and the second is like unto it, Thou shalt love thy Neighbour as thy self.* The *Apostle* St *John*, after his Master's example, lays the same stress upon this excellent Virtue; declaring, that without this Love towards *Men*, there can be no such thing as a sincere Love towards *God*; 1 Joh. iv. 20; *If a man say, I love God, and hateth his Brother, he is a Liar; For —— This commandment have we from him, that he who loveth God, love his Brother also.* His meaning is; All pretences of Love towards *God*, which produce not true Virtue, and particularly Love and Charity towards our Brethren; are nothing more than *mere Enthusiasm.* Again: he tells us, That without this universal Charity, no pretended zeal for Religion can be sincere; *ch.* ii. 10. *He that loveth his Brother, abideth in the Light;*——*but he that hateth his Brother, is in darkness, and walketh in darkness*; that is, he is altogether *ignorant* of the true Nature and Spirit of Christianity. Lastly; That the want of this Virtue, and the prevalency of the contrary imperious Spirit, is one principal Mark and Character of Antichrist, *ch.* iii. 10. *In this the children of God are manifest, and the children of the Devil; whosoever doth not righteousness, is not of God, neither he that loveth not his Brother; For this is the Message that ye heard from the beginning, that we should love one another.* St *Peter* in like manner, 1 Pet. iv. 8, *Above all things*, saith he, *have fervent Charity among yourselves; for Charity shall cover the Multitude of Sins*: The sense is; not that any one *particular* Virtue, such as that which we Now call *Charity to the Poor*, shall excuse men *from* the practice of *other* Duties, or *in* the practice of *any* Vices or Immoralities; but that That *general* Christian Temper and good Spirit of Love and sincere Desire of doing good to all men, which he here calls *having fervent Charity among yourselves*, shall cover Many Errours, many *such* imperfections and failings, as a truly good Christian, who has this excellent root of Virtue in him, can be supposed to be guilty of. The very same Notion is likewise perpetually inculcated by St *Paul*, Col. iii. 14, *Above all these things put on Charity, which is the Bond of Perfectness:* The word which we here render *Charity*, is in *This*, as in *all other* places, Ἀγάπη *Love, Universal Love* towards Mankind. Again; 1 Tim. i. 4, 5; *Neither give heed*, says he, *to Fables and endless Genealogies*, (that is, to matters of mere *Form*, Order of *Successions*, and the like, which the *Jews* were apt to lay so great a Stress upon;) But *The End of the Commandment*, (the Great Design of the *Christian* Law,) *is Charity.* Lastly, and to conclude: In That Noble Discourse, whereof my Text is a part, he thus, eloquently and affectionately, inculcates the same Doctrine. *Though I speak*, says he, *with the Tongues of Men and of Angels, and have not Charity; I am become as sounding Brass, or a tinkling Cymbal. And though I have the gift of Prophecy, and understand all Mysteries, and all Knowledge; and though I have all Faith, so that I could remove Mountains; and have no Charity; I am nothing. And though I bestow all my Goods to feed the Poor, and though I give my Body to be burned, and have not Charity; it profiteth me nothing.* In St *Paul*'s opinion therefore; though a man could *preach* like an *Angel*, and had the *Knowledge* of an *inspired Prophet*; Though he had the *Faith* of an *Apostle*, and the *Zeal* of a *Martyr*, and gave away in *Alms to the Poor*, even his *whole Substance*: yet, if his Religion

consisted

SERM. confifted in *Party and Faction*, and promoted *uncharitablenefs, imperioufnefs*, and
XLVII. *ill-treatment* of *Other men*; even notwithftanding all thofe Great Excellencies, it would
profit him nothing. The *Reafon* of this lofty affertion, follows in the 8th verfe: For,
all *other* excellent Gifts, and even *Virtues themfelves*, are only of temporary continuance; But *Charity* Alone, *never faileth: Whether there be Prophecies, they fhall fail*;
*whether there be Tongues, they fhall ceafe; whether there be Knowledge, it fhall vanifh
away: Faith* fhall be fwallowed up in *Vifion*, and *Hope* fhall terminate upon *Injoyment*;
But the *Love of God and of our Brethren*, fhall, when *This World* is *paffed away*,
continue and increafe *for ever*. That every *man*, and every *Number of men*, who
call themfelves *Chriftians*, may ferioufly confider this important Truth; God of his
infinite Mercy grant, *&c.*

SERMON XLVIII.

Of the Virtue of CHARITY.

1 COR. XIII. 3.

*And though I beftow all my goods to feed the poor, and though I
give my Body to be burned, and have not Charity, it profiteth
me nothing.*

SERM. IN difcourfing upon thefe words of the Apoftle, I propofed 1ft, To explain *What*
XLVIII. That Virtue is, which he here calls *Charity*; and *What* its oppofite *Vice* is:
2*dly*, To confider the excellent *Effect*, which the general Practice of this Virtue
would have in the World; and the great *Strefs* which our Saviour and his Apoftles
accordingly do conftantly lay upon it, as being the *Principal Part* and the *Main End*
of Religion: 3*dly*, To take Notice of the incredible *Mifchiefs* arifing to Mankind,
from the *Want* of the Practice of this Great Virtue: And *laftly*, To draw fome ufeful *Inferences* from the Whole.

THE *Two Former* of thefe Heads, I have already gone through: And have fhown;
That the word *Charity* here, does not fignify the *particular Virtue* of giving *Alms* to
the Poor; For 'tis expreffly diftinguifhed from *That*, in the very words of the Text
itfelf; But, that it is here made ufe of to exprefs a more *general* and extenfive Virtue,
even That *Chriftian Temper and Difpofition*, That general *Love and Good-Will towards
Mankind*, which is the Great Foundation of *All* Virtues and good Habits; teaching
men with Meeknefs and Patience, with Tendernefs and Affection, with Gentlenefs and
Kindnefs, after the Example of Chrift, to labour and be follicitous for Nothing elfe,
comparatively fpeaking, than the promoting univerfally the *Knowledge of Truth* and the
Practice of Righteoufnefs in the World.

That the contrary *Vice* therefore, or the proper Sin of *Uncharitablenefs*, is That
Spirit of Violence and Impofition, which reigns too much amongft Mankind; That

I　　　　　　　　　　　　　　　　　　Love

Love of Imperiousfnefs and Dominion, That prefumptuous Hating and ill-treatment S E R M. of each other, which prevails fo much in the World, upon account of Matters either XLVIII. of *indifferent Practice* or of *fincere Opinion.*

That the *Effect*, which the *General Practice* of the *Charity* or *Christian Temper* here recommended by the Apoftle, would produce in the World, could not fail to be *The univerfal Spreading of the Gofpel of Truth and Peace*, over all the Nations of the Earth.

AND *That* for *This reafon* it is, that our Saviour and his Apoftles accordingly do conftantly lay fo *Great and fingular a Strefs* upon *This* Virtue, as being the *Principal Part*, and the *main End* of Religion.

III. I PROCEED now, in the *Third* place, to confider diftinctly the incredible *Mifchiefs* arifing to Mankind, from the *Want* of the practice of this excellent Virtue. And here opens itfelf to our View, one of the moft melancholy Scenes, that ever was beheld upon the face of the Earth. Our Bleffed Saviour came to teach Mankind a Doctrine of Truth and Purity, of Simplicity and Plainnefs; A Doctrine of Religion, which All men might eafily underftand, and which 'tis infinitely every man's Intereft to practife; A Doctrine, the Whole of which, as he himfelf affures us, is fummed up in Two particulars, the Love of God, and of our Neighbour; the Worfhip of the One True God, the Father and Lord of all things, thro' the One True Mediatour whom he himfelf has appointed, in oppofition to every kind of Idolatry; and a conftant fincere endeavour of doing Good to all men, in oppofition to every degree of Unrighteoufnefs, Iniquity and Uncharitablenefs. To the Happinefs of Mankind even in *This* Life, 'tis manifeft Thefe are the Means which would contribute incomparably more, than any other Methods whatfoever. But the *principal* View wherewith our Lord gave thefe Commands to his Followers, was that they might practife them in expectation of God's having appointed a day, wherein he would judge the World in righteoufnefs by his Son Jefus Chrift; and reward every man finally, in the *future and eternal* State, according to their Works. And becaufe 'twas thus principally with regard to the *Life to come*, that our Lord gave all his Commandments; therefore with great earneftnefs he continually cautioned his Difciples, that as *he* had declared his *own Kingdom* was not to be of This World, fo *They* fhould continually take ftrict heed *after him*, never to make their *preaching of* His *religion* a pretence for afpiring after *temporal Authority.* In a Parable framed on purpofe, he commands his Followers not to take upon them to pull up the *Tares, left they root up alfo the Wheat with them.* The meaning of which is not, that Magiftrates are not to cut off *Malefactors*; but that in matters merely *religious*, Chriftians are not to prefume to judge the Confciences of each other, before the day of the Lord cometh. *The Princes of the Gentiles*, fays he, *exercife Dominion over them, and they that are Great, exercife Authority upon them: But it fhall not be fo among You; but whofoever will be great among you, let him be your Minifter; and whofoever will be chief among you, let him be your Servant; Even as the Son of Man came not to be miniftred unto, but to minifter, and to give his Life a Ranfom for many,* Matt. xx. 25. So *long*, and fo *far*, as Chriftianity was planted according to This Standard of its Great Author; in plainnefs and Simplicity of uncorrupt Doctrine; and in meeknefs, and Humility, Love and Charity, in Practice: When Chriftians *continued* Acts ii. 42, 46. *ftedfaftly in the Apoftles doctrine and fellowfhip, and in breaking of Bread and in Prayers;——continuing daily with one accord in the Temple,——eating their Meat with gladnefs and finglenefs of Heart, praifing God, and having favour with all the people;* When *the Multitude of them that believed, were of one Heart, and of One Soul; and great Grace was upon them All*; Acts iv. 32, 33. *Then* did their *Light* fhine forth *indeed* before men, and caufe them to praife and *glorify the God of Heaven: Then* were they in reality and indeed, *acceptable to God, and approved of Men: Then* was the Gof-

SERM.
XLVIII.

pel truly and confpicuoufly, like a City upon an Hill, *a Light to lighten the Gentiles,* *and the Glory of God's people Ifrael:* It was the *Praife* and *Wonder* of thofe who beheld its Bleffed *Effects,* and *might have been the Joy of the whole Earth.* Had Chriftians continued, as St *Paul befeeched* them, Eph. iv. 1; *to walk worthy of the Vocation wherewith they were called; with all lowlinefs and meeknefs, with long-fuffering, forbearing one another in Love;* indeavouring *to keep the Unity of the Spirit in the Bond of Peace:* Had they confidered the Argument he urges, that there could be but *One Body and One Spirit, even as they were called in One Hope of their Calling; One Lord, One Faith, One Baptifm; One God and Father of all, who is Above All:* Had they continued, (according to the exhortation and inference he draws from this Argument;) to *fpeak the Truth in Love,* that they *might grow up into Him in all things, who is the Head, even Chrift; From whom the whole Body fitly joined together, and compacted by that which every Joint fupplieth, according to the effectual working in the meafure of every part, maketh increafe of the Body unto the edifying of itfelf in Love:* The Church of God eftablifhed upon This *Foundation of the Apoftles and Prophets, Jefus Chrift himfelf being the chief corner-ftone;* might in its Whole *Building fitly framed together,* have *grown up* into One *Holy Temple of the Lord.*

ver., 6.

ver. 15.

BUT an *Enemy* foon *fowed Tares among this Wheat,* and contentious men very early began to build *Hay and Stubble* upon the *Foundation of Chrift.* Not content with the Simplicity and Plainnefs of the Gofpel, which could poffibly furnifh no Materials for Strife and Contention, vain men foon began to mix their own uncertain Opinions with the Doctrine of Chrift; and had no other way to give them Weight and Authority, but by indeavouring to force them upon the Faith of Others. And out of This *Bramble,* as *Jotham* foretold the men of *Shechem, Jud.* ix. 15, out of this *Bramble* hath a *Fire* proceeded, which hath *devoured the Cedars of Lebanon;* Or, as the Prophet *Ezekiel* expreffes himfelf concerning the Vine of *Ifrael,* ch. xix. 14. A *Fire is gone out of a Rod of her Branches, which hath devoured her Fruit.* For, from a defire of being *Many Mafters;* from a Defire of forcing mutually our *own* Opinions upon Others, inftead of exhorting them to ftudy and obey the Gofpel of *Chrift;* have arifen Strifes and Contentions, Hatred and Uncharitablenefs, Schifms and Divifions without End. *From whence,* fays St *James, come Wars and Fightings among you? come they not hence, even of your Lufts that war in your Members?* From a zeal for the Religion and for the Commandments of *Chrift,* from a Concern for the promoting of Truth, Righteoufnefs and Charity, 'tis evident in the nature of things, and in the experience of All Ages, that Wars and Fightings, Hatred and Animofities, never have, nor can proceed. *Thefe* precious Fruits have always fprung from That Root of Bitternefs, a zeal for the Doctrines and Commandments of *Men,* a Striving for *temporal Power and Dominion.* At the *firft beginning of the working of the Myftery of Iniquity,* the *Builders of Hay and Stubble upon the foundation of Chrift* went no farther than to *Cenforioufnefs* and *Uncharitablenefs* towards their Brethren. Againft whom, St *Paul* argues, *Rom.* xiv. 10; *Why doft thou judge thy Brother, or why doft thou fet at nought thy Brother? for we fhall all ftand before the judgment-feat of Chrift.* But in procefs of time; as Water, at a further Diftance from the Fountain, divides itfelf continually into *more* ftreams, and becomes lefs pure, and more mixt, and more different from the Nature of the Fountain itfelf; fo, when men had once departed from the Simplicity and Purity of the *Doctrine,* and from the Charitablenefs and Goodnefs of the *Spirit* of Chrift, their Hatred and Animofities againft each other increafed continually, till they literally fulfilled That remarkable Prophecy of our Saviour, in which is contained a moft Severe Reproof of thofe Corrupters of the Gofpel of Truth and Charity, who he forefaw would arife in following Ages, St *Luk.* xii. 49; *I am come to fend Fire on the Earth;* And *Matt.* x. 34; *Think not that I am come to fend Peace on Earth; I came not to fend Peace, but a Sword: For I am come to fet*

Ch. iv. 1.

I

a man

a man at variance againſt his Father, and the Daughter againſt her Mother; ——
and a man's Foes ſhall be they of his own Houſehold. Nay, even that deſcription which
he gives of the Perſecution which the *Jews* ſhould bring upon his Diſciples, *Joh.* xvi. 2;
The Time cometh, that whoſoever killeth *you, will think that he doth* God *Service;*
even *This,* in Time, came to be fulfilled by *one* Chriſtian, (ſo they ſtill *called* themſelves;)
it was fulfilled, I ſay, by *one* Chriſtian upon *another.* Till at laſt, when the Meaſure
of iniquity was become full, and the Power of Popery was compleatly ſeated and eſtabliſhed in the Temple of God; then, in like manner as our Lord declared concerning
That generation of the *Jews* in which He himſelf lived, that *the Blood of all the prophets, which was ſhed from the foundation of the World,* ——from the *Blood of righteous
Abel* even unto that day, ſhould be *required of That Generation;* ſo likewiſe, and for
the very ſame Reaſon, concerning That Body of men, which calls itſelf the *Chriſtian*
and the *Catholick Church,* does the Scripture wonderfully foretell, that *in Her* ſhould be
found the Blood of Prophets and of Saints, and of all that are ſlain upon the Earth. Since
the Reformation, and *in Places where* it has happily prevailed, this wicked and unchriſtian Spirit has in very great meaſure abated: But ſtill, ('tis to be feared,) even a-
mong too many *Proteſtants themſelves,* Zeal for particular Forms and Ceremonies,
more than for Virtue and Religion itſelf; A Concern for the diſtinguiſhing Doctrines of
Parties, more than for the Commandments of our Common Lord; A Deſire of compelling each Other's Faith, more than of reforming our Own Manners; continues to
hinder the growth of Chriſtian Charity, and, like the Worm at the Root of *Jonah's*
Gourd, to eat out the Vitals of true Religion. We read every day in St *John,* that
whoſoever doth not Righteouſneſs, is not of God, neither he that loveth not his Brother;
and that *if any man ſay, I love God, and hateth his Brother, he is a Liar :* And yet we
are ſtill ſo weak, as frequently to reverſe the Text, and think we can no way ſo zealouſly ſhow forth our *Love* towards *God,* as by *Hatred* and *ill treatment* of our *Brethren.*
Our Lord ſeverely rebuked his Diſciples, telling them *they knew not what Spirit they
were of,* when they would have called for Fire from Heaven upon the *Samaritans :*
And yet men are ſtill ſo fooliſh, as to be continually deſirous of uſing Methods of
Force, even *Chriſtians* againſt *each other.* The *immediate and neceſſary Effects* of This
Uncharitableneſs and Bitterneſs of Spirit, is, that the true Fruits of Virtue and Righteouſneſs and real Goodneſs are (comparatively ſpeaking) neglected and lightly eſteemed;
that Superſtition and Bigottry and abſurd Notions of Religion prevail among the *Weak;*
and thoſe who have *more diſcernment,* who have diſcernment enough to *ſee,* and yet
not enough to *ſee Through* theſe Abſurdities, are tempted to Atheiſm, Scepticiſm, and
Infidelity. All which things being obſerved by thoſe who are *without;* inſtead of being
moved to *glorify our Father which is in Heaven,* as our *Light ſhining before them* ought
to cauſe them to do; they are on the contrary, by our *Works of* Darkneſs which they
behold, confirmed in their Unbelief; and *the Name of God is blaſphemed among the
Gentiles, through Us, as it is written.* This is the Great Reproach to Chriſtians, and
the Great Impediment to the Progreſs of Chriſtianity. This is that which makes the
Pagan and *Mahometan* World ſtill ſuperior in Number to the Chriſtian; and that even
in the midſt of the Light of the Goſpel itſelf, yet Infidelity prevails beyond meaſure.

But 'tis an eaſy thing to ſee the *ill conſequences* of Uncharitableneſs, and to complain of the *Miſchiefs* that ariſe from the Diviſions among Chriſtians. The Difficulty
is, and the more uſeful part is, to find how to *remedy them.* Now 'tis very evident
there are but *Two* poſſible Ways by which the Diviſions among Chriſtians can have an
End put to them. The *one* is, what all parties of Men are generally very fond of, but
which can never poſſibly be accompliſhed; and if it could, 'twould be the Deſtruction
of Chriſtianity itſelf. The *other* is, what would very eaſily and effectually cure the
Evil, but what All parties are always very unwilling to put in Practice. The Method of
curing

SERM. curing Divifions, which Every party of men are very fond of, is, that thofe of all *other*
XLVIII. *opinions* would at a venture unite in fubmitting to *Them* : The Effect of which, if it
could be accomplifhed, would be, not the Eftablifhment of the Gofpel of Chrift, but
of fome Worldly Power and Dominion in the ftead of it ; as is more particularly notorious, in all Places where Popery has prevailed. But indeed *This* method of Union is altogether impoffible to be accomplifhed. For as every party of Chriftians reproaches all
others, with caufing Schifms and Divifions by not coming into *Their* opinions ; fo the
others reciprocally caft the fame reproach upon *Them*, for not coming into *Theirs* : And
thus the Fire of mutual Uncharitablenefs is blown up for ever, while Both fides are perhaps equally, or perhaps unequally, in Fault. For the cafe is exactly the fame, in
Moral matters, as in things *natural*. In Nature and Truth, *real Motion* belongs only
to That Body, which changes the *Abfolute Place* it was in ; but *relative Motion*, or
the parting of one body from another, belongs equally to the *Body from which another
is removed*, as to *That which itfelf moves*. Thus likewife in *Morality* ; the *Real* Sin, or
Guilt, of *caufing Schifms and Divifions*, lies always at the door of Him who departs
from the *Truth*, and who lays the *Strefs* of Religion where Chrift has not laid it : But
the *relative Schifms or Divifions themfelves*, by which Chriftians are parted from each
other, are always, by All Parties equally, laid to the Charge of their Adverfaries ; And
it muft not be expected, that they can ever be cured, by any *One Party* fwallowing up
all the reft. The *Other* therefore, and the *Only True* Method, of remedying Divifions ; but which All parties are generally very unwilling to put in Practice is, that every
party of Chriftians, forbearing to infift and to lay too much Weight on their own diftinguifhing Doctrines or Inventions of Men, fincerely endeavour to unite upon the foundation of the Gofpel itfelf, that is, the original undifputed Doctrines and Commandments of Chrift ; and in all *other* things, by mutual Charity and Forbearance, Tendernefs and Goodwill, preferve the Unity of the Spirit in the Bond of Peace ; according to
St *Paul*'s direction, *Rom.* xiv. 3. *Let not him that eateth, defpife him that eateth not ;
and let not him which eateth not, judge him that eateth.*

IV. It remains, in the *Laft* place, that I draw fome ufeful Inferences from what
has been faid, and fo conclude. And

1*ft*, From what has been faid concerning the Nature of the *Virtue of Charity*, and
its *oppofite Vice* ; we may fee clearly whence it comes to pafs, that St *Paul* in his Catalogue of great Wickednefes, *Gal.* v. 20 ; among *uncleannefes, idolatry, murders,
drunkennefs and revelling*, reckons alfo *hatred, variance and ftrife, feditions* (or Schifms,)
herefies and fuch like, as being *Works of the Flefh*. 'Tis evident, *differing in judgment
or opinion*, is not a work of the *Flefh*, but of the *Underftanding*. *Difapproving* the
opinions of thofe whom a man fincerely thinks to be in the *wrong*, is not a work of
the *Flefh*, but the *neceffary* Duty of a *Chriftian*. The Crimes therefore which St *Paul*
fpeaks of, are the prefumptuous affecting of worldly Power, and the caufing of Strifes
and uncharitable Divifions among Chriftians, by laying the *Strefs* of Religion upon particular diftinguifhing Doctrines and Practices, on which our Saviour himfelf has laid *No
Strefs*. Thefe are *indeed*, Works of the *Flefh* : Thefe are deftructive of That Love and
Charity and Chriftian Temper, which is fo fundamental in Religion, that, whofoever
wants it, though *he beftows all his goods to feed the poor, and though he gives his Body to
be burned*, yet, the Text tells us, *it fhall profit him nothing*. The expreffion is of the
fame kind with That in *Gal.* v. 2. *Behold, I Paul fay unto you, that if ye be circum-
cifed, Chrift fhall profit you nothing* : Circumcifion, was in its own Nature a thing of
indifference ; *Circumcifion*, as he elfewhere tells them, *is nothing, and Uncircumcifion is
nothing*. But if they forced it upon the *Gentile* Converts as a *Neceffary part of Chriftianity*, This was a deftroying of Charity, and their Religion (he declares) would be
in vain.　　　I

2*dly*, From

2dly, FROM what has been above said concerning the true Nature and Spirit of Christianity, we may easily answer That Question usually put by those of the Church of *Rome*; *Where was the Reformed Religion, before the Times of the Reformers?* The Answer is: 'Twas *Then*, just where it is *Now*, even in the *Gospel of Christ*; studied and obeyed by all Sincere Followers of *Truth and Charity*. Which *Rule*, whosoever in *Any* Age, or in *Any* Country of the World, has walked by; That person was a true Disciple of Christ: And whosoever follows any *Other* Rule, is in *No* Age and in *No* Country a good Christian. *Gal.* vi. 16. *As many as walk according to This Rule, Peace be on them, and Mercy, and upon the Israel of God.* For *wheresoever two or three are gathered together in the Name of Christ*, (whether they be two or three *thousands*, or two or three *single* persons;) *There* (says our Lord) *am I in the midst of them.*

3dly, FROM what has been above said, we may easily understand in what Sense it is, that *Zeal* and *Moderation* are *Both of them* in Scripture equally recommended as Virtues. When the Question is concerning things *indifferent* in their own nature, concerning matters of *Party* and Divisions among *Men*, concerning any *Doctrines or Practices* of *Human* Appointment; then the Rule is, *Let your Moderation be known unto all men*, Phil. iv. 15: And *Ephes.* iv. 2. *With all lowliness and meekness, with long-suffering, forbearing one another in Love.* But when the matter in question is a *Moral Virtue*, or a *plain and express Command of God*; Then, *it is good to be* zealously *affected always in a good thing*, Gal. iv. 18. For Christians, are to be a people zealous *of* good *Works*, Tit. ii. 14. And to be *careless* or *indifferent* in the cause of *Virtue and Righteousness*, is being in the case of the Church of *Laodicea*, Rev. iii. 13. *I know thy Works, that thou art neither cold nor hot; I would thou wert cold or hot; So then, because thou art luke-warm, and neither cold nor hot, I will spue thee out of my Mouth.* In matters of *Party and Factions*; in questions relating to the Powers and to the Doctrines of *Men*; God knows, men are apt to be *Hot enough*: But for enquiring impartially after the Knowledge of *Truth*, and for promoting the Practice of universal *Righteousness and Charity*; 'twere well if the Warmest among Christians in these corrupt Ages, were in their Zeal even so much as *luke-warm*.

4thly and *Lastly*, FROM what has been said, we may learn the true Meaning of that Exhortation of St *Paul*, 1 Cor. i. 10. *I beseech you, brethren, by the Name of our Lord Jesus Christ, that——there be no divisions among you, but that ye be perfectly joined together in the same mind, and in the same judgment.* His Meaning is not, that they must be all exactly of *one opinion* in every thing: For *such* an Unity cannot possibly arise, but either from *perfect and infallible Knowledge*, which is *not attainable* in This World; or from *gross Ignorance and Darkness*, which is an effect of great Corruption. But the plain meaning of St *Paul* is, that they ought to be *joined together in the same* charitable *mind, and in the same* charitable *judgment* towards each other, *notwithstanding* any differences in Opinion. Thus he expresly explains himself, *Rom.* xv. 5. *God grant you to be like-minded one towards another:* He does not say, *like-minded* or of like judgment, concerning *Things*; For That is in no man's Power: But *like-minded*, or *alike well-affectioned*, towards each *Other's Persons*. So likewise, *Eph.* iv. 3. *Endeavouring to keep the Unity of the Spirit, in the Bond of Peace:* And how was That to be done? Was it by compelling men to pretend that they All think alike? No: For This, instead of Unity of Spirit in the Bond of Peace, is indeed nothing else, but either Unity of Opinion in the Bond of Ignorance, or Unity of Practice in the Bond of Hypocrisy. But the Apostle's meaning is, Keep the Unity of the Spirit, *With all lowliness* (says he) *and meekness, with long-suffering, forbearing one another in Love.* Again: *Phil.* ii. 2. *That ye be like-minded*; how? why, *having the same love, being of one accord, of one mind*; *let nothing be done through strife or vain-glory, but in lowliness of Mind.* St *Peter* also explains himself after the same manner, 1 *Pet.* iii. 8. *Finally be ye all of one mind.*

SERM. How? Is it by following each other ignorantly and implicitly? No: but, *having com-*
XLVIII. *paffion* (fays he) *one of another, love as Brethren, be pitiful, be courteous.* This is
That *Charity*, which whofoever *has not*, the Text clearly affirms he cannot be a good
Chriftian: And whofoever *has it*, cannot eafily fail in any *Other* inftances of Virtue;
For *Love, is the Fulfilling of the Law.*

SERMON XLIX.

The Nature of Relative Duties.

COL. III. 20, 21, 22.

Children, obey your Parents in all things; for This is well-pleafing
unto the Lord. Fathers, provoke not your children to anger, left
they be difcouraged. Servants, obey in all things your Mafters
according to the flefh.

SERM. IT is the conftant Method of St *Paul* in all his Epiftles, firft to inlarge upon and
XLIX. explain diftinctly the *particular* point or queftion, which was the occafion of his
writing at That time to *That particular Church*; and then to add fuch *general*
exhortations to the practice of *all* Chriftian Duties and Virtues, as might at all times be
of Ufe to *All Churches*, and to *every Chriftian* in all Ages and in every part of the
World. Thefe *general* Exhortations are, in the main, the *fame* in *All* his epiftles; eafy
and plain, univerfal and unvaried, fuited to all Capacities, and containing the moft important and fundamental Principles of Religion. The *former part* of the feveral Epiftles ufually relates to fome *particular Controverfy* between the *Jewifh* and *Gentile Con-*
verts, which at That time gave Trouble to the Apoftles: And *Thefe* parts of his Writings *cannot* be rightly underftood any other way, than by attending carefully to the *oc-*
cafion and *State* of the *particular queftion* which he is there determining. And therefore it has been a great Error in thefe latter Ages of the World, and the Caufe of many
vain difputes among Chriftians, that, without attending to the Defign and Scope of a
Difcourfe written in an argumentative manner, Men have frequently picked out and
applied *to Themfelves* fingle Paffages, which, in the courfe of the Apoftle's Argument,
had plainly a View only to the State of the then *Jewifh* or *Gentile Church.* From this
One miftake, it is evident, have fprung *all* the vain Controverfies concerning *Faith* and
Works, concerning *Juftification* and *Sanctification*, concerning *Election* and *Reproba-*
tion, and the like: wherewith while the Minds of Men have been needlefsly diftracted,
they have been the *lefs apt* to attend to the *great and weightier* Matters of the Law, to
the *moral* and *general Exhortations*, repeated and inculcated univerfally in *every* epiftle,
as things by *every* Chriftian *indifputably eafy to be underftood*, and *indifpenfably neceffary*
to be practifed.

THE

THE Words of my Text are part of the *general Exhortation*, which concludes the SER M.
epiftle to the *Coloffians*. In the *Beginning* of This chapter the Apoftle exhorts them to XLIX.
fet their Affections on *heavenly* things, to *mortify* every *vicious* and *inordinate appetite*,
to lay afide all *Malice* and *Contentioufnefs* among themfelves, and to live in the practice
of univerfal *Love*, *Charity* and *Good-Will*: And in the *Latter* part of the chapter, he
recommends to them the *Relative* Duties of life; the Duties of *Husbands* and *Wives*,
of *Children* and *Parents*, of *Mafters* and *Servants*, of *Superiors* and *Inferiors* in *all*
Relations. *Children, obey your Parents in all things; for This is well-pleafing unto the
Lord: Fathers, provoke not your children to anger, left they be difcouraged: Servants,
obey in all things your Mafters according to the Flefh.*

IN difcourfing upon thefe words; I fhall, *Firft, diftinctly* take Notice of the feveral *Particulars* contained in the Text; And, *Secondly*, I fhall thence deduce this *General* Obfervation; that the due Performance of the *Relative Duties* of Life, is a principal Means of obtaining both the Bleffings of the *prefent World*, and the Happinefs
of *That which is to come.*

I. IN the *Firft* place, That which ftands *firft and moft obvioufly* obfervable in the
Text, is this *Precept; Children obey your Parents*. In his epiftle to the *Ephefians*, the
fame Apoftle expreffes this Precept Thus: *Children, obey your Parents in the Lord;
for This is Right: Honour thy Father and Mother, which is the firft Commandment
with Promife;* ch. vi. 1. In which expreffion, there is an allufion to the *Order* or
Placing of the Commandments in the Law of *Mofes;* This being the Firft in the Se-
cond Table, the Firft of thofe Commandments which declare our *Duty towards* Men;
the Firft to which is annexed expreffly a *particular Reward;* the Firft *Commandment with Promife.* The natural obfervation arifing from which particular, is, the *reafonablenefs* and *goodnefs* of the *Great Commandments of God* both in the *Law* and the
Gofpel. God begins where *Nature itfelf* does, making the *fame* things to be the *prime*
Foundations of *His Law*, which in the nature of things themfelves, without *Any* Law,
were moft reafonable to be practifed. The Gofpel carries indeed This and all other
Moral Precepts to a much *higher* degree of improvement, requiring us to extend our
Love toward *all* men, and our defire of doing good even unto *Enemies* themfelves.
But the *prior* obligation, is That of *Gratitude* to *Benefactors;* and of making *juft Re-
turns* to Thofe, from whom we have received the Benefits of Life. Neverthelefs, as
clear as this Obligation is, both in the Nature of Things and in the Command of God;
yet, not Irreligion and Atheifm only, but *Superftition* alfo has found means to evade
This in like manner as it does all *other* moral and eternal Obligations. *God*, (fays our
Saviour; *Matt.* xv. 4; God,) *commanded, faying, Honour thy Father and Mother: But
Ye fay, Whofoever fhall fay to his Father or his Mother, it is a Gift by whatfoever thou
mighteft be profited by Me*, (that is, it is given to the Service of the *Temple*, or to fome
other of what they then called *pious* Ufes) *he fhall be free;* he fhall be difcharged from
all Obligation to relieve his neceffitous Parents. *Thus* (fays our Lord) *ye have made the
commandment of God of none Effect by your Tradition.* Notions fomewhat of the fame
nature have, in *All Ages* of the World, prevailed over fuperftitious and corrupt Minds;
teaching them to value things that promote outward Pomp and Show, and Diftinctions
of Men under Party-Denominations, more than Obedience to the eternal and unchangeable Duties of God's *Moral* Law.

2dly, THE Next thing proper to be taken notice of in the Text, is, that the Particulars here mentioned of the Duty of *Children* and *Servants*, are Only *Inftances* of the
General *Exhortation*, defigned to extend proportionably to perfons in *All* Relative Stations and Circumftances of Life *whatfoever*. As Rom. xiii. 7; *Render to All, their Dues;
Tribute, to whom tribute is due; cuftom, to whom cuftom; fear, to whom fear; honour,*

to

S E R M. *to whom honour.* To *Magiftrates,* there is due from the Subjeƈt *Obedience* according to
XLIX. the Laws of the Country, in matters not oppofite to the Law of God; *Peaceableneſs*
and Quietneſs under Government, and a willing *Contribution* towards the *Support* of it.
To *Teachers,* or *Spiritual* Superiors, there is due from the People *Such* Refpeƈt, as to
Stewards of the Myſteries of God, appointed to exhort Men continually to the Praƈtice
of Virtue, and to affift in all the Adminiftrations of Religion: Towards *Theſe,* there
ought to be in men a Willingneſs to hear and be informed by them, and a readineſs
to obferve and praƈtice what they teach; not blindly and implicitely, (which is the
Doƈtrine of *Rome*) but in all things which they can *ſhow* to be the *Doƈtrine and Commands of God.* To *Maſters,* there is due from Servants *Diligence* and *Induſtry, Honeſ-
ty* and *Fidelity, Submiſſion,* and *Obedience,* according to the direƈtion in the Text; *Servants, obey ——— your Maſters according to the Fleſh; not with eye-ſervice, as men-
pleaſers, but in ſingleneſs of Heart, fearing God: And whatſoever ye do, do it heartily
as to the Lord, and not unto men.* In like manner; Eph. vi. 7; *With good Will* (fays
he) *doing Service, as to the Lord, and not to men; Knowing that whatſoever good thing
any man does, the ſame ſhall he receive of the Lord, whether he be bond or free.* The
only difference here to be obferved, is, that whereas the *Servants* mentioned by the
Apoftle, were, in thofe days, *Slaves,* under the abfolute Power of their Mafters, without Any Relief under the greateft oppreffions; (for which reafon St *Peter* exhorts Such
to be patient under the fevereft hardfhips, confidering that *it is thank-worthy, if a man
for conſcience towards God endure grief, ſuffering wrongfully:* Whereas (I fay) in the
Apoſtles days the ftate of *Servants* was abfolute *Slavery,* · it is *Now* on the contrary always to be Underftood, that the Duty and Obligation of thofe in the loweft Station towards their refpeƈtive Superiors in *This* kind, is fuch only as arifes from *Law* and *Con-
traƈt,* and is wholly limited by thofe Meafures. And This concerning the *feveral
particular relative Perfons,* to whom the Apoftle defigned his exhortation to extend.

3*dly,* T H E *Third* Particular obfervable in the Text, is, the unbounded manner
in which the Apoftle expreffes the *General* Duty of *Subjeƈtion* to Superiors, in *every*
Relative Station of Life: *Children, obey your Parents in* all *things: Servants, obey in*
all *things your Maſters according to the Fleſh.* So elfewhere: *Let the Wives* (fays he)
be ſubjeƈt to their own Husbands in every thing: And Tit. ii. 9; *Exhort Servants to be
obedient unto their own Maſters; and to pleaſe them well in* all *things.* Reafon, and
the Nature of things, and the general Ufage of all language, ſhoweth, that in thefe
and all other the like Expreffions, the phrafe, *in* every *thing,* and *in* all *things,* muft
neceffarily be underftood to mean only, *in* all *things* juft, *in* all *things* lawful,
in all *things that are* honeft *and* fit *to be done.* In *Human* Writings, thefe *general* manners of expreffion, arifing from the known and vulgar ufe of Language, are *never* mifunderftood: And therefore to mifunderftand them in the *Sacred*
Books *only,* is mere Perverfeneſs. The Gofpel neither *inlarges* nor *diminiſhes* any Superior's *Power;* it neither *adds to,* nor *takes from* any *Inferior's Right.* In *Theſe* Cafes,
it only confirms and explains the Obligations of Nature; and inforces the *Praƈtice*
of the refpeƈtive Duties, with ftronger and more powerful *Motives.* As therefore in
all *other* Writings, fo in *Scripture* likewife; the true, the natural, and evident Meaning of fuch Phrafes as thefe, *in* all *things, in* every *thing,* and the like; is not what the
word, *all,* fuggefts in its *ſingle* Signification; but what the *vulgar* fenfe of it is, in
fuch expreffions and fentences. When we are taught that the Commands of *God,* or
the Laws of *Truth and Right,* are to be obeyed *in* all *things;* the *nature* of the *Thing,*
not the *force* of the *ſingle words,* ſhows that the Obedience is to be *univerſal* and *without exception.* In *other* cafes, where the very *ſame words* are ufed; (as, in the Text,
Servants obey your Maſters in all things) the nature of the Thing *There* likewife no leſs
plainly ſhows, that this *obedience in all things* is to be *limited,* by its *conſiſtency with*

3　　　　　　　　　　　　　　　　　　　　　　　　　　　　　　　　　　the

the Commands of any *Superior Master* either on Earth or in Heaven. In *All* language,
the fignification of *every word* neceffarily depends upon the *other* words with which it
is connected: And where no *Controverfy* is concerned, nor *Prejudice* interpofes, it is
always underftood, and cannot but be underftood to be fo, by all Underftandings, and
by all Capacities equally, from the Higheft to the Meaneft. When the Scripture mentions *The* Everlafting *God*, it is not the force of the word *Everlafting*, but the application of it to the *Firft Caufe and Author of all things*, that makes it denote a true and
abfolute *Eternity*: For when the fame Scripture mentions the *everlafting Mountains*,
it is underftood by all men both of the greateft and of the fmalleft Underftandings, that
it there fignifies only *fuch* a Duration, as is proper to the Subject of which it is fpoken.
Thefe things are, *in their own Nature*, exceedingly evident: And yet where *Party*,
or *Intereft*, or *Controverfy* is concerned, it is wonderful to what a degree men have
fometimes, even in fo *plain* a cafe, impofed upon the *ignorant*, and upon the *learned* too. I fhall mention but *One* Inftance, and leave *Others* to be judged of by the
fame proportion. In the queftion about *Tranfubftantiation*, the Writers of the Church
of *Rome* alledge with great confidence, that the *natural*, the *literal*, the *firft and obvious* fenfe of the words, *This is my Body*, is plainly in favour of *Their* fide of the
Queftion. And yet in reality, the very contrary to This, is evidently true. For the
natural, the *literal*, the *firft*, and *obvious* fenfe of the *phrafe*, is not that which arifes
from the fignification of the word *Body* fingly, but That which arifes from its natural
fignification in *fuch* an expreffion, wherein *commemorative Bread* is affirmed to be the
Body of Him who is commemorated thereby. When a *Picture* is fpoken of, as being the
perfon it reprefents; the *natural*, the *literal*, the *firft* and *obvious* fenfe of the expreffion,
is not that it is *really*, but that it is *reprefentatively*, That perfon. When our Lord
fays, *I am the true Vine*; the queftion is not what the word, *Vine*, naturally fignifies
in *other* cafes; but what it *There* moft *naturally and obvioufly fignifies*, when a *Teacher*
calls *Himfelf* a *Vine*, and his *Followers* its *Branches*. When *Wifdom* declares concerning herfelf, Eccluf. xxiv. 2 1 ; *They that eat me, fhall yet be hungry, and they that drink
me, fhall yet be thirfty*; the *natural* and *obvious*, nay, the *literal* fignification of the
whole Sentence, arifes from what the terms, *eat* and *drink*, do *Then* moft *naturally*
and *obvioufly* fignify, when a perfon is fpeaking, not concerning Food, but about *im-
bibing* and *digefting* a Doctrine. But to return from This Digreffion.

4thly, T H E *Next* Particular obfervable in the Text, is the *Reafon* or *Motive* annexed by the Apoftle in order to inforce his exhortation: *For This* (fays he) *is well-pleafing
unto the Lord*. In his Epiftle to the *Ephefians*, (as I before obferved;) after having
laid down the fame exhortation as in the text; inftead of inforcing it, as he does here,
with telling them that *This is well-pleafing unto the Lord*; he cites the words of the
Commandment itfelf, *Honour thy Father and thy Mother*; and adds, by way of obfervation, that This *is the Firft Commandment with Promife*, ch. vi. 2. The *Promife* he means,
is; *That thy days may be long, in the Land which the Lord thy God has given thee*. By
which *Promife*, as delivered in the *Commandment to the Jews*, God by a wife and
fuitable Difpofition of Things, very aptly annexed the Bleffing of *Long Life*, to *Them*
that paid due Regard to Thofe who were the Means of *giving them Life*. But then,
even under the *Law*, (very *certainly*, though not fo *explicitly* as in the Revelation of
the *Gofpel*) it is always to be underftood, that in all Promifes of This nature, there
was a *further Reference* to a *Future* and a *Better Life*. Thus in the 11*th* to the *Hebrews*, the Apoftle affures, that *Abraham* underftood the promifed inheritance, to be
laid up for him in that heavenly *city which has foundations, whofe Builder and Maker is
God*. Thus the prophetick Tradition among the antient *Jews*, that *Jerufalem fhould
be built up with Saphirs*, Tobit xiii. 16 ; is by St *John* made the defcription of That
City *of God* which *cometh down from Heaven*. Thus our Saviour's Promife, that *the*

S E R M. *Meek shall inherit the Earth*, Matt. v. 5; may well have *Reference* at leaft, if it be not
XLIX. expreffly applied by him in his firft intention, to That *New Heaven and New Earth*,
〰〰〰 *wherein Righteoufnefs* is to *dwell* for ever. Thus, to mention but One Inftance more;
That Expreffion of *Ezekiel*, ch. xiii. 9; They fhall not be in the *Affembly of my people*,
*neither fhall they be written in the Writing of the Houfe of Ifrael, neither fhall they en-
ter into the Land of Ifrael;* cannot be doubted but that implicitly means the fame thing,
as, in the New-Teftament-language, being not *written in the Book of Life.*

5thly, and *Laftly,* F R O M the *relative Antithefis* in the refpective parts of the text;
Children, obey your Parents in all things; and, *Fathers, provoke not your Children to
anger:* It is obfervable, that as in *Nature,* in the frame and conftruction of this *material* Fabrick of the Univerfe, all *operations* of the parts of *Matter* are *mutual* upon each
other, for the Support and Prefervation of the Whole; fo in *morality* and *religion,* All
Duties are of reciprocal Obligation. Where-ever the Duty of the *Inferior* is mentioned,
it is always to be underftood that the Duty of the *Superior* is proportionably fuppofed.
Parents are to fupport, and be gentle towards their Children; *bringing them up in the*
Eph. vi. 4. *Nurture and Admonition of the Lord.* *Mafters* are to exact Service, not rigoroufly and
cruelly, but with Mildnefs, and according to the Terms contracted for. *Governors in
the* Church are not to *lord it over the Heritage of God,* nor to affume to themfelves dominion over the Confciences of Men; but, as faithful Stewards of the Myfteries of
God, to affift men in *underftanding* the Will of God, and to exhort them continually
to *practife* it in Peace and Love. *Magiftrates* are to govern according to thofe Inftructions of *Job,* ch. xxix. 14; *I put on righteoufnefs, and it clothed me; my Judgment
was as a Robe and a Diadem. I was eyes to the blind, and feet was I to the lame. I
was a Father to the Poor; and the Caufe which I knew not, I fearched out.* Laftly,
Princes, or Supreme Civil Governors, are to ufe Power within the limits of Law and
Reafon: Confidering the admonition of the Author of the Book of *Wifdom,* ch. vi. 2,
*Give ear, you that rule the People, and that glory in the multitude of Nations; For Power
is given you of the Lord, and Sovereignty from the Higheft; who fhall try your Works,
and fearch out your Counfels:——For he which is Lord over All fhall fear no man's perfon, neither fhall he ftand in awe of any man's greatnefs: For he hath made the fmall
and great, and careth for All alike.*

II. H A V I N G thus at large confidered the feveral diftinct *Particulars* contained in
the Text: I fhall now briefly from the Whole, deduce this *General* Obfervation; that
the Due Performance of the *Relative Duties* of Life, is a principal Means of obtaining
both the Bleffings of the *prefent* World, and the Happinefs of *That which is to come.*
As to the Happinefs of the *Life to come;* the Promife of that being annexed to the Obfervance of *All* God's commandments in general, needs not here be particularly enlarged
upon: It is fufficiently implied in thofe words of the Text, *This is well-pleafing unto
the Lord.* But what in This cafe is peculiarly remarkable, is, that the Bleffings and
Happinefs of the *prefent Life,* are *not only* by the Promife of God *annexed to,* but even
in the Nature of things do effentially *confift in,* the due Performance of thefe *Relative
Duties.* As, in the *natural Body,* the Health and Prefervation of the *Whole* depends
upon *every Part's* performing its proper office; So, in every *political Society, Inferiors
and Superiors* in all the various ftations of Life depend *mutually* upon each other, and
the Welfare of the *Whole* upon the Duties of *Both.* *Superiors,* in the confcientious
performance of *their Duty,* are the *Protectors and Guardians* of the Rights and Properties of *Thofe below them:* And *Inferiors,* acting under a Senfe of Duty, moved by *Love
and Reafon* more than by *Compulfion* or *Fear,* are the moft folid Support of the Authority and Peace and Happinefs of *Thofe above them.* The *Corruption and Depravity* of
Mankind makes it *neceffary,* by the intervention of Human *Laws,* to *compel* men *in
fome meafure* to perform thefe refpective Duties: But a true fenfe of *Religion,* and of

the *Reafonablenefs* and *Ufefulnefs* and *effential Obligation* of the Duties themfelves, would
cblige them by a much ftronger and fecurer Tie, to do all the fame things *freely and*
willingly, *heartily and fincerely*, *in publick and in private*; which the beft and wifeft
Laws can but compel thofe who want fuch a fenfe of Religion, to do *unwillingly*,
flightly and fuperficially, *in publick Appearance only*, *and in the Sight of Men*. Religion
therefore and true Virtue, if they prevailed in the World, would obtain the fame happy Ends *fully and effeEtually*, which the beft and wifeft Laws can do but *in part*; and
Laws are made only to fupply, in the beft manner they can, the Want of true Religion
and Virtue among Men. *The Law is not made for a righteous Man*, *but for the law-
lefs and difobedient*, *for the ungodly and for finners*, *for the unholy and the profane*;
1 Tim. i. 9. Did men univerfally, from a *fenfe* of the *Right* and *Reafon* of the *thing itfelf*, live in an uniform and confcientious Performance of the *Relative Duties of Life*;
the Prophecies of That Great Happinefs which under *typical* Reprefentations is foretold
as coming in the days of the *Meffias*, would be *literally* fulfilled: If. ii. 4; *They fhall
beat their fwords into plough-fhares, and their fpears into pruning hooks; nation fhall not
lift up fword againft nation, neither fhall they learn war any more*: And ch. lx. 18,
*Violence fhall no more be heard in thy land, wafting nor deftruEtion within thy borders;
but thou fhalt call thy Walls Salvation, and thy Gates Praife:* ——— *Thy people alfo
fhall be All Righteous*. But however, even as things *Now* are; would *Superiors*
in all Times and Places, who are the Great *Example* and *DireEtion* to the World,
endeavour each in their refpeEtive ftations, to make ufe of That Power wherewith God has intrufted them, always to the ProteEtion and Support of *Right*; the
Benefits which would thence accrue to Mankind, even in this prefent imper-
feEt and corrupt State, would be inconceivably Great. 2 Sam. xxiii. 3; *He that
ruleth over men muft be juft, ruling in the Fear of God: And he fhall be as the Light
of the Morning, when the Sun rifeth, even a morning without clouds; as the tender Grafs
fpringing out of the Earth, by clear fhining after Rain*. And Pf. lxxii. 4; *He fhall
judge the People according unto Right, and defend the Poor,*———*and punifh the wrong-
doer*———.*He fhall come down like Rain into a fleece of Wool, even as the Drops that
water the Earth: In His time fhall the Righteous flourifh, yea, and abundance of Peace
fo long as the Moon endureth*.

SERMON

SERMON L.

The Inconsistency of the Love of God with the Love of the World.

1 JOH. II. 15.

Love not the World, neither the things that are in the World : If any man love the World, the Love of the Father is not in him.

SERM.
L.

THE Great End and Design of Religion, is, by the Tryal of mens Virtue and Integrity in the present World, to qualify them for the Happiness of That which is to come: That they who have been *Faithful* in a small and *temporary Trust*, committed to them *Here*; may *hereafter* be put in Possession of a never-fading *Inheritance*, which shall be *their Own* for ever. As our Saviour has largely and distinctly set forth this matter, in his Parable of the Unjust Steward, *Luke* xvi.

MISTAKING this True End and Design of Religion, men have fallen into Two contrary Extremes: Some having framed to Themselves *such* a notion of Religion, as is *consistent* with the *Vices* of this present World; and Others, on the contrary, *such* a one as is *not consistent* with some of the most considerable and important *Duties* of *Life*. Some have placed the highest Excellency of Religion in *retiring* wholly *from* the World, so as to render themselves altogether *useless* in it: And Others, on the contrary, imagining Religion principally to consist in certain *Forms* and *Ceremonies*, or in the Profession of certain *Systems* of *empty Opinions*; indulge themselves in the Practice of known *Immoralities*, at the same time that they are most zealously religious. The proper Remedy for Both these Mistakes, is to endeavour to give men a *just* idea of the *Nature* of True Religion; and of the Influence it ought to have upon mens whole Behaviour, with regard to the *World*, and to the things that are in it. For which Purpose I have chosen these words of the Apostle: *Love not the World, neither the things that are in the World; If any man love the World, the Love of the Father is not in him.*

IN discoursing upon which words, I shall endeavour to show, *1st, What* the Apostle here means by *the World, and the Things that are in it*; which he exhorts us, *not to love*. *2dly, What* That *Love of the Father* is, with which the *Love of the World* is inconsistent. And *3dly, What* are the principal *Reasons and Motives*, upon which the Apostle here so earnestly cautions men against That *Love of the World*, which he thus describes as inconsistent with the *Love of God*.

I. WHAT the Apostle here means by *the World*, and by *the Things that are in it*, which he exhorts us *Not to love*, he himself expressly and distinctly explains in the words next following the Text; *For all that is in the World*, saith he, *the Lust of the Flesh, and the Lust of the Eyes, and the Pride of Life, is not of the Father, but is of* the World. That is to say: Not *That World* which *God* has *created*, or any of the things that *he* has made in it; but *That World* which *Sin-*

2   *ners*

ners have fafhioned to themfelves, and which is entirely the Work of their own Inven- S E R M.
tion. *Every Creature* of God is *Good*; and every thing that *he* has made may be made ufe   L.
of with Thankfgiving: But there is an *imaginary World,* which corrupt Minds have
framed to themfelves in Perverfenefs, by *Abufe* and *Mifapplication* of the good Creatures
of God. And concerning the *World* in *This fenfe* of the word, this *Wicked* Form and
Fafhion of a World, it may very well and properly be faid, what the Author of the Book
of *Wifdom* fays concerning *Death,* ch. i. 13, that *God made it not:* 'Tis made entirely
through *Enmity* to *Him,* and in direct Oppofition to *His* Commands. The *Particulars* of which *the World* in *This fenfe* confifts; the *wicked* and *corrupt World,* which is
not of the Father, which is no part of the creation of God; *all the things that are in* it,
as the Apoftle here expreffes himfelf, are reducible under *Three* Heads.

THE *Firft,* is the Defire of *unlawful* Pleafures; all *Intemperance and Debauchery,
Luxurioufnefs, Drunkennefs and Uncleannefs.* And Thefe are ftyled by the Apoftle, *the
Luft of the* Flefh, becaufe they are the things into which men are hurried by *Paffion
and Appetite,* which is what the Scripture ftyles *Flefh;* in oppofition to the Dictates of
Reafon and Religion, which is what the Scripture calls being *led by the Spirit.* All the
Good things of Life, which God has created to be *injoyed* with *Temperance* and *Thankfgiving,* according to the Ends and Meafures of *Nature,* within the Limits of *Reafon, Sobriety* and *Good manners,* and confiftent with the more noble Views and Improvements of *Religion:* All *Thefe* things, I fay, are the Gifts and Bleffings of *God, who
giveth us richly all things to enjoy,* 1 *Tim.* vi. 17. But when men, inftead of *governing* their *Paffions and Appetites* by *Reafon,* do on the contrary fuffer their *Reafon* to be
over-ruled by *Paffions and Appetites;* fubverting the natural Order of God's Creation,
and giving no attention to thofe Superior Faculties, which were defigned to diftinguifh
men from the Beafts that perifh: their Injoyments in This cafe are of Such a nature,
that they can neither *pray for* them *beforehand,* nor *return Thanks for* them *afterwards,* as *Bleffings* of God; but are forced to reflect upon them with *Shame,* whether
they will or no; as being confcious that thefe things proceed *not* from *the Father* and
Creator of the Univerfe, but from what the Apoftle here ftyles *the World* by way of
oppofition; *That World,* which is an *Enemy* to God; and concerning which St *Paul*
fpeaks, when he fays of Wicked men, that *the God of* This World *has blinded their
minds,* 2 Cor. iv. 4.

THIS is the *Firft* Particular; *the Luft of the Flefh.* The *Second* Head, under which
the Apoftle here reduces *all the things that are in the World,* in the *wicked and corrupt*
World, is the *unlawful* Defire of *Riches;* the Defire of *Riches* by *unjuftifiable Means,* and to
no valuable Purpofes. And thefe are here ftyled *the Luft of the* Eyes; becaufe the Love
of *Riches,* as *fuch,* and as it ftands here diftinguifhed from *Other* vitious affections; the
Covetous Defire of *Riches* for *Riches fake,* without any regard to the True and Beneficial Ufes of them; is but *feeding the* Eyes with a mere fruitlefs View of unprofitable
Treafure, with the empty Shows of Vanity and Deceit. *What Good is there,* fays the
Wife man, *Ecclef.* v. 11, *What Good is there to the Owners thereof, faving the beholding
of them with their* Eyes? *There is One alone,* fays he, *and there is not a Second,* ch. iv. 8,
*yea, he hath neither Child, nor Brother; yet is there no end of all his Labour, neither is his
Eye fatisfied with Riches; neither faith he, for whom do I labour, and bereave my foul
of good? This is alfo Vanity.* The Phrafe, *neither is his* Eye *fatisfied with Riches* is the
fame as what he elfewhere expreffes, *Prov.* xxvii. 20. *Hell and deftruction are never
full; fo the* Eyes *of man are never fatisfied.* And from hence have been derived thofe *particular manners of fpeaking* in Scripture, where *Liberality* is ftyled a *Bountiful* Eye, and Prov. xxii. 9.
a *Single* (or *Open*) Eye; and *Covetoufnefs,* an *Evil* (or *niggardly*) Eye; and the like.
Whenever *Riches* are defired and employed as Inftruments of *Good,* they are Then in-

S E R M. deed *real Bleffings of Providence*; *Bleffings* to the *Poffeffors* of them, whom they enable
L. to have *Great Influence* in promoting Juftice, Righteoufnefs, Charity, and every Other
good Work in the World; And *Bleffings* to *Others*, who are Partakers of the *Effects* of
thofe good *Influences*. But when they are only what the Apoftle here ftyles the *Luft
of the* Eyes; the Food either of *Covetoufnefs* merely, *without* Ufe; or of *Vanity* and
Folly, in an *ill* Ufe of them: The Defire of them, in That cafe, is not an *Appetite* of
God's creating; 'Tis not *of the Father*, but *of the World*; 'Tis the *creature* merely of a
perverted Imagination, and of a *corrupt Will*; 'Tis a *Defire* that will perpetually put
men upon *obtaining* Wealth by *ill* Methods, and upon *employing* it in *nothing Good*.
The *Temptations* that *This Appetite* expofes men to, are the Foundation of great Corruption. *They that will be rich*, (fays the Apoftle,) *fall into Temptation and a Snare,
and into many foolifh and hurtful Lufts, which drown men in deftruction and perdition:
For the Love of Money is the Root of all Evil: Which while Some coveted after, they
have erred from the Faith, and pierced themfelves through with many Sorrows*: That is,
they have expofed themfelves to be feduced into fuch corrupt Practices, the avoiding
whereof is That Part of true Religion, which St *James* calls a man's *keeping himfelf unfpotted from the World*.

THE *Third* Head, under which the Apoftle here reduces *all the things that are in
the World*; in the *wicked and corrupt World*, confidered as oppofite to *God*; is *Ambition*, or the *unlawful* Defire of *Dominion and Power*. And This is here ftyled by the
Apoftle the Pride *of Life*, becaufe both the *Defire of obtaining Power*, by *unrighteous*
methods, and the *Pleafure of exercifing* it in ways of *Infolence* and *Oppreffion*, have their
whole Foundation in *Pride*; in a *prefumptuous* Imagination, that *Right* and *Reafon* and
Equity are things of *No reality*, and which may at any time give place to *Our Wills
and Pleafures*. *Power*, confidered in itfelf, as derived from *God* the *Fountain* of Power,
and as being the *Great Inftrument* of fecuring *Right and Juftice* in the World; is indeed
juftly valuable, and moft reafonably attended with the Higheft Marks of *Dignity and
Efteem*. Upon which account, not only *Angels in Heaven*, but *Magiftrates* alfo upon
Earth, are in fome paffages of Scripture called *Gods*; and *God himfelf* is, upon the
fame ground, ftyled by *Antient Writers* the * *Fountain of Divinity*: Not, the *Fountain of the Deity*, as the words were in after-times *ignorantly* mifapplied: (For That,
is ftyling *God* the *Fountain of Himfelf*:) But the Fountain of *Divinity*, meaning all
That *Dignity, Authority and Power*, which is in Scripture at any time afcribed either
to *Angels* or to *Men*. *Power*, I fay, in *This fenfe*, as derived from God, and exercifed
to His Glory, and to the Benefit of the World; is indeed greatly valuable, and moft
juftly attended with all poffible Marks of Honour and Regard. But the *Defire of
Power* for the Purpofes of *Ambition* only, and for the *Pleafure* of bearing *Rule*; is
what the Apoftle here, with great propriety and ftrictnefs calls *The Pride of Life*; which
is not of the Father, but of the World. 'Tis *That Pride*, or *That* fetting up of *Self-
Will* in oppofition to *Reafon and Equity*, which is the Ground and Foundation of almoft *every* Immorality. The *Intemperances* and *Debaucheries* Men are guilty of, for
want of *Government of Themfelves*, are moft properly indeed included under the *Firft
Head*, which is the *Luft of the Flefh*. The *Second Head*, which is the Luft *of the Eyes*,
or the *Covetous Defire of Riches* for *Riches* fake, is alfo frequently the occafion of *much
Corruption*, of many and great *particular Acts* of *Injuftice* and *Hardfhip* towards
Others. But the moft *general* and *extenfive* caufe of an *habitually injurious* and *oppreffive*
Temper, is This *Pride of Life*; this Love of *Power*, *Domination*, and *Self-Will*.
From hence ufually arife *Wars*, *Defolations*, *Tyrannies*, and all the Great, *Extenfive*,
and *Mercilefs Oppreffions*, which totally extinguifh that univerfal Benevolence towards

---

* πηγὴ Θεότητος, not πηγὴ τῆ Θεότ. See, *Reply to Dr*. Waterland's *Defence*, p. 5, 48, 49, 219. And, *Obfervations on*
Dr. Waterland's *2d Defence*, p. * 53.

Mankind,

Mankind, which is the *Charity* reprefented in Scripture as *the Fulfilling of the* whole S E R M. *Law.* To the fame Caufe alfo are owing generally, all the *Great* Breaches of our Duty L. towards *God.* For, *Whence* arifes That ftrange *Negligence* and *Unconcernednefs* for the Difcovery of *Truth*, which is the Caufe of almoft all the Irreligion and Superftition in the World; but from this *Pride* of imagining, that our own *Wills, Pleafures* and *Paffions*, are *Guides* preferable to the *Reafon* and *Truth* of things? And whence comes it to pafs, that fo many *monftroufly abfurd Opinions* and *Idolatrous Practices* have prevailed in the Nations of the World; contrary to all the common *Senfe* and *Reafon* of Mankind, contrary to the *natural* Dictates of every man's own *Confcience*, and in oppofition to the proteftations and perpetual Endeavours of all *Rational* and *Virtuous* Men: Whence, I fay, has This come to pafs; but that it has beft ferved the Purpofes of *Ambition* and *Tyranny*, to keep Men in fuch *Ignorance* by all poffible *Frauds*, and in the continuance of fuch *Practices* by all the cruel Methods of *Violence?* And This may abundantly fuffice for explication of the *Firft* Particular; *What* the Apoftle here means by the *World* which he exhorts us *not to love*; and by *the Things that are in the World*, which (he faith) are *not of the Father, but of the World.*

II. I A M to confider *What* That *Love of the Father* is, with which the *Love of the World* is here declared to be inconfiftent. Many there are, who by this phrafe of *loving God*, feem to have meant nothing more than a mere *fpeculative imagination*, an *unintelligible enthufiaftick Warmth of Affection*, a *notional abftract Zeal*; fometimes *withdrawing* Men wholly into a retirement from the moft *ufeful Duties of Life*, and fometimes *not withdrawing them* from the *Vitious Practices of the World.* But the Scripture-fenfe of *loving God*, is exprefsly declared to be the *Keeping his Commandments*, the looking upon *Him*, as our *Supreme Governour*, and moft *Bountiful Benefactor* ; as a *Reafonable* Governour, whofe Commands are to be obeyed not only out of *Neceffity*, but out of *Choice*, with *cheerfulnefs* and *affection*, in *Preference* to every thing that would entice us to tranfgrefs them. And This being the cafe, the reafon immediately and evidently appears, why, *if any man love the World*, the *World* in the fenfe already explained, *the Love of the Father* cannot be *in him.* For, in the Nature of Things, where-ever two inconfiftent Objects offer themfelves *in competition*, the *Object preferred* is the *Object loved* ; and the preferring or choofing one before the other, is manifeftly inconfiftent with preferring the Other before That. *If any Man* therefore *loves the World*, *That World* here defcribed by the Apoftle, which *is not of the Father* ; the *Love of the Father* cannot poffibly be *in him* : For *no man can ferve Two Mafters.* Of neceffity he muft *either hate the one, and love the Other* ; *or elfe* he muft *hold to the* other, *and defpife* the firft: He *cannot ferve God and Mammon*, Matt. vi. 24. Whatever be a man's ultimate View and Aim ; (as every man always has *fome* principal and ultimate View ;) by *This* will the generality, at leaft of the *Material* Actions of his life, always be determined. If the Love of *Truth* and *Reafon* and *Right*, (or, which is the fame thing, a Regard to the *God* of Truth and Right,) be his *governing Principle* ; his *Defires* after, and his *Ufe* of, the *Pleafures, Riches, and Power* of *This World*, will, according to the natural Order and Defign of God's creation, always be *regulated by*, and *made fubfervient to*, thofe Greater and more Noble Ends. On the contrary, if thefe things, not as they are *In* the *world*, but as they are *Of* the *world, and not of the Father* ; if thefe things, in the manner they are here defcribed by the Apoftle, *the Luft of the Flefh, the Luft of the Eyes, and the Pride of Life* ; be the Object of a Man's Defires, principally and ultimately, as the main End which he has continually in View ; it cannot be but he will purfue his *Pleafures*, without regard to the limitations of Reafon and Religion ; he will heap up unto himfelf, *Riches*, by Methods inconfiftent with Juftice, Equity and Charity ; he will indeavour to raife himfelf to *Honour* by mean and unworthy Compliances ; and he will make Ufe of *Power* to arbitrary and unreafonable Purpofes.

S E R M. poſes. And for *This Caufe*, theſe things are in Scripture repreſented as being Enemies
L.   to God: So that, *if any man love the World, the Love of the Father is not in him.* With
Rom. xii. 1. regard to *Pleaſure* in particular, the Apoſtle St *Paul* exhorts: *I befeech you, brethren,*
            by the Mercies of God, that ye preſent your Bodies a living Sacrifice, holy, acceptable
Rom. viii. 7. *unto God, which is your reaſonable Service*; *And be not conformed to This World*: For
            the *Carnal* mind *is enmity againſt God*; *for it is not ſubject to the Law of God, neither*
            indeed can be: *So then they that are in the Fleſh, cannot pleaſe God.* And St *Peter*,
            1 Pet. i. 13, 14. *Be ſober,*——*as obedient children*; *Not faſhioning yourſelves according*
            to the former Luſts, in your ignorance; *But, as He which hath called you is holy, ſo be*
            Ye Holy in all manner of converſation. And St *James*, ch. iv. 4: *Ye Adulterers and*
            Adultereſſes; *know ye not, that the Friendſhip of the World is Enmity with God*; *Who-*
            ſoever therefore will be a Friend of the World, is the Enemy of God. In like manner
            with regard to *Riches*: In the paſſage before-cited, *They that will be Rich*, faith
            St *Paul*; that is, they who make *Riches* their ultimate *End* and *View*, will *fall into*
            Temptation and a Snare, and into many Fooliſh and Hurtful Luſts, which drown men
            in deſtruction and perdition, 1 Tim. vi. 9. And therefore in the ſame chapter, *ver.* 17.
            he mentions *Truſting in Riches* and *Truſting in the Living God*, as direct *Oppoſites* to
            each other. Laſtly, with Regard to the *Honours and Eſteem* of Men, and the corrupt
            and unworthy Compliances, by which the *Pride of Life* leads Men to aim at *Falſe*
            Reputation and *Power*; *Do I* (ſays the Apoſtle) *ſeek to pleaſe men? for if I yet pleaſed*
            Men, I ſhould not be the Servant of Chriſt, Gal. i. 10.

            IN *This* ſenſe therefore, and for *theſe Cauſes*, it is, that the *Love of the World*, and
            the *Love of God*, are in the Text declared to be inconſiſtent with each other. And as
            He who *loves the World*, the *Wicked World* in the ſenſe now explained, cannot have
            the *Love of the Father in him*: So, on the reverſe, if any Man has *the Love of the*
            Father in him, that is, acts ſteddily and immoveably upon the Principles of Truth
            and Virtue; to *Him* will the *World*, the *wicked and corrupt* part of the World, neceſ-
            ſarily bear a *Hatred*, Joh. xv. 19. *If ye were of the World, the World would love his*
            own; *but becauſe ye are not of the World, but I have choſen you out of the World,*
            therefore the World hateth you. And ch. xvii. 14. *The World hath hated them, becauſe*
            they are not of the World. The *Reaſon and Ground* of which Procedure, is excellently
            expreſſed by the Author of the Book of *Wiſdom*, ch. ii. 12. *Becauſe the Righteous is*
            not for Our Turn, and he is clean contrary to our Doings; *he upbraideth us with our*
            offending the Law, and objecteth to our Infamy the Tranſgreſſions of our education. He
            profeſſeth to have the Knowledge of God, and——*was made to reprove Our Thoughts.*

            III. THE *Third* and Laſt thing I propoſed, was to conſider the *Reaſons and Motives*
            upon which the Apoſtle here ſo earneſtly cautions Men againſt that *Love of the World*,
            which he thus deſcribes as inconſiſtent with the *Love of God.* Its *Inconſiſtency with the*
            Love of God, that is, of our *Supreme Good* and *ultimate Happineſs*; is itſelf One princi-
            pal and ſufficient *Motive.* But *This* and *all other Motives* whatſoever, are *included in,*
            o: *reducible to*, what the Apoſtle alledges in the words following my Text, *ver.* 17.
            The world paſſeth away, and the Luſt thereof; *but He that doth the Will of God, abid-*
            eth for ever. There *can* be *nothing* in *This World* worth purchaſing at the Expence
            of incurring the Divine diſpleaſure. For all the things that are in the World, even
            thoſe that are *innocent*, much more the *Sinful* ones here mentioned by the Apoſtle,
            are *obtained* with uneaſineſs and much Uncertainty, are *poſſeſſed* with much Mixture
            of Diſſatisfaction, are *preſerved* with continual Fear and Hazard of loſing them; And,
            when poſſeſſed in the higheſt Perfection, and for the longeſt Period, muſt of neceſſity
            paſs away in a very few years, to return no more for ever. That Habit of Mind, which
            is founded in the *Love of Truth*, and in the *Practice of Virtue*, is the only Thing that
            will continue and improve for ever into a compleat felicity in the eternal Kingdom of
            God.   3   SERMON

SERMON LI.

The Folly of Mocking at Sin.

PROV. XIV. 9.

Fools make a Mock at Sin.

THERE is nothing, concerning which Men of great Spirits are more apt to make a wrong Judgment, than concerning the Notion and true Extent of *Courage* and Magnanimity. Courage, is a Bravenefs of Mind, confifting and fhowing forth itfelf in a juft *Contempt of Danger*. And becaufe this is a Virtue moft ufually found in men of *better condition*, and of a *good education*; it is therefore generally accompanied with more *reputation and honour*, with more *Value and Efteem* in the World, than moft Other fingle Virtues. For this reafon, thofe who *are not* indued with this Virtue, are yet very defirous of being *thought to be* fo; and, as That which is moft *efteemed* is always moft in danger of being *counterfeited*, Falfe *Courage* is very apt to fupply the Place and the Want of *True*. For there *is* a Courage, which deferves not That Name; and there *is* a Hardinefs, which is *not* a *Virtue*, but a *Vice*. Something of this nature there may be obferved in the inftance of almoft *every* Virtue. *Superftition*, and *Forms*, and outward *Ceremonies*, too ufually fupply the place of true *Piety towards God*. *Covetoufnefs* calls itfelf *Frugality*; and the *name* of *Generofity* often covers the *real* crime of *Profufenefs*. The moft unchriftian Vices of *Uncharitablenefs* and *Perfecution* frequently pafs under the Title of *Zeal*; and *Love* towards *God*, is (in fome men's opinion) excellently expreffed by *Hatred* towards their *Brethren*, towards Men very often much more pious than themfelves. Thus likewife in the cafe of *Courage*; *Fool-hardinefs* too often puts on the Garb of this Virtue; and a fenfelefs *pretending* to *defpife*, what ought not and cannot be defpifed, ferves inftead of *really contemning* fuch Dangers, as ought to be contemned. Now the way to *diftinguifh* rightly, *when* Courage *is* really that Virtue which the name denotes, is to confider carefully its true Definition: Which, (as I before obferved) is This; It is a Greatnefs or Bravenefs of Mind, confifting and fhowing forth itfelf in a juft *Contempt of Danger*. Where therefore the Contempt of Danger is *juft* and *well-grounded*, there fuch Contempt is the True Virtue of Courage, a true Greatnefs and Bravery of Mind: But where the Contempt of Danger is *neither reafonable nor juft*, there it is *not* Courage, but *Fool-hardinefs* and *Madnefs*. For want of obferving this plain diftinction it comes to pafs, that whereas it is True Greatnefs and Bravery of Mind, for a Man to hazard his Life in the Defence of his *Country*, in Defence of the *common Rights and Liberties* of Mankind, in oppofition to the unjuft Invafions of ambitious *Tyrants*, and the Great *Oppreffors* of the World; *contempt of Danger*, in This cafe, being *juft and well-grounded*, becaufe a Man hazards Himfelf for the *Publick Benefit*, and for the *preventing* a much *greater and more extenfive Evil*, than the Lofs of his own fingle Life: From hence paffionate and unreafonable Men ignorantly call it *Courage*, to hazard their Lives in their *own* private *Quarrels*; where *Contempt of Danger* is, on the contrary, neither

S E R M. *reasonable nor just* ; becauʃe, neither is the Danger at all needful to be run into,
LI. nor is the Benefit propoʃed to be obtained by it, in any manner equal to the Evil
hazarded. Again: Whereas it is True Greatneʃs of Mind, to be *above* all vain
Superʃtitions, to *deʃpiʃe* all falʃe and groundleʃs *Imaginations*, not to be terrified
with *empty Phantoms* nor fear *where no Fear is* ; hence weak and profane Men
have ridiculouʃly attempted, to cauʃe it to be looked upon as a piece of Courage
and Gallantry, to *deʃpiʃe* the *real* Differences of Good and Evil ; to *mock* at *Truth*
in common with *Error*, and at *Religion* and *Virtue* equally with *Superʃtition* ; to
affect to be *above* the Obligations even of the moʃt *reaʃonable* and *neceʃʃary Laws*,
without which no *Order*, no *Government*, no *Peace* could poʃʃibly ʃubʃiʃt in the World;
laʃtly, to dare *undauntedly to revile the Maker of all things*, and ʃhow their *Fearleʃʃneʃs*
even of *God himʃelf*, by openly trampling upon his *Commandments* in their *Lives*, and
reproaching his *Name* by *vain Oaths and profane Speeches*. The Fortitude of theʃe
Men, is like *that* Courage of a Soldier, who not daring to do his common Duty againʃt
the publick Enemy, ʃhould be perpetually ʃhowing his Proweʃs in bravely refuʃing to
obey the Orders of his proper Commander. And the *Liberty* Theʃe Heroes in Vice
promiʃe to their Followers, in diʃcharging them from all Obligations of Virtue, and
from all fear of God, is excellently deʃcribed by St *Peter*, in his 2d epiʃtle, ch. ii. 18.
When they ʃpeak great ʃwelling words of Vanity, they allure through the Luʃts of the
Fleʃh, thoʃe that were clean eʃcaped from Them who live in Error ; While they promiʃe
them Liberty, they themʃelves are the Servants of Corruption ; For of whom a man is
overcome, of the ʃame is he brought in bondage. Theʃe are the perʃons, who, in the *worʃt*
and *higheʃt* Senʃe of the phraʃe, *make a Mock at Sin* ; and who are accordingly in Scripture
repreʃented as being guilty of the *worʃt* and *higheʃt* degree of *Folly. Fools*, that is, thoʃe
who in a *ʃingular* manner, and by way of *emphaʃis* or diʃtinction *above* all Others, de-
ʃerve the Name of Fools, are They which *make a Mock at Sin. Weakneʃʃes* there are
in *all* Men ; and the *Moʃt* are too often guilty of ʃuch Actions, as would in ʃtrictneʃs
rank them, in thoʃe *particulars* at leaʃt, among the *Unwiʃe*. But the *compleat* character of Folly, or that which renders a Man in his *whole* denomination, according to
the Scripture-ʃenʃe, a *Fool* ; is the *making a mock at Sin*. Not, being deluded into it
by *Ignorance* or *Miʃtake* ; Not, being ʃeduced into it by *Inadvertency* or *Surprize* ; But,
knowingly and deliberately looking upon it as *trivial matter* ; mocking at it as a thing
harmleʃs, and of *no great Danger* ; This is the proper *Eʃʃence*, This (if I may ʃo ʃpeak)
is the *Perfection of Folly*. Nevertheleʃs, becauʃe even of *This*, there are *Differences*
and Degrees ; and of the *Mockers* here ʃpoken of by the Wiʃe-Man, there are *Diverʃe*
kinds ; I ʃhall therefore in the following Diʃcourʃe endeavour briefly, but diʃtinctly, to
ʃhew ; 1ʃt, What is *meant* more *particularly*, by *making a* Mock *at Sin* ; 2dly, Upon
what *grounds or reaʃons*, Men are tempted to be guilty of the ʃeveral degrees of This
Vice ; and 3dly, How *weak* all thoʃe Grounds really are, and how *great* the *Folly* of
upon them.

I. In the *Firʃt* place, as to the explication of the Phraʃe, *making a* Mock *at Sin* ;
there are three ʃorts of Sinners, who, in their ʃeveral Degrees, may juʃtly be charged
Acting with This Guilt. Of the

1ʃt and *higheʃt* Degree, are thoʃe whom I have partly *already* deʃcribed, who eʃteem
it a piece of *Courage* to deʃpiʃe all Religion, and a *Greatneʃs of Mind* to deride all the
Obligations of Virtue. Theʃe are the Perʃons the Pʃalmiʃt means, when he elegantly
riʃes by *Steps* in his deʃcription of Sinners, from the loweʃt degree of Wickedneʃs to the
higheʃt ; Pʃ. i. 1 ; *Bleʃʃed is the man, that hath not walked in the Council of the ungodly,*
nor ʃtood in the way of Sinners, and hath not ʃat in the Seat *of the* Scornful. The Scornful, are thoʃe whom the Prophet *Jeremy* repreʃents under the *ʃame* Character, and in
the Uʃe of the *ʃame* word, as the Wiʃe Man in the Text ; Jer. xv. 17 ; *I ʃat not in the*

2　　　　　　　　　　　　　　　　　　　　　　　　　　　　　　*Aʃʃembly*

Affembly of the Mockers. To fit (the word ufed both by *Jeremiah* and by the *Pfalmift,)* fignifies a *fixed, determinate, fecure, refolute* eftablifhment in a *Habit* of Wickednefs; whereas *walking,* or *ftanding,* in the way of Sinners, reprefents only *particular* wicked *Actions.* And the Seat of the Scornful (which is the *Pfalmift's* phrafe) fignifies the *Higheft Power* and *Dominion* of Impiety. Juft as *our Saviour,* in the *Revelations,* elegantly defcribes the Tyranny of the Antichriftian Church, by calling it *The Throne of Satan;* Rev. ii. 13; *I know thy works, and where thou dwelleft, even where Satan's Seat* (in the Original it is, *where Satan's* Throne) *is.* The Perfons who, in *This* fenfe, *make a Mock at Sin,* are the *Atheifts,* and the *openly Profane;* Thofe who think it *Wit,* to turn the moft *ferious* matters into *Ridicule;* and commit the moft *unjuft and unrighteous Actions,* without Any reluctancy or *Abhorrence.* Thefe are the Perfons whom *Solomon* defcribes, Prov. x. 23; *It is as* Sport *to a Fool, to do mifchief;* and ch. xxvi. 18; *As a Mad-man who cafteth Firebrands, Arrows and Death; fo is the man that deceiveth his Neighbour, and faith, Am not I in fport?* The *fame* fort of Perfons, are in the New *Teftament* mentioned by St *Jude,* ver. 17. of his Epiftle; *Remember,* faith he, *the words, which were fpoken before of the Apoftles of our Lord Jefus Chrift, how they told you there fhould be* Mockers *in the laft time, who fhould walk after their own ungodly Lufts.*

T H E Y who think it an *Objection* againft the Truth of Chriftianity, that there fhould be found, even in the World that calls itfelf *Chriftian,* fo much open Profanenefs and Impiety as there is; may do well to obferve, how diftinctly thefe things are *foretold* in the New Teftament; and confequently that the *Fulfilling of them* is not an Argument *againft,* but a ftrong Evidence *for,* the truth of revealed Religion.

2dly; T H E *next* fort of Sinners, who may juftly be charged with *making a Mock at Sin,* are thofe, who do not indeed in *Words,* like Thofe before-mentioned; but yet, in their *Actions,* do equally bring Contempt upon Religion. In their *Profeffion* they pretend to *believe in God,* but their *Practice* is the fame with that of *Atheifts and Infidels.* Thefe are elegantly defcribed by St *Paul;* Tit. i. 16; *They* profefs, *that they know God; but in* Works *they deny him; being abominable, and difobedient, and unto every good work reprobate.* This *practical Infult* upon Religion, This *Contempt* of Virtue and Goodnefs in men's *Lives and Actions,* is as *really* in the Sight of *God,* though not fo *offenfively* in the Eye of the *World,* a *making a Mock at Sin,* in the Senfe of the Text; as the moft *profane Speeches* even of *profeffed Atheifts.*

3dly; T O *make a Mock at Sin,* may, in the *laft* place, fignify, entertaining fo *flight* an Opinion of the *Evil and Danger* of Sin, as makes men who are *not* entirely profligate, yet content themfelves with *diftant* refolutions of future Repentance, and in the mean time fpeak Peace to themfelves in the Practice of Unrighteoufnefs, or in the Injoyment of unlawful Pleafures. This may properly enough be called, though not in fo *high* a fenfe as the forementioned Inftances, *a making a Mock at Sin.* It is a *feeming* to be *afraid* of it, and yet *not really* abhorring it. It is entring voluntarily into the Snare of the Devil, and yet not daring to refolve to continue in it. It is running into a Danger, with a Defign to come out of it again; *as a Bird hafteth to the Snare, and knoweth not that it is for his Life.* In a word; it is *playing* with the Inftruments of *Death,* and *fporting* with *Deftruction;* for want of *ferioufly* and *in earneft* confidering, what a dreadful thing it is to fall into the hands of the Living God, whofe Wrath is a confuming Fire. The Defcription of *Leviathan* in the Book of *Job;* ch. xli. 5; may very naturally be applied to This Purpofe; *Wilt thou play with him as with a Bird? or wilt thou bind him for thy maidens? Shall the Companions make a Banquet of him? fhall they part him among the Merchants? Canft thou fill his fkin with barbed irons, or his Head with Fifh-fpears? Lay thine hand upon him, remember the Battle, do no more.*

II. A N D

SERM. II. A N D now, having shown particularly, *what* is meant by this phrase of *making*
LI. *a mock at Sin*; I proceed, in the 2d place, to consider *upon what Grounds or Reasons*
men are tempted to be guilty of the several degrees of this Vice. And

1st, As to those *Sitters in the Seat of the Scornful*; those *profane* Spirits, who esteem
it a mark of *Courage* to despise all Religion, and a *Greatness of Mind* to deride all the
Obligations of Virtue: The *only* Ground *These* have to go upon, is *Atheism* and *Infidelity.* Either they must disbelieve the *Being of God,* and disclaim all difference of
good and evil, and renounce in general all expectation of a future State; or at least they
must reject all divine *Revelation,* casting behind them all the Promises and Threatnings
of God, and denying that he will ever judge men according to their Works. This
is excellently represented to us by St *Peter,* in his Second Epistle; ch. iii. 3 ; *There shall
come,* saith he, *in the last days Scoffers, walking after their own Lusts, and saying,
Where is the Promise of his coming? For since the Fathers fell asleep, all things continue
as they were, from the Beginning of the Creation.* The Persons the Apostle here describes, looked upon all things as going on, it seems, in a constant and necessary
Course of Nature: One generation of men passed away, and another came in the room
of it; but the World remained still as it was; And thus, for ought *They* knew, things
Eccl. i. 9.   might hold on for ever. *The thing which Hath been,* they thought, *is That which
Shall be; and that which Is done, is That which shall be done; and there is no New thing
under the Sun.* Upon This foundation, the same kind of Debauchees argue with
themselves in *All* Ages; *Let us eat and drink, for to morrow we die. Come ye,* say they,
I will fetch wine, Is. lvi. 12, *and we will fill ourselves with strong drink, and to morrow shall be as This day, and much more abundant.* There is a most elegant description
of This sort of Sinners, in the 2d chapter of the Book of *Wisdom*; ver. 1 ; *The Ungodly
said, reasoning, with themselves, but not aright;—We are born at all adventures, and
we shall be hereafter as though we had never been; for the Breath in our Nostrils is as
smoak, and a little Spark in the moving of our Heart:———Come on therefore, let us enjoy the good things that are present, and let us speedily use the creatures like as in youth:
Let us oppress the poor righteous man, let us not spare the widow, nor reverence the gray
hairs of the aged; Let our Strength be the Law of Justice, for that which is feeble is
found to be nothing worth.* Thus the *only* foundation *This kind* of *Mockers* build upon,
is the Hope that there will be *no* future state, *no* judgment to come.

2dly; T H E *second* sort; those who pretend to *believe* a God, and *another life* after
this, and yet live as viciously as if they believed it *not.* The manner of *These,* is to
flatter themselves with a Notion, that *Sin* is *not* of so dangerous a nature, as the Preachers of the Gospel represent it: that *Morality,* or Righteousness of Life, is not absolutely
of indispensable importance; and that God will be very well satisfied with a *Form* of
Godliness, with a *Zeal* for *Names and Distinctions* of Religion, though not accompanied with *Moral Virtue.* And then

3dly; As to the *last* sort of Men, who (I said) might also justly be charged with being in some degree guilty of the same Vice of *making a Mock at Sin*; namely, those
who are really sensible of the Necessity of true Repentance and Amendment, and yet at
the present speak Peace to themselves in the Practice of Unrighteousness, or in the Injoyment of unlawful Pleasures: The *only* Foundation *These* can possibly go upon, is an
artificial Design of securing to themselves Both *Worlds,* and of ingrossing *more* Happiness than either God or Nature designed them; by injoying securely the Pleasures of
Sin for a Season, and at the End by Repentance obtaining the Reward of *Virtue* likewise. This what the Apostle calls, *mocking of* God; *Gal.* vi. 7 ; and is indeed more truly
a *mocking* or *deceiving* of Themselves. As will appear, if we proceed now, in the *Third*
place,

III. T o

III. To confider, how *Weak* all the forementioned *Grounds or Reafons* are, upon S E R M. which men are tempted to be guilty of the feveral Degrees of this Vice; and confe- LI. quently how *Great* the *Folly* is of Acting upon thofe Grounds: Fools *make a mock at Sin.* And;

1*ft*; As to that *higheft* degree of *Profane Mockers*, who have *no other* Hope to reft upon but that of *Atheifm and Infidelity*; *Their* Folly is *greater* than can be exprefied in words, or that can rightly be conceived by any Imagination. For; *What* is the State of fuch a perfon, when God taketh away his Soul? Can he be *fure* that there is *no God?* or can he *demonftrate* to himfelf, that there will be no future ftate? The Hardieft *Un-believer* never yet pretended to have *demonftration* in this cafe. And if he had, yet al the Comfort, all the Hopes, that could be built even upon *That*, would be but the Hope of a Beaft, the Expectation of perifhing as if he had never been. But fince there *can be no* fuch demonftration; on the fide of Atheifm; the confequent Poffibility on the *other* fide, that there may *be* a *God*, proves the Folly of the profane Mocker to be *in-tolerable*; the *Probability* that there *is* a God, ftill *increafes* That Folly; the *Certainty*, the *Demonftration*, that there *cannot but be* a God, fhows it to be what *Solomon* elegantly fets forth in that accumulative expreffion; *Ecclef.* vii. 25: the Wickednefs *of Folly*, *even of Foolifhnefs and* Madnefs. For if there *is* a God, as the Works of Nature demonftrate that there is; both *Reafon itfelf* declares, and *Revelation* fully confirms, that he *will* govern the World in Righteoufnefs, and in the End judge every man according to his Works. That *poor* Objection of the Scoffers mentioned by St *Peter*, that all things *hitherto* continue as they were from the Beginning of the Creation, and that therefore they *never* will be otherwife; difcovers the extreme Shortnefs of Thofe men's Underftandings, who confider not that God with much long-fuffering gives men Space of Repentance; and can as eafily judge the World after a Thoufand years as after One day's fpace: Upon which delay of his Lord's Coming, if any wicked Servant flatters himfelf that he will not come at all; and upon that Affurance of Impunity hardens himfelf in his Impiety; *the Lord of That Servant* will *come in a day when he looketh not for him, and in an hour that he is not aware of, and will cut him afunder, and appoint him his portion with the Hypocrites; there fhall be weeping and gnafhing of Teeth.* For, *as in the days that were before the Flood, men were eating and drinking, marrying and giving in marriage, until the day that Noah entered into the Ark; And knew not until the Flood came; and took them all away:* And, *as it was in the days of Lot, they did eat, they drank, they bought, they fold, they planted, they builded; But the fame day that Lot went out of Sodom, it rained fire and brimftone from Heaven, and deftroyed them all: Even thus* (fays our Lord) *fhall it be, in the day when the Son of Man is revealed*; St *Luke* xvii. 30; Then fhall the Lord *convince* ungodly men of all *their hard* and profane *Speeches which they have fpoken againft him:* And the wicked, feeing the Salvation of the righteous, *fhall with anguifh of Spirit fay within themfelves*, (as it is elegantly expreffed in the Book of *Wifdom*, ch. v. 4;) *We* Fools *accounted his Life Madnefs, and his End to be without Honour; How is he numbred among the children of God, and his Lot is among the Saints!*

2*dly*, As to thofe who cannot argue themfelves into Infidelity, but *believe* the Certainty of a Future State and of a Judgment to come; and yet live vicioufly, and continue Impenitent, upon a *general, loofe*, and *inconfiderate* expectation, that Sin is lefs *dangerous*, and God more *merciful*, than the Preachers of the Gofpel reprefent him: The Folly of making a Mock at Sin in *This* Senfe, and upon *This* Ground; (which is indeed nothing elfe, but refolving to *neglect* a *mortal Difeafe* as of *no Danger*, and to fhut *one's* Eyes upon the Mouth of *Deftruction:*) The *Folly of This*, I fay, is well reproved by the Author of the Book of *Eccluf.* ch. xxi. 2; *My Son,——flee from Sin as from the Face of a Serpent; for——the Teeth thereof are as the Teeth of a Lion, flaying*

S E R M. *the Souls of Men, and, All iniquity is as a two-edged sword, the wounds whereof cannot be*
LI. *healed.* To imagine that God will be pleased with an empty Form of Godliness, and
accept a *Zeal* for *mere* Names *and Distinctions of Religion,* without true *Virtue and Holiness* of Life, is, to be so foolish as to think *God* more easily deceived, even than mortal *Men*; and that the *Searcher of Hearts* will be imposed upon with an outward *Profession* of Service, which even an *Earthly Superior* would with indignation reject. *Little
children,* saith St *John, let no man deceive you: He that* Doth *righteousness, is righteous.*
The Vain Hope of those who rely on any Other Foundation, is affectionately described
in the 5th chapter of the Book of *Wisdom*; ver. 14; *The Hope of the Ungodly, is like
Dust that is blown away with the Wind; like a thin Froth, that is driven away with the
Storm; like as the Smoke which is dispersed here and there with a Tempest; and passeth
away as the Remembrance of a Guest, that tarrieth but a day: But the Righteous live
for evermore; their Reward also is with the Lord, and the Care of them is with the most
High.*

3*dly* and *lastly*; As to those who are truly sensible of the indispensable Necessity of
a Virtuous life, and yet *at the present* speak peace to themselves in the Practice of Unrighteousness and in the injoyment of Unlawful Pleasures, upon an Intention of Repenting and Amending *hereafter*: The *Folly* of making a mock at Sin in *This* sense, is the
Folly of Playing *with Death,* and Sporting *with Destruction*: It is the *Folly* of letting
slip opportunities, which possibly, nay, very probably, may never be retrieved: It is
the *Folly* of provoking God to cut us off in his Wrath, and to assign us our Portion a-
mong Hypocrites and Unbelievers. To conclude; It is the *Folly* of *incapacitating* a
man's self *more and more* for the doing of That, which yet is of absolute Necessity not
to be left undone. For except we do effectually repent and amend, and That speedily
too, so as to bring forth the Fruits of Virtue and Righteousness, we must inevitably
perish: And yet the longer any man continues in Sin, the more difficult it becomes for
him to leave it off. For he grows *hardened* at length through the Deceitfulness of
Sin; and by being long *accustomed to do Evil,* it becomes in a manner (figuratively and
comparatively speaking) as difficult for him to *learn to do well,* as for the *Ethiopian to
change his Skin, or the Leopard his Spots.* The Prophet *Jeremy* most elegantly sets forth
the *same* Difficulty in *another* Comparison, wherewith I shall conclude; ch. xii. 5; *If
thou hast run with Footmen, and They have wearied thee, then How canst thou contend
with Horses? And if in the Land of Peace, wherein thou trustedst, they wearied thee,
then How wilt thou do in the Swelling of Jordan?*

THAT every One of *Us,* may in Time set about the Practice of our Duty, before
our Feet stumble upon the dark Mountains, and the things that belong to our Peace
be hid from our Eyes; God of his infinite mercy, grant, &c.

SERMON

SERMON LII.

Of that Belief which is neceſſary to Baptiſm.

St MARK XVI. 16.

*He that believeth and is baptized, ſhall be ſaved; But he that be-
lieveth not, ſhall be damned.*

THESE Words, together with the Verſe foregoing, are an *Abridgment* of
our Saviour's laſt inſtructions and directions to his Diſciples, a little before his
Departure from them and Aſcenſion into Heaven: *He ſaid unto them, Go
ye into all the World, and preach the Goſpel to every creature: He that believeth and
is baptized, ſhall be ſaved; But he that believeth not, ſhall be damned.* And that they
are nothing more than ſuch a brief Summary or *Abridgement* of his Diſcourſe, is evident, both from the *whole Tenor* of the Goſpels in *general*, wherein almoſt *All* his Diſcourſes are recorded after This manner, in One more briefly, in Another more at
large; and *particularly* from comparing the Account the ſeveral Goſpels give us, of
this very particular.

For *St Matthew* in *His* Goſpel, has left us upon record ſome *other* parts of the
ſame Diſcouſe, ch. xxviii. 18, *All Power,* ſays our Lord, *is given unto me in Heaven
and in Earth: Go ye therefore and teach all Nations, baptizing them in the Name of
the Father, and of the Son, and of the Holy Ghoſt; Teaching them to obſerve all Things
whatſoever I have commanded you; and lo, I am with you always, even unto the end of
the World.* The Words, *Teaching them to obſerve all things whatſoever I have commanded you,* ſhow that even *This* alſo, is but another ſhort Abridgment of the ſame
Diſcourſe.

St *Luke,* in *His* Goſpel, gives us a ſtill *more particular* Account, how our Lord appeared to his Diſciples in the way to *Emmaus,* and *beginning at Moſes and all the
Prophets, expounded unto them in all the Scriptures the things concerning himſelf,*
ch. xxiv. 27. And afterwards at another Appearance before his Aſcending, ver. 45,
*Then opened he their Underſtanding, that they might underſtand the Scriptures; And ſaid
unto them; Thus it is written, and thus it behoved Chriſt to ſuffer, and to riſe from the
dead the third day; And that Repentance and Remiſſion of Sins ſhould be preached in his
Name among all Nations, beginning at Jeruſalem; And ye are Witneſſes of theſe
things.*

St *John* adds ſeveral other Circumſtances; of his particularly convincing St *Thomas;*
of his appearing at ſeveral other times to his Apoſtles; and of his uſing the following
Words to them in his laſt Inſtructions, ch. xx. 21, *As my Father hath ſent me, even
ſo ſend I you;——Whoſoever Sins ye remit, they are remitted unto them; and whoſoever Sins ye retain, they are retained.* That is; whoſoever receiveth the Doctrine I
ſend you to preach, for the Remiſſion of Sins, and complieth with the Terms thereof,
his Sins ſhall be forgiven: Or, as the ſame Senſe is expreſſed by other Words in the
Text, *He that believeth, and is baptized, ſhall be ſaved.* But whoſoever rejecteth your
Doctrine, and complieth not with the Conditions therein offered him from God; his

SERM.
LII.

Sins

SERM.
LII.
Sins ſhall be retained, and he muſt conſequently periſh. In the Phraſe of the *Text*; *he that believeth not, ſhall be damned.*

St *Luke*, in his Hiſtory of the *Acts*, tells us yet further, that our Lord was ſeen of his Diſciples after his Paſſion for *forty days* together, *Acts* i. 3; and that That time was ſpent in inſtructing them in *the Things pertaining to the Kingdom of God.*

FROM theſe ſeveral Paſſages compared together, 'tis evident, that St *Mark* did not intend the Words of the Text ſhould be taken to be the *very* Words, and the *whole* of the Words, which our Saviour ſpake; but on the contrary, that they ſhould be underſtood only as an *Abridgement* of his laſt inſtructions to his Diſciples; and ſo not to be taken in their bare literal Signification, but as well known by common Uſe, in a ſhort and abbreviate manner of ſpeaking, to comprehend more than they might otherwiſe ſeem at firſt ſight to expreſs. In order to underſtand therefore their full meaning, we ought to take Notice, that to the Words *Believe* and *be Baptized*, St *Luke*, in relating our Saviour's giving theſe very ſame Inſtructions to his Apoſtles, adds *Repentance* for the Remiſſion of Sins; And St *Matthew* adds further, Obſerving *all things whatſoever I have commanded you.* And thence it will appear, that by *believing* and *being baptized*, St *Mark* plainly means, *Believing, Repenting, and Obeying the Goſpel.* All which, there was no need to expreſs at length; becauſe it was perfectly well underſtood in the common Uſe and Acceptation of each of thoſe Words among Chriſtians, that the part was always ſuppoſed to be put, in a brief way of ſpeaking, for the whole; and that, where-ever any *One* of theſe Words was uſed, it always ſignified the ſame as if all *Three* were expreſſed. The Reaſon whereof is plain; Becauſe in reality theſe things cannot be ſeparated from each other; To *believe* the Goſpel, without *repenting* and *obeying* it, being *not* indeed *believing* it, but only *pretending* to do ſo. And hence it is, that, throughout the whole New Teſtament, *Faith* generally ſignifies, not bare abſtract Belief, but the whole Obligation of the Chriſtian Religion, including *Repentance, Fidelity, and Obedience*; juſt as *Repentance* likewiſe ſignifies, not the bare Sorrow for Sin, but the actual *forſaking* it alſo, and the effectual *reforming* our manners. *Baptiſm* alſo muſt always be underſtood to ſignify, not the bare Rite, the outward Form or Ceremony, *the waſhing away of the Filth of the Fleſh*; but *the Anſwer of a good Conſcience towards God*: Not the being baptized with *Water* only, but the being *born of Water and of the Spirit*: Not the being baptized only into the Name *of the Father and of the Son and of the Holy Ghoſt*; but the being *taught* alſo *to* obſerve *whatſoever I have commanded you*; as our Saviour adds in the very Words of Inſtitution, St *Matt.* xxviii. 20. To *believe* therefore, and to *be baptized*; is to believe *the Goſpel*, and to enter into a *ſolemn Obligation to* obey *it*. And as, under the *Law*, to him that tranſgreſſed the Law, his *Circumciſion* (ſays the Apoſtle) *is made Uncircumciſion*; ſo under the *Goſpel*, to him that obeys not the Goſpel, his *Baptiſm* is *no Baptiſm* to any ſpiritual Purpoſe, but a mere natural Waſhing of the Body, without Fruit or Efficacy. In like manner on the other ſide, the *Unbelief* of them who in Scripture are condemned for *Not believing*, is not the bare Negative Disbelief of what men do not clearly Know, or have not ſufficient Means of coming to the Knowledge of; but always, either an obſtinate rejecting of what is diſtinctly propoſed to them, and, through the Love of Vice, refuſing to conſider what might be ſufficiently proved to them; or elſe, and indeed more uſually, it ſignifies, the Diſobedience of thoſe who hypocritically profeſs, or perhaps careleſſly fancy themſelves, to be Believers. In either of theſe Senſes, *He that believeth not*, ſaith our Saviour, *ſhall be damned.* And there was no need of adding in this ſecond Clauſe, as he had done in the firſt, any mention of *Baptiſm*: Becauſe, in the *firſt* Caſe, *Believing* is *not* ſufficient without entering into the Obligation to obey, and therefore *Both* were neceſſary to be diſtinctly mentioned; but, in the *latter* caſe, *Unbelief* implies *in courſe* the Neglecting or the renouncing of Baptiſm, and therefore

I

it was ſufficient that That alone was expreſſed. The full meaning therefore of the Words of the Text, compared with the paſſages in the *other* Goſpels, wherein the ſame Hiſtory is recorded, is This. He that believes the Doctrine of the Goſpel when preached to him, and by Baptiſm enters into an Obligation to live ſuitably to that Belief, and verifies that Obligation by his following Practice, in a Life of Virtue, Righteouſneſs and Charity; the ſame ſhall be ſaved: But he that rejects the Doctrine of the Goſpel, when duly and reaſonably propoſed to him; or pretending to embrace it, yet obeys it not; (Both which, in Scripture-phraſe, are equally ſtiled *Unbelief*;) the ſame ſhall be damned.

T H E general Meaning of the Words being thus briefly explained, I ſhall in the following Diſcourſe, for the more particular juſtifying the ſeveral Parts of This Explication, and for the more clearly illuſtrating ſo univerſal and important a Doctrine, endeavour to ſhow diſtinctly, *1ſt*, What the *Thing to be believed*, or what the *Subject-matter* of that Belief is, which our Saviour here declares to be ſo neceſſary to Salvation. *2dly*, What the *Manner* of the Belief, or what the *Nature and Extent* of that *Act* of Believing is, which is here ſo indiſpenſably required. *3dly*, Whence it comes to paſs, that *Believing*, which in other caſes is a Matter of Indifference, of Prudence or Underſtanding only, and not of Morality; yet in the Caſe of Religion, is ſo highly eſteemed: And Theſe with regard to the *former* part of the Words; *He that believeth, and is baptized, ſhall be ſaved.* Then with regard to the latter part of the Words; *He that believeth not, ſhall be damned*; I ſhall inquire *1ſt*, What is the full and proper meaning of this Phraſe of *not believing*; and *2dly*, Whence it comes to paſs, that *Unbelief* is in Scripture always ſo ſeverely cenſured, as being the greateſt of Crimes.

I N the *1ſt* place, It is a matter of the greateſt importance, to inquire *What* the *Thing to be believed*, or what the *Subject-matter* of that Belief is, which our Saviour here declares to be ſo neceſſary to Salvation. And becauſe it *is* neceſſary to every man's Salvation, to whom the Goſpel is duly preached; 'tis therefore evident at firſt Sight, that it muſt of Neceſſity be ſomething, which every man is equally capable of underſtanding. For that God ſhould make any thing neceſſary to any man's Salvation, which That man, to whom it is neceſſary, is not made capable of underſtanding and knowing; is contrary to common Senſe, and to the Nature of God the righteous Judge. The Doctrine of the Goſpel therefore, on the Belief whereof our Saviour in the Text makes *all* men's Salvation to depend; (that is, the Salvation of *all* men to *whom* that Doctrine is duly and reaſonably propoſed;) is not, cannot be, any Matter of Intricacy and Difficulty, any thing that requires Learning or Subtilty to apprehend; but 'tis a Doctrine of *Practice*, a Doctrine of *Virtue* and *Righteouſneſs*, propoſed as of Neceſſity to be embraced by All men alike; by the Learned and the Ignorant, by the Rich and the Poor, by the Wiſe and the Simple, by the Teacher and by the Meaneſt of Them that are taught. For ſince they All have Souls alike to be ſaved, and muſt All appear equally before the Judgment-Seat of Chriſt; 'tis plain they muſt All underſtand the Rule by which they are to be judged; and That Rule muſt conſequently be level to the Capacities of them All. *Degrees* indeed of Knowledge there are; and accordingly to whom much or little is given, of him proportionably will much or little be required. But as to the main *Body* of the Rule, the great and *Fundamental* Doctrines of Religion, the things *covenanted about* at Baptiſm, the things to be known and believed as of *general* abſolute *Neceſſity* to Salvation; theſe cannot but be equally intelligible to perſons of all Capacities. And accordingly the Character the Scripture gives us of the Doctrine of the Goſpel, is This; that it is made *plain, that he that runs may read it*, Hab. ii. 2. And in the Prophecy of *Jeremiah*, ch. xxxi. 33. applied by St *Paul*, Heb. viii. 11. *I will put my laws into their mind, ſaith the Lord, and write them in their Hearts; ——and they ſhall not teach every man his Neighbour, and every man his Brother, ſay-*

 ing,

SERM. *ing, Know the Lord; For all ſhall know me from the leaſt to the greateſt.* And again,
LII. *Deut.* xxx. 11. exprefsly applied by the Apoſtle to the Doctrine of Chriſt, *Rom.* x. 6.
The commandment which I command thee This day, is not hidden from thee, neither is it far off; it is not in Heaven, that thou ſhouldſt ſay, Who ſhall go up for us to Heaven, and bring it unto us, that we may hear it and do it? Neither is it beyond the Sea, that thou ſhouldſt ſay, Who ſhall go over the Sea for us, and bring it unto us, that we may hear it and do it? But the Word is very nigh unto thee, even in thy mouth and in thy heart, that thou mayeſt do it. And here, 'tis very obvious to ask; if the Doctrine, of which our Saviour declares, that *he who believes and is baptized* into it, *ſhall be ſaved,* be ſo very plain, and nigh unto us; *Where* then is it *exprefsly* and *explicitly* to be found? and *what* is it, that every ſincere, every well-diſpoſed perſon, may ſo eaſily underſtand; and, by embracing and being guided by it, be undoubtedly ſaved? I anſwer: 'Tis as to its ultimate and moſt eſſential parts implanted in our very nature and reaſon. 'Tis more diſtinctly and authoritatively delivered to us in the Diſcourſes of our Saviour, and in the Writings of the Apoſtles; and repeated over and over again, and inculcated perpetually throughout the whole Scripture. The Sermons of our Saviour himſelf in the Goſpels, are ſo plain and intelligible, that hardly any well-diſpoſed perſon *can* miſunderſtand them. In the Epiſtles of the Apoſtles, the plain and univerſally neceſſary Doctrines, are intermixed indeed with particular and more difficult determinations of certain points of Controverſy, peculiarly neceſſary and well-known in Thoſe Times; uſeful and inſtructive at *all* times to All that have Capacities and Abilities to conſider the ſeveral Occaſions of their being written; but not abſolutely and indiſpenſably needful to be exactly underſtood by every ſingle Chriſtian for his own Salvation. The Primitive Church therefore, uſed to ſelect out of Theſe, the univerſally neceſſary and Fundamental Doctrines, wherein to inſtruct All perſons, who, by believing and being baptized, were deſirous to ſecure to themſelves the Promiſe in the Text, that, by ſo doing, they ſhould be ſaved. In which Matter, that the Authority of the Doctrines revealed immediately from God, might be diminiſhed as little as poſſible by any mixture of human Fallibility; they kept as near as could be, to the very Words themſelves, the undoubted and indiſputable Words of Scripture. And the Sum of the Doctrines ſo expreſſed, as of Neceſſity to be believed by All to whom they were preached, was after This or the like manner. That there is One God, the Father and Lord of All things, the Maker of Heaven and Earth; the Preſerver, Governour, and Judge of All; who is above All, and through All, and in us All. That by the Sins and Impieties of Men, this Supreme Governour of the World, who is of purer Eyes than to behold Iniquity, was juſtly offended; and They conſequently, become the Objects of his Anger and Diſpleaſure. That yet compaſſionating the Frailty of our Nature, he reſolved to have Mercy upon ſinful Man, in ſuch a manner, as not to give countenance or incouragement to Sin; and accordingly ſent forth his own Son, the Brightneſs of his Glory, and the expreſs Image of his Perſon, both to condemn Sin in the Fleſh, and at the ſame time to obtain pardon for it, by the ſhedding of his own blood. That, to this end, the Son of God freely and willingly left the boſom of his Father, was incarnate and made in the likeneſs of Man, became ſubject to all the infirmities and weakneſſes of our Nature; lived therein holily and purely, without ſpot of Sin; preached and declared the Will of his Father to Mankind; ſet an Example of all Virtue, Righteouſneſs and Patience in his Converſation; gave himſelf up into the Hands of Wicked Men, to be crucified and ſlain for our Sins; roſe again the third day from the Dead; aſcended up into Heaven, and ſat down on the right Hand of the Throne of God; and ſent forth his Holy Spirit, (the ſame Spirit of God, which ſpake of old by the Prophets,) to inſpire his Apoſtles in like manner, and inable them with Power and Authority to preach Repentance and Remiſſion of Sins in his Name, to all
Nations.

Nations. That by the ſame Spirit, he now governs and ſanctifies his Church, and will continue to do ſo unto the End of the World. At which Time he ſhall come again in the glory of his Father, and raiſe the whole World from the Dead, and ſhall judge every One according to his Works. The Devil, and all thoſe Angels which followed him in his firſt Tranſgreſſion ; and all wicked Men, who have ſuffered themſelves to be ſeduced by him ; the impious and the profane, the unrighteous and unjuſt, the unholy and the impure ; theſe he ſhall condemn to be caſt into the furnace of Fire ; where they ſhall every one be puniſhed with exact Juſtice according to their ſeveral Deſerts. But all holy and good Men ; who under the ſeveral Diſpenſations of God's true Religion in all Ages and in all Nations from the beginning of the World, either in Obedience to the Light of Nature, with *Enoch* and *Noah* and *Job* and the Patriarchs ; or under the Law, with *Moſes* and the Prophets ; or under the Goſpel, after the Example of the Apoſtles and Diſciples of our Lord, have in Piety and Devotion, in Righteouſneſs, Equity and Charity, in Holineſs and Purity of Life, ſerved God and kept his Commandments, either from the beginning of their Lives, or from the time of their forſaking their Sins by Repentance ; theſe he ſhall reward with everlaſting and inexpreſſible Happineſs, each in their ſeveral Degree, in the eternal Kingdom of his Father ; in that general Aſſembly and Church of the Firſt-born, where the Spirits of juſt men made perfect, together with the innumerable company of Angels, and with Jeſus the Mediator and great High-Prieſt of the New Covenant, ſhall ſtand continually in the preſence of God the Judge of All, and ſhall ſerve him before his Throne for ever. This is that Form of Sound Words, that Summary of neceſſary Truth, which the Apoſtle exhorts all men to hold faſt. This is that univerſal Doctrine, in the Profeſſion of which conſiſts the Unity of the Catholick Church of Chriſt under all Differences of external Forms, and under all Variety of Opinions in other and leſs important matters, in all Ages and thorough all Nations over the Face of the whole Earth. This is that Doctrine, which whoſoever ſincerely believes, and verifies that belief by a ſuitable Practice, ſhall be ſaved. *Other* Doctrines there are, delivered in Scripture, uſeful *for reproof, for correction, for inſtruction* in many particular Caſes ; but not indiſpenſably neceſſary to be underſtood by every man. And ſtill other Doctrines there are, and Explications of Doctrines, delivered by the Authority of *Men* ; ſometimes profitable indeed and helpful for the underſtanding of Scripture, but more frequently occaſioning nothing but vain Contentions and empty Diſputes, which hinder rather than promote mens Salvation. At leaſt *Neceſſary to Salvation*, there cannot any thing be, beſides that general Doctrine before-mentioned ; which All men can as univerſally underſtand, as they are univerſally concerned to look after their own Salvation ; and of which our Lord declares, that *He that believeth and is baptized* into it, *ſhall be ſaved*.

T H I S therefore may ſuffice concerning the 1ſt Particular, *viz.* What the *Thing to be believed*, or what the *Subject-Matter* of that belief is, which our Saviour here declares to be ſo neceſſary to Salvation. 2dly, I am to conſider in the next place, what the *Manner* of the Belief, or what the *Nature and Extent* of that *Act* of Believing is, which is here ſo indiſpenſably required. And to him that ſeriouſly conſiders the Scriptures upon this Head, it will plainly appear, that therein is always intended ſuch a firm and rational Perſwaſion, as is *founded* upon reaſonable and good *grounds*, and *produces* ſuitable and proper *Effects*. There have been ſome ſo unreaſonable, as, from theſe Words of our Saviour, *He that believeth ſhall be ſaved* ; and from other paſſages of Scripture, wherein men are ſaid to be *juſtified by Faith* ; and, *believe on the Lord Jeſus* Acts xvi. 31. *Chriſt, and thou ſhalt be ſaved* ; to conclude that *mere Credulity*, how *inconſiderate* ſoever, and how *little effect* ſoever it has upon their lives, will entitle them to Salvation. But tho' in a ſhort and conciſe manner of ſpeaking, the Part is indeed ſometimes thus

put

S E R M.
LII.

put for the Whole, yet very often the Whole is fully expreſſed; and where it is not, yet Reaſon and the general Tenor of Scripture ſhows, that it is always underſtood. I ſay therefore, that to *Believe*, conſtantly implies theſe two Things, 1ſt, a Firm Per-ſwaſion, *founded* upon reaſonable and good *grounds*. And This in oppoſition to ſuch a careleſs Credulity, as, like a Foundation in the Sand, quickly ſuffers whatever is built upon it to fall to the Ground. *The Simple believeth every word, but the prudent man looketh well to his going*, Prov. xiv. 15 The *Bereans* are commended, *Acts* xvii. 11, for *ſearching the Scriptures* of the Old Teſtament *daily, whether the things* taught them by the Apoſtles *were ſo or not*. (Far from That Popiſh Notion of believing at a venture as the Church believes; they are commended, for not having an implicit Faith even in the *Apoſtles* themſelves, but *ſearching the Scriptures daily, whether thoſe things were ſo*.) And St *Thomas*'s careful and inquiſitive Faith, was by our Saviour himſelf thought fit to be confirmed in the following ſingular and moſt affectionate manner, St *Joh.* xx. 27. *Reach hither thy finger, and behold my hands; and reach hither thy hand, and thruſt it into my ſide; and be not faithleſs, but believing*. He does indeed, in the next words, pronounce *Them ſtill More* bleſſed, *who have not ſeen, and yet have believed*. But his meaning therein, is not to recommend a careleſs and inconſiderate Credulity, which he elſewhere compares to Corn ſown upon a Rock, which ſprings up indeed ſuddenly, but ſoon withers for want of Root; but his Deſign on the contrary, is highly to recommend the Diligence of thoſe, who, having not the opportunity which St *Thomas* had; and conſidering, that

Heb. xi. 1.
Rom. viii. 24.

Faith is moſt properly the *Subſtance of things hoped for, the Evidence of things not ſeen*; and that *Hope that is ſeen, is not Hope; for what a man ſeeth, why doth he yet hope for?* his Deſign, I ſay, is to commend the Diligence of thoſe, who *hoping for that they ſee not, do with Patience wait for it*, Rom. viii. 25; who beholding *the Promiſes afar off*, and *being perſwaded of them, endure* with *Moſes*, (Heb. xi. 13, 27.) *as* ſeeing *him which is inviſible*; in a word, who, by *inquiring and ſearching diligently* (as St *Peter* expreſſes it, 1 *Pet.* i. 8,) attain to a ſatisfactory and rational conviction of the Truth of the Doc-trine of our Lord and Saviour Jeſus Chriſt; *whom having not ſeen*, they *love; in whom, though now they ſee him not, yet believing*, they *rejoice with joy unſpeakable, and full of Glory*. They conſider, the Purity and Excellency of the Doctrine itſelf, and its agreeableneſs to Reaſon, and to the Nature and Attributes of God: They ponder the Evi-dence of the Miracles he worked; which, though they behold not Themſelves, yet they find atteſted by the greateſt and moſt remarkable Teſtimony that was ever given to any Fact in the World: They examine the Prophecies which went before concern-ing him, and compare all the Actions of his Life with thoſe antient Predictions; *Search-ing what* Things, and *what manner of Time the Spirit of Chriſt which was in* the Pro-phets *did ſignify, when it teſtified before-hand the ſufferings of Chriſt, and the Glory that ſhould follow*, 1 Pet. i. 11. They conſider alſo the Prophecies that he himſelf delivered, and his Apoſtles after him; and compare them with the whole Series of Events, and general Diſpenſations of Providence through all the Ages of the World. And by theſe means they work in themſelves a Firm Perſwaſion, *founded* upon reaſonable and good *grounds*; which is the 1ſt thing, that I ſaid *Believing*, in the Scripture-ſenſe, conſtant-ly implies. The 2*d* is, that it be ſuch a Perſwaſion of Mind, as *produces* ſuitable and proper *Effects*: He *that believeth, and is baptized*. But This; together with the Rea-ſons, why *Believing*, in this caſe, is ſo highly eſteemed and rewarded; *He that believ-eth, and is baptized, ſhall be ſaved*; and the conſideration of its contrary, *Unbelief*; and the reaſons why that is declared ſo criminal and ſo ſeverely condemned; *He that be-lieveth not ſhall be damned*; muſt be referred to a farther Opportunity.

S E R M O N

SERMON LIII.

Of that Belief which is neceſſary to Baptiſm.

St MARK XVI. 16.

He that believeth and is baptized, ſhall be ſaved; But he that believeth not, ſhall be damned.

IN a Former Diſcourſe upon theſe Words, I propoſed to conſider, *1ſt*, What the *Thing to be believed*, or what the *Subject-matter* of that Belief is, which our Saviour here declares to be ſo neceſſary to Salvation. *2dly*, What the *Manner* of the Belief, or what the *Nature and Extent* of that *Act* of Believing is, which is here ſo indiſpenſably required. *3dly*, Whence it comes to paſs, that *Believing*, which in other caſes is a matter of Indifference, of Prudence or Underſtanding only, and not of Morality; yet in the Caſe of Religion, is ſo highly eſteemed. And theſe with regard to the *1ſt* part of the Words; *He that believeth, and is baptized, ſhall* be ſaved. Then with Regard to the Latter part of the Words; *he that believeth not, ſhall be damned;* *1ſt*, What is the full and proper meaning of this Phraſe of *not believing*; and *2dly*, Whence it comes to paſs, that *Unbelief* is in Scripture always ſo ſeverely cenſured, as being the greateſt of Crimes. In the *1ſt* place, What the *Thing to be believed*, or what the *Subject-Matter* of that Belief is, which our Saviour here declares to be ſo neceſſary to Salvation, I have already explained. *2dly*, As to the *Manner* of the Belief, or what the *Nature and Extent* of that *Act* of Believing is, which is here ſo indiſpenſably required; I obſerved that in Scripture-ſenſe, it always imports ſuch a firm and rational Perſwaſion of Mind, as is *founded* upon reaſonable and good *grounds*, and *produces* ſuitable and proper *Effects*. The Explication of the former part of this Propoſition, I have already gone through; *viz.* that *Belief*, in Scripture-ſenſe, always imports ſuch a firm and rational Perſwaſion of Mind, as is *founded* upon reaſonable and good *grounds*. It remains that I proceed at this Time, to ſhow that it alſo conſtantly ſignifies ſuch a Perſwaſion, as *produces* ſuitable and proper *Effects*.

AND This is evident in the firſt place, from the very *Nature* and *Reaſon* of the Thing. For, as the Shadow or Image of a Man, is not the Man himſelf; nor a dead Corpſe, the Perſon, whoſe Body only it is: And, in all other Caſes, Things are valued only by their Power and Efficacy; and are what they are, not by the mere denomination or external Appearance, but by their real Nature and inward Virtues or Qualities: So *Faith*, is not a bare empty Aſſent to the Truth of the Goſpel, a Means conſidered ſeparate from its intended End; but it is ſuch an *Effectual* Aſſent to the *Underſtanding*, as by a regular Operation influences and determines the *Will*, and thereby governs the Man's *Life and Actions*; ſhewing forth itſelf in the Fruits of true Virtue. And He of whom our Saviour declares in the Text, that he *ſhall be ſaved* becauſe *he believeth*; is not he who propoſes to believe, what in his Actions he has no regard to; but he who by the

S E R M. Fruit and Effects of a Chriſtian and Good Life, ſhews that he really has within himſelf
LIII. That Faith, which is the Root, the Spring, and the Cauſe of ſuch Actions.

    ALL which, as it is evident from the *Nature* and *Reaſon* of the thing itſelf, ſo it is
farther apparent from our Saviour's adding thoſe Words, *And is baptized.* He that
believeth, and is baptized; That is, which believeth the Goſpel and entereth into a
ſolemn Obligation to obey it, and verifies That Obligation by a ſuitable Practice in the
following Courſe of his Life; *He ſhall be ſaved.* For ſo the Apoſtle expreſſly explains
it; that the *Baptiſm* which *ſaves us,* is *not the putting away the filth of the Fleſh, but
the Anſwer of a good Conſcience towards God,* 1 Pet. iii. 21. And our Saviour himſelf
paraphraſeth his own Command, (*baptizing them in the Name of the Father and of the
Son and of the Holy Ghoſt,*) by the Words immediately following; Matt. xxviii. 20,
Teaching them to Obſerve *all things whatſoever I have commanded you.* And in his
Diſcourſe with *Nicodemus,* St Joh. iii. 5, *Except a man be born,* ſaith he, *of Water and
of the* Spirit, *he cannot enter into the Kingdom of God.* The Baptiſm of Water, is but
the Sign or Emblem; the Baptiſm of the *Spirit,* is the reality or thing ſignified. And
what *That* means, *viz.* the being *Baptized* or *Born* of the *Spirit,* the Apoſtle tells us,
2 Th. ii. 13, *God has from the beginning choſen you to Salvation, through* Sanctification
of the Spirit, and Belief of the Truth. What our Saviour in the words of the Text,
calls *believing* and being *baptized;* and in St *John's* Goſpel, being *baptized with Water
and the Spirit;* St *Paul* here ſtyles *Belief of the Truth,* and Sanctification *of the Spirit.*
And what *That* Sanctification is, he explains ſtill more diſtinctly, 1 Cor. vi. 11, *Know
ye not that the unrighteous ſhall not inherit the Kingdom of God?——And ſuch were
ſome of you; But ye are waſhed, but ye are ſanctified, but ye are juſtified, in the Name
of our Lord Jeſus Chriſt, and by the Spirit of our God.* Hence Baptiſm is called, *the
Baptiſm of* Repentance *for the Remiſſion of Sins;* And Baptized perſons who anſwer
Rev. vii. 14. their Profeſſion, are ſaid to have *waſhed their Robes, and made them white in the Blood
of the Lamb.* The literal meaning of which figurative expreſſion, is thus ſet down by
the Prophet; Iſ. i. 16, *Waſh you, make you clean, put away the evil of your doings from
before mine eyes; ceaſe to do evil, learn to do well;* —— Then *though your Sins be as
ſcarlet, they ſhall be white as ſnow; though they be red like crimſon, they ſhall be as wool.*
Now, as the Scripture thus fully explains *This* part of our Saviour's Words, *he that is
Baptized,* to ſignify a man's entring into a ſolemn Obligation to obey the Goſpel, and
his verifying That Obligation by a ſuitable Practice; ſo does it in numberleſs places, as
clearly explain thoſe *other* Words *alſo, he that Believeth,* to ſignify always ſuch a Perſwaſion of Mind, as ſtops not without producing its proper *Effects.* What is here called
Believing, is elſewhere expreſſed more diſtinctly, Repent *ye, and believe the Goſpel,*
St *Mar.* 1. 15. In another place, 'tis ſtyled *believing with the* Heart *unto Righteouſneſs,
and with the* Mouth *making confeſſion unto Salvation,* Rom. x. 10, In other places,
it is called believing and perſevering; Heb. x. 39, *We are not of them who draw
back unto perdition, but of them that believe to the ſaving of the Soul;* where
believing being oppoſed to *drawing back,* muſt of neceſſity ſignify That *Perſeverance*
which is the effect of True Faith. And 1 Cor. xv. 2, *By which ye are ſaved, if ye keep
in memory what I preached unto you, unleſs ye have believed in vain.* In the ſixth chapter of St *John's* Goſpel, what our Saviour ſays, ver. 40 and 47, *He that* believeth *on me,
hath everlaſting Life;* is at the 54th verſe repeated in another form of Expreſſion, *Whoſo*
eateth my fleſh and drinketh my blood, *hath eternal Life:* That is; He who in a
conſtant Imitation of me and Obedience to my Commands, continues united to me
by a Vital Participation, as Members of the Body with their Head; *he* has the promiſe
of eternal Life remaining in him. In *other* paſſages of Scripture; what is meant by *believing,* ſufficiently appears from the parallel Expreſſions, by which it is deſcribed.
Rom. x. 6. *Acts* vi. 7, it is being obedient *to the Faith;* and again, *Rom.* i. 5, the Obedience *of*

    3

Faith.

Faith. Ch. ix. 30, it is called *the* Righteouſneſs *of Faith*; and *Phil.* iii. 9, *the* righteouſneſs *which is of* God *by Faith.* 1 *Tim.* i. 19, it is *Faith and a good Conſcience*; and
ch. iii. 9, *Faith in a* pure *conſcience.* *Gal.* v. 6, it is *Faith which worketh by Love*;
and *Tit.* iii. 8, *They which have believed in* God, *muſt be careful to maintain* good Works.
In theſe and numberleſs other the like places, ſufficient Care is taken to ſatisfy all reaſonable Perſons, that *Belief* is in the Goſpel always valued, not by its *Denomination*,
but by its *Effects.* And yet, to prevent all Poſſibility of Miſtake in a matter of ſuch
extreme importance, there is ſtill a clearer and more expreſs way of ſpeaking, for explication of this Doctrine, made uſe of by St *James*, ch. ii. of his Epiſtle; where he
tells us, that *Faith without Works* can no more ſave a man, than good Words without
Deeds can feed the Hungry, or cloath the Naked, ver. 14. 15; that even the *Devils*
themſelves *believe*, and tremble, ver. 19; that *Abraham our Father was juſtified by
Works*, or (which is the ſame thing) was *therefore* juſtified *by* Faith, becauſe *by Works
was his Faith made perfect*, ver. 21, 22; that, *as the Body without the Spirit is dead,
ſo Faith without Works is dead alſo*, ver 26. And by our Saviour himſelf, *St* Matt. vii.
21; *Not every one that ſaith unto me, Lord, Lord, ſhall enter into the Kingdom of
Heaven*; but he that Doth *the Will of my Father which is in Heaven*; and ver. 26. he
that heareth theſe ſayings of mine, and doth them not, *ſhall be likened unto a fooliſh man,
that built his Houſe upon the Sand.* From which clear and deciſive Expreſſions it appears moſt evidently, that when St *Paul* ſays *we are juſtified by Faith without the Deeds
of the Law*, he muſt be underſtood to mean by Faith, not a *bare ſpeculative Belief*,
but ſuch *Belief and Moral Obedience* to the Commands of the *Goſpel*, as are oppoſed to
the *ceremonial Works* of the *Moſaic Law*: And that, when 'tis ſaid, *Acts* xiii. 39, that
by Chriſt, All who believe, *are juſtified from all things, from which they could not be
juſtified by the Law of Moſes*; it muſt be underſtood, All who *ſo* believe, as to *repent
and forſake* thoſe Sins, *from* which they hope to be juſtified *by* that Faith. And that
when it is ſaid, *Acts* xv. 9, that God *purified* the *hearts* of the Gentiles, *by Faith*; it
muſt needs be underſtood of *ſuch* a Faith, as St *Peter* deſcribes in his Firſt Epiſtle,
ch. i. 21, 22, when he ſays, *you who by* Chriſt *do* believe *in God,——have purified your
ſouls in* obeying *the Truth.* All which explications of the Word, *Believing*; are further confirmed, by the like Uſe of *other* Phraſes in Scripture; where *Other* ſingle Virtues,
as *Hope, Love, Fear*, the *Knowledge of God*, and *calling upon the Name of the Lord*, are by
a like Figure put for the whole of Religion: As they are plainly declared to be, either by
the *Manner of Expreſſion* itſelf in the places where they are mentioned, or by *diſtinct Explication* in other paſſages. *Hope*, when it is uſed to ſignify a *Virtue*, can for That only Reaſon be ſuppoſed to be ſo, becauſe the Ground or Foundation on which it is built, is the
having obeyed the Commandments of God. *Fear*, in like manner, when it is not a
Paſſion, but a *Virtue*, evidently ſignifies ſuch a filial or reverential Fear, as is the ſame
with Obedience. Our *Love* of God, is by our Saviour himſelf diſtinctly defined,
St *Joh.* xiv. 21, *He that hath my* Commandments *and* keepeth *them, he it is that* loveth
me; and by the Apoſtle, 1 Joh. v. 3, *This is the Love of God, that we keep his* Commandments. In like manner, the *Knowledge of God*, 1 Joh. ii. 3, 4; *Hereby we know
that we* know *him, if we* keep *his* Commandments. *He that ſaith, I know him, and
keepeth not his Commandments, is a Liar, and the Truth is not in him.* And what is
affirmed, *Acts* ii. 21, that *whoſoever ſhall* call *on the Name of the Lord, ſhall be ſaved*;
is by our Saviour fully explained in the place before-cited, *Not every one that ſaith unto me, Lord, Lord, ſhall enter into the Kingdom of Heaven*; but he that Doth *the Will
of my Father which is in Heaven.* By the ſame Analogy therefore, *Belief* alſo muſt
always be underſtood to ſignify; not, barely an empty Aſſent, but ſuch a Conviction
of the Underſtanding, as fails not to operate by a ſuitable Obedience of the Will
and Actions.

and *ver.* 15, 23.

AND

SERM.   AND This may ſuffice for Explication of the *ſecond* particular in the Text, What
LIII.   the *Manner* of the Belief, or what the *Nature* and *Extent* of that *Act* of Believing is, which is here ſo indiſpenſably required ; namely, that it is ſuch a firm and
rational Perſwaſion of Mind, as is *founded* upon reaſonable and good *grounds*, and produces ſuitable and proper *Effects*.

THE 3*d* Particular to be conſidered, was, whence it comes to paſs, that *Believing*
which in other caſes is a Matter of Indifference, of Prudence or Underſtanding only,
and not of Morality ; yet in the caſe of Religion is ſo highly eſteemed ; *He that believeth, and is baptized, ſhall be ſaved.*   And the Reaſons are ;

1*ſt*, BECAUSE, in practical Matters, it is an Act, not of the *Underſtanding* only,
but partly of the *Will* alſo, to attend and be willing to ſubmit to reaſonable Evidence ;
lay aſide the Prejudices of Luſts and Paſſions ; to ſuffer Reaſon and Argument to prevail over worldly Intereſts ; and to embrace a Doctrine of Truth and Right, merely
upon the Evidence of its being ſuch, without regard to temporal Conſiderations.   *Believing*, in matters of ſtrict Demonſtration, is an Act, not of Choice, but of Neceſſity.
In Queſtions of uncertain Speculation, 'tis a thing merely indifferent, neither good nor
evil, or, at moſt, a part of Prudence or Imprudence only.   But in matters of Practice,
to Believe and be guided by Reaſon and Evidence, not by Inclination and Paſſion ;
as 'tis the moſt proper and natural, ſo 'tis one of the moſt commendable and excellent
Actions of a rational Being.   Hence in Scripture, the ſingular Commendation given the
Bereans, Acts xvii. 11. is founded upon This, that *they ſearched the Scriptures daily,
whether thoſe things were ſo or not.*   And the high Encomium beſtowed upon *Abraham*'s
Faith is upon this ground, *Heb.* xi. 19, that he *Accounted*, (the word in the original is,
he *Reaſoned within himſelf*, and was *ſatisfied,*) that God *was able to raiſe up* his Son
Iſaac again, even from the Dead : And our Saviour's Approbation of the *Canaanitiſh*
Woman, *O Woman, great is thy Faith*, Matt. xv. 28. was occaſioned by her arguing
reaſonably, that as *even the dogs eat of the Crumbs that fall from the childrens table*, ſo
ſhe, though an Alien from the Commonwealth of *Iſrael*, yet might hope for ſome
ſmall portion of Bleſſing from the Meſſiah, who was ſent into the World by the common Creator of All men.   And the extraordinary Character he gives the *Centurion* ; *I
have not found ſo great Faith, no, not in Iſrael*, Matt. viii. 10, was upon This account,
that he *reaſoned himſelf* into a Belief of Jeſus's power to heal Diſeaſes at a *Diſtance*, by
conſidering that even *he himſelf* alſo, though, a Perſon infinitely inferior to our Lord,
yet had *Servants* under him, ſo that he needed not to go in his own Perſon, but could
ſay to This man, Go, and he goeth, and to another, Come, and he cometh.   The Particular Commendation given to theſe Perſons Faith, was, that it was not a raſh Credulity, but a reaſonable, conſiderate, and well-grounded Belief.   And accordingly the
Scripture, in other places, directs us to try *the Spirits, whether they are of God*, 1 Joh. iv. 1.
and exhorts us to *be ready always to give an anſwer to every man that asks* us a reaſon *of
the hope that is in* us, 1 Pet. iii. 15.   And *the Sluggard* on the contrary, who *conſiders*
nothing carefully, is juſtly reproved for being *wiſer in his own Conceit, than ſeven men
that can render a* Reaſon, *Prov.* xxvi. 16. *God himſelf*, in his Dealings with mankind,
appeals to them by the Prophet, to *conſider* and *ſhow themſelves men :* Mic. vi. 2, *The
Lord has a controverſy with his people, and he will* plead *with Iſrael :* And, *Come now,
and let us reaſon together, ſays the Lord*, Iſ. i. 18.   He expects of them, a *reaſonable
ſervice*, founded upon a juſt and *reaſonable Belief* ; and Both theſe, are the proper and
moſt commendable Acts of *reaſonable Creatures*.

Iſ xlvi. 8. (margin)

2*dly*, ANOTHER reaſon, why Faith is in Scripture always ſo highly commended, is becauſe, in the Scripture-Senſe of the Word, it is always ſuppoſed to *ariſe* and
begin from a Willingneſs of knowing and being informed in the Will of God, and

ends

ends in actual Obedience to his Commands fo made known. Which being both the Foundation and the higheſt *Improvement* of Virtue, 'tis no wonder if upon *That Part,* which by way of eminence is frequently put for the *Whole,* fo great Commendations are beſtowed in Scripture. 2 Chr. xx. 20. *Believe in the Lord your God, fo ſhall ye be eſtabliſhed ; Believe his prophets, fo ſhall ye proſper.* The meaning is, *Obſerve* and *obey* them ; obey the commandments, which *They* deliver you from God ; (in like manner as our Saviour in the Text, *Believe and be baptized,* and verify that Obligation in the Senſe before-explained ;) So ſhall ye be Partakers of the Promiſe annex'd.

A N D This, concerning the *former* part of the Words, *He that believeth, and is baptized, ſhall be ſaved.* In the *latter* part of the Words, *He that believeth not, ſhall be damned* ; it is to be conſidered, 1ſt, What is the full and proper meaning of this Phraſe of *not believing* ; and 2dly, Whence it comes to paſs, that *Unbelief* is in Scripture always fo ſeverely cenſured, as being the greateſt of Crimes.

T H E latter of theſe will be cleared by the Explication of the former, *viz.* what is the full and proper meaning of this Phraſe of *not believing.*

A N D This is indeed a very great and important Inquiry ; becauſe there is no Sin, againſt which ſeverer Judgments are denounced in Scripture, than againſt *Unbelief.* Among thoſe who are to have their part in the Lake that burneth with Fire and Brim- ſtone, the *unbelieving* are placed in the firſt Rank, *Rev.* xxi. 8. The *fearful and un- believing and the abominable aud murderers,* and fo on. And when our Saviour ex- preſſes his higheſt indignation againſt that evil Servant, who began to beat his fellow- ſervants, and to eat and drink and be drunken ; as if he had nothing *more ſevere* to terrify him withal, he threatens to *cut him in ſunder, and appoint him his portion with* Unbelievers, as with the worſt of Offenders ; St *Luke* xii. 46. 'Tis evident therefore, that by *Unbelief,* in this and other places of Scripture, cannot be meant that bare nega- tive *want of Belief,* which, with regard to the Whole *Goſpel,* is the caſe of all thoſe to whom it never was preached ; and, with regard to any particular *Doctrine whatſoever,* is the Caſe of thoſe to whom that Doctrine was never clearly made known and reaſon- ably explained. For, *not to believe* what a Man has not *good and ſufficient* Reaſon to believe, can never be fo much as any Crime at all. And *the Judge of all the Earth will do what is right,* and *with Equity will he judge the Nations.* And, *to whom little is given, of him will not be much required.* And St *Paul* expreſsly declares, that *when the Gentiles which have not the Law, do by nature the things contained in the Law, theſe, having not the Law, are a Law unto themſelves* ; and that their *uncircumciſion ſhall be counted for circumciſion,* Rom. ii. 14, 26 : So that tho' there is indeed *no other Name given under Heaven, by which he muſt be ſaved,* but that of *Chriſt* only ; yet by that very Name may thoſe poſſibly have Benefit, who never had any explicit Knowledge of him. But by *Unbelief* therefore in Scripture, is always meant one of the two fol- lowing things ; Either 1ſt, in *general,* ſuch an obſtinate Rejecting of the Whole Goſ- pel and of the gracious Terms thereof, as ariſes from a vitious and wilful refuſing to attend to and examine the Evidence of it ; Or 2dly ſuch a Diſbelief of the *Particulars* of God's Promiſes, in thoſe who profeſs to embrace the *Whole,* as hinders them from *obeying* the Doctrine, which they would ſeem to receive. The *firſt was* the Caſe of the Phariſees, in our Saviour's time ; and *is Now* the Caſe of all vitious Infidels in Chriſtian Countries, who refuſe to examine and conſider the Reaſonableneſs of the un- corrupted Doctrine of the Goſpel, as delivered by Chriſt and his Apoſtles, ſeparate from the uncertain Doctrines and Comments of *Men.* The *latter, was* the Caſe of the *Jews* of old, who in the Wilderneſs were fo often charged with *Unbelief* ; and *Now is* the Caſe of all profeſſed Chriſtians, whoſe Works do not prove their Faith to be real.

A s to thoſe who *wholly* reject the Goſpel, when duly and reaſonably preached to them ; That the *Unbelief* They are charged with in Scripture, is always a vitious Re-

S E R M. fuſing to examine; appears from all the Texts, wherein ſuch Unbelief is mentioned.
LIII. For ſo our Saviour, when he had declared to *Nicodemus*, that *he who believeth not in the*
Name of the only begotten Son of God, is condemned already; immediately explains it
Job xxiv. 13. by adding, *And this is the Condemnation, that* Light *is come into the World, and men*
loved darkneſs rather than Light, becauſe their Deeds were evil, St Joh iii. 18. And
again, ch. xii. 46. *I am come*, ſaith he, *a Light into the World, that whoſoever believeth*
on me, ſhould not abide in Darkneſs; *And if any man hear my Words, and believe not,*
I judge him not; ——*the* Word *that I have ſpoken, the ſame ſhall judge him in the laſt*
Joh. x. 37. *day*. And *ch*. xv. 24. *If I had not done among them the Works that none other man did,*
they had not had Sin; but now they have both ſeen and hated, both me and my Father.
And the ſame thing is expreſſed in thoſe other places of Scripture, where men are ſaid
therefore *to caſt God's Words behind them*, becauſe *they hate to be reformed*; and that
they *believe not the Truth*, becauſe *they have* pleaſure *in unrighteouſneſs*, 2 Th. ii. 12.

AND hence it is, that the Word, *not believing*, comes in the *ſecondary* Senſe to be
uſed frequently, not only for Rejecting the *Whole* Goſpel, but alſo to ſignify ſuch a partial Diſbelief of the *Particulars* of God's Promiſes, in thoſe who profeſs to embrace
the *Whole*, as hinders them from *obeying* the Doctrine, which they would ſeem to receive. So that in Scripture nothing is more common, than in like manner as He is
ſtiled *Fool*, who *acts* not according to what he *knows and underſtands*; ſo to call Him
Unbeliever, who *practiſes not* what he profeſſes to believe. What our Saviour threatens,
St *Luk.* xii. 46. *ſhall appoint him his portion with the* Unbelievers, is in St *Matthew* thus
expreſſed, *ch.* xxiv. 51. *ſhall appoint him his portion with the* hypocrites. In like manner, *Eph.* v. 6. What in the *margin* is tranſlated, *cometh the Wrath of God upon the*
children of Unbelief, is in the *Text* itſelf, *the children of* Diſobedience. The *Jews*
in the Wilderneſs, though they could not poſſibly diſbelieve what they ſaw with their
own Eyes, yet for their Diſobedience they are in Scripture called *Unbelievers*: Jude 5.
The Lord having ſaved the People out of the land of Egypt, afterwards deſtroyed them
that believed not. And *Heb.* iii. 19. *We ſee they could not enter in, becauſe of* Unbelief; And *ver.* 18. *To whom ſware he, that they ſhould not enter into his Reſt, but to*
them that believed not? That is, as 'tis explained in the *verſe* before; *them that had*
ſinned. Again, *ch.* iv. 6. They *entered not in, becauſe of* Unbelief; *i. e.* of *Diſobe-*
dience. And the ſame Phraſe is uſed concerning their Poſterity in the days of *Hoſhea*,
2 Kings xvii. 14. *They would not hear*, i. e. would not obey; *but hardened their neck,*
like to the neck of their Fathers, who did not believe *in the Lord their God*. And the
Apoſtle applies it in the ſame Senſe to Us Chriſtians, *Heb.* iv. 11. *Let Us labour there-*
fore to enter into that Reſt, leſt any man fall after the ſame example of Unbelief; in the
margin it is, after the ſame example of *Diſobedience*. And ch. iii. 12. *Take heed bre-*
thren, leſt there be in any of You *an evil Heart of* Unbelief *in departing from the living*
God; i. e. as he explains it in the following verſe, in being *hardned* (as *The* Others
were) *through the Deceitfulneſs of Sin*.

AND now, the Nature of *Unbelief* being thus explained, it thence ſufficiently appears (which was the *Laſt* thing propoſed) how it comes to paſs, that *not believing* is
always in Scripture ſo ſeverely cenſured, as being the greateſt of Crimes. For, the
Doctrine of Chriſt being extremely reaſonable in itſelf, (the Doctrine of Chriſt, I ſay,
as delivered in Scripture in its original Simplicity, and ſeparate from the uncertain additional Doctrines and Comments of *Men*,) *This* doctrine being extremely *reaſonable in*
itſelf, and being *proved* moreover by the ſtrongeſt *Evidence* in the World; All thoſe to
whom That *Evidence* is fairly propoſed, and the *Reaſonableneſs* of the Doctrine truly
repreſented, if they obſtinately reject it, and the gracious Terms thereof; they plainly
do deſpite to the Spirit of God; And their Love of Vice being the only Cauſe of their
Unbelief, 'tis conſequently of the ſame Nature, and accordingly called in Scripture promiſcuouſly

4

miſcuouſly by the ſame Name, with the *Diſobedience* of Believers.　And therefore they are joined together, as in their Crime, ſo in their Puniſhment ; they that know *not God*, and they that obey *not the Goſpel*.　And 'tis very reaſonable, that as *He that believeth and is baptized, ſhall be ſaved* ; ſo he that *believeth not*, in the Senſe which has been now explained, *ſhould* on the contrary *be damned*. S E R M.　LIII.

T H A T which remains is, by way of Inference, *1ſt*, to exhort thoſe who call themſelves *Deiſts*, or Followers of *natural* Religion only, without regard to the Goſpel, to conſider ſeriouſly what it is they reject ; and when they have ſeparated the undiſputed *Doctrines of Chriſt* from the uncertain *Opinions of contentious Men*, Then to judge, whether deſpiſing this gracious Offer of the divine Goodneſs, be not *rejecting the Counſel of God againſt themſelves*, and fooliſhly *forſaking their own Mercies*.　*2dly*, To exhort all thoſe who profeſs themſelves *Chriſtians*, above all things to live *worthy of* their *holy profeſſion* ; to *let their light ſhine before men, that others ſeeing their good works, may glorify their Father which is in heaven* ; at leaſt, to *give no Offence to Them that are without*, leſt *through* Them *the Name of God be blaſphemed among the Gentiles, as it is written*, Rom. ii. 24.　And *Laſtly*, to exhort thoſe who *Teach* Chriſtianity to others, that, ſince hindring others from believing, is of the ſame guilt as not believing ourſelves ; therefore we be very diligent to repreſent the Doctrine of Chriſt as reaſonable and plain, as he himſelf has repreſented it ; deſiring with *Moſes*, that *All the Lord's people were Prophets* ; and not imitating the Romiſh and Scholaſtick Writers, who make their own Doctrines, Traditions, and Explications of Doctrines, of the ſame Authority with the Word of God ; and, inſtead of teaching all men (after the Apoſtle's example) to be *ready to give an Anſwer to every man that asketh* them *a* Reaſon *of the Hope that is in them*, perſwade them on the contrary to believe ſo much the more implicitly and with the greater Confidence, as the things they impoſe on them are the more *unreaſonable* and abſurd to be believed.　From ſuch Follies and Impieties, which promote nothing but Scepticiſm and Infidelity, let *Us* turn away ourſelves ; Always remembring our Saviour's Admonition, that we *are the Salt of the Earth* ; *But if the Salt itſelf has loſt its ſavour, wherewith ſhall things be ſeaſoned* ; *It is neither fit for the land, nor yet for the dunghil, but to be caſt out and to be trodden under foot of men*. Numb. xi. 29.

Matt. v. 13.
Lu7. xiv. 34
Col. iv. 5, 6.

S E R M O N

S E R M O N LIV.

The Defign and End of Baptifm is Newnefs of Life.

R O M. VI. 3, 4.

Know ye not, that fo many of us as were baptized into Jefus Chrift, were baptized into his Death? Therefore we are buried with him by Baptifm into Death, that like as Chrift was raifed up from the Dead by the glory of the Father, even fo We alfo fhould walk in Newnefs of Life.

SERM. LIV.
T HE Apoftle having in the foregoing chapter, with great variety of emphatical expreffions, fet forth the excceding goodnefs and compaffion of God towards Mankind, in caufing the Righteoufnefs of the *Second Adam* to become in its confequences *more* effectual towards the *recovery and falvation* of Sinners, than the introducing of Sin into the World by the *Firft Adam* had been inftrumental towards their *Deftruction*; He in *This* chapter proceeds to anfwer a very great and dangerous Objection, and to prevent a moft fatal Corruption and Abufe, which he forefaw would arife in ill minds upon the Doctrine he preached; and which in Fact, to great Numbers of thofe who call themfelves Chriftians, has caufed the Gofpel itfelf, inftead of being *the Savour of Life unto Life*, to become on the contrary the *Savour of Death unto Death.* ver. 1, *What fhall we fay then? Shall we continue in Sin, that Grace may abound?* The *Inference* to vitious and corrupt minds is very natural and obvious. If God has fent his Son into the World to die for the Sins of Men; if Chrift has given himfelf a fufficient Sacrifice, Oblation, and Satisfaction, for the Sins of the whole World; is it not a rendring *honour* to Chrift, to rely entirely upon *his* Merits; and to depend more upon *his* Satisfaction, than upon *Any* Virtuous Practice of our own? Is it not (they will fay) a *Magnifying* of the Mercy of God, to think that a Vitious Life will be eafily pardoned to thofe who *fully rely* upon the *Merits of Chrift?* and may we not therefore *continue in Sin, that Grace may abound?* To this the Apoftle, not without juft indignation, replies, ver. 2, *God forbid: how fhall we that are dead to Sin, live any longer therein?* A Chriftian (he fuppofes,) *as* Such, even *effentially* to his being a Difciple of Chrift, has *put off* That *Body of* Sin which Chrift came to deftroy; and can no more, with Any Confiftency to his profeffion, live in the practice of any known Vice, than a man *naturally dead* can perform any *natural action* of life. *Know ye not, that fo many of us as were baptized into Jefus Chrift, were baptized into his Death? Therefore we are buried with him by Baptifm into Death, that like as Chrift was raifed up from the dead, by the Glory* (that is, by the *glorious Power*) *of the Father, even fo We alfo fhould walk in Newnefs of Life.*

In which words there are *Three* Particulars principally remarkable, 1ft, The Apoftle here fuppofes, that the Great *End* and *Defign* of the Gofpel is to bring men to

Amendment

4

Amendment and *Newnefs of Life.* 2*dly,* He urges the confideration of the *Death* and S E R M.
Refurrection of Chrift, as a Great *Argument* to promote This End. And 3*dly,* He LIV.
alleges, that the Great Defign of *Baptifm* in particular, is to *remind* us perpetually of
This Argument, and to *inforce* it upon us.

I. *Firft,* THE Apoftle here fuppofes, that the Great *End* and *Defign* of the Gofpel,
is to bring men to *Amendment* and *Newnefs of Life: Even fo We alfo fhould walk in
Newnefs of Life.* The only reafon why God, who ftands in need of Nothing, and
is infinitely Self-fufficient to his own Happinefs, ever created any rational Creatures at
all, is, that by following the Light of the Reafon he has given them, and by imitating the moral Perfections of God, and by obeying his Commandments in the Practice
of Virtue and Righteoufnefs; they might (as St *Peter* expreffes it) *become Partakers
of the Divine Nature,* that is, might have fuch Degrees communicated to them of
their Creator's Happinefs as *irrational* Beings are by their nature incapable of. Now
the Perfections of God being abfolutely unchangeable, and the nature of Good and Evil
effentially invariable; 'tis manifeft that That Practice of Virtue and Righteoufnefs,
That Worfhip of God who ruleth over All, and That Juftice and Goodnefs due from
One Creature towards Another, in which the Effence of True Religion confifts; muft
among *All* rational Beings, in *All* parts of the Univerfe, and in *All* periods of Time,
be eternally and univerfally the Same. Had *All* creatures therefore *Always* continued
innocent and virtuous, the Form and Method of Religion could never have admitted
of Any Change. And for the fame reafon, when, upon the account of *Sin,* the
Mercy of God has vouchfafed to appoint any particular method or inftitution of Religion, in order to the acceptance and reconciliation of *Sinners;* 'tis evident that the ultimate *End* and *Defign* of every fuch method or inftitution of Religion can poffibly be
no Other, than the recovery or bringing back of fuch Perfons to the fame State, in
whch they would originally have been fixed, had there been No Tranfgreffion. Our
Saviour expreffes this Notion very emphatically, St *Luke* v. 3 5, *They that are whole,
need not a Phyfician, but they that are fick; I came not to call the Righteous, but Sinners to Repentance.* Virtue is the *Life* and *Health* of the Soul: And as, in *all* cafes in
general, the ultimate End of whatever is intended for *reftoration* or *recovery,* is always
the attaining of that firft and natural State, the Lofs of which occafions a *Want* of Reftoration or Recovery; fo in *particular,* the End and Defign of that Religion, which
the Gofpel has appointed for the reconciliation of Sinners, is fummed up in what the
Text here ftyles *Newnefs of Life.* For, *for* This purpofe, fays the Apoftle, *the Son
of God was manifefted, that he might deftroy the Works of the Devil,* 1 Joh. iii. 8:
The Works of the Devil; that is, all thofe *Sinful Habits* and *Vitious Practices of Men,*
which they commit either through the *Temptation,* or after the *Example,* or agreeably to the *Inclinations and Defires* of the Wicked One. Again: *Tit.* ii. 14, *Our Saviour Jefus Chrift,* fays St *Paul, gave himfelf for us* (to This End) *that he might redeem
us from all iniquity, and purify to himfelf a peculiar people, zealous of good works.*
And the fame thing he elfewhere expreffes in a very elegant and fublime figure;
Eph. ii. 10. *We are his Workmanfhip,* created *in Chrift Jefus unto good Works, which
God hath before ordained that we fhould walk in them.* And fo particular a *Strefs* is
laid upon this Great Truth, that the Scripture expreffly declares, it had been better for
men *never* to have heard the Gofpel *at all,* than that it fhould not produce in them
the Fruit of a Virtuous Life, 2 *Pet.* ii. 20. *It had been better for them not to have
known the way of righteoufnefs, than after they have known it, to turn from the holy
Commandment delivered unto them.*

FROM what has been faid upon *This* Head, evidently appears the Folly of making
a comparative *oppofition* (as Some have done) between *Chriftianity* and *Morality.* For
if the Great *End* and *Defign* of the Gofpel, is to bring men to *Amendment* and *New-*

S E R M. *nefs of Life*; and *Newnefs of Life* is only another Name for the *Practice of Virtue*,
LIV. which is *Morality*; 'tis plain there can be no other oppofition made between *Chriftiani-*
ty and *Morality*, than between the *Means* and the *End*. Much lefs ought true Virtue to be *lightly fpoken* of, when compared with any *pofitive* Duty, or *ritual* Performance whatfoever: Becaufe this is the fame Abfurdity, as preferring the *Means* which
are in order to any *End*, before the *End* itfelf to be obtained by thofe *Means*.

ALSO from what has been faid upon *This* Head, appears the Vanity of fubftituting
any thing *elfe* in matters of religion, upon which finally to build our Hopes, befides
the Fruits of true *Virtue* and *Righteoufnefs* of Life. For if the great and ultimate
End of the Gofpel, is to bring men to *Repentance*, and *Amendment* of manners; 'tis
evident that whatever falls fhort of this End, and proves ineffectual to it, cannot be finally *good and profitable unto men*. *Profeffing* the Religion of Chrift is nothing, if
men be not thereby made *better* than if they profeffed it *not*. Having *prophefied in the*
Name of Chrift, and *in his Name* having *caft out Devils*, and *in his Name done many*
wonderful Works, is of no importance, if at the fame time the Perfon be a Practifer
of thofe *Works of Iniquity* which the *Works of Chrift* were intended to deftroy. Laftly,
Laying hold upon Chrift, and *depending upon him* with a *ftrong and confident Faith*, is of
no Benefit, if *That Faith* which is the *Root*, or *Tree* that ought to bring forth the
Fruits of Righteoufnefs, be *itfelf* mifunderftood as fupplying the *Want* of That
Fruit, which is it the *only Excellency* of the Root to produce.

AND thus having explained the *Firft* Particular in the Text, that the Great *End*
and Defign of the Gofpel, is to bring men to *Amendment and Newnefs of Life*; I proceed now to obferve in the

II. *Second* place, That the Apoftle here urges *particularly* the confideration of the
Death and Refurrection of Chrift, as a Great *Argument* to promote this End: *That,*
like as Chrift was raifed up from the Dead by the glory (that is by the *glorious Power*)
of the Father, even fo We alfo fhould walk in Newnefs of Life. The Doctrine of Chrift
is *one continued Exhortation*, and his Life a perpetual *Example* of *Goodnefs, Righteouf-*
nefs and all Virtue. And the Defign of his *Death and Refurrection*, is, by making an
Atonement for paft Sins, and eftablifhing for *the future* a gracious *Covenant of Repen-*
tance, to prevail with men effectually, by all the Arguments of *Life* and *Death*, to
turn from the ways of *Sin and Deftruction*, into the Paths of *Virtue and everlafting*
2 Cor. v. 15. *Happinefs*. *He died for All* (faith St *Paul*) *that they which live, fhould not henceforth*
live unto themfelves, but unto Him which died for them, and rofe again. And St *Peter*
in his Firft Epiftle, ch. iv. 1, *Forafmuch then as Chrift* (fays he) *has fuffered for us in*
the flefh, arm yourfelves likewife with the fame mind; for he that hath fuffered in the
Flefh, hath ceafed from Sin; that he no longer fhould live the reft of his time in the
Flefh, to the Lufts of men, but to the Will of God. By the *Death of Chrift*, God has
made the fevereft Declaration poffible, of his *Hatred againft Sin*; and at the fame
time given the ftrongeft atteftation to the Truth of that Evangelical Doctrine, which
indifpenfably requires *Amendment* for the *future*, upon the *forgivenefs* of what is *paft*.
Heb. ix. 14, *The Blood of Chrift,——purges your confcience from dead works, to ferve*
the Living God. It eafes the confcience, by giving men affurance of pardon; not
that thereby they may become acceptable to God, without the Practice of Virtue;
but that they may more effectually be encouraged, by true Repentance and Amendment, to ferve God for the future in Newnefs of Life. Before the Coming of Chrift,
the *Whole World*, in a manner, *lay in Wickednefs*: The *Heathens*, generally fpeaking,
being involved in the moft enormous Vices; and the *Jews* alfo having far departed
from true Virtue, by placing their Religion more in *typical* Purifications, than in that
real Purity which thofe types were intended to reprefent. The Reformation of *Both*
Thefe, through the Preaching of that Doctrine which our Lord fealed with his *Death*,

and

and confirmed by his *Refurrection*; the Apoftle fets forth in a moft lively and elegant S E R M. manner, in his *Epiftle to the Ephefians*, ch. ii. As to the converted *Heathens*; *Ye* (fays LIV. he) *being in times paft Gentiles in the Flefh,*——*were without Chrift, being Aliens from* ver. 11. *the commonwealth of Ifrael, and Strangers from the Covenants of Promife, having no Hope, and without God in the World*——*walking according to the courfe of this World, according to*——*the Spirit that now worketh in the children of difobedience:*——*But* ver. 2. *Now,*——*ye who fometimes were far off, are made nigh by the Blood of Chrift.* And ver. 13. as to the converted *Jews: We alfo* (fays he) *had our converfation in times paft, in the* ver. 3. *lufts of our flefh, fulfilling the Defires of the flefh and of the mind; and were by Nature the children of wrath, even as Others; But God, who is rich in mercy,*——*hath quickned us together with Chrift.* Thefe latter words, *and were by* Nature *the children of Wrath*, have by Some been very abfurdly underftood, as if men were Born *children of Wrath*, and were *of God* created *originally wicked*: Whereas the evident Meaning of the Apoftle is, that wicked and debauched men, before their converfion to Chriftianity, were by the Practice of thofe Vices which *Habit* had made as it were *natural* to them, become Enemies to God, and *children of Wrath*. But *Chrift*, by his *death*, obtained pardon for as many of them, as, by putting away thofe Vices, would *die unto Sin*; and, by his *refurrection*, he gave affurance of eternal *life* to All, who in the *moral* fenfe, would firft *rife with him unto Newnefs and Holinefs of Life*. According to the Analogy of which figurative expreffions, *all* Sins in general are in Scripture frequently ftyled dead *works*; and *wicked* men are defcribed as being *dead* in *Sin*; and they who have *forfaken* their Vices, are *dead to Sin*; and converted *Jews* are *dead* from *the rudiments of the World*, and *dead to the Law*, that they may *live to God*: And all Sinners who have *reformed* their lives, are faid to be *crucified with Chrift*, and to have *crucified the flefh with the affections and Lufts*; and that they are *dead, and their Life is hid with Chrift in God*; and that they are *quickned with Chrift*; and *rifen with Chrift*, and the like. And upon thefe figures of Speech, are grounded the following Exhortations; 2 *Tim.* ii. 11, *It is a faithful Saying; if we be dead with him, we fhall alfo live with* him: And *Rom.* viii. 10, *If Chrift be in you,* (that is, if ye be Chriftians indeed,) *the Body is dead* [διὰ] *as to Sin, but the Spirit is life becaufe of* [or, as to] *Righteoufnefs*: And in the words immediately following my Text; *If we have been planted together in the likenefs of his Death, we fhall be alfo in the likenefs of his Refurrection: Knowing this, that our old man* (that is, our former vitious courfe of life) *is crucified with him, that the body of Sin might be deftroyed, that henceforth we fhould not ferve Sin:*——*Now if we be dead with Chrift, we believe that we fhall alfo live with him: Let not Sin therefore reign in your mortal body, that ye fhould obey it in the Lufts thereof.*

From what has been faid upon *This* Head, there naturally and plainly arifes This important Inference; that one of the *greateft* and moft *pernicious corruptions* poffible of the Chriftian Religion; is, *That kind of Reliance upon the Merits of Chrift*, in which *wicked Chriftians* place their Hopes of Salvation, inftead of *obeying* the *Commandments* of Chrift delivered in his Gofpel. Next to Total Infidelity, the greateft Enemy of true Religion is *Superftition*: And of all Superftitions, the moft pernicious is That which *turns the Grace of God into Wantonnefs*; which (as the Apoftle elfewhere expreffes it) makes *Chrift the Minifter of Sin*, that is, makes even the Gofpel itfelf an Incouragement to Wickednefs. Now This is directly the cafe of all thofe profeffed Chriftians, who, while they live vitioufly, ftill *rely upon the Merits of Chrift* for Salvation; or, as the Apoftle expreffes it, *continue in Sin that Grace may abound*. Which is fubverting intirely the whole Defign of Religion. For Chrift came into the World to procure pardon of *paft* Sin, for *no other* reafon but that he might more effectually prevent it for the *future*. And there can be no greater *Mockery* of God and Religion,

than

than to turn That *Goodnefs* of God declared in the Gofpel, which was intended as the Great Motive to lead men to Repentance; to turn it into an argument for *Security* in continuing in Sin. *Rom.* ii. 4. *Defpifeft thou the Riches of his goodnefs, and forbearance, and long fuffering; not knowing that the goodnefs of God leadeth thee to Repentance? But after thy hardnefs and impenitent heart, treafureft up unto thyfelf wrath againft the day of wrath, and revelation of the righteous judgment of God.*

THIS therefore is the *Second* Particular remarkable in the Text; namely the confideration of the *Death* and *Refurrection of Chrift*, here infifted upon as an *Argument*, to perfwade men to *Repentance and Amendment of Life.* The

III. *Third* and Laft thing I propofed to take notice of in the words, is the Apoftle's here urging finally, that the Great Defign of Baptifm in particular, is to *remind* us perpetually of *This* Argument, and to *inforce* it upon us: *Know ye not, that as many of us as were baptized into Jefus Chrift, were baptized into his Death? Therefore we are buried with Him by Baptifm into death, that like as Chrift was raifed up from the dead by the glory* (by the glorious Power) *of the Father, even fo we alfo fhould walk in Newnefs of Life.* Our Lord, when he fent forth his Difciples to preach the Gofpel to all Nations, commanded them to Baptize every one that was converted, *in the Name of the Father, and of the Son, and of the Holy Ghoft :* That is, to caufe them to enter by Baptifm into a folemn obligation, to dedicate themfelves to the Service of *God* in *That* Method of religion, which the *Son of God* came into the World to eftablifh, and confirmed by Prophecies and Miracles of the *Holy Ghoft.* The Sacrament of *Baptifm* therefore, according to this inftitution of our Lord, is emphatically *fignificant* of our Duty, and moft aptly fitted to *remind* us of it perpetually, in the *three following refpects.* 1*ft*, As being *in general* a folemn *initiation* into the Profeffion of *That Religion,* the Great *End of which* is Holinefs of Life. 2*dly*, As *typifying* in a *particular* manner, the neceffity of *moral* Purity and Righteoufnefs of *life*, by the fimilitude of wafhing the *Body* with *water.* And 3*dly*, (which is what the Apoftle peculiarly infifts upon in the Text;) Baptifm, as being an *emblem* or *reprefentation* of Men's *dying* with Chrift, and *rifing* with him again; is a continual memorial of our obligation to *put off the Body of Sin,* and to *put on* the *new man*, (that is, a virtuous courfe of life;) *which after God,* (that is, according to the example and commandments of God,) *is created in righteoufnefs and true Holinefs.*

1*ft*, Baptifm is *in general* a folemn *initiation* into the Profeffion of *That Religion,* the Great *End of which* is Holinefs of Life. If therefore *That End* be not attained, there is then no Benefit in having been initiated into That Religion, the Only Ufe whereof is for the obtaining That End.

2*dly*, BAPTISM *typifies*, in a *particular* manner, the neceffity of *Moral* Purity and Righteoufnefs of *life*, by the fimilitude of wafhing the *Body* with *Water.* And as, in *all* cafes, a *type* or *reprefentation* is nothing, without the *reality* of the thing intended to be *fignified* thereby; fo in this *prefent* point the Scripture is always *particularly careful*, to exprefs wherein the *Real efficacy* of this Sacrament confifts. In the *Prophetick* Defcription, *Ezek.* xxxvi. 25, 27. after the figurative phrafes, *then will I fprinkle clean water upon you, and ye fhall be clean;* immediately follows the explication, *from all your Idols will I cleanfe you, and——caufe you to walk in my ftatutes, and ye fhall keep my judgments and do them.* Our Lord *himfelf*, in the very *words of inftitution; Go ye* (fays he) and *baptize all nations,——teaching them to do whatfoever I have commanded you :* And again; *Except a man be born of the* Spirit, as well as *Water, he cannot enter into the Kingdom of God.* The Apoftle St *Paul* accordingly, defcribing Chrift's *fanctifying* and *cleanfing* his Church *with the wafhing of water by the Word*; immediately adds, by way of explication, *that he might prefent it to himfelf——* Holy, and
1 Cor. vi. 11. without Blemifh, *Eph.* v. 26. And elfewhere, fpeaking of *particular Chriftians*, he

puts,

4

puts, *wafhed, fanctified, juftified,* as Synonymous Terms. And in his Epiftle to *Titus,* he mentions the *wafhing of regeneration* and the *renewal of the Holy Ghoft,* as two phrafes equally, and without any *difference* of fignification, expreffing the *effect* of That *Kindnefs and Love,*——*which* God *our Saviour fhed on us abundantly through Jefus Chrift our Saviour,* ch. iii. 4, 5, 6. In the epiftle to the *Hebrews, having our Bodies wafhed with pure Water,* and our *Hearts fprinkled from an evil confcience,* are ufed as Phrafes of the fame import, *ch.* x. 22. And St *Peter,* ftill more exprefsly, (1 *Pet.* iii. 21.) declares the *Baptifm,* which *faves us,* to be, *not the putting away of the filth of the Flefh, but the anfwer of a good confcience towards* God.

3*dly,* (WHICH is the Argument peculiarly infifted upon in the text;) *Baptifm,* as an *emblem* of men's *dying with Chrift* and *rifing with him again,* is a continual memorial of our obligation to *put off* the *body of Sin,* and to *walk* with Chrift in *newnefs of life.* This Argument the Apoftle purfues at large, through the whole chapter. And in *Other* of his epiftles; *Col.* ii. 12. Buried *with him in* Baptifm, *wherein alfo ye are* rifen *with him.* Gal. iii. 27. *As many of you as have been* baptized *into Chrift, have put on Chrift.* And Eph. iv. 22. *That ye put off, concerning the former converfation, the old man,* (that is, your antient manner of living,) *which is corrupt according to the deceitful Lufts; And be renewed in the fpirit of your Mind.*

THE *Application* of what has been faid upon this *Laft* General head, is; that, at the *firft* Preaching of the Gofpel, the perfons brought to Baptifm being fuch as had been converted from among the Jews or Heathens; whereas *Now* they are generally fuch as have been born of Chriftian Parents; 'tis always to be underftood, that all the fimilitudes and comparifons, all the reafonings and arguments, drawn *in Scripture* from the nature and Form, from the defigns and obligations of Baptifm; muft *Now* be applied to Chriftians, at fuch time as they profefs themfelves to be Difciples of Chrift, and followers of his Religion, with *underftanding, knowledge* and *choice.* Which matter, if duly confidered, would have a great Effect upon the Hearts and Lives of all reafonable perfons. And that it *may* have fuch Effect, God of his infinite Mercy grant, *&c.*

S E R M O N LV.

Of being baptized into the Name of any Perſon.

1 COR. I 13.

—————*or were ye baptized in the name of Paul ?*

SERM. LV.

THE Apoſtle is in this Chapter reproving the *Corinthians*, for their unreaſonable Animoſities and Diviſions among themſelves, ſo contrary to the nature and obligations of their Holy Profeſſion, ſo unbecoming the Name and Character of Chriſtians. They had *all* been inſtructed in one and the ſame *Faith*; They had *all* been baptized with one and the ſame *Baptiſm*; They had *all* profeſſed themſelves Diſ-ciples of One only *Lord and Saviour*, Jeſus Chriſt: And yet afterwards, falling into Parties, and laying ſtreſs upon particularities, and valuing themſelves upon adhering, one to *One* Form or Method of teaching, and Others to *Another*; they by degrees for-got the *Great* and *Fundamental* Obligations of Chriſtianity, and departed from the Sim-plicity of their *common* Religion. One was for following *Paul*, Another for *Apollos*, and a third for *Cephas*. This Beginning of Fooliſh Diviſions and needleſs Animoſities, This Breach of Chriſtian Charity and univerſal Love, the Apoſtle very largely and ſe-verely reproves in This and the following Chapters: And no where with greater elegance and more affectionate ſharpneſs, than in the words of the Text: *Is Chriſt*, ſays he, *divided? was Paul crucified for you ? or were ye baptized in the Name of Paul? I thank God that I baptized none of you, but Criſpus and Gaius ; Leſt any ſhould ſay, that I had baptized in my own Name.*

IN Diſcourſing upon which words, I ſhall conſider, 1ſt, What the Meaning of *This Phraſe* is in general, being *baptized in*, or *into the Name* of any Perſon. 2*dly,* What Effect, the conſideration of our being All baptized particularly into the Name of *Chriſt*, ought to have upon us. And 3*dly*, What the *Nature* of *That Corruption* is, and what the *ill conſequences* of it, which St *Paul* here reproves in the *Corinthians* by This ſharp and ſevere Queſtion; *Were ye baptized in the Name of Paul?*

1ſt, As to the Meaning of this Phraſe in general, of being *baptized in*, or *into the Name* of any perſon; 'tis to be obſerved, that Baptiſm, by an expreſſive emblem, or figure, of waſhing the *Body* with Water, ſignifies and repreſents a Change in the *Mind* of the baptized Perſon, from *One* ſort of Profeſſion or Practice to *Another*. And be-cauſe This Change in the Perſon's Mind, This reſolution of *forſaking* One State of life, one ſort of Profeſſion or Practice, and *entring upon Another*, is, in This caſe, ſuppoſed to be worked and effected, by the Preaching, Admonition, or Exhortation of Some *Teacher*, who either by Reaſon and Argument and Doctrinal Perſwaſion, or by Evidence of Au-thority and Divine Commiſſion, convinces Men that the Change he indeavours to work in them, will be acceptable and well-pleaſing to God; hence the Action of *Baptiſm*, or the external Signification of this inward Change, is ſtiled a *being baptized in*, or *into the Name* of the *Teacher*, whoſe *Diſciple*, or the *Follower* of whoſe Doctrine, the baptized perſon hereby profeſſes himſelf to be. Thus the children of *Iſrael*, becauſe when they paſſed thro' the ṛed Sea, and were conducted in the Wilderneſs by a Cloud,

3

they

they in this whole matter profeffed themfelves to be Followers of That Religion which S E R M.
God taught them by *Mofes*; therefore they are faid by the Apoftle to have been *All*   LV.
baptized unto *Mofes, in the Cloud and in the Sea*.   And they who by the preaching of
John the Baptift, were prevailed upon to repent and amend their lives, through a firm
Belief of the Promifes God had given them of the Meffiah then fpeedily to appear;
were *baptized*, as the Scripture expreffes it, *into John's Baptifm*; and called *The Difciples of John*.   In like manner, they who afterward by the Preaching of *Chrift* and *his
Apoftles*, were converted to the Belief and Profeffion of the Gofpel; were baptized *in
the Name* or *into the Name, of the Father, and of the Son, and of the Holy Ghoft*. That
is, They made a folemn Profeffion of their Believing the Doctrines, and of their Refolving to obey the Precepts of That Religion, which *God the Father Almighty* revealed and taught by his *Son Jefus Chrift*, and confirmed by the miraculous Teftimonies of
the *Holy Ghoft*.   Which being the fame thing as, briefly and in Other words, profeffing
themfelves *Chriftians*, or *Difciples of Chrift*; they are therefore elfewhere fpoken of,
in a general and lefs diftinct manner of expreffion, as having been baptized *in the Name* Acts viii. 16.
of the Lord Jefus, or, *in the Name of Jefus Chrift, for the remiffion of Sins*, Acts ii. 38.   xix. 5.
And thofe numerous places in the New Teftament, where we read, that *whofoever* Acts ii. 21.
fhall call on the Name *of the Lord, fhall be faved*; and where Chriftians are diftin-   Rom. x. 13.
guifhed by the character, of thofe who call *on the* Name of the Lord Jefus; are, ac- Acts ix. 14, 21.
cording to the true fenfe of the Original, plainly of the fame import with That Other 1 Cor. i. 2.
expreffion, *Acts* xv. 17.   *All the Gentiles*, upon *whom my* Name is called, *faith the
Lord*; that is, all thofe who have fincerely embraced the Profeffion of Chrift's religion,
and are accordingly baptized into an obligation to obey it.   And thus therefore in the
Text likewife; the Queftion here put by the Apoftle, *Were ye baptized in the Name
of Paul?* is as much as if he had faid, Am *I* your Mafter?   Are ye *My* Difciples? do
ye profefs a religion of *Mine?* have *I* taught you any *doctrine* of my *Own?*

A N D This may fuffice for explication of the *firft* particular; what the Meaning of
this Phrafe is in *general*, of being *baptized in* or *into the Name of* any perfon.

2. T H E *Second* thing I propofed, was, to inquire *What Effect*, the confideration of
our being All baptized *particularly* into the Name of *Chrift*, ought to have upon us.
And *This* evidently is, that we ought to look upon ourfelves as *His* Difciples, obliged to
hearken to *His* Doctrine, to follow *His* Inftructions, to obey *His* Commandments.

T H E *Original* Authority and Dominion of *God* over the Univerfe, over *All rational*
Creatures; and *Their* confequent Duty and Subjection to *Him*; St *Paul* elegantly expreffes, by ftiling *Them* the *Family in Heaven and Earth*, and *Him* the *Father, of
whom* That *whole Family is named*, Eph. iii. 15.   They bear *his Name*; that is, they
are *His* Property, they derive from him, they depend upon him, they acknowledge
him as their Head, their Father, the Author of their Being, and their Supreme Governour; In virtue of which relation, All Honour, All Obedience, All Subjection is neceffarily and uniformly due to him from Them.   And This in their *natural* capacity, as
they are *in general* his Creatures, or the Work of his Hands.   In the *religious* fenfe, and
where there comes *more particularly* a *diftinction* to be made, between thofe who are only
fubject by *neceffity* to God's kingdom of *Nature*, and thofe who are fubject by *Choice* to
his Kingdom of *Grace*; the Scripture fpeaks of thefe latter, as, in a fpecial and more peculiar manner, bearing the *Name* of God, or ftanding in a nearer and more proper relation
to him.   *Him that overcometh*, faith our Saviour, *will I make a pillar in the Temple of
my God, and I will write upon him the* Name *of my God*, Rev. iii. 12.   And elfewhere,
the whole Body of our Lord's fincere Followers are diftinguifhed, as *having his Father's*
Name *written in their Foreheads*.   And in the defcription of the Happinefs of their final ch. xiv. 1.
ftate, one principal character made ufe of is, that they fhall *fee the Face* of God, *and*

his Name shall be in their foreheads. The Meaning is; they shall be received and acknowledged by him as his Sons and his Servants, as being in a more particular manner his Family or Houshold. *The Tabernacle of God shall be with them, and he will dwell with them, and they shall be his people, and God himself shall be with them, and be their God*, Rev. xxi. 3.

By the same Analogy, bearing likewise the Name of *Christ*, or having been *baptized in* His Name, signifies a constant acknowledgment and profession of *His* relation to *Us*, and *Ours* towards *Him*. That *He* is our Saviour and Lord, our Mediator and Advocate, the only Revealer of the Will of God to us in the present time, and by him constituted our Judge at the last day. And that consequently *We* are his Disciples and Followers; who are to receive from *him* the doctrine of true Religion; to look upon *him* as the Way, the Truth, and the Life; to adhere stedfastly to what *he* has taught us, and to practise carefully what *he* has commanded. St *Luke*, in his history of the *Acts*, tells us, that *the Disciples were called* Christians *first in Antioch*, ch. xi. 26. By their *Adversaries*, it was intended as a Name of *Reproach*; By *Themselves*, it was esteemed as a Title of the highest *Dignity*: By *Both*, it was understood not to be a bare empty Name; but to be expressive and declarative of their adhering to Christ's Doctrine, and of their observing his Laws. Our Lord himself, speaking of those, who, whether few or many in number, should in their Teaching adhere strictly to the Rule and Doctrine of Truth; insomuch that *whatsoever they should bind on earth, should be bound in Heaven, and whatsoever they should loose on Earth, should be loosed in Heaven*; (as in the case of men's preaching the *Sincere and uncorrupt Doctrine* of Truth it must needs be;) He expresses it, by their being gathered together *in his Name*: Matt. xviii. 20. *Where two or three are gathered together* in my Name, *there am I in the midst of them.* He does not mean, Where-ever men *call themselves Christians*, or *say unto him, Lord, Lord*; but where-ever they really *are* what That *Name* signifies; and *Do*, as he has taught them, *the Will of his Father which is in Heaven*. That *professing* the Name of Christ, or being baptized into Jesus Christ, is nothing, without being sincerely sollicitous to understand what his Doctrine truly is, and careful to obey the Laws he has given us, St *Paul* declares to us in a very affectionate manner, *Rom.* vi. 3. *Know ye not that so many of us as were baptized into Jesus Christ, were baptized into his Death!——knowing this, that our old man is crucified with him, that the Body of Sin might be destroyed, that henceforth we should not serve Sin.* And again, *Gal.* iii. 27, *As many of you as have been baptized into Christ, have put on Christ*; that is, have put yourselves under an obligation of laying aside all other Distinctions, and of being united upon the foot of obedience to his alone Commands: *There is henceforth neither Jew nor Greek, there is neither bond nor free;——for ye are all One in Christ Jesus:* One, not in Title and Denomination only, but in reality of sincere affection; One, in Faith; One, in Charity; One, in uniform Obedience to the Commands of Christ; without which, 'tis of no moment to have been called by his Name. The same method of arguing, is again insisted upon by the same Apostle, 2 *Tim.* ii. 19. *Having this Seal,——Let every one that nameth the name of Christ, depart from iniquity.* The manner of expression, *having This Seal*, is a remarkable allusion to certain figurative passages of Scripture, some of which I have already mentioned. For as St *John* in his Vision, saw the Servants of God *sealed in their foreheads*; and the true Disciples of Christ, *having his Father's Name written in their foreheads*; and St *Paul* himself, in some other of his epistles, speaks of sincere Christians as being *sealed by the Holy Ghost unto the day of redemption*; so here likewise, *The Foundation*, says he, or the *Covenant, of God, standeth sure, having This Seal,——Let every one that nameth the name of Christ, depart from iniquity*: His meaning is; Let no man think, that his title to God's covenanted mercies, depends upon his bearing the *Name* of a Christian; but upon his being constantly influenced

4

fluenced by That confideration, to be *in reality* what That Name denotes, a practifer S E R M. of univerfal righteoufnefs, meeknefs and charity. As a fort of *Memorial* of This obli- LV. gation, a Cuftom has long prevailed in the Chriftian Church, that every perfon, at the time he is baptized, fhould have given him what we call a *Chriftian Name*. And the Defign was prudent; that our very *Name* fhould remind us of our Holy Profeffion; And becaufe Chriftians received their *own Name* at the time they were baptized into the *Name of our Lord*; that therefore they fhould never hear their *own* Name mentioned, without being put in mind of their being dedicated to *his*. The very *Name* therefore and *Title* of a Chriftian, is a great Reproach to every man, who, in his Life and Converfation, takes no care to *anfwer the fignification*, and to *verify the intention* of it; but intirely forgets or difhonours the *Thing*, while the *Word* or *Name* is perpetually in his mouth.

A N D thus having at large explained *What Effect* the confideration of our being *All* baptized into the Name of *Chrift*, ought to have upon us; It remains now in the

3d and *laft* place, T H A T I proceed to fhow what the *Nature* of *That corruption* is, and what the *ill confequences* of it, which St *Paul* here reproves in the *Corinthians* by this fharp and fevere queftion; *Were ye baptized* in the Name of *Paul*? And This, from what has been already faid, is very apparent. For if being baptized in the Name of *Chrift*, fignifies being Difciples and Followers of *Him*; by the fame reafon, being baptized in the name of *any other* perfon or perfons, fignifies likewife being Followers of *Him* or *them*. And for Chriftians, who were baptized in the Name of *Chrift*, to behave themfelves neverthelefs in fuch a manner, as if they took themfelves to have been baptized in the Name of *other* Teachers; evidently denotes all fuch mutual *Schifms* and *Differences*, as arife among Chriftians from their following and being fond of the *Doctrines of Men*; the Doctrines either of *particular* men, or of any *Numbers* or *Bodies* of men whatfoever. *It has been declared unto me of you, my Brethren*, fays the Apoftle in the words juft before my Text, *that there are Contentions among you*, ver. 11. *What* thofe contentions were, he explains in ver. 12; My Meaning (fays he) is This; I hear, *that every one of you faith, I am of Paul, and I of Apollos, and I of Cephas, and I of Chrift*. Some were for following *one* man's Doctrine, and fome *another's*. To This Folly of theirs, he gives a very fharp Reproof, in the 13th verfe, in which are the words of my Text: *Is Chrift* (fays he) *divided? was Paul crucified for you? or were ye baptized in the Name of Paul? I thank God that I baptized none of you, but Crifpus and Gaius; Left any fhould fay, that I had baptized in my own Name*. Had thefe their Differences (which St *Paul* calls *Schifms*;) had they regarded, not *fingle perfons*, but *Bodies of Men*; the cafe would ftill have been exactly the fame. Had every one of them faid, *I am of the Church of Corinth, and I of Ephefus, and I of Philippi, and I of Rome*: St *Paul* would ftill have given them the very fame reproof; *Is Chrift divided? was the City or People of Corinth crucified for you? or were ye baptized into the City or People of Corinth?* In like manner, could St *Paul* hear men contending and pleading, that One of them was *for the Council of Trent*, Another *for the Synod of Dort, and a* Third, *for that of Conftantinople*; he would ftill make the very fame Reply; *Is Chrift divided? was the Council of Trent crucified for you? or were ye baptized into the Synod of Conftantinople or Dort?* Were it lawful for *Any* man, or any Number *of Men*, to have Any *Doctrines* of their *own*, or any Followers to be diftinguifhed by *Their* Denomination; it would be reafonable to think, that the *Apoftles* certainly might, of All others, beft have claimed That privilege. Yet St *Paul*, we find, was very careful, was very follicitous, not to give any occafion to have it thought, that there was any fuch thing as the *Doctrine of Paul*, much lefs any fuch thing as the *Doctrine of the Church of Corinth* or *Rome*, or of Any other than *Chrift* only, who *Alone* was *crucified for us*, and in *whofe name* only we *were baptized*, and not in the *Name* or into the *Doctrines*, of *any other* Teach-

S E R M. ers whatfoever. For my *own* part, fays he, *I determined, not to know any thing among*
LV.   *you, fave Jefus Chrift, and him crucified :———And my fpeech, and my preaching, was
not with inticing words of man's wifdom;———that your faith fhould not ftand in the wifdom of men, but in the power of God,* ch. ii. 2. He difclaims all power in *himfelf,* to
add any thing to the Doctrine of Chrift; *any* notions, *any* particularities, *any* diftinguifhing doctrines of his *own.* The Doctrine of *Chrift,* who alone *was crucified for
them,* and *in whofe name they were* All *baptized;* he *fuppofes,* they *All* underftood and
embraced: Otherwife they were not capable of being Members of Chrift's Church, in
the Senfe that perfons of riper years were admitted fo to be. The doctrine of *Chrift,*
I fay, into which they were baptized, he *fuppofes* they *All* underftood; namely, the
Doctrine of *Repentance from Dead Works,* and of *Faith towards God;* of the *Refurrection of the Dead,* and of *eternal Judgment.* And as to any *additional* doctrines, by
which *One* party of Chriftians might be diftinguifhed from *another;* which he elfewhere

'Αναιδιυτοι, calls, *unlearned* queftions, in the original it is, *untaught,* things which were no part of
2 Tim. ii. 23, the inftruction of a *Chriftian;* As to *thefe,* he *Thus* expreffes his Sentiments; *I fear,*
not taught at *fays he, left by any means, as the Serpent beguiled Eve through his Subtilty, fo your minds
Baptifm,2Cor.*
xi. 3.1Cor. iii. *fhould be corrupted from the* Simplicity *that is in Chrift.* For, *Other foundation can no
11. *man lay, than That is laid, which is Jefus Chrift.* And though *We* ourfelves, fays he, *or
an Angel from heaven, preach any other Gofpel unto you, than that which we have preached unto you, let him be accurfed.* By *preaching another Gofpel,* he does not mean fetting
up a new Religion in oppofition to Chriftianity; but, as he expreffly explains himfelf in
the verfe foregoing, *Gal.*i. 6, 7, he directs his difcourfe againft Thofe, who *called men
to another Gofpel, which is not another;* That is, who to the Gofpel of Chrift *added*
their *own* peculiar Doctrines as *Marks of diftinction* among Chriftians, thereby giving
unavoidable occafion to Divifions and mutual Schifms in the Body of Chrift; Directly
contrary to that Great Precept of our Lord, Matt. xxiii. 9, *Call no man your Father upon
the Earth, for One is your Father which is in Heaven, Neither be ye called* Mafters, *for
One is your Mafter, even Chrift.* As Chrift alone was *crucified* for us, fo in *His* Name *only,*
(fays the Apoftle) into *His* Doctrine *only,* were we *baptized;* and not into the particular
doctrines of any *other* man, or any *Sect of men* whatfoever. This is the Root of Chriftian
Unity, the *Unity of the Spirit in the Bond of Peace,* the Unity of the One undivided and
undefiled Spoufe of Chrift; which is the Temple, the Houfe, the Church of the Living
God; difperfed in All Ages, and in All places, over the face of the whole Earth; and
yet united in One Holy Bond, in One indiffoluble Tie, of Truth and Charity. For
notwithftanding the numberlefs mutual *Schifms* and *Differences,* among the various
worldly Sects or Bodies of men, who place the Sum of their religion in following
the doctrines and ceremonies each of their own Sect; yet concerning all real and fincere
Chriftians in every place, who, without laying any Strefs on the Traditions of men,
endeavour carefully to ftudy and underftand the Doctrine, and to obey the Laws and
Commandments of *Chrift,* into whom alone they were baptized; (and who confequently are the True *Church* of Chrift;) concerning *Thefe,* I fay, the fimilitude ufed
by St *Paul* is ftill and always true, that *as the Body* (of a man) *is One, and hath
many members, and all the members of that one body, being many, are One body, fo alfo
is Chrift; For by one Spirit are we all baptized into One body, ——— and have been all

**Εν πνεῦμα, *made to drink into* * *One Spirit:* So that, as to the Fundamentals of religion (upon
or ἐν πόμα; which alone Thefe perfons lay any confiderable ftrefs,) they are all of them entirely
compare 1 Cor. *One body and One Spirit, even as they are called in One hope of their calling; having
x. 2. *One Lord, One Faith, One Baptifm, One God and Father of all, who is above all, and
through all, and in them all,* Eph. iv. 4. Men of evil and corrupt minds, even in
St *Paul's* days, began to depart from this *Simplicity* of the doctrine of Chrift, and to
form themfelves into Sects and Parties under different denominations, occafioning mu-

tual

tual Schifms and uncharitable Divifions among Chriftians: Ch. iii. of this, 1 *Cor.* ver. 3, S E R M.
Whereas, fays he, *there is among you envying and ftrife and divifions; are ye not carnal,*   LV.
and walk as men? That is, do ye not behave yourfelves more like the profane and
corrupt Infidels of This prefent World, than like Difciples of Chrift? *For while One*
fays, I am of Paul, and Another, I am of Apollos, are ye not carnal? That is, Do ye
not fhow yourfelves more concerned for particular *Parties,* than for propagating univerfally the *Truth* of Chrift, and the *Practice* of That Doctrine which is according to
Holinefs. In *later* and more corrupt Ages, this evil Spirit has continually increafed
among thofe who call themfelves Chriftians. And the *Confequences,* the *natural*
and *neceffary* Confequences of it, have been Animofities, Contentions, Hatred,
Schifms, Wars, Fightings, Perfecutions, Ravages, and Devaftations of the World.
The *Remedy* is *One* only ; a *very obvious* remedy, and the *only poffible one*; even *This,*
prefcribed by the Apoftle in the Text; that *All Chriftians,* every *fingle* Chriftian, and
All *Bodies* of Chriftians, whether fmall or great, would ferioufly confider, that as *Chrift*
alone was *crucified* for them, fo in His *Name only* were they All baptized, and not in
the Name of *Paul,* or of any *other* man, or of any *Sect of men,* whatfoever: And
that confequently they ought all to continue in the *Simplicity* of the Profeffion and
Practice of That Gofpel, into which they were All baptized; without contentioufly
adding, each of them their *own* peculiar Doctrines, to the Doctrine of *Chrift*; which
muft unavoidably be the occafion of never-ceafing divifions. In the *Great Foundations*
of *Faith and Practice,* they do already agree. In *other* matters, if every one would
but allow to *Others,* what he knows and expects fhould in Chriftian Charity be by
them allowed to *Him*; however men might and cannot but differ about many *Things,*
yet with regard to each other's *perfons* they might eafily (according to St *Paul*'s ad-   Rom. xii. 16.
vice) be *of the fame mind one towards another, perfectly joined together in the fame*
mind and in the fame judgment, 1 Cor. i. 10; *holding the unity of the Spirit in the*
bond of peace. So the Apoftle expreffes it with great accuracy : Holding, not *unity*
of *opinion* in the bond of *ignorance,* nor unity of *practice* in the bond of *hypocrify*;
but *the Unity of the Spirit,* the unity of a *Chriftian* and *Charitable* Spirit, in the
bond of *Peace.*

SERMON

S E R M O N LVI.

The Nature, End and Defign of the Holy Communion.

1 C O R. XI. 25.

After the fame manner alfo he took the cup, when he had fupped, faying, This Cup is the new Teftament in my Blood; This do ye, as oft as ye drink it, in remembrance of me.

SERM.
LVI.
ONE great End of our Saviour's coming into the World, was to deliver men from that yoke of ceremonious performances, which *neither they nor their Fathers were able to bear*: and to eftablifh Religion upon the Foot of Virtue and everlafting Righteoufnefs. The World had from the beginning been fo addicted to ritual and external obfervances, and laid fo great ftrefs on fenfitive and outward parts of Worfhip; that God, in condefcenfion to their infirmity, and confidering the hardnefs of their Hearts, had for feveral ages thought fit to prove the obedience of his peculiar people the Jews, by giving them fuch pofitive precepts, as had not in themfelves any real or intrinfic worth; but their obligation depended wholly, upon their being pofitively commanded. Thefe rites, were external and fenfible; fuited to the capacity of fuch perfons, whofe minds could not immediately relifh the more fublime and fpiritual parts of Religion. A willing and diligent obfervance of them, was indeed an evident proof of an obedient and fincere Mind; and a wilful neglect of them, when commanded, a manifeft token of a ftiff-necked, ftubborn, and perverfe generation; but yet they were not, *in their own nature*, Acts of Piety; or conduced any thing, *of themfelves*, towards the perfecting of the Soul, and making it like unto God. Hence, though thefe things *were not to be left undone*; yet the *weightier matters of the Law*, were always *judgment, mercy, and truth*. To *thefe*, God continually exhorted his people by the Prophets; and declared upon all occafions, that their ritual obfervations, *in comparifon of* thefe more important Duties, were of no value; and *without* them, were even abominations in his Sight. *Thinkeft thou that I will eat Bulls flefh, or drink the blood of Goats? No, But offer unto God thankfgiving, and pay thy vows unto the moft High*, Pfal. l. 13. God did therefore, by a Succeffion of Prophets, wean the Jews by degrees, as they were able to bear it, from their too high efteem of ritual and ceremonious performances; and inculcated to them the true and fpiritual nature of Religion; till at laft, in the fulnefs of time, when the World was prepared for the reception of the Gofpel, he wholly abolifhed thofe rites by the coming of his Son, whom he *fent forth* into the World *made under the Law, to redeem them that were under the Law, that we might receive the adoption of Sons*. Our Religion therefore *Now* confifts not in fuch outward and ceremonial parts of Worfhip, whofe obfervance was difficult, and their fignification oft-times obfcure. We know that *God is a Spirit; and they that will worfhip him* acceptably, *muft worfhip him in Spirit and in Truth*. The Perfection of our Religion, is to imitate the Life of God in Holinefs, and *having efcaped the*

I   *corruption*

corruption that is in the World through luſt, i. e. through the Temptations of Ambi-tion, Covetouſneſs and Senſuality; having eſcaped Theſe, *to become Partakers of the divine nature.* The *Promiſes* of the Goſpel are almoſt wholly ſpiritual; and its Pre-cepts accordingly are ſo excellent, as, not only by virtue of God's promiſe and ap-pointment, but even in their *Own Nature* alſo, to fit and prepare us for that truly ſpi-ritual life in Heaven. But then, as we are not *yet* actually in the ſtate of Perfection, but only in a ſtate of preparation for it; as we are here confined to theſe earthly Bo-dies, and to converſe with ſenſible and corporeal objects; ſo the inward devotion of our Minds, muſt be excited and expreſſed, by outward acts of Religion. *We muſt glorify God both in our Body and in our Spirit, which are God's*, 1 Cor. vi. 20. No leſs therefore do *They* err, who would exclude *all* outward Acts of Worſhip from true Re-ligion, than they who place Religion (as the greateſt part of Men are apt to do) al-moſt wholly in them. Our Minds muſt be filled with a due honour and reverence towards God; and that diſpoſition muſt be maintained and ſhow forth itſelf, in proper Acts of external worſhip. And here our Saviour has not confined us, to difficult and burdenſom forms; but only that *all things be done decently and in order.* We are not obliged to ſuch poſitive and ritual obſervances, as the Jews of old; but only to ſhow forth the religious affections of our minds in ſuch outward acts, as are in their own na-ture apt to *excite* that devotion, and to *expreſs* it. There are no more than two po-ſitive inſtitutions in the Chriſtian Church, as of neceſſity *generally* to Salvation; Bap-tiſm and the Lord's Supper; And theſe, ſo extremely ſignificant, and the connexion between the Sign and the thing ſignified ſo evident, that they can hardly be called barely poſitive inſtitutions. By the *One*, we are admitted into the Society of Chriſtians, and made members of the myſtical Body of Chriſt; By the *Other*, we are confirmed and eſtabliſhed in that ſtate; and receive ſpiritual nouriſhment, as members united to the Head; being made partakers of the benefits of his Death and Paſſion.

THE Words of the Text, are part of the Hiſtory St *Paul* gives us of the inſtitu-tion of this latter Sacrament; exactly agreeable to the Account that three of the Evan-geliſts give us, of the ſame inſtitution. The Occaſion of the Apoſtle's repeating it in this place, was the diſorderly manner of the *Corinthians* communicating; who, by rea-ſon of many diviſions among themſelves, and through the pride of the rich deſpiſing the poor, received this Holy Sacrament without a Devotion ſuitable to ſo ſacred an in-ſtitution; *not diſcerning*, (as the Apoſtle expreſſes it, *ver.* 29.) *the Lord's Body;* not diſtinguiſhing it ſufficiently from a worldly or common feaſt; not conſidering the So-lemnity, and Deſign of the Action; not having their minds prepared with worthy Qualifications, to approach with due Reverence the Table of the Lord. In order to remedy this their careleſsneſs, and prevent the like unbecoming behaviour for the future; the Apoſtle thought no Argument more proper, than to repeat to them the *very words* of our Lord's inſtitution: Which containing in *themſelves* a plain account of the End and Deſign of this Holy Sacrament, could not but put them to ſhame, and be a ſtrong reproof of their unworthy behaviour; that they ſhould ſo ſoon forget the *main and prin-cipal* intent of their coming together; and err, not in an external circumſtance, or in a matter of form; but in ſuch a particular, as ſhew them to have neglected that admo-nition and precept, which in expreſs words, was a part, and a principal part, of the *in-ſtitution itſelf; This do in remembrance of me.* For it was not poſſible, they ſhould at the very time of their religious aſſembly have run into *exceſs*; if they had conſidered, that what they were then doing, was in *remembrance* of the *Death and Paſſion of Chriſt*, who gave himſelf a Ranſom for them to that very End, that he might redeem them from all worldly and inordinate deſires: It was not poſſible, they ſhould at the very time of their receiving the Holy Communion, have deſpiſed their poor Brethren, and treated them uncharitably and with contempt; if they had conſidered, that the Action

they were then about, was a Solemn *fhewing forth the Lord's Death*, a folemn profeffion of their belief in a crucified Saviour, a publick declaration of their Hope of Salvation only through the merits of *his* Death, who died equally for poor and rich, for
the mean and for the honourable; and made it his laft Defire and Commandment
before his Death, that they who would be *his* Difciples, fhould love one another
without diftinction of worldly confiderations, and be Examples of Charity to the whole
World. Nothing therefore could be a jufter and ftronger reproof, to the *prefent* carelefs and uncharitable behaviour of the *Corinthians*; nothing more inftructive to them,
how to behave themfelves worthily and becomingly for the *future*; than to repeat, as
St *Paul* here does, the folemn words themfelves of our Lord's own inftitution; which
fo plainly and with fuch Authority exprefs the nature and defign of his Holy Sacrament. *For I have received,* (faith he) *of the Lord, that which alfo I delivered unto
you; that the Lord Jefus, the fame night in which he was betrayed, took bread; and
when he had given thanks, he brake it, and faid, Take, Eat; This is my Body which is
broken for you; This do in remembrance of Me: After the fame Manner alfo he took the
cup, when he had fupped, faying, This Cup is the New Teftament in my Blood; This do
ye, as oft as ye drink it, in remembrance of me: In remembrance of me;* i. e. in commemoration of my Death and Paffion; *fhewing* forth, (as the Apoftle expreffes it in
the following verfe,) *the Lord's Death till he come.*

IN difcourfing upon thefe Words, the

1ft Thing proper to be obferved in them and confidered, is the *general Nature,
End, and Defign* of this Holy Communion: expreffed by our Saviour in thefe Phrafes, *This is my Body, which is broken for you;* and *This Cup is the New Teftament in
my Blood; This do ye, as oft as ye drink it, in remembrance of Me:* Do it *in remembrance of Me:* i. e. Let it be a *perpetual folemn Commemoration* of my Death and Paffion; and a continual Occafion of your meditating upon the fpiritual Benefits purchafed to you thereby: Meditate ferioufly and devoutly, upon the wonderful Love of *God*,
the Supreme Lord and Father of all, in fending freely into the World no meaner a
perfon than his own Son, to become a Sacrifice and Propitiation for all Sins forfaken
and amended. Meditate upon the Love alfo of *Chrift*, in fubmitting willingly to this
good pleafure of his Father; in fubmitting willingly to *Death*, even the Death of the
Crofs, to accomplifh this merciful and gracious Defign: *For greater Love has no man
than this, that a man lay down his life for his Friends*, St John. xv. 13. Think with a
Juft Senfe upon the Humility and Condefcenfion of *him*, who *being in the Form of
God*, i. e. who being the perfon by whom God from the Beginning created and governs all things, yet *did not affect to appear in that form*, to appear *like unto God*, to
appear (as he might have done) in the glory of his Father; but voluntarily *made himfelf of no reputation, and took upon him the form of a fervant, and was made in the
likenefs of men, and being found in fafhion as a man, he humbled himfelf, and became
obedient unto Death, even the Death of the Crofs.* Confider, with due affection of mind,
the vile and heinous nature of *Sin*; confider it with the higheft indignation, and with the
firmeft refolutions againft it; which, in the Wifdom of the Almighty's Government,
was the Occafion of fuch a Humiliation to the beloved Son of God, in order to expiate and purchafe pardon for it: And let your frequent *eating this Bread, and drinking
this Cup,* be a conftant Remembrancer to your Thoughts, an Affiftance to your Devotion, and a perpetual renewing of thefe fpiritual meditations. *Do this, in remembrance of Me.* The *Mind* of Man, in this prefent State, is fo conftantly and fo ftrongly affected by the impreffions of Senfible Objects which perpetually furround it, that
it can very difficultly conceive of things fpiritual, purely and abftractedly by themfelves:
It is fo clofely united with Matter, and its attention fo continually and powerfully follicited by external and corporeal objects; that to meditate with any clofenefs and application

plication of mind on things remote from fenfe, (though indeed the moft natural and S E R M.
proper operation of the Soul,) is yet become one of the hardeft parts of our Duty, and   LVI.
the want of it one of the greateft occafions of Sin. The chief Reafon, why men, who
feem convinced in their minds of the Truth and Importance of Religion, of the certainty of a Judgment to come, and who will readily acknowledge the infinite difpropor-
tion between things temporal and eternal, between fpiritual and earthly concerns; yet
at the fame time, in their practice prefer things earthly before fpiritual, and temporal
concerns before eternal; the Reafon of This, I fay, is want of frequent and ferious Confideration; And the reafon why they do not confider, is, becaufe the capacity of their
Mind is fo wholly taken up, and their Attention fo conftantly employed, about fenfible Objects; that either they turn not their thoughts at all towards things moral and fpiritual; or, if they do, yet Thefe take fo little hold, that they are prefently diverted;
and make fuch flight impreffions, that they are immediately fwallowed up and loft,
among the deeper impreffions made by the Objects of Senfe. In confideration of this
weak and depraved ftate of man's Soul it is, that God, who is a Spirit infinitely removed from Senfe, the King immortal, invifible, whom no man hath feen nor can
fee, has in all his Revelations and Difcoveries of himfelf to mankind, reprefented himfelf, not by any fublime defcriptions of his nature and effence, (which are commonly
barren and unfruitful Speculations,) but reprefents himfelf affectionately under the character of being Author of fome great and memorable Work worthy of God, for the
good and benefit of Mankind: That fo men might neither on the one hand have any
occafion given them to frame to themfelves any likenefs or fimilitude of God; (which is
the greateft Indignity;) nor yet on the other fide want fuch a juft idea of him, as they
might fix their Thoughts and Meditations upon. Thus to the Patriarchs he ftyled himfelf, *God who created the Heavens and the Earth, and all things that are therein.* To
the Nation of the Jews, *God who brought them out of the Land of Egypt, out of the
houfe of bondage*; To us Chriftians; *God, even the Father of our Lord Jefus Chrift.*
And becaufe the great End and Effence of Religion is to imitate the nature and life of
God, in Holinefs, Juftice, Mercy, Truth, and the reft of his commendable Attributes;
therefore he has exemplified that life to us, in his Son Chrift Jefus; clothing him in
flefh, and fending him to dwell among us, that he might *leave us a* vifible and fenfible
Example, that we fhould follow his fteps. Further; becaufe men are ufually as unapt to
Remember, as they are at firft flow to *Apprehend,* things of a fpiritual nature; God has
therefore generally been pleafed to ufe the fame means, as in *conveying* fpiritual Notions firft into our minds, fo in *keeping them up* there likewife after we have once received them, by the help of *continued* outward and fenfible Signs. For fuch is our
Frame, that *Any* fenfible Memorial makes naturally a deeper and more lafting impreffion upon us, than a mere hiftorical narration of the Fact to be remembred : And the
more proper and fignificant, the more exprefs and pertinent the Memorial is, the *more*
ftrongly does it ftill affect us. When God entered into Covenant with *Abraham,* to be
a God unto Him and to his Seed after him; he inftituted the Rite of Circumcifion, as
a perpetual memorial of it to after-generations; and *it fhall be,* fays he, *a* Token *of the
Covenant between Me and You,* Gen. xvii. 11. In like manner under the *Mofaical*
Inftitution, the Jews had feveral fenfible Signs and pofitive Rites appointed them;
for the keeping up in their minds a continual *Remembrance* of God's commands, or for
lafting memorials of fome peculiar bleffings; *That ye feek not after your own Heart, and
after your own Eyes,* but may remember *and do all my Commandments, and be holy unto*
the Lord *your God,* Numb. xv. 40. Of this, we have feveral inftances in the Books of
the Law; But the moft remarkable one of all, and that which bears moft Analogy to
our Sacramental remembrance of the Death of Chrift in the Eucharift, is the Feaft of
the *Paffover*; appointed (as is fet down at large in the xiith of *Exodus,*) for a per-

petual

SERM. petual *commemoration* of the miraculous deliverance of the people of the Jews out of
LVI. *Egypt*, when *the Lord* paffed over *the Houfes of the children of Ifrael, but fmote all the
firft-born of the Egyptians* with Death. This bringing up the *Ifraelites* out of the land
of *Egypt*, was the greateft and moft wonderful deliverance that had ever been vouchfafed to any Nation. They had been long kept in fervitude, and oppreffed by a
mighty and potent People, without any poffibility of deliverance in all humane appearance; and their work was exacted *with rigor*, fo that it was called by way of
eminence *the houfe of bondage*, and *the iron furnace wherein they were made to ferve:*
Yet did God bring them forth *with a ftrong hand and with an out-ftretched arm*, with
figns and wonders and with *mighty works*. This was fuch a deliverance, as it might
reafonably have been prefumed, there could be no danger it fhould be ever forgot by
them: It was fuch a convincing and aftonifhing proof of the immediate prefence of
God amongft them, that 'tis not eafy to imagine, how the deep impreffions it muft
of neceffity make upon their minds, of the Power and peculiar Providence of God o-
ver them, fhould ever after come to be worn out. For there is nothing apt to affect
men in fo ftrong and lafting a manner, as the beholding fuch works, as they cannot
but judge to be above the Power of natural caufes, and to be the immediate effect of
the finger of God. Yet we find that *That* very people, even *that* very generation,
who had feen all thefe things with their own Eyes, (as *Mofes* often upbraided them;)
*forgat God's works, and his wonders which he had fhewed among them; They kept not the
Covenant of God, but refufed to walk in his law; They finned yet more againft him, and
provoked the moft Higheft in the wildernefs*, Pf. lxxviii. 17. How much more would
the Memory of that great work have been loft in *After*-generations, had not God appointed fuch a memorial of it, as, by its conftant return, and by its fitnefs to reprefent
the thing fignified, might always preferve it frefh in their memories, and oblige them
to *teach their Children the fame?* For *This* caufe therefore was the Feaft of the *Paffover* inftituted; an inftitution moft proper for That End to which it was defigned: Men,
in fuch a feftival Solemnity, being conftantly obliged to recollect and rehearfe particularly the Matter they gratefully commemorate; and by rejoicing together, with humble Devotion, to imprint it more and more deeply upon their minds for ever. And accordingly we find in the Hiftories of All Nations, that fomething like This was their
ufual manner of keeping up in their Minds a Senfe of great and remarkable bleffings;
of preferving the Memory of their moft eminent Benefactors; and of making effectual
the Laws and particular Precepts, fuch Benefactors have thought fit fhould be perpetually obferved.

AND now, This is the Method which God has been pleafed to make ufe of with
Us Chriftians likewife. The Sacrifice of the Death of Chrift, (which is the Foundation of God's accepting Repentance, confiftently with the Honour of his divine Laws,)
was ineftimably the greateft bleffing that was ever conferred upon the Sons of Men;
yea, the fountain and fpring, the original and foundation of all other bleffings: For fo
the Apoftle juftly argues, *He that fpared not his own Son, but delivered him up for us
all, how fhall he not with him alfo freely give us all things?* It was a Bleffing, of which
the deliverance of the People out of *Egypt*, and their paffage through the *Red Sea*,
was but a Type and a Figure; And therefore if that *Shadow* was to be fo folemnly commemorated by the Paffover, how much more does the *Subftance itfelf* of this eternal
Bleffing, deferve to be perpetually kept in mind with the higheft veneration, and commemorated with the greateft thankfulnefs, that can poffibly be expreffed. That This
might be done the more effectually; our Saviour in confideration of the weaknefs of
mens apprehenfions, and the flownefs of their memories in fpiritual matters, has thought
fit to inftitute *fuch* fymbols or reprefentations of what he has done and fuffered for
us, as might *beft* conduce to the fpiritual ends he defigned in the Sacrament; that is,

such Symbols, as might reprefent him to our Minds rather than to our bodily fenfes; and might affift the meditating faculties of the Soul; yet fo, as at the fame time not to affect the Senfes in fuch manner as to give any occafion to the outward actions to drown or thruft out the fpiritual affections of the mind; *fuch* fymbolical Reprefentations as might be naturally ufeful to excite Devotion; and yet at the fame time not be apt to degenerate into occafions of Superftition. There is no corporeal *Image*, (fuch as vain and corrupt men are apt to affect, and have found the great mifchief of it;) there is no Object to *terminate the Senfe*; but the Bread is appointed to be broken, and the Wine to be poured out; to remind us in an *abftract and fpiritual* manner, how his Body was broken, and his Blood fhed for us. And this he has commanded us to do *always* in *remembrance of him*; *fhowing forth the Lord's Death*, through all Generations, until his Second *Coming*.

WE are to do it *at all times*; to fhow forth his Death, by a perpetual commemoration, until his fecond coming: But more *efpecially*, at the folemn return of thofe great Feftivals, fet apart in remembrance of his *Nativity*, *Paffion*, and *Refurrection*. His *Birth* in human Flefh, was the humbling himfelf to a Capacity of fuffering *Death* for our fakes; and his *Refurrection* after Death, was the evidence and demonftration, of his Sufferings, being accepted in the fight of God. He *died for our Sins*, that he might expiate them by his Blood; *and he rofe again for our juftification*, that he might in his Glory communicate to us the full Effect and Fruit of that Atonement. He *offered himfelf* once *a Sacrifice for Sin*; and then *for ever fat down on the right hand of God*; *having by one offering for ever perfected them that are fanctified*. But now in order to make ourfelves capable of fo ineftimable a Benefit, it is neceffary on *our* part, that we fo commemorate *his* Death, as to die *ourfelves* alfo unto Sin; and fo to rejoyce in *his* Refurrection, as to rife *ourfelves* likewife, unto newnefs of life. *Chrift our Paffover is facrificed for us*; *Therefore let* us *keep the Feaft, not with old leaven, neither with the leaven of malice and wickednefs, but with the unleavened Bread of fincerity and Truth*, 1 Cor. v. 7. To fuch as are fincerely and heartily defirous fo to do, there can be no better Affiftance than the frequent and worthy receiving this Holy Communion: The *general Nature, End and Defign* of which, I have *Now* fhown to be a folemn commemorating of the Death of Chrift, *(Do this in Remembrance of Me;)* and the *particulars* contained under this *general* Head, fhall *hereafter* more fully be explained.

LET us therefore, with Hearts full of fincere Refolutions to forfake every Sin, partake of this Holy Feaft in the Manner our Lord himfelf has appointed: And that it may have an effectual influence upon us to imitate him in his *Life*, whom otherwife we do but mock when we commemorate his *Death*; *God of his infinite mercy grant*, &c.

SERMON LVII.

The Nature, End and Design of the HOLY COMMUNION.

1 COR. XI. 25.

After the same manner also he took the cup, when he had supped, saying, This Cup is the new Testament in my Blood; This do ye, as oft as ye drink it, in remembrance of me.

SERM.
LVII.

I HAVE from these words, in a *foregoing* Discourse, considered the *general* Nature, End, and Design, of the Institution of the Sacrament of the Lord's Supper. I proceed *at this time*, to reduce to Practice the *several particulars*, included in that *One general* direction given us by our Lord, *Do this in Remembrance of Me.*

AND 1*st*, To do *This* in remembrance *of Christ*, signifies *fixing and imprinting* in our minds with a more lasting and *permanent* Impression, the remembrance of his Death and Passion; as an effectual *Motive to universal Obedience*: That is, to the Practice of Virtue, upon the Principles of the Doctrine of Christ. There can be no stronger Argument, to perswade Men to the practice of Virtue and Holiness, than a due consideration of the exemplary *Life* and meritorious *Death* of our Saviour; His Life as a Pattern of all Virtue, and his Death as an Evidence of God's Hatred against Sin. His *Life* was so complete a *pattern* of pure Religion: and his *Death* so affectionate a *perswasive* to imitate That example; that whosoever frequently and seriously meditates upon these things, can neither readily *err* from the right way, for want of due *instruction* and sufficient *direction*; nor *faint* for want of powerful *Motives* to proceed in it. For, *What* temptation can prevail upon That person to sin deliberately against God, to run into *any* Acts of Debauchery or Impiety; who by Faith continually beholds our Lord shedding his most precious Blood, to redeem him from the dominion and punishment of that Sin, which he is now tempted to commit? What Heart can be so obdurate, what Breast so ungrateful, as to run knowingly and willingly into the commission of Sin; when he has his *dying* Saviour habitually before his eyes, intreating and beseeching him to avoid those Sins, which were the cause of his cruel and ignominious Death? In matters of *temporal* Concern, Men always indeavour to remember the instructions of a *dying* Friend; and think nothing more sacredly obliges them, than his *last* and most affectionate Desires: How much *more* religiously ought we to observe those Precepts, which we find our *Saviour* injoyning us not only when *dying*, but when dying *for our sakes*; when dying even *for that very end*, that he might enable us the more effectually to perform them! Now the *Means* to preserve these Impressions constantly fresh upon our Minds, and in their full force; is to partake frequently of those elements, which our Lord himself has appointed to be received, as the most proper remembrances of himself. Whosoever keeps up in his mind a constant remembrance of Christ, of what he has done and suffered for us, will not easily fall into gross and habitual Sins: and he that frequently and devoutly, with understanding and know-

I   ledge

ledge of what he does, partakes of the Holy Communion, cannot fail to keep up in S E R M. his Mind fuch a conftant Remembrance of our Lord. When we fee the Bread broken, LVII. and the Wine poured out; we cannot but contemplate how his Body was broken, and his Blood fhed for our fakes; and the oftner we renew thefe thoughts by frequent communicating, the ftronger and more vigorous, the deeper and more lafting impref-fions muft thefe things neceffarily make upon our Minds. One principal reafon why Men in thefe latter Ages of the World, who profefs themfelves Chriftians, are yet fo loofe and fenfual, fo carelefs and indifferent in matters of Religion, fo cold and lifelefs in their devotion, and fo little affected with things fpiritual and of a heavenly nature, is becaufe they feldom allow themfelves Time, from the Cares and Bufinefs and Pleafures of the World, to recollect their Thoughts, and meditate ferioufly upon the great Motives and Arguments of Religion : And one reafon why they fo feldom think on thefe Arguments, is, becaufe they neglect thofe means, which God has gracioufly appointed to awaken and withdraw their Minds from earthly and temporal confidera-tions; thofe means, to which God has annexed the Affiftance of his Holy Spirit, to enable us to raife our Thoughts and fix our Meditations upon things fpiritual and re-moved from Senfe. Hence it comes to pafs, that though they *believe* indeed the Hif-tory of Chrift's dying for them, as a bare relation of Matter of Fact; yet they feldom remember or think at all upon it; or if they do, yet it is fo flightly and fuperficially, with fo little due apprehenfion of the great concern and importance of it to themfelves, or of the true defign of it with regard to their own real Amendment; that it leaves upon their minds none of thofe impreffions, which are neceffary in order to have an effectual influence upon their lives and actions. One great and principal End therefore of the inftitution of the Sacrament of the Lord's Supper, is, by means of outward and vifible Signs, apt and decent, proper and fignificant, to imprint and fix in our minds with a more lafting and permanent impreffion, the remembrance of Chrift's Death and Paffion; that, having always before our Eyes thofe admirable inftances of his unparal-lelled Love, and being conftantly reminded of the true End and Defign of his Suffer-ings, we may be the more ftrongly fortified againft all temptations, that would feduce us to fin againft fo great a Benefactor; and that we may go on the more effectually in the ways of *his* commandments, who has done and fuffered for us things of fo great and fo ineftimable a value.

2. *Doing this in remembrance of Chrift*, is making *fuch* a commemoration of his Death, as is with all Humility a continual *acknowledgment* of its being to *Sinners* the *only Ground of Hope and Affurance of Pardon. This Cup*, faith he, *is the New Tefta-ment in my Blood, which is fhed for you, and for many for the remiffion of Sins*; There-fore *do this in remembrance of me.* The Sacrament of the Lord's Supper is not *itfelf*, like Baptifm, a Rite appointed for the Remiffion of Sins; but 'tis a *commemoration* only of that All-fufficient Sacrifice, which was *once* offered for an eternal Expia-tion. To imagine that the Lord's Supper, which is to be repeated *perpetually*, has fuch a promife annexed to it of taking away all paft Sins, as *Baptifm* had, which was to be adminiftred but *once*, is a dangerous and fatal Error; Becaufe fuch an Opinion would be plainly an encouragement for Men to *continue in Sin*, that *the Grace* of Forgivenefs *might* be perpetually repeated and *abound.* But the receiving *This* Sacrament is a continual *acknowledgment*, that *That* Pardon which God vouchfafes us, not as a neceffary confequent of the outward Action, but upon the condition of our true and unfeigned Repentance; even that *That* Pardon, is the purchafe of the Blood of Chrift, and the Effect of that great and eternal Sacrifice, once offered for the Expiation of Sin. The Church of *Rome*, by pretending that Sacrifice to be perpetually repeated upon the Altar; as they give men too great incouragement to continue in Sin, fo they exprefly contradict the Apoftle St *Paul*; who affures us, *Heb.* ix. 25, that

S E R M. Chrift is not to *offer himfelf often, as the High Prieft entered into the Holy place every*
LVII. *year with blood of others*; For then muft he often have *fuffered fince the foundation of the*
〰   *World*; But now Once *in the end of the World has he appeared to put away Sin, by the*
Sacrifice of himfelf. The Sacramental *remembrance* of which great Propitiation, the
antient Writers of the Church do indeed frequently ftile, by a figurative expreffion,
the unbloody Sacrifice; But for that *very reafon*, and by that *very Expreffion*, it is declared *not to be properly* itfelf *a Sacrifice*, but only a grateful *commemoration* of one; becaufe *without Blood*, as there is *no remiffion*, fo there is properly *no Sacrifice*. It is a Sacrifice, only in a *figurative* Senfe, and by way of allufion; juft in the fame manner of
fpeaking, as *Chriftians* are ftiled in the *New Teftament the Circumcifion made without*
hands. Neverthelefs, to *thofe* who truly and fincerely repent and amend; and who humbly
and devoutly beg of God the pardon of their paft and forfaken Sins, through the interceffion of Chrift; to *fuch* perfons, tho' there is indeed no *new Sacrifice*, no *new Foun-*
dation of Remiffion; there is neverthelefs fufficient ground for hope and affurance of
Pardon, in the merit of that one All-fufficient Sacrifice Once offered for ever: And
fincere Penitents can never with more reafonable and well-grounded Faith, hope to
have applied to themfelves the benefit of the grace and forgivenefs, purchafed once for
them by that great Expiation; than when they are with true Devotion and with full
purpofe of Amendment of Life, commemorating their Saviour's fufferings in that folemn manner, which *He himfelf* has appointed, *who* was the Perfon that gave himfelf
to be the reconciliation for us, that through him we might have accefs with confidence
to the throne of grace; and *whom God has fet forth to be a propitiation* for us, *thro'*
Faith in his Blood; *to declare his righteoufnefs*, (that is, his *mercy*; for fo *the righte-*
oufnefs of God fignifies in the *New Teftament*;) to declare, I fay, his righteoufnefs
for the remiffion of Sins that are paft, *through the forbearance of God*. They can never with better and more lively Hope, exprefs their full Truft and humble dependance
upon God, that he fhall *freely give* them *all* Other *things*; than at That Time when
they are worthily and devoutly commemorating, according to our Lord's inftitution,
how *he fpared not* even *his* own *Son, but delivered him up for us all*. How ill therefore does it become Men who call themfelves Chriftians to neglect this Ordinance with
a carelefs indifferency; and upon flight pretences, to deprive themfelves of the benefit
of fo reafonable a duty! The Blood of Chrift, is, in the Scripture-language, *a foun-*
tain open for Sin and for Uncleannefs, that is, for Sin repented of, and utterly forfaken;
and the benefit thereof is never more likely to be effectually applied, than when Men,
with determined refolutions of better Obedience, are difpofed to become worthy
partakers of thefe Holy Myfteries.

3. *Doing this in remembrance of Chrift*, is *declaring publickly* to the World our
Faith in him; and indeavouring to *continue down* the Memory of his Love to *all gene-*
rations. Thus St *Paul*, 1 Cor. xi. 26. in the words immediately following the Text;
As oft, fays he, *as ye eat this bread and drink this Cup, ye do* fhow *the Lord's death till*
he come. We here profefs *publickly* our Faith in his Death; and declare folemnly to
the World, that we expect remiffion of our Sins, only through the Virtue of his blood
fhed for us. We commemorate his unfpeakable Love to Mankind; and extol and
magnify in our Praifes thofe great Acts, which were the Effects of that ineftimable
love. We rehearfe and proclaim the benefits he has procured for us; and, as much as
in us lies, *make known to all men* the glory of his Love and Power: *that one genera-*
tion may praife his works to another, and declare his mighty acts; that *men may fpeak of*
the glorious honour of his Majefty, and of his wondrous works.

I N the inftitution of the Paffover, when the *children of Ifrael were commanded to*
eat unleavened bread feven days, in remembrance of their deliverance out of *Egypt*; 'tis
exprefsly added in the command, that they fhould Declare or tell forth unto their children

4

dren the mercy of that deliverance: *Thou fhalt* fhow thy *Son in that day, faying, This* S E R M. *is done becaufe of that which the Lord did unto me when I came forth out of Egypt: And* LVII. *it fhall be a Sign unto thee upon thine Hand, and for a memorial between thine eyes, that* *the Law of the Lord may be in thy mouth;* for, *with a ftrong hand hath the Lord brought thee out of Egypt,* Exod. xiii. 8. Hence they called the Pafchal Leffon *the Annuntiating* or *Declaring;* Which is a word exactly anfwering to St *Paul's* expreffion of *fhewing forth,* or declaring, the *Lord's Death till he come.* To communicate therefore *in re-membrance* of Chrift, is to *declare publickly,* and keep up amongft Men the memory of his Death, and of the ineftimable benefits purchafed for us thereby: 'Tis to teftify our firm belief of the virtue and efficacy of that great Sacrifice; and to profefs ourfelves publickly in the number of thofe, who, by partaking of the Feaft inftituted in *Re-membrance* of the Sacrifice, expect to be made partakers of the Sacrifice itfelf.

4. To *do this in remembrance of Chrift,* implies, that with the greateft *joy,* and higheft expreffions of *gratitude,* we return *Thanks* to God for his unfpeakable Mercy, in fending into the World his Son, the Son of his *Love,* out of his Bofom, for the re-demption of mankind. It was a precept in the Law of *Mofes,* Deut. xvi. 11. *Thou fhalt* rejoyce *in thy feafts before the Lord.* And particularly in the Pafchal Supper, be-fides the ufual forms of Bleffing and Thankfgiving, they fung a peculiar Hymn, in memory of their deliverance out of the land of *Egypt.* In compliance with which cuftom we find it recorded by two of the Evangelifts, that our Saviour and his Difci-ples, immediately after the inftitution of the Lord's Supper, fung an *Hymn* of Praife unto God; probably the *fame,* or *part* of That Hymn which the *Jews* ufed to fing after the Pafchal Supper; *Their* deliverance from the *Egyptians,* being a type of *our* de-liverance from the power and dominion of Sin; and the Thankfgiving proper upon *That* occafion, being much *more* emphatically applicable to *This.* Befides; in the in-ftitution itfelf, the Evangelift takes notice, that when our Saviour took the Bread, he *gave Thanks,* or Bleffed and Praifed God; Whence the *whole Action* is ufually called the *Eucharift,* that is, the Solemn *Thankfgiving;* and, by St *Paul, the Cup of Bleffing which we blefs,* or, as the word may no lefs properly be rendered, *the Cup of Praife and Thankfgiving.* The fame is alfo obfervable in St *Luke's* defcription of the Practice of the moft primitive Chriftians, *Acts* ii. 46. *And they continuing daily with one accord in the Temple, and breaking bread from houfe to houfe,* (in *the houfe,* the words fhould be tranflated, *i. e.* in the place of their religious affemblies;) did *eat their meat with gladnefs and finglenefs of heart;* Praifing God, and having favour with all the people. Frequent Forms of Praife and Thankfgiving upon this occafion, we meet with in the moft ancient Chriftian Writers; and none more affectionate than That we ftill make ufe of; *We praife thee, we blefs thee, we worfhip thee, we glorify thee, we give thanks to thee for thy great Glory, O Lord, God, heavenly King, God the Father Almighty. We give thanks to thee for thy great Glory;* i. e. for the wonderful *manifeftation* of thy Glory and Power, thy Mercy and Goodnefs towards Mankind, in *fending* thine own Son to die for our Sins, and to *give himfelf* a ranfom and propitiation for Sinners.

T H I S reconciliation of Penitent Sinners to God by the Death of his Son is the Higheft Inftance of Love and Goodnefs, that was ever fhown to Mankind: For, fcarce-ly for a *righteous* man, faith St *Paul,* will one die: But *God* commendeth his love to-wards us, in that while we were yet *Sinners,* Chrift died for us, *Rom.* v. 7. God could in a moment have deftroyed the whole race of Sinners; and, as St *John Baptift* affecti-onately expreffes it, *was able out of the Stones to have raifed up Children unto Abraham.* But *he turned away his wrath from them, and fuffered not his whole difpleafure to arife.* Wherefore, if at *all* times we are bound to return Thanks to God for *all* his mercies, for the mercies of every *day* and of every *hour;* with how much *greater* earneftnefs and ftronger affection, ought we to exprefs the fame thankful difpofition of mind, when we are commemorating *That* mercy, which is not only the greateſt of all others, but the fountain alſo and foundation of them all ? and how zealous ought we to be of expreſſing our thankfulneſs to him by ſuitable *Obedience* ; when the conſideration of the *firſt* mercy, that *he ſpared not his own Son, but delivered him up for us all*, gives us reaſon to hope, that, if we behave ourſelves in any meaſure worthy of ſo great a Salvation, much more *ſhall he with Him alſo freely give us all things?* and that if, *while we were yet Sinners, Chriſt died for us ; much more, being now juſtified by his blood, we ſhall be ſaved from wrath through Him ? For if, when we were enemies, we were reconciled to God by the Death of his Son ; much more, being reconciled, we ſhall be ſaved by his Life,* Rom. v. 9. Wherefore, let us ſay with the Holy Pſalmiſt, *Pſ.* cxvi. 12, 13, *What ſhall I render unto the Lord for all the benefits that he has done unto me ? I will receive the cup of Salvation, and call upon the Name of the Lord.* And *Pſ.* ciii. 1. *Praiſe the Lord, O my Soul, and all that is within me, praiſe his holy Name ; Praiſe the Lord, O my Soul, and forget not all his benefits ; Who forgiveth all thy Sin, and healeth all thine infirmities ; Who ſaveth thy life from deſtruction, and crowneth thee with mercy and loving kindneſs.* There is no poſſibility, but he who duly contemplates the unſpeakable love of Chriſt, in giving himſelf freely to *bear our Sins himſelf in his own body on the tree*, and ſeriouſly meditates on the original and eſſential Goodneſs of God, which firſt moved and diſpoſed him to *find out* this method of recovery for us ; muſt wiſh he had the tongues of *Men and Angels*, to ſhow forth the praiſes of *him that has loved us*, and ſent his Son to *waſh us from our Sins in his own blood, and to make us Kings and Prieſts unto God even his Father, to whom be glory and dominion for ever.*

5. *Doing this in remembrance of Chriſt*, implies on *our* part a *confirming* of our *Covenant* with God, a thankful *acceptance* of thoſe *Conditions* of Pardon he has offered us in the Goſpel, and an *acknowledging* and *renewing* our Obligations to obey him. *This Cup*, ſays our Saviour, *is the New Teſtament*, or (as the word equally ſignifies) *the new* Covenant, *in my Blood* : Now *every Covenant*, in the Nature of the thing, ſuppoſes *conditions* to be performed on either part. God has commanded Repentance and Remiſſion of Sins to be preached to all Nations in the Name of Chriſt ; and the condition on *his* part of the Covenant, the remiſſion of Sins, is always ready to be verified ; if we fail not in *our* part, of having worthily repented, and reformed our Lives. But if we continue in our Sins ; the Commemoration *of the Death* of Chriſt can do us no ſervice, where the Effect of his *Death itſelf* takes no place : The partaking of this *Feaſt in* remembrance *of the Sacrifice*, can be of no benefit to us, when we have no part nor lot in the *Sacrifice itſelf.* The Sacrament of the Lord's Supper is not properly an *Expiation* of Sin, even to thoſe who *truly repent* ; but only a *thankful* remembrance of that great Atonement, by virtue of which our Repentance is made acceptable : Much leſs, can it be of any efficacy, or power to do away ſuch *Sins*, as are *never forſaken.* Religion is no way capable of a greater corruption, nor can *any* Superſtition be of more deſtructive conſequence, than to make *That* Ordinance an eaſy method of obtaining *perpetual* Pardon of repeated Tranſgreſſions, which in reality was intended to remind us continually, that the Pardon of Sin could not *at all* be obtained, but by the ſhedding the precious blood of the Son of God.

THERE are many pious and religious perſons, who, on the *other* hand, are unreaſonably *ſcrupulous* ; and notwithſtanding their ſincere Endeavours to obey God's commandments, ſtill *fear, where no fear is* : But, as ſuch perſons have all the reaſon in the World to reſt ſatisfied, that the general courſe of a virtuous and religious life, is an abundant ſecurity againſt the danger of *not diſcerning the Lord's body* ; ſo, on the contrary, *vicious* perſons ought to be well aſſured, that there is *no external* part whatſoever of religious worſhip, by which they can receive *any* benefit, without actual amendment and reformation of life. The Arguments of Religion are ſtrong and powerful, to

invite

invite them to Repentance; The gracious Motions of the Spirit of God are ready to S E R M. assist and strengthen their sincere endeavours; and especially, where it finds them with LVII. seriousness attending his holy Ordinances: But their Obedience to *this one* command-ment of Christ must be with an intention of obeying *the rest*, and not with a design to supply that Neglect. He that *does* this worthily in *Remembrance of Christ*, must mean to express his gratitude to God for the Death of his Son, by *such* a Repentance, as the Death of Christ has enabled and obliged him to make perfect. He must *so* com-memorate the Love of his Saviour, as thereby to excite in himself a suitable return of Love to him that died for him; and our *Love* to Christ, the Scripture tells us, *is This*, that we *keep his Commandments*. We must *shew forth the Lord's Death till he come*, by *so* dying *ourselves* unto Sin, as to declare evidently to the World, that we have a well-grounded Hope, of being made like him also in his *Resurrection*. We must con-sider, that when the Blood of Christ is stiled in the prophetick language, *a fountain opened for Sin and for Uncleanness*; the Meaning is, (as St *Paul* explains it,) *for the for-giveness of Sins that are* past, not for our incouragement to continue in them for the time *to come*. We must remember that we *are bought with a* price; and *therefore* must *glorify God in our Body and in our Spirit, which are God's; Knowing that* we *were re-deemed, not with corruptible things, but with the precious blood of Christ, as of a Lamb without blemish and without spot.* We must with firm and effectual resolutions of fu-ture Obedience, *offer and present ourselves, our Souls and Bodies, a reasonable, holy, and lively Sacrifice unto God*; as often as we commemorate that great Sacrifice, which was once offered for us in the Death of his Son. Otherwise, instead of *doing this in* remem-brance *of Christ*, we shall be found to do it in *Contempt* of him; *accounting the blood of the Covenant, wherewith we ought to be sanctified, an unholy thing*; *denying the Lord* who *bought* us with the precious blood of his dear Son; *and doing despite unto the Spirit of Grace.*

Lastly, *Doing this in remembrance of Christ*, is a Profession of our *Communion* one with another, and a strong Obligation to Mutual *Love, Charity, and Good-will.* This is a Subject much insisted on by St *Paul* in this whole Epistle, and particularly in this chapter, and in this very Argument, of which the Text is a part; and therefore de-serves to be discoursed upon more largely.

SERMON

S E R M O N LVIII.

The Nature, End and Defign of the HOLY COMMUNION.

1 C O R. XI. 25. latter part.

_____*This do ye, as oft as ye drink it, in remembrance of me.*

THE due Obfervance of this Precept of our Saviour, *Do this in remembrance of Me*, I have fhown to imply the following particulars.

1. A *fixing* and *imprinting* in our minds more laftingly, the remembrance of his Death and Paffion; as a *Motive to Obedience.*

2. A Commemorating his Death in an humble *Acknowledgment*, of its being the *only Ground of our Hope of Pardon.*

3. A *declaring publickly* to the World, our Faith in him; and indeavouring to *continue down* the Memory of his Love to *all generations.*

4. A returning *Thanks* to God with the greateft *Joy*, and higheft expreffions of Gratitude, for his unfpeakable *Mercy* in fending his Son into the World for the *redemption of Mankind.*

5. A *confirming* on *our* part, our Covenant with God; a thankful *acceptance* of thofe conditions of Pardon he has offered us; and an *acknowledging* and *renewing* our Obligations to obey him.

A N D thefe I have *already* difcourfed upon.

Laftly, (and to conclude what I have to offer on this Head;) *Doing this in remembrance of Chrift*, is a Profeffion of our *Communion* one with another, and a ftrong Obligation to mutual *Love, Charity and Good-will.*

A PRINCIPAL part of the defign of this *whole* 1ft Epiftle of St *Paul* to the *Corinthans*, is to fhow the Neceffity of Love and Unity among Chriftians; and all that he difcourfes particularly in the 10th and 11th chapters concerning the Sacrament of the Lord's Supper, is chiefly with intent to draw Arguments from the nature and defign of that Holy Inftitution, to fhow the unreafonableneſs and unchriftianneſs of Animofities and Divifions among themfelves. With *This* he begins the Epiftle, ch. i. ver 10. *Now I befeech you, brethren, by the name of our Lord Jefus Chrift, that ye all fpeak the fame thing, and that there be no divifions among you; but that ye be perfectly joined together in the fame mind and in the fame judgment.* His meaning is not, that Chriftians are bound to *be*, or to *pretend* to be, in all things of the fame opinion. For to *be fo*, is *impoffible*; and to *pretend* to be fo, is *hypocrify.* But his meaning is, that *notwithftanding* all fuch differences of opinion, as are abfolutely unavoidable, yet, by mutual forbearance, meekneſs and charity, they fhould be as free from ftrife and contention, as if they were really in all refpects of One Mind. *This* exhortation, he carries on through the whole Body of his Difcourfe, ch. iii. ver. 3. *Whereas there is among you envying and ftrife and divifions, are ye not carnal, and walk as men?* To

3

This,

This, all his difcourfe concerning the Communion, ch. **x.** has refpect; *For, we being* S E R M.
many, are one Bread and one Body; for we are all partakers of that one Bread, ver. 17. LVIII.
With regard to *This* more efpecially it is, that in the xith chapter he paffes fo fevere a
cenfure on thofe who *eat this bread and drink this cup of the Lord unworthily.* For
fo he introduces his difcourfe, ver. 18. a little before the Text; *Firft of all, when ye
come together in the Church, I hear that there be divifions among you, and I partly believe it.* And by the help of this obfervation, the connexion of the Apoftle's difcourfe in thefe two chapters will appear very eafy, which otherwife may feem fomewhat difficult to be underftood. In the tenth chapter, the divifions referred to, are
fuch as arofe among the *Corinthians* upon the queftion concerning the lawfulnefs of
eating things offered unto Idols, That an *Idol* was nothing in the World, and that the
good creatures of *God* could receive no defilement from the vanity and fuperftition of
men, the Apoftle knew and plainly enough declared: But leaft Offence fhould be
given to weaker brethren, who could not fo clearly diftinguifh; he exhorts them to
forbear joining themfelves with fuch affemblies of *Gentiles*, as might make them feem
(at leaft to the weaker brethren) to be partakers of the Heathen Idolatry. For, *faith
he*, in *like manner as* a man's receiving the communion with *Chriftians*, is a publick
declaration of his being a Chriftian himfelf; and *as* a Man's partaking of the Sacrifices
at the Altars of the *Ifraelites*, is openly profeffing himfelf to be a *Jew* by religion;
fo, for a Chriftian to eat of things facrificed to *Idols*, though he *has* in himfelf that
knowledge that an Idol is nothing in the World, yet may by others be interpreted as
if he joined with them in their idolatry. This is plainly the true connexion of the A-
poftle's difcourfe; ver. 14, &c. *My dearly beloved, flee from Idolatry: I fpeak as to
wife men, judge ye what I fay*, i. e. judge and obferve, while I explain this to you by
an eafy comparifon: *The Cup of bleffing which We* Chriftians *blefs, is it not the Communion of the blood of Chrift? The Bread which we break, is it not the Communion of
the Body of Chrift?* that is; Is it not a publick declaration of our *mutual agreement* and
fellowfhip, in commemorating *together* the love of our *common* Saviour? (*For we being
many, are one bread and one body; for we are all partakers of that one bread;*) And in
like manner, fays he, continuing the fame fimilitude, Ifrael *after the flefh; are not
they which eat of the facrifices partakers of the Altar?* i. e. Are they not partakers of
the *Jewifh* religion? do they not thereby profefs their Communion with *Them? So* alfo,
the things which the Gentiles *facrifice, they facrifice to devils and not to God, and I
would not that ye fhould have fellowfhip with devils.* The Words are not abrupt and
incoherent exhortations, as (without carefully attending to the defign of the Apoftle's
argument,) they at firft Sight may feem to be; but they are directly connected with
what went before, and are clearly a continuation of one and the fame fimilitude; that,
as among both *Jews* and *Chriftians* the partaking in the fame folemn religious acts, is
a declaration of Unity, communion and agreement; *fo* to eat with *Heathens* of things
facrificed to Idols, would be an affording too great a ground of fufpicion, of agreeing
with them in their Idolatry. In the *following* chapter, the divifions referred to, are of
another kind; namely, fuch as arofe in the Church, upon occafion of the *rich* defpifing the *poor*, and not allowing them to partake equally in their religious feftival.
This was their *eating and drinking unworthily*; This was their *not difcerning the Lord's
Body:* They did not fufficiently difcern and diftinguifh, at leaft they did not act as if
they were fenfible, that this folemn act of Religion was effentially a ftrong and indifpenfable Obligation, to mutual Love, Unity, and Charity. To remedy this diforder
therefore, the Apoftle thought no Argument could be more proper and powerful, than
to repeat to them at large the hiftory of our Saviour's inftituting his laft Supper. He
thought it was not poffible, if they worthily remembred their *common Lord*, that
they could be fo forgetful of their *Duty one towards another.*

S E R M. IN *Both* thefe paffages therefore, he fuppofes (what I am *now* infifting upon,) that
LVIII. commemorating of Chrift in the manner he himfelf has appointed, is a Profeffion of
our *Communion* one with another, and a ftrong Obligation to mutual Love, Charity
and Good-will. *The Cup of Bleffing which we blefs, is it not the Communion of the Blood
of Chrift? The Bread which we break, is it not the Communion of the Body of Chrift?*
For, faith he, *we being many, are one bread and one body; for we are all partakers of
that one bread*; ch. x. ver. 17. And he *therefore* declares, ch. xi. ver. 20. that *when*
the Corinthians *came together into one place, this* was *not to eat the Lord's Supper*; becaufe faith he, *I hear that that there be divifions among you, and I partly believe it.*
One great part of the Defign of the Gofpel of Chrift, was to eftablifh a Religion, which
as it might teach us how to be *reconciled* to God, fo it might *reconcile* us likewife unto
one another: which, as it was to oblige us to *love the* Lord our God *with all our Heart*,
fo to *love our* Neighbours *alfo as ourfelves.* By *This fhall all men know*, faith our Saviour, *that ye are my Difciples, if ye have Love one to another*, St Joh. xiii. 35. To
This, the very Nature and Conftitution of the univerfal Church of Chrift, the very Notion of its being a Body whereof Chrift is the Head, does itfelf naturally lead and direct us; *For, as* (in the literal fenfe) *we have many members in one body*, faith St
Paul; fo (in the *fpiritual* fenfe likewife) We *being many are one Body in Chrift, and
every one Members one of another*, Rom. xii. 4, 5. To *This*, the due confideration of *every
part* of the Chriftian inftitution will have a powerful influence to oblige us; Let us
endeavour, as the fame Apoftle expreffly argues, *to keep the unity of the Spirit in the
bond of Peace;* For, fays he, *there is One Body and One Spirit, even as ye are called
in One hope of your calling; One Lord, One Faith, One Baptifm, One God and Father
of all, who is above all, and through all, and in you all*, Eph. iv. 3. And ver. 15.
Speak the truth in Love, that ye *may grow up into him in all things, who is the Head,
even Chrift; From whom the whole Body fitly joined together, and compacted by that which
every joint fupplieth, according to the effectual working in the meafure of every part,
maketh increafe of the Body, unto the edifying of itfelf in Love.* Through the Wickednefs of *Men* indeed, and by the Fraud of the *Devil*; thro' falfe Notions of the great
End and *Defign* of Religion; through unchriftian contentioufnefs, and more eager Zeal
for the imaginations of *Men*, than for the commands of *God*: this Body of Chrift, this
one univerfal Church, intended by our Lord to have been fpread uniformly over all the
Earth; has been for many Ages divided by many Parties, and into numerous Factions.
But, as we all believe in the fame God and Father of all, as we are all redeemed by
the fame *Lord Jefus Chrift*, as we are all baptized into the profeffion of the fame *Creed*,
(the Apoftles *Form of Sound words*,) and are all partakers of the fame *Communion* at
the Table of our Lord; fo by this one unchangeable and fundamental root of Unity,
ought we to ufe our utmoft endeavours to *hold faft the Head, from which all the Body
by joints and bands having nourifhment miniftred, and knit together, increafes with the
increafe of God*, Col. ii. 19.

AND as this great Duty of mutual Love and Charity, is thus inforced upon us by
the *general* Defign and Tendency, by the *whole Tenor* of the Gofpel; fo is it ftill *more
particularly* and *moft ftrongly*, by the Example of that unparallelled inftance of ama-
zing Love, the Death of Chrift for our fakes, which we profefs to commemorate as
often as we communicate at his Holy Table: Where 'tis not poffible for us to approach
with Hearts duly fenfible of, and worthily affected with, the Greatnefs of the Love of
Chrift towards us; but it muft at the fame time excite in us a difpofition to *imitate*
him, according to the proportion of our Abilities; and to exprefs our Gratitude to *him*,
by following that Example of loving and doing good to *our brethren*, which he has in
fo eminent a manner fet before us. 'Tis particularly taken notice of by St *Luke*, that
the primitive Difciples, as they continued ftedfaft in the Apoftles doctrine and in break-

3   ing

ing of bread and in prayer, so they did all things unanimously, *with one accord, Acts* ii. S E R M.
46, with mutual Love, Charity, and Good-will. Our Lord himself, in that last and LVIII.
most affectionate Discourse, which he made to his Disciples a little before his Death,
at the time of his instituting the Sacrament of the Lord's Supper; insists upon This,
as the thing of all others the most acceptable to him, and most desired by him: *This
is my commandment, that ye love one another, as I have loved you*, St *Joh.* xv. 12; and
ch. xiii. 34, *A new commandment, I give unto you, that ye love one another*; even *as I
have loved you, that ye also love one another.* And the Apostle St *John*, who leaned
upon his Master's Breast, and seems in a particular manner to have been partaker of his
kind and loving Spirit, the Spirit of meekness, gentleness, and goodness; presses this
Duty accordingly, with a like earnestness: *Herein*, says he, *is Love; not that we
loved God, but that he loved Us, and sent his Son to be the propitiation for our Sins. Beloved, if God so loved us, We ought also to love one another*, 1 *Joh.* iv. 10; And ch. iii.
16, *Hereby perceive we the Love of God, because he* (because Christ) *laid down his life
for us; and* We ought to lay down our lives for the Brethren: To *lay down our lives* for
them; *i. e.* to love them, comparatively speaking, even as our own Lives; to love them
as ourselves; to do every thing that is in our Power reasonably, for their benefit and
advantage. *This* is the true Spirit of Christianity; *This* is the full and proper Effect of
the Gospel of Christ: By *This* we are to judge of ourselves, whether we be truly and indeed his Disciples, and have made any considerable progress and improvement in his
religion. And By *This* we are in a more especial manner to examine ourselves, whether we be duly qualified, to be made worthy partakers of *his* Body and Blood, who
died for this end, that as he might reconcile us to *God*, so he might *also* reconcile us to
each other. And indeed in *other* particulars, men are not so very apt to mistake. There
is *no Man* who approaches the Lord's Table with *any* Reverence, with *any* Sense of
Religion upon his Mind; but is desirous at that time, to strengthen his *Faith* in *God*, to
express his *Gratitude* to his Saviour, to obtain *Pardon* of his past and forsaken Sins
through the Merits of *his* Blood who loved us and gave himself for us, and to make
solemn resolutions of perfecting his *Repentance* and renewing his *Obedience* towards
God: There is no man, I say, who has *any* Sense *at all* of Religion upon his Mind,
but must needs come affected with such Thoughts and Intentions as these: But in the
matter of mutual Love and Good-will towards *each other*; in the exercise of Christian
Charity and universal Benevolence; in that readiness to forgive offences, to overlook
little provocations, to promote speedy reconciliation, which the Gospel requires and
insists upon as of so great importance; in *This* we are very apt to be careless and defective; and to imagine that external zeal in devotion towards *God*, may compensate
for the want of real Charity and doing good to our *Brother.* For, notwithstanding *all*
the unreasonable Heats and Animosities among Christians, *all* the useless and contentious disputes, *all* the peevish and needless provocations, *all* that difficulty of forgiving
and being reconciled to each other, which is so obvious to observe in the World; yet how
few do we find, whose *Consciences* are apt to be affected with *these* things? whose scruples
concerning their own unworthiness to communicate, are founded upon *these* considerations? And yet 'tis very evident, that to be *in love and charity with our* Neighbours,
(*i. e.* with *all mankind*, as far as is possible in that infinite variety of different circumstances,) is no less necessary a Qualification for communicating worthily, than 'tis necessary that we *truly and earnestly repent* us of our Sins committed more immediately a-
gainst *God*. 'Tis as evident that the design of our Saviour's instituting the Sacrament of
the Lord's Supper, was to be a declaration of our Communion *one with another*; a declaring, that, according to the Apostle's expression, *we, being many, are one Bread
and one Body*, signified by our being *all partakers of that one Bread*; as that it was intended to be a Profession of our Communion with *Him*; a professing, that *the Bread
which*

S. E R M.
LVIII.

which we break, is the Communion of his Body; and *the Cup which we blefs, the Communion of his Blood.* 'Tis no lefs evident, that the Connexion and Sympathy of the Members one *with another*, is neceffary to the Life and Prefervation of the Body; than that the Union of them all with the *Head*, and their common dependence upon it, is neceffary to the fame End. Our Saviour, in all his difcourfes, lays fo great and remarkable a ftrefs upon *This* duty; as if therein confifted almoft the *whole* of Religion: *Thou fhalt love the Lord thy God with all thy heart*, is *the firft and great commandment*, the beginning and foundation of all Religion; *and the fecond*, faith he, *is like unto it, Thou fhalt love thy neighbour as thy felf.*

THE particular *Expreffions*, or *manners, of fhewing forth* which Love, moft earneftly and peculiarly infifted upon in Scripture, are thefe two. 1ft, A willingnefs to forgive injuries and offences; and 2dly, a readinefs to fhew mercy to the poor. 1ft, A willingnefs to forgive injuries and offences, is particularly recommended to us by the *Example*, as well as injoined by the *Commandment* of our Lord: The *whole* Chriftian difpenfation, the *general* grace and mercy of the Gofpel, the *great* pardon purchafed by the Death of Chrift, whereof the Sacrament of the Lord's Supper is a perpetual folemn commemoration; being entirely founded in God's gracious readinefs, for Chrift's fake, to forgive *Us*: and being no lefs *intended* to be fet before us as an *Example* to imitate, than as an ineftimable *Bleffing* to be received with all poffible Thankfulnefs. For which reafon, that great and original Grace of God in the Gofpel, the Remiffion of Sins fet forth even in Baptifm itfelf, feems by our Lord to be *reverfed* upon failure of this *condition* of *our forgiving one another*; in that Parable wherein he compares the Kingdom of Heaven to a certain *King*, who having forgiven one of his Servants a debt of ten thoufand Talents, yet afterwards, when that fervant refufed to forgive one of his fellow-fervants an hundred pence, the King *was wroth* with him again, *and delivered him to the Tormentors, till he fhould pay all that was due unto him*; faying unto him, *O thou wicked fervant, I forgave thee all that debt, becaufe thou defiredft me: Shouldft not Thou alfo have had compaffion on thy fellow-fervant, even as I had pity on thee?* Which our Saviour thus applies to *Us* in the conclufion of the Parable; *So likewife*, fays he, *fhall my heavenly Father do alfo unto you, if ye from your hearts forgive not every one his Brother their trefpaffes*, St *Matt.* xviii. 35. (He does not mean *Publick Malefactors*: For this would deftroy all Government: Neither are fuch ftiled *Brethren*: But, forgive every one his *Brother* their *private* Offences, and be reconciled upon reafonable and eafy Terms: This is the Meaning of the *Parable*.) And in that Form of Prayer, which our Saviour was pleafed to teach his Difciples for perpetual Ufe, he fo interpofes the acknowledgment of our Obligation to this Duty; that every man, even in his *daily Prayer*, is obliged to declare himfelf unworthy of Pardon, and to have forfeited all title to the forgivenefs of *God*, for his *own* Sins; if at the fame time he is not willing and ready, upon the moft *reafonable* terms, to forgive all his *Brother's* trefpaffes and offences againft *him*. How much *more*, at that moft folemn commemoration of the Death of Chrift in the Sacrament; when we are acknowledging in the moft publick manner, all our hopes of Salvation, all our expectation of Pardon, to be owing to that free and undeferved Goodnefs of God, which fent his Son to die for us, and to obtain remiffion of Sin; How much more (I fay) at *That* time, muft the very Nature of the Duty we are performing, the Solemnity of our confeffing our own Unworthinefs, the publicknefs of our acknowledging the freenefs of God's Goodnefs to us in forgiving us through Chrift our ten thoufand talents; of neceffity remind us, how abfolutely fit and reafonable and indifpenfable it is, that we fhould be very willing to forgive each other our hundred pence! Even *fo* neceffary does our Lord make it, that he advifes a man, if he has *brought his gift to the altar, and there remembers that his Brother has ought againft him*; he advifes him *to leave there his gift before the altar, and*

4

and go his way, first be reconciled to his Brother, and then come and offer his gift, St *Matt.* v. 23. He makes it, not indeed of *more* importance, than offering his gift; as if it might be an excuse for neglecting *That*; but he declares it to be of so *much* importance, that the Gift or Service is not acceptable to *God*, without the foregoing reconciliation with *Man*. The Apostles likewise are perpetually urging this Argument, upon the same ground: *Col.* iii. 13. *Forbearing one another, and forgiving one another, if any man has a quarrel against any; even as Christ forgave you, so also do ye.* And again; *Be ye kind one to another, tender-hearted, forgiving one another, even as God for Christ's sake has forgiven you*, Eph. iv. 32; and in the following chapter, *ver.* 2. *Walk in Love, as Christ also has loved us, and given himself for us, an offering and a sacrifice to God, for a sweet-smelling savour.* 'Tis *impossible* that any man who considers these exhortations, and has a just Sense of his own unworthiness, and of the Goodness of God, and of the great Remission purchased for him by the Death of Christ, of which he hopes to partake in attending with a fit disposition of Mind upon the ordinances of Divine appointment; 'tis *impossible* that any man, with *These* thoughts about him, can continue peevish and contentious, merciless and uncharitable, easy to be provoked, and difficult to be reconciled. The Sacrament of the Lord's-Supper therefore, so far as 'tis a memorial of the Death of Christ, of his Love towards us, and of his purchasing forgiveness for us; so far 'tis a most strong and powerful Argument, to oblige us to *mutual* Love, Charity and Good-will; to Forgiveness, Gentleness, and Easiness to be reconciled. And yet even *This* also, ought not to be made a Matter of Scruple and groundless Doubts, as if no man could be a worthy Communicant without being in actual Agreement with all Mankind; But 'tis to be understood only as an *Argument* of Duty, within its just bounds and proper limitations: For 'tis by no means impossible but Controversies concerning mens Rights and Properties *may* arise, even among *good* Christians; nay, 'tis not possible, in the present state of human Nature, but they *will* sometimes arise: And our Saviour must not be understood to forbid us making use of *such* means, for the preservation of our just rights, and for preventing the increase of injuries, as the Laws of Wise and Christian Countries, and the Usages of good and pious men direct us to make use of. But the intent of what has been said, is; that the consideration of the Death of Christ, of his great Love and Forgiveness to us, which we solemnly commemorate in the Holy Sacrament, cannot fail to dispose us, if we partake thereof worthily, to be very *willing* and *ready* upon the most *reasonable* terms, to forgive injuries and offences; to be difficult to be provoked, easy to be reconciled, apt to interpret things in the best manner; rather to recede somewhat from our right, than exceed in insisting upon more; and, if at any time we are unavoidably engaged in controversy about our Just Rights, yet never to carry it further than is absolutely necessary for the Preservation of Peace and Order and good Government in the World, as becomes the Society or Communion of Christians. *2dly*, The other branch of that Love and Charity, to which (I said) the commemoration of the Death of Christ obliges us, is a ready disposition to shew mercy to the *Poor*. The Primitive Christians, as they always celebrated the Praises of God, upon this solemn occasion, with the greatest zeal and earnestness of affection, *with gladness and singleness of Heart*, Acts ii. 46; so they as constantly expressed this their joy and thankfulness, by liberal contributions, to relieve the necessities of the poorer Saints. Which custom is, with great reason, continued to this day. And indeed 'tis very natural, when we seriously meditate on the stupendous love of Christ, in *giving himself freely* a Sacrifice for us, and *his own self bearing our Sins in his own body on the tree*; 'tis very natural, (since we cannot make any return to *him*,) that we should desire to express our gratitude in that way, which he is pleased to accept, as done immediately to himself; that is, in showing mercy and charity to the Poor. That *Their* hearts being rejoiced with *our* Bounty, may zealously

S E R M. joyn with us in sending up praises and thankſgivings to our common Father; and *that,*
LVIII. *abounding to every good work, we may be inriched in every thing to all bountifulneſs,*
which cauſeth through us thankſgiving to God. For the adminiſtration of this Service (as
St *Paul* expreſſes it, 2 *Cor.* ix. 12.) *not only ſupplyeth the wants of the Saints, but is*
abundant alſo by many thankſgivings unto God; While by the experiment of this miniſtra-
tion, they glorify God for your profeſt Subjection unto the goſpel of Chriſt, and for your
liberal diſtribution unto Them and unto all men.

S E R M O N   LIX.

The Nature, End and Deſign of the H O L Y C O M M U N I O N.

1 C O R. XI. 27.

Wherefore, whoſoever ſhall eat this bread, and drink this Cup of
the Lord unworthily, ſhall be guilty of the Body and Blood of the
Lord.

SERM. I HAVE lately, from our Saviour's words of inſtitution, *(This do in remembrance*
LIX. *of Me,)* diſcourſed concerning the *Nature, End and Deſign,* of the Sacrament of
the Lord's Supper. I ſhall now from theſe words of St *Paul,* proceed to ſome
other conſiderations, neceſſary to be underſtood, in order to our partaking worthily of
that Holy Sacrament: *Whoſoever ſhall eat this bread, and drink this cup of the Lord un-*
worthily, ſhall be guilty of the Body and Blood of the Lord. Which words do plainly
ſuppoſe in them, 1ſt, *a Duty enjoined;* to eat this bread and drink this cup: 2dly, A
Benefit ariſing from the due performance of the duty; implied in the contrary danger of
doing it unworthily. 3dly, *A certain Care and Preparation neceſſary,* in order to perform it worthily; leaſt by negligence and want of Devotion, we become *guilty of the*
Body and Blood of the Lord. In the following diſcourſe therefore, I ſhall briefly conſider, 1ſt, The *Obligation* we lie under to perform the Duty enjoined. 2dly, What
Benefits we may expect to be made partakers of, by performing it in a due and worthy
manner. 3dly, What *Qualifications or Preparation* is neceſſary, in order to ſuch a due
and worthy receiving. In which Matter, becauſe Men have ſometimes on the one hand,
been perplexed with many and unreaſonable ſcruples, as well as on the other hand been
too negligent and void of Devotion; I ſhall therefore in the 4th place conſider the
groundleſſneſs and vanity of the greateſt part of thoſe Reaſons, which Men uſually allege for their abſtaining from the Communion, under pretence of Want of due Preparation. And *Laſtly,* I ſhall conclude what I think proper to offer to your meditations
upon this Subject, with taking notice of ſome of the great and ſcandalous Corruptions,
                                                                        wherewith

wherewith the Church of *Rome* have difhonoured this folemn commemoration of our Lord, and of his dying for us.

I. I AM to confider what *Obligation* lies upon us, to perform this Duty at all. And upon *This* Head there needs little inlargement; it being acknowledged by Chriftians of *all* Communions, (excepting perhaps *One only* Sect,) to be the exprefs and pofitive commandment of our Lord. So that tho' we *could not* have underftood fo much of the reafonablenefs and ufefulnefs of the precept, as we do; tho' we could not have perceived diftinctly, the Benefits that we receive thereby; nor have at all apprehended the particular grounds and reafons of the fitnefs of the command; (which *Now* is by no means the cafe;) yet the clearnefs and expreffnefs of the injunction itfelf, would neverthelefs have made the Obligation fufficiently evident; and it would well have becomed us, without further inquiry, to have fubmitted with all Humility to the Will and Authority of our Lord. *Take, eat*; and, *Drink ye all of this*; and, *This do in remembrance of me*; are words containing as clear and exprefs a command, as are any where to be met with, upon any other occafion in the whole New Teftament: and they are recorded by three of the four Evangelifts. And they are repeated by St *Paul*, in the words a little before the Text, as a commandment enforced diftinctly, by a new and particular Revelation to himfelf; *I have received*, faith he, *of the Lord, that which I alfo delivered unto you, that the Lord Jefus, the fame night in which he was betrayed, took bread, and when he had given thanks, he brake it, and faid, Take, eat; this is my body, which is broken for you: this do in remembrance of me. After the fame manner alfo he took the cup, when he had fupped, faying, This Cup is the New Teftament in my blood: this do ye, as oft as ye drink it, in remembrance of me. For as often as ye eat this bread, and drink this cup, ye do fhew the Lord's death till he come. I have received of the Lord*; that is, he received it, not by tradition from thofe who were before him, but by immediate Revelation from Chrift himfelf. For fo he exprefsly affures us, concerning the manner of his own inftruction in all the precepts of the Gofpel: *Gal.* i. 16, 17, 12. *I conferred not*, faith he, *with Flefh and Blood, neither went I up to Jerufalem to them which were Apoftles before me;——neither received I it of man, neither was I taught it; but by the Revelation of Jefus Chrift.* This added fingular Weight and Authority, to *all* St *Paul*'s admonitions and exhortations; and it made his reproof to the *Corinthians*, (in *this particular* inftance of their unworthily receiving the Holy Communion,) to be doubly powerful and effectual: becaufe it was in the cafe of their neglecting fo *exprefs* a Command, not only delivered to them at the firft preaching of the Gofpel, but *received* alfo by St *Paul* with particular inforcement, in a new Revelation from *the Lord* himfelf. And fuitable to the expreffnefs and importance of the *Command*, is the account the Scripture gives us of the *Practice* of the primitive Difciples: *Acts* ii. 42, 46. *They continued ftedfaftly in the Apoftles doctrine and fellowfhip, and in breaking of bread, and in prayer; And continuing daily with one accord in the Temple, and breaking bread from houfe to houfe, they eat their meat with gladnefs and finglenefs of Heart.* In which account is remarkable, not only their obfervance of the Duty, but the *conftancy* alfo and *frequency* of their doing it; They continued *ftedfaftly* in the Apoftles doctrine, and were *daily* in the Temple, breaking bread with one accord. Which *frequency* of Communicating, (tho' not as to the precife *Time* indeed, yet in general the doing it *frequently*) is plainly *implied* to be our Duty, and *fuppofed* in thofe words of our Saviour; *Do this*, as oft as *ye drink it, in remembrance of me*, 1 Cor. xi. 25. and in thofe of St *Paul*, As oft as *ye eat this bread, and drink this Cup, ye do fhew the Lord's death till he come.* And indeed, if there *could* be *any difference* in the degree of the Obligation of our Lord's commands, (I mean, of *fuch* commands as are not moral and eternal, but of a pofitive nature only;) it would be natural almoft to lay the *greateft* ftrefs, upon *that* which he gave us *a little before his*

death;

SERM. *death* ; upon *that* which he commanded us to *do* particularly *in remembrance of him* ;
LIX. upon *that* which he commanded us to do in remembrance of the *greatest inftance of Love and Compaffion*, that ever was in the World. For, *Greater Love has no man than this, that a man lay down his life for his* Friend ; But our Lord refufed not to die for *Us*, while we were yet *Enemies*. And *fcarcely for a* righteous *man*, as St *Paul* exprefles it, *will one* dare to *die* ; *But* God *commendeth his Love towards us, in that while we were yet* Sinners, *Chrift died for Us*, Rom. v. 8. The Meaning is : God was never, in point of *Juftice*, under Any *Obligation*, to pardon continually All the Sins of All Penitents ; But this *gracious* and *free* Compaffion, his divine Wifdom and Goodnefs has thought fit to manifeft, in the Method of That Redemption purchafed by the Death of Chrift. In point of *Gratitude* therefore, no lefs than in *Duty*, are we bound frequently to commemorate this unparallelled Love of our Lord ; and our neglecting to attend this facred Ordinance, is breaking thro' the ftrongeft ties of a double Obligation. I *might* add, further, that not only in *Duty and Gratitude*, but in *Intereft* alfo are we obliged to attend thefe pofitive Inftitutions ; God having appointed them as *external* Means, to promote and improve in us (that which is the great End of all outward Performances,) the *real* Virtue and *inward* Religion of the Mind. But This is the

2*d*, Thing I propofed to confider, namely, What *Benefits* we may expect to be made partakers of, by the due and worthy performance of this Duty. And here, as I before obferved, tho' we did not diftinctly know what thofe Benefits were ; yet in all reafon ought we with an implicit Faith to have obeyed the commandment of *Him*, who, as he cannot deceive, fo neither can he impofe any thing upon us, that is not for our advantage. But, in reality, the *Benefits* we partake hereby are manifeft and evident. For, though the *Sacrifice* of the Death of Chrift, is not daily repeated ; as the Church of *Rome* has fondly and prophanely imagined : Though the *Subftance* of the Body and Blood of Chrift, is not in an unintelligible manner produced anew, out of the elements of Bread and Wine : Though the *grace of God* is not confined by any neceffary connexion to the material action ; that the mere formal and external participation, fhould, without true devotion of mind, and without real amendment of life, operate fecretly and unintelligibly any fpiritual advantage, according to fome Men's vain and fuperftitious expectation : Yet, when with Hearts *full* of Piety and true Devotion, with *ftedfaft Faith* in God, and *firm refolutions* of fincere Obedience, Men thankfully and frequently, in that manner which God has appointed, commemorate the Sacrifice of the Death of Chrift once offered for ever ; is it not evidently a great and ineftimable Benefit, if, through the affiftance of the Spirit of God, annexed *not* to the material elements, or to the outward action, but to the Ordinance partaken of by truly devout and welldifpofed minds ; their *Faith* in God, be increafed ; their *Hope and Truft* in him be ftrengthened ; their *Charity* towards their brethren be enlarged, in proportion to that Love they are commemorating of their common Lord ; their *good refolutions* be confirmed ; *themfelves inabled*, to *fulfil* thofe refolutions in a more effectual Obedience ; and *comforted* with fuller affurance of pardon of their paft Sins, upon true Repentance and Amendment, through the interceffion of Him who *died* for them ? Thefe (I fay,) are evidently great and ineftimable *Benefits* : And very clearly arifing, from a due and worthy frequenting of the Holy Communion. For, if, even to *private* Prayer our Saviour has annexed fuch a promife, that with far greater readinefs than Men *give good gifts unto their Children*, will our *heavenly Father give* good things, St *Matt.* vii. 11. (*fpiritual* good things even his *Holy Spirit*, as St *Luke* in the parallel place exprefles it,) 'to them that ask him ; and if all *publick* Devotions, being Ordinances of God's own appointment, as Means and Inftruments of Religion, have ftill a greater affurance of God's Bleffing attending them ; how much more in this moft folemn of all religious actions, in this great commemoration of the Sacrifice of the Death of Chrift, is it reafonable to believe, that pious and well-difpofed Minds, are, by the affiftance of the Spirit of

God,

God, which delights to dwell in Heavenly and devout Hearts, improved in all religious SERM. Affections, and ftrengthened unto the acceptable Obedience of a Holy Life? But all LIX. this depends, as I before obferved, and as Chriftians can never be too frequently re-, minded; It depends (I fay) entirely, not on any fecret Virtue annexed to the external Action, (which is one of the moft pernicious of all Errors in matters of Religion;) but it depends wholly on the right Difpofition and worthy Qualification of a pious and de-vout Mind.

WHICH was the 3d thing I propofed to confider; namely, What *Qualifications* or *Preparation* is neceffary, in order to the making us worthy partakers of the Holy Com-munion. *That*, in *general*, there *is* a diftinction to be made between things facred and profane; is allowed by all men. *That* men are not to approach to the table of the Lord, with the fame carelefnefs and indifferency of Mind, with the fame unattentive-nefs and unconcernednefs of Spirit, with the fame worldly Thoughts and Difpofitions about them, as they do to a common Feaft: *That*, feeing (as St *Paul* argues) we *have Houfes to eat and to drink in*, therefore we ought not to *defpife the Church of God*, by be-having ourfelves careleffly in *Both places* alike: *That* if we come unworthily and with-out *any* due Preparation of Mind, this is *not to eat the Lord's Supper*; But, inftead thereof, we become *guilty of the Body and Blood of the Lord*, i.e. guilty of profanenefs, in not *difcerning the Lord's Body*, in not diftinguifhing fufficiently a folemn Act of Re-ligion, by the difference of our behaviour from that in Common Life: *That* hereby we *eat and drink our own condemnation*, that is, as St *Paul* expreffly inteprets himfelf, we provoke God to inflict *feveral* kinds of *judgments* upon us: All this is acknowledged by every one. But *wherein* particularly confifts *that due Preparation*, by which we may be fure to avoid thofe evils and dangers, and to obtain the benefits of worthy receiving; this is what the Confciences of well-difpofed Perfons, are always defirous to be efpecial-ly inftructed in. Now the only rule the Scripture gives us in this cafe, is that advice of the Apoftle, in the Words immediately following the Text; ver. 28, *Let a man examine himfelf, and fo let him eat of that Bread and drink of that Cup.* And *This Examination* can only be of two forts: Either an Examination into the *whole* ftate and general courfe of a man's Life, whether he be at all a fincere Chriftian, or not; or elfe an Examination into the *prefent* difpofition of his mind, whether he be at *this particular Time* in a devout frame and temper, or not. The *former* of thefe is indeed of exceed-ing great *importance*, but of no *difficulty* at all; the latter is of great *difficulty* and full of fcruple, but by no means of fo great *importance*. 1ft, A man is to examine into the *whole* ftate and *general* courfe of his life, whether he be at all a fincere Chriftian, or not. In this fenfe, St *Paul* ufes the word; 2 Cor. xiii. 5, Examine *yourfelves, whe-ther ye be in the Faith, prove your own felves: Know ye not your own felves, how that Jefus Chrift is in you, except ye be reprobates?* And *this* Examination, is not a matter of great difficulty: For, as St *John* tells us, *the children of God are manifeft, and the children of the Devil; Whofoever doth not righteoufnefs, is not of God, neither he that loveth not his Brother.* If any man be a Blafphemer of God, or a profane Mocker and Difpifer of Religion; if he has no Senfe of the Majefty of God upon his Mind, but habitually profanes that facred and adorable Name by Oaths and vain Imprecations; if any man lives in the practice of *fecret* Fraud and Deceit, of cheat-ing and over-reaching his Neighbours; or by acts of *open* violence and Cruelty, of Paf-fion and blood-thirfty Revenge, fhows that he *hates* his Brother whom God commands him to *love*; if any man indulges himfelf in Sins of brutifh uncleannefs, or gives him-felf over to Drunkennefs and bafe Debauchery; there is no great Difficulty in fuch a perfon's Examination of himfelf; for his Confcience at the firft Thought condemns him without controverfy, and his *Sins* apparently *go before unto judgment.* He is unfit, not only to approach the Table of the Lord; but unfit to join himfelf in

SERM. the aſſemblies of the Saints; unfit to bear the Name and Profeſſion of a Chriſti-
LIX. an; unworthy to lift up his Eyes towards Heaven, towards the throne of *him*
who *cannot behold iniquity*. Such a perſon has no other courſe to take, but immediately with ſhame and confuſion of face to acknowledge his unworthineſs, and
repent in duſt and aſhes; to turn himſelf unto the Lord by a total Change of his Courſe
of Life, and an effectual Reformation of manners; and to *cry mightily unto him that
is able to ſave*, if perhaps the Wickedneſs of his paſt life may be forgiven him. But
without ſuch a thorough Change of the whole courſe of his life, to imagine that by
the formal Preparation of a few days devotion, he can become worthy to partake of the
Holy Communion, and then return to his former vicious Practices; this is openly *mocking* the Authority of God, who hateth the Hypocrite; 'tis as it were *challenging* the
Almighty to make good his threatnings. But now on the other hand, if a man in the
general courſe of his life has made it his ſincere endeavour to obey the commandments
of God, to live in the habitual Practice of Sobriety, Righteouſneſs, Piety and Charity; if
he has either been ſo happy as to have avoided all great crimes, or at leaſt has truly repented of them by utterly forſaking them; and his conſcience accuſes him of no other
unrepented and unforſaken Sins, but the daily incurſions of humane frailty; the frailties
that virtuous and good men always complain of, but can never wholly eſcape; the little
deviations of inadvertency and want of attention; the ſmall ſurprizes of Paſſion and
ſudden temptation in things not of the higheſt importance, the careleſneſs of an un-
guarded word, the Vanity of an indecent thought, the want of conſtant warmth and
affection in devotion, or the like: When *this*, I ſay, is the caſe; then the Preparation
of ſuch a Perſon for the Holy Communion, is only that *ſecond* ſort of Examination
I mentioned; an Examination into the *preſent* diſpoſition of his mind, whether he be
at this particular time in a devout frame and Temper or not. And This, as I ſaid,
is indeed, to pious perſons of melancholy diſpoſitions, a matter very often of great difficulty and full of Scruple; but, in reality, by no means of ſo great importance as the

Ecclef. v. 1. other. For, though we *are* indeed always to *keep* our *feet, when we enter into the
Houſe of God*; that we *offer* not *the Sacrifice of fools*: yet the ſlowneſs and indiſpoſition,
the want of warmth and affection, the troubleſom and uneaſy or even irreligious
Thoughts coming ſuddenly into their minds, which ſuch melancholy pious perſons are
apt to complain of; are by no means things that unqualify them for religious duties.
Such perſons, ſeeing they conſtantly endeavour to obey the commandments of God,
and to live in the habitual Practice of true Virtue, are always *ſincerely religious*, though
they be not always *equally ſenſible of it* to their own ſatisfaction. Their Lamps, though
not always alike *trimmed*, yet are always *burning*. They have always *upon* them what
our Saviour ſtiles the *wedding-garment*, although *not* always in *equal order*. Wherefore though it becomes us highly, upon every ſolemn occaſion, to trim our lamps, to
ſet our garments in order, to excite our moſt affectionate devotion, to lay aſide for the
preſent all ſecular and worldly Thoughts, and to examine more ſtrictly and particularly
into the ſtate and diſpoſition of our Souls, as Time and Opportunity offers, without
anxious and ſuperſtitious ſollicitude; yet, where this is by any accident prevented,
good men are, by the habitual courſe of a virtuous life, in a continual general Preparation; and may at *all times* as ſafely communicate without Scruple, as it is certain
that a vicious and debauched perſon can at *no time* be fit to do it, by any formal
preparative of a few days Devotion. For after all that *can* be ſaid upon this Subject, there is *no other* certain and infallible mark, to judge whether we have prepared ourſelves duly, and communicated worthily, or not; but only by the conſequent
effect. If we improve more in Virtue, and more diligently avoid every kind of Sin;
if we ſerve God more devoutly, and love our Brother with a more univerſal Charity,
and endeavour more ſincerely and ſteddily to obey the commandments of God in the

                                                                           following

following courfe of our lives; it is very certain our Preparation was good, and our S E R M.
Communion acceptable: But if we continue to live vicioufly, in *Any* inftance of un- LIX.
righteous Practice; our Preparation at beft was but a formal hypocrify; and our Offering, was without Incenfe. This is the only Rule that may certainly be depended
upon; This is judging of the Tree by its Fruit; Which both in *Nature* and in *Religion,* is the only unerring way of Trial. And all *other* marks whatfoever, are but
perplexing difficulties, full of doubts and fcruples and endlefs Superftition. And now
from hence 'tis very eafy to fhow, in the

4*th* place, T H E Groundlefnefs and Vanity of moft of thofe reafons, which men
ufually allege for their abftaining from the Communion, under pretence of want of
due Preparation. For, *if* their unpreparednefs arifes from a vicious and debauched
life, which they are unwilling to reform; they *are* unworthy indeed, and they ought
to abftain; but not from the Communion only, but from *Prayers* alfo, and from *all
Profeffion* of Religion; they being fuch perfons whom Chriftian Difcipline ought to
feparate from the Communion of Saints, as their own confcience feparates them from
the hopes of Heaven. All religious Actions to *fuch* perfons, being like watering a
plant, whofe very roots are dead. In which ftate fo long as they continue, they have
no great reafon to be uneafy at their unworthinefs to receive the Holy Communion
here; feeing they have no regard for their own Souls, and no Care of being worthy to
partake of the Happinefs of the Righteous *hereafter.* But *if* the unworthinefs they allege, be only a *prefent* Want of Warmth of Devotion, or a *general* Senfe of their being frail and finful creatures, notwithftanding their beft and moft fincere endeavours to
avoid all known Sin; this I have already fhown, not to be a real Unworthinefs, but
merely an ungrounded and melancholy imagination, which ought to be flighted and
refifted. *If* they be terrified at the feverity of the Penalty, that *they who eat and
drink unworthily, eat and drink condemnation to themfelves*; 'tis to be obferved, that
when this is underftood of the unworthinefs *only of a fingle Action*, the condemnation denounced is not eternal damnation, but temporal judgment, as St *Paul exprefsly* explains his own Words in That very Text. But when the unworthinefs
is *habitual,* and fo liable to a feverer condemnation; it is evident the penalty annexed, is not to the fingle *Action* of *eating and drinking*, but to the *habitual ftate*
of *Unworthinefs*; in which evil ftate *That man* equally continues, who, being habitually Unworthy, *eats not*; as he who *eats*, being likewife unworthy: And
confequently he cannot, by abftaining, efcape that condemnation, which is *however* due to his Unworthinefs, whether he communicates or no. For 'tis not poffible,
that he who *now* continues unworthy to partake of the *Lord's Supper*, fhould *hereafter*
be found worthy to participate of the *eternal Supper of the Lamb.* Wherefore, *whilft*
any man really continues unworthy; as it is no benefit to him to *communicate*, fo to
abftain is no advantage, and there is no other way for him to efcape the judgment he
fears, but by immediately preparing himfelf in the way of righteoufnefs, to become
worthy to *ferve* God here, and *injoy* him hereafter. Laftly, if men abftain out of an
apprehenfion that Sins committed afterwards will become unpardonable; I anfwer,
there is not the leaft ground or hint in Scripture for any fuch apprehenfion. That the
Sins of Chriftians againft the clear light of the Gofpel fhall *more difficultly* be pardoned,
than the Sins of thofe who want that light; the Scripture *does indeed* frequently affure
us: And it were well if men would think of it more than they do: But *this* Aggravation of Sin is equally the fame, in thofe who receive the Communion, and in thofe
who receive it not. For not, if we Sin wilfully after we have received the *Sacrament,*
but if we fin wilfully after we have received the *knowledge of the Truth,* (faith the A-
poftle) there remains *no new* Sacrifice for Sin. And *this* confideration indeed is a good

S E R M. reafon, not to deter men from the Communion, but to deter them from pretending
LIX. to be Chriftians at all, fo long as they refolve to live vicioufly and irreligioufly.

5. And now nothing remains of what I propofed upon this Subject, but in the *laft
place* juft to mention fome of the grofs corruptions, wherewith the Church of *Rome*
have highly difhonoured this folemn commemoration of the Death of our Lord. And

1*ft*, Whereas *our Saviour* has thought fit to inftitute no other memorial of his
Death and Paffion, but only the Euchariftical Feaft of the Sacrament; 'tis a great and
unpardonable prefumption, for men to imagine that they *themfelves* can invent *better*
reprefentations and *more fenfible* helps to Devotion, than that which God has appointed:
Such as are the ufe of *Images*, and the like, in religious Worfhip. Wherein, as they
have departed from the Simplicity and fpiritual Purity of the Chriftian worfhip; fo
they have found by experience, that the addition of any fuch human inventions in the
Worfhip of God, has tended only to corrupt mens manners, and bring in great and
endlefs Superftitions.

2. Whereas our Saviour inftituted this Holy Sacrament exprefsly for a perpetual
Remembrance or *Commemoration* of his Death and Paffion; 'tis a very great corruption,
to teach that the elements are *changed* into the *Subftance of the Body and Blood of Chrift*,
and that the Sacrament is properly a continual *repetition* (not commemoration) of that
expiatory Sacrifice once offered upon the crofs. Our Lord's command, is, *Do this in*
remembrance *of Me*. Now in the *Nature of things*, the *remembrance* of any thing, is
not the *repetition* of the thing itfelf. And fuch a *repeated* offering up continually
the *real* fubftantial Body and Blood of Chrift, (if any fuch thing could be,) would
not be a *commemorating* the Sacrifice *once* offered upon the crofs, but *obliterating* the
memory of it by offering perpetually *new* ones. And *then muft Chrift oft have fuffered
fince the foundation of the World; whereas now Once only in the end of the World* (as
the Scripture exprefsly affirms) *has he appeared to put away Sin by the Sacrifice of himfelf.* The Arguments drawn by thofe of the Church of *Rome*, from the figurative expreffions, by which the *elements* are called *Chrift's Body and Blood*; and the *Sacrament*
itfelf a *Sacrifice*; (in like manner as Chrift figuratively calls himfelf, a *Door*, a *Way*,
a *Vine*, and the like; and the Apoftles call *Praife* and *Alms* a *Sacrifice*; and St *Paul*
ftiles the *Chriftian Church* the True *Circumcifion* :) The Arguments, I fay, drawn from
thefe figurative expreffions for the Popifh doctrine, are as abfurd and contrary to common fenfe, as their Practife of worfhipping a piece of Bread for God, is idolatrous and
abominable.

3. Whereas our Saviour commands his Difciples exprefsly, to *eat* of this *Bread*
and *drink* of this *Cup*; 'tis a moft unjuftifiable innovation in the Church of *Rome*, to
with-hold the *Cup* from the people. St *Paul*, in the plaineft words that can be, declares it to be the people's Duty, to partake in *both* kinds; *As oft as ye eat this bread
and drink this* cup, *ye do fhew the Lord's Death till he come:* And our Saviour's command to his Difciples, was, Drink *ye all of this*, as well as, *Take, eat, this is my Body.*
To which if it be replied (as they fometimes abfurdly do) that all thofe Difciples
whom our Saviour commanded to *drink* this, were Priefts, and none of them Lay-men;
'tis evident they were the fame perfons only, to whom he adminiftred the *Bread* alfo:
and then it will follow, by the fame reafon, that the people are denied the Cup, that
they may be denied partaking of the Sacrament at all: Which is the higheft Impiety.
But then *We alfo* of the reformed Church, ought always to be put in mind, that though
we are allowed to communicate in *Both* kinds, yet we may ftill lofe the Advantage of
Both, if the Holinefs of our Lives be not anfwerable to the Obligations which This
Communion lays upon us.

SERMON

SERMON LX.

Of the Catholick Church of Christ.

HEB. XII. 22, 23.

But ye are come unto mount Sion, and unto the City of the Living God, the heavenly Jerusalem, and to an innumerable company of Angels, To the general Assembly and Church of the first-born which are written in Heaven, and to God the Judge of All, and to the Spirits of just men made perfect, and to Jesus the Mediator of the new Covenant.

THESE words contain the liveliest and most noble Description of the *Church* of God, and of the *Communion* of all its Members both with each other and with their Head; that is any where to be found in the whole Scripture. The Name of *God's Church*; and the *Fellowship* of the *Saints*, or the *Communion* of the *Faithful*; are words perpetually in the Mouths of *All*, who call themselves *Christians*: But the true *Intent* and *application* of them, according to the *Scripture-sense* of the words, is attended to and understood by *Few*. The Love of *Power, Authority,* and *worldly Dominion*, has made *Some* abuse the sacred Name of the *Church of God,* to serve Purposes of Tyranny, Ambition, and Cruelty: And This is what the Scripture calls, *The Man of Sin sitting in the* Temple (or Church) *of God. Others,* through a *mean, peevish,* and *uncharitable* Spirit; fond of *imposing* upon their Brethren *particular Modes and Notions*; and *blending* Doctrines and Ceremonies of mere *human Authority*, as of the same importance with the *essential Laws* of our *Saviour's* kingdom; have profanely and sacrilegiously made use of the same *venerable* Name of *the Church of God,* to cover the Worldly Designs and Interests of particular *Parties, Factions,* or *Bodies* of Men: And This, in the proper and highest Sense of the word, is an Instance of the Sin of *Schism*; the Sin of *rending the Body of Christ*; the Sin of *causing Divisions* in the *universal Church*, through the Ambition of Men inclosing to themselves by *temporal Power,* those *spiritual Privileges*, which our Saviour intended to confer upon his *Church universal.* The Church of *Rome* has been the great Author and Example of this *fundamental Corruption*: Which has been of such pernicious consequence to the Christian Religion, that sometimes even for several Ages together, the very *Notion* of the *Church of Christ* has been in a manner wholly worn out and obliterated among those who called themselves Christians; and there has succeeded in its place a mere *Temporal Polity* and *worldly Dominion*, in the room of *That Kingdom* which our Lord himself so expressly declared *was not* to be *of This World.* Insomuch that Christians have too generally behaved themselves in such a manner, as if they thought that at That Great and Tremendous day, when we must All appear before the Tribunal of Christ, men were to be judged in *Nations* and *Bodies Politick,* in *Parties* and *Societies of human establishment,* according to certain *Forms of Government* and particular

SERM.
LX.
〜〜〜

Syſtems of Notions, and Rights and Ceremonies; and not that every ſingle Man ſhall then perſonally be acquitted or condemned, according to the Great and Univerſal Rules of the Goſpel; according to what he himſelf in his own perſon has actually done in the Fleſh, whether it be good, or whether it be evil; that is, according to his *Obedience* or *Diſobedience* to the Commands of God, the *Morality* or *Immorality* of the Actions of his Life. The Want of *This* conſideration, has incredibly perplext Men's Notions concerning the *Church of God:* And though *no Two Things* are in Scripture conſtantly repreſented ſo directly oppoſite to each other, as the *Love of God* and the *Love of the World*; yet in all *Popiſh* times *principally*, and in all *Other corrupt* Ages *(proportionably,) Dominion and Pomp and Power*, inſtead of *Truth and Righteouſneſs and Charity*, have been eſteemed as Marks and Characters of Chriſt's *Holy Catholick Church.* But undoubtedly the *true Church of God* here upon *Earth*, conſiſts of the *ſame Perſons*, is made up of the very *ſame Members*, of which *hereafter* it ſhall be conſtituted in *Heaven.* And therefore as, at the *day of judgment*, our Saviour has no where given us any the leaſt Intimation, that in order to determine any Man's final Sentence, inquiry will be made concerning *Nations* and *Parties*, concerning a man's relation to *one body politick or another*, concerning *Rites and Ceremonies or Forms of Government* and the like; which are now the Great Objects of Men's Zeal, and the Main Cauſes of their reviling, hating and perſecuting each other: but every Man's future and eternal State will Then be appointed him by the Impartial and unerring Judge, according to his behaviour in every ſtation and circumſtance wherein Providence has placed him, *i. e.* according to the virtuouſneſs or viciouſneſs of his paſt life: So *Now* alſo, if we would make a right Judgment concerning ourſelves or Others, whether we be real and Living Members of the Body of Chriſt, Children of God, and Heirs of His Kingdom; we muſt take our Eſtimate from the ſame divine Rules and Meaſures, by which we ſhall at laſt be judged; and not from our preſent human Paſſions, and worldly Marks of Diſtinction. They who *worſhip the Father in Spirit and in Truth*, as our Saviour deſcribes the *True Worſhippers*, Joh. iv. 23; that is, who live with an habitual Senſe of Religion upon their Minds; in a conſtant Exerciſe of *Piety* towards *God*, through *Jeſus Chriſt*; in a *ſober* and *temperate* injoyment of the things of this preſent World, with an abhorrence of all Vice and Debauchery; and in a regular Practice of *Juſtice, Righteouſneſs, Equity, Meekneſs, Charity*, and *univerſal Good-will* towards Mankind; *looking for*, and waiting unto, *the Bleſſed Hope, and the glorious Appearance of the Great God and of our Saviour Jeſus Chriſt*; who, according to his Promiſe, ſhall give them an inheritance in That *New Heavens and New Earth*, wherein *Truth* and *Righteouſneſs* are to *dwell* for ever: Theſe, and Theſe only, are the true and living Members of *the Body of Chriſt; of his Fleſh, and of his Bones*, (as St *Paul* by a bold and lively Figure moſt elegantly expreſſes it, *Eph.* v. 30;) of *One Body*, and of *One Spirit* with him: Theſe are *indeed* the *Holy Church*, and *City*, and *Temple*, of God: Theſe are they, of whom the Apoſtle in the Text by one of the nobleſt and moſt expreſſive Metaphors that ever was uſed by Any Writer, affirms that they are *already* come *unto Mount Sion*; Even while they ſtill continue here upon Earth, in this mortal and tranſitory ſtate; yet becauſe their converſation is in Heaven, and they live according to the righteous Laws of That ſpiritual Country, wherein they expect their portion of Inheritance, and into which *there ſhall in no caſe enter any thing that defileth, neither whatſoever worketh Abomination, or maketh a Lie*; therefore they are already, ſaith he, *come unto mount Sion, and unto the City of the Living God, the heavenly Jeruſalem, and to an innumerable Company of Angels, To the general Aſſembly and Church of the firſt-born which are written in Heaven, and to God the Judge of All, and to the Spirits of juſt men made perfect, and to Jeſus the Mediator of the New Covenant.*

IN

IN the further treating upon which words, I shall first consider distinctly the several S E R M. *Persons*, whom the Apostle here supposes to have a *relation to*, and *communion* with, LX. each other: And from thence, *secondly*, there will naturally appear the true Scripture-notion of the *Catholick Church of Christ*, and of That *Unity*, or *Communion*, which is between the Members of it, as Members of the *One Body of Christ*.

1st, As to the several *Persons*, whom the Apostle here supposes to have a *relation* to and *communion* with, each other; 'tis to be observed that the Kingdom of God, is in Scripture described under the Notion or Similitude of a *royal City* : Heb. xi. 10. *Abraham looked for a* City *which hath foundations, whose builder and maker is God* : In the words of the Text, 'tis *Mount Sion, the City of the Living God, the heavenly Jerusalem*. Now as in *every* City or Kingdom, *All* who in Any station belong unto it, have a mutual *relation to*, and some sort of *communication with* each other, by which they are *All* esteemed as *One political Body* ; The *Prince*, who governs All ; The *Persons by whom* he governs ; The *Subjects*, who live under That Government : and *Those* who, through travelling in *foreign* parts, yet still continue under the same Dominion : So with regard to this heavenly City, the Apostle St *Paul* tells all Christians, that they are *no more strangers and foreigners, but fellow-Citizens with the Saints, and of the houshold of God ; being built upon the foundation of the Apostles and Prophets, Jesus Christ himself being the chief corner-stone, in whom the whole building is fitly framed together*. And in describing the constitution of this *City* or *Kingdom of God*, and the *persons* with whom every one that becomes a Subject of That Kingdom, enters consequently into some *relation* ; the same Apostle, in the Text, distinctly enumerates the following particulars. There is, says he, *God, the Judge of All* : There is *Jesus the Mediator of the New Covenant* : There is *an innumerable Company of Angels* : There are *the Spirits of just men made perfect* ; And there is *the general Assembly and Church of the first-born, which are* written *in Heaven*, though they be not yet actually *arrived* there. In the

1st place, says the Apostle, *ye are come* to *God, the Judge of All*. Ye are come to a *right Knowledge* of the *One True God*, the *Author and Maker* of all things, the *Father* of all rational Beings, and the Supreme *Judge* of every one's behaviour. By *Nature*, we are his *Subjects* and his *Creatures* ; by *Sin*, we are become *Enemies* to him, and *Objects of his Displeasure* ; by *Repentance and true Religion*, we have again *Access* to him, and are admitted to bear *relation* to him as our *God*, and our *Father*. He is the *Father* ; of *whom, by Nature the whole Family in Heaven and Earth is named* ; and through whose *Grace and Goodness*, even *Sinners*, upon their Amendment and Reformation, are again favourably received into their *Father's house*, into the *Family or City of God*. *Behold*, saith St *John*, *what manner of Love the Father has bestowed upon us, that we should be called The* Sons of God, 1 Joh. iii. 1. In the description of the *heavenly Jerusalem*, the *City of the Living God* ; (in allusion to which, the *Earthly Jerusalem*, or Congregation of true Worshippers, is by our Saviour stiled, *The City of the Great King* ;) In the description, I say, of the *heavenly Jerusalem*, the relation of God to his faithful Servants is thus set forth, *Rev.* xxi. 3. and xxii. 4. *Behold, the Tabernacle of God is with men, and he will dwell with them, and they shall be his people, and God himself shall be with them, and be their God ; And they shall see his Face, and his Name* (the Father's Name, *ch.* xiv. 1.) *shall be in their foreheads* : And of *him that overcometh*, saith God, *ch.* xxi. 7. *I will be his God, and He shall be my Son*. Upon account of *which Promise*, though to the Patriarchs, and to all other good Men, it was made at a *great Distance* ; yet the Apostle justly draws his inference even with regard to the *present* time, *Heb.* xi. 16. *Wherefore God is not ashamed*, is not *Now* ashamed, *to be called* Their God ; *for he hath prepared for them a City*. To *this relation* between *God* and righteous *Men*, St *John* has respect ; when he tells us, 1 *Joh.* i. 3. *Our Fellowship is with the Father*. The word, *Fellowship*, signifies in the original, *Com-*

2 *munion*

SERM. *munion* or *mutual Relation*; The Saints, are the *Saints of the most High*; and Good
LX.   Men, the *Children of the Living God*.

THE Use, or practical Application of *This Head*, is the Inference St *John* has drawn
for us, 1 *Joh.* iii. 3. *Every man that has This hope in him*, (every Man that is truly
sensible of this *Love which the Father has bestowed upon us*,) *purifies himself even as He
is pure*: Always remembring the Admonition of our Saviour, *Blessed are the pure in
Heart, for they shall see God*: And That solemn declaration made to St *John*, at the
Conclusion of his prophetick Vision of the new Jerusalem, the City of God; *Rev.* xxii. 14.
*Blessed are they that do his commandments, that they may have Right to the Tree of Life,
and may enter in thro' the Gates into the City*.

2dly, Ye are come, saith the Apostle, *to Jesus, the Mediator of the New Covenant*;
to *the Blood of sprinkling, that speaketh better things than that of Abel*. 'Tis by *Christ*,
that repenting Sinners, having *received the Atonement* and reconciliation; are brought
back unto God; have *Access unto the Father*; are *presented as faultless before the presence of* His Glory, *who has gathered together in One All things in Christ, both which
are in Heaven and which are on Earth*, Eph. i. 10. From henceforth therefore, *our
fellowship*, as St *John* tells us, *is with the Father, and with his Son Jesus Christ*: And
God is faithful, saith St *Paul*, 1 *Cor.* i. 9. (that is, if *we* continue obedient, *God* for
His part will certainly perform *His* Promise *faithfully*,) *by whom ye were called unto the
fellowship of his Son Jesus Christ our Lord*. *Christ* has an everlasting Kingdom given
unto him; wherein he rules, as a *Son* in his *own house*, under his *Father* the Supreme
Housholder; *Angels, and Principalities, and Powers, being made subject unto him*: And
He is the Head of the Body, the Church, Col. i. 18. He is the *Head; from whom the
whole Body fitly joined together, and compacted by That which every joint supplieth, according to the effectual working in the measure of every part, maketh increase of the Body
unto the edifying of itself in Love*, Eph. iv. 16. He is *the chief corner-stone, in whom all
the Building fitly framed together, groweth unto an holy temple in the Lord: in whom Ye
also are builded together for an habitation of God through the Spirit*, ch. ii. 21. He is
the *Vine*, and his Disciples are the *Branches*, Joh. xv. 1. God looks upon *us*, not as
what we were originally *in ourselves*, but as being *Now*, by regeneration and Adoption,
planted together in Christ; as redeemed and purchased, by *His* Blood: as *made accepted
in the Beloved*; as *Members*, of *His Body*; as *Subjects*, of the *Kingdom* given unto *Him*.
Insomuch that St *Paul* tells us, upon account of This our relation to Christ, that *God
hath raised us up together, and made us sit together*, (has *already* made us sit together)
in heavenly places in Christ Jesus, Eph. ii. 6. speaking, in an elegant and figurative
manner, as of a thing already *accomplished*, what our Lord expresses by way of Promise, with regard to a *Future State*, Rev. iii. 21. *To Him that overcometh, will I grant
to sit with Me in my Throne, even as I overcame, and am sat down with my Father in
His Throne*. This is in the highest and most exalted Sense, what the Text calls, *being
come unto Jesus the Mediator of the New Covenant, and unto God the Judge of All*. This
is the Accomplishment of our Saviour's Prayer, *Joh.* xvii. 21. *that They all may be One,
as Thou, Father, art in Me, and I in Thee; that they also may be One in Us:*——*And
the glory which thou gavest me, I have given Them; that They may be One, even as We
are One: I in Them, and Thou in Me: that they may be made perfect in One*. Lastly,
This is what the Apostle tells us, *Heb.* ii. 11. *Both he that sanctifieth, and they who
are sanctified, are all of One; for which cause he is not ashamed to call them Brethren*.

THE proper Application of what has been said upon *This* Head, is to Those who
understanding *literally* some of the fore-cited expressions of Scripture, look upon themselves to be in *such* a manner Members of the Body of Christ, as that *His* Righteousness and Acceptableness to God is *imputed* to *Them*, and This merely by Virtue of their

                                                                confident

confident Reliance upon *His* Merits, without being much follicitous whether they *them-*
felves be perfonally indued with the Fruits of Righteoufnefs or no. Which is one of
the *greateſt Corruptions,* that was ever introduced into the Chriſtian Religion. For indeed, all thoſe expreſſions, of being *Members of Chriſt,* of being *One with him,* of being *in him,* and the like; are merely *figurative* and *moral;* denoting the *Subjection* of
Members to their *Head,* and the *Unity* or *Likeneſs* which ariſes from *Imitation* and *Obe-*
dience. If we have been planted together, faith St *Paul, into the* Likeneſs *of Chriſt's*
death, we ſhall be alſo in the likeneſs of his Reſurrection, Rom. vi. 5. And what *That*
means, he explains, *ver.* 4 and 6 ; *like as Chriſt was raiſed up from the Dead by the*
glory of the Father, even ſo We alſo ſhould walk in Newneſs of Life ;——that the Body
of Sin might be deſtroyed, that henceforth ye ſhould not ſerve Sin. Let no Man therefore deceive himſelf with vain words : Being *Members of Chriſt,* and *Sons of God;*
means nothing elſe but *Obedience to the Goſpel,* and thereby conſequently obtaining *re-*
conciliation with God. 2 Cor. v. 17. *If any Man be in Chriſt, he is a new Creature ;*
that is, his Life muſt be actually amended and reformed. So likewiſe *Rom.* xiii. 14.
Put ye on the Lord Jeſus Chriſt, is joined in the ſame verſe as an equivalent exhortation
with, *make not proviſion for the Fleſh, to fulfill the Luſts thereof.* Having the *Spirit of*
Chriſt, that is, a *moral likeneſs* to him ; is the only thing, that can make us truly belong to him : *If any man have not the Spirit of Chriſt, he is None of His,* Rom. viii. 9.
And *ver.* 14. *As many as are led by the Spirit of God,* (that is, who *bring forth the*
Fruits of the Spirit, or live in the Practice of all moral virtues,) *they,* and they only,
are the Sons of God. Jeſus, the Text tells us, *is the Mediator of the New Covenant ;*
of *That* Covenant, wherein are declared the gracious Terms of Pardon and Forgiveneſs to all thoſe who repent and amend ; and which, upon *That* account, is oppoſed in the foregoing verſe, to the Terrors of the Law, *to the Mount that burned with*
Fire, joined with *blackneſs, darkneſs and Tempeſt.* To *Come* therefore *to Jeſus the Me-*
diator of the New Covenant, ſignifies, by true Repentance and effectual Amendment of
Life, (not by *groundleſs Confidence* and *vain Reliance on Chriſt,* but by ſincere *Obedi-*
ence to his *Commands,* by *true Repentance and Amendment of Life)* made available to
the Forgiveneſs of paſt Sin through the *Interceſſion of Chriſt ;* To *come to Chriſt,* I ſay,
ſignifies, by That Repentance which the Goſpel teaches, to be reconciled, and have
Acceſs again, as a returning Prodigal Son, through *Chriſt* to God the *Judge of All,* the
Supreme Lord and Father of the Univerſe. Thus this whole point is at large ſet forth
by St *Paul,* Col. i. 19. *It pleaſed the Father, that in Him ſhould all Fulneſs dwell ;*
And by Him to reconcile all things unto himſelf;——And you that were ſometimes alie-
nated, and Enemies in your Mind by wicked Works, yet now hath he reconciled, In the
body of his Fleſh through Death, to preſent you holy and unblameable and unreproveable
in his Sight ; If ye continue in the Faith, grounded and ſettled, and be not moved away
from the Hope of the Goſpel.

HAVING thus briefly explained the *Two Firſt* Particulars in the Text, (the *firſt* in
order of Nature, though not in the *placing of the words ;) Ye are come, to God the*
Judge of All, and *to Jeſus the Mediator of the New Covenant :* It might here ſeem
natural to have been expected in the next place, that in like manner as in ſome *Other*
paſſages of Scripture, with the *Grace of our Lord Jeſus Chriſt,* and *the Love of God,*
is joined likewiſe the *Fellowſhip of the Holy Ghoſt ;* ſo *here* alſo, I ſay, it might ſeem
naturally to have been expected, that the Apoſtle ſhould have added, the *Communion* or
Fellowſhip of the Holy Ghoſt ; Which with the Two before-mentioned are the True-
Scripture-*Trinity. Ye are come,* unto God the Judge of All, *and to* Jeſus the Mediator
of the New Covenant, and (it might naturally have been expected he ſhould here have
ſubjoined, *and)* unto *the Holy Ghoſt the Comforter.* But This *laſt* particular, the
Apoſtle does not add : And the *Reaſon* of his omitting it, ſeems to be This. The *Holy*

SERM. *Spirit*, is in Scripture reprefented as being to the Church in the place *of Chrift*; and,
LX. *for That very reafon*, is ftiled the *Comforter*, becaufe his proper Office is, *in the Abfence*
of Chrift, to comfort the Faithful with his Gifts and Graces, with his Holy Influence
and Affiftance. *Joh.* xvi. 7. *I tell you the Truth*, faith our Lord, *it is expedient for*
you, that I go away; For if I go not away the Comforter will not come unto you : but
if I depart, I will fend him unto you ;——and *He will guide you into All Truth ; for he*
fhall not fpeak of himfelf, but whatfoever he fhall hear, That fhall he fpeak ; and he will
fhew you things to come. The proper Office therefore of the *Holy Spirit*, being in
Chrift's ftead to fupport and comfort, to guide and direct the Church, until our Lord's
fecond Coming ; *for this reafon*, the Apoftle in the Text, fpeaking of good Chriftians
in a very fublime and figurative manner, as being *already* come unto the True Mount
Sion, the City of the Living God, the heavenly *Jerufalem* ; and being, by fpiritual relation, communion, and unity, as it were *already* actually prefent with *God the Judge*
of All, and with *Jefus the Mediator of the New Covenant* ; for *This* reafon (I fay) it
feems to be, that the Apoftle omits in this place the *Fellowfhip of the Holy Ghoft*, as a
thing *fulfilled* and *accomplifhed*, as having *already* obtained its full Effect ; as being now
fuperfeded by the immediate prefence of *God the Judge of All*, and of our *Mediator*
Jefus Chrift. During our *Abfence* from whofe Beatific prefence, while we continue in
this mortal Life, good Men are under the direction and influence of the *Holy Spirit*.
And the Proof, by which only it can appear that they really are fo, is not a pretending
to *Enthufiaftic influences*, but their bringing forth *the Fruits of the Spirit.* Which
Fruits of the Spirit, (if we will follow St *Paul's* Authority, rather than the imaginations of Enthufiafts) are *Love, joy, peace, long-fuffering, gentlenefs, goodnefs, faith, meek-*
nefs, temperance, Gal. v. 22. That is, the Practice of all moral and eternal Virtues.

THE remaining particulars of the Text, are ; Ye are come *to an innumerable Com-*
pany of Angels, to *the Spirits of juft men made perfect*, and to *the general Affembly or*
Church of the firft-born which are written in Heaven.

SERMON

S E R M O N LXI.

Of the Catholick Church of CHRIST.

HEB. XII. 22, 23.

But ye are come unto mount Sion, and unto the City of the Living God, the heavenly Jerusalem, and to an innumerable company of Angels, To the general Assembly and Church of the first-born which are written in Heaven, and to God the Judge of All, and to the Spirits of just men made perfect, and to Jesus the Mediator of the new Covenant.

IN discoursing upon these words, I have proposed *First* to consider distinctly the several *Persons*, whom the Apostle here supposes to have a *relation* to, and communion *with*, each other: And from thence, *Secondly*, to deduce the true Scripture-notion of the *Catholick Church of Christ*, and of That *Unity* or *Communion* which is between the Members of it, as Members of the *One Body of Christ*.

I. *First*, As to the several *Persons*, whom the Apostle here supposes to have a *relation* to, and *Communion* with, each other; I observed that the *Kingdom of God*, is in Scripture described under the Notion or Similitude of a *royal City*; wherein *All*, who in Any Station belong unto it, have a mutual *relation to*, and some sort of *communication with* each other; by which they are *All* esteemed as *One political Body*. In the prosecution of which Similitude, the Apostle in the Text *distinctly enumerates* the following *Particulars*; of which is constituted the True *Mount Sion, the City of the Living God, the heavenly Jerusalem*. There is, first, says he; (first, in order of *Nature*; though not in the order, wherein the *words are placed*;) There is, in the *first* place, *God the Judge of All*: There is, *secondly, Jesus the Mediator of the New Covenant*: *Thirdly*, There is, *says he*, an *innumerable Company of Angels*: *Fourthly*, There are *the Spirits of just men made perfect*: And *Lastly*, There is the *general Assembly and Church of the first-born which are* written *in Heaven*, though they be not yet actually *arrived* there.

THE *two first* of these particulars I have already gone through: *Ye are come unto God the Judge of All*, and to *Jesus the Mediator of the New Covenant*. It remains that I proceed now to the

3d particular; *Ye are come*, saith the Apostle, *unto an innumerable Company of Angels*. *Angels*, are in Scripture declared to be ministring Spirits, which go in and out continually before the Throne of God. And *our relation* to them, as members of the same heavenly *Jerusalem*, the City of the Living God, is *manifold* in the *present*, as well as in the *future* state. They are Worshippers together with *Us*, of the *same* God and universal Father, *of whom the Whole Family in* Heaven *and* Earth *is named*. Rev. xxii. 9, *I am thy fellow-servant*, said the Angel to St *John*; *I am Thy fellow-servant*, and the fellow-servant *of thy brethren the Prophets, and of them which keep the Sayings of*

2   *this*

SERM.
LXI.

this Book: Worſhip God. Nor are they *only,* in common with Us, *Subjects* of the *natural Kingdom* of God; but they are alſo moreover *Subjects and Miniſters* of the *mediatorial Kingdom of Chriſt.* Heb. i. 6. *When he bringeth in the firſt-begotten into the World, he ſaith, And let all the Angels of God worſhip him.* By *Chriſt,* God has *gathered together in One,* Eph. i. 10, (into One *Family,* into One *Kingdom,* under One Head,) *all things both which are in Heaven and which are on Earth: Angels, and Authorities, and Powers, being made ſubject unto him,* 1 Pet. iii. 22. They are *miniſtring Spirits, ſent forth to miniſter to thoſe who ſhall be Heirs of Salvation,* Heb. i. 14. Our Saviour, ſpeaking of *little children,* literally; and, figuratively, of *good men,* who are of the ſame harmleſs diſpoſition; tells us, *Matt.* xviii. 10, that the Angels, are Their *Angels* or Miniſters; that is, have the *Care* of them committed to them by God; even

* Compare
Matt. xxviii.
10. with
Eſth. i. 14.
and Tobit
xii. 15.

thoſe * *principal* Angels, *who always behold the Face of* his *Father which is in Heaven.* In *other* places, the Scripture aſſures us, that they as Subjects of the ſame heavenly Kingdom, are continually obſerving the Providences of God towards his Church; *Theſe things, the Angels deſire to look into,* 1 Pet. i. 12: and Eph. iii. 10, *To the intent, that now unto the principalities and Powers in heavenly places, might be made known by the Church,* (by the Church, that is, by the various diſpenſations of Divine Providence towards good men,) *the manifold Wiſdom of God.* It aſſures us; that *there is* joy *in the preſence of the Angels of God,* over every *Sinner that repenteth,* Luk. xv. 10; that the *Souls* of righteous men, as of *Lazarus, Luk.* xvi. 22, are, at their departure out of this World, *carried by the Angels into Abraham's boſom;* that, at the general Reſurrection at the laſt day, *the Angels ſhall come forth,* Matt. xiii. 49, *and ſhall ſever the Wicked from among the Juſt;* and laſtly, that *they which ſhall be accounted worthy to obtain That World, and the reſurrection unto Life, Luk.* xx. 35, 36, ſhall *themſelves* be equal unto the Angels, and be the children of God. Which final Union, of *Angels* and righteous *men,* into one heavenly Society, St *John* excellently ſets forth, in the ivth and vth chapters of the *Revelation:* Where, beginning the Worſhip *originally* paid to

ch. iv. 8, 9,
11.

God by all his creatures in general, (who, in their *giving glory and honour and thanks to him that ſitteth on the Throne, who liveth for ever and ever; reſt not day and night, ſaying, Holy, Holy, Holy, Lord God Almighty, which was and Is, and is to come;* —— *Thou art worthy, O Lord, to receive Glory and Honour and Power; for thou haſt created all things, and for thy pleaſure they Are, and were created:* And thence proceeding to deſcribe the *particular* Worſhip, which *began* to be paid to *Chriſt* upon his exaltation to the right hand of God; (when the Saints who were redeemed from the Earth,

ch. v. 9.

began a New Song, ſaying, *Thou art worthy;* —— *for thou waſt ſlain, and haſt redeemed us to God by thy Blood,* —— *and haſt made us unto our God Kings and Prieſts;*) he at length concludes with uniting in one univerſal Chorus the Voices of *Angels* and of *Men,* giving praiſe at the ſame time to *God* who ſat on the Throne, and to the *Lamb* who had been ſlain for men: *And I heard the Voice of many Angels round about the Throne, and the Living Creatures and the Elders, and the Number of them was ten thouſand times ten thouſand, and thouſands of thouſands, Saying with a loud Voice, Worthy is the Lamb that was ſlain, to receive Power and Riches and Wiſdom and Strength and Honour and Glory and Bleſſings; And every Creature which is in Heaven and on the Earth,* —— *heard I ſaying, Bleſſing and Honour and Glory and Power, be unto him that ſitteth upon the Throne, and unto the Lamb for ever and ever.*

THE *Uſe* which the Church of *Rome* has made of This Doctrine, of good *men's* being in Scripture joined together with the *innumerable Company of Angels,* as Members of the ſame *heavenly Jeruſalem, the City of the Living God;* The *Uſe,* I ſay, which the Church of *Rome* has made of this Doctrine, has been very *perverſe,* as well as *impious.* For, inſtead of directing their Prayers uniformly to *God the Judge of All,* through *Jeſus the Mediator of the New Covenant,* whom the Scripture declares to be Alone our *Advocate*

I

vocate

vocate with the Father; They, by a *false* inference from a *True* doctrine, of *Angels* being *ministring Spirits*, have, of their *own* Authority, presumed to establish a *Worship of Angels*, in contradiction to the *express Command of God*. For, whereas the Scripture solemnly declares, that as there is but *One God*, so there is also but *One Mediator between God and Men*; they, on the contrary, have, by Angel-worship, set up Many *Mediators*; which is direct *Idolatry* against *Him* who is the *Only True One*. To charge them with giving to *Angels* the proper Worship of *God Almighty*, is charging them with a Fact which they *deny*; and therefore is not the best and most proper way to convince them of their Error: But the setting up of *Many* Mediators, is a Fact they do not, and cannot, deny: And yet the Worship of *False* Mediators, is as *true and formal Idolatry* against the *One Mediator* appointed by God; as the Worship of *False* Gods, is Idolatry against the *One* God and Father of the Universe. St *Paul* therefore seems prophetically to describe their practice, and to condemn it directly upon such a a Principle, as cuts off from them all possibility of Evasion or Excuse; when, speaking of *things which have a Shew of Wisdom in Will-worship and Humility*, 2 Col. ii. 23; he Thus argues, ver. 18, *Let no man beguile you of your Reward, in a voluntary Humility and Worshipping of Angels, intruding into those things which he hath not seen, vainly puft up by his Fleshly mind, And not holding the Head*; that is, not keeping stedfast to *Christ* the *One Mediator*, upon whom alone the whole Church depends, as the Members of a Body on their Union with the Head.

4thly, Ye are come, saith the Apostle in the Text, *to the Spirits of just men made perfect*. The True Members of Christ's invisible Church here upon *Earth*, known unto God only, who searches the Heart, and judges of every man's sincerity; are in Scripture always represented, as being One and the same Body, or Society, with the Saints in *Heaven*: Just as persons travelling in *foreign* parts, are still always esteemed to continue Members of the same Community, with those who remain at home in their native country. *Jerusalem which is above*, saith St *Paul*, Gal. iv. 26, *is the Mother of us All*. Those who are not actually arrived there, yet, if they be *meet to be partakers of the inheritance with the Saints in Light*, their Treasure, their Portion is laid up for them in Heaven, and their *Names* are already *written* There. Their Faith, their Hope, their Conversation, their Citizenship is in Heaven: They live *Now* according to the Laws of that Spiritual Country; and therefore expect *hereafter* to be admitted there as obedient, at least as penitent and returning Children, into their Father's house. Though their *natural* habitation is upon *Earth*; yet, in the *moral* sense, having relinquished things *Earthly*, that is, all the *Wickedness* wherein the World generally lies; they are (as St *Paul* expresses it, Eph. ii. 19.) *no more Strangers and Foreigners, but fellow-citizens with the Saints, and of the Houshold of God*. St *John* expresses the same thing in a still *more sublime* and elegant figure of speaking, according to the manner of the Prophetick style, *Rev.* xiii. 6; where he Thus describes Antichristian tyranny, persecuting the True Worshippers of God; *He opened his mouth*, saith he, *in Blasphemy against God, to blaspheme his Name and his Tabernacle, and them that* dwell in Heaven; *and it was given unto him to make war with the Saints, and to overcome them*: The same persons who, in the *Latter* part of the Sentence, are called *Saints* under *Persecution*, are, in the *former* part of the same sentence, *they that dwell in Heaven*; that is, who, by the practice of Virtue and true Holiness, are qualified for, (and are therefore with great elegance said *actually to have*, what by the Promise of God they have a *certain Title to*,) an inheritance in *that new Heaven and new Earth, wherein righteousness* is to *dwell* for ever.

THE *Use*, which the Church of *Rome* has made of the Doctrine contained under *This* Head likewise, as well as the foregoing; has been extremely *corrupt*, and *irreligious*. For instead of *imitating* the *Virtues and Examples* of the *Saints*, who have

SERM.
LXI.
gone before them in the *Worship of the True God*, and in the Practice of *Righteouf-ness* and all *Holiness*; they have on the contrary turned *This very thing* into an Occasion of *Apostatizing* from *Christ*; and made *Idols* of the Saints, by causing *Them* after their Death, to become *Objects* of That Worship, which, while they *lived*, they both by their Doctrine and by their Practice taught, should be paid *only to their common Lord*. Nor is there *any Colour* of Reason, in That *Excuse* alleged by the Church of *Rome*; that they worship the Saints *no otherwise*, than by defiring the Affiftance of *Their Prayers* to *God*. For undoubtedly the *Heathen* of old, when they worshipped *Dæmons* and *Heroes* or the *Souls of their departed Kings*, did not take those *Dead* men to be *God Almighty*: And yet the Worship they paid them, *whatsoever* it was, because it was paid to a mere *Fiction*, to an Object which either had *no Being* at all, or (however) which had *no Right to the Honour* they paid it; was always justly charged as the Crime of *Idolatry*. An *Idol*, faith St *Paul*, *is Nothing in the world*: A mere *Fiction* of the Imagination of Vain Men; Either *totally* such, if the Object has *no real existence at all*; or *so far* such, as there is paid to it any *religious Honour which does not* belong to it. That the *Saints departed* have *Any Knowledge at all* of our Affairs here upon Earth, is what no Argument can be brought to prove, either from Reason or Scripture: But if they could *know* and *hear the Prayers of Men*, yet that *They* who have not as yet been judged *themfelves*, (and of whom the *most righteous*, as St *Peter* tells us, *shall scarcely be saved*, that is, shall owe their *own* Salvation merely to God's free *Pardon* of their Sins through Christ,) should be allowed to mediate and be intercessors for *Others*; is what *can* be *no* otherwise looked upon by serious persons, than as an impious Fiction. *Angels*, who are *ministring Spirits sent forth to minister to them who shall be Heirs of Salvation*, we are sure, *have* knowledge of our Affairs, and Always *behold the Face of our Heavenly Father* in That State of Glory, which the *Saints* shall *not* be instated in till the Great day of Retribution: And yet even of *Angel*-worship St *Paul* declares, that it is *an intruding into things which men have not seen, vainly puffed up by their fleshly mind*, falling away from *Christ* the *only Head* of reconciliation, and *beguiling themfelves of their Reward*: All which therefore, must *still much more* be chargeable upon the Practice of *Saint-worship*. God has appointed *One only Mediator* between God and Men, who has perfect knowledge of our Infirmities, and is abundantly able to succour them who come unto God by him: And for men to *idolize* either *Saints* or *Angels*, by setting them up, merely in their own imaginations, as *Intercessors* for them with God, whom God never appointed to That Office; is a manifest derogation from the Honour of our *Lord*. This is evidently the State of the case, even though it were true, what some of the *Romanists* allege, that they went no further than barely requesting the Prayers of the Saints departed, to be offered unto God for them. But indeed they go much further; taking it for granted, that the Prayers of the Saints are undoubtedly very much available for their devout Votaries: And whereas our Saviour expressly tells his Disciples, that the *Greatest Saints* are at the best *but unprofitable Servants*; these men teach on the contrary, that besides working out their own Salvation, they have moreover a Stock of superabundant Merit deposited in the Church, to be applied for the Benefit of those who want it. Which Notion has been carried to such a Heighth of Extravagancy, in some Ages and Nations which call themfelves *Christian*; that the deluded people, instead of loving the Lord their God with all their Heart and with all their Soul, have been taught to rely with a more constant and more entire confidence, upon the powerful Prayers and Merits of the *Holy Virgin* and the *Saints*; than upon the intercession of *Jesus the Mediator of the New Covenant*, or the acceptableness of Virtue and True Holiness in the presence of *God the Judge of All*.

THE *only Text* that I am sensible of in the whole New Testament, that can possibly be perverted to give so much as the least appearance, even to the meanest Understand-ing,

ing, of countenancing the Doctrine of the *Merit of the Saints*: is That of St *Paul,* Col. i. 24. *I rejoyce in my Sufferings for you, and fill up that which is behind of the Afflictions of Christ in my Flesh, for his Body's sake, which is the Church.* From which words it has been collected, that the afflictions and pious Works of particularly eminent Saints, are meritorious towards obtaining remission of Sin, not only for *themselves,* but for *Others* also; in *some* proportion as the Sufferings of Christ, were for the redemption of the *whole Church.* But the true meaning of St *Paul's* words, is plainly *This* only; that in like manner as it was foretold and appointed that *Christ,* the *Head* of the Church, should *first* suffer; so it was appointed that his *Body* also, the *Members* of his Church, should in many degrees suffer *after* him; being *conformed to the Image of the Son of God,* and *through much tribulation entring into the Kingdom of God.* This is *filling up that which was Behind of the Sufferings of Christ;* accomplishing that which remained to be *fulfilled,* of the fore-appointed *Sufferings,* first of *Christ,* and then of his *Church.*

THE *real* Ground and Foundation of this *whole* Invention, of the *Saints in Heaven* being *helpful* to *Sinners upon Earth;* was nothing else, but the *Worldly profit* arising from this Doctrine to Those, who claimed to themselves the Power of dispensing out the *Merits* of the Saints *for Money,* and of enjoying the *rich Gifts and Presents* offered to the Saints (in a grateful Return for their Prayers) by Superstitious Votaries.

'TIS likewise upon the very same foundation, with these *imaginary* Prayers of the *Dead* for the *Living;* that on the reverse, great Endeavours have been used, to make the Prayers also of the *Living* thought available for the *Dead:* Men having been taught to believe, that Prayers purchased with Money to be said for them after their *Death,* might avail instead of their having perfected True Repentance and Reformation in their *Lives.* Which being therefore indeed more *effectual* than the intercession of *Christ himself,* who obtains forgiveness for *those only* who *actually* repent and amend; hence it has come to pass, that among men of wicked and corrupt minds, the imaginary Prayers of *Dead Saints* interceding for the *Living,* and *Masses said by the Living* in behalf of the *Dead;* Fictions of vain and deceitful *Men,* have been more relied on, than the *everlasting Gospel* of *Christ.*

THIS is the perverse and *corrupt* Use, which the Church of *Rome* has made of this plain Doctrine of the Apostle, that *good men on Earth* are Members of the *same City of God,* with the *Spirits of just men already made perfect in Heaven.* The *True and Christian* Use of this doctrine, is That which the Apostle himself teaches us to make of it; that, if we look upon ourselves as *Fellow-citizens with the Saints, and of the Houshold of God;* if we esteem ourselves as Members of the same Society with them, and belonging to the same heavenly country, the *Jerusalem* which is above; then ought we *to set our affections on things above, not on things in the Earth,* Col. iii. 2; that our *Hearts* may be, where we believe is our *Treasure;* considering, in every *important* action we go about, what influence it will have upon our *future and eternal,* rather than our *present and temporal estate;* having *our* conversation *in Heaven,* as being *partakers of the same* Hope with those who have gone before us, and who have already attained to *the inheritance of the Saints in Light;* Praising God, for *Their deliverance* from the Miseries of this sinful World; setting before us Their *Good Examples,* imitating their *Virtues,* and respecting their *Memories; Looking for,* and waiting unto, *the Blessed Hope,* and *the Glorious Appearance of the Great God, and our Saviour Jesus Christ;* when *We* together with *Them,* who have gone before us in Christ, shall have our perfect Consummation and Bliss *both in Body and Soul,* in the eternal Kingdom of God: *We,* I say, *together with* Them, shall then receive our *perfect* Consummation and Bliss. For though, in the Text, *They* are stiled *already,* the *Spirits of just men made* perfect; yet This is spoken only with regard to their having *perfected*

or

SERM.
LXI.

or *finished their course*, and having escaped all the Dangers and Temptations of this present World. For, as to the actual possession of the *complete* Happiness laid up for them in the Kingdom of God, in *This* they are *not* to be instated till the Resurrection from the Dead: As the Apostle in the xi*th* chapter of This Epistle to the *Hebrews*, speaking of the Patriarchs and Martyrs of old, expressly tells us, ver. 39. *These all* (says he) *having obtained a good Report through Faith, received not the Promise*; God *having provided some better thing for us, that they without us should not be made perfect*.

5thly and *Lastly*; *Ye are come*, saith the Apostle in the Text, *to the general Assembly and Church of the first-born which are written in Heaven*. The word, *first-born*, carries along with it, in common Speech, the Notion of a *Right of Inheritance*; and to be *written in Heaven*, or, *in the book of Life*, signifies being *qualified*, by a Life of *Virtue and true Righteousness*, to be made *Partakers* of That Inheritance. (Thus, *Rev.* xxii. 14. *Blessed are they that do his* Commandments, *that they may have* Right *to the Tree of Life, and may enter in through the Gates into the City*.) I say, To be *written in Heaven*, signifies; not, being unalterably *predestinated* unto Life; (for, *Him that sinneth against me, will I* blot, saith God, *out of my Book*; and even *Judas* himself, before his Apostacy, was one of those, to whom our Lord said, *Luk.* x. 20, that *their Names were written in Heaven*;) but it denotes, men being *at present* true *children of God*, and, if they *continue* such unto the End, *actual Heirs of his Kingdom*. When therefore the Apostle says, *Ye are come unto the general Assembly and Church of the first-born which are written in Heaven*; the Meaning is, as if he had said; Ye are become Members of That Blessed, but at present Invisible Society, which consists of all the righteous and good men, who fear God and keep his Commandments, or who *have done* and *shall do so* through All Ages, and in all Nations over the Face of the Whole Earth. This is the True *Catholick Church of God*, the Spouse and Body of Christ. The Scripture-notion of which universal Church, having been much mistaken by the ignorance of Some, and much perverted by the wickedness of Others; I shall therefore still further and more distinctly endeavour to set That matter in a clear Light in a following Discourse.

SERMON

SERMON LXII.

Of the Catholick Church of CHRIST.

HEB. XII. 22, 23.

But ye are come unto mount Sion, and unto the City of the Living God, the heavenly Jerusalem, and to an innumerable company of Angels, To the general Assembly and Church of the first-born which are written in Heaven, and to God the Judge of All, and to the Spirits of just men made perfect, and to Jesus the Mediator of the new Covenant:

IN difcourfing upon thefe words; I have already,

I. In the *First* place, confidered diftinctly the feveral *Perfons*, whom the Apoftle, in this his Defcription of the City of the Living God, the heavenly *Jerufalem*, fuppofes to have a *relation* to, and *Communion* with each other. There is, 1ft, fays he, *God the Judge of All:* 2dly, *Jefus the Mediator of the New Covenant:* 3dly, *An innumerable Company of Angels:* 4thly, *The Spirits of juft men made perfect:* 5thly, *The general Affembly and Church of the firft-born which are written in Heaven:* Written in Heaven; that is, not, *predeftinated* unalterably unto Life; (for, *Him that finneth against me, will I blot,* faith God, *out of my Book*; and even *Judas* himfelf, before his Apoftacy, was One of Thofe, to whom our Lord faid, *Luke* x. 20, That *their Names were written in Heaven*;) But *written in Heaven,* are they, who *at prefent* are *true children* of God, and, if they *continue* fuch unto the End, fhall be *actual Heirs of his Kingdom.*

Now this *laft* Particular, *the general Affembly and Church of the firft-born which are written in Heaven,* being an exprefs *Definition* of the *True Catholick Church of God,* the Spoufe and Body of Chrift; the right Notion of which univerfal Church, has been much miftaken by the ignorance of Some, and much perverted by the Wickednefs of Others: My

II. *Second* general Head therefore, (to which I am to proceed at This time,) was, from thefe words of the Apoftle, to deduce the true Scripture-Notion of the *Holy Catholick Church of Chrift,* and of That *Unity,* or *Communion,* which is between the Members of it, as Members of the *One Body of Chrift.*

Now though the word *Catholick* is well known to fignify, in general, the *Whole* or *Univerfal* Church; yet are there *feveral different* Senfes, wherein even this *general* Expreffion, is taken in *greater* or in *lefs* Latitude of fignification. The

1ft and *largeft* Senfe of the term *Catholick Church,* is that which appears to be the moft obvious and *literal* Meaning of the words of the Text, *The general Affembly and Church of the firft-born which are written in Heaven*; that is, the *whole Number* of thofe who fhall finally attain unto Salvation. According to that lively defcription St *John* gives of them, *Rev.* vii. 9, *I beheld, and lo, a great multitude, which no man*

SERM.
LXII.

could number, of all Nations, and kindreds, and people, and tongues, stood before the Throne, —— and cried with a loud voice, saying, Salvation unto our God which sitteth upon the Throne, and unto the Lamb. Men being corrupted and depraved by Sin, could not *of themselves,* consistently with the infinite Holiness of the Divine Nature, and the Honour of God's Righteous Laws, be admitted to have Access unto *Him,* who *dwelleth in Light inaccessible,* and *is of purer Eyes than to behold iniquity.* But, through the *intercession* of the *Lamb stain from the Foundation of the World;* whom *God* from the Beginning promised by All his Holy Prophets, and in the fulness of Time actually *raised from the Dead,* and exalted into Heaven to the *right hand of the Throne on the Majesty on High,* and *gave him a Name which is above every Name,* and *a Kingdom which should never be destroyed:* Through *His* intercession, I say, All who forsake their Sins and amend their Lives, shall, consistently with the Honour of the Divine Laws, be admitted to the Grace and Favour, of having their Repentance accepted unto Pardon. To *Him* God has given, (to become Subjects of that Kingdom which the Father has appointed him, and to be Partakers with him of his eternal Glory and Happiness,) *All Those* who by sincere Repentance and true renewed Obedience, shall be found capable of applying to themselves the Redemption purchased by the Blood of Christ. *Behold,* saith he, *I and the Children which God has given me,* Heb. ii. 13. And *Luke* xxii. 29, *I appoint You a Kingdom, as my Father hath appointed unto Me.* These are, in the *largest* and most *extensive* Sense of the word, the *Catholick Church of God; the General Assembly and Church of the first-born which are written in Heaven:* All Holy and Virtuous Men, who in All Ages and in All Nations, have feared God and kept his Commandments, from the Beginning of the World. In *This* Blessed Assembly of the Sons of God, are comprehended all Those, who, under the original and general Law of *Nature* only, through the *Love* of *Truth* and *Right,* of *God* and *Goodness,* have after the example of *Enoch* and *Noah,* of *Melchisedec* and *Job,* of the *Patriarchs* and other Antient Heroes, *of whom the World was not worthy,* separated themselves from the corrupt Practices of the idolatrous and unrighteous Nations of the Earth; and they *shall* therefore, as our Saviour declares, *come from the East and from the West and from the North and from the South, and shall sit down with Abraham, Isaac and Jacob, in the Kingdom of God,* Matt. viii. 11; when *the Son of man shall send forth his Angels, and shall gather together his Elect from the four Winds, from one end of Heaven to the other,* Matt. xxiv. 31. For *God is no respecter of persons,* Acts x. 34; *but in every Nation, he that feareth God and worketh righteousness, is accepted of him.* These therefore, together with All such, as, under the *Jewish* Dispensation in particular obeyed the Law of *Moses, waiting for the Hope and Redemption of Israel;* and all Those in the *last* place, who, under the *Gospel*-state, sincerely believe in the Name of Christ, and, *by patient continuance in well-doing,* according to the Commands of God delivered to them in the Gospel, *seek for glory and honour and immortality:* These *All,* considered *together,* as One united Body, or Assembly of God's faithful Servants, are, in the most *true* and *primary* notion, in the *highest* and *largest* sense of the word, *the Catholick* or *Universal Church of Christ;* his *Spouse,* and his *Body;* his *Brethren,* and his *Members;* his *Sheep,* his *Inheritance,* and the *Subjects of his Kingdom. This* is that *Church,* which *Christ loved and gave himself for* it; that he might *sanctify and cleanse it, by the word of God;* that he might *wash it from its Sins, in his own Blood;* that he might *present it* to his Father *a glorious Church,* not having *spot or wrinkle or any such thing,* but that it should be *Holy and without Blemish,* even *undefiled and faultless before the Throne of God. These* are They, who shall *finally,* at their arrival in the *True Mount Sion, the City of the Living God, the heavenly Jerusalem;* make one complete and Blessed Society, with an *innumerable Company of Angels,* and with *Jesus the Mediator of the New Covenant,* and with *GOD the Judge of All:* And

And in the *mean time*, the *Unity* or *Communion* which is between the Members of S E R M. *This Universal Church* or *Family* of God, confifts in This; that they are All, Servants LXII. of the fame Supreme King, the One *God* and *Father of the Univerfe*; all, redeemed by the Blood of the *fame Saviour*, whether they *explicitly* knew of him, or *no*; all, guided and fanctified by the *fame Spirit*; all, Heirs of the *fame Promifes*, and have laid up for them a fhare of the *fame Glory*, not in the fame *Degree*, but in different *degrees of the* fame *Glory*, in the eternal *Kingdom of God*.

I F then we fincerely *believe* This, as we all *pretend and profefs* to believe it; *what manner of perfons ought we* confequently *to be, in all Holinefs and Godly Converfation*; (not regarding, in matters of Religion, the doctrines and commandments of *Men*, but the Laws of *God* only;) that we may be worthy to be found *written in the writing of God's people*, Ezek. xiii. 9; (that is, as St *John* expreffes it, *in the Book of Life*;) and to have our portion of inheritance among thofe Saints of the moft High; being numbred together, in that general Affembly and Church of the firft-born, with the Patriarchs and Prophets, with the Apoftles, Martyrs and Confeffors, and all righteous and juft Men, who have lived and died in the Fear of God from the Foundation of the World.

2dly, T H E *Catholick* or *univerfal* Church, fignifies in the *next* place, and indeed more *frequently*, the Chriftian *Church* only: The *Chriftian* Church, as *diftinguifhed* from that of the *Jews* and *Patriarchs* of old: the Church of *Chrift*, fpread *univerfally* from our Saviour's Days over *all the World*; in contradiftinction to the *Jewifh* Church, which was *particularly* confined to *One Nation* or People. And in *This* fenfe, the *Holy Catholick Church* fignifies *That inftitution of Chriftianity*, or *Society of men profeffing the Doctrine of the Gofpel*; which being built upon the *Foundation* of Chrift and his Apoftles, (in which fenfe our Saviour emphatically ftiles St *Peter* a *Rock*, or principal *Foundation-ftone*;) is by a continued Succeffion of their Difciples and Followers, propagated in the *Preaching of Truth* and in the *Practice of Righteoufnefs* through All Ages, without any total Interruption, unto the End of the World. *This* is That Church, which Chrift has promifed to be Always with, and to preferve it, that the *Gates of Hell*, that is, *Perfecution* and *Tyranny* and even *Death itfelf*, fhall never be able to prevail againft it. *This* is That Church, which though continually *oppofed* by *Unbelievers* on the *one* hand, and on the *other* hand *perfecuted* by the feveral *Religions* and *Powers* of the *World* that calls itfelf *Chriftian*; though corrupted by *falfe Doctrines* and *Determinations* of *Men*, diftracted by *mutual Impofitions* and *Schifms*, and moft of all deformed by *temporal Profperity*, by the mixture of *Ambition* and *worldly Power*, and by the *vitious Lives* of thofe who pretend to be its Members; yet fhall finally fo prevail, that at length the *Kingdoms of the World*, *fhall become the Kingdoms of our Lord and of his Chrift*; and the *Knowledge of God fhall fill the Earth, as the Waters cover the Sea*; and the *everlafting Gofpel* fhall be preached to all Nations, *faying*, Rev. xiv. 6, 7, *Worfhip him that made Heaven and Earth and the Sea*, and all that is therein.

T H E *Unity* or *Communion* which is between the Members of *this Church of* Chrift, fpread over the World from the days of our Saviour to the Confummation of all things, and confidered as *diftinct* from the *Jewifh Church*, and *That of the Patriarchs of old*; I fay, the Unity of *its* Members confifts further in This; that they are, not only Servants of the *fame God*, and Heirs of the *fame Promifes*, (for fo were the *Jews* and *Patriarchs*, and All the *Worthies* of Antient Ages;) but Thefe have Communion moreover, in *profeffing* particularly the *fame* explicit *Faith in Chrift*, of whom the Antients had but an *obfcure* expectation as of Him that was to come; they have a Communion or Unity, as being *Members* of Chrift's *peculiar myftical Body, of his Flefh and of his Bones*, Eph. v. 30. as being united, under the fame *Head*; as being governed,

2   by

SERM. by the fame *Laws* ; as communicating, (though they live in very *different Ages* and
LXII. *Countries* of the World,) in the fame *Ordinances of the Gofpel*, in the offering up of
Prayers to God through Chrift, in the *Miniftration* of the fame *Word*, and the *Participation* of the fame *Sacraments* : According to that elegant defcription given by St *Paul*,
Eph. ii. 20. *Ye are built upon the Foundation of the Apoftles and Prophets, Jefus Chrift himfelf being the chief corner-ftone, In whom all the Building fitly framed together, groweth unto an Holy Temple in the Lord.*

3*dly*, THE *Catholick Church* fignifies very frequently, in a ftill more *particular* and
reftrained fenfe, *that Part* of the *univerfal* Church of Chrift, which in the *prefent Age*
is *Now* living upon Earth ; as diftinguifhed from thofe which have been *before*, and
fhall come *after*. And in *This* fenfe, the word fignifies the Prefent *True Members of
Chrift*, wherefoever they be difperfed, or howfoever diftinguifhed, over the Face of the
whole Earth. *This* is the *Prefent Church Militant*, the *Invifible* Church known only
to God the fearcher of Hearts ; who, among Chriftians of all Nations, and of different
Rites and Ceremonies and Forms of Government, and of great Diverfity of Opinions in
matters not fundamental, that is, not covenanted for at Baptifm ; knows *who* they are
that worfhip him in Spirit and in Truth, and obey the Gofpel with Simplicity and Sincerity of Heart. This is the *invifible* Catholick Church, the only *true Church upon
Earth* in the Sight of *God* ; but not diftinguifhable by *Us*, who know not each others
Hearts, and therefore very often cannot poffibly diftinguifh between the hypocrite and
the fincere.

FOR which reafon, between the Members of this True *Invifible* Church, there cannot poffibly be, in this prefent Life, any *diftinct* and *feparate Communion* ; till, at the
great day of Retribution, the All-feeing and Unerring Judge, fhall finally and for ever
feparate the Sheep from the Goats.

4*thly and laftly*, THE Term, *Catholick Church*, fignifies in the *laft* place, and *moft
frequently of all*, That Part of the Univerfal Church of Chrift, which in the prefent
Generation is *Vifible* upon Earth, in an *Outward* Profeffion of the Belief of the Gofpel,
and in a *vifible external* Communion of the Word and Sacraments. *This* is That
Church, which, in our prefent imperfect State, we are forced very improperly and promifcuoufly to judge and fpeak of, as if the *Vifible* and *Invifible*, the *Apparent* and the
Real Church of Chrift, were one and the fame Body of Men, actually united in the
Communion of Saints. This is That Great *Field*, fo ftyled by our Saviour in his Parable, wherein grows together the *Corn* and the *Tares* : This is that *Net*, defcribed by
him in another parable ; wherein are inclofed both *Good Fifh* and *Bad*. This is the
mixt Society of *fincere Chriftians* and *Hypocrites*, who fhall not be feparated till the End
of the World.

THE Church of *Rome*, pretends herfelf to be *This Whole Catholick Church*, exclufive of All other Societies of Chriftians. Which is the very *fame* contradiction, as for a
fingle Member, nay, for a Member after it has *cut itfelf off* from the Body, confidently
to call itfelf the *Whole Body*.

Marks alfo, or *Notes*, they pretend to give ; whereby, as by a certain Teft, Men may
eafily diftinguifh the *True* Catholick Church, from all that are *erroneous*.

One of thefe *Marks* of Theirs, is *Vifibility* ; that is, *Temporal Grandeur* and *Profperity*, founded upon *Worldly Power* and *Dominion* : Which the *Scripture*, on the contrary makes one of the *Great Marks* of *Antichrift*, compelling by Force of Perfecution
all the World to worfhip him, that is, to make profeffion of *His* Religion : *Rev.* xviii.
7, 3. *She hath glorified herfelf, and lived delicioufly ;——fhe faith in her Heart, I fit a
Queen,——and fhall fee no forrow :——All Nations have drunk of the Wine of——her
fornication, and the Kings of the Earth have committed fornication with her*, (that is,

have

have fupported her idolatrous religion;) and the Merchants of the Earth are *waxed rich* S E R M. *through the abundance of her Delicacies.* LXII.

Another Mark they give us of the *True* Church, is *Univerfality*; By which they mean, a *large Extent of Country*: Not confidering, that *Mahometanifm* and *Paganifm* are much fuperior to them in *This* refpect: And if they were *not*, yet our Saviour feems to have had no great Opinion of This way of judging of *Truth* by *Numbers*; when he tells us that *Wide is the Gate, and Broad is the Way that leadeth to Deftruction, and Many there be that go in thereat.*

Another Mark of the True Church, they tell us, is *Antiquity*: By which they mean, not *Antiquity indeed*, not the *Primitive Antiquity* of Chrift and his Apoftles; but only feveral *paft* corrupt Ages; which, with refpect to *Us Now* indeed, are *Antient*; but, with refpect to the *Gofpel itfelf*, were very *late Innovations.*

Laftly; *Another* Mark they give us of the *True* Church, is *Miracles*: Which were indeed *Authentick Evidences* of our *Saviour's* divine Commiffion, and of his *Apoftles* after him: But *miraculous Powers*, extended not any further than to *Their* perfons; and to thofe immediately impowered by them in the firft Age: And as to the *pretend-ed Miracles*, which began in the *Fourth Century* about the Time of St *Anthony* the Monk, and have continued ever fince in the Church of *Rome*; the Character the Scrip-ture gives of *Them*, is This; 2 *Th.* ii. 8. *Then fhall that wicked one be revealed,——whofe coming is after the working of Satan, with all Power and Signs and lying Wonders, and with all deceivablenefs of unrighteoufnefs in them that perifh; becaufe they received not the Love of the Truth;——for this caufe God fhall fend them ftrong delufion, that they fhould believe a Lye*: And Rev. xiii. 13. *He doth great Wonders,——and deceiveth them that dwell on the Earth, by the means of thofe Miracles which he had Power to do*: According to that original Prophecy of our Saviour, *Matt.* xxiv. 24. *There fhall arife falfe Chrifts and falfe Prophets, and fhall fhew great Signs and Wonders.*

ALL things therefore of This kind, are mere cheats and delufions. And indeed *Marks*, or *Notes*, of the *true Church*, there are *None* other, but *This One only*; the adhering ftedfaftly to the plain and uncorrupted Doctrine of *Chrift* and his *Apoftles*, as delivered in their *own* Difcourfes and Writings. *Where-ever* This is the Cafe, *There* is the *True Church*; even though but *Two* or *Three* be *gathered together*, to worfhip God in *Chrift's Name*, and according to *his* Command. And *where-ever* This is *not* the Cafe, *There* is no *True Church*; even though it were as *Catholick* or Univerfal as the *whole World.*

THE Church of *Rome* therefore, and, in proportion, all its Followers, whether in whole or in part, by mixing the Authority of *Popes*, and *Councils*, and *Vain Men*, with the pure Doctrine of Chrift; have, like the *Jews* of old, by the *Traditions of Men*, made void the *Commandments of God*; and are thereby become That *Man of Sin*, (of whom the Apoftles have foretold us,) *fitting* blafphemoufly *in the Seat* and *Temple of God*, and *changing Laws and Times*, and *commanding all Men to worfhip* his Temporal Authority.

THE *True* and *Real* Authority of the Church of Chrift, is to be a *Witnefs and Keeper of Holy Writ*; to tranfmit it down uncorrupted from generation to generation, as the *only Rule* of *Faith* and *Manners*; and in matters of indifference, in Rites and Ceremonies and Forms of external Government, to take care that *all things be done de-cently and in Order.* In which matters, the *univerfal Church* being too large to have any poffibility of confulting together, *the Church in every Nation* Therefore has the fame Right and Authority to determine for *itfelf*, as the *Catholick Church*, if it were poffible for it to come together in One, would have to determine for the *Whole.* Which *Power* or *Authority*, in Matters of *Doctrine* indeed, that is, in appointing the Terms

SERM.
LXII.

or Conditions of Salvation, is *none at all* ; Not only in any *particular* Church, but even in the *Whole Catholick Church collectively* ; nay, even in the *Apostles* themselves ; nay, if we will believe St *Paul*, even in an *Angel from Heaven*, it is *absolutely None at all* ; For *if any man shall add to These things, God shall add unto Him the Plagues that are written in His Book* ; and *if any man shall take away* therefrom, *God shall take away his part out of the book of Life, and out of the Holy City.* But in *Rites* and *Ceremonies*, in the *Manner* and Circumstance of *Governments*, and *all matters of external Form*, which God hath left *indifferent* ; in *These* things, the Authority of *Men* takes properly place : And *herein* every good man ought to comply willingly, with the Laws and Customs of the Government he lives under : Always remembring this one Rule, that, with regard to these *outward and indifferent* things, they who make Divisions in the Church of Christ, either by needlesly separating *Themselves*, or, through needless and imperious impositions, giving to *Others* any Ground or Occasion of Separating ; are on *Both sides equally* guilty of a *Schismatical Spirit*. For so St *Paul* admonishes, Rom. xvi. 17. *Mark them which cause Divisions and Offences.* He does not say, Mark *Them only*, who *divide* ; Which is the Fault on *One* side : But also, *Mark them who give* occasion to Divisions ; Which is equally the Fault on the *Other* side.

For the *Unity* or *Communion*, which ought to be between the Members of the *Visible Church Catholick*, consists in This ; that, with universal Love and Charity, with mutual Forbearance and Good-Will, they assist, instruct, comfort, reprove, forgive one another ; and, in a word, (notwithstanding any Differences of Opinion in smaller matters,) perform all the Offices of Kindness and Goodness, that becomes Members of One and the Same Body to do for each other. That the *Members should* all have the *same Care one for another* ; *and if one member suffer, all the members should* by Compassion *suffer with it*, 1 Cor. xii. 25. That the *Eye cannot say to the Hand, I have no need of Thee* ; *nor again, the Head to the Feet, I have no need of you*, ver. 21. That Great Care should always be taken, not to lay a *Foundation* for *Schisms and Divisions*, by assuming Authority to *impose* upon each other as *Necessary*, such Matters either of *Opinion* or *Practice*, as Christ has *not* made *necessary*. The *attempting* of which, has in all Ages been the fulfilling of That Prophecy of our Saviour, *I come not to send Peace, but a Sword.* For the *True Unity* of Christians does not depend, (as some have vainly imagined) upon procuring by Force an *Uniformity of Opinions* ; (which to be *real*, is absolutely impossible in *Nature* ; and the *Appearance* of it, can never be any thing else than *Ignorance* or *Hypocrisy* :) But the *True Unity* of Christians depends upon their Agreement in the sincere *Love of Truth*, and *Practice of Charity* ; *bearing each others Infirmities* in all things that are of an *indifferent* nature, and being *stedfast* and unmoveable in things *fundamental*, that is, in the *Faith and Obedience* for which they *covenanted at Baptism* ; *holding the Head*, Col. ii. 19. *from which all the Body by Joints and Bands having Nourishment ministred, and knit together, increaseth with the Increase of God.* If we *walk in the Light* of the Gospel, we *must* have This *Fellowship* one with another. For he that saith, he *loves God*, and *loveth not his Brother*, St *John* tells us, *is a Lyar*. Nay, St *Paul* goes farther, and declares, that if a man could *speak with the Tongues of Men and Angels*, and *had all Faith so that he could remove mountains*, and *gave his Body to be burned*, and bestowed *all his goods to feed the Poor*, and *had not Charity*, (that is, had not that good and Christian Spirit, which would hinder him from putting *impositions* upon his Brethren, which are the *Occasions* of dividing the Body of Christ ;) all the rest would *profit him Nothing*. With *one thing* indeed, with *Vice and Immorality* only, we are to have *No Charity* : *Have No Fellowship with the unfruitful Works of Darkness* ; *neither be Partakers of other men's Sins* ; *For what Communion has Light with Darkness, or what fellowship has Christ with Belial?* But beyond This, our Saviour has given us no Authority to go ; least by a mistaken zeal, we *needlesly pluck up*

the

the Wheat with the Tares. For *good* men are not hurt, by living *in Communities,* with S E R M. the *Wicked,* but only by joining with them in any *Sin.* In all *other* refpects, we are LXII. to fhow tendernefs to all men; to inftruct, rebuke, or bear with them as *Brethren:* Confidering, that as there is *One Body and One Spirit,*——*and one Hope of our Calling, One Lord, One Faith, One Baptifm, One God and Father of All, who is above All;* fo we ought to *indeavour* with all *forbearance* towards one another *in Love, to keep the Unity of the Spirit in the Bond of Peace:* That we may *grow up into Him in all things, which is the Head, even Chrift; From whom the whole Body fitly joined together, and compacted by That which every joint fupplieth, according to the effectual working in the meafure of every part, maketh increafe of the Body unto the edifying of itfelf in Love. Till we all come in the unity of the Faith, and of the Knowledge of the Son of God, unto a perfect man, unto the meafure of the ftature of the fulnefs of Chrift.* By *This* Rule, if we walk here upon *Earth;* we may hope finally to be numbred in That *general Affembly and Church of the firft-born, which are written in Heaven:* with *Angels,* and with Jefus the *Mediator of the New Covenant,* and to *come to* God *in whofe prefence is fulnefs of Joy,* and at *whofe right hand are pleafures for evermore.*

S E R M O N LXIII.

Of the Number of thofe that fhall be Saved.

R E V. III. 4.

Thou haft a few Names even in Sardis, that have not defiled their Garments; and they fhall walk with me in white, for they are worthy.

WHETHER thefe Epiftles of our Saviour to the Seven Churches of *Afia,* are S E R M. to be underftood *literally* only, as Exhortations to thofe Seven particular LXIII. Churches; or whether, according to the Analogy of the reft of This Book, they are to be applied in the prophetick ftyle to Seven different States, Succeffions, or Periods, of the Whole Church of Chrift; is not material to our prefent Purpofe to inquire. The Matter contained in thefe Admonitions, may, by a Moral Application, become equally ufeful to us, upon *either* Suppofition. For, what St *Paul* affirms concerning the State of the ancient *Jewifh* Church; that the things which befel *them,* were *our* Examples, and were writ for *our* Admonition, upon whom the Ends of the World are come; is undoubtedly much *more* true, of the things relating to the Antient *Chriftian* Church, whether particular or univerfal. Thefe Exhortations therefore of our Saviour, whether given to the *fingle* Churches of *Afia,* or intended to be applied to the feveral Succeffive Periods of the *Catholick* Church; are either way worthy of our moft ferious meditations. The Subject-matter of each of the feven Epiftles is very nearly the

same;

SERM. fame; confifting of three parts; A Commendation of the Faith and Patience of the
LXIII. Saints, a Reproof of their Defects, and an Exhortation either to Amendment, or Perfeverance. The State of the Church of *Sardis* is reprefented as one of the *moft* reprove-
able of the feven; and therefore the Epiftle to *This* Church does not begin, as moft of
the others do, with a Commendation of their Faith and Patience, but on the contrary
with a very fevere Reproof; *ver.* 1. *I know thy Works, that thou haft a Name, that
thou liveft, and art dead.* Then follows the Exhortation to repent, ver. 2. *Be watchful and ftrengthen the things which remain, that are ready to die; for I have not found
thy Works perfect before God: Remember therefore how thou haft received and heard, and
hold faft, and repent.* After which he adds in the laft place that fmall Commendation
which could be allowed to fo imperfect a Church, in the Words of the Text: *Neverthelefs thou haft a Few Names even in Sardis, that have not defiled their Garments, and
They fhall walk with me in white, for they are worthy.* It might reafonably be hoped,
that, in a carelefs and corrupt Age, it fhould be an awakening Confideration to All
who have any true Concern for the Glory of God, and for the Honour and Purity of
Religion; to think within themfelves, if in the beft and pureft Times of the Gofpel, if
in thofe Primitive Ages, and among thofe moft eminent Churches of *Afia*, there was
One to which no better Commendation could be afforded, than that there were in it a
Few Names which had not defiled their Garments; what Apprehenfions will it become
Us to have of ourfelves, in thefe laft and degenerate Ages, when our Works are *not only
Ready to die*, but actually *dead*; nay, when we fcarce have fo much as a *Name that
we live?* when on the One hand by open Atheifm, Irreligion and Profanenefs, and on
the Other hand by ignorant and fuperftitious Contentions about vain, needlefs and un-
intelligible Opinions, the Life and Soul of Religion, true Devotion and Piety towards
God, and Univerfal Righteoufnefs, Love and Good-will towards Men, is in a manner
wholly eaten out and confumed? If in the Primitive Church itfelf, *Judgment* thus *began at the Houfe of God, what muft the End be of them that obey not the Gofpel* at all;
And if the Righteous fcarcely be faved, where fhall the Ungodly and the Sinner appear?
But This I intimate only, as a *general* Obfervation upon the *Whole*. In the *Words themfelves* we may more diftinctly obferve the following *Particulars.* 1*ft*, The *Number* or
Proportion of thofe, who fhall inherit Salvation; *Thou haft a* Few *names even in Sardis*:
2*dly*, The *Qualification* by which they are entitled to that inheritance; *Which have not
defiled their Garments*: 3*dly*, The *Nature* or Defcription of the Reward promifed them;
They fhall walk with me in White: And 4*thly*, The *Character* or Encomium given to
the perfons who fhall obtain this inheritance; *For they are Worthy.*

1*ft*, HERE is expreffed the *Number* or Proportion of thofe who fhall inherit Salvation; *Thou haft a* Few *names even in Sardis*: The ftrict and proper intention of which
Words in this place, feems to be to declare, that even in *Sardis*, tho' one of the moft
corrupt of all the Seven Churches, yet even in *That* Church there were *fome* who fhould
be Heirs of Salvation: Implying, that in the other Churches there were *more*, and in
a much *greater Proportion*, when there were a *Few* found even in that, which was
one of the worft of all. But yet, fince the evil things which are fpoken of the Church
of *Sardis*, are but comparative with regard to the Purity of the other more uncorrupt
Churches; and That primitive Church, with all its Faults, was ftill one of the golden
Candlefticks, and of the feven Stars in our Saviour's right Hand; with which the
Things that are moft highly commended in thefe later and more degenerate Ages of
the Chriftian World, muft hardly prefume to be compared: Therefore our Saviour's declaring that in *One*, even of *Thefe* Churches, there were *but Few* who fhould walk
with him in White, may juftly give us occafion to confider the feveral Texts of Scripture, wherein feems to be contained that melancholy Doctrine, that there are *Few
only* which fhall attain unto Salvation. In the fecond Apocryphal Book of *Efdras*,

there

there is a very ftrange expreffion to this Purpofe, ch. viii. 1, *The moft High*, fays he, **S E R M.**
has made this World for many, but the World to come for Few: For as *the Earth giveth* **LXIII.**
much mold whereof Earthen Veffels are made, but little duft that gold cometh of; *even fo*
is the Courfe of this prefent World; *there be many created, but Few fhall be faved*:
And ch. ix. 15, *There be many more of them which perifh, than of them which fhall be*
faved, Like as a Wave is greater than a Drop. Our Saviour himfelf, when *one asked* Luk. xiii. 23.
him, *Lord, are there few that be faved*; took that occafion to exhort his Difciples, faying, *Enter ye in at the ftrait gate*; For, *ftrait is the Gate, and narrow is the Way that* Matt. vii. 14.
leadeth unto Life, and Few there be that find it: And at the Conclufion of two of his
Parables, he fums up his Doctrine twice in the very fame Words; *For many are called,* Matt. xx. 16.
but Few chofen. The Apoftle St *Peter* compares our being faved by the Gofpel, to ²ˣˣⁱⁱ· ¹⁴·
the prefervation of *Noah* and his Family from the Flood; and makes *Baptifm* a *like*
Figure to the Ark, wherein Few, that is, eight Perfons, were faved by Water, 1 Pet.
iii. 20. And *Rev.* xiii. 8, *All that dwell upon the Earth fhall worfhip him, whofe names*
are not written in the book of life of the Lamb flain from the foundation of the world: That
is; the Generality of Chriftians who are not fincerely fuch, will always run after the
Religions of this World, inftead of ftudying the Doctrines which Chrift himfelf taught
them. St *Paul, Rom.* ix. 27, applies to the Salvation of the *Gofpel*, that paffage of
Ifaiah, Though the Number of the children of Ifrael be as the Sand of the Sea, a remnant
fhall be faved. And as in *Elijah*'s time there were in all *Ifrael feven thoufand men, who*
had not bowed the knee to the Image of Baal; *Even fo,* faith he, *at this prefent time alfo*
there is a remnant, according to the election of Grace, ch. xi. at the 4th verfe. Thefe
may juftly feem to be *hard fayings,* and *Who can bear them?* For if thefe thngs be fo,
Who then fhall be faved? And how fhall this be reconciled with thofe Divine Attributes, the Goodnefs, the Mercy, and Compaffion of God; of whom the Scripture declares, that he *would have* all *men to be faved,* that he *would not that* Any *fhould pe-*
rifh, and that his *tender mercies are over* all his *Works?* Now to This Difficulty it
might be fufficient to anfwer in general, that at the great day of Retribution, God
will abundantly vindicate himfelf before Men and Angels, and *all Mouths fhall be ftopped*
before him: Stopped, not by Power and fupreme Authority, but by conviction of the
Juftice, the Reafon, the Equity, the Neceffity of the Cafe: By all which things, God
will *be juftified in his faying*; *and clear,* both *when he judges* and when *he is judged.*
This, I fay, is in the whole a fufficient ground of Satisfaction, (even though nothing
further could be alledged,) to a rational, pious, and modeft Mind, who can *truft* God
till the final event of Things, to make it appear at laft, that *the Judge of all the Earth*
will do what is right. And indeed it may univerfally be looked upon as a never-failing Rule, which may in all cafes fafely be depended upon ; that where-ever any Notion we entertain, is in any degree inconfiftent with any of the natural and unchangeable Attributes of the Divine Nature, there is always either fome latent Error in the
Notion itfelf, which at prefent perhaps we cannot diftinctly difcover; or at leaft, there
is fome great Defect in our Knowledge of feveral very material *Circumftances,* which
in reality alter the nature of the whole Queftion. Upon the Whole therefore, we
ought in all reafon to reft fatisfied, with being able to affirm, that God will finally juftify his own proceeding to every man's Confcience, and *with righteoufnefs will he judge*
the World. Yet in the matter at prefent before us, there is fomething *farther* both *in*
general, of confiderable moment, that we are capable of obferving; and alfo *in parti-*
cular fomething remarkable, with regard to *each* of the fore-mentioned Texts of
Scripture.

In general: We know it was reafonable God fhould create Beings, endued with
Freedom of Will, that they might be capable of rendring him a *Free-will-offering* of
voluntary *Obedience*; which is the only thing that can poffibly be acceptable to a Su-

S E R M. preme Governor. Now by the very fame *Liberty*, which rendred them capable of
LXIII. paying a voluntary *Obedience*, they muft needs be capable likewife of *refufing to obey*:
And thence came Sin and Mifery into the Creation of God. Further: It was fit,
that infinite Power and Wifdom fhould difplay itfelf in making great *Variety* of fuch
Creatures. In which *Variety*, it could not be, but of thofe which were the loweft
and fraileft and moft fallible of all rational Beings, *greater Numbers* fhould prove inca-
pable of the Heavenly ftate; and confequently muft perifh. *Muft perifh*: Not by the
Appointment of God; (For God made not Death; neither hath he pleafure in the deftruction of the Living; but invites all men to come and take of the Water of Life freely;)
but they perifh, by their own Carelesfnefs and Senfuality, by their own Difobedience,
Wilfulnefs and Impenitency; being unfit for, and incapable of the Happinefs of Heaven.
And yet even of thofe who fo perifh, not *All* are condemned to the fevere Punifhment
of *Thofe*, concerning whom it is faid that it fhall be more tolerable for *Sodom* aud *Go-
morha* in the day of Judgment than for *Them*; But every one fhall be punifhed according to the exact *Degree only* of his own demerit; fome with *few* ftripes, (as our Saviour declares to·us,) and others with *many*; according as the Juftice and *Wifdom* of God
in his Supreme Government of the World neceffarily requires, for the fupport of his
Authority, and the honour of his righteous and eternal Laws.

THIS, *in general*. There *is* in *particular* fomething proper to be remarked, with
regard to *each* of the forementioned paffages in Scripture.

IN the *firft* place, the Smallnefs of the Numbers there mentioned, is not *abfolute*,
but *comparative*. The Righteous are *Few*, not abfolutely fpeaking; but *in Comparifon only* with thofe who are Wicked. For otherwife, where the Expreffions are not
comparative, the Scripture fpeaks after a very different manner: *I beheld*, fays St *John*
in his Vifion, Rev. vii. 9, *and lo a great multitude which no man could number, of all
Nations and Kindreds and People and Tongues, ftood before the throne and before the Lamb,
clothed with white robes, and palms were in their hands*. And yet this great Multitude
were of Thofe only, who were faved out of the Antichriftian State, out of that great
and univerfal Corruption, which was to overfpread the Church in its loweft and moft
Rev. xiii. 8. oppreffed Condition; ver. 14, *Thefe are they which came out of great Tribulation*, (out
of The *great Tribulation*, it fhould be rendred,) *and have wafhed their robes, and made
them white in the Blood of the Lamb*.

IN the next place; 'tis to be obferved, that feveral of the Texts before-cited, are
parts of Parabolical Difcourfes; in which Parables, there muft not be a ftrict Application made of every fingle Expreffion, but of That only, or principally, wherein the
Similitude confifts, and which is the main Intent of the Parable. Thus the intent
of thefe Two Parables, which our Saviour concludes with thefe Words, *Many are called, but few chofen*; is not to exprefs the Proportion of the *Numbers*, of thofe that fhall
be faved, and of thofe that perifh; but to declare, that *as* the Perfon who came without a Wedding-garment, was caft out from the Marriage-Feaft, *fo* no man who comes
not clothed with the Works of Righteoufnefs, fhall be admitted into the Kingdom of
Heaven, to the Marriage-Supper of the Lamb: And that, *as* the Labourers who came
into the Vineyard in the Morning, were not preferred to thofe who came in later, but
on the contrary reproved for their envying and complaining at the Favour fhown to
others; *fo* the Jews who were firft and originally the people of God, fhould not be preferred before the Gentiles who were converted later; but on the contrary many of
them fhould be rejected for their ill behaviour, while others from the Eaft and from
the Weft, from the North and from the South, of all Nations, Kingdoms and Tongues,
fhould come and fit down in *Their* places, with *Abraham, Ifaac* and *Jacob* in the
Kingdom of God. From whence our Saviour draws, by way of Inference, this warning to his Difciples, that they fhould not depend upon the bare outward Profeffion of

the

the true Religion; for that *Many of thofe who were called, were not chofen.* And from S E R M. his manner of expreffing this Warning at the Conclufion of thefe Parables, *(Many are* LXIII. *called, but Few chofen)* it ought no more in ftrictnefs to be inferred, that, abfolutely fpeaking, *Few* only fhall attain unto Salvation; than from what he elfewhere fuppofes, that of *Ten* Virgins *Five* were wife, and *Five* foolifh, it can be concluded that the Numbers of Both are *equal:* Or from the Parable of the Talents, wherein to one Servant were committed *Five* Talents, to another *Two*, to a third *One*; and of thefe This *Laft only* misbehaved himfelf; that therefore the Righteous are *more* in number, than the Wicked: Or from the Parable of the Marriage-Feaft, wherein of Thofe who were invited and called out of the high-ways and ftreets of the City, and even compelled to come in, *One only* among them all is reprefented as not having on a Wedding-garment; that therefore it can be concluded the Number of thofe who fhall finally be rejected, is extremely fmall. All thefe Arguments, I fay, from Parabolical Difcourfes, are without juft Foundation: The Defign of our Saviour being evidently, not to exprefs the *Proportions* of *Numbers*, but the *Qualifications* of the *Perfons* that fhall attain unto Salvation; and to warn his Difciples, againft depending, like the Pharifees, upon the bare *Profeffion* of the true Religion, without the *Practice* of it; For that many of the Children of the Kingdom, fhould *themfelves* be caft out; and *many* of them that *are called*, are not *chofen*. And 'tis worthy of Remark, that it is at the End of that *very* Parable, wherein *One Perfon only* is reprefented as not having on a Wedding-garment, that our Saviour expreffes his Caution in thofe particular Words, *Many are called, but Few are chofen*. Which therefore muft by no means be underftood to be a Difcouragement, as if any Sincere perfon were, by any Act of *God*, excluded or rejected from Salvation; but it muft be interpreted as a Complaint, of the Wickednefs and Perverfenefs of *Men*; that of thofe who are *called* to the greateft Advantages and Means of Salvation, fo *Many* prove unworthy of being finally *chofen*.

A s to the paffages in the Apocryphal Book of *Efdras*, which is the Book that has the *leaft* Authority even of all the Apocryphal Books themfelves; they feem to be the Expreffions of a Jewifh Writer, who thought that as the Jews were in *This* World the peculiar People of God, fo no others but They were to have any fhare likewife in the World *to come*. Which was a Notion the Jews fo far retained even till our Saviour's time, that there was nothing in the Gofpel more difficult for them to be perfwaded of, than that even *unto the Gentiles, alfo God had granted Repentance unto Life.* And yet even This very *Same* Author elfewhere expreffly acknowledges, that not by the Appointment of *God*, but by the Wickednefs only and Incapacity of *Men*, is their own Deftruction brought upon them. Ch. viii. 41, *As the husbandman foweth much Seed upon the ground, and planteth many Trees, and yet the thing that is fown good in his Seafon cometh not up, neither doth all that is planted take root; even fo is it of them that are fown in the World, they fhall not all be Saved.* And ch. ix. 20. *So I confidered the World, and behold there was peril, becaufe of the Devices that were come into it; And I faw and fpared it greatly; and have kept me a Grape of the Clufter, and a Plant of great People.*

T h e Paffage in St *Peter*, wherein he makes *Baptifm* a *like Figure to the Ark, wherein Few, that is, Eight Perfons, were faved by Water*, may reafonably be underftood of that *particular Time* of Perfecution and Difficulty, wherein the Apoftle lived. For in like manner as at the Time of the Flood, *God faw that the Wickednefs of Man was great in the Earth, and that every Imagination of the thoughts of his heart was only evil continually*, Gen. vi. 5: Which character 'tis very unreafonable to apply (as fome have done) to the whole Race of Mankind, when it was plainly fpoken of that particular corrupt generation only: So 'tis reafonable to fuppofe St *Peter*'s Application

of

SERM. of the fimilitude, to be made not to the whole Bulk of Mankind, but to that particular LXIII. generation, wherein *Few* entertained the firft preaching of the *Gofpel*, even like the *Few* that hearkned to *Noah*'s preaching of Righteoufnefs. And the fame is to be underftood concerning that Text in the *Revelation*, ch. xiii. 8.

In like manner St *Paul*'s applying to the Salvation of the *Gofpel*, that paffage of *Ifaiah*, *Though the Number of the children of Ifrael be as the Sand of the Sea, a remnant fhall be faved*; and his affirming, that as in *Elijah*'s time there were in all *Ifrael feven thoufand men, who had not bowed the knee to the Image of Baal*, even *fo at this* prefent Time *alfo there is a remnant according to the election of Grace*; This, I fay, is by the Apoftle's own exprefs Words limited to that *particular Time then prefent*, wherein *Few* in comparifon embraced the Gofpel; *Even fo at* this prefent Time, fays he, *alfo there is a remnant according to the election of Grace*; i. e. of thofe who embrace the gracious Terms of the Gofpel. And as in the *Old Teftament* there were exprefs Prophecies, that things fhould not always be in fuch a melancholy ftate, but on the contrary the Time fhould come when God's *People* fhould *be All righteous*, If. lx. 21; that he would *make* even their *Officers Peace*, and their *Exactors Righteoufnefs*, ver. 17; that the *Earth* fhould *be full of the Knowledge of the Lord, as the Waters cover the Seas*, ch. xi. 9; that God would *put his Law in their inward parts, and write it in their* Hearts; and that *they* fhould all *Know* him, *from the leaft of them to the greateft*, Jer. xxxi. 33; So in the *New Teftament* alfo 'tis expreffly declared, that the Time will come, when all *Ifrael fhall be faved*, Rom. xi. 26; *i. e.* the Whole, or main Body, of the People fhall be converted unto God; and *Rev.* xi. 15, *The Kingdoms of this World fhall become the Kingdoms of our Lord, and of his Chrift; and he fhall reign for ever and ever*. And therefore 'tis probable, that even thofe Words likewife of our Lord himfelf, *(ftrait is the Gate and narrow is the Way that leadeth unto Life, and Few there be that find it,)* are fpoken principally of thofe Times of Difficulty and Perfecution, wherein no man could embrace the Gofpel of Chrift, without immediately parting with all he had in the World. For fo the Word which we render, Narrow *is the way*, in the Original fignifies *Afflicted*, or *Perfecuted* is the way, that leadeth unto Life. And then it will be of the fame import with that Affertion of the Apoftle, that *we muft through much Tribulation enter into the Kingdom of God*.

Laftly, THERE is one thing further to be obferved upon thefe Expreffions of our Saviour : and That is, that what in St *Matthew*'s Gofpel is fet down in thefe Words, (*Enter ye in at the ftrait gate ;——Becaufe ftrait is the Gate——that leadeth unto Life, and Few there be that find it,*) is in St *Luke*'s Gofpel otherwife expreffed thus; *Strive to enter in at the ftrait gate; For many, I fay unto you, will feek to enter in, and fhall not be able*, St *Luk.* xiii. 24. And why fhall they *not be able?* The reafon follows in the next Words, *When once the Mafter of the houfe is rifen up and has fhut to the door, and ye begin to ftand without and knock,——he fhall anfwer and fay unto you, I know you not whence you are,—— depart from me All ye workers of Iniquity*. From whence it appears, that the Difficulty of Entring, is not fo much the Appointment of *God*, as the Negligence and Delay of *Men*: They *feek* to enter, and they are not able; becaufe they *feek* negligently, they feek *too late*, they *feek* when the Door is fhut. And fo This Paffage becomes parallel to thofe other Texts of Scripture, St *Matt.* xxv. 10; After the Bridegroom was come and the door fhut, *came the foolifh Virgins, faying, Lord, open to us*; But he anfwered and faid unto them, *I know you not*. Again: St *John* vii. 34, *Ye fhall* feek me, *and fhall not find me*. The reafon is expreffed, ch. viii. 21, *Ye fhall feek me, and fhall die in your Sins*; therefore, *whither I go, ye cannot come*. Prov. i. 28, *Then fhall they call upon me, but I will not anfwer; they fhall feek me——, but they fhall not find me*; *For that they hated Knowledge, and did not chufe the Fear of the Lord*. Pf. xviii. 41, *They cried, but there was none to fave them; even unto the*

Lord,

4

Lord, but he anfwered them not. If. i. 15. *When ye fpread forth your hands, I will* S E R M. *hide mine eyes from you; yea, when ye make many Prayers, I will not hear;* For your LXIII. *hands are full of Blood.* Jer. xiv. 12, 10, *When they faft, I will not hear their cry;* *and when they offer burnt-offering and an Oblation, I will not accept them;* For *they have loved to wander, they have not refrained their feet, therefore the Lord doth not accept them.* Hof. v. 6, *They fhall go———to* feek *the Lord, but they fhall not find him, he hath withdrawn himfelf from them;* For *they have dealt treacheroufly againft the Lord.* Mic. iii. 4, *Then fhall they cry unto the Lord, but he will not hear them; he will even hide his Face from them at that Time, as They have behaved themfelves ill in their doings.* St *Jam.* iv. 3, *Ye afk and receive not, becaufe ye afk amifs.* And, to mention but *one* paffage more ; *Rom.* ix. 31, *Ifrael which* followed *after the law of righteoufnefs, hath not attained to the Law of Righteoufnefs: Wherefore? Becaufe they fought it not by Faith;* that is, by *That* way which God had thought fit to appoint. From thefe and numberlefs other paffages in Scripture it appears, that the Rejection of men, is not from God, but of themfelves; and that the Difficulties in the way of their Salvation, are not fo much the Appointment of God, as the Effects of their own Negligence and Delay: Excepting only in the Cafe of great Perfecution; And *there* God has promifed a proportionably great Affiftance, which will, together with the Temptation, alfo make a way to efcape, that we may be able to bear it. Whether therefore the Number of thofe who fhall be faved, be in proportion Many or Few, makes no Alteration in the Concern of *any One* particular perfon ; And therefore *Every One* ought to endeavour, by following the plain Rules that are fet before him, to make his *own* Calling an Election fure, and to work out his *own* Salvation with Fear and Trembling, without inquiring too curioufly into the Affairs of *Others,* wherein God the great Judge of All will at the general Day of Account take care abundantly to juftify his own Proceedings, much better than we are now able to conceive or apprehend. For fo our Saviour, when One put that Queftion to him, *Lord, are they Few that be faved?* inftead of making him a direct reply to the Queftion propofed, anfwered him with This more pertinent Exhortation, St *Luk.* xiii. 24, *Strive* Ye *to enter in at the ftrait Gate.*

Upon the whole; The Paffages in Scripture, which feem to reprefent to us as if *Few* only fhould be faved, are on the one hand fuch, as ought by no means to be any occafion of Defpair or Diffidence to melancholy pious Perfons; becaufe the reafon why fo great Numbers perifh, is always in thofe very Texts exprefly afcribed to the Wickednefs and Carelefsnefs of *Men,* not to any Appointment of *God:* And yet on the other hand *the* fame Texts are, by the Wifdom of the Spirit of God, expreffed in fuch a manner, as to excite the carelefs, and thofe who are apt to be too negligent and remifs; by giving them to underftand, that except their Righteoufnefs exceeds the Righteoufnefs of the carelefs and worldly Multitude, they fhall in no cafe enter into the Kingdom of Heaven.

And this may fuffice concerning the 1ft Particular ; *viz.* the *Number* or *Proportion* of thofe who fhall inherit Salvation: *Thou haft a Few Names even in Sardis.* I fhould now have proceeded to the 2d Head, namely, the *Qualification* by which they are intitled to that Inheritance: *Which have not defiled their Garments.* But This muft be deferred to another Opportunity.

SERMON LXIV.

The Qualification of Thofe that fhall be Saved.

REV. III. 4.

Thou haſt a few Names even in Sardis, that have not defiled their Garments; and they ſhall walk with me in white, for they are worthy.

IN theſe later and corrupter Ages of Chriſtianity, wherein Prophanenefs and Impiety have not only *from without* aſſaulted and indeavoured to deſtroy Religion, but alſo *crept in* and even *openly appeared* within all Parts of the Church of God; and when among thoſe who are not without ſome Degrees even of *ſincere* Deſire to become truly Religious, yet Speculations entring in the Room of Practice, and vain Contentions prevailing about Human Opinions, inſtead of Diligence to obey the plain Commandments of God, have almoſt eaten out the very Heart and Life of Religion, which conſiſts in Piety and Righteouſneſs, in Juſtice and univerſal Charity, in Sobriety and Temperance, and the Practice of all Virtue and Holineſs: During this Degenerate State, I ſay, of the Chriſtian World, in theſe later and corrupter Ages of the Church; there is nothing more likely to be of Effect in reviving the true Spirit of Chriſtianity, and reſtoring in the Minds of well-diſpoſed Perſons right and worthy Notions of Religion; than putting them upon conſidering, what Chriſtian Religion was in the Primitive and pureſt Times, when Chriſtians were of One Heart and One Mind, ſerving God with Simplicity and Sincerity of Devotion, loving one another with Perfect Charity and an undivided Affection, and keeping themſelves Pure and unſpotted from the World. This latter Character of the Church of Chriſt, its Purity and Holineſs; and the Neceſſity of all its true Members anſwering that Character; is no where more affectionately deſcribed, than in the Epiſtles to the ſeven Churches of *Aſia*, ſet down in This and the foregoing Chapter. Wherein the excellent Character that is given to moſt of them by our Saviour himſelf, and yet the Reproof added at the Concluſion of that Character; will give us juſt Occaſion to conſider, what ſeverer Admonitions and Exhortations to Repentance *we* ſtand in need of, who have not *Their* Excellent Qualifiations to extenuate our Defects. To *One* of theſe Churches, our Saviour gives this Character, *ch. ii. 2, I know thy Works, and thy labour and thy Patience, and how thou canſt not bear them which are evil; ——And haſt born and haſt patience, and for my Name's ſake haſt laboured, and haſt not fainted.* And yet even of *This* Church he adds, *Neverthelefs I have ſomewhat againſt thee, becauſe thou haſt left thy firſt love.* To a *Second* he declares, ver. 9. *I know thy Works and Tribulation and Poverty, but thou art rich:* —— *Fear none of the things which thou ſhalt ſuffer.* To a *Third*, ver. 13, *I know thy Works, ——and* that *thou holdeſt faſt my Name, and haſt not denied my* Faith. And yet even of *This* he adds, *But I have a Few things againſt Thee.* To a *Fourth*, ver. 19, *I know thy Works, and Charity, and Service, and Faith, and thy Patience and thy Works, and the laſt to be more than the firſt.* And yet of *This* alſo

3

he

he adds; *Notwithftanding I have a few things againft Thee.* Of a *Fifth*, he gives the S E R M. following character, ch. iii. 8, *I know thy Works; Behold, I have fet before thee an open* LXIV. *door, and no man can fhut it:* —— *Becaufe thou haft kept the Word of my Patience, I alfo will keep thee from the hour of Temptation, which fhall come upon all the World, to try them that dwell upon the Earth.* No Man, that has a true Senfe of Religion upon his Mind, can read thefe Characters, without confidering immediately within himfelf, *How* are they *Now* applicable to the Chriftian World? And in what Proportion do we *Now* imitate the Piety and Holinefs of thofe Primitive Churches? And if fome even of *thefe* were charged with falling in fome meafure from their firft Love; and commanded to confider and remember from whence they were fallen, and repent; what Reflexions ought this to excite in our Minds, when we compare the Failings of fuch bright Examples of Piety, with the open Prophanenefs and Debauchery, with the irreligion and wickednefs of later Ages? The *Two* remaining Churches of the *Seven* are reprefented as falling extremely fhort of the Character of the other *Five*. Concerning *One* of them our Saviour declares, ver. 1*ft*, of this iii*d* chapter, *I know thy Works, that thou haft a Name that thou liveft and art Dead; Be watchful and ftrengthen the things which remain, that are ready to die.* To the *other* he fays, ver. 15, *I know thy works, that thou art neither cold nor hot,* i. e. art grown carelefs and indifferent in the great Works of Piety and Righteoufnefs; *Thou fayeft, I am rich and increafed with goods, and have need of nothing; and knoweft not that thou art wretched and miferable, and poor, and blind, and naked;* i. e. very defective in the weightier matters of Religion, in Works of Goodnefs, Charity, and true Holinefs. And yet even of *Thofe* our Saviour in the very fame place fo expreffes himfelf, as of Churches not wholly caft off, or under his entire and final Difpleafure: *As many as I love, I rebuke and chaften; Be zealous therefore and repepent,* ver. 19. If fome of thofe *Primitive* Churches, for whom our Saviour declares fo great a Concern of Love, were worthy of fuch fevere Reproofs for the decay of their Piety even in thofe Purer Times; what concern muft it needs raife in the Breaft of every fincere Chriftian, to confider how much greater Corruption of Manners, how much more open Prophanenefs and Impiety, how much more uncharitablenefs and unreafonable Animofities, how much more general Unrighteoufnefs and Iniquity of all Kinds, has in thefe later Ages overfpread the Face of the Chriftian World? What feverer Reproofs *We* have too juft reafon to fear from the Hands of God; and how much *more* remarkable a Repentance and more *univerfal* a Reformation of Manners, 'tis incumbent upon *Us* to fet about; leaft *when the Son cometh,* there remain not fo much as Room for that Queftion, *fhall he find Faith upon the Earth?* The Things which were threatned to fome of the Primitive Churches, that our Lord would remove their Candleftick out of its place, and that he would *fpue* them out of his Mouth; and which, upon their further Decay in Virtue actually came upon them; befel *them,* not only upon *their own* Account, but for *Examples* alfo to Others; and they are written for *Our* Admonition, upon whom the Ends of the World are come.

T H E Words of the Text, are taken out of our Saviour's Admonition to the former of thofe two Churches, which fell under his more particularly fevere Reproof; and they may ferve for a perpetual direction in *all* Ages, to fuch Perfons as, in the midft of a degenerate and contentious World, are defirous to underftand and practife that Religion, which at its firft inftitution was fo defervedly eminent, for Amending Men's Manners and Reforming their Lives. *Thou haft a few Names even in Sardis, that have not defiled their Garments; and they fhall walk with me in white, for they are worthy.*

W H I C H Words, I in a former Difcourfe obferved to contain in them the four following Particulars. 1*ft*, An intimation of the *Number* or Proportion of thofe, who fhall inherit Salvation; *Thou haft a Few Names even in Sardis.* 2*dly,* The *Qualification*

S E R M. *tion* by which they are intitled to that inheritance : *Which have not defiled their Gar-*
LXIV. *ments.* 3*dly,* The *Nature* or Defcription of the Reward promifed them ; *They fhall*
walk with me in White. And 4*thly,* The *Character* or Encomium given the perfons,
who fhall obtain this Inheritance, *For they are Worthy.* The 1*ft* of Thefe, we have
already confidered, namely, The *Number* or Proportion of thofe, who fhall inherit
Salvation ; *Thou haft a Few names even in Sardis.* Without repeating therefore what
has been before faid upon That Head, proceed we now in the 2*d* place, to confider
the *Qualification* mentioned in the Text, by which thofe who fhall be faved, are reprefented as being prepared or intitled to a Share in that glorious Inheritance. And
This is, their having *not defiled their Garments.* Could a man for the prefent lay afide
the Scripture, and, forbearing to look into the Characters There given of true Chriftians,
view the prefent Face of the Chriftian World, and judge from thence what the Defign and Nature of our Religion was, he could not but be tempted to imagine, that
Chriftianity was rather a Contentious and uncharitable Art of difputing about needlefs
Ceremonies, and unintelligible Opinions, than a Rule of Life and Practice, an Obligation to Virtue, Holinefs, and univerfal Charity. But in the Scripture itfelf, the great
Strefs of Religion, is always laid upon the Influence it has upon Men's Manners ; And
the higheft Character of a true Difciple of Chrift, is That given in the Text, that he
has not defiled his Garments. The Expreffion is figurative, but yet of a very Obvious
Signification ; And by confidering on the contrary what the Scripture calls *Defilement,*
we may moft eafily and fully underftand what it is *not to be defiled.* St *Matt.* xv. 18.
Not that which entreth *into* the Mouth, fays our Saviour, but thofe things which proceed *out* of the Mouth, and come forth from the Heart, *thefe defile* the man ; *For out*
of the Heart procceed evil thoughts, murders, adulteries, fornications, thefts, falfe wit-
nefs, blafphemies; Thefe are the things which defile a man; But to eat with unwafhen
hands, defileth not a man. The fame may be faid of all *other* external Denominations
whatfoever : No difference of Meats ; No variety of outward Rites, Forms or Ceremonies ; No fimple Errors of the Underftanding, in fuch matters of Opinion as affect not Moral Practice : But whatfoever *worketh Abomination or maketh a Lie* ; Whatfoever corrupteth the *Heart* of Man, and is inconfiftent with fincere and virtuous Intention ; Whatever is contrary to the Practical Law of God, and deftructive of Charity
and Good-will among Men ; *That* is it, which in the religious Senfe of the Word, *de-*
fileth the Man. And to abftain from all Appearance of fuch Evils, in the midft of a
degenerate and corrupt World ; *This* is *pure Religion and undefiled before God* ; *This* is
keeping a man's *felf unfpotted from the World* ; This is, *having not defiled his Garments.*
Originally, and in the ftrict and moft proper fignification of the Phrafe, it denotes an
entire Freedom from Sin : But in That Senfe, the Character would belong, not to a
Few Names, as is affirmed in the Text ; but abfolutely to *None* at all. For *how fhould*
man be juft before God? Job ix. 2. *What is man, that he fhould be clean? and he that*
ch. xv. ver. *is born of a woman, that he fhould be righteous? Behold, he putteth no truft in his*
14. *Saints ; yea the heavens are not clean in his Sight :* or as the fame thing is expreffed in
ch. iv. ver. another paffage of the fame Book ; *Behold, he put no Truft in his Servants, and his*
18. *Angels he charged with Folly.* Again : *ch.* xxv. 4. *How then can man be juftified with*
God? or how can he be clean, that is born of a Woman? Behold, even to the moon, and
it fhineth not, yea, the ftars are not pure in his Sight ; how much lefs Man that is a
Worm, and the Son of Man that is a Worm? The Scripture is full of declarations of
This Kind. *Prov.* xx. 9. *Who can fay, I have made my Heart clean? I am pure from*
my Sin? Pf. cxxx. 3. *If thou, Lord, fhouldft be extreme to mark iniquity; O Lord,*
who fhall ftand? And ftill more directly, Pf. cxliii. 2. *Enter not into judgment with*
thy Servant, for in thy fight fhall no man living be juftified. The Wife man, even
yet more expreffly, Ecclef. vii. 20. *There is not a juft man upon Earth, that doeth good*

and finneth not. Accordingly *Job*, that moſt righteous perſon, whoſe Character God S E R M.
himſelf joyns with that of *Noah* and *Daniel*, as the moſt irreproveable of all mortal LXIV.
men; yet even *he* confeſſes of himſelf, *Job* ix. 20. *If I juſtify myſelf, my own Mouth
ſhall condemn me*; *if I ſay I am perfect, it ſhall alſo prove me perverſe.* And the
manner of ſpeaking of the Apoſtles in the New Teſtament, is the very ſame: *In many
things we offend all,* St *Jam.* iii 2. And *if we ſay, we have no Sin, we deceive ourſelves,
and the Truth is not in us,* 1 Joh. i. 8. 'Tis evident therefore, that by this phraſe in
the Text, having *not defiled their Garments,* is not, cannot be meant, ſtrictly and abſolutely, being *without Sin.* No, This is the peculiar Character of our Saviour alone,
and cannot be truly affirmed of any other Perſon that ever dwelt upon the Face of the
Earth. Another ſignification therefore of this Phraſe may naturally be ſuggeſted to us
by the uſe of a like expreſſion in the ſame Book; *Rev.* vii. 14. *Theſe are they who
— have waſhed their robes, and made them white in the Blood of the Lamb.* Here,
having *waſhed their robes in the Blood of the Lamb,* is uſed as an equivalent expreſſion
to that of *having* never *defiled them*; ſignifying, that under the gracious Covenant of
the Goſpel, Thoſe who by Baptiſm have waſhed away their Sins, and return not to
them any more, are thro' Chriſt reputed in the Sight of God, as having never committed them. And becauſe, by Baptiſm, in Scripture is always meant, *not the waſhing
away the filth of the Fleſh, (not the bare Form or external Ceremony,) but the Anſwer
of a good Conſcience towards God*; therefore thoſe who have *broken off their Sins
by Repentance,* and *their Iniquities by ſhewing Mercy to the Poor,* (which bears the beſt
Analogy *to,* and is ſignified *by* the Baptiſm of riper years;) ſuch perſons (I ſay) are in
Scripture ſpoken of, as being (in the Goſpel Senſe) perfectly juſt and righteous. *Noah
was a juſt man, and* perfect *in his generation, and Noah walked with God,* Gen. vi. 9.
Zacharias and Elizabeth were *righteous before God, walking in* all *the Commandments
and Ordinances of the Lord* blameleſs, *St* Luk. i. 6. All *Chriſtians* in general are exhorted to be, *diligent, that* they *may be found of* our Lord *in peace,* without ſpot and
blameleſs, 2 Pet. iii. 14: that they may be blameleſs *in the day of our Lord Jeſus Chriſt,*
1 Cor. i. 8. that their *hearts* may be *ſtabliſhed* unblameable *in Holineſs, before God even
our Father, at the coming of our Lord Jeſus Chriſt with all his Saints,* 1 Theſ. iii. 13:
that their whole Spirit and Soul and Body may be preſerved blameleſs *unto the coming
of our Lord Jeſus Chriſt,* 2 Theſ. v. 23. *that they may be preſented* faultleſs *before the
preſence of his glory, with exceeding joy,* Jude 24. And accordingly in the deſcription
of them in their heavenly State, 'tis ſaid that *in their Mouth was found no guile,
for they are without Fault before the Throne of* God, *Rev.* xiv. 5. The Conſiſtency of
theſe high Encomiums with the declarations in the paſſages before-cited, concerning
the Impoſſibility of any man's being juſtified before God; The manner (I ſay) how
theſe two different kinds of Expreſſion are to be reconciled, is moſt clearly and diſtinctly ſet forth by St *Paul,* Col. i. 21; *You that were ſometime alienated, and Enemies in
your Mind by wicked Works, yet Now hath he reconciled, In the Body of his Fleſh thro'
Death, to preſent you holy, and unblameable, and unreproveable in his Sight*; and Eph. i.
4, 6. *That we ſhould be holy and without blame before him in love;* —— *to the praiſe
of the glory of his grace, wherein he has made us accepted in the beloved; In whom we
have Redemption thro' his blood, even the* Forgiveneſs of Sins. Theſe and the like Expreſſions of the Apoſtle do with ſufficient clearneſs explain to us, both how it is *poſſible* on the one hand, in the gracious and merciful Senſe of the Goſpel, for frail and
ſinful Men to attain unto this Character, that they *have not defiled their garments*; and
at the ſame time how abſolutely *neceſſary* it is likewiſe on the other hand, notwithſtanding all the Favour and Indulgence of the Goſpel, that they ſhould preſerve themſelves *ſo undefiled.*

S E R M.   3dly, The *Third* particular, observable in the Text, is the *Nature* or *Description* of
LXIV.   the *Reward* promised to them that *defile not their Garments ; They shall walk with me*
   in White.   And here 'tis obvious to observe, how in the nature of the *Thing itself,* as
well as by the *Decree and Appointment of God,* the *Reward* promised to good men in
Scripture is agreeable to the nature of the *Qualification,* to which that *Reward* is annexed.   To them that keep their *Garments undefiled,* 'tis promised that they shall *walk
with Christ in White :*   To them *that hunger and thirst after Righteousness,* that *they
shall be filled* and clothed with *Righteousness.*   To them that take delight in serving God
here ; that *hereafter* also they *shall be before his Throne, and shall serve him day and
night in his Temple.*   Whether a wicked Person, if admitted into Heaven, could not
possibly be made happy there, (as some have presumed to affirm,) is but a vain and
needless Question.   That which is certain, and all that concerns *us* to know, is ; that
whatsoever *defileth,* whatsoever *worketh* any *abomination* or unrighteousness, *shall in no
wise* be permitted to *enter therein.*   And 'tis a powerful recommendation of the necessity of a religious Life, and worthy the most serious consideration of careless Sinners ;
that Virtue is, not only, by the Appointment of God, the Way to Happiness ; but itself also, in the nature of Things, an essential part of it.   And that, as God is Himself
of essential Holiness, and *cannot behold iniquity ;* so he has made the Happiness of
Heaven to consist, not indeed in *That only,* (for, the *Whole* of those *things, which God
has prepared for them that love him, neither has eye seen, nor ear heard, neither has it
entred into the Heart of Man to conceive ;*) but in *great measure* he has made it to consist in the Perfection of *Virtue,* or at least to be in necessary Conjunction with it.   There
is nothing more earnestly and more constantly inculcated in Scripture than this Notion,
that Righteousness *here,* is *therefore* necessary to Happiness *hereafter ;* because a great
Part even of that *Happiness* itself, is to be made up of the Perfection of *Righteousness.*
One principal Particular of the great Promises made in the *Old Testament* to the Jews
after their final Restoration ; which, if it does not directly signify, yet is at least a Type
of the Heavenly state ; is, that their *people* should *be All righteous,* If. lx. 21 ; that they
should delight to *come to worship before the Lord* perpetually, *ch.* lxvi. 23 ; and should
not do iniquity, nor speak lies, neither should *a deceitful Tongue be found in their mouth,*
Zeph. iii. 13. And in the *New Testament* the future Happiness of the Church of Christ,
is described after the same manner ; that it shall be *a glorious Church, not having spot
or wrinkle or any such thing, but holy, and without blemish,* Eph. v. 27. and that *we,
according to his Promise, look for new heavens and a new Earth, wherein dwelleth Righteousness,* 2 Pet. iii. 13.   Now This Righteousness, is figuratively represented in the
Text, and in other places of Scripture, by *White Garments.*   The Purity and Holiness
of *God* himself, is expressed *Pf.* civ. 2. by his being *covered with Light as with a garment ;* and by his *garment* being *white as the Snow,* Dan. vii. 9. And *That* of our *Saviour ;* by his appearing at his *Transfiguration,* in *a raiment* as *white as the Light ;* even
shining, exceeding white as Snow, so as no Fuller on Earth could white them, St *Mark*
ix. 3. and, after his *Resurrection,* in the same Habit, *Matt.* xxviii. 3. and again, after
his *Ascension,* Rev. i. 14.   In pursuance therefore of the same Figure, the *Saints in
Heaven* are in the Text described as *walking in white :* The Church in the Prophecy,
Pf. xlv. 13. is represented *as all glorious within,* and that *her clothing is of wrought Gold.*
He that overcometh, saith our Saviour, *the same shall be clothed in white raiment,* Rev.
iii. 5.   *The four and twenty* Elders, sitting about the Throne, were clothed in *white
raiment, ch.* iv. 4 : To them that were *slain for the Word of God,* were *given white
robes, ch.* vi. 11. The great multitude that no man could number, that were redeemed
from the Earth out of all Nations, were *clothed with white robes,* and palms in their
hands, *ch.* vii. 9. *The Armies in heaven were clothed in fine linnen, white and clean,
ch.* xix. 14. And the *literal* meaning of all these expressions is unfolded, *ver.* 8. that,

at

at the *marriage of the Lamb, To Her (viz.* to the Church,) *was granted, that fhe* S E R M. *fhould be arrayed in fine linnen, clean and white; for the fine linnen is the righteoufnefs* LXIV. *of the Saints.* And this explains to us the Parable of the Man who was caſt out into utter Darkneſs, becauſe he had not on a *Wedding-garment,* St *Mat.* xxii. 11. *i. e.* was not clothed with Works of Righteouſneſs; and illuſtrates thoſe Admonitions of our Saviour, *Rev.* iii. 18. *I counſel thee to buy of me——white raiment, that thou mayeſt be clothed, and that the Shame of thy nakedneſs do not appear:* and ch. xvi. 15. *Bleſſed is he that watcheth and keepeth his garments, leſt he walk naked, and they ſee his Shame.* The Sum of all is, that into Heaven ſhall be admitted no Impurity, no Wickedneſs, nothing that defileth. Wherefore *Bleſſed are they that do his commandments, that they may have right to enter in;——For without are dogs and ſorcerers and whoremongers,* Rev. xxii. 14. *and murderers and idolaters, and whoſoever loveth and maketh a Lie.* 15.

4thly, and *Laſtly;* The Text concludes with a *Character* or *Encomium* given of thoſe perſons, who were to walk in white with our Saviour: *For they are* Worthy. The Church of *Rome* has, upon thoſe Words, founded the Doctrine of *Merit;* and Others, through Fear of falling into that Error, have run into the contrary extreme, and decried All neceſſity of Virtue and *Good Works.* The Truth in This, as in moſt other caſes, lies plainly between the two extremes. Our beſt Virtues or Works are ſo imperfect, as to need *Pardon* rather than deſerve a *Reward;* and if they were never ſo perfect, we ſhould ſtill be *but unprofitable* Servants, having done only what was our Duty to do. Yet thro' the Interceſſion of Chriſt, God is pleaſed to accept them, as if they were really meritorious; and by the gracious *Promiſe* of God, we have as juſt a claim to the Reward, as if it had been originally due to us of proper *Right.* Our improvement in Virtue, is the *Ground of Proportion,* tho' not the *Meritorious cauſe* of the Reward. So that tho' the Happineſs of Heaven, be given us, not indeed *for* our Works; yet it will be in *proportion to* them; and tho' not *upon account* of our Virtue, yet exactly *according to* our improvement therein. The beſt of Men are ſo far from being able (properly and ſtrictly ſpeaking) to *merit* any thing for themſelves and others, (which is the *Romiſh* Doctrine of Merit;) that on the contrary even the Patriarch *Jacob* declared himſelf *not worthy of the leaſt of God's mercies,* Gen. xxxii. 10. And St *Paul,* concerning Himſelf, that tho' he was not *conſcious* of any thing againſt himſelf, *yet was he not thereby juſtified,* 1 Cor. iv. 4. And, of all Chriſtians in general, that *not by works of righteouſneſs which we have done, but by his Mercy he ſaved us,* Tit. iii. 5. that *he has ſaved us, not according to our Works, but according to——his grace——given us in Jeſus Chriſt,* 2 Tim. i. 9. that our Salvation *is the Gift of God; not of works, leſt any* Rom. vi. alt. *man ſhould boaſt,* Eph. ii. 9. *That by the deeds of the Law there ſhall no Fleſh be juſtified in his Sight,* Rom. iii. 20. that *Abraham* himſelf *had whereof to glory, but not before God,* Rom. iv. 2. that even in thoſe things we actually do, we have no ſufficiency *of ourſelves, but our ſufficiency is of God,* 2 Cor. iii. 5. that *it is God which worketh in us both to will and to do of his good pleaſure,* Phil. ii. 13. and that 'tis he that makes us *perfect in every good Work to do his Will——through Jeſus Chriſt,* Heb. xiii. 21. The meaning of all theſe Paſſages is, that the Offer of the Happineſs of Heaven to us at all, is the free and undeſerved Gift of God in Chriſt; and that the Ability of performing the conditions neceſſary to the obtaining even that Free Gift, is continually the Effect of the Divine Aſſiſtance: and that therefore (properly ſpeaking,) the very beſt of our Works have no Merit in them. Even in the *Old Teſtament* where the Scripture affirms *it ſhall be our* Righteouſneſs, *if we obſerve to do all the Commandments,* Deut. vi. 25. 'tis obſervable that the Word which we render *Righteouſneſs,* is by the *Seventy* tranſlated ἐλεημοσύνη, *our Way of obtaining* Mercy only. And they who would make More of it, are ſeverely reproved, *Prov.* xxx. 12. *There is a generation that are pure in their own Eyes, and yet is not waſhed from their Filthineſs.* Which Cenſure is ſtrongly confirmed by our

Saviour's

SERM.
LXIV.
Saviour's declaration, that the *Publican* in the Parable *went down to his House justified*, *rather than* the *Pharisee* who was *righteous in* his *own eyes*. These are sufficient Evidences, that our Works (in Strictness of Speech) have *no Merit*. Yet on the other side, taking the Expression in its right Sense, (which will best be done by comparing it with those already mentioned;) and understanding it according to the gracious Tenor of the Gospel, it *may* be Truly said of virtuous and good men, because the Scripture frequently says it, that *they* are *Worthy*. Not properly and strictly, but according to God's gracious acceptation and Promise in the Gospel. They to whom God has promised, upon an easy condition, a very great and disproportionate Reward, may Truly be said, though not by the Merit of the Work itself, yet by virtue of the Promise when they *have performed* That condition, to have *deserved* the Reward. Our Saviour himself expresses himself in This manner, not only in the Text, but also in other places of Scripture; St *Luke* xx. 35. *They*, saith he, *that shall be accounted* Worthy, *to obtain that World*, And St *Matt.* x. 37. *He that loveth Father or Mother more than Me, is not* Worthy *of me*; implying, that he who did the contrary, might be said to be *worthy* of him. And accordingly the Apostle exhorts, *Col.* i. 10. to *walk* Worthy *of the Lord*; and 1 *Th.* ii. 12. to *walk* worthy *of God who has called* us, *unto his Kingdom and Glory*. St *Peter* declares, that *if a man, for conscience towards God, endure grief, suffering wrongfully, this is* Thank-worthy, 1 *Pet.* ii. 19. and St *Paul* affirms of the Saints who suffered of old, that they were such persons, *of whom the World was not worthy*, *Heb.* xi. 38. And he calls God's *Performance* of his own *free Promises* given in the Law and in the Prophets, the Righteousness *of God which is by Faith of Jesus Christ, unto All, and upon All them that believe*, *Rom.* iii. 22. and again *ver.* 25.— *his righteousness for the remission of Sins that are past*, and argues, *Heb.* vi. 10. that *God is not* unrighteous, *to forget our Work and labour of love*: And concerning *himself* in particular, he professes his firm assurance, that *henceforth there* was *laid up for him a crown of* Righteousness, *which God the* Righteous *Judge* should *give him at that Day*, 2 Tim. iv. 8. and Rev. xxii. 14. *Blessed are they that do his commandments, that they may have right to the tree of life, and may enter in through the gates into the city*. Such as allow themselves to pick single Texts of Scripture without comparing them with the whole and with each other; may from these places collect the *Romish* Doctrine of *Merit*; or from those before-cited may draw just the *contrary* Doctrine, of the *Usefulness of good Works*: But they who compare the several passages, and consider them Together; will easily see the meaning, and the consistency of them all; and particularly what it is that our Saviour intends in the Text, when he declares concerning those who keep their *garments undefiled*, that they *shall walk with* him *in white, for they are* Worthy.

SERMON

SERMON LXV.

That the Terms of Salvation are offered to all Men.

REV. II. 29.

He that hath an Ear, let him hear, what the Spirit saith unto the Churches.

THESE words are fo *frequently* and fo *emphatically* repeated by our Saviour, at the End of *feveral* of his Difcourfes in the *Gofpel*, and again at the general Conclufion of each of thefe *Epiftles* to the Seven Churches of *Afia*; that no one can doubt but they contain fomething in them, of very weighty and fignificant importance. In the xi*th* chapter of St *Matthew*, ver. 15, after his explication of the Nature of *John Baptift's* Office, he adds, *He that hath ears to hear, let him hear*. And in the xiii*th* chapter of the fame Gofpel, at the end of his Parable of the *Sower*, ver. 9. and at the end of his explication of the Parable of the *Tares* of the Field, *ver*. 43; (Both which Parables, are moft full and emphatical Defcriptions of the whole State and Nature of the Chriftian Difpenfation,) he again concludes with repeating the fame Words, *Who hath Ears to hear, let him hear*. In the ii*d* and iii*d* chapters of the *Revelation*, are contained *feven* Epiftles to the *feven* Churches of *Afia*; full of very earneft and preffing Exhortations to Repentance and Amendment of life, and moft lively, and affectionate Defcriptions of the True Nature of Chrift's religion: And at the conclufion of *every One* of thefe Epiftles, are diftinctly and at length repeated, no lefs than *feven* feveral times, the words of the Text; *He that hath an Ear, let him hear, what the Spirit faith unto the Churches*. And in chapter the xiii*th*, of the fame Book; after having given a large Prophetick defcription of Antichriftian Power fitting in the Seat and Temple of God, and making War with, (that is, perfecuting) the True Worfhippers of God, and having all Nations given into his hands, fo that all the World fhould worfhip him, whofe Names are not written in the Book of *Life*; To fhow that This is a Matter wherein All Sincere Chriftians are more or lefs concerned, to take heed to themfelves that they be not impofed upon by Delufions of worldly Power and Ambition, and by empty Shows in matters of Religion; he *ftill again* repeats the fame exclamation, *ver*. 9. *If any man have an Ear, let him hear*.

THE words are a ftrong and general Appeal, to the Reafon and Underftanding of all unprejudiced and impartial men. And they are highly expreffive, of the *Authority and Goodnefs* of God who *fpeaks*; of the *Reafonablenefs, Truth and Excellency* of the *Things that are fpoken*, and of the *Capacity* men have, and the *Obligation* they are under, to hearken to, and obey, what God thus delivers to them.

THE Phrafe, Let *him hear*, is an *Authoritative* expreffion, becoming the Majefty of God, and the Weight and Dignity of what is fpoken by his Command. It denotes, that All the Commands of God, are given men, not for his *own* fake or Benefit, but for *Theirs*: Being founded in the nature and reafon of Things, and effentially

SERM. conducive both to mens prefent and future Happinefs. And if they *refufe*, or *neglect*,
LXV. to *Hear*; if they be *carelefs and negligent to underfland* the word of God, and will be
at No Pains to *examine* into the *True* Nature and End of *Religion*; 'tis *No Hurt* to
Him, but to *Themfelves* only. When therefore *He* has done all that was reafonable for
him to do, and has given them plain and frequent Warnings, and admonifhed them
of the Ufefulnefs and Neceffity of Virtue, and yet *They* continue *deaf* to his inftructions; he proceeds *no* further, he ufes *no* Compulfion, he draws them *only with the
Cords of a Man*, and will apply to them no otherwife than as to *moral Agents*. Thus
the Prophets in the *Old Teftament*: Ezek. iii. 27, *Thus faith the Lord God, He that
heareth, let him hear; and he that forbeareth, let him forbear; for they are a rebellious
houfe.* And Thus the Great Prophet of the *New Teftament*, Rev. xxii. 11, *He that is
unjuft*, (after the repeated Admonitions and Invitations to Repentance given him in the
Gofpel,) *let him be unjuft ftill; and he that is Filthy, let him be Filthy ftill.* Upon the
fame Ground, and after the fame manner of fpeaking, St *Paul*, in 1 *Cor.* xiv. 38, *The
things*, fays he, *that I write unto you, are the Commandments of the Lord; But if any
man be ignorant, let him be ignorant.* And the fame Apoftle, after having long preached in vain to the obftinate and prejudiced *Jews*, Acts xiii. 46, *It was neceffary*, fays
he, *that the word of God fhould firft have been fpoken to You; but feeing ye put it from
you, and judge yourfelves unworthy of everlafting Life, lo, we turn to the Gentiles.* Of
the fame nature and kind, though in the way of a *gentler* and more *tender* Reproof,
are thofe words of our Saviour to his Difciples; when, after *Two* admonitions, in a
time of extreme danger, he found them the *Third* time fleeping; *Sleep on Now*, fays
he, *and take your Reft*, Matt. xxvi. 45. This therefore is the *Firft* notion, which
thofe words in the Text, *let him hear*, do obvioufly carry along with them; They are
expreffive of the *Authority* of God, and of the *Weight and Importance* of what is fpoken
by his Command.

    BUT This is not All. For as they exprefs the *Authority* of God, in *requiring* men
to *attend*; fo they do further denote his *Goodnefs* likewife, in *propofing* to men, univer-
fally and plainly, *the Doctrine and the Way of Life.* In *This* fenfe, the words of our
Lord in the Lext, *Let him hear what the Spirit faith unto the Churches*; are well para-
phrafed by *Solomon*, Prov. i. 20, *Wifdom crieth without, fhe uttereth her Voice in the
Streets; She crieth in the chief place of Concourfe in the opening of the Gates,——faying,
How long, ye fimple ones, will ye love Simplicity!—— Turn you at my Reproof; Behold,
I will pour out my Spirit unto you, I will make known my words unto you.* And by
the Author of the Book of *Wifdom*, ch. vi. 16, 14, *She goeth about*, feeking *fuch as are
worthy of her; fhe fhoweth herfelf favourable unto them in the Ways, and meeteth them
in every Thought; Whofo feeketh her early, fhall have no great Travel; for he fhall find
her fitting at his doors.* St *Paul* in a very emphatical and lofty figure of fpeaking, carries this matter ftill further, 2 *Cor.* v. 20; God, not only *propofes* to us the Means of reconciliation, but *as tho' God did* Befeech *you* (fays he) *by us, we pray you*——, *be ye
reconciled to God.* His manner of expreffion in That *whole* Verfe, is extremely remarkable: *We are* (fays he) *Ambaffadors* for *Chrift*; He does not fay, We are the Ambaffadors *of* Chrift, (though That alfo *might* properly enough have been faid;) but we
are, fays he, Ambaffadors *for* Chrift. *Chrift*, is the Great Ambaffador of the Father;
(*the Apoftle and High-Prieft of our Profeffion, Chrift Jefus*, Heb. iii. 1.) And, in *His*
abfence, *We* (fays the Apoftle) *are Ambaffadors* for *him*, Ambaffadors *in his ftead*, Ambaffadors *from God* to men, if we deliver his words faithfully; And therefore, *as though
God did Befeech you by Us, We* (fays he) *in Chrift's ftead*, (in the Abfence of Chrift
the Great Ambaffador of the Covenant, *We in his ftead*) *pray you, be ye reconciled to God.*
This is the *Second* notion included in the words, Let *him hear*; They denote the *Goodnefs* of God, in *propofing* to men, univerfally and plainly, *the Doctrine and the way of
Life.*

Life. Whofoever hath *Ears*, let him *hear*; and whofoever *heareth*, let him *obey*; S E R M. and whofoever *obeyeth* already, let him *perfevere* in fo doing unto the End: *Rev.* xxii. LXV. 11, *He that is righteous, let him be righteous ftill*; *and he that is Holy, let him be* Holy *ftill.*

THE *other* phrafe in the TEXT, *He that hath an* Ear; fignifies, he that hath *Under-ftanding*, that hath *Ability*, that hath *Capacity* to apprehend what is fpoken. Thus *Matt.* xix. 12. when our Saviour had given a Defcription of Some Excellent Perfons, who had chofen to abftain from many even of the *Innocent* Enjoyments of Life, that they might have more Time and Opportunities to promote the Intereft of Religion and Virtue, which is the Kingdom of God; he adds, *He that is* Able *to receive it, let him receive it.* And in like manner, ch. xi. 14, after having given a large Character of the Perfon and Office of *John the Baptift*; *And if ye will* receive *it*, fays he, *This is Elias which was for to come*: *He that hath Ears to hear, let him hear.* To have an Ear therefore, fignifies to have *Underftanding* and *Apprehenfion.* By which, however, is meant, *not* mere *Natural* Parts and Abilities; (For the Gofpel is preached to the *Poor* and *Mean*, as well as to the *Learned*; Neither are Many of the *Wife* men of *This World*, called; Nor are *mere natural Parts and Abilities* of *Any* confideration in *Moral* and *Religious* Eftimation;) But to *have an* Ear, in the Scripture-fenfe, means, to have an *Underftanding free* and *unprejudiced, open* to *attend* unto, and *apt* to *receive* the *Truth.* Which is a Qualification including *Probity* and Fairnefs of Mind, and is therefore highly *commendable* in the *moral* Senfe. *Matt.* xiii. 16, *Bleffed are* your *Eyes, for they* fee; *and your* Ears, *for they* hear. And the *Want* of it, is not, like the Want of *natural* Parts and Abilities, *pitiable* and compaffionable; but *faulty*, and deferving of fevere *Reproof:* Mar. viii. 17, 18, *Perceive ye not* yet, fays our Lord to his Difciples by way of Expoftulation; *perceive ye not* yet, fays he, *neither underftand? Have ye your Heart* yet *hardened? Having Eyes, fee ye not? And having Ears, hear ye not, and do ye not remember?* From which *Rebuke* given by our Lord to his Difciples, in fo earneft and affectionate a manner, for not making Ufe of their *Reafon* and *Underftanding*; we cannot fail to infer this *important Obfervation* in matters of Religion; that the *Tafte* or *Relifh*, the *Judgment*, the *Underftanding*, by which men are to difcern and chufe, and by which they are to form their Sentiments concerning the Truth or Error of any religious doctrines; muft never be, any *Enthufiaftick Fancy*, any *ftrong Imagination*, or *unaccountable impreffion of Mind*, which is the *Spirit of Delufion*; but it muft always be, an *impartial Attention* to the *Right* and *Reafon* of the Cafe, and to the *Nature* and *Evidence* of the Thing. This is in the Gofpel-fenfe, having *Ears* to *hear*, and *Eyes* to *fee*, and *Underftandings* wherewith to *Underftand.* According to which *explication* of the words; This Phrafe, fo often ufed by our Saviour, *he that hath Ears to hear*, does plainly contain a very affectionate and ftrong Appeal to the unprejudiced Senfe of Mankind, for the *Reafonablenefs*, *Truth*, and *Excellency* of the *Things fpoken*, or the *Doctrines delivered by him.*

AND as *This* Challenge, *Whofo hath an Ear*, contains thus a declaration of the Reafonablenefs of the *Doctrine propofed*; and the *other* part of the Words, *let him hear*, are expreffive of the *Authority and Goodnefs* of God who fpeaks: So *Both of* them together, plainly infer and fet forth the *Capacity* men have, and the indifpenfable Obligation they are under, to hearken to, and obey, what God delivers to them. *He that hath an Ear, let him hear, what the Spirit faith unto the Churches.*

THE Words being thus explained, we may from hence in the enfuing Difcourfe naturally deduce the *four* following Doctrinal Obfervations. *1ft*, That *God*, the Great Creator, and righteous Governor, and merciful Judge of the whole Earth, offers to *All men* the gracious Terms and Poffibilities of Salvation: *Let him hear*, (let *every man* hear,) *what the Spirit faith unto the Churches.* 2*dly*, That, This Offer, though gra-

3   cioufly

S E R M. ciouſly made to *All*, yet in Event becomes *Effectual* to *Thoſe only*, who are *qualified*
LXV.   and *capable* to *receive* it : *He that hath an Ear, let him hear.* 3*dly*, That they who
~~~~ *want an Ear*; they who *want* the *Diſpoſitions neceſſary* to their receiving and embracing
this gracious Offer of Salvation, or are prevented by any of the *Hindrances* which render it ineffectual, are always very ſeverely reproved in Scripture; plainly denoting it
to be their *own Fault*, their own *Perverſeneſs* only, that they have not *Ears to hear.*
4*thly* and *Laſtly*, That hence conſequently All thoſe paſſages of Scripture, wherein *God*
is at any time repreſented as *blinding* mens *Eyes*, or *cloſing* their *Ears*, or *hardning* their
Hearts, or *taking away* their *Underſtanding* from them; muſt of neceſſity be underſtood to be *figurative* Expreſſions only; not denoting literally what God actualy effects
by his Power, but what by his Providence he juſtly and wiſely permits.

I. *Firſt*, GOD, the Great Creator, and righteous Governor, and merciful Judge of
the Whole Earth, offers to *All men* the gracious Terms and Poſſibilities of Salvation :
Let him hear, (let *every man* hear,) *what the Spirit ſaith unto the Churches.* God
ſpeaks to men *Originally* by the *Light* of *Nature*, by the *Order* and *Proportions* of
Things, by the *Voice* of *Reaſon*, by the *Dictates* of *Conſcience.* 'Tis *every* man's Duty,
and 'tis in every man's Power to *hearken* to this *Voice* of *Reaſon* and *Conſcience*; to this
Candle of the Lord, as the Wiſe man ſtiles it, *Prov.* xx. 27. And concerning *Them*
who *do* ſo, St *Paul* declares, that, *having not the Law*, (that is, having no *revealed*
Law given them, yet) *they are a Law unto themſelves.* And *by that* Law, by the
Law of *Reaſon*, of *Nature* and *Conſcience*, ſhall they finally be judged. For every
man is accepted according to what he *Hath*, and not according to what he *Hath
not.* This *Light of Reaſon*, is *univerſal*; the *Firſt*, and *Great* Gift of God; *implanted*
in the minds of *All* men; *acknowledged* by the *Conſcience*, even of the *Unrighteous*
themſelves; atteſted to by the *neceſſary judgment and approbation* even of the moſt a-
bandoned and *Corrupt*, in all Caſes wherein their *own particular Intereſt* is not concerned. The acting *contrary* to This Light, by any profane, unjuſt, fraudulent, or
debauched Practices whatſoever, is in *All* perſons, under *All Diſpenſations*, the higheſt
and moſt inexcuſable Fault; as being deſtructive of the very *Foundation of All* Religion. And the acting *agreeably* to it, is in *All* perſons *Always* acceptable to God; and,
in Thoſe to whom no Light of Revelation hath been afforded, 'tis All *that is required*
of them. For *in every Nation, he that feareth God and worketh Righteouſneſs, is accepted of him.* When, thro' the growing Corruptions and Idolatry of many Ages, Cuſtom
and Example and bad Education had almoſt univerſally extinguiſhed the natural Light
of Conſcience; and cauſed *Reaſon*, That Great Gift and Witneſs of God, to be almoſt
totally neglected; God raiſed up the *Patriarchs*, both before and after the Flood, to
be *Preachers of Righteouſneſs* to the World, to be as *Lights ſhining in a dark place*, to
invite *All men to Repentance*, to the *Acknowledgment of the Truth* and to the *Practice
of Virtue*, in their ſeveral and reſpective *Generations.* After which, by the giving of
the *Law* to the *Iſraelites*, he placed That people as a *City on a Hill*, an eminent and
ſtanding Witneſs to all the Nations around, calling them off from impious and abominable Idolatries to the Worſhip of the God of Heaven: *Iſ.* xlix. 22, *Thus ſaith the
Lord, Behold, I will lift up mine hand to the Gentiles, and ſet up my ſtandard to the
people; and they ſhall bring thy ſons in their arms, and thy daughters ſhall be carried
upon their ſhoulders.* And by a Succeſſion of *Prophets* for Many Ages, he declared
continually to the whole People of the Jews, and by Them to All Others who were
willing *to retain God in their Knowledge*, and had not wholly given themſelves up to a
reprobate Mind; he declared his readineſs to accept That Repentance and Amendment
of Sinners, which even the Light of Nature itſelf, if they had attended to it, would
in a good degree have led them to; *God having never left himſelf wholly without Witneſs, in that he did good, and gave men rain from heaven, and fruitful ſeaſons, filling*

their

their hearts with food and gladneſs; and their *own conſciences* in the mean time, accord-S E R M.
ing to their moral or immoral Behaviour, *accuſing or elſe excuſing one another.* God, I LXV.
ſay, by a continual Succeſſion of *Prophets,* declared (what the Light of Nature itſelf
gave reaſonable but obſcurer Hopes of,) his readineſs to accept the Repentance and
Amendment of Sinners, and to receive *All men* to his Mercy, upon their returning into
the way of Righteouſneſs. *Ezek.* xxxiii. 11, *As I live, ſaith the Lord God, I have no
pleaſure in the Death of the Wicked, but that he turn from his way and live.* And
Iſ. lv. 1, 3, 6, 7, *Ho, every one that thirſteth, come ye to the Waters: And he that
hath no money; come ye, buy, and eat; yea, come, buy wine and milk without Money
and without Price.* —— *Incline your ear and come unto me; hear, and your Soul ſhall
live; and I will make an everlaſting Covenant with you, even the ſure mercies of David.*
——*Let the wicked forſake his way, and the unrighteous man his Thoughts, and let him
return unto the Lord, and he will have Mercy upon him; and to our God, for he will
abundantly pardon.* By the *Goſpel of his Son,* God has ſtill *more expreſsly and explicitly* declared, and commanded to be preached to *every Nation under Heaven,* the merciful Offer of Salvation made unto *All Mankind,* upon the moſt reaſonable and neceſſary
Terms of Faith and Repentance, That is, of ſincere renewed Obedience; Excluding
None from this gracious Invitation; but commanding his Servants to go out into All
places, and to *exhort* men, to *beſeech* them, to *urge* them, to be *inſtant with* them,
nay even to *compel* them, (by the moſt kind and earneſt Intreaties, by the moſt affectionate and preſſing Importunities, *compel them*) *to come in,* that his houſe may be filled.
Accordingly, *their Sound* has *gone forth into all the Earth, and their Words unto the
Ends of the World.* And no man, to whom this Doctrine has been preached, can
ſay, that his Duty and the Way to Happineſs has not been clearly made known to
him; unleſs he wilfully cloſes his *Eyes* that he may not ſee, and his *Ears* that he may
not *hear.* Our Saviour *himſelf,* who was in the *Boſom* of his *Father,* (and who knew
perfectly, and was ſent by him on purpoſe to reveal to us his Whole Will concerning
the Salvation of Mankind;) thus teſtifies in the moſt expreſs words: *God* (ſays he)
ſo loved the World, that he gave his only begotten Son, that whoſoever *believeth in him
ſhould not periſh, but have everlaſting Life;* and *that the* World *through him might be
ſaved,* Joh. iii. 16, 17: He does not ſay, he was ſent *that a few particular perſons,*
but *that the* World, if they would hearken to him, and be prevailed upon to return
into the ways of Righteouſneſs, *thro' him might be ſaved.* And accordingly when he
ſat about this great Work for which he was ſent; he applies himſelf to *All men* without reſerve; *Matt.* xi. 28, *Come unto me* All *ye that labour and are heavy laden, and I
will give you reſt:* And *Joh.* vii. 37, *If* any *man thirſt, let him come unto Me, and
drink.*

IN *one* place indeed, we find him affirming, that *he was not ſent, ſave unto the loſt* | Joh. xvii. 9.
Sheep of the Houſe of Iſrael. But the occaſion, and manner, of his affirming this; | Luk. iv. 23 ---
and his Treatment of the perſon afterwards, to whom he had ſaid this; and the whole | 27.
Hiſtory and Tenour of Scripture, plainly ſhow, that his Meaning herein was not to | Matt. xv. 24.
affirm, that he was not ſent to Others *at all*; but only that, in order of *Time,* he
was not ſent to Others ſo *ſoon,* as to *the loſt ſheep of the Houſe of Iſrael.* The
Goſpel was to be preached *firſt* to the Jews; and our Lord was *firſt* to be the
Glory of God's people Iſrael: But *afterwards* he was to be alſo a *Light to lighten the
Gentiles,* and to be their *Salvation unto the Ends of the Earth.* The *Apoſtles themſelves,*
at the Beginning, were under very ſtrong Prejudices concerning this Matter: But they
were convinced afterwards by frequent Admonitions from our Lord; And then they
Fully and Clearly teſtified this Great Truth. *The Grace of God,* ſaith St *Paul, which
bringeth Salvation, hath appeared to* All *men,* Tit. ii. 11: And 1 *Tim.* ii. 4, *Who will
have* All *men to be ſaved, and to come to the Knowledge of the Truth.* St *Peter* in like
manner, in his *Second Epiſtle,* ch. iii. 9. The Lord, ſaith he, is *not willing that* Any

SERM. *should perish, but that* All *should come to repentance :* To *Repentance ;* That is, to a re-
LXV. al and *affectual Amendment and Reformation of Life ;* Which is Always the meaning
of *Repentance* in Scripture. Some Writers have contended, that, in these several Texts,
the words, *All men,* must be understood to signify only, *Some of All sorts* of men, *Some*
from among the *Jews, Some* from among the *Gentiles, Some* from among the *Rich, Some*
from among the *Poor ;* and the like. But This interpretation arises merely from a great
Unskilfulness in Language. For tho' the words *All men,* do indeed in Scripture, as in
vulgar Speech, signify very frequently, not *All* men *absolutely,* but in a limited sense,
All against whom no exception is plainly understood ; yet in no *language,* according to
Any vulgar manner of speaking, can they mean, *Some* only *out of every Sort of men ;* and
consequently in *Scripture,* which always expresses itself in the language of the Vulgar,
the words cannot possibly have *That Meaning.* But the Sense plainly is, that God really and sincerely intends the Salvation of *All Men ;* and that 'tis for his *Own* Fault
only, for *Wickedness* only, and *deliberate Unrighteousness,* that Any man shall be condemned. Besides the places before-cited, This great and fundamental Truth is still
more clearly (if more clearly it *can* be,) expressed in the xxiid chapter of the *Revelations,* ver. 16, 17 ; *I Jesus have sent mine Angel to testify unto you these things in the
Churches :* ——— *And the Spirit and the Bride say, Come ; And let him that heareth,
say, Come : And let him that is athirst, come ; And whosoever will,* (*i. e.* whosoever
will live a virtuous life,) *let him take the Water of Life freely.* And, to add still greater Weight to this solemn declaration ; *God,* even the *Father* himself in Person, is introduced as affirming the same thing from the Throne of his Glory ; ch. xxi. 5, 6,
And he that sat upon the Throne, said ; ——— *these words are true and faithful ;* ———*I
will give unto him that is athirst, of the Fountain of the Water of Life freely : He
that overcometh,* (that is, who resists the temptations of a wicked and debauched
World,) *shall inherit all things, and I will be his God, and he shall be my Son.* The
Sense is the same, as in the words of my Text ; *He that hath an Ear, let him hear
what the Spirit saith unto the Churches.*

THIS therefore is the *First* Particular. God offers to *All* men the gracious Terms
and Possibilities of Salvation.

II. THE *Second* is : That This Offer, though graciously made to *All,* yet in Event
becomes *effectual* to *Those only,* who are *qualified* and *capable* to *receive* it. But referring This to a further Opportunity, I shall conclude at present with This *One* Inference from what has been already said ; *viz.* That from hence all *unrighteous,* all
wicked and *debauched* persons, being convinced that the destruction is *of themselves,*
if they continue in the Practice of Unrighteousness ; and not from any Appointment
of *God ;* may be prevailed with to reform their Lives, while they have yet Time.
That *so* they may escape the Wrath of God, from which there is *no other* possible
Means of escaping.

SERMON

SERMON LXVI.

The Qualifications neceſſary to receive the Terms of Salvation.

REV. II. 29.

He that hath an Ear, let him hear, what the Spirit ſaith untó the Churches.

IN diſcourſing upon theſe words of our Saviour, I have propoſed to deduce from them the four following Doctrinal Obſervations. 1ſt, that God the Great Creator, and righteous Governor, and merciful Judge of the whole Earth, offers to *all men* the gracious Terms and Poſſibilities of Salvation: *Let him hear;* (let *every man* hear,) *what the Spirit ſaith unto the Churches.* 2dly, that This Offer, tho' graciouſly made to *All,* yet in Event becomes *effectual* to *Thoſe only,* who are *qualified* and *capable* to *receive it: He that hath an Ear, let him hear.* 3dly, That they who *want* an *Ear;* they who *want* the *diſpoſitions neceſſary* to their receiving and embracing this gracious Offer of Salvation, or are prevented by any of the *Hindrances* which render it ineffectual; are always very ſeverely reproved in Scripture, plainly denoting it to be *their own Fault,* that they have not *Ears to hear.* 4thly and *Laſtly;* That hence conſequently All thoſe Paſſages of Scripture, wherein God is at any time repreſented as *blinding* men's *Eyes,* or *cloſing* their *Ears,* or *hardening* their *Hearts,* or *taking away their Underſtanding* from them; muſt of neceſſity be underſtood to be *figurative* Expreſſions only; not de-noting literally What God actually effects by his Power, but what by his Providence he juſtly and wiſely permits.

THE *Firſt* of theſe, I have already gone through; that God offers to *All men* the gracious Terms and Poſſibilities of Salvation: Let *him hear,* (let *every man* hear,) *what the Spirit ſaith unto the Churches.* I proceed Now to the *Second* General Head:

II. THAT this Offer of Salvation though graciouſly made to *All,* yet in Event becomes *effectual* to *Thoſe only,* who are *qualified* and *capable* to *receive* it: *He that hath an* Ear, *let him hear. Light* introduced upon Any Object, ſuppoſes always that there be *Eyes* to view, and to diſcern it *by that Light.* The *Sound* of a *Voice,* or the Uſe of *Speech* ſuppoſes always that men have *Ears* to hear, what the Speaker uttereth. *Truth* and *Right Reaſon* and *Argument, Theſe* likewiſe ſuppoſe always that men have *Senſe* and *Underſtanding,* to judge of what is offered to their conſideration. And, in matters of *Religion;* God's offering to men certain *Terms* or *Conditions* of Salvation, ſuppoſes in like manner a certain *moral Diſpoſition* in the Mind, which cauſes it to have a *Regard* to things of That nature, to have a *Senſe* and *Reliſh* of things relating to *Mo-rality:* Otherwiſe *Men* would, in their *Nature,* be no more *capable* of Religion than Beaſts. *Sweetneſs* is No *Sweetneſs* to a perſon whoſe Palate has no *Taſte: Light* is No *Light,* to him who has put out his own *Eyes:* And *Religion,* or the *Preaching of the Goſpel,* is as *Nothing* to That Man, whoſe Mind has *no Regard* to, nor *Care* to make any *Diſtinction* between, what in the nature of things is *moral* and *immoral.* St *Paul*

3   ſets

SERM. ſets *This* obſervation in a very clear light, 1 *Cor.* ii. 14: *The* natural *man* (ſays he) re-
LXVI. ceiveth not *the things of the Spirit of God*; *for they are fooliſhneſs unto him*; *neither*
can he *know them, becauſe they are ſpiritually diſcerned.* The words are not rightly
rendred, *The* Natural *man*; as if God had made Men, *naturally*, incapable of Religion. Which is the very ſame thing, as it would be to find Fault with a Man for
not Seeing, when he was *Born Blind.* But the *true meaning* of the Apoſtle, is, *The*
Senſual *man*; He who, by habitual Debauchery, by a courſe of Any vitious or corrupt Practice, has extinguiſhed the Eyes of his own Underſtanding; ſuch a one *can*
have no true Senſe of things relating to Religion, of things which are only ſpiritually
diſcerned. Our Saviour repreſents the ſame notion to us, in a very lively and expreſſive
ſimilitude, St *Matt.* xi. 17; where he compares the *Phariſees*, who hated to ſee Truth
in *Any* Light, and refuſed to hear Reaſon under *Any* form; (who were neither moved
by *John Baptiſt's* preaching, who had come in the more *reſerved* and *auſtere* way;
nor by our Saviour's *own* preaching, who came in the more *free* way of converſation
and inſtruction;) he compares them to *children ſitting in the Markets, and calling
unto their Fellows, and ſaying; We have piped unto you, and ye have not danced; we
have mourned unto you, and ye have not lamented:* They had *No Ear*; they heard not;
they gave *no Attention*; they *knew nothing of the Tune* which their Fellows plaid to
them, in *what* manner ſoever they diverſified it. The *Application* our Lord makes of
the ſimilitude, is; that to argue with the Phariſees about *morality*, about the *true* nature of *religion* and *virtue*, in *what* manner ſoever it was done; whether in *John Baptiſt's* more *ſevere* way, or in his own more *mild* way; it was All One; it was talking to them about a matter they had no ſenſe of; it was ſpeaking to them in a ſtrange
Tongue, in a Language they underſtood nothing of. There is an Alluſion to the *ſame*
Similitude, in *Rev.* xiv. 3. *No man* could *learn That Song, but the one hundred and
forty four thouſand, which were redeemed from the Earth:* No man *can* Underſtand and
Practiſe the Religion of *Heaven*, but they who by a worthy diſpoſition of Mind, by
an habitual Love of Truth and Virtue, are qualified to be redeemed from the *Earth.*
Theſe are the Perſons, whom our Lord calls his *Sheep*; which *hear* and *know* his Voice,
Joh. x. 27: Who readily perceive the excellency of his Doctrine, and its perfect agreeableneſs to eternal Truth and Reaſon: Who receive inſtruction in the ways of Truth
and Righteouſneſs with the *ſame kind* of Pleaſure, as the Eye is entertained with at the
Approach at Light: Who *come unto Chriſt* becauſe the Father *draws them*; That is,
becauſe their Love of Right and Equity, which is *natural* religion, recommends to
them That which is *revealed*; and, thro' the Love of Righteouſneſs and true Virtue,
they are *led* to believe and embrace the Goſpel of Chriſt. Theſe are They, of whom
our Lord declares, *Matt.* xiii. 12, *Whoſoever hath, to Him ſhall be given, and he ſhall
have more Abundance.* But, on the contrary, *Whoſoever hath not, from Him ſhall be
taken away even That he hath:* Whoſoever is ſo inſenſible of the eſſential and eternal
Differencs of Good and Evil; whoſoever hath ſo *little Diſcernment* in matters of religion, as to think *Any thing whatſoever* can be an equivalent for the neglect or Breach
of the *leaſt Moral Virtue*; *whoſoever ſhall break one of theſe* leaſt *commandments, and
ſhall teach men ſo; he ſhall be called the leaſt in the Kingdom of Heaven:* That is, he
ſhall be the *Laſt perſon* that ſhall be admitted there, or ſhall be very far from ever entring therein at all. Thus, tho' the Offer of Salvation is graciouſly made to *All*, yet
in event it becomes *effectual* to *Thoſe* only, who are *qualified* and *capable* to *receive* it.

IN order to make which Doctrine more uſeful to us in Practice, I ſhall proceed to
ſhow diſtinctly, *1ſt, in general*, that That Diſpoſition of Mind, which qualifies and
makes Men capable to receive and embrace effectually the Terms of Salvation, is ſomewhat which the Scripture always ſpeaks of, as a matter of *ſingular excellency*, and
worthy of *Great Commendation.* *2dly*, In what *Particulars* this excellent temper and

diſpodifpofition principally confifts. And *3dly*, What are the *oppofite* Qualities, or chief *Hindrances*, which generally *prevent* the Offers of Salvation from being *effectually* embraced.

Firft; I obferve *in general*, that That Difpofition of Mind which qualifies and makes Men capable to receive and embrace effectually the Terms of Salvation, is fomewhat which the Scripture always fpeaks of, as a matter of *fingular Excellency*, and worthy of *Great Commendation*. 'Tis an eminent *Gift*, or *Grace* of God; not in the fenfe of *Thofe*, who think God works upon men *mechanically*, as upon mere *Machines*, but in fuch a Senfe, as *Reafon* is the Gift of God, which makes us to be *Men*, to be *rational* and *intelligent* Creatures. Which we receive indeed wholly from God the Author of our Being; and yet 'tis a commendable and praife-worthy Excellency in him that has it, becaufe, in the *Ufe* and *Exercife* of it, it depends intirely upon the *Free Will* of the perfon himfelf, either to *ufe* or to *abufe* it, either to *improve*, or to neglect and *lofe* it. Upon which account, St *Peter*'s Admonition is both very elegant and very exact; 2 *Pet.* iii. 18, *Grow in Grace*. The Thing to be acquired, is the Free *Gift* of God; and yet his Exhortation fuppofes it to be their own Duty, and confequently in their own Power to *receive*, to *ufe*, and to *improve* That Gift. And becaufe, though *all* men are created *rational*, yet *Few* actually make ufe of their *reafon*; though *all* men are indued with the Senfe of *Hearing*, yet *Few* (as our Saviour in the Text expreffes it) *have an Ear* to *hear*; therefore That Temper, That Spirit, That Difpofition of Mind, which is in Scripture denoted by this *figurative Phrafe*, is therein always fet forth, under characters of the *Higheft Excellency* and *fingular Diftinction*. 'Tis That, which caufes men to prefer *God* and Virtue before the finful injoyments of a vitious and corrupt World; to choofe *Truth* and *Right* and *Reafon*, before *popular Error* and *prevailing Wrong*; to ftrive to enter in at the *ftrait gate*, rather than accompany the *Power*, and the *Numbers* of an unrighteous and debauched Age. 'Tis *This*, that, even in the *Heathen* world, caufed *Socrates* to choofe *Death* rather than not maintain the Knowledge of *the One True God* againft his fuperftitious and idolatrous Countrymen. 'Tis *This*, that made the *Patriarchs* of old, to go out from their native Country, not knowing whither they went. 'Tis *This*, that, in *Elijah*'s time, when the whole Houfe of *Ifrael* had departed from God, and introduced almoft univerfally a falfe Religion, caufed feven thoufand men to diftinguifh themfelves, by forbearing to bow the knee to *Baal*. They *loved*, and *hearkned to* Truth: They had an *Ear* to difcern the Voice of God, even in the midft of the moft corrupt Times and Nations: and they *chofe*, to *follow* That *Call*. And by *adhering to* That Choice, with Courage, Patience, and Perfeverance; they acquired to themfelves the Character of thofe whom the Prophet *Malachi* fpeaks of, *ch.* iii. 17, *They fhall be mine, faith the Lord of Hofts, in that day when I make up my* Jewels: And whom our *Saviour* defcribes, as perfons *thought* worthy *to obtain* That *Life, and the Refurrection from the Dead*: And calls them his elect, *which fhall be gathered together from the four winds, from every corner under Heaven*: And whom St *Paul* means when he applies to *Chriftians* That Paffage of the Prophet, *Though Ifrael be as the Sand of the Sea, yet a* Remnant *fhall be faved*: And of whom, *Laftly*, St *John* fpeaks, *Rev.* xv. 2, when he faw in his vifion *Them that had gotten the Victory over the Beaft*: In the Original it is, *which from out of the* midft of the *Beaft*, that is, from the midft of the moft idolatrous and wicked, the moft corrupt and perverfe Generations, had *faved themfelves*, and *overcome* the Temptations of a corrupt World. But This in *General:* I proceed now in the

Second place, to confider *more* particularly, *Wherein* confifts This excellent Temper and Difpofition of Mind, which qualifies Men to receive thus effectually, and to em-

SERM. brace ſtedfaſtly, the Terms of Salvation propoſed to them; and in *What Particulars*
LXVI. This Diſpoſition principally ſhows forth itſelf. And

1ſt; THE *firſt* Inſtance wherein this Good Diſpoſition ſhows forth itſelf, is *Atten-tiveneſs* or *Conſideration*. Without *Attention* and *Conſideration*, a Man's Mind is in the ſame State with regard to *religious* Knowledge, as it would be with regard to the Know-ledge of things in the *World*, had his *Eyes* always been *cloſed*, and his *Ears* always *ſtopped*. God has given us *Faculties* of the *Mind* to *underſtand*, juſt as he has given us *Senſes* in the *Body* to *perceive*. Neither the *One* nor the *Other* are of Any Uſe, unleſs *applied* and *attending to* their proper Objects. He that hath *an Ear*, muſt *hearken*: And he that hath *Underſtanding*, muſt *attend*. *Behold*, (ſays our Saviour to his Diſci-ples, when he had foretold them how *falſe Prophets* and falſe Teachers ſhould ariſe and deceive the whole World;) *Behold*, ſaith he, (*take Notice*,) *I have told you before*, Matt. xxiv. 25. And *Moſes*, when he had delivered to the *Iſraelites* the *Moral* part of the *Law*; *See*, ſaith he, *Deut.* xxx. 15. *See*, (that is, *Obſerve* and *Attend*,) *I have ſet be-fore thee this day Life and Good, Death and Evil*.

2dly, THE *ſecond* particular, wherein This excellent diſpoſition of Mind ſhews forth itſelf, (and which is the *natural* Conſequence of *Attention and Conſideration*,) is a *De-light in Examining into Truth and Right*; a *taking pleaſure* at all times in *beholding the Light*, and in *hearing the Voice of Reaſon*. Among *ignorant* and among *ſuperſtiti-ous* men, Nothing is more *neglected* than *Reaſon*; That Great Gift of God, That bright and ſingular Ornament of our Nature; which diſtinguiſhes us on the *one* hand from *ir-rational* natures, ſuch as are the *Beaſts* that periſh; and on the *other* hand from *unrea-ſonable* and *perverſe* natures, which is the character of *Devils*. But how far ſoever this Gift of *Reaſon* may be neglected by *corrupt* Minds; yet 'tis (as *Solomon* elegantly ex-preſſes it, *Prov.* xx. 27; 'tis) *the candle of the Lord, ſearching all the inward parts of the Belly*. Nor is there any ſeverer Puniſhment in This Life threatned any where in Scripture, than God's taking away men's Reaſon and Underſtanding from them; *Job* xviii. 5. *The Light of the Wicked ſhall be put out, and the ſpark of his Fire ſhall not ſhine; The Light ſhall be dark in his Tabernacle, and his Candle ſhall be put out with him*. To *This Light* God *requires* us to attend; and They who do ſo, are *acceptable* to him. And he *appeals* to men to judge thereby, even concerning his *own* Proceed-

Micah vi. 2, 3. ings with them: *Iſ.* i. 18. *Come now, and let us* reaſon *together, ſaith the Lord*; and, *Iſ.* v. 3. *Let us* plead *together*, ch. xliii. 26. *Judge, I pray you, betwixt Me and my Vineyard*. Which *Appeal* of God to the *Reaſon* of *Mankind* for the *Equity* of his Dealings with them, is alluded to in That Paſſage of the *Pſalmiſt*, cited by St *Paul*, *Rom.* iii. 4. *That thou mighteſt be* juſtified *in thy Sayings, and mighteſt overcome when thou art* judged. Now if we are required to *judge* in this manner concerning *God's* dealings with *Us*; much *more* muſt it needs be criminal in us, to neglect to make uſe of this Light in judging what *we* are to do *Ourſelves*. Our Saviour *reproves* the *Jews*, Luke xii. 57. *Why even of* yourſelves (ſaith he) *judge ye not what is right?* And St *Paul* ſpeaks in like manner to *Chriſtians*, 1 Cor. xi. 13. *Judge in* yourſelves, *is it comely?* and again, ch. x. 15. *I ſpeak as to wiſe men*, that is, to *reaſonable and intelligent* per-ſons; *judge ye what I ſay*.

FROM the Texts cited under This Head, I cannot but obſerve here by the way, that the Scripture (in direct oppoſition to the *Romiſh* doctrine) every where *ſuppoſes*, that men muſt of neceſſity *judge for themſelves* in matters of Religion: And that there is *never* any *Infallible Guide, There* recommended; *never* any *Credulity*, or *Implicit Faith* in *Men, There* required or incouraged. As indeed, in the very *nature of things*, how is it at all *poſſible*, that ignorant and unlearned men ſhould be able to look over the World, and to ſee and judge *Which* of all Nations is the fitteſt to be relied on implicitly? On the contrary, men are always in Scripture *ſuppoſed* to have *an Ear*; and they are *com-*

3　　　　　　　　　　　　　　　　　　　　　　　　　　　*manded*

manded to *hear*, and to *confider* : To *call no man Mafter upon Earth*, but *themfelves* to prove *all things*, and to Try *the Spirits whether they be of God* : To fatisfy their *Own minds* ; as *Abraham*, Heb. xi. 19. accounted, (in the original it is, Reafoned *with him-felf,*) that God *Could* raife his Son from the dead : And to be able alfo to give Satisfaction to *Others*, who at any time *ask them a Reafon of the Hope that is in them*, 1 Pet. iii. 15. In the Great and Weighty Matters of Religion, the forming of This Judgment is not a Bufinefs of Skill, of Parts and Learning ; but of Integrity and Simplicity of Mind. Which whofoever is indued with, though otherwife of mean Abilities, will judge better concerning any religious and moral Truth, than the moft Learned Philofopher in the World. But if this Simplicity of Judgment, this natural Eye and Guide of the Mind, be *itfelf* corrupted and depraved by Vice or Superftition, no wonder if men fall into endlefs and inextricable Errours. Our Saviour excellently reprefents this to us, *Matt.* vi. 22 ; *The Light of the Body is the Eye* : *If therefore thine Eye be fingle, thy whole Body fhall be full of Light* : *But if thine* Eye *be Evil, thy whole Body fhall be full of Darknefs* : *If therefore the* Light *that is in thee be darknefs, how great is That darknefs !* The Mind of a Man, whofe moral judgment is thus vitiated by departing from the Guidance of Reafon and from the Love of Truth, is, in the *fpiritual* fenfe, *a land of Darknefs as Darknefs itfelf, and of the fhadow of Death, without any order, and where the Light is as Darknefs*, Job x. 22.

3*dly,* Therefore ; The *Third* and *Principal* Particular, wherein confifts That excellent Temper and Difpofition of Spirit which fits and qualifies men to embrace effectually the Terms of Salvation, is *Moral Probity, Sincerity, and Integrity of Mind.* If any *man will do his Will, he* fhall *know of the Doctrine, whether it be of God*, Jo. vii. 17. *If thou defire Wifdom, keep the Commandments, and the Lord fhall give her unto thee ; For he that* keepeth *the Law of the Lord, getteth the Underftanding thereof*, Eccluf. i. 26. xxi. 11. This is what our Saviour, in his Parable, calls the *Good Ground*, which brings forth *fixty* and an *hundred fold.* Thefe are the perfons which our Lord calls his *Sheep* ; which *hear and know* his *Voice.* Thefe are they, of whom we read that they are *ordained*, or (as the *Greek* fignifies,) *prepared* and *fet in Order to* receive the Means of *eternal Life.* Thefe are they to whom 'tis promifed, that *the Wife* fhall *underftand* ; that *the Meek, God will guide in judgment* ; and *fuch as are gentle, Them* he will *teach his Way.* Of this kind was *Nathaniel* ; of whom our Saviour declared, when he *firft* faw him ; *Behold, an Ifraelite indeed, in whom there is No Guile.* Of the fame kind feems to have been That *Other* perfon, to whom our Saviour faid, *Mar.* xii. 34. (though indeed it is not recorded in the Gofpel, what *further* Progrefs he afterwards made ;) *Thou art not far from the Kingdom of God. Laftly,* of This kind are All Thofe, who come unto *Chrift*, becaufe the *Father* draws them ; that is, who through the *Love* of God, through the *Love* of *Righteoufnefs* and true *Virtue*, are led to believe and embrace the *Gofpel of Chrift.* For

Joh. x. 27.
Acts xiii. 48.
Dan. xii. 10.
Pf. xxv. 9, 14
Jo. i. 47.

4*thly,* The *fourth* and *laft* Inftance, wherein this Good Difpofition I am fpeaking of, fhows forth itfelf, is a *Readinefs* to *hearken* to the Voice of Revelation, as well as of *Reafon.* A well-difpofed mind prefently feels the *Goodnefs*, and is ftruck with a fenfe of the *Beauty* and *Excellency*, and acknowledgeth the *agreeablenefs* of the *Doctrine of Chrift*, to the *eternal Truths* of *Nature.* And This *real* Harmony of Reafon and Revelation, not any Enthufiaftick *Fancy*, is the true *internal* evidence of Scripture ; is God's *Spirit*, bearing Witnefs with *Our's.* St *Paul*, Rom. x. 8. applies to the *Gofpel*, what *Mofes* had faid of the *Moral Law*, The *Word is Nigh thee, even in thy Mouth and in thy Heart* : 'Tis, in a manner, almoft *connatural* to a reafonable and well-difpofed Mind. *The Sound* of the Apoftle's Preaching, faith he again, *ver.* 18. (what by the *Pfalmift* was fpoken concerning the Motion of the *Stars of Heaven*,) *Their Sound*, fays he, is *gone forth into all Lands, and their Words unto the Ends of the World.* He that hath *Ears* to *hear, cannot but hear* their Doctrine ; He that has *Eyes* to *fee*, even

Hab. ii. 2.

tho'

S E R M.
LXVI.
Pſ. xix. 1.
Rom. x. 18.

Joh. xii. 46.

tho' he *runs*, may *read* it; He that has *Underſtanding* and *Probity of Mind* to *appre-hend*, cannot but *embrace* it, when propoſed to him fairly and uncorruptly. As the re-gular *Motions* of the *Stars* in the Heavens, are an undeniable Proof of the *Power* and *Wiſdom of God*, and of the conſequent Obligations of Natural *Religion*; ſo the *Doctrine of the* Goſpel carries along with it, to reaſonable Minds, by its intrinſick Excellency, bright Evidences of *Divine Truth* in what it *reveals*. Chriſt is *come a* Light *into the World*: And the *Goſpel* is the Light *of the Knowledge of the Glory of God in the Face of Jeſus Chriſt, ſhining in our Hearts*, ſaith St *Paul*, as conſpicuouſly in the *Moral* Senſe, as in the *natural* ſenſe God originally, at the creation of the World, cauſed the *Light to ſhine out of Darkneſs*, 2 Cor. iv. 6. Again, Our Saviour himſelf uſes the ſame Si-militude, *Luke* xvii. 21. *The Kingdom of God*, ſays he, *is* within you:——*And if they ſhall ſay to you, See here, or See there; go not after them, nor follow them: For as the Lightning that lightneth out of the one part under heaven, ſhineth unto the other part under heaven; ſo ſhall alſo the Son of Man be in his day*. This univerſal Light of re-vealed Truth is to be found by all men, not by following This or the Other *particular man* or *Body of men* as a *Guide*; which is the *very thing* our Lord forbids in the Paſ-ſage now cited: but 'tis to be found only by attending to the *Revelation itſelf*: Ac-cording to our Saviour's direction, *Search the Scriptures*; And after the Example of Thoſe, whom we find particularly commended, *Acts* xvii. 11. for *ſearching the Scrip-tures daily, whether the things that were* taught them, *were ſo* or no: The conſequence of which, was, that they *received the word* (ſo the Text expreſſes it,) *with all readi-neſs of Mind*.

THESE are the Principal *Particulars*, wherein conſiſts that excellent Temper and Diſpoſition of Mind, which qualifies and makes men capable to receive and embrace effectually the Terms of Salvation. The

Third and *Laſt* thing I propoſed to conſider under *This* Head, was; what are the *op-poſite* Qualities, or chief *Hindrances*, which generally *prevent* the Offers of Salvation from being effectually embraced. Of theſe, the

1ſt is *Careleſſneſs*, and *Want of Attention*. Which Temper cannot poſſibly be de-ſcribed in any livelier and more expreſſive manner, than it is by our Saviour in the fol-lowing Similitude, *Luke* viii. 5. *A Sower went out to ſow his Seed; and as he ſowed, ſome fell by the way's ſide, and it was trodden down, and the Fowls of the Air devoured it.* The

2d Hindrance, is *Prejudice* or *Prepoſſeſſion*. This was the Caſe of the *Jews in gene-ral*, concerning whom St *Paul* ſays, that *the Veil was upon their Heart*, 2 Cor. iii. 15. And of thoſe *Phariſees* more *particularly*, to whom our Lord ſaid, *Matt.* ix. 13. *Go ye and learn what That meaneth, I will have Mercy and not Sacrifice.* Falſe and ſuperſti-tious Notions; or groundleſs, unreaſonable, unintelligible Opinions in religion, taken up upon *Prejudice*, are a greater Impediment to Truth, than even the moſt Profound Ignorance. The

3d Hindrance, is *Perverſeneſs* and *Obſtinacy*. This Temper is admirably expreſſed in Scripture by That Phraſe of a *ſtony Heart*, Zech. vii. 12. *They ſtopped their Ears that they ſhould not hear; yea, they made their Hearts as an* Adamant-ſtone, *leſt they ſhould hear the Law*. This was eminently the Temper of thoſe Jews, who becauſe *John the Baptiſt* came *neither eating nor drinking*, they ſaid, *He hath a Devil*; and be-cauſe *Chriſt* came *both eating and drinking*, they ſaid he was *a wine-bibber and a glut-ton*: But in *Both theſe* and in all *other* various circumſtances, *Wiſdom is juſtified of all her children*. The

Wiſd. i. 4.
Dan. xii. 10.

4th and *laſt*, and of all Others the *Greateſt* Impediment, is a *Love of Vice. Into* a Malicious *Soul*, ſaith the Scripture, *Wiſdom will not enter*; and *None of the Wicked ſhall underſtand*. Concerning ſuch a Perſon, St *John* elegantly expreſſes himſelf, that

I   *Darkneſs*

Darkneſs has blinded his Eyes. 1 *Joh.* ii. 11. St *Paul*, by a like figure of Speech, calls it S E R M.
Blindneſs of Heart, *Eph.* iv. 18 : and tells us that *the God of this World has* blinded the LXVI.
minds *of* ſome men, 2 *Cor.* iv. 4; and deludes them with *all deceivableneſs of unrigh-*
teouſneſs ; becauſe they have not a *Love of the Truth, that they might be ſaved*; but take
pleaſure *in unrighteouſneſs*, 2 Th. ii. 10, 12; placing their Religion in *any* thing rather
than in true Virtue.   And our Saviour, in a phraſe very like to That in the Text, up-
braids the Phariſees, *Joh.* viii. 43, *Why do ye not underſtand my Speech ? even becauſe ye*
cannot hear *my word: Ye are of your Father the Devil; and the Luſts of your Father*
ye will do.   They had a ſtrong Love to ſome Great Vices, which they were very unwilling to reform ; and therefore they had *No Ear*, to *hear his Words.*

T H U S have I largely ſhown, (which was my IId General Head of Diſcourſe,) that
the Offer of Salvation, tho' graciouſly made to *All*, yet in Event becomes *effectual* to
Thoſe only who are *qualified* and *capable* to *receive* it: *He that hath an* Ear, *let him hear.*
The

IIId Propoſition was, that they who want an *Ear*; they who *want the Diſpoſitions*
neceſſary to their receiving and embracing this gracious Offer of Salvation, or are prevented by any of the *hindrances* which render it ineffectual, are always very ſeverely
reproved in Scripture, plainly denoting it to be their *own Fault*, that they have not
Ears to hear.

S E R M O N LXVII.

Mens not accepting the Terms of Salvation is from Themſelves.

R E V. II. 29.

He that hath an Ear, let him hear, what the Spirit ſaith unto the
Churches.

T H E Obſervations or Doctrines I have propoſed to diſcourſe upon from theſe S E R M.
words of our Saviour, are Four. 1ſt, That God, the Great Creator, and LXVII.
righteous Governor, and merciful Judge of the whole Earth, offers to *All men*
the gracious Terms and Poſſibilities of Salvation : Let *him hear*, (let *every man* hear,)
what the *Spirit ſaith unto the Churches.* 2dly, That This Offer, though graciouſly
made to *All*, yet in Event becomes *effectual* to *Thoſe only*, who are *qualified* and *capable*
to *receive* it : *He that hath an* Ear, *let him hear.* 3dly, That They who *want an Ear*;
they who *want* the *diſpoſitions neceſſary* to their receiving and embracing this gracious
Offer of Salvation, or are prevented by any of the *Hindrances* which render it *ineffec-*
tual, are always very ſeverely reproved in Scripture, plainly denoting it to be their

SERM. *Own Fault*, that they have not *Ears to hear*. 4*thly* and *Laftly*, That hence confe-
LXVII. quently All thofe Paffages of Scripture, wherein God is at any time reprefented as *blind-*
ing mens *Eyes*, or *clofing* their *Ears*, or *hardning* their *Hearts*, or *taking away* their
Underftanding from them, muft of neceffity be underftood to be *figurative* Expreffions only; not denoting literally what God actually effects by his Power, but what by
his Providence he juftly and wifely permits.

THE *Two former* of thefe Propofitions I have already difcourfed upon: That God of-
fers to *All men* the gracious Terms and Poffibilities of Salvation: And yet, that in Event
This Offer becomes *effectual* to *Thofe* only, who are *qualified* and *capable* to receive it:
He that hath an Ear, *let him hear*.

I am now to proceed to the

III*d* general Obfervation: That they who want an *Ear*; they who *want* the *Dif-*
pofitions neceffary to their receiving and embracing This Gracious Offer of Salvation, or
are prevented by any of the *Hindrances* which render it *ineffectual*, are always *very*
feverely reproved in Scripture; plainly denoting it to be entirely their *Own Fault*, that
they have not *Ears to hear*. The *Reafon* is, becaufe thefe *neceffary Difpofitions* are not
natural but *moral* Qualifications; and the contrary *Impediments* are not *natural* but
moral Defects. Did *Religion* depend upon the ftrength or weaknefs of mens *natural*
Parts and Abilities of Mind, as Quicknefs of *Hearing* or *Seeing* depends upon the
Goodnefs of the *Bodily Organs of Senfe*; (Neither of which are at all in mens *Own*
Power;) It would follow, that *Want of Religion* was no more blame-worthy, than the
Want of *good Eyes* or the Want of *deep Underftanding*. But *Religion* depends *entirely*
upon fuch Qualities as are *Moral*; and the Capacity of *Hearing* mentioned in the Text
hath evidently relation to the *Heart*, and *Will* of the Hearer. Of this we have a moft
exprefs and undeniable Evidence, in that eloquent and fharp Reproof given by St *Ste-*
phen to the Jews, *Acts* vii. 51, *Ye ftiff-necked and uncircumcifed in Heart and* Ears, *ye*
do always refift the Holy Ghoft. Every one that heard him *well* underftood, that his
calling them *uncircumcifed in Heart and* Ears, was no more meant as a Cenfure upon
their *natural Underftanding*, than upon their *Bodily Organs*; but that it was a fevere
Rebuke upon them for *Another* kind of Defect, whereof they could by no means lay
the Blame either upon God or Nature. Perfons of the *Meaneft* natural *Capacities* may
have a Mind *Attentive* to inftruction; may have a *Love to Truth and Right*; may
have a great *Probity* and *Integrity* of Heart: Which *weak things of the World* (as
St *Paul* elegantly ftiles them) are in religion much fuperior to *the things that are Mighty*.
And on the contrary; men of the *Greateft Abilities* in *other* refpects, may yet very poffibly have *no* Relifh of *moral* Truths; may lie under powerful *Prejudices*; may be very
Perverfe in their Tempers; or may have violent *Paffions*, and ftrong Affections to particular *Vices*. Upon which Account, St *Paul* tells us that *not many Wife men after*
the Flefh, not many Mighty, not many Noble are called: It being very poffible, that fuch
perfons, notwithftanding *All Other* Advantages both of *Mind* and *Fortune*, yet, as to
the matter of *Religion*, may be in the State our Saviour reprefents the Church of *Lao-*
dicea, Rev. iii. 17, *Thou fayeft, I am rich,—— and knoweft not that thou art wretched,*
and miferable, and poor, and blind, and naked. Whoever has once carefully confidered
This, will find *no* difficulty in underftanding fuch expreffions as Thefe; *If.* xliii. 8,
Bring forth the Blind people that have Eyes, and the Deaf that have Ears: And *Jer.*
v. 21, *Hear now This, O foolifh people, and without Underftanding; which have Eyes*
and fee not, which have Ears and hear not. Again, *If.* xlii. 18, 19, 20, *Hear, ye*
deaf; and look, ye blind, that ye may fee: Who is Blind, but my Servant; or deaf, as
my Meffenger that I fent?——Seeing many things, but thou obfervedft not; opening the
ears, but he heareth not. 'Tis evident from the *Manner* in which thefe Expreffions are
introduced in the refpective Contexts, and from the *whole Tenor and Phrafeology* of

2

Scripture,

Scripture, and from *particular additional Circumstances* in *Other* Paffages wherein the S E R M. *like* Expreffions are ufed; that none of thefe Phrafes fignify *natural* Want of Capacity, LXVII. which is an Object of Compaffion; but a wilful *indifpofition to hear Reafon*, which is a moft juft ground for the fevereft Reproof. In *Ezek.* xii. 2, 'tis *Thus* expreffed: *Son of Man, Thou dwelleft in the midft of a* rebellious *houfe, which have Eyes to fee, and fee not; they have Ears to hear, and hear not; for they are a* rebellious *houfe.* He does not fay, they wanted *Capacity*, or *natural Underftanding*; but they were a *Rebellious* houfe. They were the fame, of whom he fpeaks, ch. xxiv. 13, *I have purged thee, and thou waft not purged.* In the *Gofpel* 'tis alledged by our Saviour, not as a *pitiable Infirmity*, but as an Argument of mens *Unworthinefs*, and of their *deferving to be caft off*: Matt. xiii. 13, Therefore *fpeak I to them in Parables*, becaufe *they feeing, fee not; and hearing, they hear not, neither do they underftand.* In the *natural* and *literal* fenfe of the words; not to *fee*, not to *hear*, not to *underftand*, is no *Fault* at all. But when men feeing, *fee not*; and hearing, *hear not; This* is the *great Reproach of humane* nature, and what makes men *worthy* even to be *left without inftruction.* Hence our Saviour could *not*, (fo the Scripture expreffes it:) *That is*, Agreeably to his general *Defign* and Mat. xiii. 58. *Method* of acting, he *could not* do *many* mighty works in his *own Country*, becaufe of Mar. vi. 5. their *Unbelief*: And he advifes his *Difciples*, after the example of his *own* Practice, *not* Mat. vii. 6. to *give that which is Holy unto the Dogs*, nor to *caft their Pearls before Swine.* In o- bedience to which Direction, St *Paul* tells the Jews who continued to reject his Preach- ing, after many repeated Admonitions, *Acts* xiii. 46, and xxviii. 28, *Seeing ye put from you the Word of God, and judge yourfelves unworthy of eternal Life, lo, we turn to the Gentiles*; and They will *hear it.* In his Epiftle to the *Hebrews*, after a more *gentle* manner of Reproof, but ftill in way of *Reproof* it was, as for fomething which was *entirely their own Fault*, that he complains of them as being *dull of Hearing*, ch. v. 11; and that They who *for the Time* onght to have been *Teachers of Others*, had ftill need of being *Taught* Themfelves. This was a *Faulty and blame-worthy Imperfection*; a *Want of* Improvement *in Religion*; a *Want of employing* thofe Talents, wherewith God had intrufted them; *a Want of* Growing *in Grace and in the Knowledge of God.* As for thofe who are *Totally* ignorant, and have no *Difcernment* at all in *Moral* Matters; of *Thefe*, the Scripture always fpeaks with ftill *Greater Indignation*, and with the utmoft *Severity of Reproof*; as of perfons labouring under a *Defect*, the Blame whereof can- not poffibly in Any wife be laid either upon *God* or *Nature*, but merely upon the *Wilful* and *Obftinate Negligence* of the *Perfons themfelves.* They are like the *Deaf Adder*, faith the Pfalmift, *which* ftoppeth *her Ears, which* refufeth *to hear the Voice of the Charmer, charm he never fo wifely:* They wilfully and obftinately *refufe* to confider the *Reafonablenefs*, and the *Proofs*, of true Religion. 'Tis not a *natural* Deafnefs, but a *Deafnefs* which proceeds from *ftopping* the Ears, and *Refufing* to hear the Voice of the Charmer. The Prophet *Jeremy*, ch. vi. 10, fets forth this Cafe to us in a very bold and lively fimilitude; *Behold*, faith he, *their* Ear *is* uncircumcifed, *and they* can- not *hearken; behold, the word of the Lord is unto them a* Reproach, *they have* no De- light *in it.* To which *beautiful* and *expreffive Figure* of Speech St *Stephen* plainly al- ludes, in that fharp and cunning Reproof beforementioned, *Acts* vii. 51, *Ye Stiff-necked, and Uncircumcifed* in Heart *and Ears, ye do always refift the Holy Ghoft.* St *John*, by *Another Comparifon* of the *Like* Nature, tells us that whofoever *hateth his Brother*, (that is, whofoever thinks *Uncharitablenefs* to be confiftent with True Religion,) *is in* Darknefs, *and* —— *Darknefs has* Blinded *his Eyes*, 1 *Joh.* ii. 11. Which being the cafe, 'tis no wonder that the Scripture here pronounces a *Woe* with a particular *Em- phafis*: Wo *be to them that call Evil Good, and Good Evil; that put Darknefs for Light, and Light for Darknefs*, Ifai. v. 20. And though in Scripture-phrafe, 'tis to the De- lufions of *Satan* that this Moral Incapacity of men is frequently afcribed; as when *Satan*

SERM. is faid to *take away* the Word out of mens Hearts; and *Satan* has filled *their Hearts*;
LXVII. and the like: Yet this is never fpoken by way of *Excufe*, but always on the contrary,
of *High Aggravation*. They, *out of whofe Heart Satan taketh away the word*, are by
our Saviour compared to, and *blamed* for being like unto, the *very worft* and *moft unfruitful* Ground. And *Ananias*, whofe *Heart Satan had filled*, was afked by St *Peter* in
way of *fevere Reproof*; Why *hath Satan filled*, (that is, *why* haft thou been fo *wicked*, fo
covetous, fo *corrupt*, as to *fuffer* Satan to fill) *thine Heart?* Acts v. 3. Nay, in all thofe
places, where *God himfelf* is reprefented as depriving men of their Underftanding; 'tis
ftill always, (which is a *Demonftration* of the True Meaning of fuch Phrafes,) 'tis always (I fay) in the way of moft *fevere Reproof* and *Blame*, to the Perfons of whom it
is fpoken. Of This, we have a fingular and very remarkable Inftance, in *Deut.* xxix. 4:
Where *Mofes*, bitterly expoftulating with the *Ifraelites* for their incorrigible rebellioufnefs,
Thine Eyes (fays he) *have feen the Signs, and thofe Great Miracles*; Yet the Lord hath
not given you an Heart to perceive, and Eyes to fee, and Ears to hear unto this day. Nothing ever was more evident, than that *Mofes* here did not mean to affirm literally, that
any thing was wanting on *God*'s part; (For he is *here* urging *That very Argument*, that
God had done all that was fit for him to do; but on the contrary his plain Intent was,
in a moft affectionate manner, to *expoftulate* with the *people* for their *Negligence, Obftinacy* and *Perverfenefs*; in not being led by the Sight of God's Great and numerous Miracles, to Repentance. *Your own Eyes have Seen thofe Great Miracles:* Yet fo unreafonably obftinate and perverfe are ye, that *the Lord hath not given you*; i. e. all the
Means he has ufed, have not caufed in you *a Heart to perceive*, even *unto This day*.
And This brings me to the

IV*th* and *Laft* General Propofition: That, fince the Scripture always thus *exprefsly* lays
the *Blame* upon mens *felves*; hence confequently All thofe Paffages, wherein *God* is at
any time reprefented as *blinding* mens *Eyes*, or *clofing* their *Ears*, or *hardning* their
Hearts, or *taking away* their *Underftanding* from them; muft of Neceffity be underftood to be *figurative* expreffions only; not denoting literally what God actually effects
by his Power, but what by his Providence he juftly and wifely permits. And becaufe
the Paffages of this kind are very numerous, I fhall, for Method's fake, diftinguifh them
under the following Heads.

1*ft*, SOME of thefe forts of expreffions denote only the *general Analogy* or *Fitnefs*
of the thing to be done.

2*dly*, OTHERS of them, are only figurative *Acknowledgements* of the *univerfal Superintendency* of *Providence* over All Events; without whofe *Permiffion*, nothing happens
in the World.

3*dly*, OTHERS of them, are only *Applications* of *Prophecies*, or *Declarations* of certain *Prophecies being fulfilled*.

4*thly* and *Laftly*, SOME others of them, are *Denunciations* or *Threatnings* of God's
juftly and in a judicial manner *leaving* incorrigible men to *themfelves*, after many repeated Provocations.

1*ft*, SOME of thofe Expreffions, wherein God may feem to be reprefented as *blinding* men, and *hardning* them to *deftruction*, do indeed in ftrictnefs denote *nothing* more,
than the *general Analogy* or *Fitnefs* of the thing to be done. Thus *Prov.* xvi. 4, *The
Lord has made all things for Himfelf*; (the true rendring is, *The Lord has made all
things, one anfwerable to another*;) *yea even the wicked to the day of Evil* : That is,
(as the Scripture elfewhere expreffes it,) *The wicked is referved to the day of Deftruction,
they fhall be brought forth to the day of Wrath* : For the Good, are good things created from
the Beginning ; fo likewife *evil things for Sinners*.

Job xxi. 30.
Eccluf. xxxix.
25. xi. 16. xl.
9.

AGAIN, 1 *Sam.* ii. 25, *The Sons of Eli hearkned not unto the Voice of their Father,
becaufe the Lord would flay them*. The reafon here affigned, *becaufe the Lord would*

flay

flay them, anſwers exactly to *That* expreſſion in *modern* language, Becauſe *they were* S E R M.
Abandoned, Profligate *or* Graceleſs. In which manner of ſpeaking, nobody underſtands LXVII.
Want of Grace to be a charging of any Defect on *God's* part, but a deſcribing of the
Perſons themſelves to be *worthy of Deſtruction.*

2*dly*, Some *other* Expreſſions of This kind, are only figurative *Acknowledgments* of
the *univerſal Superintendency of Providence* over all events ; without whoſe *Permiſſion*,
nothing happens in the world ; without whom, not a *Sparrow* falls to the Ground, or
a *Hair of our Head* periſhes. Thus, in Scripture-language, God *delivers into his Neighbour's hand*, that is, Providence *permits to fall*, every perſon who happens to be *ſlain*
by Chance. Thus *the* Lord ſmote *Nabal, that he died*; where the Hiſtory is not re- 1 Sam. xxvi.
corded a *Miracle*, but only the man's being ſtruck with a mortal diſeaſe. And, *the* 38.
Acts xii. 23.
Lord ſmote *the Ethiopians before Aſa*, that is, in the courſe of Providence they were 2 Chron xiv.
defeated by him in Battle. And what *Moſes* ſays concerning the King of *Heſhbon*; *the* 12.
Lord God hardned *his Spirit, and made his Heart obſtinate, that he might deliver him* Deut. ii. 30.
into thy hand; and *Joſhua* concerning the *Canaanites, it was of the Lord to* harden Joſh. xi. 20.
their Hearts that they ſhould come againſt Iſrael in battle, that he might deſtroy them
utterly; is plainly of the ſame import only, as if he had ſaid, *it pleaſed God to let their*
Obſtinacy deſtroy them. Thus, *God's hardning Pharoh's heart*, evidently means no Exod. iv. 21.
more than that the Miracles God worked before him, inſtead of convincing him as they
ought to have done, made him only more obſtinate and ſtubborn. And when God
ſays of him, *Rom*. ix. 17, *Even for this purpoſe have I raiſed thee up, that I might ſhew*
my Power in thee; St *Paul* thus explains it expreſſly, ver. 22, *What if God willing to*
ſhow his Wrath, and to make his Power known, endured with much long-ſuffering, *the*
Veſſels of Wrath, fitted to Deſtruction? Pharaoah was by his Own Wickedneſs *fitted to*
Deſtruction: God *endured him with much* long-ſuffering, and waited long for his Repentance: But he appearing incorrigible, God therefore choſe him as a proper Inſtrument, and *raiſed him up* into an *eminent Example*, upon whom he might *ſhow forth*
his Wrath, and make his Power known; for a Terror to ſuch as ſhould imitate his Obſtinacy, in all ſucceeding generations. And exactly the ſame, was the Caſe of *Judas.*
And *in general*, he *Hath mercy on whom he will have mercy, and whom he will he hard-*
neth; That is, *not* arbitrarily, irreſpectively, and without regard to mens behaviour:
But the Meaning is; *God*, who knoweth the *Heart*, and not *We*, is the only Proper
Judge, *who* are fit Objects of his Mercy, and *who* of his Wrath. Even in *Humane* Ju-
dicatures, a *Judge* may very reaſonably be ſuppoſed to ſay to an ignorant multitude,
not *arbitrarily*, but as having himſelf a moſt perfect knowledge both of the *Law* and
of the *Fact*; *I* will *acquit whom I* will *acquit*; *and I* will *condemn whom I ſee fit to con-*
demn. And that *This* is indeed the *whole* meaning of the word, *harden*, appears clearly
from hence; that 'tis uſed, not only of *Pharoh* and *Other Enemies*, but alſo of God's
own people. Iſ. lxiii. 17. *Lord why haſt thou* made *us to err from thy ways, and* hardned *our Heart from thy Fear?* Undoubtedly the Prophet in This Prayer, did not
mean to charge God with the Sins of the People; but merely to expreſs his Sorrow for
their being, in *fact*, corrupted. And, in the place before-cited, *Deut*. xxix. 4, *The*
Lord, ſays *Moſes* by way of expoſtulation to the people, *hath not given you an Heart to*
perceive; that is, his many wondrous Works have not yet had their due Effect upon
you. And concerning our Lord's *Diſciples themſelves*, 'tis written in the Goſpel, *Mar.*
vi. 52, viii. 17, that *they conſidered not the Miracle, for their Heart was* hardned:
Which is thus explained, *Luke* ix. 45, xviii. 34, *They underſtood not this Saying, and*
it was hid from them, that they perceived it not.

To give but *One* inſtance, or Two, more. By comparing 2 *Sam*. xxiv. 1, with
1 *Chron*. xxi. 1 ; it appears evidently, that God's moving *David*; or Satan's provoking
him ; or *his* own *diſtruſtful Heart* tempting him to number the People ; are All Phra-

SERM. ſes, that have one and the ſame Meaning. In like manner The men of *Shechem*'s falling
LXVII. out with, and *dealing treacherouſly* with *Abimelech*, Judg. ix. 23, is ſtiled, God's *ſend-*
ing an Evil Spirit between Abimelech and the men of Shechem. The Princes of *Egypt*
acting *fooliſhly*, in *Iſ.* xix. 14, is; *The Lord has mingled a perverſe Spirit in the midſt*
thereof. The *Hypocriſy* of the *Jews*, in *drawing near with their mouth, and honouring*
God with their Lips, when they had removed their Heart far from him, Iſ. xxix. 13,
is Thus expreſſed juſt before, ver. 10, *The Lord hath poured out upon you the Spirit of*
deep Sleep, and hath cloſed your Eyes. And the Prophet *Jeremy*'s Prayer, ch. iv. 10, *Ah*
Lord God, ſurely Thou *haſt greatly deceived this people*; evidently was not intended as
charging *God* with cauſing the people to err, but merely as an expreſſion of his Sorrow
for their being juſtly ſuffered to err.   But

   3*dly*, Some *Other* Expreſſions of this kind are Only *Applications* of *Prophecies*, or
Declarations of certain *Prophecies being fulfilled.* Thus *Jude* 4; *Ungodly Men, who*
were before of Old ordained *to this condemnation; whereunto alſo they were* appointed,
1 *Pet.* ii. 8.   Not, appointed of God to be Wicked, but *foretold* by the Antient Prophets, that ſuch perſons would ariſe.   Of the like ſenſe, are the following expreſſions,
Dan. xii. 10, *The wicked* ſhall *do wickedly.* 2 Tim. iii. 13. *Evil men and Seducers* ſhall
wax worſe and worſe, deceiving and being deceived. And *Rev.* xvii. 17, God *hath* put
it in their Hearts to fulfill his Will, (that is, hath cauſed them, not by influencing of
their Wills, but by his all-wiſe Conduct of Providential Events, he hath cauſed them to
accompliſh the Prophecies,) *and to agree, and give their Kingdom unto the Beaſt, un-*
til the Words of God ſhall be fulfilled. And *Rom.* xi. 7, 10, *The election*, (that is, the
elect people, thoſe who believe in Chriſt,) *have obtained it, and the reſt (i. e.* the Unbelievers) *were blinded:* According as *it is written, God has given them the Spirit of*
ſlumber, Eyes that they ſhould not ſee, and Ears that they ſhould not hear.——And Da-
vid ſaith,——Let their Eyes be darkned, that they may not ſee.

   But the moſt remarkable Text to This purpoſe in the Whole Scripture, is That in
the xiith of St. *John*, ver. 37, 39, 40, *Though he had done ſo many Miracles before them,*
yet they believed not on him:——Therefore they could not *believe, becauſe that Eſaias*
ſaid, He hath blinded their Eyes, and hardned their Heart, that they ſhould not ſee
with their Eyes, nor underſtand with their Heart, and be converted, and I ſhould heal
them. Evidently the Meaning of theſe words is; not, that *Iſaiah*'s *Prophecy* was the
Reaſon or *Cauſe* of the *Jews Unbelief*; but only that the *Jews Unbelief* was the *Accom-*
pliſhment of *Iſaiah's Prophecy.* For as, in *many other* paſſages of the Goſpels, according to the Nature and Phraſeology of the Jewiſh language, 'tis written that ſuch a
thing was done, that it might be fulfilled *which was ſpoken by the Prophet*; and yet 'tis
certain the thing was not *therefore done* becauſe it *had been foretold*, but had *therefore*
been foretold becauſe it *would certainly be done*; and the words, that it might *be fulfilled*,
mean nothing more than, *thereby* Was *fulfilled:* So it is likewiſe in the *preſent* caſe;
They could not *believe, becauſe that Iſaias had ſaid* it: That is, Their Unbelief was not
to be wondred at; 'twas nothing more than what *Iſaiah* had foretold; and it could not
indeed be expected of ſo corrupt a people, that they ſhould do better.   That This is
the true and only ſenſe of the Paſſage, will appear undeniably, by conſidering the *Ori-*
ginal Prophecy itſelf, and the manner how it is quoted in *Many Other* places of the
New Teſtament.   The words of *Iſaiah* are, ch. vi. 9, *Go and tell this people, Hear ye*
indeed, but underſtand not; and ſee ye indeed, but perceive not; make the Heart of this
people fat, and make their Ears heavy, and ſhut their Eyes; leſt they ſee with their Eyes,
and hear with their Ears, and underſtand with their Heart, and convert and be healed.
Our Saviour himſelf, citing theſe words, applies them by way of *Reproof*, Mat. xiii. 13,
Becauſe they ſeeing, ſee not; and hearing, they hear not;——and in Them is fulfilled the
Prophecy of Eſaias. St *Paul* cites and applies them in the way of a ſtill *ſharper Rebuke*

to thofe who rejected his Preaching; *Acts* xxviii. 26, Well *fpake the Holy Ghoft by* S E R M.
Efaiah unto our Fathers, faying, Hearing ye fhall hear, and fhall not underftand. In LXVII.
St *Mark* and St *Luke*, they are *Thus* cited; That *feeing, they might not fee; and hear-* Mar. iv.
ing, they might not underftand: Expreffing, as is evident from the parallel Texts, not 12.
the *Defign of God*, but the *Event* of the *Thing:* In the fame fenfe, as our Saviour fays Luke viii. 10.
concerning *Himfelf, I come not to fend Peace, but a Sword:* And to the *Pharifees,* Joh.
ix. 39, *For judgment I am come into this World;* that *they which fee not, might fee;
and* that *they which fee, might be made blind.* By comparing together all which feveral References to that one Prophecy of *Ifaiah*, and the manner how it is always alledged in the way of a moft fevere *Reproof* to the perfons to whom it is applied; it
moft manifeftly appears, that there is never in Scripture any Intention to afcribe to God
any actual efficiency in the making men hard and wicked; but only a perpetual declaration of God's *juft Judgments*, and of the *Wifdom of his Providence*, manifefted in
the *Truth of the Prophecies*, and in the exact *Fitnefs* of the refpective *Applications*.
The moft that is ever *literally* and *ftrictly* afcribed to God, is what Thofe Expreffions
amount to, which I obferve in the

4*th* and *Laft* place, To be *Denunciations* or *Threatnings* of God's juftly and in a judicial manner *leaving* incorrigible men to *themfelves*, after many repeated Provocations.
Of This kind is That of *Ezekiel*, ch. xxiv. 13. *Becaufe I have purged thee, and thou
waft not purged; thou* fhalt not *be purged from thy filthinefs any more.* And *If.* xxix. 13.
*Forafmuch as this people has removed their Heart far from me ;———therefore———the
Wifdom of their Wife men fhall perifh, and the Underftanding of their prudent men fhall
be hid.* The *Heathen-world*, becaufe, departing from the Light of natural Confcience,
they *liked not to retain God in their Knowledge;* therefore God gave them up *unto vile
Affections*, Rom. i. 24. The *Jews*, after long provocations, God gave up *unto their own
hearts luft*, Pf. lxxxi. 12 ; *and let them follow their own imagination;* even fo far as to
worfhip the Hoft of Heaven, Acts vii. 42. And of *Chriftians*, in the Times of great
Corruptions of the Church, St *Paul* prophecies, 2 *Theff.* ii. 11, that fince they *loved not
the Truth*, God *fhould* fend them ftrong Delufion, *that they might believe a Lye.* 'Tis a
fevere, but *very juft* Threatning, which we read in *Ezek.* xiv. 3, 9; *Since thefe men
have fet up their Idols in their Heart,———if the Prophet be deceived when he hath fpoken
a thing,* I the Lord *have deceived That Prophet,———and they fhall bear the Punifhment
of their iniquity.* Of the *fulfilling* which Threatning we have a remarkable inftance in
the Cafe of Idolatrous *Ahab :* Concerning whom, the Scripture in a *figurative* indeed,
but very *emphatical and expreffive* manner, defcribes the Prophet in a Vifion beholding
the Lord fitting upon his Throne, and *all the Hoft of Heaven ftanding about him*, and
the Lord *giving Leave* to an Evil Spirit to *deceive* the Prophets of *Ahab.* Yet even
here 'tis very obfervable, that, as a Laft Warning to *Ahab*, if it had been *poffible* to bring
him to Repentauce ; *this very thing*, even the deceiving *of his Prophets*, was itfelf told
him beforehand by *Micaiah.* But he was under the ftrong Prejudice of an idolatrous
Mind, and therefore he *had not Ears to hear.* More than This, God was not *obliged*,
nor was it *fit*, to Do for him. Nor will God to *Any man*, after he has ufed all *reafonable* Motives, and *irrefiftible* Means, to convert him whether he will or no. When the
Jews, after our Saviour had worked *Many* Miracles, ftill called for a *Sign from Heaven;*
he told them, there fhould *no Sign* be given to an *adulterous and perverfe generation.*
And *after his Refurrection*, he fhowed himfelf alive, not to *all the people*, but to *chofen*
and fufficient *Witneffes.* And when his unbelieving Countrymen, perverfely, and not
with any real Defire of being fatisfied, urged him to *repeat* the fame Miracles among
Them, as he had already worked in *other* places; he made them this fharp Reply, (the
Senfe whereof is a Paraphrafe on the words of my Text, and wherewith I fhall conclude ;) *Luke* iv. 25. *I tell you of a Truth, many Widows were in Ifrael in the days of*

Elias,

S E R M. *Elias,——but unto none of them was Elias ſent, ſave unto Sarepta a City of* Sidon, *unto*
LXVII. *a woman that was a widow. And many Lepers were in* Iſrael *in the time of* Eliſeus *the*
Prophet; and none of them was cleanſed ſaving Naaman *the* Syrian. The Manifeſtations God was pleaſed to make of Himſelf, were abundantly ſufficient; and they that
had *Ears* to hear, could not fail of underſtanding them. The caſe is the ſame *Now,*
and in *All* Ages: God has made abundant Manifeſtations of Himſelf, both by *Reaſon*
and *Revelation*; and no man can excuſably be ignorant of Him.

S E R M O N   LXVIII.

Of the Nature of true Chriſtian Zeal.

R E V. III. 15, 16.

*I know thy Works, that thou art neither cold nor hot : I would thou
wert cold or hot. So then, becauſe thou art luke-warm, and neither
cold nor hot, I will ſpue thee out of my Mouth.*

S E R M. **R**ELIGION is the Great Ornament and Glory of Humane Nature; that
LXVIII.   which principally diſtinguiſhes *Men* from the inferior Orders of Creatures;
    and upon which Alone are grounded all Hopes of Life and Happineſs hereafter,
when this ſhort and tranſitory World ſhall be paſſed away. In a matter of ſo great importance therefore, 'tis very wonderful, that any man who calls himſelf a reaſonable
Creature ſhould be careleſs, and indifferent; careleſs, whether he has *Any* Religion, or
None; indifferent, whether his religion, when he *does profeſs* any, be *True* or *Falſe*; careleſs, when he *has* embraced the *True* Religion, whether he makes Any Improvement
in his *Practice* anſwerable to it, or no. The Words of the Text are a Reproof ſent
by our Saviour to the Church of *Laodicea*, upon account of their remiſſneſs and
lukewarmneſs in this *laſt particular*. The Church of *Laodicea*, ſignifies either *literally*
one of the Seven primitive Churches of *Aſia*, or *figuratively* one of the ſeven ſucceſſive
States or Conditions of the Primitive Church Catholick, before its falling into That Univerſal Antichriſtian corruption deſcribed in the following chapters of This Book. In
whichſoever of theſe two ſenſes we underſtand the Church of *Laodicea* to be meant,
yet ſtill, it being part of the *Primitive Church* before the times of That Great and Total Apoſtacy; 'tis plain the lukewarmneſs here charged upon them, cannot ſignify a
general careleſſneſs whether they had *Any* Religion or *None*; nor an indifferency whether the Religion they profeſſed was *True* or *Falſe*; (for Theſe are the Crimes of *later*
Ages, not of the *Primitive* days:) But *Their* luke-warmneſs was a remiſſneſs or neglect
of making improvement in *Practice*, anſwerable to the excellency of the Religion they
profeſſed. *I know thy* Works, *that thou art neither cold nor hot.* The Defect was in

2   their

their *Works,* or *Practice:* They would not lay aſide the *Profeſſion* of Religion, and yet they would not live anſwerable to it by being *zealous of good works.* This is what our Saviour reproves them for in the Text: And to add Weight and Dignity to the Reproof, 'tis introduced with a Solemn deſcription of the Greatneſs and Excellency of the Perſon who ſent it: *Unto the Angel* (ſays he) *of the Church of the Laodiceàns, write; Theſe things ſaith the Amen, the faithful and True Witneſs, the Beginning of the creation of God. I know thy works, that thou art neither cold nor hot: I would thou wert cold, or hot: So then, becauſe thou art luke-warm, and neither cold nor hot, I will ſpue thee out of my Mouth: Becauſe thou ſayeſt, I am rich, and increaſed with goods, and have need of nothing;* They proſpered, (it ſeems,) in all worldly appearance, and had much Form of religion; but *knoweſt not that thou art wretched and miſerable, and poor, and blind, and naked: Naked,* that is, deſtitute of the works of righteouſneſs; and *Blind,* that is, inſenſible of the dangerouſneſs of their condition. The words therefore are a Reproof to the *Laodiceans* for their *Want of* Zeal; and an intimation *wherein* the nature of *True Zeal* conſiſts. *Thou art luke-warm, and neither cold nor hot,* is the Reproof for *want of Zeal;* And, *I know thy* Works, *that—thou art blind and naked,* is an intimation of *What* was the *Zeal* they wanted. Now ſince *Theſe* things are *Our* Examples; and the Scriptures are written for *Our* Admonition, *upon whom the Ends of the World are come;* and the Faults of which the *Primitive* Church was guilty, are much more increaſed in the *Ages of Apoſtacy:* It cannot but be very proper for us, from the conſideration of theſe affectionate words of our Saviour, to inquire, for our Own inſtruction, into the nature of True *Zeal,* which the *Laodiceans* are here reproved for wanting; and alſo of that Falſe *Zeal,* which is apt to make Chriſtians think themſelves to be *rich* in the ſpiritual ſenſe, and to *have need of nothing,* when indeed they are moſt *wretched, and miſerable, and poor, and blind, and naked.*

T R U E *Zeal* then, which is the *Virtue* of a *Chriſtian,* may be diſtinguiſhed from Falſe-*Zeal,* which is the Character of private *Parties* or *Factions;* principally by *Three* ways: By the *Object* about which it is employed, by the *Manner and Circumſtances,* in which it expreſſes itſelf; and by the *End,* to which it is directed.

I. T H E *Firſt* Mark, by which True *and* Chriſtian *Zeal* may be diſtinguiſhed from that which is Falſe *and* Unchriſtian, is the *Object* about which it is employed. The Object of *True Chriſtian Zeal* is the *Study of* Truth, and the *Practice of* Right: The continued, impartial, unprejudiced *Inquiring* after Truth *ourſelves;* and the giving conſtant *encouragement* to *All Others* to ſearch for it after the ſame manner: The conforming conſtantly *our own Practice,* to the unqueſtionable eternal Rules of *Right and Equity;* and uſing continually all juſt, honourable, and Chriſtian means, to prevail with *Others* likewiſe to do the ſame. On the contrary: The Object of *Falſe and Unchriſtian Zeal,* never is an *Impartial Inquiring What* and *Where* the *Truth* is; but always the *promoting* violently, *eſtabliſhing,* and *forcing men into* the Profeſſion of ſome *Imagined Truth,* without ever conſidering carefully whether it be *really a Truth* or no: in like manner, the *inſiſting on* the *practice,* not of ſuch things as are unqueſtionable and undiſputed Acts of *Virtue* and *Righteouſneſs;* but of ſuch things principally as are the *diſtinguiſhing* practices, or practices built upon the *diſtinguiſhing* opinions, of particular Sects or Parties.

T o explain this matter more particularly: The primary and proper Object of a *Chriſtian and good Zeal,* is the promoting the Practice of *Virtue and Righteouſneſs.* But becauſe *right Practice* can hardly be built, at leaſt can never be built with any certainty and ſteddineſs, but upon the Foundation of *Truth;* therefore the *Object* of Zeal *firſt* in the *Order* of Nature, is the *Knowledge of Truth.* And *Zeal* for ſearching after and diſcovering of *Truth* can *never* poſſibly be *exceſſive. The Price of Wiſdom,* Job xxviii. 18, *is above Rubies; The Topaz of Ethiopia ſhall not equal it, neither ſhall*

S E R M.
LXVIII.

SERM.
LXVIII.

it be valued with pure Gold. Buy the Truth, (faith Solomon,) and ſell it not; alſo Wiſdom, and Inſtruction, and Underſtanding, Prov. xxiii. 23. The like phraſe is uſed by our Saviour in the words immediately following my Text; I counſel thee to buy of me gold tried in the Fire, (that is, to inquire diligently after the uncorrupted Doctrines of the Goſpel, which will bear the Trial of the moſt impartial examination;)——and anoint thine eyes with eye-ſalve, that thou mayeſt ſee; that is, lay aſide blind prejudices and corrupt affections, which hinder men from diſcerning the Truth; And ſearch the Scriptures with an unbiaſſed underſtanding, that in Them you may find the words of eternal Life. This Zeal therefore, Zeal for inquiring and ſearching after the Truth, Zeal to know perfectly the Will of God, can never poſſibly be faulty in Exceſs. All Faultineſs upon This Head, is always and only on the Defective ſide: A want of Zeal, a Coldneſs and Luke-warmneſs, a Careleſſneſs and Indifferency in men, whether the things they profeſs to believe, be true or not. They receive things ignorantly and negligently at all adventures; They take their Religion upon Truſt, upon the Authority of common Repute; without being at all ſollicitous to underſtand it, or to know whereof they affirm: As if it was nothing more than the Cuſtom of the Country, or the Faſhion of the place they live in. Hence, though the Doctrine of Chriſt is ſo plainly and clearly expreſſed in the Goſpel, that he who runs may read it; and All Chriſtians, at all Times and in all Places, have been baptized into the Profeſſion of the Same Faith, and into an Obligation to obey the Same Commandments; yet for all this, what hath vulgarly been called Chriſtian Religion, has been at different Times, in the Same Country, and is Now in different Countries at the Same Time, as different from itſelf, as Light is from Darkneſs: God having (in great Juſtice) ſent men ſtrong Deluſion, that they ſhould believe a Lie, 2 Theſſ. ii. 11; that they ſhould entertain innumerable and incredible abſurdities; becauſe they received not the Truth in the Love thereof, and according to the Simplicity of the Goſpel of Chriſt. The firſt, therefore, and original cauſe of all corruptions in religion, is Want of Zeal for inquiring after Truth; a coldneſs or luke-warmneſs, a careleſſneſs or indifferency in men whether the things they profeſs to believe, be true, or not. But then further; if we have never ſo much Zeal for inquiring after the Truth, and never ſo much Succeſs in That Inquiry; yet ſtill even This is nothing without virtuous Practice: And therefore, as I before obſerved, the Great, the Principal, the Proper Object of Zeal, is the Practice of Virtue and True Righteouſneſs. And here likewiſe, as well as in the caſe of Searching after Truth, there is no room for our Zeal to be too Great. Men may miſtake the Object, and be zealous for ſomething elſe inſtead of Virtue; or, when the Object is right, the manner and circumſtances in which it expreſſes itſelf, may be very faulty: But the degree of the Zeal itſelf; the Zeal for Virtue, Righteouſneſs, and Equity, can never poſſibly be too Great. It is good (faith St Paul) to be zealouſly affected always in a good matter, Gal. iv. 18. And the Zeal of the Corin

＊ Cor. ix. 2.　thians in their liberality to the Poor of other Churches, is by the ſame Apoſtle commended as highly exemplary. And in his Epiſtle to Titus, ch. ii. 14, he declares that Chriſt gave himſelf for us, and redeemed us to this very end, that we might be a people zealous of good Works. Our Lord himſelf, by a figure of Speech expreſſing a Zeal which cannot be exceſſive, Bleſſed, ſays he, are they that hunger and thirſt after righteouſneſs. And deſcribing his Own Practice, My Meat, ſays he, is to do the Will of him that ſent me, and to finiſh his Work. And again, Joh. ii. 17, The Zeal of thy Houſe has eaten me up. And when, in the words of the Text, he had ſeverely rebuked the Laodiceans, for being luke-warm and neither cold nor hot; for making profeſſion of his Religion, and yet being remiſs and negligent to improve themſelves in virtuous practice, anſwerable to the excellency of the Religion they profeſſed; he adds immediately in the 19th verſe, Be zealous therefore, and repent. This is the

2　　　　　　　full

full Notion of *Chriſtian and good Zeal*, with reſpect to the Object about which it is S E R M.
employed: 'Tis a *Zeal* for the *Knowledge of Truth*, and for the *Practice of Right*; LXVIII.
And This *Zeal*, if it be not faulty in *Other* Circumſtances, the *Degree of it* can never be *exceſſive*; men can never be *too zealous* for *inquiring* impartially into *Truth*, or
for *doing* what is confeſſedly and unqueſtionably *Right*.

BU T what has been ſaid upon *This* head, will be ſtill further illuſtrated, by conſidering, on the *Other* hand, the nature of *Falſe and unchriſtian Zeal*, with regard to
the Object about which *That alſo* is employed. And the *Object* of *That*, as I obſerved at the Beginning, is always *Some Imagined Truth*, never carefully examined
whether it be *really* ſuch; Or elſe ſome *Form or Ceremony*, of no great moment to
Religion and Virtue; Or perhaps ſome *diſtinguiſhing* Practice, or Practice founded upon ſome *diſtinguiſhing* Opinion, of ſome particular Sect or Party. To explain this,
by *Inſtances*: St *Paul* relates that the *Corinthians* were *zealous*, ſome of them for *Paul*,
ſome of them for *Apollos*, and ſome for *Cephas*; and This their *Zeal*, he tells them,
was not *ſpiritual*, but *carnal*; that is to ſay, 'twas not for the *Religion of Chriſt*, but
for *Parties among Men*. Again: *Some* (he tells us,) upon the foundation of Chriſt,
inſtead of gold, ſilver, and precious ſtones, built *wood, hay* and *ſtubble*; materials which
would not bear the Teſt of the Fire: The Meaning is; They were zealous for *opinions*, of which they had never carefully examined the Truth; for *Doctrines*, which had
no uſeful Influence upon Practice; for *Forms and Ceremonies*, which made men not at
all the more careful to lead a virtuous Life. And of this ſort of things it is, that our
Saviour ſpeaks, in the words following my Text, ver. 17, *Thou ſayeſt, I am rich, and
increaſed with goods, and have need of nothing; and knoweſt not that thou art wretched,
and miſerable, and poor, and blind, and naked.* Again: we read, 2 *Sam.* xxi. 2, concerning the *Gibeonites*, to whom *Joſhua* and all *Iſrael had ſolemnly ſworn* they ſhould
not be deſtroyed, that yet *Saul* long after *ſought to ſlay them, in his* Zeal *to the children of* Iſrael and Judah. The *Object* of his Zeal was *Falſe*, as well as the *Manner*
of it *Cruel*: It was a Zeal for the *Power and Intereſt* (as *He* fanſied) of the *children
of* Iſrael and Judah, in oppoſition to the *Reaſon of the Thing*, and to the *Oath of God*.
To mention but one Inſtance more: The whole Body of the Jewiſh Nation in our
Saviour's days, were extremely *zealous* for the Obſervation of the Law: But 'twas a
Zeal, without Knowledge; 'twas a *Zeal*, without careful *Examination*; 'twas a *Zeal*
for the *ceremonial* part of the Law, more than for the *moral*; 'twas a *Zeal* for the *Traditions of the Elders*, and for the *Doctrines* each of their *own particular Sect*, more
than for the *Law* of God: And the Zeal which they had even for the *Law itſelf*,
was without conſidering, that the very *End and Deſign* of the *Law* was to lead men
to the *Goſpel*; that it was *itſelf*, in its own nature, but a *Type* of Chriſt; and that God
by the *Prophets* had all along clearly enough intimated, that there was to be ſuch a
Change in the *Diſpenſation*. For want of conſidering theſe things carefully and impartially, even thoſe Jews who were *converted*, continued ſtill, generally ſpeaking, *all
zealous of the Law*, Acts xxi. 20: And were *very earneſt* to *enforce* the obſervation of
it upon other Chriſtians: Concerning whom St *Paul* thus ſpeaks, *Gal.* iv. 17, *They
zealouſly affect you, but not well.* And Thoſe of them who *were* not *converted*, were Rom ix. 31,
infinitely zealous, in their oppoſing the Goſpel: *I bear them record*, ſays St *Paul*,
Rom. x. 2, *that they have a zeal of God, but not according to knowledge; For they being
ignorant of God's righteouſneſs,* (of That Method of Salvation which *God* has appointed,) *and going about to eſtabliſh their own righteouſneſs, have not ſubmitted themſelves
unto the righteouſneſs of God; For*, Chriſt (ſaith he) *is the End of the Law*. Of theſe
St *Paul* himſelf, before his converſion, was One. *According to the perfect manner of
the Law of the Fathers, I was* zealous (ſays he) *towards God, as ye all are this day*,
Acts xxii. 3; *being more exceedingly* zealous *of the traditions of Fathers*, Gal. i. 14.

touching

SERM. *touching the righteouſneſs which is in the law, blameleſs; concerning zeal, perſecuting the*
LXVIII. *Church,* Phil. iii. 6. becauſe *I verily thought with myſelf, that I ought to do many things*
contrary to the Name of Jeſus, Acts xxvi. 9. For when the *Object* of Zeal, is not the
Searching after Truth and the *Practice of Moral Virtue,* but the inconſiderately *and*
raſhly promoting, violently and by all means, ſome *unexamined or imagined Truth;* it
often comes to paſs that even *Zeal itſelf* for *Truth,* degenerates into the moſt *inveterate*
Prejudice, and moſt *incurable Obſtinacy* againſt *it,* and puts men upon the moſt *un-*
righteous Methods, of *propagating* (as they think, but indeed of *oppoſing*) it. *They ſhall*
put you out of the Synagogues, ſaith our Saviour, *Joh.* xvi. 2. *yea, the time cometh, that*
whoſoever killeth you, will think that he doth God ſervice. The *Reaſon* follows, *ver.* 3;
Theſe things will they do unto you, becauſe *they have not known the Father, nor Me;*
that is, becauſe they have no true Notion, either of *Natural* Religion, or of *Chriſtian.*
The *Malignity* of this ſort of *Prejudice* is ſet forth to us under a moſt lively and expreſſive figure, *Acts* vii. 57. *They ſtopped their Ears, and ran upon Stephen,——and*
ſtoned him. They took effectual care, not to be convinced by what he ſhould ſay. *They*
were, as the *Pſalmiſt* expreſſes it, *like the deaf adder that ſtoppeth her Ears; which re-*
fuſeth to hear the Voice of the Charmer, charm he never ſo wiſely. Our Saviour deſcribes
the *unreaſonable Prejudices* of the *Phariſees,* by the ſame figure of ſpeech, *Joh.* viii. 43.
Why do ye not underſtand my Speech? even becauſe ye cannot hear my word. His Meaning is, Their vitious and corrupt inclinations, would not ſuffer them to hearken to the
Truth. And elſewhere in the ſame Goſpel, he more than once expreſſes the ſame thing
again, by ſtiling them *Blind.* But

   2*dly;* THE *next* mark, by which True *and* Chriſtian *Zeal* may be diſtinguiſhed
from that which is Falſe *and* Unchriſtian, is the Manner and Circumſtances in which
it expreſſes itſelf. 'Tis manifeſt that *Zeal* cannot be at all a *Chriſtian Virtue,* except
it be imployed about its true and proper *Object,* the *Search after Truth* and the *Prac-*
tice of Right. But This *alone* is not ſufficient. For, be its *Object* never ſo good, ſo
that the Zeal cannot poſſible be exceſſive in its *Degree;* yet ſtill by the *Manner and*
Circumſtances in which it expreſſes itſelf, it may eaſily, if great Care be not taken, degenerate into a Falſe *and* Unchriſtian *Zeal. Wrath and Fierceneſs, Contentiouſneſs and*
Animoſity, Violence and Hatred, are *vitious* and *ungodly* Practiſes, whether the *Object* of
a man's zeal be *good* or *bad.* St *Paul* was not only faulty for perſecuting the *Chriſtians,*
when Himſelf was a *Jew;* but he would alſo ſtill have continued to have been equally
faulty, if he had perſecuted the *Jews,* when Himſelf was a *Chriſtian.* The character
of the *great Author* of our Religion is This, *Matt.* xii. 18. *Behold,——my beloved, in*
whom my Soul is well pleaſed, I will put my Spirit upon him, and he ſhall ſhow judg-
ment unto the Gentiles; He ſhall not ſtrive, nor cry, neither ſhall any man hear his voice
in the ſtreets; A bruiſed reed ſhall he not break, and ſmoaking flax ſhall he not quench,
till he ſend forth judgment unto victory. And when ſome of his own diſciples, beginning to depart from this example, would have called for Fire from Heaven upon the
Samaritans, he rebuked them, ſaying, *Ye know not what manner of Spirit ye are of.*
According to this Great Pattern, St *Paul* directs, 2 *Tim.* ii. 24, that *the Servant of the*
Lord muſt not ſtrive, but be gentle unto all men, apt to teach, patient, in Meekneſs in-
ſtructing thoſe that oppoſe themſelves. And he adviſes All Chriſtians, to *let their Mode-*
Phil. iv. 5.   *ration be known unto all men:* Their *Moderation:* that is, *not* a luke-warmneſs or in-
difference in *religion,* an indifference in the great and *weightier matters of the Law,*
(which is the *luke-warmneſs* reproved in the Text, and, which is very conſiſtent with
men's being *infinitely zealous* about *Trifles;*) but, by *Moderation,* St *Paul* means *That*
Meekneſs, Calmneſs, and *Equitableneſs* of Spirit, which very well agrees with, and indeed uſually accompanies, the *higheſt poſſible Zeal* for *Truth and Virtue.* The Want of
This Spirit it was, that the ſame Apoſtle complains of in the *Corinthians,* in the follow-
                                                                                      ing

                                                                                        4

ing manner; *Whereas there is among you envying and ſtrife and diviſions, are ye not car-* **S E R M.** *nal, and walk as men?* His Meaning is, do ye not act like men who are more con- **LXVIII.** cerned for *your own private parties* and *paſſions,* than for the *religion of Chriſt? Now* ~~~ *ye are full, now ye are rich, ye have reigned as Kings without us;* that is, ye are puffed 1 Cor. iii. 3. up, and grown inſolent and domineering, in your ſeveral Parties and Diviſions, one 1 Cor. iv. 8. againſt another. The manner of expreſſion, is exactly like That in the Text; where our Saviour, having rebuked the Church of *Laodicea* for being *lukewarm* and *careleſs* as to the *Works* or Fruits of true religion, immediately adds, Yet *thou ſayeſt, I am rich, and increaſed with goods, and have need of nothing; and knoweſt not that thou art wretched, and miſerable, and poor, and blind, and naked.*

B U T to proceed: How right ſoever the *Object* of our Zeal be, yet if That Zeal be accompanied with the *Wrath of man,* the nature of it (St *James* tells us) is entirely al- Jam i. 20. tered, and it *worketh not the righteouſneſs of God.* For *Wars and Fightings,* Jam. iv. 1. (that is, *Hatred, Animoſities, Contentiouſneſs,* and *Deſire of Rule over each other,*) can proceed from nothing but from *your Luſts,* that is, from worldly paſſions, not from Zeal for true Religion. And whoſoever takes pleaſure in injuring his *Brother,* 'tis abſurd and ridiculous (St *John* aſſures us) for ſuch a one to pretend he does it out of Zeal towards *God: If a man ſay, I love God, and hateth his Brother, he is a liar,* 1 Joh. iv. 20.

3*dly* and *Laſtly.* T H E *Laſt* particular, by which a *religious Zeal* is diſtinguiſhed from a *human paſſion,* and by which it becomes truly and properly a *Chriſtian virtue,* is the End or Intention towards which it is directed. A *Zeal* for inquiring after *Truth* may poſſibly be nothing but *Curioſity;* and a Zeal even for *doing what is right,* may poſſibly ſometimes proceed merely from *Temporal Views.* In which caſes, poſſibly indeed it may be an *uſeful and commendable Paſſion;* provided the *Manner and Circumſtances,* in which it expreſſes itſelf, be not faulty. But nothing makes it properly a *Chriſtian virtue,* but when, *together with* all the forementioned *requiſites,* the End alſo or Intention, to which it is ultimately directed, is the *Honour and Glory of God.* By the *Honour and Glory of God,* always taking care that we mean not any thing *imaginary and enthuſiaſtick,* which often turns *religious zeal* into ſome of the *worſt* and moſt *pernicious* of all *vices;* but that thereby be conſtantly meant the *eſtabliſhment of God's Kingdom of* righteouſneſs *here,* in Truth and Peace and Charity; in order to the *ſalvation of men's ſouls hereafter in his eternal Kingdom of* Glory. I conclude therefore with the words of the wiſe Son of *Sirach,* Eccluſ. vii. 36. *Whatſoever thou takeſt in hand, remember the* End, *and thou ſhalt never do amiſs.*

SERMON LXIX.

The miraculous Birth of CHRIST.

[Preached on Chriſtmas-Day.]

MATT. I. 22, 23.

Now all this was done, that it might be fulfilled which was ſpoken of the Lord by the Prophet, ſaying; Behold, a Virgin ſhall be with Child, and ſhall bring forth a Son, and they ſhall call his Name Emmanuel, *which being interpreted is God with Us.*

SERM. LXIX. IT is a very *uſual Method* with *Unbelievers* ;——And yet here, before I proceed, it may be proper and neceſſary to premiſe, that by *Unbelievers* I would at This Time be underſtood to mean, *not*, men of ſuch a diſpoſition as St *Thomas* was before his Converſion ; rational and inquiſitive perſons, Lovers of Truth and Virtue, men deſirous to know and to obey the Will of God, and careful to keep a Conſcience void of Offence both towards God and towards Men ; yet at the ſame time, ſenſible of the Difficulties wherewith the Divine Providence has thought fit to permit even very important Truths to be ſometimes attended ; and careful, for That Reaſon, not to be impoſed upon, nor to receive things without good Evidence, either of Reaſon, or of Revelation : Theſe, I ſay, are *not* the *Unbelievers* I would at preſent be underſtood to have in View. For concerning ſuch perſons as theſe, our Saviour ſeems to ſpeak, when he ſays, they are *not far from the Kingdom of God.* But there is *another* ſort of *Unbelievers*, who, having no right ſenſe of the Liberty of Human Actions, of the natural and eſſential Difference of Good and Evil, of the Moral Government of God over the World, of a Judgment to come, and of a Future State of Rewards and Puniſhments ; do therefore ſeek all poſſible opportunities, not of enquiring into, and impartially examining, but of *cavilling* againſt the Authority of Chriſt and the Truth of his Religion, as being the great Support and Confirmation of theſe Doctrines of Nature, with the Belief of which all Notions of Fatality or Neceſſity, and all Licentiouſneſs either of Sceptical Opinions or of Vicious Practice, is altogether inconſiſtent.

Now of *This* ſort of *Unbelievers*, I ſay, the *uſual Method* is to attack ſome particular uncertain Doctrines in the *Syſtems* of diſagreeing Sects of Chriſtians, and then conclude that they have deſtroyed *Chriſtianity* itſelf : Or they ſet themſelves to expoſe particular *Weak* Writers ; and then leave it to be ſuppoſed, that *All* Defenders of the Doctrine of Chriſt are *Fools* : Or they pick perhaps out of *Better* Writers *ſome* inconcluſive Reaſonings, and *weak* Arguments ; truſting it will thence be inferred, that there is *no Strength* in the *Strongeſt* : Or they repreſent Chriſtianity as *relying* upon ſome *Foundation*, upon which it *does not rely* ; and then conclude that it has *no Foundation* at all : Or they demonſtrate ſome *Facts* to be *no Proofs* of the *Truth* of the Goſpel, which *never* were *intended* for Proofs ; and then infer, that there is *no Proof* of it at all : Or

I   they

they dreſs up particular Facts or Doctrines, in *ridiculous Circumſtances* ; and then repre- S E R M.
ſent the *Things* themſelves, as Objects of *Ridicule* : Or they lay *great Streſs* upon ſome LXIX.
very *obſcure,* or more *difficult Prophecy* : and thence infer, that *no Streſs* is to be laid
upon *Any* : Or becauſe, in the nature of the Thing, almoſt *Any ſingle* Prophecy may
poſſibly be *imagined* applicable, in ſome ſenſe or other, to Some *Other* perſon ; therefore *all of them together,* centring uniformly in *Chriſt* and in *Him alone,* yet are not
rightly *in Fact* applied to *Him.*

T H E words of *my Text* are a particular and very remarkable *Inſtance* of Some of the
Caſes in the foregoing Obſervation.　It has been ſuppoſed by Many, that this *ſingular*
and *miraculous* Fact, of the *manner* of our Lord's *Birth,* recorded thus in the *Begin-*
ning and *firſt Entrance* of the Goſpel-Hiſtory, both by St *Matthew* and St *Luke* ; and
urged moreover by St *Matthew* as an unqueſtionable Verification of an Antient and (at
firſt Sight) as remarkable a Prophecy, as any is to be found in the whole *Old Teſta-*
ment : It has been ſuppoſed (I ſay) by Many, that *This Miraculous Fact,* thus circum-
ſtantiated, and thus uſhering-in the whole following Hiſtory of the Goſpel, muſt needs
have been intended by the Evangeliſt, as a primary and fundamental Part of the *Proof*
of our Lord's divine Commiſſion.　Which ſince in reality it *could not poſſibly* be ; as being a Fact which, in the nature of things, could not *itſelf* be proved, till the Truth of
Chriſt's Miſſion and the Veracity of his Followers had *firſt* been clearly eſtabliſhed:
Hence they have endeavoured to deſtroy the Authority of the Sacred Writer, as inſiſting (at the very Beginning of his Hiſtory) upon a *Proof* which could not poſſible be of
any *Uſe* towards the Conviction of Unbelievers ; and as confirming it by a *Prophecy,*
which they think cannot be ſhown to be rightly applied, ſince the Words may be capable of another Interpretation.

F O R the removing therefore of This Prejudice, and to clear more fully the Meaning and Intent of my Text, I ſhall endeavour diſtinctly to make out the *three* following Particulars.

I. T H A T this Hiſtory of our Lord's *miraculous Birth,* evidently in fact *was not,*
and in the nature of Things *could not poſſibly* be, intended by the Evangeliſt in this
place, as any *Proof,* for the Conviction of Unbelievers, either of the Dignity of
Chriſt's Perſon, or of the Truth of his Doctrine, or of the Reality of his Divine Commiſſion.

2. T H A T yet nevertheleſs, in the Nature of the Thing, when a Perſon of ſuch
Dignity as our Lord profeſſed himſelf to be, and with ſuch a Divine Commiſſion,
was to come into the World ; this one particular Diſtinction, the *miraculous* manner of his *Birth,* was in itſelf a very *reaſonable, proper,* and *not incredible* Circumſtance.

3. T H A T conſequently the Sacred Writer of the *Life* of our Saviour, had *juſt rea-*
ſon, when aſſured of the Truth of the Fact from things which *followed,* to inſert this
miraculous Circumſtance into the *Beginning* of his *Hiſtory* ; and, in That Manner and
to That Purpoſe for which he relates it, had a *juſt Right,* and *good and ſufficient*
Grounds, to *apply the Prophecy* here cited, as a Prediction of it.

I. I ſay, This Hiſtory of our Lord's *miraculous Birth,* evidently in fact *was not,*
and in the Nature of Things *could not poſſibly* be, intended by the Evangeliſt in this
place, as any *Proof* for the conviction of Unbelievers, either of the Dignity of Chriſt's
Perſon, or of the Truth of his Doctrine, or of the Reality of his Divine Commiſſion.
That it *could not poſſibly* be alledged in way of *Proof* of any of theſe things to be Unbelievers, is moſt evident for This Plain Reaſon ; becauſe in the Nature of Things the
Fact was *itſelf* incapable of being proved, till the Truth of Chriſt's Miſſion and the
Veracity of his Followers had *firſt* been eſtabliſhed.　And that *in fact* it was *never* by
the Evangeliſt *intended* as ſuch, appears no leſs evidently from hence　that though both

by

S E R M. by St *Matthew* and St *Luke* it be laid down as the *Beginning and Foundation* of their
LXIX. Account of the *Life* of Chrift, yet in the Account they give us of his *Preaching*, it is
never once mentioned by Either of Thefe very Evangelifts, or by Either of the Two
Other Evangelifts, as ever alledged by *Chrift* in proof of his being the true Meffiah.
Nor in the Book of the *Acts*, is it ever mentioned as urged by the *Apoftles*, in *Their
Preaching* at any time either to *Jews* or *Gentiles*. Nor in any of the *Epiftles* of *Paul*,
or of any other of the Apoftles, is it ever referred to under That View. It would have
been *abfurd* to alledge, in preaching to Unbelievers, a Fact which *itfelf prefuppofed* the
Truth of Chrift's Miffion ; and which could not have been proved, without firft taking
for granted the Truth of That very Doctrine, in Proof of which This Fact was to have
been alledged. But the *Beginning* of the *Hiftory* of the *Life* of Chrift, is a very different thing from the *Hiftory* of his *beginning* to *Preach* the Gofpel. What happened
Firft in *Time*, could not but of neceffity be *Laft* in *Proof*: The *Credibility* of the
Invifible Miracle of his *Birth*, depending entirely on the *Vifible* miraculous Proofs, by
which our Lord afterwards gave Evidence of *his* own Commiffion, and by which his
Apoftles afcertained *Their own* Veracity, and the *Truth* of the Accounts they gave concerning *Him*.

    2. THOUGH it could not indeed be alledged properly, in *Proof* of the Truth of his
Doctrine to Unbelievers ; yet neverthelefs, in the *nature of the Thing*, when a Perfon
of fuch Dignity as our Lord profeffed himfelf to be, and with fuch a Divine Commiffion, was to come into the World ; this one particular Diftinction, the *miraculous*
manner of his *Birth*, was *in itfelf* a very *reafonable, proper*, and *not incredible* Cir-
1 Cor. xv. 47. cumftance. We are taught in Scripture, that as *the firft man* and his Pofterity, *were
of the Earth, Earthy ; the fecond man was the Lord from Heaven*. And our Lord himfelf frequently declared to his Difciples, that he *came down from Heaven* ; that he *came*
Joh. iii. 13. *forth from the Father, and came into the World*. The Meaning of thefe Expreffions is
xvi. 28. explained to us in Other places ; where it is declared that he *was in the Beginning The
Word of God*, the *original* Revealer of the Will of the Almighty to his Creatures, long
before he *was made Flefh and dwelt among Us*, even from the Creation of the World :
Having been (as St *Paul* expreffes it) *in the Form of God*, that is, in the Prophetick
Language, the *Angel* or *Meffenger* of the *Covenant*, before he *took upon him the Form
of a Servant, and was made in the Likenefs of Men, and found in fafhion as a Man* ;
Phil. ii. 8. Now This being the Cafe ; The moft *obvious* manner in which it might
naturally be *expected* that fo extraordinary a Perfon, a Perfon of fuch Dignity as to
Joh. xvii. 5. have had *glory with God before the World was* ; I fay, the manner in which it was moft
natural to have *expected* that fuch a Perfon fhould come into the World, was in a way
different from *the Sons of Men*. It was the Appointment of Divine Wifdom, for *Reafons of Government* in the infinite and eternal Kingdom of God over the Univerfe, that
his Mercy and Compaffion towards Penitent Sinners fhould be difpenfed in a particular
Method through the Atonement made by the Blood of Chrift. In order to make This
Atonement, and to become capable of Suffering as a Sacrifice by the fhedding of his
Blood, it was neceffary for the Son of God to have *a Body prepared for him* ; Heb. x. 5.
and to be *born* after the *Likenefs of Men* : Ch. ii. 14 ; *Forafmuch as the children are
Partakers of Flefh and Blood, he alfo himfelf likewife took part of the fame, that through
Death he might deftroy him that had the Power of Death, that is, the Devil*. Yet, being *fuch* a Perfon as the Scripture defcribes him, fent down immediately *from Heaven* ;
his *Birth* could not *naturally*, if I may fo fpeak, but be, *miraculous*, as the Text reprefents it. And *miraculous* as it was, it was yet really, in the *nature of the Thing*, nothing *more miraculous*, excepting only that God has not thought fit to do the like *continually* ; it was *in itfelf*, I fay, not at all *more miraculous*, than what we vulgarly call
(without *Any Meaning* or *Signification* in that Phrafe,) *the Courfe of Nature* ; that is,

the

the Courfe of a *mere empty Word*, or *abſtract Notion*, which has no *Being* or Reality of S E R M. *Exiſtence*, and confequently cannot be the efficient *Caufe* of any thing.   LXIX.

3. THIS *miraculous Birth* of Chriſt, the Evangeliſt had *juſt Reaſon*, when affured of the Truth of the Fact from things which *followed*, to infert at the *Beginning* of his *Hiſtory* of our Saviour's *Life*; and, in That Manner, and to That Purpofe for which he relates it, had a *juſt Right*, and *good and ſufficient Grounds*, to *apply* the *Prophecy* here cited, as a Prediction of it.

WHEN our Lord firſt told his Difciples that he *came down from Heaven*, that *he* Joh. iii. 13; *came forth from the Father, and came into the World*; they did not clearly under- xvi. 28. ſtand his Meaning; nor probably did the *Bleſſed Virgin* herſelf comprehend the *Reaſon* of That miraculous Work which God worked in *Her*. But, as St *Luke* tells us, *Mary kept all theſe things, and pondered them in her Heart*; ch. ii. 19: And fo did his Difciples, both with regard to *This*, and to *Many Other* things that Jefus did and faid; Mar. ix. 32. Which at firſt they *underſtood not, and were afraid to aſk him*. But *when Jefus was* Luke ii. 50. *glorified*; Joh. xii. 16, and *Luke* xxxiv. 8; *then remembred they* and underſtood many ix 45. xviii. things that *were written of him*, and done and ſpoken by him. Again; *Joh*. ii. 22; John. viii. *When Jefus was riſen from the Dead*, then his Difciples remembred that he had faid 27. x. 6. theſe things *unto them: And they believed the Scripture, and the Word, which Jefus had faid*. When our Lord, by his *Refurrection from the Dead*, had *confirmed* to his Dif-ciples all the *Miracles* which he had worked, and all the Doctrines which he had taught in his *Life-time*; and particularly, before his *Afcenfion* into Heaven, had explained to them the manner of his *Defcent* from thence; which, among other things, *inſured* them of the *Truth*, and *unfolded* to them the *Reaſon*, of the *Miraculouſneſs* of his *Birth*: Then had they juſt grounds to *declare* the *Dignity* of his *Perſon*, and to expect that *Credit* fhould be given by *Believers* to the Accounts they had received of this miracu-lous *Nativity*; though it was what, in the Nature of the Thing, could never properly be alledged in their Preaching, among the Proofs they were to urge for the Conviction of Infidels.

FURTHER: When our Lord, after his Refurrection, *beginning at Moſes and all the Prophets*, had *expounded unto* his Apoſtles *in all the Scriptures the things concerning himſelf*, and *opened their Underſtanding, that they might underſtand the Scriptures*; Luke xxiv. 27, 45; Then they faw plainly, (and any one *Now*, who will trace the whole Thread of the Old Teſtament, may plainly fee) that there is a continued Series and Connexion, one uniform Analogy and Defign, carried on for many Ages by Di-vine Prefcience thro' a Succeffion of Prophecies; which, as in their proper *Centre*, do *All* meet together in *Chriſt*, and in *Him only*; however the *ſingle lines*, when confi-dered *apart*, may many of them be imagined to have another Direction, and point to intermediate Events. Nothing is more *evident*, than that the *Whole Succeffion of Pro-phecies*, can poffibly be applied to *None* but *Chriſt*. Nothing is more *miraculous*, than that they fhould all of them be *capable* of being poffibly applied to *Him*. And what-ever *intermediate* Deliverances or Deliverers of God's People, may *ſeemingly* or *really* be fpoken of upon *particular* Occafions; nothing is more *reaſonable* than to believe; (in the *Apoſtles* certainly, who converfed perfonally with our Lord after his Refurrection, nothing could be more *reaſonable* than to believe,) that the *Ultimate* and *General* View of the *Prophetick Spirit* Always was fixed on *Him*, of whom in *Some* of the Antient Prophecies it is *expreſsly* affirmed, that God's *Servant David ſhall be the Prince* over Ezek. xxxvii. his People *for ever*; that *his Dominion* fhall be *an everlaſting Dominion, which ſhall* 25. Dan. vii. 14. *not paſs away; and his Kingdom, that which ſhall not be deſtroyed*. The Apoſtle St *Mat-thew* therefore had a *juſt Right*, and *good and ſufficient Grounds*, to *apply* to our Lord the *Prophecy* cited by him in my Text. Nor is it of any moment, to what perfon *Ahaz* perhaps might think it confined; or in what fenfe even *Iſaiah* himfelf, poffibly,

SERM.
LXIX.

2 Pet. i. 20.

might underſtand the words. For the Prophets themſelves *ſaw* Theſe things, but *as through a Glaſs darkly*; even as the *Apoſtles* afterwards did, and *We* ſtill do, things that are yet future. For which reaſon, *no Prophecy of the Scripture is* (as St Peter tells us) *of any private Interpretation*; that is, it relates not to things within the Prophet's *own* [ἰδίας] *perſonal* Knowledge; *For the Prophecy came not in old time by the Will of Man, but Holy men of God ſpake as they were moved by the Holy Ghoſt.* So that

1 Pet. i. 10.

even the Prophets themſelves could do nothing more, but *enquire and ſearch diligently*; as the ſame *Apoſtle* expreſſes it: *Searching what, or what manner of time, the Spirit of Chriſt which was in them did ſignify, when it teſtified beforehand the Sufferings of Chriſt, and the glory that ſhould follow.*——*Which things*, not only the Prophets, but even *the Angels* (ſays he) *deſire to look into.* All that was *poſſible*, and all that was *intended*, and all that was *needful* to be underſtood by Thoſe who lived in the Ages *before* our Saviour, was, that God deſigned by his Prophets to keep up in the world a perpetual Expectation and Reliance upon his Promiſes in general, that his True Worſhippers ſhould be ſure finally to meet with an *everlaſting Deliverance*; and a Saviour, of whoſe Kingdom there ſhould be *no End.* This is what *Abraham ſaw afar off*, and rejoiced and *was glad.* And This is what *All the Prophecies* in the Old Teſtament moſt evidently *end* in, whatever intermediate Events ſometimes they may occaſionally *begin* with. *That Prophecy* particularly, cited here by the Evangeliſt in my Text, has *at leaſt thus much* in it; what conſtruction *ſoever*, be put upon the Words. Whatever can be *imagined* to have been in this Prediction promiſed perſonally to *Ahaz*, was fulfilled in its Seaſon: But that the words in the Text had *principally*, if not *ſolely*, a Reference to ſome far greater and more laſting Event; cannot (I think) be doubted by any rational perſon, who conſiders the Solemn *Apoſtrophe* from *Ahaz* to the *whole*

Iſ. viii. 13.

Houſe of Judah, wherewith they are introduced: *Hear ye now, O Houſe of David;—the Lord himſelf ſhall give you a Sign*, (that is, not a Sign to *That generation* then preſent; but to Them a *Promiſe* of what ſhould *finally* be a Sign or Evidence of God's everlaſting Care of his People,) *Behold, a Virgin ſhall conceive, and bear a Son, and ſhall call his Name Immanuel.* And This is ſtill the more reaſonable to be ſo underſtood, if it be compared with what the ſame Prophet ſays concerning the ſame perſon

Iſ. ix. 6.

in a chapter nearly following: *Unto Us a Child is born, unto Us a Son is given, and the Government ſhall be upon his Shoulder*——*Of the Increaſe of his Government and Peace there ſhall be no End,*——*from henceforth even for ever.*

THE Application of what has been ſaid, is; that We who are perſwaded of the Truth of Chriſt's *Miſſion*, and conſequently of his *Doctrine*, muſt endeavour to live ſuitably to That Holy Religion, of which we make Profeſſion: Always remembring, that the End and Deſign of the Goſpel is to *Teach us, that denying Ungodlineſs and worldly Luſts, we ſhould live ſoberly, righteouſly, and godly in this preſent World*; looking *for that bleſſed Hope, and the glorious appearance of the Great God, and of our Saviour Jeſus Chriſt.* And particularly that at This time when we commemorate his Birth, we *keep the Feaſt, not with the Leaven of Malice and Wickedneſs*, or of Rioting and Debauchery; *but with the unleavened Bread of Sincerity*, Soberneſs, *and Truth.*

SERMON

SERMON LXX.

The Prediction of the MESSIAH.

[Preached on Chriſtmas-Day.]

ISAIAH IX. 6.

Unto Us a Child is born, unto Us a Son is given, and the government ſhall be upon his ſhoulder; and his Name ſhall be called Wonderful, Counſellor, The mighty God, the everlaſting Father, the Prince of Peace.

GOD, the Supreme Governor and Lord of the Univerſe; who *worketh all things* SERM. *after the Counſel of his Will*; having appointed, in the unſearchable Wiſdom LXX. of his Government that the Method by which ſinful men ſhould be brought un- to Salvation ſhould be by his Son's Appearing and Suffering in the Fleſh; thought fit, from the Beginning of the World, to give men at firſt obſcure Notices, and afterwards by degrees clearer and clearer Predictions, of a Saviour who ſhould come in the fulneſs of Time, to be their Redeemer, Mediator, Interceſſor and Judge. In which whole Diſpenſation, as in all other Matters, when we affirm that God diſpoſes things *after the Counſel of his own Will*, we muſt always take care ſo to underſtand this, and other the like Expreſſions of Scripture, that it may ſignify, not what vain and preſumptu- ous *men* are apt to mean, when *They* talk of acting according to their *own Will and Pleaſure*; that is, arbitrarily and without reaſon; but the meaning of this ſort of Ex- preſſions, when applied to *God*, who can never *pleaſe* to do any thing but what is beſt, is This only; that *his* mere Will and Pleaſure ought abundantly to ſatisfy us, that tho' *we* do not perhaps know in particular *what* all the reaſons are, yet *in rea- lity* there always *are* in the *things themſelves* the greateſt and ſtrongeſt reaſons, upon ac- count of which every thing that *He* does, is *in itſelf* the beſt and fitteſt to be done. Having therefore in perfect Wiſdom, as Supreme Governor and Lord of all, deter- mined to bring ſinful Man to Salvation by this particular Method; he opened his divine Intention at firſt obſcurely to *Adam*, by promiſing that *the Seed of the Woman ſhould bruiſe the Serpent's Head*: And afterwards a little further to *Abraham*, by ſhowing him that *in His ſeed ſhould all the Nations of the Earth be bleſſed*: Then, with ſtill more diſtinct circumſtances, to *Moſes*; under the numerous types and ſhadows of the Law. And laſtly, more and more plainly and explicitly, as the Time drew nearer, by full and clear Predictions of many ſucceſſive *Prophets*. Under all which ſeveral Diſpenſa- tions, they who obeyed the word of God, according to the manner in which it was Then reſpectively revealed to them, were each of them entitled to the Benefit of the whole Salvation; and, notwithſtanding their different degrees of Knowledge, are all of them finally to be gathered together into One in Chriſt; ſo that He, to whom

2 much

much is revealed, ſhall have nothing over; and He, to whom was revealed but little, ſhall have no lack; when, at the conſummation of all things, they ſhall all meet in one great and general Aſſembly of the firſt-born which are written in Heaven; Patriarchs, Prophets, and Apoſtles; and whoſoever have in all Ages, after the pattern of theſe great Examples, obeyed the Commandments of God as made known to them, whether by the Light of Nature, or by the Law of *Moſes*, or by the Goſpel of Chriſt.

OF all the Prophecies in the Old Teſtament, concerning this Method which the divine Wiſdom has appointed, of bringing men to Salvation; there is none that contains a clearer and more diſtinct, a fuller and more particular prediction, than the words now read unto you for the Subject of our preſent Meditations: *Unto us a Child is born, Unto us a Son is given, and the Government ſhall be upon his ſhoulder; and his Name ſhall be called Wonderful, Counſellor, The mighty God, The everlaſting Father, The Prince of Peace.* In diſcourſing upon which words at This Time, the Method ſhall be, to conſider and explain diſtinctly the ſeveral particulars, whereof the Text conſiſts, in the Order they lie; and from each particular ſo explained, to infer in its place, as we go along, what may be uſefully and practically deduced therefrom.

Unto Us a Child is born: Theſe words, as they ſound in the *Engliſh*, may ſeem at firſt ſight to expreſs nothing more, than the natural Birth of ſome eminent perſon. But in the ſtrict ſenſe of the original, and according to the intention of the whole Prophecy, it is plain they muſt be ſo underſtood, as if they had been thus rendred; *Unto us is born* The *Child*, abſolutely and by way of eminence; That *Child*, whom *all* the Prophecies from the beginning of the World, in their final intention pointed at; whom *this* Prophecy of *Iſaiah*, thro' every part of it, deſcribes under different Characters; and whom the Text may reaſonably be ſuppoſed to refer to as *particularly before-mentioned*; ch. vii. 14. *The Lord himſelf ſhall give you a Sign; behold, a Virgin ſhall conceive and bear a* Son, *and ſhall call his Name Immanuel.* This Birth of Chriſt; as its being of a *Virgin*, was a mark of Dignity more than human; that He, who by the Will of his Father was the *Author* of Nature, might be diſtinguiſhed by being born not after the *Courſe* of Nature; ſo the *Birth itſelf*, his *being born at all*, and coming into the World as *a Child*, was an evidence of the reality of his Incarnation. He was *found* (ſaith St *Paul*) *in faſhion as a Man*, and was *made in the likeneſs of Men:* The meaning is; not in the likeneſs of our *nature*, in the *appearance* only, as oppoſed to the *reality*; but he was made after the likeneſs of *other* Men, by *really* partaking of our infirm *Nature*.

IN order to *redeem* mankind after *that* Method which the Wiſdom of God had from the beginning appointed, it was neceſſary that Chriſt ſhould *ſuffer*; and in order to *That Suffering*, it was neceſſary that he ſhould be *born* after the likeneſs of Men. *Foraſmuch as the children* (ſaith the Apoſtle) *are partakers of Fleſh and Blood, he alſo himſelf took part of the ſame, that through Death he might deſtroy him that had the Power of Death, that is, the Devil;——Wherefore in all things it behoved him to be made like unto his Brethren,* (tempted in all points like as we are, only without ſin, and capable of being touched with the feeling of our infirmities;) *that he might be a merciful and faithful High-Prieſt in things pertaining to God, to make reconciliation for the Sins of the people; For in that He himſelf has ſuffered being tempted, he is able to ſuccour them that are tempted;* Heb. ii. 14. And from hence the ſame Apoſtle in another place, though *There* indeed he ſpeaks *figuratively* concerning Chriſt's *myſtical* Body the Church, yet from *hence* it is that the *Ground* of his *manner of expreſſing himſelf* is taken; *We are members* (ſaith he) *of his Body, of his Fleſh and of his Bones.*

THE proper *Uſe* of this *firſt* Obſervation in the Text, the humiliation of Chriſt in his Birth, is what St *Paul* infers from the ſame obſervation; *Phil.* ii. 5; *Let This mind, the ſame humble mind, be in You, which was alſo in Chriſt Jeſus; who tho' he was in*

the

the form of God, invefted with Divine Authority and Dominion, *yet was not greedy* S E R M.
of appearing as God (fo the words are in the Original;) *but——took upon him the form* LXX.
of a fervant, and was made in the Likenefs of Men; and *glorified not* Himfelf *to be made*
an High-Prieft, but was glorified by *Him that begat him*; Heb. v. 5; and honoured
not *Himfelf*, but was honoured by him that fent him; *Joh.* viii. 54.

IT follows; *Unto Us a Son is given.* And thefe words alfo, like thofe fore-going,
muft be underftood abfolutely and by way of Eminence; *Unto us is given* The
Son; That *Son of Man*, who was *fo*, as *no other* ever was, the Son of *Man*; who
was *fo*, as *no other* ever can be, the Son of *God: That* divine Perfon, who was
the Subject of all the Prophecies, from the foundation of the World, and the Expectation of all Nations. The original of the *former* character, his being the Son
of *Man*, is that fublime defcription which the Prophet *Daniel* gives of his Vifion;
ch. vii. 13; *I faw in the Night-Vifions, and behold, one like* the Son of Man, *came*
with the clouds of Heaven, and came to the Antient of days, and they brought him near be-
fore him; *and there was given him dominion and glory and a Kingdom.* From this prophetical defcription it is, that our Saviour in the Gofpels is fo conftantly characte-
rized by That Title of *the Son of Man:* Mat. xxiv. 30; *Then fhall appear the Sign of*
the Son of Man in Heaven, (the Signal given you by the Prophet *Daniel,* the Signal
of That *Son of Man* there defcribed,) *and they fhall fee him coming in the clouds of Hea-*
ven with Power and great Glory. And *Joh.* iii. 13; *The Son of Man which is in Hea-*
ven. And in the Book of the *Revelation,* ch. i. 13; the very *words* of *Daniel* are
tranfcribed; *one* like *unto the Son of Man*; and ch. xiv. 14; *Upon the cloud one fat*, like
unto the Son of Man. The *other* character of our Saviour, his being the Son of *God,*
was given him *firft* upon account of his being *born miraculoufly* of the Virgin by the
immediate Power of God, *Luc.* i. 35; Then again, upon account of his being *raifed* Luc. i. 32.
from the dead by the like miraculous Power of the Almighty; *Rom.* i. 4: *Acts* xiii. 33. Mar. v. 7.
And laftly, upon account of his being revealed to be That divine Perfon, who, deriving his Being from the Father in a fingular and incomprehenfible manner; and having
been with the Father, from the Beginning; and having had Glory with Him, before the
World was; and having originally exercifed the Father's Power, in the Creation of the
World; and having fince in all ages appeared *in the form of God,* as the Word, the
Meffenger, the Reprefentative, the *Image, of the Invifible God*; at length, in the Fulnefs
of Time, was *made Flefh* and *dwelt among us, and we beheld his glory, the glory as* Joh. i. 14.
of the only-begotten of the Father, full of grace and truth.

UNTO Us, fays the Prophet in the Text, is this Son of God given: unto *Us,* as it
was *Then* literally underftood, the *pofterity of Abraham,* the Nation of the *Jews*; but,
as it is *Now* diftinctly revealed in the Gofpel, and as it was even *Then* obfcurely predicted, unto Us *Gentiles* alfo is he given; unto us that are *far off,* as well as to them
that are *near*; unto us *Sinners,* of all Nations and of all Ages; even unto *all Mankind,*
who are willing to repent, and reform their manners, and make acknowledgment of
the Truth ; For God *would have all men to be faved,* and wills *not that any fhould perifh,*
but that all fhould come to repentance : Nay even to *Them* therefore which never heard of
him, muft the Benefit of his Coming extend, according to the proportion of their Capacities unknown to us ; For *the Mercy* of God is, without exception, *over all his works.*

TO Us is This Son *given.* It is not without reafon, that the word *given* is fo carefully and conftantly inferted, and fo great an emphafis and ftrefs laid upon it, in almoft all the Texts of both the Old and New Teftament, which mention the coming
of Chrift into the World. The intent of it is, to exprefs to us diftinctly the refpective parts, which the Father and the Son bore in the redemption of the World ; that
neither the One, nor the Other, neither he that gave, nor he that was willing to be
given for us, fhould be defrauded of their proper Honour. That God *gave* his Son,

out of his bofom; is expreffive to us of the *Father's Supreme Authority*, and of his original, effential, and eternal *Goodnefs*: That the Son gave *himfelf* for us, or was *willing* to be *given*, denotes the *Love* of *Chrift* towards Mankind; and explains the *Juftice* of his being appointed to fuffer, tho' he was an *innocent* perfon; becaufe *That* appointment, as it was by the Will of the Father, fo it was alfo by his own free confent. The *firft* of thefe, *viz.* the *Supreme* Authority of the *Father*, is fet forth in thofe Texts of Scripture, where it is affirmed that *in the fulnefs of Time God* fent *forth his Son*, Gal. iv. 4; *that he faved us according to his* own *purpofe and grace in Chrift Jefus*, 2 Tim. viii. 9; even *according to the* purpofe *of him who worketh all things after the counfel of his own Will*; Eph. i. 11. And indeed in the Nature of things it is evident, that the Supreme Power *to* whom the fatisfaction is to be made, muft appoint *what* fatisfaction he will be pleafed to accept. The *Second* of thefe, *viz.* the *original* Goodnefs of the *Father*, is fet forth in thofe Texts, where the Scripture teaches us, *that God fo loved the World, that he gave his only begotten Son, that whofoever believeth on him fhould not perifh, but have everlafting life*; Joh. iii. 16; and 1 Joh. iv. 9; *In this was manifefted the* Love *of God towards us, becaufe that God fent his only-begotten Son into the World, that we might live through Him*; and ver. 10; *he loved us, and fent his Son to be the propitiation for our Sins*. The *third* particular, *viz.* the Love of *Chrift* in being *willing* to be thus fent or given for us, is expreffed in thofe Texts, wherein we are taught, that Chrift *gave himfelf a ranfom for all*; 1 Tim. ii. 6; that he gave himfelf *for us, that he might redeem us from all iniquity*; Tit. ii. 14. And Both thefe together, (the Authority and Goodnefs of the *Father* in giving his Son, and the Love of *Chrift* in being willing to be given for us,) are expreffed in one, *Gal.* i. 4; *who gave* himfelf *for us, according to the Will of* God, *and our Father.*

THE *Ufes* of *This particular*, are; 1*ft*, that we acknowledge *primarily* the original effential *Goodnefs* and *Compaffion* of *God our Father*, as the *firft* Caufe and Author of our Salvation; upon which account, St *Paul* frequently ftiles the Father, *God our Saviour*; and that therefore we look not upon him as a cruel and implacable Judge; but on the contrary extol with all thankfulnefs our *Redemption through* Chrift, *to the praife of the glory of* His *Grace, who has made us accepted in the beloved*, and has given us *the Adoption of children by Jefus Chrift to* himfelf, *according to the good pleafure of his own Will*; Eph. i. 5. 2*dly*, That in the next place we thankfully exprefs our Gratitude alfo to our *Saviour himfelf*, who condefcended for our fakes to become Man;

Eph. v. 2.
Rev. i. 5.

who *loved us, and gave himfelf for us*; and *wafhed us from our Sins in his own blood, and has made us Kings and Priefts to God and his Father*. 3*dly*, That from *This Great* Inftance of the divine Grace and Goodnefs, we learn to depend upon the fame Beneficence for all *other* good things likewife: For He *that fpared not his own Son, but delivered him for us all, how fhall he not with Him alfo freely give us* all things; *Rom.* viii. 32. Not, a Liberty to *fin*, that *Grace* may further abound; God forbid; but all *good* things, all things really profitable to our prefent and future Happinefs. *Laftly*, that from this wonderful Love of God towards *Us*, we learn our *Own* Obligation to love *one another*; 1 Joh. iv. 11; *Beloved, if God fo loved Us, we ought alfo to love one another.*

AND thus much concerning the firft part of the words, *Unto us a Child is born, Unto us a Son is given.*

IT follows; *And the Government fhall be upon his Shoulder.* The *Jews*, though they acknowledged thefe words were to be applied to the *Meffiah*, yet they underftood them of the Dominion only of a *temporal* Prince, who fhould fubdue their enemies for them. But the opening of this Prophecy by degrees in further predictions, was fuch as ought to have given *Them* better Notions of this matter; and the Account *We* have in the New Teftament of the accomplifhment of all thofe predictions has from *Us* removed all appearance of difficulty in the underftanding them. The true meaning

meaning of the words, is begun to be opened in the very next verfe immediately following the Text; *Of the increafe of his government and peace there fhall be no end, upon
the Throne of David, and upon his Kingdom, to order it, and to eftablifh it with judgment and with juftice from henceforth even for ever*; ver. 7. In the Prophecy of *Daniel*, it is explained a little further; ch. ii. 44; *The God of Heaven fhall fet up a Kingdom which fhall never be deftroyed, —— and it fhall ftand for ever*. And ftill more
clearly; ch. vii. 13; *I faw in the night-vifions, and behold, one like the Son of man came
with the clouds of Heaven, and came to the Antient of days, and they brought him near
before him; And there was given him dominion and glory and a Kingdom, that all people,
nations and languages fhould ferve him; his dominion is an everlafting dominion, and
his Kingdom that which fhall not be deftroyed.* This was a fufficiently plain intimation,
that the Kingdom of the Meffiah was not to be a worldly temporal Kingdom. The
Application of thefe Prophecies to *Chrift*, is made exprefsly by the Angel to the Bleffed
Virgin; *Luke* i. 32: *He fhall be great, and fhall be called the Son of the Higheft, ——
and he fhall reign over the houfe of Jacob for ever, and of his Kingdom there fhall
be no end.* What *manner* of Dominion this was to be, our Saviour himfelf began *more
clearly* to explain; Matt. xxviii. 18: *All Power is given to me in Heaven and Earth.*
This difcovered that it was to be a *fpiritual* Kingdom, more *extenfive*, as well as more
lafting, than Earthly Dominions. The Principal *Afts* of Power in this fpiritual Kingdom, are expreffed by St *Peter*; *Afts* x. 42: *He is ordained of God to be Judge of Quick
and Dead; and that through his Name whofoever believeth in him fhall receive remiffion of Sins.* And the full *Extent* of this *whole Dominion* is fet forth by St *Paul*, in
thofe paffages of his Epiftles, where he tells us that Chrift *fitteth at the right hand of*
the Throne of God, being *Head over all things*; *exalted far above all principality, and
power, and might, and dominion, and every name that is named not only in This World,
but alfo in that which is to come*; *Angels and Authorities and Powers being made
fubjeft unto him*, and *all things put under his feet.* To which defcription the Apoftle yet
thought it neceffary to add the following caution; 1 Cor. xv. 24, 27; *But when he faith
all things are put under him, it is manifeft that he is excepted which did put all things
under him; And (in the end) when all things fhall be fubdued unto him, then fhall the
Son alfo himfelf be fubjeft unto Him that put all things under Him, (having delivered
up the Kingdom to God even the Father,) that God* even the Father *may be all in all.*
Which *delivering up of the Kingdom*, if any one afked *how* it is confiftent with thofe
forementioned prophecies of his *reigning for ever*; the Anfwer is plain, That as of the
Saints, under Chrift their Head and Lord, it is affirmed, *Rev.* xxii. 5, that *they fhall
reign for ever and ever*; fo of *Chrift* in an infinitely higher fenfe, even *after* his delivering up the Kingdom to the Father it will ftill be true, that of his Dominion *with*
and *under* the Father, *there fhall be no End.* And This is the full meaning of *That*
Expreffion, *The Government fhall be upon his fhoulder.*

Heb. xii. 2.
Eph. i. 22.
Col. ii. 10.
Phil. ii. 11.
Eph. i. 21.
1 Pet. iii. 22.
1 Cor. xv. 27.
Eph. i. 22.
Heb. ii. 8.

THE remaining part of the Text, is a further Defcription of the *Perfon*, upon *whofe
fhoulder* it was prophefied *This Government fhould be*; it is a further defcription of his
Perfon, under four diftinct Names or Characters. The *Firft* is; *And his Name fhall be
called Wonderful, Counfellor.* The term, *Wonderful*, fignifies, that the Perfon was to
be of *Secret* and Greater *Dignity*, than the *Jews* expected: And fo the Word is of the
fame import, with that more antient intimation given to *Jacob*, when he wreftled with
him; *Gen.* xxxii. 29; *Wherefore is it that thou doft afk after my Name?* and to *Manoah*;
Judg. xiii. 18; *Why afkeft thou thus after my Name, feeing it is fecret?* The other term,
Counfellor, fignifies the *Revealer of the Secret* Counfel *of God*; For fo the Gofpel is
frequently ftiled in Scripture, the whole *Counfel of God*; the *hidden wifdom*; the *myftery
which has been hid from ages and from generations, but now is made manifeft to his
Saints*; the *myftery which was kept fecret fince the World began, but now is made manifeft*:

Μεγάλης βελῆς
ἀγγελ©-,
Afts xx. 27.
1 Cor. ii. 7.
Eph. iii. 9, 10.
11.
Col. i. 26.
Rom. xvi. 25.

SERM. *nifeſt: and by the Scriptures of the Prophets, according to the commandment of the e-*
LXX. *verlaſting God, made known to all Nations for the obedience of Faith.* Upon *This*

Joh. i. 1.
Rev. xix. 13.
Mal. iii. 1.

account it is, that Chriſt is called *The* Word *of God,* the Revealer of his Will, the *Angel* or *Meſſenger of his Covenant,* and, in the words of the Text, *Wonderful, Counſellor.*

THE *Second* Character is, He ſhall be called *The mighty God,* or *mighty Lord.* The meaning of which phraſe, has been already in good meaſure explained under that foregoing character, *The government ſhall be upon his ſhoulder*; And the compleat import of it is more fully expreſſed to us in thoſe places of the New Teſtament, wherein Chriſt is

Heb. i. 2.
Acts x. 36.
Rom. x. 12.
xiv. 9.
Rev. i. 5.
xvii. 14.
xix. 16.
Heb. i. 8.
John i. 1.
xx. 28.

ſtiled *Heir of all things,* Lord *of all* or over *all,* Lord *both of the Dead and Living, the Prince of the Kings of the Earth, the Lord of Lords and King of Kings,* and, in one word, (by the appointment of the Father,) *our Judge, our Lord, and our God :* The Sum and Intent of all which Titles together, is accurately ſet forth by St *Paul* in that moſt lively deſcription; *Phil.* ii. 9; *God has given him a Name which is above every Name ; that at the name of Jeſus every knee ſhould bow,* (every Creature ſhould ſubmit to *His* Authority,) *of things in Heaven, and things in Earth, and things under the Earth ; and that every tongue ſhould confeſs that Jeſus Chriſt is Lord, to the glory of God the Father.*

THE *Third* Character is, *He ſhall he called the everlaſting Father.* Which Phraſe, as it lies in our Tranſlation, is very apt to be miſtaken. For if thereby be underſtood, that the *Son* is the *Father* ; this would be plainly *confounding the Perſons* of the Father and the Son, and (by a manifeſt Abſurdity) making *the Son* to be *the Father of Himſelf.* Which manner of ſpeaking is ſo much the worſe, becauſe there were in the Primitive times certain Falſe Teachers who did ſo ſpeak, and whoſe Doctrine (being of worſe conſequence than at firſt ſight appeared) was ſeverely reproved by the Apoſtles. *He is an Antichriſt,* ſaith St *John, that denieth the Father and the Son,* 1 *Joh.* ii. 22. And *they ſhall bring in,* ſaith St *Peter, damnable hereſies, even denying the Lord that bought them ;* 2 Pet. ii. 1; ſpeaking of *thoſe,* who in reality denied our Saviour to have

Beſt Copies of
LXX.
Πατηρ μελλον-
τος αιων-.
*Pater ſeculi
futuri* Vulgg.

any Being at all, by making the Son to be nothing elſe but merely another Name for the Father. The true rendering therefore of theſe words of the Prophet, is, not *the everlaſting Father,* but the *Father* or *Lord of the future everlaſting Age,* the *Age of the Goſpel ;* concerning which the Apoſtle declares, *Heb.* ii. 5. that to *Chriſt* only, and not to *Angels,* hath God *put in ſubjection* this *Age to come.*

Laſtly, THE *Fourth* and *Laſt* Character here given to our Saviour, is, that He ſhall be called *The Prince of Peace.* The meaning of which Title, was firſt in ſome degree explained by the Angels to the Shepherds, when they ſung that Hymn; *Luke* ii. 14 ; *Peace on* Earth, *good will towards* Men ; which was well anſwered with That *Hoſannah,* the Diſciples ſung to our Saviour, ch. xix. 38 : *Peace in* Heaven, that is, reconciliation with *God.* More diſtinctly afterwards by St *Peter ; Acts* x. 36, 43. *God ſent unto the children of Iſrael, preaching peace by Jeſus Chriſt, he is Lord of All* ; (that is, eſtabliſhing Peace and Unity between *Jews* and *Gentiles,* under *Jeſus Chriſt* their Common *Lord,) that through his Name whoſoever believeth in him, ſhould receive remiſſion of Sins.* Moſt fully and clearly of all, by St *Paul,* Rom. v. 1 : *Being juſtified by Faith, we have* Peace *with God through our Lord Jeſus Chriſt* : and *Eph.* ii. 14. *He is our* Peace, *who hath made Both One,* that is, both *Jews* and *Gentiles* ; and hath——*reconciled Both unto God in one Body by the Croſs, having——preached Peace to you which were afar off, and to them that were nigh :* and *Col.* i. 19. *It pleaſed the Father——by Him, (having made Peace through the Blood of his Croſs) to reconcile all things unto himſelf ;——and you that were ſometimes alienated, and Enemies in your mind by wicked works, yet Now hath he reconciled.* The *Uſes* of this laſt particular are ; *Firſt,* Since God has graciouſly been pleaſed to ſend us this Word of reconciliation by the Prince of

3

Peace,

Peace, that therefore *We on our part* be also willing to be reconciled to *Him*, by for- S E R M.
saking thofe Sins which are the caufe of his difpleafure; *Now then,* faith St *Paul, we*   LXX.
are ambaffadors for Chrift ; *as though God did befeech you by us* ; *we pray you in Chrift's*
ftead, be ye reconciled to God ; 2 Cor. v. 20. *Secondly,* Having fo great an Interceffor
for us, as the Prince of Peace Himfelf, the Son of the living God ; that therefore we
come boldly unto the Throne of Grace, having *accefs with confidence through the Faith of* Heb. iv. 16.
him, Heb. x. 19. *Having therefore, brethren, boldnefs to enter into the Holieft by the* Eph. iii. 12.
blood of Jefus, by a new and living way which he hath confecrated for us ;———and ha-
ving an High-Prieft over the houfe of God ; let us draw near with a true Heart, in full
affurance of Faith. Thirdly, That yet we be careful to confider, that this peace and
reconciliation purchafed for us by Chrift, is only upon condition of our future obedience : For fo the Apoftle adds in the words next immediately following thofe now
cited ; *let us draw near———in full affurance of faith, having our Heart fprinkled from*
an evil confcience, and our bodies wafhed with pure Water ; that is, having our minds
cleanfed with that purification from wickednefs, the Sign and Emblem of which is the
Baptifm of Water : And *Col.* i. 23. God hath now *reconciled* you to himfelf, faith
St *Paul, if ye continue in the faith, grounded and fettled, and be not moved away from*
the hope of the Gofpel. Fourthly, That having fo great a *Mediator* as the Prince of
Peace appointed us of *God,* we fuffer no others to be joined with him by *human inven-*
tion. For as worfhipping any other *God,* befides the *Father Almighty,* is Idolatry a-
gainft *God,* or fetting up *Idols* in the place of *God :* So worfhipping any other *Mediator,*
befides his only *Son* our Lord, is Idolatry againft *Chrift,* or fetting up *Idol-Mediators.*
They who worfhip Saints and Angels, *beguile themfelves of their reward,* faith the
Apoftle, *not holding the Head,* which is *Chrift, Col.* ii. 18. *Laftly,* Upon this particular great occafion of commemorating thankfully the *Birth* of the Prince of Peace,
let us keep the Feaft worthily and as becometh Chriftians ; *not with old leaven, neither*
with the leaven of malice and wickednefs, or of rioting and debauchery, but *with the*
unleavened bread of Sincerity, Sobernefs *and Truth.*

SERMON LXXI.

The Character of the MESSIAH.

[Preached on Chriſtmas-Day.]

GAL. IV. 4, 5.

But when the fulneſs of time was come, God ſent forth his Son made of a woman, made under the law ; To redeem them that were under the law, that we might receive the adoption of Sons.

SERM.
LXXI.

THE principal Deſign of St *Paul* in this Epiſtle, is to vindicate the truth and juſtice of God in aboliſhing the *Jewiſh* religion ſo far as concerned the *Gentile* Converts, and eſtabliſhing the *Chriſtian* alone in its room : againſt thoſe who contended that even the *Gentile* Diſciples were obliged to obſerve the law of *Moſes*, and that the Religion of Chriſt was to be added to That of *Moſes*, and not That of *Moſes* to be taken away by Chriſt. Amongſt many Arguments which the Apoſtle makes uſe of to confute theſe falſe Teachers, he begins this ivth chapter with the Similitude of a young Heir's being under Tutors and Governours; *ver.* 1 and 2 ; *Now I ſay, that the Heir, as long as he is a child, differeth nothing from a Servant, though he be lord of all ; But is under Tutors and Governours, until the time appointed of the Father.* Which Similitude he applies in the 3d verſe, and in the words of the Text ; *Even So We*, ſays he, *when we were children*, We of the *Jewiſh* diſpenſation, *were in bondage under the elements of the world ; But when the fulneſs of time was come, God ſent forth his Son made of a woman, made under the law, to redeem them that were under the law, that we might receive the adoption of Sons.* The Meaning is : Before the World was prepared for the reception of the Goſpel, God thought fit to oblige men to obſerve thoſe firſt and more imperfect rudiments, which were inſtituted in the *Jewiſh* law ; But when the time was come that the *Meſſiah* ſhould appear, God did by him aboliſh *That* inſtitution of religion, (at leaſt as to the Neceſſity of its being embraced by the *Gentiles*) and redeemed or freed men from the ſervile obedience thereof ; requiring from them thenceforward, only That free, That manly and rational obedience, which is the duty and privilege not of Servants but of Sons ; *That we might receive the Adoption of Sons.*

IN the Words we may obſerve, 1ſt, The Character of the perſon ſent into the World ; *God ſent forth his Son.* 2dly, His Condition and Manner of Converſation among men ; *he was made of a woman, made under the law.* 3dly, The Deſign of this his coming ; it was *To redeem thoſe that were under the law, that we might receive the adoption of Sons.* And 4thly, The particular Time of his appearing ; *When the fulneſs of time was come.*

1ſt, HERE is the Character of the perſon ſent into the World ; *God ſent forth his Son.* The Phraſe is of the ſame import, with thoſe other expreſſions we meet with in Scripture ; *God ſo loved the world, that he gave his only begotten Son, that whoſoever*
                                                                    believeth

believeth in him should not perish, but have everlasting life ; Joh. iii. 16 : and, *God who* *at sundry times and in divers manners spake in times past unto the fathers by the prophets,* *hath in these last days spoken unto us by his Son,* Heb. i. 1. The Meaning is : God ha- ving of old established several Forms of Religion among men, by divers ways of reve- lation, by discovering himself to the Patriarchs, by the delivering of the law to *Moses,* and by the preaching of the prophets; and all these Methods having proved severally in- effectual to make men truly virtuous, to recover God's Creation from the *Corruption and Bondage* of Sin, and much *more* insufficient to afford any effectual means of redeeming them from the *Guilt* thereof; he did at last in mercy and compassion to mankind vouchsafe to afford them one more clear and perfect revelation of his Will, by the preaching of a person of far greater excellence and authority than *Any before*; even by his *own Son.* This expression therefore *of God's sending forth his Son,* implies plainly these two things ; *first,* that the person here declared to be sent forth into the World, was in a singular and peculiar manner the Son of God; and 2*dly,* that he was *with* God, before he was sent into the World. 1*st,* The person here declared to be sent in- to the World, was in a peculiar manner the Son of God. Many Senses there are in which a person may be said to be the Son of God ; and in great variety of significa- tion does the Scripture itself make use of this expression. The *Angels* are styled the *Sons of God,* Job xxxviii. 7 ; and *Adam* is said to be the *Son of God,* Luke iii. 38; be- cause immediately created by him : They who are *sanctified* by the *Spirit of God,* are called the *Sons of God,* Rom. viii. 14; because they live in obedience to his govern- ment, and so are Members of his Family or Household ; They who shall be thought worthy to obtain *that life which is to come,* are called the *Sons of God,* Luke xx. 36 ; because they are as it were anew created of God, being the Children of the resurrec- tion, to eternal Happiness : They who are appointed to any *high Office* by the special and immediate Will of God, are also called *Gods,* or the *Sons of God,* because they act in his stead, or as his Vicegerents ; and in this Sense our Saviour himself uses the phrase in his Reply to the *Jews,* John x. 34 ; *Is it not written in your law, I said ye are Gods ? If he called them Gods, unto whom the word of God came, and the Scripture can- not be broken, Say ye of him whom the Father hath sanctified and sent into the world, thou blasphemest, because I said I am the Son of God ?* These therefore and some other Senses there are, in which the Scripture gives men that great title of being *the Sons of God.* And the *reason why* any person is so called, is generally expressly added, or at least plainly included in the words ; as in the instance of *Adam*; of those who shall be raised from the Dead ; and of Princes, or sanctified Men and Prophets being stiled *the Sons of God.* But when the title is given to our Blessed Saviour, it is given him either absolutely and by way of eminence, or with some high and particular Note of distin- ction. It is sometimes given him *absolutely* and by way of *eminence* ; as in the Text he is called *The* Son of God ; and then 'tis plain from the manner of the expression, that it is to be understood in a high and peculiar Sense : For when a title which may be given men upon different respects, and frequently is so in very different significations, accord- ing to the occasion upon which it is conferred, and with manifest reference to that oc- casion ; when I say such a title is given to any particular person *absolutely and by way of eminence,* it is manifest it is then to be understood in the highest and most excellent Sense. In *other* passages of Scripture, this title is given him with some high and par- ticular Note of *distinction,* as *only begotten, beloved,* God's *dear* Son, his *own* Son, and the like : *Rom.* viii. 3. *What the law could not do in that it was weak through the flesh, God sending his* own *Son in the likeness of sinful flesh, and for Sin, i. e.* as the Words may more properly be rendred, *by being a* Sacrifice *for Sin, condemned Sin in the flesh :* and *Joh.* i. 14. *The Word was made flesh, and dwelt amongst us, and we beheld his glory, the glory as of the* only begotten *of the Father, full of Grace and Truth.* The Angels (as I before obferved) are called *the Sons of God*; Job xxxviii. 7. But unto which of the Angels faid he at any time with fo peculiar an Emphafis, *Thou art my Son, this day have I begotten thee?* Heb. i. 5. This therefore is fo diftinguifhing an expreffion, that it neceffarily implies our Saviour to be the Son of God in a different and more exalted fenfe than the Angels themfelves are; For in the next verfe the Apoftle brings *Them* in as his Minifters, fubjected unto him, and paying honour to him; ver. 6; *When he bringeth in the firft begotten into the World, he faith, And let all the* Angels *of God worfhip him.* And ch. ii. ver. 16; 'Tis faid, *He took not on him the nature of Angels,* (which fhows that it would have been a great condefcenfion in him to have done even *That) but he took upon him the feed of Abraham,* i. e. the nature of *Man*: But becaufe this was written to the *Jews*, among whom Chrift was born, and to whom he firft preached, therefore it is not faid the Nature of *Men*, but the Seed of *Abraham.* Further; even in that fingular and peculiar application of it to *our Lord only,* there is alfo fome variety: For he is fo ftiled, on account of his miraculous conception, *Luk.* i. 35; then, of his Office, *Joh.* x. 34; then, of his Refurrection, *Acts* xiii. 33, and *Rom.* i. 4; then, of his being appointed Heir of all things, and as a Son in his own houfe; *Heb.* iii. 6. But beyond all this, there is ftill fomething further implied in the Ufe of this Phrafe: For the Text fuppofes, fecondly, that he was *with* God, in the bofom of the Father, before he was fent into the World; *God fent forth his Son*; For though the word which we here render, *fend forth,* be alfo applied in Scripture to God's fending his Prophets to the *Jews,* and our Saviour's commiffioning his Apoftles to preach the Gofpel; and fo may properly fignify in *general, only* the *appointing* a perfon to execute any office or commiffion, yet when it is applied to our Saviour's *coming into* the *World,* (or coming forth from the Father into the World) as in the words now mentioned, it clearly implies, that he who was thus fent *into the World from God,* was *with* God, in the glory of the Father, before he was fent into the World: As appears both from the natural Force of the expreffion itfelf, and more fully from thofe parallel places of Scripture, which mention to us the fame thing. *Joh.* xvii. 5; Our Saviour prays thus to his Father, *And now, O Father, glorify me with thine own felf, with the glory which I had with thee before the world was:* Again, *Joh.* iii. 13; *No man hath afcended into Heaven, but he that came down from Heaven, even the Son of man which is in Heaven:* And again, ch. xvi. 28; he faith unto his Difciples, *I came forth from the Father, and am come into the world; again, I leave the world, and go to the Father.* Which words his Difciples thought fo plainly to fignify his having been *with* God, in the glory of the Father, before he was fent into the World; that they immediately anfwered him; ver. 29; *Now fpeakeft thou plainly, and fpeakeft no parable: By this we believe that thou cameft forth from God.* The *Ufe* the Scripture makes of This confideration, *of the Dignity of the Perfon,* by whom God hath been pleafed to declare his Mercy in the Gofpel; that it was *the only begotten Son of God,* fent down from Heaven to take our Nature upon him; I fay, the *Ufe* which the Scripture makes of This confideration, is This: *Heb.* ii. 2; *If the word fpoken by Angels was ftedfaft, and every tranfgreffion and difobedience received a juft recompence of Reward; How fhall we efcape, if we neglect fo great Salvation, which at the firft began to be fpoken by the* LORD!

Secondly, HERE is a defcription of this divine Perfon's *condition,* and his manner of *converfation* in the World; *He was made of a Woman, made under the Law.* He was made of a Woman, i. e. he became truly and really a Man; not taking upon him only the fimilitude of our Nature, and appearing in the form and appearance of a Man, but being really and truly fuch; *fubjected to all the infirmities of humane nature, and tempted in all points like as we are, yet without fin;* Heb. iv. 15. For (as the Apoftle obferves, *Heb.* ii. 17;) *in all things it behoved him to be made like unto his brethren, that he might be a merciful and faithful High-prieft, in things pertaining to God, to*
make

make reconciliation for the sins of the people: For in that he himself hath suffered, being
tempted, he is able to succour them that are tempted. 'It follows; *he was made under the law;* i. e. he was subject and obedient to it. By the *law,* some understand here the moral law of God; and that, by our Saviour's being made under the law, is meant his performing perfect and complete obedience to the law of God: that so, by having in his own person unsinning obedience to the law of God, he might become the Author of eternal Salvation, to all those that should believe and repent; and that by having first obeyed those commandments himself, to which he required obedience from others, he might become an example of obedience to his Disciples. All which is indeed very true: But yet, because by *the law* the Apostle in this Epistle means generally the ceremonial law, or that part of the *Mosaick* institution which is opposed to the Christian religion, and superseded by it; and because 'tis most probable he must in this place concerning our Saviour's submitting to *that* law, which in the words immediately following 'tis said the design of his coming into the World was to redeem men from; therefore 'tis more reasonable to conclude, that, by his being *made under the Law,* the Apostle intends in this place, that our Saviour was born in the nation and under the religion of the *Jews;* that he was circumcised according to the commandment of *Moses;* that he submitted to and performed the whole ceremonial law, (fulfilling even in *that* sense all righteousness;) that having perfectly obeyed the law in his Life, he might for ever abolish that part of it at his Death, and free his followers from the Servitude thereof.

3*dly,* HERE is the *End* and *Design* of his coming thus into the World, set forth in the last part of the words; *To redeem them that were under the law, that we might receive the adoption of Sons.* The same phrase the Apostle again makes use of in the Epistle to the *Romans,* ch. viii. ver. 15; *Ye have not received the Spirit of Bondage again to fear, but ye have received the Spirit of* adoption, *whereby we cry, Abba, Father;* i. e. God deals not with Us as a Master with his Servants, but as a Father with his Sons, requiring of us not any hard and burdensome service, but only a rational and sincere obedience. Our Lord came *to redeem them that were under the law;* i. e. to abrogate the burdensome ceremonies of the *Jewish* institution; *That we might receive the* adoption *of Sons ;* i. e. that he might establish with men a New Covenant, which should be most *easy* to observe, and most *sufficient* to justify those that should observe it. Most *easy* to observe, is this Covenant of the Gospel; because its precepts are not positive and carnal Ordinances, but the great duties of the moral and eternal law of God, which are absolutely and in their own nature most acceptable to God, and most perfective of men; and 'tis most *sufficient* to justify those who shall live according to it, because their works shall not be judged with strictness and rigour, but through the intercession of Christ, their sincerity shall be accepted instead of perfect obedience: In the *former* respect (its being easy to observe;) the Christian institution is called the *law of Liberty;* Jam. i. 25; and the *glorious Liberty* of the Sons of God; *Rom.* viii. 21; and *Gal.* iv. 7; *Wherefore thou art no more a Servant, but a Son.* In the *latter* respect, namely, in respect of its sufficiency to justify those that shall live suitably to it, the Christian institution is called the *righteousness of God,* Rom. iii. 20, 21. *By the deeds of the law there shall no flesh be justified. But now the* righteousness of God *without the law is manifested, being witnessed by the law and the prophets; even the* righteousness of God, *which is by Faith in* Jesus Christ, *unto all and upon all them that believe;* And, *by it all that believe are justified from all things, from which they could not be justified by the law of Moses;* Acts xiii. 39. There being several great Crimes, for which no regular Expiation was allowed under the law; from which Curse, men are now by true Repentance and Amendment, delivered under the Gospel: Which is *therefore* stiled the Righteousness of God to men. This is the Adoption, whereby we become Sons of God, and Heirs of Salvation: This is the Liberty wherewith Chriſt has made us free : We are not obliged to any impoſſible performances, nor to any grievous and burdenſome rites; but if we ſincerely repent, and return to the obedience of God's Commands, according to the gracious Terms and Conditions of the Goſpel; we ſhall, through the interceſſion of Chriſt, be accepted by our heavenly Father.　But then we muſt always remember that *without* this obedience we ſhall ſtill be rejected, notwithſtanding what our Saviour has done for us; nay we ſhall be condemned with ſo much a *ſeverer* Sentence, as he has afforded us greater means and opportunities of Salvation.　Chriſt has given us the adoption and the liberty of Sons; but if we abuſe that liberty to rebel againſt God and diſobey his Commandments, living viciouſly and profanely in this preſent World ; *it had been better for us not to have known the way of Truth, than after we have known it, to turn from the holy commandment delivered unto us.*　Our Saviour has purchaſed redemption for us upon the gracious terms of Faith and Obedience; but *without* this Obedience, we can have no benefit, even of *That* moſt perfect redemption.　Chriſt has ſuffered for us, that we might receive the adoption of Sons; but if we continue not to live virtuouſly as becomes the children of God, it will nothing profit us to have received this adoption.　*They only who are led by the Spirit of God, are the Sons of God*; Rom. viii. 14.　Wherefore if we reſiſt and grieve that good Spirit by *any* vicious practices, we have no part in him, neither will God receive us either as his Sons or his Servants.　*Whoſoever is born of God*, ſaith St *John, doth not commit Sin, for his ſeed remaineth in him, and he cannot ſin becauſe he is born of God: In this the children of God are manifeſt and the children of the devil: whoſoever doth not righteouſneſs, is not of God, neither he that loveth not his brother*; 1 Joh. iii. 9 : Again; ver. 2. *Beloved, now are we the Sons of God, and it doth not yet appear what we ſhall be; But we know that when he ſhall appear, we ſhall be like him, for we ſhall ſee him as he is*; *i. e.* God doth in *This world* acknowledge us as his children ; how much *more* hereafter, ſhall he that thus *ſpared not his own Son, but delivered him up for us all*, receive us to the more immediate injoyment of himſelf? But then he adds immediately, ver. 3 ; *Every man that hath this hope in him, purifieth himſelf even as he is pure.*　This is the only *poſſible* condition, upon which we can obtain the Salvation of the Goſpel.　Nay, on the contrary, we cannot eſcape being condemned to a ſeverer puniſhment, if we neglect the offer of ſo great a Salvation.　For if *he that deſpiſed Moſes law, died without mercy*, Heb. x. 28 ; *of how much ſorer puniſhment ſhall he be thought worthy, who hath troden under foot the Son of God, and hath counted the blood of the Covenant, wherewith he was ſanctified, an unholy thing, and hath done deſpite unto the Spirit of Grace?*

S E R M O N   LXXII.

Of the Fulneſs of Time in which C H R I S T appeared.

[Preached on Chriſtmas-Day.]

G A L. IV. 4, and 5.

But when the fulneſs of time was come, God ſent forth his Son, made of a woman, made under the law; To redeem them that were under the law, that we might receive the adoption of Sons.

IT remains, that I proceed now in the 4th and laſt place, to conſider the Time of our Saviour's appearing in the fleſh; *When the fulneſs of time was come.* Now here, By the *fulneſs of time,* we muſt underſtand *that* time, which God in his infinite Wiſdom thought fit to appoint; And we may conſider it either with reſpect to God's Fore-determination: and then it was therefore the *fulneſs of time,* becauſe determined and fore-appointed of God; or we may conſider it abſolutely as the fitteſt and moſt proper ſeaſon; and then it was fore-appointed by the Wiſdom of God, becauſe it was in itſelf the *fulneſs of time.* 1ſt, We may conſider it with reſpect to God's Fore-determination; and then it was therefore the Fulneſs of time, becauſe determined and foretold by the prophets.

ACCORDING to that antient prediction of *Jacob;* Gen. xlix. 10; the Meſſiah was to appear before the total diſſolution of the *Jewiſh* Government. *The ſcepter ſhall not depart from Judah, nor a law-giver from between his feet, till Shiloh come; and unto him ſhall the gathering of the people be.* By the word, *Shiloh,* the antient *Jewiſh* interpreters conſtantly underſtood the Meſſiah; and the *Jews* at this day are not able to interpret it to any other tolerable Senſe: Now it is certain, that after our Saviour's Coming; as ſoon as the *gathering* of the people, (or as the word may no leſs properly be rendred, the *obedience* of the people) was come *in* to him; *viz.* as ſoon as he had ſettled that inſtitution of Religion, which he came into the World to eſtabliſh; *Jeruſalem was de-ſtroyed,* the whole nation of the *Jews* diſperſed, and ſcattered among *all* people; and the conſtitution of their government entirely diſſolved. Our Saviour therefore *did* appear exactly at that period of Time, which the Prophecy of *Jacob* had ſo many ages before expreſſly determined. Again; the Prophecy of *Malachi,* ch. iii. 1, determines the Coming of our Saviour to be before the deſtruction of the Second Temple; *Behold, I will ſend my meſſenger, and he ſhall prepare my way before me, and the Lord whom ye ſeek ſhall ſuddenly come, he ſhall ſuddenly come to his temple; even the meſſenger of the co-venant, whom ye delight in, behold he ſhall come, ſaith the Lord of hoſts.* And *That* no leſs remarkable prediction of *Haggai;* ch. ii. ver. 6, 7, and 9; *Thus ſaith the Lord of hoſts, Yet once it is a little while and I will ſhake the heavens and the earth, and the ſea and the dry land; And I will ſhake all nations, and the deſire of all nations ſhall come,*

2 *and*

and I will fill This houfe *with glory, faith the Lord of hofts* ; *The glory of* this latter *houfe fhall be* greater *than of the former ; and in this place will I give peace.*   The folemn and *fublime introduction* with which this prophecy is ufhered in, fhows plainly that fomething of very great moment is therein foretold and promifed ; And the *Words* of the Prediction *itfelf* fufficiently intimate, *when* and *in whom* they were to be fulfilled.

The defire, or (as the word may more properly be rendred,) *the* expectation *of all nations* ; is a clear and undifputed character of the Meffiah : And as to the *filling That Houfe with* greater *Glory than the former*, it is well known that That Second Temple was very *far* from equalling the Glory of Solomon's, in the magnificence of its *Building*, or in its *rich ornaments :* And befides the *Jews* themfelves confefs, that the Second Temple always wanted thofe five things, which were juftly efteemed the great Glory and Excellence of the firft.   It wanted *the Urim and Thummim, the Ark of the Covenant, the Fire from heaven which burnt continually on the Altar, the Shecinah or vifible appearance of the glory of God, and the Spirit of Prophecy.*   It remains therefore that the Glory wherein this Second Temple was to exceed the Firft, could be no other than This; that it was to be honoured with the Prefence of the *King of Glory*, even *the promifed Meffias* ; Which would indeed be a far *greater* Glory, than all the riches of *Solomon*'s Temple.   Accordingly our Saviour *did* appear, during the ftanding of that Second Temple ; he was prefented therein by his parents, and acknowledged by *Simeon* and *Anna*, who praifed God for him, and *fpoke of him to all thofe that looked for redemption in Ifrael*; He alfo frequently *Taught* therein, and by his Gracious prefence filled that houfe with *glory* ; with the *Glory*, as of the only-begotten Son of God, full of Grace and Truth ; with the *Glory of God*, manifefted in the moft illuftrious *miracles*; with the *glorious Doctrine* of Peace and Salvation, of Grace, Righteoufnefs, and Truth.   And to demonftrate that this prophecy was fulfilled in *him*, and could not poffibly belong to any other, God, in his righteous judgment, not many years after our Saviour's Paffion, fuffered this Temple, at the final deftruction of the City and People, to be fo utterly overthrown and deftroyed, that *not one ftone was left upon another*, nor could it ever by any induftry be built again.   *Laftly*, That moft clear prophecy of *Daniel*; ch. ix. ver. 24; *Seventy weeks are determined upon thy people, and upon the holy city, to finifh the Tranfgreffion, and to make an end of fins, and to make reconciliation for iniquity, and to bring in everlafting righteoufnefs, and to anoint the moft Holy*; (who in the next verfe is called *by name*, Meffiah the Prince;) This prophecy, I fay, determines the time from the rebuilding of the city after the captivity to the coming of the Meffias, to be feven times Seventy, *viz.* Four hundred and ninety years : Exactly after which period of time, (the different computations of Chronologers in this point, being but fmall Niceties;) exactly, I fay, after this period of time, the Hiftory of our Saviour fhows us that he appeared in the World. It is evident therefore that the incarnation of Chrift was *in the fulnefs of time* ; that is, exactly at the time foretold and fore-determined by the Prophets.   And indeed thefe Prophecies were fo plain, that about the time of our Lord's appearance, the *Jews*, and from them the *Romans*, and all the Eaftern parts of the World, were in great expectation of fome extraordinary perfon to arife, who fhould be Governor of the World.   This made *Herod* fo inquifitive and follicitous, about *him that was born King of the Jews*; St *Mat.* ii. 2 : And this gave occafion to the impoftors, *Theudas and Judas of Galilee*, (of whom we read, *Acts* v. 36.) to profefs themfelves to be fome great perfons, and to draw away much people after them.   The *Jews* were at that Time *filled* with expectation of the appearance of their promifed Meffiah; and from thence thefe Deceivers took occafion to fet up for themfelves; But as they managed their impofture in Such manner, as to fuit with the *prejudices* and *falfe* notions the *Jews* had then conceived of their expected

I

Meffiah,

Messiah, so they acted directly contrary to his *True* Character; and their designs came accordingly to a deserved end.

BUT 2*dly*, Though it be evident that our Saviour came into the World *in the fulness of time*, *viz.* at the time foretold by the Prophets; yet the question may still return, *why* was *That* time determined rather than any other, and accordingly foretold by the Prophets; for, without doubt, it was in itself *absolutely* the fittest and the properest season; and the Incarnation of our Lord was *therefore* by the Prophets fixed beforehand to that time, *because* it was the *full*, or most *proper* Season. And to This question it might be sufficient to answer, that the time of our Saviour's incarnation, as all *Other* times and seasons which the Father has put in his own power, was *therefore* the fittest, and the properest season, because it was the time chosen by the infinite and unerring Wisdom of God: But yet it cannot be denied to be an argument worthy our consideration, to enquire into the *reasons* of our Saviour's Coming into the World at such a particular time rather than any other, so far as the history of the *Scripture*, which is what God has thought fit to open to us of his Divine Counsel; and so far as the *design* itself of our Lord's coming, will suggest to us. Now *Two* reasons there seem to have been more especially, of our Saviour's appearing at That time: The first is, because the insufficiency of the *Jewish* dispensation, as well as of natural religion, was then after a long trial, become sufficiently apparent: Apparent; not to *God*, who knows all things at Once, and makes accordingly Provision for all things from the Beginning; and who is able to judge all men with justice and equity, according to their respective Circumstances under Every Dispensation: but to *Men* to whom the Counsel of God is opened by degrees, and by the Events of things; to *Them*, the insufficiency of the *Jewish* Dispensation was by that Time become apparent. What *the law* could not *do*, saith St *Paul*, *in That it was weak through the flesh, God sending his own Son in the likeness of sinful flesh, and for Sin condemned sin in the flesh*; Rom. viii. 3. And in the Epistle to the *Hebrews*, the same Apostle all along insists on the *insufficiency* of the *Jewish* institution, as an Argument to demonstrate the *necessity* of introducing the *Christian: For if that first covenant*, saith he, *had been faultless, then should no place have been sought for the second*; Heb. viii. 7; and ch. vii. ver. 18; *There is verily a disannulling of the commandment going before, for the weakness and unprofitableness thereof.* In the old World, when men had entirely corrupted themselves, and almost wholly lost that natural and traditional Knowledge of God, which was at first the foundation of their Religion, and the rule of their lives; God began to reveal himself to *Abraham* and the Patriarchs; and chose their Posterity to give them afterwards his Laws by *Moses*, and to make them the Standard of true Religion, and of the Worship of the One God, to all Nations. Again, when this *new* Dispensation of Providence began likewise to grow ineffectual as the former had done, through the Vanity and Superstition wherewith it was by degrees over-run; when the commandments of God were almost wholly swallowed up by the traditions of Men, and the weightier matters of the law forced to give place to the superstitious doctrines of the *Scribes* and *Pharisees*; then was the time for him to appear, who, as the prophet *Malachi* describes him, *was to be like a refiner's fire, and like fullers soap; who was to sit as a refiner and purifier of silver, and to purifie the sons of Levi, and purge them as gold and silver, that they might offer unto the Lord an offering in righteousness*; Mal. iii. 3.

2*dly*; THE Second reason, *why* we may suppose our Saviour appeared just at the time he did, was because the World was at that time by many extraordinary circumstances, peculiarly prepared for his reception. The great design of his Coming, (we know,) was to establish a Religion, which as it was to continue for ever without any further alteration, so it was not (like the *Jewish* dispensation) to be confined to one particular Nation or People, but to be *preached to all the nations of the earth*

S E R M. *from one end thereof unto the other : His Dominion ſhall be alſo from the one Sea to the*
LXXII. *other, and from the Flood unto the World's end: All Kings ſhall fall down before him,*
all nations ſhall do him Service; Pſ. lxxii. 8, 11. The Goſpel of Chriſt, was to be an
univerſal Religion ; *a light to lighten the Gentiles,* as well as to be *the glory of his
people Iſrael*; According to that remarkable prophecy of *Iſaiah,* ch. xlix. ver. 6 ; *It
is a light thing, that thou ſhouldſt be my ſervant to raiſe up the tribes of Jacob, and to
reſtore the preſerved of Iſrael ; I will alſo give thee for a light to the Gentiles, that thou
mayeſt be my ſalvation unto the ends of the earth.* Now about the time of our Saviour's Birth, it is obſervable there was a concurrence of many things in the World,
to promote and further the propagating of *Such* a Religion. The *Romans* had then
conquered almoſt all the *known* parts of the World ; they had ſpread and ſettled their
language among all the nations of their conqueſts, and had made the communication
eaſy from one part to another. They had moreover improved *moral* Philoſophy to its
greateſt height ; and by having framed better notions of God and of the nature of things,
than were uſual in the idolatrous Heathen World, they were in ſome meaſure prepared
for the Reception of the Truth. This appears plainly from the vaſt number of *Proſelytes,*
which were about this time converted to the *Jewiſh* Religion ; ſo far converted, as to
believe in and worſhip the One only true God, and to obey the moral Law, yet without obſerving the ritual and ceremonial performances of the *Moſaick* inſtitution. Theſe
Proſelytes are they which in the Hiſtory of the *Acts of the Apoſtles* are ſtiled *devout
men, worſhippers of God,* and men *fearing God* ; Of whom how great numbers there
were at That time, may be ſeen in the iid chapter of the *Acts,* ver. 5, *&c.* where
it is ſaid *that there were dwelling at Jeruſalem devout men out of every nation under
heaven* ; *Parthians, and Medes, and Elamites, and the dwellers in Meſopotamia, and in
Judea, and Cappadocia, in Pontus, and Aſia, Phrygia, and Pamphylia in Egypt, and
in the parts of Libya, about Cyrene, and ſtrangers of Rome, Jews and proſelytes, Cretes
and Arabians, we do hear them ſpeak in our tongues the wonderful works of God.* Further ; the great improvement and increaſe of *Learning* in the World about this time,
(according to that prophecy of *Daniel, Many ſhall run to and fro, and knowledge ſhall
be increaſed* ;) gave occaſion to the *Jewiſh* books to be diſperſed through the World :
And particularly, the tranſlating of the Bible ſome few Ages before the Birth of Chriſt,
into one of the then moſt known and univerſal languages upon Earth, which had before been confined in a peculiar language to the *Jews* only ; was a ſingular preparative to the reception of that great Prophet and Saviour of mankind, whoſe Coming
was in that Book ſo plainly and ſo often foretold. Indeed this ſeems to have been the
firſt ſtep of God's diſcovering himſelf further than by the Light of Nature to *other*
nations as well as to the *Jews,* and of his giving the *heathen alſo* the knowledge of his
revealed laws ; And remarkably inſtrumental it afterwards appeared to be, in the propagating the Chriſtian religion through the *Gentile World.*

   B u t I barely mention theſe things, as only brief intimations to inquiſitive and conſiderate perſons ; and haſten in the laſt place, to draw ſome more univerſally *uſeful* and
practical inferences, from the particulars of the doctrine contained in the Text. And
1ſt, If our Saviour came into the World preciſely at the time determined and foretold
by the prophets ; then have we from hence an unanſwerable proof of our Saviour's
being the true Meſſias. For if our Lord appeared exactly at that time, which God
by his Holy prophets had before appointed ſhould be the time when the promiſed Meſſias, the deſire and expectation of nations, was to appear ; and no other perſon did
ariſe *near* that time, to whom that Character could poſſibly belong ; then have we an
undeniable evidence that our Saviour was that Perſon, whom the prophets did point at
and deſcribe. And this evidence is ſo convictive and unanſwerable, that the *Jews* at
this day have no other way to elude the force of it, but by pretending that though

                                                        God

God had indeed foretold pofitively by his Prophets that the Meffias fhould appear S E R M. about that time, yet for the Sins of that nation he has deferred the *fending* of the LXXII. Meffiah, and the *fulfilling* of thofe prophecies, for above Seventeen hundred years. But there are moreover *two* peculiar circumftances, which make this argument yet more ftrong and concluding; the *firft* is, that as our Saviour appeared exactly at the time determined by the prophets, fo his *character* agreed perfectly with all the defcriptions, which the prophecies had given of *That* perfon, whofe Coming was foretold. I need not enlarge upon This particularly; the Evangelifts having in their gofpels, with all clearnefs and evidence, applied to the Hiftory of our Saviour all the feveral paffages of the prophets, which fpeak of the *time* and *place* of the birth of the Meffiah; the *manner* of his education; the *courfe* of his life; the *nature* and extent of his *doctrine*; the peculiar *circumftances* of his paffion and death; and That moft remarkable inftance of the divine power, his Refurrection from the Dead. The *Other* obfervable circumftance is, that as the character of our Saviour was exactly agreeable to the prophets defcription of the true Meffiah, fo it was very different *from, and almoft contrary to, the character of* that imaginary Meffiah whom the *Jews* expected. And This particular circumftance, is a demonftration that our Saviour had no defign of impofing upon the people. The *Jews* expected a temporal Prince, to appear in all the Splendor, glory and power of this World; to deliver them from their Subjection to the *Roman* yoke, and to reftore again the kingdom to *Ifrael*. 'Tis manifeft therefore that whatever Deceiver would have fet up himfelf for the Meffiah, and hoped to be owned as fuch by the people of the *Jews*, muft have endeavoured to have appeared in fuch a Character, as the *Jews* expected; he muft have blown the trumpet to fedition, and by gathering men after him, have endeavoured to make himfelf their Prince and King: And in Fact, this method we find thofe impoftors did take, whofe Attempts are mentioned, *Acts* v. 36. But *our Saviour*, directly contrary to the expectation of the *Jews*, was a man, with refpect to all *worldly* grandeur, of no form or comlinefs; a man of Sorrows and acquainted with grief; a perfon of feemingly mean extraction, and of greater humility: So that when fome of the multitude would by force have made him a King, he was content even to work a Miracle, to efcape out of their hands. 'Tis manifeft therefore that he had no ambition, to exalt himfelf among the people. Now when in fuch a perfon, whofe character was entirely contrary to the humour and expectation of the people, it appeared yet manifeftly, that in him was really fulfilled every thing, that was fpoken in the law and in the prophets concerning the Meffias that was to come; it is no lefs than a demonftration that this was the very perfon, to whom thofe prophecies did exprefsly point. 2*dly*, If our Saviour, (the perfon fent into the world to be the Author of our Religion,) was, notwithftanding his taking upon him that humble Form, yet in reality no meaner a Perfon than the only begotten Son of God; this may convince us of the divine Authority of our Religion, and the indifpenfable neceffity of paying Obedience to its laws. The *Natural knowledge* of the difference of Good and Evil, which even the *heathen* World was capable of attaining, was truly and properly a Difcovery of the Will of God; But becaufe this difcovery was very obfcure, and very hardly fufficient to prevail over the corruptions of Men's depraved Nature; therefore the times of that ignorance *God winked at*; Acts xvii. 30: But now that the *wrath of God* is clearly and exprefsly, and by a meffenger of fuch Dignity as his own Son, revealed from heaven againft all *ungodlinefs and unrighteoufnefs of men*; now that he hath fully and diftinctly declared that *he hath appointed a day in the which he will judge the world in righteoufnefs by that man whom he hath ordained*; Now he commandeth all men abfolutely, every where to repent. God hath now fent his *laft* meffenger to warn Men of their fin and danger; even his own *beloved Son*; and if they will not

hear

SERM.
LXXII.
hear and obey *him*, they muft expect to fall under fo much a more fevere punifhment, as they defpife a clearer Revelation of the Will of God, and trample under foot a more glorious *Meffenger of his covenant*. *If the word fpoken by* Angels, faith the Apoftle; *if the* Mofaick law, *was ftedfaft*; *and every tranfgreffion and difobedience received a juft recompence of reward*; *How fhall we efcape, if we neglect fo great falvation, which at the firft began to be fpoken by* the Lord? Heb. ii. 2 and 3; And ch. xii. ver. 25; *See that ye refufe not him that fpeaketh*; *For if* They *efcaped not, who refufed him that fpake on earth*; *much more fhall not* We *efcape, if we turn away from him that fpeaketh from heaven*. And again, in the Epiftle of St *Jude*; the danger of impenitent Chriftians under fuch clear means of Knowledge is reprefented by the Apoftle under this fevere fimilitude, ver. 5 and 6; *I will therefore put you in remembrance,——that the Angels which kept not their firft eftate, but left their own habitation, he has referved in everlafting chains under Darknefs, unto the judgment of the great Day.*

3*dly,* IF this *Divine perfon*, the Author of our religion, notwithftanding the exceeding dignity of his nature, *yet* condefcended to become truly and really a man; fubjecting himfelf to all the infirmities of human nature, *and being in all things made like unto his brethren, fin only excepted*; This may convince us of the reafonablenefs of our Holy Religion; and of the poffibility of our paying obedience to its laws. Had God fent his Son in great *Glory*, and in the *Form of God*, to reveal his Will to us by his abfolute *command* only; fuch an extraordinary Revelation, like *the Mountain that burned with Fire*, would indeed have fufficiently convinced us of the neceffity of Religion and the indifpenfablenefs of obedience. But when this great perfon vouchfafed to become, not only the Author of our Religion, but in our own nature the *pattern* alfo of our duty; this demonftrated to us, that our Obedience was to be as reafonable, as it was indifpenfable. For by this means we have a perfect and familiar example of Holinefs and Obedience fet before us; by which we plainly fee, that God requires nothing of us, but what our Saviour himfelf, when he fubmitted to become Man, did think reafonable to practife. Indeed, we *cannot* be in all things perfect, as he, who is our pattern and example, was perfect: But to follow a moft perfect Pattern, is, even to an imperfect Copier, a fingular Advantage; and our Duty, is not to *equal*, but to *imitate* fo far, as the infirmities of our nature will permit, with Sincerity and Conftancy. We fhall in our proportion be made as like him in our *happinefs* as we have been in the performance of our *duty*.

SERMON

SERMON LXXIII.

Of the meaning of, The Name of G O D.

[Preached on Epiphany.]

MAL. I. 11.

For from the rifing of the Sun, even unto the going down of the same, my Name fhall be great among the Gentiles; and in every place, Incenfe fhall be offered unto my Name, and a pure Offering; for my Name fhall be Great *among the Heathen, faith the Lord of Hofts.*

IN difcourfing upon thefe words of the Prophet, I fhall 1ft explain diftinctly the principal acceptations, or the moft remarkable of thofe feveral different Senfes, in which this Phrafe, the *Name of God*, is ufed in Scripture; From whence in courfe will appear, what is meant *in general* by its being *Great* among *Men.* And This being explained, I fhall then in the 2d place, confider, *What* That glorious Event *in particular* is, which we find predicted in thefe fublime prophetick Expreffions: *From the rifing of the Sun, even unto the going down of the fame, my Name fhall be Great among the Gentiles; and in every place, Incenfe fhall be offered unto my Name, and a pure Offering, faith the Lord of Hofts.*

I. IN the 1ft place, the *Name of God*, according to the nature of the *Jewifh* language, fignifies fometimes *God himfelf.* Thus *praifing* or *bleffing* the Name of God, is praifing *God himfelf*; and calling upon the Name of the Lord, is the very fame, as calling upon the *Lord.* Something anfwerable to which manner of fpeaking, there is in many *other* inftances of the *Hebrew* language, and in the *Analogy of expreffion* in *all* languages. Thus, *Heb.* viii. 1; *The Throne of the* Majefty *in the heavens*, is, the Throne of *God*: And *Pf.* cxlv. 5. *I will fpeak of the glorious Honour of thy* Majefty, *and of thy wondrous works.*

N o w when the *Name* of God, or any other phrafe of the like nature, is thus made ufe of to fignify *God himfelf*; it is plain that by his *Name* being Great among Men, is meant Their acknowledging or profeffing *him* to be the True God, and their Adhering to the Worfhip of *Him* only, in oppofition to all Idolatry and Falfe Religions. *Mic.* iv. 5. *All people will walk every one in the* Name *of* His *God; and* We *will walk in the* Name *of the Lord our God for ever and ever*: *Will walk in his* Name, that is, we will continue ftedfaft in his True Religion and Worfhip; *fanctifying the Lord God in our Hearts*, (as St *Peter* expreffes it,) *and not being afraid of* Their *Terrour*, not fearing Their *Falfe Gods*, who fill the Minds of their Worfhippers with endlefs Dread, and vain imaginary Superftitions. According to the fame Analogy of Speech; That Precept in the Law, *Thou fhalt not profane the* Name *of thy God*, is as much as to fay, Thou fhalt not incourage Idolatrous Practices, *by letting thy children pafs through the*

SERM. *Fire to Moloch,* Lev. xviii. 21. And in the Pfalmift's expreffion, forgetting *the* Name
LXXIII. *of God,* means, for the fame reafon, *falling into Idolatry:* Pf. xliv. 20. *If we have
forgotten* the Name *of our God, or ftretched out our hands to any Strange God.* Nay,
even *mentioning* the *Name* of other Gods, denotes, in Scripture-phrafe, a tendency to
Idolatry; *In all things that I have faid unto you, be circumfpect, and make no* mention *of the* Names *of Other Gods, neither let it be heard out of thy Mouth,* Exod.
xxiii. 13.

THIS is the firft and moft ufual Signification of this phrafe, *The Name of God;*
'Tis ufed to denote *God himfelf.* And becaufe his Name, in *This* fenfe, is Then *Great*
among Men, when they moft univerfally acknowledge him to be the True God, and
adhere to the Worfhip of *Him* only; hence, in a fenfe ftill more figurative, the *Name
of God* is fometimes ufed,

2*dly,* To fignify his *True Religion and Worfhip.* Thus, *Deut.* xii. 5. *The place which
the Lord your God fhall chufe out of all your Tribes, to put his* Name *there.* The
Meaning is: The Place where he fhall appoint his Servants, the Profeffors of the true
Religion, to appear before him with the External Tokens of their Homage and Worfhip. And in *This* fenfe, the Name of God is *then Great* in the World; when they
who profefs his True Religion, and adhere to the Worfhip of *Him* alone, and to That
manner of Worfhip which He has appointed, do Honour to this their profeffion, by a
fuitable practice in the whole courfe of their lives; fhowing forth the Effect of their
Religion, in the Fruits of Righteoufnefs and true Virtue; and *letting their Light fo
fhine before men, that Others feeing their good Works, may glorify their Father which is
in Heaven.* The Apoftle St *Paul,* in his 2 *Thef.* i. 12, ufes exactly the fame manner of
fpeaking; *We pray always for you,* fays he, *that our God would fulfil all the good pleafure of his goodnefs, and the work of Faith with Power; That the* Name *of our Lord
Jefus Chrift may be glorified in you:* His Meaning is, that the *Religion* of our Lord
Jefus Chrift may by your Practice be recommended to the World, and the excellency
of it made manifeft before Men. Again, *Rom.* ii. 24; fpeaking of Such as, on the
contrary, *difcredited* their Holy Profeffion by an unfuitable and unworthy behaviour;
Thou (fays he) *that makeft thy Boaft of the Law, through breaking the Law difhonoureft
thou God? For the* Name of God *is blafphemed among the Gentiles, through you.* The
Name of God, that is, the *Religion* and true *Worfhip* of God, is reviled and ill fpoken
of among Infidels, upon account of the ill lives of its unworthy Profeffors.

3*dly,* IN *other* places of Scripture, this phrafe, *The* Name *of God,* is made ufe of to
exprefs thofe adorable *Perfections* or *Attributes,* which are as it were the proper *Denomination* and *Character* of the divine Nature. Thus, *Exod.* xxxiv. 5, *The Lord defcended in the cloud, and ftood there with Mofes, and proclaimed* the Name *of the Lord:
The Lord paffed by before him, and proclaimed; The Lord, the Lord God, merciful and
gracious, long-fuffering and abundant in goodnefs and truth: Keeping mercy for thoufands, forgiving iniquity and tranfgreffion and Sin, and that will by no means clear the
guilty: vifiting the iniquity of the Fathers upon the children, and upon the childrens
children, unto the third and to the fourth generation.* Here the Name *of God,* fignifies
the Character or Defcription of God, contained in a *fummary* recapitulation of the Divine *Perfections in general.* The Same, at *other* times, denotes more diftinctly fome
fpecial and *particular* Attribute, to which the occafion peculiarly refers. Thus, *Pf.* xx. 2.
The Name, (that is, the Power,) *of the God of Jacob defend thee.* And *Pf.* ix. 10.
They that know thy Name, (that is, who have a juft Notion of thy Veracity *and* Goodnefs,) *will put their Truft in Thee.*

AND in *Thefe* fenfes of the phrafe, the *Name* of God is then truly *Great* among
Men, when, having juft and worthy Notions of the Divine Perfections, and living
under the continual influence of thefe impreffions upon their Minds, they fhow in their
whole

whole Behaviour that they really and habitually *fear* his *Power*, admire his *Wisdom*, *revere* his *Justice*, *love* his *Goodness*, and *rely upon* his *Truth*: In all their Words and Actions, acknowledging *Him* to be the *only Potentate*; Him, *only Holy*; Him, *only Wise*; and that, absolutely, and strictly speaking, *there is none* Good, but *One, that is God*.

4thly, There is still *another* sense of the phrase; in which the Name *of God* signifies in Scripture the *Authority* of God, or his *divine Commission*. Thus, *Exod.* xxiii. 20; *Behold, I send an Angel before thee*; *Beware of him, and obey his Voice*; *provoke him not*; *For my* Name *(that is, my Authority,) is in him.* Again, *Joh.* v. 43; *I am come,* says our Saviour, *in my Father's* Name, that is, with his Divine *Commission.* In like manner the Apostles, when they were examined before the High-Priest concerning their having healed a lame man; *Acts* iv. 7; *By what Power, or by what* Name *have ye done This?* immediately they replied, *By the* Name *of Jesus Christ of Nazareth, whom Ye crucified, whom God raised from the dead*; even *by H.m* (by his *Name and Power,* by his *Authority and Commission* delivered to Us) *does this man stand here before you Whole.*

And according to *This last* sense of the phrase, the Name *of God* must be *then* understood to be *Great* among Men, when a just Regard and cheerful Obedience is paid to whatever appears vested with *His* Authority: when the Laws of *Nature* are obeyed, as being established by his Supreme Authority in the *Creation* of things; And the Precepts of the *Gospel* likewise, as being by *Revelation* authorized from the same Supreme Power.

And Thus having at large explained the principal Acceptations, or the most remarkable of those several different Senses, in which this phrase, *The Name of God,* is used in Scripture; and what accordingly is meant *in general* by its being *Great:* It remains in the

II. *2d* place, that I proceed to consider, *what* that glorious Event *in particular* is, which we find predicted in these sublime Prophetick Expressions: *From the rising of the Sun, even unto the going down of the same, my Name shall be great among the Gentiles; And in every place Incense shall be offered unto my Name, and a pure Offering; For my Name shall be great among the Heathen, saith the Lord of Hosts.* Now in this prediction there is evidently contained, *1st,* Something *comminatory,* or by way of *Threatning,* with regard to the *Jews*; And, *2dly,* a particular *Promise* in relation to the *Gentiles*; joined with a general Declaration concerning the State and Condition of the *Universal Church* in the future and latter Ages of the World.

1st, With regard to the *Jews,* there is contained in the Text, Something *Comminatory,* or in the way of *Threatning*; as is evident from the *Connexion* of the words. For the *former part* of the chapter, is a severe expostulation with That people, upon account of their unworthy behaviour in the Service of God: And this Complaint against the *Jews,* is immediately followed with God's declaring in the Text, that his Name should be Great among the *Gentiles.* The Advantages which the *Jewish* Nation enjoyed, were very extraordinary; in that *to Them were committed the Oracles of God. He showed his Word unto Jacob, his Statutes and Ordinances unto Israel; He had not dealt so with any Other Nation, neither had the Heathen Knowledge of his Laws.* Answerable to these high privileges, it was reasonable to expect, that their improvements in Virtue and all Holiness, should have been proportionably Great: For *to whom much is given, of Him,* according to the Rule of Equity, *will be much required.* But so contrary to this expectation was the Behaviour of That people, that with a just Severity God complains of them by the Prophets, ver. 6. of this chapter; *If I be a Father, where is mine Honour? If I be a Master, where is my Fear?*——*If ye offer the blind for Sacrifice, is it not evil? and if ye offer the lame and sick, is it not evil?*——*I have*

no

SERM. *no pleafure in you, faith the Lord of Hofts, neither will I accept an Offering at your hands.*
LXXIII. And then it follows in the words of the Text, *For from the rifing of the Sun, even unto the going down of the fame, my Name fhall be great among the* Gentiles. The Threatning contained in This expoftulation, is exactly the fame with that of our Saviour in the Gofpel; *The Kingdom of God fhall be taken from you, and given to a Nation bringing forth the Fruits thereof.* The Accomplifhment of which Threatning upon the people of the *Jews*, both for the unparallelled manner of its execution, and for the unexampled length of the time of its continuance, has been fo confpicuous; that now, near feventeen hundred years after the deftruction of *Jerufalem*, they remain at this very day a living and ocular demonftration of the Truth of all the antient Prophecies which concern their State. But

 2dly; The Text contains a particular *Promife* in relation to the *Gentiles*; joined with a general Declaration concerning the State and Condition of the *Univerfal Church* in the future and latter Ages of the World: *In every place, Incenfe fhall be offered unto my Name, and a pure Offering; For my Name fhall be Great among the Heathen, faith the Lord of Hofts.* Notwithftanding That ftrong and fettled Prejudice among the *Jews*, of which we find great Remains even among our Saviour's own Difciples, that That Nation was always to be the Alone peculiar people of God; yet we find in the Prophecies of the Old Teftament many very clear intimations, like This in the Text, that, in the days of the Meffiah, the Favour of God fhould be extended to the *Gentiles*, and his Knowledge fpread among the Nations of the Earth; *If.* lx. 3. *The Gentiles fhall come to thy Light, and Kings to the brightnefs of thy Rifing:* And ch. xlix. 6; *It is a light thing that thou fhouldeft be my Servant to raife up the Tribes of Jacob, and to reftore the preferved of Ifrael; I will alfo give thee for a Light to the Gentiles, that thou mayeft be my Salvation unto the Ends of the Earth.* Thefe Prophecies plainly *began* to be fulfilled, at the time when the Apoftles were commanded to preach the Gofpel to the *Gentiles* as well as to the *Jews*; and the *full accomplifhment* of them will then take place, when the fame everlafting Gofpel fhall either effectually prevail, or at leaft fhall have been preached and tendered in its purity among all Nations. *In every place, Incenfe fhall be offered unto my Name, and a pure Offering.* Incenfe, (which is the *Prayers of the Saints*, Rev. v. 8.) and this phrafe, *a pure Offering*, are plainly intended to exprefs That *Spiritual Religion*, That *Worfhip of the Father in Spirit and Truth* according to the Gofpel of *Chrift*, which is oppofed to the *carnal Ordinances* and *literal Sacrifices* of the *Jews*, and of which thofe Sacrifices and external Purifications were but Types and Figures. Hence the Chriftian Worfhip, the Worfhip of God *out of a pure heart, and of a good confcience, and of faith unfeigned*; is elegantly ftiled a Spiritual Sacrifice; 1 *Pet.* ii. 5: *the* Sacrifice *of Praife to God continually*; Heb. xiii. 15: *the prefenting* ourfelves *a living* Sacrifice, *holy, acceptable to God, which is our reafonable Service*; Rom. xii. 1. The Metaphor is exactly of the fame fort, as That whereby Chriftians are called *The* true *circumcifion, the circumcifion made without hands*; as being *That* in *reality*, in the *true and fpiritual Effect*, of which the *circumcifion in the flefh made with hands* was but a *fhadow* or figurative Reprefentation. For *circumcifion*, fays the Apoftle, Rom. ii. 28, *is not that which is outward in the flefh; but——circumcifion is That of the Heart, in the Spirit, and not in the letter; whofe praife is not of men, but of God.* The *character* therefore of the *Chriftian* Worfhip, fet forth in the Text under the prophetick figures of *Incenfe* and a *Pure Offering*, is, that it confifts in what St *Paul* calls *Lifting up Holy Hands*, 1 Tim. ii. 8. *Without Wrath and Doubting*; It confifts in approaching God, not with the Sacrifice of *Beafts*, or Offerings of the *Fruits of the Earth*; but with the offering up of *Ourfelves* to his Service, in all holinefs and righteoufnefs of Life; Approaching him with *Minds* duly fenfible of the inexpreffible Excellency of the Divine Majefty, with *Hands* clear from all iniquity and

                         unjuft

unjuſt Practices, with *Hearts* free from all Impurity and Moral Turpitude. This is the *Pure Offering*, truly acceptable unto God: And This, he foretells by the Prophet, ſhall in due time be offered unto his Name *in* every *place, from the riſing of the Sun, even unto the going down of the ſame*; for *my Name ſhall be great among the Heathen, ſaith the Lord of Hoſts.* The *Promiſe* is indeed here made *particularly* to the *Gentiles*: But from ſeveral other paſſages of Scripture, parallel to This, there ſeems reaſon to expect that God's *Antient people* alſo ſhall be converted, when once the fulneſs of the *Gentiles* is come in, *If.* xlix. 22; and xi. 12, and lx. 10; *Thus ſaith the Lord God; Behold, I will lift up my hand to the Gentiles, and ſet up my ſtandard to the Nations; and they ſhall bring thy Sons in their arms, and their Daughters ſhall be carried upon their ſhoulders. And he ſhall ſet up an enſign for the Nations, and ſhall aſſemble the Outcaſts of Iſrael, and gather together the diſperſed of Judah from the four Corners of the Earth. And the Sons of Strangers ſhall build up thy Walls, and their Kings ſhall miniſter unto thee; For in my wrath I ſmote thee, but in my Favour have I had mercy on thee.* Our Saviour himſelf predicts ſomething of the ſame nature, *Luke* xxi. 24; *Jeruſalem ſhall be troden down of the Gentiles, till the time of the Gentiles be fulfilled.* And St *Paul* ſeems to intimate the *ſame* thing; *Rom.* xi. 25; *Blindneſs in part is happened to Iſrael, until the Fulneſs of the Gentiles be come in.* After which Great Event, the Scripture is full of very Sublime Deſcriptions of a State of extraordinary Happineſs to enſue; *If.* xi. 6, and lx. 18. *The Wolf alſo ſhall dwell with the Lamb, and the Leopard ſhall lie down with the Kid;——and a little child ſhall lead them. They ſhall not hurt nor deſtroy in all my Holy Mountain; for the Earth ſhall be full of the knowledge of the Lord, as the Waters cover the Sea: And——thou ſhalt call thy Walls Salvation, and thy Gates Praiſe:——Thy people alſo ſhall be All righteous, they ſhall inherit the Land for ever.*

WHATEVER be the true Meaning of Theſe and the like Prophecies; Whether there be a time ſtill to come, wherein they ſhall be accompliſhed literally; Or whether they are intended only to expreſs the natural and genuine *Tendency* of the univerſal and ſincere Practice of Chriſtianity in the *preſent* World, and the *real Effect* which ſhall be obtained by it in the World *to come*: Whatever, I ſay, be the ſtrict and literal Meaning of theſe Prophecies; it becomes not *Us* to be too curious and inquiſitive after the particular *Times and Seaſons which the Father has put in his own Power*; But in *general*, the *Uſes* we are to make of all theſe Predictions, are very obvious. In the

1ſt place, IT is *Our* Duty, in our whole Behaviour and Practice, to promote, as much as in *Us* lies, the Knowledge of God, and the Intereſt of True Virtue and Righteouſneſs amongſt Men. This is contributing *Our* Part, towards the introducing That happy State and Conſtitution of things, which is the Accompliſhment of the fore-mentioned Prophecies. And when we have thus done our *Own* Duty, we are then to remember the Admonition of our Saviour, *Luke* xxi. 19; *In your patience poſſeſs ye your Souls*; and rely upon the Providence of *God*, to accompliſh the Great Events which he has promiſed, in his own *Manner* and at his own *Time*. In matters of *This* nature, which have not a conditional dependence upon the Behaviour of *ſingle* perſons, but relate to the *General* Scheme of Providence in the Government of the World; In *Theſe* things, I ſay, *the Gifts and Calling of God are without Repentance*; Rom. xi. 29. The Promiſes of God will certainly be accompliſhed, and his Purpoſe ſhall not fail. But becauſe it is not for *Us* to know beforehand, the exact *Times and Seaſons* which God has appointed; the Duty therefore of every particular Chriſtian, whatever be the Circumſtances of Time and Place in which Providence has fixed him, is to take care that He himſelf be in the Number of thoſe, who, *in all Holy converſation and godlineſs, look for, and haſte unto, the Coming of the day of God*; 2 Pet. iii. 12.

S E R M.   2*dly*, ANOTHER Inference arising from the confideration of fuch Predictions as
LXXIII. This in the Text, is, that we may hence learn to *juftify* to ourfelves the various Methods, in which the Wifdom of God has chofen at divers times to reveal itfelf to the
World. With regard to *fingle perfons*, to whom Providence has given very different
natural capacities, or different *Means and Opportunities of Knowledge*, or different Manners of *Revelation*, the divine Juftice and Equity confifts in judging them finally according to their refpective Abilities, accepting every one *according to what he has, and
not according to what he has not.* With regard to *Whole Nations*, the juftification of the
Divine Wifdom, is his fo doing what he pleafes with his own, as, through a Succeffion of various and great Events, to accomplifh *General Defigns* of Mercy and Goodnefs. Of This, St *Paul* has given us an admirable Inftance, in his account of God's
fetting up firft the Nation of the *Jews*, and afterwards the Churches of the Chriftian
Gentiles, to be the Standard of true Religion to the World; intending to finifh the whole
Difpenfation, by having Mercy upon Both: *Rom.* xi. 30; *For as* ye (Gentiles) *in
times paft have not believed God, yet have* Now *obtained Mercy through* Their (the *Jews*)
Unbelief: Even fo have Thefe *alfo now not believed, that through your mercy* They *alfo
may obtain mercy. For God hath concluded them All in unbelief, that he might have mer-
cy upon All. O the depth of the Riches both of the Wifdom and Knowledge of God!
How unfearchable are his Judgments, and his Ways paft finding out!*

3*dly* and *Laftly*, THE *Laft* Inference I fhall draw from what has been faid, is This.
In the words *before* my Text, the reafon given of God's rejecting the *Jews*, is the unworthy manner in which they had behaved themfelves, while unto them were committed the Oracles of God. In the *Text itfelf*, the acceptablenefs of the *converted Gentiles* unto God, is expreffed by their offering up unto his Name a *Pure Offering*. Which
Pure Offering, denotes the *Holinefs* and *real Purity* of the *Gofpel-difpenfation*, in oppo-
pofition to the *external Ceremonies* of the *Jewifh Law*. If therefore *We*, under the
greater Light of the *Everlafting Gofpel*, ftill live *vicioufly* and *corruptly*, as the *Jews*
did under thofe *carnal Ordinances*; how much *more fevere* Judgments fhall we have
reafon to expect, than what fell even upon That People! For (as St *Paul* excellently
argues, *Rom.* xi. 20;) *Becaufe of Unbelief* They *were broken off*, and Thou *ftandeft by
Faith: Be not high-minded, but fear : For if God fpared not the natural Branches, take
heed left he alfo fpare not Thee.*

SERMON

SERMON LXXIV.

The Doctrines of Religion reasonable to be believed.

[A Passion Sermon.]

M A T T. XII. 39, 40.

An evil and adulterous generation seeketh after a Sign, and there shall no Sign be given to it, but the Sign of the prophet Jonas. For as Jonas was three days and three nights in the whale's belly; so shall the Son of Man be three days and three nights in the Heart of the Earth.

WHEN our Saviour first preached to the *Jews* the Gospel of the Kingdom, he proved to them his divine Commission and the Truth of his Doctrine, not only from the *Prophecies* of the Old Testament, from the things written in the Law, and in the Prophets, and in the Psalms, concerning him; but also by the *mighty Works* which he himself performed, as direct and immediate Evidences of his being the Promised Messiah. The *Doctrine* he taught, being a Doctrine of Purity and Great Holiness, absolutely requiring a Reformation of Manners, and such an effectual Amendment of Life, as must show forth itself in the real and habitual Practice of true Virtue and Righteousness; *This Doctrine* was therefore extremely disagreeable to the *Pharisees* and Chief men among the *Jews*, who were persons of a haughty and tyrannical Spirit, covetous and ambitious, and, in order to serve the Purposes of temporal Power and spiritual Pride, infinitely zealous of all the external Forms and Ceremonials of Religion. For This reason, they hated, above all things, the Spirit with which our Saviour taught; the Spirit of Meekness and Humility, the Spirit of Goodness and Equity, the Spirit of Love and universal Charity. And accordingly they set themselves, upon all occasions, to revile his Doctrine and calumniate his person. In which matter, it was no great difficulty for them to meet with Success; because the prejudiced Vulgar, who could very hardly distinguish between the *Traditions of their Elders* and the *Commands of God*, must needs be prone to look upon our Lord as an Enemy to the *One*, because he preached against the *Other*. But the *Miracles* which our Saviour worked, were *harder* to withstand: For the people could not easily be persuaded, that God would give a *Deceiver* Power to perform as *mighty Works*, as those by which the Law of *Moses* had itself been at first established. Here therefore the malice of the *Pharisees*, was to exert itself in a more extraordinary manner. And when they could not deny the *miraculous Facts themselves*, they pretended that the *Power* which worked them was the Power of Satan: Ver. 24th *of this chapter*, They said, he *doth not cast out Devils, but by Beelzebub the Prince of the Devils.* And whensoever he

SERM.
LXXIV.

3

taught,

SERM. taught, *without* working some immediate Miracle; *then* they presently called upon
LXXIV. him again, to show them a *Sign*: Ver. 38, *Then certain of the Scribes and Pharisees*
answered, saying, Master, we would see a Sign *from thee.* Thus against wilful perverseness there is No remedy. If he spake to them with so much *reason* and *goodness,*
as *never man spake;* still his Doctrine wanted to be confirmed by a *Miracle.* And if
he confirmed what he taught, by undeniable *Miracles;* then the *Power* which worked
them, was the *Power of Satan.* For This reason, to the *Pharisees* who called upon
him to show them a Sign, he gave this severe Reply in the words of the Text; *An*
evil and adulterous generation seeketh after a Sign, and there shall no Sign be given to
it, but the Sign of the Prophet Jonas: For as Jonas was three days and three nights
in the whale's belly, so shall the Son of man be three days and three nights in the heart
of the Earth. The declaration here made by our Lord, is of the same nature with
That in the Prophet *Isaiah;* ch. vii. 13; *Hear ye now, O house of David; is it a small*
thing for you to weary Men, but will ye weary my God also? Therefore the Lord him-
self shall give you a Sign; Behold, a Virgin shall conceive and bear a Son, and shall
call his Name Immanuel. The *Jews* in *Isaiah's* time, like the *Pharisees* in our *Savi-*
our's, after all the mighty works that God had done for them, still continued *impe-*
nitent: And as often as they were called upon to repent, they presumptuously demanded *more Signs.* In way of Reproof for this Perverseness of theirs, and as a
standing Declaration of God's having done, on *His* part, what was fit for *Him* to do;
the Divine Wisdom, both in the days of *Isaiah,* and in the days of *Christ,* refers such
persons to the *settled* and *universal* Evidence of Revelation; *viz. the miraculous ful-*
filling of the *Antient Prophecies* concerning the *promised Messias.* The Sign referred to
by *Isaiah,* is the Birth *of Christ; Behold, a Virgin shall conceive.* That referred to by
our Saviour in the Text, is his Resurrection; *The Son of man shall be three days and*
three nights in the heart of the earth.

THERE is in these words *one* Difficulty; how our Lord is here said to have been
three days and three nights in the heart of the Earth, when in the History of all the
Gospels it appears, that having been buried the *first* day in the *evening,* and rising
again the *third* day in the *morning,* he consequently remained in the Sepulchre but
two whole nights, and *one* whole day. Now in order to understand this rightly, it is
to be observed that the *Jews* in *Their* language, as *We* also frequently do in *Ours,* by
the word *(day)* mean the Space of *twenty four hours.* And in *all languages* Nothing
is more common, than for the Name of the *Whole* to be made use of to express a
Part. Whatever therefore is *begun* on the *first* day, and *finished* on the *third,* may in
usual and vulgar Speech (which is always the language the Scripture speaks in) be
rightly said to be *three days* in doing. But *This* may perhaps seem a matter of *smaller*
importance; Though, indeed, it can never be without its Use, to show the consistency of such Texts of Scripture, as at first sight may appear not to agree together.

Another Inquiry therefore, naturally arising upon these words, is, for *what reason*
our Saviour continued in the Sepulchre just such a *determinate time* before his Resurrection. Now, besides that This was necessary for the *fulfilling of the Prophecies* that
went before concerning him, (which is the reason alledged in the Text;) it was moreover necessary in the *nature of the thing itself,* that he should continue so long *a time*
in the grave, to show that he was *really dead;* and he was to continue there *no longer,*
that (as the Scripture expresses it) *the Holy One might not see corruption.*

THE words of the Text being thus explained; the matter of instruction therein
contained, may be reduced to the following Heads.

1*st,* THAT

1st, THAT the Doctrine of religion is in itself reasonable to be believed, and suffi- S E R M. ciently evidenced by the *standing* and *universal Signs* or *Marks* of Truth. It is LXXIV. *supposed* in the words, that, what our Saviour here calls the *Sign of the Prophet* ⌢⌢ *Jonas,* was sufficient to render That generation of the *Jews* inexcusable in their Unbelief.

2dly, HERE is a Description given of wicked men, in one particular and re-markable part of their character; that they are apt continually to require *more* and *more* Signs, and to tempt God without reason and without end. *An evil and adulterous generation seeketh after a Sign.*

3dly, THE declaration our Saviour here makes, plainly implies, that there are just and good reasons, why God should not gratify the unreasonable expectations of prejudiced and corrupt Minds. *There shall no Sign be given to it, but the Sign of the Prophet Jonas.*

1st, THE Doctrine of religion is in itself reasonable to be believed, and suffi-ciently evidenced by the *standing* and *universal Signs* or *Marks* of Truth: It is *supposed* in the words, that what our Saviour here calls the *Sign of the Prophet Jonas,* was sufficient to render That generation of the *Jews* inexcusable in their Un-belief.

Religion is *in its Nature* a Trial or Probation of men's Hearts; and is therefore es-sentially inconsistent with all compulsive Motives, with *such* Motives as destroy the na-ture of a Trial or Probation, *Deut.* viii. 2. *The Lord thy God led thee these forty years in the Wilderness, —— to prove thee, to know what was in thine heart, whether thou wouldest keep his commandments or no.* The Meaning is, not that God wants any in-formation with regard to *Himself:* But he puts men in a probation-state, in order to their *Own* Benefit; that by virtuous *Actions* they may obtain an *habitual* Love of Vir-tue; and by labouring in the rational *Search* after *Truth,* and persevering patiently in the *Practice* of *Right,* they may be *purified and made white and tried,* Dan. xii. 10. For, as the Apostle St *James* expresses it, *the Trying of our Faith worketh Patience*; ch. i. 3. God could, if he pleased, *even out of the stones of the Street, raise up chil-dren unto Abraham*; or irresistibly compel the most obdurate Sinner to obey his Com-mandments. But This, is not dealing with *Them* as *rational Agents*; nor could such an Obedience be any more acceptable to *Him,* than the absolute Subjection of the *ma-terial* World to his Omnipotent Will, gives *irrational* Beings any Title to the Esteem and Character of Moral Goodness or Virtue. Were God by his Almighty Power to over-rule and prevent all Possibility of Disobedience or Moral Evil, as some men fancy it would be glorious for him to do; it would indeed have the contrary effect, and de-prive him of the Glory of all his Moral Attributes. For though he would still continue to be a Mighty Creator and All-Powerful Lord, yet he could in no sense be a *Moral Governor* or *Judge* of the World, nor have Any Exercise of his Moral Perfections. All Religion or Virtue, consists in the Love of Truth, and in the Free Choice and Practice of Right, and in being influenced regularly by rational and moral Motives. By *These* things therefore God tries or proves men's Obedience; and under various Circum-stances, and by various Methods of manifesting himself to them, he exercises their Faith and Patience and Virtue. By induing men originally with *Reason and Under-standing,* with a *natural Knowledge* of Good and Evil, and a *Conscience* of the differ-ence between Virtue and Vice; By the Witness that God bears to himself in the Works of *Nature,* and by the various Dispensations of his All-wise *Providence*; in which *Visi-*

SERM. *ble Effects*, the Power and Government of the *Invisible God* are clearly and continually
LXXIV. seen, *so that they*, who attend not to them, *are without excuse* : By *these* things, does
God perpetually call men to religion ; and hold out unto them an *universal Light*, in
all Places and at *all* Times. And had men *no other* Discovery of the Will of God, than
This ; yet their choosing to depart from the *natural* Law of *everlasting Righteousness*,
would justly denominate them *an evil and adulterous generation* of Mankind.   But *besides* this Voice of *Nature* in the visible works of God, and in the mind and conscience
of every particular person ; the divine Providence has moreover, in compassion to the
ignorance of the Weak, and *for a Testimony* against the perverse and corrupt, in almost
every Age of the World, raised up Eminent *Preachers of Righteousness* ; such as was
Enoch before, and *Noah at* the time of the Flood, and *Job* and the *Patriarchs after*
it ; to excite and call men to the practice of their Duty.   And to the Nation of the
Jews, he gave a *standing Revelation* of his Will ; inviting them continually to Repentance by his Messengers *the Prophets*, and at last by his Son *Jesus Christ*, their promised
and long expected Messiah : Manifesting his manifold Wisdom, *at sundry times and in
diverse manners* of Revelation ; as he had before done in the *various distribution* of the
Natural *Talents* of men's *rational Faculties, Capacities, and Abilities*, intending finally
to judge *All* his Servants, *according to what* every one in particular *has, and not according to what he has not* : And in each of these various Dispensations, giving such degrees of *evidence and testimony* to the Truth, as might be a proper Tryal of good and
well-disposed Minds, neither credulous *beyond* reason, nor prejudiced *against* reason, but
prepared always to *receive* the Truth, and to *obey* it.   Thus, to That generation of the
Jews who lived in our Saviour's time, the proper and sufficient evidence of our Lord's
being the promised Messias, to all such as impartially searched the Scriptures, was the
fulfilling of the Prophecies that went before concerning him, and particularly That most
miraculous One of his Resurrection from the Dead.   Which was a *Sign* not possible to
be resisted by Any, but by a very corrupt and *adulterous generation* ; by a generation of
such men, of such *perverse and incorrigible* Sinners, the description of whom, (which
was the

2d Particular I observed in the text,) the *description* of them, in one *remarkable*
part of their character, is, that they are apt continually to require *more* and *more* Signs,
and to tempt God without reason and without end : *An evil and adulterous generation
seeketh after a Sign*.   The wickedest of men cannot bear the Thoughts of fighting
openly against God ; and therefore, to give some degree of Ease to their Minds, they
generally take great pains to impose upon themselves, with some slight objections either
against the *Being of God*, or against the *evidence of his Laws and Commands*.   *The Jews*,
says St *Paul*, *require a Sign, and the Gentiles seek after Wisdom*, 1 Cor. i. 22.   The humour of the *Gentile* World, was to value themselves upon their *Logick and Philosophy* ;
and therefore the corrupt part of *Them* could always reject *any* religious Truth, by
drawing objections against it from the *received Maxims of their Schools*.   The *Jewish*
nation valued themselves upon the *miraculous* things, which God had done for their
Fathers ; and therefore the corrupt part of *Them*, could always reject *any* religious
Truth, by continually requiring *more* and *greater Miracles* to be worked in confirmation of it.   Of This, the behaviour of That people in the *Wilderness* is a remarkable
and very marvellous Instance.   By a continued series of Miracles, God had rescued them
from *Egyptian* Slavery and Idolatry, and was guiding them in the Wilderness like a
Flock, to the possession of the good land which he had promised to their Fathers.
Marvellous things (as the Psalmist represents this matter in a most elegant and affectionate description, *Ps.* lxxviii. 13,) *Marvellous things did he in the fight of our fore-
fathers, in the land of Egypt, even in the field of Zoan.   He divided the Sea, and let
them go through ; he made the waters to stand on a heap.   In the day-time also he led them*
with

with a cloud; and all the night through, with a light of fire. He clave the hard rocks S E R M·
in the wilderneſs, and gave them drink thereof, as it had been out of the great depth. LXXIV.
He brought waters out of the ſtony rock, ſo that it guſhed out like the Rivers. Further,
ver. 24; *He commanded the clouds above, and opened the doors of heaven. He rained
down manna alſo upon them for to eat, and gave them food from heaven. So man did
eat Angels food, for he ſent them meat enough. He cauſed the eaſt-wind to blow under
heaven, and thro' his power he brought in the ſouth-weſt wind. He rained fleſh upon
them as thick as duſt, and feathered fowls like as the ſand of the Sea. He let it fall a-
mong their tents, even round about their habitation.* And again, ver. 53, *He led them
forth like ſheep, and carried them in the wilderneſs like a flock. He brought them out
ſafely, that they ſhould not fear; and overwhelmed their enemies with the Sea. He
brought them within the borders of his ſanctuary, even to his mountain which he purchaſed with his right hand. He caſt out the heathen alſo before them; cauſed their land
to be divided among them for an heritage, and made the tribes of Iſrael to dwell in their
tents.* Sufficient *Signs* Theſe, any unprejudiced perſon would judge, to convince even
the moſt obſtinate and perverſe, the moſt *evil and adulterous generation.* But ſo familiar were theſe *Marvels* become to them, that (it appears) they had no more influence
upon *Them,* to bring them to true Amendment and Reformation of Manners, than
the Works of *Nature,* (which are in Truth the continual miraculous operation of the
omnipotent Power of the *God* of Nature,) have upon *Us.* This alſo is moſt *pathetically*
ſet forth in the ſame lxxviiith *Pſalm,* ver. 18, *Yet for all this they ſinned more againſt
him, and provoked the moſt Higheſt in the Wilderneſs : They tempted God in their hearts,
and required meat for their Luſt. They ſpake againſt God alſo, ſaying, Shall God prepare a Table in the Wilderneſs? He ſmote the ſtony Rock indeed, that the water guſhed
out, and the ſtreams flowed withal; but can he give Bread alſo, or provide fleſh for his
people ?* (Their Argument was exactly the ſame, as that of the *Phariſees* to whom our
Lord replies in my Text : They acknowledged that he had healed many diſeaſed perſons here upon *Earth;* But could he ſhow them *alſo a Sign from Heaven ?)* Further,
ver. 32, of the ſame Pſalm, *For all this they have ſinned yet more, and believed not his
wondrous works :* ver. 11. *They kept not the Covenant of God, and would not walk in his
law; But forgat what he had done, and the wonderful Works that he had ſhowed for
them,* ver. 42. *They turned back and tempted God, and moved the Holy One in Iſrael :
They thought not of his hand, and of the day when he delivered them from the hand of
the Enemy; How he had wrought his Miracles in Egypt, and his Wonders in the field of
Zoan.* And again, ver. 57, *They tempted and diſpleaſed the moſt High God, and kept not
his Teſtimonies; But turned their backs, and fell away like their forefathers, ſtarting a-
ſide like a broken Bow. For they grieved him with their hill-altars, and provoked him to
diſpleaſure with their Images.* A more lively and affectionate deſcription of the perverſeneſs of incorrigible Sinners, cannot poſſibly be given. Other Accounts of the ſame nature, we find in the hiſtory which the Old Teſtament gives us of the behaviour of
That people. When the *Egyptians* purſued after them into the Wilderneſs; *then,* as
if he who had brought them out of *Egypt* with a mighty hand was not able to protect
them in their journey; they ſaid, *Wherefore haſt thou thus dealt with us, to carry us
forth out of Egypt?* Exod. xiv. 11. When the *Egyptians* were all deſtroyed, and they
had nothing to oppoſe their progreſs but the ſolitary Wilderneſs; *then,* as if he who had
delivered them from the Hoſt of *Pharoah,* was not able to feed them in the Deſert,
they ſaid, *To have brought us forth into this Wilderneſs to kill this whole Aſſembly with
hunger,* Exod. xvi. 3. When God miraculouſly ſupplied them with Bread from Heaven;
then, there was *nothing at all beſides this manna,* Num. xi. 6 : And when, by *another*
miracle, he had quenched their Thirſt; *then,* he *ſmote the ſtony rock indeed, that the
waters guſhed out; but can he provide* Fleſh *alſo for his people?* Pſ. lxxviii. 21. And
when,

S E R M. when, by a *third* miracle, he fed them to the full with quails ; *for all* This, *they finned*
LXXIV. *yet more, and believed not his wondrous works,* ver. 32. When *Moses* tarried longer in
the Mount than They expected ; *then,* they could not live without their Leader, but
muſt *make Gods to go before* them ; *for as for This Moſes,* they knew *not what was become of him,* Exod. xxxii. 1 : When he continued with them, and put himſelf conſtantly at the Head of them ; *then,* ye *take too much upon you ; wherefore lift ye up
yourſelves above the congregation of the Lord?* Numb. xvi. 3. When God commanded
them to go up, and take poſſeſſion of the good Land which he had provided for them ;
then, the *people of the land* were *ſtrong,* and *the Cities walled,* and *the children of Anak
there,* and *we be not able to go up againſt the people,* and *the land is a land that eateth
up the inhabitants thereof,* and *we ſaw Giants there,* and *would God we had died in the
land of Egypt, or would God we had died in this Wilderneſs ;* and *wherefore has the Lord
brought us unto this land, to fall by the ſword?* Num. xiii. 28, &c. But when the Lord
hereupon commanded them not *to go up ; then, Lo we be here, and* will *go up unto the
place which the Lord has promiſed,* ch. xiv. 40.

I ſ h o u l d *proceed* to *Other* Inſtances of the unreaſonable behaviour of ſinful men
in this reſpect : But the time not permitting me to finiſh this Subject Now, I ſhall at
preſent add only a word of *application,* and ſo conclude.

I b e l i e v e there are very few perſons, who read theſe portions of Scripture,
without cenſuring in their own minds the behaviour of the *Jews,* and ſaying within
themſelves, as did thoſe whom our Saviour deſcribes, *Matt.* xxiii. 30. *If* We *had been
in the days of our Fathers, we would not have been partakers with them* in Theſe things.
But to every impenitent Sinner, in the *preſent* as well as in *former* times, the experience of the World, and the reaſon of things, and the judgment of conſcience, and the
Scripture of Truth ſays, *Thou art the man.* For all theſe things are *examples* unto Us,
and they are written for our *admonition, upon whom the ends of the World are come.*
God calls Us to Repentance, by the continual Witneſs which he gives to himſelf in the
Works of Creation, in the Reaſon and Nature of Things, in the eſſential Differences
of Good and Evil, in the voice of Conſcience, in the diſpenſations of Providence, in his
Mercies and Judgments, in the completion of Prophecies, in the Works and Preaching of Chriſt and his Apoſtles, in the Promiſes and Threatnings of the Goſpel. And
if all *Theſe* things move men not, the Scripture declares *there ſhall no Sign be given to*
us, but the *Sign* of the Nations who were deſtroyed by the *Flood,* and the Cities who
periſhed in the Overthrow of *Sodom.* For as in the days before the *Flood,* and before
the deſtruction of *Sodom,* men were *eating and drinking,* and *knew not* until the
Waters came and *took away* the one, and the Fire the other ; *ſo alſo,* ſays our Lord,
ſhall the Coming of the Son of Man be.

SERMON LXXV.

Unreafonable Expectations not to be gratified in Religion.

[*A Paffion-Sermon.*]

MATT. XII. 39.

*An evil and adulterous generation feeketh after a Sign, and there
fhall No Sign be given to it, but the Sign of the Prophet Jonas.*

GOD, who is the Supreme Governour of the Univerfe, fhows forth his infinite S E R M.
Wifdom and Goodnefs, in creating a Variety of rational Creatures in different LXXV.
Circumftances, and expecting from them a proportionable Ufe of the Talents
committed to them, according to their different degrees of Light and Knowledge, and
according to their refpective Capacities and Abilities. To *Angels*, having given Knowledge and Powers far fuperiour to thofe of Men; he expects of them accordingly an
Angelical Obedience. To *Men*, having difpenfed various Talents and various Degrees of
Knowledge, at fundry times and in divers manners, according to his own good pleafure;
after the fimilitude of the Great King in our Saviour's Parable who, in the diftribution of Employments among his Servants, without injury to any one, did what he
pleafed with his own: To *Men*, I fay, God having difpenfed various Talents and various degrees of Knowledge, he expects of them a Return proportionable to what is
given them; Not over-ruling their Actions by the Force and Power of an irrefiftible
Light; but trying their Obedience by the Willingnefs of their Endeavours to feek after
Knowledge, and to guide themfelves by That degree of Light (whatfoever it be)
whereby his Will is in any meafure made known unto them.

IN the State of *Nature*, God made himfelf known to Men by the Arguments of
Reafon, by the Works of Creation, and by the difpenfations of Providence; *having
never left himfelf wholly without witnefs, but fending men rain and fruitful Seafons, and
filling their Hearts with Food and Gladnefs;* the *invifible things of God from the creation of the World being clearly feen and underftood by the things that are made, even his
eternal Power and Godhead,* Rom. i. 20. If the *Nations of the World*, forfaking *this
univerfal Light*, fall into the abfurdeft and moft unreafonable Idolatries, and into confequently vicious and corrupt Practices of all kinds; *they are* evidently (as St *Paul* declares) *without Excufe*; and there is no injuftice with God, if to fuch *evil and adulterous generations* of men there be *no other Sign given*, but the *Signs of Nature* and *Reafon* and *Confcience*, and the perpetual univerfal *Works of God.*

UNDER the *Gofpel*, God has made himfelf known to Men by the Revelation of his
Son, confirmed by Signs and Wonders and *Miracles* of the *Holy Ghoft*, by the Completion of *Prophecies*, and by the Analogy of the *Whole Series of Events* from the

SERM. Beginning of the World. If under this *greater* and *clearer light of Revelation*, men
LXXV. still continue impenitent; not bringing forth the suitable Fruits of Righteousness, nor
living *worthy of their holy vocation*, and as *becometh* the *Gospel of Christ*; *the wrath of*
God is more severely *revealed from Heaven, against all unrighteousness and ungodliness of*
Such *men*; and there shall *no* further *Sign be given to* such *an evil and adulterous gene-*
ration, but the Sign of the Son of man coming with the clouds of Heaven, in flame of fire
taking Vengeance on them that know not God, and that obey not the Gospel.

Under the *Jewish* state, God manifested himself to That People by the Law of
Moses, by the continual Preaching of the *Prophets*, and finally by the accomplishment
of the whole dispensation in the *Life and Death and Resurrection of Christ*. And when
they who saw *These* manifestations of God, were not thereby prevailed upon to *bring*
forth Fruits meet for Repentance, and answerable to the *Light* that was then *come into*
the World; but, on the contrary, *cavilled* at our Lord's Doctrine and Miracles, and
continually required *More* Signs; our Lord, with just indignation, gives them the reply
in the Text; *An evil and adulterous generation seeketh after a Sign, and there shall No*
Sign be given to it, but the Sign of the Prophet Jonas: For as Jonas was three days and
three nights in the Whale's Belly, so shall the Son of Man be three days and three nights
in the Heart of the Earth.

In discoursing upon which words, I have before observed, that the matter of instruction therein contained, may be reduced to the following Heads.

> 1*st*, That the Doctrine of Religion is in itself reasonable to be believed, and suf-
> ficiently evidenced by the *standing* and *universal Signs* or *Marks of Truth*. It is
> *supposed* in the words, that, what our Saviour here calls the *Sign of the Prophet*
> *Jonas*, was sufficient to render That generation of the *Jews* inexcusable in their
> Unbelief.

> 2*dly*, Here is a description given of wicked men, in one particular and remarka-
> ble part of their Character; that they are apt continually to require *more* and *more*
> Signs, and to tempt God without reason and without End. *An evil and adulte-*
> *rous generation seeketh after a Sign.*

> 3*dly*, The declaration our Saviour here makes, plainly implies, that there are just
> and good reasons, why God should not gratify the unreasonable expectations of
> prejudiced and corrupt Minds. *There shall No Sign be given to it, but the Sign*
> *of the Prophet Jonas.*

The *First* of these, I have already gone through; and have shown, that the Doctrine of Religion is in itself reasonable to be believed, and sufficiently evidenced by the
standing and *universal Signs* or *Marks of Truth*. According to our Saviour's Supposition in the words of the Text; that, what he here calls the *Sign of the Prophet Jonas*,
was sufficient to render That generation of the *Jews* inexcusable in their Unbelief.

The *Second* Observable, was, the Description here given of wicked men, in one
particular and remarkable part of their Character; that they are apt continually to require *more* and *more* Signs, and to tempt God without reason and without End: *An*
evil and Adulterous generation seeketh after a Sign. And This Observation I at large
illustrated by That *remarkable Instance* the Scripture gives us, of the behaviour of the
people of the Jews in their passage through the *Wilderness*; which is so distinctly recorded
in the Books of *Moses*, and so frequently alluded to in the *Psalms*, and in St *Paul's* Epistles to the *Corinthians* and to the *Hebrews*, as a standing Admonition and Caution to
perverse Minds, in all succeeding generations.

I SHALL

I SHALL *Now* proceed to some *Other* Instances of the like Sort, in which the Unreasonableness of tempting God in this manner, will still further appear. In our *Saviour's time,* the *same* Spirit of Perverseness, which the Scripture calls an *evil Heart of Unbelief,* (meaning always by *Unbelief,* not a *reasonable Caution* in *with-holding the Assent,* but a *captious Desire* of *evading the reasons of conviction;*) In our *Saviour's time,* I say, the *same* perverse Spirit, which appeared so remarkably in the *Jews of old* in the Wilderness, continued *still* in the corrupt part of That Nation; So that *whatever* Method the divine Wisdom thought fit to make use of, in order to bring them to Repentance; they could *Always* render it ineffectual. *John the Baptist came* unto them, *neither eating Bread, nor drinking Wine*; Luke vii. 33; that is, *he* came in the more *severe* way of *austerity and mortification*; and they *said, He hath a Devil*; that is, they *charged* him with being *enthusiastick and mad.* On the other hand, *the Son of man is come eating and drinking*; ver. 34; that is, in the more *familiar* way of a free conversation; and they *said, Behold, a gluttonous man and a wine-bibber, a friend of Publicans and Sinners.* The Methods of Proceeding were *Both* of them right, in their proper Time and Place; and *Wisdom is justified of all her children*; But incorrigible men could equally find Objections against *Both.* Our Saviour therefore, in a most elegant parable, compares them to cross and perverse children, whom neither Mirth nor Seriousness could please: Ver. 31; *Whereunto shall I liken the men of This generation? and to what are they like? They are like unto children sitting in the market-place, and calling one to another, and saying, We have piped unto you, and ye have not danced; we have mourned to you, and ye have not wept.* When the men of *Nazareth* heard what mighty works our Lord had done at *Capernaum,* they said, *Whatsoever we have heard done in Capernaum, do also here in thy own country*; Luke iv. 23; On the other hand, when he did Wonders in his own country, then their Answer was, *Depart hence, and go into Judea, that thy Disciples also may see the works that thou doest* ;——*If thou do these things, show thy self to the world*; Joh. vii. 3. When our Lord had miraculously healed many diseased persons here upon *Earth,* then the *Pharisees* said unto him, *Master, we would see of thee a Sign from* Heaven: And when there came unto him a *voice from* Heaven, Joh. xii. 28; the Evangelist tells us, ver. 37, that *yet they believed not on him.* When the Chief Priests and Elders saw our Saviour crucified, they said, *Matt.* xxvii. 42; *He saved others, himself he cannot save; if he be the King of Israel, let him now come down from the cross, and we will believe him*: But when he was risen from the Dead, to the Terror of their own Soldiers, whom they had set to watch him; then they gave them money to report, that *his Disciples had come by night, and stolen him away*; ch. xxviii. 13. Thus, of tempting God; and of continually requiring more and greater Signs, and of finding Means to elude the Arguments and Motives of Religion, there is no End. The *Temper* from which all This proceeds, is of the *same* kind with That *Tempting of Providence,* which the Gospel emphatically represents to us in the history of *our Saviour's temptation*; Where *Satan* placing him upon a *pinnacle of the temple,* argues with him, that, if he was the *Son of God,* he might safely venture to *cast* himself *down* from thence: For if God owned and declared him to be his *Son,* and had so peculiar a Favour for him; *why* should not he preserve him from being hurt in his Fall; *Matt.* iv. 6. The Ground upon which incorrigible Sinners reject all the Arguments and Motives of Religion, is generally of *the like* Nature. If it be the *Will* of God, that men should *believe* and *act* in such or such a particular manner; *why* does not he *compel* them so to do? *why* does not he perpetually *give them Signs from Heaven? why* does he not *turn their Hearts,* which way soever he pleases? for *Who has resisted his Will?* The Answer is very plain; that God does not absolutely *will* such and such things to be done, but his Will is that men should *chuse* to do them upon reasonable Motives: In which alone consists the essence of all *Virtue,* and of all *Religion.*

God

S E R M. God does not therefore by irresistible Motives *compel* men to *obey* him; because, if he
LXXX. did, it would for that very Reason be in *Them No* Act of *Obedience*. But he *tries*
their Obedience, by the *proper* Instruments of *Persuasion*; and by Motives suited to the
nature of *rational* and *free* Agents. Of These, *Some* love the knowledge of *Truth*; and
are always ready, according to the degree of the Light afforded them, to do what is
Right: And these our Saviour, in his parable of the Sower, very significantly compares to *Good Ground.* *Others* love *Darkness rather than Light*, and Arguments of
Reason make no Impression upon them, and their *Hearts are as hard as the Nether-
millstone*. To *These*, the exquisite *Works of Nature* prove not the *Being of God*; the
Revelation of the Gospel, discovers not to them his *Will*: And should God vouchsafe
them still *Other Calls* to Repentance, they would prove equally ineffectual; *neither
would they be perswaded*, even *though one rose from the Dead*. Of This we have a remakable Instance; *Joh.* xii. 9, 10; *Much people——came, not for Jesus sake only, but
that they might see Lazarus also, whom he had raised from the Dead: But the chief
Priests consulted, that they might put Lazarus also to Death.* These were, in the
strongest Sense of the words in my Text, *an evil and adulterous generation*; altogether
unworthy of having any further Signs given them; and whose behaviour abundantly
justifies our Lord's declaration in the following part of the Text, (which was the

   Third and *Last* thing I proposed to speak to; *viz.* the *Declaration* our Saviour here
makes,) plainly implying that there are *just and good reasons*, why God should not gratify the unreasonable expectations of prejudiced and corrupt minds: *There shall no Sign
be given to this generation, but the Sign of the Prophet Jonas.* Now the reasonableness of this Proceeding, is very evident from what has been already said. Eternal Life,
is the Gift of God: And the Design of God, (his *just* and *reasonable* Design,) is to bestow this *free Gift*, upon those who by an habitual *Practice of Virtue*, shall have their
Minds qualified for That Happy State. The *Practice of Virtue* consists, in the *willing
Choice* of what is *good*, and *avoiding* what is evil: And the *Time* of this Choice, is the
present state of *Probation*. God could, if he had pleased, by giving *no free Will* to his
Creatures, have prevented *all possibility* of *Moral Evil*. But then the whole *Creation
of God*, would have been only a great *Machine*; in which the *Omnipotence* indeed of
the Maker, would have appeared; but he would have been no *King*, no *Judge*, no
Moral Governor; nor could have displayed *any* of those *more excellent Perfections*,
of *Justice*, *Mercy*, and the like, in which the *Glory* of the Almighty principally consists.
These have *no place*, but where there are *Subjects* capable of *obeying* or *disobeying*. The
proper Tryal of which obedience, is That *Freedom of Will*, which, according as it is
determined in different Circumstances by the *reasonableness of what is good*, or the *inticements of what is evil*, renders the *Agent* morally *good or evil*. God therefore, according to his own good pleasure, places men in all variety of Circumstances in this probation-state; And the Justice, and Wisdom, and Goodness of his Government consists
in finally judging them All with Equity, according to their respective degrees of Light
and Knowledge. The first *Root* and *Foundation* of Virtue, is the sincere Desire of *knowing* the Will of God, and impartially *searching* after the Truth: And, as a proper Tryal
of This disposition, the Wisdom of God has been pleased so to order the *Notices* given
of himself to Mankind both by *Nature* and *Revelation*, that *if any man will do his Will,
he shall know of the doctrine*; and, if he *desires not to practise* it, even the *knowledge* of
it shall be *hid from him*: *To Him that hath, shall be given*; and *from Him that hath
not, shall be taken away even That which he hath.* By the Light of *Nature*, God manifests himself to men in the *works of Creation*; Visibly enough, to those who, as St
Paul expresses it, *seek the Lord, if haply they may feel after him, and find him*: But
yet at the same time in *such a manner*, as that vicious and ill-disposed men, *seeing, may
still not see*; and *hearing, may still not hear*; but may go on to ascribe the most perfect

   I

                                                                         works

works of infinite Wifdom, to *Fate*, to *Chance*, to *Nothing*. By *Revelation*, God has S E R M. declared his *Mercy* towards Sinners: Signifying unto them, that as a Great King over LXXV. numerous Nations, confiftently with the Laws of his univerfal Kingdom, pardons, in fome rebellious City, by the interpofition of his beloved Son, as many as, by his Son's invitation and perfwafion, return to their Duty; fo alfo will *God*, the Supreme Governour of the Univerfe, accept all thofe, whom the Spirit of Chrift, (inviting them either under the ftate of *Nature*, by fuch *Preachers of righteoufnefs* as was *Noah* and the *Patriarchs*; or under the *Law*, by *Mofes* and the *Prophets*; or under the *Gofpel*, by our *Lord himfelf* and his *Apoftles*,) whom (I fay) by *Any* of thefe means, the Spirit of Chrift fhall bring to Repentance. And the *Evidences* of this *Revelation*, (in the fame manner, and for the fame reafon, as the Evidences of God in the Works of *Creation*,) are fitted to fatisfy an unprejudiced Mind, and yet are not fuch as cannot be refifted. When the *Jews* demanded of our Saviour *fuch* a Sign, as was given to their Fathers when the *Heavens* rained down *Manna* for them to eat, *Joh.* vi. 6; he would not gratify them with a *new* miracle, but gave them the true interpretation of the *antient* one: *I am, fays he, the Bread of Life; the Bread of God is He which cometh down from Heaven, and giveth Life unto the World.* Again, When the Pharifees afked of him a *Sign from Heaven*, his An- Matt. xvi. 1. fwer was; *Luk.* xii. 56, *Ye hypocrites, ye can difcern the face of the fky and of the earth; but how is it, that ye do not difcern this Time?* referring them to the *Prophecies*, which much more plainly pointed out the *Time* of his Coming, than ever the *face of the Sky* forefignified the Weather. Thefe Prophecies he fulfilled, in his *Life* and by his *Death*; by many miraculous *Actions*, and miraculous *Sufferings*. And when he was *raifed up the third day, God fhewed him openly; not to all the people*, Acts x. 41, *but unto Witneffes chofen before of God*, and *commanded to preach unto the people*: God *here* likewife doing, not every thing that *could be* done, not every thing that unreafonable men might expect *fhould* be done, but what he himfelf faw *fit* and *proper* to be done. According to that affectionate obfervation of our Saviour, *Luk.* iv. 25, *I tell you of a truth, many widows were in Ifrael in the days of Elias, but——unto none of them was he fent, fave unto——a widow of Sarepta: And many Lepers were in Ifrael in the time of Elifeus the Prophet, and none of them was cleanfed, faving Naaman the Syrian.* God has given us Faculties, to enable us to fearch after and to find the Truth; and he expects we fhould *attend* with an impartial and unprejudiced mind (which is the proper Duty of Rational Creatures,) to the *Light* he thinks fit to afford us. *Why, even of yourfelves, fays our Saviour, judge ye not what is right?* Luk. xii. 57. They who *do* thus judge; who, with a mind defirous to do the Will of God, receive and embrace the doctrine of Truth; not careleffly, creduloufly, and implicitly; but with reafon, with examination, with attention, with fuch impartial confideration and inquiry, as enables men to find (by obfervation and care) what Others are blind to, and to *be ready always to give a reafon of the Hope that is in them*; Thefe are the perfons whom the Scripture commends for their *Faith*; for having the Virtue of *Faith*; in oppofition to to the Vice of *Infidelity*, and to the Folly of *Credulity*. For, *we walk by Faith, not by Sight*, 2 Cor. v. 7: by a *rational perfwafion*, not by *Neceffity*: Seeing* (as St *Paul* elegantly defcribes it; *Seeeing*) through *a glafs* (through a *defcrying Glafs*) *εσ οπτρον*. *darkly*; 1 Cor. xiii. 12; not *beholding, as in a glafs* (as in * a *looking-glafs*,) *with open* *κατοπτρον*. *face*; 2 Cor. iii. 18. And This is That which makes *Faith* and *Hope* to be *Virtues*: For *Hope that is feen, is not Hope; for, what a man feeth, why doth he yet hope for? But if we hope for That we fee not, then do we with patience wait for it*; Rom. viii. 25. The *God of* Nature, in whom *we live and move and have our Being*, and who *is not far from every one of us*, is not *vifible* to mortal eyes: But the Light of Nature affords reafonable men, very great Arguments to believe and truft in him; And This, is a commendable and well-grounded Faith. For *Faith is the Subftance of things*

SERM.
LXXV.

Matt. xii. 41.

hoped for, the evidence of things not feen: And the commendation of *Mofes's* patience in *Egypt*, before God's revealing them himfelf to him, was, that *he indured, as feeing him who is invifible,* Heb. xi. 27. The Evidences of natural reafon and of the moft demonftrable Truths, do not force themfelves upon *All* men; But to the *impartial* and *attentive*, to the *unprejudiced* and *confiderate*, they appear in their full Strength; and, for That reafon, 'tis an Act of *Virtue* to be guided by them. For the *fame* reafon, in matters of Revelation likewife; *Bleffed*, fays our Saviour, *are they that have not feen, and yet have believed*; Joh. xxi. 29. That is: Not, they who are *credulous*, and believe *without reafon*; but they who, like the *Bereans*, are convinced of the Truth by *Searching* into the grounds of it. *The Trial of* whofe *Faith*, faith St *Peter, will be found unto Praife and Honour and Glory at the appearing of Jefus Chrift: Whom having not feen, ye love; in whom, though Now ye fee him not, yet believing ye rejoice with joy unfpeakable and full of glory*; 1 Pet. i. 7. This is the *character* the Scripture gives us of the Virtue of *Faith*, and the *commendation* of thofe who are eminent for having it. On the contrary, they who by prejudices and vicious inclinations are prevented from fearching after the Truth, and, inftead of attending to and examining what is Right, feek rather for Cavils induftrioufly to evade the evidence and conviction of it; *thefe* are the perfons whom the Scripture with the greateft feverity condemns for their *infidelity*, as being an *evil and adulterous generation*. *The uncircumcifion which is by nature*, faith St *Paul, if it fulfil the Law, fhall it not judge thee, who by the letter and circumcifion doft tranfgrefs the Law?* Rom. ii. 27. And our Saviour; *The men of Nineveh*, fays he, *fhall rife in judgment with this generation, and fhall condemn it; becaufe they repented at the preaching of Jonas, and behold a greater than Jonas is here.* Perfons thus *refifting* the Truth, our Lord, after the firft and fecond admonition, rejected; and refufed to give them any further *Signs:* and commanded his *Difciples* in like manner, *to fhake off the duft of their feet for a teftimony againft them,* and not continue *to caft their pearls before fwine.* God hath dealt with the *Jews of old,* after the fame manner: Pf. lxxxi. 12; *My people would not hear my voice, and Ifrael would not obey me; So I gave them up unto their own hearts lufts, and let them follow their own Imaginations.* And to men in *future Ages,* who fhall be found of the fame temper, the Scripture threatens that God, in juft anger, fhall even fend them *ftrong delufion, that they may believe a Lye*; 2 Th. ii. 11. The *Effect* of men's being in this manner given up for their Abufing the divine patience, is thus expreffed by the Pfalmift: Pf. lxxviii. 60; *When God heard this, he was wroth, and took fore difpleafure at Ifrael: So that he forfook the tabernacle in Shilo, even the tent that he had pitched among men: He delivered their power into captivity, and their beauty into the enemy's hand: He gave his people alfo over unto the fword, and was wroth with his inheritance.* And by our Saviour in his affectionate lamentation over *Jerufalem*; Matt. xxiii. 37; *O Jerufalem, Jerufalem, thou that killeft the prophets, and ftoneft them which are fent unto thee! How often would I have gathered thy children together, even as a hen gathereth her chickens under her wings, and ye would not! Behold, your houfe is left unto you defolate.*

SERMON

SERMON LXXVI.

How the Law is faid to be the Strength of Sin.

[*A Paffion Sermon.*]

1 COR. XV. 56 and 57.

The fting of Death is fin, and the ftrength of fin is the law; but thanks be to God which giveth us the victory, through our Lord Jefus Chrift.

THE Apoftle having in the former part of this Chapter, proved at large the truth of the refurrection of Chrift, and the certainty of the future refurrection of Chriftians; and having from thence taken occafion to give a full and particular account of the order and manner of the refurrection of the body; he concludes his whole difcourfe with this triumphal exclamation; *So then when this corruptible fhall have put on incorruption, and this mortal fhall have put on immortality, then fhall be brought to pafs the faying that is written, Death is fwallowed up in victory,* i. e. utterly and for ever; *O death, where is thy fting? O grave, where is thy victory? The fting of death is fin, and the ftrength of fin is the law; but thanks be to God which giveth us the victory, through our Lord Jefus Chrift.*

I SHALL endeavour 1*ft*, To explain the words briefly, and fhew in what Senfe Sin is faid to be *the fting of death, and the law the ftrength of fin.* 2*dly,* I fhall indeavour to fhow how and by what means Chrift gives us the victory, over the law *which is the ftrength of fin,* over Sin which *is the fting of death,* and finally over Death it felf; And *laftly,* I fhall draw fome practical Inferences from the whole.

Firft, I SHALL indeavour to fhew in what Senfe Sin is faid to be *the fting of death, and the law the ftrength of Sin.* That by Sin's being the *fting of death,* is meant that Sin is the *caufe* of Death, and that 'tis Sin only that makes Death terrible, is evident. *The firft mention* we find of death's being in the World, is upon *Adam's* committing the firft tranfgreffion; *In the day thou eateft thereof, thou fhalt furely die;* Gen. ii. 17. And the caufe of the continuance of its dominion ever fince in the World, is the conformity of the reft of mankind to that of their Forefather; *As by one man fin firft entered into the world, and death by fin;* and *fo death has fince paffed upon all men, for that all have finned;* Rom. v. 12. The Apoftle lays it down as a maxim, that the caufe of the dominion of death, is fin; and becaufe it might be objected that fince Sin is not imputed where there is no law, therefore thofe who lived between *Adam* and *Mofes,* without any exprefs revealed Law, fhould feem not to be concluded under the fentence of death; he adds, that even in *that* time, men *had* fome difcovery of the Will of God; So that before the delivery of *Mofes's* law Sin *was* in the World;

SERM. World; and therefore death *did* reign from *Adam* to *Mofes*, even over them that had
LXXVI. not finned after the fimilitude of *Adam*'s tranfgreffion; that is, who had not indeed
like *Adam* finned againft a pofitive and immediate Revelation of the Will of God, with
an exprefs threatning of death annexed; but yet had finned againft fuch a law, as they
had fufficient reafon to be affured was a difcovery of the Will of God.   The Scripture
is very exceeding full in this point; inculcating every where, that as the knowledge of
God and Obedience to his commands *is life*, fo the immediate and neceffary confequence of Sin is *death*.   *When luft has conceived, it bringeth forth Sin, and Sin when it
is finifhed, bringeth forth death*; St *James* i. 15.   *What fruit had ye then in thofe things,
whereof ye are now afhamed? for the end of thofe things is death*, Rom. vi. 21 : and
ver. 23; *the wages of fin is death*.   Moreover, as Sin is the *caufe* of death, fo alfo is it
That only which makes Death itfelf terrible.   'Tis not barely the feparation of Soul and
Body, which is the terrour of death; but that feparation, as inflicted *by*, and accompanied *with*, the wrath of God.   Death may poffibly be otherwife fo far from terrible,
that it may be and often *is* expected by good men with joy and comfort, as an entrance
into life and happinefs.   'Tis Sin only which is the horrour of death, and which gives
it that fting, which makes it really infupportable even to the moft diftant thought.
When the death of the Body is the forerunner of that death of the Soul, from which
there is no hopes of releafe, but the wrath of God muft abide on it for ever; then is
it that death appears truly dreadful and terrible.   This is that which makes wicked men,
confcious of their own guilt, and fenfible of the wrath of God hanging over their
heads, fo amazed at the approach and even the thoughts of death: They cannot bear to
think on fo affrighting a profpect, but are even overwhelmed and fwallowed up with
aftonifhment and defpair: Not that they fo dread death barely and in itfelf, (*for they
could call on the hills to fall on them, and to the mountains to cover them; they could feek
death when they cannot find it, and defire to die when death fhall flee from them*, Rev.
ix. 6.) but it is the *confequences* of death, That fting which Sin gives it, that they are
fo terribly *and fo juftly afraid of*.

BUT to proceed: *The ftrength of Sin*, faith the Apoftle, *is the law*; The ftrength
of Sin, *viz*. that which gives it its power and efficacy.   'Tis evident that Sin is the
tranfgreffion of the law, and that *where there is no law there is no tranfgreffion*, Rom.
iv. 15.   *By the law therefore is the knowledge of fin*, Rom. iii. 20 : or as the Apoftle
more fully expreffes himfelf, ch. vii. ver. 7 and 8.   *I had not known fin but by the law;
for I had not known luft except the law had faid, Thou fhalt not covet; But fin taking
occafion by the commandment, wrought in me all manner of concupifence; For without
the law fin is dead* : that is, the knowledge of Sin muft needs be, by the knowledge
and promulgation of the law that forbids it.   But this is not all; For in this fenfe, by
every declaration of the Will of God, by every command and prohibition, is the knowledge of Sin; and fo the Gofpel itfelf might as properly be ftiled the ftrength of fin, as
the law.   Since therefore by the *Law*, the Apoftle plainly means That difcovery of the
Will of God which was made to mankind before the Coming of Chrift; and particularly that which was given to the *Jews*; in oppofition to the Chriftian or Gofpel-difpenfation : it is certain that by its being the *ftrength of fin*, muft be underftood Something more, than barely its being the occafion of the knowledge of Sin.   It remains
therefore, that it muft fignify the making *fuch* a difcovery of the heinous nature and
guilt of Sin, as yet either not to afford a poffibility of avoiding it, or not to difcover any
fufficient means of recovering from it.   Now in what fenfe, and how far this may be
truly applicable to the *Jewifh* Law, is of fome difficulty to determine : (For if the *Jews
under the law* had neither any poffibility of avoiding Sin, nor yet any fufficient means of
recovering from the guilt of it, it would follow that people were in much harder circumftances than the reprefentations which the Scripture makes to us of God's difpenfations
and

and dealings with them allows us to fuppofe :) I fhall therefore for the clearing this whole matter, and to fhow both in what fenfe the Law is called the Strength of Sin, and how our Saviour has given us the victory over it, (which was the firft thing I pro- pofed to fpeak to,) endeavour briefly to prove thefe following Propofitions. 1ſt, That the Original Law of God requires exact, perfect, and unfinning obedience ; which fince Man through the weaknefs and corruption of his nature is not capable of performing, men are all thereby neceffarily concluded under Sin. 2dly, That that Law, under which the Jews were, fo far as it is diftinguifhed from, and oppofed to, the Grace or Gofpel of Chrift ; is the fame with the Original Law of God, in its full force and feverity. 3dly, That yet God never dealt with men according to the ſtrictnefs and rigour of that Law, but always anticipated the favour of the Gofpel, and dealt with men according to the Gracious Terms of the New Covenant. 4thly, That our Saviour at his appear- ance, openly promulged and declared to all the World the lefs fevere Terms of this Covenant of Grace, and by that means totally freed men from the fear and bondage of that rigorous Law, which was really in force until the time of his appearing ; excepting only as God was pleafed to anticipate the Grace and Favour of the New Covenant, at firft by the fecret difpenfations of his Mercy, and the obfcure promifes of a Redeemer to come ; and afterwards, as the time of the promife drew near, by the more open and plain declarations of the prophets. 1ſt, The Original Law of God requires exact, per- fect, and unfinning Obedience ; which fince man through the weaknefs and corrup- tion of his nature, is not capable of performing, men are all thereby neceffarily concluded under Sin. This is evident from the confideration of the Nature of *God*, and of the true and Original notion of a *Law*. The Authority of *God* being fupreme, and the condition of his creatures abfolutely dependant ; Obedience entire and conftant, univer- fal and perpetual, is plainly and naturally due to his commands : The nature alfo of a *Law* being to require obedience ; and provifion for reconciliation after a violation of it, not being originally in the condition of a Law, but only an after-provifion of Favour and Mercy : it is plain that originally to the Laws of God, there is due a perfect and unfinning Obedience. That therefore which the original law of God declares, is this ; that as God is himfelf a Being of infinite purity and holinefs, fo he cannot be pleafed with any creature, that imitates not that purity according to the utmoft capacity of its nature ; that as there are eternal meafures of Good and Evil, Right and Wrong, which are as unchangeable as the nature of God and the conftitution of things, fo God cannot poffibly delight in any creature that obferves not thefe effential and fundamental laws of his Kingdom ; that therefore men who are made capable of knowing God, are bound to worfhip him *as* God, without giving any part of that honour to another which is due only to *him*, or paying *him* that honour which is due to him, in a way not becoming the excellency of his nature ; And in brief, that knowing the eternal rules of juftice and equity, honefty and fidelity, temperance and fobriety, to be the laws of his Kingdom, they are bound to be true and juft in all their dealings one with another with all fimpli- city and fincerity of mind, and to live in Sobriety, Temperance and Chaftity, with all Purity and Holinefs : And this they are bound to do, conftantly and at all times ; the original law of God affuring indeed thofe that obey it in all points, of a reward and the favour of God ; but not providing any expiation, nor pointing with any certainty at the means of reconciliation, for thofe who fhall at any time have tranfgreffed and incurred God's difpleafure. It is true the World always had great and reafonable hopes, that God would be merciful to returning Sinners, and accept repentance inftead of perfect innocence ; But then thefe hopes were not founded on the Original condition of the law of God ; but either on men's natural notion of the mercifulnefs and placabi- lity of the Divine nature (fuch as the Heathen World has always depended upon ;) and thefe were only probable and hopeful prefumptions ; or elfe on the obfcure promifes

SERM. made to *Adam* and the Patriarchs of a Meffias to come, (fuch as the holy and devout
LXXVI. men before the giving of the Law of *Mofes* grounded their expectations of mercy upon ;)
and thefe were the firft beginnings of the declaration of the Covenant of Grace. The
Original Law of God therefore, required perfect unfinning obedience; and thereby,
fince no man was able to perform it, neceffarily concluded all men under Sin. 2*dly*, That
Law, under which the *Jews* lived, fo far as it is diftinguifhed from, and oppofed to,
the Grace or Gofpel of Chrift; is the fame with the original Law of God in its full
Force and Severity. This is evident from its retaining and confirming all the moral
precepts of Nature, with exprefs promife indeed *that the man which* doth *thefe things
fhall live by them*, Rom. x. 5; but with moft rigorous threatnings alfo, *that Curfed
fhould be every one that continued not in all things which were written in the book of the
Law to do them*, Gal. iii. 10; not affording any expiation for great and wilful fins paft,
but denouncing death without mercy againft them; nor indeed allowing any atonement even for fmaller Sins, but fuch as plainly owed all their efficacy, to their being
types of the mercy of the Covenant of grace. The fame alfo is clear from the Apoftle's
attributing all thofe feverities to the *Jewifh* Law, which are properly true only of the
Original Law of God; and his oppofing it directly to the grace and mercy of the Gofpel-
Covenant. *The law*, faith he, *is holy, and the commandment holy, and juft and good*,
Rom. vii. 12; it was fuch as if it were exactly obeyed, would certainly juftify a man,
i. e. make him appear righteous in the Sight of God, and entitle him to the reward of
obedience; *the doers of the law fhall be juftified*, Rom. ii. 13. But the corrupt eftate of
humane nature being fuch, that no man can obey this law in all points without finning,
but that in *many things we offend all, for all have finned and come fhort of the glory of
God*, Rom. iii. 23: hence the law which was ordained to the end that men obeying it
might attain life and happinefs, ferved only to their Condemnation, by working in
their Confciences a Conviction of their duty which they ought to have performed, and
of the Wrath of God hanging over their heads for not performing it: *The commandment*,
faith he, *which was ordained to life, I found to be unto death*, Rom. vii. 10. And upon
this account (I fuppofe) are thofe fo frequent expreffions of the Apoftle; *that the law
worketh wrath*, Rom. iv. 15; *that by the deeds of the law there fhall no flefh be juftified
in the fight of God*, Rom. iii. 20: *that as many as are of the works of the law are under
the curfe*, Gal. iii. 10. *And that the Law entered that the offence might abound*, Rom.
v. 20: that is to fay, not that it was defigned to that end, but that in fact and by confequence it *did* become a means of aggravating fin and rendering it more exceedingly
criminal; It is true the law did indeed appoint certain facrifices of expiation for fin;
but fuch as had not in themfelves *Any* efficacy to expiate fin, any otherwife than as
they typified that great facrifice which was once to be offered for the Sins of the whole
World: The Tabernacle was a figure for the time then prefent, in which were offered
both gifts and facrifices, that could not make him that did the fervice perfect, as pertaining to the confcience; *For the law having a fhadow of good things to come, and not
the very image of the things, can never with thofe facrifices, which they offered year by
year continually, make the comers thereunto perfect*, Heb. x. 1. Hence though thofe
good men who lived before the coming of Chrift, were indeed juftified; yet they are
faid to be juftified, how? not by the works of the law, but by faith; as St *Paul* rea-
foneth in his whole fourth Chapter to the *Romans*; His meaning is; They trufted not
to ritual and ceremonious performances, but looked through the types and fhadows of
the law to the promifed Meffiah, being fully perfwaded that what God had promifed
he would affuredly perform; and this was counted unto them for righteoufnefs. Thus
of *Abraham* particularly it is faid by the Apoftle, *that he was not juftified by the works
of the law, fo as to have wherewith to glory before God; but that he was juftified by
Faith*: and in like manner all the holy men, who lived under the law, did not expect

to be juftified in the fight of God by the works of the law, but by their faith in God, **S E R M.**
and truft in his promifes. So the law was their Schoolmafter to bring them unto Chrift; **LXXVI.**
and though they knew that nothing in the law could of itfelf avail effectually to the
forgivenefs of fins, yet they continued with patience walking in the Commandments of
God, and waiting for the confolation and redemption of *Ifrael*; *and accordingly when*
the fulnefs of time was come, God fent forth his Son, made [of a Woman, made] under
the law, that he might redeem thofe that were under the law. The *Jewifh* Law therefore, fo far as it was diftinguifhed from, and oppofed to, the grace or gofpel of Chrift,
was the fame with the original law of God in its full force and feverity; and no flefh
could be juftified thereby.

3*dly*, Yet God never dealt with men according to the ftrictnefs and feverity of that
Law, but always anticipated the favour of the gofpel, and dealt with men according to
the gracious terms of the new Covenant. Thus though no flefh could be juftified by
the law, yet both the Patriarchs who lived *before* the law (as I have already obferved,)
and all Holy men who lived *under* the Law, were juftified; and this their juftification
was by Faith, i. e. by the terms of that new Covenant, *which in the fulnefs of time*
was to be promulged openly and plainly to the whole world. Wherefore, though the
Law appointed no expiation for great and prefumptuous Sins, yet God always pardoned
Sinners upon their true repentance, (as appears in the cafe of *David* and others;) and
as the times of the gofpel drew nearer and nearer, began by degrees to *declare* by his
Prophets, that he would do fo. *David*, when he had committed thofe crying Sins
of Adultery and Murder, acknowledges that the feverity of the law allowed no Sacrifice of expiation for him; *Thou defireft not facrifice, elfe I would give it thee, but thou*
delighteft not in burnt-offerings; Pf. li. 16: Yet he hoped that upon his hearty repentance, forgivenefs would not be impoffible to be obtained at the Hands of God; *A*
broken and contrite heart, O God, faith he, *thou wilt not defpife*, ver. 17: and the event
difcovered that he did indeed obtain it. And God afterward by the Prophet *Ezekiel*
declared publickly to the whole people of the *Jews*, that *when a wicked man turneth*
away from his wickednefs, and doth that which is lawful and right, he fhould *fave his*
foul alive. Thus though the Law, ftrictly fpeaking, was in force with its full feverity
until the appearing of our Saviour, yet God never dealt with men according to that
feverity, but always anticipated the Favour of the Gofpel, and judged men by
the terms of the Covenant of grace. The *Law* was by *Mofes*, Grace and Truth by
Chrift.

4*thly*, This new Covenant of grace, which, before the coming of our Saviour,
lay hid in the fecret difpenfations of God's mercy, and began in part by degrees to
be difcovered, firft by the obfcure promifes of a Meffiah to come, and afterwards by
the more plain declarations of the Prophets; was at our Saviour's Appearance openly
eftablifhed, and the terms of it publickly promulged to the whole World; fo as to
deliver men entirely from all fear of that rigour of the Law, which the Apoftle ftiles *the*
ftrength of Sin. This deliverance of men by the Gofpel from the burden and feverity of
the Law, the Apoftle in the Text calls a Victory; and This Victory our Saviour obtained for us, principally by thefe two things: 1*ft*, By giving himfelf a facrifice and
propitiation for fins paft, from which men could not be juftified by the Law; and
2*dly*, By propofing openly the gracious terms of Faith and Repentance to thofe who
believed and were defirous to obey him. 1*ft*, He gave himfelf a facrifice and propitiation for fins paft, from which men could not be juftified by the law, *viz.* When it
was not confiftent with the wifdom of God in his government of the world, to let fin
go unpunifhed, and yet he would have mercy upon finful man, *he fent his own Son into the*
world in the likenefs of finful flefh, to bear our punifhment, and fo for fin (or as the words

4

may

S E R M. may moſt properly be rendered, *by being a ſacrifice for ſin*) *condemned ſin in the fleſh*;
LXXVI. Rom. viii. 3.   Hence Chriſt is ſaid to have *obtained redemption for us*, Heb. ix. 12:
to have put away ſin by the ſacrifice of himſelf, Heb. ix. 26: *to have given his life a ran-*
ſom for many, St Matt. xx. 28. for many: that is, *for all thoſe that ſhould believe and*
obey him; as it is explained by St *Paul*, 1 Tim. ii. 6: *to have bought us with a price*,
1 Cor. vi. 20: *to be the propitiation for our ſins*, Joh. ii. 2. *and to have purchaſed a*
church with his blood, Acts xx. 28 : with many the like expreſſions, which do all plainly
ſignify, that Chriſt by his death and the ſhedding of his moſt precious blood, has made
full and ſufficient ſatisfaction to the juſtice of God for the ſins of the whole world,
that is, for as many as ſhall out of the world flee unto him, and ſubmit themſelves to
the terms of the new Covenant, whereof he is made the mediator. *For if the blood of*
bulls and of goats, and the aſhes of an heifer ſprinkling the unclean, ſanctifieth to the pu-
rifying of the fleſh; How much more ſhall the blood of Chriſt, who through the eternal
Spirit, offered himſelf without ſpot to God, purge your Conſcience from dead works to ſerve
the living God; Heb. ix. 13, 14.   2*dly*, Our Saviour has openly propoſed to all the
world, the gracious terms of Faith and Repentance ; of Faith, that men believe on him
as the Saviour of the world and the Meſſiah that was to come, profeſſing themſelves ſubjects of his Kingdom ; and of Repentance, that men turn from the evil of their ways,
and conform their lives to the laws of that Kingdom, whoſe ſubjects they profeſs themſelves to be : That they believe on him whom God hath ſent ; and that they live ſuitably to that belief, with ſincere endeavours to obey the whole goſpel, and hearty ſorrow, and perpetually labouring after amendment, for all their failures in that obedience.
Theſe are now the gracious terms of the Goſpel, which in the *New Teſtament* are
every where preached as the conditions of Salvation.   This was the Sum of *John*
Baptiſt's preaching, who was ſent to prepare the way before Chriſt ; *Repent ye, for*
the Kingdom of heaven is at hand; St Matt. iii. 2 : with this our Saviour himſelf began
his miniſtry ; *The time is fulfilled, and the kingdom of God is at hand, Repent ye and be-*
lieve the Goſpel; Mar. i. 15 : with This he concluded his charge to his Diſciples after
his reſurrection ; *Go ye into all the world, and preach the goſpel to every creature; He*
that believeth and is baptized, i. e. he that believeth and enters into an obligation to
live ſuitably to that belief, ſhall be ſaved; *Mar.* xvi. 15 and 16. This his Diſciples after his aſcenſion publiſhed to all the world, *preaching repentance and remiſſion of ſins*
in his name among all nations, beginning at Jeruſalem; Luk. xxiv. 47.   Laſtly, this
is the Sum of all their exhortations, contained in their epiſtles to the ſeveral churches
which had before believed through their preaching.   And becauſe this Repentance or
turning from a life of ſin unto a life of righteouſneſs, is the ſumm of Religion under
the goſpel-diſpenſation, therefore is it in Scripture expreſſed by great variety of phraſes, to the different capacities and underſtandings of men.   Sometimes it is called *turn-*
ing to the Lord, that thoſe who by a courſe of ſin had been enemies to God, might
by forſaking their ſins and following after righteouſneſs, be reconciled to him :
Sometimes it is called *Converſion*, a word of the ſame import with that *of turning*
to the Lord: Sometimes it is called *the renewing of our mind*; Sometimes *putting*
on the new man, elſewhere *the new Creature*, to ſignify an entire change and reformation of life: and moſt frequently it is ſtiled *Regeneration, the new birth, new-*
neſs of Life, and the like; All which phraſes are made uſe of to imply this one
thing, that *thoſe who have been dead in treſpaſſes and Sins*, thoſe who by any means
have been engaged in a wicked courſe of life, muſt as it were by a new birth, by a
thorough and entire reformation of life and manners, enter into a new courſe of life,
and begin a life of righteouſneſs and holineſs.   So careful has the Spirit of God been,
that no one ſhould be ignorant of that which is ſo much his neceſſary and indiſpenſable

Duty,

Duty. Nothing is now required of us but that λογικὴ λατρεία, that reasonable service, of forsaking our Sins, and obeying in our lives and actions those commands of God, which are so reasonable in themselves, and so evidently perfective of our nature, so necessarily, approved by the minds of men, and the reason of their obligation so immediately acknowledged by the conscience, *that they may truly be said to be written in our Hearts*; Heb. viii. 10; Yet to incourage our practice, they are moreover most fully explained, most earnestly inculcated, and most strongly inforced by the most powerful motives in the New Testament. We are not now obliged to those numberless ritual performances, which in the Scripture are called *weak and beggarly elements, and a burden which neither we nor our Fathers were able to bear* : Our religion consists not now in such outward Ceremonies, whose observance was difficult, and their signification oftimes obscure: *But the righteousness which is of faith speaketh on this wise, Say not in thine heart, Who shall ascend into Heaven to bring Christ down from above? Or, Who shall ascend into the deep to bring up Christ again from the dead? But what saith it? The word is nigh thee, even in thy mouth, and in thy heart*; Rom. x. 6, 7 and 8 ; that is; the Gospel-Covenant consists not of such strict, difficult terms, as are above the reach of our knowledge or our strength ; but such as may easily be understood by us, and performed also by the assistance of Christ that strengthneth us. A sincere endeavour to perform our whole duty, is the condition of the Gospel; and he that so desires to do the Will of God, can neither want knowledge to understand his duty, nor power to perform it ; He shall know of Christ's doctrine, whether it be of God; and when he comes to practise it, shall find *his yoke easy and his burden light*. In a word, the Terms that Christ by his death has purchased for us, are plainly these; that whereas by the transgression of the Original law of God, which required perfect and unsinning Obedience, all men were become guilty before God; and whereas by the addition of the Ceremonial rites and sacrifices of the *Jewish* law, which in their own nature could not avail to expiate Sin, men could not be justified from the transgressions they had committed; it is now declared by the Gospel-Covenant that whosoever believing in the name of Christ shall repent him heartily of his former Sins, and for the future endeavour with all his might to obey sincerely, though not without infirmities, all the Commandments of God; shall through the redemption purchased by the Blood of Christ have his sincerity accepted instead of perfect obedience, and thereby be justified from all things from which he could not be justified by the law ; And this is that *justification by faith only*, which St *Paul* in his Epistle to the *Romans* so often opposes to *being justified by the works of the law*. Having thus endeavoured briefly to explain what is meant *by the Law being the strength of Sin* ; and by what means our Saviour has delivered us from it, or given us the victory over it ; I should proceed now in the 2d place to consider how he *gives us the victory over Sin which is the Sting of Death*: And this he does, by delivering us 1*st* from the dominion, and 2*dly* from the guilt and punishment of Sin. First, he frees men from that bondage and thraldom, into which Sin has reduced them ; and then those who are so freed he delivers from that punishment, which must have been the necessary consequence of their being inthralled to Sin. But the time not permitting me to enter upon this, I shall only draw an inference or two from what has been already said, and so conclude. And 1*st* from what has been said, we may understand why St *Paul* in his writings concerning the *Jewish* Law, always describes it as of such severity by which *no flesh could possibly be justified*: when yet it is plain God never dealt with men according to *that severity* : and why he so exceedingly magnifies the grace and mercy of the Gospel, notwithstanding it be evident that God always dealt with men according to *that indulgence*. Now the plain solution of this difficulty is this. The Apostle speaking of the Law, is not to be understood complexly of God's whole dispensation and dealing with the *Jews*, but of the Law properly

S E R M. perly and ftrictly, as it is diftinguished from and oppofed to the Gofpel; *viz.* fuch as
LXXVI. it was in itfelf, and fuch as it really would have been, if the Gofpel-Covenant had never been eftablished.   For though there *was* indeed indulgence *under* the Law, yet that
indulgence was not *from* the Law, but an anticipation, as I have faid, of the mercy of
the Gofpel.   The Law itfelf was not therefore the lefs fevere, becaufe the indulgence
of the Gofpel extended itfelf backward even under the times of the Law; neither is
the mercy of the Gofpel to be therefore the lefs magnified, becaufe it is no other than
what had in effect before been indulged under the Law.   For fince the one was in itfelf
really as fevere as it is defcribed, and had no indulgence but what was borrowed from
and founded upon the other, there is no reafon at all why this fhould be confidered when
the one is fpoken of in oppofition to the other; which is the ftate of the Apoftle's argument; and therefore he moft reafonably aggravates the feverity of the Law, and upon the comparifon moft juftly magnifies the mercy and favour of the Gofpel: Gal. ii.
21; *If righteoufnefs came by the Law, then Chrift is dead in vain.*

2*dly*, FROM what has been faid, we may learn, that the wole defign and effect of
the Gofpel *was not to deftroy, but to fulfil the Law.*   The whole defign of all God's difpenfations with mankind, is to prevent or deftroy Sin.   This the Law was to do originally, by requiring perfect and unfinning obedience: But when inftead of this, it only
concluded all men under Sin; the defign of the Gofpel was to effect the fame, by requiring and by accepting Repentance; which being no other than renewed obedience,
it is plain the Gofpel does not deftroy, but eftablish the Law.   The feverity indeed of
the Law was fo far to be qualified by the indulgence of the Gofpel, that it might not
be any longer the *Strength of Sin:*   But the Gofpel did not take away the obligation
of the Law, fo as to be itfelf the caufe and the occafion of finning.   The moral Law
denounced a Curfe againft every one that continued not in all the works thereof to do
them; and the Gofpel delivers all thofe from this Curfe, who by true Repentance renew their Obedience: The Ceremonial Law was an infupportable burden of rites, in-
fufficient of themfelves to make any expiation for fin; and the Gofpel, by exhibiting
the true and fufficient expiation, has delivered all men from the burden of this yoke.
As therefore thofe perfons [Judaizing Chriftians] in the primitive times were very unreafonable, who contended that any of thefe ritual obfervations were of neceffity to be
kept up after the coming of Chrift; fo thofe Perverters of Chriftianity in later ages
are on the other fide much more unreafonable, who contend that the moral Law has
been abolished by Chrift.   The Gofpel accepts indeed the terms, of *Faith and Repentance;* but 'tis only for the fake of the *Fruit and Effect* of them, which is *renewed obedience.*   So that nothing can be more abfurd, than for Chriftians to think themfelves excufed from holinefs of life and thofe duties of religion, which as the unchangeable Nature of God and of the things themfelves had made the neceffary requifites, fo the Gofpel alfo has made the exprefs condition of their being acceptable to God.   Our Saviour
himfelf tells us, that *Not every one that faith unto me, Lord, Lord, fhall enter into the
Kingdom of Heaven, but he that doth the Will of my Father which is in Heaven.*   The
Gofpel itfelf fpeaks aloud, and tells us, that we *muft deny ungodlinefs and worldly lufts,* that
*we fhould live foberly, righteoufly, and godly in this prefent world, looking for that blefsed
hope, and the glorious appearing of the great God, and our Saviour Jefus Chrift, Who
gave himfelf for us, that he might redeem us from all iniquity, and purify unto himfelf
a peculiar people, zealous of good works.*   The Apoftle St *Paul,* That great vindicator
of the liberties of Chriftians, warns and perfwades us, and repeats it with great earneftnefs over and over again; *Be not deceived; and let no man deceive you with vain words;
neither fornicators, nor idolaters, nor thieves, nor covetous, nor drunkards,* and fo on;
i. e. no one that allows himfelf and continues in any one known vice; fhall according
to the terms of the Gofpel of Chrift, *inherit the Kingdom of God, For, Not every one*

I

that

that faith unto me, Lord, Lord, shall enter into the Kingdom of Heaven, faith our Saviour, *but he that doth the Will of my Father which is in Heaven.*

Lastly, From what has been said, we may learn to reconcile the *Severity* and the *Compassion* of God; the *Severity,* in giving a Law, which required finless obedience; and the *Compassion* in mitigating it, by the Grace and Mercy of the Gospel; Which Grace extended itself backwards to good men under the Law; and the Severity would reach forward to the impenitent under the Gospel. *O the depth of the riches both of the wisdom and knowledge of God! how unsearchable are his judgments, and his ways past finding out!* To conclude therefore, Let us then heartily set about the reformation of our lives, and by obedience to God's commands endeavour to walk worthy of that religion we profess, adorning the doctrine of God our Saviour in all things. Let us consider and admire the infinite wisdom and mercy of God, in restoring men to a capacity of attaining that happiness by the obedience of the second Covenant, which they utterly forfeited by the transgression of the first; and let us not frustrate the grace of God by the disobedience of our lives, least there remain no more Sacrifice for our Sin: *For if the word spoken by Angels was stedfast, and every transgression and disobedience received a just recompence of reward; how shall we escape if we neglect so great Salvation, which at the first began to be spoken by the Lord, and was confirmed unto us by them that heard him? For if we sin wilfully after we have received the Knowledge of the Truth;* that is, if Christians live as those who know not God, in the Practice of any vice or debauchery whatsoever: *there remains no more Sacrifice for Sin,* no new Dispensations; *but a certain fearful looking for of judgment, and fiery indignation, which shall devour the adversaries.*

SERMON

SERMON LXXVII.

How Christ has enabled us to conquer Sin.

[*Preached on Easter-Day.*]

1 COR. XV. 56 and 57.

The sting of Death is sin, and the strength of sin is the law; But thanks be to God which giveth us the victory, through our Lord Jesus Christ.

SERM.
LXXVII.

WHEN he who was the desire and expectation of Nations appeared first in the World, it highly concerned all those who looked for redemption in *Israel*, rightly to understand the end and design of his coming: And if we who live at this distance of time after his appearing in the flesh, expect yet to be par- takers of the common Salvation which he has purchased for us; it highly concerns *Us* also to understand wherein that Salvation consists, and how and on what conditions he has purchased it for us. The *Jews* who lived about the time of his coming, misled by a partial application and wrong interpretation of the prophecies that went before concerning him, expected *a temporal prince to appear in the power and splendour of this world, who should deliver their nation from that slavery into which the Romans had subdued them, and restore again the kingdom to Israel;* They expected that *Jeru- salem* should have become once again the Head of the nations, and the glory of the whole Earth; *They expected that Messiah the prince should have come to sit upon the throne of David for ever, and to have established a kingdom among them which should have had no end.* And so indeed he did; though in a sense far different from what they expect- ed. Nay, his Disciples themselves were for a great while so blinded with the splendour of this opinion, that they understood none of those prophecies that related to his Hu- miliation, Sufferings, and Death; As appears from St *Peter's* undertaking to rebuke him when he began to foretel *how many things he should suffer of the Jews;* and from his Disciples asking him even *after* his resurrection if he would at this time restore again the kingdom to *Israel.* But as he himself a little before his death witnessed be- fore *Pontius Pilate* that good confession, *that his kingdom was not of this world;* so his Disciples, after his resurrection and ascension, began to have their eyes opened, and to understand that the design of his coming into the World was wholly Spiritual. And as at the descending of the Holy Ghost they were more perfectly instructed in the nature and end of That his Spiritual kingdom, so did they afterward in their inspired writings deliver to *us*, what they then received from that unerring instructor: Namely, that the true end and design of Christ's coming into the World, was to deliver men, not from their Temporal Enemies, but to save them from their Sin. Now This he does, by delivering us 1*st*, from the power and dominion of Sin; and 2*dly*, from the guilt and punishment thereof. 1*st*, he delivers men from that Bondage and Slavery

2

into

into which the practice of Sin has reduced them; and then those who are so freed, he delivers from that *punishment* which must have been the necessary consequence of their being enslaved to Sin. These are the two great designs which exhaust the whole history of our Saviour; there being nothing that he either said or did, which was not directed to one of these great ends. 1*st* then, We are to show, how Christ delivers us from the *dominion* or *practice* of Sin. That the service of Sin is an intolerable thraldom, All who are so unhappy as to be engaged in any habit of Vice, do sadly experience; and it may also easily be observed by others. This deplorable state, is fitly described by *Solomon* under the person of a foolish young man, drawn away with the enticements of a Strange woman; *Prov.* vii. 22, *He goeth after her straightway as an ox goeth to the slaughter, or as a fool to the correction of the stocks, till a dart strike through his liver, as a bird hasteth to the snare, and knoweth not that it is for his life.* This is the case of all who are under the dominion and habit of *any* Sin; they know not whither they are going, but are hurried away blindfold with every temptation, being intangled in the snare of the Devil, and taken captive by him at his will. Hence such a state of Sin is stiled in Scripture a *yoke, burden, captivity, bondage, thraldom,* and the like; and habitual Sinners are described to be *dead in Sin,* to let Sin *reign* in their mortal bodies, to be *sold* under Sin, to be in *captivity* to the law of Sin and Death, to be hardned through the deceitfulness of Sin, to be such as *cannot cease* from Sin, and, by a phrase which includes all these, to be *Servants* of Sin; being constrained to obey it in the lusts thereof, even against the dictates of their reason and conscience; *for to whom ye yield yourselves servants to obey, his servants ye are to whom ye obey,* Rom. vi. 16. Now that which Christ has actually done for us in order to the delivering us from the dominion of Sin, may briefly be expressed in these two propositions; 1*st,* that he has made a most clear discovery of the Will of God to mankind; and 2*dly,* that he has enabled them to obey the Will of God according to that discovery. 1*st,* He has made a most clear discovery of the Will of God to Mankind. He has plainly and fully made known to us, the heinousness of Sin, and the necessity of Repentance; he has most exactly defined the bounds of our duty, and given us an example of the practice of it in his own life; he has more clearly revealed the great motives of religion, and urged them upon men with much stronger advantage. To show these things at large, would be to repeat the whole history of our Saviour; and no man can read the New Testament wherein That history is contained, without observing that all his discourses and all the actions of his life, were directed principally to These ends: To convince men that Sin is so hateful to God, and so inconsistent with the honour of his laws, that he would not pardon it even in those whom he designed to have mercy upon, without first inflicting the punishment that was due to it, upon his only Son. To assure men, that a life of Virtue and true Righteousness, is the only and indispensable condition of *That* Covenant, wherein God has promised to save them from everlasting destruction. That therefore *unless we repent, we must perish,* Luke xiii. 5. That *without Holiness, no man shall see the Lord,* Heb. xii. 14. That no man who continues in the practice of any known Sin, *shall in any wise enter into the kingdom of God,* 1 Cor. vi. 9; and that, however vain men may deceive themselves, no pretence whatsoever, no not of having *preached or worked miracles in the name of Christ,* shall be accepted instead thereof, *Matt.* vii. 21. Further; is it not a very Advantagious stating of the bounds of our duty, to have given us such a compleat and perfect rule of Life and manners, as the Holy Scriptures cannot but be acknowledged to be? Is it not a sufficient Security against ignorance and mistake in our duty, to have such a Rule given us as contains in the plainest words all things needful for our information in all necessary truth, and for the confuting of all pernicious errour; for correcting and reclaiming us from all Sin, and for our instruction and encouragement in all Righteoufnefs? to have fuch a Rule, wherein our duty is fet down both in general and in particulars; with great variety of expreffion, repeated, urged, and inculcated upon the meaneft capacities, and exemplified in the lives of holy men, as patterns propofed to our imitation? The Hiftory of our Saviour's life, is a compleat example of all virtues; but more efpecially of Patience, Charity, and Contempt of the World: His Sermons contain fuch excellent and perfect rules of Morality, as have raifed the admiration even of the moft implacable enemies of his Religion; and his Parables are Declarations of the nature and defign of the Gofpel-difpenfation by fuch plain and eafy fimilitudes, as the vulgar were able to bear, and thofe who were well-difpofed were capable of underftanding. The Sermons of the Apoftles contain fuch proofs of the truth and certainty of the Chriftian Religion, as were neceffary to the converfion of Infidels; and their Epiftles are filled with the inforcements of fuch Chriftian Duties, as are neceffary to the Salvation of believers; containing alfo Exhortations to the practice of fpecial duties, upon particular and emergent occafions. So that every man that fincerely defires to know the will of God and to obey it, without being prejudiced with Partiality and Difputes, with Paffions and Intereft, may here find his duty written in fuch legible characters, *that he that runs may read it: Laftly*, Men's duty being thus made known, is it not a moft clear and advantagious revelation of the powerful Motives and Inforcements of that duty; to be affured that there is a future ftate of Rewards and Punifhments, wherein *God will judge the world in righteoufnefs, and render to every man according to what he has done in the body, whether it be good or evil*; and to be affured of the certainty of that ftate, not by the uncertain and difagreeing conjectures of fuch men, as undertook to prove it probable by difficult and abftrufe reafonings, but by the teftimony of one, who by that convincing proof of his Refurrection from the Dead, did undeniably demonftrate that he had himfelf been in that invifible ftate?

B U T 2*dly*, As Chrift has thus made a moft clear Difcovery of the Will of God to Mankind, fo hath he alfo enabled them to obey the Will of God according to that difcovery. As he has provided a fufficient remedy againft Ignorance of our duty, fo he has likewife made a fufficient provifion againft our Inability to perform it. Now this he has done, 1*ft*, By requiring eafier conditions of us, than could without his mediation have been accepted. And 2*dly*, By gracioufly affording us his affiftance, to perform what he fo requires. 1*ft*, He requires eafier conditions of us, than could without his mediation have been accepted. It is the great and peculiar privilege of the Gofpel-difpenfation, that whereas the original law of God required perfect unfinning obedience, and confequently men in this corrupt eftate were thereby of neceffity concluded all under Sin; the covenant of mercy eftablifhed by the Death of Chrift, has relaxed that rigour which the Apoftle calls the *ftrength of Sin*, and reduced the condition of Salvation to fuch terms, as are not impracticable, nay nor indeed *grievous* to human nature, even in this prefent ftate; He has reduced it to the gracious terms of Faith, and unfeigned Repentance; a Repentance, and fincere Endeavours to obey his Commandments to the beft of our Ability for the time to come. But if Chriftians will ftill continue in the practice, and under the dominion of Sin, notwithftanding this way which Chrift has opened for them to Salvation; it is their own fault and their extreme folly here, and will be their condemnation and mifery hereafter. It is true, fuch is the corruption of our nature and the weaknefs of our faculties, that we are not indeed *fufficient of ourfelves to do or think any thing as of our felves*, 2 Cor. iii. 5. But then it is true alfo, that we have a much greater Sufficiency, even that Sufficiency which is from God, as the Apoftle immediately adds: which is the fecond thing whereby I faid our Saviour enables us to obey the will of God, according to that difcovery of it which he has made to us in the Gofpel; he enables us, by gracioufly affording us his affiftance, to per-

from

form what he requires of us. Though we have indeed contracted much Weakness and Impotency by our wilful degeneracy from Goodness, yet That Grace which the Gospel offers us for our assistance, is sufficient for us; *I can do all things*, faith St *Paul*, *through Christ that strengthneth me*, Phil. iv. 13. Though we are indeed encompassed with many and potent enemies, whose business it is to tempt us and to deter us from our duty; yet are we indued with a power, by which we are enabled to resist and to conquer all these temptations; *For greater is he that is in us, than he that is in the world*; 1 Joh. iv. 4: *So that in all these things we are more than conquerors through him that loved us*, Rom. viii. 37. God knoweth the frailty of our nature, and considereth how many temptations we are continually liable to; he *remembreth whereof we are made, and confidereth that we are but Dust*; He knoweth our enemy's strength and our own weakness, and therefore he affords us the *continual* assistance of his Holy Spirit to supply our natural want of power. He has promised to succour all those who sincerely desire to obey his will; and, if we be not wanting in our own endeavours, we may rely upon *him*, that he will be faithful to his promise, and not *suffer us to be tempted above what we are able; but will with the temptation also make a way to escape, that we may be able to bear it*; 1 Cor. x. 13. Thus in order to the delivering us from the habit and power of Sin, our Saviour by making a most clear Discovery of the Will of God to Mankind, and by enabling them to obey the Will of God according to that Discovery, has put us in our own power, if *we* for our part will but accept this deliverance, and, by the way which he has opened for us, retreat out *of the bondage of Sin and Satan into the glorious liberty of the children of God.* Christ has compleatly performed *his* office for us; *he has paid the price*; *he has redeemed us out of captivity*: It is our part to take care that we continue not wilfully in the service of Sin, *lest we be found to do despite unto the Spirit of Grace, crucifying to ourselves the Son of God afresh, and putting him to an open shame.* Now this is what Christ has done for All *those* in general, to whom the Gospel is *preached*: But then 2*dly*, Those who *accept* of this deliverance from the dominion of Sin, that is, who by Repentance and true Amendment of life embrace the terms of the Gospel; those, and those only, he further delivers from the guilt and punishment of Sin: And in order to this; 1*st*, He hath vindicated the honour of God's laws by taking upon himself the punishment of their Sins; and 2*dly*, *He fits at the right hand of God*, ready to come in *the glory of his Father, with his holy Angels*, actually to deliver them from That punishment of Sin which *shall* finally be inflicted on them that would not be delivered from the dominion of it; even on those *who know not God and obey not the Gospel*; *i. e.* who either embraced not the Gospel at all, when it was preached to them; or pretending to embrace it, yet obeyed it not. 1*st*, He has vindicated the honour of God's laws, by taking upon himself the punishment of *their* Sins, who repent and embrace the terms of the Gospel. He condescended to *be made Sin for us, who himself knew no Sin, that we might be made the righteousness of God in him*, 2 Cor. v. 21: *to be made Sin for us, i. e.* to be made a *Sacrifice* for our Sins, that we through that expiation might become subjects *capable of the mercy* of God. He took upon him our Nature, and was clothed in flesh, partly indeed that he might preach the Will of God to mankind in a nearer and more condescending conversation with them; but principally, that he who in the form of God could not suffer, might become capable of suffering by being made in the likeness to Man. He lived a most innocent and spotless life, that he might indeed set us an example that we should follow his steps; but chiefly, because as it was required that the typical Sacrifices under the law should be whole and without blemish; so it was necessary that he, who was to be the real expiatory Sacrifice for the Sins of others, should have none that needed expiation of his own; *For such an High priest became us, who is holy, harmless, undefiled, separate from sinners,*

and

SERM. *and made higher than the heavens*; Heb. vii. 26. He fuffered a fhameful and ignomi-
LXXVII. nious Death upon the Crofs, that he might indeed give us an example of patience
and readinefs to fuffer ; but the principal defign of it was, that he might put away
Sin by the facrifice of himfelf, and obtain eternal redemption for us *through Faith in
his Blood.* His Refurrection, was the demonftration of this Sacrifice's being accepted
by God ; and his Afcenfion into Heaven, was in order to plead the merits of his Sufferings before God, and intercede for thofe, who according to the terms of the Gofpel-
Covenant fhould be capable of receiving the gracious Benefits purchafed by his Death :
Wherefore 2*dly,* He now fits at the right hand of God, ready to appear in the glory
of his Father with the Holy Angels, actually to deliver all thofe from the punifhment
of Sin, who have before been delivered by him from the dominion thereof. This
fitting at the right hand of God, fignifies his having fubdued all his enemies, and his
being fully inftated in his Regal power ; *All things being actually made fubject unto.
him, always excepting* him, *as* St *Paul* directs, *who did put all things under* him. *All
power both in heaven and earth is now committed unto* him ; *being exalted far above all
principality, and power, and might, and dominion, and every name that is named not
only in this world, but alfo in that which is to come* ; *God having put all things under
his feet, and given him to be the head over all things to the Church.* When therefore
this his Mediatorial kingdom fhall be finifhed, and the number of his Elect accomplifhed, then *unto them that look for him fhall he appear the fecond time without Sin
unto Salvation,* Heb. ix. 28. Then fhall he redeem his Elect ·from death, and ranfom
them from the power of the grave : *Then fhall the Sea give up the dead that are in
it, and Death and Hell fhall deliver up the Dead that are in* them, *and death fhall be
fwallowed up in victory* ; *O Death, where is thy fting* ! *O Grave, where is thy victory* !
But this deliverance from the *firft* and *natural* Death, fhall be common both to the Juft
and Unjuft. It is the *Second death,* that fhall be properly and finally the punifhment
of Sin ; and from This, the *Juft* only fhall be delivered. *Whofoever believeth on me,
fhall never die,* Joh. xi. 26 : that is, (as the words may more properly be rendred,)
fhall not die for ever. On the Juft the Second death fhall have no power, but they
fhall be priefts of God and of Chrift ; they fhall be made compleatly happy both in
Body and Soul, and fhall reign with him for ever and ever.

THE application I fhall make of what hath been faid, fhall be only in thefe two
brief inferences: 1*ft,* If Chrift delivers no man from the punifhment of Sin, who is
not firft delivered from the fervice and dominion of it ; then no man who continues in
the fervice and dominion of Sin, can expect to be delivered from the punifhment thereof. Chrift *has* indeed given himfelf a propitiatory Sacrifice, a full, perfect, and fufficient Oblation for the Sins of the whole World ; but it is not that the whole World,
or that any particular perfons fhould abfolutely and unconditionately be thereby excufed from the punifhment of Sin ; but that all thofe who by true Repentance turn
from Sin and become righteous, fhould obtain Remiffion and Reconciliation with God :
For he did not die that he might indulge men *in* Sin, but that he might fave them
from it. Chrift *has* indeed brought Life and Immortality to light, and opened an a-
bundant entrance into the Kingdom of God ; but it is not that any unreformed and
unrenewed nature fhould be made partaker of that Spiritual Happinefs, or be admitted
to have a fhare in thofe pure and undefiled Rewards ; but that thofe who have broken
off their Sins by Repentance, and their Iniquities by Righteoufnefs and fhewing mercy
to the poor, (which is the Wedding-garment required by our Lord in the Parable,)
fhould be entertained at the eternal Supper of the Lamb : For as impoffible as it is for
God to ceafe to be holy, or for the purity of the Divine Nature to be reconciled to
Sin, fo impoffible is it for a wicked man to obtain remiffion whilft he continues wicked,
or for a Sinner to be admitted into the kingdom of Heaven. *Be not deceived,* faith

St

St *Paul, neither fornicators, nor idolaters, nor adulterers, nor effeminate, nor abusers*
of themselves with mankind, nor thieves, nor covetous, nor drunkards, nor revilers, nor
extortioners, that is, no unrighteous person that continues in the practice of any known
Sin, *shall inherit the kingdom of God*; 1 Cor. vi. 9. Again, *Gal.* v. 21, having reckoned
up the like catalogue of Sins, he adds, *of the which I tell you before, as I have*
also told you in time past, that they which do such things, shall not inherit the kingdom
of God. And *Ephes.* v. 6; *Let no man deceive you with vain words, for because of these*
things cometh the wrath of God upon the children of disobedience. 2dly, If Christ delivers no man from the dominion of Sin any otherwise than by giving him a clear
knowledge of his duty, and a sufficient power to perform it, then no man who makes
not use of that knowledge and power to an actual performance of his duty, can be
delivered from the dominion of Sin. Christ hath completely performed *his* office for
us; but if *We* will not also perform what remains for *us* to do for ourselves; if we
will yet chuse rather to continue in the service of Sin, than to come forth into the
glorious liberty to which we are called; we must, notwithstanding all that Christ has
done for us, continue still under the dominion of Sin, and shall at last fall into the
punishment thereof. The Imputation of the Righteousness of Christ, (which some have
vainly depended upon, while they themselves continue to live in open contempt of his
righteous laws,) is a false and groundless imagination: 'Tis the unalterable Nature of
Things, and the Will of God; that if we expect to be made happy for ourselves,
we *must* also become righteous for ourselves. Righteousness is not an outward imaginary quality, but an inward and real disposition of the heart and soul, which must
show forth itself in real and substantial acts of Holiness and Piety. *Little children,*
let no man deceive you; he that doeth *righteousness, is righteous*; 1 Joh. iii 7: And
St *James*, ch. i. 27; *Pure religion and undefiled before God and the Father is this, to*
visit the fatherless and widows in their affliction, and to keep himself unspotted from
the world. Let no man therefore deceive himself with vain imaginations, in hopes of
being accounted righteous any other way, than by that which God has proposed to us
in his holy Scriptures: Let us consider how great things Christ has done in order to
our Salvation; and let us shew forth our thankfulness for what *he* has done for us, by
heartily setting about what he has absolutely required that *we* should do for *ourselves*:
Let us sincerely endeavour to obey the Will of God as discovered to us in the Gospel;
and then we may firmly hope for (and shall certainly obtain) remission, not through
the merits of that our Righteousness which is imperfect, but through the redemption purchased by the Blood of Christ, wherein we are by that sincere, though imperfect Righteousness, made capable of having a share.

SERMON LXXVIII.

How CHRIST has given us the Victory over Death.

[*Preached on Easter-Day.*]

1 COR. XV. 56 and 57.

The sting of Death is sin, and the strength of sin is the law ; but thanks be to God which giveth us the victory, through our Lord Jesus Christ.

SERM.
LXXVIII.
I Proceed now to the third and last Thing I proposed, which was to show how Christ gives *us the Victory over Death, which is the last enemy to be destroyed*, 1 Cor. xv. 26. *Death* is either natural and temporal, which is the Death of the body; or eternal, which is the Death and the Destruction of the Soul. In the Old Testament, Death generally signifies that *temporal* Death, which is the dissolution of the body; tho' when it is threatned as the punishment of Sin, it præfigures and includes in it *eternal* Death. Which is also sometimes expresly threatned even in the Old Testament; thus Ezek. xviii. 26 ; *When a righteous man turneth away from his righteousness, and committeth iniquities, and dieth in them, for his iniquity that he hath done shall he die* ; the manner of expression is very observable : If he repent not of his iniquity but *dieth* in it, *then* for the iniquity that he hath done shall he die. In the *New Testament*, Death, when 'tis threatned to Sinners, signifies almost always *eternal* Death ; the Gospel containing, as a more clear discovery of life and immortality, so also a more express revelation of the wrath of God from Heaven, against all unrighteousness and ungodliness of men. Now over *both* these kinds of Death, Death temporal and eternal, Christ gives us the victory, or delivers us from the power of them : The power of *temporal* Death is universal, as the punishment threatned to *Adam*'s transgression was extensive ; and the deliverance from it shall be also universal ; *For as in* Adam *all die,* all are become subject to mortality ; *even so in Christ shall all be made alive,* 1 Cor. xv. 22. *Eternal* Death is the punishment of unrepented Sin, and from This all those who repent and obey the Gospel, shall be delivered by Christ.

I SHALL consider 1*st* the victory that Christ gives us over *temporal* Death ; and for the clearer explaining the nature of this victory, shall endeavour to show 1*st*, That there shall be a resurrection of the body, and 2*dly*, in what manner the body shall be raised.

1*st*, THAT there shall be a resurrection of the body. That the soul should survive the dissolution of the body, and be capable of receiving in a future State the reward or punishments due to the good or evil it had done in *this* life, was clearly enough deducible from the light of nature, and proved by undeniable reasonings : But that the body should be again formed out of the dust, and reunited to the Soul, from which it was separated by Death, was a Doctrine, which as it could not be proved merely by reason

and

and argument, fo the Philofophers, who pretended to be the great mafters of reafon, S E R M.
looked upon it as the moft impoffible thing in nature. Some of them reckoned it a- LXXVIII.
mong thofe things, which they thought were not in the power even of their Gods
themfelves to effect; and we read of certain Philofophers, *Acts* xvii. 18, who en-
countred St *Paul*, and when they heard of the refurrection, they mocked him, faying,
*that he feemed to be a fetter forth of ftrange Gods, becaufe he preached unto them Jefus
and the Refurrection.* Yet is there nothing in any wife impoffible, or contrary to reafon, in this great Myftery: *For why fhould it be thought a thing impoffible that God
fhould raife the dead?* Why fhould it be more impoffible for God to gather together
the difperfed parts of a corrupted body, and reunite them to their former Soul, than to
create matter at firft out of nothing, and then form it into a humane body, *and breathe
into it the breath of life?* Why fhould any man be fo weak as to imagine, that he,
who at the creation feparated the confufed mafs of matter into fo many different forts of
bodies, cannot with the fame eafe at the general Refurrection feparate again the fame
confufed matter, and affign to each particular body its own parts? If it is not difficult
for him *to number the Stars of Heaven and call them all by their names*; it can be no
difficulty to him to keep an exact account of all our fcattered parts; and to recollect and
reunite them when he pleafes. 'Twas not therefore becaufe the thing is in itfelf at all
impoffible, but only becaufe the manner of it is a myftery not difcoverable barely by
the light of nature, that the Heathen World was utterly ignorant of the Refurrection
from the dead. The proof therefore of this great truth muft be founded in Revelation,
and fought for only in the Holy Scriptures. And here it muft be confeffed, that the
Jews had not a clear and exprefs revelation of this matter: Yet were they by no means
wholly ignorant of it; there being feveral paffages in the Old Teftament, from whence
the hope of a refurrection might very reafonably be collected. The tranflation of *Enoch*
and *Elijah* into Heaven with their bodies, was an earneft of what might finally be expected, by thofe who fhould follow their example in pleafing God; and the ftrict
command that *Jacob* and *Jofeph* gave, not to be buried in *Egypt*, but to have *their
bones carried up into the land of Canaan and laid in the Sepulchres of their Fathers*;
was to many of the antient *Jews* an argument or type of their hope of a Refurrection.
That the thing was not in itfelf impoffible, the inftances of fuch as were actually raifed
from the dead by the Prophets, was a fignal proof. And *Ifaiah* xxvi. 19; *Thy dead
men fhall live, together with my dead body fhall they arife: awake and fing, ye that dwell
in duft: for thy dew is as the dew of herbs, and the earth fhall caft out the dead.* And
the vifion of *Ezekiel*, fet down in the 37*th* Chapter of his Prophecy, tho' it fignified
indeed primarily the Reftauration of *Ifrael* to their own land, yet in all probability,
confidering the peculiar Emphafis and particularity of the defcription, it was intended
remotely to point at a greater and more general Reftauration; *Behold, a valley full of
dry bones, and there was a noife, and behold a fhaking, and the bones came together, bone
to his bone, the finews and the flefh came up upon them, and the skin covered them above,
and their breath came into them, and they lived and ftood upon their feet, and behold a
great multitude.* But that paffage in the Prophet *Daniel*, tho' by fome it be, with
great violence to the Words, otherwife interpreted; is moft exprefs, and by the antient
Jews underftood of the Refurrection, *Dan.* xii. 2 and 3, *Many of them that fleep in
the duft of the earth fhall awake, fome to everlafting life, and fome to fhame and everlafting contempt; and they that be wife, fhall fhine as the brightnefs of the firmament, and
they that turn many to righteoufnefs, as the ftars for ever and ever, and thou fhall reft
and ftand in thy lot at the end of the days,* Dan. xii. 13. Laftly, that folemn Prophecy of *Job*, ch. xix. ver. 23; *Oh that my Words were now written! Oh that they
were printed in a book! That they were graven with an iron pen and lead, in the rock
for ever! For I know that my Redeemer liveth, and that he fhall ftand at the latter Day*
upon

SERM. *upon the earth: And tho' after my skin worms destroy this body, yet in my flesh shall I see*
LXXVIII. *God :* These words, I say, tho' by many of the ancient *Jews* they were interpreted
concerning a future State without respect in particular to the Resurrection of the body,
and by some later Interpreters are understood only of his restitution to his temporal
greatness; yet because of their being introduced with so very solemn and weighty a preface, as containing somewhat of the highest moment and importance; they are by
others, not without great reason, thought to be spoken concerning the Resurrection of
the body. And that the *Jews* did believe, that the bodies, at least of such remarkably
pious men, should rise again, appears plainly from the translation of the last Verse of
the book of *Job* according to the Seventy, which in their Version runs thus; *So Job
died, being old and full of days; But 'tis written that he shall rise again with those
whom the Lord raises up.* The *Jews* therefore had at least an obscure and indetermi-
nate expectation of the Resurrection of the body; Nay, the later *Jews* more certain:
For so one of the seven Brethren, 2 *Macc.* vii. 9, 11; when his hands were to be cut
off; *These,* says he, *I had from Heaven, and for his laws I despise them, and from him
I hope to receive them again: For the King of the World shall raise us up, who have
died for his Laws, to everlasting life.* But now in the *New Testament* this Doctrine is
so clearly revealed, that it may justly be wondered how it was possible for any one that
believed the Gospel at all, to doubt of the certainty of it. Yet we read that there were,
even so very early as in the days of the Apostles themselves, *who concerning this truth,
did err, saying that the resurrection is past already; and overthrow the faith of some,*
2 Tim. ii. 18. But as their opinion was so absurd as to need no confutation, so in a little time it entirely vanished of itself. I shall not therefore insist on any other argument
for the proof of this doctrine, than that which the Apostle makes use of in this Chapter; which is the Resurrection of Christ: *For,* saith he, *if there be no resurrection of
the dead, then is Christ not risen; And if Christ be not risen, then is our preaching vain,
and your faith also is vain; But now Christ is risen from the dead, and become the first-
fruits of them that slept,* ver. 13, 14. The force of which argument is plainly this: If
there be no resurrection of the dead, then is that doctrine, which the Apostles preached
concerning it, erroneous and false; and if that doctrine be false, then the resurrection of
Christ, which is the proof of that doctrine, must likewise be false: If therefore the resurrection of Christ be true, as he had before proved *by a cloud of Witnesses* at the beginning of the Chapter, then the Apostles doctrine, of which that his resurrection was
the evidence, must also be true; and if the Apostles preaching, and the promises of
God made known by the Gospel, be true, then *shall the dead certainly rise again.*
That is: As certain as the resurrection of Christ is true, as certain as the Christian Religion is a revelation credibly attested to be from God; so certain is it, that there shall
be a resurrection of the dead: *If Christ, who is our Head, be risen; then shall we also
rise with him unto glory.* I am the resurrection and the life, saith our *Blessed Saviour,*
Joh. xi. 25; *and this is the Will of him that sent me, that every one which seeth the Son
and believeth on him, may have everlasting Life, and I will raise him up at the last day,*
Joh. vi. 40; which last words, that there might be no room for doubt concerning
them, are repeated *no* less than *four* times in that Chapter. Now that this promise
shall certainly be fulfilled, God has given us assurance by raising up *him* before-hand to
be the *first-fruits from the dead: He hath appointed a day, in the which he will judge
the world in righteousness, by that man whom he hath ordained; whereof he hath given
assurance unto all men, in that he hath raised him from the dead,* Acts xvii. 31. The
Resurrection of Christ is such an earnest and pledge of our resurrection, as not only de-
monstrates the *possibility* of the thing, but gives assurance also of the *certainty* of it:
For, that the same power that raised up him, *can* also raise up us, is evident; and that
it *will* do so, we are assured by *his* promise, who raised up Christ to that very end, that

I
he

he might give us affurance that he would alfo *raife up us*. But here fome man will fay. *How are the dead raifed up, and with what body do they come?* Which is the

2*d* Thing I propofed to fpeak to, namely, the *manner how the dead fhall be raifed*; and to *this queftion* we may anfwer in the Words of St *Paul*, 1 Cor. xv. 36 ; *Thou fool, that which thou foweft is not quickned except it die; And that which thou foweft, thou foweft not that body that fhall be, but bare grain, fuppofe of wheat or of fome other grain; But God giveth it a body as it hath pleafed him, and to every feed his own body.* From which fimilitude of the Apoftle, we may fafely colled thefe two things ; 1*ft*, That in the whole the fame body which died, fhall be raifed again ; 2*dly*, That yet it fhall rife with very great alterations. 1*ft*, That in the whole, the fame body which died, fhall be raifed again, appears in general from the Apoftle's ufing the fimilitude of Corn : *For as Corn groweth not indifferently out of any ground, but there muft be feed fown out of which it may fpring, and therefore every fort of grain produceth Corn of its own likenefs and peculiar form*; So at the refurrection, the bodies of them that arife, fhall not be formed indifferently out of any matter, but the bodies that die, thofe mortal and corruptible Bodies, fhall be in a figurative fenfe as it were the feed and material principle of thofe immortal and incorruptible ones, into which we fhall then be quickened. Indeed whether in equity, and in order to a juft retribution, it be neceffary abfolutely in the nature of the thing, that the fame Body fhould be raifed again, we cannot certainly tell; becaufe we know not diftinctly how far the fame body is neceffary to conftitute the fame perfon. But though it cannot be proved that God is abfolutely bound in juftice to unite the Soul to the fame body from which it was feparated by death, yet that in fact he *will* do fo, the expreffions of Scripture concerning this matter do fufficiently intimate: When the Apoftle affures us, *that the body fhall rife again, and that He that raifed up Chrift from the dead fhall alfo quicken our mortal bodies*, he does not fay only that the Soul fhall be again united to matter, but alfo that the *body* which died fhall be quickened or made to live again; *For this corruptible muft put on incorruption*, and *This* mortal *muft put on immortality*; which is not faying only that the Soul, which was before united to a *mortal and corruptible body*, fhall at the refurrection be clothed with an *immortal and incorruptible one*; but that *This fame body*, which is now mortal and corruptible, *fhall then put on immortality and incorruption.* To which purpofe it is affirmed in Scripture, *that the fea fhall give up the dead that are in it, and death and the grave fhall deliver up the dead that are in them, and they that fleep in the duft of the earth fhall hear the voice of Chrift and rife*: And indeed, having one example of it in the refurrection of Chrift, and knowing that in all cafes it is as eafy for God to raife the fame Body as to frame a new one, no reafon can be imagined why it fhould not be fo. But it is true, the *parts* of one body may poffibly be fo fcattered and perhaps incorporated among the parts of another body, that it fhall not be poffible for every particular body to arife with juft the fame parts, of which it confifted at the time of its diffolution: Neither is there any neceffity at all either in nature or Scripture that it fhould do fo. How far therefore each body fhall confift exactly of the fame matter, or what change of parts may be admitted, is a vain, empty and needlefs fpeculation; a nicety, which as it is not poffible for us to determine, *fo* neither is it neceffary for us to know; *Sufficient* it is to all wife and good purpofes, that we believe and affirm with St *Paul, that as out of a grain of corn fown in the earth there fprings an ear of the fame kind; fo from a mortal and corruptible body buried in the ground, there fhall be raifed an immortal and incorruptible one.* For 2*.dly*, Though in the whole the fame body that died fhall be raifed again, yet fhall it rife with very great alterations : *As thou foweft not that body that fhall be, but bare grain, fuppofe of wheat or of fome other grain, but God giveth it a body as it hath pleafed him; fo alfo is the refurrection of the dead.* What thefe alterations fhall be, the Apoftle tells us

SERM. in the 42, 43 and 44*th* Verſes of this xv*th* Chapter of 1 Cor. *It is ſown in corruption,*
LXXIX. *it is raiſed in incorruption ; it is ſown in diſhonour, it is raiſed in glory ; it is ſown in*
weakneſs, it is raiſed in power ; it is ſown a natural body, it is raiſed a ſpiritual body.
1ſt, *It is ſown in corruption, it is raiſed in incorruption ;* i. e. The body which has
now in it ſuch manifeſt principles of mortality and corruption ; which conſiſts now of
ſuch brittle and tender parts, that every the leaſt violence diſturbs and unfits them
for their operations ; which is now ſubjeℭ to ſo many caſualties, and has its continuance depending upon the fit diſpoſition of ſo many little and eaſily diſordered parts, that
it is a greater wonder how we continue to live a day, than why we die after ſo few
years.ſpace ; *this* body ſhall at the reſurreℭion be perfeℭly refined and purged from
all the ſeeds of mortality and corruption : ſhall be made up of ſuch parts, and ſo conſtituted, as ſhall neither in themſelves have any tendency to diſſolution, nor be capable of being any way diſordered and unfitted for their proper funℭions ; in a word, ſhall
ſpring up into an incorruptible and immortal ſubſtance, which ſhall be fitted to endure
as long as the Soul to which it is to be united, even to all eternity. Again, *it is ſown*
in diſhonour, it is raiſed in glory ; i. e. That body, which at death ſeems ſo baſe and
abjeℭ, ſo vile and contemptible, ſhall at the reſurreℭion be transformed *into* a bright
and beautiful and glorious body. Neither ought it at all to ſeem ſtrange to us, that
it ſhould be capable of receiving ſo great a change ; For if even in this mortal life the
motions of the Soul, joy and hope, innocence and an aſſurance of the favour of God,
can ſhew forth themſelves with ſo remarkable a Vigour, and as it were with a luſtre,
in the countenances of men ; if St *Stephen*'s innocence and joyful aſſurance, could *make*
his face to appear as it had been the face of an Angel ; and Moſes's *converſing with God*
upon the Mount, could make his face ſo ſhine, that the Children of Iſrael *were not able*
to look upon him for the brightneſs and glory of it ; how much greater change muſt the
ſtrong and powerful operations of a glorified Soul, raviſhed with the beatifick viſion of
God, make in a ſubtle, immortal and incorruptible body? But beſides this, we are
moreover aſſured, that Our Saviour ſhall alſo by his immediate power, even by that
mighty working *whereby he is able to ſubdue all things unto himſelf, change this our*
vile body that it may be faſhioned like unto his *glorious body ;* Phil. iii. 21. And what
ſort of body his glorious body is, may in ſome meaſure be gathered from the Hiſtory of
his transfiguration, where his face is deſcribed *to have ſhined like the Sun, and his raiment*
to have become ſhining, exceeding white as ſnow, ſo as no fuller on earth could white them ;
St Matt. xvii. 2: compared with *Mar.* ix. 3 : and from the deſcription of his appearance to St *John ;* Rev. i. 14: *His head and his hairs were white like wool, as white as*
ſnow, and his eyes were as a flame of fire, and his feet like unto fine braſs, as if they burn-
ed in a furnace. Such therefore ſhall be the glorified bodies of the Saints at the reſurreℭion ; namely, made like unto the glorified body of Chriſt. And this perhaps is
what is intimated by our Saviour in that promiſe ; St Matt. xiii. 43 ; *Then ſhall the righ-*
teous ſhine forth as the Sun in the Kingdom of their Father ; and in that Prophecy of
Daniel, ch. xii. v. 3 : *They that be wiſe ſhall ſhine as the brightneſs of the firmament, and*
they that turn many to righteouſneſs as the Stars for ever and ever : and by the Author
of the Book of *Wiſdom ;* ch. iii. 6, 7 : *As gold in the furnace has he tried them, and re-*
ceived them as a burnt-offering : They ſhall ſhine, and run to and fro like ſparks among
the ſtubble : They ſhall judge the nations, and have dominion over the people ; and their
Lord ſhall reign for ever. Further, *it is ſown in weakneſs, it is raiſed in power ;* i. e.
that body, which is now ſo weak and feeble, ſo ſubjeℭ to diſeaſes and indiſpoſitions, ſo
ſlow, heavy and unaℭive, that it clogs the ſoul, and retards its ſpiritual flights and o-
perations ; ſhall then become ſo ſtrong and powerful, ſo aℭive and vigorous, as even
to be aſſiſting to the moſt ſpiritual motions of the Soul, to become every way a fit
Organ and Inſtrument of its moſt exalted operations, and ſhall continue in that perfeℭ

health, ſtrength and vigour for ever: *For God ſhall wipe away all tears from their eyes;* S E R M.
and there ſhall be no more death, neither ſorrow, nor crying, neither ſhall there be any LXXIX.
more pain; for the former things are paſſed away; Rev. xxi. 4. Laſtly, *it is ſown a*
natural body, it is raiſed a ſpiritual body; i. e. That body, which is now fitted only
for this animal life; which conſiſts of ſuch groſs ſubſtance, and that in continual change,
as needs perpetually to be repaired with the ſuitable nouriſhment of meats and drinks,
to be ſuſtained and kept in order with labour and exercife, and to be refreſhed with
ſuch pleaſures as are ſuitable indeed to this animal life, but are far beneath the excellent nature of the ſoul, and prove oft-times hurtful and injurious to it; *This body*, I ſay,
ſhall at the reſurrection become of a more refined and ſpiritual nature, ſhall be wholly
delivered from all thoſe wants and incumbrances which are now ſo neceſſary to the
preſervation of the animal life; and ſhall be entirely freed from all appetites to ſuch
pleaſures, as are now the *ſnares* and temptations of the Soul. All which, our Saviour
ſeems plainly to intimate, in that anſwer of his to a captious queſtion propoſed by the
Sadducees; St *Luc.* xx. 35: *They which ſhall be accounted worthy to obtain That world*
and the reſurrection from the dead, neither marry nor are given in marriage; neither
can they die any more, for they are equal or like unto the Angels. Having thus explained
the nature of the victory that Chriſt gives us over temporal death,

2dly, I proceed now in the *2d* place to conſider the Victory which Chriſt ſhall give
to all his faithful Servants over that death which is *eternal*: And of this, very briefly.
The victory over temporal death ſhall be in ſome meaſure (as has been already obſerved)
univerſal; For all ſhall riſe again from the dead, and all both juſt and unjuſt ſhall be
clothed with immortal and incorruptible *bodies* which ſhall never be diſſolved any
more: But though there ſhall be no more diſſolution of the body, nor ſeparation of
the ſoul, yet is there a greater deſtruction, into which they who *believe not God and*
obey not his Goſpel ſhall at laſt fall; and that is, the ſecond death; Rev. xxi. 8. *The*
fearful, the unbelieving, the abominable, and murderers, and whoremongers, and ſor-
cerers, and idolaters, and all liars, ſhall have their part in the lake that burneth with
fire and brimſtone, which is the ſecond death. Now from *this* death, thoſe and thoſe
only ſhall be delivered by Chriſt, *who hear the Word of God and keep it; who hearken*
unto the commands of God, and in their lives obey them; They that overcome, ſhall not be
hurt of the ſecond death, for on them the ſecond death hath no power, but they ſhall be
Prieſts of God and of Chriſt, and ſhall reign with him for ever; Rev. ii. 11: compared
with *Ch.* xx. *ver.* 6. And of this we muſt underſtand that promiſe of our Saviour;
St *Joh.* xi. 26: *whoſoever liveth and believeth in me ſhall never die,* or (as the words
may more properly be rendered) *ſhall not die for ever;* i. e. ſhall never fall into eternal death. That which Chriſt hath already done towards delivering his Servants from
the power of this death, is his making proviſion for their deliverance from the dominion and from the guilt of Sin, of which this death is the conſequence and puniſhment.
That which ſtill remains, and which he will yet do for them, is to acquit them publickly at the great day of judgment, and then in purſuance of that ſentence of abſolu-
tion, actually *to* inſtate them in his Kingdom of Glory. The reſurrection of the dead
is only in order to that final judgment, which ſhall paſs upon all mankind; *for God*
hath appointed a day in the which he will judge the World in righteouſneſs, by that man
whom he hath ordained, even our Lord Jeſus Chriſt; at whoſe appearance all that are in
the graves ſhall hear his voice, and live, and ſtand before his judgment-ſeat, and he ſhall
judge them according to their works: The ſolemnity of which great day, cannot be
more lively expreſſed, than in thoſe prophetick words of *Daniel*; Chap. vii. ver. 9: *I*
beheld till the thrones were caſt down, and the antient of days did ſit, whoſe garment was
white as the ſnow, and the hair of his head like the pure wool; his throne was like the
fiery flame, and his wheels as burning fire; A fiery ſtream iſſued and came forth from
before

SERM. *before him, thousand thousands ministred unto him, and ten thousand times ten thousand*
LXXIX. *stood before him; the* judgment *was set, and the books were opened:* From which place
most of the expressions which are made use of in the New Testament to signify the
Second coming of Christ, are plainly borrowed. At this great Solemnity, all those
who have embraced the gracious terms of the Gospel, and through the mercy of God
have by Repentance and Obedience delivered themselves from the Power and Dominion of Sin, shall by their Saviour and Judge be publickly acquitted before Men and
Angels, and pronounced free from the Guilt and from the Punishment of Sin: *For
whosoever shall confess me before men,* faith our Saviour, *i. e.* whosoever shall not be
ashamed of the Religion of Christ, but notwithstanding all the Discouragements he
may meet with in the World, shall persist in it and obey it, him *shall the Son of man
confess before his Father which is in heaven, and before the angels of God, i. e.* he shall
acknowledge him for his true and faithful Disciple, and shall pronounce that blessed
Sentence upon him, *Well done, good and faithful servant, enter thou into the joy of thy
Lord.* The Servants of Christ being thus publickly acquitted at the general Judgment,
shall in pursuance of this Sentence enter with him into Heaven, and be actually instated
in his Kingdom of *glory*; and so shall they ever be with the Lord. *This* is the consummation of the Gospel-œconomy, and the *accomplishment* of the Kingdom of Christ:
Thus Christ, having totally subdued all his Enemies, *shall for ever be glorified with his
saints; and they shall be before the throne of God, and shall serve him day and night in
his temple; and he that sitteth on the throne shall dwell among them: they shall hunger
no more, neither thirst any more, neither shall the sun light on them nor any heat: for
the lamb which is in the midst of the throne shall feed them, and shall lead them unto living fountains of water, and God shall wipe away all tears from their eyes; and they shall
for ever sing that joyful song of praise;* Rev. i. 5: *Unto him that loved us and washed
us from our sins in his own blood, and hath made us kings and priests to God and his Father, to him be glory and dominion for ever and ever.* Amen.

Having thus at large explained how Christ gives his Servants the Victory over their
last enemy, which is Death, I shall only draw an inference *or two* from what has been
said, and so conclude. And 1*st*, If these things be so, then let us, as the Apostle infers in the words immediately following the Text, *be stedfast, unmoveable, always a-
bounding in the work of the Lord, forasmuch as we know that our labour shall not be in
vain in the Lord.* Our Saviour has assured us that if we be stedfast in our Religion,
and persevere in our Obedience to it, nothing shall by any means hurt us, but *we shall
be more than conquerors over all our enemies, even over death itself. I am,* saith he,
*the resurrection and the life; he that believeth on me, though he were dead, yet shall he
live;* Joh xi. 25. Now what greater encouragement can any man desire than to be
assured that his *labour shall not only not be in vain,* but that it shall also meet with a
great and inexpressible reward? And what greater reward can possibly be proposed,
than deliverance from death and an entrance into life eternal? If then we in earnest
believe these things, as by our Religion we profess and pretend to do, let us also consider them and urge them upon our selves; let us by frequent meditation, convince our
selves of the truth and importance of them; and let us always so *live*, as being under
the power of these convictions. Let not the terror of short and temporary evils drive
us into Sin, who are convinced that the consequence of that sin, will be misery and
death eternal; *and let not* the allurements of short and transitory pleasures withdraw *us*
from our duty, who are convinced that the performance of that duty, will be life and
happiness for ever. The religion of Christ requires nothing of us but what is extremely
reasonable and manifestly for our advantage, namely, *to live soberly, righteously, and
godly in this present World*; yet does it promise to obedience such an infinite reward,
as life from the dead, even life eternal; and he that will not by such a motive be

per-

perſwaded to be ſtedfaſt in ſuch a religion, muſt have loſt all ſenſe, I do not ſay only of **S E R M.** virtue and goodneſs, but alſo of his own intereſt and happineſs. *2dly*, If Chriſt has taken **LXXVIII.** away the *ſting of death*, and gives us the victory over it; then good Chriſtians ought not to be afraid and terrified at death, any more than at an enemy that is already conquered, and can do them no hurt. *Chriſt hath both died for us, and is riſen again*, and one great reaſon why he did ſo, was to aſſure us that as it was not poſſible for *him to be holden of death*, ſo neither ſhould we be detained by it; *for he took part of fleſh and blood, that through death he might deſtroy him that had the power of death*, i.e. the Devil, and *deliver them who through fear of death were all their life-time ſubject to bondage*, Heb. ii. 14 and 15. Chriſt has made death to be nothing elſe but a paſſage unto life eternal, to all thoſe who ſhall obey his commandments; Let us then ſincerely endeavour to obey the commands of God, and death ſhall have no ſting, nothing that is terrible in it. He that has either from the beginning, or after true Repentance, made it the principal buſineſs of his life, to live ſoberly, righteouſly, and godly; may without fear expect the approach of *death*, nay even with joy and comfort hope for it. And this the generality of mankind are ſo ſenſible of, that tho' they deſire not to *be like the Servants of God in their lives*, yet they cannot but wiſh with *Balaam* to be like them in their deaths, Num. xxiii. 10, *Let me die the death of the righteous, and let my laſt end be like his*. *3dly* and *laſtly*, If Chriſt will give all his Servants victory over death, then we ought not to grieve immoderately at the death of our friends who die in the Lord. *I would not have you ignorant*, ſaith St *Paul, concerning them that are aſleep, that ye ſorrow not even as others that have no hope; For if we believe that Jeſus died, and roſe again, even ſo them alſo which ſleep in Jeſus, will God bring with him*, 1 Theſſ. iv. 13. If we believe that there ſhall be a reſurrection from the dead, we ought not to ſorrow immoderately for the departure of thoſe, who have left this wicked and miſerable world, *and are gone to reſt from their labours?* For ſo ſaith the Spirit of God, *Rev.* xiv. 13. *Bleſſed are the dead that die in the Lord, from henceforth; yea, ſaith the Spirit, that they may reſt from their labours, and their works do follow them*.

SERMON LXXIX.

The Inexcufableneſs of rejecting the Gofpel.

[Preached on Whitſunday.]

HEB. II. 3 and 4.

How ſhall we eſcape, if we neglect ſo great ſalvation, which at the firſt began to be ſpoken by the Lord, and was confirmed unto us by them that heard him; God alſo bearing them witneſs, both with ſigns and wonders, and with divers miracles and gifts of the Holy Ghoſt, according to his own will?

SERM.
LXXIX.

THESE words contain an Account, how utterly inexcuſable all men are, who neglect the Salvation of the Gofpel; either by rejecting it through Unbelief, when offered unto them; or by living unworthily of it, after they have pretended to embrace it. Many confiderations there are, which highly aggravate the fault of ſuch perſons as contemptuouſly neglect the propoſal of a Favour, which 'tis both their duty and their greateſt intereſt to accept; and many circumſtances make them more and more inexcuſable, and juſtly to deſerve the ſevereſt puniſhment, for their ingratitude and contempt. The intrinſick *Goodneſs* and *Excellency* of the *Thing itſelf*, which they deſpiſe and neglect; the great *value*, the *neceſſity* and ſingular *importance* of it; the exceeding great *benefit*, which, by being duly received, it would bring along with it; and the Extreme *Evils* which are conſequent upon the neglect of it: The *Power* and *Authority*, the *Greatneſs* and *Goodneſs* of the Perſon, whoſe Favour we make light of; our Subjection to him and Dependence upon him, as our abſolute *Governour*; or our Obligations to him, as our greateſt *Benefactor*: The Dignity and Excellency of the *Perſon*, by whoſe *interpoſition* the Benefit is procured, and by whom it is conveyed or ſent to us: The great *Difficulties* that were neceſſary to be underwent in order to obtain it, or the great Coſt that was requiſite to purchaſe it: The Strength and Clearneſs of the *Evidence*, and the Number and Greatneſs of the *Proofs*, made uſe of to aſſure us of the *Certainty* of it: All theſe are Circumſtances which greatly increaſe our Obligation, to accept with Thankfulneſs the Advantage propoſed, to make that due Uſe of it for which it was conferred, and be influenced by it in all the Actions of our Lives. And if we neglect or deſpiſe it, or behave ourſelves ill and unworthily under it; all the ſame circumſtances do highly aggravate our guilt, render us very inexcuſable, and make us juſtly to deſerve the ſevereſt of puniſhments for our ingratitude and contempt. To reject That, which in the nature of the *thing itſelf* is of the higheſt *Excellency and intrinſick Goodneſs*, is a Mark of the greateſt Depravity and Corruption of Manners. To deſpiſe That, which is of the laſt and utmoſt *importance* to us; on the due receiving, or on the neglecting whereof, depends the greateſt Happineſs or the ex-

2 tremeſt

tremeft Mifery our Nature is capable of; is the greateft Folly and Stupidity imaginable.
To difobey the Commands of our Supreme *Governour*, whofe Power is abfolute, and
his Authority uncontroulable; is the higheft Infolence; and to oppofe the Will of our
greateft *Benefactor*, is the bafeft Ingratitude: To flight and reject a gracious Propofal
of Mercy, procured for us by the interpofition, and conveyed to us by the hands, of a
Perfon of the greateft Dignity and Excellency; and who was likewife in order thereunto, neceffarily to condefcend and fubmit to undergo great Sufferings and Indignities;
is the higheft degree of *Perverfenefs* poffible. And to withftand and not be convinced
by fuch Proofs, as both in Number, Strength, and Clearnefs, are the beft and greateft
Evidence that can be expected or in reafon defired; is the utmoft Obftinacy, and moft
inexcufably wilful Oppofition to Truth. Now all thefe aggravating Circumftances attend the rejecting, or (which is the very fame thing) the difobeying the Gofpel; and
they are moft of them contained in thefe words of the Apoftle; *How fhall we efcape, if
we neglect fo great falvation, which at the firft began to be fpoken by the Lord, and
was confirmed unto us by them that heard him; God alfo bearing them witnefs, both with
figns and wonders, and with divers miracles and gifts of the Holy Ghoft, according to
his own will?* In the words,

1ft, H E R E is the intrinfick Goodnefs and Excellency of the Thing itfelf, which
wicked men reject; intimated as a juft ground why they fhould not efcape unpunifhed.
It is in itfelf or in its own Nature a *great Salvation*; a Salvation from Sin and Mifery,
from the Power and Tyranny of the Devil, and from the punifhment of Death.

2dly, H E R E is a great Aggravation of the Sin of rejecting the Gofpel; in that it is
a Salvation not only *great in itfelf*, but alfo offered unto us by exprefs revelation from
God himfelf.

3dly, H E R E is the Dignity and Excellency of the Perfon, *by* and *through* whom
this Salvation is propofed to us; mentioned as a further Aggravation of the Sin of rejecting it. It was *at the firft began to be fpoken by the Lord.*

4thly and *Laftly*, T H E Strength and Clearnefs of the Evidence, and the Number
and Greatnefs of the Proofs, made ufe of to affure us of the Truth and Certainty of the
Gofpel; is of all others the *higheft* Aggravation, of the Guilt of thofe who neglect or
difobey it; and that which of all other circumftances renders them the moft utterly inexcufable: *God alfo bearing them witnefs, both with figns and wonders, and with divers
miracles and gifts of the Holy Ghoft, according to his own will.* The principal and moft
remarkable of all which Signs and Wonders, being that plentiful Effufion of the Holy
Spirit upon the Apoftles, which we *this day* commemorate; I fhall therefore be very
brief upon all the former Heads.

1ft, H E R E is the *intrinfick Goodnefs and Excellency of the Thing itfelf*, which
wicked men reject; intimated as a juft ground why they fhould not efcape unpunifhed.
It is *in itfelf*, a *great Salvation*; a Salvation from Sin and Mifery, from the Power and
Tyranny of the Devil, and from the punifhment of Death. Sin, in its own Nature,
even feparate from the confideration of its being an obftinate difobeying the revealed
Will of God, is in itfelf utterly unreafonable and inexcufable: 'Tis acting in oppofition
to the known reafon and proportion of things; contrary to that eternal Order and Equity,
which God has eftablifhed in the original conftitution of Nature; oppofite to the Light
of Reafon, the dictates of Confcience, the unprejudiced Judgment of our own Minds,
the agreeing Opinion of all wife and good men, nay and even of bad men themfelves
too; contrary to all our natural Notions and Apprehenfions, of the Attributes and Will
of God; deftructive to the publick Welfare and Happinefs of Mankind, the Health of
our own Bodies, the Peace of our Minds, and the Support of our good Name and Reputation amongft wife and reafonable men: 'Tis a fubjecting our reafon to vile affections, to inordinate and brutifh appetites, to diforderly and ungoverned Paffions; Which

S E R M. is the greateft and the worft flavery in the world; to fee and approve what is good, LXXIX. and yet not be able to prevail with ourfelves to practife it; to be fenfible of the deftructive confequences of Sin, and yet, through the Strength of evil Habits, continue under the power and dominion of it; To feel ourfelves deprived of our prefent Happinefs, and of our beft hopes of all that is to come; and yet continue in the practice of fuch Vices, as are the only Caufes of all this Mifery: This is evidently the greateft Mifery, and moft flavifh Bondage that can be. Now to have a way propofed to us, of being delivered from this Body of Sin, into the glorious Liberty of the Children of God; to have a method laid before us, of being refcued from this Mifery, and put into a way of fecuring both our prefent Happinefs and that which is to come: This is the Offer of a *great Salvation*; This whoever fhall neglect, is abfolutely inexcufable, and juftly deferves to fall into that Mifery, from which he would not accept a deliverance. The Light of Nature itfelf directs us thus far, and that which all true Philofophy pretended to, was to convince men of the reafonablenefs and neceffity of *endeavouring*, by all the helps of Reafon and natural Religion, to deliver themfelves from this bondage and flavery of Sin. The Gofpel propofes to us an infinitely more effectual way of obtaining this end, than any Philofophy under the Light of Nature was ever able to do; fhowing us moft clearly the heinous Nature of Sin, and the dreadful Confequences of it; all the Obligations of our Duty in a more clear and particular manner, and the infinite Advantage of complying with them; the true expiation of Sin, and the certainty of our Repentance being acceptable in the fight of God, and effectual to obtain Pardon; and affording us fufficient Helps and Affiftances, to enable us to perform what it requires of us, in order to our future and eternal Happinefs. This is, in the Nature of the Thing itfelf, a *great Salvation*; and the neglecting of which, (even feparate from the Confideration of the particular Difhonour done to God by rejecting an immediate Revelation of his Will,) is intrinfically in itfelf a moft inexcufable Neglect, and juftly deferving the fevereft of Punifhments.

BuT then 2*dly*, This further Confideration, that the Gofpel is an *exprefs and pofitive revelation of the Will of God*, is a very high Aggravation of the Sin of neglecting *fo great a Salvation*. He that defires not to be delivered from the *Dominion* of Sin, and has no thirft after a Life of *Righteoufnefs*; for *That very reafon* deferves not to be faved from the punifhment of Sin, and is in his Nature unqualified for the Rewards of Holinefs. But when to this choice of Wickednefs, there is added moreover a direct Contempt of God; when God has declared to men his Will by an immediate Revelation, and confirmed the Obligations of Nature by his pofitive Command; when he has offered us pardon upon our fincere Repentance, and vouchfafed us the Affiftance of his Spirit to enable us to perform it, and promifed us eternal Life upon our performance of it, and has obliged us to accept this Salvation under pain of the fevereft penalties; the wrath of God being now moft exprefsly revealed from Heaven againft all ungodlinefs and unrighteoufnefs of men; After *all* this, to continue ftill to defpife fo great Salvation, is adding Rebellion to our Sin, and with a high hand exalting ourfelves againft God; it is an avowed defpifing and contemning his Authority, and exprefsly declaring that we *will not have him to reign over us*. If therefore Sinning barely againft the *Law of Nature*, was fufficient to confign men to unavoidable Deftruction; how fhall *We* efcape, if we continue to Sin both againft Nature and Revelation? If the Servant that *knew not* his Lord's Will, was yet to be beaten with ftripes, becaufe he did things in themfelves worthy of ftripes; how much more feverely muft They expect to be punifhed, who do the fame things in direct oppofition to the exprefs Will and known Command of their Mafter? This was the Reafon why God punifhed the Sins of his own people the *Jews*, with greater Severity than thofe of the Heathen: And fo *Now* in like manner, whereas *the times of Ignorance God winked at*, as
the

the Apoftle expreffes it, *Acts* xvii. 30; that is, he was lefs ftrict and fevere with men
before the Revelation of the Gofpel; *Now*, on the contrary, under pain of his fevereft difpleafure, he peremptorily commands all men every where to repent; There
being no excufe left, nothing that can alleviate their condemnation, if men, *after that
the cleareft Light is come into the World*, will ftill obftinately continue in their
works of Darknefs.

3*dly*, T H E *Dignity and Excellency of the perfon*, *by* and *through* whom this great
Salvation is propofed to us, is a further Aggravation of the Sin of rejecting it. It *was
at firft begun to be fpoken by the Lord*; that is, as the fame Apoftle expreffes it in
the foregoing chapter, *God who at fundry times and in divers manners fpake in time
paft unto the fathers by the prophets, hath in thefe laft days fpoken unto us by his Son.*
The Dignity of the Perfon, by whofe interpofition any Favour is procured, and by
whom it is tranfmitted, fhows both the Greatnefs and Importance of the Thing itfelf,
and the Love and Condefcenfion of the Original Author of it; And the neglecting
it in this cafe, implies not only Folly, Infolence, and Rebellion, but moreover, the
greateft Obftinacy alfo, which no Authority can prevail over; and the bafeft Ingratitude, which no Kindnefs or Condefcenfion can overcome: Which therefore whofoever is guilty of, muft be confeffed moft juftly to deferve the fevereft of Punifhments.
This (the Ingratitude of rejecting a Mercy, offered with fo much Love and Condefcenfion, by the hands of a Perfon of fo great Dignity,) is what Our Saviour compelled the *Jews* to acknowledge, and made them condemn themfelves for it with their
own mouths, in the Parable of the Houfeholder; St *Matt.* xxi. 33; *who having planted a vineyard, and let it out to hufbandmen, firft fent his fervants to receive the fruits
of it; and when the hufbandmen had refifted and flain the fervants, he afterwards fent
his own* Son *to them, faying, Surely they will reverence my Son; But him alfo they
refifted and flew :* Whereupon when our Saviour appealed to the Pharifees themfelves,
to judge *what it was fit for the Lord of the vineyard to do unto thofe hufbandmen;*
They immediately replied, *He will miferably deftroy thofe wicked men, and let out his
vineyard unto other hufbandmen, which fhall render him the fruits in their feafons:* Un-
warily paffing a juft fentence againft Themfelves; that for rejecting the Gofpel preached by Chrift himfelf, they deferved a feverer condemnation, than their Fathers who
had before rejected the preaching and admonitions of the Prophets. The fame Argument is ufed by the Apoftle, in the words immediately preceeding the Text; *If the
word,* faith he, *fpoken by Angels was ftedfaft, and every tranfgreffion and difobedience
received a juft recompence of reward; how fhall we efcape, if we neglect fo great falvation, which at the firft began to be fpoken by* the Lord? And ch. x. ver. 28, *He that
defpifed Mofes's law, died without mercy: Of how much forer punifhment, fuppofe ye,
fhall he be thought worthy, who hath trodden under foot the* Son *of God?* and ch. xii. 25.
*See that ye refufe not him that fpeaketh: For if They efcaped not, who refufed him
that fpake on Earth, much more fhall not we efcape, if we turn away from him that
fpeaketh from Heaven.*

4*thly* and *Laftly*, T H E *Strength and Clearnefs* of the *Evidence*, and the *Number
and Greatnefs* of the *Proofs*, made ufe of to affure us of the Truth and Certainty of
the Gofpel; is the higheft Aggravation of the guilt of thofe, who neglect or difobey
it; and that which of all other things renders them the moft abfolutely inexcufable.
The Gofpel *was at firft begun to be fpoken by the Lord, and was* afterwards *confirmed to
us by them that heard him;* God *alfo bearing them witnefs both with figns and wonders, and with divers miracles and gifts of the Holy Ghoft;* whereof that which we *This
Day* commemorate, was both the Foundation of all the reft; and in itfelf alfo of the
greateft Efficacy and of the largeft Extent.

SERM. THE ftronger the Evidence of any Truth be, the more inexcufable is the making
LXXIX. oppofition to it. And the higheft Aggravation of this crime, is, to continue to oppofe a Truth, after the beft and greateft Evidence has been given of it, that the Nature
of the Thing was capable of. Oppofition in this cafe, againft the greateft Evidence
that is reafonably to be expected, can proceed from nothing but either incurable Obftinacy and Perverfenefs; or a Love of fome things, and a refolution not to part with
them, the keeping of which is inconfiftent with the acknowledgment of the Truth.
And this is plainly the Cafe of thofe who reject the Gofpel, after the undeniable Evidences that have been given of the Truth of it by the *Teftimony of the Spirit*. Their
rejecting it, cannot proceed from want of fufficient Conviction, but only from a love
of Vice, and a refolution not to be reformed; which is a degree of incorrigiblenefs,
in which there is no *hope* of excufe, and for which there remains no remedy; and
which there is no hopes of amending. When clear Light is come into the World,
and men ftill continue their works of Darknefs; then it becomes evident that their
wickednefs proceeds not from Ignorance and want of Inftruction, but from Will and
Choice; they love Darknefs rather than Light, and ftand in open defiance to God and
his fupreme Authority. This is what our Saviour fays of the *Jews*; St *Joh.* xv. 22;
If I had not come and fpoken unto them, they had not had Sin; but now they have no
cloak for their Sin; If I had not done among them the works which no other man did,
they had not had Sin; but now they have both feen and hated both me and my Father.
This is the reafon of his declaring to the Cities of *Judæa, that it fhould be more tole-*
rable for Sodom and Gomorrah in the day of Judgment than for Them; becaufe *if the*
mighty works that were done in Them, had been done in Sodom, it would have repented
in fackcloth and afhes. This is the reafon of his declaring to thofe Pharifees, who blafphemed the Holy Spirit, that *they fhould never have forgivenefs neither in this World,*
nor in that which is to come; becaufe they refifted the laft and greateft means, that
God would ever make ufe of to bring them to repentance; and not refifted it only,
but reviled it alfo: They faw with their own eyes the cleareft and ftrongeft proofs of
the Truth of the Gofpel, that could poffibly be given; and yet they not only with-
ftood the Evidence of thofe mighty works, but alfo blafphemed the Holy Spirit by
which they were worked. Their Crime was fingular and unexampled; and their
Condemnation was likewife fingular. But all others alfo, who reject the Gofpel,
are, in proportion to the greatnefs of the Evidence they refift, and according to the
degree of their Obftinacy and Wickednefs in fo doing, inexcufable in like manner,
and Defpifers of the *Teftimony of the Spirit*.

THE *Teftimony* which the Spirit of God has given to the Truth of the Gofpel,
contains a great Variety of undeniable Proofs, which St *Paul* calls *the Power and*
Demonftration of the Spirit. The many large and particular Prophecies, which from
the beginning of the World were dictated by the *Spirit*, concerning the Perfon of our
Saviour, and the Nature, Succefs, and Effects of his Doctrine: The Conception of
our Lord by the Miraculous Operation of the *Spirit*, and the manifold Wonders which
attended his Birth: The Vifible Defcent of the *Spirit* upon him at his Baptifm, accompanied with a Voice from Heaven, declaring him to be the beloved Son of God:
The Miracles which he worked during the courfe of his Miniftry, by the *Spirit of*
God; as the Scripture frequently expreffes it: His refurrection from the Dead, which
likewife the Scripture afcribes to the Power of the fame Spirit; *Rom.* viii. 11; and
1 *Pet.* iii. 18. But above all, that moft plentiful Effufion of the *Spirit* upon the A-
poftles at *Pentecoft*; whereby they were indued with Power from on high, to preach
the Gofpel with Authority and Efficacy; being enabled particularly to fpeak with
tongues, and to do even greater Works than our Saviour himfelf had worked upon
Earth, according to his Promife which he made to them before his departure. Thefe

Teftimonies, (I fay) *of the Spirit of God*, contain fuch demonftrative Proof of the Truth S E R M. of the Gofpel, as leaves *Them* who reject it, capable of no excufe; fince they defpife LXXIX. the *laft* and *greateft* means, that *fhall* be, or indeed *could* be made ufe of for their conviction and reformation. This laft Miracle in particular, the *Gift of Tongues* to the Apoftles, was of all others the ftrangeft, and in its nature and circumftances the greateft and moft affecting that could be conceived. The Apoftles, on whom this Gift was beftowed, were men, whofe Parentage and Education were well known to all that dwelt in *Jerufalem*; They were known to be illiterate and mean perfons; perfons whofe Employment had been laborious, and their manner of life from the beginning, fuch as afforded them neither Time nor Opportunities, of being fkilled in the Learning and Cuftoms of their *own* Country, much lefs of having ftudied the languages of other Nations. Had they been men of a polite and learned education, brought up in the ftudy of their own Law, and in the fchools of the Scribes and Pharifees; it might have been imagined that this their fkill in foreign languages might be the Effect of Study and Induftry, of Art and Defign, in order to gain Applaufe from the people, and fet themfelves up as Heads of new Sects, and Teachers of popular Doctrines. But fo far from This was their cafe, that on the contrary they were defpifed and contemned by their own countrymen for that very reafon, becaufe being well acquainted with their Education and manner of Life, they did not think it poffible that any Wifdom could be found in *Them*, or any Knowledge proceed from their lips. Exactly as they had formerly faid of their Mafter, when he went up into the Temple and taught: St *Joh.* vii. 14; *How knoweth this man letters, having never learned?* And St *Mar.* vi. 2; *From whence has this man thefe things? and what wifdom is this which is given unto him? Is not this the carpenter, the Son of Mary, the Brother of James and Jofes, and of Juda and Simon? and are not his fifters here with us?* Herein therefore confifted the Greatnefs of the Miracle, that Men of no Education fpake different languages *perfectly*; and that they did it *immediately and at once*, without any Time, Inftruction, or Study. Neither was there any room for any Fallacy or Deceit in this matter: For this thing was not done in a Corner, but publickly in the midft of *Jerufalem*, and in the prefence of innumerable witneffes; and that not *once* only, but with a continued and permanent Effect. The Witneffes alfo that were prefent, were the beft and moft competent Judges that could be; being perfons of different Nations, gathered together at *Jerufalem* upon account of the Feaft, to whom all the languages which the Apoftles fpoke, were feverally natural; fo that they could not be deceived, or impofed upon in this whole proceeding. The Natives of *Jerufalem*, who underftood not the tongues which were fpoken, nor knew whether they were really any languages at all; might indeed mock, and fay that *thefe men* were *full of new wine*, Acts ii. 13; but the foreigners, who heard each his own proper language, could not but be juftly filled with wonder and amazement. The Inhabitants of *Jerufalem*, were witneffes that the Apoftles were illiterate men, and underftood no language but their Mother-tongue, nor were capable of ufing any Art or Fraud in this matter; and the *Strangers* were witneffes, that what they uttered were true and real languages, and therefore could not be the effect of wine or madnefs. The Teftimony therefore of Both together, made the miracle certain, unqueftionable and manifeft; and accordingly the Effect of it, was proportionably great. For fo we read; *Acts* ii. ver. 41; that *the fame day, there were converted about three thoufand Souls.* This was the *immediate Effect* of the gift of Tongues at that very Time; and the *Ufefulnefs* of it *afterwards*, was peculiar and more remarkable, than of all other Miracles whatfoever. For this enabled the Apoftles to preach the Gofpel to all Nations, with fuch fpeed and incredible fuccefs, that though men of other Religions endeavoured to make Converts as well as they, and fome Sects of the *Jews* particularly were infinitely induftrious

duftrious and would compafs Sea and Land to gain a Profelyte; yet the Preaching of the Apoftles, *like the day-fpring from on high, like the morning-light, which in a moment difpels the darknefs from under one end of Heaven to the other*, propagated the Gofpel in a very few years to a vaftly larger extent, than ever any other religion was propagated in the compafs of many Ages. This gift of Tongues ceafed indeed after fome time, as other Miracles did; becaufe all thefe fort of gifts were beftowed not for their own fake or intrinfick worth, but only in order to the propagation of the Gofpel, and to convince men of the Truth of that Religion, whofe principal end and defign confifted in thofe gifts and graces of the Spirit which were to continue for ever. Which end being once obtained, and the Gofpel eftablifhed in the World, thefe miraculous gifts ceafed; having been given, as St *Paul* expreffes it, *not for them that believe, but for them that believe not.* But thofe gifts of the Spirit, in which confifts the renewal of the mind of man, and which are the Springs of all virtues which make us like unto God; thefe are to continue through all Ages; and are fo much more excellent and more defirable than the former, as the End is better and more excellent than the Means. In our Saviour's and in the Apoftle's time, it was very natural to the Weaknefs of Men, to be moft ambitious of fuch gifts, as made the greateft appearance, and could not but gain the greateft efteem and applaufe in the eyes of the World: But our Saviour himfelf cautioned his Difciples, *not to rejoice fo much at their being indued with a power of working Miracles, as at their Names being written in Heaven:* And St *Paul* afterwards took great pains to convince his hearers, *that though it was indeed lawful to covet miraculous gifts, yet he could ftill fhow unto them a more excellent way;* that it was a greater and far more defirable thing, to inftruct men in their plain and neceffary duty, than to work the moft ftupendous miracle; *and that Love and Goodnefs, Righteoufnefs and Holinefs, Meeknefs and Charity, were things more excellent and valuable in themfelves, than to be able to fpeak with all the Tongues, either of Men or Angels.* The reafon is plain, becaufe the one is beneficial only to *Others*, but the other to *ourfelves* likewife; He that works a Miracle or fpeaks with Tongues to convince another, may yet poffibly himfelf have no title to the rewards of the Gofpel; but He that is indued with thofe gifts which are the end and defign of the Gofpel, and for the fake only of which all the reft were given, does thereby fecure his own Salvation, as well as promote the Salvation of others. Let us then by Charity and Goodnefs and the practice of all virtues fecure to our felves that which is moft excellent; and then though the gifts of Miracles, be not continued to us, yet we fhall obtain the End for which alone thofe gifts have ever been given to Others. For, he that fpeaks with Tongues for the converfion of others, may (without the *Virtues* of Meeknefs and Humility, Love and Charity,) himfelf poffibly become a Caft-away: But he whofe Mind is indued with thofe *inward* Virtues, which are the *more* excellent gifts and fruits of the Spirit, has attained that *End*, for the promoting of which, the other *outwardly brighter* and more refplendent Gifts, were all intended but as *Means*.

SERMON

S E R M O N   LXXX.

Different Tempers judge differently of Religion.

[Preached on Eafter-Day.]

1 C O R. I. 22, 23, 24.

For the Jews require a Sign, and the Greeks feek after Wifdom: But we preach Chrift crucified, unto the Jews a ftumbling-block, and unto the Greeks foolifhnefs: But unto them which are called, both Jews and Greeks, Chrift the Power of God, and the Wifdom of God.

IN the following Difcourfe upon thefe Words, I fhall *1ft* explain diftinctly the feveral Expreffions contained in the Text; and *2dly*, I fhall deduce fome ufeful Inferences therefrom.

I. In order to explain diftinctly the feveral Expreffions made ufe of in the Text, it is to be obferved that the Doctrine therein contained, confifts plainly of the *three* following Heads. *1ft*, That the Great and general Difference, between the Humours or Tempers of the Nation of the *Jews* on *one* hand, and the *Greeks* (who were Then the principal and moft polite part of the *heathen* World) on the *other* hand, was This; That the *Jews*, in *Their* examination into the Truth of any Doctrine propofed to them, were always apt to infift prefently upon fome *Miracle*, upon fome *Token* to be fhown them, in proof of the Doctrine's coming from *God*; Whereas the Temper of the *Gentiles* was, to expect conviction by *Difputation and Argument*, according to the *Philofophy* of the Times they lived in, which was efteemed the *Wifdom* of the Age, then prefent: The *Jews require a* Sign, *and the Greeks feek after* Wifdom. *2dly*; That Perfons of *Both* thefe Tempers, and that pretended to make ufe of each of thefe ways of judging, were generally extremely prejudiced againft the Doctrine of the Gofpel: Infomuch that the coming of Chrift into the World, in the manner he did, in a mean, humble and lowly appearance, teaching a Doctrine of Morality, Plainnefs and Simplicity; was both a great Difappointment to the *Jews*, who expected one that fhould in a miraculous and pompous manner deliver them from their Enemies; and at the fame time was no lefs difagreeable to the then prevailing fafhion and method of the *Gentiles*, who judged of Doctrines by the Eloquence, and Oratory, and Artfulnefs in Difputing, of Thofe who taught and maintained them: *We preach Chrift crucified, unto the* Jews *a* ftumbling-block, *and unto the Greeks* Foolifhnefs. *3dly*, That neverthelefs, in Truth and Reality, fetting afide Prejudices and Corrupt Notions, the Doctrine of Chrift was accompanied with the *higheft* and *moft compleat Evidence*, according to *Both* thefe *Methods* of judging: It was attended with the fulleft Demonftrations of Divine *Power*, in the *Miracles* God worked by him; And it had all real marks of *Wifdom*, in its perfect agreeablenefs to the Dictates of True and Impartial *Reafon*: But

SERM. *unto them which are called, both* Jews *and* Greeks, *Chrift the Power of God, and the*
LXXX. *Wifdom of God.*

1*ft,* THE Great and general Difference, between the Humours or Tempers of the
Nation of the *Jews* on one hand, and the *Greeks* (who were then the principal and
moft polite part of the *Heathen* World) on the *other* hand, the Apoftle obferves, was
This; That the *Jews* in *Their* examination into the Truth of any Doctrine propofed to
them, were always apt to infift prefently upon fome *Miracle,* upon fome *Token* to be
fhown them, in proof of the Doctrine's coming from *God*; Whereas the Temper of
the *Gentiles* was, to expect conviction by *Difputation and Argument,* in Methods anfwering to the *Philofophy* of the Times they lived in, which was the Standard of *Wifdom* of the Age then prefent: *The Jews require a* Sign, *and the Greeks feek after* Wifdom. As to the Temper of the *Greeks* in this matter; nothing is more notorious in
Hiftory, than that about the Times of our Saviour and his Apoftles, the things principally efteemed among them were *Oratory* and the *Art of Difputing : Oratory,* by
which Things were fet forth in a beautiful Light, adorned with proper figures, made
pleafing and acceptable to the Hearers by a Variety of agreeable expreffions; And the
Art of Difputing, by which every thing could be *fupported* with *fome* plaufible *Arguments,* every thing could be *oppofed* with *Some* feeming *Difficulties,* and every *Difficulty*
could by men of Parts and Ingenuity have *Something* offered in *Reply* to it. Thefe Inftances of Skill, in themfelves, and when applied to good Purpofes, were *Both of them*
really ufeful and valuable. By *Oratory,* Truth and Right reprefented in a good View,
and clothed in proper and agreeable expreffions, appeared with a Greater Luftre, and
made more Advantagious Impreffions : And by *Skill in arguing, Reafon* was taught to
exert itfelf in its full *Strength,* and *Truth* to fhine forth in its peculiar and inimitable
Clearnefs. But *more frequently,* among vicious and corrupt Men, thefe Inftruments
and Ornaments of Reafon were perverted to very wrong and contrary Purpofes. By *Oratory,* the *Deformity* of *unrighteous Practices* was covered with the deceitful Appearance,
and painted over with the beautiful Colours of *Juft and Right :* And by *Skill in difputing,* the plaineft *Truths* were *perplexed* with fuch *Intricacies,* and the groffeft *Errours*
concealed under fuch *Forms of Arguing,* as altogether confounded, to common Underftandings, the Difference between Truth and Errour. This was what the corrupt Part
of the *Greeks* called *Wifdom.* As to the Temper of the *Jews;* They, having received
their Law by Revelation from *God,* were never much accuftomed either to value in
themfelves, or to regard in *Others,* That nice and abftract Reafoning, which was all that
the *Gentile* Philofophers had to depend upon ; The *Jews,* I fay, never much attended
to This fort of Learning ; But, whenever any Doctrine was propofed to them which
appeared to be New, immediately they infifted, that the Author of it fhould, by working fome *Miracle,* give evidence of his being fent from *God.* Thus *Joh.* iv. 48. *Except ye fee Signs and Wonders, ye will not believe :* And *Matt.* xvi. 1. *The Pharifees defired him, that he would fhow them a Sign from Heaven.* Nor were they to blame in fo
doing, when the Doctrine to which their Affent was expected, was propofed to them as
of *Divine Revelation* ; and when their demanding fuch evidence, did not proceed
from any unreafonablenefs or perverfenefs of Temper, but from a fincere Defire of having fuch Satisfaction, without which a reafonable Perfon could not juftify his Affent
from being credulous and weak. But *more frequently,* under pretence of expecting Further Satisfaction, an obftinate and malicious Temper perfifted continually in requiring
more and more Signs, for no other reafon but becaufe they refolved *not to be convinced,*
being *like the Deaf Adder which ftoppeth her ears, which refufeth to hear the Voice of
the Charmer, charm he never fo wifely.* Which Sort of perfons, our Saviour reproves
therefore with a very juft and proper Severity, *Matt.* xii. 39 : *An evil and adulterous
generation feeketh after a Sign, and there fhall no Sign be given it, but the Sign of the*
Prophet

Prophet Jonas: For as Jonas was three days and three nights in the Whale's belly, so shall *the Son of man be three days and three nights in the heart of the Earth: The men of* *Nineveh shall rise up in judgment with this generation, and shall condemn it; because* *They repented at the preaching of Jonas, and behold a greater than Jonas is here: The* *Queen of the South shall rise up in judgment with this generation, and shall condemn it;* *for she came from the uttermost parts of the Earth to hear the wisdom of Solomon, and be-* *hold a greater than Solomon is here.* The Meaning is: God had given them *Signs* a-
bundantly sufficient, to convince any reasonable and unprejudiced persons; wherewith
if they would not be satisfied, he would leave them to themselves. And This may
suffice for explication of the *first* part of the Text, the *General Observation* concerning
the *different Temper* or *Humour* of the *Jewish* and *Gentile* Nations: *The Jews require*
a Sign, *and the Greeks seek after* Wisdom.

2*dly,* T H E *Second* Particular in the Text, is the Observation, that Persons of *Both*
these Tempers, and that pretended to make use of *Each* of these ways of judging,
were generally extremely prejudiced against the Doctrine of the Gospel: Insomuch that
the coming of Christ into the World, in the Manner he did, in a mean, humble, and
lowly appearance, teaching a Doctrine of Morality, plainness and simplicity; was both
a great Disappointment to the *Jews,* who expected one that should in a miraculous and
pompous manner deliver them from their Enemies; and at the same time was no less
disagreeable to the then prevailing Fashion and Method of the *Gentiles,* who judged of
Doctrines by the Eloquence, and Oratory, and Artfulness in Disputing, of Those who
taught and maintained them: *We preach Christ crucified, unto the* Jews *a Stumbling-*
Block, and unto the Greeks *Foolishness.* The *Jews* thought that no other *Sign* was a
Mark of the true Messias, but *Delivering them from their Temporal Enemies;* and that
the *Power of God* could no otherwise be manifested in him, than by establishing him
a *Kingdom in this World.* When therefore our Lord came in *Another* manner, preaching *humility* and *meekness, patience* and *charity;* calling them to *virtue* and *goodness,* instead of *Earthly Power and Dominion :* Though they were astonished at the Excellency
of his Doctrine, and at the Greatness of his Works; and wondered, *whence has This*
man this wisdom, and those mighty works; yet presently they say, *Is not this the Car-*
penter's Son? Is not his Mother called Mary? and his Brethren, James and Joses and
Simon and Judas? and his Sisters, are they not all with us? whence then has this man
all these things? and they were offended in him, Matt. xiii. 15. Nay, Even his own *Dis-*
ciples; whenever he began to speak to them of his *Sufferings* and Death, immediately they *rebuked him, saying, Be it far from thee, Lord; This shall not be unto thee.*
And when he had actually suffered, they said with a desponding heart, *We trusted that*
it had been He which should have redeemed Israel, Luke xxiv. 21. And even after they
were satisfied of the Truth of his *Resurrection,* yet still their antient Prejudices put
them upon seeking after the same *Sign* or Token as before; *Lord, wilt thou at this*
time restore again the Kingdom to Israel? Acts i. 6. So that, considering how great a
Stumbling-block This Circumstance was to the whole Nation of the *Jews,* it was with
very good reason that our Lord pronounces, *Matt.* xi. 6. *Blessed is he whosoever shall not*
be offended in me. As to the *Gentiles;* They, as I now observed, being used to judge
of Doctrines by the *Eloquence,* and *Oratory,* and *Artfulness in Disputing,* of those who
taught and maintained them; it is no wonder that the Plainness and Simplicity of the
Gospel, which took no care to please and entertain them with artificial compositions,
nor to try their Parts and gratify their Vanity with nice and subtle Disputations, but
aimed wholly at reforming their Manners, and withdrawing them from idolatrous Imaginations to the Service of the One Living and True God, in Holiness, Righteousness
and Charity; it is no wonder, I say, that this Plainness and Simplicity of Doctrine was
offensive to *Them,* as it is *Now* to *All* sorts of men who place religion in Forms and

Ceremonies,

SERM. Ceremonies, and in certain Syftems of Opinions of which they underftand little; Nor
LXXX. ought it at all to feem ftrange, that the *Epicureans* and the *Stoicks*, Acts xvii. 18,
fhould encounter St *Paul* with That contemptuous queftion, *What will this Babler
fay?* This therefore is the *Second* Obfervation contained in the Text; that Perfons of
fuch different *Tempers*, and that made ufe of fuch different *ways of judging*, as the *Jews*
and *Gentiles* did, were yet both of them under very *Great Prejudices* againft the Doctrine of the Gofpel: *We preach Chrift crucified, unto the* Jews *a Stumbling-block, and
unto the* Greeks *Foolifhnefs.*

3*dly,* THE *Third* and Laft Obfervation contained in the Text, is; that notwithftanding thefe pretended Objections, yet, in Truth and Reality, fetting afide Prejudices
and corrupt Notions, the Doctrine of Chrift was accompanied with the *higheft* and *moft
compleat evidence*, according to *Both* the fore-mentioned *Methods* of judging: It was attended with the fulleft Demonftrations of Divine Power, in the *Miracles* God worked
by him; And it had all real Marks of *Wifdom*, in its perfect Agreeablenefs to the Dictates of True and impartial *Reafon: But unto them which are called, both Jews and
Greeks, Chrift the* Power *of God, and the* Wifdom *of God.* As to the *Jews*; (who,
in judging of the Truth of any Doctrine always infifted principally upon *Proofs* or *Tokens*
of the Teacher's *Authority*, upon *Signs* or *Evidences* of his being *fent from God*;) To
the *Jews*, I fay, The numerous particular and diftinct *Prophecies* which were fulfilled
in the Perfon of our Saviour, and in Him Only; befides all fuch as were typical, and
had any Ambiguity in them: And the *Miracles* which he worked during the Courfe
of his Miniftry, nothing inferiour nor lefs confpicuous than thofe by which *Mofes* of
old proved the Truth of his Commiffion; Thefe were *abundant Evidence*, in their *Own
way*; Evidence, to Them, who *required a Sign*, than which no greater Sign could
poffibly be given, of the immediate Interpofition of the *Power of God.* For whereas
our Lord's coming in a *mean Eftate*, was fo great a *Stumbling-block* to them; and the
principal *Sign* they expected, was his fetting up a *temporal Kingdom* with Great *Power
and Glory:* This, in Truth and Reality, would have been but a *fmall* manifeftation of
the Power of God, in comparifon of that which has and will be fhown forth by the
fpiritual Kingdom he has eftablifhed. For how *poorly* would the great Promifes of God
made to *Abraham*, and the *Patriarchs*, and to good men in all Ages; how *poorly*, and
in how *low* a fenfe, would thofe Promifes have been fulfilled to *Them*, barely by giving
their *Pofterity*, Many Ages after *Their* Deceafe, a *temporary* Kingdom; in comparifon
of That glorious accomplifhment of them in Chrift's *fpiritual* Kingdom, wherein *Abraham, Ifaac* and *Jacob*, and all the faithful Servants of God who have lived in all Ages,
fhall *themfelves literally* and *perfonally* inherit the Promifes. Upon which account, the
Apoftle to the *Hebrews* elegantly obferves, *Heb.* xi. 16: *Wherefore God is not afhamed
to be called Their God; For he hath prepared for Them*, (not for their *Pofterity* only,
when they themfelves were to be no more; but) *for* Them *hath he prepared a City.*
On the other hand, as to the *Gentiles*, who affected to depend entirely on *Reafon and
Arguments*; the Gofpel, though it defpifed the Vanity of *Oratory*, and chofe not to
recommend itfelf in the fet Forms of artificial and perplexing *Difputation*; (for which
caufe it feemed *Foolifhnefs* to conceited Philofophers;) yet in point of *True Reafon,
Wifdom* and *Goodnefs*, it approved itfelf to be a Doctrine in all Refpects Excellent, and
truly worthy of God: *Chrift, the Wifdom*, as well as the *Power*, of God. By the *Gofpel*, All the Great Truths of Natural Religion, difcoverable by Reafon and Argumentation; the Being and Attributes, the Government and Providence of God, the Unalter-
ablenefs of Moral Obligations, the Immortality of the Soul, and the Expectation of future Rewards and Punifhments; all thefe Great Truths (I fay) difcoverable in good
meafure by Argumentation and Reafon, were by the *Gofpel* more plainly and exprefsly
revealed, more diftinctly and clearly explained, more ftrongly and powerfully inforced.

I

And

And the *additional* Revelation, of *Chriſt's* being appointed an *Interceſſor* for penitent S E R M. Sinners, and the *Judge* of the World; was an advantagious confirmation of all the ſame LXXX. Truths, and a moſt wiſe and proper encouragement to the practice of Virtue. By This means, a well-atteſted Interpoſition of Divine *Authority*, became unto All men a juſt ground of Aſſent to thoſe Truths, which to make out by the Help of Reaſon only, was a work of Difficulty, Time, and Study. By This 'means, Inſtruction in matters of Religion became very *ſhort* and *eaſy*, even to the Meaneſt Capacities. And whereas the *Beſt and greateſt Philoſophers* were in continual Diſputes, and in many degrees of Uncertainty, concerning the very fundamental and moſt important Doctrines of Truth and Reaſon; Among thoſe, on the contrary, who have embraced the Goſpel of *Chriſt*, there never was the leaſt room for Diſpute about Any *Fundamental*; All Chriſtians, at all Times, and in all Places, having ever been baptized into the Profeſſion of the Same *Faith*, and into an Obligation to obey the Same *Commandments*. And it being notorious, that all the Contentions that ever aroſe in the Chriſtian World, have been merely about the ſeveral *Additions*, which every Sect or Party, in direct contradiction to the expreſs Command of their Maſter, have endeavoured preſumptuouſly to annex, by their *Own* Authority, to *His* Doctrines, and to *His* Laws. How *much* therefore, and how *juſt* ground ſoever, has been given by thoſe who Call *themſelves Chriſtians*, to the Reproach of *Them which are without*; yet *Chriſt himſelf*, that is, the Goſpel in its native Simplicity as delivered by *Him*, has abundantly, to all *Reaſonable* perſons among the *Gentiles*, manifeſted itſelf to be the *Wiſdom* of God; as well as it appeared to be the *Power* of God, in Signs and Wonders unto the *Jews*. *Unto them which are called, both Jews and Greeks, Chriſt the* Power *of God, and the* Wiſdom *of God*.

II. The Words and Doctrine of the Text being thus largely explained, it remains that I conclude with drawing two or three uſeful Inferences from what has been ſaid.

And 1ſt, From hence it appears, how Fooliſh it is to endeavour, as ſome have done, to oppoſe *Reaſon* and *Revelation* to each other. For *both* of them, are the glorious Gifts of God; and *Each* of them eſtabliſhes and confirms the Other. The Quibbling indeed, and vain Methods of Diſputing, among the greater part of the Heathen Philoſophers; were only *Shadows of Reaſoning*, falſely ſo called. But *True Reaſon*, is the Great Glory of Humane Nature: And upon account of the *Goſpel's* Agreeableneſs to *This*, it is, that the Apoſtle in the Text gives it that High Character, of being the *Wiſdom* as well as the *Power* of God. To imagine *Reaſon* and *Revelation* at variance with each other, is the like abſurdity, as ſuppoſing the *Eye* to *ſee* contrary to what the *Ear hears*, or that God ſhould make *One* Senſe, or Faculty, to contradict *another*. Vain *men* may poorly and weakly fancy, that they can ſometimes promote *One* Truth at the Expence of *Another*: But the Works of *God*, are uniform and conſiſtent, of a piece from One end to the other: And what our Saviour ſays concerning *Perſons*, acting wiſely and uſefully in *different* ways; that *Wiſdom is juſtified of All her* Children; may equally be applied to *Things* likewiſe, that *Wiſdom is juſtified in All her* Diſpenſations.

2dly, If the *Power and Authority*, as well as the *Wiſdom* of God; that is, if *Divine Revelation*, as well as *argumentative Proof*; be a juſt Ground of Aſſent, or Evidence of Truth: Then ought we always to take great heed, leaſt at any time we *weaken* the Strength of that Authority, by blending things of *Humane* invention with thoſe whoſe Inſtitution is *Divine*. For whereas weak men think, by means of ſuch confuſion, to *ſtrengthen* their *Own* Authority with the mixture of *Divine*; the Real Effect, on the contrary, always is, that the things of *Divine Authority* are inſenſibly *weakned*, by being made leſs diſtinguiſhable from what is merely *Humane*.

SERM.   3*dly* and *lastly*, F R O M the manner in which *Christ* is here called *The Wisdom* and
LXXX.   *The Power* of God, we may learn rightly to understand *Other* the like figurative ex-
〰   pressions frequently found in Scripture.   For as Christ is here stiled the *Wisdom* of God,
because his Gospel is agreeable to True *Reason*; and the *Power* of God, because his
Doctrine was confirmed by mighty *Works and Miracles:* So, in Other places, he is
stiled The *Word* of God, because he is the *Revealer* of his Will to Men; and he is the
Way, the *Door*, the *Truth* and the *Life*, because he has distinctly made known to us
the Terms and Means of Salvation.   And by the like figure of speech, the Sacramental
Bread and Wine is stiled the *Body and Blood of Christ*, because it is a Solemn *commemoration of his Death*.   And *Christians* are by the Apostle said to be the *Circumcision
made without hands*, because they *spiritually* are, what the *Jews* were *typically* by *Circumcision which was literal*.   And *Praise* or *Thanksgiving* has the name of *Sacrifice*
given to it, because it is a Signification of the same Temper and Disposition of Mind,
which Sacrifices were intended to express, and which alone made those Sacrifices acceptable before God.   With many other the like Instances: In which, a careful consideration of the ground and reason of the Manner of Expression, may easily prevent
Great Misunderstandings of Many Passages in Scripture.

SERMON

SERMON LXXXI.

Of the Refurrection of CHRIST.

[Preached on Eafter-Day.]

1 COR. XV. 14.

And if Chrift be not rifen, then is our Preaching vain, and your Faith alfo is vain.

THE great Foundation of our Hope of Immortality, is the Revelation of the Gofpel; and the great Evidence of the Truth of that Revelation, is the Re-furrection of Chrift. Without the Revelation of the Gofpel, our Hope of Immortality, according to mens different Abilities in philofophical Speculations, had continued difputable; and without the Refurrection of Chrift, the Proofs of the Truth of the Gofpel-Revelation had been finally fruftrated. As therefore the Truth of the Chriftian Revelation, is of the greateft importance to mens Souls, *in the whole*; fo the Proof of the Refurrection of Chrift, is of the greateft importance towards fecuring the Certainty of that Revelation, *in particular*. By the Light of *Nature*, the Being and Attributes of God, were certain and demonftrable; the Probability of a Future State, was great and undeniable; the Expectation of God's dealing mercifully with penitent Sinners, was reafonable and hopeful. But by the Revelation of the *Gofpel* only, was this great Hope *fecured* to us; the Pardon of Sin declared *authentickly*, by the Autho-rity of God; Life and Immortality brought to light by *Teftimony*, as well as by rational Arguments; the Rewards and Punifhments of Eternity, *diftinctly* fet forth; and the particular Method of the final Judgment, *affectionately* reprefented to us.

In like manner, as to the *Evidence* of the *Truth* of this Revelation; By the Prophe-cies of the Old Teftament, it was long before predicted; By the reafonablenefs of the Doctrine itfelf, it was made very credible; By the Witneffes of our Lord and his Apo-ftles, it was ftrongly attefted; By the conviction and filencing of its Adverfaries, it was confirmed and eftablifhed; By many Signs and Wonders and mighty Works done by Chrift in his Life, it was *for the prefent* proved beyond contradiction; But by this *laft* Evidence only, by the *Refurrection of our Lord from the Dead*, was it for ever afcer-tained to all generations. For had this *laft* Proof failed, all the reft muft in courfe have fallen with it. The Prophecies would have appeared wonderful, but never fulfilled; The Doctrine would have continued reafonable, but its Author perifhed; The Mira-cles of his Life would have remained aftonifhing, but ftill confuted by his Death; His *Enemies* would have continued to infult him, as did the *Jews*; *he faved others, him-felf, he could not fave*: And his *Friends*, that loved his Doctrine, and hoped for the Salvation of God, could *but* have joined with his defponding Difciples; *we trufted it had been he which fhould have redeemed Ifrael*. In a word, as St *Paul* expreffes it in

the

SERM. the Text, had *not Chrift rifen* again, then had *our* whole *Preaching been vain, and*
LXXXI. *your Faith alfo in vain.*

THE Refurrection of Chrift therefore, being a Fact of fo great importance,   on
which the Evidence of the Truth of the *whole* Revelation finally depended; it was
neceffary, in the Wifdom of Providence, and in the Reafon of Things, that the Proof
of this great Fact fhould be made unanfwerably ftrong.   In the following Difcourfe
therefore, I fhall 1*ft* endeavour to fet before you briefly, and in one view, the particulars of that great and fingular Care, which was taken to make the *Proof* of the Fact
undeniable, that our Saviour *did really* rife from the Dead. 2*dly*, I fhall confider what
were the *Effects* of This his Refurrection, with refpect to *Chrift himfelf*; and 3*dly*, what
were the Effects of it with regard to *Us*.

1*ft*, As to the extraordinary Care that was taken, to make the *Proof* of the Fact
itfelf undeniable, that our Saviour *did really* rife from the Dead; there was (1*ft*,) in the
firft place Notice given of it *antecedently*, by the Prophecies of the Old Teftament delivered long before. *Pf.* xvi. 10; *Thou wilt not leave my Soul in Hell*, that is, in the State of
the Dead; *neither wilt thou fuffer thy Holy One to fee Corruption.* That this was an
exprefs Prediction of our Saviour's Refurrection; the Apoftles, in their application of it
in the Book of the *Acts*, fhow by the following Argument.   The words thus fpoken by
David, muft of neceffity be meant, either of *Himfelf*, or of fome *Other Perfon*.   Of
Himfelf, they could not literally be meant, becaufe it was not *true* that *He* was raifed
before he faw corruption.   And if they were meant of any *other Perfon*, the *Jews themfelves* (notwithftanding all their Prejudices) would readily acknowledge, that That
other Perfon fo mentioned by way of Eminence, could, according to the Analogy of the
Prophetick writings, be *no other* than the Meffiah.   This Argument is ftrongly urged
by St *Peter*; Acts ii. 29; *Men and Brethren, let me freely fpeak unto you of the Patriarch David, that he is both dead and buried, and his Sepulchre is with us unto this
day*; That is, *He* did certainly fee corruption : *But being a Prophet, and knowing that
God had fworn with an Oath to him, that of the fruit of his Loins according to the
Flefh, he would raife up Chrift to fit on his throne; He, feeing This before, fpake of
the Refurrection of Chrift, that his Soul was not left in Hell, nor his flefh did fee corruption.* And by St *Paul* in the fame book; *ch.* xiii. 36; *David* (fays he,) *after he
had ferved his own generation by the will of God, fell on fleep, and was laid unto his
Fathers, and faw corruption : But he whom God raifed again, faw no corruption :* Therefore thefe words of the Pfalmift, *Thou fhalt not fuffer thine Holy one to fee corruption*, were
fpoken, not of *David* himfelf, but of the Refurrection of Chrift.   After This, and o-
ther antient Prophecies; there were, (2*dly*,) in the *next* place plain Notifications given
by our *Lord himfelf*, to his Difciples before his Suffering; that they fhould *expect* his
Rifing from the Dead.   And becaufe it was a matter of the *greateft Importance*, he
therefore *repeated* This Admonition to them feveral times.   Firft, *before* his Transfiguration; (Matt. xvi. 21;) *From that time forth began Jefus to fhow unto his Difciples,
how that he muft――fuffer many things,――and be killed, and be* raifed again *the third
day.* Then again, *after* his Transfiguration; (*ch.* xvii. 9;) *As they came down from the
Mountain, Jefus charged them to tell no man the vifion, till the Son of man be* rifen
again from the dead. Again, at his *laft* going up to Jerufalem; (*ch.* xx. 17) *he took
the twelve difciples apart in the way, and faid unto them.――The Son of man fhall be
betrayed unto the chief Priefts,――and they fhall condemn him to death,――and the third
day he fhall* rife *again.* Befides which plain admonitions to his *Difciples*, he gave fome
obfcure Hints of it to the *whole People* alfo; when, upon the *Jews* requiring of him a
Sign, at *one* time he faid unto them, (Joh. ii. 19;) *Deftroy this Temple, and in three
days I will raife it up*; and at *another* time; (Matt. xii. 39;) *To an evil and adulterous
generation, there fhall no Sign be given, but the Sign of the Prophet Jonas; For as Jonas*

was

was three days and three nights in the Whale's belly, so shall the Son of Man be three days S E R M. *and three nights in the Heart of the Earth.* The *Design and Use* of which Predictions, LXXXI. though not at all understood at the time they were spoken, is declared to us by the Evangelist; Joh. ii. 22; *When therefore he was risen from the dead, his disciples remem-bred that he had said this unto them; and they believed the Scripture, and the word that Jesus had said.* And, Luke xxiv. 6; *Remember,* said the Angel to the persons which came first to the Sepulchre, Remember *how he spake unto you,——saying,* the Son of *Man must be delivered into the hands of sinful men, and be crucified, and the third day rise again;* And *they remembred his words.* Further; (3*dly,*) in order to make the Proof of his Resurrection still more evident, the *Place* and *Manner* and *Circumstances* of his Burial, were by Providence directed to be particularly remarkable. Mark xv. 42; *Joseph of Arimathea, an honourable Counsellor, begged his Body, and wrapped it in fine linnen, and laid it in his own Sepulchre;* And this in the presence of several of *Jesus's* Followers; who thereupon resolving to come and embalm him, were providentially di-rected to become Witnesses of many Circumstances attending his *Resurrection.* *Lastly,* The Method which his *Adversaries* themselves took, to find evidence (as *they* thought) of the *Imposture; making the Sepulchre sure, sealing the Stone, and setting a Watch;* (Matt. xxvii. 66;) was by Providence designed on the contrary, to become a strong Proof of the *Truth* of his Resurrection; taking away all pretence or possibility of that plausible Objection, that *his Disciples came by Night and stole him away.*

THESE are the principal Instances, of the Care that was taken in the Circumstan-ces *going before* our Lord's Resurrection, to render the Proof of the Fact certain and undeniable. *After* his Rising again, the accumulative Evidence of the Truth of his being risen, is much greater, not only than what Unbelievers, but even than Believers themselves, without putting *together* the numerous Circumstances recorded in different places of Scripture, can easily imagine. (1*st,*) In the *first* place, an *Earthquake* terri-fied the *Watch,* and the Appearance of an *Angel made them become as dead men;* Matt. xxviii. 2. Then, (2*dly,*) the persons who came with a design to *embalm* the Bo-dy, saw likewise an Angel, and were told by him that their Lord was risen from the Dead, ver. 6. Immediately after this, *Jesus himself* appeared to them, and comforted them; ver. 9. To which St *John* adds this particular circumstance, ch. xx. 17; that when one of them embraced his *Feet,* rejoicing and worshipping him upon his Discovering himself who he was, he said unto her, *Touch me not, for I am not yet ascended to my Father.* Which words most Interpreters so understand, as if they signified, *Do not detain me now, as if you thought I was immediately leaving you; For I shall continue with you some time, and am not presently ascending to my Father.* But I think the truer meaning of them is, *Do not expect I should continue with you* Now; *for it is expedient and necessary, that I first ascend to my Father.* And therefore he adds in the very next words; *But go to my brethren, and say unto them, I ascend to my Father and your Father, to my God and your God,* Tell them, *that I am risen from the Dead, never to die any more; that I am about to return to my Father and your Father, to my God and your God, to receive full Power over all things both in Heaven and Earth, and to prepare a place for* you; *and* Then, *where I am, there shall ye be also.* After This, (3*dly,*) he appeared to *Two* of his Disciples going to *Emmaus;* Luk. xxiv. 13. and talked with them, and *expounded unto them in all the Scriptures the things con-cerning himself.* Then again (4*thly,*) he showed himself to *Peter* alone, ver. 34; and 1 *Cor.* xv. 5. Then (5*thly,*) to St *James,* ver. 7. After that, (6*thly,*) to *Seven* of the Apostles together; *Joh.* xxi. 2. Then (7*thly,*) to *Ten* of Them, *Thomas* only being absent, *Joh.* xx. 19. And (8*thly,*) a week after to *all the Eleven;* ver. 26; *Thomas* being *present* with them; whose doubting Faith he vouchsafed to confirm, by suffering him to handle him; yet at the same time pronouncing a greater Blessing upon thofe who fhould *not fee*, and yet would *believe* ; Not that *Credulity* or *Believing with-out reafon*, is in any cafe commendable ; but, that believing, upon reafonable and good evidence, things not obvious to Senfe ; fuch as are the Being of the *Invifible* God, the Rewards and Punifhments of a future State which now are likewife *invifible*, and the Coming of our Saviour to Judgment, though he does not prefently appear ; are the moft valuable Acts of Religious Faith and Dependence upon God. *Laftly*, After thefe feveral more *private* appearances of our Lord to his Apoftles, *he was feen* (faith St. *Paul) of above five hundred brethren at once*; 1 Cor. xv. 6 ; *of whom though fome were fallen afleep*, yet *the greater part remained* alive *unto* that *prefent* time, when St *Paul* wrote this Epiftle to the *Corinthians*. And in This manner continued he for *forty days* together, *fhowing himfelf alive after his paffion by many infallible Proofs, and fpeaking of the things pertaining to the Kingdom of God*, Acts i. 3. After which, at mid-day, in the prefence of all the Apoftles, he was taken up from them vifibly into Heaven ; *ver.* 9. And they were told by Angels, *ver.* 11, what *he* alfo *himfelf* had before told them in his Life time, that in like manner as they faw him *go* into Heaven, fo from thence likewife fhould they fee him *come*, at the end of the World, with Power and great Glory, even in the Glory of his Father, and all his Holy Angels with him, to judge the Quick and Dead with a righteous and unerring Sentence, rendering to every man impartially according to his Works. Put all This Evidence now together, and let it be confidered fairly in one View ; Evidence given by fo many different *Perfons*, repeated at fo many different *Times*, diverfified with fuch variety of *circumftances*, yet all agreeing in fuch a perfect Uniformity as to the *Thing itfelf*. And was there ever more undeniable Proof given, of any matter of Fact in the World ? Ne-

Acts xi. 3.
1 Cor. ix. 1.
Gal. i. 15.

verthelefs, after All This, he appeared again to St *Stephen* : Acts vii. 55. And again to St. *Paul*, as he himfelf teftifies, 1 *Cor.* xv. 8, *Laft of all* (fays he) *he was feen of* Me *alfo, as of one born out of due Time*. Befides all which *Cloud of Eye-witneffes*, the Truth of our Lord's Refurrection continued moreover to be proved, by the *Miracles* which the *Apoftles* worked in his Name; *i. e.* through *his* Power and Authority ; Alfo by the *Prophecies* he himfelf delivered, both before and after his Suffering ; The gradual fulfilling of which Prophecies in all fucceeding times, has been and *is* a ftanding Proof of our Lord's being truly rifen, and that he *is* invefted with all Power, to accomplifh whatever he has foretold. He clearly predicted, in the fulleft and moft diftinct manner, the Deftruction of *Jerufalem*, and the Defolation of the whole *Jewifh* Nation : Which Nation fhould yet neverthelefs continue in Being, (as we fee in fact it does at this day,) *till the times of the Gentiles be fulfilled*, Luk. xxi. 24. He foretold, that his Difciples fhould be hated both by *Jews* and *Gentiles*, and perfecuted from one City to another. That neverthelefs their Doctrine fhould fpread over the whole Earth, and, by the mere Force of Truth and Reafon, of Goodnefs and Charity, fhould prevail over all the Violence, and be eftablifhed againft all the Oppofition of humane Authority. That after having fo prevailed over all *outward* Enemies, it fhould, by an unaccountable corruption within *itfelf*, be over-run with almoft a total Apoftacy ; the Power and Authority of *Men*, taking upon themfelves to fit in the Seat of *God* ; and compelling all men by Force and Violence, to fubmit to Doctrines of their own Invention; and turning Chrift's Religion of Peace and Love, of Meeknefs and Charity, into a worldly Religion of Dominion and Power, of Contentioufnefs, Hatred and Oppreffion. All which predictions having been already exactly and particularly fulfilled, in the plaineft and moft remarkable manner ; give abundant reafon to expect, that what ftill remains, fhall likewife in its time be no lefs punctually accomplifhed. That when the juft pleafure of God has been performed, and the Chriftian World fhall for its great Corruptions have been juftly punifhed by thofe Corruptions themfelves ; at length the Kingdoms of the Earth, fhall become the Kingdoms of our Lord, and of his Chrift;

and

and men leaving off to contend about their own vain Notions and unreafonable Pre- S E R M.
tences of Power and Dominion, fhall agree in the original Simplicity of that pure and LXXXI.
undefiled Religion, the Sum of which, our Lord himfelf tells us, confifts in *loving*
the Lord our God with all our Heart, and our Neighbours as ourfelves.

THE Truth of our Lord's Refurrection being thus *attefted* by fuch a Multitude of
Witneffes, and *confirmed* by fuch a Number of confequent *Facts*, that it is hardly poffible the firft Preachers of his Doctrine fhould either Themfelves have been deceived,
or be Deceivers of Others; we may now eafily Anfwer that obvious Objection, fuggefted *Acts* x. 40: *why* Chrift after his Refurrection *fhowed himfelf openly, not to* all
the people, but unto Witneffes *only, chofen before of God.* And the Reafon hereof is the
fame, as why in all other cafes God does not all that he is *able* to do, but all that is
fit and right for him to do. There is in every *Means*, a certain *Fitnefs and Proportion*
to the *End* it leads to; wherewith if Men will not be fatisfied, there are no limits to
unreafonable expectations, and no bounds where groundlefs imaginations may ftop.
The Wifdom of God provided as many unqueftionable Witneffes of the Refurrection
of Chrift, as the Nature of the Thing required; as was fufficient, to make the Fact
uncontestable; as was fatisfactory, to any reafonable and unprejudiced perfon. To
work *more* miracles for the fake of obftinate and vicious Unbelievers, God was not
obliged. And, if he *had* done it, the Objection would ftill have increafed without
End. For if it was not fufficient, that Chrift fhowed himfelf openly to a *Number of*
Witneffes; but it had been neceffary that he fhould appear perfonally to the *whole* City
of *Jerufalem*; for the fame Reafon it might be fanfied neceffary, that he fhould have
fhown himfelf alfo to the whole *Jewifh* Nation: and for the fame Reafon, to all other
Nations likewife; and to Thefe, in *Every* Age *of the World,* as well as in One *Age*;
and that, to *every fingle* Perfon, if one miraculous appearance was not fufficient, he
might have fhown himfelf *oftner* and with *more* miraculous circumftances; and fo on,
without End. Which fhows plainly the unreafonablenefs of all *Such* Expectations;
when men are not fatisfied with that Evidence which is fit and fufficient in its
kind.

I SHALL conclude This Head, concerning the *Evidence of the Fact* of Chrift's
being rifen from the Dead, with only One Obfervation about the *Manner* of his
Rifing. Which is, that in more than thirty paffages of the New Teftament, it is expreffly affirmed that *God* raifed up our Lord from the Dead, or that he was raifed by
the Power of the *Father*; and yet in two or three other places it is no lefs plainly
afferted, that *Chrift* raifed up *himfelf.* Which different expreffions might have feemed
very difficult to be reconciled, but that our Saviour himfelf has in a moft remarkable paffage upon this Subject, (as it were *on purpofe,*) explained them to us with the
greateft accuracy and exact diftinctnefs: *Joh.* x. 18; *No man,* faith he, *taketh my*
Life from me, but I lay it down of myfelf; I have Power to lay it down, and I have
Power to take it again; This Commandment, (that is, This Commiffion, This Power,)
have I received of my Father. I proceed Now in the

II*d* place, To confider what were the *Effects* of Chrift's Refurrection, with refpect
to our *Lord himfelf.* And they were, 1*ft*, that thereby he was effectually, and in a
moft convincing manner, declared to be *the Son of God; Declared to be the Son of God*
with Power, faith St. *Paul, by the Refurrection from the Dead,* Rom. i. 4. Infomuch
that even thofe words of the Pfalmift, *Thou art my Son, this day have I begotten thee,*
are by the fame Apoftle, in his Sermon to the People of *Antioch,* applied to this very
purpofe; *Acts* xiii. 32; *The Promife which was made unto the Fathers, God has ful-*
filled (fays he) *unto Us their children, in that he has* raifed up *Jefus again; as it is alfo*
written in the fecond Pfalm, Thou art my Son, this day have I begotten thee. Not that
Chrift Then *began* to be the *Son of God,* but that he was Then *declared* to be fo,

2   by

S E R M. by a moſt powerful and effectual Proof; having *looſed the pains of Death*, and ſhown
LXXXI. that *it was not poſſible he ſhould be holden of it.* 2dly, Another *Effect* of Chriſt's Reſurrection, with regard to our *Lord himſelf*, was his being thereby declared the *Judge
of Quick and Dead:* Acts x. 40, 42; *Him God raiſed up the third day, —— and commanded us —— to teſtify, that it is He which was ordained of God to be the Judge
of Quick and Dead.* And ch. xvii. 31; *God hath appointed a day, in the which he will
judge the world in righteouſneſs by that man whom he hath appointed, whereof he hath
given aſſurance unto all men, in that he has raiſed him from the Dead.*

IF it be here aſked, the appointing a day of general Judgment, being a Truth of
ſo great importance to Mankind; why then was it not declared *Sooner* and *Univerſally*,
in *All Ages*, and to *All People?* The true Anſwer (I think) is, that in the Whole,
the *Rule of Righteouſneſs* and the *great Expectation of a Judgment to come*, is in all
Times and in all Places the ſame; and yet the ſeveral *Diſpenſations*, or *particular
Methods and Degrees* of God's manifeſting theſe Truths to Mankind, by the Light
of *Nature* and *Reaſon*, by revelations to the *Jews and Patriarchs*, and by the *Goſpel
of Chriſt*, are and may as juſtly be very different, as, in other Caſes, it is lawful for
God, the Author of All, to make people of different Capacities and in different Circumſtances. And accordingly, what God when he comes to judgment, will *finally
require* of Men under theſe different circumſtances, will be proportionally different.
For the Judge of the whole Earth, will do what is right, and with *Equity* ſhall he
judge the Nations. *The Goſpel* was preached before, ſays the Apoſtle, even in the
days of *Abraham, Gal.* iii. 8. And even *the Gentiles, which have not the Law* revealed, *are yet a Law unto* themſelves, *ſhowing the work of the Law* written in their
hearts, *Rom.* ii. 14. So that, upon the whole, *God is no reſpecter of perſons; but in
every nation, he that feareth Him and worketh righteouſneſs, is accepted with him:*
For, *not the* Hearers *of the Law are juſt before God, but the* Doers *of the Law ſhall
be juſtified:* ver. 13. And on the contrary, *as many as have ſinned without law, ſhall
alſo periſh without law,——in the day when God ſhall judge the Secrets of Men by Jeſus Chriſt;* ver. 16.

Acts x. 34.

IT remains that I proceed in the

IIId and *Laſt* place, To conſider what are the *Effects* of our Lord's Reſurrection,
with reſpect to *Us*. And they are; 1ſt, our *Juſtification*. That is to ſay; The Reſurrection of Chriſt from the dead, was on God's part a publick and authentick Declaration of his *accepting* the Sacrifice of the Death of Chriſt, as an Atonement for the
Sins of all that truly repent. This is the Meaning of thoſe Paſſages of St *Paul*, where
he tells us, that *Chriſt was delivered for our Offences, and raiſed again for our Juſtification;* Rom. iv. 25. That *We*, that is, *wicked men*, both among *Jews* and *Gentiles*,
having been *dead in Sin*, that is, having been in a State of condemnation; *God, who
raiſed* Chriſt *from the dead, hath quickened* Us *together with Him*, (has reſtored us to
the hope of eternal life,) *having forgiven us all Treſpaſſes;* Col. ii. 13. And that, *if
Chriſt be not raiſed, we are yet in our Sins:* 1 Cor. xv. 17; that is, if Chriſt be not riſen,
we have *Then* no evidence of *God*'s having accepted Chriſt's Mediation for us; nor conſequently of *our* being juſtified, or having our Repentance accepted; to ſuch *degrees* and
Purpoſes at leaſt, as God has now declared that it ſhall be accepted through Faith in Him.

2dly, THE *ſecond* Effect of the Reſurrection of Chriſt, with regard to *Us*; is our
Sanctification and *Regeneration:* That is, our riſing from the death of Sin, unto a Life
of Righteouſneſs; *Rom.* vi. 4; *We are buried with him by Baptiſm into Death, that like
as* Chriſt *was raiſed up from the Dead by the glory of the Father, even ſo we alſo ſhould
walk in Newneſs of Life; That having been planted together in the likeneſs of his Death,
we ſhould be alſo in the likeneſs of his Reſurrection.* The Meaning of the Apoſtle is;
that the Death and Reſurrection of Chriſt, into which we are Baptized, and whereof

I

Baptiſm

Baptifm is an Emblem, ought to be a perpetual obligation upon us, to rife from the S E R M. Death of Sin unto the Spiritual Life of Righteoufnefs and Holinefs; *Col.* ii. 12, and LXXXI. iii. 1; *Buried with him in Baptifm, wherein alfo ye are* rifen *with him.* —— *If ye then* (faith he) *be* rifen *with Chrift, feek thofe things which are above; For ye are dead,* that is, *dead to* Sin, (as the fame Apoftle explains it; *Rom.* vi. 2:) *and your Life is hid with Chrift in God.* And what he means by That Phrafe, *hid with Chrift in God,* is explained in the next verfe, ch. iii. 3: *When* Chrift, *who is our life, fhall appear, then fhall* ye *alfo appear with him in glory.*

For 3dly, The *Third* and *Laft* Effect of the Refurrection of *Chrift,* with refpect to *Us,* is the Affurance of *Our* Refurrection likewife, unto *Glorification,* 1 *Cor.* xv. 20. *Now is Chrift rifen from the Dead, and become the* firft-fruits *of them that flept.* And therefore This is conftantly ufed by the Apoftles, as a perpetual Argument of Confola-lation to good Chriftians; 1 *Pet.* i. 3; *Bleffed be the God and Father of our Lord Jefus Chrift, who according to his abundant mercy has begotten us again unto a lively hope,* by *the refurrection of (Jefus) Chrift from the Dead:* Rom. viii. 11; *If the Spirit of him that raifed up Jefus from the Dead, dwell in you; he that raifed up Chrift from the Dead, fhall alfo quicken* your *mortal bodies, by his Spirit that dwelleth in you.* And 1 *Th.* iv. 14; *If we believe that Jefus died and rofe again, even fo Them alfo which fleep in Jefus will God bring with him.*

Blessed and Happy are they, *who fhall be thought worthy to obtain* That *Life, and the Refurrection from the Dead;* For from thenceforth *they fhall be before the Throne of God, and fhall ferve him day and night in his Temple; And God fhall wipe away all Tears from their Eyes; and there fhall be no more Death, neither forrow nor crying; neither fhall there be any more pain: For the former things are paffed away.*

VOL. I.   60   SERMON

SERMON LXXXII.

Of CHRIST's Defcent into Hell.

[Preached on Eafter-Day.]

PSALM XVI. 9, 10.

Wherefore my Heart was glad, and my glory rejoiced; my Flefh alfo fhall reft in Hope. For why? Thou fhalt not leave my Soul in Hell; neither fhalt thou fuffer thy Holy One to fee corruption.

THE Afflictions and Calamities which fall upon Many men in this prefent State, are of fuch a nature, that, were it not for the Hopes which True Religion and the Knowledge of God affords, their only Comfort would be That expectation of *Death*, which *Job* thus elegantly expreffes, ch. iii. 17; *There the wicked ceafe from troubling, and there the Weary be at Reft : There the Prifoners reft together, they hear not the Voice of the Oppreffor : The Small and Great are There, and the Servant is free from his Mafter.* But *True Religion* affords virtuous and good Men a very *different* Profpect; and teaches them to expect, that, if God *does not* think fit to deliver them out of their Troubles *Here,* (which yet he fometimes *does* in a very extraordinary and unexpected Manner ;) yet even the *Grave itfelf* puts not an end to his Power of Redeeming them ; but he *can* and *will* raife them up again, to a *future* and a *better* Life. So that they may look upon *Death itfelf,* not barely as a *putting an end* to their prefent Afflictions, but as a *Paffage* to a *Glorious and Immortal* State. *Wherefore my Flefh alfo,* fays the Holy Pfalmift, *fhall reft in Hope : For why? Thou fhalt not leave my Soul in Hell; neither fhalt thou fuffer thy Holy One to fee corruption.*

THE *Pfalm,* of which thefe words are a part, feems to have been written by *David* in the time of fome particular *perfonal Calamity.* Ver. 1. *Preferve me, O God; for in thee have I put my Truft.* The *Ground* of This his Truft, he expreffes to be his *Adherence to the True Religion,* in oppofition to the *Idolatry* of the *Nations* about him: Ver. 4, 6. *They that run after another God, fhall have great Trouble ;——but The Lord himfelf is the Portion of Mine inheritance, and of my Cup.* The *particular* affliction, which he here refers to, *whatfoever* it was; he acknowledges, proved *beneficial* to him, in *fixing* his Mind *more fteddily* upon things relating to his *fpiritual eftate:* Ver. 8. *I will thank the Lord for giving me warning ; my Reins alfo chaften me in the night-feafon : I have fet God always before me ; for he is on my right hand, therefore I fhall not fall.* And then he adds, in the words of the *Text,* the *Comfort* arifing to him from the *fenfe* of this Improvement: *Wherefore my Heart was glad, and my Glory rejoiced; my Flefh alfo fhall reft in Hope: For why? Thou wilt not leave my Soul in Hell; neither fhalt thou fuffer thy Holy One to fee corruption.*

'TIS

'Tis remarkable here, that the *former* part of these words; *My Heart was glad,* and *my* Glory *rejoiced*; are cited, *Acts* ii. 26; according to the Rendring of the LXX. *My Heart rejoiced, and my* Tongue *was glad.* Which not only, in *other words,* expresses the very *same sense*; but shows us also *what* it is, that the *Psalmist,* in *Other* Passages, means by his *Glory.* Psal. xxx. 12; *To the end that my* Glory, (that is, that my Tongue,) *may sing Praise to thee, and not be silent.* And Psal. lvii. 9; *Awake up, my* Glory; *awake, Lute and Harp; I my self will awake right early:* That is; Both with my *Voice,* and with Instruments of Musick, will I sing Praise unto thee.

THE *latter* part of the words; *My Flesh also shall rest in Hope: For why? thou wilt not leave my Soul in Hell, neither shalt thou suffer thy Holy One to see corruption:* are by many understood to be a *highly figurative* expression in the Psalmist, of his earnest expectation of a *literal* and *temporal* Deliverance from the Affliction he was at present under. In like manner as St *Paul,* speaking of his own Escape from a very dangerous Persecution, calls it a deliverance from a *great Death;* 2 Cor. i. 9; *We should not trust,* says he, *in ourselves, but in God which raiseth the Dead: Who delivered us from so great a Death, and doth deliver: In whom we trust that he will yet deliver us.* And so likewise Those remarkable Words of *Job;* ch. xix. 25; *I know that my Redeemer liveth, and that he shall stand at the latter day upon the Earth; And though, after my Skin, Worms destroy this Body, yet in my Flesh shall I see God; Whom I shall see for myself, and mine eyes shall behold, and not Another, though my reins be consumed within me:* Even *These* words, I say, are by some Interpreters understood as a Prediction, in *highly figurative* and *prophetical* expressions, of his Restoration to his *Temporal* Greatness and Prosperity. But as This is a very *forced* Sense of the words, and, if it were their *True* Meaning, would still be at least the *borrowing of a Figure* from the Notion and Expectation of a *Resurrection from the Dead;* it is more *reasonable and natural* to understand them in that *obvious* and *literal* sense, wherein they are clearly and plainly the Expression of a *better* and *more certain Hope.* And, for the same reason, the words of *my Text* likewise, if they are *at all* to be applied to the *Psalmist himself;* may with a better emphasis, and as a more assured Ground of Hope, be understood to signify his expectation of a *Future State,* than of a *Temporal* Deliverance. But indeed, in their *real* and *most proper* Sense, they are not applicable to the *Psalmist himself,* but to *Him* of whom *David* was both a *Prophet* and a *Type;* The *same Spirit* of God, which through the *whole Period* of the Old Testament from the Beginning of the World pointed perpetually to *Christ* through an innumerable variety of Types and Prophecies, *here likewise* directing the inspired Penman to such Expressions, as might be a *strict* and *literal* description of the *Resurrection* of *Christ,* but could not with the same propriety be applied to *David.* Thus the Apostle observes, *Acts* xiii. 36; *David, after he had served his own generation by the Will of God, fell on Sleep, and was laid unto his Fathers, and saw corruption; But he whom God raised again, saw no corruption.* And chap. ii. 29; *The Patriarch David is both dead and buried, and his Sepulchre is with us unto This day: Therefore being a Prophet, and knowing that God had sworn with an Oath to him, that of the Fruit of his Loins, according to the Flesh, he would raise up Christ to sit on his Throne; He, seeing this before, spake of the Resurrection of Christ, that his Soul was not left in Hell, neither his Flesh did see Corruption.* And it is remarkable, by the way; that, as the fore-cited words of *Job,* which are much more emphatically descriptive of the *Resurrection of the Dead,* than of his *Restoration to his Temporal Prosperity;* are, in order to excite our more particular Attention, introduced with That extraordinary and most solemn exclamation, *Oh that my words were now written, that they were printed in a Book! that they were graven with an iron pen, and lead, in the Rock for ever!* so *This Psalm,*
which

SERM. which contains in it fo *important* a Prophecy of Chrift, is diftinguifhed by a * *Title*
LXXXII. prefixed at the Head of it, which *in the Original* fignifies a *Memorial engraved* on
Stone or Marble for perpetuity of Ages.

* *Michtam*

BUT to proceed,

CONCERNING that *particularly remarkable* Phrafe, *Thou fhalt not leave my Soul in
Hell*; 'tis to be obferved, that though in our prefent language, the word *Hell*, in common Speech, does *Now* always fignify *The State of the Damned*; yet in This Text, it
is evident, it cannot be underftood in that fignification. For, that *David* was not
condemned to That Place of Torment, is agreed on All hands: And that *Chrift*, of
whom *David* was a *Type and Prophet*, did not, by *defcending into Hell*, enter into the
Place appointed for the Final Punifhment of the wicked, is very evident both from
Scripture and *Reafon*.

IN the *Scriptures* of the *Old Teftament*, the word which we render *Hell*, frequently fignifies only *The State of the Dead* in general. Thus *Pf.* lxxxix. 47 ; according to
the Tranflation in our *Common Prayer*; *What man is he that liveth, and fhall not fee
Death; and fhall he deliver his Soul from the hand of* Hell? is, in our Tranflation in the
Bible, fhall he deliver his Soul from the hand of the Grave? And what *Solomon* affirms,
Prov. xxvii. 20; that Hell *and deftruction are never full*, is plainly the very fame in
fenfe, with what in *ch.* xxx. 15; is *Thus* expreffed ; *There are three things that are never fatisfied, yea four things fay not, it is enough: The* Grave, and fo on.

IN the *New Teftament*; the word, *Hell*, fometimes fignifies the *Place appointed for
the Final Punifhment of the wicked*, and at other times it denotes only *the State of the
Dead* in general. But This ambiguity, is in *our own* language only, and not in the O-
riginal: For whenever the *Place of Torment* is fpoken of, the word *Hell*, in the Original, is always *Gehennah*: But when *only the State of the Dead in general* is intended,
'tis always expreffed by a quite *different Name*, which though *We* render by the *fame*
word *Hell*, yet its fignification is *at large The Invifible State*. Thus when St *James*

Jam. iii. 6. fays, that *the Tongue*, meaning a *wicked and profane* Tongue, is *a world of iniquity,—
and fetteth on Fire the courfe of Nature, and is fet on Fire of* Hell: And when our Sa-

Mat. xxiii. 33. viour fays to the Pharifees; *Ye ferpents, ye generation of Vipers, how can ye efcape the
Damnation of* Hell? and tells them, that when they have gained a *Profelyte*, they

ver. 15. *make him twofold more the child of* Hell, *then themfelves*: And when he admonifhes his

ch. x. 28. Difciples to *fear Him, who*, after he has killed, *is able to deftroy both Soul and Body in*
Hell, and warns them, that *whofoever fhall fay unto his Brother, Thou Fool, fhall be in*

Matt. v. *danger of* Hell-Fire; and advifes them, *If thy right Eye offend thee*, (that is, if the
22, and ver. Defire of any thing as dear to thee as thy Eyes, be in danger to draw thee into Sin,)
29. *pluck it out and caft it from thee; for it is profitable for thee that one of thy Members
fhould perifh, and not that thy whole Body fhould be caft into* Hell: In all *Thefe* Paffages,
I fay, the word *Hell* is, in the Original, *Gehennah*; which always fignifies *The State
of the Damned*. But in *Other Places*, where *we*, in *our* Rendring, ftill make ufe of

* Ἀδης. the *fame* word, *Hell*; the Original has a *very different* word, which fignifies only *The Invifible State*, or the *State of the Dead* in general. Thus *Matt.* xi. 23 ; *Thou Capernaum, which art exalted unto Heaven, fhalt be brought down to* Hell: The Meaning is;
That Great and Proud City fhould be levelled with the Duft, and difappear utterly as
Thofe who have been long buried in the Grave. Again: When the Rich man *in* Hell,
lift up his eyes, being in Torments, Luke xvi. 23; the word in the Original denotes *at
large* That *Invifible State* of the Dead in general, wherein were both *Abraham* and
Lazarus in his Bofom, (and the *Paradife* wherein the *Penitent Thief* was to be *with
our Saviour*,) as well as the *Souls of the Wicked* in their *Torments*. Again: When
our Lord promifes, *Matt.* xvi. 18; that *the Gates of* Hell *fhould not prevail againft*

* πύλαι ᾁδε. his Church; the * words, (*Gates of Hell*,) properly and ftrictly rendred, fignify *The*

Paffage

Paffage *to the Invifible State*, that is, *Death*: And the Senfe of his Promife is, that S E R M. even *Death itfelf*, (which is the utmoft Extent of all Perfecution from *thofe who kill* LXXXII. the Body, and, *after That, have no more that they can do*,) fhould never be able to fup- prefs his Doctrine, and extinguifh his Religion in the World. Laftly; When 'tis de- clared in the Prophecy concerning the end of the World; *Rev.* xx. 13 *and* 14; that *Death and* Hell *delivered up the Dead which were in them*; and that, after the Judg- ment, *Death and* Hell *were caft into the Lake of Fire*; 'tis very evident, that *Hell* in Thefe Paffages cannot poffibly fignify *The State of the Damned*; but That *State of departed Souls in general*, from whence All fhall be fummoned at the Great Day of Ac- counts; and which *State of Death*, or *Death itfelf*, after the final Judgment, fhall *be no more*. And thus therefore likewife in the words of *my Text*, as they are cited out of the *Pfalm* by the Apoftle St *Peter*, *Acts* ii. 27; *Thou wilt not leave my Soul in* Hell; the True and complete fenfe is plainly This; *Thou wilt not relinquifh me, thou wilt not fuffer me to continue, in the State of the Dead*; but wilt certainly raife me up again, *at the appointed time*.

FROM This explication of *all* the *Texts* relating to This matter, 'tis very clear that the *Scriptures* no where teach, that our Lord, by *defcending into Hell*, ever entred into the Place appointed for the Final Punifhment of the Wicked. Nor is there any thing in *Reafon*, from whence it can by any juft *Confequence* be *inferred*, that it was at all requifite for him fo to do.

IT has been conceived by *Some*, that it was needful for our Lord to go down into the place of Torment, in order to render his *Satisfaction* complete, by undergoing him- felf the very fame Sufferings, which were due to Thofe for whom he made Satisfaction. But This notion is founded entirely upon a Miftake. For the Satisfaction of Chrift, does not depend upon the *Samenefs of the Sufferings*, but upon the *good pleafure of God* who ruleth over all; who has been pleafed to declare himfelf appeafed by the volun- tary condefcenfion and Sufferings of our Lord, as a fufficient Vindication of his Supreme Authority; fo that he can, upon the Merit of That Sacrifice, confiftently with the Ho- nour and Dignity of his Laws, accept the *Repentance* and *Amendment* of returning Sinners, and freely forgive them their paft Sins. But, befides This, Neither was it indeed *poffible* in the Nature of Things, that our Lord fhould *at all* undergo the Tor- ments of the Wicked. For the Sting of *their* Punifhment is the *Worm that never dieth*, and an endlefs *Defpair of the Favour of God*; Which are things altogether impoffible to have fallen upon *Him*.

OTHERS therefore have fancied, that our Lord defcended into *Hell*, not indeed to *fuffer* any thing there *himfelf*, but to *deliver Others* out of that Place of Torment. But *This* alfo is plainly an erroneous opinion. For fince the Scripture every where teaches, that *as the Tree falleth, fo it fhall lie*; and that for thofe who die impenitent and un- reformed, there is no Redemption; 'tis certain the *Wicked*, when once condemned, are no more capable of being delivered at all. And as to *Virtuous* and *Good* men; it is no lefs certain that *the Souls of the righteous are in the hand of God, and there fhall no Torment touch them*. They are in Scripture reprefented as being in *Paradife*, or in *Abraham's Bofom*; but never as being in the *place of Torment* at all.

LASTLY, therefore it has been fuppofed by *Others*, that Chrift defcended into the place appointed for the final Punifhment of the Wicked, to *triumph* There over *Satan* in his *own Kingdom*. But neither is This opinion, in any wife, agreeable to Scripture. For the Devil and his Angels are not *yet* confined to the Pit of Deftruc- tion, before the Day of Judgment. And if they were, yet *That* is *not* their *King- dom*, but their Place of *Punifhment*. The *Kingdom* of the *Devil*, is the Prevalency and Dominion of *Sin* in *this* World: And here Chrift *triumphs* over him, by con- verting men from their Sins and Debaucheries, from their Unrighteoufnefs and Iniquities, which are the *Works of the Devil*; to the Practice of Virtue, Juftice, Goodnefs, Temperance, Charity and Truth, which are the eftablifhment of the *Kingdom of God* upon Earth.

UPON the *Whole* therefore, there is no fufficient Foundation, either in the *Reafon* of the *Thing*, or in the *Declarations* of *Scripture*, to fuppofe that our Lord ever defcended at all into the *Place of Torment*, into the place appointed for the final Punifhment of the Wicked. But the Full Meaning, both of thofe words in my *Text*, *Thou fhall not leave my Soul in Hell*; and of all the *Other* Paffages in Scripture, relating to That matter; is, that our Lord continued in the *State of the Dead*, in the *Invifible State of departed Souls*, during the Time appointed; but that, it not being *poffible for him to be holden of Death*, he was raifed again *without feeing corruption*.

THE *natural Inference* from which Doctrine, both of our *Lord's* overcoming Death, and of *good mens* being affured confequently that *They* fhall overcome it alfo; is *That Hope* and *Comfort* to virtuous and religious Minds under all *Temporal Afflictions* whatfoever, of which the Pfalmift expreffes his Senfe in the words whereof my Text are a part. *I have fet the Lord always before me*; *becaufe he is at my right hand, I fhall not be moved. Therefore my Heart is glad, and my Glory rejoiceth*; *my Flefh alfo fhall reft in Hope. For thou wilt not leave my Soul in Hell, neither wilt thou fuffer thine Holy One to fee corruption. Thou wilt fhow me the path of Life*; *In thy prefence is Fulnefs of Joy, at thy right hand are Pleafures for evermore.*

THE *Refurrection of Chrift*, is the Great *Evidence* of the Truth of his *Doctrine*. And a *Principal Part* of his *Doctrine*, is, the *bringing Life and Immortality to Light*; or, the giving us an Affurance, that, as *Chrift* is *rifen* from the Dead, fo *We* alfo, if we imitate him in the Obedience of his Life, fhall, after Death, rife with him unto Glory. The Condition and Circumftances of this prefent tranfitory Life are fuch, that, without the expectation of a future and a better State, the Satisfactions of *Life* are very uncertain and precarious, and in *Death* there is no foundation of Hope. They who enjoy the *Greateft Affluence* of the Good things of this prefent time, yet have them mixed with fo many Interruptions, with fo many Fears, with fo many Anxieties and Vexations of Life, if in *Thefe Things alone* their Profpect of Happinefs is terminated; that, upon the whole it can hardly be faid, that their *Pleafures compenfate* for their *Uneafineffes*: But with regard to *far the greateft part* of Mankind; what St *Paul* affirms concerning *Chriftians in particular*, that, *if in this Life only* they *have Hope*, they *are of all* Men *the moft miferable*; may, with equal Truth, be afferted *generally* concerning Men; if *in This Life only* they *have Hope*, they are of All *Creatures* the moft miferable. The *wifeft* and *beft* men therefore, even in the *Heathen* World, have, in all Ages and in All Nations, from the confideration of the *Natural reafon* of *Things*, from their *Idea* of the *Attributes* and *Perfections* of *God*, and from the *unequal Diftribution* of things in the *prefent* Life; juftly and ftrongly argued themfelves into a Belief and Expectation of a *Future* and a *Better* State. They argued, that nothing can be imagined more vain and empty, nothing more void of all Marks of Wifdom, than the Fabrick of the World and the Creation of Mankind; if all This was done without any further Defign, than only for the maintaining a perpetual Succeffion of fuch fhortlived Generations of Mortals, as we at prefent are; to live in the utmoft Confufion and Diforder for a very few Years, and then perifh eternally into Nothing. They argued, that, fince This *could not rationally* be the cafe, there *muft* confequently be a *Future* State. And if fo; then the Calamities and Afflictions, which in this World often fall upon the Beft of men, cannot but be intended fome way for their Benefit, if not *Here*, yet certainly *Hereafter*.

THE *Patriarchs* of old, who, befides *this general Light of Nature*, had moreover fome *particular* Manifeftations of God, carried this matter ftill further: And though

Life

Life and Immortality was not *compleatly* revealed to them, yet from the *Manner* of God's dealing with them they affuredly gathered, that his Promifes did not terminate in This Mortal Life. Accordingly, they *fo* behaved themfelves in this *prefent World*, as fhowed plainly that they fought a *better country, that is, an heavenly* ; *Looking for a City which hath foundations, whofe Builder and Maker is God.* They *endured* by Faith, *as feeing Him who is Invifible* ; and often *were tortured, not accepting Deliverance, that they might obtain a better Refurrection.* Saying with the Pfalmift in the Text, even in *Death* itfelf ; *My Heart was glad, and my Glory rejoiced* ; *my Flefh alfo fhall reft in Hope* ; *For thou wilt not leave my Soul in Hell, nor fuffer thy Holy One to fee corruption.*

And if *This* was the Behaviour of Thofe who faw the Promifes *only afar off*, and had them revealed to them *only in Types and Figures* ; What manner of perfons ought *We* to be, to whom *Life and Immortality are* now clearly and diftinctly *brought to Light* by the Gofpel! And if we live *worthy* of the *Vocation wherewith* we are called ; how gladly may we fay with St *Paul*, under *Any Troubles* of life whatfoever ; that *our light affliction which is but for a Moment, worketh for us a far more exceeding and eternal Weight of Glory : While we look not at the things which are feen, but at the things which are not feen ; for the things which are feen, are temporal, but the things which are not feen, are eternal.*

SERM.
LXXXII.

SERMON

SERMON LXXXIII.

Of Christ's fitting on the Right Hand of GOD.

[Preached on Afcenfion-Day.]

HEB. VIII. 1.

Now of the things which we have fpoken, This is the Sum: We have fuch an High-Prieft, who is fet on the right hand of the Throne of the Majefty in the Heavens.

SERM.
LXXXIII.
IN the foregoing chapter, the Apoftle fets forth at large the Excellency, of our Saviour's *perpetual and unchangeable* Priefthood; by comparing it with That *mutable* and *fucceffive* one among the *Jews*. Ver. 23. *They truly were many Priefts, becaufe they were not fuffered to continue by reafon of Death: But this man, becaufe he continueth ever, hath an unchangeable Priefthood. Wherefore he is able alfo to fave them to the uttermoft, that come unto God by him, feeing he ever liveth to make interceffion for them. For fuch an High Prieft became us, who is holy, harmlefs, undefiled, feparate from finners, and made higher than the Heavens. Who needeth not daily, as thofe High Priefts, to offer up Sacrifice, firft for his own Sins, and then for the peoples;* but has, by *One* Offering of himfelf, *for ever*, perfected them that are fanctified. The *full explication* of This Doctrine, and of the Confequences of it, is the Subject of this *Whole Epiftle*: And a *brief Summary* of it, is given us in the words of the *Text*; *Now of the things which we have fpoken, This is the Sum: We have fuch an High Prieft, who is fet on the right Hand of the Throne of the Majefty in the Heavens.*

Our Lord, *after his Refurrection,* as we find it recorded in the *Gofpels* and in the Hiftory of the *Acts, fhowed himfelf alive to his Difciples by many infallible Proofs, being feen of them forty days, and fpeaking of the things pertaining to the Kingdom of God;* converfing with them familiarly, opening their Underftandings, expounding to them the Scriptures, explaining to them in all the Prophets the things concerning Himfelf, directing them in what manner they fhould preach the Gofpel to all Nations, and promifing to be with them by the Affiftance of his Spirit even unto the end of the World. By which means when they were fully inftructed for the execution of their Office, he departed from them, afcending vifibly into Heaven, in fuch a manner as is defcribed by St *Paul* under the prophetick words of the Pfalmift, *When he afcended up on high, he led captivity captive, and gave gifts unto men: Now——He that defcended, is the fame alfo that afcended up far above all heavens, that he might fill all things.* From thenceforth therefore, *we have* (as the Text expreffes it) *fuch an High Prieft, is fet on the right hand of the Throne of the Majefty in the Heavens.*

The word, Heaven, when applied to the *Omniprefent God;* as in that expreffion of *Solomon, God is in Heaven, and thou upon Earth, therefore let thy words be few;* and in that compellation wherewith our Lord begins his prayer, *Our Father which art*

1   *in*

in Heaven; The word, *Heaven,* I fay, when thus applied to *God,* does not fignify S E R M.
literally a particular *place,* in point of *Situation*; but *figuratively,* a State of *Higheft* LXXXIII.
Dignity and *Supreme Dominion.* For God, being *effentially* prefent *every where,* cannot be *really and literally* in *One place* more than in *Another.* But he can make *particular manifeftations* of his *Glory,* when and where and how he pleafes: And where
he does This in the moft *confpicuous* manner, *That place* is called, by way of Eminence,
his *Habitation,* his *Throne,* his *Prefence.* Now becaufe the *Heavens,* are *higher* than the
Earth; becaufe *Thence* are derived all beneficial Influences, upon this lower World;
becaufe *There* is the Habitation of Angels, attending upon the Commands of God;
therefore God, who is *really and effentially* Prefent *every-where* alike, yet, with regard
to the *Exercife of his Power* and the *Manifeftation of his Glory,* is to Us reprefented as
being particularly in *Heaven.* And *Thither* therefore did our Lord *Jefus Chrift* accordingly afcend, to the Higheft place of Glory and Dignity, to the moft immediate Prefence of the Majefty of God, to *His* Father and *Our* Father, to *His* God and *Our*
God; and is *fat down* (as the Text with great elegance expreffes it) *on the right hand
of the Throne of the Majefty in the Heavens.*

THIS phrafe, The *Majefty,* ufed thus abfolutely and indefinitely, without mentioning the perfon to whom it belongs; is, in a very fublime and empatical manner, expreffive of the *Supereminent* Glory and Majefty of *God.* It fets forth to us in *fuch*
a fenfe, the *fingular* and *tranfcendent* Glory of the Divine Majefty; as that, *comparatively* fpeaking, there is No *other* Majefty but *His.* Thus, in *Other* places of Scripture,
when God is ftiled abfolutely and by way of Eminence, The Holy *One*; *The* Bleffed,
(as *Mar.* xiv. 61; *Art thou the Chrift, the Son of* the Bleffed?) *The* Power, (as in the
verfe next following, *Ye fhall fee the Son of man fitting on the right hand of* Power;)
The Excellent Glory, (as 2 *Pet.* i. 17. *There came fuch a voice to him from The* Excellent
Glory;) The fenfe of thefe expreffions is, that, *comparatively* fpeaking, there is None
Holy, None *Bleffed,* None *Powerful,* None *Glorious,* but *He* Alone. Good *Men,*
are in Scripture frequently ftiled *Holy*; and *Angels,* are the Holy *Angels of God*; and
yet *of* him and *to* him *alone* it is faid, *Thou* Only *art Holy. Angels* and the *Souls of
Men* are *immortal*; and yet of *Him* it is in a moft juft fenfe affirmed, that *He only hath
Immortality. Others* have Wifdom afcribed to them in their Degree and Order, and
yet *He* neverthelefs is *God* Only *Wife. Others* are, in their rank and proportion, truly
and juftly called Good; and yet our Lord, with peculiar Emphafis and High Propriety,
declares, *There is None* Good, *but One, that is, God.* The Scripture, without Any
Scruple, calls *Temporal* Deliverers, *Saviours*; Nehem. ix. 27. And our Lord *Jefus
Chrift,* in the *fpiritual* and infinitely *higher* fenfe, is, by way of Eminence, ftiled *Our
Saviour:* And yet the *Father Almighty,* (who in St *Paul's* language, *Tit.* iii. 4, 5, is
God *our Saviour* which *faves us through Jefus* Chrift *our Saviour,*) declares concerning
Himfelf, *Ifai.* xliii. 11; *Befides Me, there is no Saviour.* The manner of fpeaking, is
very *juft,* as well as lofty and fublime; and it is ufeful and proper, in order to keep
up in mens minds a due and awful fenfe of the Supreme and unapproachable Greatnefs
of God. *Others* have *Power* afcribed to them, and *Dominion* and *Majefty*; There are,
as St *Paul* tells us, *Gods many, and Lords many, in Heaven and in Earth,* 1 Cor. viii.
v. Some *falfely* fo called; *Others* rightly, in *fuch* a fenfe as the Scripture gives the
Title of *Gods* and *Lords* to *Angels* and to *Men*: Yet, for all that, *there is ftill really
no other God but One*; and The *Majefty,* abfolutely fpeaking, is *His* alone. Our *High
Prieft,* is *fet on the right hand of the Throne, of* The Majefty *in the Heavens.*

THE term, Right Hand, when applied to God, is not to be underftood *literally,*
as denoting a particular *Situation* with regard to *Place,* (for God has no *Hands,* no
Shape or *Parts*;) But it fignifies *figuratively* a *State* of High *Dignity, Dominion* and
Power, next and immediately after God the Father himfelf. Our Saviour's being ad-

S E R M.　vanced to the Right Hand of *God*, is his being actually invested with That *Glory and*
LXXXIII.　*Dignity*, for the *Joy* of which, when it was *set before him*, he willingly *endured the*
　〜〜　*Cross*, (Heb. xii. 2:) *despising the Shame, and is set down at the right hand of the Throne*
of God; That is, has overcome Death, and entered into his *Kingdom of Glory*. And
therefore, in *other* places of Scripture, the very same Notion is set forth under the parallel expressions, that *Him hath God exalted* with *his right hand, to be a Prince and a*
Saviour; to be *Lord both of the Dead and Living*; to be the *Head of all Principality and*
Power, the *Head over all things to the Church*: That he hath given him *All Power*
both *in Heaven and Earth*, and *put all things in subjection under his feet*; *Angels and*
Authorities, and Powers, being made subject unto him: That he *has appointed him Heir*
of all things, and, *according to the working of his mighty Power, has set him far above*
all principality and power and might and dominion, and every name that is named, not
only in This World, but also in that which is to come; *That at the Name of Jesus every*
knee should bow, of things in Heaven, and things in Earth, and things under the Earth;
and that every tongue should confess that Jesus Christ is Lord, to the Glory of God the
Father. All which exalted characters, are emphatically included in this one figurative
expression; *the* right hand *of God*, the right hand *of the Throne of the Majesty in the*
Heavens.

　　Lastly, The word, fitting, or *being* set, is likewise to be understood, not *literally*,
as denoting a *particular* corporeal *Posture*; (for in *other* places of Scripture it is expressed that our Lord *Is* at the right hand of God, or that he *Stands* at the right hand of
God;) But the word, *fitting*, is *for This Reason* more frequently used in the case before
us, because it implies, in its *figurative* Use and Signification, Fulness of *Possession*, and
perpetuity of retaining the Glory possessed; *Heb.* x. 12: *After he had offered One Sa-*
crifice for Sins, he for ever *sat down on the right hand of God*; *From henceforth expect-*
ing, till his Enemies be made his footstool; *For by One Offering, he hath perfected* for
ever *them that are sanctified*. From the time of our Lord's ascending into Heaven, till
his Second coming to Judgment, there were *Many Ages* to pass over: And therefore
St *Peter* in his Sermon to the *Jews*, Acts iii. 19, tells them, that *when the times of re-*
freshing shall come from the presence of the Lord, he shall send Jesus Christ which before
was preached unto them; *whom the* Heaven must receive, *until the times of restitution*
of all things.

　　The *Office* which our Saviour executes during this his continuance in Heaven, is signified to us in the Text under the character of *High Priest*: *We have such an* High
Priest, *who is set on the right hand of —the Majesty in the Heavens*. And the explication of the Nature of *This Office*, as applied to our Lord, is the principal subject of
this whole Epistle. Upon which account the words of the Text are *thus* introduced
by the Apostle: *Of the things which we have spoken, This is the Sum: We have such an*
High Priest, *who is set on the right hand of the Throne of the Majesty in the Heavens*.
As, among the *Jews*, the *High Priest* in the *Temple* entred *once* a year *into the Holy*
Place, with the Blood of *Others*; so *Christ* having *once in the End of the World put*
away Sin by the Sacrifice of Himself, it was necessary that He *with his Own blood* should
enter once likewise *into the Holy Place*, into *That within the Veil, having obtained eter-*
nal redemption for us: That is, it was necessary that he should ascend into Heaven, to
finish and present his most acceptable oblation before God, for the propitiation of the
Sins of the World. For so the Apostle interprets it: *Christ* (says he) *is not entred into*
the Holy Places made with hands, *which are only the Figures of the True*; *but into Hea-*
ven itself, now to appear in the presence of God for us.

　　The first and immediate Effect of this his Appearing in the Presence of God for us,
was the *Mission* of the *Holy Ghost*. *Before* our Saviour's Exaltation, the *Holy Ghost*,
says the Evangelist, (speaking comparatively,) *was not yet given, because that Jesus*

was

was not yet glorified; Joh. vii. 39. And our Lord himself: *I tell you the Truth,* says S E R M. he; *it is expedient for you, that I go away; for if I go not away, the Comforter will* LXXXIII. *not come unto you: But if I depart, I will send him unto you;* and——*he will guide ye into all Truth.* Accordingly, at the Pentecoft after Chrift's Afcenfion, the Holy Ghoft fell upon the Apoftles in a fingular and moft miraculous manner, beyond the Examples of former Infpirations. And by the continual affiftance and ordinary operations of the fame Spirit, has our Lord promifed to *be with us* his true Difciples, to *be in the midft of them* where-ever *two or three are gathered together in his Name,* even unto the End of the World.

But further: The Scripture reprefents this our Great *High Prieft,* as continually *interceeding* for us at the right hand of God, from the time of his Afcenfion till his final coming to Judgment. *We have an* Advocate *with the Father, Jefus Chrift the righteous; and he is the propitiation for our Sins: For* our Sins; that is, for the Sins of all thofe who *truly repent* and *effectually amend* their Lives, according to the gracious Terms of the Gofpel; and who are therefore accordingly reprefented as having *wafhed their robes, and made them white in the Blood of the Lamb.* For perfons of *This* difpofition, our Saviour is a perpetual and effectual Advocate, to obtain perfect forgivenefs of their paft Sins, and to cleanfe them by the perpetual affiftance of his Spirit, from all unrighteoufnefs. They *have an High Prieft, not who cannot be touched with the feeling of their infirmities, but who was* himfelf *tempted in all points like as* They *are, yet without Sin.* And he *is* able *alfo,* as well as willing, *to fave them to the uttermoft, that come unto God by him, feeing he* ever *liveth to make interceffion for them;* Heb. vii. 25. And becaufe he thus lives *for ever,* and has an *unchangeable Priefthood,* therefore he is faid in Scripture to be a Prieft, not after the Order of *Aaron,* which was a perpetual Succeffion of Priefts *not fuffered to continue by reafon of death;* but after the Order of *Melchifedec,* who was both *Prince* and *High Prieft,* and of whom is recorded neither Predeceffor nor Succeffor, that he might be a Type and Emblem of Him who ever *liveth to make Interceffion for us.*

Some Unbelievers there have been in All Ages, and ftill are, who, in oppofition to this Great Doctrine of Chriftianity, alledge, that God being always Omniprefent and ready to hear the Prayers which every one offers for himfelf, therefore there was *no need* of appointing a Mediator; and that God always acting, in his own nature, according to the exact Right and Reafon of the Cafe; therefore he cannot be *changed,* or have Any *Affection moved,* by the interpofition of Any Interceffor whatfoever. But in This matter they greatly miftake. For if God's being himfelf every where prefent, were a fufficient reafon why *no Mediator* fhould be appointed to intercede for *Men;* it would by the fame argument be alfo a fufficient reafon, why men fhould neither pray nor intercede for *themfelves:* For God *knows* their Wants as perfectly, even without their ever praying for *Themfelves,* as without a *Mediator* interceding for them. If therefore, notwithftanding God's Omniprefence and Omnifcience, it be ftill reafonable to require that men fhould pray for *Themfelves;* in order to keep up in their Minds a conftant fenfe of God, and that they may make continual Acknowledgment of their Dependence upon him: It may in like manner be very reafonable, in order to keep up in their Minds a juft fenfe of their own *Unworthinefs* and of the true *Demerit of Sin,* to require of them, that through fuch a *Mediator* only, as he has thought fit to appoint, fhould they have Accefs to *Him who is of purer Eyes than to behold Iniquity.* And though it be indeed very true, that by No interceffion whatfoever, can God ever be moved to act otherwife than is agreeable to perfect Right and Reafon; yet in cafes of *Mercy and Compaffion,* where the *whole* of what he does, proceeds from mere *Free Bounty;* 'tis evident he may convey thofe his *Free Gifts,* in what *Manner,* and upon what *Terms or Conditions,* and through what *Inftruments* he pleafes; and may

3 require

require their being accepted in *that* particular *Method*, or not at all. For however *otherwise* it be in all such cafes, where there is any Claim of *Juſtice*, or Demand of *Right*; yet undoubtedly, in Diſpenſations of *mere* Mercy, that which is true of every *Owner* even among frail and mortal *Man*, may with much greater propriety be ſaid of *God*; ſhall he not do *what* and *how* he will with *his own?*

THAT which remains, is, to draw two or three *practical Inferences* from the whole of what has been ſaid.

AND 1*ſt*, From the doctrine of our Lord's ſitting at the Right Hand of God to intercede continually for us, and to govern his Church by the miſſion of the Holy Ghoſt the Comforter, the Apoſtle's inference is very natural. *Heb*. iv. 16; *Let us therefore come boldly unto the Throne of Grace, that we may obtain mercy, and find grace to help in time of need*: Again, ch. x. 19; *Having boldneſs to enter into the holieſt by the blood of Jeſus*, (*i. e.* having acceſs to God through Him,) *by a new and living way which he has conſecrated for us; and having an High Prieſt over the houſe of God; let us draw near with a true heart, in full aſſurance of faith*. For *He that ſpared not his own Son*; Rom. viii. 32; *how ſhall he not with him alſo freely give us all things?* —— *Who is he that condemneth? it is Chriſt that died, yea rather that is riſen again, who is even at the right hand of God, who alſo maketh interceſſion for us*.

2*dly*; IF *We* follow the *example* of our Lord's Humility and Righteouſneſs here upon *Earth*, we may hope through Him to be made Partakers alſo of his exaltation in *Heaven*. *I go*, ſays he, *to prepare a place for you, and* —— *I will come again, and receive you unto myſelf, that where I am, there Ye may be alſo*. Again: *To Him that overcometh*, that is, who perſeveres in reſiſting the temptations of Sin: *unto Him will I grant to ſit with Me in My Throne, even as I alſo overcame, and am ſet down with my Father in His Throne*. Theſe Promiſes cauſed St *Paul* ſo to expreſs himſelf, as if *God had* already *raiſed us up together* with Chriſt, and *made us* already *ſit together in heavenly places in Chriſt Jeſus*; Eph. ii. 16. The *manner of expreſſion*, is highly *figurative*; But the *literal* and proper Senſe of it is what he elſewhere thus explains: *We have hope*, ſays he, *as an Anchor of the Soul, both ſure and ſtedfaſt, and which entreth into that within the Veil, whither our fore-runner is entred for us*. And if we *have* this Hope in us, then ought we accordingly to *ſet our* affections *on things above, not on things on the Earth*; that *where our Treaſure is, there may our* Heart *be alſo*; that we may ſeek *thoſe things which are above, where Chriſt ſitteth on the right hand of God*, and where *our life is hid*, (that is, depoſited, laid up for us in the determinations of the divine good pleaſure, 'tis hid) *with Chriſt in God*: that *our* Converſation, (the Thoughts of our Home and final Abode,) *may be in Heaven, from whence alſo we look for the Saviour, the Lord Jeſus Chriſt*; who, at his coming, ſhall *ſo change* Us, that *we* ſhall become like him, when *we ſhall ſee him as he is*; and, *as we have born the image of the Earthly, we ſhall alſo bear the Image of the Heavenly*. By imploying our Meditations in *This* manner, upon our Lord's State of exaltation in Heaven; ſo as to make it a *continual Motive* to us, to *prepare* ourſelves to become finally Partakers of that promiſed inheritance; we ſhall contribute what in *Us* lies, towards fulfilling that Prophecy which he ſpake before his Death; *Joh*. xii. 32; *And I, if I be lifted up from the Earth, will draw all men unto me*.

3*dly*; *Another* proper and moſt *important* Uſe of the Doctrine before us, is as follows. If our Lord came down upon *Earth to* put away Sin *by the Sacrifice of himſelf*; and if, in his State of Exaltation in *Heaven*, the Deſign of his continual interceſſion with God, and of his whole Government of the Church by his Spirit, be ſtill always one and the ſame, even the putting away of *Sin*: Then from hence we may learn how great and fatal a Corruption it is of Chriſtian Religion, for men who *live wickedly* in a courſe of *Debauchery*, or in the habitual practice of *any known Sin* whatſoever, to ex-

I   pect

pect to obtain Salvation by relying *presumptuously upon the* Merits *of Christ*, or upon S E R M.
His Interceffion, inftead of *obeying* his *Commands* delivered in the Gofpel. *The Blood* LXXXIII.
of Chrift, who through the eternal Spirit offered himfelf without fpot to God, was fhed,
not to render men fafe in unrighteous Living, but to *purge the confcience* of fuch as
truly repent and amend, to *purge them from dead works to ferve the living God;*
Heb. ix. 14; The *End* why our Lord *gave himfelf for us*, being, *that he might* purify *to himfelf a peculiar people, zealous of good works.* If this great End be attained;
if (according to the language of St *John*) *we walk in the Light*, (that is, in the practice of true virtue and holinefs,) even as *God is Light, and in Him is no darknefs at
all*; then indeed *the blood of Jefus Chrift his Son cleanfeth us from all* paft *Sin.* But
if we fay we have fellowfhip with Him, *and* (ftill) *walk in darknefs;* (that is, continue to live wickedly, and yet hope for Benefit from the profeffion of God's true religion from what Chrift has either done or fuffered for us;) *we lie, and do not the Truth;*
1 Joh. i. 6.

4thly, and *laftly:* As from what has been faid, appears the *Reafonablenefs* of mens
applying to God through That *One* Mediator, whom *he* has appointed; fo at the fame
Time appears likewife the *Folly* of their fetting up *Other* Mediators, of their *own* invention; fuch as are Angels, Saints, the Bleffed Virgin, and the like. For *there is one
God*, fays the Apoftle, and *One Mediator between God and Men.* And as departing
from *the One God and Father of All, who is above all, and through all, and in us all*, is
the firft and higheft Species of Idolatry; fo another fort of the fame Sin, is the fetting
up falfe and imaginary *Mediators, by will-worfhip, by a voluntary humility*, as St *Paul*
ftiles it, *and worfhipping of Angels;* when men *intrude into things which they have
not feen, vainly puffed up by their flefhly mind, and not holding the Head, from which
all the body by Joints and Bands having nourifhment miniftred, and knit together, in-
creafeth with the increafe of God.*

SERMON LXXXIV.

The Converfation of Chriftians is in Heaven.

[Preached on Afcenfion-Day.]

PHIL. III. 20.

For our Converfation is in Heaven; from whence alfo we look for the Saviour, the Lord Jefus Chrift.

S E R M.
LXXXIV.

IN difcourfing upon Thefe words of the Apoftle, I fhall 1*ft* endeavour briefly to fhow, *what* is the full *meaning* of this Phrafe, of *having our Converfation in Heaven*; and 2*dly*, *what* are the principal *Benefits* and *Advantages*, which may arife to good men from This confideration.

I. As to the Signification of the Phrafe, *having our converfation in Heaven*; it may properly be underftood to imply, three things.

1*ft*, OUR *Meditating* frequently upon That Heavenly State, That Kingdom of Truth, Virtue and Happinefs, which is propofed to us as the Reward and End of our Chriftian Warfare. To *converfe* with any Perfon *prefent*, fignifies *delighting* in his *Company*, or being *concerned* in his *Affairs*. To be converfant with any perfon *abfent*, fignifies holding mutual *intercourfe* and *correfpondence* with him; being *follicitous* about what is *done by* him, or *happens to* him. To have our converfation in a diftant Place, fignifies being *much There* in our *Minds*; defiring to *have an influence* or *intereft*, in what is done There; and judging, that What paffes There, has an *influence* upon Us, *affects* us *nearly*, or *relates* to us more *immediately*. When therefore the Apoftle affirms, as in the Text, that our *Converfation is in Heaven*; his meaning is, that though *our Perfons* at prefent dwell on *Earth*, yet our *greateft Intereft* and *Concerns* are in *Heaven*. Like a Merchant trading in a diftant Country; his *prefent Abode* may be in *foreign parts*, but his *Eftate*, his *Family*, his *fettled Habitation*, is at *home*; and it is of *much more importance* to him, what the *lafting* State of his Affairs is *at Home*; than what happens to him *Abroad*, with regard to fuch Accidental *temporary* Circumftances, as do not much affect his *main Concerns in his own Country*. Thus *Chriftians*, have their *great*, their *lafting* Intereft, in *Heaven*. And though they *cannot*, they *ought not*, any more than other men, to be *infenfible* of what happens to them in this *fhort and tranfitory* life, according to the *true proportion* of things, and their *real value*; yet every thing *here*, ought *chiefly* to be confidered, with regard to the influence 'tis likely to have, upon our *future and eternal State*. Which right Judgment and Eftimation of things, 'tis impoffible men fhould make; unlefs by frequent and ferious *meditation*, they fo *behold* the things *invifible*, as to bring them to make *proportionably* as ftrong an impreffion upon the *Mind*, as *Earthly* Objects do upon the *Senfes*. Many men, like the Brute Creatures which have No Underftanding, feem hardly to think at all

1   upon

upon any thing, but what is *preſent* and *ſenſual.* But *Reaſon* in general, and *Chriſtianity* in particular, teaches us, and requires of us, to judge of things according to their *true and real Value*; and to be more concerned about things at preſent *inviſible*, if they be really of *greater* and more *laſting importance* to us, than about things which do *Now* more *immediately affect our Senſes.* St *Paul*, the great Buſineſs of whoſe Life was the Care of the Churches; thus writes to the *Corinthians*, when at a diſtance from them; *I verily*, ſays he, as *abſent in Body*, *but preſent in Spirit*; 1 Cor. v. 3; and to the *Coloſſians*, ch. ii. 5; *Though I be abſent in the Fleſh*, *yet am I with you in the Spirit*, *joyning and beholding your Order*, *and the Stedfaſtneſs of your Faith in Chriſt.* The Deſcription the Apoſtle here gives of himſelf with regard to the employment of his Thoughts upon his main Concern in *This life*; is what every ſincere Chriſtian ought to make good, with regard to his expectations in the *Life to come.* Though he be *in his Body* an Inhabitant upon Earth; and, ſo long as he continues ſo, ought not, after a Monkiſh, Superſtitious and Enthuſiaſtick manner, to neglect the Affairs of *Himſelf*, his *Family*, his *Friends*, or his *Country*; yet at the ſame time in *Spirit*, in the *bent* and *habitual diſpoſition of his Mind*, in the *direction* of the ultimate *View and Aim* of all his Actions, he may properly be ſaid to *converſe*, and to *Be*, in *Heaven.* Whoever *fears God* and *works Righteouſneſs*, and lives with a conſtant Senſe of Religion upon his Mind; how little *Time*, or how ſmall *Abilities* ſoever he has for abſtract Meditation, may yet, even in the midſt of his worldly affairs, be truly ſaid, in *This* ſenſe, to have his *Converſation in Heaven*: Becauſe he lives according to the *Laws* of *Heaven*; has in his Mind the *Temper* of Heaven; and, by the Love of Truth, and Practice of Virtue, is in a continual Preparation for the *State of Heaven.* Nevertheleſs, though the *Practice of Virtue and Goodneſs* is indeed the *End* of all religion, yet frequent and ſerious *Meditation* is valuable as a *Means* to *promote* That *End*, and to *encourage* That *Practice.* SERM. LXXXIV.

THE proper Subjects *in particular* to be *meditated upon*, as being moſt likely to have an *immediate Influence* upon the Courſe of our Lives, and to cauſe our *Converſation* on *Earth* to be effectually preparative for that in *Heaven*; are, in the *firſt* place, the *Nature* of God, and of his *Relation to* Us: the conſideration of his being *himſelf* a Perſon infinitely *Holy*; a Lover of *Virtue* and all *Goodneſs*; a *Hater* of *Iniquity*, of *Debauchery*, and of every *Corrupt Practice*; a *Juſt* and *Righteous Governour* of all things; and a *bountiful Rewarder* of them who ſerve and obey him; *in whoſe Preſence* there will finally be *fulneſs of Joy*, and *at his right hand Pleaſures for evermore.*

IN the *next* place is the Conſideration of Chriſt our *Great High-Prieſt*, the *Mediator of the New Covenant*; who *gave himſelf for us*, that by the *Doctrine and Example* of his *Life*, and by the *Merit* and Influence of his *Death*, he *might redeem us from all iniquity*, *and purify to himſelf a peculiar People zealous of good works*: Who is *now ſat down on the right hand of the Throne of God in the heavenly places*, to intercede for all thoſe that truly and effectually repent: And who, *at the end of the World*, unto all them *who with patient continuance in well-doing look for him*, *ſhall appear the ſecond time*, *without Sin*, *unto Salvation.*

THE next part of this Contemplation, tending to make us *hunger and thirſt after Righteouſneſs*, by having *at preſent* our *Converſation in Heaven*; is the conſideration of the Company, by whom that region of Happineſs is poſſeſſed. The Society of Good *Angels*, who *never departed* from their firſt eſtate; and of Good *Men*, who by true Repentance are *returned* unto it. The Society of Holy *Angels*, who *going in and out before the Throne of God*, *do always behold the Face of our Father*; even the *Father*, *of whom the whole Family in Heaven and Earth is named*: And the Society of Holy *Men*,

SERM. *Men, who, having washed their Robes in the Blood of the Lamb, are* by Him *presented*
LXXXIV. *faultless before the Presence of his Father's Glory with exceeding Joy.*

T H E *last* part of this Contemplation, is the consideration of the Happiness of this
State itself, with regard to Ourselves. And in *This respect* indeed, *it doth not yet appear
what we shall be: But we know, that when he shall appear, we shall be like him; for we*
shall see him as he is. At present *we see* only, *as through a glass, darkly;* For *Eye hath
not seen, nor ear heard, neither hath it entred into the Heart of Man to conceive, the
things that God has prepared for them that love him:* But Then, *we shall see face to face;
and know, even as we are known,* 1 Cor. xiii. 12. In *general* only, *This* we are *Now* assured of, and a sufficient employment it is for our *Meditations* upon This Head; that
the Happiness of Heaven, tho' the *particulars* of it are not yet revealed, is a *Great* and
exceeding Weight of Glory; to which the Apostle *reckons,* that nothing in *this present
World* is *worthy to be compared,* 2 Cor. iv. 17; that it is a *Kingdom, which cannot be
moved;* a *Treasure, which neither moth nor rust doth corrupt,* and to which *Thieves do
not break through and steal:* that it is a Happiness *pure and unmixed;* For *all tears shall
then be wiped from* our *Eyes; and there shall be no more Death, neither sorrow nor crying; neither shall there be any more Pain; for the former things are passed away:* Lastly, that it is an enjoyment which will *satisfy* all our *Desires,* an employment which
will *improve* to the utmost all our *Faculties;* and, which is the Crown of all, will continue *for ever;* being, as St *Peter* expresses it, an *inheritance incorruptible, undefiled,
and which fadeth not away.* I conclude This Head, with the words of a most excellent
Writer of our own: " O blessed Time, *saith he,* when Mortality shall be swallowed

Archbishop
Tillotson. " up of Life, and Death and Sorrow shall be no more;——when we shall be eased of
" all our Pains, and resolved of all our Doubts, and be purged from all our Sins, and
" be freed from all our Fears, and be happy beyond all our Hopes, and have all this
" Happiness secured to us beyond the Power of Time and Change!" Let every man
who lives in the Practice of Any known Vice, consider seriously with himself, how for
one morsel of meat he sells this Birthright.

T H I S is the *first* thing implied in the Phrase of having *our Conversation in Heaven;
meditating frequently and seriously upon the Happiness of That State.*

2*dly;* H A V I N G *our Conversation in Heaven,* signifies, not only meditating upon
the Happiness of that State, but *practically and effectually setting our* Hearts and Affections *thereon.* Speculative *Meditations* within our *own Minds,* or *moving Discourses*
and *fine Descriptions* to *Others,* are of no Use; unless the things *meditated upon by us,*
or *described to us,* affect our *Hearts,* and operate in their influence upon our *Lives and
Actions,* as *Realities,* and not as *Imaginations.* The Persons *Opposite* to those whose
conversation is in Heaven, (as they are described in the *Verse before* my Text) are those
whose God is their Belly, who mind *earthly things,* ver. 19. By way of *contraries*
therefore, they whose conversation *is* in *Heaven,* are Those only who *mind,* (not who
can *imagine* or *describe,* but who *mind,*) that is, who in earnest *attend to,* as to their
proper and most important Concern, the things which are in *Heaven:* Rom. viii. 5;
They that are after the Flesh, do mind *the things of the Flesh; and they that are
after the Spirit,* do mind *the things of the Spirit.* The meaning is; As *worldly* and
corrupt Minds, are much more concerned about their *Temporal,* than about their *eternal* Affairs; so, on the contrary, Persons *truly religious,* though they *by no means neglect*
the Concerns of this present Life, yet they are really *more sollicitous,* they are *more rejoiced* or *grieved,* at the Prospect of their *Eternal,* than of their *Temporal State.* This
is what St *Paul* exhorts us to, *Col.* iii. 1; *If ye be risen with Christ,* seek *those things
which are above, where Christ sitting on the right hand of God: Set your* Affection *on
things above, not on things upon Earth: For ye are dead, and your Life is hid with
Christ in God.* Ye are *dead;* that is, ye are by your Profession in Baptism, *dead* with

Christ;

Chriſt ; *dead with Chriſt from the rudiments of the World*; *buried with him by Bap* S E R M.
tiſm, into Death; *dead*, to all the vicious Deſires, to all the *ſinful* enjoyments of the LXXXIV.
World. *And your* Life (ſays he) *is hid with Chriſt in God*; that is, your *Hope*, (as it
is expreſſed, *ch.* i. 5.) the Hope of eternal Life, is *laid up for you in Heaven*, with
Chriſt our Saviour ; laid up, *reſerved* for you, in the determinate Counſel of God, a-
gainſt the day of retribution : At which time, *when Chriſt, who is our Life, ſhall appear,
then ſhall ye alſo appear with him in Glory.* The *only poſſible Means*, by which we
can in This ſenſe fix our *Affections*, by which we can in This ſenſe come to have
our *converſation* habitually *in Heaven*; is, that we take care, by works of Righteouſneſs and true Holineſs, by a life of Virtue and real Goodneſs, to ſecure to ourſelves
an *Intereſt* and a *Portion* There. *Lay not up*, ſays our Saviour, *treaſures upon Earth, but
lay up for yourſelves treaſures in Heaven*; *For where your Treaſure is, there* will *your
Heart be alſo*, Matt. vi. 21. The words next following to theſe, are difficult to be underſtood ; unleſs *compared* with Theſe, by which their Senſe and Connexion may be
explained : ver. 22. *The Light of the Body*, ſays our Lord, *is the Eye*; *if therefore
thine Eye be ſingle, thy whole Body ſhall be full of Light*; *But if thine Eye be Evil,
thy whole Body ſhall be full of Darkneſs*; *If therefore the* Light *that is in thee be
Darkneſs, how great is that Darkneſs!* The Meaning is : That *True Judgment*
and *Right Diſcernment* of the Difference of things, by which *Treaſure in Heaven* is
more valued than *Treaſure upon Earth*; the Rewards of Virtue, than the Pleaſures
of *Sin*; This *true Judgment*, I ſay, is to the *State* of the *Soul*, what the *Eye* is to
the *Guidance and Direction* of the *Body.* If That which ſhould be our *Guide* and
our *Rule*, be itſelf *dark*, be itſelf *fundamentally erroneous*; how miſerable muſt our
Errors be !

3*dly*, H A V I N G *our Converſation in Heaven*, ſignifies in the laſt place, according to
the moſt ſtrict and proper Import of the word in the Original ; having our Citizenſhip,
our *Home*, our proper *Country* and *Habitation* there. The State of *Heaven*, the *Happineſs* which God has promiſed in the Life to come, to thoſe who ſhall qualify themſelves for it by the Habits of Virtue *here*; is in Scripture repreſented under the deſcription of a glorious *City*; Rev. xxi. 10 : *He ſhewed me that great City, the Holy Jeruſalem, deſcending out of Heaven from God*; *having the Glory of God*, and ſo on. And
even the *Antient* Prophets, uſed from the beginning the ſame expreſſions ; As appears
in many paſſages of *Iſaiah*; And *Tobit* xiii. 16 ; *Jeruſalem*, ſaith he, *ſhall be built up
with Saphires, and her Walls——with pure Gold.* Of this *new* and heavenly *Jeruſalem*, the Apoſtle deſcribes the *Patriarchs of old* to have been *Citizens*, while their
dwelling on Earth was but as in a *foreign Country*, Heb. xi. 9. *By Faith, Abraham
ſojourned in the land of Promiſe, as in a* ſtrange *Country*;——*For he looked for a* City
which hath Foundations; (in the original it is, *he expected* The *City which hath* The
Foundations; that is, the Foundations *of precious Stones*, alluding to the Prophetic expreſſions ;) *whoſe Builder and Maker is God* : And *ver.* 13 : *Theſe all*, that is, the Patriarchs, *died in Faith, not having received the Promiſes, but having ſeen them afar off*;
*and were perſwaded of them and embraced them, and confeſſed that they were Strangers
and Pilgrims on the Earth*; *For they that ſay ſuch things, declare plainly that they ſeek
a Country*, even a——*better Country, that is an heavenly*; *Wherefore God is not aſhamed
to be called their God*; *for he hath prepared for them a* City. And *All* who imitate the
Obedience of theſe Patriarchs, in all Ages and in all Nations of the World, by a Life
of Virtue and true Goodneſs ; are in like manner repreſented in Scripture, as being
Members of the ſame heavenly *City* : Eph. ii. 19. *Ye are no more Strangers and Foreigners, but* Fellow-citizens *with the Saints, and of the houſehold of God*; *and are built*

SERM.
LXXXIV.

1 Pet. ii. 11.

upon the Foundation of the Apoſtles and Prophets, Jeſus Chriſt himſelf being the chief corner-ſtone ; In whom all the Building fitly framed together, groweth unto an Holy Temple in the Lord. In the *preſent* world, upon account of the tranſitorineſs of This mortal life we are ſtyled *Strangers* and *Sojourners,* 1 Chr. xxix. 15; and are exhorted, as *Pilgrims,* to *paſs the Time of our* ſojourning *here in Fear,* 1 Pet. i. 17. For *here we have no continuing City, but we ſeek One to come,* Heb. xiii. 14. *A city to come;* that is, the *New,* the heavenly *Jeruſalem :* For ſo St *Paul* tells us, *Gal.* iv. 26; *Jeruſalem which is above, is the Mother of us all;* that is, our proper *Home* and *Country.* Heb. xii. 22; *Ye are come unto Mount Sion, and unto the* City *of the Living God, the heavenly Jeruſalem, and to an innumerable company of Angels, To the general Aſſembly and Church of the firſt-born that are written in Heaven, and to God the Judge of All, and to the Spirits of juſt men made perfect, and to Jeſus the Mediator of the New Covenant.* In purſuance of which elegant Deſcription, virtuous and good men, *raiſed and quickned together with Chriſt* from the *Death of Sin,* are, by a lively figure, ſaid to *ſit together* (even *Now*) *in* heavenly *places, in,* (or *with*) *Chriſt Jeſus,* Eph. ii. 6. And to *dwell in Heaven :* Rev. xiii. 6. *he,* (that is, Antichriſtian Tyranny) *opened his mouth in Blaſphemy againſt God, to blaſpheme his Name and his Tabernacle, and them that* dwell in Heaven. To *blaſpheme them that dwell in Heaven* ; that is, as it is explained in the following Verſe, to *make War with* and *overcome* the *Saints* ; to perſeſecute the true Worſhippers of God, whoſe *Converſation is in Heaven.*

II. HAVING thus at large explained the *Meaning* of this Phraſe, of having *our Converſation in Heaven* ; It remains that I proceed, in the 2d place, to conſider the *Uſes* and *Advantages* which may ariſe to us therefrom. And

1ſt, IF we take the Phraſe in Either of the *Two former* Senſes, as ſignifying that we *Meditate* frequently upon the Heavenly State, or (which is the natural *eonſequence* of delighting in ſuch Meditation,) ſet our *Hearts and Affections thereon* ; the Advantage and Benefit of ſo doing, is, that it will *continually* put us upon *preparing* and *qualifying* ourſelves, by the Practice of Virtue, for the enjoyment of That Bleſſed State : *Eccluſ.* vii. 36; *Whatſoever thou takeſt in hand, remember the* End ; *and thou ſhalt never do amiſs.* The Great reaſon, why the World is generally ſo vicious ; is becauſe men ſeldom *meditate* upon the final Conſequences of Wickedneſs, and ſeldom ſeriouſly reflect upon the real State of their own Souls. They are like one, who, walking towards a Precipice, ſhuts his Eyes, and perceives not that there is Any Danger. *Conſideration* is the *Eye* of the Soul : And if this *Light* that is in us, be itſelf Darkneſs ; if our *Meditations* be never fixed upon the things which can no otherwiſe be diſcerned but by ſerious and impartial *Meditation* ; how great muſt the Darkneſs and Blindneſs of our Minds be ! Men upon a Bed of Sickneſs, and at the Approach of Death, generally have very right Notions of this Matter ; And ſince what will *Then* be True, we are ſure cannot but be equally True *Now* ; wiſe men will always endeavour, to fix thoſe Thoughts upon their Minds by timely Attention, and make them uſeful *at preſent* ; which *hereafter* will fix *themſelves* upon the Mind, whether a man will or no, when perhaps it may be too late for them to be of Any Uſe to him. *Conſiderate* Chriſtians *wait* continually *for the coming of our Lord Jeſus Chriſt,* 1 Cor. i. 7; *Denying ungodlineſs and worldly luſts ; living ſoberly, righteouſly, and godly in this preſent world ; looking for that bleſſed Hope, and the glorious Appearance of the Great God, and of our Saviour Jeſus Chriſt.* Thus did the *Apoſtles themſelves* ; and to This did they continually exhort *Others,* as in the Text ; *Brethren,* ſaith St *Paul, be Followers together of Me, and mark them which walk ſo, as ye have us for an example ;——For* Our *Converſation is in Heaven, from whence alſo we look for the Saviour, the Lord Jeſus Chriſt.*

MORE

MORE *particularly.* Having *our converfation in Heaven,* as it fignifies *meditating* S E R M. upon the *Prefence and Attributes of* God, will naturally be upon our Minds a *ftrong* LXXXIV. *Motive* and a *conftant Affiftance,* to *Purity* and *Holinefs* of Life. For if hereafter we fhall therefore *be like him,* becaufe *we fhall fee him as he is;* at prefent alfo in propor- tion we cannot but imitate him, if by ferious *meditation* we accuftom ourfelves to live *as Seeing him who is invifible.* And therefore St *John* rightly infers, 1 *Joh.* iii. 3; *Every man that hath This Hope in him, purifies himfelf even as he is pure.*

AGAIN: *Converfing in Heaven,* as it fignifies *meditating* on the Company by whom that region of Happinefs is poffeft; *an innumerable Company of Angels, and the Spirits of juft men made perfeĉt,* living together in compleat and uninterrupted Love; and *Jefus* himfelf, *the Mediator of the New Covenant,* who *loved us, and gave himfelf for us* All: under *This* View, it cannot but be a powerful Argument perpetually upon our Minds, to live *here* alfo, as a preparative to That more perfeĉt State, in mutual *Love, Forbear- ance, and univerfal Charity.*

Laftly, As it fignifies *meditating* on the *Greatnefs and Duration of the* Happinefs itfelf, which we fhall There enjoy; it is the great Security, to preferve us from being overcome at any time by the Temptations of worldly *Profperity,* or by the Fears of Temporal *Adverfity.* *I reckon,* faith St *Paul, that the Sufferings of this prefent world,* Rom. viii. 18. *are not worthy to be compared with the glory which fhall be revealed in us.* *For which caufe we faint not; but though our outward man perifh, yet the inward man is renewed day by day.* *For our light affliĉtion which is but for a moment, worketh for us a far more exceeding and eternal weight of glory.* *While we look not at the things which are feen, but at the things which are not feen; for the things which are feen, are temporal; but the things which are not feen, are eternal;* 2 Cor. iv. 16. By this Faith the Martyrs of old *fuffered themfelves to be* tortured, *not accepting deliverance, that they might obtain a better Refur- reĉtion;* Heb. xi. 35. By This Faith, *Mofes chofe rather to fuffer affliĉtion with the people of God, than to injoy the Pleafures of Sin for a Seafon; efteeming the reproach of Chrift greater Riches than the Treafures in Egypt; for he had refpeĉt unto the recompenfe of Reward;* ver. 25, 26. And our Saviour himfelf; ch. xii. 2; *for the Joy that was fet before him, endured the crofs, defpifing the Shame, and is fet down at the right hand of the Throne of God.* But

2dly, AND to Conclude. If we underftand the Phrafe, *having our Converfation in Heaven,* to fignify in the *latter* Senfe (according to the moft *ftriĉt* and proper Mean- ing of the words in the Original,) *having our* Citizenfhip, our Home, our proper Coun- try or Habitation in Heaven, and confequently *looking upon ourfelves as Members and Subjeĉts of That City or Kingdom which is above:* If we confider it under *This* View, the obvious Inference from hence is, that then we ought conftantly to endeavour to obey the *Laws of That* Kingdom, that is, the Commandments of God; leaft if, du- ring our Pilgrimage here in a *foreign* Country, we live contrary to the Laws of Heaven, we be hereafter rejeĉted at our return, and refufed admittance into our *own* City: *Rev.* xxii. 14; *Bleffed are they that do his commandments, that they may have Right to the Tree of Life, and may enter in through the Gates into the City; For without, are dogs and forcerers, and whoremongers and murderers and Idolaters, and whofoever loveth and maketh a Lie.* For *there fhall in no wife enter into it any thing that defileth; neither whatfoever worketh Abomination, or maketh a Lie.* And the fame thing is expreffed by our Saviour in the Gofpel; *Luc.* xiii. 26. When *ye begin to fay, Lord, open unto us; for——we have eaten and drunk in thy prefence, and thou haft taught in our Streets; he fhall fay, I know you not whence you are; depart from me, all ye Workers of Iniquity.* The Laws of our heavenly Country, and the Cuftoms of a vicious World, are con- trary to each other, *Rom.* vii. 22; *I delight in the Law of God after the inward man;*

2

but

SERM. *but I fee another Law in my Members, warring againft the Law of my mind: For the*
LXXXIV. *Flefh lufteth againft the Spirit, and the Spirit againft the Flefh; and Thefe are contrary*
the One to the Other, Gal. v. 17. This being the Cafe; it follows therefore, as St
James concludes, ch. iv. 4; that *whofoever will be a Friend of the World*, of the *finful*
and *debauched*, of the *vicious* and *corrupt* World, muft needs be *an Enemy of God:*
Becaufe the Carnal mind is enmity againft God; for it is not fubject to the Law of God,
neither indeed can be; Rom. viii. 7. For This reafon the Apoftle *befeeches us*, as being *Strangers and Pilgrims* here, *to abftain from flefhly Lufts, which* war *againft the Soul;*
that is, which unfit us for our heavenly Country, the habitation of everlafting Righteoufnefs and Peace; 1 *Pet.* ii. 11: and exhorts us, *not to be conformed to This World;*
Rom. xii. 2; but *to be transformed by the renewing of our Mind; that is, to prefs for-*
ward towards the Mark of the Prize of our High Calling, forgetting thofe things which
are behind: After the example of the Patriarchs, *Heb.* xi. 15; who *truly if they had*
been mindful of That Country from whence they came out, they might have had opportu-
nity to have returned; But now they defire a better Country, that is, an Heavenly. Where,
if *We* alfo have our converfation *Now*, we fhall together with *them* be glorified likewife
hereafter.

SERMON

SERMON LXXXV.

Of the Spiritual Nature of the GOSPEL.

[*Preached on Whitsunday.*]

2 COR. III. 17, 18.

Now the Lord is That Spirit; and where the Spirit of the Lord is, there is Liberty; But we all with open face, beholding as in a glass the Glory of the Lord, are changed into the same Image, from glory to glory, even as by the Spirit of the Lord.

THE Holy Ghost having been poured forth upon the Apostles at Pentecost in so very singular and plentiful a manner, as that, *before* that time, 'tis said, comparatively, *not to have been given at all*; Joh. vii. 39; and Those who were not yet acquainted with *That* day's Miracle, are represented as not having *heard* so much as whether *there* was *any Holy Ghost*, Acts xix. 2; that is, whether there had *yet* been *any* such *plentiful Effusion* of it, as the Prophets had foretold: For This reason, St *Paul* in the 8*th* verse of this chapter, whereof my Text is the Conclusion, elegantly stiles *the Gospel*, by way of Eminence, the *Ministration of the* Spirit. And from That consideration, through the *whole* chapter, he magnifies the *Doctrine of Christ*, as being more clear and plain, more powerful and efficacious, more illustrious and glorious, than the *Law of Moses*. Ver. 3; *Ye are*, saith he, *the epistle of Christ, ministred by Us, written not with ink, but with the* Spirit *of the living God; not in tables of stone, but in the fleshly tables of the heart:* His meaning is, The Power and Efficacy of the *Gospel*, is as much greater than that of the *Law*, as can be expressed by *comparing* that which is written in a *Book*, with that which is imprinted inwardly in the very *Heart and Soul itself*. The same Argument he pursues; ver. 6; *God hath made us able ministers of the New Testament, not of the letter, but of the* Spirit; *for the letter killeth, but the Spirit, giveth life*; That is, The Gospel gives us those *spiritual* precepts whereof the *legal* Ordinances were but *types and shadows*; (that is the meaning of their being called the *letter* or *dead letter*;) and teaches us the way to *eternal life*, whereas the rigour of the Law could end only in mens *condemnation*. And from hence he proceeds to *magnify* the glorious manifestation of the *Gospel*, by *comparing* it with the Glory that shined in *Moses*'s countenance; which, though so bright that the children of *Israel* could not stedfastly behold it, yet was but temporary and transient, and only a type or figure of that permanent glory of the Gospel, which was to continue for ever; ver. 7; *If the ministration of* Death, *written and engraven in stones, was glorious, so that the children of Israel could not stedfastly behold the face of Moses for the glory of his countenance, which glory was to be done away; How shall not the ministration of the* Spirit *be rather glorious? For if the ministration of* condemnation *be glory, much*

SERM. *more doth the ministration of* righteousness, (of *justification,* it should be rendred,) *exceed*
LXXXV. *in glory;——For if That which is done away was glorious, much more That which remaineth* (That which is perpetual) *is glorious.* And hereupon he takes occasion elegantly to describe the Blindness of the *Jews* after our Saviour's time, in not seeing
through the types and figures and imperfect notices of the Old Testament; he describes
it elegantly, by comparing it to the *Veil* which *Moses* put upon his Face to conceal
the Brightness of it: Ver. xiv; *Their Minds* (saith he) *were blinded: For until This
day remaineth the same Veil untaken away, in the reading of the Old Testament; which
Veil is done away in Christ: But even unto This day, when Moses is read, the Veil is
upon their Heart. Nevertheless, when it shall turn to the Lord,* (that is, when they
shall believe in Christ,) *the Veil shall be taken away.* And then he sums up and concludes his whole Discourse, in the words of the Text: *Now the Lord* (says he) *is That
Spirit; and where the Spirit of the Lord is, there is Liberty. But we all with open face,
beholding as in a glass the glory of the Lord, are changed into the same Image, from glory
to glory, even as by the Spirit of the Lord.* The words are in themselves somewhat
difficult, and have in them several phrases very different from our present manner of
expressing things: But the *general* design of them appears in some measure, from the
brief explication now given of the foregoing part of the chapter, whereby they are
introduced; and I shall now proceed to explain them more *particularly,* by considering
distinctly the several expressions in the Order they lie.

THE *Lord,* says the Apostle, is *That Spirit.* That is, *Christ,* the *Gospel* or *Doctrine* of Christ, is *That Spirit* I have been speaking of in this whole Discourse; That
Spirit, or *end and design* of the Law, which giveth *life,* or shows men the way to
justification; in opposition to the *dead letter* and to the *rigour* of the law, which leads
only to *condemnation:* That *Spirit* or final *intent* of the law, which is to continue *for
ever,* in opposition to those mere *types and shadows,* which were soon *to be done away:*
That *Spirit* or full *Meaning and signification* of the law, which is opposed to the *Veil
of ignorance* and *partial understanding* of it.

THE *Lord, is that Spirit:* The word, *Lord,* is used here to signify the *Gospel* or
Doctrine of Christ, by the same figure of speaking, as St *Paul* elsewhere uses, when
he advises Christians to marry *only* in *the Lord,* that is, to *Christians,* to such only as
have *received the Gospel;* and when he speaks of the *dead in Christ; i. e.* of those who
died in the profession and practice of the true Religion; and commands us *to put on
Christ, i. e.* to obey his Doctrine.

THE phrase, That *Spirit,* is made use of to signify the *True Meaning,* and *final
Intent* of the Law; because the opposite words, *Flesh* and *Letter,* signify on the con-
trary the mere *Shadow or Appearance* of a thing, without the *real Substance* and *true
Intention.* Thus *Joh.* vi. 63; *It is the* Spirit, saith our Saviour, *that quickneth, the
Flesh profiteth nothing; The words that I speak unto you, they are Spirit and they are
Life.* Again, ver. 6; of This chapter in which the Text is, *Able ministers of the New
Testament, not of the Letter, but of the* Spirit: And *Rom.* vii. 6; *That we should serve
in Newness of* Spirit, *and not in the oldness of the* Letter: The meaning of which is explained; ch. ii. 29; *He is a Jew, which is one* inwardly, *and circumcision is that of the
Heart, in the* Spirit, *and not in the* Letter, *whose praise is not of Men, but of God.* As
therefore the Law of *Moses,* upon account of its many ritual observances, is by a very
significant Figure, in several places of St *Paul's* epistles, called *Flesh;* so here on the contrary, concerning the *Gospel* of Christ, which was the end of those types, it is with no
less propriety and significancy affirmed, that *the Lord is that Spirit.*

IT follows, *And where the Spirit of the Lord is, there is Liberty: Liberty,* in the
first place, from that *Veil* of *ignorance and obscurity,* which remained upon the *Hearts,*
and perplexed the *Understandings* of the unbelieving *Jews,* when the Old Testament

I

was

was read to them: In oppofition to which, the Apoftle argues, ver. 12 of this chap- S E R M.
ter, that We *ufe great* plainnefs *of Speech, and not as Mofes which put a Veil over his* LXXXV
Face; And upon this account he ftiles the Gofpel, *the Manifeftation of the Truth,*
ch. iv. 2 ; and *the Spirit of* Wifdom and Revelation; *Eph.* i. 17.

THEN, in the next place, *Liberty* from the bondage of that *yoke* of Ceremonies,
which neither our Fathers nor We, fays St. *Peter, were able to bear*; Acts x. 15. Concerning which numerous and burdenfome rites, St *Paul* alfo is to be underftood, when
he rejoices that we *are now delivered from the law*; Rom. vii. 6; and compares the
Jews, who were under thefe legal Obligations, to Servants or to Children yet under
Age, *Gal.* iv. 3 ; and exhorts thofe, who by embracing the Gofpel were difcharged from
that Law, to *ftand faft in the* Liberty *wherewith Chrift had made them free, and not to
be intangled again with the yoke of bondage*; ch. v. 1. Which liberty neverthelefs, left
any man fhould fo mifinterpret, as to think himfelf difcharged thereby from *moral* as
well as *ritual* obligations, (which is the abfurd Ufe Some in modern times have made
of thefe Texts,) he takes care to add a very exprefs caution; ver. 13; *Brethren, ye*
have *indeed been called unto Liberty ; only ufe not Liberty for an occafion to the Flefh:*
That is; Do not, under pretence of being fet free from the *Mofaic Obfervations,* run
into *immoralities,* which are Breaches of God's everlafting Law: And St *Peter* in like
manner; 1 *Pet.* ii. 16; *As free, yet not ufing your Liberty for a cloke of malicioufnefs;*
(or, *as an Excufe for Immoralities,) but as the Servants of God.*

ADD to This, that by the *Liberty* which the Text affirms *is* always *There, where is
the Spirit of the Lord; i. e.* where-ever the Gofpel prevails in Faith and Practice ; is
meant alfo a Liberty from that *Fear* and *Terrour,* which under the Law, could not but
make men (as the Apoftle to the *Hebrews* expreffes it) *all their life-time fubject to bondage*; till they were affured of Pardon by the reconciliation of Chrift, for fuch *things
from which they could not be juftified by the law of Mofes.* In This fenfe it is, that St
James ufes the word, when he ftiles the Gofpel *the perfect Law of Liberty*; Jam. i. 25.
And by this is eafy to be underftood That otherwife difficult expreffion of St *Paul*; Rom.
viii. 15; *Ye have not received the Spirit of bondage again to Fear, but ye have received
the Spirit of Adoption, whereby we cry, Abba, Father*; The meaning is, we have Now,
through the reconciliation of Chrift, free Accefs to God, not as Servants to a ftrict Mafter,
but as Sons to a merciful and compaffionate Father. Which reconciliation itfelf, ought
neverthelefs to be always carefully fo underftood, not as if God was in Himfelf fevere
and cruel *before* the interpofition of Chrift; but that God, of his own original and eternal Goodnefs, freely provided for us That reconciliation *through* Chrift, which his
infinite Wifdom judged to be the propereft Method of extending his Compaffion to
us.

Laftly, *where the Spirit of the Lord is, there is* Liberty; not only from the Terrour
of *paft* Sins, through the Redemption of Chrift; but alfo Liberty from the *Power and
Dominion* of Sin for the time to come, through the affiftance of his Spirit. In This
fenfe our Saviour ufes the word; St *Joh.* viii. 36; *If the Son* (fays he) *fhall make you
free, ye fhall be free indeed; free,* in oppofition to what is expreffed in the 34*th* verfe,
Servants *of Sin.* St *Paul* in like manner; Rom. viii. 2 ; *The Law of the Spirit of Life
in Chrift Jefus, hath made me* free *from the Law of Sin and Death*; free from the
Slavery and Dominion of Wickednefs; *delivered from the bondage of corruption, into
the glorious liberty of the children of God.*

THE words next following in the Text, But *we all with open Face,* are not to
be underftood by way of *oppofition* to what went before ; For *That* takes away the
Clearnefs of the Senfe : But the Connexion is, by way of explication of, or Inference
from, the words immediately foregoing : *Where the Spirit of the Lord is,* where the
Gofpel prevails effectually, *There is Liberty* ; And *We all,* or, *And* therefore *we all,*

all

SERM.
LXXXV.
all true Chriſtians, do *with open Face*, not thro' an *obſcure Veil* as the *Jews*, but with *open face behold the glory of the Lord.*

THE phraſe, *with open Face*, ſignifies as much as, *clearly, plainly*, and *diſtinctly*; not in *types* and *ſhadows*, not in *obſcure glympſes* and *faint repreſentations*, not in *remote hints* and *diſtant proſpects*; but with a *full and direct* view, an immediate intuition as of the *Subſtance* and *reality* of things *preſent* and *actually before us.* We behold the myſtery of God in Chriſt, *not* as the children of *Iſrael* ſaw the brightneſs of *Moſes*'s countenance *thro' the Veil*, (which is what the Apoſtle here alludes to;) *but* with *open face*, as *Moſes himſelf* is deſcribed to have ſeen the Lord: *Exod.* xxxiii. 11; *The Lord ſpake unto Moſes face to face, as a Man ſpeaketh unto his Friend*: And *Num.* xii. 8; *With Him will I ſpeak mouth to mouth, even apparently, and not in dark ſpeeches; and the ſimilitude of the Lord ſhall he behold.* Thus to Us *Chriſtians*, the Myſtery of God's reconciliation to Sinners by the Method of the Goſpel, *the Riches of the glory of this myſtery* (as St *Paul* ſtiles it,) *Col.* i. 27; *even the myſtery which had been hid from Ages and from Generations; is now made* plain and *manifeſt*; ſo plain and open, as to be called by way of Eminence, 2 *Cor.* iv. 2; *The* Manifeſtation *of the Truth.*

WE *all, with open Face, beholding* the Glory of the Lord: That theſe words, the *Glory of the Lord*, are to be underſtood, not in the literal, but in a figurative ſenſe, to ſignify the *clear and* glorious *manifeſtation of the Will of God by the Goſpel*; is evident, as from the whole connexion of the Apoſtle's diſcourſe in *this* place, ſo from the many *other* paſſages of Scripture, wherein the Goſpel is ſtiled in like manner *the riches of God's Glory, Rom.* ix. 23; *the riches of the* Glory *of this myſtery*, Col. i. 27. *the* Glory *as of the only-begotten of the Father, full of Grace and Truth*, Joh. i. 14. *the Light of the* glorious *Goſpel of Chriſt, who is the Image of God*, 2 Cor. iv. 4. and ver. 6; *the Light of the Knowledge of the* Glory *of God, ſhining in our Heart.* The words of that whole verſe, are very remarkable; *God, who commanded the Light to ſhine out of Darkneſs*, (that is, who manifeſted his Glory *originally* in the *firſt Creation* of Things) the ſame God *hath ſhined in our hearts* (has manifeſted his Glory the *ſecond* time no leſs conſpicuouſly in our *redemption*;) *hath ſhined in our hearts, to give the Light of the Knowledge of the Glory of God, in the Face of Jeſus Chriſt.* And theſe two laſt expreſſions, *Chriſt's* being the Image *of God*, and the *Light of the Knowledge of God's Glory, ſhining upon us in the* Face (or in the *Perſon*) of *Chriſt*; open to us the Ground and Meaning, of that *Similitude* the Apoſtle interpoſes in this part of the Text,

Beholding, as in a Glaſs, *the Glory of the Lord.* That which he hereby intended to expreſs, is, that in *Chriſt*, who is the *Image of the inviſible God*, and the *Great Revealer of his Will*, we *clearly and plainly* behold the *whole pleaſure of God towards us.* For, *the Father, no man hath ſeen at any time; no man* hath *ſeen, nor* can *ſee*; but *the only-begotten Son, which is in his Boſom*, He *has declared him*; and has declared him *ſo plainly*, that *he who has ſeen* me, ſaith our Saviour, *has ſeen the* Father, *Joh.* xiv. 9. There is a phraſe, very *like* to This in the Text, uſed in a *contrary* ſenſe by the ſame Apoſtle, in his former Epiſtle to the *Corinthians*, ch. xiii. 12. Now (ſays he) *we ſee through a glaſs darkly, but* Then *face to face.* In which paſſage, *ſeeing through a* glaſs, ſignifies ſeeing *darkly* or *obſcurely*, in *oppoſition* to beholding *plainly, face to face*: But here in the Text, the phraſe ſignifies on the contrary, ſeeing *clearly or plainly*; and is the very *ſame* as, *beholding face to face: We all with open face, beholding as in a* glaſs *the Glory of the Lord.* The words in the Original, are in Both places more expreſſive, than in the Tranſlation; and ſhow plainly the Reaſon of this different Signification. In *one* place, the word, which we render, *glaſs*, ſignifies a

per ſpective-

perfpective-Glafs; which brings diftant things into the reach indeed of our Sight, but S E R M. ftill very *obfcurely, imperfectly, and indiftinctly*; and does therefore very aptly and by LXXXV. a moft proper fimilitude exprefs That View of a future ftate, which we have by Faith and not by Sight. But now in this *other* paffage in the Text, the word which we render, *glafs*, fignifies a *Mirrour* or *Looking-glafs*, which on the contrary reprefents things *plainly and diftinctly, face to face*; and therefore it no lefs aptly reprefents that clear *Light of the Knowledge of the Glory* and Will *of God*, which *fhines to us* (faith the Apoftle) *in the* Face *of Jefus Chrift. We all, with open face, beholding as in a* glafs *the glory of the Lord.*

I T follows, *Are changed into the fame Image*: The meaning is, As *Chrift* is, by nature, the perfect *Image* of God; fo *We*, by communication of *Light* and *Knowledge* from him, and by the practice of *Righteoufnefs* and true *Holinefs*, in Obedience *to* him and Imitation *of* him, are transformed *into the fame Image.* As *Chrift* is, by nature, the *Son of God*; fo *We*, by *Adoption* and by the *Fruits of his* Spirit *dwelling in us*, have *this Love beftowed upon us*, that *We* alfo, *fhould be called the Sons of God.* For *of his Fulnefs have we all received, and grace for grace*, Joh. i. 16. That is, Through the *Fulnefs* of thofe Divine Perfections, and of that *Grace* which was conferred upon *Him* without meafure; God has communicated to *Us* a *proportionable* Fulnefs of Divine Knowledge and Virtue, according to *our* capacities; and *Grace*, that is, Mercy and Favour, *according to the meafure of the Gift of Chrift.*

B U T more particularly; Being *changed into the fame* Image *with Chrift*, fignifies, Two things; *Firft*, being made like to him in *Holinefs here*; and *Secondly*, being made like him in *Glory hereafter. Firft*, being *changed into the fame* Image *with Chrift*, fignifies, being made like to him in *Holinefs here.* The *Image of God* in the mind of *Man*, is *Virtue and true Righteoufnefs*; and therefore, when the Scripture fpeaks of mens reforming from Vice, or improving in Virtue; it is a very lively defcription of the Excellency of their State, to exprefs it by their being transformed into the *Image* of God, or being made after his *Similitude or Likenefs.* Thus the Pfalmift; *As for me*, faith he, *I will behold thy prefence in righteoufnefs; and when I awake up after thy* Likenefs, *I fhall be fatisfied with it*, Pf. xvii. 16. And the Apoftle St *Paul*, Rom. viii. 29; *Whom he did foreknow, he alfo did predeftinate, to be conformed to the* Image *of his Son, that he might be the firft-born among many brethren.* That God's *predeftinating men to be conformed to the Image of his Son*, does not here fignify, decreeing concerning the *Perfons*, what they neceffarily fhould *do*; but decreeing concerning the *conditions*, what he would have *them do*; is evident from the parallel place, *Eph.* ii. 10, where the fame Apoftle tells us what it was, not the *perfons*, but the *good works*, which *God* before ordained, *that we fhould walk in them.* Again, *Eph.* iv. 23, Exhorting men to the practice of Virtue, he *Thus* expreffes himfelf; *Be ye renewed* (fays he) *in the Spirit of your Mind*, —— after God, (after the example and fimilitude of God,) ——*in Righteoufnefs and true Holinefs; After* the *Image* of Him that created you; as it is, *Col.* iii. 10. Transformed *by the renewing of your Mind*; as he expreffes it, *Rom.* xii. 2.

O U R Saviour himfelf in his Prayer, delivering the fame Notion, fpeaks after the following manner, *Joh.* xvii. 22; *The Glory which thou gaveft Me, I have given Them, that They may be One even as We are One*: His Meaning is the fame as That in the Text, *We beholding as in a glafs the Glory of the Lord*, (the *Light of the* Knowledge *of the Glory of God in the face of Jefus Chrift*, as it is explained immediately after,) *are changed into the fame* Image, are made partakers of *his Glory*, are *made* (as St *Paul* elfewhere fpeaks) *the* righteoufnefs *of God in Him.* This is the *firft* fignification of the phrafe, our being made like to Chrift in works of *righteoufnefs here.*

SERM.
LXXXV.
Col. iii. 4.
Phil. iii. 21.

2*dly*, BEING *changed into the same* Image *with Chrift*, fignifies alfo being made like him in *Glory hereafter.* Thus 1 *Cor.* xv. 49; *As we have born the* Image *of the Earthy, we fhall alfo bear the* Image *of the Heavenly: For, when Chrift who is our life fhall appear, then fhall We alfo appear with him in glory:* And *He fhall change* this our *vile Body, that it may be fafhioned* like *unto his glorious body, according to that* mighty *working, whereby he is able even to fubdue all things unto himfelf.* St *John* adds *another particular reafon, why* we fhall in this fenfe be changed into the fame Image with Chrift; 1 *Joh.* iii. 2: *We know, that when he fhall appear, we fhall be like him;* For, fays he, *we fhall fee him as he is:* The words are a perfect Explication of thofe in the Text; *We all with open face* beholding *the glory of the Lord, are changed into the fame Image.*

THE *Next* expreffion, *from Glory to Glory,* may be underftood to fignify the manner *of* Communication of *Chrift's* Glory to *Us,* whether in the way of *Righteoufnefs* here, or of *Happinefs* hereafter. *We beholding the Glory of the Lord, are changed into the fame Image* from Glory to Glory; that is, by Communication of *Glory* to Us, from His *Glory:* According to that Expreffion of our Saviour, before cited, *Joh.* xvii. 22: *The Glory which thou gaveft Me, I have given Them;* and that of the Evangelift, *Of his Fulnefs have we all received* Fulnefs, *and Grace for* (or *from*) His *Grace.*

BUT the *more* natural and obvious Meaning of the words, *from Glory to Glory,* is, from *one degree of Glory to another:* We *are changed into the fame Image* from Glory to Glory: That is, from our Likenefs to Chrift in works of Righteoufnefs and true Holinefs *here,* we fhall improve and go forward unto a further and more glorious Likenefs to him in the Enjoyment of eternal Happinefs *hereafter.* And this is the *more* probable to be the true Senfe of the words, becaufe it is the Nature or Idiom of the *Jewifh* language, to exprefs any improvement in *degree,* by a *repetition* of the fame word. Thus *Pf.* lxxxiv. 7; *They fhall go* from ftrength to ftrength; that is, from one degree of ftrength to another: And *Rom.* i. 17; *In the Gofpel, the Righteoufnefs of God,* (or the *Mercy of God,) is revealed* from Faith to Faith; that is, from one degree of Faith to another; from one degree of Clearnefs of revelation, to another; from a lefs clear difpenfation under the *Law,* to a clearer one under the *Gofpel.* And Thus therefore in the Text likewife, *from Glory to Glory,* may well be underftood to fignify, *from one degree of Glory to another;* from a *lefs* degree *here,* to a *greater* and more perfect degree *hereafter.*

Laftly, THE Apoftle concludes the Whole, with the addition of thefe words, *even as by the* Spirit *of the Lord.* The meaning of which is, that all thefe things he had hitherto been difcourfing upon, were accomplifhed in fuch a *manner,* in fo wife, fo effectual, fo glorious a manner, as became the Dignity of the Great Agent, and were worthy the Operation of the *Spirit of God.* The *clear revealing* the Gofpel, to be the *Spirit* and End of the Law: The *Liberty* procured men by this merciful Difpenfation, from the Burden and from the Terror of the Law; from the Guilt of paft Sin by Pardon, which is *Juftification;* and from the Dominion of Sin for the time to come, which is *Sanctification:* The full and diftinct *Manifeftation* of the glorious *Purpofe* of God in Chrift, of bringing men through him to everlafting Salvation: The *Communication* of this Glory of *Chrift* to *Us,* by our being *conformed* to *his Image* in *Righteoufnefs here,* and in *Glory hereafter:* All Thefe, are the Fruits of that *One and the fame Spirit,* which *worketh all in all,* and *diftributeth Gifts to every man feverally according to the Will of God: That* Spirit, which infpired the Predictions of the Prophets, which worked Miracles by the Apoftles, which fpread the Gofpel by the Gift of Tongues, which rejoices when men embrace the Doctrine of Chrift, and affifts them in practifing it, and fupports them in fuffering for it, and brings them finally unto Glory by it. As St *Paul* excellently argues, *Rom.* viii. 10, 11; *If Chrift be in you,*

the

the Body is dead, because of Sin; but the Spirit is Life, because of Righteousness, And S E R M·
if the Spirit of him that raised up Jesus from the Dead, dwell in you; he that raised LXXXV·
up Christ from the Dead, shall also quicken your mortal bodies, by his Spirit that dwelleth
in you.

THE Application of what has been said, is: *First*, from the true Explication of
these words, *The Lord is That Spirit*, we may take occasion to observe, that in all
other places likewise of St *Paul's* Epistles, where the word, *Spirit*, is opposed to,
The letter or *the Dead letter*, to *Flesh* or *carnal Ordinances*; it always signifies the
Gospel, or the *spiritual* and *moral* Precepts of Christ, in opposition to the *Ceremonies*
of the Law of *Moses*. Which Observation is of great Use, against those who would
make Religion to consist, not in the Practice of Virtue and true Righteousness, but in
unintelligible, mystical and enthusiastick Notions.

Secondly, FROM the right understanding of these next words, *Where the Spirit of
the Lord is, there is Liberty*; we may learn the true interpretation of those *many*
passages, wherein the Apostle contends earnestly for the *Liberty* of Christians, or for
their being *free from the Law*. In all which places, his Meaning is not, (as some in
Modern times have most unreasonably argued,) that Christians are discharged from
any part of the Obligation of the *moral* Law, or that the Gospel-dispensation (as
some Enthusiasts have imagined) sets men *above* the confinements of common Morality : But his plain Meaning, is This only ; that by the abolition of *Ceremonies*, we
are discharged from the *Burden* of the Law; By the *Pardon* declared in Christ to
Penitents, we are delivered from the *Terror and Severity* of the Law; and by the
Assistance of his *Grace* we are made, not *free* to *Sin*, but *free* from *Sin*, for the time
to come.

Thirdly, IF we now *with open face behold the glory of the Lord*, *i.e.* understand
his Will *clearly and distinctly*, not in types and shadows; then ought we above all
things to endeavour to walk as *children of Light*, as becometh those who have such
clear Knowledge of their Duty, in all Holiness and righteous Conversation.

Fourthly, IF by *this means we are changed into the same Image, from Glory to
Glory, i. e.* from a Likeness with Christ here, to a Likeness with him hereafter ;
then ought we always to remember, that by no other way can we arrive at a conformity with Christ in *Glory*, but by a conformity with him first in *Righteousness
and true Holiness*.

Lastly, IF all this be worked in us *as by the Spirit of the Lord*; if all these Benefits be the Operation of that One and the same Spirit, which always works with
us in proportion to our own Endeavours, and will not dwell in a Soul that is polluted
with Sin : Then ought we above all things to take heed, lest by any vicious practice
we quench and grieve this good Spirit of God, and drive him from us, and thereby
be found to have done despite unto the Spirit of Grace.

SERMON

SERMON LXXXVI.

Of the Sin againſt the HOLY GHOST.

[Preached on Whitſunday.]

MATT. XII. 31, 32.

Wherefore I ſay unto you, All manner of Sin and Blaſphemy ſhall be for-
given unto men ; But the Blaſphemy againſt the Holy Ghoſt ſhall not
be forgiven unto men : And whoſoever ſpeaketh a Word againſt the
Son of Man, it ſhall be forgiven him ; but whoſoever ſpeaketh againſt
the Holy Ghoſt, it ſhall not be forgiven him neither in this World,
neither in the World to come.

SERM.
LXXXVI.

WE are met together This day, thankfully to commemorate the greateſt and
moſt important Gift, that was ever ſent down from Heaven upon the Sons of
Men ; the Gift of the Holy Ghoſt at Pentecoſt ; that plentiful Effuſion of
the Holy Spirit, which was the Accompliſhment both of the Predictions of all the *An-*
tient Prophets, and of all the *later* Promiſes made by our Saviour to his Diſciples ; that
Gift of Tongues, which was ſo peculiarly proper and neceſſary a *Means* to the great
End for which it was deſigned, and the *Effects* whereof have been of ſuch univerſal
Extent over the Face of the whole Earth. The Goſpel of *Chriſt*, was not, like the
Religion of *Moſes*, to be confined to One Nation or People ; but to be preached, as the
general Doctrine of Salvation, to All Mankind : And the Gift of Tongues, wherewith
the firſt Preachers of it were indued, was equally both a *neceſſary Means* to enable them
to preach to all Nations, and a *ſtrong Proof* of the Truth of that Doctrine which they
were ſo miraculouſly enabled to ſpread. 'Twas a *neceſſary Means*, without which the
Goſpel could by no labour whatſoever ; no, not by the moſt indefatigable Induſtry, in
compaſſing Sea and Land to make a Proſelyte ; have in the Courſe of *many Ages* been
propagated thro' ſo many different and ſo remote Countries, as by This means it was
ſpread in the ſpace of *not many years*. And at the ſame Time that it ſo *ſwiftly* conveyed the *Knowledge* of the Goſpel, 'twas likewiſe a *ſtrong Proof* of the *Truth* of the
Doctrine itſelf, both upon account of the *Greatneſs* of the Miracle in its own Nature,
and the *Clearneſs* of the Evidence wherewith the Miracle was ſet forth. The *Greatneſs*
of the Miracle in its own Nature, conſiſted in This ; that it was worked upon *many*
Perſons, at one and the ſame Time ; that it was a producing in them ſuch an Effect, as
was equivalent to the Reſult of a *long Habit* ; and that it was not a ſhort and tranſitory
Effect, but of a *permanent Duration* ; and, in its *whole Continuance*, equally miraculous, as in the firſt Operation. Upon the whole therefore, 'twas ſuch a Miracle in all

its

4

its Circumſtances, as there had been no Example of any like it before; and probably referred to by our Saviour in that Promiſe, *Joh.* xiv. 12; *He that believeth on me; the works that I do, ſhall he do alſo, and greater Works than theſe ſhall he do.* The *Clear-neſs of the Evidence* wherewith the Miracle was ſet forth, conſiſted in This; that Matters were ſo diſpoſed by the Wiſdom of Providence, that the bittereſt Enemies of the Apoſtles, did themſelves, by their own Teſtimony, remove the only Objections that could be brought againſt it. For, all that could poſſibly be alledged againſt the Truth of the Miracle, was, either that the New Tongues wherewith the Apoſtles began to ſpeak, were *not real languages*; or, if they were, that then the Apoſtles, who ſpake them, had *ſtudied* and *been taught* thoſe *Languages* before. But now the former of theſe Suſpicions, was removed by the *Strangers* then preſent; and the latter was taken off, by the *Inhabitants of Jeruſalem* themſelves. The *Strangers* then preſent, who underſtood the Languages, took off that fooliſh Objection, *Acts* ii. 13. that the Apoſtles were *full of new Wine*; for they *heard* and underſtood them *ſpeaking in their* own *Tongues, the wonderful Works of God,* ver. 11. And the *Inhabitants of Jeruſalem* themſelves, removed the *other* Suſpicion, of their having been *taught* the Languages; for they knew them to be illiterate men, and ſaid, *Are not all theſe, that ſpeak Galileans?* ver. 7; juſt as they had formerly ſaid concerning Jeſus himſelf; *How knoweth this man letters, having never learned?* Joh. vii. 14: And, *whence has this man theſe things?* —— *Is not this the Carpenter, and Son of Mary? the Brother of James and Joſes and Juda and Simon? and are not his Siſters here with us?* St Mar. vi. 2. Both the *Strangers* therefore, and the *Inhabitants of Jeruſalem* themſelves, bore Teſtimony to the Truth of the Miracle, even at the ſame Time and with the ſame Arguments by which they oppoſed it; And they were of all Others the *beſt* and moſt *competent* Witneſſes, for that *very* Reaſon, becauſe they were *prejudiced* againſt the *Thing,* and *Enemies* to the *Men.* Beſides all which; the Miracle itſelf (as I before obſerved) was *permanent* in its *Continuance,* as well as *publick* in the *manner* of its being worked: So that in all reſpects, it was both the *Greateſt* in the *Nature* of the *Thing itſelf,* and the *Cleareſt* in the *Evidence* of its being *really performed*; that can poſſibly be imagined. To *Us* indeed, who live at This Diſtance of Time, the Evidence of a Fact done ſo many Ages ſince, cannot be ſo perfectly and entirely clear, as to thoſe who were themſelves Eye-Witneſſes and Ear-Witneſſes of it. But if there *are* Matters of Fact ſo atteſted, even at much *greater* Diſtances of Time, as that no reaſonable Perſon can in the leaſt queſtion the Truth of them; and *This,* of all Other diſtant Facts that are recorded in any Hiſtory, has the greateſt and moſt remarkable Atteſtations; the Evidence of it even to *Us,* can with as little Reaſon be rejected, as that which was offered to thoſe very Perſons who lived at the Time. Nay, in *ſome* reſpects, we may ſeem even to have the *Advantage* over them, in Point of Certainty of our not being deceived. For, beſides that we are Now free, from many of thoſe inveterate Prejudices, which both *Jews* and *Gentiles* then laboured under; and which we cannot aſſure ourſelves we ſhould leſs obſtinately have adhered to, than They did; We have moreover, what They at that Time could not have; We have the concurrent *Examination* of *many Ages,* and the Advantage of conſidering and comparing the *Objections of Adverſaries* on all Sides; We have the *additional* Proofs, ariſing from the *continued Effects* of this miraculous Power, in different Times and Places; We have ſeen the Truth of the Apoſtles Doctrine confirmed, by the accompliſhment of ſeveral Prophecies; by the Deſtruction of *Jeruſalem*; by the final ſcattering of the whole Nation of the *Jews*; by the incredible Succeſs, and univerſal Propagation of the Goſpel, over all the World.

SERM.   Now Theſe *additional* Confirmations, of the Truth of the Doctrine delivered by the
LXXXVI. Holy Ghoſt in the Revelation of the Goſpel, are to *Us*; (what the Strength of the Evidence ariſing from the Nearneſs of the Time, was to *Them* who lived in the firſt Ages;)
a proportionable *Aggravation* of the Guilt of Unbelief, in thoſe who, notwithſtanding
all reaſonable Proof, yet obſtinately reject the Council of God againſt Themſelves,
by *disbelieving* or (which is the ſame thing) *diſobeying* the Goſpel. For the Sin of
Unbelief, does not conſiſt in *not believing* what men have *no* ſufficient Reaſon *to believe*; but in refuſing to attend to reaſonable Evidence; in being unwilling to examine
into a Doctrine, which would oblige them to amend their Lives; in *hating the Light*,
and fearing to come into it, *leſt their Deeds ſhould be reproved* thereby. *This is the Condemnation*, ſaith our Saviour, *that Light is come into the World, and men loved Darkneſs rather than Light, becauſe their Deeds were evil*, Joh. iii. 19. *They are of thoſe*
(as *Job* elegantly expreſſes it) *who rebel againſt the* Light; *they know not the Ways
thereof, nor abide in the Paths thereof*, ch. xxiv. 13. Upon *this* Account; (that
Knowledge, or, which is all one,) the Means *of Knowledge* fairly propoſed to men, is
the great Aggravation of the Sin of Unbelief; ſhewing plainly, that in ſuch Caſe nothing but Obſtinacy and the Love of Sin, is the real Cauſe of their rejecting the Truth:
Upon this Account, I ſay, it is, that our Saviour thus declares concerning the *Jews*,
St *Joh.* xv. 22. *If I had not come, and ſpoke unto them, they had not had Sin; but now
they have no cloke for their Sin*: and ver. 24. *If I had not done among them the Works
which none other man did, they had not had Sin; but now they have both ſeen and hated,
both me and my Father.* And to the Cities, *wherein moſt of his mighty Works were done*,
Matt. xi. 21; *Wo unto thee, Chorazin; Wo unto thee, Bethſaida, For if the mighty
Works which were done in you, had been done in Tyre and Sidon, they would have repented
long ago in Sackcloth and Aſhes: But I ſay unto you, It ſhall be more tolerable for Tyre
and Sidon at the day of judgment, than for you. And thou, Capernaum, which art exalted unto Heaven, ſhalt be brought down to Hell; For if the mighty Works which have
been done in Thee, had been done in Sodom, it would have remained until this Day; But
I ſay unto you, that it ſhall be more tolerable for the land of Sodom in the day of judgment,
than for you.* And upon the ſame Ground it is, that the Apoſtle in like manner ſo
highly aggravates the Sin of rejecting the Goſpel, *Heb.* xii. 25. *See that ye refuſe not
him that ſpeaketh: For if They eſcaped not, who refuſed him that ſpake on Earth; much
more ſhall not we eſcape, if we turn away from him that ſpeaketh from Heaven.* And
ch. ii. 2. *If the Word ſpoken by Angels, was ſtedfaſt; and every tranſgreſſion and diſobedience received a juſt recompence of reward; How ſhall we eſcape, if we neglect ſo great
Salvation, which at the firſt began to be ſpoken by the Lord, and was confirmed unto us
by them that heard him: God alſo bearing them witneſs, both with Signs and Wonders,
and with divers miracles and gifts of the Holy Ghoſt, according to his own Will?* A careful Conſideration of the Senſe of theſe Paſſages, will lead us to the true meaning of the
like, but more difficult, and ſeemingly more ſevere Expreſſions in the Text. For, if
the great *Aggravation of Sin*, be the *Knowledge of our Duty*; and the *Condemnation of
the World*, be the *Light that is come into it*; and the *Guilt of the Jews* was proportionably greater than that of other men, for *this* reaſon, becauſe our Saviour *did among them
the Works which no other man did* elſewhere; and thoſe particular *Cities* of the *Jews*,
wherein *moſt of* our Lord's *mighty Works were done*, were condemned with a more particularly ſevere judgment; and in general, *every* Sin *againſt the Word ſpoken by our
Lord* himſelf *from Heaven*, and confirmed with *Signs and Wonders, and with divers
Miracles and gifts of the Holy Ghoſt*, can leſs expect to eſcape unpuniſhed, than thoſe
committed againſt the Law given *by Angels* and delivered by *Moſes* upon *Earth*: It
follows, that if there be Any Sin, more heinous than All others; if there be Any Guilt,

I

which

which in Event will terminate in final Perdition; if there be any Crime, of which it may beforehand be judged that it will never be expiated; it muſt be Mens obſtinately ſinning againſt That Light, a greater and clearer than which, will never be afforded them; it muſt be mens hardning themſelves in ſuch a Diſpoſition, as in the Nature of the Thing cuts off from itſelf the Means of Recovery; it muſt be ſuch a Corruption and Depravity of Mind, as, like a Mortal and incurable Diſeaſe, precludes all Methods of applying a Remedy. And This, it is evident, cannot be any *particular* Sin, but a *general and total* Rejection of the only Means of recovering *from* Sin. The Generation that lived at the Time of the Flood, ſinned unpardonably; not by any of the *particular* Crimes they were guilty of; but by rejecting the preaching of Righteous *Noah*, which was the laſt Call God vouchſafed them to Repentance: For he reſolved, that whoſoever blaſphemed the preaching of *Noah*, ſhould never be forgiven, but be deſtroyed by the Flood. The Inhabitanrs of *Sodom* ſinned unpardonably; not by any of their *particular* Wickedneſſes, which yet were extremely heinous; but by refuſing to hear *Lot*'s Exhortations to Repentance; who was the laſt Monitor God intended to ſend them; and he determined judicially, that whoſoever blaſphemed the preaching of *Lot*, it ſhould never be forgiven him, but he ſhould be deſtroyed in the Deſolation by Fire. The Phariſees in our Saviour's Time, ſinned likewiſe unpardonably; not by any of the *particular* Iniquities, with which they are charged in the Goſpel; (For the whole *Deſign* of our Lord's preaching, was to exhort them to *repent* of theſe, that they might be forgiven:) But they ſinned unpardonably, by opprobriouſly rejecting our Lord's Invitation to Repentance; and by ſcornfully reviling the greateſt and the laſt Miracles, which he intended to work in that Place amongſt them; And therefore, after This God reſolved to leave them to themſelves, to live and die in their Sins without further conviction, and *never to be forgiven*, or to have any New Means of Pardon offered them, *either in this World or in the World to come.* Verily *I ſay unto you, All manner of Sin and Blaſphemy ſhall be forgiven unto men; but the Blaſphemy againſt the Holy Ghoſt, ſhall not be forgiven unto men: And whoſoever ſpeaketh a Word againſt the Son of Man, it ſhall be forgiven him; but whoſoever ſpeaketh againſt the Holy Ghoſt, it ſhall not be forgiven him neither in this World neither in the World to come.* The Words are the ſevereſt Words in the whole New Teſtament; and therefore ought very carefully to be conſidered and explained, in their true and proper meaning; that neither melancholy pious perſons may, on the one hand, be terrified with Fears of what they have not the leaſt reaſon to apply to themſelves; nor wilful and incorrigible Sinners, preſumptuouſly imagine themſelves to be in leſs danger than they really are.

THE Occaſion of the Words, was This. Our Saviour having caſt out a Devil, and healed the diſeaſed perſon, ſo that he who had been dumb and blind, immediately both ſpake and ſaw; the People, aſtoniſhed at the greatneſs of the Miracle, began to expreſs their opinion, that he muſt needs be the Meſſias, *ver.* 23; Upon which, certain Phariſees, hardned by their Malice and Hypocriſy beyond all Conviction, ſuggeſted to the People, that poſſibly it might be by Confederacy with the Prince of the Devils, that Jeſus thus caſt out Devils; *ver.* 24. To This our Saviour replies; Whatever is done by Confederacy with evil Spirits, muſt be ſomething that promotes the *Intereſt* of the Kingdom of Satan, and not any thing directly *contrary* thereto; unleſs a Kingdom can be ſupported by Diviſions within itſelf; *ver.* 25; *Every Kingdom divided againſt itſelf, is brought to Deſolation; and every City or Houſe divided againſt itſelf, ſhall not ſtand.* If therefore caſting out Devils, and that in Proof of a Doctrine directly *oppoſite* to the *Intereſt* of the Kingdom of Satan, be a thing not to be done by Confederacy with Evil Spirits; then nothing, ſays he, can be more abſurdly malicious, than this your Accuſation of me; *ver.* 26; *If Satan caſt out Satan, he is*

divided

SERM. *divided againſt himſelf; how then ſhall his Kingdom ſtand?* But if the thing itſelf be
LXXXVI. apparent; and ye cannot without extreme Unreaſonableneſs and the utmoſt Degree
of Malice, deny it, that what I do, is by the immediate Power of God; then here
is a convincing Proof offered you, that I am truly ſent from God, and that the Doctrine I preach is for the eſtabliſhment of *His* Kingdom; *ver.* 28; *But if I caſt out
Devils by the Spirit of God, then the Kingdom of God is come unto you.* For, as one's
entring into a ſtrong man's houſe, and forcibly diſpoſſeſſing him of his Goods is an
evident Demonſtration, that he who ſo enters, is ſtronger and comes with greater Authority, than he that had the firſt Poſſeſſion: So my breaking the Power of Devils by
caſting them out of the Bodies, and deſtroying their Dominion over the Minds of
Men, is an undeniable Proof of my being ſent by a Power and Anthority greater than
theirs; *ver.* 29; *Or elſe how can one enter into a ſtrong man's houſe and ſpoil his goods,
except he firſt bind the ſtrong man, and then he will ſpoil his goods?* The connexion
of the following Words, *ver.* 30, is more difficult to be underſtood; for they may
ſeem at firſt ſight to be abrupt, and independent on what went before; *He that is
not with me is againſt me; and he that gathereth not with me, ſcattereth abroad:* But
the True intent of them, is, to illuſtrate and confirm what went before, in ſome ſuch
Manner as This: When two great Powers are at [open and] irreconcileable Enmity
againſt each other, even he who *only forbears* joining with one ſide, is thereupon reputed to be againſt it; according to the uſual Proverb, *He that is not with me,
is againſt me:* How much more therefore (infers our Saviour) ought ye to believe
that *I,* who have actually done *ſo much* towards deſtroying the Power and Kingdom
of the Devil, am really and in Truth acting in oppoſition againſt him, and not by
confederacy with him! And then he adds in the Words of the Text; Wherefore
*I ſay unto you, All manner of Sin and Blaſphemy ſhall be forgiven unto men; but
the Blaſphemy againſt the Holy Ghoſt, ſhall not be forgiven unto men.* The meaning
is: Since it is as evident, as it is poſſible for any thing to be, that the Works which
I do, are by the immediate Authority of God, and by the Power of his Holy
Spirit; *Therefore* whoſoever ſhall reſiſt this great Conviction, by ſo unreaſonable
and obſtinate a degree of Malice, as to aſcribe theſe very Works, theſe greateſt
and higheſt Evidences of Divine Authority, to the Power of the Devil; To ſuch
a Perſon God will never afford any further Means of Conviction: And therefore
though all other Blaſphemies and all *particular* Sins whatſoever, may be repented of
and forgiven; yet He who is guilty of *this Total* corruption of Mind, this maliciouſly
perverſe and deſperate Rejecting of the greateſt and higheſt Conviction that God vouch-
ſafes to afford men, ſhall never have granted him any further Means, of Repentance
and Forgiveneſs. Every particular Kind, or Sort of Sin, whatſoever; and all other
Blaſphemies whatſoever, ſhall be forgiven men: Even he that ſpeaks againſt *Me,* (ſays
our Lord,) in all *other* reſpects; or calumniates *me,* upon any *other* account whatſoever; and is not at firſt convinced by *my* preaching and Exhortations; may yet afterwards be convinced by the mighty *Works* he ſhall ſee, and by the *Power* of the
Holy Ghoſt; and ſo repent and be forgiven: But he who obſtinately reſiſts even this
greateſt and moſt extraordinary Method, which God has thought fit to make uſe of
for the Converſion of Mankind; and maliciouſly reviles the moſt evident Operations
of the Spirit of God; ſuch a One has no further Means left, by which he might
be convinced and brought to Repentance, and conſequently he can never be forgiven. *Whoſoever ſpeaketh a Word againſt the Son of Man, it ſhall be forgiven him;
but whoſoever ſpeaketh a Word againſt the Holy Ghoſt, it ſhall not be forgiven him,
neither in this World, neither in the World to come.*

2

THE

THE Connexion and *general* Meaning of the Words being thus explained, I ſhall for the further and more *particular* clearing of what difficulties may remain in them, and for removing ſuch Scruples as may be apt to ariſe from them, take leave to add the following Obſervations; *1ſt*, That Our Saviour does not ſay, *The* Sin *againſt the Holy Ghoſt*, but *the* Blaſphemy *againſt the Holy Ghoſt*, ſhall not be forgiven. Neither in *This*, nor in any *other* Paſſage of Scripture, is there *any* mention *at all* of a Sin *againſt the Holy Ghoſt*. For indeed our Saviour is not here ſpeaking of *a Sin*, of a particular *Act of Sin*; ſeeing on the contrary he expreſſly declares, that *All Manner of Sin*, nay, and all Blaſphemy *alſo wherewith ſoever* men *ſhall blaſpheme*, ſhall *be forgiven unto them*: But he ſpeaks of a certain incurable *malicious Diſpoſition of Mind*, which by venting itſelf under ſuch peculiar Circumſtances in Blaſphemy againſt the *greateſt* of our Lord's Miracles, plainly diſcovered itſelf to be incapable of Amendment, by *any* Means which God would vouchſafe to make uſe of. And it was not the *particular Act of Blaſpheming*, that itſelf rendred the Men unpardonable; But *That* particular *Blaſphemy*, in thoſe particular Circumſtances, was a *Sign* only or an *Evidence*, which our Saviour knew and declared to proceed from an *incurable* and therefore *unpardonable* malicious Diſpoſition of Mind. And This is evident from the Words immediately following the Text, whoſe *connexion* uſually is not ſufficiently taken Notice of. For thus, when our Saviour had declared the Phariſees Blaſpheming againſt the Holy Ghoſt, to be *unpardonable*; he adds, as a Reaſon, in the very next Words, *ver.* 33; *Either make the Tree good, and his Fruit good; or elſe make the Tree corrupt, and his Fruit corrupt: For the Tree is known by his Fruit. O generation of Vipers, how can ye, being evil, ſpeak good things? For out of the Abundance of the Heart, the Mouth ſpeaketh.* It is evident therefore, that not for the particular *Act* of Blaſphemy, but for That *incurably wicked Diſpoſition of Mind*, of which Blaſpheming in thoſe Circumſtances was a plain Indication, were theſe *Phariſees* declared to be unpardonable. Nothing therefore can be gathered from this paſſage, concerning any particular *Sin againſt the Holy Ghoſt*, (as Many have without Reaſon imagined,) in its own Nature unpardonable. For in reality *All wilful* Sin *whatſoever* is *againſt the Holy Ghoſt*; againſt the good Motions, againſt the guidance and direction of the good Spirit of God; Yet not *every*, nay not *any* wilful Sin is upon that account abſolutely unpardonable; as appears from the whole Tenour of Scripture: Much leſs are blaſphemous *Thoughts*, which melancholy pious perſons are apt to complain of, and which therefore are not wilful at all; much leſs (I ſay) are uneaſy blaſphemous Thoughts, of This higheſt Malignity; when, generally ſpeaking, they are not ſo much as *choſen* or *wilful* Sins *at all*. Even thoſe *wilful* Sins *againſt* or in oppoſition to *the Holy Ghoſt*, (which yet is a Phraſe never uſed in Scripture-language,) are in the Goſpel always ſuppoſed pardonable upon true Repentance. The Blaſphemy our Saviour here ſpeaks of, is a thing of another Nature; it is not ſingly ſinning *againſt the Perſon of the Holy Ghoſt*, or *againſt his* good Motions, but preſumptuouſly *reviling* the greateſt *Works* of the Holy Ghoſt, and ſo obſtinately *rejecting* the laſt and ſolemneſt Call to Repentance. And This is further evident from what our Saviour adds, that *he who ſpeaks againſt the Son of Man*, might *be forgiven*; as the *Jews*, who reproached him as being *the Carpenter's Son*, as *a wine-bibber and a glutton*, as a *Friend of Publicans and Sinners*, might be forgiven, if they repented upon the further Conviction that ſhould afterward be afforded them: But he that blaſphemed againſt the *Holy Ghoſt*, againſt the higheſt Evidence of our Lord's *greateſt* Miracles, was never to be forgiven; Not becauſe even *This was in itſelf*, and in the Nature of the Thing, abſolutely unpardonable; (For no reaſon can be given why ſpeaking againſt the *Perſon* of the *Holy Ghoſt*, ſhould be *in itſelf* of greater Malignity,

SERM. lignity, than ſpeaking againſt *Chriſt*, or againſt *God the Father Himſelf*;) but be-
LXXXVI. cauſe it was an obſtinate rejecting the laſt means of Conviction, and an evident
Token of incorrigible Malice. Among the Antient *Jews*, Heb. x. 28; *He that
deſpiſed Moſes's Law, died without Mercy:* Our Saviour in like manner declares,
that he who by blaſpheming againſt the Works of the Holy Spirit, deſpiſes and
rejects the final Offer of *the Goſpel*, he alſo ſhall periſh without Mercy. And
This poſſibly may be the meaning of the other Phraſe; that ſuch a malicious Temper ſhould not be pardoned, *neither in this World, neither in the World to come*;
namely, neither in that preſent Age, which was the Time of the *Law*, nor in
the Age to come, which is the Times of the *Meſſiah*. 2*dly*, It is reaſonable to
ſuppoſe that this peremptory declaration of our Saviour, concerning the unpardonable Wickedneſs of thoſe who thus blaſphemouſly rejected the higheſt Evidence
of the Goſpel, ought to be applied and underſtood of *thoſe Perſons* only, who themſelves *ſaw* his Miracles, and rejected them purely out of a wicked Diſpoſition; namely,
the Phariſees, and unbelieving *Jews*. For, though thoſe who live in after Ages, and are
not Eye-witneſſes of his mighty Works, have indeed nevertheleſs ſufficient Evidence
of the Truth of the Goſpel; and in ſome few reſpects, as I before intimated, have even
the Advantage over the greater Part of thoſe who lived at That Time; yet, Theſe Advantages ariſing from Arguments of Abſtract Reaſon, Conſideration, and Enquiry;
which work differently upon Men at different Times; and may prevail afterwards, upon more mature conſideration, over the ſame Perſon who at preſent rejects them;
therefore no man's rejecting the Goſpel Now, can be known or ſuppoſed to proceed
from the like incurable Malignity, as the Blaſphemy of thoſe who themſelves *ſaw* our
Lord's Miracles. 3*dly*, It may yet further be conceived, not without probability, that
theſe ſevere words of our Saviour, are applicable, not even ſo much as to *All* Thoſe
Phariſees, who ſaw and rejected his Miracles; but to thoſe only, who ſaw *That*
particular *great Miracle* recorded in This chapter, and who reviled it with *That* particular *malicious Blaſphemy*, of aſcribing it to the Power of the Unclean Spirit. For
ſo St *Mark* intimates, by adding in the Words immediately following the Text: *Mar.*
iii. 30; that Jeſus ſpake thus ſeverely of them, becauſe *they ſaid, he hath an unclean
Spirit.* And indeed, ſince we do not find that any Perſons whatſoever were ever
rejected from Baptiſm; it is reaſonable to ſuppoſe, that many of the *other* Phariſees,
who had *ſeen* and perhaps alſo *ſpoken againſt* our Saviour's Miracles, might yet afterwards repent, be baptized, and obtain forgiveneſs. But *Theſe*, who blaſphemed in
This *particular* manner, he *knew* were *incorrigible*, and perhaps *judicially* alſo reſolved
that no farther means ſhould be offered them. And then the Words of the Text
will be prophetical, and equivalent to thoſe other expreſſions; *Joh.* x. 26; viii. 21,
24; *Ye are none of my ſheep, ye ſhall die in your Sins:* which is the ſame as to ſay,
Ye will never be forgiven neither in this World, neither in the World to come. 4*thly*,
If this Threatning is to be extended to any *other* Perſons, it may ſeem moſt properly
to reach the caſe of ſuch, as, after the giving of the Holy Ghoſt at *Pentecoſt*, ſhould
in like manner revile that miraculous Diſpenſation. But there is no reaſon to think
(as ſome have done,) that it belongs *only* to ſuch as ſhould blaſpheme *after That:*
For the Power of the Holy Ghoſt did as viſibly appear to the Phariſees with whom our
Saviour Now converſed, as to thoſe who ſaw that wonderful gift at *Pentecoſt*; and
the Words themſelves ſeem *more naturally* to confine it to *thoſe Phariſees only:* At
leaſt, it can be applied to Both, *only* upon account of their *ſeeing* the Miracles;
which was the higheſt Evidence that could poſſibly be given them. And if there had
been any ſuch thing as any *other* Sin againſt the Holy Ghoſt, which Chriſtians in
after-times could be in danger of falling into; it cannot be imagined, but the

Apoſtles

Apoſtles in their Epiſtles, wherein they are diligent to caution men againſt all *other* SERM.
Crimes, would have been much fuller and more preſſing in their warnings to LXXXVI.
take heed of *This*, as being of more deſperate conſequence than any *other* whatſoever: Whereas, on the contrary, we find not in their writings any direct mention
of any ſuch Sin at all. 5*thly* and *Laſtly*, Yet This we may obſerve, that the A-
poſtles frequently warn Men to take heed of the *Approaches* towards the like Guilt,
and of Sins which may ſeem next in Malignity; ſuch as wilful Apoſtacy from the
Profeſſion, or from the whole Practice of Religion; Concerning Perſons guilty of
which Crimes it is ſaid, that it is *impoſſible* [exceeding difficult] *to renew them to Repentance*; that there *remains no more Sacrifice for* their *Sin*; Heb. x. 26,——29;
that like *Eſau*, they *for one morſel ſell* their *birth-right*; and, when it is joined
with obſtinacy, that their *Sin* is *unto Death*, i. e. that it is like a Diſeaſe which appears to be *mortal*, with little or no Hopes of Recovery. From which God of his
infinite Mercy, *&c.*

SERMON

SERMON LXXXVII.

Of receiving the HOLY GHOST.

[Preached on Whitsunday.]

ACTS XIX. 2, 3.

He said unto them, Have ye received the Holy Ghost since ye belived? And they said unto him, We have not so much as heard whether there be any Holy Ghost. And he said unto them, Unto what then were ye baptized?

SERM. LXXXVII.
IN the following Discourse upon these words, I shall *first* endeavour briefly to explain the full Meaning of the several *particular* expressions here made use of by the Apostle, and by the new Converts with whom he discoursed; and then, *secondly,* I shall consider the *general* doctrine, concerning the Nature and Gifts of the Holy Spirit, which was the Foundation and Occasion of the *particular* incidents referred to in the Text. It was the Method of the Apostles, when they had preached the Gospel in a Number of places, to return after a certain Time through the same places where they had formerly preached; to confirm, and strengthen the Believers; to set in order, the several Churches; to redress, what was amiss; to exhort and comfort them, under the Persecutions they were likely to meet with; and to examine how far they preserved pure and uncorrupt, That Doctrine which had been delivered unto them, with regard both to Faith and Practice. *Acts* xv. 36. *Paul said unto Barnabas, Let us go again and visit our Brethren, in every City where we have preached the word of the Lord, and see how they do.* Ver. 41. *And he went though Syria and Cilicia confirming the churches.* And ch. xvi. 5. *And so were the churches established in the Faith, and increased in Number daily.* The Text, with the foregoing and following verses, is an account of part of this Progress of St *Paul* in visiting the Churches, and of the Design and Effect of that his journey amongst them. *Paul having passed through the upper coasts, came to Ephesus,* ver. 1. *And finding certain Disciples, he said unto them, Have ye received the Holy Ghost since ye believed?* As the Apostles were themselves baptized with the Holy Ghost at *Pentecost,* so it pleased God at the *first preaching of the Gospel,* generally to endue *others* likewise, who were baptized by the Apostles, with some visible gifts of the Holy Ghost, such as speaking with tongues, prophesying, and the like. Not that This was the principal and most valuable Effect of Baptism; For *That* consisted in the *internal* Benefit on the Mind of the persons *themselves,* Remission of past Sin, and Sanctification of the Spirit for the future: But in order to a more effectual conviction of *Others* to whom the Gospel was to be preached, and for the speedier propagating of the Doctrine of Christ, it pleased God that the Power of the Holy

1

Ghost

Ghoft in Them who were baptized, difcovered itfelf in thofe firft times by *external* Evidences and miraculous Operations: *Tongues*, fays the Apoftle, *are for a Sign, not for them that believe, but for them that believe not*; 1 Cor. xiv. 22. Tho' therefore thefe miraculous Effects of the Spirit conferred in Baptifm, were not the *principal* with regard to the perfons *themfelves* on whom they were conferred; yet being the moft *vifible* to *others*, and at that Time generally attending the other more fecret and invifible Gifts, it was very natural for the Apoftle, when he came to examine into the State of fuch Difciples as had been converted in his abfence, to exprefs himfelf after this manner, *Have ye received the Holy Ghoft fince ye believed?* The Matter he was *chiefly* concerned to know, was the *thing fignified*; whether they were true Believers, and had received the Gofpel in the Truth and Purity thereof. But the thing demanded in his queftion, was the *Evidence* or *external Sign*; Has God beftowed upon you thofe vifible Gifts of the Spirit, which are now the ufual Characterifticks of the Difciples of Chrift? To this Queftion, they returned a very furprizing Anfwer indeed, if our Tranflation exprefs'd it rightly; *We have not fo much as* heard *whether there* be *any Holy Ghoft:* As if any either *Jew* or even *Gentile*, much lefs Chriftian Convert, could poffibly have been fo ignorant, as to know nothing at all, nor ever have heard any thing, either of the Being or Influences of the Spirit of God. The Meaning evidently is, (and fo the words ought to have been rendred,) *We have not heard that there has been any* fuch *Giving of the Holy Ghoft*; We have neither received any of thefe extraordinary Gifts *ourfelves*, nor been informed of their being beftowed on *others*, or that we were to *expect* any fuch thing upon our believing. And indeed it may feem very wonderful, how it fhould happen they *could* be, even *fo far* ignorant as This. But *the reafon* appears, in what follows. For when the Apoftle hereupon afks them again; *Unto what then were ye baptized*, if not unto the expectation of the Gifts of the Holy Ghoft? they reply, ver. 3; *Unto John's Baptifm.* Which Baptifm of *John the Baptift* being *preparatory* only to the Reception of Chrift, and intended only as a *Means* to a further *End*; 'tis no wonder it was not accompanied with the Effufion of thofe perfective Gifts of the Spirit, which would have made needlefs that Baptifm into the Name of Chrift, which was to follow. This therefore is the Meaning of what the Apoftle thereupon anfwers them again, *ver.* 4; *John* (fays he) *verily baptized with the Baptifm of Repentance*; *faying unto the people, that they fhould believe on* Him *which fhould come after* him, *that is, on Chrift Jefus.* The Intention of which Reply, is; *John indeed baptized you* (faith he) *into the* expectation *of the Meffiah that was to come*; But before you injoy the Benefit of his *actual Coming*, you muft verify that *expectation* by *receiving* him now he *is come*; and fulfil the *intention* of *John's* Baptifm, by being confequently baptized into the Name of *Chrift.* *John's* Baptifm was but a *Promife* or Declaration of your *Intention*, of being afterwards baptized into *Chrift*; And the Advantage you expect from being baptized by *John*, can be made good to you only by *fulfilling* that Promife, in embracing the Doctrine and the Religion of *Chrift.* *When they heard This*, ver. 5. *they were baptized in the Name of the Lord Jefus*; *And when Paul had laid his hands upon them, the Holy Ghoft came on them, and they fpake with tongues and prophefied.*

The Occafion and Meaning of the words being thus explained, we may from this Hiftory, whereof the words of the Text contain the principal circumftances, make the following Obfervations.

1ft, That the Nature and Spirit of the Chriftian Religion, is to lay as little Strefs as poffible upon all *external* Rites; and to have the greateft Regard that can be, to the *moral* Qualifications of mens Minds. The *Perfons* to whom St *Paul* puts the Queftion in the Text, are, in the verfe before, ftiled *Difciples* or Believers, that is, *Chriftians*; though they had been inftructed in nothing yet, but in the Doctrine of *John the Baptift.*

SERM. Repentance from dead works, and Reformation of Life, and a preparatory Difpofition
LXXXVII. to receive the Will of God when made known to them by the Meffias to come, was
here judged fufficient to denominate men *Difciples*; even *before* they had been *baptized*
into the Name of *Chrift*, or had received any of the *external Gifts* of the Holy Ghoft,
or had fo much as *heard* that fuch Gifts were to be beftowed upon them. There is *no
external Rite* in matters of Religion, more pofitively and expreffly commanded by God,
or more indifpenfably and without any exception required by our Saviour, than that of
Baptifm: Except a man be born, faith he, *of Water and of the Spirit, he cannot enter
into the Kingdom of God:* And yet even in *This very cafe* of fo exprefs a command, (to
fhow how much Religion is judged of in the fight of God by the moral and virtuous
Difpofition of the Heart, more than by the outward Form,) there are *many* inftances
in Scripture, where the *inward* Difpofition has been accepted inftead of the *outward*
Form; but *no* cafe, where the *Form* or *Ceremony* has in any wife fupplied the want
of the *inward* Difpofition. The Thief upon the Crofs was affured by our Saviour, that
he fhould be with him That day in Paradife; becaufe in the Difpofition of his Heart
he was fitly qualified for Baptifm, though there was no poffibility of his having the
Ceremony performed upon him. The Perfons mentioned in the Text, had they
died before their being baptized in the Name of Chrift; it cannot be queftioned, but
that thofe whom the infpired Writer calls *Difciples here*, would by our Lord have been
acknowledged for his true Difciples *hereafter*. *Cornelius* the good Centurion, was
before his Baptifm filled with the miraculous Gifts of the Holy Spirit : And *no reafon* can be conceived why that Teftimony of the Divine Favour fhould be conferred
upon him juft *before* his Baptifm, which the Apoftles themfelves expected could not
have been beftowed till *after* it; but only that the Spirit of God thought it of importance to declare in fo extraordinary a manner, that even where to the Ufe of a Form
or Ceremony God *has* annexed his Gifts, yet even there, not *upon account of* the
Form, or the Rite itfelf, but upon account of the *inward Qualifications* of the *Mind*,
does he beftow his fpiritual Bleffings. In the regular Adminiftration of Baptifm itfelf,
'tis not the *wafhing away of the Filth of the Flefh*, that faveth us; but *the Anfwer of
a good Confcience towards God*; 1 Pet. iii. 21. Many *Martyrs* in the Primitive times,
upon their profeffing their Faith in Chrift, were *immediately* hurried away to bear
Teftimony for him with their Blood : And no man doubted, but that they who *in reality* were buried *with him* and *for him* into Death; were at leaft equalized with thofe,
who by Baptifm died with him only *in a Figure*. *Infants*, who die unbaptized; unavoidably, and not poffibly by any fault of their own; cannot with reafon be worfe and
more hardly thought of, than *grown perfons* in the like condition. For concerning *Infants, as Infants*, and merely upon Account of their Innocency, it is, that our Saviour
affirms, that *of fuch is the Kingdom of Heaven*. And the *reafon why* they are faved,
is not *becaufe* they are *baptized*; but they are *therefore* baptized, *becaufe* they are capable of *Salvation*; They are *therefore* fit to be admitted into the Body of God's Church
on *Earth, becaufe* they are by their Innocence qualified to become Members of his
eternal Kingdom in *Heaven*. Neverthelefs, though the *thing fignified itfelf*, is always
of much more importance than the *Sign*; and often accepted by God in the ftead of
and without the external Form; yet this is always fo to be underftood, when the external Form *cannot* be had. For where, by the Perfon's own wilful and contemptuous
neglect, any Ceremony of God's exprefs Appointment is omitted; there *he that defpifeth,
defpifeth not Man, but God*; who has alfo annexed to what means he pleafeth, the
Gift of his Holy Spirit. *Except a man be born of Water and of the Spirit*, faith our Saviour; except he that has the Means and Opportunity of doing it, makes ufe of thofe
Means of Grace which God has been pleafed to appoint; 'tis reafonable he fhould fall
fhort of the Grace itfelf, and *he cannot enter into the Kingdom of God. Except ye Eat*

my

my Flesh and Drink my Blood, saith our Lord in another place; His *principal* Meaning **S E R M.** is, except ye receive my *Doctrine,* and, by obeying it, incorporate yourselves into my **LXXXVII.** spiritual Body ; *ye have no Life in you:* This (I say) is plainly his *principal* Meaning, because the words were spoken *before* any *external Symbols* of his Body and Blood were instituted : Yet, *when* such Sacramental Symbols *were* appointed; *then* it became the Duty of every sincere Christian, not only to eat our Lord's Flesh and drink his Blood *spiritually*; not only so to imbibe his Doctrine, as to make it the Support and Nourishment of a Spiritual Life, the Spring and Ground-work of a Holy and Virtuous Conversation; but it became their Duty also to participate of the *External Sacrament,* and to make use of the *Means,* as well as desire the *End,* of Christ's own Appointment. The *Disciples* in the Text, when they heard St *Paul* preach about the Gift of the Holy Ghost, immediately they were baptized *in the Name of the Lord Jesus*; And *without* so doing, they would not have received the Gifts of the Spirit, notwithstanding that the Text does *before* call them *Disciples,* upon their having been baptized with the Baptism of Repentance by *John.* This shows how well consistent, the *Necessity* of observing any Rite or Ceremony of God's own Appointment is, with the Christian Religion's laying at the same time *no stress at all* upon the *external* Form or Ceremony itself, but only on the *internal* moral Disposition or virtuous Qualification of the Mind. To which *inward* Qualification of Mind, great regard is always shown in Scripture, even where *all external* Advantages have been wanting. Thus to the *Scribe* who was so well-disposed, as to judge that the Love of God and of our Neighbour, was more valuable than all whole burnt-offerings ; our Saviour immediately replies, *Thou art not far from the Kingdom of God*; Mar. xii. 34. Of the *young man* who had observed the Commandments from his youth, 'tis recorded that *Jesus beholding him, loved him* ; Mar. x. 21. To the *Syrophænician woman,* whom at first our Lord seemed to reject with great severity, for not being of the house of *Israel*; yet at length he replies, *O woman, great is thy Faith, be it unto thee even as thou wilt*; Matt. xv. 28. And of the *Gentiles themselves,* St *Paul* makes no scruple to affirm, that their Uncircumcision, if they keep the Righteousness of the Law, shall be counted unto them for Circumcision; *Rom.* ii. 26. But now, on the *other* side, no *external* Advantages, no *Rites* or Observations whatsoever, are ever accepted in the stead of, or without, the *inward* Moral and virtuous Disposition of the Heart and Mind. Not *Baptism* itself; not the Sacrament of the *Lord's Supper* ; not even the *miraculous Gifts* and Graces of the Holy Ghost, are of any avail to an unrighteous person. *Many will say to me in that day, Lord, Lord, have we not prophesied in thy Name, and in thy Name have cast out devils, and in thy Name done many wonderful works? And then will I profess unto them, I never knew you; depart from me, ye that work iniquity*; Matt. vii. 22.

2. THE next Observation we may draw from the words of the Text, is, that *every* Disciple of Christ is here *supposed* to have received the *Gift of the Holy Ghost.* For so St *Paul,* as in words equivalent to asking them whether they had been *baptized* or no, thus puts the Question to them, *Have ye received the Holy Ghost since ye believed?* And *what* was then meant by *receiving the Holy Ghost,* appears from the following words, *ver.* 6. *And when Paul had laid his hands upon them, the Holy Ghost came on them ; and they spake with Tongues and prophesied.* This was the immediate Effect of the Holy Ghost's *first* coming upon the *Apostles* at Pentecost; And This was generally the Effect of its coming *afterward* upon *new Converts* at their Baptism. And when this miraculous Effect ceased, yet still the receiving of the Holy Ghost was as constant and as necessary as ever : because *Except a man be born of the Spirit,* as well as *of water, he cannot enter into* the Kingdom of Heaven. 'Tis *Now* true, as well as it was *Then,* that *if any man has not the Spirit of Christ, he is none of his ;* and that *the Spirit of Christ dwelleth in us, except we be reprobates.*

THE

SERM. LXXXVII.

THE way to *know* whether any perfon *has* this Spirit dwelling in him, or *no*; is by the *Fruits* of the Spirit; For *the Tree is known by its Fruit*, Matt. xii. 33. Now the *Fruits* of the Spirit, are either *temporary* or *perpetual*. *Temporary*; fuch as are the *miraculous* Gifts *of fpeaking with tongues, prophefying, healing difeafes, and the like*. Or *Perpetual*; fuch as are the *moral* Difpofitions and Habits of the Mind, worked in us by the Spirit of God, improved in us by his continual Affiftance, and acceptable to him in the Performance; Namely, *goodnefs, righteoufnefs, and Truth*, as St *Paul* reckons them up, *Eph.* v. 9; and more largely, *Gal.* v. 22. *The Fruit of the Spirit is love, joy, peace, long-fuffering, gentlenefs, goodnefs, faith, meeknefs, temperance.* Thefe are the *permanent* Fruits of the Spirit, neceffary to be found *at all times* in every baptized Perfon; Otherwife his Baptifm is nothing elfe, but merely the wafhing away the Filth of the Flefh; fo that, being born of *Water* only, and not of the *Spirit, he cannot enter into the Kingdom of God.* In whomfoever thefe *moral* Fruits of the Spirit *are found*, the other *miraculous and extraordinary* ones are *Now* unneceffary; And even *Then*, at the firft preaching of the Gofpel, when they were the *moft needful* of all, yet were they ufelefs and unprofitable to thofe very perfons in whom they moft abounded, if the *moral Fruits* of the Spirit were not found in conjunction with them. By the Habits of Piety and true Holinefs, men may *Now* fhow themfelves as full of the Holy Ghoft as ever, *without* any miraculous Gifts; *with* the greateft abundance of which, they were ftill void of the Holy Ghoft even *Then*, if not indued with Piety and true Holinefs. For, *miraculous Gifts*, were but *Signs* of the Holy Spirit working *by* them, not *in* and *upon* them. And therefore fuch Gifts were ufeful, rather to *Others* than *themfelves*; to convince *beholders*, rather than to fanctify the *perfons*: *Tongues*, faith St *Paul, are for a Sign, not to them that believe, but to them that believe not.* But *moral Virtues*, are Evidences of the Spirit's dwelling *in* men, and *fanctifying* mens Hearts and Lives: Which *to themfelves* is the *End* and the *Effect* of That *Belief*, the producing but the *firft Beginnings* whereof in *Others*, is all that is intended by *miraculous Gifts.* Thefe extraordinary Gifts therefore, were only *Operations* of the Spirit; But Righteoufnefs and Holinefs are properly called its *Fruits*. *Fruits of the Spirit*; becaufe worked, not as the others, extrinfecally, neceffarily, and without the concurrence of the Perfons themfelves; but worked *in* the mind, and *with* the free choice and *Will* of the Perfon, by the *approbation, affiftance*, and *help* of *the Spirit* of God, *concurring with* him, not barely operating *by* him. For which reafon, *Thefe* are never found but in *Good* men; being indeed the Qualifications which *denominate* men fuch: But the *Others* were often beftowed even upon *hypocritical* perfons; whom our Saviour, though they had done in his Name many wonderful Works, yet declares he will reject from him, as being at the fame time Workers of iniquity. And hence it is, that our Lord makes that remarkable Diftinction; St *Luke* x. 20. *In This rejoice not, that the Spirits are fubject unto you; but rather rejoice, becaufe your Names are written in Heaven:* That is, 'tis a thing much more valuable, to be a good man, than to be able to caft out Devils. Hence alfo it is, that St *Paul* gives fo manifeft a preference to works of *righteoufnefs*, before *miraculous* Gifts; 1 Cor. xii. 30; *Have All, the gifts of healing? do All fpeak with tongues? do All interpret? But covet earneftly the beft Gifts, and yet fhow I unto you a more excellent way*; a way *yet more* excellent, even than the *beft* Gifts. And what *That* is, he tells us in the next words; *Though I fpeak with the Tongues of Men and of Angels, and have not Charity, I am become as founding brafs or a tinkling Cymbal: And tho' I have the Gift of Prophecy, and underftand all myfteries and all knowledge; And tho' I have all Faith, fo that I could remove mountains, and have no Charity, I am nothing.* If I have no Charity; that is, if I am not indued with a Spirit of Univerfal Love and Goodnefs towards Men. For fo it is remarkable in the whole New Teftament, that the word *Charity* never fignifies, as it does Now in common fpeech, the

3

mere

mere *giving of Alms to the poor*; but it always means, in a larger Signification, That
Love and Defire of doing good to all men, which is oppofed to Uncharitablenefs, Peevifhnefs, Hatred, Animofity and Factioufnefs. As is particularly evident in the Verfe next
following; where *Charity* is exprefsly diftinguifhed from *giving Alms to the Poor*, as
the *whole* of a Duty from its *part* : *Though I give* (faith he) *my body to be burned, and
though I beftow all my goods to feed the poor*, *and have not Charity*, (that is, have not an
univerfally good and righteous Spirit, *it profiteth me nothing*.

3*dly*, FROM the character of the perfons defcribed in the Text, we may obferve that
thofe words, *we have not fo much as heard whether there* be any Holy Ghoft, cannot poffibly be a right tranflation ; but that they ought to have been rendred thus, *we have not
fo much as heard whether there* be any Giving *of the Holy Ghoft*; any *fuch* Gift or Diftribution of it, as the Apoftle inquired after. (There is a like expreffion, *Joh.* vii. 39.
The Holy Ghoft was not yet; fo 'tis in the original; which in the Tranflation we very
rightly exprefs, *The Holy Ghoft was not yet* given, *becaufe that Jefus was not yet glorified*.) Now of *This* indeed, of the extraordinary *Gifts* and miraculous *Effufion* of the
Holy Ghoft, the perfons mentioned in the Text *might* in their prefent circumftances be
ignorant : But, *whether there* be any Holy Ghoft, This is what they could not poffibly
make a Queftion of. For, not to fay that even the *Gentiles themfelves* were not without *Some* Notion of a *divine Afflatus*, 'tis well known that the *Jews* had in the Writings of the Prophets perpetual mention of the *Spirit of God* : And therefore the Perfons
in the Text, who were of all other Jews or Profelytes the *beft inftructed*, as having
been baptized with *John*'s Baptifm, 'tis plain could not poffibly be ignorant of *That*,
however they might not yet have heard of the extraordinary and miraculous Effufion of
it fince the Afcenfion of Chrift.

4*thly*, FROM the *manner* of the Apoftle's putting the Queftion, *Unto* What *then
were ye baptized?* unto *what*, if not unto the expectation of the Gift of the *Holy
Ghoft?* from This *manner* of the Apoftle's putting the Queftion, it appears, that the
following words, ver. 5; *when they heard This, they were baptized in the Name of the*
Lord Jefus ; and the like Expreffions in other parts of this Book, *ch.* viii. 16; *they were
baptized in the Name of the* Lord Jefus ; and *ch.* ii. 38; *be baptized every one of you in
the* Name of Jefus Chrift ; and *ch.* x. 48; *he commanded them to be baptized in the
Name of the* Lord ; it appears (I fay) that thefe Expreffions do by no means fignify, as
if any one was ever baptized *barely* into the Name of *Chrift* ; but on the contrary, that
they are an abbreviate way of fpeaking, (fuch as is every where very ufual in matters
fuppofed to be already perfectly well known,) to put the *part* for the *whole*. Baptizing
into *Jefus Chrift*, was well known by all Chriftians, to fignify baptizing in *That Form*,
which our Lord *Jefus Chrift* had appointed ; that is, in the Name of the Father, and
of the Son, and of the Holy Ghoft : And where-ever *part* of this Form is exprefs'd,
the *whole* is always underftood to be implied. Had it been ufual, according to the *Letter* of thefe expreffions, to baptize men into the Name of *Chrift* only ; the Apoftle
could not properly have afked thofe who had not yet heard of the Gift of the *Holy
Ghoft, unto what then were ye* Baptized? but his queftion fhould have been, *after what
manner have ye been* inftructed? But putting the Queftion in the manner he does; *if ye
are ignorant of the Gift of the Holy Ghoft, unto what then were ye* Baptized? fhows
plainly, that not only in the doctrinal *inftruction* of a Chriftian, but alfo in the *Baptifm* itfelf, there muft have been mention of the *Holy Ghoft*, notwithftanding that abbreviate manner of fpeaking, wherein they are faid only *to have been in the Name of
the Lord Jefus*, in contra-diftinction to *John's Baptifm*. And from hence alfo it appears further, *what* was then underftood by thofe words in the form of Baptifm, *And
of the Holy Ghoft*, or *in the Name of the Holy Ghoft* : Namely, that the perfon, as he
was baptized into the Knowledge of *God*, and into the Death of *Chrift*, fo he was bap-

S E R M.
LXXXVII.

tized alfo into the Expectation of the Gifts of the *Holy Ghoſt*; whether thoſe Gifts were *extraordinary*, as the miraculous Powers conferred at that particular Time; or *ordinary*, as the Sanctification of mens Hearts for ever.

Laſtly, FROM the Hiſtory in the Text, we may learn the difference between the Baptiſm of *John* and that of *Chriſt*, how they were Both really but one thing, the former being imperfect without the latter, and the latter perfecting only what the former had begun, and therefore not being called a Re-baptizing. When the Diſciples, to the queſtion, *Unto what then were ye baptized?* made this Anſwer, *Unto John's Baptiſm*; The Apoſtle replies, ver. 4, *John verily baptized with the Baptiſm of Repentance, ſaying unto the people, that they ſhould believe on* Him *which ſhould come after him, that is, on Chriſt Jeſus: And when they heard This, they were baptized in the Name of the Lord Jeſus; and when Paul had laid his hands upon them, the Holy Ghoſt came on them. John* baptized into the *Expectation* only, of Him that was to come after; And therefore *This* his Baptiſm was *imperfect*, till the *intention* of it was fulfilled by the ſame Perſons being afterwards baptized into the Name of Chriſt when he *was* come, and *receiving* actually *his* Gifts, of which the Former Baptiſm was but declaring a *preparatory Expectation*.   And This is what is ſet forth in thoſe Texts where *John the Baptiſt* expreſsly acknowledges and declares, *I indeed* (ſaith he) *baptize you with Water unto Repentance; but he that cometh after me, is mightier than I, whoſe ſhoes I am not worthy to bear; he ſhall baptize you with the Holy Ghoſt and with Fire*, Matt. iii. 11. Mar. i. 7, 8. Luk. iii. 16, 17: Acts i. 5, and xi. 16; *With the Holy Ghoſt and with Fire*; that is, with the *Gifts* of the Holy Ghoſt, both *ordinary* and *extraordinary*: Which was *literally* fulfilled upon the *Apoſtles* at Pentecoſt; and, in the *virtual Effect*, upon all the *other* Diſciples who were baptized afterwards.   And again: *John bare record, ſaying*, Joh. i. 31, 32; *that He* [*viz.* that *Chriſt*] *ſhould be made manifeſt to Iſrael, therefore am I come baptizing* [only] *with Water*: According to the Account the Angel prophetically gave *before* of his Office; *Luk.* i. 16; *Many of the children of Iſrael ſhall he turn to the Lord their God; and he ſhall go before him in the ſpirit and power of Elias, to turn the hearts of the Fathers to the children, and the diſobedient to the wiſdom of the juſt, to make* ready *a people* prepared *for the Lord*.   Theſe are the *particular* Obſervations I thought uſeful to draw from the Hiſtory in the Text: It remains that we conſider in the next place the *general* Doctrine concerning the Nature and Gifts of the Holy Spirit, which was the Foundation and Occaſion of the *particular* Incidents referred to in the Text.

SERMON

SERMON LXXXVIII.

Of receiving the HOLY GHOST.

[Preached on Whitfunday.]

ACTS XIX. 2, 3.

He faith unto them, Have ye received the Holy Ghoft fince ye be-
lieved? And they faid unto him, We have not fo much as heard
whether there be any Holy Ghoft. And he faid unto them, Unto
what then were ye baptized?

IN a former Difcourfe upon thefe Words, I have endeavoured briefly to explain the meaning of the feveral *particular* expreffions here made ufe of by the Apoftle, and by the new Converts with whom he difcourfed. It remains at this time, according to the Method propofed, that I proceed in the next place to confider the *general* Doctrine, concerning the *Nature* and *Gifts* of the Holy Spirit, which was the Foundation and Occafion of the *particular* Incidents referred to in the Text. And

I. WHEN *John the Baptift* came preaching and baptizing with Water; with whofe Baptifm *only*, the Difciples in the Text having been baptized, had neither received the Gift of the Holy Ghoft *themfelves*, nor fo much as *heard* of its miraculous Gifts being beftowed on *others*; he modeftly and plainly confeffed, *Matt.* iii. 11. *I indeed baptize you with Water unto Repentance; but He that cometh after me, is mightier than I, whofe Shoes I am not worthy to bear; he fhall baptize you with the Holy Ghoft and with Fire.* According to This Declaration of *John the Baptift*, our Saviour, a little before his Afcenfion, promifed his Difciples, *Acts* i. 5. *John truly baptized with Water, but ye fhall be baptized with the Holy Ghoft not many days hence.* And This his Promife was effectually made good to them, in that miraculous Effufion of the Holy Spirit at Pentecoft, which we this day commemorate, and which is particularly defcribed in the fecond chapter of the *Acts*. Where that *Circumftance* of *there appearing* unto the Apoftles, *cloven tongues, like as of* Fire, *ver.* 3; explains the meaning of that prophetical Phrafe ufed by *John the Baptift* concerning our Lord, *He fhall baptize you with the Holy Ghoft and with* Fire; He fhall baptize you with the *Holy Ghoft*, defcending at firft *vifibly* in the appearance of *Fire*; and continuing with you afterwards, in purfuance of what That Emblem reprefented, by an Affiftance as much more powerful and efficacious than what *John Baptift* pretended to, as *Fire* is more powerful and more purifying than Water. To the Apoftles and firft Difciples, who were to fpread the Gofpel over the World, this their being baptized with the Holy Ghoft, was accompanied with miraculous Gifts and Powers; fuch as fpeaking with tongues, healing difeafes, and the like: But when the reafon of thefe miraculous Operations ceafed, yet

ftill

SERM. *still* every Christian is baptized with the *Holy Ghost* as well as with *Water*; and his *in-*
LXXXVIII. *ternal* sanctifying Gifts and Graces, are to continue with us always even unto the end
of the World. If any one has not received *these* Gifts of the Holy Ghost, it may still be
asked him with the same propriety as in the Text, *Unto what then was he baptized?*
If any man has not in him the Spirit of Christ; if he does not show forth in his
Life the Fruits of the Spirit, by Works of Righteousness and true Piety; if his Heart be
not sanctified by this Spirit of Holiness; if his Mind approves not, and delights not in
things spiritual; if his Will obeys not the good Motions of this Divine Assister; if the
Actions of his Life are not guided by the Commands of God, revealed to us in Scripture by the Inspiration of the Holy Ghost; *to what purpose then was such a Person*
baptized?

IT may here perhaps be inquired, *Does not the Spirit of God distribute to every man*
severally as he himself willeth? Does not the wind blow where it listeth, and so (saith
our Saviour) *is every one that is born of the Spirit? Are we not justified freely by God's*
grace? And does not the Apostle accordingly require us humbly to acknowledge, *Who*
maketh thee to differ from another? How then can it be objected to any man as a *Fault*,
or as a *Defect* in *himself*, that he has not received the Holy Ghost, or that he is not indued with those Gifts and Graces, which are not his own acquirements, but free diftributions of the Spirit of God? To give a clear and satisfactory Answer to this Difficulty, it is necessary that we attend to the following Distinction.

SOME Gifts of the Spirit are mere external miraculous Powers; such as speaking
with Tongues, healing Diseases, and the like: And of these it is, that the Apostle declares, that the Spirit *so* divides to every man severally as he willeth, and *so* maketh
One to differ from another, that nothing at all of these kinds of Gifts depends in any
measure upon the Will of the Persons themselves. And therefore as by *having* these
Gifts, no man was the better Christian; so no man by *wanting* them, was the worse;
these Gifts being bestowed, not for the Benefit of the *Persons themselves*, but for the
Conversion of *Others*.

OTHER Gifts of the Spirit, are particular Powers and *Qualifications* for particular
Offices; Of which the Apostle speaks, *Eph.* iv. 7, 11. *To every one of us is given grace*
(or *a gift,*) *according to the measure of the Gift of Christ*; who *gave some Apostles, and*
some prophets, and some evangelists, and some pastors and teachers; for the perfecting of
the Saints, for the work of the Ministry, for the edifying of the Body of Christ. And,
with respect to *These*, the Goodness of a Christian did not consist in his having *This*
or *That* particular Gift, but in making a right *Use* of his Talent, whatever it was.
Rom. xii. 3; 'Twas God *that dealt to every man the measure of Faith*; that is, (as it
appears from the words immediately following;) God, according to his own good
pleasure, distributed to each one a *particular Trust* or Employment: That is in this
place the meaning of the *Measure of Faith*; 'Tis a *Trust* committed to each one's *Fi-*
delity or *Faithfulness*. *Having therefore Gifts* (adds the Apostle, ver. 6.) *differing ac-*
cording to the grace that is given to us; whether it be prophecying, let us prophecy, ac-
cording to the proportion of Faith, (according to the proportion of the *Gift entrusted*
to our *Fidelity*; so the words properly signify;) *Or if it be Ministry, let us wait on*
our ministring; or he that teacheth, on teaching; or he that exhorteth, on exhortation;
He that giveth, let him do it with Simplicity, (that is, liberally;) *he that ruleth, with*
diligence; he that showeth mercy, with cheerfulness.

AGAIN, *Other* Gifts of the Spirit, are *particular and personal Advantagious Cir-*
cumstances in the peculiar *Constitution* of Men's *Bodies*, the natural *Frame and Temper*
of their *Mind*, or their external *State of Life* and *Condition* in the World; by which
they are peculiarly fitted for the Exercise of some particular Offices, or for the continuing in some particular *Manner* and *Course* of *Life*. Of *These* the Apostle speaks,

I　　　　　　　　　　　　　　　　　　　　　　　　　　　　　　　　1 *Cor.*

1 *Cor.* vii. 7 ; *I would,* fays he, *that all men were even as I myſelf*; *but every man hath* S E R M.
his proper gift of God, (a *natural Qualification* or *Fitneſs* for certain *particular Duties* LXXXVIII.
or *States* of Life,) *one after This manner, and another after That.* And with reſpect
to *Theſe,* the Goodneſs of a Chriſtian does not conſiſt in his being indued with *This*
or *That* particular Qualification ; but in his behaving himſelf *ſuitably* to *Theſe* Qualifications wherewith God *has* endued him.

L a s t l y, *Other* (and indeed the *Principal)* Gifts or Fruits of the Spirit, are *moral Virtues* ; Righteouſneſs, Peace, Goodneſs, Meekneſs, Temperance, and the like.
And in *Theſe* lies the only difficulty of the Queſtion. If they be Fruits of the *Spirit,*
and worked in us by the Power of the *Grace* of God ; how then can it be objected
to any man as a *Fault* or as a *Defect* in *himſelf,* that he has not *Thus* received the
Holy Ghoſt ? The True Anſwer is ; that theſe *moral* Graces are not, like thoſe others
before-mentioned, worked on men neceſſarily by an external operation, but depend
on the endeavours of their own *Will,* at the ſame time that they are promoted by the
Aſſiſtance of the *Holy Spirit.* Every perſon that embraces the Goſpel and is baptized,
has received the Promiſe of the Holy Ghoſt ; and 'tis wholly his own Fault, and his
own Wickedneſs only, if, with That Aſſiſtance, he brings not forth the Fruits of
the Spirit. The Aſſiſtance of the Spirit, is indeed neceſſary to *inable men* to bring
forth Fruits meet for the Kingdom of God ; But then, becauſe 'tis the *Aſſiſtance* only,
and not (like the miraculous operations) the *entire* Work of the Spirit ; and becauſe
That Aſſiſtance is always afforded men in proportion to the ſincere endeavours of
their own *Will* co-operating ; therefore 'tis juſtly charged upon a man as his own
Fault, if he wants thoſe Virtues and Graces of the Spirit, which, were it not for his
own wilful rejecting its good Motions, the good Spirit of God would never be wanting in aſſiſting him to practiſe. *Examine yourſelves,* (ſaith St *Paul) whether ye be in
the Faith : Prove your own ſelves : know ye not your own ſelves, how that Jeſus
Chriſt is in you,* (or, as it is elſewhere expreſſed, *the Spirit of Chriſt dwelleth in you,)
except ye be reprobates,* that is, except by your own perverſe wickedneſs ye drive
him from you, 2 *Cor.* xiii. 5. And for this reaſon (I ſuppoſe) it is, that whereas the
miraculous operations, are generally in Scripture ſtiled the *Gifts* of the Spirit ; the *moral* Virtues are on the contrary called, not the *Gifts,* but much more uſually the *Fruits*
of the Spirit, *Fruits* ; to the production of which, it is as neceſſarily requiſite, that
there be *good ground* in which the root is planted ; as that the *root* be good which is planted in that ground. 'Tis as neceſſary in order to bringing forth the *Fruits* of the Spirit, that
the Will and good Diſpoſition of the Perſon himſelf, concur with the good Motions of
the Spirit ; as 'tis neceſſary that the Spirit affords his Aſſiſtance, to enable the Perſon effectually to fulfil his own good Diſpoſitions. Our Saviour has illuſtrated This to us, in
the Parable of the Sower ; where the Fruit brought forth in ſeveral places, is repreſented
exactly proportionable to the Goodneſs of the Ground. The Seed ſown, is the Word of
God ; and the Rain which cauſed it to grow, is the Aſſiſtance of the divine Spirit. Now
tho' without Seed ſown in the Earth, and without Rain from Heaven, no Fruit indeed
could have been produced ; yet to the Badneſs of the *ground* only, is all the Failure
juſtly aſcribed in this Parable by our Lord, becauſe the other Neceſſaries were ſupplied
from above. In like manner, though Chriſtian Virtues are indeed the Fruits of the
Spirit, and could not, without the Aſſiſtance of the divine Spirit, be acceptably and
effectually produced ; yet becauſe This Aſſiſtance from above is never wanting but
through our own unworthineſs, therefore moſt juſtly is every wicked perſon blamed
and puniſhed, for being void of thoſe Virtues, which are the Fruits of the Spirit. The
ſame thing is expreſſed to us in the Parable of the Vineyard, *Iſ.* v. 2 ; where God complains by the Prophet concerning the people of the *Jews,* whom he compares to a
vineyard ; that he had *fenced it, and gathered out the Stones thereof, and planted it*

SERM. *with the choiceſt Vine; and he looked that it ſhould bring forth grapes, and it brought*
LXXXVIII. *forth wild grapes.* The planting and dreſſing the Vineyard was neceſſary to its bringing forth good Grapes; but when it failed to do ſo, the Fault was in the Vineyard
itſelf: ver. 4. *What could have been done more to my vineyard, that I have not done in
it? Wherefore, when I looked that it ſhould bring forth grapes, brought it forth wild
grapes?* God does on *his* part, always what is neceſſary for our Aſſiſtance; and no
more denies his Holy Spirit to ſuch as worthily aſk him, than a tender Father, *if his
Son aſk an Egg, will give him a Scorpion*; Luk. xi. 12. But men by their own unworthineſs, and reſiſting his good Motions, do quench and grieve and drive him from
them; and then moſt juſtly is it charged upon them as their *own Fault*, if they have
not in them the Spirit of God, which yet at the ſame time is God's *free Gift* when
beſtowed at all. Free; becauſe originally God had no obligation, but his own mere
Goodneſs to confer it on *any*; and yet nevertheleſs it is every man's *own* Fault, if he
receives it not; becauſe God never with-holds this his Free Gift, but from Thoſe only
who are not ſincerely willing to co-operate with it; in bringing forth thoſe Fruits of
Righteouſneſs and true Holineſs, which, upon account of That concurrence, are, at
the ſame time both the *Virtues* of the *Man*, and the *Fruits* of the *Spirit*. When therefore the Scripture affirms that we are *juſtified* freely *by his Grace*; the meaning is not,
that the Grace of God operates upon Men as Machines; and that *he* ſo acts upon
them, as to make needleſs their acting for *themſelves*. But the intention of the Phraſe,
is to declare, that it is owing to the free Grace, or undeſerved Favour of God, made
known in the Goſpel; that the imperfect Fruits of Righteouſneſs which by our beſt
endeavours we are able to bring forth, are *accepted* of him unto juſtification; and
that the *Aſſiſtance* of the good Spirit of God is always at hand, to ſtrengthen and enable us to bring forth thoſe Fruits. In like manner, when our Saviour declares, that *the
Wind bloweth where it liſteth, and we hear the Sound thereof, but know not whence it
cometh, nor whither it goeth*; and that *ſo is every one that is born of the Spirit*; the
meaning is not, that the Spirit regenerates Men without any care or co-operation of
their own; (for That would make all the Exhortations of the Goſpel vain and abſurd;)
but the Intent of the paſſage is, that the *Manner* and *Degrees*, by which the Grace of
the Goſpel enables a man to reform the whole moral Frame and Temper of his Mind,
are as imperceptible to Senſe, as the ſecret Cauſes of many great Effects and Operations in Nature. That Regeneration is *owing* to the Aſſiſtance of the *Holy Ghoſt*,
our Saviour plainly ſhows in this argument, both by the ſimilitude itſelf, and by expreſſly calling it our being *born of the Spirit*; Yet that at the ſame time it depends
upon the man's own Will, whether that divine Aſſiſtance ſhall take effect in him; he
no leſs plainly declares in the very ſame diſcourſe, by *requiring* it of Us as an indiſpenſable *Duty*, that we *be born of the Spirit: Except a man*, ſaith he, *be born of Water and of the Spirit, he cannot enter into the Kingdom of God*. From hence we may
underſtand how it comes to paſs, that uſually in Scripture-Phraſe, both all the good
that *men do* is aſcribed to *God*, and all the good that *God works in them* is ſtill nevertheleſs aſcribed to *themſelves*. It is *God* that *worketh in us both to will and to do of his good
pleaſure*; and yet in the very ſame verſe we are commanded to *work out own Salvation*
ourſelves; nay, we are commanded to do it for that very reaſon, becauſe God has
given us the Power both of Willing and performing it. As *every man is tempted,
when he is drawn away of his* own *Luſt, and enticed*; and yet at the ſame time all
Sin is aſcribed to the Temptations of the *Devil*, becauſe the Devil is the Head of
Apoſtacy, and delights in the Sins of Men, and lays before them opportunities of being enticed and drawn away by their *own* Luſt and Wickedneſs, without which he
could otherwiſe have no Power over them; ſo, becauſe *God* is the original Author of
all good, and the Giver of all the Powers by which we *do* good, and *encourages and*
                                                                                          aſſiſts

affifts us in the performance of it; therefore moft juftly in Scripture is all the good we do, afcribed to *Him*; and yet, becaufe without our *own* Care and Concurrence to put them in *Action*, all thefe *Powers* and Affiftances are in vain; it is therefore very reafonably urged as a *Duty* incumbent upon *Ourfelves*, to *grow in grace*, 2 Pet. iii. 18; and it is required of us by an indifpenfable Obligation, that *We* bring forth the Fruits of *the Spirit*. And This is implied to us in the very Form of Baptifm: For when we are baptized in the *Name* of the *Holy Ghoft*, *into what is it that we are fo baptized*, but into the *expectation* of the *Affiftance* of the Holy Spirit, and into a folemn *Promife* of *fubmitting* ourfelves accordingly to his holy *Guidance and Direction?* As, being baptized in the Name of *the Father*, is declaring our *Affurance of Reconciliation* and *Return* to his Favour, who had been juftly offended with us; and a folemn *Dedication* of ourfelves to His Service for the future, as the One fupreme Governour and Lord of the Univerfe: And being baptized in the Name of *the Son*, is being baptized into the *Remiffion* of Sins by his Blood, and into a folemn *Obligation*, on our own part, of dying with him unto Sin, and rifing again unto Newnefs of Life: So, being baptized in the Name of *the Holy Ghoft*, is at the fame time a folemn Declaration both of our *Hoping* for his Guidance, and of our *Refolving to* obey it.

I HAVE been the longer upon This *firft* Head concerning the *Gifts* of the Spirit, becaufe it is a Doctrine of the Higheft Importance to us, and of great Moment in Practice. That which remains in the *2d* place, concerning the *Nature and Offices* of the Holy Spirit, being more fpeculative, I fhall explain very briefly in few words. As to the proper *Nature* of this divine Spirit, the Vanity and Pride of learned men has often confounded their Underftandings, while they have prefumed to be wife above what is written, intruding into things which they have not feen, and attempting to explain what God has not revealed. The Effence and inmoft Nature of the fmalleft *Body*, we cannot fully underftand: The Life of the meaneft *Animal*, is beyond all our Philofophy to explain: The Nature of the *Soul of Man*, is ftill a more unfeatchable Myftery: The Nature and Effence of *Angels*, is yet far more unfathomable than any of Thefe: How then fhould vain man prefume to fearch out the Nature of the *Spirit* of God? the Nature of the *only begotten Son* of God? the Nature of the *Father* himfelf, the incomprehenfible God and Father of all things? What the Scripture expreffly declares to us, is all we can ever know concerning thefe Matters; and this the meaneft Chriftian is as capable of underftanding, as the learnedeft Difputers in the World. Concerning the *Nature of the Holy Spirit* therefore, That which the Scripture teaches us, is, *This* only; that He is a Divine Perfon, in an ineffable manner deriving his Being, proceeding from, or being fent forth from, the Father; *whereby he is*, and *upon which account* he is ftiled, in a fingular and peculiar manner, *The Spirit of God*. And becaufe after the Afcenfion of Chrift, the Gifts attributed by the fame Spirit, were, according to the Promife of the Father, poured forth in *much greater plenty and abundance* than before; therefore he is frequently ftiled likewife, *The Spirit of Chrift*: And before that *Jefus* was *glorified*, it is affirmed therefore of the fame Spirit in the Gofpel, (comparatively to that *much larger Effufion* which was to follow after,) that he *was not yet given* at all, St *Joh.* vii. 39; In which Paffage it is very remarkable, that the words in the Original are, *The Holy Ghoft was not yet*; meaning, was not yet *given*; juft as in the Text the Difciples are faid *not to have heard whether there* was *any Holy Ghoft*; meaning, that they had not heard whether he was yet *given*. There have been *Some*, both in Antient and Modern times, who have taught that the *Holy Ghoft* was nothing but a *mere Power*, and Operation or Action of the Father: But though it is True, that *Powers* are indeed fometimes in Scripture, according to the nature of the *Jewifh* Language, fpoken of figuratively as *Perfons*; yet in the prefent cafe it is plain on the contrary, that the *Perfon* of the Holy Spirit is often reprefented

SERM. ſented and ſpoken of as the *Power* of the Father, only becauſe *By Him* it is that the Fa-
LXXXVIII. ther works all Miracles and beſtows all Gifts. Nor can thoſe Texts be underſtood any
otherwiſe, than of a real Perſon; in which it is expreſſed that *He*, (in the original it is,
That Perſon,) the Spirit of Truth is come, Joh. xvi. 13; that *he maketh interceſſion for
us,* Rom. viii, 26; that he *divideth* ſpiritual Gifts, *to every one ſeverally as he willeth,*
1 Cor. xii. 11; and that *he ſhall not ſpeak of himſelf, but what he ſhall hear*, or receive
from the Father, *That ſhall he ſpeak*; Joh. xvi. 13. Theſe, and other the like Texts,
do plainly declare the Holy Spirit to be, not a mere Power or Operation, but a real
Perſon ſent forth from the Father and the Son, for the perpetual Government and Direction of the Church.

In which Miſſion, the ſeveral *Offices* which the Scripture teaches us he performs,
are as follow; that it was He who inſpired the Prophets of old, to teſtify before-hand
the Sufferings of Chriſt, and the Glory that ſhould follow: that he was afterwards ſent
forth in a more particular and extraordinary manner, to be the Comforter, Director, and
Guide of the Apoſtles; to lead them into all Truth: to bring to their remembrance all
things whatſoever Chriſt had before ſaid unto them; to ſupport them againſt the Power
of the World; to inſtruct them what to anſwer to their Perſecutors; to be the great
Witneſs of our Saviour's Reſurrection, by working Signs and Wonders and mighty
Works, by inſpiring the Apoſtles with the Gift of Tongues, and dividing to their Followers Diverſities of Gifts; Finally, to continue with all good Chriſtians even unto the
End of the World, as the great Sanctifier of the Hearts of Men; ſanctifying them, not
by working upon them mechanically as Machines, but by moral Motives as rational
Beings; aſſiſting them with his Grace, admoniſhing them with his Holy Influences,
working with them and inſpiring them with his good Gifts, and helping the Infirmity
of their Prayers with an Energy that cannot be expreſſed.

3. HAVING thus briefly diſcourſed concerning the *Nature* and *Offices* and *Gifts* of
the Spirit; the *Application* of what has been ſaid, is, what *Returns* we are bound
to make for the Benefit of thoſe Divine Gifts beſtowed upon us. And 1ſt, it will become us to return continual and hearty Thanks to *God* as the original Author and
Fountain of all Good; becauſe it is *He*, who has thus *given* unto us *His* holy Spirit;
1 Theſſ. iv. 8.; and who has *ſent forth* the Spirit of his Son into our Hearts; *Gal.* iv. 6.
2*dly*, As we are to return hearty Thanks for the Gifts already received, ſo we are continually to pray to God in the whole Courſe of our Lives, that *This* his holy Spirit, into
whoſe Name we were at firſt baptized, *i. e.* dedicated wholly to his Guidance and Direction in the work of our Salvation; may never be withdrawn from us, but may continue to guide us by his perpetual influence, communion and fellowſhip. 3*dly*, With
regard to the Holy Spirit himſelf, it becomes us to endeavour to frame right and worthy Notions concerning him; that we acknowledge him to be the Inſpirer of the
Prophets and Apoſtles; the Author and Worker of all Signs and Miracles; the Sanctifier of all Hearts, and the Diſtributer of all Spiritual Gifts: that we believe and receive
his Teſtimony, as delivered by the Inſpired Writers; that we obey his good Motions;
be ſollicitous to obtain his gifts and graces; and infinitely careful not to grieve and
quench and drive him from us, leſt we be found to do deſpite unto the Spirit of grace;
which in Scripture is repreſented as a more unpardonable fault, than offending againſt
the Perſon even of our Saviour himſelf. *How is it* (ſays the Apoſtle,) *that ye have a-
greed together to* tempt *the Spirit of the Lord?* Acts v. 19; To *tempt*; that is, in Scripture-language, to *provoke* him: *In the day of Temptation in the Wilderneſs, when your
Fathers tempted me*; the meaning is, provoked *me to anger*; Pſ. xcv. 9. Again, *Epheſ.*
iv. 30; *And grieve not the Holy Spirit of God, whereby ye are ſealed unto the Day of
Redemption*: The word, *ſealed*, is a figuraitve expreſſion; the meaning of which may
be underſtood from *Rev.* vii. 3; *Hurt not the Earth,*——*'till we have* ſealed *the Ser-

vants of our God in their Foreheads, i. e. diftinguifhed them by a peculiar mark, in order to preferve them from a general deftruction. In Allufion to which, good Chriftians are faid to *be fealed by the Spirit unto the Day of Redemption* ; *i. e.* diftinguifhed by the Fruits of the Spirit, in order to be delivered from the Wrath to come. And in purfuance of this figure, is the like expreffion, 2 *Cor.* i. 22; *who hath alfo* fealed *us, and given the* Earneft (in the original it is, the *Pledge* or *Token) of the Spirit in our Hearts:* And. 2 *Tim.* ii. 19; *The Foundation of the Lord ftandeth fure, having this* Seal, *The Lord knoweth them that are his,* and, *Let every one that nameth the name of Chrift, depart from iniquity.*

THERE is one thing more upon this Head, which deferves particular obfervation, wherewith I fhall conclude: And That is, that following the Guidance of the Spirit, is not following Enthufiaftick Imaginations; but taking care to obey the Doctrine which the Spirit infpired. The *Apoftles* were directed by a miraculous Affiftance of the Spirit, upon every particular occafion: But we have *Now* no promife of any fuch miraculous direction: Obeying the Spirit *Now,* is nothing elfe but obeying his dictates, as fet down in the infpired Writings: And to enable us to do This, we *may,* upon our fincere endeavours, expect his continual bleffing and affiftance.

SERMON LXXXIX.

Of the Power and Authority of CHRIST.

[Preached on Trinity-Sunday.]

St MATT. XXVIII. part 18, 19, 20.

*All power is given unto me in Heaven and in Earth : Go ye therefore,
and teach all Nations, baptizing them in the Name of the Father,
and of the Son, and of the Holy Ghost : Teaching them to observe all
things whatsoever I have commanded you ; and lo, I am with you always even unto the End of the World.*

SERM.
LXXXIX.

OUR Saviour in his last Discourse with his Disciples *before* his suffering; after
he had instituted the Sacrament of the Lord's Supper, and was going out with
them towards the *Mount of Olives* in order to be betrayed; and had warned
them of their approaching Sorrow, ch. xxvi. 31; *All ye shall be offended because of Me
this Night ; for it is written, I will smite the Shepherd, and the Sheep of the Flock shall
be scattered abroad;* proceeds in the next verse to allay their Grief, and support them
against Despair, by giving them a remote prospect of Light after Darkness, and of Comfort that should succeed That melancholy Scene: *But after I am risen again,* saith he,
I will go before ye into Galilee. What he intended to *Do* in *Galilee,* he did not then
think fit to explain to them more distinctly ; But *Galilee* being the place wherein they
had used to converse most freely with him, and where they had with pleasure heard
the greatest part of his divine Discourses, it gave them a general Hope or Expectation,
that after the present Time of Trouble, and after their leaving *Jerusalem* the constant
place of Persecution; when he should be risen again, (the *meaning* of which, whether
it was literal or only figurative, they seemed not then fully to understand; but when it
were fulfilled,) they thought they should again converse with him freely and safely, in
their antient places of retirement in *Galilee.*

AFTER his Resurrection, This Promise was renewed and confirmed to them, by the
Angel appearing to the Women at the Sepulchre, and saying, *Mar.* xvi. 7; *Go,——tell
his Disciples,——that he goeth before you into Galilee; there shall ye see him, as he said
unto you.* And the *Fulfilling* of it, is recorded in the words immediately before the
Text; *Then the eleven Disciples went away into Galilee, into a Mountain where Jesus
had appointed them ; And there they saw him,——and he spake unto them.* What it was
that he spake unto them; or what the Design was of his meeting them there ; St *Luke*
tells us, *Acts* i. 2; *He gave Commandments unto the Apostles whom he had chosen, and
spake to them of the things pertaining to the Kingdom of God ;* He gave them full instructions concerning the Nature of his spiritual Kingdom, which before his Resurrection they did not rightly understand; and, in several Conversations during the forty

I

days

days between his Refurrection and Afcenfion, he furnifhed them with all proper Directions relating to the Doctrine of the Gofpel, which they were to preach and propagate over the whole World. A Summary or fhort Abridgement of which Inftructions, is delivered down to us in the Words of the Text: *All Power is given unto me in Heaven and in Earth: Go ye therefore, and teach all Nations, baptizing them in the Name of the Father, and of the Son, and of the Holy Ghoft: Teaching them to obferve all things whatfoever I have commanded you; and lo, I am with you always, even unto the End of the World.*

THE words contain in brief, the whole Syftem of Chriftian Doctrine: And, for Method's fake, we may obferve in them diftinctly the following particulars; *1ft*, An Account of the Extent, of our *Saviour's Power*; that he is invefted with all *Power*, both *in Heaven and Earth*. *2dly*, A Declaration, of the *Original* of that unlimited Power and Authority; *All Power*, faith he, *is given me*, *i. e.* from the *Father*. *3dly*, The *Commiffion* he thereupon grants his Difciples; *Go* Ye *therefore*, and *teach all Nations*. *4thly*, The *Doctrine*, which all Nations were to be taught, and into which they were to be baptized; *Baptizing them in the Name of the Father, and of the Son, and of the Holy Ghoft*. *5thly*, The *Practice*, of thofe who were to be baptized into this Faith; *Teaching them to* obferve all things *whatfoever I have commanded you*; And Laftly, The *Promife of effectual Affiftance*, to the Difciples fent forth upon This Commiffion; *And lo, I am with you always, even unto the End of the World*.

1ft, HERE is an Account, of the *Extent* of our Saviour's Power and Authority; that he is invefted with All *Power*, both in *Heaven and Earth*. The *Jews*, in their expectations of the Meffiah, imagined to themfelves the Character of a Temporal Prince, who fhould deliver them from the Yoke of their Enemies, and reduce all the World under their Dominion; who fhould *fubdue the People under them, and the Nations under* their *Feet*: who fhould *choofe out an Heritage for* them, *even the Excellency of Jacob whom he loved*; Pf. xlvii. 3. And *This* indeed our Saviour *has* begun, and will continue to accomplifh; according to the *True Intent* of the Prophecy, though not after the manner of *Their* Interpretation. *Unto* Them, though they know it not, *a Child is born*; *unto* If. ix. 6. Them, *a Son is given*; *and the government Is upon his Shoulder*; *and his Name Is Wonderful, Counfellor, The Mighty God*; (Not, *the everlafting Father*; For it is the *Son* here fpoken of, and *not the Father everlafting*; But) the *Governor*, the *Father or Lord of the Age to come*, (fo the Phrafe ought to be rendered;) *The Prince of Peace: And* Luc. i. 33. *he* fhall reign *over the Houfe of Jacob for ever, and of his Kingdom there fhall be no end*. The *Jews*, at the time of our Lord's appearing in the Flefh were extremely difappointed and prejudiced againft him; becaufe his *feeming* meannefs fell fo much fhort of that Grandeur, wherein they expected their Meffiah fhould have fhown himfelf: And yet in reality his *True* Power and Authority was as much Superior even to that *expected* Grandeur; as his feeming Meannefs, for which they defpifed him, was inferior to it. They expected a *Temporal* Deliverer, and he propofed to them a Salvation *eternal*: They looked for a Prince of *Men*, and he appeared to be the Lord of *Angels*; They expected a Meffiah endued with *great* Power on *Earth*, and he fhowed himfelf to be invefted with *All* Power borh in *Earth and Heaven*. Thus did the Wifdom of God put to filence the ignorance of foolifh men: And while the Lovers of Worldly Grandeur defpifed and reviled our Lord for his appearing Meannefs; under that Meannefs there lay concealed, and to all well difpofed Perfons (who looked for Redemption in *Ifrael*) there difcovered itfelf a Power, infinitely fuperior even to the higheft Expectations, of thofe whofe Hearts were bent on nothing but Worldly Greatnefs. *O the depth of the Riches both of the Knowledge and Wifdom of God! How unfearchable are his judgments, and his ways paft finding out!* Our Saviour, as he miniftred to the Father in creating the World; (For by him the Scripture declares, *God created all things*) So in
governing

SERM. *governing the* World, he likewise *supports all things by the Word of his Power.* He does
LXXXIX. what he pleases, *in the Armies of Heaven, and among the Inhabitants of the Earth;*
He is *King of Kings, and Lord of Lords;* and judges, punishes, or rewards, as he pleases: *For as the Father raises up the dead, and quickneth them; even so the Son quickneth
whom he willeth;* St Joh. v. 21; He *searches the Hearts and Reins, and declares that
he will give to every man according to his Work,* Rev. ii. 23. He *hath the Keys of
Hell and of Death,* Rev. i. 18; *the Key of David, that openeth and no man shutteth,
and shutteth and no man openeth,* Rev. iii. 7. The words are of the same import with
those in *Job,* ch. xii. 14, where compleat and irresistible Power is thus described; *Behold he breaketh down, and it cannot be built again; he shutteth up a man, and there
can be no opening:* And they are an Application of that antient Prophecy, to our Saviour; *Is.* xxii. 22: *The Key of the House of David will I lay upon his shoulder; so
he shall open, and none shall shut; and he shall shut, and none shall open.*

AND This, as it is a full Declaration of the *Extent* of our Saviour's Power, that it
is *universal,* All *Power* both *in Heaven and Earth;* which was the 1*st* particular observable in the Text; so it leads us in the 2*d* place, to the consideration of the *Original* of this unlimited Power and Authority. *I will lay upon his shoulder the Key of the
House of David.* I will invest him with *All Power,* saith God in *the Prophecy;* And,
at the Accomplishment *of the Prophecy,* All Power is *Given unto me,* saith our Saviour
in the Text, *i. e.* given unto me *by the Father.* Underived Power, is peculiar to the
Person of the Father; the incommunicable Property of Him alone, *who is made of
None, neither created, nor begotten, nor proceeding,* nor in any manner whatsoever derived from Another. All Power is derivative from *Him;* derivative from the Father,
to the Son; and from the Son, by the Spirit, to all Creatures. In our Saviour therefore, is vested all Dominion and Authority; because *in Him dwelleth the Fulness of the
Godhead,* (the Fulness of Divine Power, the Glory of the Father,) bodily, *visibly,* as
in the Person of a Man: And therefore he is stiled, *the* Image *of the* invisible *God;* because (as the Apostle expresses it,) *it pleaseth the Father, that in him should all Fulness,*
the Fulness of all Power, *dwell.* This is, in a most lively Figure, represented to us by
the Prophet *Daniel,* ch. vii. 13; *I saw in the Night-visions, and behold, One like the
Son of Man, came with the Clouds of Heaven, and came to the Antient of Days, and
they brought him near before him; And there was* given *him Dominion, and Glory, and
a Kingdom; that all people, nations and languages should serve him; His Dominion is
an everlasting Dominion, which shall not pass away; and his Kingdom, that which shall
not be destroyed.* And the Expressions in the New Testament, wherein is recorded the
Fulfilling of this Prophetick Vision, are exactly agreeable to it. The Angel at the An-
nunciation, thus declares concerning him, before his Conception, *He shall be great, and
shall be called the Son of the Highest; and the Lord God shall* give unto him *the Throne
of his Father David; and he shall reign over the House of Jacob for ever,* Luke i. 32.
Concerning *Himself* he professes accordingly, *Matt.* xi. 27; *All things are* delivered unto me *of my Father:* And again, *Joh.* xiii. 3; *Knowing that the Father had* given *all
things into his hands:* And yet more expressly, *Joh.* v. 22; *The Father judgeth no man,
but hath* committed *all judgment unto the Son:* and ver. 26; *As the Father hath Life
in himself, so hath* he given *to the Son to have Life in Himself; and hath given him Authority to execute judgment also, because he is the Son of Man:* and ver. 19; *Verily I
say unto you, The Son can do nothing of Himself, but what he seeth the Father do; for
what things soever He doth, these also doth the Son likewise.* In the same manner with
these declarations of our *Lord* concerning *himself,* do the *Apostles* also speak of Him
in their Epistles. *Whom God hath* appointed *Heir of all things.* saith St *Paul,* Heb.
i. 2: and ch. ii. 8; *Thou hast* put *all things in Subjection under his Feet.* And still more
largely and particularly, *Phil.* ii. 9; *Wherefore* God *also has highly* exalted *him, and*

I

given

given *him a Name which is above every Name; that at the Name of Jesus every knee should bow,* (should become subject to His Dominion,) *of things in Heaven, and things in Earth, and things under the Earth; And that every tongue should confess* (in acknowledgment of That Subjection,) *that Jesus Christ is Lord, to the glory of God the Father;* and *Eph.* i. 20; *he* raised Christ *from the dead, and set him at his own right hand in the heavenly places; Far above all Principalities and Powers, and Might and Dominion, and every Name that is named, not only in this World, but also in that which is to come; And hath* put *all things under his Feet, and* gave *him to be the Head over all things to the Church.* And accordingly upon account of this derivation of our Lord's Power, by way of Delegation from the Father, it is, that the same Apostle declares, 1 *Cor.* xv. 24; that at *the End, he shall deliver up* again *the Kingdom to God, even the Father, when he shall have put down all Rule and all Authority and Power: For ——when he* saith, *All things are put under him: it is manifest that He is excepted, which did put all things under him: And when all things shall be subdued unto him, then shall the Son also himself be subject unto Him that put all things under him, that God* (even the Father) *may be all in all.* It may here justly be thought a Difficulty, how in *This* place it is declared, that our Lord shall at *the End deliver up the Kingdom to the Father*; and yet in *other* Passages before-mentioned it is expressly affirmed, that *he shall rule for* ever, *and of his Kingdom there shall be* no *End.* But the Answer is obvious; that, when it is said, *his Kingdom shall have* no *End,* and that *it is a Kingdom which shall* never *be destroyed*; the meaning is, that it shall never be prevailed over by any *opposite* Power, but shall subdue all things to itself; In which Subjection of *all things* to him, it is yet manifest that *He* cannot be included, by whose original Power they were 1 Cor. xv. 27. *All* made subject to him: But as our Lord was at first sent forth by the good Pleasure of the Father, so unto Him shall he at last return again; and when, by the Power of Judgment committed unto him, he shall have *brought many Sons unto glory,* he shall, together with *Them,* deliver up again the *Power itself* also into the hands of the Father, when he *presents* them *faultless before the presence of his glory,* and instates them in the eternal Kingdom of their heavenly Father: *In* which Kingdom of the Father, He himself shall continue to *reign* over them that are saved, as King of Kings and Lord of Lords, for ever and ever. The *Socinian* Writers, from these and some other the like Texts of Scripture, have *very unreasonably* presumed to collect, that our Saviour was no greater a Person than a mere Man, born of the Virgin *Mary* without any former Existence, and exalted by the Power of God to this State of Dignity in Heaven: But This their Inference (I say) is *very unreasonable:* For though the Derivation of our Lord's Power from the Father, must and ought to be acknowledged; that all mens *confessing Jesus to be Lord,* may be (as St *Paul* directs) *to the glory of God the Father;* yet from those other Texts of Scripture, wherein it is affirmed that *by Christ God created all things;* that he was in the *Form of God,* before he appeared in *the Form of a Servant;* that he *was with God,* and *had Glory with* God *before the World was;* from these Texts, I say, it undeniably appears, that our Lord's having *all Power* given him both in Heaven and Earth, cannot signify the *original* Exaltation, of One who had no Being before he was born of the Virgin; but the Exaltation of *Him* into the Form of God, who voluntarily emptied himself of that Glory he had *before,* and with unparallelled Humility took upon himself the Form of a Servant, and suffered in that Form for our Sakes; and *Therefore* was *worthy to receive Power and Riches and Wisdom, and strength and honour, and glory and blessing,* because he *was slain, and redeemed us to God by his own Blood, out of every Tongue and Kindred and People and Nation.*

3*dly,* THE next thing observable in the Text, is the *Commission* our Saviour grants Rev v. his Disciples, upon his having received all Power in Heaven and Earth: *Go Ye there-* ver. 9 and 12. fore, *and Teach all Nations.* The Word, therefore, is the Ascertaining of *Their* Authority,

S E R M. thority, from the Security of his *own*. All Power is given unto *Me* ; Go *Ye* therefore,
LXXXIX. and teach all Nations. This particular is more fully expreſſed by St *John*, ch. xx. 21 ;
*As my Father hath ſent me, even ſo ſend I you :——— whoſeſoever Sins ye remit, they are
remitted unto them ; and whoſeſoever Sins ye retain, they are retained :* Not that the
Apoſtles were intruſted with any Power, to pardon or condemn any man according to
their *own Pleaſure :* For *This* even our Saviour *himſelf*, does only according to the Will
of the Father which ſent him : But the meaning is, that they were intruſted to preach
That Doctrine of Repentance, by the Terms of which it was to be determined, *whoſe*
Sins ſhould be pardoned and *whoſe* retained. A like Expreſſion is uſed by our Saviour
to St *Peter*, Matt. xvi. 19 ; *I will give unto thee the Keys of the Kingdom of Heaven ;
and whatſoever thou ſhalt bind on Earth, ſhall be bound in Heaven ; and whatſoever thou
ſhalt looſe on Earth, ſhall be looſed in Heaven :* Not that St *Peter*, or Any, or All the
Apoſtles, had Power to let whom they pleaſed into Heaven ; but that they were appointed and commiſſioned to preach *That* Doctrine, by the Terms of which, Men
were to be admitted into, or excluded out of Heaven.

 Go ye, and Teach *All Nations :* The Word, *Teach*, ſignifies in the original, *Make
Diſciples :* In like manner, as *Acts* xiv. 21 ; *When they had preached the Goſpel to that
City, and had* Taught *many* ; in the original it is, *and had made many Diſciples.*

 TEACH, All *Nations :* The words, *All Nations*, ſignify *primarily*, the Nations of
the *Roman* Empire ; and *then*, in a *larger* Senſe, all the Kingdoms of the World. In
St *Mark* it is, *Preach the Goſpel to* every Creature. And, in the 1ſt chapter to the
Coloſſians, what in the 6*th* verſe is expreſſed, the Goſpel came into *All the* World, is
at the 23*d* verſe ſaid to have been *preached to* every Creature under Heaven. The
meaning of which is ſo obvious, that it would hardly need to be mentioned, but that it
helps to illuſtrate a more difficult paſſage in the viii*th* to the *Romans* ; where, when the
Apoſtle had ſaid at the 21ſt verſe, *The* creature itſelf *alſo ſhall be delivered from the
bondage of Corruption, into the glorious Liberty of the children, of God :* He adds, ver. 23 ;
And not only they, but ourſelves *alſo which have the* Firſt-fruits *of the Spirit, even we
ourſelves groan within ourſelves, waiting for the Adoption, to wit, the Redemption of our
Body.* So that the words, *Creature* or *whole Creation*, ſeem to ſignify thoſe many Nations, or the *Bulk* of Mankind, to whom the Goſpel was afterwards to be preached ;
in contradiſtinction to the *Firſt-fruits*, who received it in the Apoſtle's Time.

 4*thly,* HERE is the *Doctrine*, which all Nations were to be taught, and into which
they were to be Baptized ; *Baptizing them, in the Name of the Father, and of the Son,
and of the Holy Ghoſt.* This is that brief Summary of Chriſtian Faith, which, in the
Apoſtle's Time, Men were taught, and profeſſed, and had explained to them at their
Baptiſm ; and the Explication of it was afterwards well expreſſed in that *Form of Sound
Words*, which is now uſually called the *Apoſtles Creed.* To be Baptized in the Name
of the *Father*, is to profeſs our Belief (as St *Paul* words it) in the *One God and Father
of All, who is Above All, and Through all, and In All*, even the *Father Almighty*, the
Maker, and Lord, and Supreme Governour of all things. To be Baptized in the Name
of the *Son*, is to profeſs our Belief likewiſe in the One Lord, *Jeſus Chriſt*, the only-
begotten Son of God, the Meſſiah that was to come, the Redeemer and Saviour of
Mankind, the Author and Purchaſer of Forgiveneſs to Sinners, or of the Acceptation
of Repentance through his Blood ; our great High Prieſt or Interceſſor with God, and
by the Appointment of the Father, our Judge at the laſt day. To be Baptized in the
Name of the *Son*, ſignifies alſo further, to be Baptized *into his Death : Know ye not,*
ſaith St *Paul*, that ſo many *of us as were baptized into Jeſus Chriſt, were baptized into his
Death?* Rom. vi. 3. And what *That* means, he tells us in the following verſe ; *We
are buried with him by Baptiſm into Death,* (that the Body of Sin might be deſtroyed,
ver. 6 ;) *that like as Chriſt was raiſed up from the Dead by the Glory of the Father,*

                    even

Rom. x. 18.
Mar. xvi 15.

Col. ii. 12.

even fo We alfo fhould walk in newnefs of Life.   Laftly, To be baptized in the Name of S E R M. the *Holy Ghoft,* fignifies our Acknowledging the *Holy Spirit of God,* to be the Infpirer LXXXIV. of the Apoftles and Prophets ; the Comforter, and the Director of Chriftians ; that we fubmit ourfelves to his Holy Guidance, receive the Doctrine infpired by him into the Apoftles and Prophets, expect to be juftified from our paft Sins by the renewing of the Joh. iii. 3, 5. Holy Ghoft, and to be preferved from Sin for the future by his Sanctification and Af- 1 Cor. vi. 11. Tit. iii. 5. fiftance ; that we obey his good motions, take great care not to grieve or quench and drive him from us ; and, forafmuch as *by one Spirit we are all baptized into one Body,* 1 Cor. xii. 13. ——*and have been all made to drink into one Spirit,* that therefore we endeavour by mutual Charity and Forbearance, to *keep the Unity of the Spirit in the Bond of Peace.* This is the Meaning, of being *baptized in the Name of the Father, and of the Son, and of the Holy Ghoft,* with refpect to the feveral *Offices* of thefe three Divine Perfons, in which Regard it is that the Scripture always fpeaks of them : As to their *Metaphyfical Nature* ; the Vanity of Men, fpeculating about *That* beyond what is written, has been the Occafion of many foolifh Errors : Some have imagined three co-ordinate Beings, which is the Impiety of *Polytheifm,* and directly contrary to that Fundamental Article, the Unity of God : Others have contended, that they are one Perfon only, with three Modes or Denominations ; Which is the Herefy of *Sabellianifm,* and deftroys the Perfonality both of the Son and Holy Spirit : Some, in the contrary extreme, forfaking likewife the Phrafes of Scripture, have prefumed to affirm, that there was a Time, when the Son and Holy Spirit had no Being, and were made out of Nothing even as the meaneft of Creatures ; which was the notion of *Arius* : And Others, diminifhing yet further the Dignity of our Saviour's Perfon, have made him a mere Man, and denied his having any Being before he was born of the Virgin ; Which is the Error of *Socinus.* And now among this multiplicity of Errors, how fhall a fincere and unlearned Chriftian behave himfelf ? Why, His Rule is ; Let him not follow vain men, in being Wife beyond what is written ; but let him adhere to what he finds plainly and exprefsly delivered in Scripture : And This, as far as poffible, in the very Scripture-Terms ; always remembring, where That cannot be done, yet fo to underftand all Phrafes of human Compofition, as to mean neither more nor lefs than the Scripture-Expreffions.   Now that which the Scripture declares concerning this Matter, is This : When one of the Scribes asked our Saviour, *Which is the firft Commandment of all ? Jefus anfwered him, The firft of all the Commandments is ; Hear, O Ifrael, the Lord our God is one Lord :* To which the Scribe replied, *Well, Mafter, thou haft faid the Truth ; For there is One God, and there is none other but He ;* Mar. xii. 29, 32 : and 1 Cor. viii. 6. *To Us there is but One God, the Father, of whom are all things :* and Eph. iv. 6 ; *One God and Father of All, who is above All, and through All, and in you All.*   Yet the fame Scripture does likewife exprefsly affirm that the *Son* alfo is God ; and to the *Holy Spirit* it afcribes Divine Powers and Attributes : How Then fhall This be reconciled ? Plainly Thus : The Power and Authority of the Son and Holy Spirit, is neither *Another* Power and Authority, *oppofite* to that of the Father ; nor *Another* Power and Authority, *co-ordinate* to that of the Father ; But it is *His* Power and Authority, communicated *to* Them, manifefted *in* them, and exercifed *by* them : And fo there is plainly preferved both an Unity of Power, and a Monarchy of Government in the Univerfe.

5thly, To the *Form* of Baptifm, our Saviour adds in the Text, the *Practice* of thofe who are to be baptized into This Faith.   *Teaching them to Obferve all things whatfoever I have commanded you.*   And This, is the Great End and Ufe of the whole.   As *Faith* without *Works* is dead ; fo *Baptifm,* without *the Anfwer of a good Confcience towards* 1 Pet. iii. 21. *God,* is but the *Wafhing away of the Filth of the Flefh.*   He that is baptized, muft Heb x. 22. Eph. v. 26. *put off, concerning the former converfation, the old man, which is corrupt according to the deceitful lufts ; and be renewed in the Spirit of his mind ; and put on the new man,*

which

4

which after God is created in Righteousness and true Holiness, Eph. iv. 22. He must, as St *Paul* elsewhere expresses it, *put on the Lord Jesus Christ.* Gal. iii. 27. *As many of you as have been baptized into Christ, have* put on *Christ.* The Meaning is: He that is baptized into the Religion of Christ, must conform himself to the same pattern, must *observe all things whatsoever* He *has commanded Us,* must obey his Laws delivered in the Gospel; otherwise his Baptism is vain, and his Profession but Hypocrisy.

6*thly* and *Lastly,* Here is the *Promise* of an *effectual Assistance,* to the Disciples sent forth upon This Commission: *And, lo, I am with you always even unto the End of the World.* Being *with them always,* 'tis evident did not signify his continuing *personally* with them; For this Promise was made to them at the very Time, when he had declared he was about to leave them and *ascend unto the Father.* But it signifies, that he would continue with them *by* the guidance and direction of *his Spirit;* which was in effect the same thing, as continuing with them *himself.* Thus God is in Scripture said to dwell in us *Himself,* when he dwells in us *by his Spirit;* and he that lies to the *Spirit* Eph. ii. 22.
Acts v. 4. *of God,* is justly accused of lying consequently to *God Himself;* and he who rejects the preaching of an *Apostle,* is charged with rejecting *Christ;* and he that rejects *Christ,* with rejecting *God Himself* who sent him.

C H R I S T's being with his Disciples *to the End of the World* therefore, is his being with them *by his Spirit.* And This imports *two* things: 1*st,* His giving them the Holy Ghost at Pentecost, to inspire them with the Doctrine of Truth, and to enable them to confirm that Doctrine with miraculous Gifts; according to the promise; St *Mar.* xvi. 17; *These Signs shall follow them that believe; In my Name shall they cast out Devils, they shall speak with* new tongues, *they shall take up Serpents; and if they drink any deadly thing, it shall not hurt them; they shall lay hands on the Sick, and they shall recover.* And 2*dly* it implies, That, after this Foundation of the Church, by the Teaching and Miracles of the inspired Apostles; the Blessing of Providence, and the Assistance of the Divine Spirit, should continue to preserve it; not by raising up infallible Guides and unerring humane Authority, which never was in any Others than the Apostles themselves; but by supporting the Doctrine once delivered by the Apostles, against all the Violence and Frauds of its Opposers. *Thou art Peter,* says our Saviour, *that is,* a Rock; *and upon this Rock will I build my Church, and the gates of Hell, i. e.* Persecution and even *Death* itself, (for so the words properly signify,) *shall not be able to prevail against it,* Matt. xvi. 18. And what is meant by St *Peter's* being a Rock, or Stone, upon which the Church is built, is explained, *Eph.* ii. 20; where the Church is compared to a Building, the Apostles to Foundation-stones, and our Saviour himself to the Head of the Building: *Ye are built,* saith St *Paul, upon the Foundation of the Apostles and Prophets, Jesus Christ himself being the chief Corner-stone; In whom all the Building fitly framed together, groweth into a Holy Temple in the Lord; In whom you also are builded together, for an habitation of God through the Spirit.*

S E R M O N

S E R M O N XC.

Of the different Gifts of the SPIRIT.

[*Preached on Trinity-Sunday.*]

1 COR. XII. 4, 5, 6.

Now there are Diverfities of Gifts, but the fame Spirit; And there are differences of Adminiftrations, but the fame Lord; And there are diverfities of Operations, but it is the fame God, which work-eth all in all.

IN thefe Words we have a diftinct account of three Divine Perfons concerned in bringing about the Salvation of Men; and a brief Declaration of the nature of their feveral Offices, in accomplifhing that great and merciful Defign. There are in the *firft* place Gifts of Miracles, of Signs and Wonders, for the Conviction of Infidels; and there are Gifts of Grace, of virtuous and holy Difpofitions, for the Sanctification and Improvement of Believers; And thefe are conftantly afcribed in Scripture to the *Spirit of God*, the Holy Ghoft, the Comforter: *There are diverfities of Gifts, but the fame Spirit.* There is in the *2d* place a wonderful Oeconomy in the eftablifhment and Government of the Church: Mankind was to be redeemed from the Power of Satan, and the Repentance of Sinners made acceptable before God, and available to the obtaining of Pardon, confiftently with the Juftice and Wifdom and Honour of the Laws of God; by the offering up of a fufficient Sacrifice, Oblation and Satisfaction, for the Sins of the Whole World: This Doctrine was to be revealed unto Men; and a Church gathered out of the whole World, of fuch as fhould embrace and obey this Revelation: An Order and Government was to be eftablifhed, for the propagating this Church and conveying down this Doctrine by a perpetual Succeffion, even unto the End of the World: Perpetual Interceffion was to be made to God by a Sinlefs High-Prieft, to make the Prayers of frail and finful men acceptable in the Sight of Him, who is of purer Eyes than to behold Iniquity: A Refurrection of the Dead was to be appointed, a final Judgment paffed, and a juft and impartial Retribution made to every man according to his Works: And Thefe things are all afcribed in Scripture to the *Son of God*, even our Lord Jefus Chrift, who, before his Incarnation, was the Word of the Father, the Angel of his Prefence, the Brightnefs of his Glory, the exprefs Image of his Perfon; and after his Incarnation, was the Redeemer and Saviour, the Mediator and Interceffor, the Lord and Judge of Mankind: *There are Differences of Adminiftrations*, fays the Apoftle, *but the fame Lord.* There is in the *3d* and *laft* place a Supreme and Abfolute, a felf-original, underived and independent Authority, from whence all thefe things primarily and originally proceed, and to which the Glory of them muft finally and ultimately be referred:

SERM.
XC.
And this is in Scripture conftantly afcribed to *God*, even the Father of our Lord Jefus Chrift; who is the Firft and Supreme Author of every good Gift; by whofe good pleafure, our Lord himfelf was fent forth to redeem us; and the Holy Spirit given, to fanctify us; *There are Diverfity of Operations, but it is the fame God, which worketh all in all:* Or, as the fame Apoftle elfewhere expreffes it; *Of him and through him and to him are all things, to whom be Glory and Dominion for ever.* This is the Account the Scripture gives us, of the feveral Offices of thefe three Divine Perfons. *There are Diverfities of Gifts, but the fame Spirit; and there are differences of Adminiftrations, but the fame Lord; and there are Diverfities of Operations, but 'tis the fame God that worketh all in all.* 'Tis *God*, by whofe Supreme Authority every thing in the Univerfe is directed; 'tis the *Son of God*, by whom the Government of the Church in particular is adminiftred; 'tis the *Spirit of God*, by whom all Gifts and Graces, for the Conviction of Infidels, and for the Sanctification of Believers, are difpenfed. The *God and Father* of our Lord Jefus Chrift, the infinite and incomprehenfible Fountain of underived Majefty, is the Spring and Original of all Good: The *Son of the Father,* is to Us the Author and Purchafer, the Conveyer of all *Communications from* that inexhauftible Fountain of Goodnefs; and by his Mediation and Interceffion, the only Means of *Accefs and Approach to* that Throne of otherwife inacceffible Glory: The *Spirit of God*, fent forth from the Father and the Son, is the immediate Difpenfer and Diftributer of thofe Benefits, which the Father grants by the Interceffion of the Son.

THIS is what the Scripture clearly and expreflly declares to us, concerning the Father, the Son, and the Holy Spirit. In which Doctrine, becaufe there are fome things difficult to be underftood, and not needful to be explained; wherein the vain Curiofity of men has often expofed its own Weaknefs, and which profane and carelefs perfons have wrefted (as they do other Doctrines) to their own Deftruction; therefore this matter ought not to be frequently and flightly treated of; but upon the moft folemn Occafions, with the greateft Care, and with the utmoft Reverence. And upon fuch Occafions; fince the whole ground and foundation of Chriftian Religion, is the Belief of our Reconciliation to God, the Father and Supreme Lord of All, thro' the Death of his Son, and by the Influence of his Holy Spirit; and fince *This is Life eternal, to know* Him who is *the only true God,* and to know *Jefus Chrift whom he hath fent,* and the *Spirit* by whom he worketh in us every good Work: Since This, I fay, is the very Foundation of Chriftian Religion; to have a right knowledge, of Him who is the Creator of the Univerfe, and Supreme Lord of the whole World; of him, who is the Saviour and Redeemer of Mankind; and of him, who is the Sanctifier of the elect people, which is the Church of God: it is therefore very fit, that upon particular folemn Occafions, This great Doctrine, which ought not to be frequently and flightly handled, fhould with great Caution and Reverence be *explained* at Once: *Explained*; that is, not unfolded according to the prefumptions of human Imagination: but *declared* fo far, as 'tis expreflly revealed in Scripture; and fo far forth, as 'tis therefore intelligible, becaufe it is revealed. For in Doctrines which are not made known by the Light of Reafon and natural Underftanding, but difcovered merely by Revelation, and which depend wholly on the Authority and Teftimony of the Revealer; in thefe things human Imagination has no place, and the Opinion of no man is of any Importance, but only the exprefs Words of the Revelation itfelf. In declaring therefore unto you, that which is clearly and without all controverfy revealed in Scripture concerning the Father, the Son, and the Holy Ghoft; I fhall 1ft confider briefly that which is *fpeculative,* concerning their *Nature*; 2dly, That which is *moral,* relating to their *Offices*; and 3dly, That which is *practical,* concerning the *Honour* we are to pay unto them.

1

1ft.

1ſt, I shall confider what is ſpoken in a *ſpeculative* manner concerning their Nature. And This part being that wherein we are leaſt concerned, and which we are the leaſt capable to underſtand ; the Scripture is very brief in this particular: It being of much more importance that it ſhould be clearly revealed to us, what they are *Relatively to Us,* than what their Nature is *abſolutely in themſelves.* Yet even upon This Head we find in Scripture, as follows. Concerning the Nature of *God the Father :* that, agreeable to the Light of natural Reaſon, there is One Supreme Abſolute Independent Cauſe and Original of all things, Eternal, Infinite, All-Powerful, Self-Sufficient ; the Maker and Lord of all things, himſelf derived from None, made of none, begotten of none, proceeding from none : *By* whom all Creatures material and immaterial, viſible and inviſible, animate and inanimate, rational and irrational, mortal and immortal, in Heaven and in Earth were made ; by whom the Land and Waters, the Air and Sun and Stars, the Heaven and the Heaven of Heavens, and all things that are therein ; Plants and Beaſts, and Men ; Angels and Arch-Angels ; were *created* out of nothing : *From* whom the Spirit of Truth, the Comforter and Sanctifier of all Holy men, *proceedeth* or is ſent forth : *Of* whom laſtly the Son himſelf, the Saviour and Redeemer of the World, in an ineffable manner, before all Ages, was *begotten.* This is the Supreme Father and Lord of all, who dwelleth in Light inacceſſible ; whoſe Majeſty, no Thought can comprehend ; Whoſe Glory, no Eye can behold ; whoſe Power, no Strength can reſiſt ; from whoſe Preſence, no Swiftneſs can flee ; whoſe Knowledge, no Secrecy can conceal itſelf from ; whoſe Juſtice, no Art can evade ; whoſe Goodneſs, no Creature but partakes of. This is the God of the Univerſe, whom even the Heathen World has always acknowledged. This is the God of *Abraham, Iſaac* and *Jacob* ; the God who brought the children of *Iſrael* out of the Land of *Egypt* ; the God and Father of our Lord Jeſus Chriſt ; of whom, and through whom, and to whom are all things ; to whom be Glory and Dominion for ever. But to proceed.

Concerning the *Nature* of the *Son,* that which the Scripture declares to us (and otherwiſe than from Scripture we can have no Light, in matters of Revelation ;) That which the Scripture, I ſay, declares to us, is this : That, in the Beginning, before the Foundation of the World, before all Ages, That Divine Perſon, who after and by his Incarnation became our Lord and Saviour Jeſus Chriſt, had a Being in the Boſom of his Father, and was Partaker of his Father's glory. *In the Beginning was* Joh. i. 1. *the Word ; and the Word was with God,* i. e. was with the Father ; *and the Word was God,* i. e. was Partaker of his Father's Glory, of his Divine Power and Authority, in Creating and Governing the World. The reaſon why This Divine Perſon was ſtiled *the Word,* has been much diſputed by Divines ; and various Opinions have at different Times prevailed. That which is moſt probable and moſt agreeable to the Scriptures, is, that he was ſo called, upon account of his being as it were the Mouth or Oracle of God, the Angel of his Preſence, the great Declarer of his Will, the Mediator between God and his Creatures ; by and thro' whom, as all Creatures have Acceſs to God, and give Glory to him ; ſo thro' him likewiſe are derived and conveyed all Communications of God to his Creatures. *In the Beginning was the Word :* That *Word,* which afterwards *was made Fleſh and dwelt amongſt us* ; to reveal to us with Authority the whole Will of God : That *Word,* concerning whom the ſame Author St *John* thus ſpeaks in another place ; when in his Viſion, ſeeing the *King of Kings and Lord of Lords,* Rev. xix. 16. coming forth *in righteouſneſs to judge and to make war,* and to *tread the wine-preſs of* 11. *the wrath of Almighty God* ; he thus deſcribes him ; that *out of his Mouth goeth a* 15. *ſharp Sword, and his Name is called, the Word of God* ; and ch. i. 16 ; he beheld *one* 15. *like unto the Son of man, out of* whoſe *mouth went a ſharp two-edged Sword.* Which 13. Deſcriptions afford great Light to that paſſage of St *Paul* to the *Hebrews,* ch. iv. ver. 12 ; *The Word of God is quick and Powerful, and ſharper than any two-edged Sword, piercing*
even

SERM. *even to the dividing afunder of Soul and Spirit, and of the joints and marrow, and* XC. *is a difcerner of the Thoughts and Intents of the Heart.* And this exactly anfwers the Defcription our Saviour gives of *Himfelf: Rev.* ii. 23; *I am he which fearcheth the Reins and Hearts.* Further, concerning the *Nature* of this Divine Perfon, the *Word* or *Son of God,* the Scripture adds; that he is *the only begotten of the Father,* and was in *Glory with* him *before the World* was; that he is the *Brightnefs of his* Father's *Glory, and the exprefs Image of his Perfon, and upholding all things by the Word of his Power;* Heb. i. 3: That he is *the Image of the Invifible God, the firft-born of every Creature:* Col. i. 15; or, as he himfelf ftiles himfelf, *Rev.* iii. 14; *the beginning of the Creation of God;* that is, who was before and above all things, being the firft Principle and Head over all; Himfelf, deriving *immediately* from the Father only; (and, as to the manner of That, *who fhall declare his generation?)* Whereas all other things, all Creatures, were produced *mediately* by *His* Operation. For fo St *John* affirms exprefily; *All things were made by him, and without him was not any thing made that was made:* St Joh. i. 2. And St *Paul* ftill more diftinctly: *Col.* i. 16; *By him were all things created, that are in Heaven, and that are in Earth, vifible and invifible, whether they be Thrones or Dominions or Principalities or Powers, all things were created by him and for him; and he is before all things, and by him all things confift.* If it be here demanded, how thefe two manners of Expreffion are to be reconciled, that God only is the Creator of all things, and yet all things are faid exprefily to be created by Jefus Chrift; St *Paul* gives a clear and direct Anfwer, *Heb.* i. 2; *By his Son* God *made the Worlds;* and again, *Ephef.* iii. 9; *Who created all things* by *Jefus Chrift.* To interpret thefe paffages, as fome have attempted to do, of a fecondary and figurative Creation, the new Creation or Renovation of things by the Gofpel; is wrefting Texts by a forced and unnatural Senfe to ferve an Opinion, when in their plain and literal Meaning there is no real Difficulty. For to conceive that God *created* all things at firft by his Son, is no more contrary to Reafon, than his *renewing* or *redeeming* all things by his Son; which is acknowledged by All. And if *it pleafed the Father,* by Chrift *to* reconcile *all things unto Himfelf, whether they be things in Earth or Things in Heaven;* as St *Paul* exprefily affirms, and all men underftand him to affirm it in the literal Senfe, there is no more reafon to doubt, but in the literal Senfe likewife, it pleafed the Father *by* Chrift to *Create* all things for Himfelf; which is as exprefily affirmed by the fame Apoftle. And even in the Old Teftament itfelf, thofe paffages which are fpoken of Wifdom, *Prov.* viii. 22, are by all antient Chriftian Writers underftood of God's creating the World by Chrift: *The Lord poffeffed me in the beginning of his Way, before his Works of old; I was fet up from everlafting, from the beginning, or ever the Earth was; When there were no Depths, I was brought forth; when there were no Fountains abounding with Water; Before the Mountains were fettled, before the Hills was I brought forth; While as yet he had not made the Earth, nor the Fields, nor the higheft part of the duft of the World; When he prepared the Heavens, I was there; when he fet a compafs upon the face of the deep; When he eftablifhed the clouds above; when he ftrengthened the fountains of the deep; When he gave to the Sea his Decree, that the Waters fhould not pafs his Commandment; when he appointed the Foundations of the Earth; Then was I by him, as one brought up with him; and I was daily his delight.* If it be here further enquired how thofe Divine Attributes and Powers, which are afcribed in Scripture to the Perfon of the Son, are confiftent with the Unity of God, which is the Foundation of all Religion both natural and revealed; the Anfwer is obvious; that the Divinity afcribed to the Son, is not another, a co-ordinate Divinity; but the Power, the Majefty, the Glory of the Father, communicated and derived to the Son. Could it be affirmed that there were two or more felf-originate, unbegotten, underived Principles; this would indeed deftroy the Unity of God, and fundamentally fubvert the very firft

I

Ground

Ground of Religion; But since the Glory of the Son is not originally his own Glory, but the Glory of the Father manifested in him, and derived to him, in a manner which neither we nor Angels perhaps can presume to understand; it is manifest still, that the *Monarchy* of the Universe, is hereby preserved entire.

CONCERNING the *Nature* of the *Holy Spirit of God*, the Scripture speaks very little in a Metaphysical manner; nor gives any encouragement to the inquisitiveness and vain Curiosity of humane Speculation. Declaring only, that he is a Divine Person proceeding or being sent forth from the *Father*; and in other places called the Spirit of the *Son*, and said to be sent forth from *Him*. Into the manner of his Derivation therefore, we ought not to presume to enquire; but be content with what the Scripture reveals to us, of his being in a singular manner, in a manner which we cannot presume to understand or explain, *the Spirit of God*. Only, because there have been some in these later Ages, who have denied the Being of this Holy Spirit, and have imagined it to be nothing but a mere Power or Attribute of God; it deserves to be taken notice of, that those Scriptures, which speak of him as being *grieved* at wicked men; as making *intercession* for us, and *helping our* infirmities; as *dividing* spiritual gifts *severally, as he* pleases; as *speaking, not of himself,* but what he *hears* or receives *from the Father*; these and numberless other Texts in the New Testament, do plainly declare Him to be, not a mere Virtue or Power, but a real Person distinct from the Father and the Son, and sent forth from Both for the perpetual Government and Direction of the Church.

THIS is what the Scripture briefly declares to us in a *speculative* manner concerning the *Nature* of the Father, Son, and Holy Ghost. And Happy had it been for the Church of God, if learned Men in all Ages had been content with what the Scriptures so declare, and had never entered further into Scholastick Speculations, from whence have arisen Endless Disputes, incurable Scepticism, and infinite Uncharitableness.

2dly, THERE is in the 2d place that which is *Moral*, concerning the several *Offices* of the Father, Son, and Holy Ghost with relation to *Us*. And here the Scripture teaches us, concerning the *Father*, that he, being absolutely supreme over all, *made* the World by the Ministration of his Son, and *governs* it by a perpetual Providence, without which not a Sparrow falls to the Ground, or a Hair of our Head perishes. That having Compassion upon sinful man, and resolving to afford them the Grace of Repentance, he sent his Son to take our Nature upon him, and therein to reveal his gracious Will; and delivered him up to an ignominious Death, that he might make Expiation and Reconcilement for our Sins; and raised him from the Dead by his mighty Power; and exalted him to his own right Hand; and appointed him to be the Judge of Quick and Dead; and has made all things subject unto Him; and by him reconciles all things unto Himself, both which are in Heaven and which are in Earth: and has appointed a Kingdom of eternal Happiness to them that serve and obey him; and will destroy the wicked with an everlasting Destruction. This is the *Office* of the *Father*. Concerning the *Office* of the *Son*, the same Scriptures declare, that he, by the Appointment of the Father, is our Saviour, Mediator, Intercessor and Judge; that having been in the Form of God, he emptied himself of that Glory, and willingly took upon him the form of a servant; and died, to make our Repentance available; and now sits at the right hand of God, to intercede for us; and governs the whole Church, according to the Will of his Father; and searches and tries the Hearts of men at present, and will finally judge them according to their Works. Lastly, concerning the *Office* of the *Holy Spirit*, the Scripture teaches, that having been the Inspirer of the Prophets of old, testifying before-hand the Sufferings of Christ, and the Glory that should follow; he was afterwards sent forth in a more extraordinary manner, to be the Comforter

Rom. iii. 25.
1 Joh. iv. 9,
14.

Acts v. 30.

2 Pet. i. 21.
1 Pet. i 11.
Joh. xiv.
1 Cor. ii. 10.

S E R M. Comforter and Director of the Apoſtles ; to lead them into all Truth ; to bring to their
XC. remembrance of all things which our Lord had ſaid unto them ; to ſupport them a-
gainſt the Power of the World ; to inſtruct them what to anſwer to their Perſecutors ;
to be the great Witneſs of our Saviour's Reſurrection, by working Signs and Wonders
and mighty Works, by inſpiring the Apoſtles with the gift of Tongues, and dividing
1 Cor. xii. 11. to their followers diverſities of Gifts, to every man ſeverally, as might beſt ſerve the
great end of their miniſtry : finally, to continue with all good Chriſtians even unto the
End of the World, as the great Sanctifier of the Hearts of men ; aſſiſting them with
his grace, admoniſhing them with his Holy Influences, working with them and inſpiring them with his good Gifts, and helping the Infirmity of their Prayers with his
own Interceſſion. This is what the Scripture teaches us *diſtinctly and ſeparately*, concerning the ſeveral Offices of the Father, the Son, and the Holy Spirit. They are alſo
in ſome few places all mentioned *together* ; as in the Form of Baptiſm, whereby we are
dedicated to the Service of God, baptized into the Death of his Son, and given up to
the guidance of his Holy Spirit : In the form of Bleſſing, wherein we are recommend-
Eph. ii. 18. ed by the Apoſtle to the Love of God, to the Favour of Chriſt, and to the Commu-
Cor. viii. 6. nion or Fellowſhip of the Holy Ghoſt : By St *Paul* again : *Eph. iv. 4, 5, 6. There is*
Tim. ii. 5. *one Spirit,——one Lord——one God and Father of all, who is above all, and through*
all, and in you all : And in the Words of the Text ; *There are Diverſities of Gifts, but*
the ſame Spirit ; and there are Diverſities of Adminiſtrations, but the ſame Lord ; and
there are Diverſities of Operations, but it is the ſame God, that worketh all in all.

    IT remains in the 3*d* and *laſt* place, that we conſider that which is *Practical*, con-
cerning the *Honour* due to the Perſon of the *Father*, and concerning that which is due
to the Son and to the Holy Ghoſt. To the Perſon of the *Father*, is to be directed that
Heb. xii. 23. abſolute and ſupreme Worſhip, by which he is acknowledged to be alone Παντοκράτωρ,
the Maker and Judge of all ; by whoſe incomprehenſible Power, the World was cre-
Acts v. 32 ; ated ; by whoſe unerring Providence, the Univerſe is governed ; by whoſe ſupreme Au-
xv. 8.
1 Theſ. iv. 8. thority, our Lord was ſent forth to redeem Us ; by whoſe good pleaſure the Holy Spirit
Heb. ii. 4. is *given*, to ſanctify us ; to whoſe glory, every tongue *now* confeſſes that Jeſus is the
2 Cor. i. 22 ;
v. 5. Lord ; and to whom, *at the Conſummation of all things*, our Lord himſelf ſhall deliver
Phil. ii. 11. up the Kingdom, and become ſubject to *Him* that put all things under him, that God
1 Cor. xv. 24 ;
xi. 3. may be all in all : To *Him* we are to pray for the Remiſſion of our Sins ; and that our
Repentance may be accepted, through the powerful Interceſſion of Chriſt our great
High Prieſt ; and that our Hearts may be renewed by the Inſpiration of his Holy Spirit :
and to *Him* we are to give Continual Thanks for his *original* and undeſerved Goodneſs
in ſending his Son at firſt to be the Saviour of the World, and to be unto us a propitiation through Faith in his Blood ; and for the *continuation* of that Goodneſs, in affording us the perpetual aſſiſtance of the Holy Ghoſt.

    To the Perſon of the *Son*, there is due this peculiar Honour ; that we offer up all our
Prayers in his Name ; (*whatſoever*, ſays he, *ye ſhall ask of the Father in my Name, he*
will *give it you*, Joh. xv. 16.) that we rely upon his Merits, depend upon his Interceſſion, obey him as our Lord, love him as our Saviour, fear him as our Judge. That
we acknowledge his great Condeſcenſion, in loving us and giving himſelf for us ; in
that, when he was *in the form of God, he was not greedy of retaining that form, but*
willingly *made himſelf of no reputation, and took upon him the form of a Servant, and*
was made in the Likeneſs of men ; and being found in faſhion as a man, he humbled
himſelf, and became obedient unto Death, even the Death of the Croſs, Phil. ii. 6. For
which reaſon, as the Apoſtle adds in the Words immediately following, *God alſo has*
highly exalted him, and given him a Name which is above every Name ; that at the Name
of Jeſus every knee ſhould bow, of things in Heaven, and things in Earth, and things
under the Earth ; and that every tongue ſhould confeſs that Jeſus Chriſt is Lord, to the

glory

glory of God the Father. And accordingly upon this Account, we find the higheft
Honour afcribed to him both by men and Angels: *Rev. v. 8. The four and twenty elders fell down before the Lamb,———and fung a new fong, faying, Thou art worthy———; For thou waft flain, and haft redeemed us to God by thy Blood, out of every kindred and tongue and people and nation :———And I heard the voice of many Angels———, faying———, Worthy is the Lamb that was flain, to receive power and riches and wifdom and ftrength and honour and glory and Bleffing : And every Creature———heard I faying, Bleffing and Honour and Glory and Power be unto him that fitteth on the Throne, and to the Lamb for ever and ever.* And ch. i. 5 ; *Unto him that loved us, and wafhed us from our Sins in his own Blood, and has made us Kings and Priefts unto God and his Father, to him be glory and dominion for ever.* This is the peculiar Addition of the Chriftian Religion ; that whereas before, *all men honoured the Father,* they fhould now *likewife Honour the Son* : St *Joh.* v. 23. Which Honour paid to the Son of God, is *therefore* no diminution to the Honour of the Father, nor derogation from the *Monarchy* of the Univerfe ; becaufe the Greatnefs and Dignity, the Divinity and Majefty of the Son, is not contradiftinct to, but derivative from, that of the Father ; and confequently muft be acknowledged to that very End, that it may be (as St *Paul* exprefsly declares) to *the glory of the Father.*

Laftly, CONCERNING the Honour peculiarly due to the perfon of the *Spirit,* that which the Scripture declares, is ; that we acknowledge him to be the divine Infpirer of the Prophets, both of the old and new Teftament ; and the immediate Worker of all thofe Signs and Wonders in proof of the Chriftian Difpenfation, which are properly ftiled the Witnefs and Teftimony, the Power and Demonftration of the Spirit ; that he is alfo the Sanctifier of all Hearts, and the immediate Diftributer of all the Gifts of God, for the Edification of his Church ; that therefore we receive and believe his Teftimony, as delivered in the infpired Writings ; obey his good Motions ; be follicitous to obtain his gifts and graces ; and infinitely careful not to grieve and quench and drive him from us, left we be found to do defpite unto the Spirit of grace ; which is in Scripture reprefented as a more unpardonable fault, than offending againft the Perfon even of our Saviour himfelf. But the Time allows me only to hint thefe things barely, and propofe them to your Meditations ; the inlarging upon which, would be to lay down the whole Syftem of Divinity. God grant that every one of Us, may fo give Honour to the Father of all things, through the Mediation and Interceffion of his Son our Saviour, and by the Affiftance and Operation of his Holy Spirit ; that by the communion and fellowfhip of the fame Holy Spirit, and through the Merits and Death of the Son of God making our Repentance available, we may be prefented faultlefs before the Throne of the Father of inacceffible Majefty, in the great Day.

Eph. v. 9.
Gal. v. 22.
v. 16.
1 Joh. ii. 27.
Eph. iv. 30.
1 Th. v. 19.
Heb. x. 29.

SERMON

SERMON XCI.

Of the Defire of Knowledge.

[Preached on Trinity-Sunday.]

DEUT. XXIX. 29.

The Secret Things belong unto the Lord our God; but thofe things which are revealed, belong unto us and to our children for ever, that we may do all the words of this Law.

SERM.
XCI.
THE Book of *Deuteronomy* contains a brief Summary, or Recapitulation of the Law; To which are added by *Mofes*, feveral earneft and moft affectionate Exhortations to the people of *Ifrael*, to perfwade them to the Obedience and Obfervation of that Law. He tells them that *he hath fet before them Life and Death, Blefjing and Curfing, Good and Evil*; and he perfwades them to chufe their *Duty, and cleave to it as their Life, and to refufe the Evil, and flee from it as from Death.* He invites them to Obedience by the moft affectionate promifes of the love, and favour, and protection of God; and he deters them from Difobedience by the moft fevere threatning of utter deftruction. He propofes to them the Law of God, as the proper fubject of their conftant Meditation; exhorting them *to bind it for a Sign upon their hand, and as frontlets between their eyes; to write it upon the pofts of their houfes, and upon their gates; to teach it diligently unto their children, and to talk of it when they fit in their houfes, and when they walk by the way, and when they lie down, and when they rife up;* Deut. vi. 7, 8. He tells them that *the commandments of God are the things* revealed *to them, to be ftudied by them and by their children for ever*; that the knowledge of other things, is in comparifon either unneceffary, or more difficult at leaft, and lefs needful to be attained; and that therefore nothing could be more unreafonable, than to purfue the knowledge of thofe things which were either wholly unneceffary, or at leaft far lefs needful to be known; by neglecting the ftudy and the knowledge of that, in which alone confifted their Happinefs and their Life. *The Secret things belong unto the Lord our God; but thofe things which are revealed, belong unto us and to our children for ever, that we may do all the words of this law.* The ultimate defign and defire of Man, is Happy; and as the only way to this Happinefs is Religion, fo the Knowledge of that Religion ought to be at leaft our principal and firft ftudy. Religion is the *doing all the Words of the Law, i. e.* the obeying of the Commandments of God; the Knowledge therefore of Religion, is the knowing particularly what are the Commands of God, and the knowing our obligation to obey thofe Commands. He that hath gained fo much Knowledge, as to underftand the Commandments of God, and to convince himfelf of his *indifpenfable* Obligation to obey them; fo as to live conftantly *in* the fenfe and under

I

the

the power of that Conviction ; The *Words of this Law*, are the Commandments of S E R M. God ; which he that has ftudied fo as to underftand and practife them, is fufficiently XCI. knowing, though he were ignorant of all other things, becaufe he knows his Happinefs, which is his main Concern, and the way to attain it. He that is ignorant of this, though he had all other Knowledge that were poffible to be acquired either by Men or Angels, is yet miferably and foolifhly ignorant, becaufe he is ignorant of that, which is indeed the only thing that is neceffary for him to know. A religious man *may* lawfully divert his thoughts, and exercife his induftry, in other Speculations; but he will not fo far engage his curiofity, in the fearch after *fecret* things, as to neglect thofe which are *open* and *revealed*, thofe on which the true Knowledge or Worfhip of God does any way depend. There are *fome* Things, which are abfolutely *beyond* the reach of our Faculties, and therefore not *poffible* to be throughly underftood by us ; and thefe a good man will not be ambitious to difcover, becaufe he confiders that God has placed them wholly out of the fphere of our capacity, and referved the Knowledge of them as a Prerogative to himfelf. There are *other* things, which if we can come at all to the Knowledge of, it muft be by unwarrantable or unlawful means ; and thefe likewife a religious man will not be inquifitive to know, nor uneafy for want of that Knowledge ; becaufe he confiders that God has hidden them from us, by forbidding the ufe of the means to difcover them. There are alfo fome *other* things, which are neither impoffible nor unlawful to be known, but the Search after them is difficult, and the Difcovery unprofitable ; they neither promote the true Knowledge, Honour, and Worfhip of God, nor the Benefit of Mankind ; and thefe, a pious man, will not be too much follicitous to find out ; becaufe they would take up too much of that Time and thofe Meditations, which may be *more* ufefully employed on the things that God has revealed. *Secret things belong unto the Lord our God ; but the things that are revealed, belong unto us, and to our children for ever.* From the words I fhall obferve thefe three things ; *1ft*, That there is naturally in Man, a very ftrong Defire of Knowledge ; *2dly*, That this Defire, ought to be regulated and limited by the Condition of our Nature, and by the Word of God ; and *3dly*, That not to regulate our Defire of Knowledge by thefe Rules, may be a very great occafion of Sin.

I. T H E R E is naturally in Man a very ftrong Defire after Knowledge. 'Tis the peculiar Attribute and Prerogative of *God*, to be infinitely perfect ; and to be originally and unchangeably fo. All *created* Beings, as far as we can judge of them, arrive at that Perfection which is the higheft pitch and excellency of *Their* nature, by *degrees*; and they have always in themfelves a natural and earneft Tendency towards that perfection. In things void of Reafon and Knowledge, the perfection of *Their* Nature is nothing elfe, but a compleat Number, a due Proportion, and a regular Compofition of parts; and *Their* natural tendency towards this perfection, is nothing but that Difpofition which arifes from the neceffary qualities of Matter, and from the fixed laws of Motion. But in Creatures endued with Reafon and Underftanding, the Perfection of *their* Nature confifting principally in the Improvement of thofe more excellent Faculties ; 'tis manifeft *They* can afpire to what degree they pleafe, and are apt to extend their Defires without limit. *I gave my Heart*, faith Solomon, *to feek and fearch out by Wifdom, concerning all things that are done under Heaven.* And the Scripture declares concerning him, *that he had Wifdom and Underftanding exceeding much, and largenefs of Heart even as the Sand that is on the Sea-fhore; fo that before him was none equal to him, neither after him fhould their arife any like him.* And yet even *He*, by departing from the ftudy of the Law of God, and giving heed to ftrange Women, was a fad Example of falling from God in his latter days. Wherefore, though there *be naturally* in men a very earneft Defire after Knowledge, yet I add,

SERM.   II. THIS our Defire of Knowledge, ought to be *regulated and limited*, by the Con-
XCI.   dition of our Nature and by the *Word* of God.

1*ft*, WE ought not to be ambitious of That Knowledge, which the *condition* and *circumftances* of our Nature make it impoffible for us to obtain. Knowledge is fo amiable a perfection, that men will not readily be perfwaded, they can poffibly be too earneft in the purfuit of it, even though it be in things which have no relation to the Honour of God, or to the Good of men. 'Tis true, God hath given us Faculties, which we not only *may*, but *ought* to improve; but then we muft always remember, that our Defires ought to terminate in *fuch* poffible and ufeful Perfections, as are to be attained by the improvement of the Faculties God has given us. Wifdom indeed *is* the principal thing, fays *Solomon, therefore get Wifdom, and with all thy getting get Underftanding*; Prov. iv. 7; and ch. xviii. 15; *The heart of the Prudent getteth Knowledge, and the ear of the Wife feeketh it.* But By *Knowledge, He* always means *religious* Wifdom, and not that which terminates only in *Pride* and *Vanity*; much lefs, that which by nature we are not made capable of attaining. In which refpect, a man's Defire after Knowledge may become faulty, either when he defires the Knowledge of fuch a *kind* of things, as the nature of the things does not permit him at all to underftand; or when he defires fuch a *fort* of Knowledge of any thing, as the nature of his Faculties does not capacitate him to come up to. There are fome *kinds* of things, of fo abftrufe a Nature, or at fuch a diftance of Place or Time, or which have fo little connexion with That Knowledge of God and of ourfelves, on which our whole Duty depends; that they are altogether beyond the reach of our Faculties; fo that we cannot poffibly underftand them at all; and in refpect of *thefe* things, 'tis evident we ought *fo* to limit our Defire of Knowledge by the *condition* and *circumftances* of our Nature, as not to attempt to underftand them at all; and not to pretend that we *can* underftand them, when indeed we can *not*. Of *other* things, which we can and ought to know according to the meafure of our Faculties, there is yet fuch a *fort* or degree of Knowledge as we cannot arrive to; and we have no more reafon to murmur, that we cannot attain to this *degree* of Knowledge, than we have to be difpleafed, that God has not made us equal to the higheft Orders of Angels; or than the Angels have caufe to be angry, that God has referved fome Attributes incommunicable from himfelf, and has not made *them* Mafters of all Perfections. God hath communicated to every fort of Creatures fuch Perfections as himfelf pleafed; and the condition of each of their Natures is the Law of God, by which they ought every one to limit and regulate their Defires. In matters of *Religion* indeed, in order to frame right Notions of God, and to ferve him acceptably; we can never be too follicitous and careful in inquiring into the Truth: But *fome* Secrets there are, the knowledge of which God hath referved to himfelf; and the higheft Angels cannot prefume to look into them: And without queftion Angels have a clear Knowledge of many things which humane Abilities cannot without the utmoft folly pretend to difcover. Remarkable to this purpofe is that Expoftulation of God with *Job*; *Haft thou entred into the fprings of the Sea? or haft thou walked in the fearch of the Depth? Have the gates of Death been opened unto thee; or haft thou feen the doors of the fhadow of Death? Where is the way where Light dwelleth? and as for Darknefs, where is the place thereof? Knoweft thou it becaufe thou waft then born? or becaufe the number of thy days is great?* ch. xxxviii. ver. 16. The Meaning is, *Not* that men may not commendably inquire into the Operations of Nature, which are the Works of God; fo far as they have Faculties and Opportunities to do it; But that they ought to contain their Defire of Knowledge within the bounds of thofe Faculties, and not be proud and imperious, *intruding into things which they have not feen, and vainly puffed up by a flefhly mind.*

2*dly*, As we ought not to be ambitious of what it is *impoffible* for us to attain; fo neither ought we to be follicitous after that, which it is unlawful for us to defire. And here, that which the Scripture determines in refpect of our Defire after Knowledge, is this; 1*ft*, That we ought not to endeavour to penetrate into things too deep for us, fuch as are the *hidden and fecret counfels, or unrevealed decrees of God.* True Notions of God, as difcoverable by Reafon, and the full Meaning of his whole revealed Will; thefe things we can never be too inquifitive after: But what cannot be known clearly by Reafon or Revelation, concerns us not. *Secret things belong unto the Lord our God, but the things that are revealed, to us and to our children for ever. Vain men would be wife*; Job xi. 12; *intruding into thofe things which they have not feen, and defiring to impofe them upon others. But can we by fearching find out God? Can we find out the Almighty unto perfection? It is as high as Heaven, what canft thou do? deeper than Hell, what canft thou know?* Job xi. 7, 8: And Acts i. 7. *It is not for you to know the time or the feafons which the Father hath put in his own power.* 2*dly*, The Scripture further forbids the defire of that Knowledge, the *means* of obtaining which are unlawful. The Tree of the Knowledge of Good and Evil, appeared to our Firft parents *to be pleafant to the Eye, and a Tree to be defired to make one wife*; Gen. iii. 6. But fince God had expreffly forbidden them *to Tafte of the Fruit of that Tree,* having referved it as a fingle inftance of Homage and Acknowledgement to Himfelf, as being the Creator and Lord of Paradife; 'tis evident the Defire of that Knowledge, which they thought the eating of that Fruit would furnifh them with, was at leaft the Occafion and the Caufe of their Sin. In like manner, the fame Defire of *fuch* Knowledge, as God has not afforded us the means of acquiring; has fince in all Ages of the world, through the deceit and temptations of the Devil, put vain and fuperftitious perfons upon fuch courfes and means to attain it, as God has abfolutely and expreffly prohibited. 3*dly*, The Scripture forbids us *fo* to fearch after the Knowledge of any thing elfe whatever, as in the too earneft purfuit of *that,* to neglect the ftudy of the Law of God. Thofe divine Truths, which influence our practice, which furnifh our minds with worthy Notions of God, and charitable Difpofitions towards our Neighbours, and *make men wife unto Salvation*; are the things which God has propofed to us to converfe with and meditate, to fix our thoughts and our ftudies upon. In *other* things, *There is a wifdom,* faith the Wife man, *that multiplieth bitternefs*; *and there is a Knowledge which bringeth nothing but wearinefs.* To ftudy the works of God and Nature *fo,* as therein to admire and adore the Wifdom of their Almighty Creator; to ftudy and fearch out the great Truths of Religion in fuch a manner, as thereby to be perfwaded to conform our practice *in earneft* to the Rules of the divine Law; *this* only is truly worthy of a Man, and acceptable to God; *this* only is a ftudy which will yield us *prefent* Satisfaction and *future* alfo; which will afford us the trueft Contentment *now,* and the folideft and moft fubftantial Joy *at the laft. David* found fuch fatisfaction in this Contemplation of the Works and of the Law of God, that he declares he could entertain himfelf with the Meditation of God's Law all the day long, *and in the* night *feafon alfo he could think upon the fame,* Pfal. cxix. 55; and *Solomon,* who had given his Curiofity the moft unbounded liberty, and had beyond comparifon the largeft extent of Knowledge that was ever attained by any mortal man; *whofe Wifdom compaffed the whole Univerfe, and his Underftanding and largenefs of Heart was exceeding great, even as the fand upon the fea-fhore*; this great man (I fay,) when he came ferioufly to compare all things that he had obferved, and to confider the laft Iffue of things, he concludes all his Meditations with this wife Reflection, *Ecclef.* xii. 13; *Let us hear the conclufion of the whole matter*; *Fear God and keep his commandments, for this is the* whole; the whole Duty, and the whole Happinefs of Man. It remains that I proceed now in the

III. *Third*

S E R M.   III. *Third* place, to fhow how great a *Sin* it is, not to regulate our Defires of Know-
XCI.   ledge, by the forementioned Rules. And 1*ſt*, To determine dogmatically in things
not clearly revealed, and to take delight in *impoſing* upon each other fuch Determinations, is in effect directly oppofing and ftriving againft that Order and Conftitution of
things, which God has appointed; and endeavouring to make *ourſelves* what God has
not made us. Inftead of being thankful for thofe Faculties and Capacities, which God
has freely endued us with, it is ungratefully murmuring againft him, becaufe he has
not given us every thing that our unreafonable Fancies may fuggeft to us to defire, but
has left us great occafions for Modefty, for mutual Charity and Forbearance. We are
made capable of knowing and imitating our great Creator, and of being made happy by
that Knowledge and that Imitation: and is not this fufficient for us, unlefs we be admitted alfo to determine with peremptorinefs, and to *impoſe* upon each other our own
Opinions concerning thofe Secrets, which infinite Wifdom has not thought fit to reveal
clearly to us? All other created Beings contain themfelves willingly within the bounds
of their Natures, and cheerfully move within the limits of the fphere that God has prefcribed them; except finful men, lovers of Power, and infolent towards each other;
and excepting alfo thofe Apoftate Spirits, *who kept not their firſt eſtate, but having re-
volted from God, are reſerved in chains under darkneſs unto the judgment of the great
day.* That a proud afpiring after fomething not attainable by them in thofe circumftances wherein God had created and placed them, was the caufe of thefe Angels
Fall, the Scripture frequently intimates to us; As in that Allufion of the Prophet
Iſaiah, ch. xiv. ver. 12; *How art thou fallen from Heaven, O Lucifer, Son of the
Morning? —— For thou haſt ſaid in thine heart, I will aſcend into Heaven, I
will exalt my Throne above the Stars of God, I will ſit alſo upon the Mount of
the Congregation, in the ſides of the North; I will aſcend above the heights of the
Clouds, I will be like the moſt High; yet thou ſhalt be brought down to Hell, to the
ſides of the pit.* Which though applied indeed in that place by the Prophet to the
King of *Babylon*, yet the Allufion feems to be borrowed from fome greater and higher
Event. What it was in particular, that this Pride prompted thofe wicked Spirits to
afpire to, the Scripture does not exprefsly acquaint us; But fince we cannot conceive
that they could afpire to the Power and Majefty of God, which it was impoffible
they could be fo weak as to imagine it could be aimed at by any created Being; it
is probable their Crime might be the afpiring proudly and imperioufly to fome degree
or kind of Knowledge, which God had with-held from them. 2*dly*, The not regulating this Defire by the fore-mentioned rules, was the occafion of our Firft Parents
Fall. This appears from the defcription of the Tree of the Knowledge of Good and
Evil: *Gen.* iii. 6; *When the Woman ſaw that the Tree was good for food, and that
it was pleaſant to the Eyes, and a Tree to be deſired to make one wiſe* or knowing,
ſhe took of the Fruit and did eat. It is alfo evident from the defcription of the
manner of the Temptation: *ver.* 5; *God doth know,* faith the Tempter, *that in the
day ye eat thereof, then your eyes ſhall be opened, and ye ſhall be as Gods, knowing Good
and Evil.* The Temptation propofed, was the *Knowledge of Good and Evil*; and
That which principally prevailed upon the Woman to eat of the Fruit of the Tree,
was its appearing defirable to make one wife. *What* is here meant particularly
by the Knowledge of Good and Evil, the Scripture does not directly explain to us.
That it was not the Knowledge of any particular *ſort* of Good and Evil, is evident;
For fince the Underftanding of our Firft Parents, as all their other Faculties were
much more perfect *before* than *after* the Fall, it is evident they could not but have a
perfect Knowledge of all *natural* Good and Evil, and a right Underftanding concerning the Nature of all *moral* Good and Evil; excepting only the *experimental*
Knowledge

Knowledge of both thefe forts of Evil, which it is impoffible to fuppofe could be a Temptation. It remains therefore that the Knowledge of Good and Evil, with which our Firft Parents were tempted, was not the Knowledge of any particular *things*, but fome particular *kind* or *manner* of knowing them: Poffibly a Defire of *fore-knowing* things to come; or fome other fuch *fort* of Knowledge, as in the prefent ftate and circumftances of their Nature they were not capable of attaining. *3dly* and *laftly*, A Defire of Knowledge not regulated and limited by the Rules before fet down, is very apt to put men upon unlawful practices, to attain what they fo defire. For that which is not to be attained but by finful and unwarrantable practices, the *Defire* of it cannot but be *alfo* finful. What remains therefore, is by way of inference to apply what hath been faid; and, by giving fome particular inftances, to reduce to practice what has been difcourfed in general, concerning our Defire of Knowledge and the Limitations of it.

AND *1ft*, From what has been faid, it follows, that the vain Defire of knowing beforehand things to come, is fuch a Defire of the Knowledge of fecret things, as is not permitted us by the prefent circumftances and condition of our Nature, or by the Word of God. It is the peculiar Attribute of God, and not communicable to any finite Being, to fore-know all things that *fhall* be, before they come to pafs; and therefore the Prophet, when he would expofe the Vanity of worfhipping Idols or falfe Gods, challenges them to foretel future Events; *Let them bring forth their ftrong reafons, and fhew us what fhall happen; fhow the things that are to come hereafter, that we may know that ye are Gods:* If. xli. 22 and 23. Yet becaufe the power of Beings fuperior to us, is great and unknown; vain and fuperftitious men have therefore in All Ages been fo apt to be feduced with Imaginations of the poffibility of fuch Difcoveries. In the time of Heathen Darknefs and Ignorance, the Devil by giving fometimes doubtful and ambiguous Anfwers, which to be fure fhould be interpreted to the trueft fenfe, which way foever the Event might happen to determine it; and fometimes by giving fuch dark and obfcure Oracles, as, though no man could make any fenfe of them, yet they infenfibly filled men's minds with an awful refpect and veneration for the Author of them; by thefe means, I fay, the Devil enflaved the *Gentile* World, and kept them in a conftant courfe of Idolatry. Or, if moft of thefe things were, as is probable enough, only the Frauds of wicked and profane *men*, to impofe upon the Ignorant; yet ftill the Event was much the fame, in abufing their Credulity and unjuftifiable Defire of Knowledge, to confirm them in their Idolatrous Practices. The *Jews*, who by the Knowledge of the true God and the Difcovery of his Will made to them in the Law, were in a great meafure freed from the bondage of fuch Superftitions; yet whenever they fell away from God, and began to neglect his Worfhip and diftruft his Providence, one inftance of their Difobedence prefently was, having recourfe to unlawful ways of inquiry after Knowledge. Thus when the Lord would not anfwer *Saul*, becaufe of his Difobedience, immediately he betakes himfelf to a Method, which *Mofes* tells the *Ifraelites* was one of thofe Abominations, becaufe of which *the Lord thy God doth drive the Nations out from before thee; For thefe Nations, which thou fhalt poffefs, hearkened unto Obfervers of times, and unto Diviners*, Deut. xviii. 10. And among *Chriftians* it is obfervable, that thofe always who have leaft Knowledge of God, and leaft Truft in his Providence, and leaft Underftanding in the true Syftem and Powers of Nature, have the greateft Confidence in groundlefs Pretences and unwarrantable Methods of purfuing Knowledge It matters not, that the Pretences to fupernatural ways of knowing things are commonly mere Cheat and Fraud; it is a degree of this Sin, if incouragement be given to fuch falfe Pretences. And to pretend to know things by the *Stars*, which introduces Fatality and deftroys Religion; is not much different from pretending to know them by Arts that have worfe Names.

2dly, From what hath been faid it follows, that a Defire of prying into the hidden and unrevealed Decrees, Counfels, and Purpofes of *God*, and defiring to impofe upon Others our Opinions concerning them; is alfo fuch a Defire of the knowledge of fecret things as is not permitted us by the Law of our Nature, or by the Word of God. The meafure of our Knowledge of divine things, is That revelation which God has been pleafed to make to us in his holy Scripture; This, we can never ftudy with too much care and exactnefs; But whatever pretends to go beyond thefe bounds, is prefumptuous and unwarrantable. Thofe things which God has revealed to us, we may know, becaufe God has difcovered them to us; and we are *bound* with all diligence to fearch after the knowledge of them, becaufe they are propofed to us as the rule of our life, and the condition of our happinefs. *More* than God has made known to us of this kind, we *cannot* difcover; and to pretend to underftand, and confidently impofe upon each other what God has not thought fit clearly to reveal, is no lefs foolifh and abfurd, than it is unreafonable and finful. *For who has known the mind of the Lord, or who hath been his Counfellor?* Rom. xi. 34. Only in general this *one* thing we may depend upon as certain, that no fecret Counfel or Purpofe or Decree of God can be contrary to his Will revealed in his Word. Upon what Conditions God hath appointed that men fhould be happy or miferable, he has clearly and fully revealed to us in his Holy Scriptures; and more than this, it is neither neceffary nor poffible for us to know.

3dly and *laftly*; An over-earneft Defire of knowing things fubtle and unneceffary to be known, fo as in the purfuit of the knowledge of thefe things, to neglect the ftudy of that which more nearly concerns us; is alfo a fort of that fearch after knowledge which is forbidden in the Scripture. Whatever hath no relation to the Honour and true Worfhip of *God*, and promotes not righteoufnefs and charity among *Men*: Whatever tends not *fo* to inform our judgments, as to rectify our practice and reform our lives, is ufelefs and unprofitable. Let us then in the firft place endeavour to attain that knowledge which may make us wife unto Salvation; and always fo regulate our inquiries after other things, as not to neglect the Study of that, which is our intereft and our life. I conclude with the words of the wife Son of *Sirach*; Eccluf. iii. 21; *Many are in high places and of renown; but myfteries are revealed to the meek. Seek not out the things that are too hard for thee, nor fearch the things that are above thy ftrength: But what is commanded thee, think thereon with reverence; for it is not needful for thee to fee with thine Eyes the things that are in fecret.*

SERMON

SERMON XCII.

Of the Teſtimony of our SAVIOUR's Doctrines.

[Preached on Trinity-Sunday.]

1 J O H. V. 8.

And there are Three that bear Witneſs in Earth, the Spirit and the Water and the Blood; And theſe Three agree in One.

THE Words of the foregoing Verſe, which have no relation to the Argument the Apoſtle is here inſiſting upon, I ſhall not take into conſideration at this time; for a Reaſon Now well-known to all who carefully ſtudy the Scriptures, and not needful to be mentioned in This place. But confining my Diſcourſe to the words of the Text itſelf, I ſhall *1ſt* endeavour to explain diſtinctly, their *connexion* with the whole Thread of the Apoſtle's Reaſoning in this chapter; and *2dly,* I ſhall conſider, the *Doctrine particularly contained* in the *words themſelves.*

I. IN the *firſt verſe* of This Chapter, St *John* lays down the *General Doctrine,* which is the Subject of this whole epiſtle: *Whoſoever* (ſays he) *believeth that Jeſus is the Chriſt, is born of God.* To be *born of God,* ſignifies by an eaſy Figure of Speech, to be what the Scripture calls a *Child of God,* a *regenerate perſon,* one that *loves God and keeps his Commandments;* living in the habitual Practice of univerſal Virtue and Righteouſneſs. And *ſuch* a perſon is every one, who *believeth that Jeſus is the Chriſt :* Not, every one who *profeſſes* to believe, but who *does* believe: Not, every one who *pretends* to be, but who *really is,* a *ſincere Chriſtian.* The *reaſon* why the Apoſtle expreſſes ſincere Chriſtianity by this particular phraſe of *believing that Jeſus is the Chriſt,* is becauſe there were even Then ſome falſe Apoſtles, in whom *the myſtery of iniquity did already work:* Who taught, that *Jeſus* was not indeed the *Chriſt :* That *Chriſt,* the *Son of God,* was not indeed incarnate, was not *made Man* and *ſuffered* for us *really,* but *in appearance only :* That *Jeſus,* the perſon born of the Bleſſed Virgin, was not *himſelf* the *Chriſt,* the *Son of God,* but that *Chriſt,* the *Son of God,* was *another perſon,* fictitiouſly and *in Name only* united to *Jeſus who was the Son of Man.* Againſt Theſe falſe Teachers, the Apoſtle argues through this whole Epiſtle; ch. ii. 22; *Who is a Liar, but he that denieth that Jeſus is the Chriſt ?* From the Context it appears evidently, that he is not there arguing againſt profeſſed Unbelievers, but againſt pretended Chriſtians, who denied the reality of our Lord's incarnation. Again, ch. iv. 1; *Beloved, believe not every Spirit,* (that is, every Prophet or Teacher,) *but try the Spirits whether they are of God ; becauſe many falſe Prophets are gone out into the World: Hereby know ye the Spirit of God ; Every Spirit that confeſſes that Jeſus Chriſt is come in the Feſh,* (that is to ſay, that the Son of God was really incarnate and made Man for us,) *is of God : And every Spirit that confeſſeth not, that Jeſus Chriſt is come in the Fleſh; is not of God.* Again, 2 Epiſt. v. 7, *Many deceivers are*

3 *entred*

SERM. *entred into the World, who confeſs not that Jeſus Chriſt is come in the Fleſh.* And in the
XCII. iv*th* ch. of this 1*ſt* Epiſtle, ver. 15; and ch. v. 1, 5; the Phraſes, *to confeſs that Jeſus is the Son of God, to believe that Jeſus is the Chriſt,* and *to believe that Jeſus is the Son of God,* are All uſed in the *like* ſenſe, to expreſs the *reality* of the incarnation of the *Son of God,* and that he *truly and perſonally,* (not in *Appearance and Name* only,) became the *Son of Man.* Hence, thro' this whole Epiſtle, theſe and the like Expreſſions are conſtantly to be underſtood as ſignifying *True and ſincere Chriſtians.* And therefore, I ſay, the *General Doctrine,* laid down by St *John* in the *firſt* Verſe of this Fifth Chapter, (and the Subject-matter indeed of the whole Epiſtle,) is this; that *every ſincere Chriſtian* is a *regenerate perſon,* one that *loves God and keeps his Commandments;* living in the habitual Practice of univerſal Virtue and Righteouſneſs.

On the other ſide: Whoſoever *loves God,* and deſires to *keep his Commandments,* and is diſpoſed to become a *regenerate perſon;* will hardly fail of being ſincerely a *Chriſtian:* For ſo the Apoſtle goes on in the *latter part* of the firſt verſe; *Every one that loveth him that begat, loveth Him alſo that is begotten of Him;* Every one that ſincerely loves *God,* every one that is of a good and virtuous Diſpoſition, will naturally love the Religion of *Chriſt.* And, that no man might miſtake, *wherein* this Love of God conſiſts; he defines it in expreſs words, ver. 3; *This,* ſays he, *is the Love of God, that we keep his Commandments: and his Commandments are not grievous.* And the *Reaſon why* his Commandments are not grievous, is *becauſe* (ſays he, ver. 4.) *whatſoever is born of God, overcometh the World;* A true Child of God, a ſincere Chriſtian, will deſpiſe and *conquer* all the Temptations of a ſinful and debauched World. And the *Means,* by which he is *inabled* to conquer theſe Temptations, is *Faith; This is the Victory that overcometh the World, even our* Faith: Our *Faith,* our firm *Belief,* of the *Being and Government of God,* and of his having *appointed a day wherein he will judge the World in Righteouſneſs;* this is what will not fail to prevail over the temptations, of a wicked and debauched World. And becauſe it is by the Revelation of *Chriſt,* by the Doctrine and Preaching of the *Goſpel,* that this Faith or firm Belief of a future Judgment is principally eſtabliſhed in the minds of men; therefore in the 5*th* verſe the Apoſtle proceeds to explain this Faith in the following manner; *Who is He that overcometh the World, but he which believeth that* Jeſus is the Son of God? that is, that he is the True Meſſiah which was to come into the World, the Perſon appointed to be the Judge of Quick and Dead.

That This is plainly the Meaning of the Phraſe, appears from the parallel places wherein the Scripture expreſſes the ſame Senſe in other Words. Thus, what in this 5*th verſe* is, *believing that Jeſus is the* Son of God; is in the 1*ſt* verſe, *believing that Jeſus is* the Chriſt. And St *Peter's* confeſſion, which in St *Matthew's* words, ch. xvi. 16; is, *Thou art Chriſt, the* Son of the Living God; is, in St *Mark's* words, ch. viii. 29; *Thou art the* Chriſt. Again: The Queſtion put to our Lord by the High-Prieſt, which in St *Matthew's* words, ch. xxvi. 63, is, *whether thou be the Chriſt the* Son of God; is, in St *Luke's* words, ch. xxii. 67; *Art thou the* Chriſt? And *Nathanael,* in *His* Confeſſion, *Joh.* i. 49, uſes theſe two, as known Synonymous expreſſions; *Rabbi, thou art the* Son of God, *thou art the* King of Iſrael.

The *Faith* therefore, which, St *John* here tells us, *overcometh the World;* is the believing that *Jeſus* is the *True Meſſiah,* the perſon appointed of God to be the Judge of Quick and Dead. Which Truth whoſoever is firmly perſwaded of, will not eaſily ſuffer himſelf to be overcome by the Temptations of *Sin,* which he knows will expoſe him to the final Wrath of God at that Great Day.

Wherefore This *Faith,* this *Belief* that *Jeſus is the Son of God,* that he is the perſon by whom God will judge the World in righteouſneſs; This, I ſay, being a Matter of ſo great importance, a Doctrine on which the Whole of Religion depends;

the

the Apoſtle proceeds to tell us, *ver.* 6; that our Lord did not *barely affirm* this of him- S E R M. ſelf, but came with powerful *Evidence and Proof*, with ſufficient and undeniable *Wit-* XCII. *neſſes* of ſo important a Truth: *This is he that came*, ſaith he, *by Water and Blood, even Jeſus Chriſt*. He *Came*; that is, he manifeſted himſelf to be the True Meſſiah, and made it appear that he was really ſent of God. For Thus the Meſſiah is deſcribed, in the Queſtion put by *John Baptiſt's* Diſciples to our Saviour; *Matt.* xi. 3; *Art thou He that ſhould* Come, *or do we look for Another?* *Before* his appearing, his Title was, *He that ſhould come*; And *after* it, the Apoſtle here ſtiles him accordingly, *This is He that came.* He came, *declaring* himſelf to be ſent from God, as his Son, the Chriſt, the Judge of the World; and *proving* the Truth of what he affirmed by the *evidence* of *Three* concurring *Teſtimonies,* The *Water,* The *Blood,* and The *Spirit: This is he that came by Water and Blood, even Jeſus Chriſt; not by Water only, but by Water and Blood; And 'tis the Spirit that beareth Witneſs, becauſe the Spirit is Truth.*

THE words, *not by Water only, but by Water and Blood*; ſeem to be an *Alluſion* to what the ſame Apoſtle St *John* records in his *Goſpel*, that, when our Lord's ſide was pierced, *forthwith there came out Blood and Water:* But it ſeems to be an Alluſion *only*; the Words in this place, having a different Senſe; and referring no otherwiſe to thoſe in the *Goſpel*, than as the Blood and Water there mentioned are recorded as an Evidence of the Reality and Certainty of our Lord's *Death :* Which *Death,* or voluntary *laying down of his Life,* the ſame Apoſtle here in his *Epiſtle*, alledges as *One Teſtimony* of the Truth of our Lord's Doctrine, ſtiling it *the Blood.*

By *Three concurring Teſtimonies* therefore, diſtinctly recited in the *ſixth verſe*, did our Lord *prove* himſelf to be the True Meſſiah. And becauſe they are the Three *Great* and moſt *undeniable* Evidences, that gave Teſtimony to our Lord and to the Truth of his Doctrine ; therefore the Apoſtle *repeats them again,* (as it were by way of *recapitulation* of the Summ of his Argument,) in the words of the Text, ver. 8; *There are Three that bear Witneſs, the Spirit and the Water and the Blood ; and theſe Three agree in One :* They are One concurring or agreeing Teſtimony. *And if we receive the Witneſs of Men,* ſays he, *ver.* 9; (that is, if *Two* Witneſſes were in the Law ſufficient Evidence of any matter of Fact among *Men*;) *The Witneſs of God is greater* ; this *Threefold* Teſtimony which God has given to the Truth of the Doctrine of Chriſt, is ſtill *more certain and undeniable.*

THE *End* and *Deſign,* for which this Doctrine of the Goſpel was preached by Chriſt, and thus *atteſted of God;* is ſet forth, *ver.* 11 ; *And This is the Record, that God hath given to us eternal life ; and this Life is in his Son :* Which words are of the ſame import with thoſe of our Saviour himſelf in the *Goſpel* of St *John*; *This is Life eternal, that they may know Thee the Only True God, and Jeſus Chriſt whom thou haſt ſent.*

THE *Application* of the Whole, follows, *ver.* 18 ; *We know,* ſaith the Apoſtle, *that whoſoever is Born of God, ſinneth not.* And *why* doth ſuch a one *not ſin ?* Even becauſe *the Son of God is come,* ver. 20 ; *and hath given us an Underſtanding that we may know Him that is True*; that is, he hath *taught* us *how* the *True God* will be acceptably ſerved and obeyed : *And we* are accordingly *in Him that is true,* (we *do* accordingly ſo obey and ſerve the True God,) *in* his Son, that is, *by* or *through his Son Jeſus Chriſt : This,* ſays he, *is the True God, and eternal Life.*

II. AND now, having explained diſtinctly the Connexion of the Text, with the whole Thread of the Apoſtle's Reaſoning in This chapter ; I proceed in the *ſecond* place to conſider the *Doctrine contained particularly* in the *words themſelves: There are Three that bear Witneſs, the Spirit, and the Water, and the Blood.* The Order in which they are ranked in the *Sixth* verſe, is the true Order of nature ; the *Water,* the *Blood,* and the *Spirit* ; And in That order, I ſhall diſcourſe upon them.

Firſt therefore; The *firſt* of the three great Teſtimonies here recorded by St *John*, as given to the Truth of our Saviour's Miſſion and Doctrine; is That which he ſtiles *The Water.* His Meaning is; *That Teſtimony,* which God gave to our Lord in ſo very remarkable and illuſtrious a manner at the Time of his *Baptiſm*, Matt. iii. 16; *And Jeſus when he was baptized, went up ſtraitway out of the Water; and lo, the Heavens were opened unto him, and he ſaw the Spirit of God deſcending——upon him: and lo, a Voice from Heaven, ſaying, This is my Beloved Son, in whom I am well-pleaſed.* St *John*, in his *Goſpel*, anſwerable to the Streſs here laid upon it in his *Epiſtle*, enlarges very particularly upon *This Teſtimony*; alledging the Account given of it by *John the Baptiſt* in the following manner, ch. i. 31; *I knew him not; But that he ſtould be made manifeſt to Iſrael, therefore am I come baptizing with Water: And John bare Record, ſaying, I ſaw the Spirit deſcending from Heaven,——and it abode upon him: And I knew him not; But he that ſent me to baptize with Water, the ſame ſaid unto me, Upon whom thou ſhalt ſee the Spirit deſcending, and remaining on him, the ſame is He which baptizeth with the Holy Ghoſt; And I ſaw and bare Record, that this is the Son of God.* Again. ch. iii. 26; The ſame Teſtimony is referred to by the *Jews*, diſcourſing with *John the Baptiſt*, and ſaying; *Rabbi, he that was with thee beyond Jordan, to whom thou bareſt Witneſs.* And again, by *our Saviour* himſelf; ch. v. 33, 37; *Ye ſent unto John, and he bare Witneſs unto the Truth: But I receive not Teſtimony from Man;—— the Father himſelf which has ſent me, hath born Witneſs of me.* This therefore was the *Firſt* great Evidence of the Truth of our Lord's Miſſion; the Teſtimony given him at his aſcending out of the *Water*, when the Spirit deſcended viſibly upon him, and there came a Voice from Heaven, ſaying, *This is my beloved Son, in whom I am well-pleaſed.*

Secondly; THE *next* that bears *Witneſs*, is what the Apoſtle here ſtiles, *The Blood:* That is; our Lord's *laying down his Life* for a Teſtimony to the Truth of his Doctrine, joined with the *Circumſtances preceding* and *attending* his *Death.* He did not only *preach* that he was the Son of God, and by his Holy and Exemplary *Life* juſtified his integrity in what he ſaid: But he *died* alſo, to make good his Doctrine; and, in his Death, was attended with many the ſtrongeſt circumſtantial Evidences of Truth. To his *Diſciples*, he frequently declared before-hand, that he ſhould be crucified and ſlain, and ſhould riſe again the third day. To the *Jews*, he propheſied long before his ſuffering, *Joh.* viii. 28; *When ye have lift up the Son of Man, then ye ſhall know that I am He; and that I do nothing of myſelf, but as my Father has taught me, I ſpeak theſe things.* To *Pilate*, he profeſſed, *Joh.* xviii. 37; *To This end was I born, and for This cauſe came I into the World, that I ſhould bear Witneſs unto the Truth.* This is what St *Paul* calls, his *Witneſſing before Pontius Pilate a good confeſſion*, 1 Tim. vi. 13: And his ſtedfaſtneſs in it, cauſed even *Pilate himſelf* to teſtify, that the putting him to death, would be a ſhedding the *Blood of a juſt perſon*; Matt. xxvii. 24. The *particular circumſtances* of his Death, were all of them the fulfilling of ſo many diſtinct Prophecies;

Zech. ix. 9.
Iſ. l. 6.
Pſ. lix. 21.
Pſ. xxii. 8.
——18.
Pſ xxxiv. 20.
Zech. xii. 10.
In which it had been predicted, that he ſhould be *ſold for thirty pieces of Silver*; that he ſhould be *ſcourged, buffeted, and ſpit upon*; that he ſhould have *Gall and Vinegar* offered him to drink; that they who ſaw him crucified, ſhould *mock* at his *truſting in God*; that the Soldiers ſhould *caſt lots for his garments*; that not *a Bone of him ſhould be broken*; and that *they ſhould look on Him whom they had pierced.* Concerning all which Circumſtances, and particularly this Laſt, of the Soldiers *piercing* him with *a Spear*, and his being really dead without having any Bone broken; St *John* thus declares, ch. xix. 35; *He that ſaw it, bare Record; and his Record is true.* Upon *Other Signs* following his Death, the *Centurion that watched him*, bore Witneſs, ſaying, *Truly This was the Son of God*, Matt. xxvii. 54. *After his Reſurrection*, (which was itſelf the Great Evidence of All;) his *Diſciples* ſealed likewiſe the ſame Teſtimony with *Their Blood:*

I

Which

Which is therefore stiled; *Rev.* xvii. 6; *the Blood of the* Martyrs *of Jesus;* That is, of those *who were beheaded*; ch. xx. 4; *for the* Witness *of Jesus, and for the Word of God*; Or as 'tis ch. vi. 9; *who were slain for the Word of God, and for the* Testimony *which they held.* To which may be added, that even his *Enemies* also, who wished that his *Blood* might *be on Them and on their children*; even Their *blood* also was made a Witness to the same Truth, by the Vengeance that came upon them at the destruction of *Jerusalem.*

Thirdly, T H E Third and Last Evidence or Witness to the Truth of our Lord's Doctrine, is the *Spirit.* And under This Head, are included *Many* particulars.

1st, T H E *Whole Body* of *Prophecies* under the Old Testament: *To Him give All the Prophets witness,* Acts x. 43: And *Rev.* xix. 10; *The Testimony of Jesus, is the Spirit of Prophecy:* So we render the Words: But the True Rendring is; *The Spirit of Prophecy, is* [only] *the* Testimony, or the Witness, *of Jesus.* For which reason, 'tis expressly stiled by St *Peter, The Spirit of* Christ *which was in the Prophets.*

2dly, T H E Purity and *Spiritual* nature of the *Doctrine itself* which he taught, and the *Innocency and Holiness* of his *Life*; by means of which, he, as *a Lamb without blemish, offered himself, through the eternal Spirit, without Spot, unto God.* 1 Pet. i. 19.
Heb. ix. 14.

3dly, The *Miracles* which he worked in his own life-time by the *Spirit* of God: *Matt.* xii. 28; *If I cast out Devils by the* Spirit *of God, then the Kingdom of God is come unto you:* And *Joh.* v. 36; *I have greater Witness than That of John; For the* Works *which my Father hath given me to finish, the same* Works *that I do, bear Witness of me, that the Father has sent me.*

4thly, H I S *Resurrection* from the Dead: Concerning which, St *Peter* tells us, that he was *quickned by the* Spirit; And St *Paul,* Rom. i. 4; that he was *declared to be the Son of God with Power, according to the* Spirit *of Holiness, by the Resurrection from the Dead.* 1 Pet. iii. 18.

Lastly, T H E *Gift of the Holy Ghost*; which, according to his Promise, he sent down upon the *Apostles* after his Ascension. The *Promise* was, *Joh.* xv. 26; *I will send unto you from the Father, the Spirit of Truth, which proceedeth from the Father; he shall testify of Me:* And the *Accomplishment* is, Heb. ii. 4. *God bore them Witness, both with Signs and Wonders, and with divers Miracles and Gifts of the Holy Ghost, according to his own Will.* So that, *with great Power gave the Apostles Witness of the Resurrection of the Lord,* Acts iv. 33. *Him,* saith St *Peter, hath God exalted with his right hand to be a Prince and a Saviour;* ———*and We are his Witnesses of these things; and so is also the* Holy Ghost, *whom God hath given to them that obey him,* Acts v. 31.

T H I S therefore is the *Third* and *Last* Great Witness to the Truth of our Lord's Doctrine; *It is the* Spirit *that beareth Witness, because the Spirit is Truth.* 'Tis this great *Variety,* this *manifold* Evidence, of the Works of the *Spirit*; which gives the most *undeniable* Attestation to the *Truth* of Christianity. This is what St *Paul* calls, *the Demonstration of the* Spirit, *and of Power,* 1 Cor. ii. 4. *For our Gospel,* saith he, *came not unto you in Word only, but also in Power, and in the* Holy Ghost, 1 *Thess.* i. 5. *Through mighty Signs and Wonders, by the Power of the* Spirit *of God,* Rom. xv. 19.

T H E Inferences I shall draw from what has been said, are:

1st, I F God has given us such abundant Evidence of the Truth of Christianity, as has been above shown; then from hence it appears, how inexcusable those are, who neglect to embrace it, when proposed to them in its true and original Simplicity. In the manner *some* have mixt it up with humane inventions; with their own unintelligible Doctrines, and corrupt Practices; it is no wonder indeed, that it has become a stumbling-block and an Offence. But as it was taught by Christ and his Apostles, in the native Purity of the Word of God; *no* heart of Man, that is willing to act the

part

S E R M. part of a *rational* Creature, can poſſibly withſtand its Evidence and Excellency.   Only
XCII. they who pretend to *embrace* it, and yet *diſobey* it; are, of the two, ſtill *more* inexcuſable. If we *receive* the Witneſs of God, which he has given us concerning his Son;
we muſt make Evidence of the Truth and Sincerity of our *Faith*, by the Teſtimony
of a ſuitable *Practice*.   We muſt verify and make good our *Baptiſm with Water*, by
the *Purity and Holineſs* of a virtuous and Chriſtian Life.   We muſt be content to be
ill-uſed (if at any time the Will of God be *ſo*,) and to *ſuffer many indignities*, for adhering to and preferring before humane inventions, the Simplicity of That Doctrine
which our Lord and his Apoſtles atteſted with their *Blood*.   We muſt take care to
bring forth the Fruits *of the Spirit*, in all meekneſs, righteouſneſs, ſobriety and virtuous behaviour; Otherwiſe the Works *of the Spirit*, the ſeveral Manifeſtations of the
Divine Power, will be of No Benefit to us.

2*dly*, I f the Witneſſes to the Truth of Chriſtianity recited in the Text, were a
ſufficient and *complete* Evidence and Atteſtation of That Doctrine which our *Saviour
himſelf* taught; then from hence we may learn what to think of thoſe Evidences,
which corrupt men in after-Ages have alledged in Proof of *their own additional Doctrines*.   The two principal Pretences of This kind, are That of the *internal guidance
of the Spirit*, and That of the *external Evidence of Miracles*.   The *former* has been
occaſionally claimed, by *Enthuſiaſts* of all Sorts: The *latter*, is the great and ſtanding Impoſture of *the Church of Rome*.   Concerning the *former*, it is ſufficient to obſerve,
that *Other Foundation can no man lay, than that which is laid, even Jeſus Chriſt*: And
that therefore the following of the *Guidance and Direction of the* Spirit of God, is not
following *vain and enthuſiaſtick imaginations*, but adhering to That Doctrine which God
at firſt revealed by the *inſpiration of his Spirit*, and is now recorded in the *Holy Scriptures* written for our Uſe.   Concerning the *latter*, namely the *Miracles* pretended to
be worked in theſe latter Ages in the Church of *Rome*; That which the Scripture ſays
of them, is, This: *Matt*. xxiv. 24; *There ſhall ariſe falſe Chriſts, and falſe Prophets,
and ſhall ſhow great Signs and Wonders;*——*Behold, I have told you before*. 2 Theſſ. ii. 9.
*Whoſe Coming is after the working of Satan, with all Power and Signs and Lying Won-
ders; and with all deceivableneſs of unrighteouſneſs in them that periſh, becauſe they received not the Love of the Truth*, (i. e. the purity and ſimplicity of the Goſpel;) *and for
This cauſe God ſhall ſend them ſtrong Deluſion, that they ſhould believe a Lie*. And, to
mention but one place more, with which I ſhall conclude: *Rev*. xiii. 13; *He doth great
Wonders, and*——*deceiveth them that dwell on the Earth, by the means of thoſe Miracles which he had Power to do*.   From which, and all Other Impoſtures and Deceits, *&c*.

SERMON XCIII.

Of our SAVIOUR's Temptation.

[A Sermon preached in Lent.]

MATT. IV. 1.

Then was Jesus led up of the Spirit into the Wilderness, to be tempted of the Devil.

THE History of our Saviour's Temptation, is a portion of Scripture, in which there are several *Difficulties*, that deserve particular Explication; and upon which may be made several useful *Observations*, to direct us in our Own Practice.

1. IN the *first* place, it may be inquired, *why* our Saviour, whom the Scripture elsewhere declares to have been *tempted in* all *points like as we are*, only *without Sin*; is yet by the Evangelists recorded, as having been tempted *only at This particular Time*: Then *was Jesus led up to be tempted*. *Then*: That is, as soon as he had been baptized. So St *Mark* explains it, ch. i. 11, 12. At his Baptism *there came a Voice from Heaven, saying, Thou art my beloved Son, in whom I am well pleased*: *And* immediately *the Spirit driveth him into the Wilderness*. The Reason is, because he *Then* began to enter upon his Office, of preaching the Doctrine of Salvation; *That Doctrine*, by which the Works and Kingdom of the Devil, the Power and Dominion of Sin over Mankind, was to be destroyed. *Before* This, we do not read of his being Tempted; because his Life being private like that of other men, his Temptations were so likewise, Sin only always excepted. Neither, *After* This, is there any mention of his being Tempted any *more*; because the Tempter being at This Time thoroughly vanquished, did not hereafter hope to prevail so much by *Tempting*, as by *Opposing and Persecuting* him. The *proper* Time of Tryal, was just after his Baptism, at the first entring into his Office. And as the Tempter might reasonably think *This* the likeliest Season, to assault him with Success; so the Wisdom of God knew on the contrary, that it was the fittest Time for his repulsing and triumphing over the Tempter. For This reason the Text takes notice, that *Jesus was led up* of the Spirit, that is, not by the Evil *Spirit*, but by the Good *Spirit* of God was he led up to his Temptation. So St *Luke* expressly, ch. iv. 1. *Jesus being full of the* Holy Ghost, *returned from* Jordan, *and was led by the Spirit into the* Wilderness. And indeed it is *observable*, that our Saviour, who *before* his Incarnation appeared to *Moses and the Patriarchs in the Form of God*, that is, invested with the immediate Glory and Power of his Father; on the contrary, *all the time of his residing here upon Earth*, appeared [κενωθεὶς] divested of That Glory, being *made in the Likeness of Man*; and is accordingly represented through the whole Gospel, as

acting

SERM. acting and working under the Conduct of the *Holy Spirit* ; God having (as our Lord
XCIII. speaks concerning Himself, *Joh.* iii. 34,) *given the Spirit unto him, not by Meafure.*

    2. IT may be enquired, *why* our Saviour continued fo long in the folitary Retire-
ment of a *Defert place*, and why he *Fafted* through all that Space of Forty Days. As
to his *Retirement in* general, and his *Fafting or Humiliation* during that Retirement ;
the Reafon of it feems to have been, that he might prepare himfelf beforehand by *Meditation and Prayer*, for the executing of that Great Office which he was about to undertake. Thus *Mofes*, the Giver of the *Law*. Thus *Elijah*, the Head of the Antient
Prophets. Thus *John Baptift*, the *Fore-runner* of our Lord, *before the day of his
fhowing unto Ifrael* ; Luke i. 80. Thus the *Apoftles* of our Lord, at the Time of their
fending forth *Paul and Barnabas* to preach, *fafted and prayed* ; Acts xiii. 3. And,
when they firft *ordained Elders in every Church*, they *prayed with Fafting*, ch. xiv. 23.
And our Saviour, admonifhing his Difciples concerning fome extraordinary miraculous
Gifts, with which they were to be indued ; *This kind* faith he, *goeth not out, but by
Prayer and Fafting*, Matt. xvii. 21. In *ordinary* cafes, it is to be underftood by Us as
a *Rule and Example* in proportion, that in undertaking any *Office*, and efpecially any
Sacred Function, we be not rafh and precipitate, carelefs, and full of *worldly* Thoughts
and Defigns ; but that, with-drawing our Minds from the World, and attending ferioufly to the promoting of God's Glory, or the Intereft of Truth and Virtue among Men,
we beg the Divine Affiftance to enable us, and by Meditation and Study ftrengthen our
own Refolutions of being Diligent, and improve our Qualifications towards being more
Succefsful, in the Performance of our Duty.

    As to the *particular Space of Time* wherein our Saviour fafted, which was *forty
days* ; This was an Accomplifhment of thofe Antient Types, when *Mofes was with
the Lord* in the Mount *forty days and forty nights, and did neither eat bread, nor drink
water* ; (Exod. xxxiv. 28 :) and *Elijah*, (1 Kings xix. 8 ;) *went in the ftrength of the
meat that he had eaten, forty days and forty nights, unto Horeb the Mount of God.* *Mofes*'s
Faft, was for the Sins of *Ifrael* in the Wildernefs ; *Deut.* ix. 18 ; *I fell down before
the Lord forty days and forty nights, I did neither eat bread nor drink water, becaufe of
all your Sins which ye finned, in doing wickedly in the fight of the Lord to provoke him
to Anger.* *Elijah's* Faft, was for the Idolatry of *Ifrael* in the days of the Kings ;
1 *Kings* xix. 13 ; *There came a voice to him, faying, What doft thou here, Elijah? And
he faid, I have been very jealous for the Lord God of Hofts ; becaufe the children of Ifrael
have forfaken thy Covenant, thrown down thine Altars, and flain thy Prophets with the
Sword.* Thefe Types therefore of the *Giver of the* Law, and of the *Chief of the* Prophets,
our Saviour who came to *fulfil the Law and the Prophets*, to fulfil all *Legal*, as well as
Moral Righteoufnefs, and to be an *Expiation* for the *Sins* of the *whole World* ; thought
fit to accomplifh. And poffibly even in his Own *Faft* alfo of forty days, there might
ftill be fomething typical, and prophetical. For, as it was told to *Ezekiel* in his Vifion ; ch. iv. 6 ; *Thou fhalt bear the iniquity of the Houfe of Judah forty days, I have
appointed thee each day for a year :* And as the Prophet *Jonah* prophefied of *Nineveh*,
yet forty days and Nineveh fhall be overthrown ; (which, though in the *literal* fenfe it
was deferred upon their Repentance, yet in the accounts of prophetical computation
it was really fulfilled, as is intimated at the conclufion of the book of *Tobit :*) So 'tis
very obfervable, that God *fuffered the Manners of the Jews in the Wildernefs* (upon
whofe Account *Mofes*'s Faft was kept ; God bore with them, I fay, in the Wildernefs)
forty years, in the time of that Great *Provocation* ; Acts xiii. 18 ; and Pf. xcv. 8, 9, 10.
And from the time of our Saviour's Death to the final deftruction of *Jerufalem*, the
fame impenitent Nation had again the fame Space allowed them of forty years.

    THE *Ufe* of fuch Obfervations as thefe, is to fhow the exact *Connexion* there is,
between the feveral prophetical *Types* made ufe of in Scripture, and the *Events* to which
                                                   thofe

thofe Types have relation. The comparing of which one with another, is a confirmation of the Truth of the infpired Writings, and confequently of the Truth of the Revelation itfelf.

THE Churches in *following* Ages, long after the Apoftles times, inftituted the Forty-days Faft of *Lent*, for fome *fort* of a Refemblance or Imitation of our Saviour's Faft: But This, being not of Apoftolical inftitution, is to be looked upon only as all Other Appointments of merely humane Authority.

3. IT may be inquired *why* our Saviour, who had Power over unclean Spirits, and could caft out Devils at his Pleafure; was yet pleafed to fubmit himfelf and condefcend fo far, as to be *Tempted* at all by the Enemy. To this Queftion, the Apoftle gives an Anfwer, *Heb.* ii. 14; that our Lord being through Death *to deftroy him that had the Power of Death, that is, the Devil;* —— took therefore *upon him, not the Nature of Angels,* wherein he could not have died; *but* the Nature of *Men. Wherefore in all things it behoved him to be made like unto his Brethren, that he might be a merciful and faithful High Prieft in things pertaining to God, to make reconciliation for the Sins of the people. For in that He himfelf hath fuffered, being* Tempted; *he is able to fuccour Them that Are Tempted.* And ch. iv. 15; *We have not an High Prieft which cannot be touched with the Feeling of our Infirmities; but one who was in all points* Tempted *like as we are, yet without Sin.* Tempted, not only by the *Great Adverfary,* as in the prefent Hiftory, whereof my Text is a part; but Tempted alfo by all the *ufual Difficulties of humane Life.* For fo he expreffes himfelf to his Difciples, *Luk.* xxii. 28; *Ye are they which have continued with me in my* Temptations. And indeed the Defign of his coming into the World, was not barely to *Die*; but in the whole Courfe of his *Life* alfo, to fet an Example of Humility and of perfect Obedience, as well as to give himfelf a Propitiation for our Sins by his *Death.* For *This* reafon he was *circumcifed,* and became obedient in all things to the Law of *Mofes.* And when he came to *John's* Baptifm; though he had No Sin to wafh away by Repentance; and *John,* knowing him, would have forbiden him, faying, *I have need to be baptized of Thee, and comeft thou to Me?* Matt. iii. 14: yet *Jefus* infifted upon it, faying, *Suffer it to be fo Now; For thus it becometh us to fulfil all Righteoufnefs.* All *Righteoufnefs;* that is, every thing which is, not only properly and ftrictly *needful in itfelf;* but every thing that is *meet,* every thing that is *decent,* every thing that is *regular, exemplary,* or *of good report.*

4. IT may be inquired, (and this is one of the greateft Difficulties of all,) *why* the Tempter *would* at all affault our Lord, or what Advantage he could poffibly hope to gain over him. Was it poffible that he could think to defeat the Counfel of God, or difappoint the Defign of his fending the Meffiah into the World? To This, it may be replied, 1*ft,* That as wicked *men* perpetually attempt *vain, unreafonable,* and *abfurd* things; fo wicked *Spirits* likewife, deferted of God, and forfaken of all Goodnefs and True Underftanding, may well be fuppofed to attempt things no lefs *unreafonable* and *abfurd.* That Evil Spirits fhould *at any time* have *hoped* to prevail againft the Almighty by *Power and Force,* as Some have fuppofed; is indeed too abfurd to be imagined. But that they fhould rebel againft the *Counfel and Will* of God, and endeavour malicioufly to overthrow *his Kingdom of Righteoufnefs;* this is no more than what wicked *men,* in a lower degree, are perpetually doing. But 2*dly,* It may be confidered further, that poffibly the Tempter was not yet *fure,* whether our Lord was indeed the *Meffiah* or no. His words, If *thou* be *the Son of God,* feem to exprefs his *uncertainty* concerning that matter. And there are feveral other things taken notice of in Scripture, the obferving of which will make This feem lefs improbable. The Evangelifts tell us, that the Devil *entred into Judas,* and put it in his Heart to betray his Mafter. By This it appears, that the Tempter did not even Then know, that the Salvation of Men was to be accomplifhed by the fhedding of the Blood of Chrift; feeing he

hoped

hoped to put an End to the Doctrine of Christ, by destroying his Life. And This will be the lefs to be wondred at, if we consider what is declared in Scripture even concerning good *Angels themselves,* who *always behold the Face of our Father which is in Heaven.* 1 Pet. i. 11 ; The Antient *Prophets,* says the Apostle, *searched What, and what manner of Time, the Spirit of Christ which was in them did signify, when it testified beforehand the Sufferings of Christ, and the Glory that should follow. Unto whom it was revealed, that not unto themselves, but unto Us they did minister the things which are now reported unto you by Them that have preached the Gospel unto you, with the Holy Ghost sent down from Heaven.* Which things, the Angels *desire to look into.* Not only Evil *Spirits* understood not, what the Prophets had foretold concerning the Sufferings of Christ, and the Glory that should follow ; but even *Good Angels* themselves, St *Peter* tells us, were *desirous to look into* Those things. And St *Paul* carries this matter still further : *Eph.* iii. 9 ; *To preach,* saith he, *the unsearchable Riches of Christ* ; *and to make all men see what is the Fellowship of the Mystery, which from the Beginning of the World, hath been hid in God, who created all things by Jesus Christ* ; *To the intent that Now unto the Principalities and Powers in* heavenly *places, might be known by the Church the manifold Wisdom of God.* By the Church ; that is, by the Dispensations of God's Providence towards his Universal Church, by the *Events* accomplishing antient *Types and Mysteries* ; and by the *clear fulfilling* of obscure *Prophecies* ; by These is the Wisdom of God, and the manifold Beauty of the Divine Counsels, made known not to *Men* only, but to *Angels* also. And This perhaps is the true meaning of That obscure Text : 1 *Tim.* iii. 16, The *Mystery* * *of Godliness* (or God) * *manifest in the Flesh,* was seen *of Angels* : Seen, not in the *literal* Sense ; for That was no mystery ; But *understood, apprehended, made plain,* to the Angels ; who were before, in That sense, *desirous to look into* it. To mention but One place more : There is a very remarkable expression in the Book of *Tobit,* ch. vi. 17 ; where the Angel *Raphael,* one of the seven Spirits that are described as going in and out before the Throne of God, is introduced thus speaking : *Moreover, I* suppose, says he, (he does not speak as with *certain knowledge,* but, *I suppose,* says he,) *that she shall bear thee Children.* He who considers These, and the like expressions of Scripture ; will not perhaps think *Evil* Spirits to be Creatures of such extensive Capacity, but that the Tempter might very well be *uncertain* whether our Saviour was the promised *Messiah* or no, at the Time of his presuming to tempt him as in the Text. But 3*dly,* Supposing the Tempter *did* know our Lord to be the promised *Messiah,* at the Time of his tempting him ; yet still it was by no means impossible for the Great Deceiver to suppose, that as, by seducing the *First Adam,* he had excluded Mankind out of That Paradise which God had planted for them ; so by endeavouring to make *some* impression or other upon the *Second Adam,* he might prevent men from being restored to Paradise again ; and so a *second time* defeat *the Counsel of God.* Defeat the *Counsel of God* ; That is, *not* prevent any thing that the Almighty had *resolved absolutely* to accomplish : For, in That sense, nothing can *resist* his *Will,* nothing can *oppose* his *Power* : But the Enemy *may* oppose *such* Counsels or Designs of God for the Salvation of Mankind, as are *conditional* only, and appointed to depend upon the Behaviour of *Others* : Such Counsels of God, as even *Men* are at liberty by their Perverseness and Obstinacy to disappoint. As when the Evangelist tells us, St *Luke* i. 30 ; that *the Pharisees and Lawyers* rejected *the Counsel of God against themselves* : That is ; *Against* their own Interest, *against* their own both Temporal and Eternal Welfare, they *rejected* the gracious Offers of the divine Mercy. *Such* Counsels of God as these, it is no wonder that He whose Works and Kingdom our Lord came to destroy, should endeavour to oppose. Nor is it at all impossible, that the Design of God in sending the *Messiah* into the World, might seem to the Tempter to be of the *same* Nature ; to be *conditional* likewise. For as *all the* Threat-

* *This is the old and true Reading.*

3

nings

nings of God, even thofe which in the *manner of* Expreffion are moft *peremptory and* S E R M.
abfolute, yet in reality muft always be underftood to be *conditional*, and to include a XCIII.
tacit *exception* upon the cafe of Repentance and Reformation ; (as is evident in the
Inftance of *Jonah's* Prophecy againft *Nineveh*; and as is declared in general by the
Prophet *Jeremy*, ch. xviii. 7, *At what inftant I fhall fpeak concerning a Nation and
concerning a Kingdom, to pluck up and to pull down, and to deftroy it ; If That Nation againft whom I have pronounced, turn from their Evil, I will repent of the Evil
that I thought to do unto them :*) As (I fay) all the *Threatnings* of God are thus undoubtedly conditional, fo likewife, all the Promifes of God to Mankind, *however peremptory and abfolute* they may feem in the prophetical Expreffions of Scripture, may
yet poffibly be fuppofed to be in reality *conditional* alfo. The Nation of the *Jews*
at This day, notwithftanding the moft *exprefs* and determinate *Predictions* in the
Old Teftament, not only concerning the Coming *of the Meffiah*, but even concerning
the *precife* Time *and* Manner *of his Coming*, in Terms the moft *pofitive and abfolute*
that can be ; yet are univerfally of Opinion, that for the Sins of That people his
Coming has been put off beyond the Time limited by the Prophets above feventeen
hundred years. Well therefore might the Tempter apprehend, by the fame manner
of Reafoning, even *after* the Meffiah had begun to appear in the Flefh, that notwithftanding the plain Predictions concerning the Salvation of Mankind by him, yet poffibly
even in all *Thofe* Promifes there might be included fuch *tacit Conditions*, as that either
by Tempting Chrift himfelf, or his Followers the Apoftles, or by exciting Wicked men
to oppofe and withftand Him and his Doctrine, he might at leaft in *fome meafure* prevent the Effect of his Coming, and hinder (at leaft in *great part*) the Salvation of Men.

Thus have I briefly endeavoured to give Some Anfwer to That difficult Inquiry,
why the Tempter would at all affault our Lord ; what Advantage he could poffibly
hope to gain over him ; and how, and in what degree, he could think it poffible to
defeat the Counfel of God, and to difappoint the Defign of his fending the Meffiah
into the World.

5. *Fifthly* and *Laftly* ; Since we read no more in the Gofpels, of Chrift's being
Tempted after This ; it may be enquired, in the Laft place, *how* and in *what Senfe*
it is faid by St *Luke*, at the Conclufion of This Hiftory of our Lord's Temptation,
ch. iv. 13 ; that the Tempter *departed from him, only* for a Seafon. The words, *for
a* Seafon, feem to imply, as if after fome Interval he *returned to tempt him again.*
Which fince we no where read that he attempted any more, in any *fuch* way of
Temptation as is recorded in the Text ; it is therefore probable that the Evangelift's
Meaning was This ; that the Tempter having failed of Succefs in his *prefent* Method,
departed from our Lord for a Time, intending *hereafter* to affault him after *Another*
manner. That is to fay : Finding there was *no poffibility* of making any impreffion
upon him by *Fraud*, he refolved for the future to *withftand* his Doctrine by *Oppofition
and Force :* And becaufe there was *no room* for his Suggeftions to take *any* place, upon
Chrift himfelf; the only remaining way, was to ftir up againft him the Hatred of profane *Men* ; and try, by making *Others* his Inftruments, to put a Stop by *Their* Malice
to That Doctrine, which *He himfelf* by his *own* Temptations could not prevent from
being preached. *After a Seafon* therefore, according to the intimation St *Luke* gives
us, he returned again : And having prevailed upon *Judas* to betray him, and upon the
Pharifees to encourage the Bafenefs of the Betrayer, and upon *Pilate* to put him to
Death upon their falfe Accufation ; he might very well think, that by the Succefs of
this *laft* Attempt, he had made fufficient Amends for his Failure in the *firft*. By which
Means not only wicked *Men*, by whofe hands our Lord was *crucified and flain* ; but Acts ii. 23.
even the *Great Deceiver Himfelf*, became an Inftrument in the hand of Providence,
to bring about, *according to the determinate Counfel and Foreknowledge of God,* the Sal-

SERM. vation of the World. *O the depth of the Riches both of the Wifdom and Knowledge of*
XCIII. *God! how unfearchable are his Judgments, and his Ways paft finding out!* The Particu-
Rom. xi. 33. lars of this laft and great Tranfaction, are thus recorded in the Gofpel: Our Saviour,
in his laft Difcourfe with his Difciples, a little before his Paffion, gives them Notice
of their great Temptation approaching; *Joh.* xiv. 30; *The Prince of this World,* faith
he, *cometh, and hath nothing in me.* The *firft* Effect of this his coming is expreffed,
Joh. xiii. 2; *The Devil having now put it into the Heart of Judas Ifcariot, Simon's fon,
to betray him:* And *Luke* xxii. 3; *Then* entred Satan *into Judas firnamed Ifcariot, being of the number of the twelve.* This *Succefs* of the Tempter was upon *Judas* only:
But *Attempts* were made upon the *reft* of the Difciples likewife; *Luke* xxii. 31; *The
Lord faid, Simon, Simon; behold* Satan *hath defired to have you, that he may fift
you as wheat;* But *I have prayed for thee, that thy Faith fail not:* And unto *all*
the Difciples, ver. 40; *Pray,* faith he, *that ye enter not into Temptation;* and again,
ver. 46; *Rife, and pray, left ye enter into Temptation.* Now at the fame time that
one of his Difciples, was thus moved to *betray him,* and the *reft* afraid to acknowledge him, and tempted to *deny* him, the *Malice and Cruelty* of his Enemies, his Enemies both *vifible* and *invifible,* wicked *Men* and wicked *Spirits,* was ftirred up a-
gainft him to fuch a degree, that he Thus fpeaks concerning *Himfelf, Joh.* xii. 27;
Now is my Soul troubled, and what fhall I fay? Father, fave me from this Hour, and
concerning *his* Enemies, *Luke* xxii. 53; *This is your Hour, and the Power of Darknefs.*
The *Effect* was, that he was delivered into the Hands of Wicked men, to be crucified
and flain. And when the *Enemy of man's Salvation,* and the *Enemies of* their own
Salvation, thought they had thus entirely put an End to the Doctrine of Chrift by
his Death; the *Wifdom of God,* on the contrary, brought it to pafs, (which was the
Heb. ii. 14. Myftery hid from the Foundation of the World,) that by *this very means,* even *through
Death, he deftroyed Him that had the Power of Death, that is, the Devil:* According
to That Prediction of his own, fpoken juft *before* his Paffion, but not underftood till
after his Refurrection, *Joh.* xii. 31; *Now is the Judgment of this World, now fhall
the Prince of this World be caft out:* And ch. xvi. 11; *Of Judgment becaufe the Prince
of this World is judged.*

    THE only Obfervation I fhall add further upon This Head is, that whereas it is
affirmed in This Hiftory, that Satan *entred into Judas,* and *put it in his Heart to betray his Mafter;* it is not to be underftod, either in *Judas's,* or in any *other* Wicked
man's cafe, that the *Devil's tempting them* is any manner of Excufe or Extenuation of
their Sin. For the Devil can *but* fuggeft, even as Wicked *men* do one to another.
And, *being tempted,* or having Evil *fuggefted* to them, is no *Sin.* Sin, confifts wholly
in the *Confent of the Will,* approving and putting in practice the Evil fuggefted. Over
which *Confent of the Will,* the *Devil* has no Power; but it is owing entirely to the *Wickednefs of the man's own Heart, chufing* to do the Evil which it ought to have *refufed.*
And therefore the Queftion is put by St *Peter* to *Ananias,* (Acts v. 3;) by way of *aggravation* and fevere *Reproof* of his Crime; why *hath* Satan *filled thine Heart?* that
is, what *Excufe can you have, for complying with fo* vile *a Temptation of the Devil,
which you* ought *to have rejected with all Abhorrence?*

    BUT concerning This, (which is a practical Inference from the whole,) I fhall have
occafion to fpeak further, in the following Difcourfe.

SERMON

SERMON XCIV.

Of our SAVIOUR'S Temptation.

[A Sermon preached in Lent.]

MATT. IV. 1.

Then was Jesus led up of the Spirit into the Wilderness, to be tempted of the Devil.

IN discoursing upon the Account the Scripture gives us of our Saviour's Tempta- S E R M. tion, I proposed 1*st*, to consider the several *Difficulties*, which, in that portion of XCIV. the Gospel-History, may seem to want more particular Explication: and 2*dly*, to deduce from thence such *Observations*, as may be useful to direct us in our *own* Practice.

I. IN the *First* place, the *Difficulties*, which in the History of our Saviour's Temptation, seemed most necessary to be explained, I have already considered particularly in a foregoing Discourse; And have shown distinctly, 1*st*, *why* our Saviour, whom the Scripture elsewhere declares to have been *tempted in* all *points as We are*, only *without Sin*; is yet by the Evangelists recorded, as having been tempted *only at this particular Time*. 2*dly*, *why* our Saviour continued so long in the solitary Retirement of a *Desert place*, and why he *Fasted* through all that Space of Forty days. 3*dly*, *why* our Lord, who had Power over unclean Spirits, and could cast out Devils at his Pleasure; was yet pleased to submit himself and condescend so far, as to be *Tempted* by the Enemy. 4*thly*, *why* the Tempter *would* at all assault our Lord, or what Advantage he could possibly hope to gain over him. 5*thly* and *Lastly*, *how* and *in what Sense*, since we read no more in the Gospels, of Christ's being Tempted after This: it is yet said by St *Luke*, at the Conclusion of this History of our Lord's Temptation, that the Tempter *departed from him*, only *for a* Season.

THESE several Questions, naturally arising in the mind of any one who carefully reads this portion of the Gospel-History, I have endeavoured to give particular and distinct Answers to them, in the foregoing Discourse. I am Now in the

II. *Second* place, to deduce from this History of our Lord's Temptation, such *Inferences* or *Observations*, as may be useful to direct us in our *own* Practice. And

1*st*, WE have from hence an intimation given us, that the Devil is always ready to Tempt men to Sin. As the Good *Spirit* of God, is always willing to assist those who sincerely desire to be religious; and the *Angels*, are with chearfulness sent forth to minister, to those who shall be Heirs of Salvation: so the Scripture every where represents the Evil *One*, as delighting and watching to entice men into Sin: (1 *Pet.* v. 8.) Be sober, *be vigilant; because your adversary the Devil, as a roaring Lion, walketh a-*

bout,

S E R M. *bout, seeking whom he may devour.* Again, *Eph.* vi. 11, 12; *Put on the whole Armour*
XCIV. *of God, that ye may be able to stand against the Wiles of the Devil.* For we wrestle not
*against flesh and blood, but against Principalities, against Powers, against the Rulers of
the Darkness of This World, against spiritual Wickedness in high Places.* And ch. ii. 2;
*According to the Course of this World, according to the Prince of the Power of the Air,
the Spirit that Now worketh in the children of Disobedience.* If it be here inquired, for
what *Reason* wicked Spirits tempt men to Sin, and what *End* they can propose in so
doing; the most probable Answer is, that they do it for the very *same* reasons, as wicked
men tempt and seduce one another. Partly, as esteeming it a sort of *Apology* or *Excuse* for *Themselves,* if they can draw *Others* into the like Condemnation; and partly as
being moved with *Envy,* that Others should enjoy That Happiness which they themselves have lost; and *hating* those, whose manners and dispositions are contrary to
their own. Concerning wicked *Men,* the Author of the Book of *Wisdom* Thus describes
the Temper I am speaking of; *ch.* ii. 12; *Let us lie in wait for the righteous: because
he is not for our own Turn, and he is clean contrary to our Doings;——He is grievous
unto us, even to behold; for his Life is not like other mens, his ways are of another Fashion.*
And concerning evil *Spirits,* ver. 24; *Through* Envy *of the Devil, came Death into the
World; and they that hold of his side, do find it.* Nevertheless; though the Scriptures
do indeed thus teach us, that the Devil is always ready to *Tempt* men to Sin, yet it is
Always carefully to be observed, that he *can do nothing more* but *Tempt us.* He has
no Power over our *Persons,* or our *Wills.* He can *only* set before us *Baits* and *Al-
lurements;* but we *cannot* be hurt by them, except we *yield* to them and *chuse* them.
The *Treachery* and *Corruptness* of our *own Hearts within,* is *much more dangerous,* than
all the Assaults of the *Enemy* from *without.* Let no man say, when he is tempted, I am
tempted *of God,* St *Jam.* i. 13; that is, let no man plead as an *Excuse* for his Sin, that
God permitted the *Devil* to *tempt* him into it. (For that This is the meaning of the
Phrase, *tempted of God;* appears plainly from 2 *Sam.* xxiv. 1; compared with 1 *Chron.*
xxi. 1; In *one* of which places, it is said, *the* Lord *moved David to number Israel and
Judah;* and in the *other,* that Satan *provoked David to number Israel.)* Let no man
(says the Apostle) plead as an *Excuse* for his Sin, that *God* permitted the Evil One to
tempt him into it. For *God,* as he *cannot* himself *be tempted with evil,* so *neither tempt-
eth he any man;* neither doth he permit the *Devil* to tempt any one further, than by
laying before him such Allurements, as it is *in the person's* Power, and it is his *Duty,*
and it is the *proper Trial and Exercise of his Virtue,* to resist. *But every man is* then,
and then only, *tempted;* then only, effectually and sinfully, *tempted; when he is drawn
away of his own Lust, and inticed.* The *Enemy* of men's Salvation can do nothing
more, but only entice the *Covetous* with Hopes of *Gain,* puff up the *Ambitious* with
Expectation of *Honour,* allure the *Voluptuous* with Prospects of *Pleasure.* Where the
Mind is not under the Power of any of these corrupt Affections, the Tempter finding
nothing in it, (as the Scripture-expression is, *Joh.* xiv. 30;) his Temptations can take
no hold, and his Power is at an End. *Resist the Devil,* says the Apostle, *and he will
flee from you.* Take heed only that your own *Heart* be sincere, sincere in the Pursuit
of Truth and Virtue; and all the *fiery darts of the wicked* One will in course be quench-
Eccluf. xv. 17. ed. If we do not, by our own Perverseness, *grieve* and drive from us *the good Spirit
of God;* greater is He that is in Us, than he that is in the World. God, saith the Son
of *Sirach,* has *set before man Life and Death; and whether him liketh, shall be given
him.* The good *Spirit* is *equally willing,* and *more able* to help us, than the Evil *one*
can be to hurt us. In vain therefore do wicked men hope to extenuate their own
Crimes, by alledging that they were tempted by the Devil. For the Scripture never
mentions it as an *Excuse,* but on the contrary as an *Aggravation* of a Fault, when
'tis of *such* a nature as may well be supposed to have been suggested by the *Evil One,*

and

and for *That Reason* ought above all things to have been carefully avoided. Why *has* Satan *filled thine Heart,* said St *Peter* to *Ananias;* Acts v. 3? by way of more *severe* Reproof, for his presumption in attempting to deceive the Holy Spirit, wherewith God had inspired the Apostles. Nor indeed is it at all impossible, but that men's wicked deeds may sometimes rightly be ascribed to the Devil, even when perhaps they proceed *only* from the corruption of their *own* Hearts, and not from any immediate suggestion of *evil Spirits.* For, as it is agreeable to the Style of Scripture, and to the Reason of Things, to ascribe every thing that is *Good* to *God;* because *he* is the original *Author* of the *Powers* by which all Good is done; and whatever Good is done, is in obedience to His *Commands,* and agreeable to his *Nature and Will:* So every *Wicked* thing that is done, may in a proportionate sense be ascribed to the *Devil;* because He is the *Head,* and the *Beginner* and *Encourager* of Evil; and whatever Evil is done, is in *imitation of* him, and *agreeable to* him.

2dly, THE 2d Observation I would draw from the History of our Lord's Temptation, is, that we are hereby taught, that no Person whatsoever is so *Great* or *Good,* as to be exempt from Temptation. If the *Captain of our Salvation* was himself *made perfect by Suffering,* let no man think himself so Good, as not to deserve Chastisement at the hand of God. If *Christ himself* was *in all points tempted like as we are,* let no man think himself so perfect, as to be above the Danger and the Fear of Temptation. We have great reason, as the Apostle admonishes; *Heb.* ii. 1, *to give earnest heed to the things that we have heard, lest at any time we should let them slip.* For the *Deceitfulness of Sin* is Great, and the *Tempter* is always *watchful* to seduce us, and the *Heart* of man is apt to grow *negligent.* So that even the *Best* Christians are by St *Paul* admonished, to *work out their Salvation with Fear and Trembling. Let him that thinketh he standeth, take heed lest he fall;* 1 Cor. x. 12; and *Rom.* xi. 20; *Thou standest by Faith; be not high-minded, but fear.*

3dly, FROM the consideration of the *Time* of our Saviour's being tempted, which was *immediately after his Baptism;* we are instructed, that when men *first* set about the Practice of Religion, they are *then* reasonably to expect the greatest Difficulties in their Duty. *Ecclus.* ii. 1; *My Son, if thou come to serve the Lord, prepare thy Soul for Temptation.* The Life of a Christian, is in Scripture compared to a State of *Warfare;* wherein he that goeth out to Battle, ought well to consider, before his setting out, what is the Strength of the Enemy that cometh against him. Whoever will lead a religious life; must begin with expecting, to find difficulty in subduing *his own* vitious Passions, and to find opposition from the *course* of a corrupt and debauched *World.* No man, saith St *Paul, should be moved by these Afflictions;* for, *yourselves know that* 1 Thess. iii.3. *we are* appointed *thereunto: Yea,* and All *that will live godly in Christ Jesus,* shall 2 Tim. iii. 12. *suffer Persecution.* For This reason, the Scripture frequently uses the Phrase of *Overcoming,* to express a Christian's Perseverance in the Love of Truth and Virtue. He must be *Tempted* with *Allurements,* and *terrified* with *Dangers;* and then, if he *Overcometh,* saith our Saviour, he *shall inherit all things.* The sooner a man *begins* the Practice of true religion, the *fewer* evil Habits and the *less strong* vicious inclinations will he have to struggle with from *within.* And when he has once got above the *Allurements of inward Temptation,* he will with much greater Advantage be able to withstand the *Force of Persecution from abroad.* When our Saviour had entirely repulsed the first Assaults of sensual Pleasure and Ambition; the Tempter, says the Text, *departed from him, and Angels came and ministred unto him.* Thus, whosoever in the practice of religion, steddily resists the *first* temptations to Vice, and suffers not himself to be corrupted with any Evil Habits; shall, after That, more easily *keep himself, and That wicked One toucheth him not. Wisdom,* that is, Virtue, *is glorious,* saith the

Author of the book of *Wisdom*; ch. vi. 12; *and never fadeth away:——Whoso seeketh her early, shall have no great Trouble, for he shall find her sitting at his Doors.*

　　4*thly,* FROM the following Expression in the Text, that *Jesus* being *led by the Spirit,* or being *full of the Holy Ghost,* went up into the Wilderness to be Tempted of the Devil; we may learn, that *Temptation to Sin* is not at all an *Argument of God's Displeasure,* but only a Trial *of us, appointed by his wise Providence.* 'Tis, in the Nature of things, a *necessary* and *essential* condition of a *Probation-state,* that there should be some Trial of mens Virtue. And, in *This* sense, the Scripture scruples not to affirm, that *God himself* tempts men. *Gen.* xxii. 1; *After these things God did tempt,* that is, did try, *Abraham.* And, *Deut.* viii. 2; *God led thee these forty years in the wilderness, to prove thee, to* know *what was in thine heart, whether thou wouldst keep his Commandments or no;* and suffered false Prophets, ch. xiii. 3; *that he might know whether you love the Lord your God with all your Heart, and with all your Soul.* The meaning is; not, that in These cases God does not *know before,* how men will behave themselves; but That they who *have in them* a true *Root* of Virtue, may *actually* bring forth the *Fruit* of it; may be *exercised,* may be *approved,* may be *made manifest,* to the *World* here, and to men *and* angels hereafter; and may be, *in* themselves, *improved, established,* and *fitted* for the State of Heaven. *The Trial of our Faith,* (saith the Apostle,)
worketh Patience, and Patience Experience, and Experience Hope. For *This* reason, we are exhorted, *not to faint,* nor to be *cast down* under Temptations; nor to *think it* strange *concerning the fiery Trials that are to try us.* Nay, on the contrary, we are encouraged even to *rejoice* under *manifold temptations;* to call *the man* Blessed, *that endureth temptation,* (Jam. i. 12;) to glory *in tribulations;* (Rom. v. 3;) to *count it all* joy, *when we fall into divers temptations,* (Jam. i. 2:) Considering, that *when we are tried, we shall receive the Crown of Life,* (ver. 12;) and that *the Trial of our Faith, is much more precious than of Gold that perisheth,* (1 Pet. i. 7:) For, *when he has tried us,* (as Holy *Job* expresses it,) *we shall come forth as Gold;* ch. xxiii. 10; And the Author of the Book of *Wisdom,* ch. iii. 5; God, saith he, proved *the Souls of the righteous, and found them worthy for himself;* as Gold in *the furnace hath he tried them, and received them as a burnt-offering: And in the Time of their visitation* (that is at the day of judgment;) *they shall shine, and run to and fro like Sparks among the Stubble; They shall judge the Nations, and have Dominion over the people, and their Lord shall reign for ever.*

　　NEVERTHELESS, 'tis here carefully to be observed, that all the things which the Scripture speaks in *This* manner concerning Temptations and our rejoicing under them, are to be understood *only* of Temptations either *already past and overcome;* or else of such, as we have *very good ground of assurance,* that, by the grace of God, they shall be *overcome.* For otherwise, as to *Temptations in general,* Temptations *unexperienced,* and of which we *know* the *Danger* but *not the Success;* concerning *These,* the Direction the Scripture gives us, is, on the contrary, that we may *lawfully,* nay, that 'tis *our* Duty to pray *against them,* and endeavour to *avoid* them. Our Saviour, who *knew* what was in Man, thus exhorts his Disciples, *Mar.* xiv. 38; *Watch and pray, lest ye enter into Temptation:* and *himself* prays, not for his *own* Sake, but as an *Example to Us; Father, if it be possible, let this Cup pass from me.* Our *Nature* is *Frail,* our *Passions strong,* our *Wills biassed;* and our security, generally speaking, consists much more certainly in *escaping* great Temptations, than in *conquering* them. For this reason, our Lord directed his Followers, when they were *Persecuted in One City, to flee unto another.* Which they who refused to do, led *themselves* into Temptation, and tempted *God:* Putting themselves upon an Expectation of an extraordinary Assistance, where God had not given any Promise of affording it. For where God *calls* us to a Trial, he *will* enable us to go through it; but there is *no Assurance* of such Assistance to the *Presumptuous.* 'Tis not lawful therefore, for Men to *go* of themselves, and *throw*

themselves

themfelves into Temptation; and we are taught to *pray* moreover, that God alfo, in his good Providence, would *not lead us into it*. This Phrafe, of God's leading *men into Temptation*, it is evident, muft be underftood according to the *Analogy* of Scripture-language; which, becaufe Nothing can come to pafs without God's permiffion, does therefore ufually, in acknowledgement of the Supreme fuperintendency of Divine Providence over all Events, afcribe *every thing*, figuratively to God. As when *God is* faid to have *delivered* a man, who is flain by chance, into the hand of his Neighbour; to have *moved* David, by means of Satan's Temptations, to number *Ifrael* and *Judah*; to have *hardened Pharaoh's* heart; to have *blinded the Eyes*, and *made fat*, or *ftupid*, the heart of the people; to have *fent forth* a lying Spirit among *Ahab's* Prophets; to have *hardned the Spirit of Sihon* King of *Hefhbon*, and *made his heart obftinate*; to have *hardned the Nations*, to *come againft Ifrael to battle*, that *he might deftroy them utterly*; to have *put* it in the Hearts of Evil Princes, to give their Kingdom unto the Beaft or Falfe Prophet; to *fend* upon men a *ftrong Delufion*; and, in the phrafe we are now fpeaking of, to lead *men into Temptation*. 'Tis plain, in *all* thefe Expreffions, the intention is not to affirm, (except perhaps in fome *judicial* cafes,) that God, *aftually* and *efficiently*, does thefe things; but only, that in the courfe of his All-wife Providence, he juftly *permits* them to come to pafs. Wherefore, when our Saviour teaches us to pray, that God would not lead *us into Temptation*; the meaning is, that he would be pleafed fo to order and direft things by his All-wife Providence in This Probation-ftate, as not to *fuffer us to be tempted above what we are able*, but that he would *with the Temptation alfo make a way to efcape, that we may be able to bear it*. And particularly, that he would not *judicially*, and *in anger*, give us up and leave us to the Power of Temptation, and to the Seducements of the Evil One; as he did *Pharaoh* and *Ahab*, and *Judas*, and the *Ifraelites in the Wildernefs*, when (as the Pfalmift expreffes it) *he gave them up unto their own Hearts Lufts, and let them follow their own Imaginations*. But that, on the contrary, he would either, by his *preventing Mercy*, keep *us* from *the Hour of Temptation*; Rev. iii. 10; or, by his gracious Support, *deliver us* out *of it*; 2 Pet. ii. 9.

5thly, FROM what St *Luke* records, at the Conclufion of this Hiftory of our Lord's Temptation, that the Tempter departed from him *only for a Seafon*; we may obferve, that though at the firft Entrance into the courfe of a religious Life, the greateft Difficulties and Temptations are generally to be expefted; and when Once thofe are clearly overcome, the *ways* of Virtue ufually become *Pleafantnefs*, and her *Paths Peace*; yet men ought *never* to look upon themfelves as *fecure* from the Returns of Temptation; but that the Evil One may again affault them under different Forms and Shapes, to feduce them into different kinds of Sins; grounding Temptations, *perhaps*, even upon their *Security itfelf*. Wherefore, *we ought* (fays the Apoftle) *to give the more earneft heed to the things which we have heard, left at any time we fhould let them flip*; Heb. ii. 1. For, Many Wife and Good Refolutions, made with great Sincerity and right Intention, have through Negligence after fome time, and want of ferious recolleftion, failed of their Effeft. *Watch ye therefore, and be ready* Always; *for ye know not what hour your Lord doth come: Bleffed* (fays our Saviour) *is that Servant, whom his Lord, when he cometh, fhall find fo doing*; Matt. xxiv. 46.

Laftly; FROM the *Particulars* of our Saviour's Temptation, we may obferve the *feveral principal Ways* by which the Tempter affaults men, and what are the moft *proper Means of refifting* each Temptation.

HIS *firft* Temptation, was founded upon *bodily and temporal Wants*: When he *was an hungred*, the Tempter faid; *If thou be the Son of God, command that thefe Stones be made Bread*. His meaning was; *If you are the beloved of God, do not fubmit to undergo any Hardfhips*; but infift *with God, that he fhow his Love to you, by fupporting*

you

S E R M. *you even miraculoufly. Want*, is the great Temptation to *murmuring* againft God: And
XCIV. therefore *Satan* is reprefented, *Job* i. 11; as thus pleading with God againft *Job* ; *Put
forth thine hand now, and* touch *all that he hath, and he will curfe thee to thy Face.*
And the Prayer of *Agur* is for this reafon given us as an example ; *Prov.* xxx. 8: *Give
me not poverty,———left I take the Name of my God in vain.* The *proper* Prefervative
againft *This* Temptation, our Saviour teaches us in his Reply ; *Man fhall not live by
Bread alone, but by every word that proceedeth out of the Mouth of God.* We muft at
all times depend upon the Protection of Providence; and confider, that as in the time
of *Plenty*, we are fupported *not* by the *things themfelves* which we enjoy, but by the
Bleffing of God which alone enables them to fupport us; fo, in the Time of *Want*, the
fame Providence, if he thinks fit, and fees that it will promote our eternal Intereft, can
ftill always find proper Means of preferving us.

THE *Second* Temptation offered to our Lord, was; *If thou be the Son of God, caft
thyfelf down* ; down from a pinnacle of the Temple ; *For it is written, He fhall give
his Angels Charge concerning thee,———left at any time thou dafh thy foot againft a Stone.*
To *This* Temptation, our Lord replies, that there being a Commandment given in the
Law, *Thou fhalt not tempt the Lord thy God*; 'tis therefore *not lawful* for any man to
throw himfelf needlefly into danger, merely to *try* whether Providence will therein protect him or no. We may *rely* upon God, that he will *give his Angels Charge over us*,
in all Dangers into which his Providence leads us; but no man ought to *tempt* God, by
running *wilfully* any prefumptuous hazards.

THE Ufe therefore of *This* part of the Hiftory of our Lord's Temptation, may be
to warn us againft *Two or Three* very dangerous Seducements of This Kind. *One* is
a prefumptuous *confidence* or vain *fecurity*, relying upon groundlefs Notions of *Predeftination*, and of God's *particular* Favour to us; or founded upon a *Falfe Application* of
conditional Promifes, as if they were *abfolute* : *Caft thy felf down*, For, *it is written, he
fhall give his Angels Charge concerning thee.*

ANOTHER dangerous Temptation which we are *here* likewife warned of; a Temptation, *contrary* at firft Sight to That now-mentioned, and yet in reality leading into
the *fame* Snare ; is *Diftruft* of God. Such a Diftruft, as the *Ifraelites* in the Wildernefs were guilty of, when they faid ; *He fmote the ftony rock indeed, that the Waters——
flowed withal ; but can he give Bread alfo, or provide Flefh for his People*; Pf. lxxviii.
21? He hath ferved thee indeed in *Other* Dangers; but *Caft thyfelf down from hence*,
and, if he has a *Favour* to thee, will he preferve thee *Then?* When God has given
men *fufficient* evidence of any Truth ; to be ftill diffatisfied, and continually requiring
Pf. xcv. 9. *Other* Signs, is *Tempting of God.* Thus the *Jews in the Wildernefs*, tho' they *faw*
God's *works* with their own eyes, yet continued to *tempt* him *ten times*; Num. xiv. 22.
Thus the Pharifees, after the *Voice from Heaven* at our Saviour's Baptifm, and after
many other miraculous Works, yet ftill defired of him a *Sign from Heaven*, Matt. xvi. 1.
Thus, after the Proof given to St *Peter*, of God's receiving the *Gentiles* into the Gofpel-
covenant ; he calls it *tempting of God*, Acts xv. 10; to endeavour to *put upon the necks
of the Difciples the yoke of* the Ceremonial Law. Thus, after the Proofs God has given of
his *exiftence*, by the works of Nature ; and of his *Will*, by the Revelation of the Gofpel ;
to call for *more* Proofs, is a *tempting* of God.

THE *Third* and *Laft* Temptation offered to our Lord, was *Worldly Power, Glory,*
and *Intereft* : *All thefe* Kingdoms *will I give thee*, and the Glory *of them, if thou wilt
fall down and worfhip Me.* The Greateft of all Temptations, is *Riches, Honour and
Power.* Thefe are the great Incentives, to *Luxury, Pride,* and *Tyranny.* The Profperity *of Fools deftroys them*, Prov. i. 32 : And, *Man being in* Honour, faith the Pfal-
Pf. xlix. 20. mift, *has no Underftanding* ; that is, is very apt to forget Himfelf; and his Duty. *They*
I   *that*

that will *be rich, fall into Temptation and a Snare, and into many foolish and hurtful* S E R M. *Lusts, which drown men in destruction and perdition,* 1 Tim. vi. 9. Insomuch that our XCIV. Saviour declares, *Matt.* xix. 23 ; *that a Rich man shall* hardly *enter into the Kingdom of Heaven: Hardly* ; that is, not that Riches *themselves* are any Fault, but because of the numerous Temptations they accidentally lead men into, in a vicious and corrupt World.

THE *Answer* our Lord makes the Tempter upon this Last Trial; *Thou shalt worship the Lord thy God, and Him Only shalt thou serve* ; teaches us, that we must prefer before all things, the Service of God, and the Practice of true Religion : being always ready to reject, whatever shall come in competition with our Duty; even the *whole World,* if offered to us at the purchase of *Sin.* If we be found of *This* disposition ; Lovers of Truth, and Doers of Righteousness; the *Tempter* will *depart from* us, as he did from our Lord; and *Angels* will *come, and minister unto us* ; and the *Spirit of God* will preserve and guide us unto eternal Life.

SERMON XCV.

The Shortnefs and Vanity of Humane Life.

[Preached in Lent.]

JOB V. 6, 7.

Although Affliction cometh not forth of the Duft, neither doth Trouble fpring out of the Ground; yet Man is born unto Trouble, as the Sparks fly upward.

SERM.
XCV.

THERE is no Book in the Old Teftament, that has in it greater and fuller Acknowledgments, of the Glory and Power of God; nobler and more lively defcriptions, of the Works of Creation and Providence; more moving and affectionate Declarations, of the Shortnefs and Vanity of Humane Life, and the Tranfitorinefs of all worldly Enjoyments; frequenter and more explicit Expreffions of all the moral obligations of Religion, in their higheft Improvement, in their moft refined and exalted Senfe; clearer and plainer Significations, of the Hope of the beft and wifeft men, in antient Ages, concerning a Refurrection to a future Life; and of their truft and reliance upon God, even after he had given them over unto Death; than are to be met with, in this eloquent Book of *Job.*

BUT that which is *more particularly* the Defign and Subject of the whole Book, is to reprefent to us the Character and Example, of a man perfect in his generation, and of unfpotted Integrity, a Man that feared God and efchewed Evil; whofe Strength God was pleafed to try with one of the greateft Calamities that is ever recorded to have fallen on any of the Sons of men; Under which, his behaviour was fuch, that in all that fevere tryal *he finned not, nor charged God foolifhly;* nor fuffered his Integrity to depart from him till he died: But he perpetually appealed from the falfe Opinion of *men,* to the unerring Judgment of *God;* and vindicated, in the whole Courfe of his affliction, the Sovereignty and Dominion of God, his Supreme Authority and Right over his creatures, to *Try them* in what manner he thought fit: Maintaining to the laft, *(againft* the Opinion of all his Friends,) that even that great and unparallelled affliction, which God was pleafed to lay upon him in fo fingular and unexampled a manner, was by no means an Evidence of his being wicked and forfaken of God; but an Effect of the Divine Power and Providence which governs the World, and brings about his own Defigns, by Wife, though oft-times (for the prefent) fecret and infcrutable Methods: And declaring his refolution to preferve his Confidence and Reliance upon God, even beyond the Grave itfelf; Even *though he flay me,* faith he, *yet will I truft in him:* For *I know that my Redeemer liveth, and that my Eyes fhall behold him; whom I fhall fee for myfelf, and not another.*

THE

THE chapter, out of which the words of my Text are taken, is part of the Reply S E R M.
of *Eliphaz* to that mournful Lamentation of *Job*, wherein he curfes the day of his   XCV.
Birth, and wifhes to have had his Affliction prevented by Death. In which Reply of
his to *Job*, he erroneoufly fuppofes, that, becaufe God frequently punifhes the Wicked
with fevere Judgments in this World, therefore great Afflictions are a certain Evidence
of Men's having been very wicked: *ver.* 3: *I have feen the foolifh taking root, but fuddenly I curfed his habitation*; *His children are far from fafety, and they are crufhed in the
gate, neither is there any to deliver them*; *Whofe harveft the hungry eateth up, and taketh
it even out of the thorns, and the robber fwalloweth up the fubftance*. From which *true*
Obfervation, he *wrongfully* intends to conclude, that, becaufe *Job* was afflicted with
the *like Misfortunes*, therefore he might juftly be charged with having been guilty of
the *like Impieties*; An Inference very derogatory to the Sovereignty and Wifdom of
Providence, and very unjuft to the Character of the pious Sufferer.   However, upon
the whole, he adds this juft and true *general* Obfervation, the confideration of which
is of perpetual Ufefulnefs, *ver.* 6; *Although affliction cometh not forth of the duft, neither doth trouble fpring out of the ground; yet man is born unto trouble, as the fparks fly
upward.*

THE words contain, 1*ft*, A *pathetical defcription of the Shortnefs and Vanity, the
Sorrows and Calamities of Humane Life : Man is born unto trouble, as the fparks
fly upward.*

2*dly*, A *Declaration, that thefe Miferies of Humane Life, do not arife from Chance
or from Neceffity, from blind Fate or unaccountable Accidents*; *but from the wife Difpofition of the Providence of God, governing the World : Affliction cometh not forth of the
duft, neither doth trouble fpring out of the ground.* Wherein,

3*dly*, I T is implied, and intended to be inferred, that *there are many juft and good,
wife and ufeful Ends*; *upon account of which, God permits fo many Afflictions to fall
upon Mankind*; *and the confideration therefore of which*, (fo far as we can difcover them
in this prefent dark and imperfect ftate,) *ought to teach us Patience, and chearful Refignation to the Divine Will.*

1*ft*, H E R E is a pathetical defcription of the Shortnefs and Vanity, the Sorrows
and Calamities of Humane Life : *Man is born unto trouble, as the Sparks fly upward.* Afflictions and Calamities of innumerable kinds, feem, in the courfe of
things, as neceffarily and conftantly to attend the Life of Man ; as it is the nature of *light* things to afcend upwards, or of things *heavy* to defcend. And of this,
Experience is fo continual an Evidence, that there needs no arguments of Reafon
to prove it, nor ornaments of Expreffion to defcribe it. We are *born* into the
world, weak and defencelefs; we *grow up*, fubject to numberlefs Cafualties ; and in the
whole courfe of our lives, are perpetually expofed to Dangers which cannot be forefeen,
and to Troubles which are not poffible to be prevented. The Weaknefs and Imperfections of *Childhood*, the Vanity and Follies of *Youth*, the Cares and Sollicitudes of
Manhood, the Uneafinefs and Infirmities of *Age*; follow each other in a clofe and fpeedy
fucceffion. And, in Each of thefe ftates, we are continually obnoxious to Pains and
Difeafes of *Body* ; and in moft of them, to the acuter Torment of Anxiety and Vexations of *Mind*. All which Evils are increafed, by the Accidents and Misfortunes of
the World, by our own Negligences and Vices, by the Wickednefs and Unreafonablenefs of other men, by the Judgments of God upon ourfelves, and by the confequences
of the Judgments he inflicts for the Unrighteoufnefs of others. All which feveral calamities are emphatically defcribed by pious men, in different places of Scripture. With
refpect to our being liable to *Pains* and *Difeafes*, Man is *chaftened*, faith *Elihu* in the
book of *Job*, *with pain upon his bed, and the multitude of his bones with ftrong pain*;
(Job xxxiii. 19:) and good *Hezekiah* complains ; *Mine age is departed, and is removed*

2   *from*

SERM. *from me as a shepherd's tent; I have cut off like a weaver my life; he will cut me off*
XCV. *with pining sickness, from day even to night wilt thou make an end of me:* ——— *like a*
crane or a swallow, so did I chatter; I did mourn as a dove; Isaiah xxxviii. 12. With
respect to the vain *Labours and Anxiety* of life; *Surely every man,* saith the Psalmist,
*walketh in a vain shadow, and disquieteth himself in vain; he heapeth up riches, and
cannot tell who shall gather them;* (Psal. xxxix. 6.) And *Solomon,* who had still greater
experience of all the Labours of men under the Sun, thus expresses it: (*Eccl.* ii. 23;)
*For all his days are sorrows, and his travel grief; yea, his heart taketh not rest in the
night: This also is vanity.* With respect to the *Oppreffions and Troubles,* that good
men suffer from the Wickednefs of *others; I considered,* saith the same Wife Obferver;
(*Eccl.* ix. 2.) *that all things come alike to all, that there is one event to the righteous and
to the wicked, to the clean and to the unclean, to him that sacrificeth and to him that sacrificeth not, to the Good and to the Sinner, to him that sweareth and to him that feareth an Oath: Moreover, I saw under the Sun the place of judgment, that wickedness
was there; and the place of righteousness, that iniquity was there;* (iii. 16.) *I beheld the
tears of the oppreffed, and they had no comforter; and on the side of their oppreffors there
was power, but they had no comforter;* (iv. 1.) But if there were none of those *external* and *superinduced* calamities which men bring upon themselves and others, to aug-
ment the neceffary and unavoidable Troubles which Humane Nature is *born to;* yet
even by *these inherent* ones alone, would the Complaint in the Text sufficiently be verified; and *Eliphaz* might have juftified his Obfervation, from the confideration only,
of the mere *natural* Vanity, and Shortnefs of Humane Life: Which the Scripture compares, to *a vapour that appeareth for a little time, and then vanishes away;* (Jam. iv. 14.)
to a tale that is told, and then remembred no more; (*Pf.* xc. 9.) to a *wind that paffeth
away, and cometh not again;* (Pf. lxxviii. 39.) Admonifhing us upon all occafions, that
our *days are swifter than a weaver's shuttle, and are spent without hope,* (Job vii. 6.)
that they *are swifter than a poft; they flee away, and see no good; they are paffed away
as the swift ships, as the eagle that hafteth to the prey,* (ix. 25, 26.) that *Man who is
born of a woman, is of a few days, and full of trouble; he cometh forth like a flower,
and is cut down; he fleeth also as a shadow, and continueth not;* (xiv. 1, 2:) that *as
for man, his days are as grafs; as a flower of the field, so he flourishes; For the wind
paffes over it, and it is gone, and the place thereof shall know it no more,* (Pf. ciii. 15, 16:)
that *our days on the earth are as a shadow, and there is none abiding;* (1 Chr. xxix. 15:)
that *all these things pafs away like a shadow, and as a poft that hafteth by; And as a
Ship that paffeth over the waves of the Water, which, when it is gone by, the trace
thereof cannot be found, neither the path-way of the keel in the waves; or as when a bird
has flown through the air, there is no token of her way to be found;* ——— *even so we in like
manner, as soon as we were born, began to draw to our end, and have no sign of virtue to show;* (Wifd. v. 8.) Upon all which accounts the Patriarch *Jacob,* when he was
introduced to the King of *Egypt,* complains, notwithftanding he far exceeded the ufual
meafure of mens prefent Age, and enjoyed much larger Poffeffions than the generality
of Mankind, that yet *few and evil had the days of the years of his pilgrimage been;*
(Gen xlvii. 9.) This Shortnefs and Vanity of Humane Life, is fo obvious to every man's
daily Experience and Obfervation, that it may feem in a manner needlefs to put men in
mind of That, which it is not poffible for them not to know. And yet fo it comes to
pafs, that even the obvioufnefs itfelf of the Obfervation, and the evident certainty of it;
is the caufe that it has no more effect upon the generality of Men, than if it were very
difficult to be obferved at all; And for this very reafon, becaufe men are already fatisfied that they know it fufficiently, they never attend to it; but live as if they knew it
not. It requires no reafoning, no arguing, no meditation, for men to difcover to
themfelves

themfelves that they muft fhortly die ; and therefore, putting away the thoughts of it, as too trivial and obvious, they live as if it would never happen. But

2*dly*, TOGETHER with this pathetical defcription of the Shortnefs and Vanity, the Sorrows and Calamities of Humane Life, that *Man is born unto Trouble, as the fparks fly upward* ; the Text contains likewife a Declaration, that thefe Miferies and Troubles do not arife from *Chance* or from *Neceffity*, from blind Fate or unaccountable Accidents ; but from the wife Difpofition of the Providence of *God*, governing the World : *Affliction cometh not forth of the duft, neither doth trouble fpring out of the ground.* And this indeed is the *only* true and folid comfort, that can poffibly be afforded to a rational and confiderate mind ; in order to fupport him both under the troubles of *Life*, and againft the Fears of *Death.* The *Only* poffible thing that can effectually enable a man, either to *bear patiently* the Afflictions and Troubles that will neceffarily attend him here, or to be *willing and contented to depart from them,* with any hopes of entring into another and better State hereafter ; is, to be able to confider that there is a God, a Powerful and Juft, a Wife and Good Being, that governs the World : By whofe Wifdom and Goodnefs all things are defigned, by whofe Providence all things are conducted, to bring about the greateft and beft Ends : by whofe Power we were created ; under whofe Care and Government we are preferved and fupported ; in whofe prefence we walk perpetually, whofe eyes are upon all our Actions, and *in whom we live and move and have our Being* ; without whom, not a *fparrow falls to the ground,* or fo much as a *hair of our head* perifhes ; without whofe direction no Evil can befal us, without whofe Permiffion no Power can hurt us, and who is able finally to make *all things work together for good, to them that love* and fear *Him.* This, and This only, if Men would take care to live *virtuoufly* ; (For to a *vicious* man there is No Comfort, neither in This life nor Another,) if men would take care to live *virtuoufly,* I fay, the Thought of God's governing the World is *fuch* a Confideration, as is fufficient to caufe to vanifh all the tragical complaints of the Miferies and Vanity of Humane Life. For, though we could not conjecture at any Reafon why he has made us thus ; though we were not able to difcern any kind and gracious defigns, in the Afflictions that he lays upon us ; though the ways of Providence had been ftill more inextricable than they are, and his Judgments far more unfearchable than we now apprehend them to be ; yet certainly infinite Wifdom and infinite Goodnefs, might well be trufted and relied upon, by any reafonable and confiderate Mind. *That* Power, which in the frame and conftruction of the *natural* World, has adjufted all things by Weight and Meafure : *That* Power, which with exquifite artifice has made every thing in the exacteft harmony and proportion, to confpire regularly and uniformly towards accomplifhing the beft and wifeft Ends, in compleating the beautiful Order and Fabrick of the *Material* Univerfe : *That* Power, might furely in his government of the *moral* World likewife, in his difpofing of intelligent and rational creatures, even though *we* could give *no account at all* of his ways, yet with the jufteft reafon be *believed* to direct all things for the beft, and in order to bring about the nobleft and moft excellent Ends. How much more, when, even in this fhort and dark State, our finite and narrow Underftanding *is* able to difcern *many* wife and ufeful defigns in the fevereft and moft difficult difpenfations of his Providence, (as in the fequel of this difcourfe fhall be particularly fhown ;) how much more, I fay, in *This cafe,* have we reafon to fubmit, not only with patience and refignation, but even with joy and fatisfaction, to his *good pleafure* in all things ; Firmly believing, that, as in the frame of nature, thofe things which by Atheiftical Philofophers were antiently looked upon as arguments of Errour and Defect, of want either of Knowledge or Goodnefs in the formation of the *material* World, are fince difcovered to be moft ufeful Contrivances, and Evidences of the moft perfect and confummate Wifdom ; fo in the government of the *rational and intelligent* World,

SERM. in the difpenfations of *Providence* towards Mankind, thofe very things, which by fome
XCV. Philofophers of old were urged as Arguments of an Evil Principle, of a Mifchievous
Supreme Caufe, co-ordinate and repugnant to God the Author of all Good ; will, at
the Great Day, (when the Reafons of things and the whole Counfel of God fhall be
more perfectly difclofed,) appear all to be moft *Wife*, and *Gracious*, and *Good*.

DID our *Afflictions come forth of the duft*, and our *troubles fpring out of the ground*;
were there no other caufe to produce them, no other Hand to direct them, no other
Counfel to defign them, no other Power to over-rule and remove them ; than the
accidental concourfe of Senfelefs Atoms, than the fortuitous refults of unguided Matter
and Motion, than the blind Effects of inevitable Fate, or the mere Jumbles of unintelligible Chance ; it is plain there could be no rational Comfort and Support to a confiderate Mind, under the various Misfortunes and Calamities of Life. For what is the
Hope of the Unbeliever, when God taketh away his Soul ; I fhould fay, when *Fate*
or *Chance* taketh away his Soul ? And on what ground can the Confidence of the A-
theift rely ? His Expectations at beft are thin as a Spider's web ; and his Hopes as the
light Chaff, which the Wind fcattereth away from the Face of the Earth. His Profperity and Mirth can be but for a moment, and his Adverfity muft of neceffity terminate in Defpair. For what Relief is to be expected from Fate or Chance, which
has no Underftanding? and what Support is *that* Man capable of in the days of Affliction, who does not believe things are guided by a wife hand, which can turn every thing finally to our Advantage ? How weak, how empty a Satisfaction is it, to be
told that our Miferies arife from the *Neceffity of Fate*, and therefore that it is to no
purpofe not to be willing to fubmit to them ! How fmall a Comfort is it, to confider
that *Others* perhaps are miferable as well as we ; and that therefore we have no greater
reafon to complain, than they ! How poor, how infipid a relief is it, to underftand
that it cannot be long before all the Miferies and Calamities of Life will have an end
put to them by *Death* ; if at the fame time our View be wholly bounded by that dark
Profpect, and there be no Expectation beyond the Grave ? And yet thefe are *all* the
Comforts that Infidelity can afford, and *all* the Hopes of him that is *without God in the
World*. In the moment of his *Profperity*, he may fay with the Fool in the Book of
Wifdom ; (ch. ii. ver. 6, 3 ;) *Come on, let us enjoy the good things that are prefent, and
let us fpeedily ufe the creatures like as in youth*; For our Life *being extinguifhed, our
body fhall be turned into afhes, and our fpirit fhall vanifh as the foft air*. But in the
days of *Sorrow*, he will be convinced of his folly ; and repent and groan for Anguifh
of Spirit, when it be too late ; and his Rejoicing will be turned into Defpair. His
paft Pleafures will be remembred but as a Dream, and feem to him as a Shadow that
departeth ; his *prefent Trouble* will be infupportable ; and his Fears of what may poffibly be *to come*, will be unmixt and without Hope. The pretences of Philofophy,
of Fortitude and Firmnefs of Spirit, of defpifing Pain, and looking upon Death as
Nothing, and as merely putting an end to our Being ; will appear to be vain Words
and mere empty Delufion ; and *He only* is capable of any true Comfort and Support,
who is convinced that all things are directed *well* and to *good Ends*, by the All-wife
Government of the Providence of God ; and who, by a life of Piety and true Holinefs, has fecured to himfelf finally, the Favour of the Supreme Difpofer of all things.

THE fame *Appearances of Nature*, the fame *Arguments of Reafon*, which prove to
us the Being or Exiftence of God ; prove alfo his Providence in governing the World,
and his infpection and directing of all Events : So that even from the *Light of Nature*
itfelf, which to impartial and well-difpofed Perfons gives fufficent Evidences of the
Being and Providence of God, it is manifeft that no Affliction, no Trouble of any kind,
can poffibly come upon us without his Appointment or Permiffion. And *the Scripture*,
to confirm and ftrengthen our Faith and Dependence upon God at all times and under

I   all

all circumftances, is very large and exprefs in this particular. *I am the Lord, and there* S E R M.
is none elfe ; —— *I form the Light, and create Darknefs* ; *I make Peace, and create* XCV.
Evil ; (not *moral*, but *natural Evil* ;) *I the Lord do all thefe things* : If. xlv. 7 ; *The*
Lord killeth, and maketh alive ; *he bringeth down to the grave, and bringeth up* :
I Sam. ii. 6 ; *He maketh fore, and bindeth up* ; *he woundeth, and his hands make whole* ;
Job v. 18 : *Out of the mouth of the moft High, proceedeth not Evil and Good?* Lam. iii.
38. And it is a very remarkable Expreffion in the Law of *Mofes*, that when a Man
was fmitten and killed by Accident, without any ill Intention at all in him that did
it, his Misfortune is thus defcribed : *Exod.* xxi. 13 ; *If a man lie not in wait, but* God
deliver him into his hand : To fignify, that even thofe things, which to *Us* feem the
moft cafual and merely accidental, yet in refpect of *God* are really Providential, and
could not happen but by his fuffering them and (for wife reafons) permitting them to
be done. That is ; they are not indeed done always by his Direction and Appointment ; but, becaufe they could not come to pafs *at all* without his Knowledge and
Permiffion, therefore we may be affured that he intends them for good, and to make
ufe of them to ferve fome wife and good Ends of Providence, in that it was not his
pleafure, and he did not think fit to over-rule and prevent them. And accordingly
the Prophet *Amos* puts the Queftion univerfally, not only concerning Judgments fent
immediately by God's Command and Appointment, but concerning *all*, even *thofe* alfo
which we call *natural* and *accidental* Evils ; *Shall there be Evil in a City, and the*
Lord hath not done it? ch. iii. ver. 6. Which Words fome have been fo very unreafonable as to interpret even of *Sin* itfelf or *moral Evil* ; (which is the higheft Abfurdity and Blafphemy :) But with refpect to all *natural* Evils, (fince fecond caufes have
no Powers but from and in fubordination to the firft,) it is ftrictly true : And therefore, even though we could not at all underftand the reafons why God is pleafed to
permit them, yet fince we are fure they cannot but be of his permiffion, we have
more reafon with all Patience and refignation to depend upon *him* that he intends and will Pfal. cxix. 75.
direct them for good, than a Child can have, in things above its apprehenfion, to
rely upon the Kindnefs of a moft affectionate Parent.

But 3*dly*, Though This might be a fufficient Satisfaction in *general* ; yet further,
We *are* able to inftance in *many particular* wife and good Ends, for which Providence permits fo many Afflictions to befal Mankind. The Confideration of which
muft be referred to another Opportunity.

SERMON

SERMON XCVI.

Of Refignation to the Divine Will in Affliction.

[A Sermon preached in Lent.]

JOB V. 6, 7.

Although Affliction cometh not forth of the Duft, neither doth Trouble fpring out of the Ground; yet Man is born unto Trouble, as the Sparks fly upward.

S E R M.
XCVI.

IN a foregoing Difcourfe, I have obferved that thefe Words contain in them,

1. A pathetical defcription of the Weaknefs and Vanity, the Sorrows and Calamities of humane Life; *Man is born unto Trouble, as the Sparks fly upward.*

2. A Declaration, that thefe Miferies of humane life, do not arife from Chance or from Neceffity, from blind Fate or unaccountable Accidents; but from the wife Difpofition of the Providence of God, governing the World. *Affliction cometh not forth of the Duft, neither doth Trouble fpring out of the Ground.* Wherein

3. IT is implied, and intended to be inferred, that there are many juft and good, wife and ufeful Ends; upon account of which, God permits fo many Afflictions to fall upon Mankind; and the confideration therefore of which, (fo far as we can difcover them in this prefent dark and imperfect State,) ought to teach us Patience and chearful Refignation to the Divine Will.

THE two former of thefe I have already difcourfed on; and fhown, that, fince *Afflictions do not come forth of the Duft,* do not arife from Chance or from Neceffity; but are all under the Difpofal of the All-Wife Providence of God, governing the World; this one *general* confideration alone, ought fufficiently to fecure our entire Truft and Dependence upon God, our Hope and Confidence in Him; fo as to be an abundant Support and Comfort to us, under all the poffible Accidents and Calamities of Life; even though we could not *at all* underftand any of the *grounds* of his Acting, and the *Reafons* of his fo dealing with us.

BUT feeing *this* is not wholly the Cafe; and that in this *general* Obfervation it feems moreover to be implied, and intended to be inferred, that there are alfo difcoverable *in particular*, many juft and good, wife and ufeful Ends; upon account of which, God permits fo many Afflictions to fall upon Mankind; and the confideration of which, ought to teach us Patience, and chearful Refignation to the Divine Will: It remains therefore, that we proceed now, in the

3d and *laft* place, To confider *what* are (fome of the plaineft and moft fatisfactory of) thofe reafons, that *we are* capable of difcovering; upon account of which, it was beft and fitteft that things fhould be fo ordered as they are; and in confideration whereof, we ought more *fully and readily* to acquiefce in the divine good pleafure in all things,

1

AND

AND *firft*, We are to confider, that fome of thofe things which we ufually efteem SERM. amongft the Troubles and Afflictions of life, are fuch as may *juftly* and muft *neceffarily* XCVI. be refolved into the *abfolute Sovereignty and Dominion* of God. Of this kind, are Mortality in general, and the Shortnefs of humane Life ; the unequal Diftribution of Riches and Honour, and the good things of this prefent Life ; the different capacities, and abilities of Mind ; the different tempers, and conftitutions of Body ; the different ftates and conditions, wherein God has originally placed men in the World. Of thefe things there *can*, there *needs* no other account to be given, than the abfolute Sovereignty and Dominion of God. For infinite Power, Wifdom and Goodnefs, may difplay itfelf in producing what Variety of Creatures he pleafes ; and in communicating to them his free Bounties, in what meafure and proportion he thinks fit. He that had no Obligation, no Want or Neceffity upon him, to give Being to any thing at all ; may give Being to his Creatures for what Duration he pleafes ; and diftribute his abfolute and unconditionate Favours, without giving *any* account of his Ways. It is no juft ground of complaint in *Men*, that they were not created in the condition of *Angels* ; any more than it is an injury to *inferior Creatures* that they are not indued with the Capacities of *Men*. Neither is it a wrong to thofe who are born with lower capacities and to meaner circumftances, that they are made inferior to others ; But they have *much more reafon* to be thankful for what they *have*, than to be difpleafed for want of what they *have not*. It is fufficient if, in matters of *Reward and Punifhment*, God in the End deals equitably with all his rational Creatures ; and difpofes of them according to the proportion of the feveral deferts of each of them, in their refpective States. But in the *original appointment* of the *State* and *Condition* of their Nature, there is no room for any other confideration, than that of the abfolute Sovereignty of infinite Power, and the various Exercife of infinite Wifdom. The Servant who gained four Talents by the improvement of two, it was *juft* that he fhould be rewarded with four Cities ; and that the reward of ten Cities fhould be allotted to *him*, who by a right ufe of five Talents had improved them to Ten. But why *originally* the one fhould be intrufted with five Talents and the other but with two ; of this there needs and *can* no other account be given, but this ; *Is it not lawful for* God, *to do what he pleafes with his own?* and *Shall the thing formed fay unto him that formed it, why haft thou made me thus? Hath not the Potter power over the clay, of the fame lump to make one Veffel to Honour and another to Difhonour?* Not one perfon unconditionately to *final Happinefs*, and another to *Mifery* ; But (as the fame Apoftle expreffly explains himfelf, 2 *Tim.* ii. 20) *In a great houfe there are not only veffels of Gold, and of Silver, but alfo of Wood and of Earth ; and fome to honour, and fome to difhonour.* That is : Hath not the Mafter a Right, to employ his Servants in what feveral Stations he pleafes, more or lefs honourable ; provided, in his final diftribution, he deals equitably with each of them, in their feveral and refpective degrees? As the Glory of the *natural* World confifts in that beautiful *Variety* of things, whereof the Whole is compofed : So in the *Moral* World, God has made rational Creatures of *various* Capacities, and placed them in *different* Stations : And it imports not to each one's final State, *what* his prefent Station is, but *how well* he behaves himfelf in That Station. The Scripture, as well as the Reafon of the Thing itfelf, frequently refers us to this Sovereign Power of God, in accounting for the unequal diftribution of both temporal and fpiritual Advantages. *He plucketh down one, and fetteth up another ; He maketh poor, and maketh rich ; he bringeth low and lifteth up :* He caufeth one Nation or Perfon to be rich and powerful, and another to be poor and weak. He reveals himfelf to one People in one manner, and to another in a different manner ; and in all

S E R M. this there is neither Reward nor Punifhment, but the various exercife of his Wifdom
XCVI. and Power over his Creatures, without wrong or injury to any of them. He chofe
the Nation of the *Jews* to be his peculiar People, to reveal his Law to them in a particular manner, and to make them the Standard of true Religion to the World; *He did
not deal fo with any other nation, neither had the Heathen knowledge of his Laws.* And
this St *Paul* afcribes to the abfolute Will and Pleafure of God, who may difpofe of
his unconditionate Favours in what manner and proportion he thinks fit: *Rom.* ix. 10,
11; *When Rebecca had conceived by one, even by our Father Ifaac; the children being
not yet born, neither having done any good or evil; that the purpofe of God according to
election might ftand, not of works, but of him that calleth; it was faid unto her, The
elder fhall ferve the younger; As it is written, Jacob have I loved, but Efau have I
hated.* Which Text, has *therefore only* feemed difficult, becaufe men have not ufually
attended *what* that purpofe of God according to Election was, which the Apoftle
There declares fhould ftand? For, was it a purpofe of electing one to eternal Happinefs, and the other to eternal Mifery? No; but of caufing the *elder to ferve the younger.* The Words themfelves are exprefs: *That the purpofe of God,* faith he, *according
to election might ftand, not of works, but of him that calleth.* God might appoint
whom he pleafed, to be the Father of the more powerful Nation, the progenitor of his
peculiar people; and yet there was plainly no unrighteoufnefs with God; no wrong
or injury done to *him* upon whom that Favour was not conferred, which could of right
be claimed by Neither. To apply this, or any other Texts of like importance, to
mens *final and eternal* eftate of Rewards and Punifhments in another World; is indeed
charging God wrongfully, and putting the greateft abufe that can be upon Holy Scripture, wherein God fo conftantly declares that he is *no Refpecter of Perfons,* and that
every man *fhall be judged* finally *according to his works.* But *which* fhall be *here* fuperior, and *which* fhall ferve; *who* fhall *in this Senfe* be hated, and *who* be loved; (all
which is comparative only, and not abfolute; and in which there is nothing of Reward or Punifhment, but merely a variety of diftribution of undeferved Favours;) in
this, God has an abfolute Right of acting by his Sovereign Power and Supreme Authority, and of doing what he pleafes with his own. And fince every thing that we All
enjoy, proceeds wholly from God's free goodnefs and bounty; no man, whether he has
received lefs or more, many advantages or fewer, has *any* juft reafon of complaint, *any*
ground to fay unto his Maker, *Why haft thou made me thus?* This is the account
St *Paul* gives, of God's firft calling the people of the *Jews;* and the fame he gives, of
his afterwards *rejecting* them again, and taking in the *Gentiles. I will have mercy on
whom I will have mercy, and I will have compaffion on whom I will have compaffion:*
That is, *God only,* and not fhort-fighted *Man,* is the proper Judge, upon *whom,* upon
what Perfons or *Nations,* 'tis fitteft and wifeft for him to beftow his Favours. *Hath
not the Potter power over the clay, of the fame lump to make one veffel unto honour and
another unto difhonour? What, if God, willing to fhow his Wrath, and to make his Power
known, endured with much long-fuffering the veffels of wrath fitted to Deftruction; And
that he might make known the Riches of his Glory, on the veffels of mercy which he had
afore prepared unto glory? Even Us, whom he has called, not of the Jews only, but
alfo of the Gentiles,* Rom. ix. 15, 21, 22. In all which, there is no declaration
of any *arbitrary* proceeding in God, with refpect to the *laft and great* judgment; as fome have very unreafonably apprehended: (For, the *long-fuffering* here
mentioned towards *the veffels of wrath,* i. e. the unbelieving *Jews,* was in expectation even of *Their* Repentance and Amendment; and the *veffels of mercy* here
defcribed,

defcribed, are not particular perfons fingly confidered, but the *whole Body of Chriftians* as oppofed to the *whole Nation of the Jews,* and as including both *Gentile* as well as *Jewifh* Believers; *Even Us,* faith the Apoftle, *whom he has called, not of the Jews only, but alfo of the Gentiles:*) But the plain and whole intention of the words, is to juftify God's dealing with the Nation of the *Jews,* in rejecting *them* and receiving in the *Gentiles*; and to fhow, that men have no juft reafon to complain againft God, for manifefting his Power and Glory in different difpenfations to different Perfons at different times, and for diftributing differently his undeferved Bounty, and allow-·ing men various and different advantages, after fuch manner as he himfelf thinks fit: Inafmuch as they who enjoy the feweft advantages, receive always more than they deferve or can claim ; and have no wrong or injury done to them, by the abound-ing of God's free Goodnefs to others. It was no injuftice at the firft to other Na-·tions, that God, out of his free Bounty, was pleafed to blefs in a fingular manner the Pofterity of faithful *Abraham* for many generations ; nor was it afterwards any injury to the *Jews,* that God was pleafed to receive the *Gentiles* likewife, into a participation of the fame Favour and Bleffings with themfelves. So far as the Ad-vantages of God's peculiar people were *temporal,* the confideration of his *Sovereign Power and Authority* is a fufficient and fatisfactory account of the Difference ; But as to mens *fpiritual and eternal* concern, the *Judge of all the Earth* knows how to do what is right ; *With Equity will he judge the Nations,* and will make an equitable and proportionable allowance, for the unequal circumftances of every man's cafe. Yet, even *here* alfo, there is no injuftice, in giving men different opportunities and different advantages; in entrufting them with different talents; and putting into the hands of Some, according to his own good pleafure, a greater poffibility of obtaining larger Rewards. Neither further in *this* likewife can there be any ground of complaint, if he fhall ftill think fit to make ufe of his fupreme Right, in giving freely as great a recompence to Some of whom he has not exacted fo fevere a Service, as to Others who may imagine themfelves, by the performance of a ftricter Duty, to have acquired for themfelves a title to a more ample Reward. Our Saviour re-prefents this to us in the Parable of the Labourers in the vineyard, who having been hired at different times of the day, and receiving each of them in the Even-ing the fame reward ; thofe which had been hired in the morning, though they re-ceived their full payment, yet were difpleafed at their Lord's free bounty, in giving the fame to thofe who had been hired laft ; and *murmured againft* him, *faying ; Thefe laft have wrought but one hour, and thou haft made them equal unto Us, which have born the burden and heat of the Day: But he anfwered one of them, and faid ; Friend, I do thee no wrong ; didft not thou agree with me for a penny? Take that thine is, and go thy way; I will give unto this laft, even as unto thee: Is it not lawful for me to do what I will with mine own? Is thine Eye evil, becaufe I am good?* St Matt. xx. 12. The Pa-rable may be underftood, to refpect God's dealings either with the *Jews* and *Gentiles* in different Ages of the World, or with Perfons converted to the belief of the Gofpel in different Periods of their lives. God's various diftribution of his free gifts and unde-ferved mercies, affords no juft reafon of complaint to thofe, who only want what no man has a right to claim, and what thofe who have, muft acknowledge to be of mere bounty. And this is plainly the cafe in moft of thofe things, which we are apt to look upon as fome of the greateft Afflictions and Calamities of Life. They often are not any real and pofitive infliction of Judgments from the hand of God, but merely the original differences of mens ftate and circumftances, the variety of God's Creation, the different Talents committed to mens charge, the different Stations God has placed men

in,

S E R M.
XCVI.

in, for their various trials, and in order to the exercise of a diversity of Duties. *Poverty* has not always the nature of an affliction or judgement, but is rather merely a state of life, appointed by God, for the proper tryal and exercise of the Virtues, of *Contentment*, Patience, and Resignation: And for *one* man to murmur against God, because he possesses not those Riches which he sees given to another; is the *wrath that killeth the foolish man*, and the *envy that slayeth the silly one*, Job v. 2. The like may be said of *want of Honour and Power*, want of *Children* to succeed in our Estates and Families, *Weakness* of *Body*, *Shortness* of *Life*, and the like; nay, and even of *Spiritual* disadvantages themselves likewise; *want of capacity* and good understanding, want of *knowledge* and instruction, want of many *opportunities* and means of improvement which others enjoy. None of all which, are any just ground of complaint against God, or any reason why we should not with all satisfaction acquiesce in his divine good pleasure; since all these things are only different distributions of such free gifts, as he, not being obliged to bestow on *any* man, may therefore without controversy divide to *every* man in what measure and proportion he himself thinks fit: Only *This* we may depend upon, that in such measure only will he *exact* our duty, as he enables us to *perform* it; and that to whom little is given, of him shall not be much required: And This brings all the *seeming inequalities* in the World, to a *real equality* at last; so that *he which gathers much, has nothing over; and he that gathers little, has no lack*. And we may justly apply to God's *general* dealings with all Mankind, the exclamation St *Paul* uses upon occasion of his wonderful *particular* dispensations to the people of the *Jews* and *Gentiles*; *O the depth of the riches both of the Wisdom and Knowledge of God; How unsearchable are his judgments, and his ways past finding out!* In *all* circumstances of Life therefore, we are not to be uneasy that God has made us inferiour to others; or that he has set before us, greater hardships and difficulties to go through; or that he has given us less abilities, and fewer opportunities than others: But we are to apply ourselves wholly, (with all acquiescence and resignation,) to the proper duties of *that* station, or of *those* circumstances, wherein God has been pleased to place us. *Poverty* is not an Argument, to envy the Rich; but a strong Obligation to study the duties of Humility, Contentment and Resignation. *Ignorance* and want of capacity, meanness of Parts and want of Instruction, is not a reason to murmur that God has not entrusted us with *more* talents; but an admonition to take care that we make a right improvement of those *few* that are given us. Weakness of *Body*, is not a just occasion to repine against God, for not giving us the Strength and Health wherewith he has blessed some others; but a continual Argument to us, to exercise and improve such Virtues as are more peculiar to the *Mind*. The consideration of the *Uncertainty* and *Shortness of Life* itself, ought not to make us spend our Time in fruitless complaints of the Vanity and Meanness of our State; but to cause us perpetually to consider, that it is not of so great importance how *long* we live, as how *well*: For (as it is excellently expressed in the Book of *Wisdom*,) *honourable age is not that which standeth in length of time, nor that is measured by numbers of years; but Wisdom is the gray hair unto Men, and an unspotted Life is old age.*

Secondly; It is to be considered, that a great part of the troubles of Life, and the Afflictions we are apt to complain of, are not the immediate and original appointment of *God at all*; but the mere *natural* Effects and consequences, of our own Sins. 'Tis true, it *is* indeed the wise constitution of *Providence*, which thus ordered and disposed the nature of things at first, that most Sins should even in the *natural* consequences of things, be some time or other attended with their proper Punishment. But I consider it not Now in *That respect*, as being, *upon the whole*, the wise Appointment of *God*, to

convince

convince us of the Folly of Sin, and to lead us to Repentance; but as being *in particular*, in the prefent ftate and order of things, the mere *natural* Effect and Confequence of our own foolifh and finful choice. Which confideration alone, ought to make us acquiefce with all Humility and Patience, under that Burden which not *God* but our *own hands* have laid upon us: For, *why fhould a living man complain, a man for the punifhment of his Sins?* Why fhould he murmur againft *God*, when he *eateth* but *the Fruit of his own Ways*, and is *filled only with* the natural confequences of *his own devices?* *The Foolifhnefs of Man* (as *Solomon* excellently expreffes it, *Prov.* xix. 3.) *perverteth* his own *way*, and then *his heart fretteth againft the Lord.* Very unreafonably and unjuftly. For, if Poverty be the Effect of extravagance and profufenefs, and a man's fubftance be confumed by riotous living: If Pain and Difeafes of Body, be the Effect of Debauchery and intemperate Courfes; and the Comforts of Age, be prevented by the Follies of Youth: If Anxiety and continual Vexation of Mind, be the Vanity of Covetoufnefs; and the *fore travel*, of him that *has neither Child nor Brother*; of whom the Scripture fays, that *there is no End of all his labour, neither is his Eye fatisfied with riches*; *neither faith he, For whom do I labour, and bereave my Soul of good*; Thefe troubles, are fuch as neither *come forth of the duft, neither* do they *fpring out of the ground*, neither can they be complained of as proceeding from the *hand of God*; but they are only the *natural* Effects of mens own Follies, and the fulfilling the prophecies fo often repeated in Scripture, that they who *plow wickednefs*, fhall *reap iniquity*; (Hof. x. 13;) and they who *fow iniquity*, fhall *reap vanity*, (Prov. xxii. 8;) And yet, even *Thefe* alfo, the Afflictions which are the confequences of our own Folly, may by a wife improvement, by bearing them as becomes us, and by exercifing ourfelves to Wifdom under them; even *Thefe* alfo, may become the matter of an excellent Virtue, and may turn into the occafion of much religious advantage.

Thirdly, It is to be confidered, that fome of the greateft afflictions and calamities of life, are the effects of God's publick judgments upon the World, for the wickednefs and impiety of *others*. Wherein if virtuous and good men be fometimes involved, it ought to be a fufficient fatisfaction to them to confider, that *this* is not the proper time for Rewards and Punifhments to take place upon particular perfons. And, fince they know God has referved to *another ftate* the final and equitable diftribution of juftice according to every man's defert; wherein he will give a perfect *Account of all his Matters*; wherein every inequality fhall be exactly fet right, and every circumftance of each perfon's cafe be confidered and adjufted; when God will perfectly juftify himfelf in all his proceedings, and *every mouth fhall be ftopped before him*; why fhould they be uneafy, that God *for the prefent* fuffers fecond caufes to take their regular courfe; and does not work perpetual miracles to deliver them from the common incidents of human nature, and from the publick misfortunes of the World? 'Tis recorded of *Jofiah* King of *Judah*, (2 Kings xxiii. 25;) that *like him was there no King before him, that turned to the Lord with all his heart, and with all his Soul, and with all his might, neither after him arofe there any like him:* Yet *the Lord fuffered him to fall by the fword, and turned not from the fiercenefs of his great Wrath wherewith his anger was kindled againft Judah, becaufe of all the Provocations that Manaffeh his Predeceffor had provoked him withal*; and *alfo for the innocent blood that he had fhed, which the Lord would not pardon*, 2 Kings xxiv. 4. And in a general denunciation of the fevereft wrath of God againft *Jerufalem*, he threatens by the Prophet *Ezekiel*, ch. xxi. ver. 3, that he would *cut off from* it *the righteous and the wicked*. In which cafe, it ought to be a fufficient fatisfaction to truly pious and religious perfons, that God has referved for them their portion in another life.

SERM.   THESE are *Some* of the *Many* confiderations, which ought to oblige us, in
XCVI.   *all* Circumftances of life whatfoever, *fully and readily* to acquiefce in the divine
good pleafure.   There are others yet behind, which are grounds not only of *ac-
quiefcence and Submiffion*, but even of *Thankfulnefs* alfo to God for fending upon us
Afflictions greatly to our Advantage : Such as are thofe which, by the more immediate appointment of God, are intended and fitted to teach us *Humility*, to lead
us to *Repentance*, to *wean* us from an *over-fond love of the World*, to make *Tryal
and Improvement of our Faith*, and to make eminent *Examples* of Patience and
Refignation, Fortitude and Contempt of the World.   But thefe I muft refer to another Opportunity.

SERMON

SERMON XCVII.

The End of GOD's afflicting Men.

[*A Sermon preached in Lent.*]

JOB V. 6, 7.

Although Affliction cometh not forth of the Dust, neither doth Trouble spring out of the ground; yet Man is born unto Trouble, as the Sparks fly upward.

THAT none of the Afflictions which befal Mankind, are the Effects either of blind Chance or of fatal necessity; but that they are all under the direction of infinite Wisdom and Goodness governing the World, and *in the general* intended by Providence some way or other for our advantage; I have already shown in a foregoing Discourse. I have also proposed *in particular* some of the many Considerations, which ought to teach us Acquiescence and cheerful Submission to the divine Good-pleasure, under the several kinds and sorts of Afflictions, which we are perpetually subject to in the present Life; Namely, that *some* of those things which we usually reckon among the Troubles of life, are not properly *Judgments inflicted* upon us, but merely the Effects of God's variously exercising his Infinite Power and Wisdom, his absolute Sovereignty and Dominion over his Creatures, in placing Men originally in such different States and Conditions as he himself thought fit; whereof *no man* has reason to complain; because what *every man* enjoys, in whatever proportion it be, is still *all* only of free Goodness and mere Bounty: That some *others* of the Troubles we are apt to complain of are nothing but the *natural* Consequences of our own Sins; and therefore not at all chargeable upon God: That *others* of them, are the effects of God's *publick* Judgments upon a sinful World; from partaking of which Calamities if *particular* good and pious persons are not exempted *at present*, is it not abundantly sufficient that God has *hereafter* appointed for them a day of exacter retribution? These are sufficient grounds of *Contentment and Acquiescence*, of willing *Submission and Resignation* to the Divine Will. But there are *other considerations* still behind, (which I am *now* to proceed to speak to,) which will appear to be Arguments, not of *Contentment* only and *patient Resignation*, but even of *Thankfulness* also; Considerations, which will show, that most of the Afflictions we are apt to be uneasy under, *far* from being Arguments of God's neglecting and disregarding us, are some of the greatest instances of his paternal Care and Affection towards us, and designed to tend very much to our particular benefit and advantage. The *Ends* of *this* kind, which we have reason to believe God generally intends in the Afflictions he is pleased to send upon us, may be reduced to these four.

2

1. To teach us *Humility*, and a juft Senfe of our own Unworthinefs.
2. To lead us to *Repentance* for our paft Errours.
3. To *wean* us from an over-fond Love of the prefent *World*. And
4. To *try, improve*, and *perfect* our Virtues; and make fome particular perfons eminent Examples of Faith and Patience to the World.

1. To teach us *Humility* and a juft fenfe of our own *Unworthinefs*. Though *Pride* evidently was not made for man, nor a haughty Spirit *for him that is born of a Woman*; Though nothing is more abfurd and unnatural, than for *Duft and Afhes* to be lift up againft its Maker; and for the thing formed, to exalt itfelf againft him that formed it; Though nothing can be more unreafonable and ridiculous, than for *Man, whofe breath is in his noftrils*, to defpife his *Brother*, and to behave himfelf infolently towards *him who is of the fame Nature and Dignity*, as well as of *like Paffions*, with himfelf; Yet in fact fo it is, that often *Man being in Honour, hath no Underftanding*; Pf. xlix. 20; and, being puffed up with Profperity, *confidereth* not *whereof* he is *made*, and *remembreth* not *that* he is *but duft*. Such is the Weaknefs of our Nature, that *when one is made rich, and when the glory of his houfe is increafed*, he is very apt to forget, that *when he dieth, he fhall carry nothing away with him*, and that *his glory fhall not defcend after him*. When *Power* is put into our hands, and a great Superiority of worldly Advantages gives us opportunity to judge in our own cafes; we are extremely apt, to make *Will* fucceed in the place of *Reafon*, and *Humour or Paffion* inftead of *Right*. And this, not only in Perfons openly profane, and defpifers of Religion; but fuch is the deceitfulnefs of mens Hearts, that in a long courfe of uninterrupted Profperity, this fecret Pride is apt to grow infenfibly, even upon thofe who do not affect to practife Iniquity. The almoft only certain and effectual remedy of which Evil, and the proper Prefervative againft it, is that mixture of *Afflictions* and Difappointments in the World, which, by the wife order and appointment of Providence, puts men in mind of their own Weaknefs and Infirmity, brings them to a right Senfe of themfelves and of their dependence upon God, puts them upon ferious confideration of the true ftate and Circumftances of things, and is therefore in Scripture called the *Difcipline* and *Inftruction* of the Lord, *Job* xxxiii. 16. *Then he openeth the ears of men, and fealeth their inftruction; That he may withdraw man from his purpofe, and hide pride from man;* —— *He is chaftened alfo with pain upon his bed, and the multitude of his bones with ftrong pain*, &c. St *Paul* himfelf, though fo eminent an Example of Piety, though fo conftant and indefatigable a Labourer in the work of his Miniftry, though fo fingular an inftance of Mortification and Contempt of the World; yet declares concerning himfelf, 2 Cor. xii. 7; that *leaft he fhould be exalted above meafure through the abundance of the Revelations, there was* fent upon him an affliction, which he calls *the meffenger of Satan to buffet* him, *leaft he fhould be exalted above meafure*. Which if fo great a Man as St *Paul*, thought to be his own cafe; Who is there in thefe later and corrupter Ages, that, in *Profperity*, can be fure of poffeffing his Soul with that Humility and Meeknefs, which Adverfity would teach him? or that, in *Adverfity*, can be fure he fhould not be puffed up by a courfe of Profperity; fo as to make it to himfelf a much greater Evil, than the Affliction he is now fo uneafy under, and the Ufefulnefs of which he is fo loath to be fenfible of?

2. Another *End* of God's fending Afflictions and Troubles upon Men, is to lead us to *repentance* for our paft Errors. This is excellently expreffed by *Elihu*; (Job xxxvi. 8;) *If they be bound in fetters, and be holden in cords of affliction; then he fheweth them their work, and their tranfgreffions that they have exceeded; he openeth alfo their ear to difcipline,*

2

discipline, and commandeth that they return from iniquity. When a wicked man prof- S E R M. pers in all his worldly affairs, and his designs are crowned with perpetual Success; XCVIII. when he is surrounded on all sides with undisturbed Plenty, and all his appetites are gratified with the constant injoyment of Ease and Pleasure; 'tis no wonder that he forgets the God that is above, and considers not that *for all these things God will call him into judgment:* Good Admonition and Advice makes no impression upon his Mind, and the serious exhortations of Religion find no room to enter: He is apt to put far from him the Evil day, and to say to his Soul, *Take thine ease, eat, drink, and be merry;* we will *fill ourselves* now *with new wine, and to morrow shall be as this day and much more abundant;* (If. lvi. 12.) Persons in *This* State, the Scripture every where represents as in the most dangerous condition: *Ye have lived in pleasure on the earth,* saith St *James, and been wanton;* ye have nourished your hearts as in a day of slaughter; Jam. v. 5. *Wo to them that are at ease in Zion;* Amos vi. 5. *I am very sore displeased at the Heathens that are at ease,* Zech. i. 15. *Moab hath been at ease from his Youth, and he has settled on his lees;* Jer. xlviii. 11; *i. e.* has gone on carelessly, in a long and uninterrupted course of Wickedness. The *greatest* Blessing and Happiness, that *can* befal such persons as these; the *greatest instance,* of the *mercy* of God towards them; is, the sending upon them some great Affliction; which, like a severe medicine in a very dangerous distemper, may awaken them out of their Lethargy and Stupidity; may cause them to *consider,* and entertain sober Thoughts; may bring them to a right understanding, of themselves and of their own Danger. The *silent* instruction, of Reason and true Wisdom; the soft voice of God, in the gentle admonitions of Conscience not yet terrified with any *great* Fear; is not attended to, by inconsiderate persons; is not heard in the Hurry of Passions, that have been long used to prevail; and among a multitude of Appetites, which have been constantly accustomed to be gratified without denial. But when the *Judgments* of God *are* abroad *in the Earth,* then *the inhabitants of the world will learn righteousness;* If. xxvi. 9; *Then* men begin to *consider* with themselves, what their State and Condition is; and *Consideration,* is the foundation of Repentance, the first motive and beginning of Religion. Of This, an eminent instance is recorded in the History of *Manasseh;* who, in his Prosperity *made Judah and the inhabitants of Jerusalem to err, and to do worse than the Heathen whom the Lord had destroyed before the children of Israel:* But in his captivity, *when he was in affliction, he besought the Lord his God, and humbled himself greatly before the God of his Fathers,* 2 Chr. xxxiii. 9, 12. And the example of his *Repentance* was afterwards as eminent, as that of his *Impiety* before had been pernicious. This is the proper effect of God's *Judgments* in the World; And if these last and severest Exhortations to repentance, have not that due effect upon Sinners; their case *then* becomes desperate and without hope. Nothing *then* remains, but that God leave them to themselves; For, *why should they be stricken any more?* they *will revolt more and more,* If. i. 5. This is the greatest and most extreme, of all the Temporal Curses of God; *I will not punish your daughters when they commit whoredom, nor your spouses when they commit adultery;* Hos. iv. 14. And 'tis the proper consequence of not being brought to Repentance by this *last* Admonition, even by *Afflictions themselves.* Thus God complains of the impenitency of the *Jews,* Am. iv. 6, &c. *I have given you want of bread in all your places, and have withholden the rain from you, and have smitten you with blasting and mildew; yet have ye not returned unto Me, saith the Lord. I have sent among you the pestilence after the manner of Egypt; your young men have I slain with the sword; I have overthrown some of you, as God overthrew Sodom and Gomorrah; yet have ye not returned unto Me, saith the Lord.* And 'tis set down as part of the character of the *Kingdom of the Beast,* the Kingdom of *Antichristian Tyranny,* the corruptest State of men that ever was in the world, *Rev.* xvi. 9, 11; that they *blasphemed the name of God, because of their pains* and their plagues, but *repented not of their deeds, to give glory to the God of Heaven:* That is, to return from their Idolatries, Superstitions and

S E R M. Follies, to the rational Worſhip of the True God, in Righteouſneſs, Charity and Truth.
XCVIII. This Incorrigibleneſs, is the worſt and moſt deſperate ſtate, that wicked men can
poſſibly arrive at in the preſent World: But the *proper and natural* Effect of God's
Judgments, if they would hearken to them, is to lead them to Repentance; *Where-*
fore doth a living man complain, a man for the puniſhment of his ſins? Let us ſearch and
try our ways, and turn again to the Lord; Lam. iii. 39, 40.

Now if Afflictions be thus fitted, in their proper Tendency, to convert the *wick-*
edeſt of men that are not utterly incorrigible; much *more* are they ſuited to convince
good men of their failings, to make them ſenſible of their Errors, to bring them to more
frequent and ſerious Conſideration, and to a more perfect Repentance and Amendment.
The very *beſt* of men, are far from being perfect; and *too many* good men, have even
great imperfections; which they are not duly ſenſible of, but in a day of Affliction;
and there are many Duties, and many Doctrines in Scripture, which men are not apt
to underſtand rightly, but in a time of Sorrow, and more ſerious Conſideration. *Da-*
vid himſelf confeſſes; *Pſ.* cxix. 71, 67; *It is good for me, that I have been afflicted,*
that I might learn thy ſtatutes; For, *before I was afflicted, I went aſtray, but now*
have I kept thy word. And That great man *Job*, after his ſevere trial, acknowledges
before God; (*Job* xlii. 5, 6;) *I have heard of thee by the hearing of the ear, but now*
mine eye ſeeth thee; wherefore I abhor myſelf, and repent in duſt and aſhes. The Sons
of *Jacob* were never truly ſenſible of the greatneſs of their Crime in ſelling their Brother, till they found themſelves in great diſtreſs in *Egypt*; *And* Then *They ſaid one to*
another (Gen. xlii. 21;) *We are verily guilty concerning our Brother, in that we ſaw the*
anguiſh of his Soul, when he beſought us, and we would not hear; therefore is this diſtreſs
come upon us. And of the *whole* Nation of the *Jews*, 'tis remarked by the Pſalmiſt,
(Pſ. lxxviii. 34;) that *when he ſlew them, then they ſought him, and returned, and in-*
quired early after God; and remembred that God was their Rock, and the High God
their Redeemer.

Upon *this* account, the Afflictions that God ſends upon his people and ſervants,
are ſo frequently declared in Scripture to be Evidences of his *Love* and *Care* towards
them. *When we are judged,* (ſaith St *Paul,*) *we are chaſtened of the Lord, that we*
ſhould not be condemned with the world; 1 Cor. xi. 32. and our Lord himſelf declares,
Rev. iii. 19; *As many as I love, I rebuke and chaſten; be zealous therefore and repent.*
Which Exhortation the Author of the Epiſtle to the *Hebrews* thus excellently paraphraſes: *My Son, deſpiſe not thou the chaſtening of the Lord, nor faint when thou art re-*
buked of him; For whom the Lord loveth, he chaſteneth, and ſcourgeth every Son whom
he receiveth: If we have had fathers of our fleſh, which corrected us, and we gave them
reverence; ſhall we not much rather be in ſubjection unto the Father of ſpirits, and live?
For they verily for a few days chaſtened us after their own pleaſure; but He for our profit,
that we might be partakers of his Holineſs. Now no chaſtening for the preſent ſeemeth to
be joyous, but grievous; nevertheleſs afterwards it yieldeth the peaceable fruit of righte-
ouſneſs, unto them which are exerciſed thereby, Heb. xii. 5, &c. The Apoſtle allows,
that Afflictions cannot indeed but be grievous to humane Nature, when they are actually *upon* us: But the Conſideration of the great advantage they *may* and are *intended*
to turn to, by religious improvement; is abundantly ſufficient to make *any* ingenuous
and conſiderate temper, (which ſuffers not paſſion and preſent uneaſineſs to prevail
wholly over Reaſon,) to ſay with *Eli, It is the Lord, let him do what ſeemeth him good;*
and with pious *Job, The Lord gave, and the Lord hath taken away; Bleſſed be the Name*
of the Lord: For, ſhall we receive good at the hand of God, and ſhall we not (patiently)
receive evil?

There is *one* way, by which Affliction of *this* kind, namely, ſuch as are ſent upon us by way of *correction*, may in great meaſure be prevented: and That is, if we
would take care *ſo* to behave ourſelves, as not to ſtand in *need* of them; *ſo to judge*

I

ourſelves,

ourselves, as *not to be judged* of the *Lord*. *Job* xxxiii. 27. God *looketh upon men; and if any say, I have sinned, and perverted that which was right, and it positeth me not; he will deliver his soul from going into the pit, and his life shall see the light.* But this must be understood *only* of *this one* particular kind of Afflictions; such as are intended for our *correction*, and to lead us to *Repentance* for some *particular Sins.*

3. ANOTHER *End* of God's sending Afflictions and Troubles upon men, is to *wean us from an over-fond love of the present World.* There is nothing that more hinders mens progress in Religion, nothing that more softens the minds, and cools the Zeal even of good and well-disposed persons, than a constant, careless, habitual enjoyment of, and affection to, even *those* pleasures of Life, which cannot perhaps be charged with being directly sinful: *O Death*, says the wise Son of *Sirach*, Ecclus. xli; 1; *How bitter is the remembrance of thee to a man that liveth at rest in his possessions; unto the man that has nothing to vex him, and that hath prosperity in all things!* As a continual Calm corrupteth the Waters; so a long and uninterrupted Prosperity, is a perpetual Danger and Temptation. Of the people of the *Jews* 'tis observed; *Deut.* xxxii. 15; that when *Jeshurun* waxed *fat*, he *kicked, and forsook the God that made him, and lightly esteemed the rock of his salvation.* And it is no less true of the *Christian* Church, that when, upon the Emperor's first becoming Christian, it began to receive worldly Encouragement; the Contentions among Christians multiplied, and the Purity of their Manners decreased. And in our *own* Nation it has been justly observed, that true Religion never had so remarkable an influence upon mens Lives and Manners; as at such times when we were most apprehensive of its being in danger to be removed from us. For this reason God has seldom chosen to make his best Servants the most prosperous in the world. The Patriarchs did but *sojourn in the land of promise, as in a strange country, dwelling in tabernacles,* and *confessing that they were strangers and pilgrims in the earth; For they look ed for a city which had foundations, whose builder and maker is God;* Heb. xi. 9, 10. And our Saviour inculcates no one Thing so often upon his Disciples, as the Danger of worldly Ease and Plenty, and the *Blessedness* of *them that mourn.*

YET, on the other side, *Afflictions* have also their proper Temptations, to Impatience, and Discontent, and Complaining against God; and *Prosperity*, if well employed, *may* become the Matter of an excellent Virtue: For, *Blessed is the rich, that is found without blemish, and hath not gone after gold;* that *hath been tried thereby, and found perfect*; that *might offend, and hath not offended*; or might *do evil, and hath not done it*; Ecclus. xxxi. 8, 10. Wherefore it is best for *us*, not to be sollicitous after either State; but, with all Submission, to leave that wholly to God; who knows much better than we, what is most convenient for us.

4*thly*, and *Lastly*; ANOTHER *End* of God's sending Afflictions upon men, is to *try, improve, and perfect* their Virtues, and make eminent *Examples* of their *Faith* and *Patience.* This was the case of *Job*, who was afflicted by the immediate hand of *God*; and this was the case of the *Apostles*, who were permitted to be persecuted by *wicked men*; and St *Paul* tells us concerning our Saviour himself: *(Heb.* ii. 10;) that he was *made perfect through sufferings.* Of such Afflictions as these, the Scripture declares that they are to be *gloried in*, because they *work Patience :* (Rom. v. 3. and Jam. i. 3.) that they *fall out unto the furtherance of the Gospel:* (Phil. i. 12;) that they are a *trial of Faith, much more precious than of gold that perisheth, though it be tried with fire;* (1 Pet. i. 7.) That, by these, *many are purified and made white and tried,* (Dan. xii. 10; and xi. 35 :) *And having been a little chastised, they shall be greatly rewarded; for God proved them, and found them worthy for himself; As gold in the furnace has he tried them, and received them as a burnt-offering; And in the time of their visitation they*
shall

SERM.*shall shine, and run to and fro like sparks among the stubble* ; *They shall judge the na-*
XCVIII. *tions, and have dominion over the people* ; *and their Lord shall reign for ever* ; (Wisd.
iii. 5, &c.)

I SHALL but juſt mention two inferences from what has been ſaid, and ſo conclude.

AND 1ſt, From what has been ſaid it appears, that it is a very wrong and unjuſt Concluſion to imagine with *Job's* friends, that whoever is much afflicted, muſt conſequently, have been very wicked, and that God is very angry with him. When a Man's *own* conſcience can apply his *own* Affliction to his paſt Sins, it is indeed very reaſonable, that he ſhould accept it as the Puniſhment of Sin, and as an Argument to Repentance ; But he muſt by no means make *another* man's Affliction, an occaſion of cenſuring his Neighbour ; For, on the contrary, the Scripture declares, that *happy is the man whom God correcteth* ; *therefore despise not thou the chastning of the Almighty* ; *for he maketh sore, and bindeth up* ; *he woundeth, and his hands make whole* ; Job v. 17. *Blessed is the man whom thou chastenest, O Lord, and teachest him out of thy law* ; Pſ. xciv. 12. And St *James*, ch. i. ver. 12 ; *Blessed is the man that endureth temptation* ; *for when he is tried, he shall receive the crown of life.*

2*dly* ; FROM what has been ſaid, there appears great Reaſon, for men to reſign themſelves with all patience to the Will of God ; and to rely upon him with full Truſt and Aſſurance, (in *all possible* circumſtances of life,) that he will direct things finally to our beſt advantage. *Ecclus.* ii. 4 ; *Whatsoever is brought upon thee, take cheerfully* ; *and be patient when thou art changed to a low estate* ; *For gold is tried in the fire, and acceptable men in the furnace of adversity.* This was the practice of *David* ; who, when he *was greatly distressed, encouraged himself in the Lord his God* ; 1 Sam. xxx. 6. And This was the Reſolution of the *Prophet*, wherewith I ſhall conclude, *Habbak.* iii. 17 ; *Though the fig-tree shall not blossom, neither shall fruit be in the vines* ; though *the labour of the olive shall fail, and the fields shall yeld no meat* ; though *the flock shall be cut off from the fold, and there shall be no herd in the stalls* ; *Yet will I rejoice in the Lord* ; *I will joy in the God of my Salvation.*

SERMON

SERMON XCVIII.

The Event of Things not always anfwerable to Second Caufes.

[*A Faft Sermon.*]

ECCLES. IX. 11.

I returned, and faw under the Sun, that the Race is not to the Swift, nor the Battle to the ftrong, neither yet Bread to the Wife, nor yet Riches to men of Underftanding, nor yet Favour to men of Skill; but Time and Chance happeneth to them All.

THERE are fome fort of perfons in the World fo flothful and negligent S E R M. in their own Affairs, fo hardly prevailed upon to undertake any thing that XCVIII. requires labour and diligence, fo eafily difcouraged by any appearance of ill Succefs, or fo heedlefs and unactive in the profecution of whatever they are about; as if they were of opinion even in *temporal* matters, what in fome Syftems of Religion has been abfurdly affirmed concerning *Spirituals,* that *God* does *every* thing *in* men and for men, leaving *nothing* for them to do for *themfelves;* or as if they thought That Precept to be *literal* and *univerfal,* which our Saviour fpake, with the *Latitude of a moral admonition,* to the *Apoftles* only, and upon an *extraordinary Occafion;* take *no Thought for the morrow, what ye fhall eat, or what ye fhall drink, or wherewithal ye fhall be clothed.* Such Perfons as thefe, the wife Man elegantly defcribes in his Book of *Proverbs: The Sluggard,* faith he, *will not plow by reafon of the Cold; there-* ch. xx. 4. *fore fhall he beg in Harveft, and have nothing: The flothful man faith, there is a Lion without; I fhall be flain in the Streets;* Prov. xxii. 13 : And ch. xxiv. 30; *I went by the Field of the flothful, and by the Vineyard of the man void of underftanding; and lo, it was all grown over with Thorns, and Nettles had covered the Face thereof, and the Stone-Wall thereof was broken down;* —— *So fhall thy Poverty come as one that tra-velleth, and thy Want as an armed man.* Nor is his *Reproof* and *Admonition* to thofe who are guilty of this Folly, lefs elegant than his *Defcription* of them; ch. vi. 6. *Go to the Ant, thou fluggard; confider her ways, and be wife; Which having no guide, overfeer, or ruler,* yet *provideth her meat in the Summer, and gathereth her Food in the Harveft.* And in the Words immediately before my Text, *Ecclef.* ix. 10; *What-foever thine hand findeth to do, do it with* all *thy Might;* do it with Diligence; do it with Attention, Induftry, and Care.

THERE are *Others* in a *contrary* Extreme; who rely with fuch confidence on the Effects of their own Wifdom and Induftry, and fo prefumptuoufly depend upon the natural and regular Tendencies of fecond Caufes; as if they thought, either there was

SERM. no Superior Cauſe at all, on which the Frame of Nature depended; or at leaſt, that
XCVIII. the Providence of God did not condeſcend to direct the Events of Things, in this lower
and uncertain World. And Theſe, are elegantly reproved in the words of my Text;
*I returned and ſaw under the Sun, that the Race is not to the Swift, nor the Battle to
the Strong, neither yet Bread to the Wiſe, nor yet Riches to men of Underſtanding, nor
yet Favour to men of Skill; but Time and Chance happeneth to them All.*

I RETURNED: That is; In that vaſt Compaſs of Knowledge which *Solomon* had,
in being able to ſurvey the whole Extent of Nature, and to obſerve the Tempers and
Diſpoſitions of men, and the different Events of Things in all variety of Times and
Circumſtances; he *turned* his Thoughts and Obſervations from *one Subject* to *another.*
In the verſe *before* the Text, he views the *careleſs* or *negligent* part of mankind, and
exhorts *them* to *diligence:* And then *I returned,* ſaith he, in the Words of the Text,
that is, he turned his View the *other* way, towards the *confident* or *preſumptuous*; And
them he bids to take notice, that the *Race* is not always to the *Swift,* nor the *Battle*
to the *Strong*; (that is,) that the *Events* of Things do not always anſwer to the *Probabilities* of ſecond Cauſes, unleſs the Wiſdom of God thinks fit by the direction of
his good Providence to make thoſe Cauſes ſucceſsful. *I returned, and ſaw* under the
Sun; that is, in the *whole Courſe* of this lower and uncertain world, in the whole
compaſs of Humane Affairs, in the Hiſtories of all Times or Ages, and in the Events
that have happened to all Nations or People; I obſerved, ſaith he, upon the largeſt
View and moſt extenſive Experience, that the *Race* is often *not* to the *Swift,* nor the
Battle to the *Strong.* The *Reaſon why* the Events of Things do frequently fail in this
manner, of anſwering to the natural Probabilities of ſecond Cauſes; is becauſe many
little and unforeſeen Accidents unavoidably interpoſing, do very often change the whole
Courſe of things, and produce an Event quite contrary to what in all reaſonable probability was to have been expected. The *ſwifteſt Racer,* upon the leaſt accidental
Slip, loſes the Prize to an Adverſary much ſlower than himſelf; and the *Potenteſt* Armies, upon the leaſt Diſorder befalling them in a day of Battle, have been forced to
leave the Victory to an Enemy whom they before deſpiſed for his inferior Force. *Accidents* theſe things appear to *men,* becauſe not poſſible to be foreſeen or prevented by
our ſhort and imperfect Underſtandings: But in the hands of *Providence,* the Cauſes
and Reaſons of theſe even the *minuteſt* Accidents are all as clearly and diſtinctly known
and determinate, as the *groſſeſt* and moſt *obvious* Cauſes are apparently diſcerned by *Us.*
And by means of theſe unforeſeen Cauſes, does God in his Great Government of the
Univerſe, conſtantly bring about his own Deſigns, in Bleſſing or Puniſhing Nations
according to his own good pleaſure. *Amos* ii. 14; *The Flight ſhall periſh from the
Swift, and the Strong ſhall not ſtrengthen his Force, neither ſhall the mighty deliver
himſelf; Neither ſhall He ſtand, that handleth the bow; and he that is ſwift of Foot,
ſhall not deliver himſelf; neither ſhall he that rideth the horſe, deliver himſelf.* Again:
Pſ. xxxiii. 15; *There is no King that can be ſaved by the multtude of an Hoſt, neither
is any mighty man delivered by much ſtrength: A Horſe is counted but a vain thing to
ſave a man, neither ſhall he deliver any man by his great Strength: Behold, the Eye of
the Lord is upon them that fear him, and upon them that put their Truſt in his Mercy.*
Solomon expreſſes the ſame Notion thus, *Prov.* xxi. 30; *There is no Wiſdom, nor Underſtanding, nor Counſel againſt the Lord; The Horſe is prepared againſt the day of Battle, but Safety is of the Lord.* And *Hannah,* in her prayer recorded, 1 *Sam.* ii. 4, 9;
*The Bows of the mighty men are broken, and they that ſtumbled are girt with Strength:
—— The Lord will keep the Feet of his Saints, and the Wicked ſhall be ſilent in Darkneſs; for by Strength ſhall no man prevail.* Theſe are all as it were, Paraphraſes upon
the words of the Text; *the Race is not to the Swift, nor the Battle to the Strong.*

I T follows: *neither yet Bread to the Wife, nor yet Riches to men of Underſtanding, nor yet Favour to men of Skill.* That is: As Strength and Agility of *Body*, are not al‑ ways ſuccefsful in proportion to the Degree of thoſe Faculties; nor Powerful Armies victorious, in proportion to the Numbers they confiſt of: So the Faculties and Abilities of the *Mind* likewiſe, Wiſdom and Underſtanding, Dexterity and Skill; are not al‑ ways ſuccefsful, as might regularly be expected, in obtaining Riches and Honour, Favour and Dignity in the World; but unſeen Accidents, *(Accidents* with regard to *Men*, but with *God* wiſe Diſpenſations of *Providence,)* inviſibly and inexplicably turn the Courſe even of *theſe* things alſo: For *Time and Chance happeneth to them All:* Iſ. xliv. 2 5; God *turneth* wiſe *men backward, and maketh their Knowledge Fooliſh.*

H A V I N G, thus, briefly explained the *Meaning* of the ſeveral Phraſes contained in the Text; the *Doctrinal Obſervations* I ſhall now draw from thence, are as fol‑ lows.

1ſt; W E may obſerve, that what men vulgarly call *Chance* or unforeſeen *Accident,* is in Scripture always declared to be the *determinate Counſel and Providence of God.* What careleſs and inconſiderate men aſcribe in common Speech to *Chance* or *Fortune;* that is, to *nothing at all,* but a mere empty word, ſignifying only their *Ignorance* of the true Cauſes of things; this the Scripture teaches *Us* to aſcribe to the all-ſeeing and all-directing Providence of God; that we may *acknowledge* Him *in all our Ways;* and be ſenſible of the True Author, from whom all the *Good* and all the *Evil* that befalls us, does either *mercifully* or *juſtly* proceed: *Dan. iv. 3 5; He doth according to his Will in the Army of Heaven, and among the Inhabitants of the Earth; and none can ſtay his hand, or ſay unto him, What doſt thou?* When a perſon is ſlain by *Chance* or *Accident,* as men vulgarly ſpeak; the Scripture more accurately expreſſes it, ſaying, that God *delivered* ſuch a one, *into the hand* of him that ſlew him without Deſign; *Exod.* xxi. 13. And in *all other* Inſtances, the ſame Notion is every where kept up in Scripture: *Prov.* xvi. 33 ; *The Lot is caſt into the Lap, but the whole diſpoſing there‑ of is of the Lord.* And when the Apoſtles *choſe by Lot* a Succeſſor to *Judas,* they ex‑ preſſed their Senſe of the divine Providence in the following words: *Acts* i. 24; *Thou, Lord, which knoweſt the Hearts of all men, ſhow whether of theſe Two thou haſt choſen.* And Thus likewiſe in the words in the Text; it is the ſupreme Superintendency of *Providence* over all Events, which *Solomon* meant to eſtabliſh, when he ſaith, *Time and Chance happeneth to them All.*

N E I T H E R is it, (as Some, with very weak Pretences to Reaſon, have in this caſe been apt to Imagine;) it is not, I ſay, merely in a *pious manner of Expreſſion,* that the Scripture thus aſcribes every Event to the Providence of God; but it is *ſtrictly* and *philoſophically true* in Nature and Reaſon, that there is *no ſuch thing* as *Chance* or *Accident;* it being evident that thoſe words do not ſignify any thing *really exiſting,* any thing that is truly an *Agent* or the *Cauſe* of any Event; but they ſignify, *merely* mens *Ignorance* of the real and immediate Cauſe. And this is ſo True, that very many even of Thoſe who have no Religion, nor any Senſe at all of the Providence of God; yet know very well, by the Light of their own natural *Reaſon,* that there nei‑ ther is nor can be any ſuch thing as *Chance,* that is, any ſuch thing as an Effect without a Cauſe; And therefore what *Others* aſcribe to *Chance,* *They* aſcribe to the operation of *Neceſſity* or *Fate.* But *Fate* alſo is itſelf in reality as *truly Nothing,* as *Chance* is. Nor is there *in Nature* Any *Other Efficient* or proper *Cauſe* of any Event; (of any *Event,* I ſay: For concerning *Truths* in Themſelves eſſentially, eternally and invariably neceſ‑ ſary, I am not ſpeaking: But of all the variable *Events* that happen in the Univerſe, there is, and can be in Nature no other proper and *efficient* Cauſe;) but only the *Free Will of rational and intelligent* Creatures, acting within the Sphere of their

S E R M. limited Faculties; and the *Supreme Power of God*, directing, by his omnipresent Pro-
XCVIII. vidence, (according to certain *Wise Laws or Rules*, established by, and entirely depending upon his own good pleasure,) the inanimate Motions of the whole material
and unintelligent World.

 2dly, F ROM the words of the Text I observe, that the all-directing Providence of
God, which governs the Universe; does not superintend only the *Great* Events in the
World, the Fates of Nations and Kingdoms; so that, without the direction of Providence, the *strongest* and most numerous Armies are not victorious in *Battle*; but its
Care extends, even to the Concerns of *single* Persons; so that, without the Blessing of
God, neither *Riches*, nor *Favour*, nor *any temporal Advantage*, can certainly be obtained by any thing that *Man* can do: Nay, that even in matters of still *smaller* moment not so much as a *Race* is gained by the *Swift*, without the hand of Providence
directing the Event. When men observe how *Our* Attention is distracted with a multiplicity of Objects, and can very hardly be fixed on more than one thing at once;
they are too carelessly apt to imagine, that Providence itself either cannot, or that 'tis
beneath its Dignity to condescend, to interpose in the numberless small events of
Nature or Chance. But the *Scripture* tells us otherwise, and *right Reason* also joins
with it herein. For as *Chance* is nothing, so *Nature* also is nothing but an empty
word. Every *Effect*, every *Event*, must have a *real Cause*; must proceed, immediately or mediately, from That which has a *True Existence* and *Active Power*. And to
an Omnipresent Mind, there is no more difficulty in attending to *every thing* at one
and the same Time, than to *any one thing*. Not only *piously* therefore, but even
with the *strictest* and *most philosophical Truth of expression*, does the Scripture tell us,
that God *commandeth the Ravens*, 1 Kings xvii. 4; that they are *His* directions, which
even the Winds and the Seas obey; that he causes His *Sun to rise on the Evil and on the
Good*; that God *prepared a Gourd*, and *a Worm to smite* it that it *withered*, Jonah iv.
7; that God *feedeth the Fowls of the Air*, Matt. vi. 26; and, *and without Him*, *not a
sparrow falls to the ground*; ch. x. 29: Nay, that he *clothes* even the *Lillies*, *and the
grass of the field*, Matt. vi. 30; and, with Him, *the very Hairs of our Head are All
numbered*.

 'Tis true; All these things are plainly owing to *Second Causes*. And so likewise
are all the *greater* Instances mentioned by *Solomon* in the Text. 'Tis as much according to the Course of *Nature*, that the *Strong* should *sometimes* lose a Battle by *Accident*, as that they should *generally* gain it by *Strength*; and that *unforeseen Hindrances* should *sometimes* cause the *swiftest Runner* to lose the Race, as that *Agility
and Nimbleness of Body* should make him *generally* win it. My

 3d O BSERVATION therefore is; that things being brought about according to
the course of *Nature* by *Second* Causes, is not at all inconsistent with their being nevertheless *justly and truly* ascribed to the *Providence of God*. 'Tis *Time and Chance*,
says the Text, that *happens to them All*; that happens frequently to prevent *all* the Probabilities there mentioned. The wise man does not hereby mean, that they are prevented by *Miracle*: For then he would not have used the vulgar words, of *Time and
Chance*. Nor does he mean on the contrary, that they are prevented by Blind and unintelligent *Fate*: For this would have been contrary to the whole Design of his Book,
and of all the rest of the Scripture, as well as to common Reason: But his Meaning
is; that the *Providence of God*, by means of *natural Causes*, which are all entirely of
His appointment, and *Instruments only* in *His* hand; does often for wise reasons in his
government of the World, disappoint the most probable expectations. Ridiculous
therefore is the Arguing of the Infidel and Irreligious; who presently thinks himself
secure of excluding the *Providence of God*, if he can but show a thing to be brought

                    I

                                                                        about

about by *Natural Cauſes*. Moſt *ridiculous*, I ſay, and *ignorant*, is this manner of rea- S E R M. ſoning : For, *what* are *Natural* Cauſes? Nothing but thoſe *Laws* and *Powers*, which XCVIII. God merely of his *own good pleaſure* has implanted in the ſeveral parts of Matter, in order to make them Inſtruments of fulfilling his ſupreme Will. Which *Laws* and *Powers*, as he at *firſt appointed* them, ſo nothing but the ſame go'od pleaſure of God *continually preſerves them*. And they neither *exiſt* nor *operate* in any moment of Time, but by Influence and Action derived to them (mediately or immediately) from his all-governing Will. So that he foreſees perpetually, what Effect every Power and Opera-tion of Nature tends to produce ; and could (if he thought fit,) exactly with the ſame Eaſe, cauſe it to produce a *different* Effect, as that which it Now does. From whence it follows inevitably, to the entire Confuſion of Atheiſts, that all thoſe things which they call *natural* Effects, are in very Truth as much the operation of God, (though per-haps not ſo immediately,) as even Miracles themſelves. And to argue againſt *Provi-dence* from the obſervation of the regular *courſe of natural Cauſes* ; is as if a man ſhould conclude from the *uniformity* of a large and beautiful Building, that it was not the work of mens hands, nor contrived by any Free Agent, becauſe the Stones and the Timber were laid *uniformly and regularly*, in the moſt conſtant, natural, and proper Order.

4thly, The *Laſt* doctrinal Obſervation I ſhall draw from the Text, is ; that ſince the whole Courſe of nature in the ordinary method of Cauſes and Effects, and all thoſe unexpected Turns of things which men vulgarly call Chance and Accident, are entire-ly in the Hand of God, and under the continual direction of His Providence ; it follows evidently, (and 'tis a Doctrine worthy the moſt ſerious conſideration of all wicked Men,) that God can, whenever he pleaſes, even *without* a Miracle, puniſh the diſobedient ; And no Swiftneſs, no Strength, no Wiſdom, no Artifice, ſhall in any manner avail, or inable them to eſcape the Vengeance, which even *Natural Cauſes* only, by the direc-tion of Him from whom they receive their Nature, bring upon Offenders. He can puniſh by Fires and Famine, by Plagues and Peſtilences, by Storms and Earth-quakes, by domeſtick Commotions or by foreign Enemies. He can, as *Moſes* elegant-ly expreſſes it, make the *Heavens over mens Heads Braſs*, and *the Earth under their Feet Iron*, or the very *Beaſts of the Field to riſe up againſt them* : Or, as 'tis in the Book of *Wiſdom* ; ch. v. 22, 23, 20 ; he can cauſe that *a mighty Wind ſhall ſtand up againſt them*, or *the Waters of the Sea ſhall rage againſt them*, and *the World ſhall fight for him againſt the unwiſe*. He can, by means of the leaſt *Accident*, as we ignorantly ſtile it, diſcomfit the greateſt Armies before a Few of their Enemies : As 2 *Chr.* xxiv. 24 ; *The Syrians came with a ſmall company of men, and the Lord delivered a very great Hoſt* (of the Iſraelites) *into their hand* ; *becauſe they had forſaken the Lord God of their Fathers*. Neither ſhall Any Swiftneſs deliver them from the Purſuer : *If.* xxx. 16. *Ye ſaid, We will flee upon Horſes* ; *therefore ſhall ye flee : And we will ride upon the Swift* ; *therefore ſhall they that purſue you, be ſwift : One thouſand ſhall flee at the rebuke of One* ; *at the rebuke of five ſhall ye flee* ; *'till ye be left as a Beacon upon the top of a Mountain, and as an Enſign on a Hill*. Nay, *without* any *viſible* external cauſe at all, to which ſuch an Effect can be aſcribed ; Providence can ſecretly blaſt, and inſenſibly cauſe to moulder away, the Greateſt Power, Riches, or other worldly Advantages whatſoever : *Pſ.* xxxix. 11. *When thou with Rebukes doſt chaſten Man for Sin, thou makeſt his Beauty to conſume away, like as a Moth fretting a garment* ; *every man therefore is but Vanity*. And 'tis the exceeding Stupidity of profane Men, not to be moved hereby to *repent*, and *give glory to the God of Heaven*, who *hath Power over theſe Plagues*, Rev. xvi. 9. The Meaning of this whole Obſervation is, not that theſe Judgments are always certain Signs of God's diſpleaſure againſt all the particular per-

S E R M. fons upon whom they at any time fall ; for This our Saviour has exprefsly warned us
XCVIII. againft, as a moft uncharitable Conclufion :) But whether they be Punifhments for
Sin, (as they generally, though not always, are ;) or whether they be only Trials of
Mens Virtue, (as they fometimes are defigned to be ;) or whether they be Means of
weaning them from this tranfitory and uncertain World : or whatever other Ends Pro-
vidence brings about thereby ; ftill they are always Effects of the fame All-wife divine
Providence ; which ought to be acknowledged and fubmitted to as fuch, and whofe
Defigns no Power or Wifdom of frail and vain men can oppofe or prevent.

THE *Practical Inferences,* arifing naturally from what has been faid, are as
follows.

1*ft*, IF thefe things be fo ; then let the greateft and moft powerful of wicked men
confider, that they have nothing in This World either to boaft of or to rely upon.
Jer. ix. 23 ; *Let not the wife man glory in his Wifdom, let not the rich man glory in
his Riches, neither let the mighty man glory in his Might :* For all thefe Advantages are
frequently defeated, and *Time and Chance happeneth to them All. I will not truft in my
Bow,* faith the Pfalmift, *neither fhall my Sword fave me ; But it is* Thou *that favzft
us from our Enemies,* Pf. xliv. 6. Wife therefore was the Anfwer of the King of *Ifrael,*
to an infulting meffage from the King of *Syria,* 1 *Kings* xx. 11 ; *Tell him, Let not him
that girdeth on his harnefs, boaft himfelf, as he that putteth it off.* The Event fhowed,
that his Admonition was reafonable ; and the *Syrian*'s Pride was but the immediate
fore-runner of his Deftruction. For the fame purpofe, it is recorded of *Nebuchadnezzar* King of *Babylon,* that when *his Greatnefs was grown and reached unto Heaven, and
his Dominion to the End of the Earth,* Dan. iv. 22 ; it was faid unto him, *ver.* 25 ;
*They fhall drive thee from Men, and thy dwelling fhall be with the Beafts of the Field,
and they fhall make thee to eat grafs as Oxen, and they fhall wet thee with the Dew of
Heaven,*——('tis the defcription of a very fevere and mortifying Diftemper of Mind ;)
*'till thou know that the moft High ruleth in the Kingdom of men, and giveth it to whom-
foever he will.* This is the plain Defign of Providence, in fuch extraordinary Events ;
to bring men to an Acknowledgement, of *Him* on whom they depend ; to bring them
to a right Knowledge, of *God* and of *themfelves : That he may withdraw Man from
his Purpofe,* Job xxxiii. 17, *and hide Pride from Man.* Well (indeed) may *Pride* be
faid to be hid from Men, when not only the Succefs of their greateft Advantages, but
even their very *Life* itfelf, is, uncertain every moment. *Boaft not thyfelf of to morrow,*
Prov. xxvii. 1. *for thou knoweft not what a day,* what an Hour, *may bring forth.* For
*as the Fifhes that are taken in an evil Net, and as the Birds that are caught in the
Snare ; fo are the Sons of Men fnared in an evil time, when it falleth fuddenly upon
them,* Ecclef. ix. 12. The rich man in the Gofpel, refolved to pull down his barns,
and build bigger ; and then it was faid unto him, *Thou Fool, this night fhall thy Soul be
required of Thee.* In the Days of *Noah ; Men eat and drank, they married and were
given in marriage, untill the day that Noah entered into the Ark : And* then *the Flood
came and deftroyed them All.* Likewife *in the days of Lot ; they did eat, they drank,
they bought, they fold, they planted, they builded : But the fame day that Lot went out of
Sodom, it rained fire and brimftone from Heaven, and deftroyed them All.* And fo alfo
fhall it finally be *in the Great Day, when the Son of Man is revealed,* Luke xvii. 30.

2*dly,* IF nothing happens in the World, without the divine Providence ; then good
Men have a fufficient Ground of Truft and Reliance upon God, at all times and under
All Dangers. Not, that God will *always* deliver them, or caufe them to profper in
the prefent World ; For he often fees it better, to determine otherwife : But they may
rely with affurance, that nothing can befall them but what *He* judges fit ; feeing all
the Powers of Nature and of fecond Caufes, are nothing but Inftruments in *His* hand,
and

3

and under *His* direction. *Truſt* therefore *in the Lord, with all thine heart,* —— and *in all thy ways acknowledge Him,* Prov. iii. 5. He can *ſave,* whenever he pleaſes, 2 *Chr.* xiv. 9, 11 : and xvi. 8, 9, 1 *Sam.* xiv. 6. with *many,* or with *Few*; cauſing all the Accidents, which *we* call *Time and Chance,* to *fulfill his Word,* Pſ. cxlviii. 8. and exe-cute his Pleaſure : So that, if *He* thinks *fit,* even *five ſhall* be able to *chaſe an hundred, and an hundred ſhall put ten thouſand to flight*; Levit. xxvi. 8; *and* Deut. xxxii. 30.

3*dly* and *Laſtly*; FROM This Notion of Providence, may be given a plain and direct Anſwer to that Queſtion of the profane Fataliſt; *Job* xxi. 15; *What is the Almighty, that we ſhould ſerve him? and what Profit ſhould we have, if we pray unto him?* Indeed, if the Courſe of Nature, and thoſe things which we call *ſecond Cauſes,* were independent upon Providence; there *would* be good Reaſon to ask, what Benefit could there be either in *Prayer* or *Thankſgiving.* But if, as has been ſhown, Nature is nothing, and ſecond cauſes are nothing, but mere Inſtruments; then it is very plain that Prayer and Thankſgivings are as much due to God for whatever is brought about by *Natural* cauſes, as if he had done the Thing by any *Other Inſtruments* inſtead of *Theſe,* even by the moſt miraculous ones; Which in That caſe, being no leſs conſtant, would have been no more miraculous than *Theſe.*

SERMON

SERMON XCIX.

The Practice of Wickedness generally attended with great Evil.

[*An Inauguration-Sermon.*]

PROV. XIII. 21.

Evil pursueth Sinners; but to the Righteous, Good shall be repaid.

SERM.
XCIX.

THE Parable which our Saviour spake concerning the Perverseness of the *Jews*, in finding fault equally on *Both* sides; both with *John Baptist's* more *severe*, and with our Lord's own more *free* manner of Conversation in the world; may be applied generally to almost *all* the Objections, which wicked and profane men *at any time* make against Religion. No *Reason*, No *Argument*, No *Method of Proceeding* whatsoever, will satisfy prejudiced and corrupt Minds. *John the Baptist came, neither eating nor drinking*; Matt. xi. 18. That is, *He*, when he was sent to preach, came solitary in the Wilderness, with great Austereness and Severity of Life, with Fasting and Abstinence, with Mortification and Self-denial; and they said, he is Mad, and hath a Devil. On the contrary, *Christ* came to preach *without* this Austerity, in a more free way of Conversation; and they called him a Loose Person, a Glutton, and a Wine-Drinker, and a Companion of the worst of men. Upon This their Perverseness, our Lord compares those *Jews* to *froward and peevish children*, who do every thing contrary to what their Companions desire and expect: Ver. 17; *We have piped unto you, and ye have not danced; we have mourned unto you, and ye have not lamented*: When *others* play and are cheerful, *they* will be sullen and ill-humoured: when *others* be sorrowful, *They* will laugh and mock. But after the Perverseness of Men has said and done all that it can; *Wisdom*, says our Lord, *is justified of all her children*; Wisdom will still vindicate itself, and appear to be Wisdom, in whomsoever it be found, and in what manner soever it be exercised.

THE Case is the *Same* in almost *all other* Instances, wherein prejudiced and corrupt minds are continually seeking Objections against Religion; Objections *contrary to* and *inconsistent with* each other. Does Providence at any time bestow *remarkable Blessings*, upon virtuous and good men? Immediately from hence an Argument is drawn against Virtue, as if it lost the Nature of Virtue, and became *mercenary*, by having *respect unto the recompence of Reward*. Most elegantly is *This Objection* set forth, in the *first* chapter of the book of *Job*; Where *Satan* is represented as arguing before the Lord, ver. 9; *Doth Job fear God for nought? Hast not thou made an hedge about him, and about his house, and about all that he hath on every side? Thou hast blessed the work of his hands, and his substance is increased in the land. But put forth thine hand now, and touch all that he hath, and he will curse thee to thy face.*

4

O N the *contrary*; Does Providence *forbear to interpose* in the prefent time, and referve Judgment to the day of Retribution? *Then* the Argument is *turned*; and the
Speech of the Scoffers is, *Where is the Promise of his Coming? For since the Fathers*
fell asleep, all things continue as they were from the Beginning of the Creation, 2 Pet.
iii. 4: *Then they say, It is vain to serve God; and what Profit is it, that we have kept*
his Ordinance? Mal. iii. 14: *Then they ask, What is the Almighty, that we should*
serve him? and what Profit should we have, if we pray unto him? Job xxi. 15.

T H E *Answer* to *Both*, is eafy and obvious. God's *Forbearance* at any time to in-
terpofe in the *prefent State* on the behalf of Virtue, is no Argument at all againft the
Benefit and *Advantage* of Serving him; becaufe he is able to make abundant Recompence in the *Life to come*: Upon which account, excellent is the Advice of *Solomon*,
Prov. xxiii. 17; *Let not thine heart envy Sinners, but be thou in the Fear of the Lord*
all the day long: For surely there is an end, (or, as we render it in the margin, *surely*
there is a Reward,) and thine expectation shall not be cut off. And on the *other* hand,
the *Rewards and Punishments* which *God* diftributes either in the *prefent* or in a *future*
ftate, do not at all alter the Nature of Virtue, or make it in Any degree become *mer-*
cenary: Becaufe a Man's Regard to his *own* Intereft and Advantage is *Then* only Faulty,
when it is a Temptation to him to do any thing that is in its own nature Evil; not
when it is in conjunction with the univerfal Right and Reafon of things, and the Happinefs of God's whole Creation.

M Y Defign at This Time from the words of the Text, is to reprefent and inculcate this great Truth, that the *Practice of Righteoufnefs* is mens *true Intereft*, even in
the *prefent* Life; and that *Wickednefs* is generally attended with *Great Mifery*, even
Here as well as *Hereafter. Evil purfueth Sinners; but to the Righteous, Good shall*
be repayed.

B E F O R E I enter upon the particular explication of which Doctrine, there is One
thing needful to be premifed; that the whole of what is to be faid upon This Subject,
muft always be underftood with an *exception* to the Cafe of *Perfecution* for Truth and
Righteoufnefs fake. For *all moral* and *univerfal Propofitions* of this kind, expreffing
the *general* Tendency of things in their natural Courfe, and the ordinary eftablifhed
Difpofitions of Divine Providence; are fufficiently verified, if they take place in all
Cafes where the *natural Order* of things is permitted to produce its *proper* Effect.
When the Nature of things is perverted or over-ruled by any extraordinary Violence,
an Exception muft be made; without any detriment to the Truth of the general Propofition. And of this fort is the cafe of *Perfecution* for Religion. *Virtue*, in the *Na-*
ture of things, and according to the *general Promife and Appointment of God*, is the
Foundation and Caufe of true Happinefs among men. Yet the Perverfenefs of a wicked and corrupt World, *may poffibly* load it, upon fome particular Occafions, with the
greateft Temporal Calamities; and inflict the fevereft Punifhments in their power,
upon that which really deferves the Higheft Commendation and Reward. In *This*
cafe, the Beft of men, *if in This life only they had hope*, might *of All* men become the
moft miferable. But Then, for *this very Reafon*, God has promifed them a Recompence in a *Future State*; and herein they may rejoice, even *not accepting Deliverance*,
that they may obtain a better Refurrection. Setting afide *This cafe* therefore, which is
of *peculiar* confideration; the Propofition I laid down, may evidently be fhown to be
a *General* Truth, that the *Practice of Righteoufnefs* is men's True Intereft, even in
the *prefent* Life; and that *Wickednefs* is generally attended with *Great Mifery*, even
Here as well as *Hereafter. Evil purfueth Sinners; but to the Righteous, Good shall*
be repaid.

I. I N the *Firft* place: If we confider Mankind *in general*, in the largeft and moft
extenfive View, under the notion of that One Univerfal Community, wherein St *Paul*

SERM confidered them, when he told the *Athenians*, Acts xvii. 26; *God has made of one*
XCXIX. *blood all nations of men, for to dwell on all the Face of the Earth*: Under *This* View, I
fay, it is very evident, that the *Only thing* which diftinguifhes *Men* from the *Wild Beafts
of the Foreft*, that devour each other according to their Strength, and have no Rights
nor Property in any thing; The *only thing* which diftinguifhes *Men* from thefe *Wild
Beafts*, with regard to any True *Happinefs of Life*; is *Religion*, or a *Senfe of Juft and
Right*, and of the Difference of *Moral* Good and Evil. For Reafon, as to *That* part
of it which denotes *Sagacity* only, or *Underftanding*, feparate from all Regard to *Moral*
Obligation; does only enable men, if they be wicked, *more effectually*, and with *greater*
Skill, to *torment* and *deftroy* each other; and to have a *deeper* and *more affecting* and
more *lafting* Senfe of the *Miferies* they endure, than *irrational* Creatures are by their
Nature capable of. It is *Reafon*, in that *Other* refpect alone, as it implies a fenfe of
Moral Obligation, (on which *Religion* is founded;) it is *This alone*, on which depends
all *poffibility of Happinefs* in Humane Life; And to the *degree of Influence* which *This*
has in the world, the Happinefs Mankind enjoys above the *Wild Beafts of the Field*,
is always exactly *proportionate*. Did not therefore the Paffions, the Ambition, the
Covetoufnefs, and other the like unnatural Vices of corrupt Minds, hinder this *Reafon* and *Moral Underftanding*, which is the peculiar Excellency and Glory of Mankind,
from producing its natural and proper Effect in the world; the Earth would even in
this *prefent* time, bating *Mortality* only, be that Scene of univerfal Happinefs, which
God hath promifed fhall take place *hereafter* in the *New Heavens and New Earth*,
wherein dwelleth Righteoufnefs. In the mean time, from this *abftract* View of the
general Nature of Things and of the Confequences which *would be* the natural Refult
of *univerfal Righteoufnefs*; it is apparent enough, to *what* Originals, to *what* Caufes and
Principles, the *various degrees and proportions* of *Happinefs and Mifery*, which are
found in the prefent mixt and confufed ftate of things, are juftly to be afcribed.

II. *Secondly*, If we confider Mankind in a fomewhat *lefs general View*; not in the
univerfal abftract Notion, but in their more reftrained political Capacity, as formed
into particular diftinct *Nations* and *Governments*: Under *This View* alfo it is no lefs
evident, that the only poffible Foundation of true and lafting Happinefs to any *Nation* or *People*, as fuch; is the Practice of *Righteoufnefs* and *True Virtue*. I infift not
at prefent, in This Argument, upon the extraordinary *Bleffings* which the *Providence
of God* thinks fit at any time to pour down in a peculiar manner upon a Religious Nation; or the *Judgments* wherewith he fometimes punifhes a degenerate people, *turning
a fruitful Land into Barrennefs, for the Wickednefs of them that dwell therein*: But what
I obferve, is, that in the *natural Tendency*, in the *regular and proper Confequence of
men's own Behaviour*; *Righteoufnefs* (as *Solomon* expreffes it) *exalteth a Nation, but
Sin is a Reproach to any people*. In proportion as *Juftice*, and *Order*, and *Truth*,
and *Fidelity* prevail; creating mutual Love and Good-will, mutual Truft and Confidence among men; which are the great Bands of Peace and Unity: In the *fame*
proportion is the *Happinefs* of the Society, and the Welfare of the Publick evidently
fecured.

WHEN *Magiftrates* rule in the Fear of God; looking upon themfelves as *fent by
Him for the Punifhment of Evil doers, and for the Praife of them that do well*; making
ufe of all the Influence and Authority they are invefted with, to promote Virtue, Righteoufnefs, and Good Manners among men: When *Laws* are *made* with one continued
View to the Good of the Publick; and *executed* with Diligence, Equity, and Fidelity:
When perfons in *all the relative* ftations of Life, perform faithfully and confcientioufly
the Duty of the refpective Stations wherein they are placed: When Bargains are regularly *contracted* upon Terms of *equitable* confideration, and *executed* with *Juftice* and
punctual *Veracity*: When in *every Exigence of common Life*, mutual *Truft and Confi-

I   *dence*,

dence, univerfal *Benevolence and Good-will*, are both the *Spring* or *Motive*, and the **S E R M.** *Rule* or *Meafure* of Action: There is no one fo abfurd as not to fee, that there hence **XCXIX.** arifes, in *neceffary*, in *evident*, in *immediate* confequence, an *Image* of Publick Happinefs, the moft *Lovely* that the Mind of Man can poffibly be prefented with. An *Image* indeed *only*, which the *Imagination* may contemplate; but which, in this prefent corrupt world, can never poffibly have a *Reality* to anfwer it. Yet it fhows abundantly the *Truth* of the Propofition I was to prove: Becaufe whatever is, in its *complete Idea*, of *perfect* Excellency; is by neceffary confequence, in *every degree* of its *Reality*, of *proportionably* good Effect. *So far* therefore as Juftice and Charity, and univerfal Virtue, prevails and is practifed in Any Nation or Community; *fo far* will That Community find thofe good Effects, which, were men's *Virtue perfect*, would be *perfect Felicity*. On the contrary: *So far* as Injuftice, Tyranny, Fraud, Luxury, and other Vices, are encouraged in Any Society of men; *fo far* will That Society feel certain degrees of thofe pernicious Effects, which, where Vice and Corruption arife univerfally to their higheft Pitch, do unavoidably end in Total Deftruction. The *only* poffible *Delufion* therefore, by which men are continually tempted into unrighteous Practices, notwithftanding the *evident* pernicioufnefs of fuch Practice in its moft naturally confequent Effects; is their fondly and unreafonably imagining, that, what is undeniably *ruinous* to the *Whole*, may yet to *Themfelves in particular* be *Advantagious*. And This I call a *Delufion*; not only upon account of the *Future Judgment*, which falls not within the compafs of my prefent Argument; but it is a *mere Delufion*, generally fpeaking, with refpect to the real and fubftantial Advantages even of this *prefent* Life. For, befides that whatever is in its natural confequence pernicious to the *Publick*, muft probably *by that very means*, in the *courfe of things*, bring a due Punifhment upon the *particular Offenders* themfelves; It is moreover ftill further true, without taking in *any* confideration of the Publick *at all*; it is, I fay, ftill further true in the

III. *Third* place, That if we confider men *fingly*, every one in his mere *private perfonal capacity*; ftill the only poffible Foundation of real and lafting Happinefs to a man even in *That View*, (always excepting, as I before faid, the cafe of Perfecution,) is the Practice of Righteoufnefs, Charity, Temperance, and univerfal Virtue. *Evil purfueth Sinners; but to the Righteous, Good fhall be repaid.* The Truth of the Propofition, will moft clearly appear in the *Particulars*.

THE *Firft Ground* and moft neceffary Ingredient of *every* Enjoyment in Life, and *without which* there can be no Relifh of any *other* Enjoyment whatfoever, is *Health*. Now though God *has* indeed made *all* men mortal; and the *Beft* are fubject to *Infirmities and Difeafes*, and the moft *vicious* feem *fometimes* almoft *entirely* to *efcape* the natural confequences of their Vices; yet *particular Inftances*, alter not the *general Truth* of Things; and *Virtue*, upon the *whole*, has undeniably the *Advantage* in this *firft Foundation* of Temporal Happinefs. For *Sobriety and Temperance* certainly caufe *no* Diftempers, and *Debauchery* is notorioufly the Caufe of *Many*. With all juftnefs therefore, are thofe general Declarations of Wifdom in Scripture, *My Son, forget not my* Prov. iii. 1, *Law, but let thy Heart keep my Commandments; For Length of days and long Life,* ver. 7. *fhall they add to thee. Fear the Lord, and depart from Evil; it fhall be Health to thy Navel, and Marrow to thy Bones. Length of days is in her right hand; fhe is a Tree* 16. *of Life, to them that lay hold upon her.* And on the contrary, concerning *Debauchery,* 18. Prov. vii. 26: *She has caft down many wounded, yea, many young men have been flain by her: Her houfe is the way to Hell,* (that is, to the Grave untimely,) *going down to the chambers of Death.*

THE cafe is the very fame likewife with regard to the *External* Advantages of Life; fuch as are *Riches, Honour, Reputation,* and the like. It cannot indeed be denied, but that by *Oppreffion* and *Violence*, by *Unrighteoufnefs* and *Corruption*, by *Deceit*

and

SERM.
XCXIX.
and *Fraud*, immenfe *Riches* have been fometimes obtained, and feemingly a very great Superiority over the reft of Mankind. But if it be impartially confidered, *how fmall a number in proportion*, have ever *fucceeded* in This manner; *how* many have been *defeated* and *blafted* in the *Attempt*, before they could at all gain their Point; how *little*, how *uncertain*, how *vexatious*, how *interrupted* the *Enjoyment* has been, of thofe who have in This method had the greateft and moft remarkable Succefs; and, after all, how frequently, and in how fhort a time the higheft Profperity of This kind has terminated in the heavieft Ruin; it will undeniably appear, that the *moderate proportion* of the good things of life, *gained* ufually by Frugality, Induftry, Honefty, and Integrity; *enjoyed* with Temperance, Contentment, and Security; and, through the Bleffing of God, *generally*, (or at leaft *much more often* than the Wages of Unrighte-oufnefs,) *continuing permanent*; are really and truly, in a right Computation and Ef-timate, even according to this *prefent World*, the moft Subftantial Riches. So that it is with great Truth, that *Solomon* affirms concerning *Virtue and Integrity* under the Name of *Wifdom*, Prov. iii. 14; *The Merchandife of it is better than the Merchandife of Silver, and the Gain thereof than fine Gold: She is more precious than Rubies; and all the things thou canft defire, are not to be compared to her: Length of days are in her right hand, and in her left hand Riches and Honour.* Nor is it without particular rea-fon, that he here mentions *Honour* diftinctly, as well as *Riches*. For though, with regard to *Honour alfo* as well as Riches, it *is* indeed undeniably *true*, that by *unrighte-ous, fraudulent, and corrupt* Practices, the *Higheft Honours and Dignities in the World* have *Sometimes* been attained to: yet whoever impartially confiders upon the whole, the *Precipices* upon which unrighteous Grandeur ftands; and compares it with that va-luable and *Lafting Efteem* in the Eyes of the Beft and Wifeft part of Mankind, which is built upon the folid Foundation of Real and True Worth; will find, that it is in moft perfect agreement with the *Nature and Reafon of Things*, that the *Scripture* de-clares that *the Righteous is more excellent than his Neighbour*; that *the Righteous fhall be had in everlafting Remembrance*; that *the Memory of the Juft is Bleffed, but the Name of the Wicked fhall rot*; that the Wicked *are exalted for a little while, but are gone and brought low; they are taken out of the way,——and cut off as the Tops of the Ears of Corn*; Job xxiv. 24. And therefore the Advice of *Solomon* is entirely well-grounded; *Prov.* iii. 3: *Let not Mercy and Truth forfake thee; bind them about thy Neck, write them upon the Table of thine Heart; So fhalt thou find Favour and good Underftanding, in the fight of God and Man.*

Prov. xiii. 26.
Pf. cxii. 6.
Prov. x. 7.

THERE is *One Particular* ftill behind, which contributes *more* to any man's Hap-pinefs even in this *prefent* Life, than *all* either *Bodily Enjoyments*, or *External Affluence of Wealth and Honours*; And That is, *Inward Peace and Satisfaction in his Own Mind*. Now in *This* Particular, there is *no Pretence* of Comparifon, between the Righteous and the Wicked. *Here*, Virtue triumphs abfolutely without Controul; and has *no Competitor*, to fhare or to conteft with it the Enjoyment of the moft valuable and moft lafting Pleafures of Life. The cafe of *Perfecution* itfelf, needs not *here* to be excepted. Nay, even the *Falfe* Coin, the very *Delufion*, the *imaginary* Satisfaction of the *mereft Enthufiafm*, has *in This refpect* the Advantage over the *greateft Pleafures of Unrighteoufnefs*. How much *more*, when the *Peace and Satisfaction of Mind* is built upon the moft *folid Foundation*, upon the moft *Rational and Real Grounds*! when it is founded upon a Senfe, of having done what, in *itfelf*, abfolutely in the *Nature* and *Reafon* of Things, is *juft and fit and right*! what, by *proper and natural confequence*, tends to the *Benefit of Mankind*, to the *Happinefs of the whole Creation*! what renders a man as certainly *acceptable* and *well-pleafing* unto God, as it is certain the World is at all governed by fuch a *Wife, Juft*, and *Good Being*! and what, confequently, in fhe laft place, gives a man a *reafonable and well-grounded* Expectation of being *happy*

hereafter,

hereafter, when the Enjoyments of *This World* shall be no more! This is indeed, in the S E R M. Sense of our Saviour's Parable, a *Pearl* of *great Price*; justly and highly magnified in   XCIX. numerous Expressions of Scripture. *Mark the perfect man, and behold the upright; for the end of that man, is peace*; Pf. xxxvii. 38. *Light is sown for the righteous, and joyful Gladness for them that are upright in heart*, xcvii. 11. *Great Peace have they that Love thy Law, and nothing shall offend them*, cxix. 165. *Her ways are ways of Pleasantness, and all her paths are Peace*, Prov. iii. 17. *The work of Righteousness, is Peace, and the effect of Righteousness, Quietness and Assurance for ever*, If. xxxii. 17. *The wicked is driven away in his Wickedness, but the Righteous hath Hope in his Death*, Prov. xiv. 32. It is true; sometimes *very pious* and *good* persons, have been extremely afflicted with Trouble of Mind: But *This Trouble* has never been the *Effect* of *Virtue*; and can with no more Justice be put to the Account of it, than Weeds which spring up among the choicest Corn, can be said to proceed from the good Seed which was sown. *This Trouble* is always owing, either to some mistaken Notion of the Perfections of God, to some ill-grounded Fear, to some implanted Prejudice of Superstition, or to a real Sense of some past Sins; and therefore never *arises from*, but is only to be *cured by*, a *right understanding* of the *Nature and Effects* of True *Virtue*. In like manner abandoned and debauched persons, on the *other* side, seem indeed sometimes for a season, to have *full Ease* and Satisfaction in their Folly: But *This Ease*, never is the *Acquiescence of Reason*: It is the *Stupidity* only, of a *Lethargy* or *Mortification*: Not at all a *Freedom* from the *Disease*, but merely a *Senselesness* of the *present Destruction*. Sooner or later, *Reason will* be heard; and *Truth will* force itself upon them. *For, what is the Hope of the Hypocrite, when God taketh away his Soul?* Job. xxvii. 8. I speak not here of the *Punishments* in a *future* State, but of the *Just Apprehensions* which attend Wickedness in the *present*. *The Spirit of a man will sustain his infirmity, but a wounded Spirit who can bear?* Prov. xviii. 14. And *If.* lvii. 20; *The Wicked are like the troubled Sea, when it cannot rest, whose Waters cast up mire and dirt: There is no Peace, saith my God, to the Wicked.*

S E R M O N C.

The Character of oppreſſive Power in Religion.

[Preached on the 5th of November.]

D A N. VII. 23.

Which ſhall be diverſe from all Kingdoms, and ſhall devour the whole Earth, and ſhall tread it down, and break it in pieces.

SERM. **M**Y Deſign in This Place, is not to enter into a *particular* Interpretation
C. of the Prophetick Language; much leſs to propoſe any uncertain Conjec-
tures, concerning the Times and the *Seaſons* which the Almighty has put in
his own Power; but to conſider only a *general Character*, which runs through a *long
Series* of Prophecy both in the Old Teſtament and in the New, of a certain *great
Power*, formidable and laſting, of large *Extent* and of long *Duration*, and, in its
Nature and *Kind*, different from all *Other* Powers and Kingdoms in the World. The
Character is ſuch, as ſhows plainly one principal *End* and *Deſign* of the Prophecy
to be This; to give men repeated Warnings to take great Heed, that they neither
fall (if poſſible) under the tyrannical Oppreſſion of this dreadful Power, nor Themſelves have any Share in exerciſing it over Others.

T H E *Character* or *Deſcription* given by the *Prophet*, of this *ſingular* and *extraor-*
ch vii. 21. *dinary* Power, is in the following Words. He ſhall *make War with the Saints, and*
ver. 25. *prevail againſt them: And he ſhall ſpeak great Words againſt the moſt High, and ſhall*
ver. 26, 27. *wear out the Saints of the moſt High, and think to change Times and Laws; And they*
ch. xi. 36, &c. *ſhall be given into his hand for a long Seaſon, even till the Judgment ſhall ſit. He
ſhall exalt himſelf, and magnify himſelf above every God, and ſhall ſpeak marvellous
things againſt the God of Gods: —— Neither ſhall he regard the God of his Fathers,
—— for he ſhall magnify himſelf above All; —— and ſhall divide the Land for
Gain.*

F R O M this *deſcription* given by the Prophet *Daniel*, is plainly taken the *character*
2 Theſſ. ii. 3, St *Paul* ſets forth, of a *Man of Sin to be revealed, the Son of Perdition: Who oppoſeth*
&c. *and exalteth himſelf above all that is called God, or that is worſhipped: So that He, as
God, ſitteth in the Temple of God, ſhewing himſelf that he is God: —— Whoſe Coming
is after the working of Satan, with all Power, and Signs, and Lying Wonders, and*
1 Tim. iv. 1, *with all Deceivableneſs of Unrighteouſneſs: Teaching men to give heed to ſeducing Spi-*
3. *rits, and doctrines of * Devils: —— Forbidding to marry, and commanding to abſtain*
* Δαιμονίων, *from Meats, which God hath created to be received with thankſgiving, of them which*
Souls departed, *believe, and know the Truth.*
Saints.

T H E

THE ſame character is likewiſe evidently intended by St *John*, when he prophecies of a *wild Beaſt*, or *Tyrannical Power*, to whom was given *Great Authority*, and *a Mouth ſpeaking Great things, and Blaſphemies: and he opened his Mouth in Blaſphemy againſt God: And it was given unto him to make War with the Saints, and to overcome them: And Power was given him over all Kindreds and Tongues and Nations; and all that dwell upon the Earth ſhall worſhip him.* —— *And he* —— *doth great Wonders,* —— *and Deceiveth them that dwell on the Earth, by the Means of thoſe Miracles that he had Power to do.* And the *Kings* of the Earth *have one Mind, and ſhall give their Power and Strength unto the Beaſt;* —— *even Peoples and Multitudes and Nations and Tongues.* —— *For God hath put in their Hearts* [in the Hearts of the Kings of the Earth] *to fulfil his Will, and to agree, and give their Kingdom unto the Beaſt, until the Words of God ſhall be fulfilled.* The Name of the Perſon, in whoſe hands the *Reins* or *Principal Direction* of the *Exerciſe* of this Power is lodged, is *Myſtery, Babylon the Great, the Mother of Harlots, and Abominations of the Earth: With whom the Kings of the Earth have committed Fornication,* (that is, have been led into idolatrous Practices,) *and the Inhabiters of the Earth have been made drunk with the Wine of her Fornication: And She herſelf is drunken with the Blood of the Saints, and with the Blood of the Martyrs of Jeſus:* And *by her Sorceries* (that is, artificial Methods of making men *Religious* without true Virtue,) *by her Sorceries are all Nations deceived: And in Her is found the Blood of Prophets, and of Saints, and of all that are ſlain upon the Earth.* And This Perſon, (the *political* Perſon,) to whom theſe Titles and Characters belong, is *That Great City,* Rev. xvii. 18, ſtanding *upon ſeven Mountains,* ver. 9, *which Reigneth over the Kings of the Earth.*

IT is hardly poſſible for any one carefully to read theſe Texts, as they lie in Scripture; but he muſt immediately apprehend, if he has any hiſtorical Knowledge of the State of the World, for many paſt Ages, that This Deſcription was either *intended* to be a prediction of That tyrannical Power, which *Popery* in its moſt flouriſhing times eſtabliſhed in the World; or at leaſt that it is as exact and complete a Picture of it, as could poſſibly have been drawn even *after* the Event. *Oppreſſive Powers* there *have been Many* in the World, by the righteous Judgment of God, both *Great and Laſting:* But *This* has been after a moſt remarkable and wonderful manner, in its whole *Nature* and *Kind, different* from all *Other Powers* wherewith men ever were oppreſſed. According to the deſcription given in my Text: *It ſhall be diverſe from all Kingdoms, and ſhall devour the Whole Earth, and ſhall tread it down, and break it in pieces.*

THE *Peculiarities,* wherein This Great Oppreſſive Power *differs* from all other Tyrannies which have been ſet up among men; and is *diverſe from all Kingdoms,* which have at any time *devoured the whole Earth;* are principally Theſe which follow.

1. IT is a *Religious* Tyranny; a Power ſitting in the Seat and Temple of *God. Other* Tyrannies, founded *originally* in *Force,* and in the *Power* of the *Sword;* have indeed frequently made uſe of Pretences of *Religion,* to ſupport themſelves *occaſionally;* and no leſs frequently *laid aſide* thoſe Pretences again, when they had no further occaſion for them. But *This* is a Tyranny, founded *originally* upon *mere* matters of *Religion;* and carried on through its *whole* Progreſs, to the utmoſt length of an univerſal arbitrary Dominion, under the Name and Title ſtill of a *merely Spiritual* Authority. The Church of *Rome* claims to be itſelf the *whole,* the *univerſal* Church of God; and to be inveſted with a *Power,* which indeed the *real univerſal* Church has *no* pretence to, even a Plenitude of *Divine Power.* By virtue of this Power, they have taken upon themſelves to *change Laws and Times;* to eſtabliſh what new *Doctrines* and *Practices*

Rev. xiii. 2, 5, 6, 7, 8, 12, 13, 14, 16, 17.

ch. xvii. 13, 15, 17.

ver. 3, 7.
ver. 5.
ver. 2.

ver. 6.

ch. xviii. 23, 24.

S E R M.
C.

tices they pleaſed, under the name of Religion ; *forbidding to marry, and commanding to abſtain from Meats which God hath created to be received with Thankſgiving.* Deſtroying men's plain and natural Notions of *God,* and of his *Worſhip* ; and thereby undermining and making unintelligible the very *Foundation* of all Religion. Introducing *new, ſuperſtitious* and *Idolatrous Objects* of Worſhip ; the *Elements* in the *Sacrament* ; and the *Mother of Chriſt,* whom (by a *profane* and *blaſphemous* ambiguity) they affect to ſtile the *Mother of God* ; and even *Images, Pictures,* and *Statues* repreſenting her. *Giving heed to ſeducing Spirits, and Doctrines of Dæmons* ; Doctrines, concerning the *Spirits of Saints departed* ; and of *Saints,* who were *no Saints,* but very *Wicked men* ; and of *Saints,* who *never lived* nor had any *Being at all,* but in the imaginations of deluded men ; invoking them, as *Mediators* and *authoritative Interceſſors* ; as inveſted with *miraculous Powers,* to *protect Men, Cities* and *Nations* ; and as having in the *Court of Heaven a corrupt Intereſt,* to *ſkreen* their Devotees, even the moſt *abandoned Sinners,* from the *Wrath of him that ſitteth upon the Throne,* from the Sentence *of the Righteous Judge of the whole Earth :* To the utter Subverſion of all *real religion and virtue,* and turning into Ridicule the *eſſential and unalterable* Difference of *Good and Evil,* and the *Eternal Laws of God and Nature* ; which are *more immoveable,* than the Foundations of Heaven and Earth. For, to *diſpenſe* with *Morality,* and to indulge men in certain ſtated *Equivalents* of *Ceremony,* in the ſtead of *real Virtue* and *Amendment of Manners* ; is a Power, which even *God himſelf* has

2 Tim. iii. 13.

never claimed ; and the doing of which, would be, (as the Apoſtle expreſſes it) to *deny himſelf :* It would be a *changing* of his *unchangeable* Nature, and making himſelf to *be* what he *is not.* Yet He who ſtiles himſelf *The Vicar of Chriſt,* has often claimed to Himſelf *This* Power ; and, in *ſome* Ages of the Church, has carried it ſo far, as even ſolemnly to *abſolve* men from the Obligation of juſt and reaſonable Compacts, and thoſe too made and confirmed upon Oath ; merely to ſet them at liberty to be guilty of the moſt unjuſt and violent Oppreſſions, conſiſtently with being very pious and Religious perſons. What is This, but *opening his Mouth in Blaſphemy againſt God,* and *ſpeaking great Words againſt the moſt High?* That is ; Not in the way of *profeſſing Atheiſm,* or openly *defying* the *Name* of *Religion* ; but by turning *Religion itſelf* into *Superſtition* and *Wickedneſs.*

A N D in order the more effectually to ſupport this abſurd and extravagant Power; the Church of *Rome* has, by the Eſtabliſhment of its New Doctrines and Practices, *fenced* itſelf *in,* and excluded abſolutely out of Communion all Chriſtians who are not willing to *make void the Commandments of God through theſe Traditions of Men.* By which means, they have formed a violent *Schiſm* ; ſeparating and dividing themſelves totally from all Chriſtians, who deſire to *hold faſt* That *Form of ſound words,* that Doctrine which *was once delivered unto the Saints* by Chriſt and his Apoſtles, and which is *now* conveyed down to *us* in the Sacred Writings : And then they confidently reproach all thoſe with the name of *Schiſmaticks,* who dare not join with them in this their *Great Schiſm.* Which is exactly the ſame thing, as if, in a *Civil* Government, a private Corporation ſhould make *By-laws* contrary to the Laws of the Country ; and then confidently caſt the reproachful name of Traitors upon all the reſt of their Fellow-Subjects, who are not willing to involve themſelves in the guilt of real Rebellion by ſubmitting to thoſe illegal By-laws.

I N conſequence of this *Great Separation,* by which the Church of *Rome* has thus *hedged* itſelf *in,* and formed itſelf into a *Sect,* excluſive of and deſtructive to all ſuch as deſire to obey *God rather than Men* ; they have in all places, where-ever they have had Power, openly ſet themſelves to deſtroy and extirpate, by all the Methods of Violence and Cruelty, all who would not *fall down and worſhip* this *Image which they*

have

have ſet up. They have *made War with the Saints*, and *prevailed againſt them*, and worn them out. They have, by Courts of *Inquiſition*, made it unſpeakably more penal to differ from them in any point of doctrine of mere humane invention, than to have been guilty of the moſt enormous Vices and Immoralities, in breach of the Eternal Laws of God. And whereas in all *Civil Governments*, where-ever there are Any Remains of *Humanity*, all Laws concerning Capital Crimes are ſo framed, as that it may be more poſſible for a *guilty* perſon to *eſcape*, than that an *Innocent* one ſhould *ſuffer*; in *This* Kingdom, on the contrary, *diverſe from all Kingdoms*, the Principle is; that *Millions*, not only of *Innocent* perſons, but even of the *Beſt* and moſt *Virtuous* men, ought rather to be expoſed to the extremeſt miſery, and to Puniſhments cruel above the worſt of Malefactors; than that any of *Their Doctrines*, however contrary to All *Senſe* and *Reaſon*, ſhould be permitted to be *examined* and *debated* whether they be true or no.

2. ANOTHER Inſtance, wherein This Great oppreſſive Power *differs* from other Tyrannies; is, that it has been raiſed and kept up, not by *Force* only, but by *Sorceries* and *Lying Wonders* peculiar to itſelf. By *Signs* and *Wonders* and Lying *Miracles*, which the Scripture calls the *deceivableneſs of Unrighteouſneſs*; by *Theſe* have they impoſed upon the *ignorant* and *credulous*. By numberleſs artificial Methods of making men very *Religious* without Any *Virtue*, which are what the Scripture calls *Sorceries*; by *Theſe* have they drawn away the *Superſtitious* and *Devout*. By eſtabliſhing a political Kingdom of Religion, *diffuſed* over many Nations, *independent* upon every Government, and yet at the ſame time cloſely and ſtrongly *united* within itſelf, under the uniform direction of *One* foreign Power; by *This* have they gradually prevailed upon *the Kings of the Earth to have one Mind*, and to give up *their Kingdom*, their *Power and Strength, unto the Beaſt*,——— even *Peoples and Multitudes and Nations and Tongues* Which laſt Circumſtance, points out to us ſtill further, a

3. THIRD Inſtance, wherein this Great Oppreſſive Power *differs* from other Tyrannies: And *That* is, that it is a Tyranny ſet up over even *Remote* Princes, over *all Kindreds and Tongues and Nations*; a Tyranny *ruling over the Kings of the Earth*, ruling in Places where it never had the leaſt pretence of any *Civil Power* or *Authority* whatſoever. This is what the Scripture calls, *exalting himſelf above all that is called God*; above all *Magiſtracy*, *Authority*, or *Dominion*, that God ever inſtituted. Diſpoſing arbitrarily of Kingdoms: abſolving Subjects from their *Allegiance*, from all Obligation to obey the *Laws* of their Country: And cauſing Kings and People, even whole Nations, to be maſſacred, by ſecret Plots or by open Violences.

THIS is the Deſcription and Character given in the *prophetick* parts of the inſpired Writings, of a great and *potent* Apoſtacy, which was largely and very diſtinctly foretold ſhould happen in the latter Ages of the Church. And the *Particularities*, wherein this Tyranny was to be *diverſe from all Kingdoms* that ever *devoured the whole Earth*, are ſo *ſingular* and *remarkable*; that it is hardly poſſible for any man to miſtake in judging, to *Whom* the Characters belong. What remains therefore, is to draw ſome *Obſervations* from what has been ſaid, proper upon the *preſent* Occaſion. And

Firſt, WHEN St *John* ſaw this ſtrange tyrannical Power repreſented to him in Prophecy, whilſt as yet there was no ſuch Power in being; when he ſaw it repreſented to him under the ſimilitude of a *Woman* of fornications, that is, in Scripture-language, an idolatrous Church; riding upon *peoples and multitudes and nations and tongues*, and domineering over the *Kings* of the Earth; *When I ſaw her*, ſays he, *I wondered with great Admiration*, Rev. xvii. 6. And even *after* the Event, whoſoever has Any *Notion* what *Virtue* or *Religion* is, muſt *ſtill* of neceſſity *wonder with great Admiration*,

Margin notes:
S E R M. C.

2 Th. ii. 9, 10.

Rev. xviii. 23.

Rev. xvii. 13, 15, 17.

Rev. xiii. 7.

2 Th. ii. 4.

Rev. xvii. 15.

SERM.   how it was ever poſſible that the *Name of Religion* ſhould be ſo prodigiouſly abuſed·
C.   *Religion* is not an *arbitrary* or *imaginary* thing, but founded upon eternal *Truth* and
Right, or it never can have any Foundation at all. *Religion* is the Practice of *Virtue*, proceeding from a regard to *God the Judge of All*, the all-ſeeing and unerring
Judge. *Good and Evil* are neceſſarily, eſſentially, and unalterably what they are:
And God neceſſarily ſees and judges them to be ſo. The *Worſhip of God*, and the
univerſal *Love of our Neighbour*, are evidently the Perfection of Moral *Good*; and the
contrary to theſe, the greateſt Moral *Evil*. Whatever *Forms* or *Ceremonies* therefore
have at any time been inſtituted either of *God* or *Good Men*, they have always been entirely ſubſervient to theſe *Moral Duties:* For *Moral Duties*, are the *End* and laſt Aim
of *All Religion*, of all Religion both *natural and revealed*. What then muſt be thought
of a Religion, filled with *Opinions* contrary to the neceſſary *Truth* and *Nature* of
things; over-run with *idolatrous Practices*, in the Worſhip of *God*; and ſupported by
Wars, Perſecutions, Maſſacres; by open *Violences*, and ſecret *Plots*; oppoſite, in the
moſt barbarous and cruel manner, to the whole Spirit of that great Duty of *Love and*
Matt. v. 16. *Charity* towards *Men! Ye ſhall know them by their Fruits*, ſaid our Saviour; admoniſhing his Diſciples, to guard themſelves againſt *Falſe Prophets*. And when he warn-
Matt. x. 17. ed them to *beware of Men*; he did not mean only of *Heathen Perſecutors*, but of *the*
ver. 21.   *Brother* alſo *delivering up the Brother to Death*.

    Secondly; From what has been ſaid, we may learn how ſincerely Thankful we
ought to be, for the happy Deliverance of the King and the Three Eſtates of this Realm,
from the bloody intended Maſſacre by *Gun-Powder*, which was to have been effected
as upon *This* Day.

    Thirdly; From hence alſo we may learn to ſet a juſt Value upon the Greatneſs of
that *Second* Deliverance, which God worked for us *again* as upon *This* Day, by the
Happy Arrival of his late Majeſty King *William*. They who rightly apprehend how
great a Calamity it is, to be deprived of all Uſe of Reaſon and Conſcience: to be obliged to profeſs in Belief the moſt abſurd Impoſſibilities, and to comply in Practice
with the groſſeſt Idolatries; and this under the Penalty of the moſt barbarous and
inhumane Cruelties: All men, I ſay, who have a juſt Senſe of the Dreadfulneſs
Θλίψεως τῆς of this Calamity, which is what the Scripture calls *The great Tribulation*, and per-
μεγάλης, petually compares it to the ancient Captivity of God's people in *Babylon*; nay, ſtiles
Rev. vii. 14. This, in compariſon of the former, by the name of *Babylon the Great*; will not
fail to be very ſincerely Thankful, for the Deliverance of his Country from this ſevereſt of all Temporal Judgments; and very fearful of taking any even remote Step,
that may tend towards bringing back ſo great a Deſtruction; and very ſollicitous to
make the Government always eaſy in the Hands of ſuch Princes, as are by Principle
and by Inclination deſirous to preſerve all the Civil and Religious Rights of the
Community.

    Fourthly; The *Laſt* Inference I ſhall draw from what has been ſaid, is; that we who
profeſs the Reformed Religion, and, upon ſtated Solemnities, pretend to return hearty
Thanks to God for the wonderful preſervations of it amongſt us; ought above all things
to avoid *thoſe corrupt Practices*, for which we ſo juſtly condemn the Church of *Rome*.
Proteſtants muſt not *hate* the perſons of *Roman-Catholicks*; nor uncharitably judge every
private perſon among them to have That Malignity of Spirit, on which the *publick*
Dominion of their Church, is founded. *Proteſtants*, I ſay, muſt not hate the perſons
of *Roman Catholicks*, or of any others who differ from them: Much leſs ought we to
offer them any Injury, Violence, or Wrong: But, on the contrary, we ought to endeavour to convince them of their Errors, by *Strength* of *Reaſon*, and by *Gentleneſs* of
Behaviour. If a man's Practice be *vicious* and *injurious* to his Fellow-creatures; what

                                                      Religion

Religion he *profeſſes,* imports little more to his *Moral* character than the *Shape* or the S E R M.
Colour of his *Cloaths.* What matters it in point of *Religion,* to deteſt the *Violences* C.
and Perſecutions of *Rome*; if men ſtill continue Lovers of *Violence* and *Contention?*
What matters it in point of *Truth,* to have rejected the *unintelligible Doctrines* of *Rome*;
if men ſtill continue fond of *unintelligible Notions?* What matters it in point of *Virtue*
and real *Goodneſs,* to have departed from the *Superſtitious Practices* of *Rome*; if men
will ſtill be fond of *Superſtitious Practices?* The *Religion of Chriſt* conſiſts, in the
Worſhip and Love and Imitation of *God,* and in univerſal Charity and Good-Will towards *Men.* The One of theſe is *the Firſt and great Commandment*; and the Other,
ſays our Lord, *is like unto it :* And on *Both* of them, depend *the Law and the Prophets,*
and the Perfection of the *Goſpel of Chriſt.* If *Proteſtants* at any time depart from This
Principle, they depart from their Profeſſion: And whenſoever they do ſo, they juſtly
provoke God to deliver them up again into That Darkneſs, from whence they have
eſcaped; and into the Power of that Tyranny from which they have often been ſo
marvellouſly delivered.

S E R M O N CI.

Providential Deliverances from Slavery.

[Preached on the 5th of November.]

P S A L. XXXIII. 10.

The Lord bringeth the Counſel of the Heathen to nought; he maketh the
Devices of the People of none Effect.

THIS Pſalm, is a Pſalm of Praiſe and Thankſgiving, upon the Subject of God's S E R M.
works of Creation and Providence; and the royal Author of it, ſeems in his CI.
enumeration of the Works of God, to equal the Wonders of *Providence* with
thoſe of *Creation.* Ver. 6; *By the word of the Lord were the heavens made, and all*
the hoſt of them by the breath of his mouth; he gathereth the waters of the ſea together
as an heap, he layeth up the depth in ſtore-houſes; Let all the earth fear the Lord, let
all the inhabitants of the world ſtand in awe of him; for he ſpake and it was done, he
commanded and it ſtood faſt : The Lord bringeth the counſel of the heathen to nought, he
maketh the devices of the People of none effect.
THE *reaſon why* the Pſalmiſt thus joins the works of Creation and Providence together, as equal Subjects of Praiſe and Thankſgiving, was the many wonderful *Deli-*
verances which God had worked for the nation of the *Jews in general,* and (if this
Pſalm

Pfalm be *his*) for the perfon of *David* in particular; many of which Deliverances were fo extraordinary and remarkable, that they could not poffibly have been brought a-bout, but by the peculiar influence of that divine Providence, which mightily over-rules all things; the Defigns of the Enemies having fometimes been laid with fuch *Secrecy*, and fometimes carried on with fuch *ftrength*, that all Hopes from natural Caufes ceafing, it feemed that no lefs Power, than that, which as it *created*, fo it *governs* all things, could be able to difappoint them. Wherefore the Pfalmift having de-clared the Weaknefs and Infufficiency of all other Caufes, and the Uncertainty of all other Hopes which men ufually depend upon, concludes, ver. 12; *Bleffed is the na-tion whofe God is the Lord, and the people whom he hath chofen for his own inheri-tance.*

Now, excepting fome *few* cafes, wherein God exerted his Almighty Power in plain and undifputed *miracles*; the Deliverances which Providence has worked at feveral times for *this our* Nation from the profeffed Enemies of its Religion and Liberty, have been in no wife inferior to the greateft Deliverances that God ever vouchfafed to the Nation of the *Jews*. We need not fearch for other inftances, nor mention the ma-ny Examples which cannot but offer themfelves to every one's thoughts. The Two great Deliverances which we This Day commemorate, and are met together to return Thanks to God for, are alone abundantly fufficient to make good the Obfervation. For whether we confider the difficulty and fmall probability there was, of preventing the Defigns laid againft our Religion and Liberty; or whether we confider the great-nefs of the Calamities that would have enfued, had thofe Defigns took effect; or the greatnefs of thofe Bleffings, which through the Mercy of God did follow upon their being difappointed; I believe we fhall not meet with any Event in Hiftory, wherein the Providence of God can feem more vifibly to have concerned itfelf, or to have given more evident Marks of its governing and over-ruling all things. Had that fecret Treafon, which was carried on in Darknefs where no Eye faw it, been as fuccefsful as it was fecretly contrived; and the Glory and Flower of the Nation been permitted to fall at once by the black malice of Implacable men; the Reformation of our Reli-gion, and the wife Conftitution of our Government had perifhed together; and what unfpeakable Confufion would have fucceeded that dreadful Blow, no mortal can tell. In like manner, had the later Defigns which have fince been carried on againft this Nation, to fubvert our Laws and extirpate our Religion, been permitted by the un-fearchable Judgment of God to have prevailed and taken effect; we had once again exchanged Religion for Superftition, and well-conftituted Government for Tyranny; and together with Us had perifhed the Liberties of all *Europe*. But though the firft of thefe Attempts was managed with fo much Caution and Secrecy, as feemed to fecure it from being difcovered by any humane Wifdom; and though later Defigns were carried on with fuch advantages of Power, and fuch appearance of Authority, as made the Enemies of the Name of Proteftant, think it impoffible they fhould be difappoint-ed; yet Providence did fo difcover the *one*, as to convince the World that there is no Darknefs nor Shadow of Death where the Workers of Iniquity may hide themfelves: and fo prevented the *others*, by the feafonable Coming of his late Majefty of happy Memory; as to fhow that with God it is all one to fave by Many or by Few; who *breaketh the arm of the wicked, and weakeneth the ftrength of the mighty, and de-livereth the poor from him that is too ftrong for him.*

But it will be proper to fpeak more *diftinctly* and *particularly* of this matter, when we come to apply the *general* Obfervations which I fhall raife from the Text, to the *Special* occafion of our affembling This Day; in fome ufeful and practical Infe-rences from the whole Difcourfe.

The

The Obfervations therefore, which may firft be raifed *in general* from the words, are thefe: *1ft*, That the Providence of God prefides over and governs all things, and has a peculiar Influence upon all the great Events that happen unto Men. *2dly*, That this, as it is obfervable in all the great periods of every particular man's Life, fo it is more efpecially and remarkably true, in refpect of fuch Events, wherein the Fates of whole Nations and Kingdoms are concerned: *The Lord bringeth the counfel of the heathen to nought, he maketh the devices of the people to be of none effect.*

I. *Firft*; The Providence of God prefides over and governs all things, and has a peculiar Influence upon all the *great Events*, that happen unto Men. Upon all the *Great Events*, I fay; not to exclude Providence from regarding even the *fmalleft* things as well as the *greateft*, but becaufe Thefe are eafieft and moft ufeful for *Us* to obferve; and in Thefe the Footfteps of Providence may with more certainty be traced.

There was a certain Sect among the Ancient Philofophers, who though they pretended to believe the Being of God, yet they denied his particular Providence and Infpection over all Events; and the Actions and Contrivances of many who call themfelves Chriftians, however contrary their Profeffion may be, give but too juft occafion to place them in the fame rank. Thefe men thought that the Life of God confifted merely in Reft and doing nothing; and that he had no regard to the Events of Things, or the Actions of men on Earth; but left all to be managed by the Chance or the Fate of Second Caufes: They thought, and fo far indeed very juftly, that God could not but be an infinitely happy Being, perfectly free from all that Care and Labour, that Toil and Anxiety, which makes a great part of the Mifery of humane Life: But muft he therefore be a mere *unactive* Being? Cannot he with the fame Eafe wherewith he *made* the World, a work of infinite Power, Wifdom, and Counfel, *govern* it alfo and prefide over it? Cannot he who at one View fees and obferves all things that are done in the world, concern himfelf for the Benefit and Well-government of his Creatures, without diminifhing from his own infinite Happinefs? efpecially fince Happinefs confifts, not in doing nothing, but in doing good; and infinite Happinefs is nothing elfe, but the perfecteft exercife, of infinite Power, Wifdom, and Goodnefs. To fee and to know all things that are done in the world, is a natural and neceffary Attribute of an Omniprefent Mind; To rule and order all things which are prefent before him, cannot but be infinitely eafy to Almighty Power; and nothing can be more abfurd, than to fuppofe that God being thus neceffarily every-where prefent, and feeing all things, and being thus infinitely able to determine all Events according to his own Will, fhould yet be only a carelefs and unconcerned Beholder of them. It is evident therefore from Reafon, that the Providence of God *can* and *muft* govern and over-rule all things. And that it *actually* and *in fact* does fo, the whole *Hiftory* and *Doctrine* of the Scripture abundantly confirms to us. It fhows us by numberlefs Inftances, that God has not only upon *fpecial* occafions made ufe of the Power of *Miracles* for the Prefervation of the Righteous, or the Deftruction of the Wicked, but that *generally* he governs the Moral World; by providentially directing Natural Caufes and Influences, to effect what he determines fhould be done: That he rewards or punifhes men by wholefome or peftilential Air, by fruitful or barren Seafons; that he promotes or difappoints their Defigns by the uncertain changes of Winds or Weather; that he employs and directs the Influences of Nature to overthrow the moft powerful Armies, to defeat the wifeft Counfels, to determine the Differences of Princes, and the Fates of Men and Kingdoms: That the unfearchable Wifdom of Providence directs and fteers the moft cafual and accidental events, to change the Fortunes of Men, and difappoint the moft proper and natural means of fuccefs; fo that *the race is not to the fwift, nor the battle to the ftrong, neither yet bread to the wife, nor riches to men of underftanding, nor favour to men of fkill*; but that *Time and Chance*, directed by the Providence of God, *happens to

SERM. *them all.* Nay further, the Scripture teaches us, that God not only directs natural Cau-
CI. ſes and over-rules the Actions of men to fulfil his own good pleaſure, but moreover influences men's minds by ſtrange Concurrences of external cauſes, or by other more ſecret and unknown ways, to bring about juſt Events: That he comforts good men and
ſupports them in their Deſigns; that he terrifies bad men with ſtrange Amazements,
to diſcover their own Conſpiracies, and to fall into the Snares which they had ſecretly
laid for others; that *he fruſtrateth the tokens of liars, and maketh diviners mad; turneth
wiſe men backward, and maketh their knowledge fooliſh: that a man's heart deviſeth his
ways, but the Lord directeth his ſteps;* that *there are many devices in the heart of man;
but the counſel of the Lord, That ſhall ſtand:* and that *the heart of the Prince is in the
hand of the Lord; as the rivers of waters, he turneth it whitherſoever he willeth.*

BY theſe and numberleſs other paſſages, illuſtrated with many hiſtorical Examples,
which no man can read the Bible without obſerving, the Scripture aſſures us that the
Providence of God governs and directs the Events of all things. It remains only to
conſider, how this Doctrine agrees with our preſent Experience of things, and is conſiſtent with that fixed courſe of Natural Cauſes, which God ſeems to have eſtabliſhed
in the world. And here indeed lies the great difficulty of all; ſince Men do and cannot but obſerve, that where Miracles are not wrought, God ſuffers the World to be
governed by the natural Operations and Efficacy of Second Cauſes. Moſt things go
on in a regular and ſettled courſe; and diligent men by ſtudying the Nature of things,
and the ordinary Series of Cauſes, have been able in moſt Events to diſcover the Connexion of the Cauſe with the Effect. Hence men of Underſtanding and Induſtry,
foreſee very many Events; and by ordering their Affairs accordingly, ſecure to themſelves in moſt of their Deſigns a great probability of Succeſs. And even where things
do not ſucceed according to the Probabilities of known Cauſes, but are diſappointed or
changed by ſtrange intervening Accidens, or ſudden and unexpected Turns of things;
yet even There it appears generally that the Alteration proceeds from ſome equally natural, though not timely foreſeen cauſe. When *the Race is not won by the Swift,* nor
the Battle by the Strong, as it ought to be in the ordinary courſe of things; yet even in
ſuch caſe men are generally able to diſcover, that the unforeſeen Accidents which altered the courſe of things, and prevented the expected Succeſs, were the Effects of
ſome Natural Cauſes, which ought to have been taken into the Eſtimate, and would,
if men could have attained a perfect knowledge of the whole Natures and Powers of
things, have entirely changed their Expectations of the Succeſs. Thus the Diſcovery of
This Day's wicked Conſpiracy, was owing to a ſtrange ſeries of Accidents, which tho'
utterly impoſſible to be foreſeen by humane Wiſdom, yet, after the Event, appeared
not to have any thing in them abſolutely above the power of Nature: And our Deliverances from later Attempts againſt our Religion and Laws, were not ſtrictly Miracles,
but plainly owing on one hand to the ill management of our Adverſaries, and on the
other hand to the Wiſdom and Conduct of his late Majeſty.

IF then things be acknowledged to be Thus, the Difficulty is, how the Interpoſition
of Providence is reconcileable with this Regularity of the Operations of Natural Cauſes;
and why (as the Scripture plainly determines) we are bound with all Thankfulneſs to
acknowledge the Goodneſs of the Divine Providence in working for us ſuch Deliverances, which yet we do not at the ſame time believe to be properly and ſtrictly miraculous. Now though to This it might perhaps be anſwered (as ſome learned men
have done) that the All-wiſe Creator of the World, when he fixed the preſent Laws
and appointed the conſtant courſe of Nature, foreſaw at the ſame time all the Diſpoſitions and Exigencies of men, and therefore accordingly ſo ordered the ſeries of Natural
Cauſes, as to make the very ſame Proviſion for all theſe occaſions in the original
Conſtitution of things, which he would otherwiſe have done by the miraculous Interpoſition

position of his Providence: Though, I say, it might perhaps silence this Objection, to
say that the Constitution of the Natural World was so settled upon God's Foresight of the Dispositions of the Moral, as that the Justice and Goodness of Providence must equally be acknowledged in all the great Events of Nature, as in miraculous Operations; and this Observation might perhaps be of great use against the Asserters of Fate: For, as it is no objection against the Skill of the *Workman*, to say that every Wheel of a Watch is moved only naturally according to the frame of its parts; so it is no Objection against *Providence*, to say that things are brought about by second Causes, since it is God who is the Author of those Causes: Yet because the Scripture every where plainly teaches that God *actually* interposes in the Government of the World; and because it is a more honourable Notion of God, to suppose him constantly inspecting and ruling all things, than that he should have fixed certain unchangeable Laws of Nature, and then left the World to be governed by them as by Fate; therefore in answer to this Difficulty about the Workings of Providence, it is more reasonable to say, that as God must be acknowledged to have upon some great occasions made *such* Alterations in the visible Course of Nature, as we call *Miracles*; so he does at other times, at least so govern and manage the first Springs of Natural Causes, as to bring about, though without any visible Alterations of Nature, whatever his infinite Wisdom sees fit. And this is so far from being contrary to true Philosophy, or inconsistent with the State of Nature and the regular Appearances of Things, that the best Philosophy that ever yet appeared in the world, has not to this day determined, whether the first Springs of the commonest and most universal Operations of Nature, be moved by some general laws impressed by God on Matter, or whether even in These things he does not continually employ the Offices of intelligent Beings: Or rather, it *has* determined, that God is immediately the Author, even of all those we call *Natural*, as well as of Miraculous Events. For to cause either the Sun or the Earth to move, is plainly an Effect of the same Power, as to cause them to stand still; and the only reason why men usually look upon One as the immediate hand of God, and the Other they fancy is done without Him; is no other but This, that what God does Once, they cannot but acknowledge is done by *Him*; but what He does Always, they therefore childishly think it is not *He* does it at all. But However This be, yet to be sure nothing can be more reasonable than to say, that God, upon whose good pleasure all the Laws and Powers of Nature perpetually depend, does at least in some great Events determine the Influences of Natural Causes to produce such or such particular Effects. Thus much we see God has put even in the Power of *Men*, that by skilful and artificial Application of Causes, they can in many Instances determine the natural Powers of things to produce such Effects, as they would not naturally have produced without that guidance and direction of Art: And nothing can be more absurd, than to imagine that God does less in the Government of the World, than even some of the meanest of his Creatures are able to do. When therefore we see Natural Causes conspire strangely and by a long series to produce some remarkable Event; we have all the reason in the world, to believe that thing brought about, by the peculiar direction of Providence; and to behave ourselves accordingly in our Prayers or Thanksgivings to God. Thus we have all possible reason to believe, that the Wisdom of Providence directed that train of Accidents by which the Great Conspiracy of This Day was discovered: And that the same Wisdom and Power since worked for us those later Deliverances, in consequence of which we still enjoy our Religion and Liberties; and governed the Springs of the first Causes of the Winds and Weather and of numberless other Circumstances of things, on which depended the Success of his late Majesty's Enterprize; in consequence of the Success of which, we still enjoy our Religion

SERM. ligion and Liberty, the happy Effects of that feasonable and neceffary Revolution,
CI. which cannot without the greateft *Ingratitude*, but be acknowledged with all Thank-
fulnefs, to have been the immediate Work and fingular Bleffing of Providence.
For

II. *Secondly*, As this Direction of the firft Springs of Natural Caufes by the Providence of God, is to be obferved and acknowledged in all other confiderable Events; fo
does it more efpecially and remarkably difcover itfelf in the Accomplifhment of fuch
Events, on which the Fates of whole Nations and Kingdoms depend. It muft indeed
be confeffed, as I have already obferved, that the fmalleft things of all, are no lefs truly
Objects of the Care of Providence, than the greateft; that *without our heavenly Father*,
not fo much as *a fparrow falls to the ground*, or *a hair of our head perifhes*: And it
was a very unworthy Notion of God in fome Philofophers to imagine, that whilft he
governed Kingdoms, he could not at the fame time attend to the guidance and direction of fmaller things. But in refpect to *Us*, the Effects of Providence are more *confiderable*, and the Footfteps of it are more eafily traced, and the Events which it produces require greater and more publick Acknowledgments, when the Fates of whole
Nations are therein concerned. There is *one* reafon alfo in the *Nature of things*, why
Providence fhould more vifibly concern itfelf with what whole Nations and People are
interefted in; and That is, that particular Perfons are to have their exact and particular Retributions in a future State; but great Confpiracies, and overflowing Tyrannies,
confidered as fuch and in a Body, muft have their defeat in this world; and National
Bleffings muft of neceffity be Temporal: Not indeed for any neceffity on account of
ftrict *Juftice*; (becaufe *That* may as well be fatisfied in the Life to come;) but for the
publick manifeftation of Providence to the World, and of God's immediate Judgments
in the prefent State.

But the Time will not permit me to enlarge farther on this head. I fhall therefore only apply briefly what has been faid to our prefent Occafion, and fo conclude.

And here I need not detain you with a particular Narrative of the dark Confpiracy
which was defigned to have been executed as upon This Day: I need not aggravate
the incredible Barbaroufnefs of this Attempt, which is not to be parallelled in all the
Hiftories of Time, and which a great many even of the Romifh Communion, have
themfelves been afhamed of and defirous to difown: I need not reprefent the great
Craft and Cunning wherewith this Defign was laid; undifcoverable, as they thought,
by any Wifdom or Chance: *They took crafty counfel againft thy people, and confulted
againft thy hidden ones; they faid, Come, and let us cut them off from being a nation,
that the name of Ifrael may be no more in remembrance*; Pf. lxxxiii. 4. I need not repeat to you with what *Secrefy* this whole matter was carried on; fo that the words of
David are moft fitly applicable to this occafion; Pf. lxiv. 5; *They fhoot in fecret at the
perfect, they encourage themfelves in an evil matter, they commune of laying fnares privily,
they fay, Who fhall fee them?* and *ver.* 6; *They fearch out iniquities, they accomplifh a
diligent fearch; both the inward thought of every one of them, and the heart is deep.*
It would alfo be fuperfluous to give a particular account how this Confpiracy was difcovered; how *God fhot at them fuddenly with a fwift arrow, and their own tongues made
them to fall*; how (as the wife man expreffes a like matter, *Ecclef.* x. 20:) *a Bird
of the air carried the voice, and that which has wings difcovered the matter.* For all
thefe tranfactions have been often fully and lively reprefented to you, and it would
be but tedious to repeat them again.

I Need not likewife enlarge upon the particulars of the *fecond* Deliverance, which
we this Day commemorate. The thing itfelf is ftill frefh in all our Memories; and

every

every one that has *any* juft Senfe of the inhumane Barbarity of the *Popifh* Religion, and of the extreme wickednefs of that great Apoftacy fo largely prophefied of in the New Teftament, cannot but be fenfible of the *Greatnefs* of every efcape from it, being a Deliverance from the worft and moft dreadful Slavery both of body and mind ; together with the *Strangenefs* of the means by which it was brought about, and the *Suddennefs* and *Eafinefs* of its Accomplifhment.

OMITTING therefore to repeat things already fo well known, I fhall chufe rather to conclude my Difcourfe with fome practical Inferences fuitable to the Occafion And

1*ft* ; IF the Providence of God has certainly a peculiar influence over all the great Events that happen to Mankind ; and if the Bleffings and Deliverances which we this day commemorate, carry upon them as vifible characters of that divine Providence, as any that were ever beftowed upon any People ; then ought the expreffions of our Acknowledgments and Thankfgivings to God upon this occafion, to be proportionably great and fervent. That in *the general* the Providence of God has a peculiar Influence over all the great Events that happen to Mankind, I have endeavoured to prove in the foregoing Difcourfe ; and that the Deliverances we this Day commemorate *in particular*, carry upon them as vifible characters of that divine Providence, as any thing lefs than a direct Miracle can poffibly do ; is evident from all the circumftances of their accomplifhment. For if the Strangenefs of Events compared with the ordinary courfe of things ; if the difproportionatenefs of means and caufes to their effects ; if weaknefs triumphing over formidable Strength, and Succeffes unufual like thofe recorded in Scripture ; if the difappointment of the greateft cunning, and infatuation of the profoundeft Politicians ; if the difcovery of the fecreteft and moft cautious Plots, by improbable means, and unaccountable accidents ; if bringing to nought the greateft and beft-laid enterprizes, at the very point of their being put in execution ; if wicked men's infnaring themfelves and blowing up their own defigns, involving themfelves in the Calamities which they defigned for others ; in a word, if *turning wife men backward, and making their knowledge foolifhnefs* ; if confounding *the devices of the crafty, fo that their hands cannot perform their enterprize* ; if taking *the wife in their own craftinefs,* and turning *down the counfel of the froward headlong* ; If all thefe things, I fay, be tokens of Providence interpofing in any great event ; then are This day's Deliverances certainly of that kind. Thus was *Pharaoh* overwhelmed, when he had juft overtaken the Children of *Ifrael* ; Thus did *Haman* perifh, when he had procured a royal decree, and had fixed a time to deftroy the *Jews* ; And thus were numberlefs other defigns, mentioned in Scripture, difappointed by ftrange, and to human Wifdom unaccountable Providences. Let us then ackowledge the hand that worked thefe things for us, and exprefs our acknowledgments in fuitable Thankfgivings : Let us *declare God's works*, that is, publickly glorify his fpecial Providence, and celebrate his adorable perfections difplayed in fuch extraordinary events ; and provoke others to confider and do the fame ; that men may *praife the Lord for his goodnefs, and for his wonderful works to the children of men* ; that they may *offer the Sacrifice of thankfgiving, and declare his works with gladnefs* ; that they may *fpeak the glorious honour of his might, and of his wondrous works* ; that they may *declare the glory of his kingdom, and talk of his terrible acts.* Let us truft and place our Affiance in God, who hath done fo great things for us already whereof we rejoice ; and learn from the confideration of former mercies, to rely upon Providence for Deliverance in future Dangers. Thus the Pfalmift, when he had praifed God for paft Deliverances, faying ; *Bleffed be the Lord, who hath not given us over for a prey into their teeth ; Our foul is efcaped as a bird out of the fnare of the fowler, the fnare is broken and we are efcaped* ; immediately he adds in the next words ; *Our help,* that

SERM. is, our Truſt and Dependance for the future, *is on the name of the Lord, who made*
CI.   *heaven and earth.*

2*dly,* SINCE God hath already vouchſafed This Nation ſo many and great Deliverances from the Attempts of Popiſh Superſtition and Cruelty, we ought to be greatly
careful to prevent the ſpreading of that Superſtition, that we again feel not the Effects
of its Cruelty. That which was ſpoken by *Ezra* upon a like occaſion, may moſt fitly
be ſaid by *Us,* at this time ; *Ezra* ix. 13 ; *After all that is come upon us for our evil
deeds, and for our great treſpaſſes, ſeeing that thou our God haſt puniſhed us leſs than
our iniquities deſerve, and haſt given us ſuch deliverances as theſe ; ſhould we again
break thy commandments, and join in affinity with the people of theſe abominations ; wouldſt
thou not be angry with us till thou hadſt conſumed us, ſo that there ſhould be no remnant
nor eſcaping ?* It highly behoves us therefore to be very vigilant in preventing the
growth of that Superſtition, which this Nation hath already ſo often felt the ill Effects
of ; and to be diligent in endeavouring to reclaim Thoſe who have been ſeduced by
it, or have been unhappily educated in the Prejudices of it. God has indeed by great
Deliverances freed this Nation from the immediate and imminent Dangers of its prevailing Cruelty ; but there are ſtill great Remains of That Superſtition in the Nation ;
and it has by great Induſtry even to This Day been ſo propagated amongſt us, that our
Superiors have almoſt every year been obliged to conſider of new means to prevent it,
and to recommend to all ſuch as have any opportunity, to endeavour heartily the
putting a ſtop to it. The *firſt* means that we ſhould uſe to this purpoſe, is to endeavour
to convince them, with all meekneſs of Temper, that the Doctrines of *Rome,* are not
the Doctrines of Chriſtianity ; and to demonſtrate to them by the Influence it hath
upon our Lives and Practice, that *our* Religion is better than *theirs.* Our very keeping
up the Remembrance of This Day, is a ſufficient Teſtimony, how contrary to the
Spirit of Chriſtianity, and how utterly unjuſtifiable we account that Zeal, which under
pretence of Religion ſubverts even common Humanity, and deſtroys Mens Lives
which Chriſt came into the World to ſave : And nothing can be more proper to convince good and well-meaning perſons of the Error of That way, than to ſhow them
viſibly how much the Principles of the Reformed Religion are more agreeable to the
common Deſign of Religion and to the Spirit of Chriſt, than the Doctrines of *Rome*
are. But above all, the greateſt and moſt effectual means that we can poſſibly uſe to
prevent the growth of Popery and Superſtition, is to be infinitely careful not to run
into that Atheiſm and profane Libertiniſm, which is the contrary extreme to Superſtition. For as unreaſonable Superſtition enſlaves the Minds of men, and makes them ſo
uneaſy under the yoke, that they often fly off into the contrary extreme of Irreligion and
Profaneneſs ; ſo the natural Effect of Profaneneſs, when men ſee the intolerable Conſequences and Miſchiefs of it, is to drive weak Minds into the other extreme of Superſtition. If therefore while we fly from the Superſtition of Popery, we run into
the Contempt of *all* Religion ; that profane Libertiniſm will probably terminate in Popery again.

WHEREFORE 3*dly* and to conclude, If we deſire to have the Bleſſings of thoſe
Deliverances, for which we This Day return our publick Thanks to God, continued
amongſt us ; let us make ourſelves capable and fit to enjoy them, by a holy and worthy Converſation : Let us in Meekneſs and Peace live agreeably to the Laws and to
the Spirit of that Reformed Religion, which God has mercifully reſtored and ſtill continues to us : For it is no advantage to us to be delivered from the tyranny of Superſtition, if we run into the madneſs of Atheiſm and Irreligion. There are not wanting
Enemies, who are yet watchful againſt us ; and the Judgments of God are ſtill abroad
in the Earth. And we have always juſt reaſon to fear, that if we repent not in time,

and

and behave ourſelves worthily under paſt Deliverances, God may yet be forced to try **S E R M.** us with heavier Calamities, than any that have hitherto come upon us. But if we   **CI.** every one heartily ſet about a Reformation ; he that would have ſpared *Sodom* for the ⌇⌇⌇ ſake of *ten* righteous perſons, and *Jeruſalem* for the ſake of any *one* man that had but executed Juſtice and Judgment in it, may be prevailed upon ſtill to avert the Judgments that threaten this our ſinful Nation. But if we cannot be ſo happy as always to obtain Mercy in the Preſervation of our *Country*, yet he that is truly religious ſhall be ſure not to fail of it in the Safety of *himſelf*. Righteous men, ſuch as *Noah, Job,* and *Daniel*, though poſſibly they may not be able to deliver a ſinful City which God has doomed to Deſtruction, yet ſhall not fail to *deliver their own Souls :* And he that ſincerely repents and reforms his Life, ſhall at leaſt have the comfort of attaining *That* Peace, which the World cannot *give*, and which it cannot *take away*.

Now unto him who hath from time to time delivered us from the mercileſs Deſigns of wicked and unreaſonable men ; *who did as upon this day reſcue us from that dreadful Deſtruction which was ready to have ſwallowed us up* ; *and who ſtill* brings to light the hidden things of Darkneſs, *and preſerves our Religion and Rights to us, in deſpite of all the malicious and reſtleſs Attempts of our Adverſaries* ; *Unto him who hath delivered us, and* doth *deliver us, and we truſt will* ſtill *deliver us, be all Honour,* &c.

SERMON

S E R M O N CII.

Of the Duty of CHARITY.

[*A Charity Sermon*]

MATT. V. 48.

Be ye therefore perfect, even as your Father which is in Heaven is perfect.

SERM.
CII.

I SUPPOSE there is little need of premiſing in this place, that by being perfect like God, is not here *meant a* perfection of degrees, but only a ſimilitude or imitation in kind. The higheſt attainable perfections of the moſt excellent creatures in the Univerſe, are infinitely mean and imperfect in compariſon of God, who *chargeth even his Angels with Folly, and the Heavens are not pure in his Sight.* How much more weak and of no value, muſt the beſt performances of frail, mortal, and ſinful Men, of neceſſity be! But though all that we can poſſibly do, muſt needs fall infinitely ſhort of our moſt perfect pattern, yet we are indiſpenſably obliged to be like it in our proportion, and according to our capacity ; and as a finite *can* reſemble infinite, ſo we are to reſemble God, by partaking of the ſame excellencies in *kind*, though they cannot but be infinitely inferior in *degree.* A Candle, though its Light bears no proportion at all to the Light of the Sun, yet it reſembles it nevertheleſs in giving Light ; whereas Darkneſs is directly contrary to both : So the Virtues of Angels and of Men, though they bear no proportion at all to the adorable Perfections of God, yet they reſemble them nevertheleſs in being of the ſame nature and kind ; whereas wickedneſs is in its whole Kind a State of contrariety, oppoſition and enmity. A perfect and moſt complete example is ſet before us for our imitation, that aiming always at that which is moſt excellent, we may *grow* continually, and make a perpetual Progreſs in the ways of Virtue ; and though we can never come up to our pattern itſelf ; yet it is ſufficient that we may juſtly be ſaid to become *like* unto God, when, as the Apoſtle expreſſes it, we *are made partakers of the Divine Nature* : And ſuch Imitation of God, as our frail and mortal nature is capable of, is truly and in a proper Senſe the comparative Perfection of our *Human Nature* ; as abſolute Perfection is the Perfection of the *Divine.*

THIS may ſuffice for explication of the words in general. But then more particularly, *Perfection*, in the Scripture phraſe, and as it is recommended to us as a Duty, to be purſued and attained to by us in imitation of God ; ſignifies uſually one or other of theſe four *ſpecial* Virtues or Excellencies.

1ſt ; IT ſignifies ſometimes *Purity* and *Holineſs* ; a being ſeparated from, and raiſed above, worldly and ſenſual deſires ; *keeping ourſelves unſpotted from the World*, as St *James*

expreſſes

expresses himself; and fixing our affections upon divine and heavenly and spiritual things. Thus, 1 *Pet.* i. 15; *As he which has called you is holy, so be ye holy in all manner of conversation; Because it is written, Be ye holy, for I am holy.* Which words are taken out of the Book of *Leviticus,* where they are repeated three several times to the children of *Israel*; and answer to that precept which God had before given to *Abraham,* Gen. xvii. 1; *I am the Almighty God, walk before me, and be thou perfect.*

2*dly*; In some other places of Scripture, the word, *Perfection,* signifies our conforming ourselves to the Example of our Saviour, in *suffering patiently,* when God calls us to it, and parting with all things willingly for *his* sake. Our Saviour himself is described to have been made *perfect* by *Sufferings*; Heb. ii. 10. In prophesying of which before-hand, he expresses it in the same phrase, *Luke* xiii. 32; *I do cures to day and to morrow, and the third day I shall be* perfected. And warning his Disciples of the persecutions they must expect to meet with, he tells them, *Luke* vi. 40; *The Disciple is not above his Master; but every one that is* perfect *shall be as his Master*; that is, as 'tis explained in the parallel place, *Matt.* x. 24; must expect to be persecuted like him. And giving instruction to the young man, who desired to know what he must do to be perfect; *If thou wilt be* perfect, saith he, *go and sell that thou hast, and give to the poor, and come and follow* me.

3*dly*; In other places of Scripture, because *universal Love* in the highest and most exalted degree; forgiving of injuries, and doing Good even to our bitterest Enemies; is one of the great Improvements and Excellencies of Duty, which the Christian Religion has introduced, and wherein it exceeds all other Institutions of Religion that ever were in the World; therefore This also is sometimes stiled *Perfection*; And the practice of this Duty is called *being perfect.* Thus the words of the Text seem in their first and most literal Sense to be understood, by their connexion with what goes before. For when our Saviour had commanded his Disciples, ver. 44; *Love your enemies, bless them that curse you, do good to them that hate you, and pray for them which despitefully use you and persecute you: That ye may be the children of your Father which is in Heaven; for he maketh his Sun to rise on the evil and on the good, and sendeth rain on the just and on the unjust:* he adds immediately in the words of the Text; *Be ye therefore* perfect, *even as your Father which is in Heaven is* perfect; that is, Imitate ye therefore this excellent perfection of God; and as *he* does good even to the unholy and unthankful, so do *ye* forgive and do good even to your enemies; For this is the *Perfection* of the Christian State.

Lastly; PERFECTION in other places signifies *Mercy and Goodness,* works of *Charity* and *Beneficence*; which the Christian Religion recommends to us with the greatest Earnestness, with the most pressing Arguments, and with the amplest Promises of an exceeding great Reward. This Interpretation of the word, St *Luke* authorises in the parallel place to the Text; where, repeating the very same Discourse of our Saviour; instead of these words, *Be ye therefore perfect, even as your Father which is in Heaven is perfect,* he expresses it thus; *Be ye therefore merciful, as your Father also is merciful*; Luke vi. 36. And St *Paul,* speaking of the same excellent Duty of Charity, calls it the *bond of Perfection*: Col. iii. 14; *And above all these things put on Charity, which is the bond of perfectness.*

In this latter Sense therefore, I shall take leave to understand the words at this time; and shall accordingly endeavour in the following Discourse, to recommend to you this excellent Duty of Charity, in the following Method.

1*st*, By showing how many and great Obligations, we are continually under, to practise this Duty.

2*dly*, **What** great Benefits and Advantages accrue to *ourselves*, by the Practice of it.   And

3*dly*, **In** what particular Methods and Instances, it may best and most usefully be performed.

I. **How** many and great *Obligations* we are continually under, to practise this Duty. And because they are great and numerous, it may be useful to distinguish them into their proper Heads, as they arise from the consideration either of God, our Neighbour, or our selves.   And

If. lviii. 6, 7.   1*st*, **With** respect to *God*. *Is it not* the thing that he has chosen, *to loose the bands of wickedness, to undo the heavy burdens, and to let the oppressed go free, and that ye break every yoke? Is it not to deal thy bread to the hungry; and that thou bring the poor that are cast out to thy house? when thou seest the naked, that thou cover him, and that thou hide not thyself from thine own flesh?* Nothing is more agreeable to the Nature of God, and renders us more conformable to the Excellencies of that most perfect pattern; than the exercise of Beneficence and Goodness. The Divine Nature is Goodness itself; and his bountiful Kindness extends itself perpetually over all his works. This is the Attribute which he principally delights to exercise; and in which, of all others, he most expects and requires we should imitate him. Our Saviour in the Text, and in all his Discourses, proposes this example to us to follow; and frequently repeats it, that hereby only we can truly become the children of our Father which is in Heaven. This imitation of God, is in Heaven. This imitation of God, is the Foundation of all Religion, and the true Spring, the inward and natural Principle and Ground of Happiness: Wherefore we are equally obliged both in Duty and Interest, as we hope to be made Partakers of that Happiness, which is the Perfection of our Nature, and for which God ultimately designed us; to prepare and fit ourselves for it, by acquiring that divine frame and temper of mind, that beneficent and good Disposition, which alone can qualify us and make us capable to enjoy it. This Argument would be equally strong, even though we had an absolute and supreme Right to the things we possess; as God has over the whole Creation. But *we* are further to consider, that this is not *our* Case. *We* are not absolute Lords of the things we possess, but enjoy them merely by the divine permission and good pleasure. We are Stewards intrusted with our portion of good things, under the Supreme Householder the Governor of the Universe; and we are to give a strict account, in what manner we dispose of them. We *may* employ them to all the necessary uses, and all the reasonable conveniences, nay and even to the innocent *diversions* also of Life; but we must not consume them upon Lusts and Follies, and *with-hold good from them to whom it is due, when it is in the power of our hand to do it*, Prov. iii. 27. Some *portions* at least of what we enjoy, are due to God, as an acknowledgement of our dependence upon him for the *whole*; and instead of costly Sacrifices and Burnt-offerings to *himself*, he requires only that we be willing to relieve the necessities of *Men like ourselves*; And he seems in the Wisdom of his Providence to have made a very unequal distribution of the Blessings of this Life *on purpose*, that we might have continual opportunities of paying this reasonable homage to him, according to our respective Abilities. Thus much were evidently due to him, even tho' we had been innocent and sinless Creatures; But now how greatly is this motive enforced, when we reflect how all the Blessings with which he daily crowns us, were not only *originally* undeserved, but in their *continuance* are perpetual instances of mercy and compassion towards us! When by Sin we had forfeited all title to his Love and Favour, yet still he *causes his Sun to rise on the Evil and on the Good, and sendeth rain on the just and on the unjust*. And not only continues to us these *temporal* Blessings; but moreover, when we by Sin had ruined

3   *ourselves*

ourſelves and muſt have been miſerable for ever, ſent his Son into the World, to re- S E R M.
ſtore us to a capacity of recovering *that* Happineſs, which is *eternal*. And now, What   CII.
ſhall we render unto the Lord, for all theſe inſtances of his Mercy towards us? *Can*
our Goodneſs extend to Him? or *can a Man be profitable to his Maker?* No; The only
way *we* have of expreſſing our Gratitude towards him, is by exerciſing ſome little Similitude of that mercy and compaſſion towards our *Brethren*, in relieving their *tempo-*
ral wants; which he has extended to *us* in an infinitely greater degree, in our neceſſities *both temporal and eternal*. This he has expreſſly commanded us by our Saviour
and his Apoſtles, and it fills almoſt every page both of the Old and New Teſtament,
that it is the return he principally expects from us *for all the benefits that he has done*
unto us. *This* he declares he will accept as the beſt expreſſion of our Love towards
him, and as if the benefit of it had accrued immediately to himſelf: *He that hath*
pity on the poor, lendeth unto the Lord; and look, what he layeth out, it ſhall be paid
him again, Prov. xix. 17 : and *inaſmuch as ye have done it to the leaſt of theſe my*
Brethren, ſaith our Saviour, *ye have done it unto me*, St Matt. xxv. 45. Concerning
This, the great Enquiry will be made at the day of Judgment; and according to our
behaviour in this particular, will the final Sentence, as our Saviour himſelf has deſcribed
to us the Solemnity of that great day, he principally determined : *I was an hungred,*
and ye gave me meat : I was thirſty, and ye gave me drink : I was a ſtranger, and ye
took me in : Naked, and ye clothed me : I was ſick, and ye viſited me : I was in priſon,
and ye came unto me. Not as if any *other* good or evil Action ſhould then be over-looked
by the eye of the All-ſeeing Judge; but to intimate to us, that a charitable or uncharitable diſpoſition, is a principal and *ruling* part of a man's character; the moſt conſiderable Teſt of the whole frame and temper of his Mind; with which all other Virtues or Vices reſpectively, will almoſt neceſſarily be connected. To the performance
of *This* Duty, God has in Scripture annexed the promiſe of more and greater rewards,
than are ſpecified in the Exhortations to any other ſingle Virtue; and to the Neglect
of it are made proportionably, the greateſt of Threatnings; that *He ſhall have judg-*
ment without mercy, who hath ſhowed no mercy, and that *whoſo ſtoppeth his ears at the*
cry of the poor, he alſo ſhall cry himſelf, but ſhall not be heard. In the Characters given
of good men in Scripture, their exerciſe of this Duty of Charity, always makes a principal part of their Commendation : *I delivered the poor that cried*, ſays *Job, and the*
fatherleſs, and him that had none to help him : The bleſſing of him that was ready to
periſh came upon me, and I cauſed the Widows heart to ſing, ch. xxix. ver. 12. and in
the New Teſtament, the Character of *Cornelius*; to whom God vouchſafed to ſend an
Apoſtle on purpoſe, with a ſingular Commiſſion; and on whom the Holy Ghoſt fell,
even before his Baptiſm; was, that he was *a devout man, and one that feared God,*
and gave much Alms to the People. To conclude this Head : As in *all* ſorts of things,
the whole kind uſually receives its denomination from that part which is moſt excellent;
ſo the word *Righteouſneſs* in *general*, is frequently uſed in Scripture to ſignify *Mercy*
and Charity in *particular*; and Charity is affirmed by St *Paul* to be the *End of the*
Commandment; and that *he that loveth his Brother, hath fulfilled the whole Law*.

    2dly; W I T H reſpect to our *Neighbour*, the Obligations we are under to practiſe
this excellent Duty, are likewiſe great and many. We are all partakers of the ſame
common nature, and are therefore under the ſame ties of common humanity. God
has made of one blood, as St *Paul* expreſſes it, *all nations of men, for to dwell on all the*
face of the Earth, Acts xvii. 26; and therefore the command in the Text is thus expreſſed, that we *hide not ourſelves from* our own Fleſh. We are All ſubject to the
ſame Infirmities, All liable to fall under the ſame misfortunes, All obnoxious to the
ſame Wants; and therefore have All of us reaſon to exerciſe that compaſſion, which
no man knows but he may ſtand in need of himſelf. *The merciful man*, ſaith *Solomon*,
doth

SERM. *doth good to his own Soul; but he that is cruel, troubleth his own Flesh*, Prov. xi. 17:
CII. and the Prophet *Isaiah*, exhorting men to the exercise of Charity, expresses it by *not
hiding themselves from their own Flesh*, Is. lviii. 7. God is equally the common Father
of us all; and in his Government of the World, *accepteth not the persons of Princes,
nor regardeth the rich more than the poor; for they are all the work of his hands. The
rich and the poor*, saith the wise man, *do meet together; the Lord is the Maker of them
all*, Prov. xxii. 2. So *we* in like manner, are to make no distinction of Persons; not
by behaving ourselves alike towards all; but by performing with like chearfulness
our respective duty towards all, according to their several Circumstances; showing
with equal readiness compassion to the poor, as we do respect to the Rich, and Honour
to those in Power and Authority. God has in the whole an equal regard to all his
Creatures; but in the present State has made an unequal distribution of temporal
Blessings, *that one man's abundance should supply another man's want, that there may
be an Equality*, 2 Cor. viii. 14. By an *Equality* the Apostle does not mean, that
Christians are obliged to bring themselves all to a Level; (though the *first* Converts indeed did so, for reasons particular to those times;) but He means that there ought to
be among them such mutual assistance and relief, as that the wants and necessities of
all, may be proportionably supplied.

THE Christian religion has super-added particular Arguments to the general
ones drawn from nature and reason, to enforce our Obligation to this Duty. We
have *one Lord, one Faith, one Baptism, one Body, and one Spirit, even as we are called
in one hope of our calling*: We are all Members of one body, and *members also one of
another*, Rom. xii. 6. We all profess to be Worshippers of that One Supreme God,
who *giveth to all men liberally and upbraideth not*. We are all redeemed by the blood
of that Saviour, and depend upon his merits, for the hope of Salvation; who voluntarily became poor, that *we* might be made rich; who *went about doing good*; who
laid down his life for our sakes; and in all this, set us *an example that we should follow his steps*; leaving it to his Disciples as his last Commandment and most earnest
request, that they would *love one another as he had loved them*; making it the Badge
and distinguishing Mark, whereby *all men* should *know that they were his Disciples,
if they had love one towards another*; and declaring it to be the Sum and End of that
Religion, which he came to establish in the World, that we should *love the Lord our
God with all our hearts, and our neighbours as our selves*. These considerations, if we
will be Christians indeed, cannot but produce in us the greatest Endearments of mutual
affection; and those, if they be sincere, must necessarily show forth themselves in
suitable effects. *We ought*, if need were, *even to lay down our lives for the Brethren*,
saith St *John*, 1 *Joh*. iii. 16: But how do we answer this character, if, when *we* see
our Brother in want, we are not willing to part with any of the Superfluities of life,
to relieve *his* Necessities, for whom Christ was not unwilling to die? In the Primitive
Times the Disciples sold all that they had, and distribution was made to every one
according as he had need: God does not *now* require, any such thing of *us*; but we
are very ungrateful to him, if, when the circumstances of things are so changed, that
far less is required of us; we be now more unwilling to contribute our *small* proportion,
than they were then to offer up their *whole* estates. The least we can do, is to give
such *experiment of this ministration*, as St *Paul* expresses himself, that men may *glorify God for our professed Subjection to the Gospel of Christ, and for our liberal distribution to our brethren and to all men*; 2 Cor. ix. 13.

3*dly*; WITH respect to *ourselves*, the Obligations incumbent upon us to be charitable and beneficent, are very considerable. Compassion is by the Wisdom of our
great Creator, implanted in the very frame of our Nature; and men cannot without

great and long habits of Wickednefs, root out of their minds fo noble and excellent an S E R M. inclination. 'Tis almoft as natural for us to feel an agreeable Satisfaction and unex-, CII. preffible Pleafure of mind, upon *fatisfying a hungry Soul with bread,* or *cloathing the naked with a garment*; as 'tis for *Them* to be pleafed with the Senfe of their being relieved from thefe natural wants. And the greater abilities and opportunities God has endued any man with, of enlarging his bowels of compaffion, and doing good to greater numbers of his Fellow-creatures, and diffufing his virtue more widely through the World in acts of bounty and beneficence, in imitation of the great Creator and Preferver of all things; the greater Capacities and Advantages has fuch a one, of obtaining higher degrees of that Satisfaction and Complacency of mind, in the perfection of which confifts in great meafure the Happinefs of God himfelf. On the contrary, *what* pleafure, *what* benefit is there in the poffeffion of thofe good things, which after fupplying our own neceffities, and making reafonable provifion for our families, are laid up as ufelefs and unprofitable fuperfluities? Concerning which, *What good,* faith the wife man, *is there in them to the owners thereof, fave the beholding of them with their eyes?* Real Good indeed, and any true advantage, there feldom is; but very many times great mifchief, and ftrong temptations. *There is a fore evil,* faith Solomon, *which I have feen under the Sun; riches kept for the owners thereof to their hurt:* And *they that will be rich,* faith St *Paul, fall into temptations and a fnare, and into many foolifh and hurtful lufts; which drown men in Deftruction and Perdition.* If we intend only to fecure ourfelves, againft future contingencies; a reafonable provifion of this kind, is neither contrary to religion, nor inconfiftent with charity; but beyond this, an unbounded defire of heaping up great riches, is by no means fo very advantagious in this very refpect, as a charitable difpenfing them in wife proportions would be. For fuch is the inftability of all temporal things, that, as the wife man elegantly expreffes it, *Riches make themfelves Wings, and fly away, as an eagle towards Heaven*; that is, we cannot with all our Care, fecure them to ourfelves for any certain time; much lefs are *Riches for ever,* or do our poffeffions *endure for all generations.* We know not how foon they may be fnatch'd from *Us,* by numberlefs unforefeen Accidents; or we may as fuddenly be taken from *them,* and our Soul be required of us this very Night. In this Cafe no other part of them will be really beneficial to us, but that which by works of Charity hath been before *lent unto the Lord,* who in the Life to come *will repay it again.* And even in refpect of our Continuance in this *prefent* World, That which has been well laid out in doing Good to Mankind, has a greater Probability of turning to our Advantage even *here*; (confidering the variety of Accidents all human Affairs are fubject to;) than that which may have been covetoufly treafured up. For, as *Solomon* excellently expreffes this matter, *Caft thy bread upon the Waters, and thou fhalt find it after many days; Give a portion to feven, and alfo to eight, for thou knoweft not what evil fhall be upon the earth,* Ecclef. xi. 1. and iii. 31. *He that doth good turns, is mindful of that which may come hereafter; and when he falleth, he fhall find a ftay.* But this leads me to the

II*d* THING I propofed to fpeak to, namely, what great Benefits and Advantages accrue to ourfelves, by the Practice of this excellent Duty. And thefe I have but time barely to mention. And

1*ft*; As has already been hinted; the Charitable man in the natural and ordinary courfe of things, lays up for himfelf a truer Security againft the Accidents of the World, in the Love and Favour, the Affection and Good-Will of Men; than he could do by hoarding up the largeft treafures. For thefe he may be robbed of by many Accidents; but *he which giveth to the poor, fhall not lack,* faith Solomon; *and he that devifeth liberal things,* faith the Prophet, *by liberal things fhall he ftand.*

SERM. *2dly*; He leaves behind him an honourable memory, which will be a benefit to
CII. his Children and Posterity after him. *He has dispersed abroad, he has given to the
poor, his righteousness endureth for ever, his horn shall be exalted with honour: His
seed shall be mighty upon earth, the generation of the upright shall be blessed*, Ps. cxii.
9, 2. And this, humanly speaking, even in the natural consequence and tendency of
things. But

3dly; Such a person has moreover special Promises of the particular Blessing and
Protection of Providence to himself and his posterity. *The liberal Soul shall be made
fat, and he that watereth shall be watered also himself*, Prov. xi. 25. *If thou draw out
thy Soul to the hungry, and satisfy the afflicted Soul; then shall thy light rise in obscurity, and thy darkness be as the noon-day. And the Lord shall guide thee continually,
and satisfy thy Soul in drought, and make fat thy bones, and thou shalt be like a watered garden, and like a spring of water, whose waters fail not*, If. lviii. 10. *Be as a
Father unto the Fatherless, and instead of a Husband unto their Mother; so shalt thou
be as the Son of the most High, and he will love thee more than thy Mother doth*,
Eccluf. iv. 10. But because now under the Gospel, temporal Blessings are not dif-
pensed with the same certainty and regularity, as in the time of the *Jews*; therefore

4thly; The Duty of Charity has likewise the largest promises of the Life to
come. He *that soweth bountifully*, saith St *Paul*, *shall reap bountifully*: And our
Saviour affirms of them that abound in this grace, that they *make to themselves bags
which wax not old*; and lay up *a treasure that faileth not, in the heavens, where neither moth nor rust doth consume, and where thieves do not break through and steal*. And,
as was before observed, in his description of the process at the great Judgment, he represents our Behaviour in this one respect, as that which will principally determine
the final and irreversible Sentence at that dreadful Day.

Lastly; The Scripture frequently intimates, that Charity is one of the best Instruments of Repentance, and of assuring to us the pardon of past Sins. *Break off thy
Sins by Repentance*, said *Daniel* to the King of *Babylon*, *and thine iniquities by shewing
mercy to the poor*. *Water will quench a flaming fire*, says the wise Son of *Sirach*,
and alms maketh an atonement for Sins, Eccluf. iii. 39. *Blessed are the merciful*,
saith our Saviour himself, *for they shall obtain mercy*. And *Charity*, saith St *Peter*,
shall cover the multitude of Sins. The meaning is not, that Charity will excuse any
man's continuance in Sin; but that it is an excellent mark and evidence of the Truth
and Sincerity of our Repentance, and will afford us greater comfort and assurance in
the expectation of the full pardon of Sins past and forsaken. And in this Sense we
are to understand those Words of the Author of the Book of *Ecclesiasticus*, ch. xxix.
ver. 9; *Help the poor for the commandments sake, and turn him not away because of his
poverty. Lay up thy treasure according to the commandment of the most high, and it
shall bring thee more profit than gold. Shut up alms in thy store-houses, and it shall
deliver thee from all affliction. It shall fight for thee against thine enemies, better than
a mighty shield and strong spear*. It remains in the

III*d* and *last* place, That we consider briefly, in what particular Methods and
Instances, this Duty may best and most usefully be performed. And here, the several
manners of performing this Duty, are as various as the necessities of those who want to
be relieved. We are to visit the sick, to relieve the needy, to feed the hungry, to
cloath the naked, to comfort the afflicted, to instruct the ignorant, to reprove the
wicked; in a word, to do every thing that we can observe will be beneficial to the
Body or to the Soul of our Brother; as the Providence of God shall offer us opportunities, or as every man's Prudence shall direct him in the choice of objects on which

to

to difpofe his Charity. Concerning which there are no certain rules to be given; but every man has his Liberty to employ his bounty in fuch manner, as to himfelf fhall feem beft, and moft ufeful to the purpofes he is defirous chiefly to promote. Only here I muft not omit to obferve, that there is one comprehenfive method of Charity, which in its extent and effects is a compendium of all the inftances of beneficence in one; and That is the education of poor children, to which your contribution is now defired. This is *feeding the hungry, and cloathing the naked with a garment*; this is inftructing the ignorant, and propagating the knowlege of the Gofpel of Chrift; This is early fowing the Seeds of virtue and piety, and preventing the firft beginnings of thofe habits of wickednefs, which afterwards perhaps no Zeal for Reformation of manners would ever be able to root out; This is preventing idlenefs and poverty, and all their confequent ill effects; and (by a double benefit) making thofe to be ufeful members of the publick, who otherwife might be a burden and a hindrance to it. This is at once relieving the neceffities of the prefent generation, and preventing the wants of thofe which are to come. To *this* therefore we are exhorted by all thofe arguments *in conjunction*, which *fingly* incite us to difpenfe our Charity in any particular inftances. To this we are invited by all the confiderations of publick benefit, and by all the Motives of Religion. To this we are encouraged by the united force of all thofe promifes at once, which in Scripture are made upon diverfe occafions to the feveral methods of exercifing Mercy and Charity. Which that they may have their full effect and influence upon us, *God of his infinite mercy*, &c.

SERMON

SERMON CIII.

Of the Neceffity of Offences arifing againft the Gofpel.

LUK. XVII. 1.

It is impoffible but that Offences will come ; but wo unto Him through whom they come.

AS, in matters of *Property and Civil Right*, it cannot be but Wars and Defolations will arife among Men ; the Caufe of which Calamities ought always to be charged, not upon Him who happens to ftrike the firft ftroke, but upon Him who by Oppreffion, Pride, and Ambition, unjuftly incroaching upon his Neighbour's Rights, makes the Breach unavoidable : So, in matters of *Religion* likewife, it is impoffible but that Offences *will* come. The Progrefs of the *Gofpel*, and the prevailing of *Truth* in the World, *will* be hindred by the ill behaviour of *Some* ; And the Practice of *Righteoufnefs*, among thofe who have already embraced the Truth in Profeffion, *will* be difcouraged by the Corruption and Perverfenefs of *Others*. But *Wo be to that Man*, fays our Saviour, through *whom thefe Offences come* : Wo be to *Him*, who by his Wickednefs hinders the Propagation of *Truth*, or the practice of *Virtue*. Concerning *Other* Sinners, and fuch as through Infirmity fall into Errors of all kinds, our Saviour always fpeaks with great Tendernefs and Compaffion ; treating them, as a Phyfician does a weak Patient, with all poffible Gentlenefs and Care. But thofe who through Pride and a Tyrannical Spirit oppofe and fet themfelves againft the Truth, or through Ambition and for worldly Ends perfift in things which neceffarily caufe Divifions and Contentions among Chriftians, or by profligate Living corrupt and debauch Mankind : againft thofe through whom *fuch* Offences come, he always denounces the moft fevere *Wo*.

THE word, *Offence*, in its *general* and moft ufual acceptation, fignifies *every Sin*, every Action whereby God is offended or difpleafed. But in the *Text*, it feems more particularly to be meant of *fuch* Sins, as are occafions either of deterring men from embracing the Gofpel, or of tempting them to difobey it. For fo our Saviour in the very next words, after he had declared *Wo be to him through whom Offences come*, explains it by adding, ver. 2. *Better were it for him, that a milftone were hanged about his neck, and he caft into the Sea, than that he fhould offend one of thefe little ones* ; that he fhould *offend* them, that is, that he fhould caft a *ftumbling-block* before them ; fo the word *literally* fignifies ; that he fhould caufe them to fin, that he fhould difcourage them in their duty, that he fhould tempt them to offend God. In the *old law*, it is written, *Deut.* xxvii. 18 ; *Curfed be He that maketh the Blind to wander out of the way* ; and *Lev.* xix. 14, *Thou fhalt not put a ftumbling-block before the Blind, but fhalt fear thy God.* In the *literal* fenfe, the Commandment is right, and, no doubt, intended in the Law : But the *fpiritual* fenfe is of more importance, and perhaps *ultimately* intended in the *Law itfelf* ; Curfed be He, that by his Example or Authority,

2 maketh

maketh the Weak to wander out of the way of Righteousness. In the *parallel* place of St *Matthew's* Gospel, our Saviour still more expressly explains This to be the meaning of the Text; ch. xviii. 6; *Whoso*, says he, *shall* offend *one of these little ones that believe in Me*; one of these *little ones*; that is, any plain and sincere Christian, such a one as in the foregoing part of his Discourse he had compared for simplicity and sincerity to a little Child; *Whoso*, says he, *shall* offend *one of these little ones*; whoso shall draw or lead such a one into Sin, *better were it for him that a milstone were hanged about his neck, and that he were drowned in the depth of the sea*. And then he goes on, ver. 7; *It must needs be that Offences come; but Wo to that man*, by *whom*, (not, by whose *occasion* perhaps, but by whose *Fault*,) *the Offence cometh.* In which passage what he means by *Offence*, he again explains, ver. 10; —— *Take heed that ye despise not one of these little ones*; take heed lest ye think it a light thing, a Matter of small consequence, to draw them into Sin; *for I say unto you, that in Heaven their Angels do always behold the face of my Father which is in Heaven*: that is, those mean and sincere persons, whom ye have so little regard for, are the Care of Angels, and under the Protection of God.

B U T to consider more distinctly the words of the Text: *It is impossible*, says our Saviour, *but that Offences will come, but Wo unto Him*, Wo to That Man, or Body of Men, through *whom they come*. In Discoursing upon these words, it will be proper to show particularly, 1*st*, *What* the principal of those *Offences* are, which hinder the propagation of the Gospel of Truth. 2*dly*, In *what* Sense our Saviour must be understood to affirm, that it is *impossible* but such Offences *will* come; or, as it is expressed in St *Matthew*, that it must *needs be* that Offences come. 3*dly*, Why a *particular Wo* is, by way of *emphasis and distinction*, denounced against the Persons *by whom* these Offences come. 4*thly* and *lastly*, I shall draw some *particular Inferences* from the Whole.

I. I N the *First* place, it will be proper to consider, *what* the principal of those *Offences* are, which hinder the Propagation of the Gospel of Truth. And though *every thing*, that is faulty in *any* kind, does in its measure and degree contribute to This Evil; yet whoever considers the State of the Christian World, and the History of the Church in all Ages from the Beginning, will find that the Great *Offences*, (or, as the original word literally signifies, the *Stumbling-Blocks*) which have all along chiefly hindred the Progress of true Christianity, are these which follow.

1*st*, *Corruption of Doctrine.* The Gospel of Christ, as taught by himself, and his Apostles in its original Plainness and Purity, is a Doctrine of Truth and Simplicity, a Doctrine so easy to be understood, so reasonable to be practised, so agreeable to the natural notions and reason of Mankind, so beneficial in its effects, if men were really governed by it; teaching them nothing but the Worship of the True God, thro' the Mediation of Christ; and towards each Other, Justice, Righteousness, Meekness, Charity, and universal Good-Will; in expectation of a future Judgment, and of a lasting State of Happiness in a better World, for them who love God and keep his Commandments: This Doctrine of Christ, I say, in its native Simplicity and Purity, is so reasonable, so excellent, and of such irresistible Evidence; that had it never been *corrupted* by Superstitions from *within*, it never could have been opposed by Power from *without*; but it must of necessity have *captivated* Mankind, *to the obedience of Faith*: 'till the *knowledge of the Lord had filled the Earth, as the Waters cover the Sea*. But *Offences* soon came, and the Enemy sowed *Tares* among this Wheat. The *Jewish* Believers, even in the Apostles own times, contended for the necessity of observing the *rites and ceremonies* of the Law of *Moses*; And This gave just *Offence* to the *Gentiles*, and deterred them from readily embracing the Gospel. Others, built *hay and stubble* upon the foundation of Christ; bringing in *mixtures* of *Jewish Fables*, and

SERM. *queſtions that miniſtred ſtrife rather than godly edifying*; and introducing (after the CIII. Example of the *Phariſees,*) *will-worſhip*, and *voluntary humilities*, and *commandments of Men*; which, like a Cloud, darkned the clear Light, and obſcured the inexpreſſible *native* beauty, of the *glorious Goſpel of Chriſt*. After This, *Other* Offences aroſe from among the *Gentile*-Converts, who by degrees corrupting themſelves after the Similitude of the Heathen-Worſhippers, introduced Saints and Images, and Pompous Ceremonies, and Grandour into the Church, inſtead of true Virtue and Righteouſneſs of Life. Concerning Theſe, our Saviour ſpeaks, *Rev.* ii. 14; *Thou haſt them that hold the Doctrine of Baalam, who taught Balak to caſt a ſtumbling-block before the children of Iſrael, to eat things ſacrificed unto Idols, and to commit fornication*: By *fornication*, meaning ſpiritual *fornication*, or corruption of the plain and uniform Worſhip of God. Theſe were *Offences indeed*: Offences which gave occaſion at length, to the riſe and growth of the *Turkiſh* Empire, in oppoſition to Chriſtianity; Offences, which have all along prevented the Remains of the Nation of the *Jews*, from univerſally embracing the Profeſſion of Chriſt's Religion: Offences, which together with the introducing of dark and unintelligible Doctrines, and the requiring of blind Submiſſion to an *Infallible Guide*, inſtead of exhorting men to ſtudy ſeriouſly the *word of God*, and to live in the Practice of all *virtue and righteouſneſs* in expectation of that Great Day when God ſhall judge every man according to his Works: ended at laſt in that Great and General Corruption, which the Scripture calls, *Myſtery, Babylon the Great, the Mother of Harlots and Abominations of the Earth*. This therefore is the *Firſt* Great Offence, which hinders the propagation of the Goſpel of Truth: *Corruption of Doctrine*; or, Deſtroying the Plainneſs and Simplicity of the Religion of Chriſt.

2dly; THE *Next* is; *Diviſions, Contentions*, and *Animoſities* among Chriſtians; ariſing from Pride, and from a Deſire of Dominion, and from building matters of an uncertain nature, and of human Invention upon the Foundation of Chriſt. Other *Foundation*, ſays the Apoſtle, *can no man lay, than that which is laid, even Jeſus Chriſt*. Upon This Foundation, *the whole Building fitly framed together, groweth unto an Holy Temple in the Lord*; ſupported by Righteouſneſs and true Virtue, and united in one Holy Bond of Charity and Love. *By This*, ſays our Saviour, *ſhall all men know that ye are my Diſciples, if ye have love one to another*. And St *John* tells us, that *God is Love; and he that dwelleth in Love, dwelleth in God*. And St *Paul* declares, that *Love is the fulfilling of the Law*, Rom. xiii. 8; *For*, all the Commandments, ſays he, *Thou ſhalt not kill, thou ſhalt not ſteal*, and ſo on; *and if there be any other Commandment*, they are all *briefly comprehended in This Saying, Thou ſhalt Love thy Neighbour as thyſelf*. Did men rightly underſtand *This* to be the Great End of Chriſt's Religion, and ſincerely endeavour to practiſe it accordingly; *whence* then could *Heats* and *Enmities, Contentions and Animoſities*, poſſibly ariſe among *Chriſtians*; among thoſe whoſe Religion teaches them nothing but Meekneſs, Goodneſs and Charity; *Charity* towards their *Brethren*, and *Meekneſs* even to *thoſe that oppoſe themſelves*? St *James* ſhows us the only Spring, from *whence* Contentions ariſe; ch. iv. 1. *From whence*, ſays he, *come wars and fightings among you? come they not hence, even from your Luſts?* from the Luſt of *Dominion*, and *Temporal Power*; from the Luſt of *Contentiouſneſs, Peeviſhneſs*, or *Ambition*; from the Luſt of being Lords over each other's Faith, inſtead of being Helpers towards the common Salvation. *Rom.* xvi. 17; *Mark them which* cauſe *Diviſions and Offences, contrary to the Doctrine which ye have learned*; (that is, contrary to the doctrine which ye have learned of *Chriſt and his Apoſtles*;) Mark thoſe, who, contrary to This doctrine, cauſe Diviſions, by laying the great Streſs in matters of Religion, upon Commandments and *Traditions of* Men, *Col.* ii. 8. Almoſt all *Heats* and *uncharitable Contentions* among Chriſtians, have in all Ages ſprung from this Root; not ſo much concerning the Commandments of *God*, which are plain

I

and

and eaſy to be underſtood by *All*; as about the *Impoſitions*, and the *Authority* of *Men.* Theſe have been the *great Offence*, which has hindred the Converſion of the World to Chriſt; while Infidel Nations obſerve, that Chriſtians who preach that their Religion is *Charity*, yet *hate* and *revile* and *perſecute* each other. The *Great Offence*, I ſay, which in all Nations and in all Ages has hindred the propagation of the Goſpel of Truth, has been a hypocritical Zeal to ſecure by Force a fictitious uniformity of opinion, which is indeed impoſſible in nature; inſtead of the real Chriſtian Unity of Sincerity, Charity, and mutual Forbearance, *which is the bond of Perfectneſs.*

3dly; T H E *Third* and *Laſt* great *Offence* I ſhall mention, by which the propagation of true Religion is hindred; is the *vicious* and *debauched Lives*, (not of *Chriſtians*, for That is a contradiction; but) of thoſe who for Form's ſake *profeſs* themſelves to be ſo. For as the good *Lives* of thoſe who ſtile themſelves the Servants of God, are a *Light ſhining before men*, cauſing them to *glorify the God of Heaven*, and to admire a Religion which is of ſuch great Benefit to Mankind: So on the contrary, the *vicious and corrupt* Practices of thoſe who call themſelves Chriſtians, cannot but raiſe a Prejudice againſt, and caſt a Reproach upon, the Religion which ſeems to have ſo little influence upon the Lives of its Profeſſors. Among thoſe who are *already Believers*, the minds of the Weak are by ſuch ill Examples corrupted, tempted, and emboldened to ſin; being by degrees made leſs *ſenſible* of the *Danger* of Wickedneſs, and edified *as it were* unto deſtruction; So St *Paul* moſt elegantly expreſſes himſelf in the inſtance of Idolatry; 1 *Cor.* viii. 10; *Shall not the conſcience of him that is Weak*, be edified, (that is the word in the original, and in the margin of our *Bibles*,) ſhall he not *be* edified, *i. e.* be led on by degrees, *to eat things offered unto Idols?* And by the ſame means, that the *Manners* of Believers are corrupted; Infidels are at the ſame time confirmed in their *Unbelief*, and emboldened to deſpiſe and mock at all Religion. *By this Deed*, ſaid the Prophet *Nathan* to *David*, reproving him for his Adultery and Murder; by This Deed *thou haſt given great occaſion to the Enemies of the Lord to* blaſpheme; 2 *Sam.* xii. 14. And by reaſon of the Wickedneſs of *Eli*'s Sons, 'tis recorded that *men* abhorred *the Offering of the Lord*, 1 Sam. ii. 17. And, ſpeaking of the Corruption of the *Jewiſh* Nation; *The Heathen*, ſays God by *Ezekiel*, profaned *my holy name, when they ſaid to them*, Theſe *are the people of the Lord.* Which paſſage of the Prophet, St *Paul* cites and applies to wicked Chriſtians, *Rom.* ii. 23; *Through breaking the Law, diſhonoureſt thou God? For the Name of God is* blaſphemed *among the Gentiles, through You, as it is written.* And the ſame Argument he urges likewiſe in *other* of his Epiſtles; Exhorting men to the practice of Righteouſneſs and Holineſs, that They of the *contrary* part *may be aſhamed*, and *that the word of God be not blaſphemed*, Tit. ii. 5, 8; and 1 Tim. vi. 1; *that the Name of God, and his Doctrine, be not blaſphemed.*

co. xxx. 20.

To conclude this Head; our Saviour in his Parable, where he compares the End of the World to the Time of Harveſt, deſcribes iniquity under the character of an *Offence* or *Scandal*, in the ſenſe I am now ſpeaking of; *The Son of man*, ſaith he, *ſhall ſend forth his Angels, and they ſhall gather out of his kingdom all things that* offend, (in the original it is, *all* Scandals,) *and them which do iniquity*, Matt. xiii. 41.

II. H A V I N G thus at large explained what is meant in the Text by the word, *Offences*; I proceed in the *Second* place to conſider in what Senſe our Saviour muſt be underſtood to affirm, that 'tis *impoſſible* but ſuch *Offences* will come; or, as 'tis expreſſed in St *Matthew*, that it muſt *needs be* that Offences come. And here there have been ſome ſo abſurdly unreaſonable, as to underſtand this of a *proper* and *natural* Neceſſity; as if God had *ordained* that Offences ſhould come, and had accordingly *predeſtinated* particular men to commit them. But This, is directly charging *God* with the Sins of *Men*; and making *Him*, not *themſelves*, the Author of Evil. The plain meaning of

our

S E R M. our Saviour, when he affirms it to be *impoſſible* but that Offences *will* come, is This
CIII. only; that, conſidering the State of the World, the Number of Temptations, the
Freedom of mens Will, the Frailty of their Nature, the Perverſeneſs and Obſtinacy
of their Affections; it cannot be *expected*, it cannot be *ſuppoſed*, it cannot be *hoped*,
but that Offences *will* come; tho' it be very unreaſonable they *ſhould* come. Men
need not, men *ought* not to *corrupt the Doctrine of Chriſt*; they *need* not *diſhonour* their
Religion, by unchriſtian *Heats*, *Contentions*, and *Animoſities* among themſelves;
much leſs is there any *Neceſſity* that they ſhould *live contrary* to it, by *vicious and
debauched Practices*: And yet, morally ſpeaking, it *cannot be* but that all theſe things
will happen. The manner of uſing the like Expreſſions in *other* places of Scripture,
does evidently and beyond contradiction ſhow This to be the true Senſe of the words.
Thus our Saviour, St *Mar.* xiii. 7, ſpeaking of Wars and Tumults, *When ye ſhall hear*,
ſays he, *of Wars and Rumours of Wars, be ye not troubled*; *For ſuch things muſt* needs
be: They muſt *needs be*; that is, not that God has laid upon men any *neceſſity* of
quarrelling; but that, from the Wickedneſs of the World, nothing better can be ex-
1 Joh. iii. 9. pected. St *John*, by a like manner of ſpeaking, tells us of *ſome* perſons ſo far im-
2 Pet. ii. 14. proved in Virtue, that they *cannot* ſin; and St *Peter*, of *Others* ſo extremely corrupted,
that they *cannot* ceaſe *from Sin*: and our Saviour himſelf, of *Rich* perſons, for whom
Matt. xix. *with* men, that is, *humanly ſpeaking*, it is *impoſſible* to enter into the Kingdom of Hea-
23. ven. All which expreſſions moſt evidently ſignify, not *natural Impoſſibilities*, but *moral Improbabilities* only. To mention but one place more; *It cannot be*, ſays our Lord,
St *Luk.* xiii. 33; *it cannot be, that a prophet periſh out of Jeruſalem*: His meaning is
This only; that *Jeruſalem* was then ſo very wicked and corrupt a place, that it would
be a very ſtrange thing, a thing hardly to be imagined, that a Prophet ſhould be ſlain
in any *other* City. And thus therefore likewiſe in the words of the Text, *It is* impoſſible *but that Offences will come*: That is to ſay; In the courſe of a World, wherein (according to the nature of a Probation-ſtate) *all* men are *free*, and among Them
ſome are *weak*, and *many will* be *wicked*; it cannot be expected but that Offences *muſt*
come. And 'tis *very reaſonable* for the Providence of God to *permit* it ſo to be, for the
Trial and Improvement of the Sincere: 1 *Cor.* xi. 19; *There* muſt *be alſo Hereſies
among you, that they which are approved may be made manifeſt*: The meaning is; There
will be Factions, Parties, and Animoſities, ariſing among worldly and contentious men
from the Love of Power and Dominion: And by Theſe, (by ſuffering Theſe ſometimes to prevail almoſt univerſally, and to exalt themſelves with great Power and Authority in the World,) the Providence of God tries and diſtinguiſhes, *who* are Lovers
of the Truth, and Goodneſs, and Meekneſs of the Goſpel, and *who* on the contrary
are of worldly, factious, and ambitious Tempers.

III. I PROPOSED to conſider in the *Third* place, why a particular *Wo* is, by way
of Emphaſis and Diſtinction, denounced againſt the Perſons *by whom* theſe Offences
come: *Wo unto Him*, Wo to That *Man*, or That *Body of Men*, whoſoever or of how
great Power ſoever they be, thro' *whom the Offences come*. That, *in general*, thoſe
who by their ill Behaviour bring reproach upon the Goſpel of Chriſt, *are worthy of Puniſhment*, notwithſtanding the *Neceſſity* of ſuch Offences coming; appears from what
has been ſhown under the fore-going Head, *viz.* that the Neceſſity of Offences
coming, is not that *God* lays *a neceſſity* upon any Man *to be wicked*, (which would
indeed excuſe the *Man*, and transfer the Fault upon God *himſelf*;) but only declares,
that mens voluntary *wickedneſs and corruption* is ſuch, that it *cannot be expected* but
Offences *will* come. We have an extraordinary inſtance of This kind in the caſe of
Judas. God *decreed* that the Son of Man ſhould be betrayed to Death; and accordingly *foretold* by the Prophets, that One of his Followers ſhould betray him. Yet

1

God

God did not predeftinate *Judas* to be *wicked* : But Chrift, in order to accomplifh the Will of God, chofe on purpofe one fuch Difciple whofe Heart he knew was *wicked,* and gave him (as might have been given to any *other* wicked man) an *opportunity to* betray him. Thus both the Will of God was accomplifhed in the Death of Chrift ; and yet *Judas,* like other wicked men, acted merely from the Wickednefs of his own Heart, and therefore had no Excufe for his Crime : *Matt.* xxvi. 24 ; *The Son of man goeth, as it is written of him* ; *but Wo unto that man by whom the Son of man is betrayed* ; *it had been good for that man, if he had not been born.* The *expreffion* is of the *fame* kind, and the *manner of arguing* the *fame,* as in the words of the Text ; *It is impoffible but that Offences will come, but Wo unto Him through whom they come* ; *It were better for him that a milftone were hanged about his neck, and he caft into the Sea* ; that is, better were it for him, that he had never been born, or that he had quickly perifhed by fome untimely Death. Thus it appears plainly *in general,* that the *Neceffity* here mentioned of Offences coming, is *no Excufe* for thofe, by whofe Wickednefs they come.

B u T then further, the reafon why a *particular* Wo, by way of *Emphafis and Diftinction,* is denounced againft the Perfons, *by whom* the Offences here fpoken of arife ; is becaufe they are Offences of an *extenfive* Nature ; Hindrances to the propagation of the Gofpel ; Sins, not only in the perfons who immediately commit them, but *Stumbling-blocks* caufing *Others* to fin likewife, and promoting in general the Caufe of Satan. Now if *they who turn many to righteoufnefs, fhall fhine* (as the Scripure affures us,) with a diftinguifhed Glory *as the Stars for ever and ever* ; and *he that converteth a Sinner from the Error of his Way, fhall hide a multitude of Sins :* for the fame reafon, they who by *corrupt Practices,* or by *abfurd and unreafonable Doctrines,* contrary to the exprefs Command of our Saviour, *Call no man Father upon Earth, for One is your Father which is in Heaven* ; and *be not ye called Rabbi, for one is your mafter, even Chrift :* They, I fay, who by introducing Doctrines upon the Authority of *men,* contrary to this exprefs Command of Chrift,) deter men from believing the Gofpel, and prevent them from coming into the way of righteoufnefs ; deferve juftly in proportion a *greater Condemnation.*

IV. T h e *Inferences* I fhall draw from what has been faid, are :

1/t, F r o m the explication which has been given of thefe words of our Saviour, *It is* impoffible *but that Offences will come* ; we may learn, not to charge God with Evil ; nor to afcribe to any Decree of His, the Wickednefs and Impieties of Men. And whenever any Text of Scripture may poffibly in the literal Senfe to a carelefs Reader feem to give countenance to any fuch Notion, we muft always be careful to compare with it, *other* Expreffions of the like nature, which will be found in other *parallel* places of Scripture ; and then the true Senfe of Both, will eafily appear, even to a mean Underftanding.

2dly, S i n c e our Saviour has forewarned us, that it *muft needs be* that fuch Offences will come, as may prove Stumbling-blocks to the weak and unattentive ; let us take care, fince we have received this Warning, not to ftumble or be offended at them. Let us not, becaufe Chriftians (as they call themfelves) *will* lead wicked lives, and *will* be contentious for dominion over each other's Faith, and *will* introduce blind, corrupt, and unintelligible Doctrines ; let us not, I fay, upon any of *thefe* Accounts, which our Saviour has fo plainly forewarned us of ; let us not think at all the worfe of *Chriftianity itfelf,* of the *true,* the *plain,* the *peaceable,* the univerfally *charitable* and *beneficent* Doctrine of our Lord and Saviour Jefus Chrift.

3dly, A n d above all ; As we ought not to *take,* fo much more ought we to be careful that we never *give* any of thefe Offences. Let not any of them who call themfelves Chriftians, live *vicious and debauched lives.* Let us not fow *Divifions,* by endeavouring to *impofe* upon each Other in matters of Faith, and by *lording it* (as the

S E R M. Apoſtle expreſſes himſelf) *over the heritage of God.* Let us not by departing from the
CIII. unerring Rules of *Reaſon* and *Scripture*, corrupt the plain and beautiful Doctrine of Chriſt;
but endeavour always to keep it in that *original Simplicity*, wherein he himſelf has delivered it in ſuch a manner, as to be level to the capacity even of the meaneſt Underſtandings. Nay, let us *not only* not *give* any of theſe Offences, but let us by all poſſible means endeavour diligently to *prevent* them. Our Saviour exhorts us, in the
words immediately following the Text, as they are recorded in St *Matthew's* Goſpel,
ch. xviii. 8 ; *If thy hand offend thee, cut it off ; and if thine Eye offend thee, pluck it
out :* that is, (as appears from the connexion of theſe words with thoſe of the Text ;)
how great worldly Temptations ſoever, any *Man* or any *Body of Men* may have, to
do any thing which will offend or hinder Others from embracing the Goſpel ; yet do
it not. Abſtain, (not indeed from any thing which is *neceſſary* in order to preſerve
either the *Truth and Simplicity of the Goſpel*, or the *Practice of Righteouſneſs* ; but abſtain,) both from impoſing and from practiſing, even things *innocent and indifferent*,
if doing otherwiſe will accidentally be a prejudice to true Religion : *Rom.* xiv. 21 ; *It
is good neither to eat fleſh nor to drink wine*, (much leſs to inſiſt on any needleſs Doctrine or Ceremony,) *nor any thing whereby thy Brother ſtumbleth or is offended, or is
made Weak.* For my own part, ſays St *Paul, if Meat make my Brother to offend,
I will eat no Fleſh while the World ſtandeth, rather than make my Brother offend.* To
conclude : *Provide things honeſt*, ſays the ſame Apoſtle, *in the ſight of all Men.* Have
a good Report from them that are without, that is, even from Unbelievers themſelves.
In a word ; *Give no offence*, ſays he, *neither to the Jews, nor to the Gentiles, nor to
the Church of God.*

SERMON

SERMON CIV.

Againſt Perſecution for Religion.

LUKE XIV. 23.

And the Lord ſaid unto the Servant, Go into the High-ways and Hedges, and compel *them to come in, that my Houſe may be filled.*

MY Deſign in the following Diſcourſe, is 1ſt, to explain diſtinctly the *true* S E R M. Meaning of theſe words of our Saviour; and 2*dly*, to ſhow, to what an CIV. *impious* ſenſe they have ſometimes been perverted by men of corrupt and ﹏ ambitious minds in the *Romiſh* Church.

I. *Firſt*; Our Saviour, in This Parable, compares the Kingdom of Heaven to a *King making a Marriage-feaſt for his Son*; To which the Gueſts *firſt invited,* were Matt. xxii. 2. the *Jews,* God's original peculiar People, to whom the Goſpel was *firſt* preached : Luk. xiv. 16. But They, upon ſundry trivial Excuſes, refuſing to come to the Feaſt; and going care-leſſly elſewhere, one to his Farm, another to his Merchandize; that is, the *Jews* ad-hering to the vain Traditions of their Elders, and refuſing to embrace the doctrine of the Goſpel; *The maſter,* thereupon *being angry, ſaid to his ſervant,* ver. 21, *Go out into the ſtreets and lanes of the city, and bring in hither the poor and the maimed, and the lame and the blind;* That is, as our Saviour elſewhere explains it, *Verily the* publi- Matt. xxi. 31. cans *and the* harlots *go into the kingdom of God before* you; For *the publicans juſtified God,* Luke vii. 29, that is, obeyed God's invitation to Repentance; *But the Phariſees and Lawyers rejected the counſel of God againſt themſelves.* After this, there being ſtill room, *the Lord ſaid unto the ſervant,* in the words of the Text, *Go out in-to the high-ways and hedges, and* compel *them to come in, that my houſe may be filled:* Go, not only into the ſtreets and lanes of the City; but alſo *out of* the City, *into the high-ways and hedges;* that is, go even among the *Gentiles,* Aliens from the commonwealth of *Iſrael,* ſtrangers as yet to the covenant of Promiſe, and invite them to come in: According to That explication given by our Saviour in another place, *Many ſhall come from the Eaſt and from the Weſt, and ſhall ſit down with Abra-* Matt. viii. 11. *ham, Iſaac, and Jacob, in the Kingdom of God, and the children of the Kingdom ſhall be ſhut out.* Go, and *compel* them to come in; that is, not by *Force of Arms,* but by the force of *Perſwaſion* and earneſt *Entreaty :* For ſo in this very parable, recorded by St *Matthew*; the words which we find *here,* compel *them to come in*; are there, only, Matt. xxii. 9. *go into the Highways, and bid them to the Marriage.* The word, *compel,* is *more em-phatical*; expreſſing very affectionately the *greatneſs* of God's *Goodneſs,* or his, *earneſt and ſincere Deſire* of men's Salvation. And becauſe in This place, it is by the Na-ture and Circumſtances of the whole Diſcourſe, an Expreſſion of ſuch *Goodneſs* only, and not of *Severity*; an invitation of men to a *Feaſt,* and not a dragging them to *Puniſhment*; This therefore evidently ſhows, what *ſort* of compulſion it is, that muſt here be underſtood to be meant. For there are many ways of *compelling,* in the figu-

2 rative

SERM. rative and moral Senſe, very different from compulſion by *Force of Arms*. *Perſwaſion*
CIV. and *Arguments*, compel men; *Importunity* and *Earneſtneſs*, compel; *Promiſes* and
〰〰 *Threatnings*, *Hopes* and *Fears*, compel; *Kindneſs* and *Gratitude*, have a compulſive
force; and *Reaſons ſtrong and clear*, though they offer *no violence*, are yet, in the *moral* ſenſe, to underſtanding and unprejudiced perſons, *irreſiſtible*. And in the *Scripture*, as well as in *common-ſpeech*, is the word, *compelling*, very frequently thus uſed.
Men are in the ſacred Writings ſaid to be *compelled*, ſometimes by *importunity*:
Gen. xxxiii. 11. *Jacob* urged *Eſau*, (in the original it is, he *forced* him,) to receive
his preſent, and he received it: 1 *Sam.* xxviii. 23; *Saul's ſervants, with the woman.*
compelled *him*, (that is, prevailed with him by their importunity,) *and he hearkned to
their Voice, and did eat:* 2 Kings iv. 8; *The Shunamite* conſtrained *Eliſha*, (in the *Hebrew* it is, *compelled him*,) *to eat bread.* So likewiſe in the *New Teſtament*, Matt. xiv.
22; *Jeſus* conſtrained *his Diſciples*, (in the original it is the very ſame word with that
in the Text, he *compelled* them,) *to get into a ſhip.* *Luk.* xxiv 29; When Jeſus *made
as though he would have gone further*, the Diſciples *conſtrained him*, (in the *Greek* it is,
forced him; that is, not by *violence*, but by *perſwaſion* they forced him,) *to go in and
tarry with them.* And *Acts* xvi. 15, the woman *conſtrained* us to go into her houſe;
It is again, in the original, the ſame word, *forced* them; which yet is directly explained in the very ſame verſe to have been done only by her importunity in *beſeeching* them.
In *other* places, *Diligence and Induſtry* is repreſented as a ſort of *Compulſion*; Matt. xi.
12; *From the days of John the Baptiſt until Now, the Kingdom of Heaven ſuffereth
Violence, and the* Violent *take it by* Force: The Meaning is, what St *Luke* expreſſes
in the parallel place, *ch.* xvi. 16; *The Law and the Prophets were until John; Since
that time, the Kingdom of God is preached, and every man* preſſeth *into it*; that is, the
Goſpel is now preached *publickly* and *univerſally*; and even the *Gentiles* as well as
Jews, are diligent to underſtand and receive it. Sometimes *neceſſary* buſineſs is deſcribed as *compelling* men; that is, *ſuch* buſineſs, as either they *cannot*, or fancy *they
cannot*, without great inconvenience, neglect. Thus in this very Parable, in the words
juſt before the Text, one of the gueſts firſt-invited is introduced making This excuſe,
I have bought a piece of ground, and I muſt needs go and ſee it; In the original it is the
very ſame word, as in the Text itſelf, *I am compelled to go and ſee it.* And another
anſwers immediately after; *I have married a wife, and therefore I* cannot (the *Greek*
is, *I am not* able, to) *come.* In *ſome* places, men are ſaid to be *compelled*, by having
an *earneſt* deſire *of mind* to do a thing; *Job* xxxii. 18; *I am* full *of matter, the Spirit within me* conſtraineth *me*: And in *other* places, they are compelled by *Fear and
Diſtreſs of mind*; 1 Sam. xiii. 12; *Saul*, being in diſtreſs, forced *himſelf therefore*,
contrary to his duty, *and offered a burnt-offering.* Sometimes ſtrong and unanſwerable *Reaſons*, compel men: *Job* vi. 25; How forcible *are right words!* Sometimes,
a *Senſe of* Duty, compels men as it were *againſt* their own Inclination: 1 *Pet.* v. 2;
Feed the flock of God, not by conſtraint, *but willingly*: And 2 *Cor.* ix. 7; give, not as
of *Neceſſity, but cheerfully.* At *other* times, men are repreſented in Scripture, as
compelled by *fair and deceitful ſpeeches*; Prov. vii. 21; *With much fair ſpeech ſhe cauſed
him to yield, with the flattering of her Lips ſhe* forced *him.* Or, by *Error, and the
Prevalency of a Falſe Opinion or Doctrine*: Gal. vi. 12; *As many as deſire to make a
fair ſhew in the Fleſh, they* conſtrain *you*, (here again the original has the very *ſame*
word, as in my Text; they compel you) *to be circumciſed, only leſt they ſhould ſuffer
Perſecution for the Croſs of Chriſt*: And *Gal.* ii. 14; *Why* compelleſt *thou the Gentiles
to live as do the Jews?* namely, by *perſwading* them of the Neceſſity of Circumciſion;
Or, by the *Perverſeneſs of* Others, men are ſometimes ſaid to be *compelled*, for the conviction of ſuch gainſayers, to do things which they would otherwiſe diſlike: *Gal.* ii. 3;
Neither Titus, who was with me, being a Greek, was compelled *to be circumciſed; And*

That

That becauſe of falſe brethren, unawares brought in, —— *to ſpie out our Liberty* ; And S E R M. 2 *Cor.* xii. 11 ; *I am become a Fool in glorying,* ye *have* compelled *me,* viz. by your ill CIV. behaviour. Or, by mere *Cuſtom* ſometimes, are men repreſented as compelled : *Luk.* xxiii. 17 ; *Of* neceſſity *he muſt releaſe One to them at the Feaſt* ; that is, as St *Matthew* expreſſes it in the parallel place, *he was* wont *to releaſe One* at That Time ; ch. xxvii 15. or, in St *John's* words, *they had a* Cuſtom, *that One ſhould then be releaſed.* Laſtly, ch. xviii. 39. by the *willing* and *agreeable* compulſion, of *Love and Gratitude* powerfully working, in the motions of a free and generous Mind ; are men elegantly ſaid to be *compelled* : 2 Cor. v. 14 ; *The* Love *of Chriſt,* conſtrained *us.* And not of *Men* only, but even concerning *God himſelf* alſo, is the like figure of ſpeaking ſometimes uſed in Scripture : *Iſ.* lxii. 7 ; *Ye that make mention of the Lord, give him* No Reſt, *till he eſtabliſh, and till he make Jeruſalem a Praiſe in the Earth.* Here the holy Spirit repreſents God, in a moſt wonderful way of condeſcenſion, ſuffering himſelf to be *compelled* as it were, by the *importunate* Prayers of good men. And the ſame thing is ſtill more lively ſet forth, in the Hiſtory of *Jacob's* ſtriving with the Angel ; *Gen.* xxxii. 24. where our Tranſlation improperly expreſſes it by his *wreſtling* with the Angel ; But the Senſe is ; the Angel made as if he would have departed from him ; but *Jacob* held him, and ſtrove with him, and preſſed him *importunately* for a Bleſſing, ſaying, *I will not let thee go, except thou bleſs me* ; Whereupon he bleſſed him, and ſaid, ver. 28 ; *As a* Prince *haſt thou Power with God and with Men, and haſt prevailed.* Which matter, the prophet *Hoſea* thus ſets forth, ch xii. 3 ; *By his* Strength *he had Power with God* ; yea, *he had Power over the Angel, and prevailed* ; *he* wept, *and made ſupplication unto him :* The Strength (ſays the Prophet,) by which *Jacob prevailed over the Angel,* was his *weeping and making ſupplication unto him.* From theſe, and numerous other the like expreſſions in Scripture, as well as from the Nature and Reaſon of the thing itſelf, it is evident beyond controverſy, that when our Lord in the Text, bids the Preachers of his Goſpel, go into the high-ways, and hedges and *compel* men to come in ; his meaning is not, *Compel them by Force of Arms* ; but, compel them by irreſiſtible Clearneſs of Reaſon, by Strength of Argument, and affectionate Admonition ; convince, perſwade, intreat them ; ſet before them the certainty of a Future Judgment, the Promiſes, and the Threatnings of the Lord ; prevail with them by your own good Example ; urge, preſs, inculcate upon them the Neceſſity of Religion ; *Preach the word, be inſtant in* 2 Tim. iv. 2. *ſeaſon, out of ſeaſon ; reprove, rebuke, exhort, with all long-ſuffering and doctrine :* According to that of St *Paul,* 1 Th. ii. 10 ; *Ye are witneſſes, how holily, and juſtly, and unblameably, we behaved ourſelves among you* ; *As you know alſo, how we* exhorted, *and* comforted, *and* charged *every one of you, as a Father doth his children* ; *That ye would walk worthy of God, who has called you unto his Kingdom and Glory.* This is evidently the *true* and *full* Meaning, of theſe remarkable words of our Saviour in the Text. It remains that I proceed now in the

II. *Second* place to ſhow, to what a wicked Senſe they have ſometimes been perverted, by men of corrupt and ambitious Minds in the *Romiſh* Church. Compel *them to come in* : That is, (in *Their* explication,) *compel them by Violence and Force of Arms,* by Racks and Tortures, by Dragoons and Inquiſitions, by Fire and Sword. As if the Religion of Chriſt was intended to diveſt men of common humanity, and the Service and Glory of God could really be promoted by the Deſtruction of Mankind : As if Religion, whoſe Great End is Peace and Love, the univerſal Reconciliation of men to God and to each other, could itſelf be propagated by the higheſt Oppreſſions, and moſt inhumane Cruelties : and be made to authorize and to ſanctify ſuch Practices, the preventing whereof is indeed the very chief Deſign, of All Religion both Natural and Revealed. But to be more particular.

**SERM.
CIV.**

1*st*; I T is originally, in the very *nature of things*, inconſiſtent and abſurd, to think that a right Senſe of Religion can be put into mens Minds by Force of Arms. For *What* is Religion, but ſuch a Perſwaſion of Mind towards God, as produces Obedience to his Commands; ariſing from a due *Senſe* of him in the *Underſtanding*, a juſt *Fear and Love* of him in the *Affections*, and a *Choice or Preference* of Virtue in the *Will*? Now to attempt to influence the *Will*, by *Force*; is like applying *Sounds* to the *Eyes* in order to be *Seen*, or *Colours* to the *Ears* in order to be *Heard*. The Abſurdity, in Both caſes, is exactly the Same; For as nothing affects the *Eyes*, but *Light*; nor the *Ears*, but *Sounds*; ſo nothing affects the *Underſtanding* and the *Will*, but *Reaſon and Perſwaſion*. A man's *external* Acts, *may* indeed be *compelled*, or may be reſtrained, by *Force*; And, in many caſes, it is very *fit* they ſhould be ſo: But the *inward* Acts of the Mind, *cannot* be forced; nor is it *poſſible* for a man to be *compelled*, *againſt* his Will, to fear God, and be ſincerely religious. A Robber or Murderer *may*, and ought to be reſtrained by Force, from killing or pillaging his Brother; And This is the very End, for which Providence appointed Magiſtracy and Government in the World: But the man is not therefore at all the more religious in the Sight of *God*, becauſe his hands are in Chains. It is the *Heart* properly, that is the Seat of Religion; and where *That* occurs not, the *outward action* is of no conſideration in the Sight of God. What is it then, that men can be compelled to by Force, in matters of Religion? Nothing but *Hypocriſy*, nothing but a *Mocking of God*. That which *our Saviour in the Text* would have men compelled to, is a *good Heart*, and a *ſincere Mind*; and therefore the compulſion here ſpoken of, muſt needs be that which compels, not the *Body*, but the *Mind*; And This, it is evident, can be no other, than *ſtrong Reaſon* and *powerful Perſwaſion*; Meekneſs, and Charity, and good Example. For which reaſon, when the Gueſts were all come in, who are here by our Lord ſaid (in this Senſe) to have been *compelled* to the Feaſt; yet the man who had not on the Wedding-garment of righteouſneſs, was not *forced* to *put one on*, but was caſt out into outer-darkneſs for coming in *without one*. God himſelf, whoſe Power is infinite, yet *compels* and over-rules no man in matters of Morality: He invites, he exhorts, he entreats; But if they will not be *drawn by theſe Cords of a Man*, theſe proper Motives

Rev. xxii. 11.

Ezek. iii. 27.

Gen. vi. 3.

Pſ. lxxxi. 12.

1 *Cor.* xiv. 38.

to rational Creatures; then, *He that is unjuſt*, ſaith he, *let him be unjuſt ſtill; and he that is filthy, let him be filthy ſtill*; And, *He that heareth, let him hear; and he that forbeareth, let him forbear*: His *Spirit will not ſtrive with them*, by any other than rational and moral Motives; by which if they *will not* be led to obey him, then he *gives them up unto their own Heart's Luſt, and lets them follow their own imagination.* All our Saviour's Preaching, was with This Declaration; *He that has Ears to hear, let him hear*; and St *Paul* in like manner, 1 *Cor.* xiv. 38; *If any man be ignorant*, (after all reaſonable means of inſtruction,) let *him be ignorant*. Nay indeed, to ſuppoſe that even the Power of God, *can* compel in moral matters; is a manifeſt inconſiſtency in the nature of the *thing*. For the *eſſence* of religion or virtue, conſiſts in the *free choice* of the Will; ſo that to *compel* a man in *this caſe*, by taking away his freedom; is indeed *deſtroying* the *Faculty itſelf*, or *removing* the *Subject*, in which Virtue was to reſide. Wherefore the utmoſt that the Scripture ever repreſents God doing in this matter, is what is expreſſed, *Pſ.* lxxxi. 13; O *that my people would have hearkened unto me! that Iſrael had walked in my Ways!* and *Iſ.* v. 4; *What could have been done more to my Vineyard, that I have not done in it?* But

2*dly*, As *Force* is *inconſiſtent* with the nature of *Religion* in *general*; ſo is it much *more* oppoſite to the Spirit of *Chriſtianity* in *particular*. Our *Saviour's whole* Life and Character was, that *he went about, doing good*; humble and lowly, meek and merciful, and *exhorting* Sinners to Repentance; 'till at laſt he was led, as a *Lamb*, to the Slaughter. *If ye will be my Diſciples*, *If any man* will *come after me*, was his ſtile in *inviting*

viting

viting men to receive the Goſpel; Will *ye alſo go away,* was his manner of *expoſtu-* SERM.
lation : Bleſſed are the meek, *Bleſſed are the* merciful, *Bleſſed are they which are* per- CIV.
ſecuted, (not they which *perſecute*;) was his conſtant *Doctrine :* A *new, a particular,*
a diſtinguiſhing *Commandment, give I unto you*; *Love* one another, *love even your E-*
nemies, *love even your* Perſecutors: *By* This *ſhall all men know that ye are my Diſci-*
ples, if ye have love *one to another :* To *love* God *with all your Heart, and your* Neighbours *as your ſelves,* theſe are *the firſt and* great *Commandments*; And if any man deſires to diſtinguiſh the Preachers of *Truth* from the Teachers of *Error,* by theſe *Fruits*
(ſaith he) *ſhall ye know them :* Laſtly, when ſome of his Diſciples, with too high a
Spirit of Zeal, would have *called for fire from heaven,* upon the *Samaritans* who contemptuouſly rejected their Maſter; though they were far from maſſacring them with
their own hands, and deſired only to have the *unerring* righteous Judgment of God
executed upon them, yet *he reproved them, ſaying, Ye know not what manner of Spirit* Luk. ix. 55.
ye are of; *for the Son of Man came not to deſtroy mens Lives, but to ſave them.* Accordingly, in the firſt and uncorrupt Ages, *ſuch* alſo was the Manner of the *Apoſtles*
teaching, in imitation of their Maſter : *Hereby know we,* ſaith St *John, that we are* 1 Joh. ii. 5.
in Him; *If a man ſay, I love God, and hateth his Brother, he is a Liar*; *for he that* iv. 20.
loveth not his Brother whom he hath ſeen, how can he love God whom he hath not ſeen?
And St *James* : *Who,* ſays he, *is a wiſe man? let him ſhew his Works with* meekneſs Jam. iii. 13.
of Wiſdom : But *if ye have bitter envyings and ſtrife in your hearts, glory not, and lie*
not againſt the Truth : For this wiſdom deſcendeth not from above, but is earthly, ſen-
ſual, deviliſh : But the Wiſdom that is from above, is firſt pure, then peaceable, gentle,
and eaſy to be intreated, full of mercy and good Fruits : For, *the* Wrath of Man, (and ch. i. 20.
much *more, the* Cruelty of Man,) *worketh not the righteouſneſs of God.* St Paul likewiſe, though in his natural Temper the moſt zealous of All the Apoſtles, yet declares,
that the very End *of the Commandment is Charity*; that though a man ſhould ſpeak 1 Tim. i. 5.
with the Tongues *of Men and of Angels,* and had Faith *to remove Mountains,* and 1 Cor. xiii. 1.
Zeal *to give his body to be burned,* and Liberality *to beſtow all his goods to feed the Poor,*
and *had not* Charity ; that is, univerſal Love, Temper and Good-Will towards Mankind;
it would *profit him nothing.* And accordingly he exhorts Chriſtians to put on *bowels of*
mercy, kindneſs, meekneſs; *forbearing one another, and forgiving one another, if any*
man have a quarrel againſt any; *And above all things put on* Charity, *which is the*
bond of Perfectneſs, Col. iii. 12. Charity, the Bond of Perfectneſs ; That is ; Not U-
nity of Opinion in the Bond of Ignorance, or Unity of Practice in the Bond of Hypocriſy, but Unity of the Spirit in the Bond of Peace. And, with regard to *Unbelievers,*
2 Tim. ii. 24, *The Servant of the Lord,* ſays he, *muſt not ſtrive, but be gentle unto*
all men, apt to teach, patient, in meekneſs (not with Fire and Sword) *inſtructing thoſe*
that oppoſe themſelves, if God peradventure will give them repentance to the acknowledg-
ment of the Truth. Particularly, in the caſe of an unbelieving *Wife,* he commands
the Huſband not to try to bring her over by ill uſage and force, but by *kindneſs only*
and good example ; for *what knoweſt thou O man, whether thou ſhalt ſave thy Wife?*
1 Cor. vii. 16 : And Huſbands *that obey not the Word,* 1 Pet. iii. 1, *may alſo without*
the word be won by the converſation and good example *of the Wives while they behold*
your chaſte converſation coupled with Fear.

   DID the Profeſſors of Chriſtianity univerſally follow theſe Precepts of their Maſter
and his Apoſtles, ſo that the *Labourers* were as *many* as the *Harveſt* is *Great*; the
whole World would ſoon be *filled with the Knowledge of the Lord, as the Waters co-*
ver the Sea : And the *Goſpel,* from a *grain of muſtard-ſeed,* according to our Saviour's
parable, would have waxed into a great Tree ; which (in the Pſalmiſt's expreſſion)
having taken deep root, had filled the Land; *The Hills were covered with the Shadow* Pſal. lxxx. 9.
of it, and the boughs thereof were like the goodly cedar-trees; *She ſtretched out her*
                                                                                    branches

S E R M. *branches unto the Sea, and her boughs unto the river:* Or in the Prophet *Daniel's* phraſe,
CIV. ch. iv. 11; *The Tree grew and was ſtrong, and the height thereof reached unto Heaven, and the Sight thereof to the End of all the Earth; The leaves thereof were fair, and the fruit much; and in it was Meat for all; The Beaſts of the Field had ſhadow under it, and the Fowls of the Heaven dwelt in the boughs thereof, and all Fleſh was fed of it.* Thus would the Goſpel certainly be propagated, did its Profeſſors every where promote it according to their Maſter's Direction, and practiſe it in the Love thereof. But if the Goſpel of Peace, be *itſelf* turned into an occaſion of hatred and violences; *the Name of*
Mat. v. 13. *God must needs be blaſphemed among the Gentiles, through Us, as it is written,* Rom. ii.
Mar. ix. 50. 24; *If the Salt itſelf has loſt its Savour, wherewith ſhall things be ſeaſoned?* If the *Eye,*
Mat. vi. 22. which is the *Light* of the Body, be *itſelf* Confuſion; *wherewith* ſhall a man's ſteps be
Job x. 22. directed? *If the very Light that is in thee, be darkneſs,* (as our Saviour expreſſes it;) *how great is that Darkneſs?* If a man's *Religion itſelf* be *wickedneſs,* how *great* muſt his Wickedneſs be?

     3*dly,* A s *Force* is inconſiſtent with the Nature of *Religion in general,* and ſtill *more* oppoſite to the Spirit of *Chriſtianity in particular;* ſo it is in Scripture, ſtill *further,* made the *diſtinguiſhing Character of the great Apoſtacy* foretold by Chriſt and his A-poſtles. As, in the *literal Babylon, Nebuchadnezzar* commanded, that whoſoever would not worſhip the King's golden Image, ſhould be caſt into the fiery furnace; ſo the deſcription of *Spiritual Babylon* is This, that *whoſoever will not worſhip the Beaſt's*
Luke xii. 49. *Image,* that is, profeſs the idolatrous religion of falſe Chriſtians, *ſhall be killed:* Rev.
Mat. x. 21, xiii. 15. Our Saviour foretold his Diſciples from the *Beginning,* that *he came not to*
34. *ſend Peace on the Earth, but Fire* and *a Sword;* that *the Brother ſhould deliver up the*
Joh. xvi. 2, *Brother to death, and the Father the Child; yea, the time cometh,* ſaith he, *that whoſo-*
3, *and* xv. 21. *ever killeth you, will think that he doth* God *Service; And theſe things will they do, be-cauſe they have neither* known Me, *nor my* Father *that ſent me;* that is, have neither underſtood the Doctrine of *Chriſt,* nor the Precepts of *natural Religion* itſelf. Theſe Prophecies began in *ſome degree* to be accompliſhed, by the *Jews* perſecuting the A-poſtles of our Lord: But the *Jews* were ſo far outdone in this Wickedneſs, by corrupt *Chriſtians* afterwards; that in like manner as our Saviour teſtified concerning the *worſt*
Luk. xi. 50. Age of the *Jews,* that the *blood of all the Prophets which was ſhed from the foundation of the world, even from the blood of righteous Abel, down to the blood of Zacharias, ſhould be required of That generation;* ſo concerning the moſt corrupt and perſecuting part of
Rev. xvii. 6. the *Chriſtian* Church, it is propheſied likewiſe, that *in Her* ſhall be *found the blood of*
xviii 24. *Prophets and of Saints, and of All that are ſlain upon the Earth.* It is very obſervable;
Deut. xxviii. that as *Moſes,* in the concluſion of the *Law,* foretold ſuch a diſperſion of the *Jews* in-
64. to All Nations, as no *Falſe* Prophet *could* have invented, becauſe it is ſuch a thing as Never happened to any *other* People, and is therefore a great Evidence of the Truth of *Moſes's* Inſpiration: So in the *New Teſtament* there is clearly foretold ſuch a Corruption of *Chriſtianity,* ſo *unnatural,* ſo *incredible,* as could not have entered into the reach of any *humane* Wiſdom, to foreſee or ſuſpect: That the Profeſſors of *That religion,* whoſe diſtinguiſhing *character,* whoſe very *Eſſence,* is univerſal *Love* and Good-will towards Mankind; ſhould ſome of them exceed, in *Cruelty,* even the moſt *barbarous* of the Heathens: That, in order to convert *Others,* they ſhould *themſelves* break the *greateſt* of God's Commandments; and overturn *all his Laws,* for the Propagation (it ſeems) of his *Religion:* That Chriſtianity, inſtead of making men Partakers of the *Divine* Nature, ſhould on the contrary become ſo corrupt, as to diveſt them of all Remains even of *Humanity itſelf;* That, inſtead of cauſing the *Sun* of Righteouſneſs to ariſe in mens hearts, it ſhould on the contrary extinguiſh That *Candle* of the Lord, which was *before* in their breaſts by the Light of Nature; and make them even *ten times more the*
          children

children of Wrath, than if they had never received the Goſpel at all, nor ever heard of *the way of Righteouſneſs.*

I T will here, no doubt, be alledged, by thoſe of the *Romiſh* Church, that *Proteſtants* alſo, have ſometimes *perſecuted* men, upon account of Religion : Which perhaps *may* indeed be True, juſt in the *ſame* ſenſe, as *good men* may be ſaid to have ſometimes committed Robberies, or Murder, or other Crimes ; that is, they have, in *ſo* doing, a-poſtatized from their Profeſſion. But *muſt* men then, (they will ſay,) be left *wholly at Liberty* whether they will be religious or not ? No certainly : We muſt exhort, convince, reprove, *be inſtant with them, in ſeaſon, out of ſeaſon* ; ſetting before them, without ceaſing, the Promiſes and the Terrors of the Lord. But *what* if all theſe things will not prevail with them ? Why, then (our Saviour tells us) they muſt be unto us *as heathen-men and publicans* ; that is, we muſt leave them to the righteous judgment of God. But muſt not the *Magiſtrate* then *puniſh* the Obſtinate ? Undoubtedly he muſt ; that is, he muſt puniſh them for every Action which is *vicious and immoral*; and conſequently *hurtful* to the *Publick*, which has a right of Self-defence againſt all Malefactors : But to abuſe the *Sword of Juſtice*, to an *unjuſt Compulſion* in matters relating wholly to God and mens own Conſciences ; this is the *Great Corruption* propheſied of in the whole *New Teſtament*.

Laſtly, I t may be alledged by the Church of *Rome*, that there are in *Scripture* approved Inſtances of men *put to death* upon account of Religion : but the plain Anſwer is, that the Caſes there mentioned, are All of them *exceeding different*, from Thoſe which They are by Popiſh Writers brought to excuſe. In the Law of *Moſes*, he that ſeduced men to worſhip other Gods, was commanded to be put to death : Becauſe he ſeduced men to worſhip Stocks and Stones, the Gods of thoſe abominable Nations whom the Lord had commanded to be extirpated; a Crime equally againſt all Natural, and all Revealed Religion ; which no man's Conſcience could innocently or erroneouſly lead him into ; and the Puniſhment moreover was grounded upon, and juſtified only by, the *particular expreſs* Command, given by God at That time to the *Jews*, under a ſevere Law, and under a *political Theocracy* even with reſpect to their *civil* Government ; and was therefore a Caſe, not to be imitated, but when exactly under *all* the *like Circumſtances*, and with the *like* particular *expreſs* Command from God. *Elijah* deſtroyed men with Fire from Heaven : But it was God's own miraculous Interpoſition, and not any Action of the Prophet, that killed them. He ſlew alſo at another time the Prophets of *Baal* : But it was upon an expreſs Command of God, warranted and proved to him by an immediate *Miracle* of Fire from Heaven upon his Burnt-offering. *Phinehas* ſuddenly killed a man and a woman in their Sin : But the Text tells us, it was according to a *ſpecial command* given to *Moſes* upon That very occaſion : And he that will do the like, muſt ſhow the like *Inſpiration* and the like *Command*. *Ananias* and *Sapphira* fell down dead at the Apoſtle's feet ; but it was by the miraculous Judgment of *God*, not by any Action of the *Apoſtles themſelves*. He that, from theſe inſtances, thinks he may *kill* all men that differ from him in Religion ; will bring in all Enthuſiaſm and all Wickedneſs into the world. Can *Chriſtians* ſhow, that *they* have any ſuch Command ? have they not the very *contrary* declared to them, in our Saviour's telling his Diſciples, when they wiſhed for Fire from Heaven, that they *knew not what Spirit they were of* ? There is not therefore, in all the Prophecies through the whole Scripture, any *One* more certain mark of Antichriſtian Corruption, than the Spirit of *Perſecution : Come out of her, my people, that ye be not partakers of her Sins, and that ye receive not of her Plagues.*

S E R M O N CV.

Againſt falſe Pretences to Religion.

MATT. XXII. 11, 12.

And when the King came in to ſee the Gueſts, he ſaw there a man which had not on a Wedding-garment : And he ſaith unto him, Friend, how cameſt thou in hither, not having a Wedding-garment? and he was Speechleſs.

SERM.
CV.

THESE Words are part of the concluſion of a Parable, in which our Lord re-preſents the *Kingdom of Heaven*, or God's gracious Declarations to Mankind in the *Goſpel*, under the Similitude of a King ſending forth his Servants at dif-ferent times, and inviting his Subjects to the *Marriage-Feaſt* of his Son. Not only by the Light of *Nature* and *Reaſon*, has God given men the Knowledge of *Himſelf*, a Senſe of the eſſential and eternal Differences of *Good and Evil*, a neceſſary and unavoid-able Expectation of a *Future Judgment*, and of *Rewards and Puniſhments* in a *life to come*; but moreover by *Revelation* alſo, at *ſundry times* and in *divers manners*, to the *Patriarchs* and the *Prophets*; and at laſt by the Preaching of *Chriſt himſelf*, and of his *Apoſtles and Miniſters* ſent forth even unto the Ends of the World; has he continually *repeated* his *Admonitions*; and without ceaſing *invites, perſwades, urges, preſſes* men, with all the *poſſible* Arguments both of *Reaſon* and *Authority*, to accept the Gracious and Neceſſary Terms of Salvation. The *inſenſibility* of men, in not underſtanding their true Happineſs; their *Negligence*, in refuſing to receive inſtruction in the ways of Virtue; and their *Perverſeneſs*, in preferring the momentary Pleaſures of Sin, before the Happineſs of Eternity; is affectionately ſet forth by our Saviour in *That part* of the Parable, where he deſcribes the Temper and Diſpoſition of the perſons invited to the Wedding, *ver. 3, and 5*, that they would not *come*, but *made light of* the invitation, *and went their ways, one to his Farm, another to his Merchandize*. The *Goodneſs* and *Long-ſuffering* of *God*, in bearing patiently with Sinners, and giving them ſpace for Repentance, and exhorting them with all earneſtneſs to flee from the Wrath to come; is, in a very lively manner, expreſſed in the *following part* of the Parable, *ver. 9*; where the King ſays to his Servants, after they who had been before invited refuſed to come; *Go ye into the high-ways, and as many as ye ſhall find, bid to the Wedding*: Or, as St *Luke* expreſſes it ſtill more pathetically, *Go out into the Streets and Lanes of the City*——*go out into the High-ways and Hedges*, and compel *them to come in, that my houſe may be filled: Compel* them; that is, be *preſſing*, be very *urgent* with them, uſe *all poſſible* Arguments of Perſwaſion, give them *no Reſt*, till they be convinced of their Folly, and prevailed upon to underſtand their own True Happineſs. The *Effect* of theſe earneſt and repeated invitations; was; *ver. 10*; that *the Servants gathered toge-ther all, as many as they found, both Bad and Good; and the Wedding was furniſhed*

with

with Gueſts : That is ; By the continual Preaching of the Goſpel, *Many* are prevailed upon to make *Profeſſion of Religion,* and to ſeek after the Happineſs of the Life to come. But though God *does indeed,* with *all* the *Earneſtneſs* and *Affection* expreſſed under theſe Similitudes in the Parable, *invite* men into his Kingdom of Glory ; Though he really would *have All men to be ſaved, and to come to the Knowledge of the Truth ; not willing that Any ſhould periſh, but that All ſhould come to Repentance :* Yet 'tis, a-bove all things, to be here carefully obſerved, that all theſe *earneſt, repeated, preſſing* Invitations, are in no degree any encouragement to any man to expect the *End* with-out the *Means,* but they are merely Invitations to the *Means* in order to the *End.* God calls no man to *Salvation,* without a Life of *Righteouſneſs :* But he *invites, perſwades, exhorts, preſſes* men, with all the *poſſible* Arguments both of *Reaſon* and *Authority,* to *live virtuouſly* in order to their *eternal Happineſs.* And This is what our Saviour teaches in the words of the Text, at the concluſion of the Parable. *When the King,* (ſays he) *came in to ſee the Gueſts, he ſaw there a man which had not on a Wedding-gar-ment : And he ſaith unto him, Friend, how cameſt thou in hither, not having a Wedding-garment ? and he was ſpeechleſs. Then ſaid the King to his Servants, Bind him hand and foot, and take him away, and caſt him into outer Darkneſs ; there ſhall be weeping and gnaſhing of Teeth. For Many are called, but Few are choſen.*

I N the following Diſcourſe, I ſhall *firſt* explain the Ground and Meaning of this figurative expreſſion, of *having on a wedding-garment :* And *Then* I ſhall make ſome uſeful and practical *Obſervations* upon the Text.

I. I N the *firſt* place ; The Original and Ground of this figurative expreſſion, of *ha-ving on a wedding-garment,* is very eaſy and natural. The *Mind* of man being *inviſi-ble,* and the *Temper* or *Diſpoſition* of a *ſpiritual Subſtance* not being diſcernible to *Senſe ;* its *Qualifications* conſequently can no otherwiſe be deſcribed in words, than under *figu-rative* expreſſions drawn from the Similitude of *corporeal Objects. Pure* and *Impure, Clean* and *Unclean* when applied to the *Soul* in the *Moral* Senſe ; owe the *clearneſs* and *expreſſiveneſs* of their Signification, to the known meaning of the ſame words when ap-plied in their *literal* Senſe to things *corporeal* and *ſenſible.* The *Habits* of the *Mind,* are very aptly and ſtrongly repreſented to our Imagination, by Figures taken with juſt-neſs and propriety from the *Habit* of the *Body.* And the conſtant, prevailing, habi-tual *Temper* or *Diſpoſition* of any man's *Spirit,* can no way be ſet forth more expreſſive-ly and affectionately ; than under the Similitude of *Bodily* garments, ſo inveſting the Perſon, as to be his *proper and diſtinguiſhing Attire.* The inviſible, and inacceſſible Glory ; the inexpreſſible Greatneſs and Majeſty ; the inconceivable Purity and Holi-neſs, of *God Himſelf ;* is in Scripture deſcribed, after This manner, by his *Putting on glorious* Apparel ; by his being Clothed *with Majeſty and Honour, and decking himſelf with Light as with a* Garment ; *Pſ.* xciii. 1 ; civ. 2. The *Good,* and the *Evil* Qua-lities, of *Men ;* the *habitual* ones, which determine and diſtinguiſh the Perſon's *Whole* Character ; are, through all the Scriptures, perpetually repreſented under the *ſame* Fi-gure. A *malicious, uncharitable, perſecuting* Spirit ; is, in the *Pſalmiſt's* deſcription, one that Clothes himſelf with *Curſing ;* To whom it is as the *Cloke that he has upon him, and as the* Girdle *that he is always girded withal ;* Pſ. cix. 17. And when, on the contrary, he is to expreſs the perfecteſt and moſt compleat character of ſpotleſs Virtue ; he does it in the *ſame* manner ; *Let thy Prieſts be* Clothed *with Righteouſneſs ;* Pſ.cxxxii. 9. In that beautiful and affectionate Apology which *Job* makes for himſelf, in That paſſage where he maintains his paſt Innocency, and deſcribes his virtuous Behaviour in the days of his Proſperity ; *he* likewiſe makes uſe of the *ſame* Metaphor : ch. xxix ; *ver.* 15, 16, 14 ; *I was Eyes to the Blind, and Feet was I to the Lame : I was a Fa-ther to the Poor ; and the Cauſe which I knew not, I ſearched out : I put on Righteouſ-neſs, and it* Clothed *me ; my Judgment was as a* Robe *and a Diadem.* The Prophet

I   *Iſaiah*

S E R M. *Iſaiah*, deſcribing the *Redeemer* of *Iſrael*, ſpeaks after the *ſame* Faſhion ; ch. lix. 17 ;
CV.   *He* put on *Righteouſneſs as a Breaſt-plate,——and was* clad *with Zeal as a Cloke.* And
concerning the People *Redeemed* by him ; ch. lxi. 10 ; *He has* Clothed *me* (ſays he)
with the Garments *of Salvation, he hath covered me with the* Robe *of Righteouſneſs, as a*
Bridegroom *decketh himſelf with Ornaments, and as a* Bride *adorneth herſelf with her*
Jewels.

    F R O M *Theſe* figurative Expreſſions ſo frequently occuring in the *Old Teſtament*, the
ſame manner of ſpeaking has deſcended to the Writers of the *New.* In the Book of
the *Revelation*, the Elders before the Throne of God, in St *John's* Viſion of the Church
Rev. iv. 4. in Heaven, are repreſented to him as ſitting, *clothed* in *white Raiment :* And the Na-
ch. vii. 9. tions of them that are ſaved, as ſtanding before the Throne, *clothed* with *white Robes.*
And our Saviour, in the ſame Viſion, is accordingly introduced pronouncing ; *Bleſſed is*
xvi. 15. *he that Watcheth, and keepeth his* Garments: And, They *that have not defiled their*
Garments, *ſhall walk with me in white, for they are worthy.* Now Theſe *Garments*,
the Text expreſſly tells us ; *ch.* xix. 8 ; are *The Righteouſneſs of the Saints.* The
Whole Paſſage is exactly parallel to the *Parable in the Goſpel*, of which *my Text* is a
Part ; and *in particular* it moſt diſtinctly explains, what is there meant by the perſon
not having on a Wedding-Garment ; ver. 7 ; *The Marriage of the Lamb is come ;* ——
and to Her (to the Church) *was granted, that ſhe ſhould be arrayed in fine linnen, clean*
and white ; for the fine linnen is the Righteouſneſs of the Saints: *And he ſaith unto me,*
Write ; Bleſſed are they which are called to the Marriage-Supper *of the Lamb.* From
this Deſcription it is evident, that the *man*, whom *the King* in the Parable, when he
came in *to ſee the Gueſts* whom he had invited to his Son's *Marriage-Feaſt*, ſaw *Not*
having on a Wedding-garment ; This *man* (I ſay) is *every perſon*, who, *making profeſ-*
ſion of the Chriſtian Religion, yet *practiſes not the Virtues of a Chriſtian Life* ; Every
perſon, who, expecting to be *Saved by Chriſt*, yet regards not the *Conditions on which*
That Salvation depends ; In a word, every *Profane*, every *Unjuſt*, every *Unrighteous*,
every *Debauched* perſon, whom the repeated Invitations of Chriſt in the Goſpel, bring
not to a timely and an effectual Repentance.

    H A V I N G thus explained the *Principal Phraſe* in the Text ; I ſhall here, before I
proceed, obſerve by the way, how great a Light may be given, from the explication of
this *One* phraſe, to *Many other* paſſages of Scripture, in which the *ſame figure* of Speech
has extended itſelf into a *variety* of *other* Expreſſions. Thus when St *Paul* exhorts,
Eph. iv. 22, 24 ; *Put ye off, concerning the former converſation, the Old man, which is*
corrupt according to the deceitful Luſts : And put ye on *the New man, which after God*
is created in Righteouſneſs and true Holineſs : 'Tis evident how by phraſes literally expreſſing a Change of the *Habit* of the *Body*, and of the external Appearance of the *Per-*
ſon, he emphatically deſcribes a Change of the *Moral Habit* and Diſpoſition of the
Mind. Again, *Col.* ii. 11 ; and ch. iii. 8, 9, 10, 12, 14. Put off *the body of the Sins*
of the Fleſh : Put off *all theſe ;* anger, wrath, malice, and the like : *Seeing that ye have*
put off *the Old man with his deeds ; and have* put on *the New man, which is renewed in*
Knowledge, after the Image of him that created him : Put on *therefore, (as the elect of*
God, holy and beloved,) bowels of mercies, kindneſs, humbleneſs of mind, meekneſs, long-
ſuffering : And above all theſe, put on *Charity, which is the Bond of perfectneſs.* His
Meaning is : *Cloath* yourſelves with all Moral and Chriſtian Virtues : Make them the
Habit of your *Minds* ; the conſtant *character*, by which ye may be known and diſtin-
guiſhed from men of different Principles. The *ſame* figure of Speech, he carries ſtill
higher ; *Gal.* iii. 27 ; *As many of you as have been baptized into Chriſt, have* put on
Chriſt : And *Rom.* xiii. 14 ; *Put ye on the Lord Jeſus Chriſt ; and make not proviſion*
for the Fleſh, to fulfill the Luſts thereof. The phraſe is highly ſignificant and expreſſive :
Let your Minds be habitually *inveſted* with all Moral and *Chriſtian* Virtues, defending

your-

yourſelves continually againſt the Approaches of Temptations, and againſt the Enticements of a vicious and debauched World.

II. *Secondly*, THIS being premiſed by way of *Explication*, I proceed now to make
ſome *uſeful and practical Obſervations* upon the words of the Text. And

1ſt, BY our Lord's repreſenting the King in the Parable, as coming in to view his
Gueſts, and to ſee whether Any of them had not on a Wedding-garment; is intended
to be ſet forth to us, how *abſolutely* and *indiſpenſably* God *expects and requires*, that
every man who hopes to be admitted into the Kingdom of Heaven, ſhould have his
Mind endued, (and as it were *cloathed)* with thoſe *habitual virtuous Qualifications*,
which can no otherwiſe be acquired than by righteous Practice. To appear in the *Preſence*
of a *Prince*, upon any publick and moſt ſolemn Occaſion, in an improper, indecent
and abſurd Dreſs; is a direct Indignity and Affront. Now *Sin*; that is, every *moral
Impurity*, every *Wickedneſs* whatſoever, is infinitely more odious in the ſight of *God*,
than *Any natural* Indecency can be offenſive before *Men.* As therefore, even in the *preſent*
time, (to uſe the words of the Author of the Book of *Wiſdom*; ch. i. 5.) *into a malicious
ſoul Wiſdom ſhall not enter, nor dwell in the Body that is ſubject unto Sin; For the Holy
Spirit of Diſcipline will flee Deceit, and remove from Thoughts that are without Underſtanding, and will not abide when Unrighteouſneſs cometh in:* So, much more, in the
future State, into the *heavenly Jeruſalem, there ſhall in no caſe enter Any thing that
defileth, neither whatſoever worketh Abomination, or maketh a Lie;* Rev. xxi. 27.

2dly, BY the *Queſtion* the King here puts, to the Man who had not on a Wedding-
garment; *Friend, how cameſt thou in hither?* upon *what Pretence*, upon *what Ground*,
with *what Aſſurance*, with *what Expectation* cameſt thou in hither, not having on a
Wedding-garment? by *This queſtion*, I ſay, our Lord plainly intimates to us, in way
of Admonition or Warning; that there *is* ſuch a thing as a Falſe or ill-grounded Hope;
that there *are* deceitful Expectations, which may betray Men into Perdition. And
'tis of the higheſt importance in the World, not to be led by them into a groundleſs
Preſumption. When men who live in the habitual Practice of Virtue, are, by any
particular melancholy and erroneous Notions, led into Great Fears and unreaſonable
Deſpondencies; the ill Effect in This caſe, provided they continue to live virtuouſly
and religiouſly, is nothing more than the Trouble itſelf which ariſes from ſuch Fears.
But on the *other* hand, when men who live not a virtuous life, have yet a preſumptuous Hope, founded upon *Other* Expedients, and built upon *Any other* Grounds whatſoever; here the Error is *Fatal*, and directly leads men to Deſtruction. And therefore
our Saviour, in *This* Point, is always very plain and explicit, that no one, even of the
meaneſt capacity, can poſſibly miſunderſtand him. The *Wedding-garment*, is a *Virtuous
Life:* Without This, whoſoever pretends to any Hope in Chriſt, upon what preſumption
ſoever it be; to *Him* is the Queſtion put by our Lord; *Friend, how cameſt thou in hither?*
Many are the Expedients which men of corrupt minds have invented, to deceive themſelves in This matter. Some ſatisfy themſelves with the *Zeal* they expreſs for the *Profeſſion*
of the True Religion, tho' they diſhonour That Profeſſion by Unrighteous Works. Others
expect to obtain Salvation by the Strength of their *Faith*; utterly miſtaking the *very
Meaning* of the word *Faith*; apprehending it to ſignify *Credulity*, inſtead of *Fidelity*;
and that they ſhall be accepted for being *Confident*, inſtead of *Faithful* Servants. Some
depend upon certain Things that can be done for them by *Others*; as if any thing
could, in the *religious* Senſe, be of Advantage to any man, which does not at all make
him the *Better* man. Others rely upon the *Merits of Chriſt*; deceiving themſelves
with an expectation that Chriſt will reſcue them from *Puniſhment*, though they reject
all the Motives by which His Goſpel propoſes to reſcue them from *Sin.* Theſe, and all
other Expedients of the like nature; all Expedients whatſoever, intended to ſupply

SERM. the Want of the One thing neceſſary, which is a virtuous Life; are what our Saviour
CV. here repreſents to us, by the Perſon *not having on a Wedding-Garment*. It is the ſame
thing, as what he elſewhere compares to a Man's *building his Houſe upon the Sand*,
inſtead of founding it *upon a Rock*. It is the ſame thing, as what he elſewhere warns
us of, when he tells us, *that Many ſhall ſeek to enter in, and ſhall not be able:* For,
when they ſhall ſay unto him, Lord, Lord, open unto us; his Anſwer will be, *I know
you not whence ye are; Depart from me, all ye workers of Iniquity.*

     3dly, By the following Obſervation; that, when the King aſked, *how cameſt thou
in hither, not having a Wedding-garment?* the Man was *ſpeechleſs*: By *This* obſervation (I ſay) our Lord teaches us, that the Judgment of God will be *according to
Right; According to Right*, in the Senſe that *We* underſtand Juſt and Right; in the
Senſe, that even the *Wickedeſt* of men ſhall not be able to deny, is according to Righteouſneſs and Juſtice. The man convicted, was *ſpeechleſs*. He had *nothing to plead* in
his own behalf. He was condemned by the Verdict of his *own conſcience*, as well as
by the righteous Sentence of *God*. This evidently ſhows, how abſurd and unreaſonable all thoſe men's notion of God is, who look upon him not as a juſt and equitable
Judge, but as an Arbitrary Lord; condemning or acquitting Men according to certain
abſolute Decrees of *his own*, and not according to *Their* Behaviour. Which Doctrine
if it had been true, the perſon here in the Parable might very juſtly have pleaded in his
own Excuſe, that it was not poſſible for him to have a Wedding-garment, becauſe the
King had not been pleaſed to give him One. And our Saviour, by laying, on the
contrary, a particular Streſs upon the man's having *no apology* to make for himſelf;
clearly warns us againſt entertaining any ſuch diſhonourable Notions of *God*. The
condemnation of Sinners, is wholly from *Themſelves*: And the Scripture, by perpetually
inſiſting that it *is* ſo, urges upon all wicked men, in the moſt affectionate manner,
the deſtructive Conſequences of their vicious Courſes, and the indeſpenſable neceſſity
of effectual Repentance and Reformation of manners; And at the ſame time, it affords
the ſtrongeſt Aſſurance to thoſe who ſincerely endeavour to live virtuouſly, that by *That*
method *certainly*, and by *That* method *only*, they ſhall obtain the eternal Favour of God.
The reaſon why even wicked *Heathens* ſhall be condemned at the laſt day, is becauſe
they *did things* (as our Saviour expreſſes it) *worthy of Stripes*; things *in their own nature*
worthy of ſtripes; things contrary to the dictates of *their own Conſciences*, contrary to the
Light of *univerſal Reaſon*, contrary to their *natural Knowledge of God: So that they are
without Excuſe*; Rom. i. 20; *Without Excuſe*; That is, in the Language of my Text,
Speechleſs. And This is what the Scripture elſewhere declares, when it tells us that *the
mouth of all Wickedneſs ſhall be ſtopped*; Pſ. cvii. 42: And, Rom. iii. 19; *That every mouth
may be ſtopped, and all the World become guilty before God*. The Meaning is: When God
ſhall finally judge the Secrets of all Hearts, he ſhall be juſtified in his Sentence, even
Sinners themſelves being Judges; and every mouth ſhall be ſtopt before him, not by
the force of arbitrary and irreſiſtible Power, but by the undeniable evidence of the Juſtice and Equity and Righteouſneſs of the Judgment.

     4thly, By the *Benignity* of the *appellation* wherewith our Saviour here repreſents
the King treating his unworthy Gueſt; *Friend, how cameſt thou in hither, not having
a Wedding-garment?* Hereby, I ſay, is affectionately ſet forth to us the *Reality* of
the Concern God has for the Salvation of men. *He*, as the Apoſtle expreſſes it, *willeth All men to be ſaved; not willing that Any ſhould periſh, but that All might come to
Repentance.* And when men continue obſtinately impenitent, he condeſcends to repreſent himſelf as *Grieved* with their iniquities. And he *argues* with them, in the moſt
affectionate manner, by his Prophets and by his Miniſters: *come now, and let us* reaſon
together, ſaith the Lord: For, why will ye die, O ye Houſe of Iſrael?

         5thly,

5thly, B y what follows in the *next words after* the affectionate expreſſion in the S E R M. Text, Our Saviour adds a *very moving Admonition*, how dreadful at laſt will be the CV. State of all Thoſe, whom the great Goodneſs and Long-ſuffering of God have not been 〰 able to bring to Repentance, and to effectual Amendment of Life and Manners. When the man who had not on a Wedding-garment, was *Speechleſs,* and had *no Excuſe* for his Total Want of the abſolutely neceſſary and indiſpenſable Qualification of Virtue and Holineſs; *Then ſaid the King to his Servants,* ver. 13; *Bind him hand and foot, and take him away, and caſt him into outer darkneſs; There ſhall be weeping and gnaſh-ing of Teeth.*

Laſtly: B y the concluding words, with which our Lord cloſes the whole Para-ble; *ver.* 14; *For Many are called, but Few are Choſen:* By theſe words, I ſay, our Lord clearly and diſtinctly declares, that the *Choſen* or the *Elect* of God, are not per-ſons originally and unconditionately from the Beginning, *decreed* to be ſaved; but all ſuch as ſhall at the End be found *having a Wedding-garment,* that is, Clothed with Righteouſneſs, having led *a Holy and a Virtuous Life.*

SERMON

SERMON CVI.

Every Man is principally to regard his own proper Duty.

J O H. XXI. 22.

Jefus faith unto him, If I will that he tarry till I come, what is That to Thee? Follow Thou me.

IN the Beginning of This chapter, our Lord appearing to his Difciples after his Refurrection, and making himfelf known to them by a miraculous draught of Fifhes, *ver.* 6, 7, 11; takes That occafion to give a *particular Admonition* to be as *diligent* for the *time to come* in propagating the *Doctrine* of *Chrift*, as he had in *time paft* been *faulty* in denying of *Chrift himfelf.* For which reafon he *repeats* his Queftion no lefs than *Three times* fucceffively; *Simon, fon of Jonas, loveft thou me?* till *Peter* was *grieved* at it, ver. 17; and his heart fmote him with Regret, at the Juft-nefs of the Reproof, and at the Earneftnefs of the threefold Repetition. Yet at the fame time it could not but be matter of *Comfort* to him, and an affured Token of his Repentance being *accepted*; that our Lord was pleafed, in fo particular and diftinct a manner, to inquire into the Sincerity of his *Love*, and to lay upon him fuch a re-peated Command to *feed his Flock.* The Church of *Rome*, has built upon thefe words a very extraordinary Confequence: That, becaufe our Saviour commanded St *Peter* to inftruct men diligently in the Chriftian Faith, and St *Peter* was afterward martyred at *Rome* by the Heathen Emperor; therefore the *Bifhop of Rome* has a perpetual Right to require what Doctrines he pleafes, to be received implicitly by the whole Chriftian Church; without being at all able to prove, that thofe Doctrines were ever taught either by Chrift or by St *Peter.* Which is juft fuch another Confequence, as their inferring the Supremacy of the Bifhop or Church of *Rome*, from our Lord's ftyling St *Peter* a Rock, or a Firm and Solid part in That *Foundation of the Apoftles and Pro-phets*, upon which the *Church of Chrift* was to be built. But though neither the One nor the Other were indeed *any* Emblem of *Authority* at all, but of *Duty* only, and of *Succefs in his Labours*; yet, as being prophetick Declarations of *great Succefs* in thofe La-bours, they could not but be matter of great *Encouragement* and *Satisfaction* to his mind. And therefore our Lord, (according to his conftant Cuftom of adding Arguments of *Humility* to all his Promifes;) as, in the *former* cafe, after the Promife of *building his Church upon this Rock*, and *giving to Peter the Keys of the Kingdom of Heaven*, (Matt. xvi. 18, 19, 21;) to prevent his Difciples being puft up with a fudden expectation of That Kingdom, he immediately proceeds to a Prediction of *his own Sufferings*, of the Suf-ferings *our Lord himfelf* was to fubmit to; fo, in this *Latter* cafe, after having given This *Command* to *Peter* to *feed his Sheep*; immediately he proceeds in the very next

words, to foretel what *Sufferings Peter himfelf* likewife fhould undergo. *Verily, verily,*

4

I lay

I say unto thee; when thou waſt young, thou girdeſt thyſelf, and walkedſt whether thou wouldeſt; (alluding to the *Readineſs,* wherewith *Peter, when he heard that it was the Lord,* girt his *Fiſher's Coat about him, and caſt himſelf into the Sea,* ver. 7;) *But when thou ſhalt be old,* faith he, *thou ſhalt ſtretch forth thy hands, and another ſhall gird thee, and carry thee whither thou wouldeſt not;* that is, ſhould carry him to be crucified. Upon This, *Peter turning about,* and *ſeeing the Diſciple, whom Jeſus loved, following* them; *he faith to Jeſus, Lord, and what ſhall this man do?* The Queſtion was a matter of mere *Curioſity;* and therefore our Lord anſwers it accordingly in the words of my Text, *If I will that he tarry till I come, what is That to Thee? Follow thou Me.* *Modern* Expoſitors have imagined, that our Lord by theſe words meant to foretel, that St *John* ſhould live till after the *Deſtruction of Jeruſalem,* which they fancy is ſometimes ſtiled *The Coming of Chriſt.* In the *Apoſtles* days, the ſame words were underſtood by ſome of the Diſciples, as a Prediction that St *John* ſhould not *die at all,* but ſhould continue alive till the *Day of Judgment;* which thoſe, who thus underſtood the words, in all probability apprehended to be much nearer than it was. *Then went this Saying abroad among the Brethren,* ver. 23; *that That Diſciple ſhould not die.* Yet *Jeſus* ſaid no ſuch thing, as that That Diſciple ſhould continue alive, either till the *Deſtruction of Jeruſalem,* or till his Final *Coming to Judgment,* or to *any other* determinate time; but only that it concerned not *Peter* to inquire *at all,* what the Divine Providence had thought fit to determine concerning his *Fellow-Diſciple.* It was foretold to *Peter* for *particular reaſons,* that he himſelf ſhould *die a Martyr:* Poſſibly to *ſupport and comfort* him under the uneaſy Thoughts, of his having before ſo ſhamefully denied his Maſter: Poſſibly alſo for a *contrary* reaſon, to *humble* him, and keep him from being *puffed up* with the preheminence that ſeemed in ſome manner to be given him above the reſt of the Diſciples: Or for any *Other Reaſon,* which the Wiſdom of God thought proper. But as to That *Other Diſciple,* ſays our Lord; whether *He alſo,* ſhall die by the hands of *Violence,* or whether he ſhall die a *Natural Death,* or *how and when* he ſhall die, or whether he ſhall *die at all; What is That to Thee? Follow Thou Me.*

THE words of the Text being thus explained; the *Obſervations* naturally ariſing from them, are briefly as follows.

I. *Firſt;* THAT every perſon, in every ſtation of Life whatſoever, wherein the Providence of God thinks fit to place him, has always ſome *plain* and *certain Duty,* which it is his preſent proper Buſineſs to attend to, *Follow thou Me.* Attend (ſays our Lord,) to the Doctrine which I am now teaching you; That, when I am aſcended into Heaven, you may inſtruct others therein with Fidelity and Diligence which is *Feeding my Sheep.* This was St *Peter's* Duty, at the time of our Lord's ſpeaking theſe words to him: And the Admonition is recorded, as the reſt of our Saviour's Diſcourſes were, upon account of the *Univerſality* and *Perpetuity* of its *Application.* 'Twas not in *One ſingle caſe* only, that our Lord gave this Intimation; *What I ſay unto you, I ſay unto All, Watch:* But, in general, the ſame was intended to be underſtood in almoſt *all* his Inſtructions. *Follow thou Me;* is an Admonition to *Every man,* at *all* Times and in *all* Places, and in *every* Circumſtance of Life, to be *intent upon* his proper duty, whatſoever it be. God has been pleaſed to diſtribute among men very different Gifts, to each one his proper Talent; and an account will be expected from every one, *according to what he hath, and not according to what he hath not.* In the right Uſe of thoſe Capacities and Faculties, thoſe Abilities and Opportunities, whatſoever they be, wherewith God has intruſted every particular perſon; in *This* conſiſts That perſon's proper and peculiar Duty. They who are indued with *Riches, Power,* and *Authority* in the World; are, by the great Weight and Influence of their Example, to promote *Juſtice, Equity,* and *Charity* among Mankind. They who are *Poor,*

S E R M. and *Afflicted*, have a particular Call to the Virtues of *Patience* and *Contentment*; which,
CVI. in their proper place, do no lefs truly and affectually promote the Glory of God, than
the more confpicuous Virtues of thofe in higher Stations. Thofe who have *Learning*
and *Knowledge*, are to fpread the Light of *Truth* with Fidelity and Diligence, and to
apply the Arguments of *uncorrupt Religion* and the Motives of *Virtuous Practice*, with
all the Clearnefs and Strength they are able. And Thofe of the *Loweft* and *Meaneft*
Capacities, even the moft *Ignorant* of all, have ftill a plain way of Duty before them;
to adhere ftedfaftly to thofe *Few Truths* they know, thofe moft *Important Truths*
which no man can innocently be ignorant of: *Living foberly, righteoufly, and godly
in this prefent world*, becaufe *God has appointed a Day in the which he will judge the
World in Righteoufnefs*: And taking heed not to be impofed upon with things they
cannot underftand; by which the World has been led into the inextricable Labyrinth
of endlefs and unintelligible Superftitions. *Before* the Will of God was made clear
by *Revelation*, the *Light of Nature* was mens *Guide*, and the *Obligations of right Reafon* were the *Rule of their Duty* and their *Guard againft Superftition*. Since That time,
whofoever has had the Doctrine of the Gofpel *reafonably* and *credibly* propofed to him,
to *Him* does our Lord fay, as to St *Peter* in the Text, *Follow Thou Me*. He is *in general* to follow Chrift, in the *univerfal Practice* of *all* Chriftian Virtues; and *in particular* he is to attend to *that proper and peculiar* Duty, whatfoever it be, which is
the right Ufe of thofe Talents wherewith Providence has intrufted him. *Every man,
faith the Apoftle, hath his proper Gift of God; one after This manner, and another
after That*; 1 Cor. vii. 7: *To one is given by the Spirit, the word of Wifdom; to another,
the word of Knowledge*; —— *to another, Faith*; —— *to another, Prophecy; to another,
——— divers kinds of Tongues*; 1 Cor. xii. 8; *Having then gifts differing, according to
the grace that is given to us; whether Prophecy, let us prophefy according to the proportion of Faith*; (That is, let us teach the Will of God *faithfully*, according to the degree of the *Ability*, the *Talent*, the *Truft* committed to us: That is the Meaning of
the word, *Faith*, in This place:) *Or* (whether it be) *Miniftry, let us wait on our
miniftring; or he that teacheth, on Teaching; Or he that exhorteth, on Exhortation;
He that giveth, let him do it with Simplicity; he that ruleth, with diligence; he that
fheweth mercy, with chearfulnefs*; Rom. xii. 6. Or in the words of St *Peter*; 1 Pet. iv.
10: *As every man has received the Gift, even fo minifter the fame one to another, as
good Stewards of the manifold grace of God. If any man fpeak, let him fpeak as the
Oracles of God: If any man minifter, let him do it as of the Ability which God
giveth.*

    T H I S is the *Firft* Obfervation I would draw from the words of the Text: That
every perfon, in every ftation of Life whatfoever, wherein the Providence of God
thinks fit to place him, has always fome *plain* and *certain* Duty, which it is his prefent
proper Bufinefs to attend to: *Follow thou Me.*

    II. T H E *Second* thing obfervable in the words of the Text, is; that when *Peter*
put a Queftion to our Lord, upon a matter which did not at all relate to his own *proper* and *particular* Duty; the Anfwer our Lord gives him, *(what is That to thee? Follow thou Me*;) is fuch an Anfwer, as he conftantly gave at all *other* Times to *any* of
his Difciples upon *any* the like occafion. It was his *General* Method, through the
whole Hiftory of the Gofpel; whatever *Difcourfe* was raifed, or whatever *Queftion*
was put to him, which had no relation to the particular *Duty* of the perfons that propofed it; it was his conftant and general Method, inftead of fatisfying their *Curiofity* by
a direct Anfwer, to turn the Difcourfe into an occafion either of inftructing them in
the *Knowledge* of their *Duty*, or of exhorting them to the *Practice* of it. Thus,
when his Difciples afked him; *Matt.* xxiv. 3; *When fhall thefe things be? and
what fhall be the Sign of thy coming, and of the End of the World?* His Anfwer

I

is, *Watch YE*, and *be ye ready* always; *for in such an hour as you think not, the Son of Man cometh*. When one asked him; *Luk*. xiii. 23; *Lord, are there Few that be saved?* instead of satisfying the person's Curiosity, he exhorts both Him that asked the Question, and as many Others as were present, to take care that *They themselves* be found in the number, *whatever That Number* be: *Strive YE to enter in at the strait gate*. And again: When his Disciples asked him; *Matt*. xviii. 1; *Who is the Greatest in the Kingdom of Heaven?* instead of naming, according to *Their* expectation, some among themselves, who had conversed with him most intimately here upon Earth, (which Expectation showed forth itself particularly in the Request of the Mother of *Zebedee*'s children, that *One of her Sons* might *sit on his Right hand,* and the *Other on his Left in his Kingdom*;) instead of This, I say, he tells them *Which* was the *Only Way*, whereby they could attain to the Kingdom of Heaven *at all*. *Setting a little Child in the midst of them*, he said; *Verily I say unto you, except ye be converted and become as little children, ye shall not enter into the Kingdom of Heaven*. Thus, *in general,* whatever Question or matter of Discourse had no relation to the proper and necessary *Duty* of the *persons themselves* who moved the Discourse; our Lord always turned it from a matter of mere Curiosity, into some real *Instruction* or useful *Exhortation*.

III. A *Third* thing to be observed in the words of the Text, is; that our Lord does here discourage *in particular,* a *Curiosity of Inquiry* into *Other mens Affairs*. 'Twas upon *Peter*'s inquiring concerning *Another Disciple* which followed him, *and what shall This man do?* that our Lord made to him the Reply in the Text, *What is That to Thee? Follow Thou Me*. The Inquiry was *innocent;* And there is no reason to suppose that our Lord was *angry* with *Peter* for making it. But he was willing to take This opportunity, (according to his Custom upon all Other occasions,) of inculcating upon *Peter his own* Duty, and of discouraging all *needless Curiosity* concerning the Affairs of Others. What was *innocent* in St *Peter* in the *present* case, and may in *numberless* Instances be *innocent* in *Any* man; is yet a matter which *may* grow into a *Vice,* and, by becoming a *Habit,* may lead to things very *detrimental* to a right Temper and Disposition of Mind. The *Evil* of *Vain Curiosity* does not appear at first sight, either to *Others,* or perhaps to the *Person himself;* but when indulged habitually, it frequently terminates in an *idle, worthless,* and *unprofitable* Temper: Such as is described by St *Paul;* 1 Tim. v. 13; *They learn to be idle, wandering about from house to house and not only idle, but tatlers also, and busy-bodies, speaking things which they ought not:* Or, as St *Peter* expresses it, 1 Pet. iv. 15; *Busy-bodies in other mens matters*. This Temper, though *in itself* it may seem only *trifling* and *worthless,* yet in its consequences it leads very naturally to *Other* and *Greater Vices;* to *Envy, Strife, Contentiousness, Pride, Censoriousness, Discontent,* and numberless other troublesome and mischievous Effects. Persons of This disposition, are extremely apt to be continually *pulling Motes out of their Brother's Eye,* while a *Beam* remains unperceived *in their Own;* That is, to be perpetually *magnifying* the *Faults* of Others, and altogether *insensible* of *their Own*. They are very apt, either to *undervalue* and *despise* the *Talents* and *Abilities* wherewith God has been pleased to endue Others; which is what St *Paul* represents under the similitude of *The Eye saying unto the Hand, I have no need of Thee;* and again the *Head* to the *Feet, I have no need of You:* Or else, in the contrary Extreme, they will *envy* and *repine* at the *Advantages* that Others enjoy; Which is what our Saviour reproves in his parable of the Labourers. *Is Thine Eye evil, because I am Good?* The same Temper it is, that moves persons of different *Sects,* to be inquisitive about the possibility of mens Salvation in *Other Communities,* rather than attentive to discover and amend any Errors in *their Own*. Whether a *Heathen,* to whom the Light of the Gospel was never made known, can be saved by obeying the Law of *Reason;* and whether Salvation is attainable in such *Christian Societies,* as are greatly corrupt in very important Doctrines;

are

S E R M.
CV.
ver. 42, 44.

1 Cor. xii. 21.

Mat. xx. 15.

S E R M. are Queſtions, to which our Saviour would have replied, *What is That to Thee? Follow*
CVI. *Thou Me.* But one thing is very certain, that no man can be ſaved, who does not ſin-
cerely endeavour to find out the *Truth* for *Himſelf*; who *wilfully* propagates *known*
Errors; and has no ſollicitude to reform his *Own* Vices, and (as far as lies in *His*
Power) the Vices of his *Companions and Friends.*

IV. *Fourthly,* As our Lord in the Text expreſsly diſcourages all needleſs Curioſity
of inquiry into other men's *Affairs*; ſo, by Analogy, the ſame Caution may in its Application reaſonably be extended likewiſe to a Curioſity about *Doctrines* not of importance to Religion. Whatever *Notions* do in their Conſequences affect the *Worſhip* of
the *True God*, or have any direct influence either in promoting or hindring the Practice of *True Virtue and Goodneſs* among *Men*; Theſe indeed can never be too carefully
inquired into, or too thoroughly examined. But Speculations which are of no ſuch
Conſequence, the Fewer of them Religion is concerned with, the better. They are
generally matter of Contention only, and uncharitable Animoſity; and have brought
great Scandal and Reproach upon Religion. A Fondneſs of determining things not at
all certain, or not clearly underſtood; and a Shame of departing from what could not
reaſonably be maintained; has been the Ground and the Support, the Cauſe both of
the Riſe and of the Continuance, of almoſt all the Sects, with which the *World* has
been *divided*, and the *Religion* of Chriſt *diſhonoured*. Could men prevail with themſelves to be more zealous about things confeſſedly of Univerſal Importance, than about
the diſtinguiſhing Notions of Particular Sects; which, in the common Methods of the
World, are ſo much the *more eagerly* contended for, as they are *leſs reaſonable* or *more
uncertain:* Could men, I ſay, prevail with themſelves to be *leſs ſollicitous* about things
uncertain, and *more diligent* in the Practice of undiſputed Virtues; the State of Religion
in the World, would ſoon have a very different Aſpect; and the Effect of its influence
upon mens Lives and Manners, would be unſpeakably great, with reſpect both to the
Happineſs of the *Preſent Life*, and of That alſo which is *to come.*

V. *Fifthly and Laſtly;* T H E Laſt Obſervation I ſhall raiſe from the words of the
Text, is; that we are not to draw *Inferences* from *particular Expreſſions* in Scripture
different from the evident *Intention* of the *Whole Diſcourſe* in which Such Expreſſions
are found. From our Lord's ſaying to St *Peter, If I will that* That other Diſciple *tarry
till I come, what is That to Thee?* immediately *This Saying went abroad among the Brethren, that That Diſciple ſhould not die. Yet Jeſus ſaid not unto him, He ſhall not die; but,*
whether he ſhall die or no, *what is That to Thee?* In like manner; he who from the
Parable of the *Ten Virgins*, whereof *Five* are repreſented as being *Wiſe*, and *Five Fooliſh*; ſhould infer that the *Number* of thoſe who ſhall be *Saved*, will be exactly *Equal*
to that of Thoſe who *Periſh*; when the Parable was not intended to deſcribe the
Number, but the *Qualifications* of Them which ſhall be ſaved; would be found to make
a very inconſequent Deduction. And the like would be the Argument, of Him who,
from the Parable of the *Talents*; (wherein the Servants, who with *Ten*, and with *Five*,
and with *Two* Talents committed to them are repreſented as being proportionally *rewarded* for their proportional Improvement of theſe reſpective Sums; while *He only* was
puniſhed, who hid in a Napkin his *One Single* Talent;) ſhould infer, that *Thoſe only*
will periſh, who have but *Small Abilities*; though the Scripture on the contrary expreſsly declares, *that to whom much is given, of Him will be the more required.* All Arguings, I ſay, of This Kind, from ſingle *incidental* Expreſſions of Scripture; are mere
groundleſs Imaginations: Nor can Any thing ever be of real Uſe in the Religion of a
Chriſtian, but our being careful in the *Profeſſion* of *Thoſe Doctrines*, and in the *Practice*
of *Thoſe Duties*, which are evidently the *intentional* Aim and View of our Lord's *whole*
Diſcourſes.

SERMON

SERMON CVII.

The Folly of losing one's Soul to gain the whole World.

MATT. XVI. 26.

For what is a man profited, if he shall gain the whole World, and lose his own Soul ?

OUR Saviour in his Parable of the Sower, represents to us the incredible *Careless-* ness of men, in the most important matters of Religion, by a very remarkable Comparison: As *some seeds, says he, fall by the way-side, and the fowls come and devour them up ; so when any one heareth the Word of the Kingdom and understandeth it not,* i. e. attends not to it, nor fixes his Mind upon it, *then cometh the wicked one, and catcheth away That which was sown in his Heart.* The Meaning is; not that the Devil has Power *literally,* to steal mens Knowledge out of their minds, and rob them of their religious Notions ; but that men are frequently so *careless,* even in things which they themselves *well know* to be of the utmost importance to them ; that the *degree* of their negligence cannot be Truly represented by any lower figure, than by supposing them to have even lost *out of their Minds* Those Notions, to which they give so little attention. St *Paul* has a Phrase no less expressive, *Gal.* iii. 1 ; *O foolish Galatians, who has* bewitched *you ; that you, before whose eyes Jesus Christ has been* evidently *set forth, yet should not obey the Truth? That* men should have the Truth *evidently* set before them, and yet *not obey* it ; is so great an Absurdity, that he represents it elegantly by That *unusual* Phrase, *Who has* bewitched *you ?*

T H A T, in *temporal* affairs, a man should accept *any thing* in exchange for his *Life,* is a Folly never heard of. *Skin for Skin, yea, all that a man hath, will he give for his Life* ; Job ii. 4. In *spiritual* Concerns, the Argument is as much stronger, as *Eternity* is of more importance than *Time,* and *Immortality* of greater Consequence than this *transitory Life.* Our Saviour, with great Propriety of expression, compares the Kingdom of Heaven to a *Treasure hid in a Field, which when a man hath found, for joy thereof he goeth, and selleth all that he hath, and buyeth that Field* ; Mat. xiii. 44 : and to a *goodly pearl of great price,* (ver. 46.) *which when a man had found, he went and sold all that he had, and bought it.* To part with this inestimable Treasure, for a *Trifle* ; and accept any thing, that the pleasures of Sin can afford a man, in exchange for his own Life, in exchange for his future and *eternal* life ; is the Folly our Saviour intended to expose in the words of the Text, *What is a man profited, if he shall gain the whole World, and lose his own Soul?*

T H A T there is *no profit* in such an Exchange, is a Proposition that wants no *Proof.* For there is no man so stupid, as not to be sensible of this Truth ; no man so ignorant, as not to think it needless for Another to go about to convince him of it. Yet so it is, that even This very *Reason,* the indisputable *Certainty* of so great a Truth, and its being without controversy and of necessity acknowledged by all, comes in the event of things to be *itself* an occasion, that makes men stand in need of *more earnest exhortations,* to

SERM. perſwade them not to forget or neglect it. For, as the *ſtrongeſt* Objects, which make
CVII. perpetually an equal and *continued* Impreſſion upon our Senſes, are apt, by reaſon of
their *conſtant* Preſence, to affect us *little* more, than if they made *no* Impreſſion upon the
Senſe at all : So the *abſolute* and *evident Certainty* of this great Truth, leaving *no room*
for Enquiry or Debate, makes careleſs men almoſt as much lay aſide the Thoughts of it,
as if the Certainty were on the *other* ſide of the Queſtion ; and as if they really thought
it a *ſufficient Profit*, to gain, not the *Whole* World, but even ſome of the moſt *inconſiderable* of its enjoyments, at the Expence of their own Souls. It is very evident, *no man*
can poſſibly ſo think : It is very evident that *every man*, who pretends to believe any
thing of religion at all, muſt of neceſſity acknowledge the inexpreſſible diſproportion between things temporary and eternal. Nevertheleſs, they are not *influenced* by this great
Truth, according to the importance of it ; but ſhake off the Thoughts of it, as if it were
of no moment to meditate upon what they think they are *already ſufficiently convinced
of* ; and look upon it as a troubleſome importunity, to be always reminding them of
That, which they *well knew* and were ſatisfied of *before*. They *know* it indeed very
well ; But *That Knowledge* of theirs, without frequent and ſerious Meditation, is *like*
unto Ignorance ; becauſe it has *no effect*, and makes *no Impreſſion*. It is like the *ſpeculative* knowledge of a Truth that concerns them not ; or like the *habitual* Underſtanding of a mathematical Demonſtration, never recollected. Moſt reaſonably therefore
does our Saviour put to us the Queſtion, and expects that we ſhould frequently put it to
ourſelves ; *What is a man profited, if he ſhall gain the whole World, and loſe his own Soul?*

THE *occaſion* of the words, was his diſcourſing to his Diſciples concerning the expectation of *Perſecution*. He had told them, *ver.* 21, how many things *he himſelf*
was to ſuffer at the hands of the *Jews* ; and he goes on to tell them, *ver.* 24, that
They alſo muſt expect to ſuffer in like manner : *If any man will come after me*, he muſt
deny himſelf, and take up his croſs, and follow me ; *For whoſoever will loſe his Life for my
ſake, ſhall find it* ; and *whoſoever will ſave his Life, ſhall loſe it* : That is, whoſoever
parts with his virtue and good conſcience, to *ſave* his *temporal* life ; ſhall *loſe* that which
is *eternal* ; and by eſcaping the *firſt* Death for a *time*, ſhall incur the penalty of the *ſecond* Death *for ever*. And This explains the meaning of thoſe difficult words which
follow in the 28th verſe, *Verily, I ſay unto you, there be ſome ſtanding here, which ſhall
not taſte of Death, till they ſee the Son of Man coming in his Kingdom*. By theſe words,
there be ſome ſtanding here, it is probable he had Regard particularly to *Judas* : And it
ſeems to have been his intention, to repreſent *natural* or *temporal* Death ſo inconſiderable, as if *They* only, who fell under the *ſecond* Death, could with any propriety be ſaid
to *Taſte* the Bitterneſs of *Death* at all. They ſhall not *taſte of Death, till they ſee the
Son of Man coming in his Kingdom*. And This *increaſes* the Strength of the Argument
he intended to inforce in the words of the Text ; *What is a man profited, if he ſhall gain
the whole World, and loſe his own Soul?*

THE *Argument* our Saviour here uſes, is one of *That* kind, which by taking into the
Suppoſition much *more* than *is* or *can be true* ; concludes ſo much the *more undeniably*,
and with the *greater Strength*, in all *caſes* which really *are* true. He puts the Suppoſition, that a man by loſing his Soul, *could* gain the *whole* World : And if he *did* ſo,
his Gain would be *nothing*. The *Concluſion* he intended we ſhould draw from hence,
is this ; How much more *fooliſh* then are ſinful men ; who *loſe* their Souls, and yet, in
the exchange, gain *not the whole World* neither ; nor indeed, any conſiderable *part*
of it ?

FOR, *what* is it, that *Sinners* generally enjoy in the World, more than the *righteous?* Not a *longer Life* : Very often a *ſhorter*, being cut off by their own Folly in the
midſt of their days. Not a *healthier Body* : Moſt uſually a more *infirm* one, made ſo,
by their own debauched and intemperate Living. Not a more *ſatisfied Mind* : On the

contrary

contrary, a Mind *very* Uneasy for the moft part, and full of *perplexity*. In a word, S E R M.
they enjoy in reality, more than the Righteous, nothing but the *bare perverfenefs*, no- CVII.
thing but the *mere irregularity* of thofe very pleafures, which really and in Truth are
much more pleafures when accompanied with innocency.

B U T to be *more diftinct and particular*, in confidering, 1*ft*, the *Suppofition*, which
our Saviour puts ; and 2*dly*, the *Conclufion*, which he intends we fhould draw from it.

I. *Firft* ; Our Saviour puts the *Suppofition*, that a man, by lofing his Soul, could, in
exchange, gain to himfelf the *whole World* : And, upon That Suppofition, propofes
the Queftion ; *What would it profit him* ? The Anfwer, *that it would profit him nothing*, is what every man's natural Senfe immediately fuggefts to him. The *Doctrine*
therefore *included* in our Saviour's *Queftion*, and *afferted* in the *Anfwer*, is This : that,
could a man, by being *wicked*, gain to himfelf abfolutely *all* the *good* things of this prefent life ; and, on the contrary, by being confcientioufly *religious*, were *certainly* to
fuffer *all* the *Evil*, that this prefent World can inflict ; (which, generally fpeaking, is
by no means the cafe : But, fuppofing it *were* ;) yet ftill the *Wicked* man's Choice
would be infinitely *foolifh*, and the *Virtuous* man's truly *Wife*.

F O R, *what* is it, that a *virtuous* man, even upon *This* Suppofition, can poffibly fuffer ? *All the Evils* of this prefent life ; All the *external* Evils, which are the *only* ones
that *can* befal a righteous man ; are *poverty* of *condition*, Contempt in the *opinion of
wicked men*, and *Pain* or Uneafinefs of *Body* : Things very grievous indeed to Flefh
and Blood, and which may and ought by all *lawful* means to be carefully avoided.
But they are all of them *natural* Calamities ; incident to the *wicked*, as well as to the
righteous : Sometimes, they can by *no means* be avoided ; neither by any *lawful*, nor
by any *unlawful* Practices. But when they *can* be avoided, by deferting our Duty ;
it is by no means worth while to do it, at the expence of our *Souls*. For *thefe Evils*,
at the *worft* that can be fuppofed, are all *Temporal* ; and, when at the greateft extre-
mity, not *Temporal* only, but even *very fhort* alfo. *My Friends*, faith our Saviour, *be Luk. xii. 4.
not afraid of them that kill the Body, and after That have no more that they can do :
But I will forewarn you, whom you fhall fear* ; *Fear Him, who, after he has killed, has
power to caft into Hell* ; *yea, I fay unto you, Fear Him*. The Argument ufed by the
Lepers in the Siege of *Samaria*, 2 *Kings* vii. 4, is very applicable to this cafe ; *If
we enter into the City, faid they, the Famine is in the city, and we fhall die* ; *and if
we fit here, we die alfo* ; *and if we fall unto the Hoft of the Syrians, and ―― they
kill us, we fhall but die*. A man in the worft of Circumftances, and under the fevereft
Perfecutions, by adhering to the Caufe of Truth and Virtue, can lofe but his temporal Life : And fo he muft *however*, perhaps by a Difeafe more painful, than the
Death his Perfecutors would inflict ; and his Mind, at the fame time, not fupported
with the Hopes of a glorious Immortality.

O N the other hand ; *what* is it, that a wicked man, even upon the *high* Suppofition
our Saviour puts, can poffibly attain ? All the *good* things of this *whole* World, are
Riches, Honour, and *Pleafure* : Now were it poffible that a man, in exchange for his
Soul, could gain to himfelf the whole Compafs of thefe fenfual Enjoyments ; (Which
yet is indeed very far from any wicked man's cafe ; But fuppofe he *could* ;) *Suppofe* he
could, in *Riches*, exceed the Glory of *Solomon* ; and, in *Power*, extend his Dominion
from one Sea to the other, and force all Nations to do him Service ; and, in his *perfonal*
capacity, enjoy a continued feries of the greateft and moft uninterrupted *pleafures* ;
And All this, even to the Age of *Methufalem* ; yet ftill thefe things would be but *Temporal* ; and, when paft, though after the *longeft* duration, they would all feem but as a
fhadow that departeth, and as a Dream when one awaketh. *Riches* would *not profit* the Prov. xi. 4
man, *in the day of wrath* ; and the Time muft at length come, when it would be faid
unto him, *Thou Fool, this night fhall thy Soul be required of thee* ; and his having been
clothed

S E R M. *clothed in purple and fine linnen, and having fared sumptuously every day*, would be *no*
CVII. *comfort* to him, when he finally *lift up his eyes in Torment*. Besides, that, even in this
present life itself, such a Possessor of the *whole* World, could enjoy *really* but a very *small*
part, of what, in *fancy and imagination only*, would be his own *property*. He who
knew and enjoyed more of it, than any other mortal man ; concluded, more than once,
that even in the highest Pitch of temporal Prosperity, *All is Vanity and Vexation of
Spirit*.

THUS have I put the Case, according to our Lord's *Supposition* in the Text, not as
things usually *are*, but to the *greatest* advantage on the side of Wickedness ; that a man,
in exchange for his Soul, could gain by unrighteousness the *whole* World ; or, by adhering to Virtue, would on the contrary *suffer*, all he can *here suffer*. By considering
the *Recompence*, which will attend the Choice of *either* part ; we may be enabled to
judge, of the *Truth* of our Lord's assertion ; that the *wicked* man's Choice, even upon
this extraordinary *supposition* of gaining the *whole* World, would be very *foolish* ; and the
virtuous man's, very *wise*. For, to enter into the *particulars* ; Suppose a religious person, is by his adh ering to the ways of Virtue, reduced to extreme *Poverty* ; (which
however is very seldom the Case, except in times of Persecution only ;) yet there is a
worse Poverty, which at the same time he *avoids* by *that very* Choice ; a State of *Ex-
clusion* from the Love and Favour of God, which Loss, even in this *present* Time,
is an anticipation of outer darkness : *Rev.* iii. 17 ; *Thou knowest not, that thou art
wretched and miserable and* poor *and blind and naked.* This *Poverty*, the *virtuous* man,
even under the *severest* Persecutions, is sure to escape ; and under the *greatest* pressure of
temporal Wants, secures to himself the *truer* and more *certain* Riches of *Virtue and*
Prov. iii. 14. *Contentment* ; the *Merchandise whereof is better than the Merchandise of Silver, and the
gain thereof than fine Gold.* He secures to himself That *Pearl* of great price, of which
our Saviour affirms, that *He* was a wise man, who *sold all that he had, and bought it.*
He is numbered with Those, concerning whom St *James* declares, that though they
Jam. ii. 5 are *poor* in *this World*, yet *they are rich in Faith* ; *and Heirs of the Kingdom, which*
Heb. xi. 26. God *has promised to them that love him.* He, with *Moses*, esteems *the reproach of Christ*,
greater Riches *than the treasures in Egypt* ; and may justly apply to himself our *Saviour's* words to the Church of *Smyrna, Rev.* ii. 9 ; *I know thy works, and tribulation
and poverty, but thou art* rich. He has *laid up for himself treasure in Heaven, where
neither moth nor rust doth corrupt, nor Thieves break through and steal*, nor any Anxiety of Mind disturbs the enjoyment of it.

AGAIN : If a truly religious Man, does, by being such, fall under the *greatest*
Contempt, in the Opinion of wicked men ; yet there is a *worse Dishonour*, which he
at the same time avoids, even the *Shame and Dishonour* of *Sin*, to his *own Conscience
here*, and in the presence of the *whole World hereafter* ; when they that sleep in the
dust of the earth, shall *awake, some to everlasting Life, and some to* Shame and Everlasting Contempt ; *Dan.* xii. 2. And, under the *highest* unjust *Reproaches* of Men,
he is secure in the Possession of true *Worth* ; of *That Worth*, which God himself the
Judge of All, will vouchsafe to honour in the presence of the Holy Angels ; when
Christ shall present those who suffer for his sake, as *Kings and Priests unto God even
his Father* ; and they *shall reign with Him for ever* ; crowned with *Glory* and *Immortality* ; being made *Sons of God*, and *equal unto the Angels* ; among whom, *they that
be wise, shall shine as the brightness of the Firmament,* and *they that turn many to
righteousness, as the Stars for ever and ever.*

Lastly, IF a virtuous and good man suffers in his *Person*, even unto *Death* itself ;
(which *very seldom* is the Case ;) yet there *is* a Calamity *greater* than Death, which
he avoids by choosing the present temporal Suffering. He avoids the Sting of a
guilty Conscience, the insupportable Terror of a wounded Spirit, and the future inex-
         pressible

preffible Pains of Hell. And he gains at prefent That Peace and Joy in the Holy **S E R M.** Ghoft; which can be exceeded by nothing but That which follows after it, even **CVII.** That Happinefs of Heaven, which *Eye hath not feen, nor Ear heard, neither hath it* entered into the Heart of man to conceive; a Happinefs prepared for them that love him, by *Him in whofe prefence there is Fulnefs of Joy, and at whofe right hand there are Pleafures for evermore.*

O n the other hand; Could a *wicked* man, by being wicked, gain to himfelf (as our Saviour here puts the Suppofition; could he *certainly* gain to himfelf) the *whole* World; yet *where* would be the Wifdom and Advantage of *His* Choice, who thus *laid up Treafure for Himfelf, and was not rich towards God?* For, by choofing *Tempo-* Luk. xii. 21. *ral* Wealth, Honour, and Pleafure, upon the Terms of unrighteoufnefs; he forfeits That unfpeakable Happinefs which is *Eternal*: and by avoiding the *fhort and tranfi-tory* Evils, of *prefent* Poverty, Contempt, and Pain; he choofes the fame *future* evils, to continue *for ever*; where the worm dieth not, and the Fire is not quenched, in which the foolifh and impenitent Sinner *fhall be punifhed with everlafting deftruction* 2 Th. i. 9. *from the prefence of the Lord and from the glory of his Power. This* Confideration, fets forth in few words, the extreme Folly of the Man that lofes his own Soul, even upon that *High Suppofition* our Saviour puts, of his gaining in exchange for it the *whole World.* Which was the *Firft* thing to be confidered. But

II. *Secondly*; T h e *Principal* Defign of our Saviour in This Argument, was, by taking into the Suppofition much *more* than *is* or *can be true*; to conclude fo much the *more undeniably*, and with the *greater Strength*, in all *cafes* which really *are* true. He puts the *Suppofition*, that a man by lofing his Soul could gain the *whole World*: And if he did fo, his Gain would be *nothing*; For, *What* would it *profit* him? The *Conclu-fion* he intended we fhould draw from hence, is; how much more *foolifh* are finful men; who *lofe* their Souls, and yet, in the Exchange, gain *not the whole World* nei-ther; nor indeed, any confiderable *part* of it? *Generally fpeaking*, they lofe, both *their own Souls*, and the beft part of the enjoyments even of this *prefent World* too. *They that have done wickedly*, (as it is elegantly expreffed in the *fecond* Book of *Efdras*, ch. vii. 18;) *have fuffered the ftrait things, and yet fhall* not *fee the wide*; that is, they *fuffer*, by their Folly in the *prefent* Life; and yet obtain not *That which is to come*. But *good* men, both fecure to themfelves *That which is to come*; and at the fame time, (excepting *always* the cafe of *Perfecution*, which hath its *peculiar Promifes*,) they en-joy the *prefent* good things, at leaft *equally*, with the wicked. To be particular: The *Religious* man, *believes in God*; *worfhips, loves, fears, and trufts in him*: What de-triment is This to his *temporal* Affairs? Nay, on the contrary, it gives him Affurance and Peace and Satisfaction of Mind in the whole courfe of his Life *here*, at the fame time that it fecures to him eternal Reft *hereafter*.

H e is *juft and righteous, equitable and charitable* in his dealings with all Man-kind: what lofes he by That, *at prefent?* Nay, generally it gains him *Truft, and Confidence*; the *Love, Honour, and Efteem*, at leaft of Wife and Good Men. In the *prefent* time, the righteous is more honourable than his Neighbour; and in the *End* he attains a glorious Immortality.

H e is not *covetous* to heap up inordinate Riches; but with Diligence and Fruga-lity, with Piety and Charity, gets and ufes them: What difadvantage is This to him in the *World?* Nay, on the contrary, by This, faith *Solomon*, fhall *his barns be filled with plenty*, and *the Soul of the liberal fhall be made fat*: The Bread that he fcattereth Prov. iii. 10; upon the Waters, fhall he find again after many days; and he lays up for himfelf, xi. 25. *befides*, in *Heaven*, an incorruptible Treafure.

Laftly, H e moderates his *Appetites and Paffions*, by the Rules of Reafon and true Religion: And what damage is that to him in the *prefent* Life? Nay, generally

fpeaking,

SERM. CVII. ſpeaking, he is Maſter of *all lawful and valuable Enjoyments*; with better Health of Body, and more Satisfaction of *Mind*: Prov. iii. 7, 8, 17: *Fear the Lord, and depart from Evil*; *It ſhall be Health to thy Navel, and Marrow to thy Bones*. The Ways of Wiſdom, even in the *preſent* time, *are Pleaſantneſs, and all her Paths are Peace*; and in the End they lead to *Fulneſs of Joy*, and *Pleaſures for evermore*.

ON the other hand; The *wicked and debauched* perſon, either *diſbelieves* all religion, or neglects and *deſpiſes* it; living in contempt of God, and in habitual profanation of the Laws of his Maker: What gains he by That *Here?* Fears and Terrors, Horror and Deſpair, Uncertainty and anxious *Doubtfulneſs* at leaſt, about what is to come hereafter. *Iſ.* lvii. 20; *The wicked are like the troubled Sea, when it cannot reſt*; *whoſe Waters caſt up mire and dirt*; *there is no Peace, ſaith my God, to the wicked*: And for *This* it is, that he exchanges his Soul *hereafter*.

HE is *unjuſt and uncharitable, falſe and unfaithful, cruel and oppreſſive*: What *Benefit* is This, even to his *temporal* affairs? Generally, it brings upon him Hatred and Diſtruſt, Shame and Diſhonour, among *Men*: And for *This*, he parts with his Soul *for ever*.

HE is *Covetous and inſatiable* in *getting*, or *profligate and profuſe* in *waſting*: What *Fruit* has he of theſe things *at preſent?* Anxiety, and no enjoyment of what he has heaped up, *ſaving the beholding it with his Eyes*; or elſe Poverty and Want, after he has waſted it in rioting and Debauchery: And for *This* it is, that he exchanges his immortal Treaſure.

Laſtly, HE is under the Dominion of ungoverned *Appetites*, diſorderly *Paſſions*, and unlawful *Pleaſures*; What Happineſs has he in this licentiouſneſs *at preſent?* Slavery and Vexation of *Mind*, always; and generally, in his *Body*, acute Diſeaſes, and a ſpeedy Death: *Her houſe is the way to Hell, going down to the Chambers of Death*; Prov. vii. 27: And for *This*, he parts with his Hope of future Immortality.

THIS *is the portion of a wicked man from God, and* This *the Heritage appointed unto him*; Job xx. 29. From all which, the Folly of chooſing the ways of Wickedneſs is ſo extremely apparent; that, as if (comparatively ſpeaking) there were *no other* Folly in the World, the Scripture with great reaſon uſes the words, *Folly and Wickedneſs*, promiſcuouſly for one and the ſame thing: And it is not a *Tautology*, but a moſt *elegant* Deſcription of the extreme Folly of Sinners, which *Solomon* gives us; Prov. xiv. 8, 24; *The Folly of Fools is Deceit, and the Fooliſhneſs of Fools is Folly.*

THE *cauſe* of ſo great a Stupidity among rational Creatures *can* be nothing, but either *Unbelief* of the Government of God, and of a Judgment to come; which is contrary to all Principles of Reaſon: or elſe ſuch *extreme Careleſſneſs*, as St *Peter* deſcribes, when he compares ſome men to *natural brute Beaſts made to be taken and deſtroyed*; 2 Pet. ii. 12: or ſuch *want of Conſideration*, as our Saviour, in the Parable of the Sower, deſcribes by a very elegant Figure, when he repreſents the Devil *ſtealing away* out of mens minds the Notions that had been taught them: Or elſe, laſtly, it muſt be ſuch an obſtinate *Madneſs*, in reſolving *knowingly* to prefer things temporal before eternal; as *Eſau* was a figure of, when *for one morſel of Meat he ſold his Birthright*; or ſuch as St *Paul* deſcibes in the 7th to the *Romans*, when he introduces a man *doing* what he *allows not*; and *what he hates*, (that is, what his *Reaſon* hates,) he in his *Folly* does. Whenever this caſe is repreſented to a wicked man in the perſon of *Another*, or ſet forth under the Circumſtances of a *worldly* affair; he can hardly believe it *poſſible*, that any rational creature ſhould act ſo abſurdly. 'Tis with him, as it was with *David*, when the Prophet *Nathan* ſurprized him, ſaying, *Thou art the Man*; or as it was with *Hazael*, when he ſaid to *Eliſha*, *Is thy Servant a Dog, that he ſhould do this thing?*

SINCE therefore, in *Reaſon and Speculation*, This whole matter is ſo clear and indiſputable; let us, in order more effectually to influence our *Practice*,

I

1st, SERIOUSLY and frequently *meditate*, upon the *True Weight* and *Importance* of Things; that we suffer not ourselves to be deceived by *perpetual Inadvertancy*, and ruined by *habitual Negligence*, after the Example of a careless and inconsiderate World.

2dly, LET us accustom ourselves to consider, *what* Notions *Other* men Now have, and we are sure *we ourselves* shall *have*, of these things; when the Deceits of this World shall be removed from before our Eyes, at the Hour of *Death*, and in the day of *Judgment*. For this is not an *imaginary*, but a *real* Event; towards which *Wise men* always look forward, that it may never surprize them unprepared.

3dly, LET us be Thankful to God, that, generally speaking, he puts upon us no *harder* Terms of Salvation. What the Servant said to *Naaman* the *Syrian*, may well be applied to *Us*: *If the Lord had bid thee do some great thing, wouldst thou not have done it? How much more when he only saith unto thee, wash and be clean!* When we consider what the *Martyrs* suffered of old for *Religion*, and what *Austerities* many in the World now undergo through mere *Superstition*; shall *we* think it much to mortify an unlawful Lust, and deny ourselves a sinful Pleasure, for the Honour of God and the Salvation of our Souls?

4thly and *lastly*; LET us consider that the prize is worthy: Let us fortify ourselves with resolutions to undergo the *hardest* conditions Providence shall think fit to lay upon us; and this will enable us *chearfully* to perform the *easier* ones.

SERMON

SERMON CVIII.

Of the Neceffity of Holinefs.

H E B. XII. 14.

Follow peace with all men, and Holinefs, without which no man fhall fee the Lord.

SERM.
CVIII.

THESE words contain a moft powerful motive, to *Holinefs* of life; drawn from the confideration of the Nature of our *Religion* and the Condition of our *Happinefs.* The abfolute and indifpenfable Condition of *Happinefs,* is the practice of true Religion; and the true nature and effence of *Religion,* is Holinefs of Life: *Without Holinefs, no man fhall fee the Lord.*

I n the words we may obferve; 1*ft,* A Reprefentation made, of the *true nature* of Religion, under the name or character of *Holinefs.* 2*dly,* An Exhortation given us, to put That Holinefs in practife; *(Follow peace, and* Holinefs.) 3*dly,* An Affurance or Connexion of Happinefs, as the proper confequence of fuch Religious Practice. And 4*thly,* A Reprefentation of the nature of that Happinefs, under the notion or character of *Seeing God.*

F ROM which Obfervations there naturally arife the following Propofitions: 1*ft,* That the true and ultimate Intent of all the Laws and Inftitutions of Religion, is to make men holy. 2*dly,* That it *is poffible* for us to be really holy, according to the true Intent and Meaning of thofe Laws. 3*dly,* That God has made it the indifpenfable Condition of our Happinefs, that we become *thus* holy. And 4*thly,* That the nature of that Happinefs is fuch, that it is not poffible to be enjoyed, but by thofe who actually *are* thus holy.

I. *Firft*; T HE true and ultimate Intent of all the Laws and Inftitutions of Religion, is to make men holy. Man is a rational creature, made capable of knowing and of obeying God, and of conforming his life to the Pattern and Imitation of the divine Perfections. This Obedience to the Commands, and Imitation of the Nature and Life of God, is the true Effence of Religion. And as it is the indifpenfable duty of all Created Beings, to *endeavour* after this Purity, fo 'tis the higheft excellency and per-fection of their nature, 'tis their greateft poffible improvement, to *attain* it. The greater degrees of fuch Holinefs any Being is endued with, fo much the higher rank does it obtain in the order of Creatures. The higheft *Angels,* fo much as they obey the Will of God *more entirely,* and imitate the divine Life *more perfectly* than *men* do; fo far are they exalted *above* men, and have a nearer approach to the immediate Pre-fence and Enjoyment of God. And fo much as *one Man* in this life arrives at a greater degree of Holinefs than another, fo much fhall he obtain a more excellent degree of Happinefs in that life which is to come.

I

To

To aſſiſt men in their Endeavours after this *Holineſs*, God has, *at ſundry times and in* S E R M. *divers manners*, appointed ſeveral forms or inſtitutions of Religion; which we ought CVIII. carefully ſo to diſtinguiſh from Religion itſelf, as we would do the *means* of obtaining any thing, from the *end* to be obtained. For *Religion* itſelf, is that Purity, or that virtuous temper and diſpoſition of mind, which exerts itſelf in a conſtant endeavour of being like unto God, and of obeying his Commands: But the *inſtitution* of Religion, is only that outward eſtabliſhment or *form* of worſhip, which is the Means of acquiring ſuch a Holy Diſpoſition. And theſe outward forms, which in their own nature are changeable, have never been valued in the ſight of God, any otherwiſe than as they promoted the End they were deſigned for; *viz.* That Holineſs, which is eternally and unchangeably the ſame. This was the original religion of Paradiſe, and before that, even of Heaven itſelf. This was the End of God's revealing himſelf to the Patriarchs, and ſeparating them from the idolatrous World. This was the End, of his giving the Law to the *Jews*; that they might be a *Holy people* unto the Lord their God. To This all their Sacrifices, all their Purifications led them; and were of no value in *compariſon with* This, but only *in order to* it. *Wherewith ſhall I come before the Lord*, ſaith the Prophet, *and bow myſelf before the high God? Shall I come before him with burnt-offerings, with calves of a year old? Will the Lord be pleaſed with thouſands of rams, and ten thouſands of rivers of oyl? Nay, but He hath ſhewed thee, O man, what is good, and what doth the Lord thy God require of thee, but to do juſtly, and to love mercy, and to walk humbly with thy God?* Micah vi. 6. And whenſoever they failed of having this deſired effect, of making the perſons lives more holy; God declares that he even abhorred all their religious Exerciſes; *He that killeth an ox, is as if he ſlew a man; he that ſacrificeth a lamb, as if he cut off a dog's neck; he that offereth an oblation, as if he offered ſwine's blood; and he that burneth Incenſe, as if he bleſſed an Idol; yea they have choſen their own ways, and their ſoul delighteth in their Abominations:* Iſai. lxvi. 3. And, concerning the *Chriſtian* Inſtitution it is ſtill more expreſſly evident, that the deſign of *the grace of God which bringeth ſalvation, i. e.* of the *Goſpel's appearing unto all men*, was to *Teach us that denying ungodlineſs and worldly luſts, we ſhould live ſoberly, righteouſly, and godly in this preſent world.* And nothing can be a greater contradiction, than the practice of ſuch perſons, as hope to anſwer the deſign of Chriſtianity by any other method whatſoever, inſtead of *purifying themſelves from all filthineſs both of fleſh and ſpirit, and perfecting holineſs in the fear of God.* The Apoſtles in their Epiſtles give us ſeveral repreſentations of Religion under figurative and metaphorical expreſſions, but all agreeing conſtantly in this; that the Subſtance and the End of all Religion, is Virtue or Holineſs of life. Sometimes it is called the *New Man*, i. e. a being changed from Wickedneſs to Righteouſneſs; *Eph.* iv. 22. Sometimes it is called *a New Creature*; Gal. vi. 15; *In Chriſt Jeſus neither Circumciſion availeth any thing, nor Uncircumciſion, but a New Creature*, i. e. a life of real Holineſs and renewed Obedience to God's commands; For ſo the Apoſtle explains his own words expreſſly; 1 *Cor.* vii. 19; *Circumciſion is nothing, and uncircumciſion is nothing; but the keeping the commandments of God.* In ſome places, a religious life is called *Sanctification*. In other paſſages it is repreſented under the titles of *Repentance* and *Converſion, Regeneration* or the *New Birth, Purification* and *Holineſs,* All which, and many other the like Terms made uſe of in Scripture, do manifeſtly tend to this; that the Life and Subſtance, the End and Deſign of Chriſtian Religion, is, that Men turn from a life of Sin unto a life of Righteouſneſs, in order to have a *Conſcience void of offence both towards God and towards Men.*

II. I PROCEED in the *ſecond* place to ſhow, that, as the main Deſign of Religion is to oblige men to Holineſs, ſo it is *poſſible* for us, to be really holy, according to the true intent and meaning of the laws of our Religion. And indeed, ſince God is not

SERM. a hard maſter, expecting to *reap where he has not ſown*, and *to gather where he has not*
CVIII. *ſtrawed*, it cannot be conceived that he ſhould impoſe any commands on us, which it
were not poſſible for us to obey. But becauſe, when we think of the infinite Purity
of God, who cannot behold Iniquity; and conſider the corrupted and degenerate ſtate
of humane nature; this may be apt to make us more apprehenſive than is reaſonable,
of the difficulty of our Duty; it is therefore here to be obſerved particularly; *1ſt*, That
God does not ordinarily require more of us, than what a ſincere mind, notwithſtanding the corruption of our nature, is well able to perform; *2dly*, That whenſoever he
requires more than this, he never fails to afford us proportionably great aſſiſtance, to
enable us to perform what he ſo requires; and *laſtly*, That if at any time we are ſurprized into the commiſſion of Sin, he accepts real Repentance and a renewed Obedience inſtead of an uninterrupted courſe of Holineſs.

　　1ſt, GOD does not ordinarily require more of us, than what a ſincere mind, notwithſtanding the corruption of our nature, is well able to perform. The condition of
the Goſpel-covenant is not perfect unſinning Obedience, but a ſincere endeavour to
obey all the Commands of God to the utmoſt of our Power. Upon which account,
St *John* juſtly affirms, that the *commands* of God *are not grievous*; and our Saviour himſelf calls his *yoke eaſy*, and his *burden light*. What the Servant ſaid to *Naaman* the Sy-
rian is very applicable upon this Argument: *My Father, if the Lord had bid thee do ſome*
great *thing, wouldſt thou not have done it? how much more, when he only ſaith unto thee,*
Waſh and be clean! The Commandments, in their general and moſt proper Senſe, are
ſo far from being impoſſible to be obſerved, that on the contrary a man cannot eaſily
tranſgreſs them, without a hardened conſcience and deliberate choice. But becauſe,
in *ſome* particular caſes and circumſtances, things *more difficult* are enjoined us, ſuch as
our Saviour compares to pulling out a right eye, or cutting off a right hand; therefore
I add,

　　2dly, THAT whenſoever God requires more of us than we are naturally able to perform, he never fails to afford us proportionably great aſſiſtance, to enable us to perform
what he ſo requires. Our Saviour aſſures us, that if a tender mother cannot deny the
ſon of her love any reaſonable requeſt, much leſs *will God deny his holy Spirit to them*
that ask him; and St *Paul* declares, that all good Chriſtians *have* the Spirit of God
dwelling in them, except by their wilful Sins they quench, and grieve, and drive it from
them. So that however weak and imperfect our *Nature* be, yet with this *aſſiſtance*
we are ſure that the Power which is for us is greater than that which is againſt us;
and a ſufficient encouragement it is, to *work out our own ſalvation with fear and trem-*
bling, to conſider that it is God that giveth us both to will and to do of his good plea-
ſure; Phil. ii. 13. There are ſome particular Temptations, which humane nature
ſeems more peculiarly unable to reſiſt; and when any of theſe aſſault us, God has
promiſed that he will with the Temptation alſo make a way to eſcape, that we may
be able to bear it; and that he will afford us a ſupport proportionable to the Difficulty
we are obliged to encounter. The primitive Chriſtians, are a wonderful inſtance of
this Truth: They were tried with the moſt cruel tortures, that either the wit of man
could invent, or the malice of the devil could prompt men to inflict: *They were*
ſtoned, they were ſawn aſunder, were tempted, were ſlain with the ſword; they wandred
about in ſheep-skins and goat-skins, being deſtitute, afflicted, tormented: Yet ſo powerfully were they ſupported by the influence of God's Holy Spirit, that they ſuffered all
the Barbarities of their inhumane Perſecutors with *leſs* concern, than we can even endure to hear or to read of them. And in the caſe of the *contrary* Temptation, of great
and uninterrupted *worldly Proſperity*; (which is almoſt as dangerous, and apt (by ſof-
tening and debaſing mens minds) to ſeduce them and withdraw them inſenſibly from

their

their Duty, as Perſecution is by violence to drive them from it;) concerning This, **S E R M.**
when our Saviour had affirmed, *that it is eaſier for a camel to go through the eye of a* **CVIII.**
needle, than for a rich man to enter into the kingdom of God : He immediately adds,
With Men *this is impoſſible, but with* God *all things are poſſible* ; i. e. By the aſſiſtance
of the grace of God, which he is always ready to afford to thoſe that *believe* and deſire
to *obey* his Goſpel, this temptation of great Proſperity *may* be overcome ; and not only
ſo, but even further, That Power and Riches which are to moſt men an occaſion of
falling, may become the matter of a more excellent Virtue, and an advantage of doing
much more good in the world. To *Us,* humanly ſpeaking, in a ſtate of great *Proſ-*
perity, the Dangers are ſo great, and the Errors ſo numerous, that *That which is*
crooked cannot be made ſtraight, and That which is wanting cannot be numbered : But
to the grace of God revealed in the Goſpel, all things are poſſible. But

3*dly,* I F through the frailty and infirmity of our Nature, we be at any time, notwithſtanding our ſincere endeavours to the contrary, ſurprized into the commiſſion of
Sin ; God accepts real Repentance and a renewed Obedience, inſtead of an uninterrupted courſe of Holineſs. *If any man ſin,* ſaith St *John, we have an Advocate with*
the Father, Jeſus Chriſt the righteous, and he is the propitiation for our Sins ; 1 Joh.
ii. 1. God takes no delight in the death of a Sinner ; but uſes great forbearance and
long-ſuffering towards us, that we may be led to Repentance ; And if we *do* ſo ſincerely
repent, as *indeed* to amend our lives and forſake our ſins, God has ſworn by himſelf
that we *ſhall* live ; for, *have I any pleaſure at all that the wicked ſhould die, ſaith the*
Lord God, and not that he ſhould rather turn from his ways and live ? Ezek. xviii. 22.
With thoſe Limitations, it is abundantly evident, that as the true and only deſign of
the laws of the Goſpel, is to make us holy and undefiled, ſo it *is* poſſible for us to be
really holy according to the true Intent and Meaning of thoſe laws. Wherefore, as
the excellent Nature and Deſign of our Religion, ſufficiently recommends it to our
judgment ; ſo the poſſibility of obeying it, is a moſt powerful encouragement to us, to
ſet in earneſt about the practice of it. But then we muſt always conſider, that as God
requires nothing *more* of us, than a ſincere obedience according to the gracious terms
of the Goſpel-covenant ; ſo he will not accept of any thing leſs : As it *is poſſible* for us
to be holy and undefiled, according to the true intent of the laws of our Religion ; ſo
God has made it the *indiſpenſable* Condition of our Happineſs, that we actually and in
reality become ſuch holy Perſons : Which was the

III. *Third* Head I propoſed to ſpeak to. Our Saviour by his Death and Sufferings
has purchaſed this grace for us, that real Repentance and ſincere renewed Obedience
ſhall be accepted inſtead of Innocence ; but *without* this Repentance and renewed Obedience, we ſhall never be accepted upon any terms. God *has* eſtabliſhed a new and
gracious Covenant with us, upon the mediation of Chriſt ; but the abſolute and indiſpenſable condition of our enjoying the benefit of this new Covenant, is our ſincerely
renewing our Obedience. *Not every one that ſaith unto me, Lord, Lord,* (ſays our Saviour) *ſhall enter into the Kingdom of Heaven, but he that* doeth *the will of my Father*
which is in Heaven. In like manner St *Paul* ; 1 Cor. vi. 9 ; *Know ye not that the*
unrighteous ſhall not inherit the kingdom of God ? Be not deceived ; *neither fornicators,*
nor idolaters, nor adulterers, nor thieves, nor covetous, nor drunkards, nor revilers, nor
extortioners, ſhall inherit the kingdom of God. Again ; *Epheſ.* v. 6 ; *Let* no man deceive you with vain words, *for becauſe of theſe things cometh the wrath of God upon the*
children of diſobedience even in the *Heathen-world.* And *Gal.* v. 19 ; *The works of the*
fleſh are manifeſt ; of the which I tell you before, as I have alſo told you in time paſt,
that they which do ſuch things, ſhall not *inherit the kingdom of God.* So *Rev.* xxi. 27 :
and xxii. 15. Notwithſtanding all which moſt expreſs and repeated declarations of
Holy

SERM.
CVIII.

Holy Scripture, there are yet two ſorts of perſons eſpecially, who are very apt to deceive themſelves in this matter. The one is of thoſe, who think their *Faith* ſufficient to ſave them, without Works of Holineſs. To whom we may anſwer in the words of St *James*; ch. ii. ver. 14; *What doth it profit, my brethren, though a man ſay he hath faith, and have not works; can faith ſave him?* And this he illuſtrates by a moſt elegant ſimilitude; *ver.* 15; *If a brother or ſiſter be naked and deſtitute of daily food, and one of you ſay unto them, Depart in peace, be you warmed and filled; notwithſtanding ye give them not thoſe things which are needful to the body; what doth it profit? Even ſo faith,* (ſays he) *if it hath not works, is dead being alone;* Dead, *i. e.* fruitleſs, without life or profit. But what ſaith the ſame Apoſtle? *Pure religion and undefiled before God and the Father is this, to viſit the fatherleſs and widows in their afflictions, and to keep a man's ſelf unſpotted from the world;* Jam. i. 27. The other ſort of perſons, who are very apt to deceive themſelves in this matter, are thoſe who living wickedly, yet deſign to repent before they die. And to theſe we may very well apply the Similitude of the ſame Apoſtle. If our ſaying to a poor man, Depart in peace, be you warmed and filled, (without giving him any thing to ſupply thoſe Neceſſities,) can ſatisfy his Hunger and relieve his Wants; then alſo in like manner may a dying man's *wiſhing* that he *had* ſo lived, *be indeed* living a holy life. But the folly of theſe pretences will be yet more manifeſt, if we conſider in the

IV. *Fourth* and *laſt* place, that the very *nature* itſelf of the Happineſs promiſed to holy and virtuous men is ſuch, that it is not poſſible to be enjoyed, but by thoſe that actually *are* holy. And this the Apoſtle St *Paul* hints to us (in the Text; *Heb.* xii. 14.) by giving us a repreſentation of that Happineſs, under the notion of *Seeing God.* And *Rev.* xxii. 4; *And they ſhall ſee his face, and his name ſhall be in their foreheads.* Now to *ſee God,* is not, ſeeing him as with bodily eyes; or underſtanding his metaphyſical nature; This, as no creature now *can,* ſo it is probable they never *will* be able to do. But to *ſee God,* is to be admitted into his glorious preſence, and to enjoy that Satisfaction which muſt neceſſarily ariſe, from the *contemplation* of his perfections, and from the *ſenſe* of his favour: For *in his preſence is fulneſs of joy, at his right hand there are pleaſures for evermore.* And *thus to ſee God,* neceſſarily implies a perfect love of him, and, as far as is poſſible, a *likeneſs or reſemblance* to him. For ſo St *John* argues, in his firſt epiſtle; ch. iii. *ver.* 2; *It doth not yet appear what we ſhall be, but we know that when he ſhall appear, we ſhall be* like *him; for we ſhall ſee him as he is.* This therefore is the Happineſs promiſed to holy and good men: They ſhall be admitted into the immediate preſence of God, and into the ſociety of Angels and of the Spirits of juſt men made perfect; *Ye are come,* ſaith St *Paul,* Heb. xii. 22, *unto mount Sion, unto the city of the living God, the heavenly Jeruſalem, and to an innumerable company of angels, to the general aſſembly and church of the firſt-born which are written in heaven, and to God the Judge of all, and to the ſpirits of juſt men made perfect, and to Jeſus the Mediator of the new Covenant. They who ſhall be thought worthy to obtain that life, and the reſurrection from the dead,* ſhall for ever behold the face of God in glory, and by that bleſſed Viſion their hearts ſhall be filled with a moſt ardent *Love* of God, and their Souls ſhall be transformed into his image and *likeneſs.* And if this be the caſe; then nothing is more evident, than that this Happineſs is of ſuch a nature, as is not poſſible to be enjoyed, but by ſuch as actually *are* holy and undefiled. For what agreement can there be, between a ſenſual, wicked, or malicious ſoul, and the pure ſociety of the Spirits of juſt men made perfect? We ſee even in *this* life, how ungrateful the Society of good men is, to ſuch as are obſtinately and incorrigibly wicked; and as it is in *this,* ſo, much more, will it be in the *other* world. Such Perſons, as have been wholly given up to

the

4

the finful pleafures of a debauched world, can never be fit company for thofe fpiritual S E R M. and refined minds, whofe Defires and Enjoyments are as far exalted above every thing CVIII. that is grofs and fenfual, as Heaven is above Earth: And *malicious* tempers, whofe delight upon *Earth* was in nothing, but Hatred, Envy, and Revenge, can never converfe in *Heaven* with thofe bleffed Spirits, who feed and live upon no other pleafures, but thofe of Goodnefs, Holinefs, and Love. Again, what can be more impoffible, than for wicked and debauched minds to be made happy by the Vifion and Fruition of God, who is Purity and Holinefs itfelf? Salvation, muft be begun *here:* Grace and Glory, are but different degrees of one and the fame ftate: and it is a very remarkable expreffion of Scripture, according to the true rendering of the Original, that *God adds to the Church daily,* not *fuch as* fhould be, but *fuch as* are *faved.* So that unlefs God fhould work a miracle for profane perfons, and when he removes them into another world, fhould transform them alfo into new Creatures; it is no more poffible for *Them* to enjoy the Happinefs of Heaven, than for *Body* to enjoy the pleafures of *Spirit,* or for *Darknefs* to have communion and agreement with *Light.* I will not prefume to affirm, (though fome have done it, not without appearance of reafon,) that if God fhould tranfplant fuch perfons into Heaven, he *could* not make them happy there; but fo long as they are thus exceedingly indifpofed for it, nothing is more certain than that he *never will:* For, *without Holinefs, no man fhall fee the Lord.*

S E R M O N CIX.

Holineſs of Life the moſt acceptable Sacrifice to God.

R O M. XXII. 1.

I beſeech you, therefore, Brethren, by the Mercies of God, that ye pre-ſent your Bodies a living Sacrifice, holy, acceptable unto God; which is your reaſonable Service.

THE Apoſtle St *Paul* in the former part of this Epiſtle, having ſhown that the *Gentiles* by departing from the Law of *Nature*, and the *Jews* by tranſgreſſing the Law of *Moſes*, had Both of them become obnoxious to the Wrath of God; from thence infers the Obligation incumbent upon *Both*, to have recourſe to the Grace and Mercy of the *Goſpel*, by believing in *Chriſt*, and returning to God in *That way* of Faith and Repentance, which the Apoſtles were ſent forth to preach both unto *Jews* and *Gentiles*. Againſt This great Doctrine of the Goſpel, the *Gentiles* had nothing material to object, any further than as the Antient Cuſtoms of their Forefathers, and the habitual Corruption of their own Manners, made them unwilling to reform. But the *Jews*, to whoſe Anceſtors God had made ſingular Promiſes of *eternal* Bleſſings, and to whom (as a peculiar People or Nation) he had been pleaſed to give a *particular Law* by immediate Revelation; Theſe were extremely averſe to believe, that he would ever put an end to That Inſtitution, and receive the *Gentiles* to his Mercy in common with the *Jews*; nay, and *reject* the nation of the *Jews*, for not receiving the Goſpel in common with the *Gentiles*. To remove this Great Prejudice therefore; the Apoſtle from the *third chapter* of this Epiſtle to the end of the *eleventh*, argues with ſingular ſtrength and earneſtneſs, that the Great Father of the *Jewiſh* Nation, even *Abraham* himſelf, received the Promiſes of God, not upon account of the *Law*, which was not then given; nor upon account of the Seal of *Circumciſion*, which had not as yet been commanded him; but upon account of the *like Faith*, and the *like obedience*, as was afterwards required by the *Goſpel*. That as God, the Maker and Lord of all, had an undoubted Right to *chuſe* the *Poſterity of Abraham* to be his peculiar people and the Standard of true Religion, without doing thereby Any Wrong or Injury to the reſt of Mankind; ſo he had evidently the very ſame Right, whenever he pleaſed, to *remove* again That partition-wall, and admit the *Gentiles* to be Partakers of the ſame external Advantages with the *Jews*; nay, and to *caſt off* the *Jews* for refuſing that Method of Salvation, which he had *now* commanded to be preached equally to *All*. *Laſtly*, the Apoſtle argues, that in *all* theſe various diſpenſations of Providence, the *Deſign of God* was merciful towards *All men*; leading them, by the Motives both of Severity and Goodneſs, to Repentance and Reformation of Life. Caſting off the *Jews* for their impenitency, and offering mercy to the *Gentiles*; intending finally, through the Fulneſs of the *Gentiles*; to bring in alſo the *Jews* again. For ſo he ſumms up his *whole* Argument, ch. xi. 39; *As* Ye *in times paſt have not believed God, yet have now obtained*

I

mercy

mercy through Their *Unbelief*; *even ſo have* Theſe *alſo now not believed, that through*
your *mercy they alſo may obtain mercy:* For God *hath concluded them* all *in unbelief,*
that he might have mercy upon All: O *the depth of the riches both of the Knowledge*
and Wiſdom of God! how unſearchable are his judgments, and his ways paſt finding
out !

Having thus concluded his *Argument,* he proceeds in the words of the Text, according to his uſual Method in all his epiſtles, to draw an *inference of exhortation* from
what he had before ſaid, to perſwade men to the *Practice* of Virtue and Righteouſneſs.
I beſeech you therefore, brethren, by the Mercies of God, that ye preſent your Bodies a
Living Sacrifice, holy, acceptable unto God ; whieh is your reaſonable Service.

I beſeech you Therefore: The word, *Therefore,* ſhows the *connexion* of the *preſent*
exhortation, with his *foregoing* Argument. God in *all* the diſpenſations of his Providence, both in the *merciful* and in the *ſevere* parts of it, has ſet forth to us the Neceſſity of Repentance and Amendment ; Therefore, (ſays he) *I beſeech you, brethren,* let
This Conſideration have its due effect upon you, that you neither deſpiſe his Mercy,
nor provoke his Severity.

And becauſe the *finiſhing point* in which his Argument terminates, is the obſervation, that *all* the Great Diſpenſations of Providence are with unſearchable Wiſdom
deſigned finally to iſſue in Events of *Mercy* ; (God *hath concluded All in Unbelief, that*
he might have Mercy *upon All :)* for This reaſon it is with great eloquence of affection,
that the Apoſtle lays the Streſs of his exhortation upon *That* particular Motive : *I be-*
ſeech you therefore, brethren, by the Mercies *of God.* The like expreſſion he again uſes,
2 *Cor.* x. 1 ; *I beſeech you by the Meekneſs and Gentleneſs of Chriſt.* His Senſe,
in Both places is : Let the Mercy and Goodneſs of God, manifeſted and declared to
you by the Goſpel of Chriſt, prevail with you to live as *becometh* the Goſpel, to live
worthy of the Grace and Benefits ye have received.

That *ye preſent your Bodies,* (that is, *yourſelves,*) a living Sacrifice ; a Sacrifice as
much more valuable in the Sight of God, than the Sacrifices of Beaſts offered up upon
the Altar, as a *Man* is more valuable than an *irrational Animal* ; as a Living *Man* is
more valuable, than a *ſlain Beaſt* ; as the Moral *Perfections* of a Man, are more excellent than a *Sacrifice free from mere* natural *Blemiſhes of the Body* ; as, laſtly, the *thing*
ſignified itſelf, is always preferable to a *Mere Repreſentation.* That ye preſent yourſelves unto God, ſuch a *Living Sacrifice* as This ; Holy, not with a mere *legal, exter-*
nal, nominal Holineſs, conſiſting purely in things being *ſet apart* (by *conſecration* or
ſolemn denomination only) to ſuch or ſuch particular Uſes ; but Holy, by a *real, moral,*
intrinſick Sanctity, of which the *Legal* Holineſs was but a Type or a Shadow ; Holy,
by *real Purity* and *Goodneſs of Manners* ; in the Senſe wherein *He is Holy,* who is of
purer eyes than to behold iniquity ; Holy, in this *true and ſpiritual* Senſe ; And conſequently, as the Text goes on, acceptable *unto God* ; acceptable, not merely by virtue
of *inſtitution and Command* ; but acceptable in the *nature of the* thing itſelf ; acceptable, as being in *Agreeableneſs and Conformity* to the *Nature of* God ; acceptable, as being a fulfilling of the *eſſential and unchangeable Law of everlaſting* Righteouſneſs.
For *thus* even the Light of *Reaſon* taught the Wiſer *Heathens,* that by *No Offering*
could God be ſo acceptably worſhipped, as by the Oblation of a *Heart* free from *Un-*
righteouſneſs and Iniquity. Thus alſo the *Prophets* among the *Jews,* in order to draw
That people, as they were able, to a rational notion of religion ; *Hath the Lord as great*
delight in burnt-offerings and Sacrifices, as in obeying the voice of the Lord? Behold, to
obey is better than Sacrifice ; and to hearken, than the Fat of Rams. And *Thus* likewiſe, our *Saviour himſelf,* who came to reſtore the Purity of uncorrupted religion ;
Thou art not far, ſays he, *from the Kingdom of God* ; expreſſing his High Approbation
of

S E R M. of a certain Scribe's profeſſion, that for a Man *to Love God with all his Heart, and*
CIX. *his Neighbour as himſelf, is more than all whole Burnt-offerings and Sacrifices.*

IN the *laſt* place therefore, the Apoſtle adds, as a *concluſion* of his *whole* exhortation in the Text; that This ſpiritual Sacrifice, this Moral Purity and Holineſs of Life,
is our Reaſonable Service: Reaſonable, in point of *Gratitude*; upon account of what
he had before alledged concerning the *Mercies of God*, or the merciful and gracious
Diſpenſations of his Providence towards men: Reaſonable, in the *nature* of *Things*; as
being *in itſelf* of eternal and unchangeable Obligation: Reaſonable, with regard to
the nature of *God*; who is a Being of eſſential Purity and Holineſs: and Reaſonable,
with Regard to the nature of *Men*; as being the *Proper* Duty and Service, of *Ratio-*
nal Creatures.

THE words of the Text being thus explained; the principal *Particulars* therein,
which deſerve to be more largely and diſtinctly conſidered, are; 1*ſt*, Whence it comes
to paſs, that the Apoſtle here expreſſes our *whole* Chriſtian Duty, by the *particular*
phraſe of preſenting our Bodies Holy, acceptable unto God: and 2*dly*, What is the
full intent, of his ſtiling this our Service *a Living* Sacrifice.

I. *Firſt*; WHENCE comes it to paſs, that the Apoſtle here expreſſes our *whole*
Chriſtian Duty, by the *particular* phraſe of preſenting our Bodies Holy, acceptable
unto God? He does not ſay, preſent *yourſelves*, but your *Bodies*, a living Sacrifice,
Holy, acceptable unto God. Now the reaſon of This, ſeems to be, that having in the
former part of this epiſtle deſcribed the great *depravity* and *corruption* of manners a-
mong the *unbelieving Gentiles*, *principally* in the inſtance of thoſe Works of the Fleſh,
to which God had judicially given them up as a conſequence of their groſs idolatries,
ſo contradictory to the plain Light of Nature and Reaſon; in the *latter* part of the
epiſtle he accordingly *ſuits* his exhortation to the *converted* Gentiles, to *purify them-*
ſelves from all filthineſs both of Fleſh *and* Spirit, *perfecting Holineſs in the Fear of God*;
and that, in the *firſt* place, they ſhould be ſure to cleanſe themſelves from thoſe *Works*
of the Fleſh, which were the Great Cauſe of God's Anger even againſt the Heathen
World; and by forſaking of which, they might in a particular manner be ſaid to preſent their *Bodies* a living Sacrifice, holy, acceptable unto God. The Sins of *This* kind,
are what ought not indeed to be once *named* among Chriſtians: *Eph.* v. 3; *Fornica-*
tion and all uncleanneſs, let it not be once named *amongſt you, as becometh Saints; nei-*
ther filthineſs, nor fooliſh talking, nor jeſting, which are not convenient; but rather,
giving of Thanks: For This ye know, that no whoremonger, nor unclean perſon, hath
any inheritance in the Kingdom of Chriſt, and of God: Let no man deceive you with
vain words; For becauſe of theſe things, cometh the wrath of God upon the children of
diſobedience; or, as it is in the margin, upon the children of *Unbelief*; that is, even
upon the *Heathen world* itſelf. Where, by the way it is very obſervable, that the
Apoſtle, ſpeaking of the *Heathen-nations*, does not ſay, as Some in *later* Ages have
done, that their being *ignorant in Unbelief* is the cauſe of all their Actions being ſinful
and diſpleaſing to God; but, on the contrary, that the Sinfulneſs and Wickedneſs of
their *Actions*, in oppoſition to That degree of Light they enjoy; is the true and only
cauſe, of their being hateful to God: *For becauſe of* Theſe *things* (ſays he,) *cometh the*
Wrath of God upon the Children of Unbelief. Now if among thoſe who *knew not God*,
that is, who had no *expreſs* Revelation, nor *any other* Declaration of the Will of God,
than what the mere Light of *Nature and Reaſon* afforded; if among Theſe (I ſay,) all Sins
of This kind were ſo juſtly puniſhable; how much more among *Chriſtians*; whom (as the
Apoſtle expreſſes it) God hath called *unto Holineſs*, that is, has by a *particular* Revelation, by *peculiar* Promiſes, and by *extraordinary* Aſſiſtances, appointed to be unto himſelf a *choſen generation, a royal Prieſthood, a Holy Nation, a peculiar people!* For, *This*
is the Will of God, 1 Th. iv. 3; *this is the Will of God, even your Sanctification; That*

I   *every*

every one of you may know how to poffefs *himfelf in Sanctification and Honour : Not in* S E R M. *the luft of concupifcence, even as the Gentiles which know not God :*——*Becaufe that the* CIX. *Lord is the avenger of all fuch, as we have alfo forewarned you and teftified:*——*He therefore that defpifeth, defpifeth not Man, but God, who hath alfo given unto us his* Holy Spirit: That is, has given us all the extraordinary *Motives,* and all the peculiar *Affift- ances* and *Advantages* of the *Gofpel,* in order to our *Sanctification.* Infomuch that the fame Apoftle, by a very elegant and expreffive fimilitude, ftiles the *Bodies* of Chriftians, *Temples of God,* and *Temples of the Holy Ghoft*; and from thence draws a ftrong and af- fecting argument, to perfwade them to the Virtues of Sobriety and Holinefs. *Know ye not* (fays he) *that ye are the Temple of God, and that the Spirit of God dwelleth in you ? If any man defile the Temple of God, him fhall God deftroy ; For the Temple of God is Holy, which Temple ye are.* And again: *Know ye not that your Body is the Temple of the Holy Ghoft, which is in you, which ye have of God, and ye are not your own? For ye are bought with a Price ; Therefore glorify God (glorify the Lord who bought you* with the precious blood of his dear Son ; glorify him) *in your Body, and in your Spirit, which are God's :* (1 Cor. vi. 19.) In *very corrupt* and *degenerate* Ages of the World, there will always be *Some profligate* perfons, who will pretend indeed they cannot *dif- cern* the Great *Wickednefs and Immorality* of fome of the Practices againft which thefe exhortations are directed ; as (they muft needs confefs,) they evidently enough do, in the Inftances of Many *Other* forts of Crimes. But how unwilling foever they are to *perceive, wherein* lies the heinous nature of thefe Vices, when they are the *guilty perfons themfelves* ; yet they are always very fenfible of it, when they *themfelves fuffer* by the Guilt of *Others* ; when any Difhonour of this kind is done to their *own Fa- milies,* or even to *remote Relations. Then* they fee plainly, how deftructive all thefe Debaucheries are, to Human Society, and to the publick Welfare ; how irreconcile- able they are with All Serious Thoughts, and worthy Actions ; how they cover men with Shame, and Bafenefs of Spirit ; how they feparate the neareft and moft clofe Re- lations, lay a ground for inextricable Confufions and implacable Diffentions in Fami- lies, and very frequently occafion Murders, Seditions and publick Devaftations: So that hardly from *Any Other* Caufe, have fprung fuch *Tragical* and calamitous Events, as from the Sins and Debaucheries of *This* fort. *One* part of thefe ill confequences, is excellently defcribed by *Solomon,* Prov. vi. 32 ; vii. 22 ; *He that doth* thefe things, *de- ftroyeth his own Soul : A wound and difhonour fhall he get, and his Reproach fhall not be wiped away. He goeth after a ftrange woman, as an Ox goeth to the Slaughter, or as a Fool to the correction of the Stocks ; 'Till a dart ftrike through his Liver ; as a Bird hafteth to the fnare, and knoweth not that it is for his Life.*——*For her houfe is the way to Hell, going down to the Chambers of Death.* This is an Argument drawn from the *natural Tendency* of things, and from the Wife *Obfervations* which *Solomon* had made upon the Courfe of the world, and upon the Ways and Practices of Men. But the Argument is *doubly* enforced, by the confiderations of the *Gofpel* ; which, to the gene- ral Motives of *Nature and Reafon,* has added this *further* peculiar Obligation, great and more powerful than all ; that having a Promife given us of an inheritance incor- ruptible and undefiled in the Heavens, we are now, as *Strangers and Pilgrims* in this prefent World, required to reftrain all inordinate Defires which *war againft the Soul* ; that is, which would tempt men to exchange their *eternal Happinefs* for the *tranfient and momentary pleafures of Sin :* Heb. xii. 16 ; *Left there be Any Fornicator, or pro- fane perfon as Efau, who for one morfel of meat fold his Birthright ; For ye know that afterwards, when he would have inherited the Bleffing, he was rejected ; for he found no place of Repentance, though he fought it carefully with Tears.* The Meaning is ; not that True Repentance, which produces real Amendment and effectual Reformation of Manners, will ever be rejected ; but that, at the time of Judgment, when the Bleffing

S E R M. comes to be inherited, and they who have fold their Hopes of it for the Pleafures of
CIX. Sin, fhall fay, *Lord, Lord, open unto us*; then will our Lord reply, *I know you not
whence ye are, Depart from Me all ye Workers of Iniquity.* I conclude *This* head
therefore with That excellent exhortation of St *Paul*, Rom. xiii. 12; *Let us caft off
the Works of Darknefs, and put upon us the Armour of Light : Let us walk honeftly as
in the day,* (that is, as becometh thofe who enjoy the Light of the Gofpel;) *not in
rioting and drunkennefs, not in chambering and wantonnefs, not in ftrife and envying; But
put ye on the Lord Jefus Chrift,* (that is, live as becomes the Difciples of Chrift,) *and
make no provifion for the flefh, to fulfil the Lufts thereof.*

II. *Secondly;* THAT which remains, is to confider in the *next* place, what is the
true and full Intent of that *Other* Phrafe the Apoftle ufes in the text; when this Duty
of *prefenting our Bodies Holy, acceptable unto God,* is here ftiled by him a *Living* Sacrifice. For the clear underftanding the ground of which expreffion, it is to be obferved, that the proper Punifhment of Sin being *Death,* and yet God refolving to have
Mercy on fuch as fhould repent and amend; he thought proper, in the Wifdom of his
Government, to declare and eftablifh, to confirm and ratify this Covenant of Mercy,
by the *Sacrifice* of the *Death of Chrift* once offered for ever. As a *Type* of which, and
as an *Emblem* of the true Demerit of Sin, and as the Sinners *Acknowledgment* of his
Guilt, and Profeffion of Repentance; God was pleafed, in the early Ages of the World,
to accept the *facrificing* of Beafts. In which matter, when impartially confidered, it
cannot be faid there was any thing unworthy of God. For fince they are all, creatures
which God has *freely* created, and *freely* given them *Life*; fince they are moreover
created *neceffarily fubject* to Death; and fitted in the very *Courfe* and original *Defign* of
their nature, to be flain for Food, to *Men* and to *each other*; it cannot be faid there is
any thing *incongruous,* in their having been appointed to be ufed as *Sacrifices* in the Service of God. Neverthelefs, fince thefe Sacrifices were never in any *other* refpect acceptable unto God, but merely as *Figures* and *Shadows*; as *Types* of *Chrift,* and as Acknowledgements or Profeffions of the Sinner's *Repentance*; it is evident, that from the
Beginning, the real and true Sacrifice moft pleafing to God, always was the *perfon's* dedicating *himfelf* to the *Service* of God, by fuch a *Death unto Sin,* as the *flaying* of the
Sacrifice reprefented; and by fuch *Amendment of Life* for the future as was typically
fignified by the Sacrifice being *without Blemifh.* From whence, even in the *Old Teftament,* the Prophet, fpeaking comparatively, *Behold,* fays he, *to Obey is better than Sacrifice, and to hearken than the fat of Rams.* The Pfalmift likewife, *Thou defireft not
facrifice,* fays he, *elfe would I give it thee, but thou delighteft not in burnt-offerings :
The Sacrifices of God are a broken Spirit, a broken and contrite heart (O God) thou
wilt not defpife.* And under the *New Teftament,* That *fpiritual* Worfhip, and That
Chriftian Practice of Moral Duties, which fucceeded in the place of *literal* Sacrifices, is
hence very elegantly ftiled *A Sacrifice* or *Offering.* By *Malachi,* it is *before-hand* ftiled
prophetically, a *Pure-Offering*; ch. i. 11. By the *Apoftle, after* its eftablifhment, it is
called a *Spiritual Sacrifice*; an *odour of a fweet fmell, a facrifice acceptable, well-pleafing to God*; (Phil. iv. 18.) And in the Epiftle to the *Hebrews,* ch. xiii. 15; we are
thus exhorted; *By him therefore,* that is, By or Through Chrift, *let us offer the* Sacrifice of Praife *to God continually, that is the Fruit of our lips, giving thanks to his Name :
Alfo to do good and to communicate, forget not; for with fuch* Sacrifices *God is well-
pleafed.* From which *manner of fpeaking,* it is very obvious to obferve, by the Way;
how abfurdly fome *Modern* Writers, from the *Antients* ftiling the *Eucharift* an *unbloody
Sacrifice,* have inferred that it is in *fome real and* literal Senfe a *Sacrifice :* Whereas the
Antients, on the contrary, ufed the word *Sacrifice* in the fame Senfe here, as the
Apoftle calls *Praife and Works of Charity* a *Sacrifice*; nay, in the fame Senfe, as by a
ftill more fublime figure, he fays of *Chriftians,* Phil. iii. 3; that *We are the Circumcifion;*

1 Pet. ii. 5.

3

fion ; That is, that *Chriſtians* are by real *Holineſs purified* unto God a *peculiar people*, more truly than the *Jews* were by the typical *Ceremony* of *Circumciſion*.

Laſtly, THE Moral Purity and Virtue of ſincere Chriſtians, is in the Text ſtiled, not only a *Sacrifice*, but a *Living Sacrifice*; to expreſs more emphatically, how much the Service of a *rational living perſon* is more valuable in the Sight of God, than the Sacrifice of a *ſlain Beaſt*. By the ſame Analogy of Speech, Chriſtians are ſtiled by St *Peter*, *Living Stones*, 1 Pet. ii. 5; to ſignify their being parts of That *Spiritual* Building or Temple of God, which is his *Church* or the Whole Body of his Faithful Servants, much more precious in his Sight than any Temple literally built with hands. After the ſame manner *Chriſt*, in oppoſition to the *Jews typical* Approach to God in the Holy Place through the Veil of the Temple, is ſtiled a *New* and Living *Way*; Heb. x. 20. A d in general, *all outward Forms and Ceremonies* whatſoever, are in Scripture called a *dead letter*; in compariſon with the *Spirit* and *reality*, of true *Virtue and Righteouſneſs*. Which *real Virtue and Righteouſneſs* in the whole courſe of mens lives, is, in the fulleſt and moſt complete Senſe of the phraſe, *preſenting themſelves unto God a* Living *Sacrifice:* Rom. vi. 11, 13; *Reckon ye yourſelves,* ſays the Apoſtle, (with which exhortation I ſhall conclude,) *Reckon ye yourſelves to be* dead *indeed unto ſin, but* alive *unto God, through Jeſus Chriſt our Lord; ——yielding yourſelves unto God, as thoſe that are* alive *from the dead; and your members as inſtruments of righteouſneſs unto God.*

SERMON

SERMON CX.

Of the unchangeable Difference of Good and Evil.

ISAI. V. 20.

Wo unto them that call evil good, and good evil ; that put darkness for light, and light for darkness ; that put bitter for sweet, and sweet for bitter.

SERM.
CX.
THE reasonableness of Religion, is the great condemnation of Sinners ; and the Folly of Wickedness is most evidently reproved, by showing it to be contrary both to the Nature of *Man* and to the Reason of *Things*, as well as to the positive Will and Command of God. The Distinction of Moral Actions is in itself as necessary and as manifest, as the Differences of natural and sensible Objects ; and it is a greater and juster reproach to the understanding of a Man, not to discern these *its* proper Objects ; than it is a weakness and defect in the Organs of the Senses, not to distinguish Theirs. Light and Darkness are so absolutely contrary to each other, and Sweetness so sensibly different from Bitter, that no man can mistake or confound these things, without having wholly lost the use of those Senses, by which they were intended to be discerned. Pain and Pleasure are so directly opposite, that nothing less than the loss of Life itself, can make us insensible of *Them*, or hinder us from preferring the one, and avoiding the other. Moral Good and Evil, Virtue and Vice, the Happiness and the Diseases of the Mind, are as truly and as widely different in their own nature ; as the Perceptions of our outward Senses : And God has endued us with Faculties of the Soul as well fitted to distinguish them, as the Bodily Senses are to discern corporeal Objects. If any man, notwithstanding this, will obstinately call Evil Good, and Good Evil, and will deny all Distinction between Virtue and Vice ; he must as much have laid aside the use of his natural Reason and Understanding, the Judgment and Discernment of his mind ; as he that would confound Light and Darkness, must contradict his Senses, and deny the Evidence of his clearest Sight. And when such a person falls finally into unavoidable Misery and the just Punishment of Sin, he will no more deserve Pity and Compassion, than one that falls down a Precipice because he would not open his Eyes to discern that Light, which should have guided and directed him in his way. Misery and Destruction must necessarily be the effect of neglecting those Rules, on which both God and Nature have made the Life and Happiness of the Soul to depend ; as certainly as the Destruction of the *Body* must be the speedy Consequence of neglecting the difference between things wholesome and poisonous. And so much the more deserved and the less pitiable is the Destruction of wilful and impenitent Sinners, by how much the clearer the difference is between Good and Evil ; and by how much the more obstinately they must shut their eyes, that they may not see the strong Light of Reason and Conscience, the Excellency and Necessity of Virtue, and the plain and only way to true Happiness. *Wo unto them that call evil good, and good evil ; that put darkness for light, and light for darkness ; that put bitter for sweet, and sweet for bitter.*

In

IN the following Difcourfe upon which words, I fhall endeavour to fhow, *1ft*, That there is originally in the very *Nature* of things, a neceffary and eternal Difference between Good and Evil, between Virtue and Vice; which the Reafon of things does itfelf oblige men to have a conftant Regard to. *2dly*, That God, by his fupreme and abfolute Authority, and by exprefs Declaration of his Will in Holy Scripture, has eftablifhed and confirmed this original Difference of things; and will fupport and maintain it by his immediate Power and Government in the World. And *3dly*, I fhall draw fome Obfervations from the whole, which may be of ufe to us in Practice.

I. *Firft*; There is originally in the very Nature of things, a neceffary and eternal Difference between Good and Evil, between Virtue and Vice; which the Reafon of things does itfelf oblige men to have a conftant Regard to. This is *fuppofed* in the Text, by the Prophet's comparing the Difference between Good and Evil, to that moft obvious and fenfible Difference of Light and Darknefs. And it is not without great Reafon, that he fuppofes this Difference of Good and Evil to be fo plain and felf-evident, as if it could not be proved by any thing more clear and manifeft than it felf. For in like manner as any man, who fhould be fo abfurd as to contend, that there was no Difference between Light and Darknefs; could not be confuted by any Argument more ftrong, than the Evidence of his own Senfes: So to any one who will perverfely deny all Difference between Good and Evil, it is not eafy to offer any better Argument to convince him of this great and fundamental Truth; than by appealing to the Reafon and Confcience of his own Mind. Not becaufe there is any real Difficulty or Obfcurity in the Thing itfelf to be proved; but on the contrary, becaufe it is fo very plain and evident, that fcarcely any foreign Argument can by the ftricteft Proof make it more clear and certain than it was before. When men will deny a Truth, which is as evident, as the Difference between Light and Darknefs; Punifhment then is the only proper remedy for fuch Obftinacy; and very juftly may thofe men be excluded from all the Benefits of humane Society, who will not have any regard to that Difference of things, on which alone all the Happinefs of Society depends. *Natural* Good and Evil, in fuch inftances wherein we are perfonally concerned, and where the Effect is not very remote, we are always fufficiently fenfible of, and abundantly able and careful to diftinguifh. Death and Life, Sicknefs and Health, Pleafure and Pain, Poverty and Riches, Honour and Difgrace, are Differences of condition, concerning which there is no difpute, and no danger that men will be carelefs or negligent. Death and Life, Pain and Pleafure, Happinefs and Mifery, men cannot but diftinguifh; and muft of neceffity always purfue the one, and endeavour to avoid the other. Yet in thefe very things is originally founded the Difference of *Moral* Good and Evil, which they are fo apt to neglect; and it is only for want of attending to the Iffues and Confequences of things, that men are ever guilty of fo fatal a Miftake. That which tends truly and univerfally, to the Perfection of humane Narure, and to the general Happinefs of Mankind; is Moral Good, as well as Natural: And Moral Evil, is that which corrupts and depraves and difhonours our Nature, and renders it truly miferable; which difquiets mens Minds, and weakens their Bodies; which ruins their Eftates and deftroys their Reputation; which breaks Laws, and difturbs good Government, and diforders and confounds the World. Thefe refpective Effects are fometimes remote indeed, and at a diftance; and This is that which deceives and impofes upon men: But they are neverthelefs moft certain, and neceffary Effects; and of direct, proper, and natural confequence: So that even in Nature, Virtue and Vice, Wifdom and Folly, are as neceffarily diftinct, and as unalterable as Happinefs and Mifery themfelves. God hath fo conftituted our Nature, that the fame things which truly and univerfally promote our Happinefs, are likewife the chief Inftances of our Duty; and the univerfal performance of our Duty, is plainly the moft natural and direct means to attain true and lafting Happinefs. The

SERM.
CX.

Accidents of this World, and the extreme Wickedneſs of Men, make it ſometimes indeed prove otherwiſe for a ſhort ſeaſon: But the *final* Event of things, is always ſuch as I have now deſcribed; and the order of Nature *tends* to make it be ſo likewiſe, even in all the *preſent* intermediate ſpaces of time. The Fear and Love of God, the Imitation of his Nature, and the Obeying of his Commands; the Senſe of *His* preſent and future Favour, who is the ſupreme Lord and infinitely powerful Governour of the whole World; is evidently the only foundation of ſolid Peace and Satisfaction of Mind, in which a rational and immortal Spirit can poſſibly acquieſce: Piety therefore towards God, is as neceſſarily good in itſelf, and of as unchangeable Obligation in Nature and Reaſon; as the Creator is of neceſſity infinitely ſuperiour to his Creatures; and as ſettled peace and ſatisfaction of Mind, which can only ariſe from the ſenſe of *his* Favour, is neceſſarily the ground and condition of our Happineſs. Temperance and Sobriety, Diligence and Patience, the due government of our Appetites, and reſtraint of our Paſſions, are the only *natural and moſt certain* means of preſerving the health of our Bodies, of improving the faculties of our Minds, and of keeping ourſelves conſtantly in ſuch Temper and Diſpoſition, as is neceſſary to qualify us for the regular performance of all other duties of Life. He that ſuffers himſelf to be deprived of his Reaſon, either by violent Paſſion, or by great Intemperance and Exceſs, has no guard left, that can ſecure him from falling into the greateſt Crimes. Such government of ourſelves therefore, is as neceſſarily good and obligatory in the nature of the thing itſelf, as it is confeſſedly uſeful and excellent in its Effects. Juſtice and Righteouſneſs, Goodneſs and Charity, Faithfulneſs and Truth, Subjection to Government, Obedience to Laws, due Reſpect to Authority, according to mens ſeveral Qualities and Stations in the World; are the only poſſible Means, of preſerving the Peace and Welfare of the Publick, the Order of Societies, and mutual Protection and Support; on which depends all our Happineſs, all our Enjoyments, and whatſoever is moſt valuable amongſt men: Theſe things therefore are as unchangeably Wiſe and Good, and the practice of them as indiſpenſably enforced upon us by the eternal Reaſon of things, and of as indiſpenſable Obligation; as it is natural and neceſſary for us to deſire both our own private Happineſs, and the publick Welfare of Mankind. Wicked and unreaſonable men, who will be governed by no rule, but their preſent Appetites; look not ſo far before them, as to make true judgments and take right meaſures concerning their proper Happineſs. Whatever gratifies their preſent Luſt or Paſſion, That they chuſe as Good and conducive to their Happineſs; not conſidering that in the courſe of things it may be the greateſt Evil in the world, either directly to themſelves, or conſequentially by being injurious to other men, deſtructive of Publick Peace, and Order, and Government, and ſo in the end pernicious even in this preſent World to themſelves alſo. For want of this Conſideration it is, that they confound the natural and eternal Differences of things; judging of Good and Evil, by no other meaſure, but by their own ſudden Paſſions, changeable Appetites, diſorderly and unreaſonable Luſts. If they get beyond this, and are forced to confeſs that the Neceſſity of things, the very Nature and Conſtitution of the world, left every thing ſhould run immediately into the utmoſt Confuſion, obliges them to be under ſome kind of Rules and Reſtraints; yet, far from having any generous and noble principles of true Virtue and Goodneſs, they will go no further than they are compelled, nor acknowledge any other Difference between Good and Evil, than what is forced upon them by the Authority of Law or Cuſtom. And yet concerning Theſe alſo, it is as evident, that Good and Evil, are things prior and ſuperiour to all humane Laws, and which they cannot alter; as that the Difference of Light and Darkneſs does not depend upon the Will and Pleaſure of men, and cannot be changed by them. The true and only reaſon of all humane Laws, is to enforce and ſecure the practice of ſuch things, as are before in their own Nature good, and uſeful, and profitable to Society.

3

For,

For, if this were not the cafe, it would not be of any importance, whether thefe
or the very contrary practices were enjoined by Laws. It is not therefore barely
the Force and Obligation of the Law, which makes a thing become good and
reafonable to be practifed; (though in all indifferent things, This is indeed a fufficient
Obligation;) but it is the Wifdom and Goodnefs of the Things themfelves, that is the
Ground and Foundation of all wife Laws; and which makes it neceffary, that men
fhould by Authority and by Laws be compelled to do that, which if there had been
no Law at all, it would neverthelefs have been reafonable and good for them to
do. We are infinitely obliged by Nature and Reafon, to worfhip God and adore, to
pray and to give thanks, to the Supreme Author and Preferver of our Being; and to
do all the Good we can to Men, in our feveral ftations; promoting univerfally the Happinefs of our Fellow-creatures, and the Peace and good Order of the World. It is
fit the Fear and Authority of Laws, fhould prevent fuch men from oppofing and
hindering this great End, who perhaps would not otherwife be reftrained by the Obligation of right Reafon, or by the Fear of God: But the Obligation of right Reafon
would ftill have been the fame, though no humane Laws had laid any fuch Compulfion upon men; Nay even, if it could be fuppofed that all pofitive Laws and all humane Authority whatfoever, fhould require us to act the contrary part; deftroy and do
all evil to each other without difference or refpect; If all the Nations in the world,
fhould confpire in having fuch a Falfe Notion of Honour and Glory, as to account it
truer greatnefs to deftroy and ruin, than to protect Mankind and preferve the Liberties
of Nations, and the common Rights of humane Societies; yet it would neither be
wife, nor good, nor reafonable, neither truly great nor honourable fo to do : any more
than men's agreeing to call poifon wholefome, would make it really be fo ; or the opinion or declaration of any number of Men, could make Darknefs put on the Nature
of Light. Wicked and unreafonable men, powerful Tyrants and Oppreffors, the greateft Debauchees and Purfuers of unlawful Pleafures; when they are above the cenfure
of all humane Laws, and have little or no reverence for thofe that are divine ; yet
often know that they do evil, and cannot deny but that it would be better to do
otherwife. They are fenfible that the practice of Virtue and Goodnefs, is infinitely
more reafonable than Debauchery and Injuftice ; And though their Lufts and Paffions
have fuch Dominion over them, that they cannot forbear doing unjuft and unrighteous
Actions; yet they fee at the fame time a more excellent Law ; they know better
things, and cannot but approve them as more wife and reafonable. This is a Obligation upon them, to return into the ways of Virtue and Religion: The Senfe of
this Obligation they cannot get rid of ; the Uneafinefs which it gives their Minds, they
cannot fhake off: It is This makes them pafs a fevere Judgment upon their own paft
Actions, whenever they reflect on them; and to chufe even the prefent Pleafure or
unjuft Acquifitions with difficulty and remorfe : The reproach of Confcience imbitters
all their finful Enjoyments ; and they fecretly condemn themfelves, where the Laws
of men have no power to condemn them. The crimes they commit, are a continual
flavery and burden upon their Minds. And were it not, that evil Habits and ungoverned
Lufts keep them by an unwilling choice in a perpetual bondage; they would infinitely
rather chufe the Satisfaction of being innocent, and wifh always that they could feparate the Pleafure or Profit from the Crime. The Actions of men that live virtuoufly
and religioufly, they cannot but approve of; and condemn in others the very fame Practices, which they are guilty of themfelves. They will truft a virtuous man in any
bufinefs of importance, much rather than the promoters and partakers of their Vices;
and defire always to have their affairs managed, by men of Uprightnefs, Righteoufnefs
and Integrity. In fine, they *at laft* wifh *themfelves* always in the *place* of the Righteous; and, however they have *lived*, yet *O that they could but* die *at leaft the* death *of*
the

the righteous, and that their laſt end *might be like his*; and thereby clearly acknow-ledge the Excellency of Virtue, its Neceſſity in order to the publick welfare of Mankind, and the Unchangeableneſs of its Obligation. By all theſe things, the wickedeſt of men do themſelves give Teſtimony to the Truth of this *1ſt* general Propoſition, *viz.* That there is originally in the very Nature of things, a neceſſary and eternal Difference between Good and Evil, Virtue and Vice; which the Reaſon of things does itſelf oblige men to have a conſtant Regard to.

II. *Secondly*; GOD has moreover, by his ſupreme and abſolute Authority, and by expreſs Declaration of his Will in Holy Scripture, by his poſitive Will and Command eſtabliſhed and confirmed this original Difference of things, and will ſupport and maintain it by his immediate Power and Government in the world. The former Propoſition, *viz.* the natural and unchangeable Difference of Good and Evil, is contained in the *Suppoſition* in the Text, wherein this Diſtinction is *preſumed* to be equally evident with that of Light and Darkneſs. The latter Propoſition, *viz.* God's interpoſing moreover his ſupreme Power and Authority, to confirm and ſupport this ſame original Difference of things; is contained in the poſitive *declaration* in the Text, wherein a ſevere *Wo* is denounced againſt all ſuch as ſhall attempt to confound them. *Wo unto them that call evil good, and good evil; that put darkneſs for light, and light for darkneſs; that put bitter for ſweet, and ſweet for bitter.* That ſuch is the Will of God, as well as the Nature of things; may in good meaſure be gathered even from what we *naturally* know concerning him. For God being the alone Author and Creator of all things; it is plain their Natures are reſpectively ſuch as he was pleaſed to make them; and their relations one to another are the reſult of that Conſtitution, which the Creator in his Wiſdom has thought fit to eſtabliſh; the *Nature* therefore of things is the *Law* of God; and whatever is agreeable or diſagreeable to right Reaſon, muſt be ſo likewiſe to the Will of the Author of Nature. Wherefore ſince Good and Evil, as has been already ſhown, are neceſſarily and eternally different in the Nature of things, as Light and Darkneſs are in the Frame of the World, and in the Judgment of our Senſes; it is manifeſtly the Will of God, that the one ſhould be the rule and determiner of our Moral Actions, as the other is the guide and direction of our Natural ones. *The Light of the Body is the Eye,* as our Saviour himſelf expreſſes it, St *Matt.* vi. 22; meaning to ſignify by an eaſy ſimilitude, that our Minds ought to be guided by Reaſon and Truth, as our Bodies are by the Sight of the Eyes. In this reſpect, the Light of Nature itſelf ſufficiently condemns all the workers of Unrighteouſneſs; making it appear that the practice of Iniquity in every inſtance, is as truly and for the very ſame reaſon a direct contempt of the Authority of God, as it is an abſurd confounding of the natural Reaſons and Proportions of things. The Order and Harmony of God's Creation, depends upon every Creature's acting according to the law of its Nature: And this Law of Nature to *Men*, is, our Obligation to govern ourſelves by that particular Underſtanding and Knowledge, whereby we are diſtinguiſhed from the inferiour part of the Creation; whereby we are enabled to diſcern between Good and Evil; and by which, as it is expreſſed in the book of *Job, God has taught us more than the beaſts of the field, and made us wiſer than the fowls of heaven.* God has endued us with Faculties, by which we are able to ſee and diſtinguiſh what will promote the Welfare and Happineſs of the World; and he has given us thoſe Faculties for that very End, that by diſtinguiſhing things rightly, we might direct our choice to ſuch Actions always as are moſt univerſally uſeful and beneficial to Mankind. God himſelf, in his government of the World, does always what in the whole is beſt; that is, what tends moſt to the Good of the whole Creation; and ſo far as we are capable of underſtanding his Attributes and manner of acting, ſo far it is manifeſt *we* are obliged to imitate *his* Nature; and in our ſeveral ſtations to conform ourſelves to the likeneſs of ſo excel-

lent

lent an Example, by the ſtudy and practice of all Goodneſs and Holineſs, Righteouſneſs and Truth. This is the firſt ground and foundation of all Religion : This is that
Knowledge of God and of his Will, which Nature implants, and Reaſon confirms,
and all the Wiſdom in the world centers in, and all the Happineſs of rational Creatures depends upon.

But becauſe the vain Curioſity and ſceptical Diſcourſes, the vicious Inclinations
and unreaſonable Paſſions, the evil Affections and perverſe Diſputings of men of corrupt minds, have ſometimes as it were raiſed a duſt to obſcure this cleareſt of all
natural Truths; Truth, concerning the neceſſary and eternal Difference of Good and
Evil; even in like manner as certain ridiculous Philoſophers of old, undertook by
ſubtil intricacies to confound the plaineſt Differences of natural and ſenſible things, to
prove that Snow was black, or, as the Text expreſſes it, that Light is the ſame with
Darkneſs, and Bitter with Sweet; therefore God in all the *ſupernatural Revelations* he
has made of his Will, and moſt expreſly in this laſt Revelation of the Goſpel, has
placed the Sum of affairs in reſtoring Virtue and Goodneſs which is the Image of
God, and in rooting out Vice in which conſiſts the Kingdom of the Devil; in aſcertaining the Difference of Good and Evil, and aſſigning to each of them their proper
Reward. *Wo unto them,* ſaith he, *that call evil good, and good evil; that put darkneſs
for light, and light for darkneſs;* If. v. 20 : *that rebel againſt the light,* Job xxiv. 13 :
that love darkneſs rather than light, becauſe their deeds are evil; St Joh. iii. 19. This
eternal Difference of Good and Evil, God has now confirmed with new Authority, illuſtrated with greater Light, diſtinguiſhed with plainer and clearer bounds, and inforced
mens Obſervation of this Rule, with new Motives and ſtronger Obligations. For this
he ſent his Son into the world, to be born, to live and to die for us; that he might
effectually deſtroy the works of the Devil, and overthrow the kingdom of Darkneſs :
For this he has expreſſly revealed his Wrath from Heaven, againſt all Ungodlineſs
and Unrighteouſneſs of Men; that the eternal Difference of Good and Evil, when
men had neglected to be moved by the voice of Nature and Reaſon, might be ſupported
by divine Authority and by God himſelf ſpeaking. To this all the precepts of the
Goſpel tend, and all our Saviour's Sermons terminate in it. To this all his mercies,
all his patience leads : and all his judgments are intended to compel us. To this all
his promiſes gently invite and draw us, and all his threatnings loudly command and
preſs us. This is the End, to which all other things are directed as the Means.
This is finally good and profitable unto Men. On this depend all the Bleſſings of the
preſent Life, and all the Happineſs of a future Eternity.

III. I proceed in the *Third* and *laſt* place to draw ſome Obſervations from the
whole, which may be of uſe to us in Practice. And

1ſt, From what has been ſaid we may obſerve, that Religion and Virtue are truly
moſt agreeable to Nature, and that Vice and Wickedneſs are of all things the moſt
contrary to it. It is naturally the part of underſtanding and reaſonable Beings, to obſerve the differences that are in the Natures of Things; and therefore if Good and Evil,
be naturally and neceſſarily different; it is manifeſt it muſt needs be agreeable to Nature (unleſs ſtrangely corrupted with evil habits,) that men ſhould live religiouſly by
diſcerning and chuſing what is good, and avoiding what is evil. Men do indeed
frequently err in this matter, and are wilfully blinded by innumerable Corruptions,
by cuſtoms and evil habits, by Pleaſure and Intereſts, by falſe Opinions and looſe
practices; and then, to excuſe and vindicate themſelves, they take refuge in the Follies of Infidelity, and preſumptuouſly call *Light Darkneſs, and Darkneſs Light;* And
as a Palate vitiated by a long diſeaſe, ceaſes to be able to diſtinguiſh between Sweet
and Bitter; ſo theſe hardned Sinners mock at all difference of Good and Evil : But
ſtill the natures of things remain unalterably what they were, and cannot but juſtify

themſelves

S E R M. themfelves to the reafon and underftanding even of thofe very men that unreafonably
CX. deny them. It is not Nature, (as they weakly and falfely reproach it,) but unnatural
and corrupt Inclinations, that lead them to Wickednefs. Nature and Reafon, as well
as Revelation, call upon Men to be religious; and Virtue and Goodnefs are as truly
agreeable to the Mind, as Light is to the Eyes, or Sweetnefs to the Tafte. Their own
Confciences reproach them as often as they act otherwife; and no worldly Advantages
whatfoever, no Power upon Earth, can ever difcharge them from this Obligation.
Solomon had greater Experience, and made more Obfervations upon thefe things, than any
other man that ever lived; And the Sum of all *his* Obfervations, is the Reflection,
Ecclef. ii. 13. *Then I faw that Wifdom excelleth Folly, as far as Light excelleth Darknefs.*

2*dly*, FROM what has been faid, it follows that the knowledge of the moft important and fundamental Doctrines of Religion, muft be very eafy to be attained;
and that grofs ignorance of our Duty, can by no means be innocent or excufable; our
Minds being as naturally fitted to underftand the moft neceffary parts of it, as our Eyes
are to judge of Colours, or our Palate of Taftes. *If any man will do his Will, he fhall
know of the Doctrine whether it be of God.* To difcover that we ought to Fear and
Love, to worfhip and obey the great Creator of all things, the Author and Preferver of
our Beings, and the Giver of all things we enjoy or hope for: To underftand that Juftice is better than Iniquity, and Love and Charity than Violence and Oppreffion; doing good to Mankind than conquering of Nations, and preferving the World than ra-
vaging and deftroying it: To find out that Temperance and Sobriety, is more excellent than Debauchery; and wife and reafonable Counfels, than the fudden impulfes of
Lufts and Paffion: Thefe things require no great depth of Knowledge, no nice and
tedious difputes, nothing that can perplex or confound the underftanding even of the
meaneft perfon: They are eafy and obvious, plain and felf-evident, and vifible as the
cleareft day-light: Yet thefe are the things of the greateft importance, and which are
of the higheft concernment for all men to know and underftand: Thefe are the things
by which the World fubfifts; by which alone all Order and Government is maintained. Men that have time and abilities may lawfully and commendably and to very
excellent purpofes, ftudy fome things of greater difficulty. There is variety enough
in the *Works* of God, to employ the whole capacity of men and angels to all eternity; There are depths and fecrets in the difpenfations of *Providence*; There are *fome*
difficulties in fome circumftances of the *Laws* of God, and in the Revelations of his
Will; And thefe are a worthy employment for the moft enlarged underftandings
upon Earth. But the things which are of abfolute and indifpenfable neceffity to the
happinefs of men, thefe, under the Government of a Juft and Wife and Good God,
it cannot be imagined but they muft be univerfally level to the capacities of all Mankind.

3*dly*, FROM hence it appears, that the judgments of God upon impenitent Sinners, who obftinately difobey the moft reafonable and Neceffary Laws in the World,
are true and juft and righteous judgments. Had God commanded us things only in
their own nature indifferent; yet *even here* Obedience to the Supreme Lord of all
things, would have been highly reafonable; and all Creatures could not but confefs
his Juftice, if they were feverely punifhed for Difobedience to *fuch* Commands. But
when the Supreme Power and Authority of God, impofes fcarcely any thing upon
us, but what the very nature of the things themfelves makes neceffary, what the
Confciences of Sinners themfelves cannot but approve as moft reafonable and excellent, and what the Happinefs of man immediately and directly confifts in, as well as
the Law of God makes it his Duty to obferve; how much more muft Sinners now

confefs

4

confefs before all the World the righteoufnefs of God's judgments manifefted in their deftruction, if they will not by his Goodnefs be led to Repentance!

4*thly*, F R o M hence we may conclude, that whatever Doctrine is contrary to the nature and attributes of God, whatever is plainly unwife or wicked, whatever tends to confound the effential and eternal differences of Good and Evil, every fuch Doctrine, how plaufibly foever it may be fupported, muft neceffarily be falfe. By this Rule the Heathens might have difcovered the Folly of that Idolatry, which taught them to worfhip fuch Gods, as they themfelves had firft feigned like to the moft wicked men. And by the fame Rule, men of Underftanding and Probity will eafily condemn moft of the corruptions both in Doctrine and Worfhip, which have in many places among Chriftians themfelves crept in under a falfe pretence of divine Revelation. And at the fame time, it is a credible and excellent evidence of the Truth of the pure and uncorrupted Doctrine of the Gofpel as delivered in Scripture; that, befides the Authority of Miracles and Prophecies, it is inwardly in the Nature of the thing itfelf, a conformity to the divine Nature and Attributes, a confirmation aud improvement of our natural Notions of Good and Evil, and of the Rewards and Punifhments in a future State, and Affurance of the Reconciliation of God to repenting Sinners through the Mediation of Chrift, and a direct Promoter of the univerfal Happinefs of Mankind.

Laftly; F R o M what has been faid it is certain, that every Perfon or Doctrine, which would feparate Religion from a holy Life; and make Religion to confift merely in fuch fpeculative Opinions, as may be defended by an ill Liver; or in fuch outward Solemnities of Worfhip, as may be performed by a vicious and wicked man; does greatly corrupt Religion. The defign and the very effence of Religion, is to make men good and happy: The defign of the Revelation of the Gofpel, is to deftroy Superftition, and to reftore the Truth of Religion, by correcting mens Opinions and reforming their Manners, by introducing Repentance, and fecuring to us the Acceptablenefs of it through the merits of Chrift. If without this, men will pretend to be religious by any other method, they wholly miftake the Nature of Religion, and the defign of the Gofpel of Chrift. If they will not add to their Faith Virtue, but think it fufficient that they hold the Truth, though it be in Unrighteoufnefs; they are like the man who, our Saviour tells us, *built his houfe upon the Sand:* Their very Faith itfelf will but increafe their Guilt; and the Truth which they profefs, will but the more feverely condemn them for being workers of Iniquity. *Which Condemnation that we may all efcape, God of his infinite mercy grant,* &c.

SERMON

SERMON CXI.

Of the Nature of Moral and Positive Duties.

MATT. XXII. 40.

On these two Commandments hang all the Law and the Prophets.

S E R M. **T**HESE words are part of our Saviour's Answer to a captious Question
CXI. proposed to him by one of the Pharisees; Which *was the great Command-*
ment in the Law? It appears from the parallel place in St *Mark*, ch. xii.
ver. 33, that *the comparison* was made between the eternal and unchangeable Duties
of Piety and Righteousness on the one hand, and the external Precepts of the Law of
Moses, burnt offerings and sacrifices, on the other. For when our Saviour had given
this Answer to the Question proposed; that the first and great Commandment of all,
was this, *Thou shalt love the Lord thy God with all thy heart, and with all thy soul,*
and with all thy mind, and with all thy strength; and that the second was like unto it,
Thou shalt love thy neighbour as thy self; and added, that *on these two commandments*
hang all the Law and the Prophets; that is, that these are the ultimate End and Design of religion; and all positive precepts, only subordinate to these, and as means to
these great Ends; The Pharisee convinced with the *clearness,* and pleased with the
goodness of the Answer, replies, ver. 32, 33; *Well Master, thou hast said the Truth;*
for there is one God, and there is none other but he; And to love him with all the heart,
and with all the understanding, and with all the soul, and with all the strength;
and to love his neighbour as himself, is *more than all whole burnt-offerings and*
sacrifices.

O u r Saviour's determination of the Question proposed to him, was plain and clear,
full and decisive; that there was no Comparison at all, between the excellency of
ritual and of moral Duties. The Love of God and of our Neighbour, are the Life and
Essence of true Religion; the highest improvement and the greatest possible perfection
of our rational Nature; The Sum and Fountain, *in* which all other moral Duties are
contained, *from* which they all spring, and *to* which they may all be reduced; and
they are the ultimate *End,* for the Security of which, all *positive* Commandments, were
ever given at all. All the precepts of the Law of *Moses,* tend to this great End; All
the Exhortations of the Prophets, are directed to the same Design; and nothing is
truly valuable in the sight of God, but what is derived from these Fountains, and terminates in these excellent Ends.

I t may perhaps justly be wondred, *how* the *Jews* in our Saviour's time *could* possibly be so ignorant of the nature of true Religion, and so possessed with false Notions
concerning it; as to make *Any* competition, between the value of mere external Forms,
and the Real Practice of True Virtue; after God had so frequently declared to them
by his Prophets, that their *Sacrifices and oblations, their washings and purifications,*
their feasts and solemn assemblies, their fasts and severest humiliations, were so far from
being acceptable in his sight, if not accompanied with the practice of Justice, *Truth,*

3 *Righte-*

Righteousness, and Charity; that on the contrary, *without* these virtues, these very rites, though of his own Institution, were the *greatest abomination in his sight*; as being only evidences of a deeper hypocrisy. *To what purpose is the multitude of your Sacrifices unto me, saith the Lord? I am full of the burnt-offerings of rams, and the fat of fed beasts, and I delight not in the blood of bullocks or of lambs or of he-goats:* But *Wash ye, make you clean, put away the evil of your doings from before mine eyes, cease to do evil, learn to do well, seek judgment, relieve the oppressed, judge the fatherless, plead for the widow*; Then *though your sins be as scarlet, they shall be white as snow; though they be red like crimson, they shall be as wool*, Isaiah i. 11.

But yet, notwithanding these plain and frequent declarations of the Prophets, it is evident in the whole History of the Gospel, that the most eminent and famous men, men of the greatest character and esteem for learning and piety among the Jews, Scribes and Pharisees, Doctors, and expounders of the Law, were, in our Saviour's time, almost universally fallen under this great and fatal mistake. They were very strict and zealous even to the highest degree of Superstition, in observing the outward rites and ceremonies of the Law; concerning which, our Saviour, with great exactness of expression, says, *that they ought not indeed to be left undone:* But at the same time *they neglected the practice, of the great and weightier and more indispensable Duties, of Truth and Righteousness and Goodness towards all men.* They were very strict and superstitious in outward Purifications, in the *washings of pots and cups, and the like;* while they took no care at all to purify their own *Minds, from unrighteousness and all uncleanness.* And if we duly consider the corrupt estate of humane Nature; it may not perhaps be very difficult, to give an account *whence* all this Evil arises. For to men of corrupt affections and indulged vicious habits, nothing is so difficult as the practice of virtue and true Religion; To mortify long-indulged Appetites, to cleanse themselves from all filthiness both of flesh and Spirit, to conquer vicious inclinations, to root out confirmed habits, to govern unruly passions; these things *are like cutting off a right hand, and pulling out a right eye;* or, as *Nicodemus* expresses it, *like a man's being born again when he is old.* And yet, in order to keep up a reputation in the World, *'tis* absolutely necessary, that Men have *some* pretence of zeal for Religion.. Corrupt Minds therefore, who will not be at the pains to practise true Virtue, and yet desire to serve themselves of the temporal advantages which the name and credit of religion is apt to gain in the World; *must* call something else, *must* call certain Forms or Opinions, by the name of religion, instead of That which really and only is so. They *must* make religion to consist, in things *more visible* to the eyes of the vulgar, and better fitted to procure the applause of the World; than the sincerest Love of God, and of our neighbour; than meekness and simplicity, Justice and Charity, Holiness and Purity of Mind, and the Practice of other the like excellent Virtues; which are so much the more sincere and of the greater value in the sight of God, as they are seated in the heart and soul itself, and are less exposed to the eye of the world. This *One* Mistake, is the great and general corruption of mankind: This has at all Times and in all Places been the First and the Last Error in matters of Religion. Thus did the *Pharisees* in our Saviour's days: and Thus among *Christians*, in all places, especially where Popery has prevailed, and in Other places in proportion as the same Spirit has gained ground, How has the worship of God been corrupted, and almost wholly turned into Pomp and Superstition? How have the empty forms and appearances of Religion, shut out the true Love of God, which consists in Imitation of his Nature, and in Obedience to his holy and divine Commands? How hath false zeal for vain and corrupt doctrines, for the doctrines and Traditions of particular *Men* or Sects and *Bodies of Men*, turned Christian Love, Meekness and Charity, those prime and fundamental Duties, into that which is

SERM. the *moſt directly oppoſite* to the whole End and Deſign of *all* Religion, even into the
CXI. greateſt and moſt inhuman Cruelties? How have vain penances, and repeated confeſſions and abſolutions, and other weak and deceitful obſervances, been ſubſtituted in the
room of true repentance and reformation of Life? In a word, how numberleſs have
been the inventions of men, and what pains have they not been willing to take, to reconcile the *Name* of religion with the *practice* of wickedneſs, and to make great zeal
for God, conſiſtent with being workers of Iniquity? And how totally have been neglected thoſe Great and Eternal Duties, which are briefly ſummed up in the *Love of*
God and of our neighbour? on which *two Commandments our Saviour* (in the Text)
affirms, *that all the Law and the Prophets depend:* That is; All Chriſtian Duties are
either *contained in* theſe; or are *ſubſervient to* them: All *moral* Duties may be reduced to
theſe Heads, and are contained *under* them; and all *poſitive* Injunctions are only ſubſervient *to* them, and but as means to theſe Ends.

I. *Firſt*; ALL *moral* Duties are contained *in*, and may be reduced *to*, theſe two
Heads; the Love of God and of our Neighbour.

GOD, is a Being of infinite and unlimited Perfections; the Fountain of all Goodneſs and Happineſs; who contains in himſelf all things that are excellent, all things
that are truly worthy of Admiration or Love; and from whom as from their only Fountain, are derived all Excellencies, that are found in the *whole* or in any *parts* of the
Creation. To *Love* God therefore, is to have always fixt upon our minds a juſt regard
to the Perfections of his Nature; and a due Senſe of his ineſtimable Goodneſs, in communicating ſo much Happineſs to his Creatures. And This, if carefully attended to,
ſo as to produce its juſt Effect and natural conſequence, muſt neceſſarily have ſuch
an Influence upon our Practice, as to cauſe us to Praiſe and to Adore him continually;
to devote our ſelves wholly to *his* Service, who is the only Author of our Being, and
of whatever Good we enjoy or hope for; to worſhip him conſtantly, and him only,
who alone has the Power of all things in his own Hands, and employs that Power
under the Direction of infinite Goodneſs, only for the Benefit and Welfare of all his
Creatures, according to their ſeveral Capacities. How inconſiſtent with this Love of
God is it, to prefer ſinful and corrupt enjoyments, ſhort and tranſitory and unrighteous
Pleaſures, before that infinite and eternal Happineſs, which God has propoſed to us in
the fruition of himſelf? and how will this naturally oblige us to govern our Paſſions,
to moderate our Appetites, to reſtrain all unreaſonable Deſires, to deſpiſe all the allure-
ments of Sin, and (in a word) to apply our ſelves wholly to the Obſervation of his juſt
and righteous Commands? Thus all the Duties of the firſt Table, which relate to
God; and alſo all thoſe Duties which reſpect ourſelves, or the Government of our
Paſſions and Appetites by the Rules of Reaſon and Religion; ſpring from the Love of
God, as from their true Fountain; and are all neceſſarily contained in it, and may
eaſily be reduced to it.

IN like manner; The Duties of the ſecond Table, are all as plainly contained *un-*
der, and may be reduced to the Love of our *Neighbour*; as the Duties of the firſt
Table, are to the Love of *God.* God created and ſent us into this World on purpoſe,
to do Good one to another; to love and to aſſiſt each other, in all the neceſſities and
exigencies of human Life. In this, all his commandments terminate; for this he propoſes to us the example of his own infinite Goodneſs; This End whoever conſtantly
aims at, and ſteddily purſues, will never greatly fail in the particulars of his Duty.
He that loves his neighbour ſincerely as himſelf; and is willing to do to all men, as he
deſires they ſhould do to him; that thinks himſelf ſent into the World on purpoſe to
do Good to others, and looks upon it as the Sum and End of his Duty, to promote
the univerſal peace and happineſs of mankind; will certainly upon this Principle regu-

larly

larly and uniformly perform all the parts of his Duty towards men; And this univerfal Love of his Neighbour, will as naturally fpread itfelf into all the branches of a truly Chriftian converfation in the world, as a root or ftock will in a fit and proper foil, re- gularly fend forth branches, leaves and fruit, agreeable to its proper nature and kind. From this Fountain of univerfal Love and Charity, will certainly flow all thofe ftreams of virtue and good works, in which confifts the Life and Beauty and Ufefulnefs, and the true Excellency and Glory of Religion. Whoever is under the guidance of this one Principle, will naturally behave himfelf well in all relations, and perform the part of a wife and good man in all the different accidents and circumftances of Life. Such a one, will not fail to make it his bufinefs, to promote the publick Good; and delight to contribute as much as poffible towards the Peace and Welfare of the World. He will naturally treat his Superiours with chearful Submiffion, his Benefactors with gratitude and all decent refpect, his Equals with affability and readinefs to do all Offices of kind- nefs, his Inferiours with gentlenefs, moderation, and charity. Thus evidently, un- der the Love of our Neighbour, are contained all the Duties of the fecond Table; and from it, as from their root or fountain, they all naturally and regularly flow. This is what the Apoftle teaches; *Gal.* v. 14; *For, all the Law is fulfilled in one word, even in This, Thou fhalt love thy Neighbour as thy felf.* And ftill more exprefsly, *Rom.* xiii. 8; *Owe no man any thing but to Love one another, for he that loveth another, hath fulfilled the Law:* For every particular precept, fuch as, *Thou fhalt not commit adultery, Thou fhalt not kill, Thou fhalt not fteal, Thou fhalt not bear falfe witnefs, Thou fhalt not covet, and if there be any other commandment, it is briefly comprehended in This faying, Thou fhalt love thy neighbour as thy felf: Love worketh no ill to his neighbour: therefore love is the fulfilling of the Law.* And our Saviour himfelf; St *Matt.* vii. 12; *Therefore all things whatfoever ye would that men fhould do to you, do ye even fo to them; for this is the Law and the Prophets;* or, as it is in the words of the Text, *on thefe command- ments hang all the Law and the Prophets;* that is, in this are contained, in this do termi- nate, all the Commandments of God.

HAVING thus fhown, which was the firft thing I propofed, that all *Moral* Duties of Life may be reduced to thefe two Heads, the Love of God and of our Neighbour. I proceed in the

II. *Second* place, to fhow that all *Pofitive* and *ritual* Injunctions, though in their pro- per place they *ought not to be left undone,* (as our Saviour himfelf expreffes it,) yet they are but fubordinate to Thefe, and fubfervient to them; And this may abundantly be made appear by the following confiderations.

1ft, THAT the *moral* Duties of life, *the Love of God and of Our Neighbour,* are things in their *own Nature* good and excellent, of eternal and neceffary Obligation; which receive not their power of obliging, merely from their being commanded; but their obligation is eternal and abfolutely unchangeable, as is the Nature of the things themfelves. Our Obligation to Love God, arifes from the Nature and Attributes of God himfelf; and therefore That Obligation can no more ceafe or be altered, than the Divine Nature and Attributes can be fubject to change. In like manner, our Obliga- tion to Love and do right to our Neighbour, arifes from the Nature of Man, and from our relation one towards another; from that ftate and condition, wherein God has created us; from the exigencies of Life, the neceffity of focieties, and the equity, rea- fon, and proportion of things. So long therefore as thefe things continue the fame; fo long this Obligation alfo muft continue unalterable. Thefe Moral Duties therefore, are by neceffity and in their own Nature, good and excellent: They are indifpenfably neceffary, to preferve the Order and Happinefs of the World; they are neceffary to the improvement and perfection of our own Minds; they are neceffary to Qualify us and make us capable of that State of Glory, to which God has defigned us hereafter; But

SERM. all ritual and ceremonial Observances, have no intrinsick goodness in the nature of the
CXI. things themselves; nor any Obligation, but what arises merely from their being positively and occasionally enjoyned. Their Obligation therefore is of a changeable Nature, depending wholly on the good Pleasure of him that commands them; and consequently though it is our Duty to perform them *when* and *where* they are enjoyned, yet they can never be compared or come in competition with Those Duties, whose Obligation is necessary and eternal; and the Practice of which, has an intrinsick goodness and unchangeable excellency absolutely, in the Nature of the things themselves.

2*dly*, A L L Positive and ritual injunctions whatsoever, can be but subordinate to the Practice of moral Virtues; because these latter are the End for which the former are commanded, and the former can be considered only as Means to the latter. In the Perfection of Virtue and Goodness, consists the Image of *God*; and in the same likewise is Placed the Chief Happiness of *Man*. In this therefore consists our Chief Good, on this depends our final Happiness, in this lies the Excellency and Perfection of our Nature. Consequently this must of necessity, be our ultimate End; this must be the principal scope of all our Actions; and nothing else can be truly valuable or worthy of Esteem, but only so far as it may be a means and assistance to attain this End. Ritual Observances in Religion, if they be such as truly increase our Devotion towards God; if they enlarge our Charity and Good-will towards Men; if they be such as are significant and remind us of our Obligation to Purity and Temperance in ourselves; they are then indeed of excellent Use, and (so far as they are commanded,) of indispensable Obligation. *Baptism*, as St *Peter* affirms, *does indeed save us:* 1 Pet. iii. 21; but if it does so by being, not barely a washing away the filth of the flesh, but the answer of a good Conscience towards God. The Sacrament of the Lord's Supper likewise confirms our Title to eternal Life; but it does so by renewing our obligation and our vows, to obey that Covenant upon which eternal Life was promised us in Christ. Circumcision in like manner, and the Purifications appointed under the Law, were means of Salvation to the *Jews*; yet not by any virtue in the things themselves, but as Instances of Obedience to the Will of God, and as representations of their Obligation to Purity and Holiness. Where these Observances are not used as Means to this End, they become altogether useless and unprofitable; *commandments which are not good, and precepts by which men shall not live*; as the Prophet expresses it. *Circumcision, to them that obeyed not the* Law, *was accounted Uncircumcision*; Baptism and the Lord's-Supper, to them that obey not the *Gospel* in the course of a virtuous life, is but as washing a dead Corpse in hopes to infuse life into it, and an attempting to please God by profaning his Feast and despising his Ordinances. *The End of the commandment*, saith the Apostle, *is* Charity, *out of a pure heart, and of a good conscience, and of faith unfeigned*; 1 Tim. i. 5. In a word; *The Kingdom of God*, saith our Saviour, *is* within *you*; St *Luke* xvii. 21: Every man's *Religion* is, not what he *professes*, or what *show* he makes in external observances; but what *influence* it *really* has upon the *Man himself*, in the habit of his mind, and in the course of his Actions, in his Family, in his Business, in his dealings with all Mankind, in his common conversation, and even in his very Diversions themselves, as well as in his more solemn Acts of Prayer and Devotion. For, in like manner, as in our Saviour's Parable, *not the eating with unwashen hands, or any thing else that cometh from* without, *can make a man morally* unclean; but only the wicked dispositions that are *within* the heart of the *man himself*: So on the contrary also, no rites or ceremonies, nor any thing else that is *without* the man, can make him truly *holy and religious*; but that *inward* habitual virtuous Disposition of *mind*, the fruits of which appearing in his Actions, determine the man's true Character and Denomination. Were this *One* Fundamental Truth sufficiently attended to; Christians could not be so absurdly imposed upon, as to make their Religion, whose *Essential*

Character

Character is univerfal Goodnefs and Charity, become on the contrary *itfelf* an occafion S E R M. of Hatred, Quarrels, and Contentions. Which is, by catching at the *Shadow*, to lofe CXI. the *Subftance* ; and by contending about the *Means*, to neglect the *End*.

3*dly*, THE fame thing appears further from hence; that Moral Duties or the Practice of true Virtue, will continue for ever; but all pofitive Commandments are but of temporary Obligation. The Love of God and of our Neighbour, are Qualifications which will remain and be perfected in *Heaven*; but all ritual Obfervances, are appointed only for the affiftance and improvement of our Religion here upon *Earth*. When that which is perfect is come, then thefe fubordinate Inftitutions are to be done away; And not thefe only, but even thofe *Virtues* themfelves alfo, which are of a fecondary rank, and whofe excellency does not ultimately terminate in themfelves. Hope, and Faith itfelf, and all other Graces and Gifts of the Spirit, which are in order to thefe, muft at the confummation of things, neceffarily and of courfe ceafe: *Whether there be Prophecies, they fhall fail; whether there be tongues, they fhall ceafe; whether there be knowledge, it fhall vanifh away: But Charity only, never faileth:* Our Love of *God*, will be as much *more* perfect in heaven than it is here ; as our knowledge of him will then be increafed, *when we fhall fee him as he is:* And our Love of our *Neighbour* will then be as much improved beyond what it can now arrive to, as the nature of Angels is at prefent more excellent than that of frail men.

VOL. I.   8 S   SERMON

SERMON CXII.

Of the Difficulty of arriving at Truth.

St JOH. IV. 11.

The Woman faith unto him; Sir, Thou haft nothing to draw with; and the Well is deep; From whence then haft thou that living Water?

SERM. CXII.

THE former part of this Chapter contains a very remarkable Hiftory of our Saviour's Converfation with a Woman of *Samaria*. The *accidental occafion* whereof, as to humane appearance, was, his retiring out of *Judæa*, to avoid the hatred of the *Pharifees*; leaft they fhould apprehend and kill him before his appointed Time: But in reality, the *gracious Intention* of Providence in difpofing That feemingly accidental Occafion, was, that the Gofpel might be preached to the *Samaritans* alfo, as well as to the *Jews*. And as, upon *other occafions*, our Saviour ufually introduced his Doctrine under the veil of a Parable, that he might open it by degrees as men were able and difpofed to apprehend it, and not furprize them with more Light at once than they were able to bear; fo *here likewife* he took occafion from things that feemed to offer themfelves in common Difcourfe, to inftruct firft the Woman, and afterwards a whole City, in the great Doctrines of the Gofpel. For, in his paffage out of *Judæa* through the Country of *Samaria*, fitting as it were by-chance, and being weary with his journey, on the fide of a Well, (near the City of *Sichar*,) called *Jacob's-well*, becaufe fuppofed to have been anciently digged by that Patriarch; he defires a Woman, who came out of the City to draw Water, that fhe would give him to drink, *ver.* 7. The Woman, perceiving *Jefus* by his Speech and Garb to be a *Jew* and not a *Samaritan*; and knowing that the *Jews* and *Samaritans* were at fuch irreconcileable Enmity againft each other, upon account of their Differences in Religion, that they had no Communication nor Converfe one with another; fhe feemed furprized with Wonder, and faid; *How is it, that Thou being a Jew, afkeft drink of Me, who am a Woman of Samaria?* ver. 9. *Jefus* replied; *If thou kneweft the gift of God, and who it is that faith to thee, Give me to drink; thou wouldft have afked of Him, and he would have given thee living Water*, ver. 10. Meaning, by an eafy fimilitude taken from the Occafion of their difcourfing together, that he would have taught her the *Doctrine of Salvation* contained in the Gofpel; which is more truly refrefhing to a Mind well-difpofed and defirous of Inftruction, than Water to a dry and thirfty Body. The Woman, not underftanding the Metaphor, but imagining that *Jefus* fpake of real Water, anfwers in the words of the Text, *ver.* 11; *Sir, Thou haft nothing to draw with, and the Well is deep; From whence then haft thou That living Water?* *Jefus*, opening and explaining the Figure to her by degrees, replies, *ver.* 13; *Whofoever drinketh of this Water*, (the natural Water of the Well, to quench his bodily Thirft,) *fhall thirft again; But whofoever drinketh of the Water that I fhall give him, fhall never thirft; but the Water that I fhall give him*, (the Doctrine of eternal

Salvation

Salvation propofed in the Gofpel,) *fhall be in him a Well of Water fpringing up into* S E R M. *everlafting Life.* And thus having prepared her by degrees, to remove her Prejudices;   CXII. he then proceeds to tell her fome of the moft fecret Actions of her Life, to convince her of his Power and Knowledge; and, after That, expreffly owns himfelf to be the Meffias; and then declares to *her*, and, upon the fame opportunity, to the *whole City*, that not the *Samaritan*, but the *Jewifh* worfhip, was, at that time prefent, the true Religion; but that both the one and the other were fhortly to be fuperfeded by the inftitution of the *Chriftian*, when *the true Worfhippers*, according to the Doctrine of the Gofpel, *fhould worfhip the Father*, neither after the way of the *Jewifh* Ceremonies, nor the *Samaritan*, but *in Spirit and in Truth*.

THE Occafion and Defign of the *whole* Hiftory being thus briefly explained; I re-turn now to that *particular* portion of it, which is contained in the words of the Text: *The Woman faith unto him; Sir, thou haft nothing to draw with; and the Well is deep; From whence then haft thou that living Water?* The words were fpoken by the Wo-man, (being yet ignorant of our Saviour's Intention,) they were fpoken by *Her* in their *literal* Senfe. But our Saviour in his Anfwer, immediately applying them to a *figura-tive* fignification; and calling his own *Doctrine*, the Doctrine of Truth and of eternal Life, by the Name of *living Water*; will juftify *Us* likewife, in confidering the words and difcourfing upon them, according to that figurative Senfe or fpiritual Interpretation, which our Saviour himfelf was pleafed to put upon them. Allegorizing of Scripture, and putting figurative Senfes upon plain and literal Expreffions, according to every man's particular Imagination or Conceit; is indeed a thing of dangerous Confequence; and has in former Ages, been the occafion of many vain Difputes in the Church of God; whilft men of warm imaginations have, by fuch a method of interpreting, found Doctrines in Scripture which never were there; and contended earneftly for their own Fancies, inftead of that Form of Sound Words which was once delivered unto the Saints. But, where our Saviour himfelf has made the Interpretation, and the Senfe is juftified by the Defign of the whole Difcourfe; there we need not fear leaft we fhould miftake in our Explication, nor fcruple to follow the guidance of fuch an un-erring Inftructor. In difcourfing therefore upon thefe words, *Sir, Thou haft nothing to draw with, and the Well is deep:* I fhall propofe the following Confiderations. 1ft, Whence it comes to pafs, that *Truth*, (for that's what our Saviour in this Difcourfe calls *living Water: Whence*, I fay, it comes to pafs, that *Truth*) which feems fo ne-ceffary for *every man* to know, fhould yet generally be fo difficult for *any man* to come at: *The Well is deep, and we have nothing to draw with.* And 2dly, By what means *every* fincere perfon, may yet certainly attain to fuch a *Degree* of Knowledge, or the Difcovery of *fo much Truth*, as is neceffary for his own particular Salvation.

I. *Firft*; Whence it comes to pafs, that *Truth*, which feems fo neceffary for *every man* to know, fhould yet generally be fo difficult for *any man* to come at: *The Well is deep, and we have nothing to draw with.* It has been an antient complaint from the beginning of the World, among the Philofophers of all Nations, who have profeffed to employ themfelves in the Study of *Nature*; that *Truth* hath lain buried in fo *deep a Pit*, that they have never been able to difcover the Bottom of it. And the like Com-plaints we meet with, even in the *Scripture itfelf*. In the Book of *Job: There is*, fays he, *a vein for the filver, and a place for gold where they fine it; iron is taken out of the Earth, and brafs is molten out of the ftone :——But where fhall Wifdom be found, and where is the place of Underftanding?—— There is a path which no fowl knoweth, and which the vulture's eye hath not feen; The lion's whelps have not trodden it, nor the fierce lion paffed by it:—But whence cometh Wifdom, and where is the place of Underftanding; feeing it is hid from the eyes of all living, and kept clofe from the fowls of the air?* ch. xxviii. 1, &c. And *Solomon*, whofe Largenefs of Underftanding
exceeded

S E R M. exceeded all that went before him, and was never equalled by any that came after
CXII. him, yet even *he* complained, *Ecclef.* iii. 11 ; *No man can find out the work that God
maketh, from the beginning to the end.* For, *as thou knoweft not the way of the Spirit,
nor how the bones do grow in the womb of her that is with Child ; even fo thou knoweft not
the works of God who maketh all* ; ch. xi. 5: and ch. viii. 16. *When I applied mine
heart,* (faith he) *to know wifdom, and to fee the bufinefs that is done upon the earth:
Then I beheld all the work of God, that a man cannot find out the work that is done under
the Sun ; becaufe though a man labour to feek it out, yet fhall he not find it ; yea further, though a* wife *man think to know it, yet fhall he not be able to find it.* But
thefe things are fpoken, of *natural* Knowledge ; of the Knowledge of the Works of
God in the Frame of Nature ; which is that part of Truth, wherein we are leaft concerned to be accurately inftructed. In that which concerns us more, and feems to be
of more importance for us to underftand ; the Works of God in the *moral* World, the
Difpenfations of his Providence towards the Righteous and the Wicked even in *This*
alfo there are Difficulties, which the Wifeft of men have very hardly been able to fur-
mount. Atheiftical and profane Spirits, have been willing to give it over, as irreconcileable with the Belief of a Divine Being ; and Holy and Pious men themfelves have
been perplexed in their own Minds, when they could not find out the Explication. *My
feet,* fays the Pfalmift, *were almoft gone ; my treadings had well-nigh flipt ;* when *I was
grieved at the wicked* ; and faw *the ungodly in fuch Profperity ; I thought to underftand
this, but it was too hard for me* ; Pf. lxxiii. 2, 15. And the Prophet *Jeremy* ; ch. xii.
ver. 1 ; *Righteous art thou, O Lord, when I plead with thee ; yet let me talk with thee
of thy judgments : Wherefore doth the way of the wicked profper ? wherefore are all they
happy, that deal very treacheroufly ?* And *Solomon* himfelf ; *Ecclef.* iv. 1 ; *I returned and
confidered all the oppreffions that are done under the Sun ; and behold, the tears of fuch as
were oppreffed, and they had no comforter ; and on the fide of the oppreffors there was power, but they had no comforter.* But This alfo is of lefs importance than that which follows. For even in that very thing, which of all others is of the higheft concernment to us, the knowledge of our *Practical Duty itfelf,* the knowledge of what is
incumbent upon *ourfelves in particular,* and of Neceffity to be done by us ; even in
This likewife there may feem at firft fight, (to perfons not very confiderate) to be no
fmall Confufion ; and to perfons not very confiderate, the *Fountain of Truth* may appear very *deep,* and that *they have nothing to draw with.* For among that vaft Variety
of *Religions* that are profeffed in the World, how fhall a fincere perfon of ordinary capacity find *Which* is alone the true one ? and if he is fatisfied that *Chriftianity* is the
true Religion, yet among Chriftian Churches damning and anathematizing each other,
and among Sects even of *Chriftians* faftening all Names of Contumely and Reproach
upon each other, how fhall he know *Which* it is his Duty to adhere to ? The Church
of *Rome* tells him, he muft blindly follow *her* Authority ; or elfe he forfakes his only
Infallible Guide : All *Other* Sects of Chriftians tell him, he muft follow the *Scripture*
only, as the complete Rule of Faith and Manners ; and yet in interpreting the meaning
of that Rule, *They* alfo differ from each other ; and Every one affures him he is not in
the way of Truth, unlefs he ftedfaftly adheres to *Their* Interpretation. The Difputes
about Religion are infinite, and yet it is of infinite importance not to be deceived :
And *what fhall* a fincere perfon *do to be faved ?* This is the ground of Complaint ; *The
Well is deep,* and we *have nothing to draw with :* And now the Queftion is, (which was
the 1ft thing I propofed ;) whence comes it to pafs, that *Truth,* which feems fo neceffary for *every man* to know, fhould yet generally be fo difficult for *any man* to
come at ? And *firft,* There is neceffarily in the Nature of *Things themfelves* fome *Difficulty,* and in *our Underftandings* much *natural Imperfection :* Which is a juft and
continual ground of Humility, and Meeknefs of Spirit. *Some* things are entirely above

the reach of our Capacities; and *others* not to be attained to, without much labour and study. *Some* things we can at moft arrive but at a *probable* Knowledge of; and even *That*, not without fuch peculiar Advantages, as very few men ever are Mafters of. And in thofe things which are the moft *level* to our Underftandings, and which in their plain and *general* acceptation are of the greateft importance for us to know, there are yet *at the bottom* fome accurate Niceties, fome fubtle Intricacies of Nature, which limit the *Degree* of our Knowledge, even in thofe very matters which we know the moft; and fet bounds to our Search even in thofe things, whofe Nature we feem to apprehend the moft thoroughly. In the cleareft and moft unbounded Profpect, there is a diftance beyond which no Eye can reach; and in the inmoft Nature even of the plaineft and moft intelligible parts of all the Works of God, there is a depth into which no finite Sagacity can penetrate. But then thefe Secrets are no *part* of *that* Truth, which it is neceffary for us to know; and therefore we have no juft reafon to complain, that they are hid from our imperfect Underftandings. There is *fome* pains and induftry, *fome* labour and ftudy, at leaft fome *attention* and ferious confideration requifite, to the underftanding even of the moft obvious and neceffary Truths; And this is a juft and reafonable Obligation upon every man, according to the degree of his Capacity, to look about him and confider with due *Attention of Mind, which* is the true way to eternal Salvation; even in like manner as the Providence of God has wifely and reafonably made *fome Labour* of the *Body* neceffary, to the prefervation and fupport of this *Temporal* Life. *With* fuch ferious Attention, how mean foever a man's Capacity be, he fhall certainly find out (as will prefently be made appear more diftinctly) *fo much* of *Truth*, as is neceffary for his own particular Salvation: But, without Care and Attention, he muft unavoidably continue *Ignorant* even of the moft *neceffary* Truths; becaufe, in the very *Nature* of Man, our Underftandings are neceffarily flow and imperfect; and in the *Nature* of Things *themfelves*, how plain foever in comparifon, yet there is always *fome* Degree of *Difficulty* to apprehend them thoroughly. And This is the *firft* occafion of *Truth's* being *difficult to be difcovered*. But then, how great Care and Attention foever men apply, and how large foever their Capacities be; yet if they amufe themfelves in fearching out things *above* their Faculties; or if, about things in the main fufficiently intelligible, they prefume unneceffarily and where *Practice* is not concerned, to enter into fuch Intricacies and fubtle Speculations, as are *beyond* their Depth; thus alfo they will run into Errour and Uncertainty. And This is a *fecond* occafion, why Truth becomes difficult to be difcovered; namely, mens *perplexing themfelves*, by aiming at things *not neceffary* to be known, that is, which relate not to Chriftian *Practice*; or at fuch *degrees* of Knowledge, as are not poffible to be arrived at. Of This, thofe perfons are a great inftance, who while they have loft themfelves in the Labyrinth of an imaginary *fecret* Will of God, have neglected to obey, or perplexed the Obligations of obeying, his *declared* Will and Commands. Which is juft as if a Mariner in a cloudy night, fhould neglect his Compafs, and refolve to fail by the Stars, which cannot be feen. Of the fame kind were the reafonings of thofe *Jewifh* Doctors, who by their vain Traditions made void the Commandments of God, and taught for Doctrines the Opinions of Men. Under the fame Denomination fall all thofe Speculations concerning the *metaphyfical Nature* of the *Liberty* of Man's *Will*, and the like; which, while *Wife* men could not explain *wherein* their *Liberty* confifted, have made *Foolifh men* doubt whether they had any *Liberty of acting* at all. The Church of *Rome*, by pretending to explain *philofophically* that which our Saviour fpoke *morally*, concerning the *Bread and Wine in the Sacrament* being *his Body and Blood*; perplexed the Truth to fuch a degree, that at laft, after many Difputes, they fixt upon That to be true, which of all other things was the

S E R M. most impossible to be so; and made all intelligent persons in their Communion, of ne-
CXII. cessity to become Scepticks, and, so long as they continue in That Profession, to look
upon Truth not only as a thing difficult to come at, and hid as it were in a very deep
Abyss, but in reality not to be found any where at all. The Scholastick Writers in the
middle and disputing Ages of the Church, by presuming to explain metaphysically,
how the *Son and Holy Spirit* of God, derived their Being from the Father, ran sometimes even into Blasphemy, against him from whom they both proceeded; instead of
taking care, by the Sanctification of the *Spirit*, and through the redemption of the *Son*,
to reconcile themselves to the *Father* and Supreme Lord of all things. *Lastly*, To
mention no more instances upon this Head; the Contentions which have disturbed the
World, about *Authority and Power* in making *Doctrines of Faith*, which yet none
could ever agree in whom it ought to be placed; have frequently so far perplexed even
those who know and profess the plain *Doctrine of Christ*, which he himself has expressly declared necessary, *to be the only Rule*; that they have hardly trusted themselves
to act upon the Security, of so plain and evident and necessary a Truth. This therefore is the *second* Occasion of Truth's being difficult to discover; namely, mens perplexing themselves perpetually, by aiming at things needless and not necessary to be
known. A *third* occasion, is, *Prejudice and Prepossession*; arising from the Custom of
Education, and from mens depending on the *Opinion* and *Authority of particular persons*, without Examination. For it is very natural, for men to be fond of such Opinions,
as they have been long accustomed to without contradiction; and which are maintained by such persons, for whom they have long been taught to have a great Veneration and Esteem. Hence in Popish and other Countries, where-ever any Errour has
generally prevailed; however *contrary*, and however *apparently* contrary, both to Reason and Scripture the Errour be; yet the greater Number of Men, always steddily adhere to it; And it is very difficult, even for *reasonable* and *considerate* persons, so far
to shake off these Prejudices, as to come to *inquire* and so much as *doubt* concerning an
Errour, which, if they had not been so prejudiced beforehand, they would hardly have
been perswaded that any man could ever be so absurd as to have entertained at all. This
is plainly the Case of *Transubstantiation*, and of all other the like unreasonable Doctrines. *Fourthly* and *lastly*; The last reason of Truth's being difficult to discover, is
the *Wickedness* and *Perverseness* of Men; who, for their own Interest and Worldly
Ends, do sometimes on purpose endeavour to conceal it. Atheistical and profane men,
have always made it their business to confound the World with Darkness and Sophistry;
to cast Mists before the eyes of the Simple, and Stumbling-blocks before the feet of the
Unwary. And even among Christians themselves, there have in all Ages been *perverse
disputings of men of corrupt minds, and destitute of the Truth, supposing that Gain is
Godliness*: 1 Tim. vi. 5. There have never wanted men, who for the support of known
Errours, and for temporal Advantages, have discouraged all Learning and sober Inquiry
after Truth, all study and diligent search into the Grounds and Reasons of things. Nay
the whole Protestant World knows *who* have openly carried this matter so far, as to
corrupt and falsify Histories, to forge some Books, and destroy or suppress others, to
take away (as much as in them lay) the Key of Knowledge, and expressly to forbid the
Reading even of the Scripture itself.

T H E S E are the several Ways, by which Errors are promoted and spread in
the World, and from whence it comes to pass (which was the *first* thing to be
explained,) that *Truth*, which seems so necessary for *every man* to know, should
yet generally be so difficult for *any man* to arrive at. It remains that I proceed now
in the

II. *Second*

II. *Second* place to fhow, by *what means* every ferious and fincere perfon, may yet certainly attain to fuch a *Degree* of Knowledge, or the Difcovery of *fo much Truth,* as is neceffary for his own particular Salvation. This is the Inquiry, of the greateft Importance in the World: And the Anfwer to it, may in good meafure be gathered, from what has been before faid. For as Truth is contrary to Errour; fo the Ways alfo by which they are propagated, are contrary to each other: And he that knows by what Means *Errour* prevails in the World, is by the fame directed in general to the beft Method of finding out the *Truth.* But to be more particular: Becaufe this is a Matter, that concerns Perfons of all Capacities; and Men of the loweft Abilities are equally under Obligation to find out the Way of Life, as the Learnedft Difputers in the the World; from whence it is evident, that the Method of finding out fo much Truth as is neceffary for every particular man's Salvation, cannot be a Matter of fubtle Speculation, but of Integrity and fincere Inquiry; I fhall therefore propofe what I think needful upon This Head, in three very plain and intelligible particulars. And

1*ft*, He that fincerely and ferioufly defires to difcover fo much Truth as is neceffary to his Salvation, muft above all things take care, that he in the firft place refolve to *do* the Will of God; and then he has a promife, that he *fhall know* of the Doctrine, whether it be of God. The greateft impediment to the Difcovery of Truth in matters of Religion, is a *vicious difpofition*; which makes men hate to come forth into the Light, left their deeds fhould be reproved. For, what St *Paul* fays of the *natural* man, holds true of the *vicious* perfon much more; that he *receiveth not the things of the Spirit of God, for they are foolifhnefs unto him, neither can he know them, becaufe they are fpiritually difcerned.* If a man deals fincerely with himfelf, and fuffers not himfelf to be blinded with the Love of any Wickednefs, there is fomething in the Frame of the Mind of Man, and fomething in the Nature of Truth itfelf, which makes them agreeable and connatural to each other, as Objects are fuited to their proper Organs; even as the Eye is fitted to diftinguifh Colours, or the Ear to judge of Sounds. Befides which; fuch a perfon is fecured moreover by the Promife of God, that he fhall by the guidance and Direction of the divine Spirit, be led into all neceffary truth: that the *Secret of the Lord* fhall be *with them that fear him, and that he* will *fhew* them *his Covenant,* Pf. xxv. 14. Which is the Foundation of that excellent Advice of the Son of *Sirach,* Eccluf. i. 26; *If thou defire Wifdom, keep the commandments, and the Lord fhall give her unto thee; For the Fear of the Lord is Wifdom and Inftruction, and Faith and Meeknefs are his delight.* This is the *firft* and principal Qualification, requifite to the Difcovery of truth in matters of Religion. The *fecond* is, that a man firmly refolve with himfelf, never to be deluded into the Perfwafion of any thing, *contrary* to plain and evident *Reafon,* which is the Truth of God's *Creation*; contrary to the known *Attributes* of God, which are the Truth of the *Divine Nature*; or contrary to the *moral and eternal Differences of Good and Evil,* which are the Truth and Foundation of all *Religion in general,* and are in *Scripture* conftantly reprefented as fuch. Had men but kept fteddily to this natural and plain Rule, this *Candle of the Lord* (as the Wife man ftiles it,) which God has implanted in their very nature; men, even of the meaneft capacities, could never have been impofed upon with the belief of *impoffible* and abfurd Doctrines, fuch as is *Tranfubftantiation*; or with *contradictory* and unintelligible Explications of *true* Doctrines, fuch as are moft of the Schoolmens fubtle and empty Speculations; Becaufe thefe are plainly contrary to the Truth of God's *Creation,* and confequently cannot poffibly be of Divine *Revelation*; for, *no Lie is of the Truth*; 1 Joh. ii. 21. Neither could they ever have been perfwaded to believe, that God *abfolutely and unconditionally,* without any regard to their Works, decreed from the beginning the

greateft

greateſt part of Mankind to *everlaſting Torments*; which is contrary to the *primary Attributes* of God, and to the *Truth* of the *Divine Nature*. Neither could it ever have entered into the Heart of Man to conceive, that *Cruelty and Inhumanity* ſhould have been *doing God good Service*; or that *Perſecution* ſhould have been ſet up in *his* Name and for *his* ſake, who came into the World *not to deſtroy mens lives, but to ſave them*; who himſelf always *went about, doing good* only; and the very *End* and the *greateſt* of whoſe Commandments, is *Charity*; that is, Univerſal Love and Good-will towards Mankind. Nor could it ever have been imagined, that *Any Wickedneſs whatſoever*, ſhould have been made part of *Any Religion*; when all ſuch things are directly contrary to the moral and eternal Differences of *Good and Evil*; which are the very *Ground and Foundation* of *All Religion in general*, and as unchangeable as the Nature of God himſelf.

THERE are indeed in the *Old Teſtament* ſome inſtances of the Actions of great and good Men, which to weak perſons may ſeem contrary to this Rule; But it is for want of ſufficient Care and Attention, to the particular Circumſtances of the Hiſtory. *David*, the Man after God's own Heart, was indeed guilty of ſome Actions which are very far from being juſtifiable; But then thoſe Actions are expreſsly excepted, as being not *Parts*, but *Blots* in that Character. *Jacob* is repreſented as gaining the Bleſſing by an *Untruth*; But neither is that *Untruth* juſtified in the Hiſtory; neither was it in reality altogether an *Untruth*, becauſe he had before actually bought that Birthright, to which was annexed the Bleſſing he then claimed; and at the buying the Birthright, though that Circumſtance is not indeed mentioned in the Hiſtory of *Geneſis*, yet it appears from what the Apoſtle aſſures us, *Heb.* xii. 16; that it was not a *real* but a *pretended* neceſſity, and merely the *profaneneſs* of *Eſau*, that made him ſell and *deſpiſe* it. *Abraham's* offering his Son, ſeems contrary at firſt ſight to the eternal Law of Nature; but he is juſtified by the *immediate* Command of God, who has undeniably a ſupreme Right over all: A *Right*, not to make Virtue to be Vice, and Vice Virtue; but a *Right* over the *Life* of every man whom he has created: A *Right*, not to make it excuſable in *Abraham* to *hate* his Son; but to make it commendable in him to be willing to part with the Son of *his Love*. In receiving which Command, the Patriarch could not be deceived, becauſe he had been long accuſtomed to the *Manner* wherein God had been pleaſed to reveal himſelf to him; And he had moreover this peculiar ſecurity, that he was ſure his own Heart was perfectly right; in which caſe he might depend God would not permit him to be inevitably deceived; the Thing that was to be done, being no gratification of any Luſt or Cruelty, or any evil Inclination whatſoever, which is always the ſubject-matter of Temptations from the Evil One. The *Jews* at their coming out of *Egypt*, are repreſented as *borrowing* jewels of the *Egyptians*, without intention to *repay* them: And this is uſually excuſed by God's expreſsly commanding them ſo to do; who, without all queſtion, has a right to take from one and give to another, as he pleaſes: But (I think) the truer Anſwer is, that the Word in the Original does not ſignify to *borrow*, but to *demand*; and that, having now the Power in their hands, they refuſed to depart without being paid for that Work, which the *Egyptians* had hitherto unjuſtly compelled them to perform without Wages. But to draw to a Concluſion:

3*dly* and *laſtly*; THE next, and the infallible means of finding the Truth in all matters relating to Religion, is, that to ſincere intention and virtuous practice, men add *diligent Study of the Holy Scripture*, as the only authoritative Guide in matters of poſitive *Revelation*. Whoſoever he be, of how large, or of how mean capacity ſoever, that ſo ſtudies the Scripture, as to reſolve that he will *obey* all the plain *precepts* of
Chriſt

Chrift and his Apoftles therein contained, and *believe* all the plain *doctrines* he clearly underftands, and *not be contentious or uncharitable* about thofe he does *not* underftand, but apply himfelf to fuch perfons as he thinks moft able to imform him better, not fo as to depend implicitly upon *any man's Authority upon Earth* in a matter of Faith, but fo as by *their* affiftance to enlighten and enlarge *his own* Underftanding of the Scriptures; This man has found an infallible Guide, that will either certainly lead him in the way of Truth, or at leaft fecure him from all fuch *pernicious* Errours, as might endanger his Salvation. This man has difcovered the *Fountain* of living Water; and has wherewith to draw, how *deep* foever it be. In a word: Notwithftanding all the Darknefs and Confufion, all the Intricacy and Difputes, which the Ignorance and Folly, the Perverfenefs and Wickednefs of Men, have introduced in the World; yet by this method, a fincere perfon may certainly avoid all the *corrupt Doctrines*, brought in by thofe who carelefsly follow *humane Guides*; and all the *needlefs Divifions*, kept up among thofe who pretend to follow only the *Word of God*: And as many as endeavour to walk according to this Rule, Peace will be on them, and Mercy, and upon the *Ifrael* of God.

SERMON CXIII.

Of the Nature of Religious Faith.

JOHN XX. 29. latter part.

Blessed are They that have not seen, and yet have believed.

SERM.
CXIII.

'TIS the Method of Scripture in *general*, and of our Lord in his Discourses in *particular*, to take all Occasions of setting before men the Happiness both of Virtue *absolutely*, and of every degree of improvement in it *comparatively*. How much more valuable, *in general*, the *Love of Truth* and the *Practice of Virtue* is, than *any external* Circumstances or Advantages whatsoever; our Saviour expresses in a very affectionate manner; when, upon occasion of a certain woman crying out, *Blessed is the Womb that bare thee, and the paps which thou hast sucked*; he thus declares himself, *Luke* xi. 28; *Yea rather, blessed are they that hear the word of God and keep it.* How much *every degree* in *particular*, of improvement in virtuous Practice, either by more extensive Habits of Goodness, or by overcoming greater or more numerous Temptations, or by doing what is Right with Fewer Helps and under greater Disadvantages, does *comparatively* increase the Blessedness of being Righteous ; is set forth to us distinctly in such Passages of Scripture, as these which follow ; *They that be wise, shall shine as the Brightness of the Firmament* ; *and they that turn many to Righteousness, as the Stars for ever and ever :* Dan. xii. 3. *There is one glory of the Sun, and another glory of the Moon, and another glory of the Stars ; for one Star differeth from another Star in glory :* So also is the resurrection of the Dead : 1 Cor. xv. 41. *In a great House there are——Vessels of Gold and of Silver,* and also *of Wood and of Earth :* 2 Tim. ii. 20. *Blessed are ye, when men shall revile you, and persecute you, and shall say all manner of evil against you falsely for my sake :* Rejoice, and be exceeding glad ; for Great is your Reward in Heaven ; Matt. v. 11. And in the words of my Text : Where our Lord having overcome St *Thomas's* incredulity by a singular condescension in permitting him to feel and handle his Body after his Resurrection, and having thereby extorted from him a Confession of his being thoroughly convinced; reproves him afterwards, with this gentle Admonition ; *Thomas, because thou hast seen me, thou hast believed ; Blessed are they that have not seen, and yet have believed.*

THE Words are plainly *comparative*, expressing the *greater Blessedness* of those who with *less Light* find the way of *Truth*, and with *fewer Helps and Assistances* do what is *Right.* Yet it is very evident, this is to be understood *only* of those, who in all *other respects* are in *like* Circumstances, and of whom are required the *like* Instances of Duty. For, *not All who have not seen and yet have believed*, have *in the Whole* the Advantage over Them who believed upon the Evidence of *Sight* ; but *so far* only as their Circumstances are in all *other respects* equal, *so far* is the Blessedness greater of those who have believed *without seeing.* St *Thomas* was one of those *Twelve*, to whom our Lord pro-

I

mised

miſed That high Preheminence, *Matt.* xix. 28; *When the Son of Man ſhall ſit in the* S E R M. *Throne of his glory, ye alſo ſhall ſit upon twelve Thrones, judging the Twelve Tribes of* CXIII. *Iſrael.* And *All* the Apoſtles, to whom this *ſingular* Promiſe of *Glory* was made; were of Thoſe who, *becauſe* they *had ſeen,* had *believed:* 1 Joh. i. 1; *That which we have heard, which we have ſeen with our eyes, which we have looked upon, and our Hands have handled of the Word of Life*; this *declare we unto you.* The Want of this *Evidence of Senſe,* which the Apoſtles enjoyed; moſt certainly our Saviour in my Text did not mean to affirm, that it ſhould give *every Believer* in the *latter* Ages of the World, a Title to a *greater* degree of Happineſs in the life to come, than the *Apoſtles* themſelves. But *ſo far forth,* as all *other* Circumſtances are equal ; *ſo far only* is it *more* advantagious, to have believed *without ſeeing.* The Apoſtles were intruſted with a High and Excellent Office, endued with ſingular and extraordinary Talents, charged with a very great and Laborious Duty, expoſed to Dangers and Sufferings above all men. Chriſtians in the *latter* Ages of the World, may very poſſibly have *ſome particular* Grounds of Bleſſedneſs, which the Apoſtles had not : And yet it will not at all from thence follow, that they *are* therefore *in the Whole* more Bleſſed than the Apoſtles. The Virtue of a *Man* may in ſome *particular Reſpects,* or in ſome *ſingle Points of View,* (as being in a State of greater ignorance, and more Temptations,) be *more* valuable than the Virtue of an *Angel*; and yet it will by no means from thence follow, that men *are,* or that they *ought to be,* more Bleſſed than Angels. The Virtue of a *Penitent,* may in ſome *particular Reſpects* be *more* commendable than That of one who *never offended*; and yet it will by no means from thence follow, that Penitents *are,* or that they *ought* to be, more Bleſſed than thoſe who need no Repentance. God intruſts all his Servants with what Talents he pleaſes, and places them in different Stations, and *deals to every man — Gifts differing* Rom. xii. 3, 6. *according to* his own good pleaſure. In the Church, he has given *Some, Apoſtles*; *and* Eph. iv. 11. *Some, Prophets*; *and Some, Evangeliſts*; *and Some, Paſtors and Teachers.* Of Theſe, St *Paul* affirms, that they are *Labourers together with God*; 1 Cor. iii. 9 : And of *All* Chriſtians in general, that they *are God's Husbandry,* that they *are God's Building.* That in This Building, one *layeth the Foundation, and another buildeth thereon.* That ver. 10. in this Vineyard, one *planteth,* and another *watereth :* And that *every man ſhall receive* ver. 6. *his Own Reward, according to his own Labour.* All, are not *Apoſtles* : All, have not ver. 8. the ſame *Gifts :* All, are not called to the ſame *Obligations,* or to the ſame *Poſſibilities.* As, in the natural Body, *all members have not the ſame Office,* Rom. xii. 4 : So in the *ſpiritual* Body of Chriſt, God who *does what he pleaſes with his own,* appoints to every man his proper *Duty* or *Truſt*; ver. 3. The words in *Our* Tranſlation are here very *abſurdly* rendered ; *God hath dealt to every man the meaſure of Faith :* But the Senſe of the Apoſtle is, *God has dealt to every man his proper* Truſt, a Truſt committed to his *Fidelity* or *Faithfulneſs.* What every man's *Truſt,* what every man's *Ability,* what every man's *Station* ſhall be; is the Appointment of *God.* But *in That* Station, *whatſoever* it be ; ſo much the *more* acceptable ſhall his Fidelity be, as he has done his Duty under *greater Diſadvantages* or with *fewer Helps.* What our Lord declares in the caſe of *Puniſhment,* that the Servant which knew his Maſter's Will, and did it not, ſhall be beaten with *Many* Stripes ; is no leſs equitable in the caſe of *Reward*; that he who, under *any* Circumſtances of *Diſadvantage,* does what is *good* and *right* ; ſhall, (not indeed *abſolutely,* but) in *his Proportion* and *Station,* whatſoever it be, whether great or ſmall, be intitled to a *greater* degree of Recompence. *Bleſſed are they that have not ſeen, and yet have believed.*

HAVING thus explained *in general* the *Senſe* of the *Words,* and the *Ground* of the *Doctrine* contained in the Text; I ſhall now proceed more *diſtinctly and particularly* to the Obſervation of certain remarkable and important Truths, either *neceſſarily ſuppoſed in,* or *clearly deduced from,* this Aſſertion of our Lord. And

Firſt,

SERM.
CXIII.

Firſt, WHAT our Lord here aſſerts, clearly ſuppoſes, that in the Nature of things, (contrary to what *Enthuſiaſts* have frequently imagined,) *Faith* or *Belief* cannot but be *leſs ſtrong* in degree of Evidence, than either the *Teſtimony of Senſe*, or *Proof by Demonſtration*. Enthuſiaſts of all kinds have been very apt to imagine, that by magnifying the certainty and aſſurance of *Faith*, even *above* the Evidence of *Senſe* itſelf, and *equal* to that of *Demonſtration*; they could greatly promote the Glory of God, and the Honour of Religion: Not conſidering, that in reality on the contrary, by ſubverting the Nature of Things, they ſubverted the Foundation of that very Faith, which they fancied they were eſtabliſhing. For *Faith* or *Belief*, in the nature of the thing, neceſſarily ſuppoſes that there is ſome *Reaſon* for believing; Otherwiſe it is not *Faith*, but groundleſs *Deluſion*. And this *Ground* or *Reaſon* of Belief, whatſoever it be, cannot poſſibly but be always Somewhat, which we already *know* either by the uſe of our *Senſes*, or by *neceſſary and demonſtrative Certainty*. The Certainty of *Knowledge* therefore, of the things which we *know* by immediate *Intuition*, either of the *Eye* or of the *Mind*; muſt neceſſarily be *prior* to the Aſſurance of *Faith*, and conſequently *more ſtrong* in the degree of Evidence; as *every Foundation*, in any caſe whatſoever, *muſt* be *of Strength* to ſupport what ſhall be built upon it. The *Credibility* of things *not ſeen*, cannot but depend upon the *Certainty* of the things that *are ſeen*: And *Faith* or *Belief*, in its higheſt poſſible degree of *Aſſurance*, can eſſentially be nothing more, than a well-grounded expeċtation of things *Future*, in conſequence of what we ſee already *paſt*; or a rational Aſſent to the Reality of things *Abſent and Inviſible*, in conſequence of what we have ſeen or known to be *Preſent*. To endeavour to raiſe the Evidence of Faith *higher* than this, is entirely to deſtroy it. For, what St *Paul* ſays concerning *Hope*, Rom. viii. 24; *Hope that is ſeen, is not Hope; for what a man ſeeth, why doth he yet hope for? But if we hope for what we ſee not, then do we with Patience wait for it*: may with equal reaſon be applied to *Faith*. In a man's aſſenting to what he *ſees*, or *knows*; there is nothing of *Faith*, but *Senſe* only. And therefore when our Saviour, in the words before my Text, ſays; *Becauſe thou haſt ſeen me, Thomas, thou haſt believed*: His Meaning was not, that *Thomas believed* what he *Saw*; but that by what he *had Seen*, he was convinced of the Truth of what he had *not ſeen*. The Scripture in *other* Places, always ſpeaks after the *ſame* manner; uniformly and conſiſtently throughout. When St *Paul* ſays, *We walk by Faith, not by Sight*, 2 Cor. v. 7; his Meaning is not, (as ſome Enthuſiaſts have imagined,) that the Evidence of *Faith* is *ſtronger* than that of *Senſe*; but on the contrary, that the Grounds of *Faith*, though ſufficient to command a reaſonable man's *Aſſent*, and to determine his *Practice*, yet are not equal to the Evidence of *Senſe*. And when he tells us, that *the things which are ſeen, are temporal; but the things which are not ſeen, are eternal*; 2 Cor. iv. 18; he plainly ballances the *greater Importance* of the One, againſt the *ſenſible* Certainty of the Other. For now, ſaith he, *we know* only *in part, and*

1 Cor. xiii. 9, 12.

we prophecy in part——*Now we ſee through a glaſs darkly, as* [δἰ Ἐσόπｂ] through a *deſcrying-glaſs*, which makes ſome ſmall and imperfeċt Diſcovery of things at a great diſtance; But hereafter, when Faith ſhall terminate in Knowledge, *Then* we ſhall ſee *face to face*; as in a *looking-glaſs*, [κατοπｍｐιζόuεɴοι, 2 *Cor.* iii. 18.] which repreſents things diſtinċtly in their full and true Dimenſions. To ſpeak *otherwiſe* of Faith, and to repreſent it as of Evidence *Superiour* to Senſe or Reaſon; is to open the Door to all the Abſurdities of Tranſubſtantiation, and all other Extravagancies of the wildeſt Fancy; inſtead of cauſing Religion to *appear* to be, what it really *is*, the moſt *Reaſonable* as well as the moſt important thing in the World. For

Secondly, THOUGH Faith *has not*; and indeed, in the nature of the thing, *cannot have* the Evidence either of Senſe or Demonſtration; yet our Saviour, in pronouncing thoſe men Bleſſed, who *have not ſeen, and yet have believed*; plainly ſuppoſes, and it

4

is

is evident in itself, that Many things are very *reasonable to be believed*, and cannot without extreme Wilfulness and Unreasonableness be rejected, which yet are neither *Objects of Sense*, nor capable of *Demonstration*. That many *invisible* things are real, is evident from the continual Effects of Nature, which are all of them produced by *invisible Powers*; And from thence the *Being of God*, is strictly *demonstrable*. But they who have *not* capacities to apprehend the *Demonstration*; have yet sufficient *Reason*, from what they *are able* to observe and understand, to be *fully persuaded* of the *Truth* of God's Being, and of his Government of the World. And every Atheist, who ridicules *This Faith*, does himself at the same time *believe*, with the most unreasonable Credulity, things that can neither be *Seen* nor *Understood*. The *Judgment to come*, and the *future* permanent State of *Happiness* or *Misery*; are things not *capable* of the Evidence of *Sense*, nor *demonstrable* in any other way than that of moral Certainty. Yet the *rational evidence* arising from the consideration of the *Perfections of God* and of the *Nature of Men*, confirmed moreover by the credible *Testimony* of Revelation; is such, in which every reasonable man ought to rest satisfied; 'Tis such, as is abundantly sufficient to justify every man's Discretion, in parting at any time with any Temporal Advantage, for the Hopes of a Happy Immortality; 'Tis such, as is really stronger, than what the wisest and most cautious men go upon, in all the *Temporal* Affairs of Life. Hence the Apostle St *Paul*, (Heb. xi. 1,) defines *Faith* to be, what we render, *The Substance*; but the word in the Original signifies, *The well-grounded confidence* or *assured expectation*, of *things hoped for*; the *Evidence* or *rational persuasion* of the Truth of *things not Seen*. And argues, that though at present *we walk* indeed *by Faith* only, *and not by Sight*; 2 Cor. v. 7; yet we have sufficient ground to be *always confident* (ver. 6.) of the Truth of God's Promises, so as to be able to support our Spirits under all Events, and in every condition of Humane Life. The Apostles who *saw* our Lord's *Miracles*, and were *Themselves* indued with *Miraculous Powers*; had indeed a *Superior Evidence* of the Truth of Christ's Doctrine, than We at This Distance of Time can have; And therefore they were sent forth upon a more *difficult* Duty. But to *Us* at This day, and to *all Christians* at *all times* to the end of the World; the *Character* of the *Persons* of the Apostles, and their *Sufferings* for their Testimony to the Truth of Facts within their own Knowledge, and the *Completion of Prophecies*, and the *Reasonableness and Excellency* of the *Doctrine*, and the *Agreement* and uniform corresponding *Series* of *Historical* Facts; and the *State* of the *Patriarchal*, and of the *Jewish* and *Christian* Church, from the Beginning of the World to this Day; does and will give *credibility* to the *Miracles* recorded in the Gospels and in the Acts of the Apostles. And the absolute *Demonstrative Certainty* both of the *Grounds* and *Obligations* of *Natural* Religion, makes it extremely *reasonable* and *commendable* in men, to have a *Disposition* to receive *That Confirmation and Improvement* of it by *Revelation*, which Christ and his Apostles so clearly taught, separate from the *Follies* and *Corruptions* wherewith it has been confounded in later Ages. *Blessed are they that have not seen and yet have believed.*

Thirdly; THIS therefore is a *Third* Observation I would make upon these Words of our Saviour. Such Belief as I am now speaking of; such in its Nature, and such in its Grounds, as I have now described; because it is *reasonable*; therefore it is *commendable*: And so much *the more so*, as there are at any time *more Temptations* arising, or *more Arguments* drawn, from *any* thing *except Reason*, in favour of *Unbelief*. A virtuous Disposition of Mind, naturally loving Truth, and desirous to do what is Right; apt to fear God, and to rely upon his Protection both present and future, as Father and Governor of the Universe; sensible of the necessary, the essential and unalterable Difference of Good and Evil, and moved perpetually with the Reasonableness of the Expectation of a Judgment to come: The *more Temptations* it meets with to Infidelity,

SERM. from such Considerations as These; that the things of another Life are remote in
CXIII. *Place*, and far distant in *Time*; that there is always a Possibility of being *mistaken*
in things which are not at all the Objects of Sense; that there are often very great
Present Advantages to be obtained, by transgressing the Rules which Religion pre-
scribes; and sometimes very great *Disadvantages* necessarily to be suffered, by adhering too strictly to the Obligations of Morality: The *more Temptations*, I say, a virtuous Mind meets with, from *Such* Considerations as *These*, to be shaken in its Faith
concerning the great Truths of Religion; *the more* valuable and praise-worthy is its
Stability in That Faith. Hence the Scripture so frequently declares, that *Blessed is the
Man which endureth Temptation*; Jam. i. 12. Hence the Example of the *Patriarchs*
Faith, is so highly recommended; in that they *saw the Promises* only *afar off*; Heb. xi.
13. and *having here no continuing City, but seeking one to come*, they *endured, as seeing
Him who is Invisible*; ch. xiii. 14; xi. 27. Hence St *Peter* exhorts *Christians* to
rejoice in *manifold Temptations*; *that the Tryal of their Faith being much more precious than of Gold that perishes, though it be tried with Fire, may be found unto Praise
and Honour and Glory at the Appearing of Jesus Christ: Whom* (says he) *having not
Seen, ye love; in whom though now ye see him not, yet believing, ye rejoice with Joy unspeakable, and full of Glory.* 1 Pet. i. 7.

Fourthly; THE *Fourth* and *Last* Observation I shall make upon the Words of
our Saviour in my Text, is; that though a Disposition to receive and believe the
Great Truths of Religion, however relating to things at present *invisible* and *remote
from Sense*, is indeed highly commendable; yet to expect at any time, under pretence of Religion, to have things *contrary to Sense or Reason*, entertained and believed; is greatly *absurd* and *impious*. The Reason is, because the *One* is founded in a *virtuous* and *good Temper of Mind*; the *Other* always proceeds either from
deep and pitiable *Folly*, or from *tyrannical and unrighteous* Views. *The Simple believeth every word, but the prudent man looketh well to his going*; Prov. xiv. 15.
Our Saviour does not say, *Blessed are the credulous*: But *Blessed are they that have not
seen, and yet have believed*: Blessed are they who believe and willingly embrace
things *reasonable*, and act honestly according to That Belief, tho' the things themselves be not at present visible to Mortal Eyes. To believe a *Judgment to
come*, such as the Gospel of *Christ* has declared; is infinitely *reasonable*, tho' we
yet *See* it *not*. To believe *Transubstantiation*, or any *Other* Absurdity, contrary either to *Sense* or *Reason*; is in the most profane manner to make Religion *ridiculous*,
by taking away the very *Foundation* of *All Knowledge* and of *All Belief*, either in
matters of Religion or in any thing else. For the Judgment of *Reason* being once
set aside, there remains no possible means of judging whether any one thing whatsoever, be more *reasonable* or more *unreasonable* to be believed, than another; or
whether, in Any case whatsoever, either Belief or Unbelief be in any degree *reasonable*
or *unreasonable* at all. The Excellency of *Abraham's* Faith, consisted in This,
that *against Hope he believed in Hope*; Rom. iv. 18. But the *Ground* of this Faith,
was; that his own *Senses* assured him, of the reality of God's *Promise*; and his * *Reason* assured him, (so the Apostle expresses it, *Heb.* xi. 19,) that the thing promised
was *possible in itself*, though beyond the Bounds of all *natural* Hope. Had the *Object* of
his Faith been either *contrary to Sense*, or *contradictory in Reason*; the Motives for
his *not believing*, had been stronger than for his *believing*; and his *Faith* had been
a *Credulity* founded upon *Nothing*. Whoever carefully considers this, will never
imagine that the words of our Saviour in my Text, give any Encouragement either
to the Impositions of Popish Tyranny, or to the Extravagancies of Enthusiastick
Folly.

* λογισά
μενος.

SERMON

I

SERMON CXIV.

In what the Kingdom of GOD confifts.

ROM. XIV. 17.

For the Kingdom of God, is not meat and drink; but righteoufnefs, and peace, and joy in the Holy Ghoft.

THE greateft part of Chriftians in the *Apoftles* days, having been educated originally, in the *Jewifh* Religion, and but newly converted from it; it is not to be wondred at, that whilft *Some* of them rightly underftood the Nature and Excellency of the *Gofpel*, *Others* of them, who were of weaker Judgments and lefs clear Underftandings, retained, for a long time after their Converfion, many of their antient *Prejudices* and *Scruples* of mind, concerning diftinctions of *Days* and differences of *Meats*, which they had been taught to look upon, not (according to the true intention of the Law) as being *typically* and *figuratively* under the then prefent difpenfation, but as being *really* and *intrinfically*, *morally* and *perpetually*, *clean* or *unclean*. Ver. 2. *One man*, (fays he) *believeth that he may eat all things; another, who* ver. 5. *is weak, eateth herbs:——One man efteemeth one day above another, Another efteemeth every day alike.* The *Method* the Apoftle takes in this cafe, to prevent any Inconveniencies arifing in the Church, from this diverfity of mens apprehenfions concerning indifferent things; is by perfwading them, that one of the Great Ends and Defigns of true Religion, is the promoting among men univerfal peace and good-will towards each other; ver. 19; *Let us follow after the things which make for peace, and things wherewith one may edify another:* And that the only way to obtain this moft defirable peace, is to forbear cenfuring each other upon account of things not in their own nature vicious or immoral: Ver. 3; *Let not him that eateth, defpife him that eateth not; and let not him which eateth not, judge him that eateth:——Let every man be fully perfwaded in his own mind: He that regardeth the day, regardeth it unto the Lord; and he that regardeth not the day, to the Lord he doth not regard it: He that eateth, eateth to the Lord, for he giveth God thanks; and he that eateth not, to the Lord he eateth not, and giveth God thanks.* And ver. 13; *Let us not therefore judge one another—; but judge this rather, that no man put a ftumbling-block or an occafion to fall, in his brother's way: I know, and am perfwaded by the Lord Jefus, that there is nothing unclean of itfelf; but to him that efteemeth any thing to be unclean, to Him it is unclean.* And then he adds in the words of the Text, as an *argument* or *reafon* for their thus bearing with each other, drawn from the *nature* and *effence* of true Religion; *The Kingdom of God* (fays he) *is not meat and drink, but righteoufnefs, and peace, and joy in the Holy Ghoft.*

S E R M. In the following Diſcourſe upon which words, I ſhall *1ſt* explain diſtinctly the
CXIV. ſeveral phraſes made uſe of in the Text: And *then* I ſhall proceed to draw ſome uſeful
Obſervations and *Inferences* therefrom.

    I. *Firſt*; This phraſe, *The Kingdom of God*, in its *original, literal,* and *proper*
ſenſe, ſignifies God's Supreme *Dominion* over the Univerſe; The whole courſe of *Na-*
ture, in Heaven and in Earth, being merely the Effect of his Will and Pleaſure; for
All things Serve Him. But becauſe the *principal* and moſt *valuable* part of Government, conſiſts in the Subjection and *willing* Obedience of *rational and moral* Agents;
hence, in Scripture, *the Kingdom of God* generally ſignifies That *State* or *Eſtabliſhment*
of true Religion or Righteouſneſs in the World, which *would* have been fixed and
ſettled in the State of *Innocence*; but which, *by Sin and Diſobedience,* was removed
from among men; and which, by *Repentance* and *Amendment,* is again in ſome degree *reſtored* upon *Earth*; and will be *perfectly* and *for ever* eſtabliſhed in *Heaven.*
And becauſe the principal *Means,* by which This recovery of ſinful Creatures is accompliſhed, is the *Goſpel of Chriſt*; therefore the *State of the* Goſpel, the Spreading
of the *Profeſſion of true Religion,* and, above all, the *real efficacy and influence of it*
upon the Hearts and Lives of Men, is by our Saviour and his Apoſtles frequently ſtiled *The Kingdom of God.* Thus when our Saviour firſt began to preach Repentance,

Matt. iv. 17.
xii. 28. *The Kingdom of Heaven* (ſays he) *is at hand*: And when he confirmed his Doctrine with miraculous works, *then the Kingdom of God* (ſays he) *is come unto you.*
When the *Phariſees,* ſollicitous, not for the promoting of *Virtue* and *true Righte-*
ouſneſs, but for the obtaining of *temporal power and grandour,* demanded of him when

Luk. xvii. 21. *the Kingdom of God ſhould come*; his Anſwer was, *It cometh not with obſervation; nei-*
ther ſhall they ſay, Lo here, or lo there; for, behold, the Kingdom of God is within
you : And in like manner the *Kingdom of* Satan, is not an *external* ſenſible Dominion,
but the power of *Wickedneſs* and *Immorality* reigning in the *Hearts* and *Lives* of

Matt. vi. 33. men. When our Lord bids his Diſciples to *ſeek* in the *firſt* place *the Kingdom of God,*
he explains his meaning by adding in the next words, *and* His righteouſneſs : And

Mar. x. 15. tells them, that *whoſoever ſhall not receive the Kingdom of God as a little child,* (whoſoever ſhall not receive the doctrine of the Goſpel with Humility and Sincerity, with
Simplicity and Probity of Mind,) *he ſhall not enter therein*; that is, he ſhall not be
acknowledged as a Diſciple of Chriſt at all. And they who *do receive* it for a *time,*
but *continue not* to live worthy of the Religion they profeſs; this *Kingdom of God* (he

Matt. xxi. 45.
xiii. 41. threatens) *ſhall be taken from them, and given to a nation bringing forth the fruits there-*
of. And if it be not *taken from* them, yet at the End, *the Son of man* (ſays he) *ſhall*
ſend forth his Angels, and they ſhall gather out of his Kingdom (out from among the Profeſſors of *His* Religion) *All that offend, and them which do iniquity; and ſhall caſt them*
into a furnace of fire; there ſhall be wailing and gnaſhing of Teeth.

    Now according to the analogy of *this figure* of ſpeaking, ſo often uſed by our
Saviour, wherein he ſtiles the Eſtabliſhment of his true religion the *Kingdom of God*;
the Apoſtle St. *Paul* in like manner in *His* epiſtles, *The Kingdom of God,* ſays he,
(1 *Cor.* iv. 20,) *is not in word, but in power* : His meaning is; The Religion of
Chriſt, does not conſiſt in mere outward Profeſſions and in Forms of Godlineſs, but
in the efficacy of a true Perſwaſion upon the minds of men, bringing forth real Virtue
and Holineſs in their Lives. And in the words of the Text, *The Kingdom of God*
(ſays he) that is, the eſſence of True Chriſtian religion, *is not meat and drink; but*
righteouſneſs, and peace, and joy in the Holy Ghoſt.

    The phraſe, *Meat and Drink,* is an alluſion to that diſtinction of Meats, of
clean and unclean, and other ſuch like external Obſervances, on which the *Jews* laid
ſo great a Streſs in *Their* religion. *Heb.* ix. 10; *The firſt tabernacle,*——ſays the A-
poſtle,

poftle, *ftood only in Meats and Drinks, and divers Wafhings, and carnal Ordinances, impofed on them until the time of reformation.* And becaufe they were impofed *only until* the time of reformation, therefore when the Gofpel of Chrift was eftablifhed, thefe things were no longer to take place. Col. ii. 16; *Let no man judge you in meat or in drink, or in refpect of an Holiday, or of the new moon, or of the fabbath-days; Which are a fhadow of things to come, but the Body is of Chrift :——Why then are ye fubject to ordinances,——(which all are to perifh with the ufing,) after the commandments and doctrines of men?* Things of *this* nature, even during the *Jewifh* difpenfation, were by all reafonable perfons underftood to be *in their own* nature indifferent, however *commanded* for a time upon *particular* reafons. Matt. xv. 17; *Do not ye yet underftand,* faith our Saviour, *that whatfoever entereth in at the mouth, goeth into the belly, and is caft out into the draught? But thofe things which proceed out of the mouth, come forth from the heart, and they defile the man: For out of the heart proceed evil thoughts, murders, adulteries, fornications, thefts, falfe witnefs, blafphemies: Thefe are the things which defile a man; but to eat with unwafhen hands defileth not a man.* St Paul in like manner; 1 Cor. vi. 13; *Meats* (fays he) *for the belly, and the belly for Meats; but God fhall deftroy both It and Them.* And again, ch. viii. ver. 8; *Meat* (fays he) *commendeth us not to God*; (The Argument is *univerfal*, and held good at *all times* and under *all difpenfations*, with regard to the *real* and *intrinfick nature* of things: *Meat commendeth us not to God*;) *for neither, if we eat are we the better; neither if we eat not, are we the worfe.* Even, therefore, under the *Jewifh* difpenfation *itfelf*, things of *this* nature, though very ftrictly commanded, in order to the more compleat feparation and legal Holinefs of that particular people; yet were not really *perfective of them that did the fervice, as pertaining to the confcience*; any otherwife than as *types*, having their fignification verified by *moral* Purity and Holinefs. Heb. xiii. 9; *It is a good thing that the heart be eftablifhed with grace, not with meats, which have not profited them that have been occupied therein.* And if, even to the *Jews themfelves*, the cafe was Thus; *much more* were thofe *Chriftians* to blame, whom St Paul writes to in this Epiftle to the *Romans*, and in his firft to the *Corinthians*; who, profeffing a religion not appointed for the feparating of *one* particular nation, but in which *all* nations were to agree, yet defired to lay too great *a ftrefs* upon fuch particular Obfervances with regard to things in their own nature indifferent, as could have no other tendency than to promote Divifions among Chriftians, and uncharitablenefs in their *judging one another*; Which are the great Hindrances of That Glory of God, which confifts in the univerfal eftablifhment of true Virtue and Righteoufnefs amongft men. Againft *thefe perfons* therefore he directs himfelf, when he fo earneftly exhorts; 1 Cor. ix. 31; *Whether ye eat or drink, or whatfoever ye do, do all to the glory of God.* And ch. iv. 20; *The Kingdom of God is not in* word, *but in* power; not in mere *forms* of Godlinefs, but in the *effectual practice* of true Virtue. And in the words of the Text; The *Kingdom of God, is not meat and drink; but righteoufnefs, and peace, and joy in the Holy Ghoft.*

Rom. xiv. 3.

THE terms, *Righteoufnefs, and Peace, and Joy in the Holy Ghoft*, are here put by way of *eminence*, as Parts for the Whole; as being the *principal* Virtues in which true religion confifts, or (as our Saviour fpeaks) *the weightier matters of the Law*. The *reafon why* the Apoftle, in reckoning up thefe weightier matters of the Law, does not here mention That *firft and great Commandment*, the *Love* or *Worfhip of God*; is becaufe *That* is included in the *Subject* of his Propofition, *The Kingdom of* God. The *Kingdom of God*, that is, the religion of the fincere Worfhippers of the True God, confifts principally and effentially, not in the obfervation of mere external Forms, but in the practice of real and true Virtue, of *Righteoufnefs, Peace, and Joy in the Holy Ghoft*. The word, *Righteoufnefs*, comprehends the practice of thofe *moral* and *eternal* Virtues, *Juftice, Equity, Truth, Fidelity, Holinefs, Purity*, and the like; the Op-

S E R M. pofites whereof, are *all Injuftice*, and *Iniquity* towards *Others*, and *all Debaucheries*
CXIV. which men practife among *themfelves.* The term, *Peace*, fignifies That good Temper, That Charitable Spirit, and kind difpofition of mind, by which Thofe who, with
regard to *things in their own nature indifferent*, have *not* exactly the fame Sentiments,
yet through mutual forbearance and love towards each other, preferve neverthelefs the
bands of chriftian unity and concord: For, Peace and Concord among men there can
poffibly be, only by one or other of the three following ways: Either by the agreement of All, in a perfect and infallible Knowledge of the Truth: Or by a compul-
five and hypocritical agreement, in the maintaining of Opinions which they underftand not: Or laftly, by an agreement of mutual Charity and Good-will, among All
who live in the fincere Enquiry after Truth, and practice of Righteoufnefs. The firft
of Thefe, is the Unity which is among Angels: The Second is That Unity, which
is among profane, atheiftical, irreligious or very fuperftitious men: The Third, is
the *Peace* mentioned in the Text; the Peace and Unity which is among Good and
Sincere Chriftians; *walking in love*, as the fame Apoftle elfewhere expreffes it; and
*giving no Offence, neither to the Jews, nor to the Gentiles, nor to the Church of God;
Even as I* (fays he) *pleafe all men in all things; not feeking my own profit, but the profit of many, that they may be faved.* *Laftly*; The phrafe, *Joy in the Holy Ghoft*, fignifies That *delight* and *taking pleafure* in *doing good*, which is the higheft *perfection* of
Chriftian virtue; and That *fatisfaction* even in *fuffering* at any time (if the Will of
God be fo) for Righteoufnefs fake, which is the higheft *Evidence* of *Chriftian fincerity.* Which affection of mind, becaufe it is (at leaft in remarkable cafes) worked in
men by the affiftance and influence of the divine Spirit, it is therefore called in Scripture
Joy of the Holy Ghoft; 1 Th. i. 6: and, in the Text, *Joy in the Holy Ghoft*; while at
the fame time, in other places, it is mentioned under the more large and unlimited
expreffions, of *rejoicing evermore, rejoicing in hope, rejoicing in the Lord*; and, in
general, doing all things (*Acts* ii. 46,) *with gladnefs and finglenefs of heart.* Nor is
there Any inconfiftency in thus reprefenting one and the fame Chriftian Virtue, as being both a good difpofition of the *mind itfelf* in the *man* who poffeffes it, and yet alfo at
the fame time an influence of the *fpirit* of God. For, as, in true Philofophy, all *natural* Actions, when purfued, with the moft fagacious exactnefs of Inquiry, through
all their feries of Second Caufes, appear *at laft* to the eye of the moft exquifite Philofopher, as they do *at firft* to the pious judgment of the meaneft Chriftian, to derive
originally from God: So in *fpiritual* actions, thofe very Virtues, which, effentially to
their being Virtues at all, muft be the voluntary operations of a man's own mind;
may yet, very confiftently, have at the fame time the *like* fort of dependence upon
the Influences of the divine Spirit, as all our *natural* actions have upon that Concurrence of God, from which our Wills themfelves, and all the Faculties of our nature, continually and every moment derive their Power of Acting. And This obfervation will very clearly account for all thofe paffages of Scripture, wherein the *Virtues*
of *Men*, and the *Gifts* of the Spirit of God, are promifcuoufly taken for each other.
The *Fruits* or *Graces of the Spirit*, in St *Paul's* Catalogue, are individually the fame
as *moral Virtues:* And *Barnabas's* being a *good man*, and *full of the Holy Ghoft*, are
joined together as expreffions of the *fame* import: And what our Saviour in St *Luke*,
ch. vii. 11. ch. xi. 13, fays of our *heavenly Father, giving his* Holy Spirit, is, in St *Matthew* re-
cording the very fame words, underftood of *his giving* good things *to them that afk
him.*

    II. *Secondly*; AND thus having diftinctly and at large explained all the *feveral*
expreffions in the Text, *The Kingdom of God, is not meat and drink, but righteoufnefs, peace, and joy in the Holy Ghoft*; The *Obfervations* I would draw from the Apoftle's affertion in the *whole*, are briefly as follows.

                                                Firft;

Firft ; THAT the Great and Principal End of true Religion, is the promoting and S E R M. eftablifhing among Men, the Practice of *moral* Goodnefs and Righteoufnefs. *God*, is CXIV. himfelf effentially a Being of infinite Purity and Holinefs; and his *future Kingdom in* Heaven, is of fuch a nature, that *there fhall in no wife enter into it any thing that de-* Rev. xxi. 27. *fileth, neither whatfoever worketh abomination, or maketh a lie.* Confequently thofe Virtues which are effentially neceffary to the enjoyment of the Happinefs of Heaven *hereafter,* cannot but be the principal Conftituents of the Kingdom of God *here.* Which Virtues, *our Saviour* therefore emphatically calls *The* weightier *matters of the* Matt. xxiii. *Law.* And the *Apoftle* accordingly, whenever he mentions *Thefe* things, always fup- 23. pofes all *other* matters to be, *comparatively* fpeaking, as nothing. *In Chrift Jefus,* (fays Gal. v. 6. he) *neither circumcifion availeth any thing, nor uncircumcifion, but faith which worketh by love.* For *Circumcifion is nothing, and uncircumcifion is nothing, but the keeping of* 1 Cor. vii. *the commandments of God. And as many as walk according to This rule, peace be on* 19. Gal. vi. 17. *them, and mercy, and upon the Ifrael of God.* For *Thefe* things (fays he) *are good,* Tit. iii. 8. (are effentially good) *and profitable unto men:* And *He that in Thefe things ferveth* Rom. xiv. 18. *Chrift, is acceptable unto God, and approved of* (all reafonable) *men.*

Secondly ; THE *Second* Obfervation I would draw from the Apoftle's doctrine in the Text, is : that though the Great and Principal End of true Religion, is the promoting and eftablifhing the Practice of *Moral Virtue and Righteoufnefs* ; yet the *Externals alfo* of Religion, Matters of Order and Decency and Particular Appointment, are neverthefs of neceffity not to be neglected. The diftinctions of *meats and drinks* alluded to in the Text, though they are *not the Kingdom of God, not* of the effence *of Religion,* yet, under the *Jewifh* difpenfation, they *were* expreffly and immediately of *divine appointment* ; And *fo long as* they were appointed, and *for the* Ends *to which* they were appointed, and *in fubordination to* thofe Ends, they *were* of neceffity to be *obferved.* The weightier matters of the Law, *ought* (as our Saviour expreffes it with the moft perfect accuracy ; they *ought)* to be *done*; and the others, *not to be left undone.* And, Matt. xxiii. *in proportion*; now, and at all times, under the *Chriftian* difpenfation likewife, matters 23. of *pofitive appointment,* of decency and external form, though *not* of the *effence* of religion, yet fo far as they are *Helps* and *Means* of Religion, ought not in any wife to be *left undone.* In proportion (I fay) This holds true, under the *Gofpel* likewife : For

Thirdly ; THE *Third* and *Laft* Obfervation I would draw from the words of the Text, is ; that *That* Form and Inftitution of religion is *proportionably* the *moft perfect,* which has the *feweft* pofitive external Rites, and lays the *leaft ftrefs* upon them; and wherein thofe Rites which *are* appointed, have the moft direct and immediate tendency to promote *real* Virtue and Holinefs. This is evident in the *nature* of *things.* For, in *all* cafes whatfoever, the *End* is *always* beft and moft certainly attained, where the Means made ufe of, are *Feweft* in *number*, and moft *direct* in their *nature*, and moft *obvious* in their *tendency,* and *leaft apt* to be *perverted,* and have *no other ftrefs* laid on them, than juft as they promote the End they were defigned for. The *End* therefore, is always principally to be had in View ; and *Means* are nothing, but with relation to the End. *The Kingdom of God, is not meat and drink; but righteoufnefs, and peace, and joy in the Holy Ghoft.*

THE *Inferences* from what has been faid, fhall be very fhort, and fuch as obvioufly follow from the foregoing Obfervations.

1ft, FROM hence appears the peculiar Excellency and Advantage of the *Chriftian* religion ; that it is not burdened, as the *Jewifh* was, with a multitude of outward Rites and Ceremonies ; with perpetual Wafhings, Purifications, Sacrifices, and other typical Obfervations, which (as the Apoftle expreffes it) *neither we nor our Fathers were able to bear* ; but requires of us, in order to eternal Salvation, only *Faith* in God and in *Jefus Chrift, Repentance* from *dead Works,* and *Obedience* to the *Laws* of Chrift in the *Gofpel,* in expectation of the *Refurrection* to *eternal Judgment.*

SERM. *2dly*, FROM what has been faid, appears the Great *Wifdom* and *Ufefulnefs* of thofe
CXIV. *few* even external Rites in the *Chriftian* inftitution; the *Preaching of the Word*, and
the *Adminiftration* of the *two Sacraments*; Thefe being fuch *Means*, as have a *direct*,
natural, and *immediate* Tendency, to promote the *Ends* of *real* Virtue and Holinefs.
For, by the *Preaching* of the *Word*, men are inftructed in the *Knowledge of* their Duty,
and continually exhorted to perform it. By *Baptifm*, they are admitted into a folemn
Obligation to *obey* it : And by the Sacrament of the *Lord's Supper*, they continually
renew and *confirm* That Obligation. Neverthelefs, *excellent* as thefe *Means* are, both
in their *natural* aptnefs to the End defigned, and moreover as being *exprefsly* and *pofi-*
tively commanded by *Chrift himfelf*; yet that they are ftill *but* Means, fubordinate *to*,
and ufeful *only as* they promote, the practice of real Godlinefs, Righteoufnefs, and
Charity; is evident from hence; that the *Virtues* which thefe Inftitutions were intended to promote, are *abfolutely, effentially, indifpenfably,* and without *Any* excepted Cafes
whatfoever, neceffary to Salvation; there being no expedient, by which an unrighteous perfon, continuing fuch, can *poffibly* enter into the Kingdom of Heaven: The
Gofpel itfelf to fuch a perfon, inftead of being a *Savour of Life unto Life,* becomes
on the contrary the *Savour of Death unto Death : Baptifm,* being merely the *wafhing*
away the filth of the flefh, and not the *anfwer of a good confcience towards God,* is of
no benefit to him; and the receiving the *Lord's Supper,* does but increafe his condemnation. But now on the other fide, in matters of *pofitive inftitution,* though by
our Lord himfelf, declared *generally* neceffary to Salvation, yet in *particular* circumftances there are manifeftly *Some* excepted Cafes. *Infants* dying fuddenly *before Bap-*
tifm, no reafonable perfon can believe fhall perifh, for what can in no fenfe be efteemed
their own Fault. The *Penitent* upon the *Crofs,* though he could not be baptized, yet
received from our Lord's own Mouth a Promife of Salvation. And in the primitive
Ages, when Many Converts, before they could be baptized, were carried immediately
to *Martyrdom;* no one doubted, but their dying *literally* with and for Chrift, was
more than equivalent to being *figuratively* buried with him by Baptifm into Death.
Which clearly fhows the *true difference,* between the things which abfolutely *muft be*
done, and the things which *ought not to be left undone.*

    3dly, FROM what has been faid, it appears, how contrary to the Spirit of Chrifti-
anity the manner of the Church of *Rome* is, in multiplying mere Forms and Ceremonies without number, and particularly in making additional *Sacraments* of their
own invention, or pretended means of conveying Grace, in order to amufe the people
and withdraw their attention from the Practice of real and true Virtue. Thus *Con-*
firmation, which is only mens publickly ratifying their baptifmal Vow; and *Ordina-*
tion, which is the Solemn appointment of particular perfons to a particular Office ; are,
with *Them, Sacraments.* Alfo, inftead of True Repentance and Amendment of Life,
they have the *Sacrament* of *Penance.* And upon a grofs mifinterpretation of a fingle
paffage in St *James's* epiftle, concerning the Sick being anointed with oil, and having
their Sins forgiven, and their bodily difeafe at the fame time miraculoufly cured ; is
built the fuperftitious *Sacrament* of *extreme Unction.* And becaufe St *Paul,* in his
comparing Matrimony with the fpiritual Union between Chrift and his Church, calls
That Similitude a great *Myftery,* which word *Myftery* the *Latin* tranflator ignorantly
and ridiculoufly renders *a great Sacrament ;* hence *Matrimony* is, with *Them,* another
Sacrament. And innumerable other things of the like nature there are among them,
of which St *Paul* would have faid, with greater earneftnefs than even of the *Jewifh*
Obfervations themfelves ; *The Kingdom of God is not meat and drink ; but righteoufnefs,*
and peace, and joy in the Holy Ghoft.

The End of the Firft Volume.

Oversize
BX
5037   Clarke, Samuel.
C5   The works, 1738.
1976
v.1

BX5037 C5 1976
Over +The works, 1738 +Clarke, Samuel,

0 00 02 0236422 0
MIDDLEBURY COLLEGE

DEMCO